Social Structure Theory	Social Process Theory	Critical Theory	Developmental Theory	
			Life Course	Latent Trait
Sociological Theory		Marxist/Conflict Theory	Multifactor Theory	
Clifford R. Shaw & Henry D. McKay; Walter Miller; Albert Cohen; Richard Cloward & Lloyd Ohlin	Edwin Sutherland; Travis Hirschi; Edwin Lemert; Howard Becker	Willem Bonger; Ralf Dahrendorf; George Vold; Karl Marx	Sheldon & Eleanor Glueck; John Laub & Robert Sampson	James Q. Wilson & Richard Herrnstein; Travis Hirschi & Michael Gottfredson
1920s to Present	1930s to Present	1960s to Present	1930s to Present	1980s to Present
Social and economic forces are the key determinants of criminal behavior patterns. Crime is the result of an individual's location within the structure of society.	Criminal behavior is a function of the interaction between individuals and society; criminality occurs as a result of group interaction and the socialization process.	Inequality between social classes (groups) results in conditions that empower the wealthy and disenfranchise the less fortunate; these are the root causes of crime. It is the ongoing struggle for power, control, and material well-being that produces crime.	As people go through the life course, social and personal traits undergo change and influence behavior.	A master trait that controls human development interacts with criminal opportunity.
Social Disorganization Theory; Strain Theory; Anomie Theory; Institutional Anomie; General Strain Theory (GST); Cultural Deviance Theory; Theory of Delinquent Subcultures; Theory of Differential Opportunity	Social Learning Theory; Differential Association Theory; Neutralization Theory; Social Control Theory; Labeling Theory; Social Reaction Theory	Critical Criminology; Instrumental Theory; Structural Theory; Left-Realism; Critical Feminism Power-Control Theory; Peacemaking Criminology	Social Development Model; Interactional Theory; General Theory of Crime and Delinquency; Age-Graded Theory	General Theory of Crime (GTC); Integrated Cognitive Antisocial Potential (ICAP) Theory; Differential Coercion Theory; Control Balance Theory
Poverty; transitional neighborhoods; concentric zones; subculture; cultural transmission; social ecology; collective efficacy; relative deprivation; anomie; conduct norms; focal concerns; differential opportunity	Socialization; peer relations; family relations; differential association; techniques of neutralization; self-concept; social bond; stigma; retrospective reading; primary and secondary deviance	Power; social conflict; marginalization; capitalism; social class; globalization; left realism; exploitation; patriarchy; restorative justice; social justice; reintegrative shaming; restoration	Problem behavior syndrome; pathways to crime; turning points; social capital	Impulsive personality; low self-control; latent traits

Cengage Learning Careers in Criminal Justice Website

Do you know what you are going to do when you graduate? Do you know what career paths are available to you in the field of criminal justice? Go to the **Careers in Criminal Justice Website** and take the interest assessment quiz to help you narrow your focus. Learn about more than 80 available careers, including 25 Video Profiles, available to you in this field. The website also features a career rolodex and a career planner with sample resumes, letter, interview questions, and more—plus, the engaging "CJ Files" videos that will help you know what to anticipate from your study of the criminal justice field.

Access to the **Careers in Criminal Justice Website** may have been packaged with your text; if so, visit **www.cengage.com/login** to register and begin using this site. If not, you may view a demo at **www.cengage.com/criminaljustice/careers** and purchase access at **ichapters.com**.

Get the best grade in the shortest time possible!
Visit **www.ichapters.com** to view more than 10,000 print, digital, and audio study tools.

For additional online resources...
Find the Companion Website for this text and much more at **www.cengage.com/criminaljustice**

FOURTH EDITION

Criminology
The Core

LARRY J. SIEGEL

University of Massachusetts, Lowell

WADSWORTH
CENGAGE Learning™

Australia • Brazil • Japan • Korea • Mexico • Singapore • Spain • United Kingdom • United States

Criminology: The Core, **Fourth Edition**
Larry J. Siegel

Senior Publisher: Linda Schreiber-Ganster

Senior Acquisitions Editor: Carolyn Henderson Meier

Senior Developmental Editor: Shelley Murphy

Assistant Editor: Megan Power

Editorial Assistant: John Chell

Media Editor: Ting Jian Yap

Senior Marketing Manager: Michelle Williams

Marketing Assistant: Jillian Myers

Senior Marketing Communications Manager: Tami Strang

Content Project Manager: Christy Frame

Creative Director: Rob Hugel

Senior Art Director: Maria Epes

Print Buyer: Paula Vang

Rights Acquisitions Account Manager, Text: Bob Kauser

Rights Acquisitions Account Manager, Images: Robyn Young and Bill Jentzen

Production Service: Aaron Downey, Matrix Productions Inc.

Photo Editor/Researcher: Linda L Rill

Copy Editor: Connie Day

Cover Designer: Riezebos Holzbaur/Tim Heraldo

Cover Illustration: Noah Woods

Compositor: Pre-Press PMG

Design photos: (Capitol bldg) © Allan Baxter/Getty Images; (businessman) © Gregory Costanzo/Getty Images; (young man with arms crossed) © Image Source/Getty Images; (woman with tattoo) © Mark Lewis/Getty Images; (Iranian businesswoman) © Jupiterimages/Getty Images; (demonstrators) © Image Source/Getty Images; (handcuffed hand) © rubberball/Getty Images

For product information and technology assistance, contact us at **Cengage Learning Customer & Sales Support, 1-800-354-9706.**

For permission to use material from this text or product, submit all requests online at **www.cengage.com/permissions.** Further permissions questions can be e-mailed to **permissionrequest@cengage.com.**

Library of Congress Control Number: 2009940270

ISBN-13: 978-0-495-80983-8

ISBN-10: 0-495-80983-7

Wadsworth
20 Davis Drive
Belmont, CA 94002
USA

Cengage Learning is a leading provider of customized learning solutions with office locations around the globe, including Singapore, the United Kingdom, Australia, Mexico, Brazil, and Japan. Locate your local office at **www.cengage.com/global.**

Cengage Learning products are represented in Canada by Nelson Education, Ltd.

To learn more about Wadsworth, visit **www.cengage.com/wadsworth**

Purchase any of our products at your local college store or at our preferred online store **www.CengageBrain.com.**

Printed in the United States of America
1 2 3 4 5 6 7 14 13 12 11 10

This book is dedicated to my grandchildren:

The brilliant and handsome Jack Macy

The talkative and beautiful Brooke Macy

The gorgeous princess and ballet dancer,

Kayla Jean Macy

About the Author

The author with his wife, Therese, in Italy

LARRY J. SIEGEL was born in the Bronx in 1947. While living on Jerome Avenue and attending City College of New York in the 1960s, he was swept up in the social and political currents of the time. He became intrigued with the influence contemporary culture had on individual behavior: Did people shape society or did society shape people? He applied his interest in social forces and human behavior to the study of crime and justice. After graduating CCNY, he attended the newly opened program in criminal justice at the State University of New York at Albany, earning both his M.A. and Ph.D. degrees there. After completing his graduate work, Dr. Siegel began his teaching career at Northeastern University, where he was a faculty member for nine years. After leaving Northeastern, he held teaching positions at the University of Nebraska–Omaha and Saint Anselm College in New Hampshire. He is currently a professor at the University of Massachusetts–Lowell. Dr. Siegel has written extensively in the area of crime and justice, including books on juvenile law, delinquency, criminology, criminal justice, and criminal procedure. He is a court certified expert on police conduct and has testified in numerous legal cases. The father of four and grandfather of three, Larry Siegel and his wife, Terry, now reside in Bedford, New Hampshire, with their two dogs, Watson and Cody.

Brief Contents

Contents

Part 1 Concepts of Crime, Law, and Criminology

Part 2 Theories of Crime Causation

Chapter 5
Trait Theory 107

Chapter 6
Social Structure Theory 135

Chapter 7
Social Process Theories 167

Part 3 Crime Typologies

Chapter 10

Violent Crime: Personal and Political   253

Chapter 11

Property Crimes   293

© AP Images/Wally Santana

© AP Images/LAPD

Chapter 12

Enterprise Crime: White-Collar Crime, Cyber Crime, and Organized Crime   315

© Jay Directo/AFP/Getty Images

Chapter 13

Public Order Crimes   349

Part 4   The Criminal Justice System

Preface

On November 5, 2009, the nation was stunned to hear that a gunman had opened fire in the Soldier Readiness Center at Fort Hood, in Killeen, Texas, killing 13 people and wounding 30 others. As the suspected gunman, Army Major Nidal Malik Hasan, exited the building, he was shot in an exchange of gunfire by civilian police officers Sergeant Kimberly Munley and Sergeant Mark Todd, who had responded to an emergency call. Sergeant Munley, hit three times, was later hailed as a hero for her cool behavior under fire.

A U.S. Army psychiatrist, Hasan had enlisted immediately after high school graduation, and he served eight years while attending college at Virginia Tech. After graduation he went on to medical school at the Uniformed Services University of the Health Sciences (USUHS), all at the expense of the U.S. government. In 2009 he was promoted to major, despite having received poor evaluations.

After the shooting, reports soon surfaced that, far from being gratified by his military and academic success, Hasan was a deeply troubled man. His relatives maintained that he had suffered harassment as a consequence of his Middle Eastern background (Hasan is of Palestinian descent). Family members also claimed he was seeking a discharge from the Army because he had been the target of religious discrimination.

More troubling were reports that military authorities had failed to act despite intelligence showing that Hasan was involved in Islamic radical groups and that he had attempted to forge ties with al Qaeda. He had attended the Dar al-Hijrah mosque in Falls Church, Virginia, at the same time that it was frequented by two 9/11 hijackers, Nawaf al-Hazmi and Hani Hanjour. The imam at that time, Anwar al-Awlaki, was a spiritual adviser to the hijackers, and Hasan has been said to have had deep respect for Awlaki's teachings. Reports circulated that Hasan was highly critical of United States policy in the Middle East and believed that it constituted a war on the Muslim religion. Yet even though the FBI informed the Army about his contacts and statements, no action was taken.

Was Hasan a terrorist or simply a disturbed individual who cracked under stress? He shouted, "Allah Akbar" ("God is the Greatest,") as he shot his way through the Readiness Center. Is this an indication that he had taken on a role similar to that of a jihadist suicide bomber? There was little indication that Hasan was part of a terror cell or had formal contacts with terrorist organizations. Can a person acting alone be considered a terrorist? On the other hand, Hasan was a doctor and psychiatrist who was in close contact with mental health professionals. If he was truly disturbed, how is it possible that none of his colleagues, trained in psychology and psychiatry, noticed his condition? Is this an indication that, rather than being mentally ill, he was a rational decision maker seeking revenge?

Considering such incidents of mass violence as the Fort Hood shootings, it is not surprising that many Americans are concerned about crime and worried about becoming victims of violent crime themselves. We alter our behavior to limit the risk of victimization and question whether legal punishment alone can control criminal offenders. We watch movies about law firms, clients, fugitives, and stone-cold killers. We are shocked when the news media offer graphic accounts of school shootings, police brutality, and sexual assaults.

I, too, have had a life-long interest in crime, law, and justice. Why do people behave the way they do? What causes someone like Major Hasan to kill people he hardly knew? Was his behavior the result of a diseased mind and personality? Or was he a cool, calculating terrorist seeking to undermine the U.S. military? Could his murderous rampage have been predicted and prevented? And what should be done with people who commit horrendous crimes? Does Hasan deserve to be executed for his misdeeds? And if not, who does? Would executing someone like Hasan deter others from terrorism? Or might his martyrdom encourage other would-be terrorists to take similar actions?

Goals of this Book

For the past 40 years, I have channeled my fascination with issues related to crime and justice into a career as a student and teacher of criminology. My goal in writing this text is to help students share the same enthusiasm for criminology that has sustained me during my teaching career. What could be more important or fascinating than a field of study that deals with such wide-ranging topics as the motivation for mass murder, the effects of violent media on young people, drug abuse, and organized crime? Criminology is a dynamic field, changing constantly with the release of major research studies, Supreme Court rulings, and governmental policy. Its dynamism and diversity make it an important and engrossing area of study.

One reason why the study of criminology is so important is that debates continue over the nature and extent of crime and the causes and prevention of criminality. Some view criminals as society's victims who are forced to violate the law because of poverty and lack of opportunity. Others view aggressive, antisocial behavior such as the Fort Hood massacre as a product of mental and physical abnormalities, present at birth or soon after, that are stable over the life course. Still another view is that crime is a function of the rational choice of greedy, selfish people who can be deterred from engaging in criminal behavior only by the threat of harsh punishments. It all comes down to this: Why do people do the things they do? How can we explain the intricacies and diversity of human behavior?

Because interest in crime and justice is so great and so timely, this text is designed to review these ongoing issues and cover the field of criminology in an organized and comprehensive manner. It is meant as a broad overview of the field, an introduction to whet the reader's appetite and encourage further and more in-depth exploration.

Several major themes recur throughout the book:

Fact versus Fiction: A main goal of this new edition is to expose some of the myths that cloud people's thinking about crime and criminals. Because the media often paint a distorted picture of the crime problem in America and focus only on the most sensational cases, it is essential to help students separate the rhetoric from the reality: Is the crime rate really out of control? Are unemployed people inclined to commit crime? Are immigrants more crime-prone than the native-born? Are high school dropouts more likely to commit crime than graduates? Distinguishing what is true from what is merely legend is one of the greatest challenges for instructors in criminology courses. The all-new *Fact or Fiction?* feature in *Criminology: The Core* helps meet that challenge head on. This feature separates myth from reality to disabuse students of incorrect notions, perceptions, and biases. Each chapter opens with a list of *Fact or Fiction?* statements highlighting common perceptions about crime that are related to the material discussed in the chapter. Then, throughout the text, these topics are revisited so the student will become skilled at distinguishing the myths from the reality of crime and criminality.

Competing Viewpoints: There are still on-going debates about the nature and extent of crime and the causes and prevention of criminality. I try to present the various viewpoints on each topic and then draw a conclusion based on the weight of the existing evidence. Students become familiar with this kind of analysis by examining *Concept Summary* boxes that compare different viewpoints, reviewing both their main points and their strengths.

Critical Thinking: It is important for students to think critically about law and justice and to develop a critical

perspective toward the social institutions and legal institutions entrusted with crime control. Throughout the book, students are asked to critique research highlighted in boxed material and to think "outside the box," as it were. To aid in this task, each chapter ends with a brief section called *Thinking Like a Criminologist*, which presents a scenario that can be analyzed with the help of material found in the chapter. This section also includes critical thinking questions to guide classroom interaction.

Diversity: Diversity is a key issue in criminology, and this text attempts to integrate issues of racial, ethnic, gender, and cultural diversity throughout. The book includes material on international issues, such as the use of the death penalty abroad, and on gender issues, such as the rising rate of female criminality. Boxed features headed *Race, Culture, Gender, and Criminology* enhance the coverage of diversity issues. In Chapter 14, for example, there is an in-depth discussion of how race influences sentencing in criminal courts.

Current Theory and Research: Throughout the book, every attempt is made to use the most current research to illustrate the major trends in criminological research and policy. Most people who use the book have told me that this is one of its strongest features. I have attempted to present current research in a balanced fashion, even though this approach can be frustrating to students. It is comforting to reach an unequivocal conclusion about an important topic, but sometimes that simply is not possible. In an effort to be objective and fair, I have presented each side of important criminological debates in full. Throughout the text, boxed features headed *Current Issues in Crime* review important research in criminology. For example, in Chapter 12, a box called "The Subprime Mortgage Scandal" helps explain this white-collar crime that nearly brought down the financial system.

Social Policy: There is a focus on social policy throughout the book so that students can see how criminological theory has been translated into crime prevention programs. Because of this theme, *Policy and Practice in Criminology* features are included throughout the text. These show how criminological ideas and research can be put into action. For example, Chapter 4 includes a *Policy and Practice in Criminology* box called "Reducing Crime through Surveillance." It examines the effectiveness of closed-circuit television (CCTV) surveillance cameras and improved street lighting—crime prevention techniques that are currently being used around the world.

My primary goals in writing this text were as follows:

1. To separate the facts from the fiction about crime and criminality
2. To provide students with a thorough knowledge of criminology and show its diversity and intellectual content
3. To be as thorough and up-to-date as possible
4. To be objective and unbiased

5. To describe current theories, crime types, and methods of social control, and to analyze their strengths and weaknesses
6. To show how criminological thought has influenced social policy

In sum, the text has been carefully structured to cover relevant material in a comprehensive, balanced, and objective fashion. Every attempt has been made to present the material in an interesting and contemporary manner. No single political or theoretical position dominates the text; instead, it presents the many diverse views that are contained within criminology and characterize its interdisciplinary nature. The text includes analysis of the most important scholarly works and scientific research reports, but it also offers a great deal of topical information on recent cases and events, such as the controversial arrest, trial, and conviction of activist cop killer Mumia Abu-Jamal and the fall of financier Bernard Madoff, perpetrator of what was probably the largest scam in the nation's history.

Topic Areas

Criminology: The Core is a thorough introduction to this fascinating field and is intended for students in introductory courses in criminology. It is divided into four main sections or topic areas.

Part 1 provides a framework for studying criminology. The first chapter defines the field and discusses its most basic concepts: the definition of crime, the component areas of criminology, the history of criminology, the concept of criminal law, and the ethical issues that arise in this field. Chapter 2 covers criminological research methods, as well as the nature, extent, and patterns of crime. Chapter 3 is devoted to the concept of victimization, including the nature of victims, theories of victimization, and programs designed to help crime victims.

Part 2 contains six chapters that cover criminological theory: Why do people behave the way they do? Why do they commit crimes? These views focus on choice (Chapter 4), biological and psychological traits (Chapter 5), social structure and culture (Chapter 6), social process and socialization (Chapter 7), social conflict (Chapter 8), and human development (Chapter 9).

Part 3 is devoted to the major forms of criminal behavior. The chapters in this section cover violent crime (Chapter 10), common theft offenses (Chapter 11), enterprise crimes (Chapter 12), and public order crimes, including sex offenses and substance abuse (Chapter 13).

Part 4 consists of one chapter, which covers the criminal justice system (Chapter 14). It provides an overview of the entire justice system, including the process of justice, the major organizations that make up the justice system, and concepts of and perspectives on justice.

What's New in This Edition?

Chapter 1, *Crime and Criminology,* now opens with a vignette on financier Norman Hsu, who pleaded guilty to ten counts of mail and wire fraud stemming from his role in an investment fraud scheme that affected investors across the United States. A *Policy and Practice in Criminology* feature addresses the important issue of whether registration of sex offenders who have served their sentences should be required. There is a review of recent research, including an article by Tatia M. C. Lee, Siu-Ching Chan, and Adrian Raine that sought to determine whether these criminals' aggressive behavior was a product of their neurological makeup or a social condition such as unemployment. A new *Profiles in Crime* feature focuses on a case involving "kiddie porn."

Chapter 2, *The Nature and Extent of Crime,* begins with a vignette on George Zinkhan, who killed his wife Marie Bruce and two other people as they left a reunion picnic of the Town and Gown Players theater group in Athens, Georgia. A *Profiles in Crime* feature called "A Pain in the Glass" tells the story of Ronald and Mary Evano, who turned dining in restaurants into a profitable—albeit illegal—activity via a scam that involved eating glass. The data in the chapter has been updated with a look at recent crime trends and patterns.

Chapter 3, *Victims and Victimization,* includes a new section on blaming the victim that shows that the suffering endured by crime victims does not end when their attacker leaves the scene of the crime. They may suffer further from innuendos or insinuations that they are somehow to blame for what happened. A new section on crime in schools shows that, unfortunately, educational facilities are the site of a great deal of victimization, because they include a concentrated population of one of the most dangerous segments of society: teenage males. A new section on victim impulsivity explores the idea that some personality traits exhibited by victims may provoke attack. A *Current Issues in Crime* feature called "Escalation or Desistance: The Effect of Victimization on Criminal Careers" discusses what happens when a criminal experiences victimization. Does it encourage further criminal activities? Or might the experience of victimization help convince a career criminal to choose another career?

Chapter 4, *Choice Theory: Because They Want To,* begins with the story of the "pump and dump" stock market scheme orchestrated by Michael Pickens, son of one of the nation's richest men. A new section on evaluating the risks of crime explores how reasoning criminals carefully select targets. For example, burglars seem to choose targets on the basis of their value, novelty, and resale potential. A *Profiles in Crime* feature called "Looting the Public Treasury" tells the tale of the corruption of Albert Robles, who served terms as mayor, councilman, and deputy city manager of South Gate, California. A *Policy and Practice in Criminology* feature called "Reducing Crime through Surveillance" updates the research of Brandon Welsh and David Farrington, who have been using systematic review and meta-analysis to assess the comparative effectiveness of situational crime prevention techniques. The chapter also examines the deterrent effects of the severity, certainty, and speed of punishment and the way those factors may influence one another. Research is presented to show that people may be deterred from committing some crimes more readily than from committing others and that the most significant deterrent effects can be achieved in minor crimes and offenses, whereas more serious crimes such as homicide are harder to discourage.

Chapter 5, *Trait Theory,* opens with the stories of 23-year-old Seung-Hui Cho, who took the lives of 32 people at Virginia Tech, and Steven Kazmierczak, a former student at Northern Illinois University who killed five people when he attacked the campus. There is an analysis of psychologist Bernard Rimland's 2008 book *Dyslogic Syndrome,* which disputes the notion that bad or ineffective parenting is to blame for troubled or disobedient children and places the blame on bad diets instead. A *Current Issues in Crime* feature titled "Teenage Behavior: Is it the Brain?" reviews new brain research that is shedding light on some of the reasons why so much conflict exists between parents and teens. There is a new section on John Bowlby's attachment theory, which holds that the ability to form an emotional bond to another person has important psychological implications that persist across the life span. Another *Current Issues in Crime* feature updates research on violence in the media and its effect on human behavior.

Chapter 6, *Social Structure Theory,* contains new information on the MS-13 gang, which originally formed as a means of self-protection. (The name is made up of three elements: *mara,* Spanish for "posse" or gang, *salvatruchas,* slang for being alert and ready to take action, and 13, a reference to the gang's beginnings on 13th Street in Los Angeles.) There is updated information on poverty in the United States and its impact on children and minority group members. Today, almost 25 percent of African Americans and 22 percent of Latino Americans still live in poverty, compared to less than 10 percent of whites. A *Race, Culture, Gender, and Criminology* feature called "More than Just Race" updates the work of William Julius Wilson, one of the nation's most prominent sociologists, with analysis of his most recent work, *More than Just Race: Being Black and Poor in the Inner City.*

Chapter 7, *Social Process Theories,* begins with the continuing saga of Genarlow Wilson, a teenager who was labeled a sexual predator and sent to prison but was later released when those in power decided that he was not really a felon and that the law was not intended to apply to his offense. A *Current Issues in Crime* feature titled "Family Functioning and Crime" reviews the work of Rand Conger, one of the nation's leading experts on family life. Recent research on peers and delinquency and the association of young offenders with friendship groups is reviewed. New evidence suggests that most juvenile offenses are committed by individuals acting alone and that group offending, when it does occur, is merely incidental and of little importance in explaining the onset of delinquency, a finding that supports Hirschi's social bond theory.

Chapter 8, *Social Conflict and Critical Criminology,* is introduced by a vignette on the Sri Lankan government's civil rights abuses in its war against the Tamil Tiger rebel group. There is a major new section on state (organized) crime—criminal acts committed by state officials, both elected and appointed, while holding their jobs as government representatives. Within this section are discussions of political corruption, illegal domestic surveillance, human rights violations, state–corporate crime, and state violence. A *Current Issues in Crime* feature titled "Torturing Terror Suspects" looks at the use of torture to gain information from suspected political criminals. There are new sections on restorative justice, including A *Policy and Practice in Criminology* feature on the Victim Offender Reconciliation Program (VORP) of Denver, Colorado.

Chapter 9, *Developmental Theories: Life-Course and Latent Trait,* opens with a vignette on the life and times of the outlaw Jesse James, a true folk hero. Loved by the "little people," James remained an active outlaw until April 3, 1882. How did his career develop? And can we identify turning points that led him to a life of crime? A *Profiles in Crime* feature on the Xbox killers covers the career of Troy Victorino and his friends Robert Cannon, Jerone Hunter, and Michael Salas, who committed one of the most brutal crimes in American history. A *Current Issues in Crime* feature called "Love, Sex, Marriage, and Crime" delves into the effect of romance on crime. According to developmental theory, romance helps neutralize crime. Does love really work wonders? Another *Current Issues in Crime* feature, "Self-Control and Drug Dealing," probes the motives for getting involved in drug dealing, a crime that seems to reflect business enterprise and cunning, rather than impulsivity and lack of self-control.

Chapter 10, *Violent Crime: Personal and Political,* updates the data on various forms of common-law violence: rape, murder, assault, and robbery. A new *Race, Culture, Gender, and Criminology* feature titled "The Honor Killing of Women and Girls" discusses culture and violence. There is new information on date rape and hate crimes. The material on terrorism has been reorganized and updated.

Chapter 11, *Property Crimes,* begins with the story of William M. V. Kingsland, an urbane upper-class gentleman, intellectual, and art expert who, after his death, was found to have been a chronic art thief who was able to amass a collection worth millions. There are new sections on cargo thieves, professional criminals who work in highly organized groups, targeting specific items and employing "specialists" who bring different sets of criminal skills to the table when they hijack cargo shipments. Another section introduces car cloning, a new form of professional auto theft that involves stealing a luxury car and then substituting the registration of a vehicle of the exact same make and model (and even the same color) as the stolen one. There is an exhibit on check fraud schemes. A new section on third-party fraud discusses schemes in which the "victim" is a third party, such as an insurance company that is forced to pay false claims.

Chapter 12, *Enterprise Crime: White-Collar Crime, Cyber Crime, and Organized Crime,* begins with a new vignette on an international child pornography ring that originated in Australia and recruited pornographers from all over the world. The chapter now discusses contract frauds that tempt people to sign long-term agreements without informing them that the small print included in the sales contract obligates them to purchase high-priced services they did not really want in the first place. A new *Profiles in Crime* feature covers the multibillion-dollar stock market fraud committed by businessman Bernard Madoff, and a *Current Issues in Crime* feature addresses the subprime mortgage scandal. There is a review of the case of Wayne Cresap, a Louisiana judge who was charged with accepting bribes from individuals who wanted to influence his bail decision making. The section on cyber crime examines the case of Lori Drew, a Missouri woman who perpetrated a MySpace hoax on a teenage neighbor who later committed suicide. The text now discusses the illegal sale of controlled substances, mostly stimulants and depressants, via Internet websites.

Chapter 13, *Public Order Crimes,* begins with a vignette on the Emperor's Club and one of its clients, New York's hard-charging Governor Eliot Spitzer, who was forced to resign when word got out that he was seeing prostitutes. A new section on social harm points out the irony that 500,000 deaths in the United States each year can be linked to the consumption of tobacco and alcohol, substances it is perfectly legal for adults to sell and use. The material on moral crusades has been expanded, and there is discussion of antismut campaigns that target books considered too "racy" or controversial to be suitable for a public school library. A new section examines the "moral crusade" aimed at preventing the legalization of same-sex marriage. There is a new section on the international sex trade and a *Race, Culture, Gender, and Criminology* feature titled "International Human Trafficking." Among the new research discussed is a recent longitudinal analysis by Cesar Rebellon and Karen Van Gundy, which found evidence that marijuana users are up to five times more likely than nonusers to escalate their drug abuse and try cocaine and heroin.

Chapter 14, *The Criminal Justice System,* begins with the story of Savana Redding, a 13-year-old eighth-grade honor student who was subjected to a strip search after being accused of possessing prescription-strength ibuprofen. The ruling in this case limited the ability of school officials to search students. The newest data on the size, cost, and scope of criminal justice is presented. A *Profiles in Crime* titled "Canine Cruelty" shows that NFL quarterback Michael Vick is not

alone in his involvement with dog fighting. Detailed analysis of the correctional population is included. Both the jail and prison populations have steadily grown despite a reduction in the crime rate, probably because the proportion of those convicted who are sentenced to prison has been increasing, along with the lengths of criminal sentences.

Features

This text contains various pedagogical elements designed to help students analyze material in greater depth and also link it to other material in the book:

▶ **Fact or Fiction?** There are numbers of myths and legends about crime and criminology. And some widely held beliefs have turned out to be false and misleading myths. Can we tell what is fact from what is merely fiction? At the beginning of each chapter, a set of statements appears describing popular beliefs about crime, criminals, law, and justice. Then, throughout the chapter, these statements are revisited in order to confirm the accurate ones and set students straight about the others. For example, many people believe that immigrants commit a lot of crime. Is that true? Find out in Chapter 2.

▶ **Current Issues in Crime** boxed inserts review important issues in criminology. For example, in Chapter 2, the feature "Explaining Trends in Crime Rates" discusses the social and political factors that cause crime rates to rise and fall.

▶ **Policy and Practice in Criminology** boxes show how criminological ideas and research can be put into action. For example, a *Policy and Practice in Criminology* feature in Chapter 7 discusses Head Start, probably the best-known effort to help youths in the lower socioeconomic class receive effective socialization and, in so doing, reduce their potential for future criminality.

▶ **Race, Culture, Gender, and Criminology** boxes cover issues related to racial, cultural, and sexual diversity. In Chapter 6, for example, the feature "More Than Just Race" discusses the work and thought of William Julius Wilson, one of the nation's leading sociologists.

All of these boxes are accompanied by critical thinking questions. In addition to these elements, the text also includes other helpful features:

▶ **Profiles in Crime** (new in this edition) present students with actual crimes that help illustrate positions or views discussed in the chapter. For example, a Chapter feature titled "Crime of the Century: Bernard L. Madoff Investment Securities, LLC" examines the greatest securities fraud in U.S. history.

▶ **Connections** are brief inserts that help link the material to other topics addressed in the book. For example, a Connections box in Chapter 11 shows how efforts to control theft offenses are linked to the choice theory of crime discussed in Chapter 4.

▶ **Checkpoints** appear at the end of each major section throughout each chapter. They review the key concepts presented in that section to reinforce the chapter learning objectives.

▶ **Chapter Outlines**

▶ **Chapter Learning Objectives**. Each chapter begins with a list of key learning objectives that correspond to the most important sections and issues contained within the material.

▶ A **running glossary** in the margins ensures that students understand words and concepts as they are introduced.

▶ A **Thinking Like a Criminologist** section at the end of each chapter presents challenging questions or issues that students must answer or confront by drawing on their knowledge of criminology. Applying the information they have learned in the text will help students begin to "think like criminologists."

▶ An end of chapter **Summary** revisits the opening chapter learning objectives and links them directly to the material covered in the text.

▶ Each chapter ends with a list of **Key Terms,** followed by **Critical Thinking Questions,** which help develop students' analytical abilities.

Supplements

An extensive package of supplemental aids is available for instructor and student use with this edition of *Criminology: The Core*. Supplements are available to qualified adopters. Please consult your local sales representative for details.

FOR THE INSTRUCTOR

Instructor's Edition Designed just for instructors, the Instructor's Edition includes a visual walk-through that illustrates the key pedagogical features of the text, as well as the media and supplements that accompany it. Use this handy tool to learn quickly about the many options this text provides to keep your class engaging and informative.

Instructor's Resource Manual with Test Bank The updated and revised *Instructor's Resource Manual* for the fourth edition, prepared by Joanne Ziembo-Vogl of Grand Valley State University, provides detailed outlines, key terms and concepts, discussion topics and student activities, and critical thinking questions that will help you more effectively communicate with your students, while allowing you to strengthen your coverage of course material.

PowerLecture This instructor resource includes Microsoft® PowerPoint® lecture slides with graphics from the text, making it easy for you to assemble, edit, publish, and present lectures customized for your course.

PowerPoint Slides These handy Microsoft PowerPoint slides, which outline the chapters of the main text in a classroom-ready presentation, will help you in making your lectures engaging and in reaching your visually oriented students. The presentations are available for download on the password-protected website and can also be obtained by emailing your local Cengage Learning representative.

eBank Lesson Plans The Lesson Plans, created by Aaron Peeks of Elon University, bring accessible, masterful suggestions to every lesson. The Lesson Plans include sample syllabi, learning objectives, lecture notes, discussion topics, in-class activities, a detailed lecture outline, and assignments. Lesson Plans are available on the PowerLecture resource and the instructor website, or you can access them by emailing your local representative and asking for a download of the eBank files.

WebTutor™ Jumpstart your course with customizable, rich, text-specific content within your Course Management System. Whether you want to Web-enable your class or put an entire course online, WebTutor™ delivers. WebTutor™ offers a wide array of resources, including media assets, test bank, practice quizzes, and additional study aids. Visit webtutor.cengage.com to learn more.

Classroom Activities for Criminal Justice This valuable booklet, which is available to adopters of any Wadsworth criminal justice text, offers instructors the best of the best in criminal justice classroom activities. Containing both tried-and-true favorites and exciting new projects, its activities are drawn from across the spectrum of criminal justice subjects (including introduction to criminal justice, criminology, corrections, criminal law, policing, and juvenile justice) and can be customized to fit any course. Novice and seasoned instructors alike will find this booklet a powerful tool to stimulate classroom engagement.

The Wadsworth Criminal Justice Resource Center, www.cengage.com/criminaljustice Designed with the instructor in mind, this website provides information about Wadsworth's technology and teaching solutions, as well as several features created specifically for today's criminal justice student. Supreme Court updates, timelines, and hot-topic polling can all be used to supplement in-class assignments and discussions. You'll also find a wealth of links to careers and news in criminal justice, book-specific sites, and much more.

FOR THE STUDENT

Companion Website, www.cengage.com/criminaljustice/siegel The new companion website provides many chapter-specific resources, including chapter outlines, learning objectives, glossary, flash cards, crossword puzzles, and tutorial quizzing.

Criminal Justice Media Library This engaging resource provides students with more than 300 ways to investigate current topics, career choices, and critical concepts.

Study Guide An extensive student guide has been developed for this edition by Bernadette Holmes of Norfolk State University. Because students learn in different ways, the Study Guide includes a variety of pedagogical aids that will help them do their best, as well as integrated art and figures from the main text. Each text chapter is outlined and summarized, major terms and figures are defined, and self-tests are provided for review.

Handbook of Selected Supreme Court Cases, Third Edition This supplementary handbook covers nearly 40 landmark cases, each of which includes a full case citation, an introduction, a summary from WestLaw, excerpts from the case, and the decision. The updated edition includes *Hamdi v. Rumsfeld*, *Roper v. Simmons*, *Ring v. Arizona*, *Atkins v. Virginia*, *Illinois v. Caballes*, and much more.

CLeBook CLeBook enables students to access Cengage Learning textbooks in an easy-to-use online format. Highlight, take notes, bookmark, search your text, and (in some titles) link directly into multimedia. CLeBook combines the best aspects of paper books and ebooks in one package.

Acknowledgments

The preparation of this book would not have been possible without the aid of my colleagues who helped by reviewing the previous editions and gave me important suggestions for improvement.

REVIEWERS FOR THE FOURTH EDITION

Yvonne Downs, Hibert College
Michael Hallett, University of North Florida

Monica Jayroe, Faulkner University
Charles Ochie, Albany State University
Kay Kei-Ho Pih, California State University Northridge

REVIEWERS OF PREVIOUS EDITIONS

John Broderick, Stonehill College
Stephen J. Brodt, Ball State University
Doris Chu, Arkansas State University
Dana C. De Witt, Chadron State College
Dorinda L. Dowis, Columbus State University
Yvonne Downs, Hibert College
Sandra Emory, University of New Mexico
Dorothy M. Goldsborough, Chaminade University
Robert G. Hewitt, Edison Community College
Catherine F. Lavery, Sacred Heart University
Danielle Liautaud-Watkins, William Paterson University
Larry A. Long, Pioneer Pacific College
Heather Melton, University of Utah
Adam Rafalovich, Texas Technology University
Ronald Sopenhoff, Brookdale Community College
Mark A. Stelter, Montgomery College
Tom Tomlinson, Western Illinois University
Matt Vetter, Saint Mary's University
Scott Wagner, Columbus State Community College
Jay R. Williams, Duke University

My colleagues at Cengage Learning have done their typically outstanding job of aiding me in the preparation of this text and putting up with my yearly angst. Carolyn Henderson Meier, my scintillating editor, helped guide this project from start to finish. Shelley Murphy, que es fabuloso y fantástico, is a terrific developmental editor I cannot live without. My BFF Linda Rill did her usual outstanding job on photo research. Aaron Downey, the book's production editor, was professional, helpful, and kind. I really appreciate the help of Connie Day, a wonderful copyeditor. The sensational Christy Frame is an extraordinary production manager, and the incomparable Michelle Williams is my favorite marketing manager.

Larry Siegel
Bedford, New Hampshire

Criminology
The Core

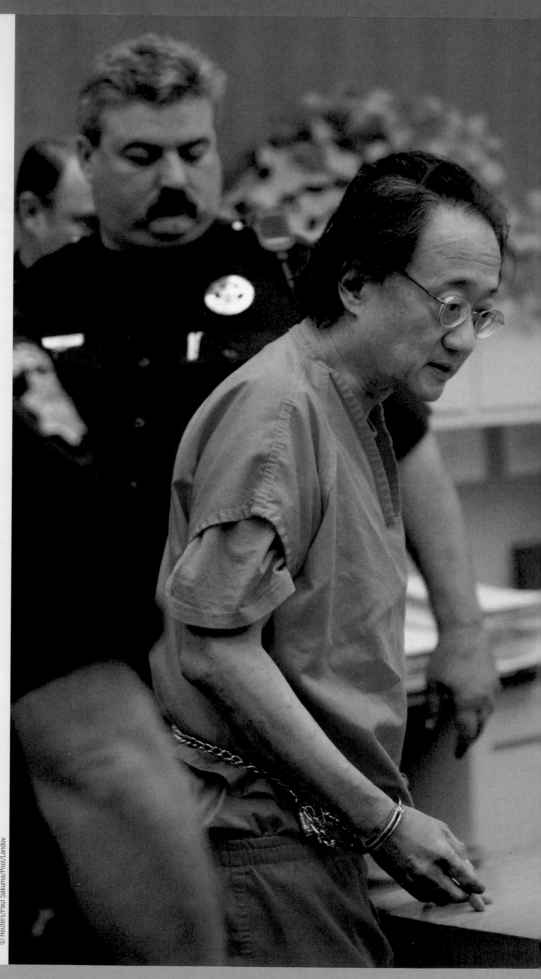

Chapter Outline

Crime and Criminology 1

On May 7, 2009, in what has become an all too familiar occurrence, businessman Norman Hsu pleaded guilty to ten counts of mail and wire fraud stemming from his role in an investment fraud scheme that defrauded investors across the United States. Hsu was the managing director of two companies, Components Ltd. and Next Components Ltd., that solicited investments by promising guaranteed short-term high returns. The companies would supposedly generate funds to pay those attractive returns by providing short-term financing to other businesses. For a time, investors were paid interest and returned principal as promised. As their trust grew, investors agreed to keep their money with the company and often recruited friends to invest with Hsu. In reality, Hsu was running what is referred to as a Ponzi scheme: He returned money to earlier investors with money received from subsequent investors. From 2000 through August 2007, Hsu convinced victims to invest at least $60 million in his fraudulent scheme. In the end, after making some payments intended to perpetuate the scheme, Hsu swindled his victims out of at least $20 million. Hsu's crimes were particularly disturbing because he mingled his business activities with his role as a major fundraiser for the Democratic Party; for example, he raised over $100,000 for Hillary Rodham Clinton's 2008 presidential campaign. Investigations into his activities revealed that he had a long history of business frauds extending back more than 20 years.[1]

Fact or Fiction?

▶ Sex offender registration lists help deter potential offenders and reduce the incidence of child molestation.

▶ Domestic violence is abnormal. Wife abusers must have abnormal brains.

▶ Terrorists are disturbed, angry people, many of whom are psychopaths.

▶ The checks and balances in the U.S. court system prevent innocent people from (a) being convicted and (b) receiving the death penalty.

▶ Criminals and victims are two totally different types of people.

▶ A person can be convicted of a crime for possessing a sexually explicit line drawing of a child.

Chapter Objectives

1. Understand what is meant by the "field of criminology."
2. Be familiar with the various elements of the criminological enterprise.
3. Know the historical context of criminology.
4. Know the difference between crime and deviance.
5. Discuss the three different views of the definition of crime.
6. Know what is meant by the term "criminal law."
7. Discuss the different purposes of the criminal law.
8. Trace the development of criminal law.
9. Describe the difference between a felony and a misdemeanor.
10. Be familiar with the ethical issues in criminology.

CONNECTIONS
We will discuss the crimes of Madoff, Lay, Skilling, and Fastow in Chapter 12 when we cover business-related enterprise crimes. Their crimes cost investors and taxpayers billions.

The fraud that Norman Hsu perpetrated, though serious, pales in comparison to similar multi-billion-dollar schemes of investment managers such as Bernard Madoff and of businessmen such as Kenneth Lay, Jeffrey Skilling, and Andrew Fastow. Enron, at one time the tenth largest company in America, is now bankrupt because of their corrupt business practices.

These and similar incidents show that today, people in positions of power have the capability of illegally obtaining not just millions but billions of dollars from people around the globe. The reach of crime has become truly international, creating new challenges for law enforcement authorities. These cases have captured headlines around the globe, have raised fascinating questions about crime and its control, and have spurred interest in **criminology**, an academic discipline that uses the scientific method to study the nature, extent, cause, and control of criminal behavior. Unlike political figures and media commentators, whose opinions about crime may be colored by personal experiences, biases, and election concerns, criminologists remain objective as they study crime and its consequences.[2]

Criminology is an **interdisciplinary** science. Criminologists hold degrees in a variety of diverse fields—most commonly sociology, but also **criminal justice**, political science, psychology, economics, engineering, and the natural sciences. For most of the twentieth century, the majority of criminologists were trained in sociology, but today criminology can be viewed as an independent approach to the study of criminal behavior, with its own literature, scholarly journals, and specialized graduate programs. How this field developed, its major components, and its relationship to criminal law and deviance are among the topics discussed in this chapter.

What Criminologists Do: The Criminological Enterprise

Criminology is a fascinating field, encompassing a wide variety of topics that have both practical application and theoretical importance: How can substance abuse rates be reduced? Does viewing violence in the media cause people to commit crime? Can punishment reduce crime? Criminologists bring to their field a wide variety of skills, education, and experience that enhance their primary professional role: applying the scientific method to the study and analysis of crime and criminal behavior.[3]

As is the case in other social sciences, several subareas exist within the broader arena of criminology. Taken together, these subareas make up the **criminological enterprise**. Criminologists may specialize in one of them in the same way in which psychologists might specialize in child development, perception, personality, psychopathology, or social psychology.

CRIMINAL STATISTICS/CRIME MEASUREMENT

The subarea of criminal statistics/crime measurement involves calculating the amounts and trends of criminal activity: How much crime occurs annually? Who commits it? When and where does it occur? Which crimes are the most serious?

Criminologists interested in computing criminal statistics focus on creating **valid** and **reliable measures** of criminal behavior:

▶ To analyze the activities of police and court agencies, they formulate techniques for collecting and analyzing institutional records and activities.
▶ To measure criminal activity not reported to the police by victims, they develop survey instruments that estimate the percentage of people who commit crimes but escape detection by the justice system.
▶ To identify the victims of crime, they create surveys designed to have victims report loss and injury that may not have been reported to the police.

criminology
The scientific study of the nature, extent, cause, and control of criminal behavior.

interdisciplinary
Involving two or more academic fields.

criminal justice
System made up of the agencies of social control, such as police departments, the courts, and correctional institutions, that handle criminal offenders.

criminological enterprise
The various subareas included within the scholarly discipline of criminology, which, taken as a whole, define the field of study.

valid measure
A measure that actually measures what it purports to measure; a measure that is factual.

reliable measure
A measure that produces consistent results from one measurement to another.

▶ To test theories (for example, the theory that income inequality produces high crime rates), they create databases that make it possible to investigate the relationship between an independent variable (such as percentage of population living in poverty) and a dependent variable (such as neighborhood violent crime rates).

Without valid and reliable measures of criminal behavior, efforts to conduct research on crime and formulate criminological theories would be futile. The development of criminal statistics and what they tell us about patterns and trends in the crime rate will be discussed in Chapter 2.

SOCIOLOGY OF LAW / LAW AND SOCIETY / SOCIO-LEGAL STUDIES

Sociology of law / law and society / socio-legal studies is a subarea of criminology concerned with the role that social forces play in shaping criminal law and the role of criminal law in shaping society. Criminologists interested in socio-legal studies might investigate the history of legal thought in an effort to understand how criminal acts (such as theft, rape, and murder) evolved into their present form.

Criminologists may use their research skills to assess the effects of a proposed legal change. Take, for instance, the crime of obscenity. Typically, there is no uniform standard of what is considered obscene; material that to some people is lewd and offensive is, to others, a work of art. How far should the law go in curbing the production and distribution of "adult" films and literature? Criminologists might conduct research aimed at determining the effect the proposed law will have on curbing access to obscene material such as "kiddie porn." Other relevant research issues might include analysis of the harmful effects of viewing pornography: Are people who view pornography more likely than others to commit violent crime? The answers to such questions may one day shape the direction of legislation controlling sexual content on the Internet. In the accompanying Policy & Practice feature, criminological research on a similar policy issue—sex offender registration—is discussed in some detail.

DEVELOPING THEORIES OF CRIME CAUSATION

Criminologists also explore the cause of crime. Some who have a psychological orientation view crime as a function of personality, development, social learning, or cognition. Others investigate the biological correlates of antisocial behavior and study the biochemical, genetic, and neurological linkages to crime. Those with a sociological orientation look at the social forces producing criminal behavior, including neighborhood conditions, poverty, socialization, and group interaction.

New York City Police Department Sergeant Rafi Ovanessian checks the contents of a commuter's backpack as he goes into the subway at 96th Street on October 6, 2005, just after New York authorities received a specific threat of a terrorist attack. Four years later on September 19, 2009, law enforcement agents arrested 24-year-old Najibullah Zazi of Denver, Colorado, the alleged ringleader of another plot to bomb the New York subway system. What motivates terrorists to take such extreme and destructive action? Some criminologists focus on a specific crime problem, such as terrorism, in order to understand its nature and extent and to help plan programs that can control or eliminate its occurrence.

Fact or Fiction?

Sex offender registration lists help deter potential offenders and reduce the incidence of child molestation.

Fiction. Research indicates that registration has little effect on either offenders or rates of child molesting.

Criminologists also evaluate the impact that new laws have had on society after they have been in effect for a while. Take the practice of sex offender registration, which requires convicted sex offenders to register with local law enforcement agencies whenever they move into a community. (These provisions are often called Megan's Laws, in memory of 7-year-old Megan Kanka. Megan was killed in 1994 by sex offender Jesse Timmendequas, who had moved unannounced into her New Jersey neighborhood. We will revisit this case in Chapter 3 in the Profiles in Crime feature on page 78.) Megan's Laws require law enforcement authorities to make information available to the public about registered sex offenders, including the offender's name, picture, address, incarceration date, and nature of

To answer this question, criminologists Kristen Zgoba and Karen Bachar recently (2009) conducted an in-depth study of the effectiveness of the New Jersey registration law and found that, although it was maintained at great cost to the state, the system did not produce effective results. On the one hand, sex offense rates in New Jersey were in steep decline before the system was installed, and the rate of decline actually slowed down after 1995 when the law took effect. The study showed that the greatest rate of decline in sex offending occurred prior to the passage and implementation of Megan's Law. Zgoba and Bachar also found that the passage and implementation of Megan's Law did not reduce the number of rearrests for sex offenses, nor did it have any demonstrable effect on the time between when sex offenders were released

Policy and Practice in Criminology Should Sex Offenders Be Registered?

crime. The information can be published in newspapers or put on a sex offender website.

In *Connecticut Dept. of Public Safety v. Doe* (2003), the U.S. Supreme Court upheld the legality of sex offender registration when it ruled that persons convicted of sexual offenses may be required to register with a state's Department of Public Safety and may then be listed on a sex offender registry that contains registrants' names, addresses, photographs, and descriptions and can be accessed on the Internet. In a 9–0 opinion upholding the plan, the Court reasoned that, because these defendants had been convicted of a sex offense, disclosing their names on the registry without a hearing did not violate their right to due process.

Thus sex offender registration laws have been ruled constitutional, are pervasive (they are used in all 50 states), and appeal to politicians who may be swayed by media crusades against child molesters (such as "To Catch a Predator" on *Dateline NBC*), and appease the public's desire to "do something" about child predators. But do they actually work? Does registration deter offenders from committing further sex offenses and reduce the incidence of predatory acts against children?

from prison and the time they were rearrested for any new offense, such as a drug offense, theft, or another sex offense.

Zgoba and Bachar's results can be used to rethink legal changes such as sex offender registration. Rather than deterring crime, such laws may merely cause sex offenders to be more cautious, while giving parents a false sense of security. For example, sex offenders may target victims in other states or in communities where they do not live and parents are less cautious.

CRITICAL THINKING

1. Considering the findings of Zgoba and Bachar, would you advocate abandoning sex offender registration laws because they are ineffective? Or might there be other reasons to keep them active?
2. What other laws do you think should be the topic of careful scientific inquiry to see whether they actually work as advertised?

SOURCES: *Connecticut Dept. of Public Safety v. Doe*, 538 U.S. 1 (2003); Kristen Zgoba & Karen Bachar, "Sex Offender Registration and Notification: Research Finds Limited Effects in New Jersey," National Institute of Justice, April 2009, www.ncjrs.gov/pdffiles1/nij/225402.pdf.

Fact or Fiction?

Domestic violence is abnormal. Wife abusers must have abnormal brains.

Fact. Research suggests that wife beaters may have an abnormal brain structure that predisposes them to respond to any provocation with violence.

Criminologists may use innovative methods to test theory. For example, some criminologists believe that the root cause of crime can be linked to an abnormal biological state or condition that predisposes people to react in an aggressive, antisocial manner to environmental stimuli that might have little effect on people without the biological irregularity. To test this view, three bio-criminoloigists—Tatia M. C. Lee, Siu-Ching Chan, and Adrian Raine—recently focused their attention on wife batterers to determine whether these criminals' aggressive behavior was a product of their neurological makeup, rather than resulting from some social condition such as unemployment. Because Lee and his associates suspected that neural makeup might be the true cause of domestic violence, they used a magnetic resonance imaging device (MRI) to assess brain function in 10 male batterers and 13 male controls matched to the batterers in terms of social conditions. Their brain scanning efforts revealed that compared to controls, batterers showed significantly higher neural hyperresponsivity to threat stimuli in a variety of regions of the brain. When these hypersensitive men experience even mild provocations from their spouses, they are hard-wired to respond with violence; in essence, some men have a neurobiological predisposition to spouse abuse.[4]

Pinning down "one true cause" of crime remains a difficult problem. Criminologists are still unsure why, given similar conditions, some people choose criminal solutions to their problems, whereas others conform to accepted social rules of behavior.

UNDERSTANDING AND DESCRIBING CRIMINAL BEHAVIOR

Another subarea of criminology involves research on specific criminal types and patterns: violent crime, theft crime, public order crime, organized crime, and so on. Numerous attempts have been made to describe and understand particular crime types. Marvin Wolfgang's 1958 study *Patterns in Criminal Homicide* is a landmark analysis of the nature of homicide and the relationship between victim and offender.[5] Edwin Sutherland's analysis of business-related offenses helped coin a new phrase, **white-collar crime**, to describe economic crime activities of the affluent.[6] Criminologists are constantly broadening the scope of their inquiry because new crimes and crime patterns are constantly emerging. Whereas 50 years ago they might have focused their attention on rape, murder, and burglary, they now may be looking at stalking, cyber crime, terrorism, and hate crimes. For example, a number of criminologists are now doing research on terrorism and the terrorist personality in order to discover why some young people are motivated to join terror groups. Among the findings:

▶ Mental illness is not a critical factor in explaining terrorist behavior. Also, most terrorists are not "psychopaths."

▶ There is no "terrorist personality," nor is there any accurate profile—psychological or otherwise—of the terrorist.

▶ Histories of childhood abuse and trauma and themes of perceived injustice and humiliation often are prominent in terrorist biographies, but these elements do not really help to explain terrorism.[7]

PENOLOGY: PUNISHMENT, SANCTIONS, AND CORRECTIONS

The study of **penology** involves the correction and sentencing of known criminal offenders. Some criminologists are advocates of **rehabilitation**; they direct their efforts at identifying effective treatment strategies for individuals convicted

© AP Images/Gerry Broome

On August 5, 2009, Sabrina Boyd, right, the wife of terrorism suspect Daniel Boyd, is shielded by her son Noah Boyd outside the Terry Sanford Federal Building and Courthouse following a hearing in Raleigh, North Carolina, during which a federal judge ordered Boyd, along with five other suspects, detained until trial. Daniel Boyd, who appeared to be an upstanding citizen of Willow Springs, North Carolina, was arrested on July 27, 2009, along with his 20-something sons Dylan and Zakariya for allegedly plotting "violent jihads." According to the indictment, Boyd spent the past three years stockpiling weapons in his rural home, recruiting and training would-be suicide bombers, and going on scouting trips to Gaza, Israel, Jordan, and Kosovo to map out potential attack sites. One job of criminologists is to understand the motivation of homegrown terrorism suspects.

white-collar crime
Illegal acts that capitalize on a person's status in the marketplace. White-collar crimes may include theft, embezzlement, fraud, market manipulation, restraint of trade, and false advertising.

The following subareas constitute the discipline of criminology.

Criminal Statistics	*Gathering valid crime data.* Devising new research methods; measuring crime patterns and trends.
Sociology of Law / Law and Society / Socio-Legal Studies	*Determining the origin of law.* Measuring the forces that can change laws and society.
Theory Construction	*Predicting individual behavior.* Understanding the cause of crime rates and trends.
Criminal Behavior Systems	*Determining the nature and cause of specific crime patterns.* Studying violence, theft, organized crime, white-collar crime, and public order crimes.
Penology: Punishment, Sanctions, and Corrections	*Studying the correction and control of criminal behavior.* Using the scientific method to assess the effectiveness of criminal sanctions designed to control crime through the application of criminal punishments.
Victimology	*Studying the nature and cause of victimization.* Aiding crime victims; understanding the nature and extent of victimization; developing theories of victimization risk.

Fact or Fiction?

Terrorists are disturbed, angry people, many of whom are psychopaths.

Fiction. Although many terrorists have experienced disturbed childhoods, most cannot be considered psychopaths suffering from a personality disturbance.

penology
Subarea of criminology that focuses on the correction and control of criminal offenders.

rehabilitation
Treatment of criminal offenders that is aimed at preventing future criminal behavior.

capital punishment
The execution of criminal offenders; the death penalty.

mandatory sentences
A statutory requirement that a certain penalty shall be carried out in all cases of conviction for a specified offense or series of offenses.

victimology
The study of the victim's role in criminal events.

of law violations. Others argue that crime can be prevented only through a strict policy of social control; they advocate such measures as **capital punishment** and **mandatory sentences**.

Criminologists interested in penology may help evaluate crime control programs in order to determine whether they are effective and how they will impact people's lives. When Samuel Gross and his colleagues sought to appraise the effect of the death penalty, they found that between 1989 and 2003, 340 people (327 men and 13 women) were exonerated after having served an average of more than 10 years each in prison. Almost half (144 people) were cleared by DNA evidence. Gross and his colleagues found that death row prisoners were more than 100 times more likely to be exonerated than the average imprisoned felon.[8] The Gross research illustrates how important it is to evaluate penal measures such as capital punishment in order to determine their effectiveness and reliability.

VICTIMOLOGY

Criminologists recognize that the victim plays a critical role in the criminal process and that the victim's behavior is often a key determinant of crime.[9] **Victimology** includes the following areas of interest:

▶ Using victim surveys to measure the nature and extent of criminal behavior and to calculate the actual costs of crime to victims
▶ Calculating probabilities of victimization risk
▶ Studying victim culpability in the precipitation of crime
▶ Designing services for crime victims, such as counseling and compensation programs

Criminologists who study victimization have uncovered some startling results. For one thing, criminals have been found to be at greater risk of victimization than noncriminals.[10] This finding indicates that rather than being passive targets who are "in the wrong place at the wrong time," victims may themselves be engaging in a high-risk behavior, such as crime, that increases their victimization risk and renders them vulnerable to crime.

The various elements of the criminological enterprise are summarized in Concept Summary 1.1. ▶ **Checkpoints**

A Brief History of Criminology

How did this field of study develop? What are the origins of criminology?

The scientific study of crime and criminality is a relatively recent development. During the Middle Ages (1200–1600), people who violated social norms or religious practices were believed to be witches or possessed by demons.[11] The use of cruel torture to extract confessions was common. Those convicted of violent or theft crimes suffered extremely harsh penalties, including whipping, branding, maiming, and execution.

CLASSICAL CRIMINOLOGY

By the mid-eighteenth century, social philosophers began to argue for a more rational approach to punishment. They sought to eliminate cruel public executions, which were designed to frighten people into obedience. Reformers stressed that the relationship between crime and punishment should be balanced and fair. This more moderate view of criminal sanctions can be traced to the writings of an Italian scholar, Cesare Beccaria (1738–1794), who was one of the first scholars to develop a systematic understanding of why people commit crime.

Beccaria believed in the concept of **utilitarianism**: In their behavior choices, people want to achieve pleasure and avoid pain. Crimes occur when the potential pleasure and reward from illegal acts outweigh the likely pains of punishment. To deter crime, punishment must be sufficient—no more, no less—to counterbalance criminal gain. Beccaria's famous theorem was that in order for punishment to be effective it must be public, prompt, necessary, the least possible in the given circumstances, proportionate, and dictated by law.[12]

The writings of Beccaria and his followers form the core of what today is referred to as **classical criminology**. As originally conceived in the eighteenth century, classical criminology theory had several basic elements:

- People have free will to choose criminal or lawful solutions to meet their needs or settle their problems.
- Crime is attractive when it promises great benefits with little effort.

This engraving from the year 1555 shows witches being burned in Derneburg, Germany. In more primitive times, people who violated the law might be considered witches or demons or assumed to be possessed by the devil.

Bibliothèque des Arts Décoratifs, Paris, France / Archives Charmet / The Bridgeman Art Library International

Checkpoints

▶ Criminologists engage in a variety of professional tasks.

▶ Those who work in criminal statistics create accurate measures of crime trends and patterns.

▶ Some criminologists study the origins and sociology of law.

▶ Theorists interested in criminal development seek insight into the causes of crime.

▶ Some criminologists try to understand and describe patterns and trends in particular criminal behaviors, such as serial murder or rape.

▶ Penologists evaluate the criminal justice system.

▶ Victimologists try to understand why some people become crime victims.

CONNECTIONS

Criminologists have sought to reconcile the differences among various visions of crime by combining or integrating them into unified but complex theories of criminality.

At their core, these integrated theories suggest that as people develop over the life course, a variety of factors—some social, others personal—shape their behavior patterns. These factors and their influence on human behavior are discussed in Chapter 9.

utilitarianism
The view that people's behavior is motivated by the pursuit of pleasure and the avoidance of pain.

classical criminology
Theoretical perspective suggesting that (1) people have free will to choose criminal or conventional behaviors; (2) people choose to commit crime for reasons of greed or personal need; and (3) crime can be controlled only by the fear of criminal sanctions.

CONNECTIONS

Many of us have grown up with movies showing criminals as "homicidal maniacs." Some may laugh, but *Freddy vs. Jason* was a big hit at the box office. See Chapter 5 for more on psychosis as a cause of crime.

positivism
The branch of social science that uses the scientific method of the natural sciences and suggests that human behavior is a product of social, biological, psychological, or economic forces.

scientific method
The use of verifiable principles and procedures for the systematic acquisition of knowledge. Typically involves formulating a problem, creating hypotheses, and collecting data, through observation and experiment, to verify the hypotheses.

▶ Crime may be controlled by the fear of punishment.
▶ Punishment that is or is perceived to be severe, certain, and swift will deter criminal behavior.

This classical perspective influenced judicial philosophy, and sentences were geared to be proportionate to the seriousness of the crime. Executions were still widely used but gradually came to be employed for only the most serious crimes. The catchphrase was "Let the punishment fit the crime."

POSITIVIST CRIMINOLOGY

During the nineteenth century, a new vision of the world challenged the validity of classical theory and presented an innovative way of looking at the causes of crime. The scientific method was beginning to take hold in Europe and North America. Scientists were using careful observation and analysis of natural phenomena to explain how the world worked. New discoveries were being made in biology, astronomy, and chemistry. If the scientific method could be applied to the study of nature, then why not use it to study human behavior?

Auguste Comte (1798–1857), considered the founder of sociology, argued that societies pass through stages that can be grouped on the basis of how people try to understand the world in which they live. People in primitive societies believe that inanimate objects have life (for example, the sun is a god); in later social stages, people embrace a rational, scientific view of the world. Comte called this the positive stage, and those who followed his writings became known as positivists.

Positivism has a number of elements:

▶ Use of the **scientific method** to conduct research. The scientific method is objective, universal, and culture-free.
▶ Predicting and explaining social phenomena in a logical manner. This means identifying necessary and sufficient conditions under which a phenomenon may or may not occur.
▶ Empirical verification. All beliefs or statements must be proved through empirical investigation guided by the scientific method. Such concepts as "God" and the "soul" cannot be measured empirically and therefore are not the subject of scientific inquiry; they remain a matter of faith.
▶ Science must be value-free and should not be influenced by the observer/scientist's biases or political point of view.

Early Criminological Positivism The earliest "scientific" studies examining human behavior now seem quaint and primitive. Physiognomists, such as J. K. Lavater (1741–1801), studied the facial features of criminals and found that the shape of the ears, nose, and eyes and the distances between them were associated with antisocial behavior. Phrenologists, such as Franz Joseph Gall (1758–1828) and Johann K. Spurzheim (1776–1832), studied the shape of the skull and bumps on the head and concluded that these physical attributes were linked to criminal behavior. They believed that the size of a brain area could be determined by inspecting the contours of the skull and, further, that the relative size of brain areas could be increased or decreased through exercise and self-discipline.[13] Although their techniques and theories are no longer applied or taken seriously, these efforts were an early attempt to use a scientific method to study human behaviors.

By the early nineteenth century, abnormality in the human mind was being linked to criminal behavior patterns. Phillipe Pinel, one of the founders of French psychiatry, coined the phrase *manie sans delire* to denote what eventually was referred to as a psychopathic personality.

In 1812 an American, Benjamin Rush, described patients with an "innate preternatural moral depravity."[14] English physician Henry Maudsley (1835–1918) believed that insanity and criminal behavior were strongly linked.[15] These early research efforts shifted attention to brain functioning and personality as the keys to criminal behavior.

Biological Determinism In Italy, Cesare Lombroso (1835–1909), known as the "father of criminology," began to study the cadavers of executed criminals in an effort to determine scientifically how criminals differed from noncriminals. Lombroso was soon convinced that serious and violent offenders had inherited criminal traits. These "born criminals" suffered from "atavistic anomalies"; physically, they were throwbacks to more primitive times when people were savages and were believed to have the enormous jaws and strong canine teeth common to carnivores that devour raw flesh. Lombroso's version of criminal anthropology was brought to the United States via articles and textbooks that adopted his ideas.[16] By the beginning of the twentieth century, American authors were discussing "the science of penology" and "the science of criminology."[17]

Although Lombroso's version of strict biological determinism is no longer taken seriously, some criminologists have recently linked crime and biological traits. Because they believe that social and environmental conditions also influence human behavior, the term **biosocial theory** has been coined to reflect the assumed link between physical and social traits and their influence on behavior.

SOCIOLOGICAL CRIMINOLOGY

At the same time that biological views were dominating criminology, another group of positivists were developing the field of sociology to study scientifically the major social changes taking place in nineteenth-century society. The foundations of **sociological criminology** can be traced to the work of pioneering sociologists L. A. J. (Adolphe) Quetelet (1796–1874) and (David) Émile Durkheim (1858–1917).[18]

Quetelet was a Belgian mathematician who (along with a Frenchman, Andre-Michel Guerry) used social statistics that were just being developed in Europe to investigate the influence of social factors on the propensity to commit crime. In addition to finding that age and sex had a strong influence on crime, Quetelet uncovered evidence that season, climate, population composition, and poverty were also related to criminality.[19] He was one of the first criminologists to link crime rates to alcohol consumption.[20]

According to Durkheim's vision of social positivism, crime is normal because it is virtually impossible to imagine a society in which criminal behavior is totally absent.[21] Durkheim believed that crime is inevitable because people are so different from one another and use such a wide variety of methods and types of behavior to meet their needs. Even if "real" crimes were eliminated, human weaknesses and petty vices would be elevated to the status of crimes. Durkheim suggested that crime can be useful—and occasionally even healthful—for society in that it paves the way for social change. To illustrate this concept, Durkheim offered the example of the Greek philosopher Socrates, who was considered a criminal and was put to death for corrupting the morals of youth simply because he expressed ideas that were different from what people believed at that time.

In *The Division of Labor in Society,* Durkheim wrote about the consequences of the shift from a small, rural society, which he labeled "mechanical," to the more modern "organic" society with a large urban population, division of labor, and personal isolation.[22] From the resulting structural changes flowed **anomie**, or norm and role confusion. An anomic society is in chaos, experiencing moral uncertainty and an accompanying loss of traditional values. People who suffer anomie may become confused and rebellious. Might the dawning of the "Internet age" create anomie in our own culture?

The Chicago School The primacy of sociological positivism was secured by research begun in the early twentieth century by Robert Ezra Park (1864–1944), Ernest W. Burgess (1886–1966), Louis Wirth (1897–1952), and their colleagues in the Sociology Department at the University of Chicago. The scholars who taught at this program created what is still referred to as the **Chicago School** in honor of their unique style of doing research.

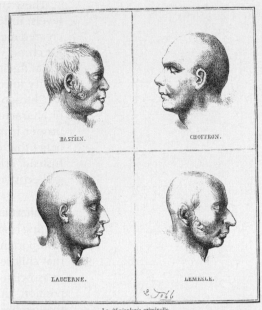

Early positivists believed the shape of the skull was a key determinant of behavior. These drawings from the nineteenth century illustrate "typical" criminally shaped heads.

biosocial theory
Approach to criminology that focuses on the interaction between biological and social factors as they are related to crime.

sociological criminology
Approach to criminology, based on the work of Quetelet and Durkheim, that focuses on the relationship between social factors and crime.

anomie
A lack of norms or clear social standards. Because of rapidly shifting moral values, the individual has few guides to what is socially acceptable.

Chicago School
Group of urban sociologists who studied the relationship between environmental conditions and crime.

These urban sociologists examined how neighborhood conditions, such as poverty levels, influenced crime rates. They found that social forces operating in urban areas created a crime-promoting environment; some neighborhoods were "natural areas" for crime.[23] In urban neighborhoods with high levels of poverty, the fabric of critical social institutions, such as the school and the family, came undone. Their traditional ability to control behavior was undermined, and the outcome was a high crime rate.

Chicago School sociologists argued that crime was not a function of personal traits or characteristics but, rather, a reaction to an environment that was inadequate for proper human relations and development. Thus, they challenged the widely held belief that criminals were biologically or psychologically impaired or morally inferior. Instead, crime was a social phenomenon and could be eradicated by improving social and economic conditions.

Socialization Views   During the 1930s and 1940s, another group of sociologists began conducting research that linked criminal behavior to the quality of an individual's relationship to important social processes, such as education, family life, and peer relations. They found that children who grew up in homes wracked by conflict, attended inadequate schools, or associated with deviant peers became exposed to forces that engendered crime. One position, championed by the preeminent American criminologist Edwin Sutherland, was that people learn criminal attitudes from older, more experienced law violators. Another view, developed by Chicago School sociologist Walter Reckless, was that crime occurs when children develop an inadequate self-image, which renders them incapable of controlling their own misbehavior. Both of these views linked criminality to the failure of **socialization**—the interactions people have with the various individuals, organizations, institutions, and processes of society that help them mature and develop.

CONFLICT CRIMINOLOGY

While most criminologists of the late nineteenth and early twentieth centuries embraced either the ecological view (stemming from Durkheim's theory) or the socialization view of crime, the writings of another social thinker, Karl Marx (1818–1883), had sown the seeds for a new approach in criminology.[24]

In his *Communist Manifesto* and other writings, Marx described the oppressive labor conditions prevalent during the rise of industrial capitalism. Marx was convinced that the character of every civilization is determined by its mode of production—the way its people develop and produce material goods. The most important relationship in industrial culture is between the owners of the means of production (the capitalist bourgeoisie) and the people who perform the labor (the proletariat). The economic system controls all facets of human life; consequently, people's lives revolve around the means of production. The exploitation of the working class, Marx believed, would eventually lead to class conflict and the end of the capitalist system.

Although these writings laid the foundation for a Marxist criminology, it was not until the social and political upheaval of the 1960s—fueled by the Vietnam War, the development of an antiestablishment counterculture movement, the civil rights movement, and the women's movement—that criminologists began to analyze the social conditions in the United States that promoted class conflict and crime. What emerged from this intellectual ferment was a **critical criminology** that indicted the economic system as producing the conditions that support a high crime rate. Critical criminologists have played a significant role in the field ever since.

DEVELOPMENTAL CRIMINOLOGY

In the 1940s and 1950s, Sheldon and Eleanor Glueck, a husband-and-wife team of criminologists and researchers at Harvard Law School, conducted numerous studies of delinquent and criminal behavior that profoundly influenced criminological theory. Their work integrated sociological, psychological, and economic elements into a complex developmental view of crime causation. Their most important research efforts followed the careers of known delinquents to determine what factors predicted

CONNECTIONS

Did your mother ever warn you about staying away from "bad neighborhoods" in the city? If she did, how valid were her concerns? To find out, go to Chapter 6 for a discussion of the structural conditions that cause crime.

socialization
Process of human development and enculturation. Socialization is influenced by key social processes and institutions.

conflict theory
The view that human behavior is shaped by interpersonal conflict and that those who maintain social power will use it to further their own ends.

critical criminology
The view that crime is a product of the capitalist system.

persistent offending; they also made extensive use of interviews and records in their elaborate comparisons of delinquents and nondelinquents.[25]

The Gluecks' research focused on early onset of delinquency as a harbinger of a criminal career: "[T]he deeper the roots of childhood maladjustment, the smaller the chance of adult adjustment."[26] They also noted the stability of offending careers: Children who are antisocial early in life are the most likely to continue their offending careers into adulthood.

The Gluecks identified a number of personal and social factors related to persistent offending, the most important of which was family relations. This factor was considered in terms of quality of discipline and emotional ties with parents. The adolescent raised in a large, single-parent family of limited economic means and educational achievement was the most vulnerable to delinquency.

The Gluecks did not restrict their analysis to social variables. When they measured such biological and psychological traits as body type, intelligence, and personality, they found that physical and mental factors also played a role in determining behavior. Children with low intelligence, who had a background of mental disease, and who had a powerful physique were the most likely to become persistent offenders.

In a photo taken on May 4, 1972, a youth shoves an unidentified girl as she tries to put on her coat and escape a group of boys who approached her on a bench in New York's Central Park. Her purse lies momentarily unprotected at left. She struck back at the youth and rushed to join friends nearby, ruffled but with herself and her property intact. Describe the life course of these kids as they emerged from adolescence into adulthood. What do you think has happened to them during the 35-plus years since this photograph was taken?

Thus the Gluecks' vision integrated biological, social, and psychological elements. It suggested that the initiation and continuity of a criminal career was a developmental process influenced by both internal and external situations, conditions, and circumstances. Their **developmental theory** model is still influential in the field today.

CONTEMPORARY CRIMINOLOGY

These various schools of criminology, developed over 200 years, have been constantly evolving.

▶ Classical theory has evolved into modern **rational choice theory**, which argues that criminals are rational decision makers: Before choosing to commit crime, criminals evaluate the benefits and costs of the contemplated criminal act; their choice is structured by the fear of punishment.

▶ Lombrosian biological positivism has evolved into contemporary biosocial and psychological **trait theory** views. Criminologists no longer believe that a single trait or inherited characteristic can explain crime, but some are convinced that biological and psychological traits interact with environmental factors to influence all human behavior, including criminality. Biological and psychological theorists study the association between criminal behavior and such factors as diet, hormonal makeup, personality, and intelligence.

▶ The original Chicago School sociological vision has transformed into a **social structure theory**, which maintains that the social environment directly controls criminal behavior. According to this view, people at the bottom of the social hierarchy, who cannot achieve success through conventional means, experience anomie, strain, failure, and frustration; they are the most likely to turn to criminal solutions to their problems.

▶ Some sociologists have adopted a social psychological orientation and now focus on upbringing socialization. These **social process theorists** believe that children learn to commit crime by interacting with, and modeling their behavior after, others whom they admire. Some criminal offenders are people whose life experiences have shattered their social bonds to society.

developmental theory
The view that criminality is a dynamic process, influenced by social experiences as well as individual characteristics.

rational choice theory
The view that crime is a function of a decision-making process in which the would-be offender weighs the potential costs and benefits of an illegal act.

trait theory
The view that criminality is a product of abnormal biological or psychological traits.

social structure theory
The view that disadvantaged economic class position is a primary cause of crime.

social process theory
The view that criminality is a function of people's interactions with various organizations, institutions, and processes in society.

The major perspectives of criminology focus on individual factors (biological, psychological, and choice theories); social factors (structural and process theories); political and economic factors (conflict theory); and multiple factors (developmental theory).

Classical/Choice Perspective	*Situational forces.* Crime is a function of free will and personal choice. Punishment is a deterrent to crime.
Biological/Psychological Perspective	*Internal forces.* Crime is a function of chemical, neurological, genetic, personality, intelligence, or mental traits.
Structural Perspective	*Ecological forces.* Crime rates are a function of neighborhood conditions, cultural forces, and norm conflict.
Process Perspective	*Socialization forces.* Crime is a function of upbringing, learning, and control. Peers, parents, and teachers influence behavior.
Conflict Perspective	*Economic and political forces.* Crime is a function of competition for limited resources and power. Class conflict produces crime.
Developmental Perspective	*Multiple forces.* Biological, social-psychological, economic, and political forces may combine to produce crime.

Checkpoints

▶ Criminology has had a long and rich history.

▶ The first criminologists believed that crime was a matter of free will. This outlook is referred to as classical criminology.

▶ In the nineteenth century, positivist criminologists began to use the scientific method to study crime. They were convinced that the cause of crime could be found in the individual offender.

▶ During the early twentieth century, sociological criminology was developed to explain the effect of the social environment on individual behavior.

▶ Critical criminologists attempted to explain how economic forces create crime.

▶ Developmental criminologists trace criminal careers over the life course.

▶ Contemporary criminology carries on and refines these traditions.

deviance
Behavior that departs from the social norm but is not necessarily criminal.

▶ Many criminologists still view social and political conflict as the root cause of crime. These **critical criminologists** believe that crime is related to the inherently unfair economic structure of the United States and other advanced capitalist countries.

▶ The Gluecks' pioneering research has influenced a new generation of developmental theorists. Their focus today is on the creation and maintenance of criminal careers over the life course.

Each of the major perspectives is summarized in Concept Summary 1.2.
▶ **Checkpoints**

Deviant or Criminal? How Criminologists Define Crime

Criminologists devote themselves to measuring, understanding, and controlling crime and deviance. How are these behaviors defined, and how do we distinguish between them?

Criminologists view deviant behavior as any action that departs from the social norms of society.[27] **Deviance** thus includes a broad spectrum of behaviors, ranging from the most socially harmful, such as rape and murder, to the relatively inoffensive, such as joining a religious cult or cross-dressing. A deviant act becomes a **crime** when it is deemed socially harmful or dangerous; it then will be specifically defined, prohibited, and punished under the criminal law.

Crime and deviance are often confused because not all crimes are deviant and not all deviant acts are illegal or criminal. For example, recreational drug use such as smoking marijuana may be a crime, but is it deviant? A significant percentage of the population has used recreational drugs (including some well-known politicians). To argue that all crimes are behaviors that depart from the norms of society is probably erroneous. Similarly, many deviant acts are not criminal, even though they may be shocking or depraved. A passerby who observes a person drowning is not legally required to jump in and render aid. Although the general public would probably condemn the person's behavior as callous, immoral, and deviant, no legal action could be taken because citizens are not required by law to effect rescues. In sum, many criminal acts, but not all, fall within the concept of deviance. Similarly, some deviant acts, but not all, are considered crimes.

In May 2006, U.S. Immigration and Customs Enforcement (ICE) intercepted a mail package coming into the United States from Japan and addressed to Christopher Handley, 39, of Glenwood, Iowa. Inside the package was obscene material, including books containing visual representations of the sexual abuse of children, specifically Japanese *manga* drawings of minor females being sexually abused by adult males and animals. Handley was indicted after U.S. Postal Inspectors searched his home and seized additional obscene drawings of the sexual abuse of children. On May 20, 2009, Handley pleaded guilty in Des Moines, Iowa, to possessing obscene visual representations of the sexual abuse of children; he faces a maximum of 15 years in prison, a maximum fine of $250,000, and a three-year term of supervised release.

What is interesting about the case is that Handley's crime involved possessing sexually explicit drawings that were not pictures of actual children but merely imaginary renderings. Given that no child was involved or harmed, is his behavior really criminal or merely deviant (though repulsive and repugnant), and therefore not subject to criminal punishment? Should Handley be protected by the First Amendment guarantee of freedom of speech because no real person was exploited or harmed by his actions? Regardless of your personal thoughts, Handley's behavior was in fact in violation of Title 18, United States Code, Section 1466A(b)(1), which prohibits the possession of any type of visual depiction, including a drawing, cartoon, sculpture, or painting, that depicts a minor engaging in sexually explicit conduct that is obscene. So according to current U.S. law his behavior was criminal and not merely deviant.

SOURCE: U.S. Department of Justice, "Iowa Man Pleads Guilty to Possessing Obscene Visual Representations of the Sexual Abuse of Children," May 20, 2009, http://omaha.fbi.gov/dojpressrel/2009/om052009a.htm

Criminologists are often concerned with the concept of deviance and its relationship to criminality. For example, when does sexually oriented material stop being merely erotic and suggestive (i.e., deviant) and become obscene and pornographic (i.e., criminal)? Can a clear line be drawn separating sexually oriented materials into two groups, one that is legally acceptable and a second that is considered depraved or obscene? And if such a line can be drawn, who gets to draw it? If an illegal act, such as viewing Internet pornography, becomes a norm, should society reevaluate its criminal status and let it become merely an unusual or deviant act? The shifting definition of deviant behavior is closely associated with our concepts of crime: Where should society draw the line between behavior that is considered merely deviant and unusual and behavior that is considered dangerous and criminal? The accompanying Profiles in Crime feature addresses this issue.

BECOMING DEVIANT

To understand the nature and purpose of criminal law, criminologists study both the process by which deviant acts are criminalized (become crimes) and, conversely, how criminal acts are **decriminalized** (that is, the penalties attached to them are reduced) and/or legalized.

In some instances, individuals, institutions, or government agencies mount a campaign aimed at convincing both the public and lawmakers that what was considered merely deviant behavior is actually dangerous and must be outlawed. During the 1930s, Harry Anslinger, then head of the Federal Bureau of Narcotics, used magazine articles, public appearances, and public testimony to sway public opinion about the dangers of marijuana, which up until that time had been legal to use and possess.[28] In testimony before the House Ways and Means Committee considering passage of the Marijuana Tax Act of 1938, Anslinger stated,

> In Florida a 21-year-old boy under the influence of this drug killed his parents and his brothers and sisters. The evidence showed that he had smoked marihuana. In Chicago recently two boys murdered a policeman while under the influence of

Fact or Fiction?

A person can be convicted of a crime for possessing a sexually explicit line drawing of a child.

Fact. It is against the law to possess kiddie porn, even if it is a rendering of an imaginary child.

critical criminologists
Members of a branch of criminology that focuses on the oppression of the poor, women, and minorities, thereby linking class conflict, sexism, and racism to crime rates. Critical criminologists examine how those who hold political and economic power shape the law to uphold their self-interests.

crime
An act, deemed socially harmful or dangerous, that is specifically defined, prohibited, and punished under the criminal law.

decriminalized
Having criminal penalties reduced rather than eliminated.

Concept Summary 1.3 Criminology, Criminal Justice, and Deviance

Criminology Criminology explores the etiology (origin), extent, and nature of crime in society. Criminologists are concerned with identifying the nature, extent, and cause of crime.	
Criminal Justice	The criminal justice system consists of the agencies of social control that handle criminal offenders. Criminal justice scholars describe, analyze, and explain operations of the agencies of justice, specifically the police departments, courts, and correctional facilities. They seek more effective methods of crime control and offender rehabilitation.
Overlapping Areas of Concern	Criminal justice experts cannot begin to design effective programs of crime prevention or rehabilitation without understanding the nature and cause of crime. They require accurate criminal statistics and data to test the effectiveness of crime control and prevention programs.
Deviance	Deviance consists of behavior that departs from social norms. Included within the broad spectrum of deviant acts are behaviors ranging from violent crimes to joining a nudist colony. Not all crimes are deviant or unusual acts, and not all deviant acts are illegal.
Overlapping Areas of Concern	Under what circumstances do deviant behaviors become crimes? When does sexually oriented material cross the line from merely suggestive to obscene and therefore illegal? If an illegal act becomes a norm, should society reevaluate its criminal status? There is still debate over the legalization and/or decriminalization of abortion, recreational drug use, possession of handguns, and assisted suicide.

CONNECTIONS

Some of the drugs considered highly dangerous today were once sold openly and considered medically beneficial. For example, the narcotic drug heroin, now considered extremely addicting and dangerous, was originally given its name in the mistaken belief that its pain-killing properties would prove "heroic" to medical patients. The history of drug and alcohol abuse and legalization efforts will be discussed further in Chapter 13.

marihuana. Not long ago we found a 15-year-old boy going insane because, the doctor told the enforcement officers, he thought the boy was smoking marihuana cigarettes. They traced the sale to some man who had been growing marihuana and selling it to these boys all under 15 years of age, on a playground there.[29]

As a result of Anslinger's efforts, a deviant behavior, marijuana use, became a criminal behavior, and previously law-abiding citizens were defined as criminal offenders. Today some national organizations, such as the Drug Policy Alliance, are committed to repealing draconian drug laws and undoing Anslinger's "moral crusade." They call for an end to the "war against drugs," which they believe has become overzealous in its effort to punish drug traffickers. In fact, they maintain, many of the problems the drug war purports to resolve are actually caused by the drug war itself. So-called "drug-related" crime is a direct result of drug prohibition's distortion of immutable laws of supply and demand. Public health problems such as HIV and hepatitis C are all exacerbated by zero tolerance laws that restrict access to clean needles. The drug war is not the promoter of family values that some would have us believe. Children of inmates are at risk of educational failure, joblessness, addiction, and delinquency. Drug abuse is bad, but the drug war is worse.[30]

In sum, criminologists are concerned with the concept of deviance and its relationship to criminality. The shifting definition of deviant behavior is closely associated with our concept of crime. The relationship among criminology, criminal justice, and deviance is illustrated in Concept Summary 1.3.

THE CONCEPT OF CRIME

Professional criminologists usually align themselves with one of several schools of thought, or perspectives. Each of these perspectives maintains its own view of what constitutes criminal behavior and what causes people to engage in criminality. A criminologist's choice of orientation or perspective depends, in part, on his or her definition of crime. The three most common concepts of crime used by criminologists are the consensus view, the conflict view, and the interactionist view.

CONSENSUS VIEW OF CRIME

According to the **consensus view**, crimes are behaviors that all elements of society consider repugnant. The rich and powerful as well as the poor and indigent are believed to agree on which behaviors are so repugnant that they should be outlawed and criminalized. Therefore, the **criminal law**—the written code that defines crimes and their punishments—reflects the values, beliefs, and opinions of society's mainstream. The term "consensus" implies general agreement among a majority of citizens on what behaviors should be prohibited by criminal law and hence be viewed as crimes.[31]

This approach to crime implies that it is a function of the beliefs, morality, and rules inherent in Western civilization. Ideally, the laws apply equally to all members of society, and their effects are not restricted to any single element of society.

CONFLICT VIEW OF CRIME

Although most practicing criminologists accept the consensus model of crime, others take a more political orientation toward its content. The **conflict view** depicts society as a collection of diverse groups—such as owners, workers, professionals, and students—who are in constant and continuing conflict. Groups able to assert their political power use the law and the criminal justice system to advance their economic and social position. Criminal laws, therefore, are viewed as created to protect the haves from the have-nots. Conflict criminologists often contrast the harsh penalties inflicted on the poor for their "street crimes" (burglary, robbery, and larceny) with the minor penalties the wealthy receive for their white-collar crimes (securities violations and other illegal business practices). Whereas the poor go to prison for minor law violations, the wealthy are given lenient sentences for even serious breaches of law.

INTERACTIONIST VIEW OF CRIME

According to the **interactionist view**, the definition of crime reflects the preferences and opinions of people who hold social power in a particular legal jurisdiction. These people use their influence to impose their definition of right and wrong on the rest of the population. They maintain their power by stigmatizing or labeling people who fall outside their definition of right and wrong. Criminals therefore are individuals that society labels as outcasts or deviants because they have violated social rules. In a classic statement, sociologist Howard Becker argued, "The deviant is one to whom that label has successfully been applied; deviant behavior is behavior people so label."[32] Crimes are outlawed behaviors because society defines them that way, not because they are inherently evil or immoral acts.

Interactionists see criminal law as conforming to the beliefs of "moral crusaders," or moral entrepreneurs, who use their influence to shape the legal process as they see fit.[33] Laws against pornography, prostitution, and drugs are believed to be motivated more by moral crusades than by capitalist sensibilities. Consequently, interactionists are concerned with shifting moral and legal standards.

A DEFINITION OF CRIME

Because of their diverse perspectives, criminologists have taken a variety of approaches in explaining crime's causes and suggesting methods for its control (see Concept Summary 1.4). Considering these differences, we can take elements from each school of thought to formulate an integrated definition of crime:

> "Crime" is a violation of societal rules of behavior as interpreted and expressed by the criminal law, which reflects public opinion, traditional values, and the viewpoint of people currently holding social and political power. Individuals who violate these rules are subject to sanctions by state authority, social stigma, and loss of status.

This definition combines the consensus view that the criminal law defines crimes, the conflict perspective's emphasis on political power and control, and the interactionist

consensus view
The belief that the majority of citizens in a society share common values and agree on what behaviors should be defined as criminal.

criminal law
The written code that defines crimes and their punishments.

conflict view
The belief that criminal behavior is defined by those in power in such a way as to protect and advance their own self-interest.

interactionist view
The belief that those with social power are able to impose their values on society as a whole, and these values then define criminal behavior.

The definition of crime affects how criminologists view the cause and control of illegal behavior and shapes their research orientation.

Consensus View	• The law defines crime. • Agreement exists on outlawed behavior. • Laws apply to all citizens equally.
Conflict View	• The law is a tool of the ruling class. • Crime is a politically defined concept. • "Real crimes" such as racism, sexism, and classism are not outlawed. • The law is used to control the underclass.
Interactionist View	• Moral entrepreneurs define crime. • Acts become crimes because society defines them that way. • Criminal labels are life-transforming events.

concept of stigma. Thus crime as defined here is a political, social, and economic function of modern life.

No matter which definition of crime we embrace, criminal behavior is tied to the criminal law. It is therefore important for all criminologists to have some understanding of the development of criminal law, its objectives, its elements, and how it evolves.

Crime and the Criminal Law

The concept of criminal law has been recognized for more than 3,000 years. Hammurabi (1792–1750 BC), the sixth king of Babylon, created the most famous set of written laws of the ancient world, known today as the **Code of Hammurabi**. Preserved on basalt rock columns, the code established a system of crime and punishment based on physical retaliation ("an eye for an eye"). The severity of punishment depended on class standing: If convicted of an unprovoked assault, a slave would be killed, whereas a freeman might lose a limb.

More familiar is the **Mosaic Code** of the Israelites (1200 BC). According to tradition, God entered into a covenant, or contract, with the tribes of Israel in which they agreed to obey his law (the 613 laws of the Old Testament, including the Ten Commandments), as presented to them by Moses, in return for God's special care and protection. The Mosaic Code is not only the foundation of Judeo-Christian moral teachings but also a basis for the U.S. legal system. Prohibitions against murder, theft, perjury, and adultery preceded, by several thousand years, the same laws found in the modern United States.

COMMON LAW

After the Norman conquest of England in 1066, royal judges began to travel throughout the land, holding court in each county several times a year. When court was in session, the royal administrator, or judge, would summon a number of citizens who would, on their oath, tell of the crimes and serious breaches of the peace that had occurred since the judge's last visit. The royal judge would then decide what to do in each case, using local custom and rules of conduct as his guide. Courts were bound to follow the law established in previous cases unless a higher authority, such as the king or the pope, overruled the law.

The present English system of law came into existence during the reign of Henry II (1154–1189), when royal judges began to publish their decisions in local cases. Judges began to use these written decisions as a basis for their decision making, and eventually

Code of Hammurabi
The first written criminal code, developed in Babylonia about 2000 BC.

Mosaic Code
The laws of the ancient Israelites, found in the Old Testament of the Judeo-Christian Bible.

a fixed body of legal rules and principles was established. If a new rule was successfully applied in a number of different cases, it would become a **precedent**. These precedents would then be commonly applied in all similar cases—hence the term **common law**. Crimes such as murder, burglary, arson, and rape are common-law crimes whose elements were initially defined by judges. They are referred to as *mala in se,* or inherently evil and depraved. When the situation required, the English Parliament enacted legislation to supplement the common law shaped by judges. Crimes defined by Parliament, which reflected existing social conditions, were referred to as *mala prohibitum*, or **statutory crimes**.

Before the American Revolution, the colonies, then under British rule, were subject to the common law. After the colonies acquired their independence, state legislatures standardized common-law crimes such as murder, burglary, arson, and rape by putting them into statutory form in criminal codes. As in England, whenever common law proved inadequate to deal with changing social and moral issues, the states and Congress supplemented it with legislative statutes, creating new elements in the various state and federal legal codes.

CONTEMPORARY CRIMINAL LAW

Criminal laws are now divided into felonies and misdemeanors. The distinction is based on seriousness: A **felony** is a serious offense, a **misdemeanor** a minor or petty crime. Crimes such as murder, rape, and burglary are felonies; they are punished with long prison sentences or even death. Crimes such as unarmed assault and battery, petty larceny, and disturbing the peace are misdemeanors; they are punished with a fine or a period of incarceration in a county jail.

Regardless of their classification, acts prohibited by the criminal law constitute behaviors considered unacceptable and impermissible by those in power. People who engage in these acts are eligible for severe sanctions. By outlawing these behaviors, the government expects to achieve a number of social goals (see Figure 1.1):

▶ *Enforcing social control.* Those who hold political power rely on criminal law to formally prohibit behaviors believed to threaten societal well-being or to challenge their authority. For example, U.S. criminal law incorporates centuries-old prohibitions against the following behaviors harmful to others: taking another person's possessions, physically harming another person, damaging another person's property, and cheating another person out of his or her possessions. Similarly, the law prevents actions that challenge the legitimacy of the government, such as planning its overthrow and collaborating with its enemies.

▶ *Discouraging revenge.* By punishing people who infringe on the rights, property, and freedom of others, the law shifts the burden of revenge from the individual to the state. As Oliver Wendell Holmes stated, this prevents "the greater evil of private retribution."[34] Although state retaliation may offend the sensibilities of many citizens, it is greatly preferable to a system in which people have to seek justice for themselves.

▶ *Expressing public opinion and morality.* Criminal law reflects constantly changing public opinions and moral values. *Mala in se* crimes, such as murder and forcible rape, are almost universally prohibited; however, the prohibition of legislatively created *mala prohibitum* crimes, such as traffic offenses and gambling violations, changes according to social conditions and attitudes. Criminal law is used to codify these changes.

▶ *Deterring criminal behavior.* Criminal law has a social control function. It can control, restrain, and direct human behavior through its sanctioning power. The threat of punishment associated with violating the law is designed to prevent crimes before they occur. During the Middle Ages, public executions drove this point home. Today, criminal law's impact is felt through news accounts of long prison sentences and an occasional execution.

Common law was created by English judges during the Middle Ages. It unified local legal practices into a national system of laws and punishments. Common law serves as the basis for the American legal system.

© A. C. Cooper Ltd., by permission of The Inner Temple, London

precedent
A rule derived from previous judicial decisions and applied to future cases; the basis of common law.

common law
Early English law, developed by judges, which became the standardized law of the land in England and eventually formed the basis of the criminal law in the United States.

statutory crimes
Crimes defined by legislative bodies in response to changing social conditions, public opinion, and custom.

felony
A serious offense that carries a penalty of imprisonment, usually for one year or more, and may entail loss of political rights.

misdemeanor
A minor crime usually punished by a short jail term and/or a fine.

Figure 1.1 Purposes of the Criminal Law

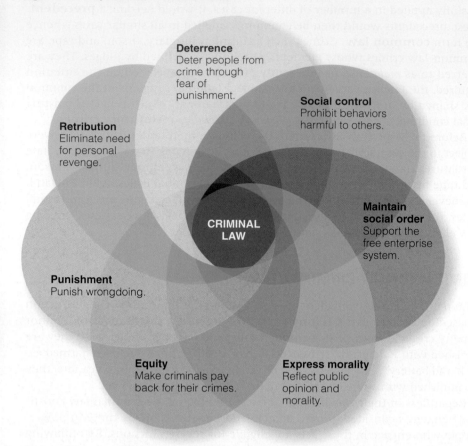

Deterrence
Deter people from crime through fear of punishment.

Social control
Prohibit behaviors harmful to others.

Retribution
Eliminate need for personal revenge.

Maintain social order
Support the free enterprise system.

CRIMINAL LAW

Punishment
Punish wrongdoing.

Equity
Make criminals pay back for their crimes.

Express morality
Reflect public opinion and morality.

▶ *Punishing wrongdoing.* The deterrent power of criminal law is tied to the authority it gives the state to sanction or punish offenders. Those who violate criminal law are subject to physical coercion and punishment.

▶ *Creating equity.* Criminals benefit from their misdeeds. People who violate business laws make huge profits from their illegal transactions; the drug dealer accumulates wealth because of his trafficking in illegal substances. Through fines, forfeiture, and other economic sanctions, the criminal law redistributes illegal gains back to society, thereby negating the criminal's unfair advantage.

▶ *Maintaining social order.* All legal systems are designed to support and maintain the boundaries of the social system they serve. In medieval England, the law protected the feudal system by defining an orderly system of property transfer and ownership. Laws in some socialist nations protect the primacy of the state by strictly curtailing profiteering and individual enterprise. Our own capitalist system is also supported and sustained by criminal law. In a sense, the content of criminal law is more a reflection of the needs of those who control the existing economic and political system than a representation of some idealized moral code.

THE EVOLUTION OF CRIMINAL LAW

The criminal law is constantly evolving in an effort to reflect social and economic conditions. Sometimes legal changes are prompted by highly publicized cases that generate fear and concern. For example, a number of highly publicized cases of celebrity stalking, including Robert John Bardo's fatal shooting of actress Rebecca Schaeffer on July 18, 1989, prompted more than 25 U.S. states to enact stalking statutes. Such laws prohibit "the willful, malicious, and repeated following and harassing of another person."[35] California's sexual predator law, which took effect on January 1, 1996, allows people convicted of sexually violent crimes against two or more victims to be committed to a mental institution after their prison terms have been served. This law has already been upheld by **appellate court** judges in the state.[36]

The criminal law may also change because of shifts in culture and social conventions and thus may reflect a newfound tolerance for behavior condemned only a few years before. For example, in an important 2003 case, *Lawrence v. Texas*, the Supreme Court declared that laws banning sodomy were unconstitutional because they violated the due process rights of citizens because of their sexual orientation.[37] The Lawrence decision made consensual sex between same-sex adults legal and paved the way for the legalization, on a state-by-state basis, of gay marriage. As of early 2010, gay marriages are performed in Massachusetts, Connecticut, Iowa, Vermont, and New Hampshire.

The future direction of U.S. criminal law remains unclear. Certain actions, such as crimes by corporations and political corruption, will be labeled as criminal and given more attention. Other offenses, such as recreational drug use, may be reduced in importance or removed entirely from the criminal law system. In addition, changing technology and its ever-increasing global and local roles in our lives will require modifications in criminal law. ▶ **Checkpoints**

Ethical Issues in Criminology

A critical issue facing criminology students involves recognizing the field's political and social consequences. All too often criminologists forget the social responsibility they bear as experts in the area of crime and justice. When government agencies request their views of issues, their pronouncements and opinions may become the basis for sweeping changes in social policy.

The lives of millions of people can be influenced by criminological research data. Debates over gun control, capital punishment, and mandatory sentences are ongoing and contentious. Some criminologists have argued successfully for social service, treatment, and rehabilitation programs to reduce the crime rate; others consider these a waste of time, suggesting instead that a massive prison construction program coupled with tough criminal sentences can bring the crime rate down. By accepting their roles as experts on law-violating behavior, criminologists place themselves in a position of power. The potential consequences of their actions are enormous. Therefore, they must be both aware of the ethics of their profession and prepared to defend their work in the light of public scrutiny. Major ethical issues include what to study, whom to study, and how to conduct those studies.

▶ *What to study.* Criminologists must be concerned about the topics they study. Their research must not be directed by the sources of funding on which research projects rely. The objectivity of research may be questioned if studies are funded by organizations that have a vested interest in the outcome of the research. For example, a study on the effectiveness of the defensive use of handguns to stop crime may be tainted if the funding for the project comes from a gun manufacturer whose sales may be affected by the research findings. It has been shown over the past decades that criminological research has been influenced by government funding linked to the topics the government wants research on and those it wishes to avoid. Recently, funding by political agencies has increased the likelihood that criminologists will address drug issues, while spending less time on topics such as incapacitation and white-collar crime.[38] Should the nature and extent of scientific research be shaped by the hand of government, or should research remain independent of outside interference?

▶ *Whom to study.* Another ethical issue in criminology concerns selection of research subjects. Too often, criminologists focus their attention on the poor and minorities, while ignoring middle-class white-collar crime, organized crime, and government crime. For example, a few social scientists have suggested that criminals have lower intelligence quotients than the average citizen and that because the average IQ score is lower among some minority groups, their crime rates are high.[39] This was the conclusion reached in *The Bell Curve*, a popular but

Checkpoints

▶ There are a number of views of what crime entails. The three major views are the consensus, conflict, and interactionist perspectives.

▶ The American legal system is a direct descendant of the British common law.

▶ The criminal law has a number of different goals, including social control, punishment, retribution, deterrence, equity, and the representation of morality.

▶ Each crime has both a physical and a mental element.

▶ Persons accused of crimes can defend themselves either by denying the criminal act or by presenting an excuse or justification for their actions.

▶ The criminal law is constantly changing in an effort to reflect social values and contemporary issues and problems.

appellate court
Court that reviews trial court procedures to determine whether they have complied with accepted rules and constitutional doctrines.

Thinking Like a Criminologist

You have been experimenting with various techniques in order to identify a surefire method for predicting violent behavior in delinquents. Your procedure involves brain scans, DNA testing, and blood analysis. Used with samples of incarcerated adolescents, your procedure has been able to distinguish with 75 percent accuracy between youths with a history of violence and those who are exclusively property offenders. Your research indicates that if all youths were tested with your techniques, potentially violence-prone career criminals could be easily identified for special treatment. For example, children in the local school system could be tested, and those identified as violence-prone could be carefully monitored by teachers. Those at risk for future violence could be put into special programs as a precaution.

Some of your colleagues argue that this type of testing is unconstitutional because it violates the subjects' Fifth Amendment right against self-incrimination. There is also the problem of error: Some children may be falsely labeled as violence-prone.

Writing Assignment

Write an essay addressing the issue of predicting antisocial behavior. Address such issues as the following: "Is it fair or ethical to label people as potentially criminal and violent, even though they have not yet exhibited any antisocial behavior?" Do the risks of such a procedure outweigh its benefits?

---

highly controversial book written by Richard Herrnstein and Charles Murray.[40] Although such research is often methodologically unsound, it brings to light the tendency of criminologists to focus on one element of the community while ignoring others.

▶ *How to study.* A third area of concern involves the methods used in conducting research. One issue is whether subjects are fully informed about the purpose of research. For example, when European American and African American youngsters are asked to participate in a survey of their behavior or to take an IQ test, are they told in advance that the data they provide may later be used to demonstrate racial differences in their self-reported crime rates? Criminologists must also be careful to keep records and information confidential in order to maintain the privacy of research participants. But ethical questions still linger: Should a criminologist who is told in confidence by a research subject about a future crime report her knowledge to the police? How far should a criminologist go to protect her sources of information? Should stated intentions to commit offenses be disclosed?[41]

In studies that involve experimentation and treatment, care must be taken to protect those subjects who have been chosen for experimental and control groups. For example, is it ethical to provide a special program for one group while depriving others of the same opportunity just so the groups can later be compared? Conversely, criminologists must be careful to protect subjects from experiments that may actually cause harm. An examination of the highly publicized "Scared Straight" program, which brings youngsters into contact with hard-core felons in a prison setting, found that participants may have been harmed by their experience. Rather than being frightened into conformity, subjects actually increased their criminal behavior.[42] Finally, criminologists must take extreme care to ensure that research subjects are selected in a random and unbiased manner.[43]

Of course, it is critical that criminological research do no harm to subjects, but criminologist Ida Dupont argues that this is not enough: Criminological research can, and should, be empowering and directly useful to research participants. To be truly ethical, she insists, criminological research must have social value to research participants rather than simply doing no harm.[44]

Summary

1. Understand what is meant by the "field of criminology."

   Criminology is the scientific approach to the study of criminal behavior and society's reaction to law violations and violators. It is an academic discipline that uses the scientific method to study the nature, extent, cause, and control of criminal behavior. Criminology is an interdisciplinary science. Criminologists hold degrees in a variety of fields, most commonly sociology, but also criminal justice, political science, psychology, economics, engineering, and the natural sciences. Criminology is a fascinating field, encompassing a wide variety of topics that have both practical application and theoretical importance.

2. Be familiar with the various elements of the criminological enterprise.

   The various subareas included within the scholarly discipline of criminology, taken as a whole, define the field of study. The subarea of criminal statistics/crime measurement involves calculating the amount of, and trends in, criminal activity. Sociology of law / law and society / socio-legal studies is a subarea of criminology concerned with the role that social forces play in shaping criminal law and the role of criminal law in shaping society. Criminologists also explore the causes of crime. Another subarea of criminology involves research on specific criminal types and patterns: violent crime, theft crime, public order crime, organized crime, and so on. The study of penology, correction, and sentencing involves the treatment of known criminal offenders. Criminologists recognize that the victim plays a critical role in the criminal process and that the victim's behavior is often a key determinant of crime.

3. Know the historical context of criminology.

   The scientific study of crime and criminality is a relatively recent development. By the mid-eighteenth century, social philosophers began to argue for a more rational approach to punishment. Classical theory was the view that crime is a function of a decision-making process in which the potential offender weighs the potential costs and benefits of an illegal act. Later, criminologists began using verifiable principles and procedures for the systematic acquisition of knowledge. Sociological criminology focused on the relationship between social factors and crime. Critical criminology reflected the view that crime is a product of the capitalist system. Developmental theory holds that criminality is a dynamic process, influenced by social experiences as well as individual characteristics.

4. Know the difference between crime and deviance.

   Criminologists devote themselves to measuring, understanding, and controlling crime and deviance. Deviance includes a broad spectrum of behaviors that differ from the norm, ranging from the most socially harmful to the relatively inoffensive. Criminologists are often concerned with the concept of deviance and its relationship to criminality.

5. Discuss the three different views of the definition of crime.

   According to the consensus view, crimes are behaviors that all elements of society consider repugnant. It is the belief that the majority of citizens in a society share common values and agree on what behaviors should be defined as criminal. The conflict view depicts criminal behavior as being defined by those in power to protect and advance their own self-interest. According to the interactionist view, those with social power are able to impose their values on society as a whole, and these values then define criminal behavior.

6. Know what is meant by the term "criminal law."

   The criminal law is a set of rules that specify the behaviors society has outlawed.

7. Discuss the different purposes of the criminal law.

   The criminal law serves several important purposes. It represents public opinion and moral values. It enforces social controls. It deters criminal behavior and wrongdoing. It punishes transgressors. It creates equity. And it abrogates the need for private retribution.

8. Trace the development of criminal law.

   The criminal law used in U.S. jurisdictions traces its origin to the English common law. In the U.S. legal system, lawmakers have codified common-law crimes into state and federal penal codes.

9. Describe the difference between a felony and a misdemeanor.

   A felony is a serious offense that carries a penalty of imprisonment, usually for one year or more, and may entail loss of political rights. A misdemeanor is a minor crime usually punished by a short jail term and/or a fine.

10. Be familiar with the ethical issues in criminology.

    Ethical issues arise when information-gathering methods appear biased or exclusionary. These issues may cause serious consequences because research findings can significantly affect individuals and groups. Criminologists must be concerned about the topics they study. Another ethical issue in criminology revolves around the selection of research subjects. A third area of concern involves the methods used in conducting research.

Key Terms

criminology 4
interdisciplinary 4
criminal justice 4
criminological
  enterprise 4
valid measure 4
reliable measure 4
white-collar crime 7
penology 8
rehabilitation 8
capital punishment 8
mandatory sentences 8

victimology 8
utilitarianism 9
classical criminology 9
positivism 10
scientific method 10
biosocial theory 11
sociological
  criminology 11
anomie 11
Chicago School 11
socialization 12
conflict theory 12

critical criminology 12
developmental
  theory 13
rational choice theory 13
trait theory 13
social structure theory 13
social process
  theorists 13
deviance 14
critical criminologists 15
crime 15
decriminalize 15

consensus view 17
criminal law 17
conflict view 17
interactionist view 17
Code of Hammurabi 18
Mosaic Code 18
precedent 19
common law 19
statutory crimes 19
felony 19
misdemeanor 19
appellate court 21

Critical Thinking Questions

1. What are the specific aims and purposes of the criminal law? To what extent does the criminal law control behavior? Do you believe that the law is too restrictive? Not restrictive enough?

2. If you ran the world, which acts that are now legal would you make criminal? Which criminal acts would you legalize? What would be the probable consequences of your actions?

3. Beccaria argued that the threat of punishment controls crime. Are there other forms of social control? Aside from the threat of legal punishment, what else controls your own behavior?

4. Would it be ethical for a criminologist to observe a teenage gang by hanging with them, drinking, and watching as they steal cars? Should the criminologist report that behavior to the police?

© AP Images/*Athens Banner-Herald*, Richard Hamm. Inset: Courtesy and by permission of the Office of Marketing and Communications, Terry College of Business, The University of Georgia

Chapter Outline

The Nature and Extent of Crime

On April 25, 2009, George Zinkhan, 57, (shown in inset) killed his wife Marie Bruce and two other people, Thomas Tanner, 40, and Ben Teague, 63, as they exited a reunion picnic of the Town and Gown Players theater group in Athens, Georgia. Zinkhan then fled the scene and eluded a police manhunt until his body was located in a rural area two weeks later. It seems that Zinkhan had dug a shallow grave, covered himself with twigs and leaves and then committed suicide by shooting himself in the head. At first the shootings seemed inexplicable, but news reports later indicated that George and Marie were having marital problems and that George suspected Tanner, a Clemson University economics professor, of being romantically involved with Marie; the third victim, Ben Teague, was simply "at the wrong place, at the wrong time."

Fact or Fiction?

▶ The official crime data is extremely accurate and can give us a valid picture of the nature, extent, and trends in crime.

▶ Most kids do not commit crime; a few hard-core delinquents are responsible for most criminal activity.

▶ Crime is out of control and is more dangerous now in the United States than at any time in history.

▶ Immigrants who are in the United States illegally commit a lot of crime, a fact that justifies limiting immigration and closing down the borders.

▶ The Old West is still pretty wild, having higher crime rates than the East.

▶ A small group of offenders is responsible for most serious crimes; they persist in crime throughout their lifespan.

Chapter Objectives

1. Be familiar with the various forms of crime data.

2. Know the problems associated with collecting data.

3. Be able to discuss recent trends in the crime rate.

4. Be familiar with the factors that influence crime rates.

5. Compare crime rates under different ecological conditions.

6. Be able to discuss the association between social class and crime.

7. Know what is meant by the term "aging out process."

8. Recognize that there are gender and racial patterns in crime.

9. Be familiar with Wolfgang, Figlio, and Sellin's pioneering research on chronic offending.

10. Know what causes chronicity.

Although romantic triangles have been the basis of violence for quite some time (when Katherine Howard had an affair with Thomas Culpepper in 1542, her husband Henry VIII had them both beheaded), what made this case unusual was the social and educational standing of those involved. George Zinkhan received his Ph.D. from the University of Michigan, became a distinguished professor of marketing at the University of Georgia, had authored numerous books and scholarly articles, and was serving as editor of a prestigious business journal. Marie Bruce, his wife, was a highly regarded attorney in Athens, Georgia. Thomas Tanner had earned a master's degree in economics at Iowa State University in Ames, Iowa, and his Ph.D. in economics at the University of Georgia; he was director of the Center for Economic Modeling at Clemson University.[1]

Stories such as the Athens shooting, splashed across the media and rehashed on nightly talk shows, help convince most Americans that we live in a violent society. If a well-known professor kills three people, including his wife, is anyone safe? Are Americans justified in their fear of violent crime? Should they barricade themselves behind armed guards? Are crime rates actually rising or falling? And where do most crimes occur and who commits them? To answer these and similar questions, criminologists have devised elaborate methods of crime data collection and analysis. Without accurate data on the nature and extent of crime, it would not be possible to formulate theories that explain the onset of crime or to devise social policies that facilitate its control or elimination. Accurate data collection is also critical in assessing the nature and extent of crime, tracking changes in the crime rate, and measuring the individual and social factors that may influence criminality.

In this chapter, we review how data is collected on criminal offenders and offenses and what this information tells us about crime patterns and trends. We also examine the concept of criminal careers and discover what available crime data can tell us about the onset, continuation, and termination of criminality. We begin with a discussion of the most important sources of crime data that criminologists use to measure the nature and extent of crime.

Primary Sources of Crime Data

The primary sources of crime data are surveys and official records. Criminologists use these techniques to measure the nature and extent of criminal behavior and the personality, attitudes, and background of criminal offenders. Understanding how such data is collected provides insight into how professional criminologists approach various problems and questions in their field.

OFFICIAL RECORDS: THE UNIFORM CRIME REPORT

Uniform Crime Report (UCR)
Large database, compiled by the FBI, of crimes reported and arrests made each year throughout the United States.

Part I crimes
The eight most serious offenses included in the UCR: murder, rape, assault, robbery, burglary, arson, larceny, and motor vehicle theft.

Part II crimes
All other crimes, aside from the eight Part I crimes, included in the UCR arrest data. Part II crimes include drug offenses, sex crimes, and vandalism, among others.

In order to understand more about the nature and extent of crime, criminologists use the records of government agencies such as police departments, prisons, and courts. The Federal Bureau of Investigation collects the most important crime record data from local law enforcement agencies and publishes it yearly in their **Uniform Crime Report (UCR)**. The UCR includes crimes reported to local law enforcement departments and the number of arrests made by police agencies.[2] The FBI receives and compiles records from more than 17,000 police departments serving a majority of the U.S. population. The FBI tallies and annually publishes the number of reported offenses by city, county, standard metropolitan statistical area, and geographical divisions of the United States for the most serious crimes. These **Part I crimes** are murder and nonnegligent manslaughter, forcible rape, robbery, aggravated assault, burglary, larceny, motor vehicle theft, and arson. Exhibit 2.1 defines these crimes.

In addition to recording crimes reported to the police, the UCR also collects data on the number and characteristics (age, race, and gender) of individuals who have been arrested for committing a crime. Included in the arrest data are both people who have committed Part I crimes and people who have been arrested for all other crimes, known collectively as **Part II crimes**. This latter group includes such criminal acts as sex crimes, drug trafficking, and vandalism.

Criminal Homicide

Murder and Nonnegligent Manslaughter The willful (nonnegligent) killing of one human being by another. Deaths caused by negligence, attempts to kill, assaults to kill, suicides, accidental deaths, and justifiable homicides are excluded. Justifiable homicides are limited to (1) the killing of a felon by a law enforcement officer in the line of duty and (2) the killing of a felon, during the commission of a felony, by a private citizen.

Manslaughter by Negligence The killing of another person through gross negligence. Traffic fatalities are excluded.

Forcible Rape

The carnal knowledge of a female forcibly and against her will. Included are rapes by force and attempts or assaults to rape. Statutory offenses (no force used but victim under age of consent) are excluded.

Robbery

The taking or attempting to take anything of value from the care, custody, or control of a person or persons by force or threat of force or violence and/or by putting the victim in fear.

Aggravated Assault

An unlawful attack by one person upon another for the purpose of inflicting severe or aggravated bodily injury. This type of assault is usually accompanied by the use of a weapon or by means likely to produce death or great bodily harm. Simple assaults are excluded.

Exhibit 2.1 Part I Crimes

Burglary

The unlawful entry of a structure to commit a felony or a theft. Attempted forcible entry is included.

Larceny/ Theft (except motor vehicle theft)

The unlawful taking, carrying, leading, or riding away of property from the possession or constructive possession of another. Examples are thefts of bicycles or automobile accessories, shoplifting, pocket picking, and the stealing of any property or article that is not taken by force and violence or by fraud. Attempted larcenies are included. Embezzlement, con games, forgery, worthless checks, and so on are excluded.

Motor Vehicle Theft

The theft or attempted theft of a motor vehicle. A motor vehicle is self-propelled and runs on the surface and not on rails. Specifically excluded from this category are motorboats, construction equipment, airplanes, and farming equipment.

Arson

Any willful or malicious burning or attempt to burn, with or without intent to defraud, a dwelling house, public building, motor vehicle, aircraft, personal property of another, or the like.

SOURCE: FBI, Uniform Crime Report, 2008.

Compiling the Uniform Crime Report The methods used to compile the UCR are quite complex. Each month, law enforcement agencies report the number of Part I crimes reported by victims, by officers who discovered the infractions, or by other sources.

Whenever criminal complaints are found through investigation to be unfounded or false, they are eliminated from the actual count. However, the number of actual offenses known is reported to the FBI whether or not anyone is arrested for the crime, the stolen property is recovered, or prosecution ensues.

In addition, each month, law enforcement agencies also report how many crimes were **cleared**. Crimes are cleared in two ways: (1) when at least one person is arrested, charged, and turned over to the court for prosecution; or (2) by exceptional means, when some element beyond police control precludes the physical arrest of an offender (for example, the offender leaves the country). Data on the number of clearances involving the arrest of only juvenile offenders, data on the value of property stolen and recovered in connection with Part I offenses, and detailed information pertaining to criminal homicide are also reported. Nationwide in 2008, law enforcement cleared 45 percent of violent crimes and 17 percent of property crimes by arrest or exceptional means (Figure 2.1).

Violent crimes are more likely to be solved than property crimes because police devote more resources to these more serious acts, witnesses (including the victim) are frequently available to identify offenders, and in many instances the victim and offender were previously acquainted.

The UCR uses three methods to express crime data. First, the number of crimes reported to the police and arrests made are expressed as raw figures (for example, in

cleared crimes
Crimes are considered cleared when at least one person is arrested, charged, and turned over to the court for prosecution or when some element beyond police control (such as the offender having left the country) precludes the physical arrest of an offender.

Figure 2.1 Crimes Cleared by Arrest

Percentage of crimes cleared by arrest or exceptional means, 2008

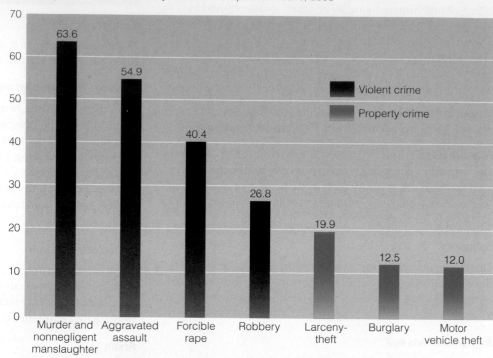

SOURCE: Uniform Crime Report, 2008, http://www.fbi.gov/ucr/cius2008/offenses/clearances/index.html

2008, 16,272 murders occurred). Second, crime rates per 100,000 people are computed. That is, when the UCR indicates that the murder rate was about 5.4 in 2008, it means that almost 6 people in every 100,000 were murdered between January 1 and December 31, 2008. This is the equation used:

$$\frac{\text{Number of Reported Crimes}}{\text{Total U.S. Population}} \times 100{,}000 = \text{Rate per } 100{,}000$$

Third, the FBI computes changes in the number and rate of crime over time. For example, the murder rate decreased by 4.7 percent between 2007 and 2008, and the 2008 murder rate was 6 percent below the 1999 level. Overall, data indicates that crime declined about 3.5 percent between 2007 and 2008.

Validity of the UCR The UCR's accuracy has long been suspect. Many serious crimes are not reported to police and therefore are not counted by the UCR. The reasons for not reporting vary:

▶ Victims may consider the crime trivial or unimportant and therefore choose not to call police.
▶ Some victims fail to report because they do not trust the police or have little confidence in the ability of the police to solve crime.
▶ People without property insurance believe it is useless to report theft.
▶ Victims may fear reprisals from an offender's friends or family.
▶ Some victims have "dirty hands" and are involved in illegal activities themselves. They do not want to get involved with police.

Because of these and other factors, less than half of all criminal incidents are reported to the police.

The way police departments record and report criminal activity also affects the validity of UCR statistics. Some departments may define crimes loosely—reporting a trespass as a burglary or an assault on a woman as an attempted rape—whereas others pay strict attention to FBI guidelines. Some make systematic errors in UCR reporting—for example, counting an arrest only after a formal booking procedure, even though the UCR requires arrests to be counted if the suspect is released without a formal charge. These reporting practices may help explain inter-jurisdictional differences in crime.

Some critics take issue with the way the FBI records data and counts crimes. According to the "Hierarchy Rule," in a multiple-offense incident, only the most serious crime is counted. Thus, if an armed bank robber commits a robbery, assaults a patron as he flees, steals a car to get away, and damages property during a police chase, only the robbery is reported because it is the most serious offense.

Although these issues are troubling, the UCR continues to be one of the most widely used sources of criminal statistics. Because data for the UCR is collected in a careful and systematic way, it is considered a highly reliable indicator of crime patterns and trends. That is, even if reporting problems inhibit the precise count of total crimes committed in a single year, measurement of year-to-year change should be accurate because these problems are stable over time. For example, if the UCR reports that the murder rate decreased 4.7 between 2007 and 2008, that assessment is probably accurate because the reporting and counting problems that influenced data collection in 2007 had the same effect in 2008.

NIBRS: THE FUTURE OF THE UNIFORM CRIME REPORT

Clearly there must be a more reliable source for crime statistics than the UCR as it stands today. Beginning in 1982, a five-year redesign effort was undertaken to provide more comprehensive and detailed crime statistics. The effort resulted in the **National Incident-Based Reporting System (NIBRS)**, a program that collects data on each reported crime incident. Instead of submitting statements of the kinds of crime that individual citizens report to the police and summary statements of resulting arrests, the new program requires local police agencies to provide at least a brief account of each incident and arrest, including the incident, victim, and offender information.

Under NIBRS, law enforcement authorities provide information to the FBI on each criminal incident involving 46 specific offenses, including the eight Part I crimes, that occur in their jurisdiction; arrest information on the 46 offenses plus 11 lesser offenses is also provided in NIBRS. These expanded crime categories include numerous additional crimes, such as blackmail, embezzlement, drug offenses, and bribery; this makes it possible to develop a national database on the nature of crime, victims, and criminals. Other collected information includes statistics gathered by federal law enforcement agencies and data on hate or bias crimes. Thus far, more than 20 states have implemented their NIBRS programs, and 12 others are in the process of finalizing their data collections. When this program is fully implemented and adopted across the nation, it should bring about greater uniformity in cross-jurisdictional reporting and improve the accuracy of official crime data.[3] Some crimes are quite complex, and a more sophisticated measurement will help to improve understanding and analysis. Consider the case discussed in the accompanying Profiles in Crime feature.

SURVEY RESEARCH

Another important method of collecting crime data is through surveys in which people are asked about their attitudes, beliefs, values, and characteristics, as well as their experiences with crime and victimization. Surveys typically involve **sampling**, the process of selecting for study a limited number of subjects who are representative of an entire group that has similar characteristics, called the **population**. To understand the social forces that produce crime, a criminologist might interview a sample of 3,000 prison inmates drawn from the population of more than 2 million inmates in the United States; in this case, the sample represents the entire population of U.S. inmates. It is assumed that the characteristics of people or events in a carefully selected sample will be similar to those of the population at large. If the sampling is done

National Incident-Based Reporting System (NIBRS)
Program that requires local police agencies to provide a brief account of each incident and arrest within 22 crime patterns, including incident, victim, and offender information.

sampling
Selecting a limited number of people for study as representative of a larger group.

population
All people who share a particular characteristic, such as all high school students or all police officers.

From 1997 to 2005, Ronald and Mary Evano turned dining in restaurants into a profitable albeit illegal scam. They used the "Waiter, there is glass in my food" ruse in restaurants and supermarkets stretching from Boston to Washington, DC. Though crude, their efforts paid big dividends. They allegedly swindled insurance companies out of $200,000 and conned a generous helping of food establishments and hospitals along the way. And to top it off, in order to look authentic, the Evanos actually did eat glass.

How did the Evanos pull off their scam? After ordering or buying food at restaurants, hotel bars, or supermarkets, either Ronald or Mary would "discover" glass in his or her food. They would then complain of the incident to management and fill out a report.

After leaving the food establishment, they would check into the emergency room at the local hospital, complaining of severe stomach pain. After presenting fake IDs and Social Security cards to hospital staff, they would allow doctors to examine them. In some cases, X-rays would show actual pieces of glass in their stomachs (none of it came from the food they purchased). Once released from the hospital, the couple would continue getting medical treatment for stomach pain. After racking up several thousand dollars in bills,

they would file an insurance claim for their extensive "pain and suffering."

The scheme unraveled when the Insurance Fraud Bureau of Massachusetts noticed a pattern of glass-eating claims in the state. The private industry organization eventually realized that most claims were being filed by the same couple and contacted federal authorities, who then traced the couple's trail of insurance fraud across three states and the District of Columbia.

On March 16, 2006, the Evanos were indicted on mail fraud, identity theft, Social Security fraud, and making false statements on health care matters. Ronald pled guilty on October 4, 2007, and received a five-year prison sentence, but Mary—his partner in crime—is still on the lam.

SOURCES: Federal Bureau of Investigation, "Bizarre Meal Ticket: The Couple Who Ate Glass," November 8, 2006, www.fbi.gov/page2/nov06/glass110806.htm (accessed May 11, 2009); "Mass. Couple Charged in Glass-Eating Insurance Fraud," *Insurance Journal*, April 17, 2006, www.insurancejournal.com/news/east/2006/04/17/67327.htm (accessed May 11, 2009); Department of Justice, "Man Sentenced to 63 Months in Glass-Eating Fraud Scheme," http://boston.fbi.gov/dojpressrel/pressrel07/fraudscheme100407.htm (accessed May 11, 2009).

CONNECTIONS

Victim surveys provide information not only about criminal incidents that have occurred but also about the individuals who are most at risk of falling victim to crime and where and when they are most likely to be victimized. Data from recent NCVS surveys are used in Chapter 3 to draw a portrait of the nature and extent of victimization in the United States.

National Crime Victimization Survey (NCVS)
The ongoing victimization study conducted jointly by the Justice Department and the U.S. Census Bureau that surveys victims about their experiences with law violation.

correctly, the responses of the 3,000 inmates should represent those of the entire population of inmates.

THE NATIONAL CRIME VICTIMIZATION SURVEY (NCVS)

Because many victims do not report their experiences to the police, the UCR cannot measure all the annual criminal activity. To address the nonreporting issue, the federal government sponsors the **National Crime Victimization Survey (NCVS)**, a comprehensive, nationwide survey of victimization in the United States conducted annually by the U.S. Census Bureau for the Bureau of Justice Statistics (BJS).

How is the NCVS conducted? In the most recent survey (2008), about 42,000 households and 78,000 individuals age 12 or older are interviewed for the NCVS.[4] Households stay in the sample for three years. New households are rotated into the sample on an ongoing basis. The NCVS collects information on crimes suffered by individuals and households, whether or not those crimes were reported to law enforcement. It estimates the proportion of each crime type reported to law enforcement, and it summarizes the reasons that victims give for reporting or not reporting. In 1993, the survey was redesigned to provide detailed information on the frequency and nature of the crimes of rape, sexual assault, personal robbery, aggravated and simple assault, household burglary, theft, and motor vehicle theft. In 2006, the techniques used were once again changed, and while some methodological problems resulted that year, the data is now considered comparable to those collected in previous years (see below for more on the changes).[5]

The survey provides information about victims (age, sex, race, ethnicity, marital status, income, and educational level), offenders (sex, race, approximate age, and victim–offender relationship), and the crimes (time and place of occurrence, use of weapons, nature of injury, and economic consequences). Questions also cover the experiences of victims with the criminal justice system, self-protective measures used by victims, and possible substance abuse by offenders. Supplements are added periodically to the survey to obtain detailed information on topics such as school crime.

The greatest advantage of the NCVS over official data sources such as the UCR is that it can estimate the total amount of annual crimes, not just those that are reported to police. Nonreporting is a significant issue: Fewer than half of all violent victimizations and about a third of all property crimes are routinely reported to the police. As a result, the NCVS provides a more nearly complete picture of the nation's crime problem. Also, because some crimes are significantly underreported, the NCVS is an indispensable measure of their occurrence. Take the crime of rape and sexual assault, of which only about 40 percent of incidents are reported to police. The UCR shows that slightly more than 90,000 rapes or attempted rapes occur each year, compared to about 200,000 uncovered by the NCVS. In addition, the NCVS helps us understand why crimes are not reported to police and whether the type and nature of the criminal event influences whether the police will ever know it occurred. With the crime of rape, research shows that victims are much more likely to report rape if it is accompanied by another crime, such as robbery, than they are if the rape is the only crime that occurred. Official data alone cannot provide that type of information.[6]

Validity of the NCVS Although its utility and importance are unquestioned, the NCVS may also suffer from some methodological problems. As a result, its findings must be interpreted with caution. Among the potential problems are the following:

▶ Overreporting due to victims' misinterpretation of events. A lost wallet may be reported as stolen or an open door may be viewed as a burglary attempt.
▶ Underreporting due to the embarrassment of reporting crime to interviewers, fear of getting in trouble, or simply forgetting an incident.
▶ Inability to record the personal criminal activity of those interviewed, such as drug use or gambling; murder is also not included, for obvious reasons.
▶ Sampling errors, which produce a group of respondents who do not represent the nation as a whole.
▶ Inadequate question format that invalidates responses. Some groups, such as adolescents, may be particularly susceptible to error because of question format.[7]

The Future of the NCVS For the past 30 years, the NCVS (along with the UCR) has served as one of the two major indicators of crime and victimization in the United States. It now faces some important challenges. A recent analysis conducted by the National Research Council found that its effectiveness has been undermined by budget limitations.[8]

To enable it to keep going in spite of limited resources, the survey's sample size and methods of data collection have been altered. Although the current sample size is valid for its purpose, victimization is still a relatively rare event, such that when they are contacted, many respondents do not have incidents to report. Consequently, the NCVS now has to combine multiple years of data in order to comment on change over time, which is less desirable than an annual measure of year-to-year change.

Reflecting these issues, in 2006 significant changes were made to the way the NCVS is collected. The methodological changes included a new sampling method, a change in the method of handling first-time interviews with households, and a change in the method of interviewing. Some selected areas were dropped from the sample, and others were added. Finally, computer-assisted personal interviewing (CAPI) replaced paper-and-pencil interviewing (PAPI). These issues are critical, but there is no substitute available that provides national information on crime and victimization with extensive detail on victims and the social context of the criminal event.

© AFP/Getty Images

This astounding photo captures two masked men as they knock down a cyclist and steal his bag during a street robbery. The robbers stole the man's backpack, which contained money that he was on his way to the bank to deposit. The man sustained a small cut to his forehead and was aided by the unidentified driver. Although serious crimes such as this robbery are routinely reported to police, many more go unreported and constitute "the dark figures of crime." The fact that so many victims fail to report crime to police has prompted the development of national victim and self-report surveys.

SELF-REPORT SURVEYS

Another tool commonly used by criminologists to measure crime is the **self-report survey** that asks people to describe, in detail, their recent and lifetime participation in criminal activity. Self-reports are given in groups, and the respondents are promised anonymity in order to ensure the validity and honesty of their responses. Most self-report studies have focused on juvenile delinquency and youth crime.[9] However, self-reports can also be used to examine the offense histories of prison inmates, drug users, and other segments of the criminal population.[10]

Most self-report surveys also contain questions about attitudes, values, and behaviors. There may be questions about a participant's substance abuse history (How many times have you used marijuana or cocaine?) and the participant's family history (Did your parents ever strike you with a stick or a belt?). By correlating the responses, criminologists can analyze the relationship between personal factors and criminal behaviors and explore such issues as whether people who report being abused as children are also more likely to use drugs as adults and whether failure in school leads to delinquency.[11]

CONNECTIONS

Criminologists suspect that a few high-rate offenders are responsible for a disproportionate share of all serious crime. Results would be badly skewed if even a few of these chronic offenders were absent or refused to participate in schoolwide self-report surveys. For more on chronic offenders, see the sections at the end of this chapter.

self-report survey
A research approach that requires subjects to reveal their own participation in delinquent or criminal acts.

Validity of Self-Reports Critics of self-report studies frequently suggest that expecting people to candidly admit illegal acts is unreasonable. This is especially true of those with official records—the very people who may be engaging in the most criminality. At the same time, some people may exaggerate their criminal acts, forget some of them, or be confused about what is being asked. Some surveys contain an overabundance of trivial offenses, such as shoplifting small items or using false identification to obtain alcohol, often lumped together with serious crimes to form a total crime index. Consequently, comparisons between groups can be highly misleading.

The "missing cases" phenomenon is also a concern. Even if 90 percent of a school population voluntarily participates in a self-report study, researchers can never be sure whether the few who refuse to participate or are absent that day constitute a significant portion of the school's population of persistent high-rate offenders. Research indicates that offenders with the most extensive prior criminality are also the most likely "to be poor historians of their own crime commission rates."[12] It is also unlikely that the most serious chronic offenders in the teenage population are willing to cooperate with criminologists administering self-report tests.[13] Institutionalized youths, who are not generally represented in the self-report surveys, not only are more delinquent than the general youth population but also are considerably more misbehaving than the most delinquent youths identified in the typical self-report survey.[14] Consequently, self-reports may measure only nonserious, occasional delinquents, while ignoring hard-core chronic offenders who may be institutionalized and unavailable for self-reports.

To address these criticisms, various techniques have been used to verify self-report data.[15] The "known group" method compares youths known to be offenders with those who are not, to see whether the former report more delinquency. Research shows that when kids are asked whether they have ever been arrested or sent to court, their responses accurately reflect their true life experiences.[16]

Table 2.1 "Monitoring the Future" Survey of Criminal Activity of High School Seniors

Crime	Percentage Engaging in Offenses	
	Committed at Least Once	**Committed More than Once**
Set fire on purpose	1	2
Damaged school property	5	7
Damaged work property	3	3
Auto theft	2	3
Auto part theft	2	2
Break and enter	12	13
Theft, less than $50	12	17
Theft, more than $50	4	5
Shoplift	12	16
Gang or group fight	9	7
Hurt someone badly enough to require medical care	7	6
Used force or a weapon to steal	1	2
Hit teacher or supervisor	1	2
Participated in serious fight	7	6

SOURCE: *Monitoring the Future, 2009* (Ann Arbor, MI: Institute for Social Research, 2009).

One way to improve the reliability of self-reports is to use them in a consistent fashion with different groups of subjects over time. That makes it possible to measure trends in self-reported crime and drug abuse to see whether changes have occurred. One important source of longitudinal self-report data is the Monitoring the Future study that researchers at the University of Michigan Institute for Social Research (ISR) have been conducting annually since 1978. This national survey, which typically involves more than 50,000 high school students, is one of the most important sources of self-report data.[17]

Table 2.1 contains data from the most recent (2009) Monitoring the Future survey. A significant number of teenagers reported involvement in criminal behavior: About 13 percent reported hurting someone badly enough that the victim needed medical care; about 29 percent reported stealing something worth less than $50, and another 9 percent stole something worth more than $50; 28 percent reported shoplifting. As Table 2.1 also shows, many kids reported committing these offenses more than once.

If the MTF data is accurate, the crime problem is much greater than UCR and NCVS data would lead us to believe. There are approximately 21 million youths between the ages of 15 and 19, and 3 percent of the students in this age group say they have used a weapon to steal one or more times in the past year.[18] At this rate, high school students must have committed a minimum of 630,000 armed robberies during the past 12 months; in comparison, the UCR tallied about 440,000 armed robberies for all age groups.

Although these studies are supportive, self-report data must be interpreted with some caution. Asking subjects about their past behavior may capture more serious crimes but miss minor criminal acts; that is, people remember armed robberies and rapes better than they do minor assaults and altercations.[19] In addition, some classes of offenders (for example, substance abusers) may have a tough time accounting for their prior misbehavior.[20]

Fact or Fiction?

Most kids do not commit crime; a few hard-core delinquents are responsible for most criminal activity.

Fiction. Self-reports show that most kids do in fact commit some crimes, ranging from shoplifting to serious felonies. Fortunately, the great majority "age out" of crime in their adolescence.

Uniform Crime Report	• Data are collected from records from police departments across the nation, crimes reported to police, and arrests. • Strengths of the UCR are that it measures homicides and arrests and that it is a consistent, national sample. • Weaknesses of the UCR are that it omits crimes not reported to police, omits most drug usage, and contains reporting errors.
National Crime Victimization Survey	• Data are collected from a large national survey. • Strengths of the NCVS are that it includes crimes not reported to the police, uses careful sampling techniques, and is a yearly survey. • Weaknesses of the NCVS are that it relies on victims' memory and honesty and that it omits substance abuse.
Self-Report Surveys	• Data are collected from local surveys. • Strengths of self-report surveys are that they include nonreported crimes, substance abuse, and offenders' personal information. • Weaknesses of self-report surveys are that they rely on the honesty of offenders and omit offenders who refuse or are unable, as a consequence of incarceration, to participate (and who therefore may be the most deviant).

EVALUATING CRIME DATA

Each source of crime data has strengths and weaknesses. The FBI survey contains data on the number and characteristics of people arrested, information that the other data sources lack. For the most serious crimes, such as drug trafficking, arrest data can provide a meaningful measure of the level of criminal activity in a particular neighborhood environment, which other data sources cannot provide. It is also the source of information on particular crimes, such as murder, that cannot be measured by survey data.[21] The UCR remains the standard unit of analysis on which most criminological research is based. However, this survey omits the many crimes that victims choose not to report to police, and it is subject to the reporting caprices of individual police departments.

The NCVS includes unreported crime and important information on the personal characteristics of victims. However, the data consist of estimates made from relatively limited samples of the total U.S. population, so even narrow fluctuations in the rates of some crimes can have a major impact on findings. It also relies on personal recollections that may be inaccurate. The NCVS does not include data on important crime patterns, including murder and drug abuse.

Self-report surveys can provide information on the personal characteristics of offenders (such as their attitudes, values, beliefs, and psychological profiles) that is unavailable from any other source. Yet, at their core, self-reports rely on the honesty of criminal offenders and drug abusers, a population not generally known for accuracy and integrity.

Although their tallies of crimes are certainly not in synch, the crime patterns and trends that all three sources record are often quite similar.[22] For example, they all generally agree about the personal characteristics of serious criminals (such as age and gender) and where and when crime occurs (such as urban areas, nighttime, and summer months). In addition, the problems inherent in each source are consistent over time. Therefore, even if the data sources are incapable of providing a precise and valid count of crime at any given time, they are reliable indicators of changes and fluctuations in yearly crime rates. Concept Summary 2.1 lists the main characteristics of these sources of crime data.

In addition to these primary sources of crime data, criminologists use other data in their studies. These are discussed in Exhibit 2.2 on page 38.

Crime Trends

Crime is not new.[23] Studies have indicated that a gradual increase in the crime rate, especially in violent crime, occurred from 1830 to 1860. Following the Civil War, this rate increased significantly for about 15 years. Then, from 1880 up to the time of World War I, with the possible exception of the years immediately preceding and following the war, the number of reported crimes decreased. After a period of readjustment, the crime rate steadily declined until the Depression (about 1930), when another crime wave was recorded. As measured by the UCR, crime rates increased gradually following the 1930s until the 1960s, when the growth rate became much greater. The homicide rate, which had actually declined from the 1930s to the 1960s, also began a sharp increase that continued through the 1970s.

TRENDS IN OFFICIALLY RECORDED CRIME

In 1981 the number of Part I crimes rose to about 13 million and then began a gradual upward trend until 1991, when police recorded almost 15 million crimes. There were sharp increases in rates of robbery, motor vehicle theft, and overall homicide from the mid- to late 1980s through the early 1990s and a disturbing increase in youth firearm homicide rates (although adult homicide rates actually fell modestly throughout the 1980s). Since then the number of crimes has been in decline; about 11.1 million crimes were reported in 2008, a drop of 4 million reported crimes since the 1991 peak, despite a boost of about 50 million in the general population. (Figure 2.2 illustrates the changes in numbers of crimes reported between 1960 and 2008.)

Especially welcome has been a significant drop in UCR violent crimes—murder, rape, robbery, and assault. About 1.4 million violent crimes are now being reported to the police each year, a rate of around 454 per 100,000 Americans. Of course, people are still disturbed by media reports of violent incidents, but in reality there are 500,000 fewer violent crimes being reported today than in 1991, when almost 2 million incidents occurred, a violence rate of 758 per 100,000. This means that the violence rate has dropped almost 40 percent from its peak.

Not only has violent crime been in decline, but so too have theft offenses. The property crimes reported in the UCR include larceny, motor vehicle theft, and arson. Property crime rates have also declined in recent years, dropping more than 10 percent during the past decade. At their peak, in 1991, about 13 million property crimes were reported, a rate of almost 5,000 per 100,000 citizens. Currently, about 9.8 million property crimes are reported annually to police, a rate of about 3,200 per 100,000 population. Nonetheless, property crimes remain a serious national problem, and an estimated 18 billion dollars in losses results from property crimes each year.

How do the crime rate trends experienced in the United States compare to what is going on abroad? The Race, Culture, Gender, and Criminology feature on page 40 discusses trends in crime elsewhere in the world.

Figure 2.2 Crime Rate Trends

1960
Total crimes: 3.4 million
Violent crimes: 288,000
Property crimes: 3.1 million

1991
Total crimes: 14.8 million
Violent crimes: 1.9 million
Property crimes: 12.9 million

2008
Total crimes: 10.7 million
Violent crimes: 1.3 million
Property crimes: 9.4 million

SOURCE: FBI, *Crime in the United States*, 2008, www.fbi.gov/ucr/08aprelim/table_1.html.

Although property crime rates have trended downward, valuable new commodities such as the iPod may encourage more theft. Thefts on New York City subway trains have risen as thieves target music-playing devices such as the iPod, game-playing cell phones, and other popular mobile electronic devices.

Fact or Fiction?

Crime is out of control and is more dangerous now in the United States than at any time in history.

Fiction. Crime rates are lower now than they were 20 years ago. The violent crime rate, including murder, has been in decline. Crime rates were much higher in the nineteenth century.

Exhibit 2.2 Alternative Crime measures

In addition to the primary sources of crime data—UCR, NCVS, and self-report surveys—criminologists use several other methods to acquire data. Although this list is not exhaustive, the methods described here are routinely used in criminological research and data collection.

Cohort Research Data

Collecting cohort data involves observing over time a group of people who share certain characteristics. Researchers might select all girls born in Boston in 1970 and then follow their behavior patterns for 20 years. The research data might include their school experiences, arrests, and hospitalizations, along with information about their family life (marriages, divorces, parental relations, for example). Data may also be collected directly from the subjects during interviews and meetings with family members. If the cohort is carefully drawn, it may be possible to accumulate a complex array of data that can be used to determine which life experiences are associated with criminal careers. Another approach is to take a contemporary cohort, such as men in prison in New York in 2009, and then look back into their past and collect data from educational, family, police, and hospital records—a format known as a retrospective cohort study. If criminologists wanted to identify childhood and adolescent risk factors for criminality, they might acquire the inmates' prior police and court records, school records, and so on.

Experimental Data

Sometimes criminologists conduct controlled experiments to collect data on the cause of crime. To conduct experimental research, criminologists manipulate, or intervene in, the lives of their subjects to see the outcome or the effect of the intervention. True experiments usually have three elements: (1) random selection of subjects, (2) a control or comparison group, and (3) an experimental condition. For example, to determine whether viewing violent media content is a cause of aggression, a criminologist might randomly select one group of subjects and have them watch an extremely violent and gory film (such as *Evil Dead 2* or *Texas Chainsaw Massacre*) and then compare their behavior to that of a second randomly selected group who watch something mellow (such as *Shrek* or *Wall-E*). The behavior of both groups would be monitored; if the subjects who had watched the violent film were significantly more aggressive than those who had watched the nonviolent film, an association between media content and behavior would be supported. The fact that both groups were randomly selected would prevent some preexisting condition from invalidating the results of the experiment.

Observational and Interview Research

Sometimes criminologists focus their research on relatively few subjects, interviewing them in depth or observing them as they go about their activities. This research often results in the kind of in-depth data that large-scale surveys do not yield. In one such effort, Claire Sterk-Elifson focused on the lives of middle-class female drug abusers. The 34 interviews she conducted provide insight into a group whose behavior might not be captured in a large-scale survey. Sterk-Elifson found that these women were introduced to cocaine at first "just for fun": "I do drugs," one 34-year-old lawyer told her, "because I like the feeling. I would never let drugs take over my life." Unfortunately, many of these subjects succumbed to the power of drugs and suffered both emotional and financial stress.

Homicide Most criminologists believe that, for obvious reasons, homicide data is the most accurate and valid UCR statistic. Figure 2.3 illustrates homicide rate trends since 1900. Note that the rate peaked around 1930 and then held relatively steady at about 4 to 5 per 100,000 population from 1950 through the mid-1960s, at which point it started rising to a peak of 10.2 per 100,000 population in 1980. From 1980 to 1991, the homicide rate fluctuated between 8 and 10 per 100,000 population; in 1991 the number of murders topped 24,000 for the first time in the nation's history. Between 1991 and 2008, homicide rates dropped more than 40 percent; about 16,000 murders now occur each year. Even though questions have been raised about the validity of UCR data, the fact that homicide rates have declined supports the fact that the overall crime rate is in remission.

Trends in Victimization

According to the latest NCVS survey, U.S. residents age 12 or older experienced about 23 million violent and property victimizations. About 16 million households now experience one or more property crimes or have a member age 12 or older who has experienced one or more violent crimes.[24]

Similar to the UCR data, NCVS data shows that criminal victimizations have declined significantly during the past 30 years. In 1973 an estimated 44 million

Meta-Analysis and Systematic Review

Meta-analysis involves gathering data from a number of previous studies. Compatible information and data are extracted and pooled together. When analyzed, the grouped data from several different studies provide a more powerful and valid indicator of relationships than the results provided by a single study. A systematic review is another widely accepted means of evaluating the effectiveness of public policy interventions. It involves collecting the findings from previously conducted scientific studies that address a particular problem, appraising and synthesizing the evidence, and using the collective evidence to address a particular scientific question.

Data Mining

A relatively new criminological technique, data mining uses multiple advanced computational methods, including artificial intelligence (the use of computers to perform logical functions), to analyze large data sets that usually involve one or more data sources. The goal is to identify significant and recognizable patterns, trends, and relationships that are not easily detected through traditional analytical techniques. Data mining might be employed to help a police department determine whether burglaries in its jurisdiction have a particular pattern. To determine whether such a pattern exists, a criminologist might employ data-mining techniques with a variety of sources, including calls for service data, crime or incident reports, witness statements, suspect interviews, tip information, telephone toll analysis, and Internet activity. The data mining might uncover a strong relationship between the time of day and the place of occurrence. The police could use the findings to plan an effective burglary elimination strategy.

Crime Mapping

Criminologists now use crime mapping to create graphical representations of the spatial geography of crime. Computerized crime maps enable criminologists to analyze and correlate a wide array of data to create immediate, detailed visuals of crime patterns. Crime mapping is a research technique that employs computerized crime maps and other graphical representations of crime data patterns. The simplest maps display crime locations or concentrations and can be used, for example, to help law enforcement agencies increase the effectiveness of their patrol efforts. More complex maps can be used to chart trends in criminal activity. For example, criminologists might be able to determine whether certain neighborhoods in a city have significantly higher crime rates than others—whether they are so-called hot spots of crime.

SOURCES: David Farrington, Lloyd Ohlin, and James Q. Wilson, *Understanding and Controlling Crime* (New York: Springer-Verlag, 1986), pp. 11–18; Claire Sterk-Elifson, "Just for Fun? Cocaine Use among Middle-Class Women," *Journal of Drug Issues* 26 (1996): 63–76; William F. Whyte, *Street Corner Society* (Chicago: University of Chicago Press, 1955) 38; Herman Schwendinger and Julia Schwendinger, *Adolescent Subcultures and Delinquency* (New York: Praeger, 1985); David Farrington and Brandon Welsh, "Improved Street Lighting and Crime Prevention," *Justice Quarterly* 19 (2002): 313–343; Colleen McCue, Emily Stone, and Teresa Gooch, "Data Mining and Value-Added Analysis," *FBI Law Enforcement Bulletin* 72 (2003): 1–6; Jerry Ratcliffe, "Aoristic Signatures and the Spatio-Temporal Analysis of High Volume Crime Patterns," *Journal of Quantitative Criminology* 18 (2002): 23–43.

Figure 2.3 Trends in Homicide Rate

Rate per 100,000 population

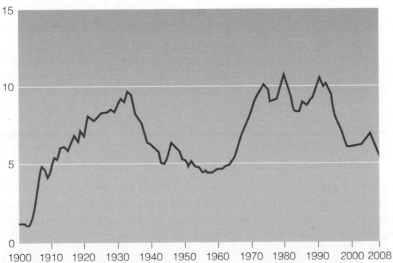

SOURCE: Bureau of Justice Statistics, *Homicide Trends in the U.S.*, www.ojp.usdoj .gov/bjs/homicide/hmrt.htm, updated with FBI data, www.fbi.gov/ucr/cius2007/offenses/ violent_crime/murder_homicide.html.

India has experienced a shocking form of violence against women known as bride burning: A woman may be burned to death if her family fails to provide the expected dowry to the groom's family or if she is suspected of premarital infidelity. Many Indian women commit suicide to escape the brutality of their situation.

The most recent data shows that the danger from various forms of violent behavior abroad, such as bride burning in India, may be trending downward abroad. However, although the United States once led the Western world in overall crime, there has been a marked decline in U.S. crime rates, which are now below those of other industrial nations, including England and Wales, Denmark, and Finland.

What do these various sources tell us about international crime rates?

Homicide

Many nations, especially those experiencing social or economic upheaval, have murder rates much higher than the United States. Colombia has about 63 homicides per 100,000 people, and South Africa has 51, compared to fewer than 6 in the United States. During the 1990s, there were more homicides in Brazil than in the United States, Canada, Italy, Japan, Australia, Portugal, Britain, Austria, and Germany taken together. Why are murder rates so high in Brazil? Law enforcement officials link the upsurge in violence to drug trafficking, gang feuds, vigilantism, and

Race, Culture, Gender, and Criminology
International Crime Trends

Making international comparisons is often difficult because the legal definitions of crime vary from country to country. There are also differences in the way crime is measured. For example, in the United States, crime may be measured by counting criminal acts reported to the police or by using victim surveys, whereas in many European countries, the number of cases solved by the police is used as the measure of crime. Despite these problems, valid comparisons can still be made about crime across different countries using a number of reliable data sources. For example, the United Nations Survey of Crime Trends and Operations of Criminal Justice Systems (UNCJS) is the best-known source of information on cross-national data. The International Crime Victims Survey (ICVS) is conducted in 60 countries and managed by the Ministry of Justice of the Netherlands, the Home Office of the United Kingdom, and the United Nations Interregional Crime and Justice Research Institute. There is also the United Nations International Study on the Regulation of Firearms. INTERPOL, an international police agency, collects data from police agencies in 179 countries. The World Health Organization (WHO) has conducted surveys on global violence. The *European Sourcebook of Crime and Criminal Justice Statistics* provides data from police agencies in 36 European nations.

disputes over trivial matters, in which young, unmarried, uneducated males are involved.

Rape

Until 1990, U.S. rape rates were higher than those of any other Western nation, but by 2000, Canada had taken the lead. Violence against women is related to economic hardship and the social status of women. Rates are high in poor nations in which women are oppressed. Where women are more emancipated, the rates of violence against women are lower.

For many women, sexual violence starts in childhood and adolescence and may occur in the home, school, and community. Studies conducted in a wide variety of nations ranging from Cameroon to New Zealand found high rates of reported forced sexual initiation. In some nations, as many as 46 percent of adolescent women and 20 percent of adolescent men report sexual coercion at the hands of family members, teachers, boyfriends, or strangers.

Sexual violence has significant health consequences, including suicide, stress, mental illnesses, unwanted pregnancies, sexually transmitted diseases, HIV/AIDS, self-inflicted injuries, and, in the case of child sexual abuse, adoption of high-risk behaviors such as multiple sexual partners and drug use.

victimizations were recorded, compared to 23 million today. Figure 2.4 shows the recent trends in violent crime, and Figure 2.5 tracks property victimizations. As these graphs show, the downward trend in the crime rate is supported by the NCVS; both property crimes and violent crimes have declined more than 30 percent in the past decade.

The factors that help explain the upward and downward movement in crime rates are discussed in the Current Issues in Crime feature on page 44.

Robbery

Countries with more reported robberies than the United States include England and Wales, Portugal, and Spain. Countries with fewer reported robberies include Germany, Italy, and France, as well as Middle Eastern and Asian nations.

Burglary

The United States has lower burglary rates than Australia, Denmark, Finland, England and Wales, and Canada. It has higher reported burglary rates than Spain, Korea, and Saudi Arabia.

Vehicle Theft

Australia, England and Wales, Denmark, Norway, Canada, France, and Italy now have higher rates of vehicle theft than the United States.

Child Abuse

A World Health Organization report found that child physical and sexual abuse takes a significant toll around the world. In a single year, about 57,000 children under 15 years of age are murdered. The homicide rates for children aged 0 to 4 years were over twice as high as rates among children aged 5 to 14 years. Many more children are subjected to nonfatal abuse and neglect; 8 percent of male and 25 percent of female children up to age 18 experience sexual abuse of some kind.

Gun Crimes

There has also been a common assumption that the United States is the most heavily armed nation on earth, but there is new evidence that people around the world are arming themselves in record numbers: Residents in the 15 countries of the European Union have an estimated 84 million firearms. Of these, 67 million (80 percent) are in civilian hands. With a total population of 375 million people, this amounts to 17 guns for every 100 people.

Victimization

The latest international victimization surveys indicate that the threat of criminal victimization has declined abroad. According to data from the most recent international crime victim survey, an estimated 16 percent of the population in the 30 participating nations have been a victim of at least one of ten common crimes (such as burglary, robbery, theft, assault) in the course of the last year. The countries with the most victimizations are Ireland, England and Wales, New Zealand, and Iceland, whereas citizens seem to be safest in Spain, Japan, Hungary, and Portugal. Just as in the United States, city residents experience the highest rates of victimization. At the top of the list are Phnom Penh, Cambodia; Maputo, Mozambique; Buenos Aires, Argentina; Johannesburg, South Africa; São Paulo and Rio de Janeiro, Brazil; London, England; and Tallinn, Estonia. In contrast, people are safest in Hong Kong, China; Lisbon, Portugal; Budapest, Hungary; Athens, Greece; and Madrid, Spain.

Although victimization rates are still high, most of the countries show a distinct downward trend in the level of victimization since 1995. The drops are most pronounced in property crimes such as vehicle-related crimes (bicycle theft, thefts from cars, and joyriding) and burglary. In most countries, crime rates are back at the level of the late 1980s. One reason is that people around the world are taking precautions to prevent crime. Improved security may well have been one of the main forces behind the universal drop in crimes such as joyriding and household burglary.

CRITICAL THINKING

1. Although risk factors at all levels of social and personal life contribute to youth violence, young people in all nations who experience change in societal-level factors—such as economic inequalities; rapid social change; and the availability of firearms, alcohol, and drugs—seem the most likely to get involved in violence. Can anything be done to help alleviate these social problems?
2. The United States is notorious for employing much tougher penal measures than European nations. Do you believe our tougher measures would work abroad and should be adopted there as well? Is there a downside to putting lots of people in prison?

SOURCES: Jan van Dijk, John van Kesteren, and Paul Smit, "Criminal Victimisation in International Perspective: Key Findings from the 2004–2005 ICVS and EU ICS, 2008," http://rechten.uvt.nl/icvs/pdffiles/ICVS2004_05.pdf;

Virendra Kumar and Sarita Kanth, "Bride Burning," *Lancet* 364 (2004): 18–19; Etienne Krug, Linda Dahlberg, James Mercy, Anthony Zwi, and Rafael Lozano, *World Report on Violence and Health* (Geneva: World Health Organization, 2002); Graeme Newman, *Global Report on Crime and Justice* (New York: Oxford University Press, 1999).

WHAT THE FUTURE HOLDS

Speculating about the future of crime trends is risky because current conditions can change rapidly, but some criminologists have tried to predict future patterns. There are approximately 50 million school-age children in the United States, and many are under age 10; this is a greater number than we have had for decades. Many come from stable homes, but some lack stable families and adequate supervision. These children will soon enter their prime crime years, and as a result, crime rates may

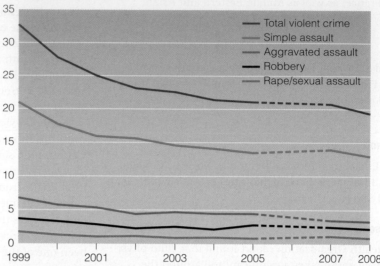

Figure 2.4 Trends in Violent Crime
The overall rate of violent crime fell by 41 percent from 1998 to 2008.
Note: Because of methodological problems, 2006 is not included.

SOURCE: Rand, "Criminal Victimization, 2007," www.ojp.usdoj.gov/bjs/pub/pdf/cv07.pdf, updated 2008.

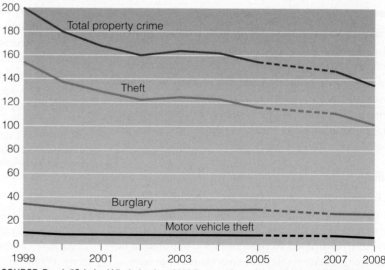

Figure 2.5 Trends in Property Crimes
Overall, property crime rates fell by 32 percent from 1999 to 2008.
Note: Because of methodological problems, 2006 is not included.

SOURCE: Rand, "Criminal Victimization, 2007," www.ojp.usdoj.gov/bjs/pub/pdf/cv07.pdf. updated 2008.

increase in the future.[25] However, whereas kids increase crime rates, seniors depress them. Even if teens commit more crime in the future, their contribution may be offset by the aging of the population, which will produce a large number of senior citizens and elderly, a group with a relatively low crime rate.[26]

Although population trends are important, the economy, technological change, and social factors may shape the direction of the crime rate.[27] The narcissistic youth culture that stresses materialism is being replaced by more moralistic cultural values.[28] Positive social values have a "contagion effect"; that is, the values held by the baby boomers will influence the behavior of all citizens, even

Part 1 Concepts of Crime, Law, and Criminology

crime-prone teens. The result may be a moderation in the potential growth of the crime rate.

Such prognostication is reassuring, but there is, of course, no telling what changes are in store that may influence crime rates either up or down. Technological developments such as e-commerce on the Internet have created new classes of crime. Although crime rates have trended downward, it is too early to predict that this trend will continue into the foreseeable future. ▶ **Checkpoints**

Crime Patterns

Criminologists look for stable crime-rate patterns to gain insight into the nature of crime. The cause of crime may be better understood by examining the rate. If, for example, criminal statistics consistently show that crime rates are higher in poor neighborhoods in large urban areas, the cause of crime may be related to poverty and neighborhood decline. If, in contrast, crime rates are spread evenly across society, and rates are equal in poor and affluent neighborhoods, this would provide little evidence that crime has an economic basis. Instead, crime might be linked to socialization, personality, intelligence, or some other trait unrelated to class position or income. In this section we examine traits and patterns that may influence the crime rate.

Bennie Crabtree, a 61-year-old homeless, poverty-sticken man, waits for lunch at Our Daily Bread on Race Street in the Over-the-Rhine neighborhood of Cincinnati on July 22, 2009. Authorities in Cincinnati say Crabtree is the most-arrested man in the county, having been arrested 146 times since 1998 for such crimes as criminal trespassing, disorderly conduct, and theft. Crabtree steals food and intrudes in places such as the University of Cincinnati, hospitals, and businesses. He has never done anything serious enough to be sent to prison. Because of jail overcrowding, he's now often released hours after arrest. Considering that more than about 40 million people live in poverty, does it surprise you that crime rates are so low?

THE ECOLOGY OF CRIME

Patterns in the crime rate seem to be linked to temporal and ecological factors. Some of the most important of these are discussed here.

Day, Season, and Climate Most reported crimes occur during the warm summer months of July and August. During the summer, teenagers, who usually have the highest crime levels, are out of school and have greater opportunity to commit crime. People spend more time outdoors during warm weather, making themselves easier targets. Similarly, homes are left vacant more often during the summer, making them more vulnerable to property crimes. Two exceptions to this trend are murders and robberies, which occur frequently in December and January (although rates are also high during the summer).

Crime rates also may be higher on the first day of the month than at any other time. Government welfare and Social Security checks arrive at this time, and with them come increases in such activities as breaking into

Checkpoints

▶ The FBI's Uniform Crime Report is an annual tally of crime reported to local police departments. It is the nation's official crime database.

▶ The National Crime Victimization Survey (NCVS) samples more than 75,000 people annually to estimate the total number of criminal incidents, including those not reported to police.

▶ Self-report surveys ask respondents about their own criminal activity. They are useful in measuring crimes rarely reported to police, such as drug use.

▶ Crime rates peaked in the early 1990s and have been in sharp decline ever since. The murder rate has undergone a particularly steep decline.

▶ A number of factors are believed to influence the crime rate, including the economy, drug use, gun availability, and crime control policies that include adding police and putting more criminals in prison.

▶ Gauging future trends is difficult. Some experts forecast an increase in crime, whereas others foresee a long-term decline in the crime rate.

Criminologists consider the explanation of crime trends one of their most important goals. Yet when they are asked, "Why have crime rates declined?" or "Why are rates increasing?" they tend to fumble around, mumble, and become lost in thought, because articulating a single explanation for crime rate change has proved elusive. And despite the fact that policymakers and politicians like simple solutions to complex problems, such as getting kids to watch less violence on TV, many different factors contribute to the ebb and flow of crime rates. The interplay of these social, economic, and demographic changes determines the crime rate. Let's look at a few of the most important influences.

Age Structure of the Population

The age composition of the population has a significant influence on crime trends: Teenagers have extremely high

specifically. In another recent study using national metropolitan-level data, Jacob Stowell and his associates found that violent crime rates, especially those for robbery, tended to *decrease* as metropolitan areas experienced gains in their concentration of immigrants.

In sum, this research indicates that as the number of immigrants in the population increases, the crime rate may actually decline; in other words, immigration has a suppressor effect on crime.

Economy/Jobs

Although it seems logical that high unemployment should increase crime rates and that a good economy should reduce criminal activity, especially theft-related crimes, there is actually significant debate over the association between the economy and crime rates.

Current Issues in Crime Explaining Trends in Crime Rates

crime rates, whereas seniors rarely commit crime. The greater the proportion of teens in the population, the higher the crime rate and the greater the number of persistent offenders. When the "baby boomers" hit their teen years in the mid-1960s, the crime rate skyrocketed. Because the number of senior citizens is expanding and the population is aging, crime rates may remain relatively low for some time.

Immigration

Immigration has become one of the most controversial issues in American society, and some people believe that immigrants should be prevented from entering the country because they have a disruptive effect on society. Research suggests the opposite, however, and some scholars, such as Harvard sociologist Robert Sampson, find that immigrants as a whole engage in criminal activities less than the general population. When Ramiro Martinez and his colleagues examined the association between drug crimes and immigration in Miami, Florida, and San Diego, California, they also found that the more immigrants in the population, the lower rate of homicides and drug-related homicides

- Some crime experts believe that a poor economy actually helps lower crime rates because unemployed parents are at home to supervise children and guard their possessions. Because there is less to spend, a poor economy reduces the number of valuables worth stealing. And it is unlikely that law-abiding, middle-aged workers will suddenly turn to a life of crime if they are laid off during an economic downturn.
- An alternative view is that over the long haul, a strong economy helps lower crime rates, whereas long periods of sustained economic weakness and unemployment may eventually lead to increased rates: Crime skyrocketed in the 1930s during the Great Depression.

One reason for this confusion is that short-term economic swings have different impacts on different segments of the population. When manufacturing moved overseas during the latter half of the twentieth century, it had a much greater impact on young minority men living in cities hit hardest by deindustrialization than on highly educated suburban dwellers who could get jobs in service and technology industries.

mailboxes and accosting recipients on the streets. Also, people may have more disposable income at this time, and the availability of extra money may encourage behaviors associated with crime such as drinking, partying, and gambling.[29]

Temperature Weather effects (such as temperature swings) may have an impact on violent crime rates. Traditionally, the association between temperature and crime was thought to resemble an inverted U-shaped curve: Crime rates increase with rising temperatures and then begin to decline at some point (85 degrees) when it may be too hot for any physical exertion.[30] However, criminologists continue to debate this issue:

Abortion

There is evidence that the recent drop in the crime rate can be attributed to the availability of legalized abortion. In 1973, *Roe v. Wade* legalized abortion nationwide, and the drop in crime rate began approximately 18 years later, in 1991. Crime rates began to decline when the first groups of potential offenders affected by the abortion decision began reaching the peak age of criminal activity. It is possible that the link between crime rates and abortion is the result of two mechanisms: (1) selective abortion on the part of women most at risk to have children who would engage in criminal activity, and (2) improved child rearing or environmental circumstances caused by better maternal, familial, or fetal care because women are having fewer children.

Gun Availability

As the number of guns in the population increases, so too do violent crime rates. There is evidence that more guns than ever before are finding their way into the hands of young people. Surveys of high school students indicate that up to 10 percent carry guns at least some of the time. As the number of gun-toting students increases, so does the seriousness of violent crime, as happens when a schoolyard fight turns into murder.

Gang Membership

According to government sources, there are now more than one million gang members in the United States. Criminal gangs commit as much as 80 percent of the crime in many communities, including armed robbery, assault, auto theft, drug trafficking, extortion, fraud, home invasions, identity theft, murder, and weapons trafficking. Gang members are far more likely to possess guns than those not affiliated with gangs; criminal activity increases when kids join gangs. Drug-dealing gangs are heavily armed, a condition that persuades non–gang-affiliated kids to arm themselves for self-protection. The result is an arms race that generates an increasing spiral of violence.

Drug Use

As drug use increases, crime rates increase. The surge in the violent crime rate between 1985 and 1991 has been tied directly to the crack cocaine epidemic that swept the nation's largest cities. Well-armed drug gangs did not hesitate to use violence to control territory, intimidate rivals, and increase market share. When crack use declined in urban areas after 1991, so too did crime rates. A sudden increase in drug use may be a harbinger of future increases in the crime rate, especially if guns are easily obtained and the economy is weak.

Media

The jury is still out, but some experts believe that violent media can influence the direction of crime rates. As the availability of media with a violent theme skyrocketed with the introduction of home video players, DVDs, cable TV, and computer and video games, teen violence rates increased as well.

Medical Technology

Some crime experts believe that the presence and quality of health care can have a significant impact on murder rates. The big breakthrough occurred in the 1970s, when technology that was developed to treat injured soldiers in Vietnam was applied to trauma care in the nation's hospitals. Ever since then, fluctuations in the murder rate have been linked to the level and availability of emergency medical services.

Aggressive Law Enforcement

Reductions in crime rates may be attributed to adding large numbers of police officers and using them in aggressive police practices that target "quality of life" crimes, such as panhandling, graffiti, petty drug dealing, and loitering. By showing that even the smallest infractions will be dealt with seriously, aggressive police departments may be able to discourage potential criminals from committing more serious crimes. Cities that encourage aggressive, focused police work may be able to lower homicide rates in the area.

Incarceration

It is also possible that tough laws imposing lengthy prison terms on drug dealers and repeat offenders can affect crime rates. The fear of punishment may inhibit some would-be criminals, and placing a significant number of potentially high-rate offenders behind bars seems to help lower crime rates. As the nation's prison population has expanded, the crime rate has fallen.

(Continued)

- ► Some believe that crime rates rise with temperature (the hotter the day, the higher the crime rate).[31]
- ► Others have found evidence that the curvilinear model is correct.[32]
- ► Some research shows that a rising temperature causes some crimes (such as domestic assault) to continually increase, whereas other crimes (such as rape) decline after temperatures rise to an extremely high level.[33]

If, in fact, there is an association between temperature and crime, can it be explained? The relationship may be due to the stress and tension caused by extreme

Prisoner Reentry

Even though putting people in prison may have a short-term positive effect on crime rates, in the long run, increasing punishments may backfire. The recidivism rate of paroled inmates is quite high, and about two-thirds of those released from state custody will eventually return to prison. Inmates reentering society may have a significant effect on local crime rates, and most reoffend shortly after being released.

Cultural Change

In contemporary society, cultural change, such as increases in the number of single-parent families, in high school drop-out rates, in racial conflict, and in teen pregnancies, can affect crime rates.

Criminal Opportunity

As criminal opportunities increase, so do crime rates. Conversely, crime rates may drop when an alternative to criminal opportunity develops. The decline in the burglary rate over the past decade may be explained in part by the abundance, and subsequent decline in price, of commonly stolen merchandise such as cell phones. Improving home and commercial security devices may also discourage would-be burglars, convincing them to turn to other forms of crime, such as theft from motor vehicles. On the other hand, new targets may increase crime rates: Subway crime increased in New York when thieves began targeting people carrying iPods and iPhones.

Each of these factors may contribute to shifts in crime rate trends. They also have theoretical implications for social policy. For example, if crime is influenced by economic and justice-related factors, then criminals must be rational decision makers who will choose to commit crime if the need arises and the threat of punishment is limited. Effective crime control efforts might then be linked to convincing perspective offenders that crime does not pay and offering them alternative methods for economic gain, such as job training and vocational education.

SOURCES: Jacob I. Stowell, Steven F. Messner, Kelly McGeever, and Lawrence Raffalovich, "Immigration and the Recent Violent Crime Drop in the United States: A Pooled Cross-Sectional Time-Series Analysis of Metropolitan Areas," *Criminology* 47 (2009): 889–928; Amy Anderson and Lorine Hughes, "Exposure to Situations Conducive to Delinquent Behavior: The Effects of Time Use, Income, and Transportation," *Journal of Research in Crime and Delinquency* 46 (2009): 5–34; The National Gang Intelligence Center, National Gang Threat Assessment, 2009, www.atf.gov/pub/gang_related/2009_nat_gang_threat_assessment.pdf; Scott Decker, Charles Katz, and Vincent Webb, "Understanding the Black Box of Gang Organization: Implications for Involvement in Violent Crime, Drug Sales, and Violent Victimization, *Crime and Delinquency* 54 (2008): 153–172; Robert Sampson and Lydia Bean, "Cultural Mechanisms and Killing Fields: A Revised Theory of Community-Level Racial Inequality," in *The Many Colors of Crime: Inequalities of Race, Ethnicity, and Crime in America*, ed. Ruth D. Peterson, Lauren Krivo, and John Hagan (New York: New York University Press, 2006), pp. 8–36 ; Ramiro Martinez Jr. and Amie Nielsen, "Local Context and Determinants of Drug Violence in Miami and San Diego: Does Ethnicity and Immigration Matter?" *International Migration Review*, 38 (2004): 131–157; Martin Killias, "The Opening and Closing of Breaches: A Theory on Crime Waves, Law Creation and Crime Prevention," *European Journal of Criminology* 3 (2006): 11–31; Matthew Miller, David Hemenway, and Deborah Azrael, "State-Level Homicide Victimization Rates in the U.S. in Relation to Survey Measures of Household Firearm Ownership, 2001–2003," *Social Science & Medicine* 64 (2007): 656–664; Alfred Blumstein, "The Crime Drop in America: An Exploration of Some Recent Crime Trends," *Journal of Scandinavian Studies in Criminology & Crime Prevention* 7 (2006): 17–35; Thomas Arvanites and Robert Defina, "Business Cycles and Street Crime," *Criminology* 44 (2006): 139–164; Fahui Wang, "Job Access and Homicide Patterns in Chicago: An Analysis at Multiple Geographic Levels Based on Scale-Space Theory," *Journal of Quantitative Criminology* 21 (2005): 195–217; John J. Donohue and Steven D. Levitt, "The Impact of Legalized Abortion on Crime," *The Quarterly Journal of Economics* 116 (2001): 379–420.

temperature. The human body generates stress hormones (adrenaline and testosterone) in response to excessive heat, and such hormonal activity has been linked to aggression.[34]

Regional Differences Large urban areas have by far the highest violence rates; rural areas have the lowest per capita crime rates. Exceptions to this trend are low-population resort areas with large transient or seasonal populations—such as Atlantic City, New Jersey. Typically, the western and southern states have had consistently higher crime rates than the Midwest and Northeast (Figure 2.6 illustrates this with data from 2008). This pattern has convinced some criminologists that regional cultural values influence crime rates; others believe that regional differences can be explained by economic differences.

USE OF FIREARMS

Firearms play a dominant role in criminal activity. According to the NCVS, firearms are typically involved in about 20 percent of robberies, 10 percent of assaults, and more than 5 percent of rapes. According to the UCR, about two-thirds of all murders

Fact or Fiction?

Immigrant who are in the United States illegally commit a lot of crime, a fact that justifies limiting immigration and closing down the borders.

Fiction. Immigrants, whether they are in this country legally or illegally, have very low crime rates. Immigration helps reduce crime rates.

Figure 2.6 Regional Crime Rates: Violent and Property Crimes per 100,000 Inhabitants

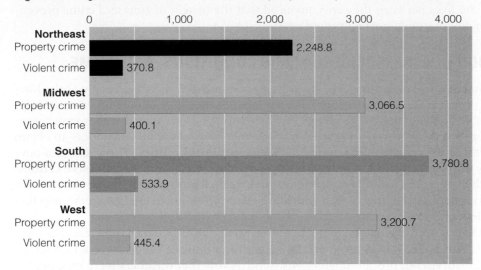

Northeast
Property crime — 2,248.8
Violent crime — 370.8

Midwest
Property crime — 3,066.5
Violent crime — 400.1

South
Property crime — 3,780.8
Violent crime — 533.9

West
Property crime — 3,200.7
Violent crime — 445.4

SOURCE: FBI, *Crime in the United States*, 2008, http://www.fbi.gov/ucr/cius2008/offenses/standard_links/regional_estimates.html.

involve firearms; most of these weapons are handguns. Criminals of all races and ethnic backgrounds are equally likely to use guns in violent attacks, and the presence of a weapon increases the likelihood that a violent incident will result in serious injury and/or death.[35]

Because of these findings, there is an ongoing debate over gun control. Some criminologists staunchly favor gun control. Franklin Zimring and Gordon Hawkins believe that the proliferation of handguns and the high rate of lethal violence they cause is the single most significant factor separating the crime problem in the United States from that in the rest of the developed world.[36] Differences between the United States and Europe in nonlethal crimes are modest at best and are getting smaller over time.[37]

In contrast, some criminologists believe that personal gun use can actually be a deterrent to crime. Gary Kleck and Marc Gertz have found that as many as 400,000 people per year use guns in situations in which they later claim that the guns "almost certainly" saved lives. Even if these estimates are off by a factor of 10, it means that armed citizens may save 40,000 lives annually. Although Kleck and Gertz recognize that guns are involved in murders, suicides, and accidents, which claim more than 30,000 lives per year, they are convinced that the benefit of guns as a crime prevention device should not be overlooked.[38]

SOCIAL CLASS, SOCIOECONOMIC CONDITIONS, AND CRIME

It makes sense that crime is a lower-class phenomenon. After all, people at the lowest rungs of the social structure have the greatest incentive to commit crimes. Those unable to obtain desired goods and services through conventional means may consequently resort to theft and other illegal activities—such as selling narcotics—to obtain them. These activities are referred to as **instrumental crimes**. Those living in poverty are also believed to engage in disproportionate amounts of **expressive crimes**, such as rape and assault, as a result of their rage, frustration, and anger against society. Alcohol and drug abuse, which are common in impoverished areas, help fuel violent episodes.[39]

Official statistics indicate that when measured with UCR data, crime rates in inner-city, high-poverty areas are generally higher than those in suburban or wealthier areas.[40] Surveys of prison inmates consistently show that prisoners were members of the lower class and unemployed or underemployed in the years before their incarceration. Nor is this relationship restricted to the United States. Cross-national comparisons show that wealthier nations, as measured by GNP, have lower violence rates than less economically developed nations.[41]

An alternative explanation for these findings is that the relationship between official crime and social class is a function of law enforcement practices, not actual criminal behavior patterns. Police may devote more resources to poor areas, and consequently apprehension rates may be higher there. Similarly, police may be more likely to formally arrest and prosecute citizens of lower socioeconomic class than those in the middle and upper classes, which may account for the lower class's over-representation in official statistics and the prison population.

Self-report data do show that kids in all levels of society and in all social classes commit crime.[42] However, the weight of recent evidence seems to suggest that serious crime is more prevalent in socially disorganized lower-class areas, whereas less serious offenses are spread more evenly throughout the social structure.[43] Middle-class kids may commit crime, but it is generally of the less serious nuisance variety, such as selling pot or committing acts of vandalism, rather than serious felony offenses. Criminologists recognize that community-level indicators of poverty and disorder—deteriorated neighborhoods, lack of informal social control, income inequality, presence of youth gangs, and resource deprivation—are all associated with the most serious violent crimes, including homicide and assault.[44]

AGE AND CRIME

There is general agreement that age is inversely related to criminality. Criminologists Travis Hirschi and Michael Gottfredson state that "Age is everywhere correlated with crime. Its effects on crime do not depend on other demographic correlates of crime."[45]

Regardless of economic status, marital status, race, sex, and other factors, younger people commit crime more often than older people, and this relationship has been stable across time.[46] Official statistics tell us that young people are arrested at a rate disproportionate to their numbers in the population; victim surveys generate similar findings for crimes in which assailant age can be determined. Whereas youths aged 15–18 collectively make up about 7 percent of the total U.S. population, they account for about 12 percent of Part I violent crime arrests and 18 percent of property crime arrests. As a general rule, the peak age for property crime is believed to be 16, and for violence 18. In contrast, adults 45 and over, who make up about a third of the total U.S. population, account for less than 10 percent of crime arrests. The elderly are particularly resistant to the temptations of crime; they make up more than 12 percent of the population and account for less than 1 percent of arrests. Elderly

CONNECTIONS

Hirschi and Gottfredson have used their views on the age–crime relationship as a basis for their General Theory of Crime. This important theory holds that the factors that produce crime change little after birth and that the association between crime and age is constant. For more on this view, see the section on the General Theory of Crime in Chapter 9.

instrumental crimes
Offenses designed to improve the financial or social position of the criminal.

expressive crimes
Offenses committed not for profit or gain but to vent rage, anger, or frustration.

Part 1 Concepts of Crime, Law, and Criminology

males 65 and over are arrested predominantly for alcohol-related matters (such as public drunkenness and drunk driving) and elderly females for larceny (for example, shoplifting).

Aging Out of Crime Most criminologists agree that people commit less crime as they age.[47] Crime peaks in adolescence and then declines rapidly thereafter. According to criminologist Robert Agnew, this peak in criminal activity can be linked to essential features of adolescence in modern, industrial societies. Because adolescents are given most of the privileges and responsibilities of adults in these cultures, they also experience

▶ A reduction in supervision
▶ An increase in social and academic demands
▶ Participation in a larger, more diverse, peer-oriented social world
▶ An increased desire for adult privileges
▶ A reduced ability to cope in a legitimate manner and increased incentive to solve problems in a criminal manner[48]

Adding to these incentives is the fact that young people, especially the indigent and antisocial, tend to discount the future.[49] They are impatient, and because their future is uncertain, they are unwilling or unable to delay gratification. As they mature, troubled youths are able to develop a long-term life view and resist the need for immediate gratification.[50] **Aging out** of crime may be a function of the natural history of the human life cycle.[51] Deviance in adolescence is fueled by the need for money and sex and is reinforced by close relationships with peers who defy conventional morality. At the same time, teenagers are becoming independent from parents and other adults who enforce conventional standards of morality and behavior. They have a new sense of energy and strength and are involved with peers who are similarly vigorous and frustrated. Adults, on the other hand, develop the ability to delay gratification and forgo the immediate gains that law violations bring. They also start wanting to take responsibility for their behavior and to adhere to conventional mores, such as establishing long-term relationships and starting a family.[52] Research does show that people who maintain successful marriages are more likely to desist from antisocial behaviors than those whose marriages fail.[53]

Age and Biology Some criminologists now believe that the key to desistance and aging out is linked to human biology. Biocriminologist Kevin Beaver and his colleagues found evidence that the **neurotransmitters** *serotonin* and *dopamine* play a role in aggression, the former limiting offensive behavior and the latter facilitating its occurrence. Levels of these neurotransmitters ebb and flow over the life course. During adolescence, dopamine increases while serotonin is reduced; in adulthood, dopamine levels recede while serotonin levels become elevated. It seems more than coincidental that change in brain chemistry parallels the aging-out process: If delinquents commit less crime (or even desist from crime) in adulthood, might not the change be linked to the level of hormone activity in the brain? And, suggests Beaver, because the activity of neurotransmitters is controlled genetically, the genes that are responsible for producing, transporting, and breaking down neurotransmitters may be able to shed light on the potential causes of the age–crime curve, including the sharp decline in delinquent involvement in young adulthood.[54]

GENDER AND CRIME

Male crime rates are much higher than those of females. Victims report that their assailant was male in more than 80 percent of all violent personal crimes. The Uniform Crime Report arrest statistics indicate that the overall male–female arrest ratio is almost 4 male offenders to 1 female offender; for serious violent crimes, the ratio is almost 5 males to 1 female; murder arrests are 8 males to 1 female. Monitoring the Future data also show that males commit more serious crimes (such as robbery, assault, and burglary) than females. However, although the patterns in self-reports

aging out
Phrase used to express the fact that people commit less crime as they mature.

neurotransmitter
A chemical substance, such as dopamine, that transmits nerve impulses from one neuron to another (neurons are specialized cells that make up the body's nervous system).

parallel official data, the ratios are smaller. In other words, males self-report more criminal behavior than females, but not to the degree suggested by official data.

Even though gender differences in the crime rate have persisted over time, there seems little question that the gender gap has narrowed and that there are now more similarities than differences between male and female offenders.[55] UCR arrest data shows that over the decade ranging from 1999–2008, total male arrests declined by 3 percent, while female arrests increased by 11 percent. Male violent crime arrests declined 6 percent during this period, while female violent crime arrests increased 1 percent; similarly, male property crime arrests declined about 6 percent, while female property crime arrests increased almost 20 percent. During the past decade have been increases in female arrests for serious crimes such as robbery (up 37 percent) and burglary (up 26 percent). So during a period of crime rate decline, the arrest data indicates that women have increased their relative participation in crime. Research using NCVS data also suggests a narrowing of the gender gap in violent crime, caused mostly by a greater decline in male offending rates than female rates.[56] How can these differences be explained?

masculinity hypothesis
The view that women who commit crimes have biological and psychological traits similar to those of men.

Trait Differences Why are there gender differences in the crime rate? Early criminologists pointed to emotional, physical, and psychological differences between males and females to explain the differences in crime rates. They maintained that because females were weaker and more passive, they were less likely to commit crimes. Cesare Lombroso argued that a small group of female criminals lacked "typical" female traits of "piety, maternity, undeveloped intelligence, and weakness."[57] Lombroso's theory became known as the **masculinity hypothesis**; in essence, a few "masculine" females were responsible for the handful of crimes that women committed.[58]

Although these early writings are no longer taken seriously, some criminologists still consider trait differences a key determinant of crime rate differences. They link antisocial behavior to hormonal influences by arguing that male sex hormones (androgens) account for the more aggressive male behavior; thus, gender-related hormonal differences can explain the gender gap in the crime rate.[59]

Socialization Differences Although there are few gender-based differences in aggression during the first few years of life, girls are socialized to be less aggressive than boys and are supervised more closely by parents. Males are taught to be more aggressive and assertive and are less likely to form attachments to others. They may seek approval by knocking down or running through peers on the playing field, while females literally cheer them on.[60] Male perceptions of power, their relative freedom, and their ability to hang with their friends help explain the gender differences in crime and delinquency.

Cognitive Differences Psychologists note significant cognitive differences between boys and girls that may affect their antisocial behaviors. Girls have been found to

© AP Images/Al Grillo

Although women still commit less crime than men, the gender gap has been narrowing. Sherry Johnston, mother of Levi Johnston, the man former Alaska governor Sarah Palin's daughter Bristol had planned to marry, right, talks to her attorney Rex Butler, left, and her daughter Mercede Johnston, center, after changing her plea to guilty in a Palmer, Alaska, courtroom on August 19, 2009. Johnston pled guilty to one count of possession with intent to deliver the painkiller OxyContin. Five other felony counts were dropped. It is possible that in the future, as women such as Johnston commit more serious crimes, gender differences in the crime rate will evaporate.

be superior to boys in verbal ability, whereas boys test higher in visual-spatial performance. Girls acquire language faster, learning to speak earlier and with better pronunciation. Girls are far less likely to have reading problems than boys, whereas boys do much better on standardized math tests. (This difference is attributed by some experts to boys receiving more attention from math teachers.) In most cases these cognitive differences are small and getting smaller, and they are usually attributed to cultural expectations. Their superior verbal skills may enable girls to talk rather than fight. When faced with conflict, women might be more likely to attempt to negotiate, rather than responding passively or resisting physically, especially when they perceive increased threat of harm or death.[61]

Social/Political Differences In the 1970s, **liberal feminist theory** focused attention on the social and economic role of women in society and its relationship to female crime rates.[62] This view suggested that the traditionally lower crime rate for women could be explained by their "second-class" economic and social position. It was assumed that as women's social roles changed and their lifestyles became more like men's, their crime rates would converge.

Criminologists, responding to this research, began to refer to the "new female criminal." The rapid increase in the female crime rate, especially in what had traditionally been male-oriented crimes (such as burglary and larceny), supports the feminist view. In addition, self-report studies seem to indicate that (1) the pattern of female criminality, if not its frequency, is similar to that of male criminality, and (2) the factors that predispose male criminals to crime have an equal impact on female criminals.[63]

Recent trends seem to support the feminist view of crime rate differences. Although male arrest rates are still considerably higher than female rates, female arrest rates seem to be increasing while male rates are in decline; it is possible that they may eventually converge.[64] Young girls are joining gangs in record numbers.[65] Although these trends indicate that gender differences in the crime rate may be eroding, some criminologists remain skeptical about the data. According to Darrell Steffensmeier and his associates, these arrest trends may be explained more by changes in police activity than by changes in criminal activity: Police today may be more willing to arrest girls for crimes.[66] Police may be abandoning their traditional deference toward women in an effort to be gender neutral. In addition, changing laws—such as dual arrest laws in domestic cases, which mandate that both parties be taken into custody—result in more women being arrested in domestic violence incidents.[67]

RACE AND CRIME

There is no more complex and controversial issue than that of race and crime. That is because UCR data indicates that minority group members are involved in a disproportionate share of criminal activity. African Americans make up about 12 percent of the general population, yet they account for about 39 percent of arrests for Part I violent crime and 30 percent of property crime arrests. They also are responsible for a disproportionate number of Part II arrests (except for alcohol-related arrests, which involve primarily white offenders).

Similarly, while data collected by the Monitoring the Future study generally shows similarity in offending patterns between African American and European American youths for most crimes, there are some significant differences in reports for some serious offenses, such as stealing more than $50 (13 vs. 7 percent), and using a weapon to steal (7 vs. 2 percent). African American youth do in fact admit more participation in the most serious crimes, a finding that is reflective of the UCR arrest data.[68]

How can these differences be explained? One view is that despite any self-reported disparity, racial bias is responsible for differences in the arrest rate. Suspects who are poor minority group members are more likely to be formally arrested than suspects who are white and affluent.[69] Some critics charge that police officers routinely use racial profiling to stop African Americans and search

CONNECTIONS

Critical criminologists view gender inequality as stemming from the unequal power of men and women in a capitalist society and the exploitation of females by fathers and husbands. This perspective is considered more fully in Chapter 8.

liberal feminist theory
A view of crime that suggests that the social and economic role of women in society controls their crime rates.

One view of the association between race and crime is that police are more likely to investigate and arrest minority group members and to treat white offenders more informally. According to this view, racial profiling and similar practices account for a significant portion of the race-based differences in the crime rate. No recent case has garnered more national attention than the arrest, on July 16, 2009, of Harvard professor Henry Louis Gates. Returning home from a trip to China, Gates found the door to his house jammed. As he and his driver attempted to gain entrance, a passer-by called police and reported a possible break-in. When Cambridge police officers arrived, a confrontation ensued, resulting in Gates being arrested and charged with disorderly conduct. Prosecutors later dropped the charges. The fact that a very prominent African American academic was suspected of breaking into his own home and then taken away in handcuffs sparked a great deal of discussion about race relations and the police. The arresting officer, police Sergeant James Crowley, an 11-year veteran of the force who had recently been in charge of impressing on police officers the importance of avoiding racial profiling, was accused of racism. In the aftermath of the incident, President Barack Obama invited Sergeant Crowley and Professor Gates "for a beer" at the White House to discuss race relations and set aside their differences.

racial threat theory
As the size of the black population increases, the perceived threat to the white population increases, resulting in a greater amount of social control imposed on blacks.

their cars without probable cause or reasonable suspicion. Findings from a national survey of driving practices show that young black and Latino males are more likely to be stopped by police and suffer citations, searches, and arrests, as well as to be the target of force, even though they are no more likely to be in possession of illegal contraband than white drivers.[70]

Others dispute the fact that racial bias alone can explain race-based differences in the crime rate. For example, while research shows that young minority males are more likely to be stopped by police, other studies have found they are also more likely to violate traffic laws.[71] Although the official statistics, such as UCR arrest data, may reflect discriminatory justice system practices, African Americans are arrested for a disproportionate amount of serious violent crime, such as robbery and murder. It is improbable that police discretion and/or bias alone could account for these proportions. It is doubtful that police routinely release white killers, robbers, and rapists, while arresting black offenders who commit the same offenses. In fact, recent research by Terrance Taylor and his associates shows that violent crime cases involving white victims and white criminals were more likely to be cleared than those involving black offenders and white victims, a finding that does not support a police bias view of racial differences in the crime rate.[72] How can these racial differences in serious crimes be explained?

Racism and Discrimination Some criminologists view black crime as a function of socialization in a society where the black family was torn apart and black culture destroyed in such a way that recovery has proved impossible. Early experiences, beginning with slavery, have left an open wound that has been deepened by racism and lack of opportunity.[73] Children of the slave society were thrust into a system of forced dependency and of ambivalence and antagonism toward one's self and group.

Racism is still an element of daily life in the African American community, a factor that undermines faith in social and political institutions and weakens confidence in the justice system. Such fears are supported by empirical evidence that, at least in some jurisdictions, young African American males are treated more harshly by the criminal and juvenile justice systems than are members of any other group.[74] According to the **racial threat theory**, as the percentage of African Americans in the population increases, so does the amount of social control that the justice system imposes on blacks, especially when police officers are given the freedom to use their discretion to arrest, unbridled by departmental rules and regulations.[75] When politicians use veiled hints of racial threat in their political campaigns, the result is excessive punishment of minority citizens.[76]

A significant body of research shows that the justice system may be racially biased.[77] Research shows that black and Latino adults are less likely than whites to receive bail in cases of violent crime and that minority juveniles are more likely to be kept in detention pending trial in juvenile court.[78]

There is also evidence that African Americans, especially those who are indigent or unemployed, receive longer prison sentences than whites with the same employment status. It is possible that judges impose harsher punishments on unemployed African Americans because they view them as "social dynamite"—that is, they consider them more dangerous and more likely to recidivate than white offenders.[79]

Economic and Social Disparity Racial and ethnic differentials in crime rates may also be tied to economic and social disparity. Racial and ethnic minorities are often forced to live in high-crime areas, where the risk of victimization is significant and social support, such as government programs, is lacking.[80]

Racial and ethnic minorities face a greater degree of social isolation and economic deprivation than the white majority, a condition that has been linked by empirical research to high rates of violence.[81] Many black youths are forced to attend essentially segregated schools that are underfunded and run down, a condition that elevates the likelihood of their being incarcerated in adulthood.[82]

Family Dissolution In the minority community, family dissolution may be tied to low employment rates among African American males, which places a strain on marriages. The relatively large number of single-female-headed households in these communities may be tied to the high mortality rate among African American males, which is due in part to their increased risk of early death by disease and violence.[83] When families are weakened or disrupted, their social control is compromised. It is not surprising, then, that divorce and separation rates are significantly associated with homicide rates in the African American community.[84]

In sum, the weight of the evidence shows that although there are few race-based differences in self-report data, Latinos and African Americans are more likely to be arrested for serious violent crimes. The causes of minority crime have been linked to the poverty, racism, hopelessness, lack of opportunity, and urban problems experienced by all too many nonwhite citizens. Research indicates that if racial and ethnic disparity in social and economic resources were to end and minority group members enjoyed the same social and educational benefits as do whites, crime rates would be significantly reduced.[85] ▶ **Checkpoints**

Chronic Offenders/Criminal Careers

Crime data shows that most offenders commit a single criminal act and, upon arrest, discontinue their antisocial activity. Others commit a few less serious crimes. A small group of criminal offenders, however, account for a majority of all criminal offenses. These persistent offenders are referred to as **career criminals** or **chronic offenders**. The concept of the chronic, or career, offender is most closely associated with the research efforts of Marvin Wolfgang, Robert Figlio, and Thorsten Sellin.[86] In their landmark 1972 study *Delinquency in a Birth Cohort*, they used official records to follow the criminal careers of 9,945 boys born in Philadelphia in 1945 from the time of their birth until they reached 18 years of age in 1963. Official police records were used to identify delinquents. About one-third of the boys (3,475) had some police contact. The remaining two-thirds (6,470) had none. Each delinquent was given a seriousness weight score for every delinquent act.[87] The weighting of delinquent acts enabled the researchers to differentiate between a simple assault requiring no medical attention for the victim and serious battery in which the victim needed hospitalization. The best-known discovery of Wolfgang and his associates was that of the so-called chronic offender. The cohort data indicated that 54 percent (1,862) of the sample's delinquent youths were repeat offenders, whereas the remaining 46 percent (1,613) were one-time offenders. The repeaters could be further categorized as nonchronic recidivists and chronic recidivists. The former consisted of 1,235 youths who had been arrested more than once but fewer than five times and who made up 35.6 percent of all delinquents. The latter were a group of

Checkpoints
▶ There are stable and enduring patterns in the crime rate.

▶ Crime is more common during the summer and in urban areas.

▶ Although the true association between class and crime is still unknown, the official data reveals that crime rates are highest in areas with high rates of poverty.

▶ Young people have the highest crime rates; people commit less crime as they mature.

▶ Males have a higher crime rate than females, but the female crime rate appears to be rising.

▶ Some criminologists suggest that institutional racism, such as police profiling, accounts for the racial differences in the crime rate. Others believe that African American crime rates are a function of living in a racially segregated society.

chronic offenders (career criminals)
The small group of persistent offenders who account for a majority of all criminal offenses.

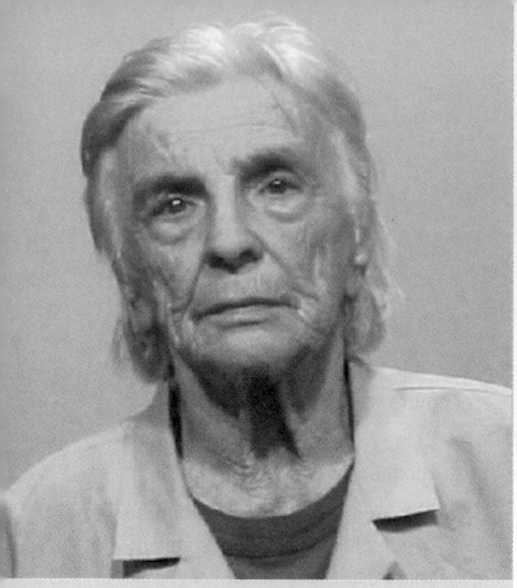

© AP Images/Chicago Police Department

Not all chronic offenders are violent teens. Ella Orko, an 86-year-old woman recently charged with shoplifting wrinkle cream and other items from a Chicago grocery store, has been arrested 61 times since 1956. Ella Orko was arrested August 2, 2009, after authorities say she stuffed $252 worth of items into her pants, including cosmetics, salmon, batteries, and instant coffee. Orko was charged with felony shoplifting, but that charge was reduced to a misdemeanor in exchange for a guilty plea.

627 boys arrested five times or more, who accounted for 18 percent of the delinquents and 6 percent of the total sample of 9,945.

The chronic offenders (known today as "the chronic 6 percent") were involved in the most dramatic amounts of delinquent behavior. They were responsible for 5,305 offenses, or 52 percent of all the offenses committed by the cohort. Even more striking was the involvement of chronic offenders in serious criminal acts. The chronic 6 percent committed 71 percent of the homicides, 73 percent of the rapes, 82 percent of the robberies, and 69 percent of the aggravated assaults.

Wolfgang and his associates found that arrests and court experience did little to deter the chronic offender. In fact, punishment was inversely related to chronic offending: The more stringent the sanction chronic offenders received, the more likely they were to engage in repeated criminal behavior.

In a second cohort study, Wolfgang and his associates selected a new, larger birth cohort born in Philadelphia in 1958, which contained both male and female subjects.[88] Although the proportion of delinquent youths was about the same as that in the 1945 cohort, the researchers again found a similar pattern of chronic offending. Chronic female delinquency was relatively rare—only 1 percent of the females in the survey were chronic offenders. Wolfgang's pioneering effort to identify the chronic career offender has been replicated by a number of other researchers in a variety of locations in the United States.[89] The chronic offender has also been found abroad.[90]

WHAT CAUSES CHRONICITY?

Criminologists believe that chronic offenders tend to be at-risk youth who are exposed to a variety of personal and social problems and who begin their law breaking at a very early age—a phenomenon referred to as **early onset.** Some of the social and personal markers that predict chronicity are set out in Exhibit 2.3.[91] Research studies have also linked chronicity to relatively low intellectual development and to parental involvement in drugs.[92]

IMPLICATIONS OF THE CHRONIC OFFENDER CONCEPT

Fact or Fiction?

A small group of offenders is responsible for most serious crimes; they persist in crime throughout their lifespan.

Fact. Chronic offenders are believed to account for the most serious and persistent crimes committed by adults.

The findings of the cohort studies and the discovery of the chronic offender have revitalized criminological theory. If relatively few offenders become chronic criminals, perhaps chronic offenders possess some individual trait that is responsible for their behavior. Most people exposed to troublesome social conditions, such as poverty, do not become chronic offenders, so it is unlikely that social conditions alone can cause chronic offending. Traditional theories of criminal behavior have failed to distinguish between chronic and occasional offenders. They concentrate more on explaining why people begin to commit crime and pay scant attention to why people stop offending. The discovery of the chronic offender 30 years ago forced criminologists to consider such issues as persistence and desistance in their explanations of crime; more recent theories account not only for the onset of criminality but also for its termination.

The chronic offender has become a central focus of crime control policy. Apprehension and punishment seem to have little effect on the offending behavior of chronic offenders, and most repeat their criminal acts after their release from corrections.[93] Because chronic offenders rarely learn from their mistakes, sentencing policies designed to incapacitate chronic offenders for long periods without hope of probation or parole have been established. Incapacitation rather than rehabilitation is the goal. Among the policies spurred by the chronic offender concept are mandatory sentences for violent or drug-related crimes; **"three strikes"** policies, which require people convicted of a third felony offense to serve a mandatory life sentence; and "truth in sentencing" policies, which require that convicted felons spend a significant portion of their sentence behind bars. It remains to be seen whether such policies can reduce crime rates or are merely "get tough" measures designed to placate conservative voters.

early onset
The view that repeat offenders begin their criminal careers at a very young age.

"three strikes"
Laws that require offenders to serve life in prison after they are convicted of a third felony.

School Behavior/Performance Factor

- Attendance problems (truancy or a pattern of skipping school)
- Behavior problems (recent suspensions or expulsion)
- Poor grades (failing two or more classes)

Family Problem Factor

- Poor parental supervision and control
- Significant family problems (illness, substance abuse, discord)
- Criminal family members
- Documented child abuse, neglect, or family violence

Substance Abuse Factor

- Alcohol or drug use (by minors in any way other than experimentation)

Exhibit 2.3 Characteristics That Predict Chronic Offending

Delinquency Factor

- Stealing pattern of behavior
- Runaway pattern of behavior
- Gang member or associate

SOURCE: Michael Schumacher and Gwen Kurz, *The 8% Solution: Preventing Serious Repeat Juvenile Crime* (Thousand Oaks, CA: Sage, 1999).

Thinking Like a Criminologist

The planning director for the State Department of Juvenile Justice has asked for your advice on how to reduce the threat of chronic offenders. Some of the more conservative members of her staff seem to believe that these kids need a strict dose of rough justice if they are to be turned away from a life of crime. They believe juvenile delinquents who are punished harshly are less likely to recidivate than youths who receive lesser punishments, such as community corrections or probation. In addition, they believe that hard-core, violent offenders deserve to be punished; excessive concern for offenders, and not enough concern for their acts, ignores the rights of victims and of society in general.

The planning director is unsure whether such an approach can reduce the threat of chronic offending. She is concerned that a strategy stressing punishment will have relatively little impact on chronic offenders and, if anything, may cause escalation in their serious criminal behaviors.

She has asked you for your professional advice.

Writing Assignment

Write an essay explaining both sides of the issue, comparing the potential effects of stigma and labeling with the need for control and security. Explain how you would handle chronic offenders, and tie your answer to the aging out process.

Summary

1. Be familiar with the various forms of crime data.

    The Federal Bureau of Investigation collects data from local law enforcement agencies and publishes that information yearly in its Uniform Crime Report (UCR). The National Incident-Based Reporting System (NIBRS) is a program that collects data on each reported crime incident. The National Crime Victimization Survey (NCVS) is a nationwide survey of victimization in the United States. Self-report surveys ask people to describe, in detail, their recent and lifetime participation in criminal activity.

2. Know the problems associated with collecting data.

    Many serious crimes are not reported to police and therefore are not counted by the UCR. The NCVS may have problems due to victims' misinterpretation of events and underreporting prompted by the embarrassment of reporting crime to interviewers, fear of getting in trouble, or simply forgetting an incident. And respondents in self-report studies may exaggerate their criminal acts, forget some of them, or be confused about what is being asked.

3. Be able to discuss recent trends in the crime rate.

Crime rates peaked in 1991 when police recorded almost 15 million crimes. Since then the number of crimes has been in decline. About 11 million crimes were reported in 2008, a drop of 4 million reported crimes since the 1991 peak, despite an increase of about 50 million in the general population. NCVS data shows that criminal victimizations have declined significantly during the past 30 years: In 1973 an estimated 44 million victimizations were recorded, compared to 23 million today.

4. Be familiar with the factors that influence crime rates.

The age composition of the population, the number of immigrants, the availability of legalized abortion, the number of guns, drug use, availability of emergency medical services, numbers of police officers, the state of the economy, cultural change, and criminal opportunities all influence crime rates.

5. Compare crime rates under different ecological conditions.

Patterns in the crime rate seem to be linked to temporal and ecological factors. Most reported crimes occur during July and August; large urban areas have by far the highest rates of violent crimes, and rural areas have the lowest per capita.

6. Be able to discuss the association between social class and crime.

People living in poverty engage in disproportionate amounts of expressive crimes, such as rape and assault. Crime rates in inner-city, high-poverty areas are generally higher than those in suburban or wealthier areas.

7. Know what is meant by the term "aging-out process."

Regardless of economic status, marital status, race, sex, and other factors, younger people commit crime more often than older people, and this relationship has been stable across time. Most criminologists agree that people commit less crime as they age.

8. Recognize that there are gender and racial patterns in crime.

Male crime rates are much higher than those of females. Gender difference in the crime rate have persisted over time, but there is little question that females are now involved in more crime than ever before and that there are more similarities than differences between male and female offenders. Official crime data indicates that minority group members are involved in a disproportionate share of criminal activity. Racial and ethnic differentials in crime rates may be tied to economic and social disparity.

9. Be familiar with Wolfgang, Figlio, and Sellin's pioneering research on chronic offending.

The concept of the chronic, or career, offender is most closely associated with the research efforts of Marvin Wolfgang, Robert Figlio, and Thorsten Sellin. Chronic offenders are involved in significant amounts of delinquent behavior and tend later to become adult criminals. Unlike most offenders, they do not age out of crime.

10. Know what causes chronicity.

Kids who have been exposed to a variety of personal and social problems at an early age are the most at risk to repeat offending. Chronic offenders often have problems in the home and at school, relatively low intellectual development, and parental drug involvement.

Key Terms

Critical Thinking Questions

1. Would you answer honestly if a national crime survey asked you about your criminal behavior, including drinking and drug use? If not, why not? If you would not answer honestly, do you question the accuracy of self-report surveys?
2. How would you explain gender differences in the crime rate? Why do you think males are more violent than females?
3. Assuming that males are more violent than females, does that mean crime has a biological rather than a social basis (because males and females share a similar environment)?
4. The UCR reports that crime rates are higher in large cities than in small towns. What does that tell us about the effects of TV, films, and music on teenage behavior?
5. What social and environmental factors do you believe influence the crime rate?
6. Do you think a national emergency would increase or decrease crime rates?

© AP Images/Tina Fineberg

Chapter Outline

Victims and Victimization

On February 25, 2006, Imette St. Guillen stopped in for a late-night drink in The Falls bar, a popular New York City nightspot. Later that evening, the bar's manager asked the bouncer Darryl Littlejohn to escort Imette out after she stayed past the 4:00 AM closing time.[1] He recalled hearing the pair argue before they disappeared through a side door. Sometime during the next 17 hours, Imette was raped and killed and her bound body left on the side of a desolate Brooklyn roadway. Police investigators soon set their sights on Littlejohn, a felon with prior convictions for robbery, drugs, and gun possession. He was indicted for murder when blood found on plastic ties that were used to bind Imette's hands behind her back matched Littlejohn's DNA.

Imette St. Guillen was a brilliant and beautiful young woman loved by her family and friends. She attended Farragut Elementary School, followed by Boston Latin School in Massachusetts, and graduated magna cum laude from George Washington University in 2003 as a member of Phi Beta Kappa. At the time of her death, she was a graduate student at John Jay College of Criminal Justice in New York City, where she would have completed her master's degree in May 2006. "New York was Imette's home," her sister Alejandra St. Guillen later told reporters. "She loved the city and its people. . . . Imette was a good person, a kind person. Her heart was full of love. With Imette's death, the world lost someone very special too soon."[2] In contrast, her killer, Darryl Littlejohn, had a long history of violent crimes, had spent more than 12 years in prison for drug possession and robbery charges, and was on parole at the time of the crime. While awaiting trial, he was convicted of abducting another woman in 2005 and received a life sentence for that crime. On July 8, 2009, Littlejohn was found guilty of murdering Imette St. Guillen and sentenced to life without parole.

Fact or Fiction?

▶ The cost of victimization to American society is in the hundreds of billions each year.

▶ Victims are passive people who would never get involved in crime themselves.

▶ Sadly, a great deal of violent crime and theft crime takes place on school grounds.

▶ Men are more likely to be victimized by strangers, women by someone they know.

▶ Most crime victims are people who are simply in the wrong place at the wrong time.

▶ Criminals are given too many rights, while their victims have few legal protections.

Chapter Objectives

1. Describe the victim's role in the crime process.
2. Know the greatest problems faced by crime victims.
3. Know what is meant by the term "cycle of violence."
4. Be familiar with the ecology of victimization risk.
5. Describe the victim's household.
6. Describe the most dominant victim characteristics.
7. Be familiar with concept of repeat victimization.
8. Be familiar with the most important theories of victimization.
9. Discuss programs dedicated to caring for the victim.
10. Be familiar with the concept of victims' rights.

The St. Guillen murder case illustrates the importance of understanding the victim's role in the crime process. Why do people become targets of predatory criminals? Do some become victims because of their lifestyle and environment? Did Imette contribute to her attack by staying out late at night, drinking, and being alone? Imette's friends, who were with her earlier in the evening, left her in the early morning hours because they considered the neighborhood around The Falls bar safe. If Imette had been with friends to guard her, would she be alive today? Or does asking these questions smack of unfairly "blaming the victim" for risky behavior? Can someone deflect or avoid criminal behavior, or is it a matter of fate and chance? What can be done to protect victims? For example, should a convicted criminal be employed in a bar and asked to escort patrons? Should lifelong violent criminals ever be let out of prison on parole before they are truly rehabilitated? And when prevention fails, what can be done to help victims in the aftermath of crime?

The Victim's Role

For many years, crime victims were viewed by criminologists as merely the passive targets of a criminal's anger, greed, or frustration; they were considered to have been "in the wrong place at the wrong time." Then, more than 60 years ago, a number of pioneering studies found that, contrary to popular belief, the victim's own behavior is important in the crime process. Victims were found to influence criminal behavior by playing an active role in a criminal incident, such as when an assault victim initially provokes an eventual attacker. Victims can also play an indirect role in a criminal incident, such as when a woman adopts a lifestyle that continually brings her into high-crime areas.

The discovery that victims play an important role in the crime process has prompted the scientific study of victims, or **victimology**. Criminologists who focus their attention on crime victims refer to themselves as **victimologists**.

In this chapter, we examine victims and their relationship to the criminal process. First, using available victim data, we analyze the nature and extent of victimization. We then discuss the relationship between victims and criminal offenders. In this context, we look at various theories of victimization that attempt to explain the victim's role in the crime problem. Finally, we examine how society has responded to the needs of victims and consider what special problems they still face.

Victimization's Toll on Society

The National Crime Victimization Survey (NCVS) indicates that the annual number of victimizations in the United States is about 23 million incidents. Being the target or victim of a rape, robbery, or assault is a terrible burden that can have considerable long-term consequences. The costs of victimization can include damaged property, pain and suffering to victims, and the involvement of the police and other agencies of the justice system. The pain and suffering inflicted on an individual by an assault or robbery can result in medical care, lost wages from not being able to work, and reduced quality of life imposed by debilitating injuries and/or fear of being victimized again, which can result in not being able to go to work, long-term medical care, and counseling.

ECONOMIC LOSS

When the costs of goods taken during property crimes is added to productivity losses caused by injury, pain, and emotional trauma, the annual cost of victimization is estimated to be in the hundreds of billions of dollars.

System Costs Part of the economic loss due to victimization is the cost to American taxpayers of maintaining the justice system. Violent crime by juveniles alone costs the United States $158 billion each year.[3] This estimate includes some of the costs

victimology
The study of the victim's role in criminal events.

victimologists
Criminologists who focus on the victims of crime.

incurred by federal, state, and local governments to assist victims of juvenile violence, such as medical treatment for injuries and services for victims, which amounts to about $30 billion. The remaining $128 billion is due to losses suffered by victims, such as lost wages, pain, suffering, and reduced quality of life. Not included in these figures are the costs incurred trying to reduce juvenile violence, which include early prevention programs, services for juveniles, and the juvenile justice system.

And juvenile violence is only part of the picture. When the cost of the justice system, legal costs, treatment costs, and so on, are included, some estimates of the total loss due to crime amounts to $450 billion annually, or about $1,800 per U.S. citizen.[4]

Individual Costs In addition to these societal costs, victims may suffer long-term losses in earnings and occupational attainment. Victim costs resulting from an assault are as high as $9,400. Costs are even higher for rape and arson, and the average murder costs around $3 million.[5] Research by Ross Macmillan shows that Americans who suffer a violent victimization during adolescence earn about $82,000 less than nonvictims; Canadian victims earn $237,000 less. Macmillan reasons that victims bear psychological and physical ills that inhibit first their academic achievement and later their economic and professional success.[6]

Some victims are physically disabled as a result of serious wounds sustained during episodes of random violence, including a growing number who suffer paralyzing spinal cord injuries. And if victims have no insurance, the long-term effects of the crime may have devastating financial as well as emotional and physical consequences.[7]

BLAMING THE VICTIM

The suffering endured by crime victims does not end when their attacker leaves the scene of the crime. They may suffer innuendos or insinuations from friends and family members who suggest that they are to blame for what happened or that the crime was somehow their fault.

Being blamed for what others perceive to be a result of risky behavior is especially painful for rape victims. Victims of date rape or acquaintance rape may be made to feel they were somehow responsible for the attack because they used poor judgment or took risks.[8] Research by Courtney Ahrens found that rape survivors are often the target of negative reactions from people who are supposed to give them support. Specifically, (1) negative reactions from professionals led survivors to question whether future disclosures would be effective; (2) negative reactions from friends and family reinforced feelings of self-blame; and (3) negative reactions from either source reinforced uncertainty about whether their experiences qualified as rape.[9]

A trauma such as the one experienced by the rape survivors whom Ahrens interviewed can have serious repercussions. Some rape victims report that the treatment they received from legal, medical, and mental health services was so destructive that they couldn't help feeling "re-raped."[10] But when the victim finds that people are sympathetic and responsive, she develops confidence and becomes more willing to turn to them and report victimizations.[11]

LONG-TERM STRESS

Victims may suffer stress and anxiety long after the incident is over and the justice process has run its course. **Post-traumatic stress disorder (PTSD)**—the symptoms of which include depression, anxiety, and self-destructive behavior—is a common problem, especially when the victim does not receive adequate support from family and friends.[12] Rape victims are particularly susceptible to PTSD, and its effects are felt whether the victim acknowledges the attack or remains in denial about what happened. In other words, there is no escaping the long-term effects of sexual assault, even if the victim refuses to acknowledge having been raped.[13]

Adolescent Stress Adolescent victims are also at risk of PTSD.[14] Kids who have undergone traumatic sexual experiences may later suffer psychological deficits.[15]

Fact or Fiction?

The cost of victimization to American society is in the hundreds of billions of dollars each year.

Fact. Some experts believe that, all told, criminal victimization costs society hundreds of billions of dollars each year, including medical, legal, and social costs.

post-traumatic stress disorder Psychological reaction to a highly stressful event; symptoms may include depression, anxiety, flashbacks, and recurring nightmares.

Relational stress can lead to violence. A recent, widely publicized instance of domestic violence involved pop diva Rihanna, left, and her singer boyfriend Chris Brown, seen here at the MTV Movie Awards on June 1, 2008, in Los Angeles. After her beating made national headlines, the pop star told authorities that Brown had a history of abusing her and that the violence was getting progressively worse.

© AP Images/Matt Sayles

Many run away to escape their environment, which puts them at risk for juvenile arrest and involvement with the justice system.[16] Others suffer post-traumatic mental problems, including acute stress disorders, depression, eating disorders, nightmares, anxiety, suicidal ideation, and other psychological problems.[17] And the stress does not end with childhood. Children who are psychologically, sexually, or physically abused are more likely to suffer low self-esteem and be more suicidal as adults.[18] They are also at greater risk of being abused as adults than those who escaped childhood victimization.[19] The reabused carry higher risks for psychological and physical problems, ranging from sexual promiscuity to increased HIV infection rates.[20] Abuse as a child may lead to despair, depression, and even homelessness in adulthood. One study of homeless women found that they were much more likely than other women to report childhood physical abuse, childhood sexual abuse, adult physical assault, previous sexual assault in adulthood, and a history of mental health problems.[21]

Relationship Stress Each crime can have a different effect on its victims. Spouse abuse takes a particularly heavy toll on victims. Numerous research efforts show that victims of spousal abuse suffer an extremely high prevalence of psychological problems, such as depression, generalized anxiety disorder (GAD), panic disorder, substance use disorders, borderline personality disorder, antisocial personality disorder, post-traumatic stress disorder, anxiety disorder, and obsessive-compulsive disorder (an extreme preoccupation with certain thoughts and compulsive performance of certain behaviors).[22] One reason for the prevalence of psychological disorders may be that abusive spouses are as likely to abuse their victims psychologically, with threats and intimidation, as they are to use physical force. Such psychological abuse can lead to depression and other long-term disabilities.[23]

FEAR

Some victims, especially the elderly, the poor, and members of minority groups, develop a persistent and paralyzing fear that they will be victimized again.[24] Victims of violent crime are the most deeply affected, fearing a repeat of their attack. There may be a spillover effect in which victims become fearful of other forms of crime they have not yet experienced; for example, people who have been assaulted may develop fears that their house will be burglarized.[25] In a moving book called *Aftermath: Violence and the Remaking of a Self*, rape victim Susan Brison recounts the difficult time she had recovering from her ordeal. The trauma of rape disrupted her memory, cut off events that happened before the rape from those that occurred afterward, and undermined her ability to conceive of a happy or productive future. Although sympathizers encouraged her to forget the past, she found that confronting it can have healing power.[26]

Even those who have escaped attack themselves may develop fears and become timid after hearing about another's victimization.[27] For example, not only are people likely to move out of their neighborhood if they become crime victims, but they are also likely to relocate if they hear that a friend or neighbor has suffered a break-in or burglary.[28] Their fear is exacerbated by lurid news accounts or crime and violence.[29] Matthew Lee and Erica DeHart found that news stories about serial killers on a rampage can cause a chill felt throughout the city. Fear of these violent crimes prompts people to protect themselves and their family by implementing some sort of protective measure, such as carrying mace or pepper spray or installing a security device in their home.[30]

ANTISOCIAL BEHAVIOR

People who are crime victims may be more likely to commit crime themselves. The process may begin early in life, because being abused or neglected as a child increases the odds of being arrested, both as a juvenile and as an adult.[31] People who were physically or sexually abused, especially young males, are much more likely to smoke, drink, and take drugs than nonabused youth. Incarcerated offenders report significant amounts of post-traumatic stress disorder as a result of prior victimization, which may in part explain their violent and criminal behaviors.[32] Some may run away, increasing their risk of becoming a crime victim.[33] Others may seek revenge against the people who harmed them, and sometimes these feelings are generalized to others who exhibit the same characteristics as their attackers.[34] The abuse–crime phenomenon is referred to as the **cycle of violence**.[35]

As adults, there is evidence that crime victims themselves are more likely than nonvictims to commit crimes. Fearing re-victimization, they may take drastic measures and arm themselves for self-protection.[36] Such measures may amplify victimization risk. ▶ **Checkpoints**

The Nature of Victimization

How many crime victims are there in the United States, and what are the trends and patterns in victimization?

Patterns in the victimization survey findings are stable and repetitive, suggesting that victimization is not random but is a function of personal and ecological factors. The stability of these patterns allows judgments to be made about the nature of victimization; policies can then be created in an effort to reduce the victimization rate. Who are victims? Where does victimization take place? What is the relationship between victims and criminals? The following sections discuss some of the most important victimization patterns and trends.

THE SOCIAL ECOLOGY OF VICTIMIZATION

The NCVS shows that violent crimes are slightly more likely to take place in an open, public area, such as a street, a park, or a field, or at a commercial establishment such as a tavern, during the daytime or early evening hours than in a private home during the morning or late evening hours.

The more serious violent crimes, such as rape and aggravated assault, typically take place after 6:00 PM. Approximately two-thirds of rapes and sexual assaults occur at night—6:00 PM to 6:00 AM. Less serious forms of violence, such as unarmed robberies and personal larcenies such as purse snatching, are more likely to occur during the daytime.

Neighborhood characteristics affect the chances of victimization. Those living in the central city experience significantly higher rates of theft and violence than suburbanites; people living in rural areas have a victimization rate less than half that of city dwellers. The risk of murder for both men and women is significantly higher in disorganized inner-city areas where gangs flourish and drug trafficking is commonplace. Even if people are not personally victimized, city dwellers, especially those living in areas with large disadvantaged populations, are more likely to observe or be exposed to violence than those living in more advantaged neighborhoods. And observing violence can contribute to stress, fear, and flight.[37]

Checkpoints
▶ Victimology is the branch of criminology that examines the nature and extent of crime victimization.

▶ The total economic loss from crime victimization amounts to hundreds of billions of dollars annually.

▶ Victims may suffer long-term trauma, including post-traumatic stress disorder.

▶ Many victims become fearful and go through a fundamental life change.

▶ People who are victims may be more likely to engage in antisocial acts themselves.

Fact or Fiction?

Victims are passive people who would never get involved in crime themselves.

Fiction. In what is known as the "cycle of violence," many victims get involved in crime after they themselves have been victimized.

cycle of violence
Victims of crime, especially victims of childhood abuse, are more likely to commit crimes themselves.

CONNECTIONS

As we saw in Chapter 2, the NCVS is currently the leading source of information on the nature and extent of victimization. It uses a sophisticated sampling methodology to collect data; statistical techniques are then applied to estimate victimization rates, trends, and patterns for the entire U.S. population.

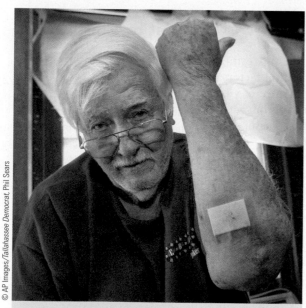

On July 20, 2009, Bradley Harvell, an 82-year-old World War II veteran, shows the spot on his arm where he was shocked with an electrical device by an invading robber at his home south of Bristol in Liberty County, Florida. Harvill said the man, who was dressed like a western-style "train robber," forced his way into Harvill's home and demanded money, shocking him with an electrical device. A scuffle ensued when Harvill didn't produce enough money. He then shot the invader twice, the second time in the head, killing him.

Crime in Schools Schools unfortunately are the scene of a great deal of victimization because they are populated by one of the most dangerous segments of society, teenage males. One reason is that adult supervision is minimal before, during, and after school activities. For example, hallways and locker rooms are typically left unattended. Kids who participate in school sports may leave their valuables in locker rooms; others congregate in unguarded places, making them attractive targets for predators who come on school grounds.[38] Currently:

▶ Among students ages 12–18, there were about 1.7 million victims of nonfatal crimes at school, including 900,000 thefts and 800,000 violent crimes (simple assault and serious violent crime).

▶ About 8 percent of students in grades 9–12 report having been threatened or injured with a weapon in the previous 12 months, and 22 percent report that illegal drugs were made available to them on school property.

▶ Currently about 86 percent of public schools report that at least one violent crime, theft, or other crime occurred at their school.[39]

THE VICTIM'S HOUSEHOLD

The NCVS tells us that within the United States, larger, African American, western, and urban homes are the most vulnerable to crime. In contrast, rural, European American homes in the Northeast are the least likely to contain crime victims or to be the target of theft offenses, such as burglary and larceny. People who own their homes are less vulnerable than renters.

Recent population movement and changes may account for recent decreases in crime victimization. U.S. residents have become extremely mobile, moving from urban areas to suburban and rural areas. In addition, family size has been reduced; more people than ever before are living in single-person homes (which now account for about 25 percent of households). The fact that smaller households in less populated areas have a lower victimization risk is a possible explanation for the decline in household victimization rates during the past 15 years.

VICTIM CHARACTERISTICS

Social and demographic characteristics also distinguish victims and nonvictims. The most important of these factors are gender, age, social status, and race.

Gender As Figure 3.1 shows, gender affects victimization risk. Except for the crimes of rape and sexual assault, males are more likely than females to be the victims of violent crime. Men are almost twice as likely as women to experience robbery. Women, however, are six times more likely than men to be victims of rape or sexual assault. Although males are more likely to be victimized than females, the gender differences in the victimization have narrowed.

One significant gender difference is that women are much more likely to be victimized by someone they know or with whom they live. Of those offenders victimizing females, about two-thirds were described as someone the victim knew or was related to. In contrast, only about half of male victims were attacked by a friend, relative, or acquaintance. However, intimate partner violence seems to be declining. One reason may be an increasing amount of economic and political opportunities for women: Research shows that economic inequality is significantly related to female victimization rates. As more laws supportive of women are passed

Figure 3.1 Violent Victimization by Gender

Adjusted victimization rate per 1,000 persons age 12 and over

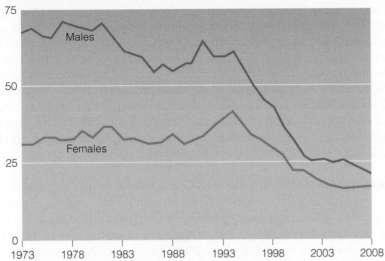

SOURCE: Bureau of Justice Statistics data, www.ojp.usdoj.gov/bjs/glance/vsx2.htm.
Note: Violent crimes included are homicide, rape, robbery, and both simple and aggravated assault.

Figure 3.2 Violent Crime Rates by Age of Victim

Adjusted victimization rate per 1,000 persons in age group

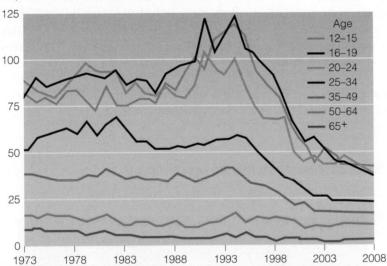

SOURCE: Bureau of Justice Statistics data, www.ojp.usdoj.gov/bjs/glance/vage.htm.
Note: Violent crimes included are homicide, rape, robbery, and both simple and aggravated assault.

and more economic opportunities become available to them, the rates of their violent victimization decline.[40]

Age Although violent crime rates declined in recent years for most age groups, victim data reveal that young people face a much greater victimization risk than older persons. Teens and young adults experience the highest rates of violent crime (see Figure 3.2), but even the youngest kids are not immune. David Finkelhor and his colleagues found that compared to older siblings, younger children were just as likely to be hit with an object that could cause injury, were just as likely to be victimized on multiple occasions, and suffered similar injuries.[41] Victim risk diminishes rapidly after

CONNECTIONS

The association between age and victimization is undoubtedly tied to lifestyle: Adolescents often stay out late at night, go to public places, and hang out with other young people who have a high risk of criminal involvement. Go back to Chapter 2 and review the association between age and crime.

age 25: Teens 16 to 19 suffer 37 violent crimes per 1,000, whereas people over 65 experience only 3 such incidents per 1,000.

Although the elderly are less likely to become crime victims than the young, they are most often the victims of a narrow band of criminal activities from which the young are more immune. Frauds and scams, purse snatching, pocket picking, stealing checks from the mail, and crimes committed in long-term care settings claim more older than younger victims. The elderly are especially susceptible to fraud because they have insurance, pension plans, proceeds from the sale of homes, and money from Social Security and savings that make them attractive financial targets. Because many elderly live by themselves and are lonely, they remain more susceptible to telephone and mail fraud. Unfortunately, once victimized, the elderly have more limited opportunities either to recover their lost money or to earn enough to replace what they have lost.[42]

Social Status The poorest Americans are the most likely to be victims of violent and property crime. This association occurs across all gender, age, and racial groups.

The homeless, who are among the poorest individuals in America, suffer very high rates of assault.[43] In contrast, the wealthy are more likely to be targets of personal theft crimes such as pocket picking and purse snatching. Perhaps the affluent, who sport more expensive attire and drive better cars, attract the attention of thieves.

Race and Ethnicity As Figure 3.3 shows, African Americans are significantly more likely than European Americans to be victims of violent crime. However, there has been a significant decline in the victimization risk of both racial groups, and the decline in violent victimization among African Americans exceeds that experienced by European Americans.

Why do these discrepancies exist? Because of income inequality, racial and minority group members are often forced to live in deteriorated urban areas beset by alcohol and drug abuse, poverty, racial discrimination, and violence. This places them in the most "at-risk" population group.

Marital Status Victimization risk is also influenced by marital status: Never-married males and females are victimized more often than married people.

Figure 3.3 Violent Crime Rates by Race of Victim

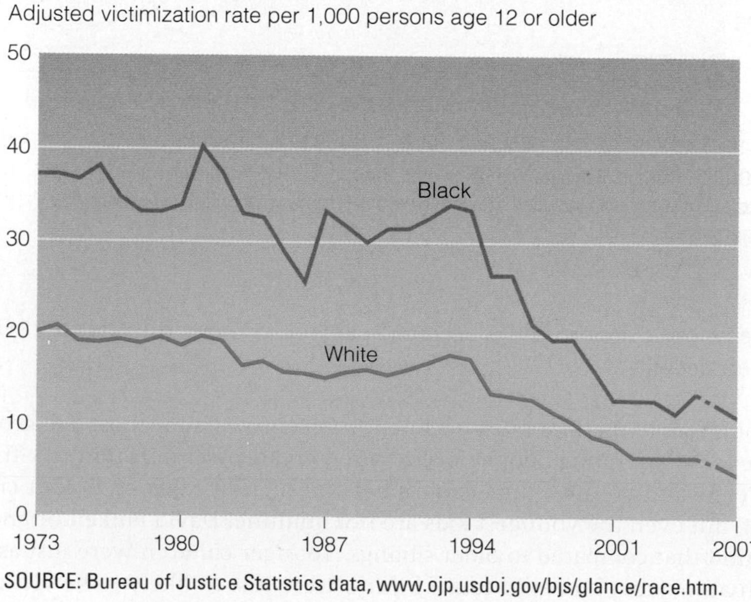

Adjusted victimization rate per 1,000 persons age 12 or older

SOURCE: Bureau of Justice Statistics data, www.ojp.usdoj.gov/bjs/glance/race.htm.

Widows and widowers have the lowest victimization risk. This association between marital status and victimization is probably influenced by age, gender, and lifestyle:

1. Many young people, who have the highest victim risk, are actually too young to have been married.
2. Young, single people also go out in public more often and sometimes interact with high-risk peers, increasing their exposure to victimization.
3. Widows and widowers suffer much lower victimization rates because they are older, interact with older people, and are more likely to stay home at night and to avoid public places.

Repeat Victimization Does prior victimization enhance or reduce the chances of future victimization? Individuals who have been crime victims have a significantly higher chance of future victimization than people who have remained nonvictims.[44] Households that have experienced victimization in the past are the ones most likely to experience it again in the future.[45]

What factors predict chronic victimization? Most repeat victimizations occur soon after a previous crime has occurred, suggesting that repeat victims share some personal characteristic that makes them a magnet for predators.[46] For example, children who are shy, physically weak, or socially isolated may be prone to being bullied in the schoolyard.[47] David Finkelhor and Nancy Asigian have found that three specific types of characteristics increase the potential for victimization:

1. *Target vulnerability.* The victims' physical weakness or psychological distress renders them incapable of resisting or deterring crime and makes them easy targets.
2. *Target gratifiability.* Some victims have some quality, possession, skill, or attribute that an offender wants to obtain, use, have access to, or manipulate. Having attractive possessions, such as a leather coat, may make one vulnerable to predatory crime.
3. *Target antagonism.* Some characteristics increase risk because they arouse anger, jealousy, or destructive impulses in potential offenders. Being gay or effeminate, for example, may provoke attacks in the street; being argumentative and alcoholic may provoke barroom assaults.[48]

Repeat victimization may occur when the victim does not take defensive action. If an abusive husband finds out that his battered wife will not call police, he repeatedly victimizes her; or if a hate crime is committed and the police do not respond to reported offenses, the perpetrators learn they have little to fear from the law.[49]

VICTIMS AND THEIR CRIMINALS

The victim data also tells us something about the relationship between victims and criminals. As stated earlier, males are more likely to be violently victimized by a stranger, and females are more likely to be victimized by a friend, an acquaintance, or an intimate.

Victims report that most crimes were committed by a single offender over age 20. Crime tends to be intraracial: African American offenders victimize blacks, and European Americans victimize whites. Victims report that substance abuse was involved in about one-third of violent crime incidents.[50]

Although many violent crimes are committed by strangers, a surprising number of violent crimes are committed by relatives or acquaintances of the victims. In fact, more than half of all nonfatal personal crimes are committed by people who are described as being known to the victim. Women are especially vulnerable to people they know. More than 6 in 10 rape or sexual assault victims stated the offender was an intimate, a relative, a friend, or an acquaintance. Women are also more likely than men to be robbed by a friend or acquaintance. ▶ **Checkpoints**

Checkpoints

▶ Males are more often the victims of crime than females; women are more likely than men to be attacked by a relative.

▶ The indigent are much more likely than the affluent to be victims of violent crime; the wealthy are more likely to be targets of personal theft.

▶ Younger, single people are more often targets than older, married people.

▶ Crime victimization tends to be intraracial.

▶ Some people and places are targets and venues of repeat victimization.

Victim precipitation theory suggests that criminal violence may be encouraged by the active or passive behavior of its target. Consider the famous case of victimization known as the Jena 6 incident. It began when Justin Barker, 18, shown here, was beaten on December 4, 2006, by six black students at Jena High School in Jena, Louisiana. There had been an undercurrent of racial tension in the town, which had led to outbreaks of violence between white and black students. The tension escalated when a black student attempted to sit under a tree where white students congregated. The next day, three nooses were found hanging from the branches of this tree. Subsequent to the incident, six black students attacked Barker, who was not involved in the incident in any way and whose attack may have been a function of passive precipitation. At trial, where five of the defendants received probation and were asked to pay restitution, their lawyer read a statement apologizing to the Barker family and to the town. This statement also addressed the rumors that the attack had been provoked by Barker's using a racial epithet: "To be clear, not one of us heard Justin use any slur or say anything that justified Mychal Bell attacking Justin, nor did any of us see Justin do anything that would cause Mychal to react." The Barker case is a good example of passive victim precipitation: Justin was victimized because of ongoing racial tension and hostility that were simply not his doing.

victim precipitation theory
The view that victims may initiate, either actively or passively, the confrontation that leads to their victimization.

active precipitation
Aggressive or provocative behavior of victims that results in their victimization.

Theories of Victimization

For many years criminological theory focused on the actions of the criminal offender; the role of the victim was virtually ignored. More than 60 years ago, scholars began to realize that the victim was not simply a passive target in crime but someone whose behavior can influence his or her own fate, who "shapes and molds the criminal."[51] These early works helped focus attention on the role of the victim in the crime problem and led to further research efforts that have sharpened the image of the crime victim. Today a number of different theories attempt to explain the causes of victimization.

VICTIM PRECIPITATION THEORY

According to **victim precipitation theory**, some people actually initiate the confrontation that eventually leads to their injury or death. Victim precipitation can be either active or passive.

Active precipitation occurs when victims act provocatively, use threats or fighting words, or even attack first.[52] In 1971, Menachem Amir suggested that female rape victims often contribute to their attack by dressing provocatively or pursuing a relationship with the rapist.[53] Although Amir's findings are controversial, courts have continued to find the defendants in rape cases not guilty if actions of the victim can in any way be construed as consent to sexual intimacy.[54]

In contrast, **passive precipitation** occurs when the victim exhibits some personal characteristic that unknowingly either threatens or encourages the attacker. Gender may play a role in the decision-making process: Criminals may target female victims because they perceive them to be easier, less threatening targets.[55] Thus, it is possible that a fearful or anxious demeanor may make a woman more vulnerable to attack.

The crime can occur because of personal conflict, such as when two people compete over a job, promotion, love interest, or some other scarce and coveted commodity. A woman may become the target of intimate violence when she improves her job status and her success results in hostility from a jealous spouse or partner.[56] In other situations, although the victim may never have met the attacker or even known of his or her existence, the attacker feels menaced and acts accordingly.[57]

Victim Impulsivity Perhaps there is something about victims that provoke an attack. It is possible that some personality trait exhibited by victims incites attacks. A number of research efforts have found that both male and female victims score high on impulsivity scales, indicating that they have an impulsive personality that may render them abrasive and obnoxious, characteristics that might incite victimization.[58] People who are impulsive and lack self-control are less likely to have a high tolerance for frustration, tend to have a physical rather than a mental orientation, and are less likely to practice risk avoidance. It is possible that impulsive people are antagonistic and more likely to become targets, but they are also risk takers who get involved in dangerous situations and fail to take precautions. Some research results suggest a strong association between victimization risk and impulsive personality, even among kids who do not have a risky lifestyle—that is, even among those who don't hang with delinquent friends or stay out late at night.[59]

LIFESTYLE THEORIES

Some criminologists believe that people may become crime victims because their lifestyle increases their exposure to criminal offenders. Victimization risk is increased by such behaviors as associating with young men, going out in public places late at night, and living in an urban area. Conversely, one's chances of victimization can be reduced by staying home at night, moving to a rural area, staying out of public places, earning more money, and getting married. The basis of such **lifestyle theories** is that crime is not a random occurrence; rather, it is a function of the victim's lifestyle.

High-Risk Lifestyles People who have high-risk lifestyles—drinking, taking drugs, getting involved in crime—have a much greater chance of victimization.[60] Take for example young runaways: The more time they are exposed to street life, the greater their risk of becoming crime victims.[61]

Teenage males have an extremely high victimization risk because their lifestyle places them at risk both at school and once they leave the school grounds.[62] They spend a great deal of time hanging out with their friends and pursuing recreational fun.[63] Their friends may give them a false ID so they can drink in the neighborhood bar. They may hang out in taverns at night, which places them at risk because many fights and assaults occur in places that serve liquor. Exposure to violence and associating with violent peers enmeshes young men in a violent lifestyle that increases their own risk of violent offending. One way for young males to avoid victimization is to limit their male friends and hang out with girls! The greater the number of girls in their peer group, the lower their chances of victimization.[64]

Those who have a history of engaging in serious delinquency, getting involved in gangs, carrying guns, and selling drugs have an increased chance of being shot and killed. Kids who have done time and have a history of family violence are the ones most at risk for becoming homicide victims.[65] Lifestyle risks continue into young adulthood. As adults, those who commit crimes increase their chances of becoming the victims of homicide.[66]

The association between victimization and criminal lifestyle is probably one of risk rather than of propensity: People who are involved simply get close to violent, dangerous people and are therefore exposed to victimization themselves.

College Lifestyle Some college students maintain a lifestyle—partying, taking recreational drugs—that makes them vulnerable to victimization.[67] One research effort by Bonnie Fisher and her colleagues surveyed thousands of college students and found that coeds face the risk of sexual assault at a higher rate than women in the general population.[68] Fisher and her colleagues found that 90 percent of the victims knew the person who sexually victimized them. Most often this was a boyfriend, ex-boyfriend, classmate, friend, acquaintance, or coworker; college professors were not identified as committing any rapes or sexual coercions. The vast majority of sexual victimizations occurred in the evening (after 6:00 PM), typically (60 percent) in the students' living quarters; many were connected to drinking. Other common crime scenes were other living quarters on campus and fraternity houses (about 10 percent). Off-campus sexual victimizations, especially rapes, also occurred in residences. Incidents where women were threatened or touched also took place in settings such as bars, dance clubs or nightclubs, and work settings. Research confirms that young women who involve themselves in substance abuse and come into contact with men who are also substance abusers increase the likelihood that they will be sexual assault victims.[69]

Fact or Fiction?

Most crime victims are people who are simply in the wrong place at the wrong time.

Fiction. Criminologists believe that victims often engage in behaviors that increase the likelihood of their being targeted for crime. Victims are more likely to engage in risky behavior than nonvictims.

CONNECTIONS

In Chapter 9 the association among impulsivity, low self-control, and crime will be covered in some detail. Research indicates that personality traits, covered in Chapter 5, make an individual vulnerable to both crime and victimization.

passive precipitation
Personal or social characteristics of victims that make them attractive targets for criminals; such victims may unknowingly either threaten or encourage their attackers.

lifestyle theories
Views on how people become crime victims because of lifestyles that increase their exposure to criminal offenders.

Criminal Lifestyle One element of lifestyle that may place some people at risk for victimization is an ongoing involvement in a criminal career. Both convicted and self-reported criminals are much more likely than noncriminals to suffer victimization.[70]

The association between criminal lifestyle and victimization risk can be assessed with data from the Rochester and Pittsburgh Youth Studies, two ongoing surveys tracking thousands of at-risk youths. Researchers discovered that kids who get involved in gangs and carry a weapon are up to four times more likely than kids who are not gang members to become victims of serious crime. About 40 percent of males involved in gang/group fights had been seriously injured themselves; among females, 27 percent of those involved in gang/group fights had been seriously injured. Carrying a weapon was another surefire way to become a crime victim. Males who carried weapons were approximately three times more likely to be victimized than those who did not; 33 percent of the weapons carriers became victims, compared to 10 percent of those who did not carry weapons.[71]

Considering the risk that criminals take and the likelihood that they will become victims themselves, what impact does victimization have on a criminal career? Does it encourage more crime and bloody retaliation or does it result in rethinking the dangers of a criminal way of life? The accompanying Current Issues in Crime feature helps answer this question.

Victim or Criminal? Thus it seems that taking risks and engaging in crime put one at risk for personal victimization. Is it possible, then, that criminals and victims are not two separate and distinct groups but rather one and the same? In other words, are victims people engaged in a criminal lifestyle whose dangerous activities backfire on them, resulting in injury or death? We noted earlier that victims tend to be impulsive people, and so are criminals.

Although that conclusion may seem plausible, recent research by Christopher Schreck, Eric Stewart, and D. Wayne Osgood finds, to the contrary, that victims and criminals fall into two separate groups. Violent encounters involve (1) criminals and (2) victims. The personal traits that produce violent criminals, such as an impulsive personality, are not the same ones that produce their victims.[72] Thus, even though many criminals suffer victimization, the Schreck research suggests that criminality is not a per se cause of victimization. Considering these contradictory findings, there is a need for further research on the personality traits of victims.

DEVIANT PLACE THEORY

According to **deviant place theory**, the greater their exposure to dangerous places, the more likely people are to become victims of crime and violence.[73] Victims do not encourage crime but are vulnerable because they reside in socially disorganized, high-crime areas where they have the greatest risk of coming into contact with criminal offenders, no matter what their own behavior or lifestyle.[74] Neighborhood crime levels may be more significant than individual characteristics or lifestyle for determining the chances of victimization. Consequently, there may be little reason for residents in dangerous areas to alter their lifestyle or take safety precautions, because personal behavior choices do not influence the likelihood of victimization.[75]

So-called deviant places are poor, densely populated, highly transient neighborhoods in which commercial and residential properties exist side by side.[76] The commercial establishments provide criminals with easy targets for theft crimes, such as shoplifting and larceny. Successful people stay out of these stigmatized areas. They are home to "demoralized ... people" who are easy targets for crime: the homeless, the addicted, the mentally ill, and the elderly poor.[77]

People who live in more affluent areas and take safety precautions significantly lower their chances of becoming crime victims, but the effect of safety precautions is less pronounced in poor areas. Residents of poor areas have a much greater risk of becoming victims because they live near many motivated offenders; to protect themselves, they have to try harder to be safe than do the more affluent.[78]

deviant place theory
The view that victimization is primarily a function of where people live.

What happens when a criminal experiences victimization? Does it encourage further criminal activities or conversely might the experience help convince a career criminal to choose another career?

Recent research by Scott Jacques and Richard Wright shows that for at least one set of criminal offenders—drug dealers—becoming a crime victim sets the stage for their breaking away from their chosen profession and transitioning into a new life course. This unexpected life event is a "break from the customary" (being in control of drugs) and may lead to "a disturbance of habit in which a customary behavior [drug dealing] can no longer be maintained." According to these investigators, serious victimizations that drug dealers define as being caused by their own law breaking increase the probability of their transitioning out of crime. Terminating their drug dealing is an adaptation that enables them to gain control over their lives and to reduce the probability of future victimization.

Just before he was victimized, Christian recognized that he had lost control of his life and said to himself, "Why . . . am I doing this? I'm about to get robbed. Why am I doing this?'" Christian could not find the strength to stop himself from doing a drug deal that he predicted would result in his own victimization. He thought about finding his attacker and getting revenge, but Christian did not want to take the chance of getting shot. He wasn't into physical violence, so he did not find retaliation to be an attractive option. Although victimization did not result in Christian's instantly terminating his illicit activity, the desistance process was set in motion, and he started to reevaluate the benefits and costs of dealing in relation to alternative lines of available action. Christian considered that he was 18 years old and thus no longer a minor, that he was going to college, that the profit of dealing was not large enough to offset the risks, and that it was time for him to go and make something of

Current Issues in Crime Escalation or Desistance? The Effect of Victimization on Criminal Careers

Jacques and Wright tested their theory by interviewing two drug sellers, Pete and Christian. Both were in their early twenties, were enrolled in college, and had never been arrested. Each tells about the incident that resulted in his terminating his drug dealing. Pete was robbed and beaten. He was forced to show up at a family member's funeral battered and sporting a black eye. When Pete's extended family saw his black eye at the funeral and consoled him, Pete experienced regret and shame. As Pete put it, "That's the thing in my life that I regret most in my life ever, having my whole entire family having to see me *all beat up because I was selling weed*" (emphasis added). Shame and regret related to victimization and drug dealing strengthened his bond to his family and thereby reduced the probability of future drug dealing.

himself. In the end, Christian decided that dealing was too hazardous and that termination was the best course of action.

CRITICAL THINKING

Jacques and Wright find that for some criminals, victimization is an eye-opening event that helps them choose to desist from crime. This transition is aided by a number of factors, including attachment to family and friends and the belief that there are alternatives to criminality. However, the victimization is the catalyst for the decision to transition out of crime. Do you agree with their assessment? Or might victimization breed anger, resentment, and vengeance?

SOURCE: Scott Jacques and Richard Wright, "The Victimization–Termination Link," *Criminology* 46 (2008): 47–91.

ROUTINE ACTIVITIES THEORY

A series of papers by Lawrence Cohen and Marcus Felson first articulated **routine activities theory**.[79] Cohen and Felson assume that both the motivation to commit crime and the supply of offenders are constant.[80] Every society will always have some people willing to break the law for revenge, greed, or some other motive. Therefore, the volume and distribution of predatory crime (violent crimes against a person and crimes in which an offender attempts to steal an object directly) are closely related to the interaction of three variables that reflect the routine activities of the typical American lifestyle:

1. The availability of **suitable targets**, such as homes containing goods that are easily sold.
2. The absence of **capable guardians**, such as police, homeowners, neighbors, friends, and relatives.
3. The presence of **motivated offenders**, such as a large number of teenagers.

routine activities theory
The view that victimization results from the interaction of three everyday factors: the availability of suitable targets, the absence of capable guardians, and the presence of motivated offenders.

suitable targets
Objects of crime (persons or property) that are attractive and readily available.

capable guardians
Effective deterrents to crime, such as police or watchful neighbors.

According to routine activities theory, motivated offenders will commit crime if they find valuable targets. The Red Line Robber is shown here during a theft he perpetrated on August 5, 2009, at the Chicago Community Bank in Chicago. On August 29 he entered the Charter One bank at about 2:30 P.M. and told a teller he wanted to open a checking account. After the teller directed him to a desk in the lobby, he said he didn't actually want an account and instead lifted his shirt to show the handle of a handgun, which he had tucked in his waistband. He asked the teller, "You don't want to get shot, do you?" Then he told her and others to put bundles of cash in a black plastic bag. One teller surreptitiously put in a dye pack. The Red Line Robber, Lance Dennie, 44, was caught later that day.

The presence of these components increases the likelihood that a predatory crime will take place. Targets are more likely to be victimized if they are poorly guarded and exposed to a large group of motivated offenders, such as teenage boys.[81] Increasing the number of motivated offenders and placing them in close proximity to valuable goods will increase property victimizations. Even after-school programs, which are designed to reduce criminal activity, may produce higher crime rates because they lump together motivated offenders, such as teenage boys, with vulnerable victims, such as teenage boys.[82] Figure 3.4 illustrates the interacting components of routine activities theory.

Crime and Everyday Life Routine activities theory helps explain why U.S. citizens suffer such high rates of victimization. According to Felson, crime began to increase in the United States as the country changed from a nation of small villages and towns to one of large urban environments. Because metropolitan areas provide a critical population mass, predatory criminals are better able to hide and evade apprehension. After committing crime, criminals can blend into the crowd, disperse their loot, and make a quick escape using the public transportation system.[83]

motivated offenders
People willing and able to commit crimes.

Figure 3.4 Routine Activities Theory

Crime and victimization involve the interaction of three factors.

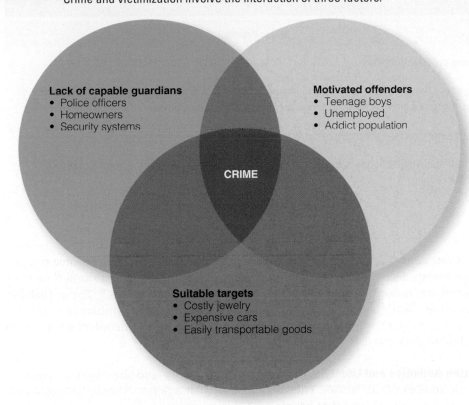

Lack of capable guardians
- Police officers
- Homeowners
- Security systems

Motivated offenders
- Teenage boys
- Unemployed
- Addict population

CRIME

Suitable targets
- Costly jewelry
- Expensive cars
- Easily transportable goods

As the population became more urban, the middle class, fearing criminal victimization, fled to the suburbs. Rather than being safe from crime, the suburbs produced a unique set of routine activities that promotes victimization risk. Both parents are likely to commute to work, leaving teens unsupervised. Affluent kids own or drive cars, date, and socialize with peers in unsupervised settings—all behaviors that are related to both crime and victimization.[84] The downtown shopping district was replaced by the suburban shopping mall. Here strangers converge in large numbers, and youths "hang out." The interior is filled with people, so drug deals can be concealed in the pedestrian flow. Stores have attractively displayed goods, encouraging shoplifting and employee pilferage. Substantial numbers of cars are parked in areas that make larceny and car theft virtually undetectable. Cars that carry away stolen merchandise have an undistinguished appearance: Who notices people placing items in a car in a shopping mall parking lot? Also, shoppers can be attacked in parking lots as they walk in isolation to and from their cars. As car ownership increases, teens have greater access to transportation outside parental control. Thus, even though victimization rates in urban areas are still higher, the routine activities in the suburbs may also produce the risk of victimization.

Research Support Research supports many facets of routine activities theory. Cohen and Felson themselves found that crime rates increased between 1960 and 1980 because the number of adult caretakers at home during the day (guardians) decreased as a result of increased female participation in the workforce. While mothers are at work and children in day care, homes are left unguarded. Similarly, with the growth of suburbia and the decline of the traditional neighborhood, the number of such familiar guardians as family, neighbors, and friends diminished.[85] Steven Messner and his associates found that as adult unemployment rates *increase,* juvenile homicide

Concept Summary 3.1 Victimization Theories

Victimization Theory	Major Premise
Victim Precipitation	Victims provoke criminals.
Lifestyle	Victims put themselves in danger by engaging in high-risk activities, such as going out late at night, living in a high-crime area, and associating with high-risk peers.
Deviant Place	Victimization risk is related to neighborhood crime rates.
Routine Activities	A pool of motivated offenders exists, and these offenders will take advantage of unguarded, suitable targets.

arrest rates *decrease*. One possible reason for this phenomenon: It is possible that juvenile arrests decreased because unemployed adults were at home to supervise their children and make sure they did not get into trouble or join gangs.[86] The availability and cost of easily transportable goods have also been shown to influence victimization rates: As the cost of goods such as mobile phones and camcorders declined, so too did burglary rates.[87]

Routine Activities and Lifestyle Routine activities theory and the lifestyle approach have a number of similarities. They both assume that a person's living arrangements can affect victim risk and that people who live in unguarded areas are at the mercy of motivated offenders. These two theories both rely on four basic concepts: (1) proximity to criminals, (2) time of exposure to criminals, (3) target attractiveness, and (4) guardianship.[88]

These theories also share five predictions: People increase their victimization risk if they (1) live in high-crime areas, (2) go out late at night, (3) carry valuables such as an expensive watch, (4) engage in risky behavior such as drinking alcohol, and (5) are without friends or family to watch or help them.[89] Young women who drink to excess in bars and fraternity houses may elevate their risk of date rape, because (1) they are easy targets, and (2) their attackers can rationalize raping them because they are intoxicated. ("She's loose and immoral, so I didn't think she'd care.") Intoxication is sometimes seen as making the victim culpable for the crime.[90] Conversely, people can reduce their chances of repeat victimization if they change their lifestyle and adopt crime-suppressing routines such as getting married, having children, or moving to a small town.[91]

The various theories of victimization are summarized in Concept Summary 3.1.
► **Checkpoints**

Caring for the Victim

National victim surveys indicate that almost every American age 12 and over will one day become the victim of a common-law crime, such as larceny or burglary, and in the aftermath will suffer financial problems, mental stress, and physical hardship.[92] Surveys show that upward of 75 percent of the general public have been victimized by crime at least once in their lives. As many as 25 percent of the victims develop post-traumatic stress syndrome, with symptoms that last for more than a decade after the crime occurred.[93]

Helping the victim to cope is the responsibility of all of society. Law enforcement agencies, courts, and correctional and human service systems have come to realize

Checkpoints

▶ Victim precipitation theory suggests that crime victims may trigger attacks by acting provocatively.

▶ Some experts link victimization to high-risk lifestyles.

▶ Some people live in places that are magnets for criminals.

▶ The routine activities approach suggests that the risk of victimization may be an interaction among suitable targets, effective guardians, and motivated criminals. Victims who have insufficient protection present motivated criminals with attractive targets.

that due process and human rights exist not only for the criminal defendant but also for the victim of criminal behavior.

Because of public concern over violent personal crime, President Ronald Reagan created a Task Force on Victims of Crime in 1982.[94] This group suggested that a balance be achieved between recognizing the victim's rights and providing the defendant with due process. Recommendations included providing witnesses and victims with protection from intimidation, requiring restitution in criminal cases, developing guidelines for fair treatment of crime victims and witnesses, and expanding programs of victim compensation.[95]

As a result, Congress passed the Omnibus Victim and Witness Protection Act, requiring the use of victim impact statements at sentencing in federal criminal cases, greater protection for witnesses, more stringent bail laws, and the use of restitution in criminal cases. In 1984, the Comprehensive Crime Control Act and the Victims of Crime Act authorized federal funding for state victim compensation and assistance projects.[96] With these acts, the federal government recognized the plight of the victim and made victim assistance an even greater concern of the public and the justice system.

VICTIM SERVICE PROGRAMS

An estimated 2,000 **victim–witness assistance programs** have been developed throughout the United States. These programs are organized on a variety of government levels and serve a variety of clients. We will look briefly at some prominent forms of victim assistance operating in the United States.[97]

Victim Compensation A primary goal of victim advocates has been to lobby for legislation creating crime victim **compensation** programs.[98] As a result of such legislation, the victim ordinarily receives compensation from the state to pay for damages associated with the crime. Rarely are two compensation schemes alike, however, and many state programs suffer from a lack of both adequate funding and proper organization within the criminal justice system. Compensation may be provided for medical bills, loss of wages, loss of future earnings, and counseling. In the case of death, the victim's survivors may receive burial expenses and aid for loss of support.[99] Awards typically range from $100 to $15,000. Occasionally, programs provide emergency assistance to indigent victims until compensation is available. Emergency assistance may come in the form of food vouchers or replacement of prescription medicines.

In 1984, the federal government created the Victims of Crime Act (VOCA), which grants money derived from fines and penalties imposed on federal offenders to state compensation boards. Each year the money is distributed to the states to fund both their crime victim compensation programs and their victim assistance programs, such as rape crisis centers and domestic violence shelters. Currently, this assistance amounts to $300 million per year.[100]

Victim Advocates Some programs assign counselors to victims to serve as advocates, help them understand the operations of the justice system, and guide them through the process. Victims of sexual assault may be assigned the assistance of a rape victim advocate to stand by their side as they negotiate the legal and medical systems that must process their case. Research shows that rape survivors who had the assistance of an advocate were significantly more likely to have police reports taken, were less likely to be treated negatively by police officers, and reported less distress from their medical contact experiences.[101]

Court advocates prepare victims and witnesses by explaining court procedures: how to be a witness, how bail works, and what to do if the defendant makes a threat. Lack of such knowledge can cause confusion and fear, making some victims reluctant to testify in court proceedings.

victim–witness assistance programs
Government programs that help crime victims and witnesses; may include compensation, court services, and/or crisis intervention.

compensation
Financial aid awarded to crime victims to repay them for their loss and injuries; may cover medical bills, loss of wages, loss of future earnings, and/or counseling.

Many victim programs also provide transportation to and from court, as well as counselors who remain in the courtroom during hearings to explain procedures and provide support. Court escorts are particularly important for elderly and disabled victims, victims of child abuse and assault, and victims who have been intimidated by friends or relatives of the defendant. These types of services may be having a positive effect: Recent research shows that victims may now be less traumatized by a court hearing than they previously were.[102]

Victim Impact Statements Most jurisdictions allow victims to make an impact statement before the sentencing judge. This gives the victim an opportunity to tell of his or her experiences and describe the ordeal; in the case of a murder trial, the surviving family can recount the effect the crime has had on their lives and well-being.[103] The effect of victim/witness statements on sentencing has been the topic of some debate. Some research finds that victim statements result in a higher rate of incarceration, but others find that victim/witness statements are insignificant.[104] Those who favor the use of impact statements argue that because the victim is harmed by the crime, she or he has a right to influence the outcome of the case. After all, the public prosecutor is allowed to make sentencing recommendations because the public has been harmed by the crime. Logically, the harm suffered by the victim legitimizes her or his right to make sentencing recommendations.[105]

Public Education More than half of all victim programs include public education to help familiarize the general public with their services and with other agencies that help crime victims. In some instances, these are primary prevention programs, which teach methods of dealing with conflict without resorting to violence. School-based programs present information on spousal and dating abuse, followed by discussions of how to reduce violent incidents.[106]

Trena Gage tries to compose herself while reading her victim impact statement during the sentencing of Roger Paul Bentley on February 24, 2006, at the Johnson County Courthouse in Iowa City. Bentley, who kidnapped, raped, and murdered Gage's 10-year-old daughter Jetseta, was convicted of first-degree murder and first-degree kidnapping and was sentenced to two consecutive terms of life in prison.

Crisis Intervention Most victim programs refer victims to specific services to help them recover from their ordeal. Clients are commonly referred to the local network of public and private social service agencies that provide emergency and long-term assistance with transportation, medical care, shelter, food, and clothing. In addition, more than half of all victim programs provide **crisis intervention** for victims who feel isolated, vulnerable, and in need of immediate services. Some programs counsel at their offices; others visit victims in their homes, at the crime scene, or in the hospital. For example, the Good Samaritan program in Mobile County, Alabama, unites law enforcement and faith-based and community organizations to train and mobilize volunteers who can help crime victims. Good Samaritan volunteers provide services such as

▶ Making repairs to a home after a break-in
▶ Conducting home safety inspections to prevent revictimization
▶ Accompanying victims to court
▶ Supplying "victim care kits" or other support [107]

Victim–Offender Reconciliation Programs Mediators facilitate face-to-face encounters between victims and their attackers in **victim–offender reconciliation programs (VORPs)**. The aim is to engage in direct negotiations that lead to restitution agreements and, possibly, reconciliation between the parties involved.[108] More than 120 reconciliation programs currently in operation handle an estimated 16,000 cases per year. Originally designed to handle routine misdemeanors such as petty theft and vandalism, such programs now commonly hammer out restitution agreements in more serious incidents, such as residential burglary and even attempted murder.

VICTIMS' RIGHTS

Because of the influence of victims' rights advocates, every state now has a set of legal rights for crime victims in its code of laws, often called a Victims' Bill of Rights.[109] These generally include the right

▶ To be notified of proceedings and the status of the defendant
▶ To be present at criminal justice proceedings
▶ To make a statement at sentencing and to receive restitution from a convicted offender
▶ To be consulted before a case is dismissed or a plea agreement entered
▶ To a speedy trial
▶ To keep the victim's contact information confidential

Ensuring victims' rights may involve an eclectic mix of advocacy groups—some independent, others government-sponsored, and some self-help. Advocates can be especially helpful when victims need to interact with the agencies of justice. For example, advocates can lobby police departments to keep investigations open and can request the return of recovered stolen property. They can demand that prosecutors and judges provide protection from harassment and reprisals by, for example, making "no contact" a condition of bail (research shows that victims who hire lawyers have a better chance of getting these orders enforced).[110] They can help victims make statements during sentencing hearings and during probation and parole revocation procedures. Victim advocates can also interact with news media, making sure that reporting is accurate and that victims' privacy is not violated. Victim advocates can be part of an independent agency similar to a legal aid society. Top-notch victim advocates sometimes open private offices, similar to attorneys, private investigators, or jury consultants.

A final, though controversial, element of the victims' rights movement is the development of offender registration laws that require law enforcement agencies to post the name, and sometimes the address, of known sex offenders. Today, almost every

CONNECTIONS

Reconciliation programs are based on the concept of restorative justice, which rejects punitive correctional measures and instead suggests that crimes of violence and theft should be viewed as interpersonal conflicts that need to be settled in the community through noncoercive means. See Chapter 8 for more on this approach.

crisis intervention
Emergency counseling for crime victims.

victim–offender reconciliation programs
Mediated face-to-face encounters between victims and their attackers, designed to produce restitution agreements and, if possible, reconciliation.

Richard and Maureen Kanka thought that their daughter Megan was safe in their quiet, suburban neighborhood in Hamilton Township, New Jersey. Then, on July 29, 1994, their lives were shattered when their 7-year-old daughter Megan disappeared. Maureen Kanka soon began to search the neighborhood and met 33-year-old Jesse Timmendequas, who lived across the street. Timmendequas told her that he had seen Megan earlier that evening while he was working on his car. The police were called in and soon focused their attention on Timmendequas's house when they learned that he, along with two other residents, were convicted sex offenders who had met at a treatment center and decided to live together upon their release. Timmendequas, who appeared extremely nervous when questioned, was asked to accompany the officers to police headquarters, where he confessed to luring Megan into his home by telling her she could see his puppy dog. There, he said, he had raped her and strangled her to death.

Timmendequas had served six years in prison for aggravated assault and attempted sexual assault on another child. Megan's tragic death, and the fact that a known sex offender was living anonymously in the Kankas' neighborhood, sparked a national crusade to develop laws that require sex offenders to register with local police when they move into a neighborhood—and laws that require local authorities to provide community notification of the sex offender's presence. New York State's Sex Offender Registration Act (SORA) is typical of these efforts, which are commonly known as Megan's Laws. SORA, which went into effect on January 21, 1996, requires that sex offenders in New York be classified in terms of the risk that they will reoffend. A court determines whether an offender is classified at level 1 (low risk), 2 (moderate risk), or 3 (high risk). The court also determines whether an offender should be given a "designation" and, if so, whether that designation should be sexual predator, sexually violent offender, or predicate sex offender. Offenders are required to register either for 20 years or for life. Level 1 offenders with no designation must register for 20 years. Level 1 offenders with a designation, as well as all level 2 and level 3 offenders, whether or not they have a designation, must register for life.

Local law enforcement agencies are notified whenever a sex offender moves into their jurisdiction. That agency may notify schools and other "entities with vulnerable populations"

Jesse Timmendequas, the accused killer of Megan Kanka.

about the presence of a level 2 or level 3 offender if the offender poses a threat to public safety. The act established a free (area code 800) Information Line that citizens can call to inquire whether a person is listed in the Registry and to access information about sex offenders living in their neighborhoods. On the federal level, the Jacob Wetterling Crimes against Children Law, passed in May 1996, requires states to pass some version of "Megan's Law" or lose federal aid. At least 47 states and the District of Columbia have complied. Jesse Timmendequas was sentenced to death on June 20, 1997. However, as you may recall from Chapter 1, research shows that Megan's Law has had little effect on sex offending rates in New Jersey.

CRITICAL THINKING

The case of Megan Kanka illustrates both the risk children face from sexual predators and the efforts being made by the justice system to limit that risk. To some civil liberty groups, such as the American Civil Liberties Union, registration laws go too far, because they do not prevent sex offenders from committing crimes and because they victimize rehabilitated ex-offenders and their families. Should the rights of possible victims take precedence over the privacy of convicted sex offenders?

SOURCE: New York State Sex Offender Registry and the Sex Offender Registration Act (SORA), http://criminaljustice.state.ny.us/nsor/; New York State Correction Law Article 6-C (Section 168 et seq.); Court TV library, *New Jersey v. Timmendequas*, www.courttv.com/archive/casefiles/verdicts/kanka.html (accessed March 28, 2006).

The director of your state's Department of Human Services has asked you to evaluate a self-report survey of adolescents aged 10 to 18. She has provided you with the following information on physical abuse.

Adolescents experiencing abuse or violence are at high risk of immediate and lasting negative effects on their health and well-being. Of the high school students surveyed, an alarming 1 in 5 (21 percent) said they had been physically abused. Of the older students, aged 15 to 18, 29 percent said they had been physically abused. Younger students also reported significant rates of abuse: 17 percent

responded "yes" when asked whether they had been physically abused. Although girls were far less likely to report abuse than boys, 12 percent said they had been physically abused. Most abuse occurs at home, it occurs more than once, and the abuser is usually a family member. More than half of those physically abused had tried alcohol and drugs, and 60 percent had admitted to committing a violent act. Nonabused children were significantly less likely to abuse substances, and only 30 percent indicated that they had committed a violent act.

Writing Assignment

Write an essay describing why being abused as a child leads to substance abuse and violence as an adult. In your essay, interpret these findings from an environmental, socialization, psychological, and biological point of view, and provide evidence supporting each perspective.

state has adopted sex offender laws, and the federal government runs a National Sex Offender Public Registry with links to every state.[111] Sex offender registration is indelibly associated with the death of Megan Kanka, a horrifying event described in the Profiles in Crime feature on page 78.

Similarly, the European Union has moved toward increasing the role of victims in the justice process. The Council of the European Union recently agreed to implement what is known as the *Framework Decision on the Standing of Victims in Criminal Proceedings*. The Framework Decision is groundbreaking in that it sets out minimum standards for the treatment of victims of crime (and their families) that apply throughout the European Union.[112]

Fact or Fiction?

Criminals are given too many rights, while their victims have few legal protections.

Fiction. Almost every state and the federal government have developed victims' rights legislation.

Summary

1. Describe the victim's role in the crime process.

   Victims may influence criminal behavior by playing an active role in a criminal incident. The discovery that victims play an important role in the crime process has prompted the scientific study of victims, or victimology. Criminologists who focus their attention on crime victims refer to themselves as victimologists.

2. Know the greatest problems faced by crime victims.

   The costs of victimization can include such things as damaged property, pain and suffering to victims, and the involvement of the police and other agencies of the justice system. The pain and suffering inflicted on an

   individual can result in the need for medical care, the loss of wages from not being able to go to work, and reduced quality of life from debilitating injuries and/or fear of being victimized again, which can result in not being able to go to work, long-term medical care, and counseling.

3. Know what is meant by the term "cycle of violence."

   People who are crime victims may be more likely to commit crimes themselves. Some may seek revenge against the people who harmed them. The abuse–crime phenomenon is referred to as the cycle of violence.

4. Be familiar with the ecology of victimization risk.

Violent crimes are slightly more likely to take place in an open, public area, such as a street, a park, or a field. The more serious violent crimes, such as rape and aggravated assault, typically take place after 6:00 PM. Those living in the central city have significantly higher rates of theft and violence than suburbanites; people living in rural areas have a victimization rate almost half that of city dwellers. Schools unfortunately are the site of a great deal of victimization because they are populated by one of the most dangerous segments of society, teenage males.

5. Describe the victim's household.

The NCVS tells us that within the United States, larger, African American, western, and urban homes are the most vulnerable to crime. In contrast, rural, European American homes in the Northeast are the least likely to contain crime victims or be the target of theft offenses, such as burglary and larceny. People who own their homes are less vulnerable than renters.

6. Describe the most dominant victim characteristics.

Except for the crimes of rape and sexual assault, males are more likely than females to be the victims of violent crime. Victim data reveal that young people face a much greater victimization risk than older persons. The poorest Americans are the most likely to be victims of violent and property crime. This association occurs across all gender, age, and racial groups. African Americans are about twice as likely as European Americans to be victims of violent crime. Never-married males and females are victimized more often than married people.

7. Be familiar with concept of repeat victimization.

Individuals who have been crime victims have a significantly higher chance of future victimization than people who have remained nonvictims. Households that have experienced victimization in the past are the ones most likely to experience it again in the future. One reason: Some victims' physical weakness or psychological distress renders them incapable of resisting or deterring crime and makes them easy targets.

8. Be familiar with the most important theories of victimization.

According to victim precipitation theory, some people may actually initiate the confrontation that eventually leads to their injury or death. Victim precipitation can be either active or passive. Some criminologists believe that people may become crime victims because their lifestyle increases their exposure to criminal offenders. People who have high-risk lifestyles—drinking, taking drugs, getting involved in crime—have a much greater chance of victimization. According to deviant place theory, the greater their exposure to dangerous places, the more likely people are to become victims of crime and violence. So-called deviant places are poor, densely populated, highly transient neighborhoods in which commercial and residential properties exist side by side. Routine activities theory links victimization to the availability of suitable targets, the absence of capable guardians, and the presence of motivated offenders.

9. Discuss programs dedicated to caring for the victim.

Victim–witness assistance programs are government programs that help crime victims and witnesses; they may include compensation, court services, and/or crisis intervention. Such programs often include victim compensation—financial aid awarded to crime victims to repay them for their loss and injuries; this assistance may cover medical bills, loss of wages, loss of future earnings, and/or counseling. Some programs assign counselors to victims to serve as advocates to help them understand the operation of the justice system and guide them through the process. Most jurisdictions allow victims to make an impact statement before the sentencing judge. Most victim programs refer victims to specific services to help them recover from their ordeal.

10. Be familiar with the concept of victims' rights.

Every state now has a set of legal rights for crime victims in its code of laws, often called a Victims' Bill of Rights. These generally include the victim's right to be notified of proceedings and the status of the defendant, to be present at criminal justice proceedings and to make statements at trials, to receive restitution from a convicted offender, and to be consulted about trial procedures, such as when a plea is offered.

Key Terms

victimology 60

victimologists 60

post-traumatic stress disorder (PTSD) 61

cycle of violence 63

victim precipitation theory 68

active precipitation 68

passive precipitation 69

lifestyle theories 69

deviant place theory 70

routine activities theory 71

suitable targets 71

capable guardians 71

motivated offenders 72

victim–witness assistance programs 75

compensation 75

crisis intervention 77

victim–offender reconciliation programs (VORPs) 77

Critical Thinking Questions

1. Considering what you have learned in this chapter about crime victimization, what measures can you take to better protect yourself from crime?

2. Do you agree with the assessment that a school is one of the most dangerous locations in the community? Did you find your high school to be a dangerous environment?

3. Do people bear some of the responsibility for their victimization if they maintain a lifestyle that contributes to the chances of becoming a crime victim? That is, should we "blame the victim"?

4. Have you ever observed someone habitually "precipitating" crime? If so, did you do anything to improve the situation?

5. What would you advise freshman girls to do to lower their risk of being sexually assaulted?

Chapter Outline

Choice Theory
Because They Want To

4

Just before Christmas in 2004, more than 150,000 fax machines around the country spat out a mysterious message from a financial planner named simply "Chris" that was addressed to a "Dr. Mitchel." The note was intriguing because it referred to a hot stock that Chris wanted the good doctor to buy immediately:

> I have a stock for you that will tripple [sic] in price just like the last stock I gave you "SIRI" did. I can't get you on either phone. Either call me, or call Linda to place the new trade. We need to buy IFLB now.

People who received this "tip" thought they were fortunate to have been on the receiving end of a wrong number and started buying shares of IFLB (Infinium Labs, a video gaming company now called Phantom Entertainment). The increased volume had an immediate effect, and the price of the shares jumped 160 percent in four days. Two other stocks mentioned in alternate versions of the fax—Data Evolution and Soleil Film—saw similar increases. Unfortunately for the investors who acted on the tip, however, there was no Dr. Mitchel, no Chris, no Linda, and no real stock tip. It was all part of a scam to get them to buy shares of stocks, so that the conspirators could pocket a tidy profit after the prices rose. It all worked according to plan: In less than two months, the conspirators who had sent out the bogus faxes made a $400,000 profit.

Eventually the Securities and Exchange Commission opened an investigation, tracing the fax calls to a Florida company run by Michael Pickens, who was arrested and charged with securities fraud. Michael pled guilty and, on December 20, 2007, was sentenced to five years of probation, ordered to take part in a substance abuse program, and directed to pay restitution of $1.2 million in connection with the fraud. One irony of the case: Michael Pickens is the son of multibillionaire oil investor T. Boone Pickens, one of the nation's richest people.[1]

Fact or Fiction?

▶ A relatively new and fresh piece of electronic equipment is highly desired by burglars.

▶ Drug dealers are violent street thugs.

▶ Neighborhood watch programs are a waste of time.

▶ Criminal behavior is essentially harmful and dysfunctional.

▶ It's possible to reduce drunk driving by installing on cars a locking device that prevents drunk drivers from starting their vehicles.

▶ Adding police on the street has no effect on crime rates.

▶ The more you punish people, the less likely they are to commit crime.

▶ Locking up millions of criminals can bring down the crime rate.

Chapter Objectives

1. Describe the development of rational choice theory.

2. Describe the concepts of rational choice.

3. Discuss how offenders structure criminality.

4. Describe how criminals structure crime.

5. Be acquainted with the evidence suggesting that crime is rational.

6. Know what is meant by the term "seductions of crime."

7. Discuss the elements of situational crime prevention.

8. Be familiar with the elements of general deterrence.

9. Discuss the basic concepts of specific deterrence.

10. Understand the pros and cons of applying an incapacitation strategy to reduce crime.

The "pump and dump" stock market scheme orchestrated by Michael Pickens involves knowledge, planning, and ingenuity. It illustrates the fact that people involved in criminal activities carefully plan their crimes, buy the proper equipment, try to avoid detection, and (if they are successful) attempt to squirrel their illegal profits away in some hidden bank account. Such calculated actions suggest that the decision to commit crime involves rational decision making, designed to maximize personal gain and avoid capture and punishment. Some criminologists go as far as suggesting that the source of all criminal violations—even those involving violence—is rational decision making. The decision to commit crime may lie in a variety of personal reasons, including greed, revenge, need, anger, lust, jealousy, thrill-seeking, or vanity. But the final decision to act is made only after the potential offender carefully weighs the potential benefits and consequences of the planned action and decides that the benefits of crime are greater than its consequences. Here are a few examples:

▶ The jealous suitor concludes that the satisfaction of punching a rival in the nose is worth the risk of punishment.
▶ The greedy shopper considers the chance of apprehension by store detectives so small that she takes a "five-finger discount" on a new sweater.
▶ The drug dealer concludes that the huge profit from a single shipment of cocaine far outweighs the possible costs of apprehension.
▶ The schoolyard bully carefully selects his next victim, someone weak and unpopular who probably won't fight back.
▶ The college student downloads a program that enables her to illegally copy music onto her iPod.

This view of crime is referred to here as **rational choice theory (choice theory)**.

In this chapter, we review the philosophical underpinnings of rational choice theory—the view that criminals rationally choose crime. We then turn to theories of crime prevention and control that flow from the concept of choice: situational crime control, general deterrence theory, specific deterrence theory, and incapacitation. Finally, we take a brief look at how choice theory has influenced criminal justice policy.

Development of Rational Choice Theory

As you may recall from Chapter 1, rational choice theory has its roots in the **classical criminology** developed by the Italian social thinker Cesare Beccaria, whose utilitarian approach powerfully influenced the criminal justice system and was widely accepted throughout Europe and the United States.[2] Although the classical approach was influential for more than 100 years, by the end of the nineteenth century its popularity had begun to decline. During this period, positivist criminologists focused on internal and external factors—poverty, IQ, education—rather than personal choice and decision making.

Beginning in the late 1960s, criminologists once again began to embrace classical ideas, producing books and monographs expounding the theme that criminals are rational actors who plan their crimes, can be controlled by the fear of punishment, and deserve to be penalized for their misdeeds. In the 1960s, Nobel Prize–winning economist Gary Becker applied his views on rational behavior and human capital (that is, human competence and the consequences of investments in human competence) to criminal activity. Becker argued that except for a few mentally ill people, criminals behave in a predictable or rational way when deciding to commit crime. Engaging in a cost-benefit analysis of crime, they weigh what they expect to gain against the risks they must undergo and the costs they may incur, such as going to prison.[3] Instead of regarding criminal activity as irrational behavior, Becker viewed criminality as rational behavior that might be controlled by increasing the costs of crime and reducing the potential for gain.

In *Thinking About Crime*, political scientist James Q. Wilson observed that people who are likely to commit crime are unafraid of breaking the law because they value the excitement and thrills of crime, have a low stake in conformity, and are willing

CONNECTIONS

In Chapter 1 we traced the history of classical theory. As you may recall, Beccaria believed that criminals weighed the benefits and consequences of crime before choosing to violate the law. They would be unlikely to choose crime if punishment were swift, certain, and severe.

rational choice theory (choice theory)
The view that crime is a function of a decision-making process in which the potential offender weighs the potential costs and benefits of an illegal act.

classical criminology
A theory of crime suggesting that criminal behavior is a matter of personal choice, made after the individual considers its costs and benefits, and that the criminal behavior reflects the needs of the offender.

to take greater chances than the average person. If they could be convinced that their actions would bring severe punishment, only the totally irrational would be willing to engage in crime.[4]

From these roots has evolved a more contemporary version of classical theory based on intelligent thought processes and criminal decision making; today this is referred to as the rational choice approach to crime causation.[5]

Concepts of Rational Choice

According to contemporary rational choice theory, law-violating behavior is the product of careful thought and planning. Offenders choose crime after considering both personal factors (such as money, revenge, thrills, and entertainment) and situational factors (such as target availability, security measures, and police presence). Before deciding to commit a crime, the reasoning criminal evaluates the risk of apprehension, the seriousness of expected punishment, the potential value or benefit of the criminal enterprise, his or her ability to succeed, and the need for criminal gain. People who believe that the risks of crime outweigh the rewards may decide to "go straight." If they think they are likely to be arrested and punished, they are more likely to seek treatment and turn their lives around than to risk engaging in criminal activities.[6]

EVALUATING THE RISKS OF CRIME

Before choosing to commit a crime, reasoning criminals carefully select targets, and their behavior is systematic and selective. Burglars seem to choose targets on the basis of their value, novelty, and resale potential. A piece of electronic gear that has been recently introduced, such as an iPhone or new laptop, may be a prime target, because it has not yet saturated the market and still retains high value.[7] The decision to commit crime is enhanced by the promise of easy gain with low risk.

In contrast, the decision to forgo crime is reached when the potential criminal believes that the risks outweigh the rewards:

▶ They stand a good chance of getting caught and being punished.
▶ They fear the consequences of punishment.
▶ They risk losing the respect of their peers, damaging their reputations, and experiencing feelings of guilt or shame.[8]
▶ The risk of apprehension outweighs the profit and/or pleasure of crime.[9]

Risk evaluations may cover a wide range of topics: What's the chance of getting caught? How difficult will it be to commit the crime? Is the profit worth the effort? How familiar am I with the target?[10]

People who decide to get inolved in crime compare the chances of arrest (based on their past experiences) with the subjective psychic rewards of crime (including the excitement and social status it brings and perceived opportunities for easy

© AP Images/Waco Tribune Herald, Jerry Larson

Some people engage in elaborate schemes to commit crime, an indication that their criminal acts are a matter of rational choice, not impulsive behavior. Here, former Downtown Waco Inc. executive director Margaret Mills cries in the courtroom on November 5, 2008, in Waco, Texas. The judge has just accepted a plea agreement that calls for her to be sentenced to serve nine years in prison. Mills was indicted last fall on a charge of first-degree felony theft. The indictment alleged that she stole more than $200,000 from the nonprofit group.

gains).[11] If the rewards are great, the perceived risk small, and the excitement high, the likelihood of their committing additional crimes increases.[12]

OFFENSE- AND OFFENDER-SPECIFIC CRIME

Rational choice theorists view crime as both offense-specific and offender-specific.[13] In the case of an **offense-specific crime**, offenders react selectively to the characteristics of an individual criminal act. Take, for instance, the decision to commit a burglary. Such potential offenders might consider

- ▶ Their evaluation of the target yield
- ▶ The probability of security devices
- ▶ Police patrol effectiveness
- ▶ Availability of a getaway car
- ▶ Ease of selling stolen merchandise
- ▶ Presence of occupants
- ▶ Neighbors who might notice a break-in
- ▶ Presence of guard dogs
- ▶ Escape routes
- ▶ Entry points and exits

In the case of an **offender-specific crime**, criminals are not simply robots who engage in unthinking and unplanned acts of antisocial behavior. Before deciding to commit crime, individuals must decide whether they have the personal needs, skills, and prerequisites to commit a successful criminal act. These assessments might include evaluation of

- ▶ Whether they possess the necessary skills to commit the crime
- ▶ Their immediate need for money or other valuables
- ▶ Whether legitimate financial alternatives to crime exist (such as obtaining a high-paying job)
- ▶ Whether they have available resources to commit the crime
- ▶ Their fear of expected apprehension and punishment
- ▶ Availability of alternative criminal acts, such as selling drugs
- ▶ Their physical ability, including health, strength, and dexterity

Note the distinction made here between "crime" and "criminality."[14] A crime is an event; criminality is a personal trait. Criminals do not commit crime all the time; conversely, even the most honest citizens may, on occasion, violate the law. Some high-risk people lacking opportunity may never commit crime; and conversely, given enough provocation or opportunity, a low-risk, law-abiding person may commit crime. What are the factors that structure (1) criminality and (2) the decision to commit crime?

STRUCTURING CRIMINALITY

Because crime is both offense- and offender-specific and also depends on a careful risk evaluation, it stands to reason that a number of personal factors and conditions must be evaluated before someone decides to choose criminality.

offense-specific crime
A crime in which the offender reacts selectively to the characteristics of a particular criminal act.

offender-specific crime
A crime in which offenders evaluate their skills, motives, needs, and fears before deciding to commit the criminal act.

Economic Need/Opportunity There may be a number of reasons why women choose to get into prostitution, but few stories are as compelling as that of the university lecturer with an Ivy League education (she had a Ph.D. in cultural anthropology) who became a call girl to help pay her bills.[15] Rather than living on her meager teaching salary, she *chose* to add to her income by becoming a highly paid sex worker. The "Ivy League Hooker's" illegal activity was shaped by her economic needs. She is not alone. Drug users report that they increase their criminal involvement when the costs of their habit rise. Once they become cocaine and heroin users, the benefits of criminal enterprise become overwhelmingly attractive, and their crime rates increase.[16] Clearly, one important decision that people make before they embark on a life of crime is whether they need the money!

Some people choose to commit crime because they are misled about its financial rewards. They may know people who have made "big scores" and/or people who are quite successful at crime. If their friend or brother-in-law can do well, they assume they will "succeed" also.[17] But in reality, the rewards of crime are often quite meager. When Steven Levitt and Sudhir Alladi Venkatesh studied the financial rewards of being in a drug gang, they found that despite enormous risks to their health, life, and freedom, average gang members earned slightly more than what they could earn in the legitimate labor market (about $6 to $11 per hour).[18] Why, then, did they stay in the gang? Members believed that there was a strong potential for future riches if they stayed in the drug business and earned a "management" position (gang leaders earned a lot more than street level dealers). In this case, the rational choice is structured by the person's weighing of the potential for future criminal gain against what they could earn if they chose conventional alternatives and opportunities.[19]

Evaluating Personal Traits and Experience Personal experience may be an important element in structuring criminality.[20] Career criminals may learn the limitations of their powers; they know when to take a chance and when to be cautious. Experienced criminals may turn away from a life of crime when they come to believe that the risk of crime is greater than any potential profit.[21] Personality and lifestyle also affect criminal choices. Criminals appear to be more impulsive and to have less self-control than other people; they seem unaffected by fear of punishment.[22] They typically are under stress or are facing some serious personal problem or condition that forces them to choose risky behavior.[23] Some are part of a street culture that shapes their criminal choices. When Bruce Jacobs and his colleagues looked at the basis for carjackings, they found that offenders may have little financial need to commit crime. Why do they do it, then? When the "right target" presents itself, they will attack it rather than squander the opportunity. Some criminal opportunities are simply too good to pass up.[24]

Criminal Expertise Criminals report that before committing crimes, they actually learn techniques to help them avoid detection while making their illegal profits. Female crack dealers learn how to camouflage their activities within the bustle of their daily lives. They sell crack while hanging out in a park or shooting hoops in a playground. They meet their customers in a lounge and try to act normal, as though they are having a casual, light-hearted good time—anything not to draw attention to themselves and their business. They use props to disguise drug deals.[25] Research conducted by Leanne Fiftal Alarid and her partners found that women drawn into dealing drugs learn the trade in a businesslike manner. One young dealer told Alarid how she learned the tricks of the trade from an older male partner:

> He taught me how to "recon" [reconstitute] cocaine, cutting and repacking a brick from 91 proof to 50 proof, just like a business. He treats me like an equal partner, and many of the friends are business associates. I am a catalyst. . . . I even get guys turned on to drugs.[26]

Note the business tone and terminology. This coke dealer could be talking about taking a computer training course at a major corporation. If criminal acts are treated as business decisions, in which profit and loss potential must be carefully calculated, then crime must indeed be a rational event. Another example is the career of Albert Robles, discussed in the accompanying Profiles in Crime feature on page 88.

STRUCTURING CRIME

According to the rational choice approach, the decision to commit crime, regardless of its substance, is structured by (1) where it occurs, and (2) the characteristics of the target.

Choosing the Place of Crime Criminals carefully choose where they will commit their crime. Criminologist Bruce Jacobs's interviews with 40 active crack cocaine street

CONNECTIONS

Rational choice theory dovetails with routine activities theory, which was discussed in Chapter 3. Though not identical, these approaches both claim that crime rates are a product of criminal opportunity. They suggest that increasing the number of guardians, decreasing the suitability of targets, or reducing the offender population should lower crime rates. Conversely, increased opportunity and reduced guardianship should increase crime rates.

After graduating from UCLA, Albert Robles served terms as mayor, councilman, and deputy city manager of South Gate, California, an industrial community about 12 miles outside downtown Los Angeles. Soon after Robles became city treasurer in 1997, he plotted to rule the city purely for his own benefit. He even proclaimed himself "King of South Gate" and referred to the city as his "fiefdom." Once in power, Robles got involved in a number of convoluted illegal schemes, including

- Using the city's treasury as his "private piggy bank for himself, his family, and his friends" (according to acting U.S. Attorney George Cardona), costing South Gate more than $35 million and bringing it to the verge of bankruptcy
- Firing city hall employees at will and replacing them with supporters who had little experience
- Recruiting and bankrolling the campaigns of unqualified local supporters for city council until he controlled the council
- Threatening anyone who stood in his way (suspiciously, one of his adversaries on the city council was shot in the head)

Robles and his corrupt cronies then cooked up schemes to line their own pockets with the public's cash. In one such scheme, Robles coerced businesses to hire a financial consultant named Edward Espinoza in order to win various city contracts, including senior housing and sewer rehabilitation projects. As part of this plan, Robles and Espinoza set up a shell corporation that raked in some $2.4 million—more than $1.4 million of which went straight into Robles's pockets. He used part of the money to buy a $165,000 beach

© AP Images/Nick Ut

condo in Baja for his mother; he also forked over $55,000 for "platinum membership" in a motivational group. In another scheme, Robles steered a $48 million refuse and recycling contract to a company in exchange for more than $30,000 in gifts and campaign contributions.

In February 2003, Robles was targeted by a federal grand jury looking into the handling of federal loans and grants. FBI and IRS investigators pored over city records to uncover his illegal schemes. The citizens of South Gate ultimately voted Robles and his cronies out of office (but not before he racked up huge legal bills at the city's expense), and he was convicted at trial in July 2005. Two of his business associates—including Espinoza—also went to prison.

Robles's illegal acts were the product of careful plotting and planning. They were motivated by greed, not need. To some criminologists, stories like these confirm that many crimes are a matter of rational choice.

SOURCES: Federal Bureau of Investigation, "Corruption in City Hall: The Crooked Reign of 'King' Albert," January 8, 2007, www.fbi.gov/page2/jan07/cityhall010807.htm (accessed March 15, 2009); Hector Becerra, "Robles Sentenced to 10 Years," *Los Angeles Times*, November 29, 2006, p. 1.

---

dealers in a midwestern city showed that dealers carefully evaluate the desirability of their sales area before setting up shop.[27] Dealers consider the middle of a long block the best choice because they can see everything in both directions; police raids can be spotted before they occur.[28] Another tactic is to entice new buyers into spaces between apartment buildings or into back lots. Although the dealers may lose the tactical edge of being on a public street, they gain a measure of protection because their colleagues can watch over the operation and come to the rescue if the buyer tries to "pull something."[29]

Choosing Targets Evidence of rational choice may also be found in the way criminals locate their targets. Burglars check to make sure that no one is home before they enter a residence. Some call ahead; others ring the doorbell, preparing to claim they had the wrong address if someone answers. Some find out which families include star high school athletes, because those that do are sure to be at the weekend football game, leaving their houses unguarded.[30] Others seek unlocked doors and avoid the ones with deadbolts; houses with dogs are usually considered off-limits.[31] Burglars also report being sensitive to the activities of their victims. They note that homemakers often develop predictable behavior patterns, which helps them plan their crimes.[32] Burglars seem to prefer "working" between 9.00 AM and 11.00 AM and in mid-afternoon, when parents are either working or dropping off or picking up children at school. Burglars appear to monitor car and pedestrian traffic and avoid selecting targets on heavily traveled streets.[33] It does not seem surprising that well-organized communities that restrict traffic and limit neighborhood entrance and exit routes have experienced significant declines in property crime.[34]

In sum, rational choice involves both shaping and structuring criminality and crime. Personality, age, status, risk, and opportunity seem to influence the decision to become a criminal; place, target, and techniques help to structure crime.[35]

▶ **Checkpoints**

Is Crime Rational?

It is relatively easy to show that some crimes are the product of rational, objective thought, especially when they involve an ongoing criminal conspiracy centered on economic gain. When prominent bankers were indicted for criminal fraud, their elaborate financial schemes not only showed signs of rationality but also exhibited brilliant, though flawed, financial expertise.[36] Similarly, the drug dealings of organized crime bosses demonstrate a reasoned analysis of market conditions, interests, and risks. But what about crimes that are immediate rather than ongoing? Do they too show signs of rationality?

IS THEFT RATIONAL?

There is evidence that theft related crimes are the product of careful risk assessment, including environmental, social, and structural factors. Target selection seems highly rational. Ronald Clarke and Patricia Harris found that auto thieves are very selective in their choice of targets. Vehicle selection seems to be based on attractiveness and suitability for a particular purpose: German cars are selected for stripping, for example, because they usually have high-quality audio equipment that has good value on the second-hand market.[37]

Burglars seem to choose targets on the basis of their value, freshness, and resale potential. A relatively new piece of electronic gear, such as an iPhone or BlackBerry, may be a prime target because it has not yet saturated the market and still retains high value.[38] While they may seek out goods that are easily resold, burglars also report that they like to work close to home. Perhaps a familiar location enables them to blend in, not look out of place, and not get lost when returning home with their loot.[39]

IS DRUG USE RATIONAL?

Did Lindsay Lohan make an objective, rational choice to abuse alcohol and potentially sabotage her career? Did Heath Ledger make a rational choice when he abused prescription drugs to the point where it killed him? Is it possible that drug users and dealers, a group not usually associated with clear thinking, make rational choices?

Research does in fact show that at its onset, drug use is controlled by rational decision making. Users report that they begin taking drugs when they believe the benefits of substance abuse outweigh its costs. That is, they believe drugs will provide a fun, exciting, thrilling experience. They choose what they consider safe sites to buy and sell drugs.[40] Their entry into substance abuse is facilitated by their perception that valued friends and family members endorse and encourage drug use and that these individuals abuse substances themselves.[41]

Drug dealers approach their profession in a businesslike fashion. Traffickers and dealers face many of the same problems as legitimate retailers. If they are too successful in one location, rivals will be attracted to the area, and stiff competition may drive down prices and undermine profits. The dealer can fight back against competitors

Fact or Fiction?

A relatively new and fresh piece of electronic equipment is highly desired by burglars.

Fact. Burglars love iPhones and BlackBerry phones, for example, because of their resale value.

Fact or Fiction?

Drug dealers are violent street thugs.

Fiction. Many drug dealers approach their profession in a businesslike fashion, offering deals, undercutting the competition, and using violence only to scare off their rivals' customers.

CONNECTIONS

As you may recall from earlier discussion in this chapter, criminals may find that despite its risks, crime can provide economic rewards that are far higher than they could hope to achieve in conventional employment. Many overestimate the profits from crime, although most seem to realize that the chances of a big payoff are remote.

Fact or Fiction?

Neighborhood watch programs are a waste of time.

Fiction. Robbers avoid areas where neighbors keep an eye out for trouble. Robbery rates are low in these watchful communities.

Woods   Riley   Elliott

Wilson   McBride

© AP Images/Alton Police Department

Is crime rational? This photo shows five of six suspects charged with first-degree murder, battery, and unlawful restraint in the January 31, 2008, killing of a pregnant, developmentally disabled woman, Dorothy Dixon, of Alton, Illinois. Dixon was beaten, shot with a BB gun, and scalded with hot liquid. Those charged are Judy Woods, 43; Michelle Riley, 35 (who has already pled guilty); Michael J. Elliott, 18; Benny Lee Wilson, 16; and LeShelle McBride, 15. Riley's 12-year-old son was given probation. While such acts of violence seem purely irrational, even the most violent criminals choose vulnerable targets who are unlikely to fight back or pose a threat, and making this cautious distinction is a clear sign of rationality.

by discounting the price of drugs or increasing quality, as long as this doesn't reduce profit margins.[42] If these "business tactics" are not working, dealers can always turn to violence. They may start drug wars on their rivals' turf and then convince customers to stay away from such a dangerous area; in retaliation, rivals may cut prices to lure customers back. Thus, drug dealers face many of the same problems as law-abiding businesspeople; they differ in the tactics they use to help settle disputes.[43]

CAN VIOLENCE BE RATIONAL?

Is it possible that violent acts are the product of reasoned decision making? Evidence confirms that violent criminals, even serial killers, select suitable targets by picking people who are vulnerable and lack adequate defenses.[44] Richard Wright and Scott Decker interviewed active street robbers in St. Louis, Missouri. Their subjects expressed a considerable amount of rational thought before choosing a robbery, which may involve violence, over a burglary, which involves stealth and cunning.[45] One told them why he chose to be a robber:

> I feel more safer doing a robbery because doing a burglary, I got a fear of breaking into somebody's house not knowing who might be up in there. . . . On robbery I can select my victims, I can select my place of business. I can watch and see who all work in there, or I can rob a person and pull them around in the alley or push them up in a doorway and rob them.[46]

Robbers generally choose targets close to their homes or in areas to which they routinely travel. Familiarity with the area gives them ready knowledge of escape routes; this is referred to as their "awareness space."[47] Robbers may be wary of people who are watching the community for signs of trouble; robbery levels are relatively low in neighborhoods where residents keep a watchful eye on their neighbors' property.[48] Many robbers avoid free-standing buildings because these can more easily be surrounded by police; others select targets that are known to do a primarily cash business, such as bars, supermarkets, and restaurants.[49] Robbers also tend to shy away from victims who are perceived to be armed and potentially dangerous.[50] However, some actually target fellow criminals—for example, drug dealers.[51] Although these fellow criminals may be dangerous, robbers recognize that people with "dirty hands" are unlikely to call police and get entangled with the law. When Bruce Jacobs interviewed armed robbers, he found that some specialize in targeting drug dealers because they believe that even though their work is hazardous, the rewards outweigh the risks: Drug dealers are plentiful, visible, and accessible, and they carry plenty of cash. Their merchandise is valuable, is easily transported, and can be used by the robber or sold to another. Drug dealers are not particularly popular, so they cannot rely on bystanders to come to their aid. Nor can they call the police and ask them to recover their stolen goods! Of course, drug dealers may be able to "take care of business" themselves, but surprisingly, Jacobs found that many choose not to carry a pistol.[52] Drug dealers may be tough and bad, the robbers claim, but *they* are tougher and badder!

In some instances, however, targets are chosen in order to send a message rather than to generate capital. Bruce Jacobs and Richard Wright used in-depth interviews with street robbers who target drug dealers and found that their crimes are a response to one of three types of violations:

- *Market-related* robberies emerge from disputes involving partners in trade, rivals, or generalized predators.
- *Status-based* violations involve encounters in which the robber's essential character or values have been challenged.
- *Personalistic* violations flow from incidents in which the robber's autonomy or sense of values has been jeopardized.

Robbery in this instance is an instrument used to settle scores, display dominance, and stifle potential rivals. And as Jacobs and Wright conclude, retaliation certainly is rational in the sense that actors who lack legitimate access to the law and who prize respect above everything else will often choose to resolve their grievances through a rough and ready brand of self-help.[53]

Why Do People Commit Crime?

Assuming that crime is rational, why—knowing its often unpleasant consequences—do people choose to commit crime? Rational choice theorists believe that crime is a natural choice people make after weighing such issues as their personal needs, their mental state, legitimate alternatives such as a job, the risks of getting caught, and the threat of punishment. All these factors are considered before the decision is made to commit crime. Consequently, even the most desperate criminal might hesitate to attack a well-defended target, whereas a group of teens might choose to rip off an unoccupied home on the spur of the moment.[54]

For many people, crime is a more attractive alternative than law-abiding behavior. It brings rewards, excitement, prestige, or other desirable outcomes without lengthy work or great effort. Whether it is violent or profit-oriented, crime has an allure that some people cannot resist. Crime may produce a natural "high" and other positive sensations that are instrumental in maintaining and reinforcing criminal behavior.[55] Some law violators describe the "adrenaline rush" that comes from successfully executing illegal activities in dangerous situations. This has been termed **edgework**: the "exhilarating, momentary integration of danger, risk, and skill" that motivates people to try a variety of dangerous criminal and noncriminal behaviors.[56]

Sociologist Jack Katz argues that there are, in fact, immediate benefits to criminality. These situational inducements, which he labels the **seductions of crime**, directly precede the commission of crime and draw offenders into law violations. For example, someone challenges their authority or moral position, and they vanquish their opponent with a beating; or they want to do something exciting, so they break into and vandalize a school building.[57] According to Katz, choosing crime can help satisfy personal needs. For some people, shoplifting and vandalism are attractive because getting away with crime is a thrilling demonstration of personal competence (Katz calls this "sneaky thrills"). Even murder can have an emotional payoff: Killers behave like the avenging gods of mythology, glorying in the life-or-death control they exert over their victims.[58]

The criminal lifestyle fits well with people who organize their life around risk taking and partying. Criminal events provide money for drugs and are ideal for displaying courage and fearlessness to one's peers. Rather than create overwhelming social problems, a criminal way of life may be beneficial to some people, helping them overcome the problems and stress they face in their daily lives. Antisocial behavior gives adolescents the opportunity to exert control over their own lives and destinies by helping them to avoid situations they find uncomfortable or repellant (such as by cutting school or running away from an abusive home) or to obtain resources for desired activities and commodities (such as by stealing or selling drugs to buy stylish outfits).[59] ▶ **Checkpoints**

Fact or Fiction?

Criminal behavior is essentially harmful and dysfunctional.

Fiction. Crime can be seductive, giving the criminal enjoyment, power, and the ability to obtain things that would otherwise be beyond their economic reach. Getting caught may be harmful, but the crime itself can be a natural high.

Checkpoints

▶ Theft crimes appear to be rational because thieves and burglars typically choose targets that present little risk, and they plan their attacks carefully.

▶ Robbers report that they select vulnerable targets who are unlikely to fight back. Some like to attack drug dealers who have lots of cash and cannot call the police when they are robbed.

▶ Drug users and dealers use elaborate ploys to avoid detection.

▶ They employ businesslike practices in their commercial enterprises.

▶ Even serial killers use cunning and rational thought to avoid detection.

▶ Crime is seductive. People may rationally choose crime because it provides them with psychological and social benefits. It helps them solve problems.

edgework
The excitement or exhilaration of successfully executing illegal activities in dangerous situations.

seductions of crime
The situational inducements or immediate benefits that draw offenders into law violations.

DON'T LET DRUG DEALERS CHANGE
THE FACE OF YOUR NEIGHBOURHOOD.
Call Crimestoppers anonymously on 0800 555 111.

According to rational choice theory, potential criminals calculate the possible benefits of committing crime and choose not to commit a crime if the disadvantages of doing so outweigh the benefits. Crime can therefore be prevented if people are convinced that it is not in their best interest to violate the law. This image from an advertising campaign uses photos that show the degenerative effects of drug addiction. This woman was addicted to methamphetamine, and her decline is depicted over a four-year period, ages 36 to 40. Would you be afraid of using speed after seeing these results? (Correct answer: Yes!)

Controlling Crime

If committing crime is a rational choice, it follows that crime can be controlled or eradicated by convincing potential offenders that crime is a poor choice—that it will bring them not rewards but pain, hardship, and deprivation. According to rational choice theory, street-smart offenders (1) calculate the potential success of committing crime; (2) select their targets on the basis of risk assessment; and (3) will choose not to commit a crime if the disadvantages, such as getting caught and punished, outweigh the benefits, such as making lots of money. A number of potential strategies for controlling crime flow from this premise. Among the most important of these are situational crime prevention strategies, general deterrence strategies, specific deterrence strategies, and incapacitation strategies.

SITUATIONAL CRIME PREVENTION

According to the concept of **situational crime prevention**, in order to reduce criminal activity, public officials interested in controlling crime must be aware of the characteristics of sites and situations that are conducive to crime, the things that impel people toward these sites and situations, what equips such people to take advantage of the criminal opportunities offered by these sites and situations, and what constitutes the immediate triggers for actual criminal actions.[60] Criminal acts will be avoided if (1) potential targets are carefully guarded, (2) the means to commit crime are controlled, and (3) potential offenders are carefully monitored. Desperate people may contemplate crime, but only the truly irrational will attack a well-defended, inaccessible target and risk strict punishment.

One way of preventing crime, then, is to reduce the opportunities people have to commit particular crimes. This approach was popularized in the United States in the early 1970s by Oscar Newman, who coined the term **defensible space**. The idea is that crime can be prevented or displaced through the use of residential designs that reduce criminal opportunity, such as well-lit housing projects that maximize surveillance.[61]

CRIME PREVENTION STRATEGIES

situational crime prevention
A method of crime prevention that seeks to eliminate or reduce particular crimes in specific settings.

defensible space
The principle that crime can be prevented or displaced by modifying the physical environment to reduce the opportunity that individuals have to commit crime.

Situational crime prevention involves developing tactics to reduce or eliminate a specific crime problem (such as shoplifting in an urban mall or street-level drug dealing). According to Derek Cornish and Ronald Clarke, situational crime prevention efforts may be divided into the six strategies described in the following paragraphs.[62]

Increase the Effort Needed to Commit Crime Tactics to increase effort include target-hardening techniques such as putting unbreakable glass on storefronts, locking gates, and fencing yards. Removing signs from store windows, installing brighter lights, and instituting a pay-first policy have helped reduce thefts from gas stations and convenience stores.[63] Technological advances can also make it more difficult for would-be offenders to commit crimes; having an owner's photo on credit cards should reduce the use of stolen cards; security products such as steering locks on cars have reduced the incidence of theft.[64] Installing on cars a locking device that prevents drunk drivers from starting the vehicle (such as the Breath Analyzed Ignition Interlock Device) significantly reduces drunk-driving rates among people with a history of driving while intoxicated.[65]

Increase the Risk of Committing Crime If the risk of getting caught can be increased, rational offenders are less likely to commit crime. Marcus Felson argues that the risk of crime may be increased by improving the effectiveness of **crime discouragers**: people who serve as guardians of property or people.[66] Discouragers can be grouped into three categories: "guardians," who monitor potential targets (such as store security guards); "handlers," who monitor potential offenders (such as parole officers and parents); and "managers," who monitor places (such as homeowners and garage attendants). If the discouragers do their jobs correctly, the potential criminal will be convinced that the risk of crime outweighs any potential gains.[67] Police are invaluable crime discouragers, and their effectiveness has been linked to reductions in the crime rates in cities such as New York and Boston.[68]

Some crime discouragers are mechanical rather than human. Efforts have been made to create and install mechanical devices, such as closed-circuit TV cameras, that may discourage crime while reducing the need for higher-cost security personnel.[69] The accompanying Policy & Practice in Criminology feature on page 94 discusses a recent evaluation of such methods in the United States and Britain.

Reduce Rewards of Crime Target reduction strategies are designed to reduce the value of crime to the potential criminal. They include making car radios removable so they can be kept in the home at night, marking property so that it is more difficult to sell when stolen, and having gender-neutral phone listings to discourage obscene phone calls. Tracking systems, such as those made by the LoJack Corporation, help police locate and return stolen vehicles.

Induce Guilt: Increase Shame Crime may be reduced or prevented if we can communicate to people the wrongfulness of their behavior and how harmful it is to society. We may tell them to "say no to drugs" or that "users are losers." By making people aware of the shamefulness of their actions, we hope to prevent their criminal activities, even if the chances that they will be detected and punished are slight.

Sometimes punishment is designed to make people ashamed and embarrass them so that they will not repeat their criminal acts. In 2008 a judge in Hudson, Kansas, ordered a man who admitted molesting an 11-year-old boy to post signs reading "A Sex Offender Lives Here" on all four sides of his home and to display the warning "Sex Offender In This Car" in bold yellow lettering on both sides of his automobile.[70]

Inducing guilt or shame might include such techniques as setting strict rules to embarrass offenders. For example, publishing "John lists" in the newspaper punishes those arrested for soliciting prostitutes. Facilitating compliance by providing trash bins might shame chronic litterers

Fact or Fiction?

It's possible to reduce drunk driving by installing on cars a locking device that prevents drunk drivers from starting their vehicles.

Fact. Research shows that ignition locks work and can reduce drunk driving.

crime discouragers
People who serve as guardians of property or people.

© AP Images/Corpus Christi Caller-Times, David Pellerin

One technique of situational crime prevention is to induce shame. Here a sign warning of danger from a registered sex offender is posted in front of a residence in Corpus Christi, Texas. Nueces County District Judge J. Manuel Banales has ordered 15 Corpus Christi sex offenders to place signs in their yards. Would that convince potential sex offenders that the shame and humiliation they face is greater than any reward they may derive from sex offending?

Brandon Welsh and David Farrington have been using systematic review and meta-analysis to assess the comparative effectiveness of situational crime prevention techniques. Recently, they evaluated the effectiveness of closed-circuit television (CCTV) surveillance cameras and improved street lighting, techniques that are currently being used around the world.

They find that CCTV surveillance cameras serve many functions and are used in both public and private settings. CCTV can deter would-be criminals who fear detection and apprehension. They can also aid police in the detection and apprehension of suspects, aid in the prosecution of alleged offenders, improve police officer safety and compliance with the law (through, for instance, cameras mounted

thus has to be buttressed by other methods, such as security fences or guards.

Another important issue is cultural context. In the UK, there is a high level of public support for the use of CCTV cameras in public settings to prevent crime. In America and other nations, the public is less accepting of surveillance technology and more apprehensive about its "Big Brother" connotations. Furthermore, in America, resistance to the use of CCTV in public places also takes the form of legal action and constitutional challenges under the U.S. Constitution's Fourth Amendment prohibition against unreasonable searches and seizures. In Sweden, surveillance cameras are highly regulated in public places, and in nearly all instances their use requires a permit from

Policy and Practice in Criminology Reducing Crime through Surveillance

on the dashboards of police cruisers to record police stops, searches, and so on), and aid in the detection and prevention of terrorist activities. Nowhere is the popularity of CCTV more apparent than in Great Britain, where an estimated 4.2 million CCTV cameras, or 1 for every 14 citizens, are in operation. It has also been estimated that the average Briton is caught on camera 300 times each day.

After reviewing 41 studies conducted around the world, Welsh and Farrington found that CCTV interventions have a small but significant desirable effect on crime, are most effective in reducing crime in car parks (parking lots), are most effective in reducing vehicle crimes, and are more effective in reducing crime in the United Kingdom than in other countries.

They found that effectiveness was significantly correlated with the degree of coverage of the CCTV cameras, which was greatest in car parks. However, the effect was most pronounced in parking lots that also employed other situational crime prevention interventions, such as improved lighting and security officers.

Notably, Welsh and Farrington found that CCTV schemes in the UK showed a sizable (19 percent) and significant desirable effect on crime, whereas those in other countries proved ineffective. One reason was that all of the sites that used other interventions alongside CCTV were in England. It is possible that CCTV on its own is not sufficient to influence an offender's decision whether to commit a crime and

the county administrative board. In Norway, there is a high degree of political scrutiny of public CCTV systems run by the police.

It could very well be that the overall poor showing of CCTV schemes in other countries is due in part to a lack of public support (and maybe even of political support) for these schemes, which in turn may result in reduced program funding, the police assigning lower priority to CCTV, and negative media reactions. Each of these factors could undermine the effectiveness of CCTV schemes. In contrast, the British Home Office, who funded many of the British evaluations, wanted to show that CCTV was effective because it had invested so much money in these systems.

Welsh and Farrington conclude that CCTV reduces crime in some circumstances. In light of the mixed results, future CCTV schemes should be carefully implemented in different settings and should employ high-quality evaluation designs with long follow-up periods.

CRITICAL THINKING

Would you be willing to have a surveillance camera set up in your home or dorm in order to prevent crime, knowing that your every move was being watched and recorded?

SOURCE: Brandon C. Welsh and David P. Farrington, *Making Public Places Safer: Surveillance and Crime Prevention* (New York: Oxford University Press, 2008).

into using them. Ronald Clarke found that caller ID in New Jersey resulted in significant reductions in the number of obscene phone calls, presumably because of the shame presented by the threat of exposure.[71]

Reduce Provocation Some crimes are the result of extreme provocation—for example, road rage. It might be possible to reduce provocation by creating programs that reduce conflict. Mandating an early closing time in local bars and pubs might limit assaults that result from late-night drinking and conflicts in pubs at closing time. Posting guards outside schools at closing time might prevent childish taunts from escalating into full-blown brawls. Antibullying programs that have been implemented in schools are another method of reducing provocation.

Remove Excuses Crime may be reduced by making it difficult for people to excuse their criminal behavior by saying things like "I didn't know that was illegal" or "I had no choice." For example, municipalities have set up roadside displays that electronically flash a car's speed as it passes, eliminating the driver's excuse that she did not know how fast she was going when stopped by police. Litter boxes, brightly displayed, can eliminate the claim that "I just didn't know where to throw my trash." Reducing or eliminating excuses in this way also makes it physically easy for people to comply with laws and regulations, thereby reducing the likelihood that they will choose crime.

THE COSTS AND BENEFITS OF SITUATIONAL CRIME PREVENTION

Situational crime prevention efforts bring with them certain hidden costs and benefits that can either undermine their success or increase their effectiveness. Before the overall success of this approach can be evaluated, these costs and benefits must be considered.

Hidden Benefits When efforts to prevent one crime unintentionally prevent another, it is known as **diffusion**.[72] Video cameras set up in a mall to reduce shoplifting can also reduce property damage, because would-be vandals fear they are being caught on camera. Police surveillance set up to reduce drug trafficking may unintentionally reduce the incidence of prostitution and other public order crimes by scaring off would-be clients.[73] **Discouragement** occurs when crime control efforts targeting a particular locale help reduce crime in surrounding areas and populations. In her study of the effects of the SMART program (a drug enforcement program in Oakland, California, that enforces municipal codes and nuisance abatement laws), criminologist Lorraine Green found that drug dealing decreased not only in targeted areas but also in adjacent areas. It is likely that the drug control program discouraged buyers and sellers who saw familiar hangouts closed. This sign that drug dealing would not be tolerated probably decreased the total number of people involved in drug activity, even though they did not operate in the targeted areas.[74]

Hidden Costs Situational crime prevention efforts may also contain hidden costs that may limit their effectiveness. **Displacement** occurs when crime control efforts simply move, or redirect, offenders to less heavily guarded alternative targets.[75] For example, beefed-up police patrols in one area may shift crimes to a more vulnerable neighborhood lacking in police.[76] **Extinction** occurs when crime reduction programs produce a short-term positive effect, but benefits dissipate as criminals adjust to new conditions; for example, burglars learn to dismantle alarms or avoid patrols. **Replacement** occurs when criminals try new offenses they had previously avoided because situational crime prevention programs neutralized their crime of choice. If every residence in a neighborhood installs a foolproof burglar alarm system, motivated offenders may turn to armed robbery, a riskier and more violent crime, to replace the income they lost from burglaries. Before the effectiveness of situational crime prevention can be accepted, these hidden costs and benefits must be weighed and balanced.

General Deterrence

According to the rational choice view, motivated people will violate the law if they do not fear the consequences of their crimes. It stands to reason, then, that crime can be controlled by increasing the real or perceived threat of criminal punishment; this is the concept of **general deterrence**. Based on Beccaria's famous equation, general

diffusion
An effect that occurs when efforts to prevent one crime unintentionally prevent another.

discouragement
An effect that occurs when crime control efforts targeting a particular locale help reduce crime in surrounding areas and populations.

displacement
An effect that occurs when crime control efforts simply move, or redirect, offenders to less heavily guarded alternative targets.

extinction
An effect that occurs when crime reduction programs produce a short-term positive effect, but benefits dissipate as criminals adjust to new conditions.

replacement
An effect that occurs when criminals try new offenses they had previously avoided because situational crime prevention programs neutralized their crime of choice.

general deterrence
A crime control policy that depends on the fear of criminal penalties, convincing the potential law violator that the pains associated with crime outweigh its benefits.

deterrence theory holds that the greater the severity, certainty, and speed of legal sanctions, the lower the crime rate.

Perception and Deterrence According to deterrence theory, not only the actual chance of punishment, but also the *perception that punishment will be forthcoming*, influences criminality.[77] A central theme of deterrence theory is that people who perceive that they will be punished for crimes will avoid doing those crimes.[78] Conversely, the likelihood of being arrested or imprisoned will have little effect on crime rates if criminals believe that they have only a small chance of suffering apprehension and punishment in the future.[79]

Because criminals are rational decision makers, if they can be convinced that crime will lead to punishment, then they will be deterred. To prove this relationship empirically, Canadian criminologists Etienne Blais and Jean-Luc Bacher had insurance companies send a written threat to a random sample of insured persons reminding them of the punishment for insurance fraud. The investigators then compared these people's claims with those of a control group of people who did not get the threatening letter. The letter was sent to all the insured persons at a time when they had an opportunity to exaggerate the value of their claims. Blais and Bacher found that those who got the letter were less likely to pad their claims than were those in the control group.[80] Clearly, the warning, which gave people the perception that they would be caught and punished for insurance fraud, deterred them from illegal activity.

CERTAINTY OF PUNISHMENT

According to general deterrence theory, if the certainty of arrest, conviction, and sanctioning increases, crime rates should decline. If certainty increases, rational offenders will soon realize that the increased likelihood of punishment outweighs any benefit they perceive from committing crimes. Crime will persist, however, when people believe that even if they are caught, they will have a good chance of escaping punishment.[81] If people believe that their criminal transgressions will almost certainly result in punishment, then only the truly irrational will commit crime.[82]

A number of research efforts do show a direct relationship between crime rates and the certainty of punishment. And although the issue is far from settled, the weight of the evidence seems to be on the side of deterrence: People who believe that they will get caught if they commit crime are the ones most likely to be deterred from committing criminal acts.[83] What happens to them after apprehension seems to have a lesser impact on their decision-making process.[84]

Police and Certainty of Punishment If certainty of apprehension and punishment deters people from engaging in criminal behavior, then increasing the number of police officers on the street should cut the crime rate. Moreover, if these police officers are active, aggressive crime fighters, would-be criminals should become convinced that the risk of apprehension outweighs any benefits they can gain from crime.[85]

The deterrent effect of police has been supported by a number of recent studies that have found that police presence does in fact reduce crime levels.[86] Evidence shows that cities with larger police departments that have more officers per capita than the norm also experience lower levels of violent crimes.[87] The mere presence of added police, however, may not be sufficient to discourage crime; the manner in which they approach their task may make more of a difference. Proactive, aggressive law enforcement seems more effective than routine patrol. Improving response time and increasing the number of patrol cars that respond per crime may be one way of increasing police efficiency and deterring people from committing crime.[88]

SEVERITY OF PUNISHMENT

According to deterrence theory, the threat of severe punishment should also bring the crime rate down. Some studies have found that people who believe that they will be punished severely for a crime will forgo committing criminal acts.[89] Nonetheless, there is little consensus that strict punishments alone can reduce criminal activities.

Fact or Fiction?

Adding police on the street has no effect on crime rates.

Fiction. Adding aggressive police officers can reduce crime, especially if they target particular offenses.

Indeed, there is evidence that the certainty of punishment has a greater deterrent effect than its severity.[90]

It stands to reason that if severity of punishment can discourage crime, then fear of the death penalty, the ultimate legal deterrent, should significantly reduce murder rates. Because no one denies its emotional impact, if the death penalty failed to deter criminals from committing violent crime, the validity of the entire deterrence concept would be jeopardized. Because this topic is so important, it is discussed in the accompanying Current Issues in Crime feature on page 98.

SWIFTNESS OF PUNISHMENT

The third leg of Beccaria's equation involves the celerity, or speed, of punishment: The more rapidly punishment is applied and the more closely it is linked to the crime, the more likely it is to serve as a deterrent.[91] The deterrent effect of the law may be neutralized if there is a significant lag between apprehension and punishment. In the American justice system, court delays brought by numerous evidentiary hearings and requests for additional trial preparation time are common trial tactics. As a result, the criminal process can be delayed to a point where the connection between crime and punishment is broken. Take for instance how the death penalty is employed. Typically, more than 10 years elapse between the time a criminal is convicted and sentenced to death for murder and that person's execution. Delay in application of the death penalty may mitigate or neutralize the potential deterrent effect of capital punishment.

Interrelationship of Factors The factors of severity, certainty, and speed of punishment may also influence one another. If a particular crime—say, robbery—is punished severely but few robbers are ever caught or punished, the severity of punishment for robbery will probably not deter people from robbing. However, if the certainty of apprehension and conviction is increased by modern technology, more efficient police work, or some other factor, then even minor punishment might deter the potential robber.

Deterrence theorists tend to believe that the certainty of punishment has a greater impact than its severity or speed. As you may recall, people who believe they will be caught and punished are less likely to commit crime regardless of what form the punishment takes.[92] Nonetheless, all three elements of the deterrence equation are important, and it would be a mistake to emphasize one at the expense of the others. For example, if all resources were given to police agencies to increase the probability of arrest, crime rates might increase because there would not be sufficient funds for swift prosecution and effective correction.[93]

CRITIQUE OF GENERAL DETERRENCE

Some experts believe that the purpose of the law and justice system is to create a "threat system."[94] The threat of legal punishment should, on the face of it, deter lawbreakers through fear. Nonetheless, crime rates and deterrent measures are much less closely related than choice theorists might expect. Despite efforts to punish criminals and make them fear crime, there is little evidence that the fear of apprehension and punishment alone can reduce crime rates. How can this discrepancy be explained?

Rationality Deterrence theory assumes a rational offender who weighs the costs and benefits of a criminal act before deciding on a course of action. Criminals may be desperate people who choose crime because they believe there is no reasonable alternative. Some may suffer from personality disorders that impair their judgment and render them incapable of making truly rational decisions. Psychologists believe that chronic offenders suffer from an emotional state that renders them both incapable of fearing punishment and less likely to appreciate the consequences of crime.[95] Research on repeat sex offenders finds that they suffer from an elevated emotional state that negates the deterrent effect of the law.[96] There is also evidence that drinking alcohol impedes a person's ability to reasonably assess the costs and benefits of crime.[97] If the benefits of crime are exaggerated, the law's deterrent effect may be deflated.

According to deterrence theory, the death penalty—the ultimate deterrent—should deter criminals from committing murder—the ultimate crime. Most Americans, even convicted criminals who are currently behind bars, approve of the death penalty. But is the public's approval warranted? Does the death penalty actually discourage murder?

Empirical research on the association between capital punishment and murder can be divided into three types: immediate impact studies, comparative research, and time-series analysis.

routinely employ the death penalty. Studies using this approach have found little difference between the murder rates of adjacent states, regardless of their use of the death penalty; capital punishment did not appear to affect the reported rate of homicide.

- **Time-Series Studies.** If capital punishment is a deterrent, then periods that have an upswing in executions should also experience a downturn in violent crime and murder. Most research efforts have failed to show such a relationship. Economic conditions, population density,

Current Issues in Crime Does Availability of the Death Penalty Discourage Murder?

- **Immediate Impact.** If capital punishment is a deterrent, the reasoning goes, then its impact should be greatest after a well-publicized execution. However, most research has failed to find evidence that an execution produces an immediate decline in the murder rate. For example, when Lisa Stolzenberg and Stewart D'Alessio examined the effect of the death penalty on the murder rate in Houston, Texas, they found that even highly publicized executions had little impact on the murder rate.

- **Comparative Research.** It is also possible to compare murder rates in jurisdictions that have abolished the death penalty with the rates in jurisdictions that

and incarceration rates have a much greater impact on the murder rate than does the death penalty.

Rethinking the Deterrent Effect of Capital Punishment

Some recent studies have concluded that executing criminals may, in fact, bring the murder rate down. These newer studies, using sophisticated data analysis, have been able to uncover a more significant association. For example, James Yunker, using a national data set, has found evidence that there is a deterrent effect of capital punishment now that the pace of executions has accelerated. Economists Hashem Dezhbakhsh, Paul H. Rubin, and Joanna M. Shepherd found

System Effectiveness As Beccaria's famous equation tells us, the threat of punishment involves not only its severity but also its certainty and speed. The American legal system is not very effective. Only 10 percent of all serious offenses result in apprehension. Half of these crimes go unreported, and police make arrests in only about 20 percent of reported crimes. Even when offenders are detected, police officers may choose to warn rather than arrest.[98] The odds of receiving a prison term are less than 20 per 1,000 crimes committed. As a result, some offenders believe that they will not be severely punished for their acts, and they consequently have little regard for the law's deterrent power. Even those accused of murder are often convicted of lesser offenses and spend relatively short amounts of time behind bars.[99] In making their "rational choice," offenders may be aware that the deterrent effect of the law is minimal.

Some Offenders—and Some Crimes—Are More "Deterrable" Than Others Not every crime can be discouraged, nor is every criminal deterrable. Research shows that deterrent measures may have greater impact on some people and a lesser effect on others.[100] Among some groups of high-risk offenders, such as teens living in economically depressed neighborhoods, the threat of formal sanctions is irrelevant. Young people in these areas have little to lose if arrested; their opportunities are few, and they have little attachment to social institutions such as school and family. Even if they truly fear the consequences of the law, they must commit crime to survive in a hostile environment. Similarly, some people may be suffering from personality disorders and mental infirmity, which make them immune to the deterrent power of the law.[101]

that each execution leads to an average of 18 fewer murders. Shepherd concludes what when a state routinely uses executions, the deterrent effect becomes significant.

These recent studies are not without their detractors. Jeffrey Fagin, a highly regarded criminologist, finds fault with the methodology now being used, arguing that "this work fails the tests of rigorous replication and robustness analysis that are the hallmarks of good science." Similarly, John Donohue and Justin Wolfers examined recent statistical studies that claimed to show a deterrent effect from the death penalty and found that they "are simply not credible." In fact, they reach an opposite conclusion: Applying the death penalty actually *increases* the number of murders.

Even if it is an effective deterrent, capital punishment has significant drawbacks: Since 1976, more than 100 people have been wrongfully convicted and sentenced to death in the United States. And according to research sponsored by the Pew Foundation, a majority of death penalty convictions have been overturned, many due to "serious, reversible error," including egregiously incompetent defense counsel, suppression of exculpatory evidence, false confessions, racial manipulation of the jury, "snitch" and accomplice testimony, and faulty jury instructions.

Thus, after years of study, the deterrent effect of the death penalty remains a topic of considerable criminological debate.

CRITICAL THINKING

Even if it is effective, the death penalty is not without serious problems. For example, when Geoffrey Rapp studied the effect of the death penalty on the safety of police officers, he found that the introduction of capital punishment actually created an extremely dangerous environment for law enforcement officers. Because the death penalty does not have a deterrent effect, criminals are more likely to kill police officers when the death penalty is in place. Tragically, the death penalty may lull officers into a false sense of security, causing them to let down their guard—killing fewer criminals but getting killed more often themselves. Given Rapp's findings, should we still maintain the death penalty?

SOURCES: Tomislav Kovandzic, Lynne Vieraitis, Denise Paquette Boots, "Does the Death Penalty Save Lives?: New Evidence from State Panel Data, 1977 to 2006," *Criminology and Public Policy*, 8 (2009): 803–843; Jeffrey Fagan, "Death and Deterrence Redux: Science, Law and Causal Reasoning on Capital Punishment," *Ohio State Journal of Criminal Law* 4 (2006): 255–320; Pew Foundation, "Death Penalty," www.pewcenteronthestates.org/topic_category .aspx?category=510 (accessed February 28, 2009); Joanna Shepherd, "Deterrence versus Brutalization: Capital Punishment's Differing Impacts among States," *Michigan Law Review* 104 (2005): 203–253; Matt Beverlin, "A Study of the Deterrence Effect of the Juvenile Death Penalty," paper presented at the Southern Political Science Association annual meeting, New Orleans, 2005, 1–34; John Donohue and Justin Wolfers, "Uses and Abuses of Empirical Evidence in the Death Penalty Debate," *Stanford Law Review* 58 (2005): 791–845; Lisa Stolzenberg and Stewart D'Alessio, "Capital Punishment, Execution Publicity, and Murder in Houston, Texas," *Journal of Criminal Law and Criminology* 94 (2004): 351–380; Thorsten Sellin, *The Death Penalty* (Philadelphia: American Law Institute, 1959); Jon Sorenson, Robert Wrinkle, Victoria Brewer, and James Marquart, "Capital Punishment and Deterrence: Examining the Effect of Executions on Murder in Texas," *Crime and Delinquency* 45 (1999): 481–931; James Yunker, "A New Statistical Analysis of Capital Punishment Incorporating U.S. Postmoratorium Data," *Social Science Quarterly* 82 (2001): 297–312; Hashem Dezhbakhsh, Paul H. Rubin, and Joanna M. Shepherd, "Does Capital Punishment Have a Deterrent Effect? New Evidence from Postmoratorium Panel Data," *American Law and Economics Review* 5 (2003): 344–376.

However, for some crimes, where a small group of chronic offenders (for example, dealers in illegal firearms) are responsible for a great majority of the criminal activity, a targeted strategy that directs a surge of law enforcement activity against repeat offenders may help reduce crime even in the most disorganized neighborhoods.[102]

It also appears that it is easier to deter offenders from some crimes than from others. A recent (2009) meta-analysis of the existing literature shows that the most significant deterrent effects can be achieved in minor crimes and offenses, whereas more serious crimes such as homicide are harder to discourage.[103] Because criminals may be more readily deterred from committing some crimes—for example, tax noncompliance, speeding, and illegal parking—future research should be directed at identifying and targeting these preventable offenses.[104]

Specific Deterrence

The theory of **specific deterrence** (also called special or particular deterrence) holds that criminal sanctions should be so powerful that known criminals will never repeat their criminal acts. According to this view, the drunk driver whose sentence is a substantial fine and a week in the county jail should be convinced that the price to be paid for drinking and driving is too great to consider future violations. Similarly, burglars who spend five years in a tough, maximum-security prison should find their enthusiasm for theft dampened.[105] In principle, punishment works when a connection can be established between the planned action and memories of its consequence; if these recollections are adequately intense, the action is unlikely to occur again.[106]

specific deterrence
The view that criminal sanctions should be so powerful that offenders will never repeat their criminal acts.

Research on specific deterrence does not provide any clear-cut evidence that punishing criminals is an effective means of stopping them from committing future crimes. In a famous study conducted in Minneapolis, Lawrence Sherman and Richard Berk evaluated the effect of police action on repeat domestic violence. They found clear evidence that when police take formal action (arrest), offenders are less likely to recidivate than when less severe methods are used (a warning or a cooling-off period).[107] Subsequent to this study, a number of states adopted legislation mandating that police either take formal action in domestic abuse cases or explain in writing their failure to act. However, when the Minneapolis experiment was repeated in other locales, evaluations failed to duplicate the original results.[108] In these locales, formal arrest was not a greater specific deterrent to domestic abuse than warning or advising the assailant.

Sherman and his associates later found that the effect of arrest quickly decays and that in the long run, arrest may actually escalate the frequency of repeat domestic violence.[109] A possible explanation is that offenders who are arrested fear punishment initially, but when their cases do not result in severe punishment, their fear is eventually replaced with anger and violent intent toward their mates. This result implies that even if punishment can produce a short-term specific deterrent effect, it fails to produce longer-term behavior change.[110]

There are other indications that specific deterrence strategies do not work as expected. Research indicates that arrest and punishment have little effect on experienced criminals and may even increase the likelihood that first-time offenders will commit new crimes.[111] About two-thirds of all convicted felons are rearrested within three years of their release from prison; the most experienced are also the most likely to commit a new offense.[112] **Incarceration** may sometimes delay **recidivism**, but the overall probability of rearrest is not reduced, and may even be increased, by serving a prison sentence.[113]

Some states are now employing high-security "supermax" prisons that apply a bare minimum of treatment and impose lockdown 23 hours a day. Certainly, such a harsh regimen should discourage future criminality. But a recent study in the state of Washington, which matched supermax prisoners with inmates from more traditional prisons on a one-to-one basis, showed that upon release, supermax prisoners had significantly higher felony recidivism rates than controls from less restrictive prisons. Those released directly into the community from a supermax prison committed new offenses sooner than supermax prisoners who were first sent to traditional institutions three months or more before their release.[114]

How is it possible that the harshest treatment increases rather than reduces crime?

▶ Punishment may breed defiance rather than deterrence. People who are harshly treated may want to show that they cannot be broken by the system.
▶ The stigma of harsh treatment labels people and helps lock offenders into a criminal career instead of convincing them to avoid one.
▶ Criminals who are punished may also believe that the likelihood of getting caught twice for the same type of crime is remote: "Lightning never strikes twice in the same spot," they may reason; no one is that unlucky.[115]
▶ Experiencing the harshest punishments, such as a stay in a supermax prison, may cause severe psychological problems because these prisons isolate convicts, offer little sensory stimulation, and provide minimal opportunities for interaction with other people.[116]
▶ In neighborhoods where everyone has a criminal record, the effect of punishment erodes and people instead feel they have been victimized rather than fairly treated for their crimes.[117]

Thus, although the concept of specific deterrence should work on paper, the reality can be far different.

Incapacitation

Even if severe punishments cannot effectively turn criminals away from crime, it stands to reason that if more criminals are sent to prison, the crime rate should go down. Because most people age out of crime, the duration of a criminal career is

Fact or Fiction?

The more you punish people, the less likely they are to commit crime.

Fiction. There is very little evidence that severe punishments reduce crime rates or individual recidivism rates.

incarceration
Confinement in jail or prison.

recidivism
Repetition of criminal behavior.

limited. Placing offenders behind bars during their prime crime years should reduce their lifetime opportunity to commit crime. The shorter the span of opportunity, the fewer offenses they can commit during their lives; hence, crime is reduced. This theory, which is known as the **incapacitation effect**, seems logical, but does it work?

In the past 20 years we have witnessed significant growth in the number and percentage of the population held in prisons and jails. The most recent data (2009) indicates that nationwide, almost 1.6 million are in prison and that the inmate population has nearly tripled in 30 years; another 700,000 people are in local jails. Because the number of American adults is about 230 million, this means that one in every hundred adults is behind bars.[118] Advocates of incapacitation suggest that this growth in the prison/jail population is directly responsible for the decade-long decline in the crime rate: Putting dangerous felons under lock and key for longer periods of time significantly reduces the opportunity they have to commit crime, so the crime rate declines as well.

Critics counter that what appears to be an incapacitation effect may actually be the effect of some other legal or social phenomenon: The police may be more effective, for example, or the crack cocaine epidemic may have waned. Crime rates may be dropping simply because potential criminals now recognize and fear the tough new sentencing laws that provide long mandatory prison sentences for drug and violent crimes. What appears to be an incapacitation effect may actually be an effect of general deterrence.[119]

CAN INCAPACITATION REDUCE CRIME?

Criminologists have long debated the effect of incarceration on the crime rate.[120] Some experts question the effect of incarceration.[121] Others find that it can reduce crime.[122] The fact that crime rates have dropped while the prison population has burgeoned supports the incapacitation concept that criminal opportunities are ended once criminals are behind bars. Although it is difficult to measure precisely, there is at least some evidence that crime rates and incarceration rates are related.[123] Economist Steven Levitt, author of the widely read book *Freakonomics,* concludes that each person put behind bars results in a decrease of 15 serious crimes per year.[124] He argues that the social benefits associated with crime reduction equal or exceed the social and financial costs of incarceration.[125]

Even though Levitt's argument is persuasive, not all criminologists buy into the incapacitation effect:

▶ There is little evidence that incapacitating criminals will deter them from future criminality, and there *is* reason to believe they may be more inclined to commit even more crimes upon release. There is a significant correlation between incarceration and recidivism. In other words, the more prior incarceration experiences people have, the more likely they are to recidivate within 12 months of their release.[126]

▶ By its nature, the prison experience exposes young, first-time offenders to higher-risk, more experienced inmates who can influence their lifestyle and help shape their attitudes.

▶ Novice inmates also run an increased risk of becoming infected with AIDS and other health hazards, and that exposure reduces their life chances after release.[127]

▶ The short-term crime reduction effect achieved by incapacitating criminals is balanced by the escalating frequency of criminal behavior upon their release.

▶ The economics of crime suggest that if money can be made from criminal activity, there will always be someone to take the place of the incarcerated offender. New criminals will be recruited and trained, offsetting any benefit that can be attributed to incarceration.

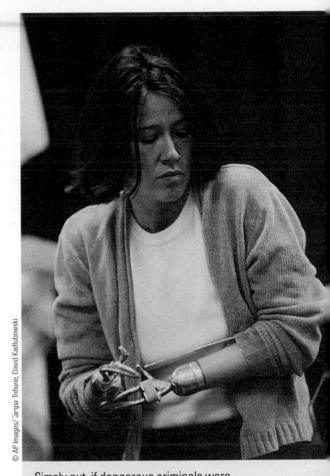

© AP Images/*Tampa Tribune,* David Kadlubowski

Simply put, if dangerous criminals were incapacitated, they would never have the opportunity to prey upon others. One of the most dramatic examples of the utility of incapacitation is the case of Lawrence Singleton, who in 1978 raped a young California girl, Mary Vincent, and then chopped off her arms with an axe. He served eight years in prison for this vile crime. Upon his release he moved to Florida, where in 1997 he killed a woman named Roxanne Hayes. Vincent is shown here as she testifies at the penalty phase of Singleton's trial for this killing; he was sentenced to death. Should a dangerous predator such as Singleton ever be released from incapacitation? Is rehabilitation even a remote possibility?

incapacitation effect
The view that placing offenders behind bars during their prime crime years reduces their opportunity to commit crime and helps lower the crime rate.

Concept Summary 4.1 Choice Theories

Theory	Major Premise	Strengths	Research Focus
Rational choice	Law-violating behavior occurs after offenders weigh information on their personal needs and the situational factors involved in the difficulty and risk of committing a crime.	Explains why high-risk youths do not constantly engage in delinquency. Relates theory to delinquency control policy. It is not limited by class or other social variables.	Offense patterns—where, when, and how crime takes place.
General deterrence	People will commit crime and delinquency if they perceive that the benefits outweigh the risks. Crime is a function of the severity, certainty, and speed of punishment.	Shows the relationship between crime and punishment. Suggests a real solution to crime.	Perception of punishment, effect of legal sanctions, probability of punishment, and crime rates.
Specific deterrence	If punishment is severe enough, criminals will not repeat their illegal acts.	Provides a strategy to reduce crime.	Recidivism, repeat offending, punishment type, and crime.
Incapacitation	Keeping known criminals out of circulation will reduce crime rates.	Recognizes the role that opportunity plays in criminal behavior. Provides a solution to chronic offending.	Prison population and crime rates, sentence length, and crime.

Fact or Fiction?

Locking up millions of criminals can bring down the crime rate.

Fiction. The evidence that incarceration can bring down crime rates is inconclusive, and it is countered by the fear that locking people up can eventually cause crime rates to increase.

▶ Imprisoning established offenders may likewise open new opportunities for competitors who were suppressed by more experienced criminals. Incarcerating gang members or organized crime figures may open crime and illegal drug markets to new groups and gangs that are even hungrier and more aggressive than the gangs they replaced.

▶ Most criminal offenses are committed by teens and very young adult offenders who are unlikely to be sent to prison for a single felony conviction. Aging criminals are already past the age when they are likely to commit crime. As a result, a strict incarceration policy may keep people in prison beyond the time when they cease being a threat to society, while a new cohort of high-risk adolescents is on the street.[128]

▶ An incapacitation strategy is terribly expensive. The prison system costs billions of dollars each year. Even if incarceration could reduce the crime rate, the costs would be enormous.

▶ A strict incarceration policy would result in a growing number of elderly inmates whose maintenance costs, estimated at about $70,000 per year, are three times higher than those of younger inmates. Estimates are that about 16 percent of the prison population is over age 50.[129]

▶ Most inmates come from a few impoverished communities. When they are released, they disrupt their neighborhoods, undermine social institutions, and create community disorganization. Rather than act as a crime suppressant, incarceration may have the long-term effect of accelerating crime rates.[130]

Concept Summary 4.1 summarizes the main features of choice theories.

▶ **Checkpoints**

Policy Implications of Choice Theory

From the origins of classical theory to the development of modern rational choice views, the belief that criminals choose to commit crime has influenced justice policy. Although research on the core principles of choice theory and deterrence theories has produced mixed results, these models have had a significant impact on contemporary crime prevention strategies.

When police patrol in well-marked cars, it is assumed that their presence will deter would-be criminals from committing crime by increasing the certainty that their criminal acts will be punished. And when tough mandatory criminal sentences are created to control violent crime and drug trafficking, the underlying vision is that the severity of punishment can control crime. These measures assume criminals are rational decision makers who will choose not to commit crime if they believe that they will be caught and severely punished for their crimes. Two current, albeit controversial, justice policies represent the influence of choice on justice policy: the three strikes laws and the death penalty.

The "Three Strikes and You're Out" Sentencing Policy In order to discourage crime and make sure that chronic offenders are incapacitated, "three strikes and you're out" laws require the state courts to hand down mandatory periods of incarceration for up to life in prison to persons who have been convicted of a serious criminal offense on three or more separate occasions.

The rationale for its use relies on both general deterrence (scaring off would-be criminals) and incapacitation (keeping repeat offenders off the streets). Can such hard-line policies work? The results are mixed. Some criminologists, using highly sophisticated research techniques, have found a significant association between the increased use of incarceration and reductions in the crime rate.[131] A strict incarceration policy may also have residual benefits. Ilyana Kuziemko and Steven Levitt found that as the number of prisoners incarcerated on drug-related offenses rose dramatically (1,500 percent) between 1980 and 2000, crime rates dropped. One reason was that the incarceration policy had an unforeseen impact on drug markets: Putting dealers in prison increased the cost of cocaine by 10 to 15 percent, and the higher prices spelled a drop of as much as 20 percent in the use of cocaine.[132]

Although get-tough policies have political appeal in our conservative society, some criminologists conclude that it is premature to embrace a three strikes policy:

► Most three-time losers are on the verge of aging out of crime anyway.
► Current sentences for violent crimes are already quite severe.
► An expanding prison population will drive up already high prison costs.
► There would be racial disparity in sentencing.
► The police would be in danger because two-time offenders would violently resist a third arrest, knowing that conviction would mean a life sentence.[133]
► The prison population probably already contains the highest-frequency criminals.

The Death Penalty Nowhere can the influence of choice theory be felt more dramatically than in the use of the death penalty as a deterrent to murder. Despite its questionable effect, advocates argue that the death penalty can effectively restrict criminality; at least it ensures that convicted criminals never again get the opportunity to kill. Many observers are dismayed because people who are convicted of murder sometimes kill again when released on parole. About 9 percent of all inmates on death row have had prior convictions for homicide. Death penalty advocates argue that if these criminals had been executed for their first offenses, hundreds of people would be alive today.[134] While critics bemoan the use of capital punishment, advocates retort that the murder rate has been in dramatic decline since its return to frequent use, and the general public approves of its use as a deterrent to murder. This "success" has prompted some members of the legal community to suggest that capital

Checkpoints

► Situational crime prevention efforts are designed to reduce or redirect crime by making it more difficult to profit from illegal acts.

► General deterrence models are based on the fear of punishment that is severe, swift, and certain.

► Specific deterrence aims at reducing crime through the application of severe punishments. Once offenders experience these punishments, they will be unwilling to repeat their criminal activities.

► Incapacitation strategies are designed to reduce crime by taking known criminals out of circulation, which denies them the opportunity to commit further offenses. The effectiveness of incapacitation strategies is hotly debated.

A Justice Department official contacts you and asks your opinion on crime control. She cites data showing that as the number of people behind bars has sky-rocketed, the crime rate has been in a steep decline. It appears that tough sentences, featuring mandatory prison stays and the use of supermax prisons, have paid dividends.

She asks you, "Could these sentencing practices be responsible for U.S. crime rates that, for the most part, have been in decline?"

Writing Assignment

Write a critical essay relating sentencing practices to crime rates. Address the issue of whether locking people up is an effective crime control policy—or might it have hidden costs that undermine its effectiveness? Is the recent crime drop in America a function of incarcerating known criminals, or might other factors be responsible for a declining crime rate?

punishment is morally justified because it is a life-saving social policy. Writing in the *Stanford Law Review*, Cass Sunstein and Adrian Vermeule conclude that "a government that settles upon a package of crime-control policies that does *not* include capital punishment might well seem, at least prima facie, to be both violating the rights and reducing the welfare of its citizens—just as would a state that failed to enact simple environmental measures promising to save a great many lives."[135]

Summary

1. Describe the development of rational choice theory.

Rational choice theory has its roots in the classical school of criminology developed by the eighteenth-century Italian social thinker Cesare Beccaria. In the 1960s, Nobel Prize–winning economist Gary Becker applied his views on rational behavior and human capital to criminal activity. James Q. Wilson observed that people who are likely to commit crime are unafraid of breaking the law because they value the excitement and thrills of crime, have a low stake in conformity, and are willing to take greater chances than the average person.

2. Describe the concepts of rational choice.

Law-violating behavior is the product of careful thought and planning. People who commit crime believe that the rewards of crime outweigh the risks. If they think they are likely to get arrested and punished, people will not risk engaging in criminal activities. Before choosing to commit a crime, reasoning criminals carefully select targets, and their behavior is systematic and selective. Rational choice theorists view crime as both offense-specific and offender-specific.

3. Discuss how offenders structure criminality.

Criminals consider their needs and capabilities before committing crimes. One important decision that an individual makes before entering a life of crime is whether to attach the highest priority to his or her need for money. Personal experience may be an important element in structuring criminality. Criminals report that before committing crimes, they actually learn techniques to help them avoid detection while making profits.

4. Describe how criminals structure crime.

Criminals carefully choose where they will commit their crime. Evidence of rational choice may also be found in the way criminals locate their targets. Rational choice involves both shaping criminality and structuring crime. If a target appears dangerous, criminals will choose another target.

5. Be acquainted with the evidence suggesting that crime is rational.

There is evidence that theft-related crimes are the product of careful risk assessment, including environmental, social, and structural factors. Target selection seems highly rational. Even drug use is controlled by rational decision making. Users report that they begin taking drugs when they believe the benefits of substance abuse outweigh its costs. Evidence confirms that even violent criminals select suitable targets by picking people who are vulnerable and lack adequate defenses. In some instances, targets are chosen in order to send a message rather than to generate capital.

6. Know what is meant by the term "seductions of crime."

According to sociologist Jack Katz, choosing crime can be seductive and pleasant. It can help people satisfy personal needs. Even murder can have an emotional payoff: The criminal lifestyle is very attractive to people who organize their life around risk taking and partying. Criminal behavior provides money for drugs and is ideal for displaying courage and fearlessness to one's peers.

7. Discuss the elements of situational crime prevention.

Situational crime prevention involves developing tactics to reduce or eliminate a specific crime problem. Such tactics include increased efforts to discourage crime, such as putting unbreakable glass on storefronts, locking gates, and fencing yards. Another approach is to increase the risks of crime through better security efforts. Reducing the rewards of crime is designed to lessen the value of crime to the potential criminal. Crime may be reduced or prevented if we can communicate to people the wrongfulness of their behavior and how harmful it is to society. Crime may be reduced by making it difficult for people to excuse their criminal behavior by saying things like "I didn't know that was illegal" or "I had no choice."

8. Be familiar with the elements of general deterrence.

Crime can be controlled by increasing the real or perceived threat of criminal punishment. According to deterrence theory, criminality is affected not only by the actual chance of punishment but also by the *perception* that one is likely to be punished. A central theme of deterrence theory is that people who believe they will be punished for crimes will avoid committing those crimes.

According to general deterrence theory, if the certainty of arrest, conviction, and sanctioning increases, crime rates should decline. The threat of severe punishment should also bring the crime rate down. The more rapidly punishment is applied and the more closely it is linked to the crime, the more likely it will serve as a deterrent. The factors of severity, certainty, and speed of punishment may also influence one another.

9. Discuss the basic concepts of specific deterrence.

The theory of specific deterrence holds that criminal sanctions should be so powerful that convicted criminals will never repeat their criminal acts. However, research on specific deterrence does not provide any clear-cut evidence that punishing criminals is an effective means of stopping them from committing future crimes. Punishment may bring defiance rather than deterrence. People who are harshly treated may want to show that they cannot be broken by the system. The stigma of harsh treatment labels people and helps lock offenders into a criminal career instead of convincing them to avoid one.

10. Understand the pros and cons of applying an incapacitation strategy to reduce crime.

According to those who endorse the incapacitation strategy, the more criminals who are sent to prison, the more the crime rate should go down. Placing offenders behind bars during their prime crime years should reduce their lifetime opportunity to commit crime. The shorter the span of opportunity, the fewer offenses they can commit during their lives; hence, crime is reduced. However, there is little evidence that incapacitating criminals will deter them from future criminality; rather, there is reason to believe that incarceration may make them inclined to commit even more crimes upon their release.

Key Terms

rational choice theory
  (choice theory) 84
classical criminology 84
offense-specific crime 86
offender-specific
  crime 86

edgework 91
seductions of
  crime 91
situational crime
  prevention 92
defensible space 92

crime discouragers 93
diffusion 95
discouragement 95
displacement 95
extinction 95
replacement 95

general deterrence 95
specific deterrence 99
incarceration 100
recidivism 100
incapacitation
  effect 101

Critical Thinking Questions

1. Are criminals rational decision makers, or are most of them motivated by uncontrollable psychological and emotional drives or social forces such as poverty and despair?

2. Would you want to live in a society where crime rates were quite low because they were controlled by extremely harsh punishments, such as flogging for vandalism?

3. Which would you be more afraid of if you were caught by the police while shoplifting: receiving criminal punishment or having to face the contempt of your friends or relatives?

4. Is it possible to create a method of capital punishment that would actually deter people from committing murder? For example, would televising executions work? What might be some of the negative consequences of such a policy?

© AP Images/Amy Carcetta

Chapter Outline

Trait Theory

5

On Monday, April 16, 2007, 23-year-old Seung-Hui Cho methodically took the lives of 32 people—27 students and 5 professors—at Virginia Tech before taking his own life.[1] In the aftermath of the tragedy, Cho was described as a loner unable to make social connections. He had been involuntarily institutionalized in a mental health facility. He had become fixated on several female students, who eventually complained to the police because he was showing up at their rooms and bombarding them with instant messages.[2] In a creative writing class, he had read one of his poems aloud, and its sinister content had so frightened classmates that some did not show up the next time the class met.[3]

Ten months later, on February 14, 2008, another tragedy occurred at Northern Illinois University. Steven Kazmierczak, a former student who was currently enrolled in the school of social work at the University of Illinois at Urbana-Champaign, entered Cole Hall, a large auditorium-style lecture hall, on the NIU campus armed with a shotgun and three handguns. Standing on the stage, he began shooting into the crowded classroom, killing 5 and wounding 16 others before taking his own life. In the aftermath of the incident, Kazmierczak was described as "an outstanding student" who suffered from depression and anxiety. His girlfriend, Jessica Baty, confirmed that Kazmierczak was taking Xanax (an anti-anxiety drug), Ambien (a sleep aid), and Prozac (an antidepressant) but that he had stopped taking the Prozac about three weeks before the shooting. "He was anything but a monster," Baty said. "He was probably the nicest, most caring person ever."[4]

Fact or Fiction?

▶ You are what you eat! "Eating healthy" can reduce antisocial behaviors.

▶ It may be because of their hormones that men exhibit more violent behavior than women.

▶ The image of the brain-damaged villain going on a violent rampage is more likely to occur in horror films than in real life.

▶ The acorn does not fall far from the tree; that is, the children of deviant parents are more likely than other kids to be anti-social themselves.

▶ The behavior of identical twins is eerily similar, but if they live apart all their lives without knowing each other, they are likely to be quite different.

▶ Watching violent TV shows makes kids behave more violently.

Chapter Objectives

1. Be familiar with the development of trait theory.

2. Discuss some of the biochemical conditions that have been associated with crime.

3. Understand the linkage between aggression and neurophysiological makeup.

4. Link genetics to crime.

5. Explain the evolutionary view of crime.

6. Discuss the elements of the psychodynamic perspective.

7. Link behavioral theory to crime.

8. Show why aggressive behavior may reflect cognitive processes.

9. Discuss the elements of personality that are related to crime.

10. Be aware of the controversy over the association between intelligence and crime.

11. Discuss the association between mental disorders and crime.

These two senseless tragedies remind us that at least in some instances, the cause of crime is linked to mental or physical abnormality. How could two college students such as Cho and Kazmierczak engage in mass murder unless they were suffering from some form of mental instability or collapse? In the aftermath of the killings there seemed to be ample evidence that both were under severe psychological stress, yet no one was able to foresee or predict their violent actions.

This vision is neither new nor unique. The image of a disturbed, mentally ill offender seems plausible because a whole generation of Americans has grown up on films and TV shows that portray violent criminals as mentally deranged and physically abnormal. Beginning with Alfred Hitchcock's film *Psycho*, producers have made millions depicting the ghoulish acts of people who at first seem normal and even friendly but turn out to be demented and dangerous. Lurking out there are deranged female (*Obsession*) and male (*Fear*) admirers and lunatic high school friends (*Scream*), who evolve into even crazier college classmates (*Scream II*) and then grow up to become deranged young adults (*Scream III*). Some of these psychos do not act alone but are part of extended demented families (*Texas Chainsaw Massacre*; *The Hills Have Eyes*). No one is safe when the psychologists and psychiatrists who are hired to treat these disturbed people turn out to be demonic murderers themselves (*Silence of the Lambs, Hannibal, Red Dragon*). Is it any wonder that we respond to a particularly horrible crime by saying of the perpetrator, "That guy must be crazy" or "She is a monster"?

This chapter reviews the theories that suggest that criminality is an outgrowth of abnormal human traits. These **trait theories** can be subdivided into two major categories: those that stress biological makeup and those that stress psychological functioning. Although these views often overlap (that is, brain function may have a biological basis), each branch has its unique characteristics and will be discussed separately.

Development of Trait Theory

The view that criminals have physical or mental traits that make them different and abnormal is not restricted to movie viewers but began with the Italian physician and criminologist Cesare Lombroso. The early research of Lombroso and his contemporaries is today regarded as historical curiosity, not scientific fact. The research methodology they used was slipshod, and many of the traits they assumed to be inherited are not genetically determined but caused by environment and diet. As criticism of this early work mounted, biological explanations of crime fell out of favor and were abandoned in the early twentieth century.[5] In the early 1970s, spurred by the publication of Edmund O. Wilson's *Sociobiology: The New Synthesis*, biological explanations of crime once again emerged.[6] **Sociobiology** differs from earlier theories of behavior in that it stresses the following principles:

▶ Behavioral traits may be inherited.
▶ Inherited behavioral traits have been formed by natural selection.
▶ Behavioral traits evolve and are shaped by the environment.
▶ Biological and genetic conditions affect how social behaviors are learned and perceived.
▶ Behavior is determined by the need to ensure survival of offspring and replenishment of the gene pool.
▶ Biology, environment, and learning are mutually interdependent factors.

Simply put, sociobiology assumes that social behavior is often genetically transmitted and subject to evolutionary processes; that is, it changes to meet existing environmental conditions. This view revived interest in finding a biological or psychological basis for crime and delinquency. It prompted some criminologists to conclude that personal traits must be what separates the deviant members of society from the nondeviant. Possessing these traits may help explain why, when faced with the same life situation, one person commits crime whereas another obeys the law. For example, living in a disadvantaged neighborhood will not cause a well-adjusted person to

trait theory
The view that criminality is a product of abnormal biological or psychological traits.

sociobiology
The view that human behavior is motivated by inborn biological urges to survive and preserve the species.

commit crime, and living in an affluent area will not stop a maladapted person from offending.[7] All people may be aware of and even fear the sanctioning power of the law, but some are unable to control their urges and passions.

Contemporary Trait Theory

Contemporary trait theorists do not suggest that a single biological or psychological attribute adequately explains all criminality. Rather, each offender is considered physically and mentally unique, so there must be different explanations for each person's behavior. Some may have inherited criminal tendencies; others may be suffering from neurological problems; still others may have blood chemistry disorders that heighten their antisocial activity. Criminologists who focus on the individual see many explanations for crime because, in fact, there are many differences among criminal offenders.

According to psychologist Bernard Rimland, what may appear to some as the effect of environment and socialization may be actually linked to genetically determined physical and/or mental traits. In his 2008 book *Dyslogic Syndrome*, Rimland disputes the notion that bad or ineffective parenting is to blame for troubled or disobedient children. To him, the culprit is more likely to be bad diets:

> [M]ost "bad" children . . . suffer from toxic physical environments, often coupled with genetic vulnerability, rather than toxic family environments. . . . America's children are not their parents, but rather the poor-quality food substitutes they eat, the pollutants in the air they breathe, the chemically contaminated water they drink, and other less well-known physical insults that cause malfunctioning brains and bodies. . . .[8]

Thus, according to clinical psychologists such as Rimland, it is personal traits and biological conditions, not parenting or social environment, that best explains behavioral choices. Trait theorists today recognize that having a particular physical characteristic does not, in itself, produce criminality. Crime-producing interactions involve both personal traits (such as defective intelligence, impulsive personality, and abnormal brain chemistry) and environmental factors (such as family life, educational attainment, socioeconomic status, and neighborhood conditions). People may develop physical or mental traits at birth, or soon thereafter, that affect their social functioning over the life course and influence their behavior choices; they suffer some biological or psychological condition or trait that renders them incapable of resisting social pressures and vulnerable to developing behavior problems.[9]

Trait theories have gained prominence recently because of what is now known about chronic recidivism and the development of criminal careers. If only a few offenders become persistent repeaters, then what sets them apart from the rest of the criminal population may be some abnormality in biochemical makeup, brain structure, genetic constitution, or some other human trait.[10] Even if crime is a choice, the fact that some people make that choice repeatedly could be linked to their physical and mental makeup. According to this view, biological makeup contributes significantly to human behavior. ▶ **Checkpoints**

Checkpoints

▶ Early criminologists, such as Cesare Lombroso, suggested that some people had crime-producing biological traits.

▶ Some contemporary criminologists believe that human traits interact with environmental factors to produce criminal behaviors.

▶ No single trait is responsible for all crime. Suspected crime-producing traits include neurological problems, blood chemistry disorders, and personality disorders.

▶ Each person is physically and mentally unique; otherwise, all people living in the same environment would act in the same way.

Biological Trait Theories

One branch of contemporary trait theory focuses on the biological conditions that control human behavior. Criminologists who work in this area typically refer to themselves as biocriminologists, biosocial criminologists, or biologically oriented criminologists; the terms are used here interchangeably.

The following sections examine some important subareas within biological criminology (Figure 5.1). First we review the biochemical factors that are believed to affect how proper behavior patterns are learned. Then we consider the relationship between brain function and crime. Next we analyze current ideas about the association between genetic factors and crime. Finally, we evaluate evolutionary views of crime causation.

CONNECTIONS

As you may recall from Chapter 1, Lombroso's work on the born criminal was a direct offshoot of applying the scientific method to the study of crime. His identification of primitive, atavistic anomalies was based on what he believed to be sound empirical research using established scientific methods.

CONNECTIONS

Although it may seem reasonable to believe there is a biological basis to aggression and violence, it is more difficult to explain how insider trading and fraud are biologically related. The causes of white-collar crime are discussed in Chapter 12.

Figure 5.1 Biosocial Perspectives on Criminality

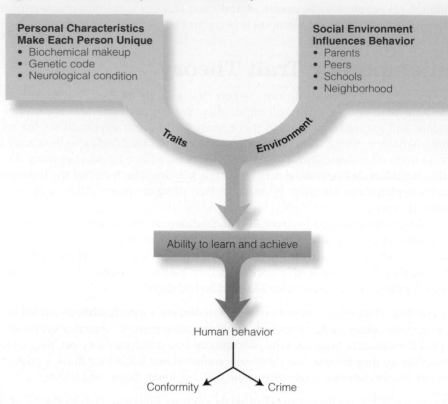

Personal Characteristics Make Each Person Unique
- Biochemical makeup
- Genetic code
- Neurological condition

Social Environment Influences Behavior
- Parents
- Peers
- Schools
- Neighborhood

Traits   Environment

Ability to learn and achieve

Human behavior

Conformity   Crime

BIOCHEMICAL CONDITIONS AND CRIME

Some trait theorists believe that biochemical conditions, including both those that are genetically predetermined and those that are acquired through diet and environment, influence antisocial behavior. This view of crime received national attention in 1979 when Dan White, who confessed to killing San Francisco Mayor George Moscone and City Councilman Harvey Milk, claimed that his behavior was precipitated by an addiction to sugar-laden junk foods.[11] White's successful "Twinkie defense" prompted a California jury to find him guilty of the lesser offense of diminished-capacity manslaughter rather than first-degree murder. (In 1985 White committed suicide after serving his prison sentence; 24 years later he was played by Josh Brolin in the film *Milk*, for which Sean Penn won an Oscar for his portrayal of Harvey Milk.)

In some cases the influence of chemicals and minerals is direct. Research now shows that people who start drinking by the age of 14 are five times as likely to become alcoholics as people who hold off on drinking until the age of 21. It is possible that early exposure to alcohol short-circuits the growth of brain cells, impairing the learning and memory processes that protect against addiction. Thus, early ingestion of alcohol may have a direct influence on behavior.[12]

In other cases, the relationship between biochemical makeup and antisocial behavior is indirect: Chemical and mineral imbalance leads to perceptual and intellectual deficits and problems, which may eventually generate antisocial behaviors.[13] In a recent international study, researchers discovered that the blood mercury levels of children diagnosed with attention-deficit/hyperactivity disorder (ADHD) were significantly higher than the levels found in the general population, indicating a clear association between an environmental pollutant and a behavior disorder.[14]

Some of the biochemical factors that have been linked to criminality are discussed in detail here.

Diet Biocriminologists maintain that a healthful diet can provide minimal levels of minerals and chemicals needed for normal brain functioning and growth, especially

Fact or Fiction?

You are what you eat! "Eating healthy" can reduce antisocial behaviors.

Fact. Biocriminologists link antisocial behavior to diet and chemical intake. You may in fact be what you eat.

in the early years of life. An improper diet can cause chemical and mineral imbalance and can lead to cognitive and learning deficits and problems, and these factors in turn are associated with antisocial behaviors.[15]

Research conducted over the past decade shows that an over- or undersupply of certain chemicals and minerals (including sodium, mercury, potassium, calcium, amino acids, and iron) can lead to depression, hyperactivity, cognitive problems, memory loss, or abnormal sexual activity.[16] Either eliminating harmful substances or introducing beneficial ones into the diet can reduce the threat of antisocial behaviors.[17]

A recent review of existing research on the association between diet and crime found that a combination of the following nutrients produced good mental health and well-adjusted behavior patterns:

▶ Polyunsaturated fatty acids (particularly the omega 3 types found in oily fish and some plants)
▶ Minerals, such as zinc (in whole grains, legumes, meat, and milk); magnesium (in green leafy vegetables, nuts, and whole grains); and iron (in red meat, green leafy vegetables, eggs, and some fruit)
▶ Vitamins, such as folate (in green leafy vegetables and fortified cereals); a range of B vitamins (in whole-grain products, yeast, and dairy products); and antioxidant vitamins such as C and E (in a wide range of fruits and vegetables).[18]

People whose diets lack one or more of this combination of polyunsaturated fats, minerals, and vitamins, and/or contain too much saturated fat (or other elements, including sugar and a range of food and agricultural chemicals) seem to be at higher risk of developing psychological disturbances, such as schizophrenia, that are directly related to antisocial acts. The association may also be indirect: Kids with faulty diets tend also to be starved for attention, and this may lead to school failure and educational underachievement, a social problem linked to subsequent antisocial behavior patterns.[19]

Because we are eating too much saturated fat, sugar, and salt and not enough vitamins and minerals, our diets may also be contributing to rising rates of mental ill-health and antisocial behavior.

Hypoglycemia When blood glucose (sugar) falls below levels necessary for normal and efficient brain functioning, a condition called **hypoglycemia** occurs. Symptoms of hypoglycemia include irritability, anxiety, depression, crying spells, headaches, and confusion. Research studies have linked hypoglycemia to outbursts of antisocial behavior and violence.[20] High levels of reactive hypoglycemia have been found in groups of habitually violent and impulsive offenders.[21]

Hormonal Influences Biosocial research has found that abnormal levels of male sex hormones (**androgens**) can produce aggressive behavior.[22] Other androgen-related male traits include sensation seeking, impulsivity, dominance, and reduced verbal skills; all of these traits are related to antisocial behavior.[23] A growing body of evidence suggests that hormonal changes are also related to mood and behavior. Adolescents experience more intense mood swings, anxiety, and restlessness than their elders, explaining in part the high violence rates found among teenage males.[24]

Testosterone, the most abundant androgen, which controls secondary sex characteristics such as facial hair and voice timbre, has been linked to criminality.[25] Research conducted on both human and animal subjects has found that prenatal exposure to unnaturally high levels of testosterone permanently alters behavior. Girls who were unintentionally exposed to elevated amounts of testosterone during their fetal development display a marked, long-term tendency toward aggression.[26]

Conversely, boys who were prenatally exposed to steroids that decrease testosterone levels display decreased aggressiveness.[27] Gender differences in the crime rate, therefore, may be explained by the relative difference in testosterone and other androgens between the two sexes. Females may be biologically protected from deviant behavior in the same way that they enjoy immunity from some diseases that strike males.[28] Hormone levels also help explain the aging-out process: Levels of testosterone decline during the life cycle, and so do violence rates.[29]

CONNECTIONS

Should a person be excused from responsibility for committing a crime if he or she suffers from a disease that impairs judgment? If eating junk foods can excuse crime, what about drinking alcohol? See Chapter 1 for more on criminal defenses.

Fact or Fiction?

It may be because of their hormones that men exhibit more violent behavior than women.

Fact. Criminologists have linked excessive levels of the male hormone testosterone to antisocial behaviors.

hypoglycemia
A condition that occurs when glucose (sugar) in the blood falls below levels necessary for normal and efficient brain functioning.

androgens
Male sex hormones.

testosterone
The principal male hormone.

Premenstrual Syndrome The suspicion has long existed that the onset of the menstrual cycle triggers excessive amounts of the female sex hormones, which stimulate antisocial, aggressive behavior. This condition is commonly referred to as **premenstrual syndrome (PMS)**.[30] The link between PMS and delinquency was first popularized more than 30 years ago by Katharina Dalton, whose studies of English women indicated that females are more likely to commit suicide and to be aggressive and otherwise antisocial just before or during menstruation.[31]

Although the Dalton research is often cited as evidence of the link between PMS and crime, methodological problems make it impossible to accept her findings at face value. There is still significant debate over any link between PMS and aggression. Some doubters argue that the relationship is spurious; that is, it is equally likely that the psychological and physical stress of aggression brings on menstruation, and not vice versa.[32] However, Diana Fishbein, a noted expert on biosocial theory, concludes that there is in fact an association between menstruation and elevated levels of female aggression. Research efforts, she argues, show that (1) a significant number of incarcerated females committed their crimes during the premenstrual phase, and (2) at least a small percentage of women appear vulnerable to cyclical hormonal changes that make them more prone to anxiety and hostility.[33]

The debate is ongoing, but the overwhelming majority of females who experience anxiety and hostility before and during menstruation do not engage in violent criminal behavior.[34] Thus, any link between PMS and crime is tenuous at best.

premenstrual syndrome (PMS)
Condition, postulated by some theorists, wherein several days before and during menstruation, excessive amounts of female sex hormones stimulate antisocial, aggressive behavior.

Lead Exposure Exposure to lead has been linked to emotional and behavioral disorders.[35] Delinquents have been found to have much higher bone lead levels than children in the general population.[36] There is also evidence linking lead exposure to mental illnesses, such as schizophrenia.[37] Locales with the highest concentrations of lead also report the highest levels of homicide.[38] Examining changes in lead levels in

© AP Images/Jim Cole

Benita Nahimana (left foreground), 3, plays with her sister Sophia and their neighbor Gloria on the chipped-paint wood floor in their old apartment, with parents Regina and Razaro nearby. Now in a new home, Benita is still recovering from lead poisoning she experienced in the apartment. Some criminologists believe that early and prolonged exposure to lead is related to antisocial behavior in adolescence.

the United States, Britain, Canada, France, Australia, Finland, Italy, West Germany, and New Zealand, economist Rick Nevin found that long-term worldwide trends in crime levels correlate significantly with changes in environmental levels of lead. Some 65 to 90 percent of the substantial variation in violent crime in all these countries was explained by lead.[39]

Environmental Contaminants Research has linked prenatal exposure to PCBs (polychlorinated biphenyls) to lower IQs and attention problems, both considered risk factors for serious behavioral and learning problems.[40] Similarly, exposure to severe air pollution has been found to cause cognitive deficits and changes in brain structure of otherwise healthy children. These destructive changes affect intelligence, influence cognitive control, and produce other neurological deficits that have been associated with school failure; educational underachievement is a condition that has long been associated with delinquency and adult criminality.[41]

NEUROPHYSIOLOGICAL CONDITIONS AND CRIME

Some researchers focus their attention on **neurophysiology**, or the study of brain activity.[42] They believe that inherited or acquired neurological and physical abnormalities control behavior throughout the life span.[43]

Brain-scanning techniques using electronic imaging, such as magnetic resonance imaging (MRI), positron emission tomography (PET), brain electrical activity mapping (BEAM), and the superconducting quantum interference device (SQUID), have made it possible to assess which areas of the brain are directly linked to antisocial behavior.[44] Studies carried out in the United States and elsewhere have shown a significant relationship between impairment in executive brain functions (such as abstract reasoning, problem solving, and motor skills) and aggressive behavior.[45] Both violent criminals and substance abusers have impairment in the prefrontal lobes, thalamus, medial temporal lobe, and superior parietal and left angular gyrus areas of the brain.[46]

Neurological impairment may also lead to the development of personality traits linked to antisocial behaviors. There is now evidence that low self-control may in fact be regulated and controlled by the prefrontal cortex of the brain.[47] Under this scenario, neurological impairment reduces impulse management and self-control, a condition that often results in antisocial behaviors.

Neurological deficits have been linked to a full range of criminal activity, including serial murder.[48] There is a suspected link between brain dysfunction and **conduct disorder (CD)**, which is considered a precursor of long-term chronic offending. Children with CD lie, steal, bully other children, get into fights frequently, and break schools' and parents' rules; many are callous and lack empathy and/or guilt.[49]

The association between crime and neurological impairment is quite striking: Nearly one in every five offenders reports some type of traumatic brain injury, and that means that for every 100,000 criminal offenders, 20,000 or more may be suffering neurological deficits. In comparison, the number of traumatic brain injuries in the general U.S. population is estimated to be 180–250 per 100,000.[50] The accompanying Current Issues in Crime feature on page 114 further explores this association.

Attention-Deficit/Hyperactivity Disorder Many parents have noticed that their children do not pay attention to them—they run around and do things in their own way. Sometimes this inattention is a function of age; in other instances it is a symptom of **attention-deficit/hyperactivity disorder (ADHD)**, in which a child shows a developmentally inappropriate lack of attention, along with impulsivity and hyperactivity. Exhibit 5.1 lists the various symptoms of ADHD. About 3 percent of U.S. children, most often boys, are believed to suffer from this disorder, and it is the most common reason why children are referred to mental health clinics. The condition has been associated with poor school performance, retention for another year in the same grade, placement in classes for those with special needs, bullying, stubbornness, and lack of response to discipline.[51]

Fact or Fiction?

The image of the brain-damaged villain going on a violent rampage is more likely to occur in horror films than in real life.

Fiction. A significant percentage of violent offenders may have sustained violent brain trauma and be suffering from neurological deficits.

neurophysiology
The study of brain activity.

conduct disorder (CD)
A pattern of repetitive behavior in which the rights of others or social norms are violated.

attention-deficit/hyperactivity disorder (ADHD)
A developmentally inappropriate lack of attention, along with impulsivity and hyperactivity.

Teenagers and adults often don't see eye to eye, and new brain research is now shedding light on some of the reasons why so much conflict exists. Although adolescence is often characterized by increased independence and a desire for knowledge and exploration, it also is a time when different areas of the brain mature at different rates, and the resulting instability can result in high-risk behaviors, vulnerability to substance abuse, and mental distress.

Recent imaging studies in humans show that brain development and connectivity are not complete until the late teens or early twenties. It is becoming clear that the status of brain chemical systems, and the connectivity between brain regions, makes teenagers different from both the young child and the fully mature adult. In other words, as if you did not already know, there really is a big difference between teenage and adult brains!

To find out why, Guido and his colleagues recruited two groups of male adolescents: one group diagnosed with "reactive-affective-defensive-impulsive" (RADI) behavior and the other group without any history of mental illness or aggression problems. While being scanned by a brain-imaging machine, both sets of teenagers were asked to perform tasks that involved reacting to age-appropriate, fear-inducing images. The tasks also tested the teenagers' impulsivity. Preliminary results revealed that the brains of RADI teenagers exhibited greater activity in the amygdala and lesser activity in the frontal lobe in response to the images than the brains of the teenagers in the control group.

Guido's research helps explain what goes on in the brains of some teenage boys who respond with inappropriate anger and aggression to perceived threats. It is possible that rather than having a social or environmental basis, such behavior

Current Issues in Crime Teenage Behavior: Is It the Brain?

Brain Structure and Aggression

One area of teen brain functioning that has piqued the interests of neuroscientists is aggression. Adolescent aggressive behavior can be divided into two types: proactive and reactive. Proactive aggressors plan how they're going to hurt and bully others. Reactive aggression, however, is not premeditated; it occurs in response to an upsetting trigger from the environment.

Research psychiatrist Frank Guido finds that aggressive teen behavior may be linked to the amygdala, an area of the brain that processes information regarding threats and fear, and to a lessening of activity in the frontal lobe, a brain region linked to decision making and impulse control. Guido's research indicates that reactively aggressive adolescents—most commonly boys—often misinterpret their surroundings, feel threatened, and act inappropriately aggressive. They tend to strike back when being teased, blame others when getting into a fight, and overreact to accidents. Their behavior is emotionally "hot," defensive, and impulsive.

is associated with brain functioning and not environment, socialization, personality, or other social and psychological functions.

CRITICAL THINKING

1. If teen aggression is linked to brain chemistry and structure, what is the purpose of such crime-reducing policies as providing summer jobs for at-risk kids or providing counseling for those who have already violated the law?
2. Do you believe that crime declines with age because changes in the structure of the brain decrease in adulthood? Could differences between the teen brain and the adult brain really explain age-related differences in antisocial behavior, or is something else to blame?

SOURCE: Society for Neuroscience News Release, "Studies Identify Brain Areas and Chemicals Involved in Aggression; May Speed Development of Better Treatment," http://www.sfn.org/index .cfm?pagename=news_110507d (accessed June 1, 2009).

Although the origin of ADHD is still unknown, suspected causes include neurological damage, prenatal stress, and even reactions to food additives and chemical allergies. Recent research has suggested a genetic link.[52] There are also links to family turmoil: Mothers of children with ADHD are more likely to be divorced or separated, and they are much more likely than others to move to new locales.[53] It may be possible that emotional turmoil either produces symptoms of ADHD or, if they already exist, causes them to intensify.

Many children with ADHD also suffer from conduct disorder (CD) and continually engage in aggressive and antisocial behavior in early childhood.[54] Children diagnosed with ADHD are more likely to be suspended from school and to engage in criminal

Lack of Attention

Frequently fails to finish projects
Does not seem to pay attention
Does not sustain interest in play activities
Cannot sustain concentration on schoolwork or related tasks
Is easily distracted

Impulsivity

Frequently acts without thinking
Often "calls out" in class
Does not want to wait his or her turn in lines or games
Shifts from activity to activity
Cannot organize tasks or work
Requires constant supervision

Hyperactivity

Constantly runs around and climbs on things
Shows excessive motor activity while asleep
Cannot sit still; is constantly fidgeting
Does not remain in his or her seat in class
Is constantly on the go like a "motor"

SOURCE: Adapted from American Psychiatric Association, *Diagnostic and Statistical Manual of Mental Disorders*, 4th ed. (Washington, DC: American Psychiatric Press, 1994).

behavior as adults.[55] Children with ADHD are also at greater risk for adolescent antisocial activity and drug use/abuse that persists into adulthood.[56]

Brain Chemistry As you may recall from Chapter 2, chemical compounds called **neurotransmitters** influence or activate brain functions. Those studied in relation to aggression and other antisocial behaviors include dopamine, norepinephrine, serotonin, monoamine oxidase (MAO), and gamma-aminobutryic acid (GABA). Evidence exists that abnormally low levels of these chemicals are associated with aggression, whereas people with an abundance are better able to withstand traumatic life events such as child abuse.[57] For example, male victims of child abuse who had low levels of MAO have been found to engage in more antisocial activity than a group of equally abused children who had above-normal MAO levels.[58] Other research efforts have linked low levels of MAO to high levels of violence and property crime, as well as defiance of punishment, impulsivity, hyperactivity, poor academic performance, sensation seeking and risk taking, and recreational drug use.[59] Abnormal MAO levels may explain both individual and group differences in the crime rate. Females naturally have higher MAO levels than males, which may contribute to gender differences in the crime rate.[60] MAO is not the only neurochemical linked to crime. Studies of habitually violent criminals show that low serotonin levels are associated with poor impulse control and hyperactivity, increased irritability, and sensation seeking.[61]

What is the link between brain chemistry and crime? Prenatal exposure of the brain to high levels of androgens can result in a brain structure that is less sensitive to environmental inputs. Affected individuals seek more intense and varied stimulation and are willing to tolerate more adverse consequences than individuals not so affected.[62] Because this link has been found, it is not uncommon for violence-prone people to be treated with antipsychotic drugs such as Haldol, Stelazine, Prolixin, and Risperdal. These drugs, which help control levels of neurotransmitters (such as serotonin or dopamine), are sometimes referred to as chemical restraints or chemical straitjackets.

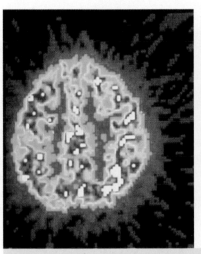 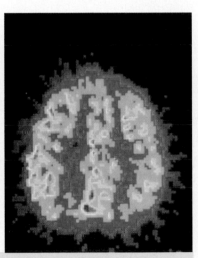

Dr. Alan Zamitkin, "Clinical Brain Imaging." Courtesy of the Office of Scientific Information, NIHM.

This scan compares a normal brain (left) and the brain of an individual with ADHD (right). Areas of orange and white demonstrate a higher rate of metabolism, whereas areas of blue and green represent an abnormally low metabolic rate. Why is ADHD so prevalent in the United States today? Some experts believe that our immigrant forebears, risk takers who impulsively left their homelands for life in a new world, may have brought with them a genetic predisposition to ADHD.

neurotransmitters
Chemical compounds that influence or activate brain functions.

Arousal Theory According to **arousal theory**, for a variety of genetic and environmental reasons, people's brains function differently in response to environmental stimuli. All of us seek to maintain a preferred or optimal level of arousal: Too much stimulation leaves us anxious and stressed, whereas too little makes us feel bored and weary. However, people vary in the way their brains process sensory input. Some nearly always feel comfortable with little stimulation, whereas others require a high degree of environmental input to feel comfortable. The latter group of "sensation seekers" looks for stimulating activities, which may include aggressive, violent behavior patterns.[63]

Although the factors that determine a person's level of arousal are not fully understood, suspected sources include brain chemistry (such as serotonin levels) and brain structure. Some brains have many more nerve cells, with receptor sites for neurotransmitters, than other brains have. Another view is that people with low heart rates are more likely to commit crime because they seek stimulation to increase their arousal to normal levels.[64]

GENETICS AND CRIME

Another biosocial theme is that the human traits associated with criminality have a genetic basis.[65] According to this view, (1) antisocial behavior is inherited, (2) the genetic makeup of parents is passed on to children, and (3) genetic abnormality is linked to a variety of antisocial behaviors.[66] The association between genetic makeup and antisocial behavior is often hard to validate. Even when a child's behavior is similar to that of his or her parents, proving whether the influence is genetic or a product of learning and socialization is difficult. How have criminologists tried to test the effects of inheritance on crime?

Parental Deviance If criminal tendencies are inherited, children of criminal parents should be more likely to become law violators than the offspring of conventional parents. A number of studies have found that parental criminality and deviance do, in fact, powerfully influence delinquent behavior.[67] The Cambridge Youth Survey, a longitudinal cohort study conducted in England, indicates that a significant number of delinquent youths have criminal fathers.[68] Whereas 8 percent of the sons of noncriminal fathers eventually became chronic offenders, about 37 percent of youths with criminal fathers were multiple offenders.[69] In another important analysis, David Farrington found that one type of parental deviance—schoolyard aggression, or bullying—may be both inter- and intragenerational. Bullies have children who bully others, and these second-generation bullies grow up to father children who are also bullies, in a never-ending cycle.[70]

In sum, there is growing evidence that crime is intergenerational: Criminal fathers produce criminal sons, who then produce criminal grandchildren. Although there is no certainty about the relationship between parental and child deviance, it is possible that at least part of the association is genetic.[71] How can this relationship be more definitively tested?

Adoption Studies It seems logical that if the behavior of adopted children is more closely aligned with that of their biological parents than with that of their adoptive parents, the idea of a genetic basis for criminality will be supported. If, on the other hand, adoptees' behavior is more closely aligned with the behavior of their adoptive parents than with that of their biological parents, an environmental basis for crime will seem more valid.

Several studies indicate that some relationship exists between biological parents' behavior and the behavior of their children, even when they have had no contact.[72] In a classic study, Barry Hutchings and Sarnoff Mednick found that in a sample of adopted youths, the biological father's criminality strongly predicted the child's criminal behavior.[73] When both the biological father and the adoptive father were criminal, the probability that the youth would engage in criminal behavior greatly increased.

Fact or Fiction?

The acorn does not fall far from the tree; that is, the children of deviant parents are more likely than other kids to be antisocial themselves.

Fact. Research shows that there is a significant association between parental and child deviance levels, although investigators are still not sure whether it is a matter of environment or genetics.

arousal theory
The view that people seek to maintain a preferred level of arousal but vary in how they process sensory input. A need for high levels of environmental stimulation may lead to aggressive, violent behavior patterns.

Twin Behavior If, in fact, inherited traits cause criminal behavior, we might expect that twins would be quite similar in their antisocial activities. And as predicted, research efforts confirm a significant correspondence of twin behavior in activities ranging from frequency of sexual activity to crime.[74] However, because twins are usually brought up in the same household and exposed to the same social conditions, determining whether their similar behavior is a result of similar biological, sociological, or psychological conditions is difficult. To control for environmental factors, criminologists have compared identical, **monozygotic (MZ) twins** with fraternal, **dizygotic (DZ) twins**.[75] MZ twins are genetically identical, whereas DZ twins have only half their genes in common. Studies of MZ twins reared apart, whom have never met, show that their behavior is nearly identical.

Studies conducted on twin behavior have detected a significant relationship between the criminal activities of MZ twins and a much lower association between those of DZ twins; these genetic effects can be seen in children as young as 3 years old.[76] Among the relevant findings:

▶ There is a significantly higher risk for suicidal behavior among monozygotic twin pairs than among dizygotic twin pairs.[77]
▶ The scores of MZ twins are more similar than DZ twins on tests measuring psychological dysfunctions such as conduct disorders, impulsivity, and antisocial behavior.[78]
▶ MZ twins are closer than DZ twins in such crime-relevant measures as level of aggression and verbal skills.[79]
▶ Both members of MZ twin pairs who suffer child abuse are likely to engage in later antisocial activity more often than DZ pairs. Because the association is stronger among MZ twins, the link between abuse and delinquency may be an inherited genetic component.[80]
▶ Callous, unemotional traits in very young children can be a warning sign for future psychopathy and antisocial behavior. Using samples of same-sex twin pairs, psychiatrist Essi Viding and colleagues found a powerful hereditary influence on levels of callous, unemotional behavior in children.[81]

Is there a genetic basis to crime? This photo shows the notorious London gangsters Ronnie and Reggie Kray. Reginald Kray and his twin brother Ronald were England's most prominent criminals in the 1950s and 1960s. The Krays were involved in robbery, arson, and extortion and did not hesitate to torture or murder their victims. In the 1960s they became celebrities, being photographed extensively and interviewed on television. They were eventually arrested and, in 1969, were convicted and sentenced to life in prison.

© Evening Standard/Getty Images

Although this evidence is persuasive, many questions still need to be answered about the association between genetics and crime. Even if the behavior similarities between MZ twins is greater than that between DZ twins, the association may be explained by environmental factors. MZ twins are more likely to look alike and to share physical traits than DZ twins, and for this reason they are more likely to be treated similarly. Similarities in their shared behavior patterns may therefore be a function of socialization and/or environment, not of heredity.[82] It is also possible that what appears to be a genetic effect picked up by the twin research is actually the effect of sibling influence on criminality, a phenomenon referred to as the **contagion effect**: Genetic predispositions and early experiences make some people, including twins, susceptible to deviant behavior, which is transmitted by the presence of antisocial siblings in the household.[83] Twin influence is everlasting: If one twin is antisocial, it legitimizes and supports the criminal behavior in his or her co-twin. This effect may

monozygotic (MZ) twins
Identical twins.

dizygotic (DZ) twins
Fraternal (nonidentical) twins.

contagion effect
People become deviant when they are influenced by others with whom they are in close contact.

CONNECTIONS

The relationship between evolutionary factors and crime has just begun to be studied. Criminologists are now exploring how social organizations and institutions interact with biological traits to influence personal decision making, including criminal strategies. See the discussion of latent trait theories in Chapter 9 for more about the integration of biological and environmental factors.

grow even stronger in adulthood because twin relations are more enduring than any other. What seems to be a genetic effect may actually be the result of sibling interaction with a brother or sister who engages in antisocial activity.

EVOLUTIONARY VIEWS OF CRIME

Some criminologists believe that the human traits that produce violence and aggression have been advanced by the long process of human evolution.[84] According to this evolutionary view, the competition for scarce resources has influenced and shaped the human species.[85] Over the course of human existence, people whose personal characteristics enabled them to accumulate more than others were the most likely to breed successfully, have more offspring, and (genetically speaking) dominate the species. People have been shaped to engage in actions that promote their well-being and ensure the survival and reproduction of their genetic line. Males who are impulsive risk takers may be able to father more children because they are reckless in their social relationships and have sexual encounters with numerous partners. If, according to evolutionary theories, such behavior patterns are inherited, impulsive behavior becomes intergenerational, passed down from parents to children. It is therefore not surprising that human history has been marked by war, violence, and aggression.

The Evolution of Gender and Crime Evolutionary concepts that have been linked to gender differences in violence rates are based loosely on mammalian mating patterns. To ensure survival of the gene pool (and the species), it is beneficial for a male of any species to mate with as many suitable females as possible because each can bear his offspring. In contrast, because of the long period of gestation, females require a secure home and a single, stable, nurturing partner to ensure their survival. Because of these differences in mating patterns, the most aggressive males mate most often and have the greatest number of offspring. Therefore, over the history of the human species, aggressive males have had the greatest impact on the gene pool. The descendants of these aggressive males now account for the disproportionate amount of male aggression and violence.[86]

Crime rate differences between the genders, then, may be less a matter of socialization than of inherent differences in mating patterns that have developed over time.[87] Among young men, reckless, life-threatening, risky behavior is especially likely to evolve in cultures that force them to find suitable mates to ensure their ability to reproduce. Unless they are aggressive with potential mates and with potential rivals for those suitable mates, they will remain childless.[88] Reproductive aggressiveness and similar evolutionary processes may explain why women of childbearing age are more attractive targets for rapists (and rapist-murderers) than women who are no longer able to bear children and therefore cannot reproduce their DNA.[89]

High rates of spouse abuse in modern society may be a function of aggressive men seeking to control and possess mates. Men who feel most threatened over the potential of losing mates to rivals are the most likely to engage in sexual violence. Research shows that women in common-law marriages, especially those who are much younger than their husbands, are at greater risk of abuse than older, married women. Abusive males may fear the potential loss of their younger mates, especially if the woman is not bound by a marriage contract, and may use force for purposes of control and possession.[90]

EVALUATION OF THE BIOLOGICAL BRANCH OF TRAIT THEORY

Biosocial perspectives on crime have raised some challenging questions. Critics find some of these theories racist and faulty in other ways as well. If there are biological explanations for street crimes such as assault, murder, or rape, the argument goes, and if, as official crime statistics suggest, the poor and minority-group members commit a disproportionate number of such acts, then by implication, biological theory says that members of these groups are biologically different, flawed, or inferior.

Biological explanations for the geographic, social, and temporal patterns in the crime rate are also problematic. Is it possible that more people are genetically predisposed to crime in the South and the West than in New England and the Midwest? Furthermore, biological theory seems to divide people into criminals and noncriminals on the basis of their genetic and physical makeup, ignoring self-reports that indicate that almost everyone has engaged in some type of illegal activity.

Biosocial theorists counter that their views should not be confused with Lombrosian, deterministic biology, which suggested that people are born either criminals or noncriminals, and nothing can alter their life course. Contemporary biocriminologists instead maintain that some people carry the potential to be violent or antisocial and that environmental conditions can sometimes trigger antisocial responses.[91] This would explain why people who appear to be at risk of engaging in crime can refrain from criminal activities. For example, when Kevin Beaver and his associates studied teens who carried a gene pathology affecting the neurotransmitter dopamine, they found that these youths were more likely than noncarriers to join a delinquent crowd. However, family life influenced behavior choices: Kids from close-knit families were less likely to seek out deviant friends than those whose family relations were more distant. It is possible, then, that although biochemical makeup influences behavior, social factors (such as nurturing parents) can mitigate its effects.[92] This study supports the interactive association between genetic influences and environment that is a feature of most contemporary trait theories.

Although these findings are impressive, biosocial theorists lament the fact that their work is sometimes not taken seriously.[93] One reason may be that some critics still believe that biosocial theory has not been subjected to sufficiently vigorous empirical testing. Most research samples have been relatively small and nonrepresentative. A great deal of biosocial research is conducted with samples of adjudicated offenders who have been placed in clinical treatment settings. Methodological problems make it impossible to determine whether findings apply to all criminals or only to offenders who have been convicted of crimes and placed in treatment.[94] There are also issues involving causal connections: If we find that kids with poor diets are more likely to commit crime, can we conclude that the diet is the root cause of antisocial behavior, or is it possible that kids already at risk for crime also have poor diets because of parental neglect, poverty, or some other social factor? More research is needed to clarify the relationships proposed by biosocial researchers and to satisfy critics.

Concept Summary 5.1 lists the major elements of biosocial theory.

▶ **Checkpoints**

Checkpoints

▶ Brain chemistry and hormonal differences are related to aggression and violence.

▶ Most evidence suggests that there is no relationship between sugar intake and crime.

▶ The male hormone testosterone is linked to criminality.

▶ Neurological impairments have been linked to crime.

▶ Genetic theory holds that violence-producing traits are passed from generation to generation.

▶ According to evolutionary theory, instinctual drives control behavior. The urge to procreate influences male violence.

▶ Biological explanations fail to account for the geographic, social, and temporal patterns in the crime rate; critics question the methodology used.

The Psychological Trait View

The second branch of trait theory focuses on the psychological aspects of crime, including the associations among intelligence, personality, learning, and criminal behavior. This view has a long history, and psychologists, psychiatrists, and other mental health professionals have long played an active role in formulating criminological theory.

Among nineteenth-century pioneers in this area were Charles Goring (1870–1919) and Gabriel Tarde (1843–1904). Goring studied 3,000 English convicts and found little difference in the physical characteristics of criminals and noncriminals. However, he uncovered a significant relationship between crime and a condition he referred to as "defective intelligence," which involved such traits as feeblemindedness, epilepsy, insanity, and defective social instinct.[95] Tarde was the forerunner of modern learning theorists, who hold that people learn from one another through imitation.[96]

Biochemical	• The major premise of the theory is that crime, especially violence, is a function of diet, vitamin intake, hormonal imbalance, or food allergies. • The strengths of the theory are that it explains irrational violence and that it shows how the environment interacts with personal traits to influence behavior. • The research focuses of the theory are diet, hormones, enzymes, environmental contaminants, and lead intake.
Neurological	• The major premise of the theory is that criminals and delinquents often suffer brain impairment. Attention-deficit/hyperactivity disorder and minimal brain dysfunction are related to antisocial behavior. • The strengths of the theory are that it explains irrational violence and it shows how the environment interacts with personal traits to influence behavior. • The research focuses of the theory are CD, ADHD, learning disabilities, brain injuries, and brain chemistry.
Genetic	• The major premise of the theory is that criminal traits and predispositions are inherited. The criminality of parents can predict the delinquency of children. • The strengths of the theory include the fact that it explains why only a small percentage of youths in high-crime areas become chronic offenders. • The research focuses of the theory are twin behavior, sibling behavior, and parent–child similarities.
Evolutionary	• The major premise of the theory is that as the human race evolved, traits and characteristics became ingrained. Some of these traits make people aggressive and predisposed to commit crime. • The strengths of the theory include its explanation of high violence rates and aggregate gender differences in the crime rate. • The research focuses of the theory are gender differences and understanding human aggression.

psychodynamic (psychoanalytic) theory
Theory, originated by Freud, that the human personality is controlled by unconscious mental processes that develop early in childhood and involve the interaction of id, ego, and superego.

id
The primitive part of people's mental makeup, present at birth, that represents unconscious biological drives for food, sex, and other life-sustaining necessities. The id seeks instant gratification without concern for the rights of others.

ego
The part of the personality developed in early childhood that helps control the id and keep people's actions within the boundaries of social convention.

PSYCHOLOGICAL THEORIES AND CRIME

In their quest to understand and treat all varieties of abnormal mental conditions, psychologists have encountered clients whose behavior falls within the categories that society has labeled criminal, deviant, violent, and antisocial. A number of different psychological views have various implications for the causation of criminal behavior. The most important of these theoretical perspectives and their association with criminal conduct are discussed in the following sections.

THE PSYCHODYNAMIC PERSPECTIVE

Psychodynamic (or **psychoanalytic**) psychology was originated by Viennese psychiatrist Sigmund Freud (1856–1939) and has remained a prominent segment of psychological theory ever since.[97] Freud believed that we all carry with us the residue of the most significant emotional attachments of our childhood, which then guides our future interpersonal relationships.

According to psychodynamic theory, the human personality has a three-part structure. The **id** is the primitive part of people's mental makeup, is present at birth, and represents unconscious biological drives for food, sex, and other life-sustaining necessities. The id seeks instant gratification without concern for the rights of others. The ego develops early in life, when a child begins to learn that his or her wishes cannot be instantly gratified. The **ego** is the part of the personality that compensates for the demands of the id by helping the individual keep his or her actions within the boundaries of social convention. The **superego** develops as a result of incorporating within the personality the moral standards and values of parents, community, and significant others. It is the moral aspect of people's personalities; it judges their own behavior.

The psychodynamic model of the criminal offender depicts an aggressive, frustrated person dominated by events that occurred early in childhood. Because they had unhappy experiences in childhood or had families that could not provide proper love and care, criminals suffer from weak or damaged egos that make them unable to cope with conventional society. Weak egos are associated with immaturity, poor social skills, and excessive dependence on others. People with weak egos may be easily led into crime by antisocial peers and drug abuse. Some have underdeveloped superegos and consequently lack internalized representations of those behaviors that are punished in conventional society. They commit crimes because they have difficulty understanding the consequences of their actions.[98]

In sum, the psychodynamic tradition links crime to a manifestation of feelings of oppression and the inability to develop the proper psychological defenses and rationales to keep these feelings under control. Criminality enables troubled people to survive by producing positive psychic results: It helps them to feel free and independent, and it offers them the possibility of excitement and the chance to use their skills and imagination.

Attachment Theory According to psychologist John Bowlby's **attachment theory**, the ability to form an emotional bond to another person has important psychological implications that follow people across the life span.[99] Attachments are formed soon after birth, when infants bond with their mothers. Babies will become frantic, crying and clinging, to prevent separation or to reestablish contact with a missing parent. Attachment figures, especially the mother, must provide support and care, and without attachment an infant would be helpless and could not survive.

Failure to develop proper attachment may cause people to fall prey to a number of psychological disorders, some of which resemble attention-deficit/hyperactivity disorder (ADHD). Such individuals may be impulsive and have difficulty concentrating—and consequently experience difficulty in school. As adults, they often have difficulty initiating and sustaining relationships with others and find it difficult to sustain romantic relationships. Criminologists have linked people who have detachment problems with a variety of antisocial behaviors, including sexual assault and child abuse.[100] It has been suggested that boys disproportionately experience disrupted attachment and that these disruptions are causally related to disproportionate rates of male offending.[101]

THE BEHAVIORAL PERSPECTIVE: SOCIAL LEARNING THEORY

Behavior theory maintains that human actions are developed through learning experiences. The major premise of behavior theory is that people alter their behavior in accordance with the response it elicits from others. In other words, behavior is supported by rewards and extinguished by negative reactions, or punishments. The behaviorist views crimes—especially violent acts—as learned responses to life situations, which do not necessarily represent abnormality or moral immaturity.

The branch of behavior theory most relevant to criminology is **social learning theory**.[102] Social learning theorists argue that people are not born with the ability to act violently; rather, they learn to be aggressive through their life experiences. These experiences include personally observing others acting aggressively to achieve some goal or watching people being rewarded for violent acts on television or in movies (see the Current Issues in Crime entitled "Violent Media/Violent Behavior?"). People learn to act aggressively when, as children, they model their behavior after the violent acts of adults. Later in life, these violent behavior patterns persist in social relationships. For example, the boy who sees his father repeatedly strike his mother with impunity is likely to become a battering parent and husband.

Although social learning theorists agree that mental or physical traits may predispose a person toward violence, they believe a person's violent tendencies are activated by factors in the environment. The specific form of aggressive behavior, the

CONNECTIONS

Chapter 1 discussed how some of the early founders of psychiatry tried to understand the criminal mind. Early theories suggested that mental illness and insanity were inherited and that deviants were inherently mentally damaged by their inferior genetic makeup.

superego
Incorporation within the personality of the moral standards and values of parents, community, and significant others.

attachment theory
Bowlby's theory that being able to form an emotional bond to another person is an important aspect of mental health throughout the life span.

behavior theory
The view that all human behavior is learned through a process of social reinforcement (rewards and punishment).

social learning theory
The view that people learn to be aggressive by observing others acting aggressively to achieve some goal or being rewarded for violent acts.

Do the media influence behavior? Does broadcast violence cause aggressive behavior in viewers? This has become a hot topic because of the persistent theme of violence on television and in films. Critics have called for drastic measures, ranging from banning TV violence to putting warning labels on heavy-metal albums out of fear that listening to hard-rock lyrics produces delinquency.

If there is in fact a TV–violence link, the problem is indeed alarming. Systematic viewing of TV begins at 2.5 years of age and continues at a high level during the preschool and early school years. The Kaiser Foundation study *Zero to Six: Electronic Media in the Lives of Infants, Toddlers, and Preschoolers* found that children 6 and under spend an average of two hours a day using screen media such as TV and computers—about the same amount of time they

portrayals of a scene. Of the 118 theatrical films monitored (every one that aired that season), 50 raised concerns about their use of violence.

On-air promotions also reflect a continuing, if not worsening, problem. Some series may contain several scenes of violence, each of which is appropriate within its context. An advertisement for that show, however, will feature only those violent scenes without any of the context. Even some children's television programming had worrisome signs, featuring "sinister combat" as the theme of the show. The characters are usually happy to fight and frequently do so with little provocation. There have been numerous anecdotal cases of violence linked to TV and films. For example, in a famous incident, John Hinckley Jr. shot President Ronald Reagan due to his obsession with actress Jodie Foster, which developed after he watched her play a

Media   Guns   Jobs   Economy

Current Issues in Crime Violent Media/Violent Behavior?

spend playing outside and significantly more time than they spend reading or being read to (about 39 minutes per day). Nearly half of children 6 and under have used a computer, and just under a third have played video games. Even the youngest children—those under 2—are exposed to electronic media for more than two hours per day; more than 40 percent of those under 2 watch TV every day. Marketing research indicates that adolescents ages 11 to 14 view violent horror movies at a higher rate than any other age group. Children this age use older peers and siblings and apathetic parents to gain access to R-rated films. Most U.S. households now have cable TV, which features violent films and shows that are not available on broadcast networks. Even children's programming is saturated with violence. A University of Pennsylvania study also found that children's programming contained an average of 32 violent acts per hour, that 56 percent had violent characters, and that 74 percent had characters who became the victims of violence (although "only 3.3 percent had characters who were actually killed"). In all, the average child views 8,000 TV murders before finishing elementary school.

The fact that children watch so much violent TV is not surprising considering the findings of a well-publicized study conducted by UCLA researchers, who found that at least ten network shows made heavy use of violence. Of the 161 television movies monitored (every one that aired that season), 23 raised concerns about their use of violence, violent theme, violent title, or inappropriate

prostitute in the film *Taxi Driver*. Hinckley viewed the film at least 15 times.

Not all experts believe that media violence is a direct *cause* of violent behavior (if it were, there would be millions of daily incidents in which viewers imitated the aggression they watched on TV or in movies), but many do agree that media violence *contributes* to aggression. Developmental psychologist John Murray carefully reviewed existing research on the effect of TV violence on children and concluded that viewing media violence is related to both short- and long-term increases in aggressive attitudes, values, and behaviors; the effects of media violence are both real and strong. Similarly, Brad Bushman and Craig Anderson have found that watching violence on TV is correlated with aggressive behaviors.

There is also evidence that kids who watch TV are more likely to persist in aggressive behavior as adults. A recent study conducted by researchers at Columbia University found that kids who watch more than an hour of TV each day show an increase in assaults, fights, robberies, and other acts of aggression later in life and into adulthood. One reason may be that TV viewing in childhood creates changes in personality and cognition that produce long-term behavioral changes. Dimitri Christakis and his associates found that for every hour of television watched daily between the ages of 1 and 3, the risk of developing attention problems increased by 9 percent over the life course; attention problems have been linked to antisocial behaviors.

There are several explanations for the effects of television and film violence on behavior:

- Media violence can provide aggressive "scripts" that children store in memory. Repeated exposure to these scripts can increase their retention and lead to changes in attitudes.
- Children learn from what they observe. In the same way that they learn cognitive and social skills from their parents and friends, children learn to be violent from television.
- Television violence increases the arousal levels of viewers and makes them more prone to act aggressively. Studies measuring the galvanic skin response of subjects—a physical indication of arousal based on the amount of electricity conducted across the palm of the hand—show that viewing violent television shows led to increased arousal levels in young children.
- Watching television violence promotes such negative attitudes as suspiciousness and the expectation that the viewer will become involved in violence. Those who watch television frequently come to view aggression and violence as common and socially acceptable behavior.
- Television violence enables aggressive youths to justify their behavior. It is possible that, instead of causing violence, television helps violent youths rationalize their behavior as a socially acceptable and common activity.
- Television violence may disinhibit aggressive behavior, which is normally controlled by other learning processes. Disinhibition takes place when adults are viewed as being rewarded for violence and when violence is seen as socially acceptable. This contradicts previous learning experiences in which violent behavior was viewed as wrong.

Debating the Link between Media Violence and Violent Behavior

Even though this research is quite persuasive, not all criminologists are convinced that watching violent incidents on TV and in the movies or playing violent video games predisposes young people to violent behavior. The observation that some kids who are exposed to violent media also engage in violent behaviors is not proof of a causal connection. It is also possible that kids who are already inclined to violence seek out violent media: What would we expect violent gang boys to watch on TV? *Hannah Montana*? There is little evidence that areas that experience the highest levels of violent TV viewing also have rates of violent crime that are above the norm. Millions of children watch violence every night but do not become violent criminals. If violent TV shows did, indeed, cause interpersonal violence, then there should be few ecological and regional patterns in the crime rate, but in fact there are many. To put it another way, how can regional differences in the violence rate be explained, considering the fact that people all across the nation watch the same TV shows and films? Nor can the link between media violence and violent behavior explain recent crime trends. Despite a rampant increase in violent TV shows, films, and video games, the violence rate among teens has been in significant decline.

One possibility is that media violence may affect one subset of the population but have relatively little effect on other groups. Sociologist George Comstock has identified the attributes that make some people especially prone to the effects of media violence:

- Predisposition to aggressive or antisocial behavior
- Rigid or indifferent parenting
- Unsatisfactory social relationships
- Low psychological well-being
- Having been diagnosed as suffering from DBD—disruptive behavior disorder

Thus, if the impact of media on behavior is not in fact universal, it may have the greatest effect on those who are the most socially and psychological vulnerable.

CRITICAL THINKING

1. Should the government control the content of TV shows and limit the amount of weekly violence? How could the national news be shown if violence were omitted? What about boxing matches and hockey games?
2. How can we explain the fact that millions of kids watch violent TV shows and remain nonviolent? If there is a link between violence on TV and violent behavior, how can we explain the fact that violence rates may have been higher in the Old West than they are today? Do you think violent gang members stay home and watch TV shows?

SOURCES: George Comstock, "A Sociological Perspective on Television Violence and Aggression," *American Behavioral Scientist*, 51 (2008): 1,184–1,211; John Murray, "Media Violence: The Effects Are Both Real and Strong," *American Behavioral Scientist*, 51 (2008): 1,212–1,230; Tom Grimes and Lori Bergen, "The Epistemological Argument against a Causal Relationship between Media Violence and Sociopathic Behavior among Psychologically Well Viewers," *American Behavioral Scientist* 51 (2008): 1,137–1,154; Victoria Rideout, Elizabeth Vandewater, and Ellen Wartella, *Zero to Six: Electronic Media in the Lives of Infants, Toddlers and Preschoolers* (Menlo Park, CA: Kaiser Foundation, 2003); Dimitri Christakis, Frederick Zimmerman, David DiGiuseppe, and Carolyn McCarty, "Early Television Exposure and Subsequent Attentional Problems in Children," *Pediatrics* 113 (2004): 708–713; Jeffery Johnson, Patricia Cohen, Elizabeth Smailes, Stephanie Kasen, and Judith Brook, "Television Viewing and Aggressive Behavior during Adolescent and Adulthood," *Science* 295 (2002): 2,468–2,471; Craig Anderson and Brad J. Bushman, "The Effects of Media Violence on Society," *Science* 295 (2002): 2,377–2,379; Brad Bushman and Craig Anderson, "Media Violence and the American Public," *American Psychologist* 56 (2001): 477–489; UCLA Center for Communication Policy, *Television Violence Monitoring Project* (Los Angeles, California, 1995), http://www.digitalcenter.org/webreport94/toc.htm (accessed September 15, 2009).

frequency with which it is expressed, the situations in which it is displayed, and the specific targets selected for attack are largely determined by social learning. However, people are also self-aware and engage in purposeful learning. Their interpretations of behavior outcomes and situations influence the way they learn from experiences. One adolescent who spends a weekend in jail for drunk driving may find it the most awful experience of her life—an ordeal that convinces her never to drink and drive again. Another person, however, may find it an exciting experience about which he can brag to his friends.

Social learning theorists view violence as something learned through a process called **behavior modeling**. In modern society, aggressive acts are usually modeled after three principal sources:

1. *Family interactions.* Studies of family life show that aggressive children have parents who use aggressive tactics when dealing with others. For example, the children of wife batterers are more likely to use aggressive tactics themselves than children in the general population, especially if the victims (their mothers) suffer psychological distress from the abuse.[103]
2. *Environmental experiences.* People who reside in areas where violence occurs daily are more likely to act violently than those who dwell in low-crime areas whose norms stress conventional behavior.
3. *Mass media.* Films, video games, and television shows commonly depict violence graphically. Moreover, violence is often portrayed as acceptable, especially for heroes who never have to face legal consequences for their actions.[104] As the Current Issues in Crime feature suggested, viewing violence is believed to influence behavior in a number of ways.

Social learning theorists have tried to determine what triggers violent acts. One position is that a direct, pain-producing, physical assault will usually set off a violent response. Yet the relationship between painful attacks and aggressive responses has been found to be inconsistent. Whether people counterattack depends, in part, on their fighting skill and their perception of the strength of their attackers. Verbal taunts and insults have also been linked to aggressive responses. People who are predisposed to aggression by their learning experiences are likely to view insults from others as a challenge to their social status and to react violently.

In summary, social learning theorists suggest that the following factors may contribute to violent or aggressive behavior:

▶ *An event that heightens arousal.* For example, a person may frustrate or provoke another through physical assault or verbal abuse.
▶ *Aggressive skills.* Learned aggressive responses picked up from observing others, either personally or through the media.
▶ *Expected outcomes.* The belief that aggression will somehow be rewarded. Rewards can come in the form of reducing tension or anger, gaining some financial reward, building self-esteem, or receiving praise from others.
▶ *Consistency of behavior with values.* The belief, gained from observing others, that aggression is justified and appropriate, given the circumstances of the current situation.

COGNITIVE THEORY

One area of psychology that has received increasing recognition in recent years is **cognitive theory**. Psychologists with a cognitive perspective focus on mental processes—how people perceive and mentally represent the world around them and solve problems. The pioneers of this school were Wilhelm Wundt (1832–1920), Edward Titchener (1867–1927), and William James (1842–1920). Today the cognitive area includes several subdisciplines. The moral development branch is concerned with how people morally represent and reason about the world. Humanistic psychology stresses self-awareness and getting in touch with feelings. **Information-processing theory** focuses on how people process, store, encode, retrieve, and manipulate information to make decisions and solve problems.

Fact or Fiction?

Watching violent TV shows makes kids behave more violently.

Fiction. The evidence shows little association between viewing violent media and acting in antisocial ways.

behavior modeling
The process of learning behavior (notably, aggression) by observing others. Aggressive models may be parents, criminals in the neighborhood, or characters on television or in movies.

cognitive theory
Psychological perspective that focuses on the mental processes by which people perceive and represent the world around them and solve problems.

information-processing theory
Theory that focuses on how people process, store, encode, retrieve, and manipulate information to make decisions and solve problems.

When cognitive theorists who study information processing try to explain antisocial behavior, they do so in terms of mental perception and how people use information to understand their environment. When people make decisions, they engage in a sequence of cognitive thought processes. First, they encode information so that it can be interpreted; next, they search for a proper response and decide on the most appropriate action; and finally, they act on their decision.[105]

According to this cognitive approach, people who use information properly, who are better conditioned to make reasoned judgments, and who can make quick and reasoned decisions when facing emotion-laden events are best able to avoid antisocial behavior choices. In contrast, crime-prone people may have cognitive deficits and use information incorrectly when they make decisions. They view crime as an appropriate means to satisfy their immediate personal needs, which take precedence over more distant social needs such as obedience to the law.[106] They are not deterred by the threat of legal punishments because when they try to calculate the costs and consequences of an action—that is, when they are deciding whether to commit a crime—they make mistakes because they are imperfect processors of information. As a result of their faulty calculations, they pursue behaviors that they perceive as beneficial and satisfying but that turn out to be harmful and detrimental.[107]

One reason for this faulty reasoning is that they may be relying on mental scripts learned in childhood that tell them how to interpret events, what to expect, how they should react, and what the outcome of the interaction should be.[108] Hostile children may have learned improper scripts by observing how others react to events; their own parents' aggressive, inappropriate behavior would have considerable impact. Some may have had early, prolonged exposure to violence (such as child abuse), which increases their sensitivity to slights and maltreatment. Oversensitivity to rejection by their peers is an outgrowth of sensitivity to rejection by their parents.[109] Violence becomes a stable behavior because the scripts that emphasize aggressive responses are repeatedly rehearsed as the child matures. In adulthood, these errors in cognition and information processing help explain the urge to sexually exploit children. Errors in cognition and information processing have been used to explain the behavior of child abusers. The distorted thinking patterns that abusers of children express include the following:

▶ *Child as a sexual being*. Children are perceived as being able to and wanting to engage in sexual activity with adults and also as not harmed by such sexual contact.[110]
▶ *Nature of harm*. The offender perceives that sexual activity does not harm the child and may in fact be beneficial to him or her.
▶ *Entitlement*. The child abuser perceives that he is superior to and more important than others and hence is able to have sex with whomever, and whenever, he wants.
▶ *Dangerous world*. An offender perceives that others are abusive and rejecting, and believes he must fight to regain control.
▶ *Uncontrollable*. The world is perceived as uncontrollable, and circumstances are outside of his control.

The various psychological theories of crime are set out in Concept Summary 5.2.

PERSONALITY AND CRIME

Personality can be defined as the reasonably stable patterns of behavior, including thoughts and emotions, that distinguish one person from another.[111] One's personality reflects a characteristic way of adapting to life's demands and problems. The way we behave is a function of how our personality enables us to interpret life events and make appropriate behavioral choices. Can the cause of crime be linked to personality?

Several research efforts have attempted to identify criminal personality traits. Surveys show that traits such as impulsivity, hostility, narcissism, hedonism, and aggression are highly correlated with criminal and antisocial behaviors.[112] Personality defects have been linked not only to aggressive antisocial behaviors such as assault and rape, but also to white-collar and business crimes.[113] For example, Hans

personality
The reasonably stable patterns of behavior, including thoughts and emotions, that distinguish one person from another.

Theory	Major Premise	Strengths	Research Focus
Psychodynamic	The development of the unconscious personality early in childhood influences behavior for the rest of a person's life. Criminals have weak egos and damaged personalities.	Explains the onset of crime and why crime and drug abuse cut across class lines.	Mental illness and crime
Behavioral	People commit crime when they model their behavior after others they see being rewarded for the same acts. Behavior is reinforced by rewards and extinguished by punishment.	Explains the role of significant others in the crime process. Shows how media can influence crime and violence.	Media and violence; effects of child abuse
Cognitive	Individual reasoning processes influence behavior. Reasoning is influenced by the way people perceive their environment.	Shows why criminal behavior patterns change over time as people mature and develop their reasoning powers. May explain the aging-out process.	Perception; environmental influences

Eysenck's PEN model contains three elements: psychoticism(P), extraversion(E), and neuroticism(N). He associates two personality traits, extroversion and introversion, with antisocial behavior:

▶ Extroverts are energetic, enthusiastic, action-oriented, chatty, glib, and self-confident.
▶ Introverts tend to be quiet, low-key, deliberate, and detached from others.

People who fall at the far ends of either trait, either extremely extroverted or extremely introverted, are at risk for antisocial behaviors. For example, extroverts who are also unstable, a condition that Eysenck calls neuroticism, are anxious, tense, and emotionally unstable.[114] They may act self-destructively—for example, by abusing drugs and repeating their criminal activity over and over.[115]

PSYCHOPATHIC PERSONALITY

Some people lack affect, cannot empathize with others, and are short-sighted and hedonistic. These traits make them prone to problems ranging from psychopathology to drug abuse, sexual promiscuity, and violence.[116] As a group, people who share these traits are believed to have a character defect referred to as sociopathic, psychopathic, or **antisocial personality**. Although these terms are often used interchangeably, some psychologists distinguish between sociopaths and psychopaths by suggesting that the former are a product of a destructive home environment, whereas the latter are a product of a defect or aberration within themselves.[117]

Studies of the antisocial personality have been conducted worldwide.[118] There is evidence that offenders with an antisocial personality are crime-prone, respond to frustrating events with strong negative emotions, feel stressed and harassed, and are adversarial in their interpersonal relationships. They maintain "negative emotionality"—a tendency to experience aversive affective states such as anger, anxiety, and irritability. They also tend to have weak personal constraints and have difficulty controlling impulsive behavior urges. Because they are both impulsive and aggressive, crime-prone people are quick to act against perceived threats.

antisocial personality
Combination of traits, such as hyperactivity, impulsivity, hedonism, and inability to empathize with others, that make a person prone to deviant behavior and violence; also referred to as sociopathic or psychopathic personality.

A number of factors are believed to contribute to the development of a criminal personality.[119] Some factors are related to improper socialization, such as having a psychopathic parent, experiencing parental rejection and lack of love during childhood, and receiving inconsistent discipline. Some psychologists believe the cause is related to neurological or brain dysfunction.[120] They suspect that psychopaths suffer from a low level of arousal as measured by the activity of their autonomic nervous system. It is possible, therefore, that psychopaths are thrill seekers who engage in high-risk antisocial activities to raise their general neurological arousal level. Psychopaths may have brain-related physical anomalies that cause them to process emotional input differently from nonpsychopaths.

Considering these personality traits, it is not surprising that research studies show that people evaluated as psychopaths are significantly more prone to criminal and violent behavior than the members of nonpsychopathic control groups. Psychopaths tend to continue their criminal careers long after other offenders burn out or age out of crime. They are continually in trouble with the law and, therefore, are likely to wind up in penal institutions. After reviewing available data, forensic psychologist James Blair and his colleagues conclude that approximately 15 to 25 percent of U.S. prison inmates meet diagnostic criteria for psychopathy. Once they are released, former inmates who suffer from psychopathy are three times as likely as other prisoners to reoffend within a year—and four times as likely to reoffend violently.[121]

Mark Brewer, a violent criminal with "psychopathic traits" and a history of alcohol and drug abuse, punched teenager Dominic Barritt to death three years and four months after being given a three-and-a-half-year prison sentence for robbery. Should dangerous criminals such as Brewer ever be released, or should they be kept in confinement until their personality disorders have been successfully treated?

INTELLIGENCE AND CRIME

Early criminologists maintained that many delinquents and criminals have below-average intelligence and that low IQ causes their criminality. Criminals were believed to have inherently substandard intelligence and thus seemed naturally inclined to commit more crimes than more intelligent persons. Furthermore, it was thought that if authorities could determine which individuals had low IQs, they might identify potential criminals before they committed socially harmful acts. These ideas led to the "nature versus nurture" controversy that continues to rage today.

Nature Theory Proponents of **nature theory** argue that intelligence is largely determined genetically, that ancestry determines IQ, and that low intelligence, as demonstrated by low IQ, is linked to criminal behavior. When newly developed IQ tests were administered to inmates of prisons and juvenile training schools in the early decades of the twentieth century, the nature position gained support because most of the inmates scored low on the tests.[122] In 1926, William Healy and Augusta Bronner tested groups of delinquent boys in Chicago and Boston and found that 37 percent were subnormal in intelligence. They concluded that delinquents were 5 to 10 times more likely to be mentally deficient than normal boys.[123] These and other early studies were embraced as proof that low IQ scores indicated potentially delinquent children and that a correlation existed between innate low intelligence and deviant behavior. IQ tests were believed to measure the inborn genetic makeup of individuals, and many criminologists accepted the idea that individuals with substandard IQs were predisposed toward delinquency and adult criminality.

Nurture Theory Proponents of **nurture theory** argue that intelligence is not inherited and that low-IQ parents do not necessarily produce low-IQ children.[124] Intelligence must be viewed as partly biological but primarily sociological. Nurture theorists discredit the notion that people commit crimes because they have low IQs. Instead, they postulate that environmental stimulation from parents, relatives, social contacts, schools, peer groups, and innumerable others accounts for a child's IQ level and that low IQs may result from an environment that also encourages delinquent and criminal behavior. Thus, if low IQ scores are recorded among criminals, these scores may reflect the criminals' cultural background, not their mental ability.

In 1931, Edwin Sutherland evaluated IQ studies of criminals and delinquents and questioned whether criminals in fact have low IQs.[125] Sutherland's research all but

nature theory
The view that intelligence is largely determined genetically and that low intelligence is linked to criminal behavior.

nurture theory
The view that intelligence is not inherited but is largely a product of environment. Low IQ scores do not cause crime but may result from the same environmental factors.

put an end to the belief that crime was caused by feeblemindedness; the putative link between IQ and crime was almost forgotten in criminological literature.

IQ and Criminality Although the alleged IQ–crime link was dismissed by mainstream criminologists, it once again became an important area of study when respected criminologists Travis Hirschi and Michael Hindelang published a widely read 1977 article linking the two variables.[126] They proposed the idea that low IQ increases the likelihood of criminal behavior through its effect on school performance. That is, youths with low IQs do poorly in school, and school failure and academic incompetence are highly related to delinquency and later to adult criminality.

Hirschi and Hindelang's inferences have been supported by both U.S. and international research.[127] In their influential book *Crime and Human Nature*, James Q. Wilson and Richard Herrnstein concluded that the IQ–crime link is indirect: Low intelligence leads to poor school performance, which enhances the chances of criminality.[128] In the controversial 1994 book *The Bell Curve*, Herrnstein with Charles Murray confirmed that adolescents with low IQs are more likely to commit crime, get caught, and be sent to prison. Conversely, at-risk kids with higher IQs seem to be protected from becoming criminals by their superior ability to succeed in school and in social relationships. To those who suggest that the IQ–crime relationship can be explained by the fact that only low-IQ criminals get caught, Herrnstein and Murray counter with data showing little difference in IQ scores between self-reported and adjudicated criminals.[129] This means that even criminals whose activities go undetected have lower IQs than the general public; the IQ–crime relationship cannot be explained away by the fact that slow-witted criminals are the ones most likely to be apprehended.

Although these reviews supported an IQ–crime link, a number of studies have found that intelligence has negligible influence on criminal behavior.[130] An evaluation of research on intelligence conducted by the American Psychological Association concluded that the strength of any IQ–crime link is "very low."[131]

The IQ–criminality debate is unlikely to be settled soon. Measurement is beset by many methodological problems. The well-documented demonstrations that IQ tests are biased against members of racial minority groups and lower socioeconomic classes would certainly influence the testing of the criminal population, which is besieged by a multitude of social and economic problems. Even if it can be shown that known offenders have lower IQs than the general population, it is difficult to explain many patterns in the crime rate: Why are there more male than female criminals? Why do crime rates vary by region, time of year, and even weather patterns? Why does aging out occur? IQ does not increase with age, so why should crime rates fall?

MENTAL DISORDERS AND CRIME

Psychologists and psychiatrists have long debated the origin of mental disorders and mental illness, linking it to a variety of sources such as genetic predisposition, traumatic family and upbringing, brain trauma, and substance abuse. For example, cognitive theories link learning to development of mental disorders. Children growing up in an abusive home may be "rewarded" by not getting beaten if they learn to be quiet, introverted, and withdrawn, a condition that often leads to clinical depression in adulthood.[132]

Regardless of its source, criminologists have connected antisocial behavior to mental instability and turmoil. Offenders may suffer from a wide variety of mood and/or behavior disorders rendering them histrionic, depressed, antisocial, or narcissistic.[133]

Some have been diagnosed with some form of **mood disorder** characterized by disturbance in expressed emotions. Children with **oppositional defiant disorder (ODD)**, for example, experience an ongoing pattern of uncooperative, defiant, and hostile behavior toward authority figures that seriously interferes with day-to-day functioning. Symptoms of ODD may include frequent loss of temper, constant arguing with adults, defying adults or refusing adult requests or rules, deliberately

mood disorder
A condition in which the prevailing emotional mood is distorted or inappropriate to the circumstances.

oppositional defiant disorder (ODD)
A pattern of negativistic, hostile, and defiant behavior, during which a child often loses her or his temper, often argues with adults, and often actively defies or refuses to comply with adults' requests or rules.

annoying others, blaming others for mistakes or misbehavior, being angry and resentful, being spiteful or vindictive, swearing or using obscene language, or having a low opinion of oneself.[134] Similarly, children who are diagnosed with conduct disorder (CD) have great difficulty following rules and behaving in a socially acceptable way.[135] They are often viewed by other children, adults, and social agencies as severely antisocial. Research shows that they are frequently involved in such activities as bullying, fighting, committing sexual assaults, and behaving cruelly toward animals.

Crime and Mental Illness The most serious forms of mental illness are psychotic disorders, such as **schizophrenia** and **bipolar disorder** (manic-depression), which affect the mind and alter a person's ability to understand reality, think clearly, respond emotionally, communicate effectively, and behave appropriately. People with psychotic disorders may hear nonexistent voices, hallucinate, and make inappropriate behavioral responses. Others exhibit illogical and incoherent thought processes and a lack of insight into their own behavior. They may see themselves as agents of the devil, avenging angels, or the recipients of messages from animals and plants.

Research efforts find that offenders who engage in serious, violent crimes often suffer from some sort of mental disturbance.[136] Female offenders seem to have more serious mental health symptoms than male offenders, including schizophrenia, paranoia, and obsessive behaviors.[137]

Mental illness dogs offenders across the life course: Delinquent adolescents have higher rates of clinical mental disorders than adolescents in the general population.[138] As adult criminals, people who have been arrested for multiple crimes are more likely to suffer from a psychiatric disorder, particularly a psychotic disorder, than non-chronic offenders.[139] Even if apprehended, the mentally ill are much more likely to experience repeated incarcerations if they continue to suffer from major psychiatric disorders (such as depressive disorder, bipolar disorder, schizophrenia, and nonschizophrenic psychotic disorders).[140] In sum, there is a body of research showing that people who suffer from severe mental illness and distress seem to be more antisocial than members of the general population and that punishment may do little to reduce their criminal offending.[141]

Although these findings are persuasive, the association between crime and mental illness must be interpreted with some caution. It is possible that the link between mental illness and crime is spurious and that, in fact, both mental illness and criminal behavior are caused by some other, independent factor:

▶ People who suffer from prior social problems (for example, child abuse) may be more likely to commit violent acts and to suffer mental illness. The original social problem is the cause of both crime and mental illness.[142]

▶ Mentally ill people may also be more likely than the mentally sound to lack financial resources. They are thus forced to reside in deteriorated high-crime neighborhoods, a social factor that may increase criminal behavior.[143] Living in a stress-filled urban environment may produce symptoms of both mental illness and crime.[144]

▶ The police may be more likely to arrest the mentally ill, which fosters the impression that they are crime-prone.[145] The accompanying Profiles in Crime feature discusses one of the better known of these cases. ▶ **Checkpoints**

Social Policy and Trait Theory

For most of the twentieth century, biological and psychological views of criminality have influenced crime control and prevention policy. The result has been **primary prevention programs** that seek to treat personal problems before they manifest themselves as crime. To this end, thousands of family therapy organizations, substance

schizophrenia
A severe disorder marked by hearing nonexistent voices, seeing hallucinations, and exhibiting inappropriate responses.

bipolar disorder
An emotional disturbance in which moods alternate between periods of wild elation and deep depression.

primary prevention programs
Programs, such as substance abuse clinics and mental health associations, that seek to treat personal problems before they manifest themselves as crime.

© David J. Phillip/Reuters/Corbis

Andrea (Kennedy) Yates was born on July 2, 1964, in Houston, Texas. She seemed to have had a successful, normal life, having been the class valedictorian, captain of the swim team, and a member of the National Honor Society. She graduated from the University of Texas School of Nursing in Houston and worked as a registered nurse at a facility run by the University of Texas. She met and married Rusty Yates, and the couple began to raise a family. Though money was tight and living conditions cramped, the couple had five children in the first eight years of their marriage. The pressure began to take a toll on Andrea, and her mental health deteriorated. On June 17, 1999, after attempting suicide by taking an overdose of pills, she was placed in Houston's Methodist Hospital psychiatric unit and diagnosed with a major depressive disorder. Even though she was medicated with powerful antipsychotics such as Haldol, Andrea continued to have psychotic episodes and was hospitalized for severe depression. Her losing battle with mental illness culminated in an act that shocked the nation: On June 20, 2001, she systematically drowned all five of her children, including her eldest, 7-year-old Noah, who tried to escape after seeing his siblings dead, but was dragged back into the bathroom by his mother and drowned also.

At trial, Yates's defense team attempted to show that she suffered from delusional depression and postpartum mood swings that can sometimes evoke psychosis. In spite of the fact that she drowned her children one by one, even chasing down 7-year-old Noah to drag him to the tub, did she really have any awareness that what she was doing was wrong? About 40 percent of all mothers experience postpartum depression. In its mildest form, it leaves new mothers feeling "blue" for a few weeks; more serious cases can last more than a year and involve fatigue, withdrawal, and eating disorders. The most serious form, which Andrea Yates is believed to have suffered, is a psychosis that produces hallucinations, delusions, and feelings of worthlessness and inadequacy. Though very uncommon, postpartum psychosis increases the likelihood of both suicide and infanticide if left untreated. Despite her long history of mental illness, and despite psychiatric testimony suggesting she lacked the capacity to understand her actions, the jury found her guilty of murder on March 12, 2002, ordering a life sentence instead of the death penalty sought by the prosecution.

Andrea's conviction was later overturned when a Texas appeals court ruled that an expert witness, Dr. Park Dietz, made a false statement during the trial. (He claimed she might have been influenced by an episode of *Law and Order*, even though no such episode ever aired; it was actually *L.A. Law* that dealt with a case of a mother killing her children.) In January 2007, Yates was moved to a low-security state mental hospital in Kerrville, Texas.

The Andrea Yates case illustrates the association between mental illness and crime. Who could claim that a woman as disturbed as Andrea *chose* to kill her own children? The jury may have reached that verdict, but it was constrained by the legal definition of insanity, which relies on the immediate events that took place, not on Andrea's long-term mental state that produced this horrible crime.

SOURCES: Andrea Yates, CourtTV Crime Library, www.crimelibrary .com/notorious_murders/women/andrea_yates/index.html (accessed April 3, 2009); *New York Times*, "Retrial to Begin for Mother of 5 in Drownings," www.nytimes.com/2006/06/26/us/ 26yates.html (accessed April 3, 2009).

---

secondary prevention programs
Programs that provide treatment, such as psychological counseling, to youths and adults after they have violated the law.

abuse clinics, and mental health associations operate throughout the United States. Teachers, employers, courts, welfare agencies, and others make referrals to these facilities.

These services are based on the premise that if a person's problems can be treated before they become overwhelming, some future crimes will be prevented. **Secondary prevention programs** provide treatment such as psychological counseling to youths

Fourteen-year-old Daphne A. is a product of Boston's best private schools; she lives with her wealthy family on Beacon Hill. Her father is an executive at a local financial services conglomerate and makes close to $1 million per year. Daphne, however, has a hidden, darker side. She is always in trouble at school, and teachers report that she is impulsive and has poor self-control. At times she can be kind and warm, but on other occasions she is obnoxious, unpredictable, insecure, and hungry for attention. She is overly self-conscious about her body and has a drinking problem. Daphne attends AA meetings and is on the waiting list at High Cliff Village, a residential substance abuse treatment program. Her parents seem intimidated by her and confused by her complexities; her father even filed a harassment complaint against her once, saying she had slapped him.

Despite repeated promises to get her life together, Daphne likes to hang out most nights in the Public Gardens and drink with neighborhood kids. On more than one occasion she went to the park with her friend and confidant Christopher G., a quiet boy who had his own set of personal problems. His parents had separated, and subsequently he began to suffer severe anxiety attacks. He stayed home from school and was diagnosed with depression for which he took two drugs—Zoloft, an antidepressant, and Lorazepam, a sedative.

One night Daphne and Chris met up with Michael M., a 44-year-old man with a long history of alcohol problems. After a night of drinking, a fight broke out and Michael was stabbed, his throat cut, and his body dumped in the pond. Daphne was quickly arrested when soon after the attack she placed a 911 call to police,

telling them that a friend had "jumped in the lake and didn't come out." Police searched the area and found Michael's slashed and stabbed body in the water; he had been disemboweled by Chris and Daphne in an attempt to sink the body.

At a waiver hearing, Daphne admits that she participated in the killing but cannot articulate what caused her to get involved. She had been drinking and remembers little of the events. She says that she was flirting with Michael and that Chris stabbed him in a jealous rage. She speaks in a flat, hollow voice and shows little remorse for her actions. It was a spur-of-the-moment thing, she claims, and after all it was Chris, not she herself, who had the knife. Later Chris testifies, claiming that Daphne instigated the fight and egged him on, taunting him that he was too scared to kill someone. Chris says that when she was drunk, Daphne often talked of killing an adult because she hated older people, especially her parents.

Daphne's parents claim that although she has been a burden with her mood swings and volatile behavior, she is still a child and can be helped with proper treatment. They are willing to supplement any state intervention with privately funded psychiatrists. Given that this is her first real offense and because of her age (14), her parents believe that home confinement with intense treatment is the best course.

The district attorney, however, wants Daphne treated as an adult and "waived" to adult court where, if she is found guilty, she can receive a 25-year sentence for second-degree murder; there is little question of her legal culpability.

Writing Assignment

Take the role of a defense lawyer in the juvenile court. Write a brief to the juvenile court judge that could be used at the waiver hearing. Use your essay to persuade the judge to keep Daphne in the juvenile court, where she could be treated rather than punished. How would you convince the court that Daphne's crime was a function of some abnormal trait or condition that is amenable to treatment? Be sure to refute the notion that she is a calculating criminal who understood the seriousness of her actions.

and adults *after* they have violated the law. Attendance at such programs may be a requirement of a probation order, part of a diversionary sentence, or aftercare at the end of a prison sentence.

Biologically oriented therapy is also being used in the criminal justice system. Programs have altered diets, changed lighting, compensated for learning disabilities, treated allergies, and so on.[146] More controversial has been the use of mood-altering chemicals, such as lithium, pemoline, imipramine, phenytoin, and benzodiazepines, to control behavior. Another practice that has elicited concern is the use of psychosurgery (brain surgery) to control antisocial behavior. Surgical procedures have

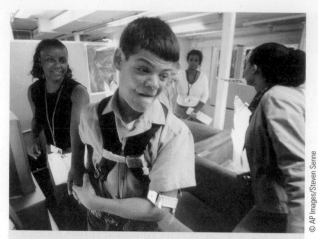

Prevention programs based on trait theory are aimed at treating the individual rather than improving the environment. Here a student identified only as Brandon leads workshop coordinator Silvia Dos Santos, left, during a class at the Judge Rotenberg Educational Center in Canton, Massachusetts, on May 25, 2006. The center is a special needs school, which teaches students with behavioral, psychiatric, and autistic-like problems ranging from moderate to lower-functioning levels. The school is unique in that it employs a low-level electric shock program to help control behavior.

been used to alter the brain structure of convicted sex offenders in an effort to eliminate or control their sex drives. Results are still preliminary, but some critics argue that these procedures are without scientific merit.[147]

The numerous psychologically based treatments that are available range from individual counseling to behavior modification. Treatment based on how people process information takes into account that people are more likely to respond aggressively to provocation if thoughts intensify the insult or otherwise stir feelings of anger. Cognitive therapists attempt to teach explosive people to control aggressive impulses by viewing social provocations as problems demanding a solution rather than retaliation. Programs are aimed at teaching problem-solving skills such as self-disclosure, role playing, listening, following instructions, joining in, and using self-control.[148] Therapeutic interventions designed to make people better problem solvers may involve measures that enhance

▶ Coping and problem-solving skills
▶ Relationships with peers, parents, and other adults
▶ Conflict resolution and communication skills, and methods for resisting peer pressure related to drug use and violence
▶ Decision-making abilities and thinking about consequences
▶ Prosocial behaviors, including cooperation with others, self-responsibility, respecting others, and efficacy in public speaking
▶ Empathy[149]

Summary

1. Be familiar with the development of trait theory.

The view that criminals have physical or mental traits that make them different originated with the Italian physician and criminologist Cesare Lombroso. In the early 1970s, spurred by the publication of *Sociobiology: The New Synthesis*, by Edmund O. Wilson, biological explanations of crime once again emerged. Trait theorists today recognize crime-producing interactions that involve both personal traits and environmental factors. If only a few offenders become persistent repeaters, what sets them apart from the rest of the criminal population may be some crime-producing trait.

2. Discuss some of the biochemical conditions that have been associated with crime.

Biochemical conditions influence antisocial behavior. Biocriminologists maintain that an improper diet can cause chemical and mineral imbalance and lead to cognitive and learning deficits and problems, and these factors in turn are associated with antisocial behaviors. Abnormal levels of male sex hormones (androgens) can incline individuals to aggressive behavior. And exposure to lead has been linked to emotional and behavioral disorders.

3. Understand the linkage between aggression and neurophysiological makeup.

Inherited or acquired neurological and physical abnormalities control behavior throughout the life span. Neurological impairment may also lead to the development of personality traits linked to antisocial behaviors. According to arousal theory, a need for high levels of environmental stimulation may lead to aggressive, violent behavior patterns.

4. Link genetics to crime.

Another biosocial theme is that the human traits associated with criminality have a genetic basis. According to this view, (1) antisocial behavior is inherited, (2) the genetic makeup of parents is passed on to children, and (3) genetic abnormality is linked to a variety of antisocial behaviors.

5. Explain the evolutionary view of crime.

Human traits that produce violence and aggression have been shaped by the long process of human evolution. According to evolutionary theory, behavior patterns are inherited and impulsive behavior becomes intergenerational, passed down from parents to children.

6. Discuss the elements of the psychodynamic perspective.

The id is the primitive part of people's mental makeup. The ego is shaped by learning and experience, and the superego reflects the morals and values of parents and significant others. Criminals are id-driven people who suffer from weak or damaged egos. Crime is a manifestation of feelings of oppression and the inability to develop the proper psychological defenses and rationales to keep these feelings under control.

7. Link behavioral theory to crime.

People are not born with the tendency to act violently; rather, they learn to be aggressive through their life experiences. These experiences include personally observing others acting aggressively to achieve some goal or observing people being rewarded for violent acts.

8. Show why aggressive behavior may reflect cognitive processes.

Crime-prone people may have cognitive deficits and use information incorrectly when they make decisions. They view crime as an appropriate means to satisfy their immediate personal needs, which take precedence over more distant social needs, such as obedience to the law.

9. Discuss the elements of personality that are related to crime.

Sociopathic, psychopathic, or antisocial people lack affect, cannot empathize with others, and are short-sighted and hedonistic. These traits make them prone to problems ranging from psychopathology to drug abuse, sexual promiscuity, and violence. The factors related to personality problems include improper socialization, having a psychopathic parent, experiencing parental rejection and lack of love during childhood, and receiving inconsistent discipline.

10. Be aware of the controversy over the association between intelligence and crime.

Proponents of nature theory argue that intelligence is largely determined genetically, that ancestry determines IQ, and that low intelligence is linked to criminal behavior. Proponents of nurture theory argue that intelligence is not inherited and that low-IQ parents do not necessarily produce low-IQ children. The debate about any link between IQ and criminality is unlikely to be settled soon. Measurement is beset by many methodological problems.

11. Discuss the association between mental disorders and crime.

Antisocial behavior has been linked to mental instability and turmoil. Offenders may suffer from a wide variety of mood and/or behavior disorders that render them histrionic, depressed, antisocial, or narcissistic. However, it is possible that the link between mental illness and crime is spurious and that both crime and mental illness are precipitated by some other, independent factor.

Key Terms

trait theory 108
sociobiology 108
hypoglycemia 111
androgens 111
testosterone 111
premenstrual syndrome (PMS) 112
neurophysiology 113
conduct disorder (CD) 113
attention-deficit/ hyperactivity disorder (ADHD) 113

neurotransmitters 115
arousal theory 116
monozygotic (MZ) twins 117
dizygotic (DZ) twins 117
contagion effect 117
psychodynamic (psychoanalytic) theory 120
id 120
ego 120
superego 121

attachment theory 121
behavior theory 121
social learning theory 121
behavior modeling 124
cognitive theory 124
information-processing theory 124
personality 125
antisocial personality 126
nature theory 127

nurture theory 127
mood disorder 128
oppositional defiant disorder (ODD) 128
schizophrenia 129
bipolar disorder 129
primary prevention programs 129
secondary prevention programs 130

Critical Thinking Questions

1. If research could show that the tendency to commit crime is inherited, what should be done with the young children of violence-prone criminals? Would it be unfair to monitor their behavior from an early age?
2. Considering the evidence on the association between media and crime, would you recommend that young children be forbidden to view films with violent content?
3. Knowing what you do about trends and patterns in crime, how would you counteract the assertion that people who commit crime are physically or mentally abnormal?
4. Aside from becoming a criminal, what other career paths are open to psychopaths?
5. Should sugar be banned from school lunches?
6. Can gender differences in the crime rate be explained by evolutionary factors? Do you agree that male aggression is linked to mating patterns developed millions of years ago?

© Reuters/Luis Rivera/Landov

Chapter Outline

Social Structure Theory 6

The tiny country of El Salvador (population 6.6 million) is home to more than 40,000 gang members. Rather than being a homegrown phenomenon, these gangs are actually a U.S. import. How did this happen? In the early 1990s, hundreds of members of two of the largest gangs in Los Angeles, the 18th Street gang and the MS-13 gang, who had illegally made their home in the United States, were deported back to El Salvador. The deportees brought Los Angeles gang culture with them to a country already swamped with weapons from an ongoing civil war. Now on their home turf, gang boys recruited thousands of local teenagers into their reconstituted gangs. Joining a gang gives these poor, urban teenagers a powerful sense of identity and belonging. They were also free now to show their courage and manhood by engaging in a never-ending turf war with one another.

Ironically, both gangs originated in Los Angeles, organized by Salvadorans fleeing a civil war. When they arrived in Los Angeles, they were preyed upon by preexisting Mexican gangs. The MS-13 gang was formed as a means of self-protection. The M in the gang's name refers to a *mara*, Spanish for "posse," or gang. The S comes from *salvatruchas*, local slang for being alert and ready to take action; the "13" is a reference to the gang's beginnings on 13th Street in Los Angeles.

Over time, the ranks of both gangs grew, and members entered a variety of rackets, from extortion to drug trafficking. When law enforcement cracked down and deported members, the deportees quickly created outposts in El Salvador and throughout Central America. The Salvadoran government has responded by criminalizing gang membership and arresting thousands. But government efforts have

Fact or Fiction?

▶ Gangs are local groups that defend their turf from outsiders.

▶ There are very few truly poor people in the United States, the wealthiest country on earth.

▶ Political, social, and economic programs such as affirmative action have erased the economic gulf between whites and minorities.

▶ People living in lower-class neighborhoods mistrust the government and believe that government programs are part of a plot to destroy their communities.

▶ Residents can help to lower community crime rates if they pull together and work to maintain public order.

▶ Crime rates always go down in a healthy economy.

Chapter Objectives

1. Be familiar with the different elements of the U.S. social structure.
2. Describe the association between social structure and crime.
3. Know the elements of social disorganization theory.
4. Be familiar with the views of Shaw and McKay.
5. Know the various elements of ecological theory.
6. Be able to discuss the association between collective efficacy and crime.
7. Discuss the concept of strain.
8. Know what is meant by the term "anomie."
9. Discuss the concept of negative affective states.
10. Discuss the elements of cultural deviance theory.

not stemmed the tide of recruitment, and the gangs appear to be more popular than ever.[1] According to the latest reports on MS-13 activity in the United States:

▶ MS-13 operates in at least 42 states and the District of Columbia and has about 6,000–10,000 members nationwide.

▶ MS-13 members engage in a wide range of criminal activity, including drug distribution, murder, rape, prostitution, robbery, home invasions, immigration offenses, kidnapping, carjacking/auto theft, and vandalism.

▶ MS-13 is expanding its membership at a "moderate" rate through recruitment and migration. MS-13 often recruits new members by glorifying the gang lifestyle (often on the Internet, complete with pictures and videos) and by absorbing smaller gangs.

▶ MS-13 members typically work for legitimate businesses by presenting false documentation. They primarily pick employers that don't scrutinize employment documents, especially in the construction, restaurant, delivery service, and landscaping industries.

▶ MS-13 originated in Los Angeles, but when members migrated eastward, they began forming cliques that for the most part operated independently. These cliques often maintain regular contact with members in other regions to coordinate recruitment/criminal activities and to prevent conflicts.[2]

Fact or Fiction?

Gangs are local groups that defend their turf from outsiders.

Fiction. Many gangs today are national organizations that contain thousands of members and may have branches in more than one state.

To criminologists it comes as no surprise that gangs develop in poor, deteriorated urban neighborhoods. Many kids in these areas grow up hopeless and alienated, believing that they have little chance of being part of the American Dream.[3] Joining a gang holds the promise of economic rewards and status enhancements that the conventional world simply cannot provide. Kids who become criminals are indigent and desperate people rather than abnormal, calculating, or evil. Raised in deteriorated parts of town, they lack the social support and economic resources available to more affluent members of society. To understand criminal behavior, we must analyze the influence of these destructive social forces on human behavior. According to this view, it is *social forces*—not individual traits—that cause crime.

Economic Structure and Crime

According to social structure theory, the key to understanding the root cause of crime can be found in the nation's socioeconomic makeup. People in the United States live in a **stratified society**. Social strata are created by the unequal distribution of wealth, power, and prestige. **Social classes** are segments of the population whose members have a relatively similar portion of desirable things and who share attitudes, values, norms, and an identifiable lifestyle. In U.S. society, it is common to identify people as belonging to the upper, middle, or lower socioeconomic class, although a broad range of economic variations exist within each group. The upper-upper class is reserved for a small number of exceptionally well-to-do families who control enormous financial and social resources. As Figure 6.1 shows, the government estimates that there are now 37 million Americans living in poverty, defined as a family of four earning about $21,000 per year. Such families have scant, if any, resources and suffer socially and economically as a result. The top 20 percent of households earn more than $90,000 per year, and the bottom 20 percent average about $19,000; the "super-rich" the top one-tenth of 1 percent (0.1%) average about $1.6 million in income each year.[4] This wealth concentration effect is not unique to the United States; it is a worldwide phenomenon. According to the most recent World Wealth Report, there are about 10 million high-net-worth individuals in the world today (people with more than $1 million in assets, excluding their primary residence); they have a net worth of more than $40 trillion.[5]

stratified society
People grouped according to economic or social class; characterized by the unequal distribution of wealth, power, and prestige.

social class
Segment of the population whose members are at a relatively similar economic level and who share attitudes, values, norms, and an identifiable lifestyle.

Figure 6.1 Number in Poverty and Poverty Rate

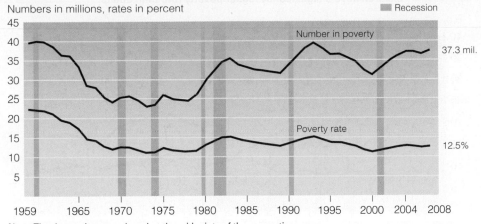

Numbers in millions, rates in percent

Note: The data points are placed at the midpoints of the respective years.

SOURCE: U.S. Census Bureau, Current Population Survey, 1960 to 2008 Social and Economic Supplements, www.census.gov/hhes/www/poverty/poverty07/pov07fig03.pdf.

PROBLEMS OF THE LOWER CLASS

In 1966, sociologist Oscar Lewis argued that the crushing lifestyle of lower-class areas produces a **culture of poverty** that is passed from one generation to the next.[6] Apathy, cynicism, helplessness, and mistrust of social institutions, such as schools, government agencies, and the police, mark the culture of poverty. This mistrust prevents the inner-city poor from taking advantage of the meager opportunities available to them. Lewis's work was the first of a number of studies that described the plight of at-risk children and adults. In 1970, Swedish economist Gunnar Myrdal described a worldwide **underclass** that was cut off from society, its members lacking the education and skills needed to function successfully in modern society.[7]

Lower-class areas are scenes of inadequate housing and health care, disrupted family lives, underemployment, and despair. Members of the lower class also suffer in other ways. They are more prone to depression, less likely to have achievement motivation, and less likely to put off immediate gratification for the sake of future gain or security. Members of the lower classes may be less willing to stay in school because the rewards for educational achievement are in the distant future.

CHILD POVERTY

Economic disadvantage and poverty can be especially devastating to younger children.[8] This is particularly important today because, as Figure 6.2 shows, children have a higher poverty rate than any other age group.

Adolescents are hit especially hard by poverty. Children who grow up in low-income homes are less likely to achieve in school and less likely to complete their schooling than children with more affluent parents.[9] Poor kids are also more likely to suffer from health problems and to receive inadequate health care. The number of U.S. children covered by health insurance is declining and will continue to do so for the foreseeable future.[10] Without health benefits or the means to afford medical care, these youths are likely to have health problems that impede their long-term development.

MINORITY GROUP POVERTY

The burdens of underclass life are often felt most acutely by minority group members. Whereas many urban European Americans use their economic, social, and political advantages to live in sheltered gated communities patrolled by security guards and police, most minorities do not have access to similar protections and privileges.[11]

culture of poverty
A separate lower-class culture, characterized by apathy, cynicism, helplessness, and mistrust of social institutions such as schools, government agencies, and the police, that is passed from one generation to the next.

underclass
The lowest social stratum in any country, whose members lack the education and skills needed to function successfully in modern society.

Figure 6.2 Poverty by Age

Children have a significantly higher poverty rate than adults.

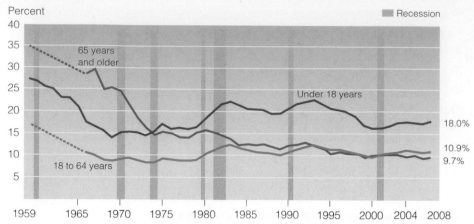

Note: The data points represent the midpoints of the respective years. Data for people 18 to 64 and people 65 and older are not available from 1960 to 1965.

SOURCE: U.S. Census Bureau, Current Population Survey, 1960 to 2008 Annual Social and Economic Supplements, http://www.census.gov/prod/2008pubs/p60-235.pdf.

Felicia Coffey and her family of 16 all live together in a mobile home in Duncan, Mississippi. Poverty rates among minority groups are still double that of European Americans. Almost 25 percent of African Americans and 22 percent of Latino Americans still live in poverty, compared to less than 10 percent of whites. The median family income of Latinos and of African Americans is two-thirds that of whites. These social problems and conditions take a toll on young Americans of these ethnic groups and make it difficult for them to achieve the American Dream.

Almost 25 percent of African Americans and 22 percent of Latino Americans still live in poverty, compared to less than 10 percent of whites. According to the U.S. Census Bureau, the median family income of Latinos and African Americans is two-thirds that of whites.[12]

Among recent findings about the plight of the minority population are these:

► The proportion of young black men without jobs has climbed relentlessly, with only a slight pause during the economic peak of the late 1990s. As of June 2009, the African American unemployment rate was 15 percent, and the Latino unemployment rate was 11 percent, compared to the white unemployment rate of 8 percent.[13]

► If they do commit crime, minority youths are more likely to be officially processed to the juvenile court than Caucasian youths. This makes it more likely that they will develop an official record at an early age, an outcome that may increase the odds of their being incarcerated as adults.[14] According to a recent report by the Pew Foundation, whereas 1 in 30 men between the ages of 20 and 34 is behind bars, for black males in that age group the figure is 1 in 9; and 1 in 100 black women in their mid- to late-30s is incarcerated compared to 1 in 355 European American women.[15]

► Even though dropout rates have declined, about 6 percent of white, 11 percent of African American, and 22 percent of Hispanic students drop out of high school each year.[16] In the inner cities, more than half of all black men do not finish high school.[17]

These economic and social disparities continually haunt members of the minority underclass and their children. Even if they value education and other middle-class norms, their desperate life circumstances, such as high unemployment and nontraditional family structures, may prevent them from developing the skills and habits that lead first to educational success and later to success in the workplace; these deficits have been linked to crime and drug abuse.[18]

Interracial differences in the crime rate could be significantly reduced by improving levels of education, lowering levels of poverty, and reducing the extent of male unemployment among minority populations.[19] The issue of minority poverty is explored further in the accompanying Race, Culture, Gender, and Criminology feature.

POVERTY AND CRIME

According to **social structure theory**, the root cause of crime can be traced directly to the socioeconomic disadvantages that have become embedded in American society. The social problems found in lower-class areas have been described as an "epidemic" that spreads like a contagious disease, destroying the inner workings that enable neighborhoods to survive; they become "hollowed out."[20] As neighborhood quality decreases, the probability that residents will develop problems sharply increases. Because they lack ties to the mainstream culture, some lower-class people are driven to desperate measures, such as crime and substance abuse, to cope with their economic plight.[21] Crime and violence may also take the form of a "slow epidemic," with a course consisting of stages: onset, peak, and decline. Violence and crime have been found to spread and then contract in a pattern similar to a contagious disease.[22] When lower-class kids are exposed to a continual stream of violence, they are more likely to engage in violent acts themselves.[23]

Aggravating this dynamic is the constant media bombardment linking material possessions to self-worth. Because they are unable to obtain desired goods and services through conventional means, members of the lower class may turn to illegal solutions to their economic plight. They may deal drugs for profit, steal cars and sell them to "chop shops," or commit armed robberies for desperately needed funds. They may become so depressed that they take alcohol and drugs as a form of self-tranquilization, and because of their poverty, they may acquire the drugs and alcohol through illegal channels.

CONNECTIONS

Concern about the ecological distribution of crime, the effect of social change, and the interactive nature of crime itself has made sociology the foundation of modern criminology. This chapter reviews sociological theories that emphasize the relationship between social status and criminal behavior. In Chapter 7 the focus shifts to theories that emphasize socialization and its influence on crime and deviance; Chapter 8 covers theories based on the concept of social conflict.

Fact or Fiction?

Political, social, and economic programs such as affirmative action have erased the economic gulf between whites and minorities.

Fiction. Minorities still have a significantly lower standard of living than whites, as well as much higher unemployment rates.

social structure theory
The view that disadvantaged economic class position is a primary cause of crime.

William Julius Wilson, one of the nation's most prominent sociologists, has produced an impressive body of work that details racial problems and racial politics in American society. In 1987, he provided a description of the plight of the lowest levels of the underclass, which he labeled the truly disadvantaged. Wilson portrayed members of this group as socially isolated people who dwell in urban inner cities, occupy the bottom rung of the social ladder, and are the victims of discrimination. They live in areas in which the basic institutions of society—family, school, housing—have long since declined. Neighborhood decline triggers breakdowns in community cohesion and loss of the ability of people living in the area to control the flow of drugs and criminal activity. For example, in a more

is pervasive and unchanging—if anything, it is steadily worsening as residents are further shut out of the economic mainstream.

Wilson focuses on the plight of the African American community, which had enjoyed periods of relative prosperity in the 1950s and 1960s. He suggests that as difficult as life was for African Americans in the 1940s and 1950s, they at least had a reasonable hope of steady work. Now, because of the globalization of the economy, those opportunities have evaporated. In the past, growth in the manufacturing sector fueled upward mobility and lay the foundation of today's African American middle class. Those opportunities no longer exist, because manufacturing plants have been moved to inaccessible rural and overseas locations where

Race, Culture, Gender, and Criminology
More Than Just Race

affluent area, neighbors might complain to parents that their children were being disruptive. In distressed areas, this element of informal social control may be absent, because parents are under stress or (all too often) absent. These effects magnify the isolation of the underclass from mainstream society and promote a ghetto culture characterized by hopelessness and lawless behavior.

Because the truly disadvantaged rarely come into contact with the actual source of their oppression, they direct their anger and aggression at those with whom they are in close contact, such as neighbors, businesspeople, and landlords. Plagued by under- or unemployment, they begin to lose self-confidence, a feeling exacerbated by the plight of kin and friendship groups who also experience extreme economic marginality. Self-doubt is a neighborhood norm that threatens to overwhelm those forced to live in areas of concentrated poverty.

In another important book, *When Work Disappears,* Wilson assesses the effect of joblessness and underemployment on residents in poor neighborhoods on Chicago's south side. He argues that for the first time in the twentieth century, most adults in inner-city ghetto neighborhoods are not working during a typical week. He finds that inner-city life was only marginally affected by the surge in the nation's economy brought about by new industrial growth connected with technological development. Poverty in these inner-city areas

the cost of doing business is lower. With manufacturing opportunities all but absent in the United States, service and retail establishments that depended on blue-collar spending have similarly disappeared, leaving behind an economy based on welfare and government supports. In less than 20 years, formerly active African American neighborhoods have become crime-infested inner-city ghettos.

The hardships faced by residents in Chicago's south side are not unique to that community. In addition to perpetuating inner-city poverty, the absence of employment opportunities has torn at the social fabric of the nation's inner-city neighborhoods. Couples are less likely to marry because minority women no longer see men as breadwinners. Epidemic unemployment among minority males also undermines the community. Work helps socialize young people into the wider society, instilling in them such values as hard work, caring, and respect for others. When work becomes scarce, however, the discipline and structure it provides are absent. Community-wide underemployment destroys social cohesion, increasing the presence of neighborhood social problems ranging from drug use to educational failure. Schools in these areas are unable to teach basic skills, and because desirable employment is lacking, there are few adults to serve as role models. In contrast to more affluent suburban households where daily life is organized around job and career demands, children in

Social Structure Theories

Criminologists who view membership in a disadvantaged economic class as a primary cause of crime are referred to as social structure theorists. As a group, social structure theories suggest that social and economic forces operating in deteriorated lower-class areas push many of their residents into criminal behavior patterns. These theories view the existence of unsupervised teenage gangs, high crime rates, and social inner-city areas are not socialized in the workings of the mainstream economy.

In *The Bridge over the Racial Divide: Rising Inequality and Coalition Politics,* Wilson expands on his views of race in contemporary society. He argues that despite economic gains, there is growing inequality in American society, and ordinary families, of all races and ethnic origins, are suffering. Whites, Latinos, African Americans, Asians, and Native Americans must therefore begin to put aside their differences and concentrate more on what they have in common—their aspirations, problems, and hopes. There needs to be mutual cooperation across racial lines.

One reason for this set of mutual problems is that the government tends to aggravate rather than ease the financial stress on ordinary families. Monetary policy, trade policy, and tax policy are harmful to working-class families. A multiracial citizens' coalition could pressure national public officials to focus on the interests of ordinary people. As long as middle- and working-class groups are fragmented along racial lines, it is impossible to exert such pressure.

Wilson finds that racism is becoming more subtle and harder to detect. Whites believe that blacks themselves are responsible for their inferior economic status because of their cultural traits. And because even affluent whites fear corporate downsizing, they are unwilling to vote for government assistance to the poor. Whites are continuing to be suburban dwellers, further isolating poor minorities in central cities and making their problems seem distant and unimportant. He believes that the marketplace, with its ever-increasing reliance on sophisticated computer technologies, continues to demand fewer and fewer low-skilled workers, which impacts African Americans more negatively than other, better educated and more affluent groups.

Wilson argues for a cross-race, class-based alliance of working- and middle-class Americans to pursue policies that will benefit them rather than the affluent. These policies include full employment, programs to help families and workers in their private lives, and a reconstructed "affirmative opportunity" program that benefits African Americans without antagonizing whites.

In *There Goes the Neighborhood,* Wilson and Richard P. Taub assess racial relations in four Chicago neighborhoods. The picture they paint is quite bleak. Racism is still an active part of people's lives, even though its motif is changing. People are unusually hostile when outsiders move into their enclave. If they have a choice, they move; if not, they are angry and sullen. In a white, middle-class neighborhood, people are angry when black and Latino newcomers arrive,

believing that their presence threatens property values and neighborhood stability. Whites and Latinos are able to reach common ground on only one social issue: preventing kids from being bused to a predominantly black school district. People seldom hesitate to use offensive racist language to express their feelings, and they feel superior to other groups and races. Racism seems to cloak social anxiety: People who are worried about jobs and health care take their frustrations out on others. As always, Wilson comes up with a prescription for positive change: Strengthen neighborhood social organizations, and people will be less likely to flee. Race relations can be improved if people from diverse backgrounds can come together to reach common goals such as school improvement. Society as a whole must be willing to help out and repair inner-city ghettos. Without such help, racial and class tensions spread throughout the city.

In his most recent work, *More than Just Race: Being Black and Poor in the Inner City,* Wilson tries to explain the persistence of poverty in black neighborhoods: Is it attributable to cultural (family, personal values) or structural values (segregation, racism)? He finds that both factors play a role. For example, a law-and-order political philosophy and fear of racial conflict have led to high incarceration rates among African American males. Although black women can get jobs in services industries, employers are less likely to hire black men, especially those with a criminal record. As a result, there has been a decline in the ability of black men to be providers, which has tended to undermine the stability of the African American family. Here we can see how structure and culture intertwine to produce stress in the African American community.

CRITICAL THINKING

1. Is it unrealistic to assume that a government-sponsored public works program can provide needed jobs in this era of budget cutbacks?
2. What are some of the hidden costs of unemployment in a community setting?
3. How would a biocriminologist explain Wilson's findings?

SOURCES: William Julius Wilson, *More than Just Race: Being Black and Poor in the Inner City* (New York: Norton, 2009); William Julius Wilson and Richard Taub, *There Goes the Neighborhood: Racial, Ethnic, and Class Tensions in Four Chicago Neighborhoods and Their Meaning for America* (New York: Knopf, 2006); William Julius Wilson, *The Truly Disadvantaged* (Chicago: University of Chicago Press, 1987); *When Work Disappears: The World of the Urban Poor* (New York: Knopf, 1996); *The Bridge over the Racial Divide: Rising Inequality and Coalition Politics,* Wildavsky Forum Series, 2 (Berkeley: University of California Press, 1999).

disorder in poor inner-city areas as major social problems. Because crime rates are higher in lower-class urban centers than in middle-class suburbs, social forces must influence or control behavior.

The social structure perspective encompasses three independent yet overlapping branches: social disorganization theory, strain theory, and cultural deviance theory. These three branches are summarized in Figure 6.3.

Figure 6.3 The Three Branches of Social Structure Theory

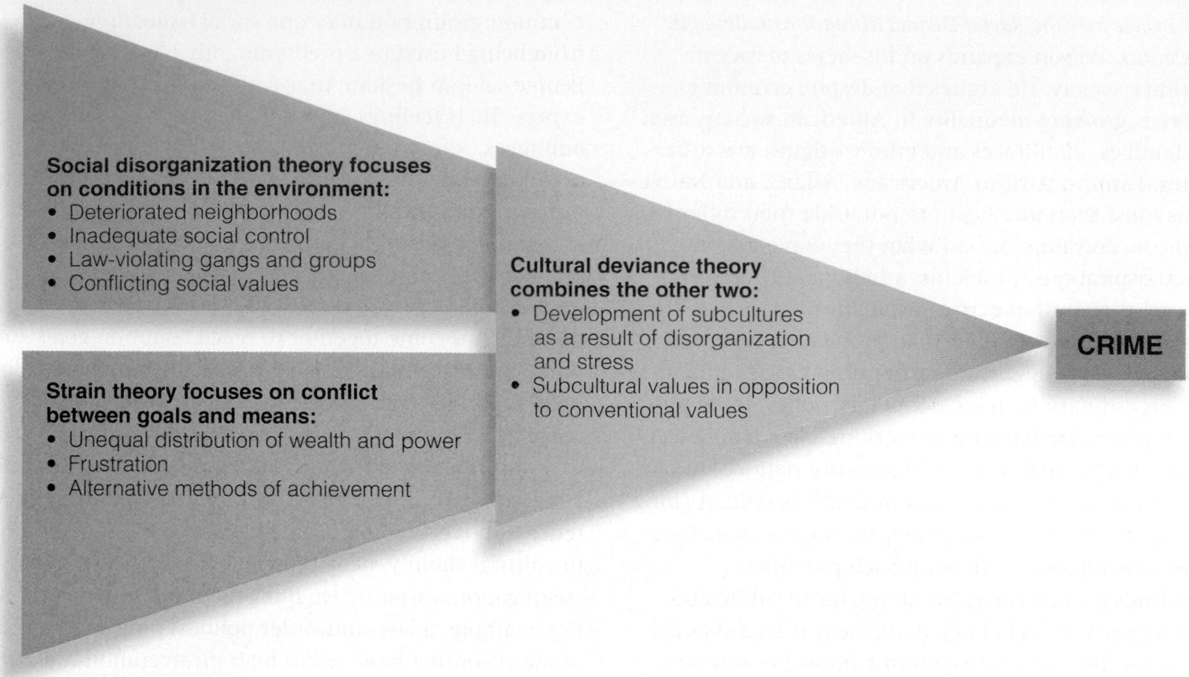

Social disorganization theory focuses on conditions in the environment:
- Deteriorated neighborhoods
- Inadequate social control
- Law-violating gangs and groups
- Conflicting social values

Cultural deviance theory combines the other two:
- Development of subcultures as a result of disorganization and stress
- Subcultural values in opposition to conventional values

Strain theory focuses on conflict between goals and means:
- Unequal distribution of wealth and power
- Frustration
- Alternative methods of achievement

CRIME

social disorganization theory
Branch of social structure theory that focuses on the breakdown in inner-city neighborhoods of institutions such as the family, school, and employment.

strain theory
Branch of social structure theory that sees crime as a function of the conflict between people's goals and the means available to obtain them.

strain
The anger, frustration, and resentment experienced by people who believe they cannot achieve their goals through legitimate means.

cultural deviance theory
Branch of social structure theory that sees strain and social disorganization together resulting in a unique lower-class culture that conflicts with conventional social norms.

subculture
A set of values, beliefs, and traditions unique to a particular social class or group within a larger society.

cultural transmission
Process whereby values, beliefs, and traditions are handed down from one generation to the next.

Social disorganization theory focuses on the urban conditions that affect crime rates. A disorganized area is one in which institutions of social control, such as the family, commercial establishments, and schools, have broken down and can no longer perform their expected or stated functions. Indicators of social disorganization include high unemployment and school dropout rates, deteriorated housing, low income levels, and large numbers of single-parent households. Residents in these areas experience conflict and despair, and as a result, antisocial behavior flourishes.

Strain theory holds that crime is a function of the conflict between people's goals and the means they can use to obtain them. Strain theorists argue that although social and economic goals are common to people in all economic strata, the ability to obtain these goals is class dependent. Most people in the United States desire wealth, material possessions, power, prestige, and other life comforts. Members of the lower class are unable to achieve these symbols of success through conventional means. Consequently, they feel anger, frustration, and resentment, which are referred to collectively as **strain**. Lower-class citizens can either accept these conditions and live as socially responsible but unrewarded citizens, or they can choose an alternative means of achieving success, such as theft, violence, or drug trafficking.

Cultural deviance theory combines elements of both strain and social disorganization theories. According to this view, because of strain and social isolation, a unique lower-class culture develops in disorganized neighborhoods. These independent **subcultures** maintain unique values and beliefs that conflict with conventional social norms. Criminal behavior is an expression of conformity to lower-class subcultural values and traditions, not a rebellion from conventional society. Subcultural values are handed down from one generation to the next in a process called **cultural transmission**.

Although these theories differ in critical aspects, each approach has at its core the view that socially isolated people, living in disorganized neighborhoods, are likely to experience crime-producing social forces. The remainder of this chapter discusses each branch of social structure theory in some detail. ▶ **Checkpoints**

Social Disorganization Theory

Social disorganization theory links crime rates to neighborhood ecological characteristics. Crime rates are elevated in highly transient, mixed-use (where residential and commercial property exist side by side), and changing neighborhoods in which the fabric of social life has become frayed. These localities are unable to provide essential services, such as education, health care, and proper housing, and as a result, they experience significant levels of unemployment, single-parent families, and families on welfare.

Residents in crime-ridden neighborhoods try to leave at the earliest opportunity. As a result they take little interest in community matters, so the common sources of control—the family, school, business community, and social service agencies—are weak and disorganized. Personal relationships are strained because neighbors are constantly moving. Constant resident turnover weakens communications and blocks attempts at solving neighborhood problems or establishing common goals (see Figure 6.4).[24]

Gang Formation Because social institutions are frayed or absent, law-violating youth groups and gangs form and are free to recruit neighborhood youth. Both boys and girls who feel detached and alienated from their social world are at risk to become gang members.[25]

Not surprisingly, then, there are now more than 27,000 gangs such as MS-13 in the United States, containing about 800,000 members.[26] Nor is ganging unique to the United States. In his recent book *A World of Gangs* (2008), John Hagedorn, a leading authority on the topic, shows that the culture that produces gangs in America is not

Checkpoints

▶ Because crime rates are higher in lower-class areas, many criminologists believe that the causes of crime are rooted in socioeconomic factors.

▶ Despite economic headway, there are still more than 30 million indigent Americans. Minority groups are more likely than the white majority to be poor.

▶ Some criminologists believe that destructive social forces in poverty-stricken areas are responsible for high crime rates.

▶ The strain and frustration inflicted by poverty are a suspected cause of crime.

▶ Indigents may become involved in a deviant subculture that sustains and supports criminality.

Figure 6.4 Social Disorganization Theory

Poverty
- Development of isolated lower-class areas
- Lack of conventional social opportunities
- Racial and ethnic discrimination

∨

Social disorganization
- Breakdown of social institutions and organizations such as school and family
- Lack of informal and formal social control

∨

Breakdown of traditional values
- Development of gangs, groups
- Peer group replaces family and social institutions

∨

Criminal areas
- Neighborhood becomes crime-prone
- Stable pockets of crime develop
- Lack of external support and investment

∨

Cultural transmission
Adults pass norms (focal concerns) to younger generation, creating stable lower-class culture

∨

Criminal careers
Most gang boys age out of delinquency, marry, and raise families, but some remain in life of crime

unique and that more than a billion people live in urban slums around the world. Gangs are a common feature in these disorganized areas. They engage in a variety of activities, including drug dealing and crime, and in some areas they are involved in political violence. Even though gangs they may be organized by race, their true purpose is to provide a platform for members to confront poverty, racism, and conflict. They have their own culture and language (such as gangsta rap) and members espouse a philosophy of survival by any means necessary. Gangs will flourish and expand if globalization continues to produce masses of the very poor and a few super-rich.[27]

THE WORK OF SHAW AND MCKAY

Social disorganization theory was popularized by the work of two Chicago sociologists, Clifford R. Shaw and Henry McKay, who linked life in transitional slum areas to the inclination to commit crime. Shaw and McKay began their pioneering work on Chicago crime during the early 1920s, while working as researchers for a state-supported social service agency.[28]

Shaw and McKay explained crime and delinquency within the context of the changing urban environment and ecological development of the city. They saw that Chicago had developed into distinct neighborhoods (natural areas), some affluent and others wracked by extreme poverty. These poverty-ridden **transitional neighborhoods** suffered high rates of population turnover and were incapable of inducing residents to remain and defend the neighborhoods against criminal groups.

In transitional areas, successive changes in population composition, disintegration of traditional cultures, diffusion of divergent cultural standards, and gradual industrialization dissolve neighborhood culture and organization. The continuity of conventional neighborhood traditions and institutions is broken, leaving children feeling displaced and without a strong or definitive set of values.

Concentric Zones Shaw and McKay identified the areas in Chicago that had excessive crime rates. They noted that distinct ecological areas had developed in the city, forming a series of nine concentric circles, or zones, and that there were stable and significant interzone differences in crime rates (see Figure 6.5). The areas beset by the most crime appeared to be the transitional inner-city zones, where large numbers of the city's poorest citizens had settled.[29] The zones farthest from the city's center had correspondingly lower crime rates.

Analysis of this data indicated a surprisingly stable pattern of criminal activity in the nine ecological zones over a period of 65 years. Shaw and McKay concluded that multiple cultures and diverse values, both conventional and deviant, coexist in the transitional neighborhoods. Children growing up in the street culture often find that adults who have adopted a deviant lifestyle (gamblers, pimps, drug dealers) are the most financially successful people in the neighborhood. Forced to choose between conventional and deviant lifestyles, many slum kids opt for the latter. They join other like-minded youths and form law-violating gangs and cliques. The development of teenage law-violating groups is an essential element of youthful misbehavior in slum areas. The values that slum youths adopt often conflict with existing middle-class norms, which demand strict obedience to the legal code. Consequently, a value conflict further separates the delinquent youth and his or her peer group from conventional society; the result is a more solid embrace of deviant goals and behavior. To further justify their choice of goals, these youths seek support for their choice by recruiting new members and passing on the delinquent tradition.

Shaw and McKay's statistical analysis confirmed that even though crime rates changed, the highest rates were always in Zones I and II (the central city and a transitional area, respectively). The areas with the highest crime rates retained high rates even when their ethnic composition changed (the areas that Shaw and McKay examined shifted from German and Irish to Italian and Polish).[30]

The Legacy of Shaw and McKay The social disorganization concepts articulated by Shaw and McKay have remained prominent within criminology for more than

CONNECTIONS

If social disorganization causes crime, why are most low-income people law abiding? To explain this anomaly, some sociologists have devised theoretical models suggesting that individual socialization experiences mediate environmental influences. These theories will be discussed in Chapter 7.

transitional neighborhood
An area undergoing a shift in population and structure, usually from middle-class residential to lower-class mixed-use.

Figure 6.5 Shaw and McKay's Concentric Zones Map of Chicago

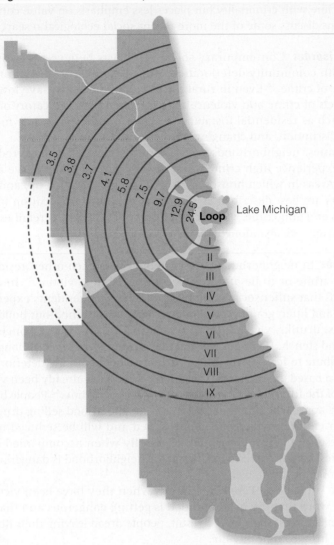

Note: Arabic numbers represent the rate of male delinquency.
SOURCE: Clifford R. Shaw et al., *Delinquency Areas* (Chicago: University of Chicago Press, 1929), p. 99. Reprinted with permission. Copyright 1929 by the University of Chicago. All rights reserved.

75 years. Although cultural and social conditions have changed over time, and today we live in a much more heterogeneous, mobile society, the most important of Shaw and McKay's findings—crime rates correspond to neighborhood structure—still holds up.[31]

Their research supported the fact that crime is a constant fixture in areas of poverty, regardless of residents' racial or ethnic identity. Because the basis of their theory was that neighborhood disintegration is the primary cause of criminal behavior, Shaw and McKay paved the way for many of the community action and development programs that have been developed in the last half-century.

THE SOCIAL ECOLOGY SCHOOL

At mid-century, social disorganization theory fell from favor after several published studies questioned its validity.[32] Criminologists turned to theories with a social-psychological orientation, stressing offender socialization within the family, school, and peer group (see Chapter 7).

Then about thirty years ago, a group of criminologists focused their attention on ecological conditions that produced high crime rates including the effects of social disorganization.[33] These contemporary social ecologists developed a purer form of structural theory that emphasizes the association of community deterioration and economic decline with criminality but places less emphasis on value conflict. The following sections discuss some of the more recent social ecological research.

Community Disorder Contemporary social ecologists believe that crime rates are associated with community deterioration: disorder, poverty, alienation, disassociation, and fear of crime.[34] Even in rural areas, which normally have low crime rates, increased levels of crime and violence are associated with indicators of social disorganization such as residential instability (a large number of people moving in and out), family disruption, and changing ethnic composition.[35]

In larger cities, neighborhoods with a high percentage of deserted houses and apartments experience high crime rates; abandoned buildings serve as a "magnet for crime."[36] Areas in which houses are in poor repair, boarded up, and burned out, whose owners are best described as slumlords, are also the location of the highest violence rates and gun crime.[37] These neighborhoods, in which retail establishments often go bankrupt, are abandoned and deteriorate physically.[38]

Community Fear In neighborhoods where people help each other, residents are less likely to fear crime or to be afraid of becoming a crime victim.[39] In disorganized neighborhoods that suffer social and physical incivilities, residents experience rowdy youths, trash and litter, graffiti, abandoned storefronts, burned-out buildings, littered lots, strangers, drunks, vagabonds, loiterers, prostitutes, noise, congestion, angry words, dirt, and stench. Having parks and playgrounds where teens hang out and loiter may contribute to fear.[40] And as fear increases, quality of life deteriorates.[41]

Fear is often based on experience. Residents who have already been victimized are more fearful of the future than those who have escaped crime.[42] People become afraid when they are approached by someone in the neighborhood selling drugs. They may fear that their children will also be approached and will be seduced into the drug life.[43] The presence of such incivilities, especially when accompanied by relatively high crime rates, convinces residents that their neighborhood is dangerous; becoming a crime victim seems inevitable.[44]

Fear can be contagious. People tell others when they have been victimized, thus spreading the word that the neighborhood is getting dangerous and that the chance of future victimization is high.[45] As a result, people dread leaving their homes at night and withdraw from community life.

Siege Mentality People who live in neighborhoods that experience high levels of crime and civil disorder become suspicious and mistrusting.[46] Minority group members may experience greater levels of fear than whites, perhaps because they may have fewer resources to address ongoing social problems.[47] They develop a sense of powerlessness, which increases levels of mistrust. Some residents become so suspicious of authority that they develop a "siege mentality," in which the outside world is considered the enemy bent on destroying the neighborhood.

Siege mentality often results in an expanding mistrust of social institutions, including business, government, and schools. Government officials seem arrogant and haughty. The police are believed to ignore crime and, when they do take action, to use excessive force.[48] As incivility increases, people lose respect for the police: They are supposed to "serve and protect," and they are not doing their job![49]

Residents' fears may not be misplaced; research does show that police are more likely to use higher levels of force when suspects are encountered in high-crime, disadvantaged neighborhoods, regardless of the suspects' behaviors or reactions.[50] When police ignore crime in poor areas, or, conversely, when they are violent and corrupt, anger flares, and people take to the streets and react in violent ways.

Community Change Recent studies recognize that change, not stability, is the hallmark of inner-city areas. A neighborhood's residents, wealth, density, and purpose are constantly evolving. Even disorganized neighborhoods acquire new identifying features. Some may become multiracial and others racially homogeneous. Some areas

Fact or Fiction?

People living in lower-class neighborhoods mistrust the government and believe that government programs are part of a plot to destroy their communities.

Fact. People in disadvantaged areas develop a siege mentality and mistrust any form of governmental involvement in their community.

Part 2 Theories of Crime Causation

Latinos show pride in their heritage at the annual Queens Hispanic Parade in Jackson Heights on September 28, 2008. The area is a bustling urban melting pot that is home to many ethnic populations, but Latino Americans predominate. Although some communities undergoing rapid change experience an upsurge in crime rates, those that attract immigrant groups often see their crime rates lowered. The reason: Immigrants have significantly lower crime rates than the native-born.

become stable and family-oriented, whereas in others, mobile, never-married people predominate.[51] Urban areas undergoing rapid structural changes in racial and economic composition also seem to experience the greatest change in crime rates.[52] In contrast, stable neighborhoods, even those with a high rate of poverty, experience relatively low crime rates and have the strength to restrict substance abuse and criminal activity.[53]

As areas decline, residents flee to safer, more stable localities. Those who can move to more affluent neighborhoods find that their lifestyles and life chances improve immediately and continue to do so over their life span.[54] Those who cannot leave because they cannot afford to live in more affluent communities face an increased risk of victimization. Because of racial differences in economic well-being, those who remain are all too often minority citizens.[55] Whites may feel threatened as the percentage of minorities in the population increases and there is more competition for jobs and political power.[56] As racial prejudice increases, the call for "law and order" aimed at controlling the minority population grows louder.[57]

Those who cannot move find themselves surrounded by a constant influx of new residents. In response to this turnover, a culture may develop that dictates, to neighborhood youths, standards of dress, language, and behavior that are in opposition to those of conventional society. All these factors are likely to produce increased crime rates.

As communities change, neighborhood deterioration precedes increasing rates of crime and delinquency.[58] Neighborhoods most at risk for increased crime contain large numbers of single-parent families and unrelated people living together, have changed from owner-occupied to renter-occupied units, and have lost semiskilled and unskilled jobs (hence the growing number of discouraged workers who are no longer seeking employment).[59] These ecological disruptions strain existing social control mechanisms and undermine their ability to control crime and delinquency.

CONNECTIONS

The racial threat theory, discussed in Chapter 2, hypothesizes that increases in the African American population will threaten the majority population and encourage more aggressive police tactics targeting minorities.

Poverty Concentration One aspect of community change may be the concentration of poverty in deteriorated urban neighborhoods.[60] William Julius Wilson describes how working- and middle-class families flee inner-city areas where poverty is pervasive, resulting in a poverty **concentration effect** in which the most disadvantaged population is consolidated in the most disorganized urban neighborhoods. Poverty concentration has been associated with income and wealth disparities, nonexistent employment opportunities, inferior housing patterns, and unequal access to health care.[61] Urban areas marked by concentrated poverty become isolated and insulated from the social mainstream and more prone to criminal activity, violence, and homicide.[62]

How does neighborhood poverty concentration produce high crime rates? White families are more likely to leave an area when they perceive that the surrounding neighborhoods have become predominantly minority.[63] As the working and middle classes move out to the suburbs, they take with them their financial and institutional resources and support.[64] The people left behind have even a tougher time coping with urban decay and conflict and controlling youth gangs and groups; after all, the most successful people in the community have left for "greener pastures." Businesses are disinclined to locate in poverty-stricken areas; banks become reluctant to lend money for new housing or businesses.[65] Unemployment rates skyrocket, destabilizing households, and unstable families are likely to produce children who use violence and aggression to deal with limited opportunity. Large groups or cohorts of people of the same age are forced to compete for relatively scarce resources.[66]

Limited employment opportunities reduce the stabilizing influence of parents and other adults, who might once have counteracted the allure of youth gangs. Sociologist Elijah Anderson's analysis of Philadelphia neighborhood life found that "old heads" (respected neighborhood residents), who at one time played an important role in socializing youths, have been displaced by younger street hustlers and drug dealers. Although the old heads may complain that these newcomers have not earned or worked for their fortunes in the old-fashioned way, they nevertheless envy these young people whose gold chains and luxury cars advertise their wealth amid poverty.[67] So the old heads admire the fruits of crime, even as they disdain the violent manner in which they are acquired.

Collective Efficacy In contrast to areas plagued by poverty concentration, cohesive communities with high levels of social control and social integration, where people know one another and develop interpersonal ties, may also develop **collective efficacy**: mutual trust, a willingness to intervene in the supervision of children, and the maintenance of public order.[68] Cohesion among neighborhood residents, combined with shared expectations for informal social control of public space, promotes collective efficacy.[69] Residents in these areas enjoy a better life because the fruits of cohesiveness can be better education, health care, and housing opportunities.[70]

In contrast, socially disorganized neighborhoods find that efforts at social control are weak and attenuated. People living in economically disadvantaged areas are significantly more likely to perceive their immediate surroundings in more negative terms (with higher levels of incivilities) than those living in areas that maintain collective efficacy.[71] When community social control efforts are blunted, crime rates increase, further weakening neighborhood cohesiveness.[72] This suggests that there are spillover effects that extend beyond the geographic boundaries of a single neighborhood.

There are three forms of collective efficacy—informal social control, institutional social control, and public social control—and all three contribute to community stability.

Informal Social Control Some elements of collective efficacy operate on the primary, or private, level and involve peers, families, and relatives. These sources exert informal control by either awarding or withholding approval, respect, and admiration. Informal control mechanisms include direct criticism, ridicule, ostracism, desertion, and physical punishment.[73]

Fact or Fiction?

Residents can help to lower community crime rates if they pull together and work to maintain public order.

Fact. According to the concept of collective efficacy, mutual aid and cooperation at the neighborhood level can in fact help lower crime rates.

CONNECTIONS

The concentration effect contradicts, in some measure, Shaw and McKay's position, discussed earlier in this chapter, that crime rates increase in transitional neighborhoods. Today the most crime-prone areas may be stable, homogeneous areas whose residents are trapped in public housing and urban ghettos.

concentration effect
As working- and middle-class families flee inner-city poverty-ridden areas, the most disadvantaged population is consolidated in urban ghettos.

collective efficacy
Social control exerted by cohesive communities and based on mutual trust, including intervention in the supervision of children and maintenance of public order.

The most important wielder of informal social control is the family, which may keep at-risk kids in check through such mechanisms as effective parenting, withholding privileges, or ridiculing lazy or disrespectful behavior. The informal social control provided by the family takes on greater importance in neighborhoods with few social ties among adults and limited collective efficacy. In these areas parents cannot call upon neighborhood resources to take up the burden of controlling children; family members face the burden of providing adequate supervision.[74] In neighborhoods with high levels of collective efficacy, parents are better able to function and effectively supervise their children. Confident and authoritative parents who live in areas that have developed collective efficacy are able to effectively deter their children from affiliating with deviant peers and getting involved in delinquent behavior.[75]

In some neighborhoods, even high-risk areas, people are willing to get involved in anticrime programs.[76] Neighbors may get involved in informal social control through surveillance practices—for example, by keeping an "eye out" for intruders when their neighbors go out of town. Informal surveillance has been found to reduce the levels of some crimes such as street robberies; however, if robbery rates remain high, surveillance may be terminated because people become fearful for their safety.[77]

Institutional Social Control Social institutions such as schools and churches cannot work effectively in a climate of alienation and mistrust. Unsupervised peer groups and gangs, which flourish in disorganized areas, disrupt the influence of those neighborhood control agents that do exist.[78] Children who reside in these neighborhoods find that involvement with conventional social institutions, such as schools and afternoon programs, is blocked; they are instead at risk for recruitment into gangs and law-violating groups.[79] As crime flourishes, neighborhood fear increases, which in turn decreases a community's cohesion and thwarts the ability of its institutions to exert social control over its residents.[80]

To combat these influences, communities that have collective efficacy attempt to use their local institutions to control crime. Sources of institutional social control include businesses, stores, schools, churches, and social service and volunteer organizations.[81] When these institutions are effective, rates for some crimes (such as burglary) decline.[82] Some institutions, such as recreation centers for teens, have been found to lower crime rates because they exert a positive effect; others, such as taverns and bars, tend to destabilize neighborhoods and increase the rate of violent crimes such as rape and robbery.[83]

©Jim West/The Image Works

Community collective efficacy can be supported by both internal and external organizations. In 1993, President Clinton signed the National and Community Service Trust Act, which established the Corporation for National and Community Service and brought the full range of domestic community service programs under the umbrella of one central organization. This legislation built on the first National and Community Service Act, signed by President George H. W. Bush in 1990. It also formally launched AmeriCorps, a network of national service programs that engage Americans in intensive service to meet the nation's critical needs in education, public safety, health, and the environment. Here, as part of their community service in an AmeriCorps program, volunteers in southwest Detroit cover up graffiti before painting murals on a building at the St. Hedwing playfield.

Public Social Control Stable neighborhoods are also able to arrange for external sources of social control. If they can draw on outside help and secure external resources—a process referred to as public social control—they are better able to reduce the effects of disorganization and maintain lower levels of crime and victimization.[84]

Concept Summary 6.1 Social Disorganization Theories

Theory	Major Premise	Strengths	Research Focus
Shaw and McKay's concentric zones theory	Crime is a product of transitional neighborhoods that manifest social disorganization and value conflict.	Identifies why crime rates are highest in slum areas. Points out the factors that produce crime. Suggests programs to help reduce crime.	Poverty; disorganization
Social ecology theory	The conflicts and problems of urban social life and communities (including fear, unemployment, deterioration, and siege mentality) influence crime rates.	Accounts for urban crime rates and trends.	Social control; fear; collective efflcacy; unemployment

The level of policing, a primary source of public social control, may vary between neighborhoods. Police presence is typically greatest when community organizations and local leaders have sufficient political clout to get funding for additional law enforcement personnel.

The presence of police sends a message that the area will not tolerate deviant behavior. Because they can respond vigorously to crime, police prevent criminal groups from gaining a toehold in the neighborhood.[85] Criminals and drug dealers avoid such areas and relocate to easier and more appealing "targets."[86] In contrast, crime rates are highest in areas where police are mistrusted because they engage in misconduct, such as use of excessive force, or because they are seemingly indifferent to neighborhood problems.[87]

In more disorganized areas, the absence of political power brokers limits access to external funding and protection. Without money from the outside, the neighborhood lacks the ability to "get back on its feet."[88] In these areas there are fewer police, and those that do patrol the area are less motivated and their resources are stretched thinner. These communities cannot mount an effective social control effort because as neighborhood disadvantage increases, the level of informal social control decreases.[89]

The government can also reduce crime by providing economic and social supports through publicly funded social support and welfare programs. Although welfare is often criticized by conservative politicians as being a government handout, there is evidence of a significant inverse association between the amount of welfare money people receive and crime rates.[90] Government assistance may help people improve their social status by providing the financial resources to clothe, feed, and educate their children, while reducing stress, frustration, and anger. Using government subsidies to reduce crime is controversial, and not all research has found that it actually works as advertised.[91]

The ramifications of having adequate controls are critical. In areas where collective efficacy remains high, children are less likely to become involved with deviant peers and engage in problem behaviors.[92] In disorganized areas, remember, the population is transient, so interpersonal relationships remain superficial. And even when an attempt is made to revitalize a disorganized neighborhood by creating institutional support programs such as community centers and better schools, the effort may be neutralized by the ongoing drain of deep-rooted economic and social deprivation.[93]

Concept Summary 6.1 lists some of the basic concepts and theories of the social disorganization view. ▶ **Checkpoints**

Checkpoints

▶ Social disorganization theory holds that destructive social forces present in inner-city areas cause the breakdown of institutions of social control and promote crime.

▶ Shaw and McKay first identified the concepts central to social disorganization. They found stable patterns of crime in the central city.

▶ The social ecology school associates community deterioration and economic decline with crime rates.

▶ Ecological factors such as community deterioration, changing neighborhoods, fear, lack of employment opportunities, incivility, poverty, and deterioration produce high crime rates.

▶ Collective efficacy can reduce neighborhood crime rates by creating greater cohesiveness.

Strain Theories

Inhabitants of a disorganized inner-city area feel isolated, frustrated, ostracized from the economic mainstream, hopeless, and eventually angry. How do these feelings affect criminal activities?

Strain theorists view crime as a direct result of frustration and anger among the lower socioeconomic classes. Although most people share similar values and goals, the ability to achieve personal goals is stratified by socioeconomic class. Strain is limited in affluent areas because educational and vocational opportunities are available. In disorganized areas, strain proliferates because legitimate avenues for success are all but closed. To relieve strain, indigent people may achieve their goals through deviant methods, such as theft or drug trafficking, or they may reject socially accepted goals and substitute more deviant goals, such as being tough and aggressive (see Figure 6.6).

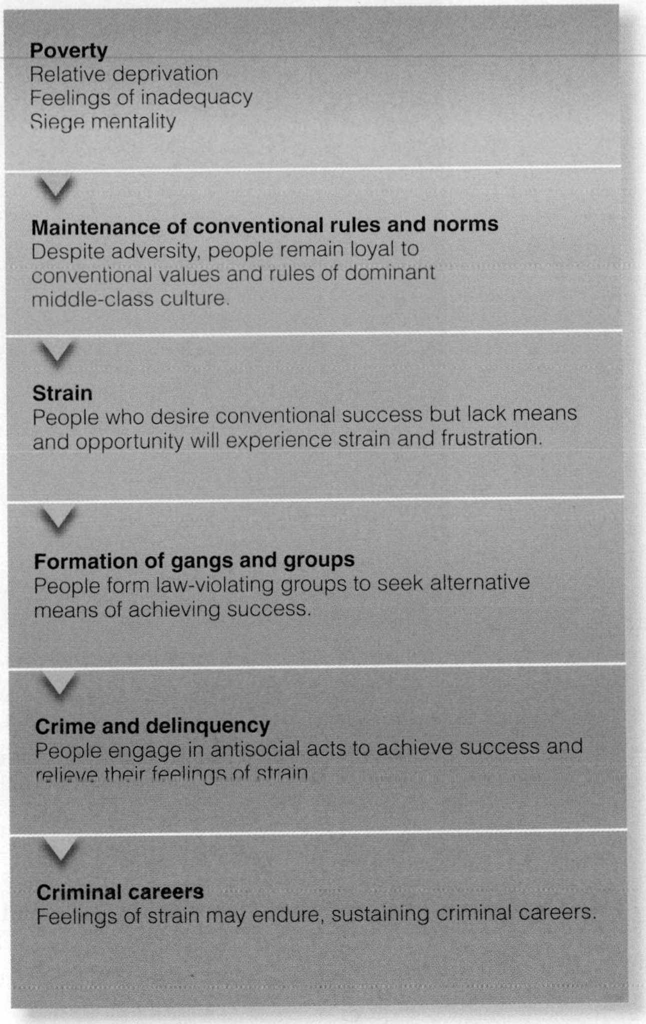

THEORY OF ANOMIE

Sociologist Robert Merton applied the sociological concepts first identified by Durkheim to criminology in his theory of anomie.[94] He found that two elements of culture interact to produce potentially anomic conditions: culturally defined goals and socially approved means for obtaining them. For example, U.S. society stresses the goals of acquiring wealth, success, and power. Socially permissible means include hard work, education, and thrift.

Merton argues that in the United States, legitimate means to acquire wealth are stratified across class and status lines. Those with little formal education and few economic resources soon find that they are denied the ability to legally acquire wealth—the preeminent success symbol. When socially mandated goals are uniform throughout society and access to legitimate means is bound by class and status, the resulting strain produces anomie among those who are locked out of the legitimate opportunity structure. Consequently, they may develop criminal or delinquent solutions to the problem of attaining goals.

Social Adaptations Merton argues that each person has his or her own concept of society's goals and his or her own degree of access to the means to attain them. Some people have inadequate means of attaining success; others, who have the means, reject societal goals. The result is a variety of social adaptations:

▶ *Conformity*. When individuals embrace conventional social goals and also have the means to attain them, they can choose to conform. They remain law-abiding.
▶ *Innovation*. When individuals accept the goals of society but are unable or unwilling to attain them through legitimate means, the resulting conflict forces them to adopt innovative solutions to their dilemma: They steal, sell drugs, or extort money. Of the five adaptations, innovation is most closely associated with criminal behavior.
▶ *Ritualism*. Ritualists gain pleasure from practicing traditional ceremonies, regardless of whether they have a real purpose or goal. The strict customs in religious orders, feudal societies, clubs, and college fraternities encourage and appeal to ritualists.
▶ *Retreatism*. Retreatists reject both the goals and the means of society. They attempt to escape their lack of success by withdrawing, either mentally or physically, through taking drugs or becoming drifters.

Figure 6.6 Basic Concepts of Strain Theory

Poverty
Relative deprivation
Feelings of inadequacy
Siege mentality

Maintenance of conventional rules and norms
Despite adversity, people remain loyal to conventional values and rules of dominant middle-class culture.

Strain
People who desire conventional success but lack means and opportunity will experience strain and frustration.

Formation of gangs and groups
People form law-violating groups to seek alternative means of achieving success.

Crime and delinquency
People engage in antisocial acts to achieve success and relieve their feelings of strain.

Criminal careers
Feelings of strain may endure, sustaining criminal careers.

John Ziebell yells at Immigration Day protest marchers as they pass by his home in New Haven, Connecticut, on May 1, 2007. Ziebell was angry because, he said, he was unemployed and had been unable to find a job. According to strain theory, conflict results when, because of rapid changes in society, a gulf develops between personal goals and the means available to achieve them. The result: alienation and conflict.

CONNECTIONS

As you may recall from Chapter 1, the roots of strain theories can be traced to Émile Durkheim's notion of anomie (from the Greek *a nomos*, "without norms"). According to Durkheim, an anomic society is one in which rules of behavior (the norms) have broken down or become inoperative during periods of rapid social change or social crisis such as war or famine.

anomie theory

The view that anomie results when socially defined goals (such as wealth and power) are universally mandated but access to legitimate means (such as education and job opportunities) is stratified by class and status.

▶ *Rebellion.* Some individuals substitute an alternative set of goals and means for conventional ones. Revolutionaries who wish to promote radical change in the existing social structure and who call for alternative lifestyles, goals, and beliefs are engaging in rebellion. Rebellion may be a reaction against a corrupt, hated government or an effort to create alternative opportunities and lifestyles within the existing system.

Evaluation of Anomie Theory According to **anomie theory**, social inequality leads to perceptions of anomie. To resolve the goals–means conflict and relieve their sense of strain, some people innovate by stealing or extorting money; others retreat into drugs and alcohol; some rebel by joining revolutionary groups; and still others get involved in ritualistic behavior by joining a religious cult.

Merton's view of anomie has been one of the most enduring and influential sociological theories of criminality. By linking deviant behavior to the success goals that control social behavior, anomie theory attempts to pinpoint the cause of the conflict that engenders personal frustration and consequent criminality. By acknowledging that society unfairly distributes the legitimate means to achieving success, anomie theory helps explain the existence of high-crime areas and the apparent predominance of delinquent and criminal behavior in the lower class. By suggesting that social conditions, not individual personalities, produce crime, Merton greatly influenced the directions taken to reduce and control criminality during the latter half of the twentieth century.

Even so, anomie theory leaves a number of questions unanswered.[95] Merton does not explain why people choose to commit certain types of crime. For example, why does one anomic person become a mugger whereas another deals drugs? Anomie may explain differences in crime rates, but it cannot explain why most young criminals desist from crime as adults. Does this mean that perceptions of anomie dwindle with age? Is anomie short-lived?

INSTITUTIONAL ANOMIE THEORY

Steven Messner and Richard Rosenfeld's **institutional anomie theory** is an updating of Merton's work.[96] Messner and Rosenfeld agree with Merton that the success goal is pervasive in American culture. For them, the **American Dream** refers to both a goal and a process. As a goal, the American Dream involves accumulating material goods and wealth via open individual competition. As a process, it involves both being socialized to pursue material success and believing that prosperity is achievable in American culture. Anomic conditions arise because the desire to succeed at any cost drives people apart, weakens the collective sense of community, fosters ambition, and restricts the desire to achieve anything other than material wealth. Achieving respect, for example, is not sufficient.

Why does anomie pervade American culture? According to Messner and Rosenfeld, it is because institutions that might otherwise control the exaggerated emphasis on financial success, such as religious or charitable institutions, have been rendered powerless or obsolete. These social institutions have been undermined in three ways:

1. Noneconomic functions and roles have been devalued. Performance in other institutional settings—the family, school, or community—is assigned a lower priority than the goal of financial success.
2. When conflicts emerge, noneconomic roles become subordinate to and must accommodate economic roles. The schedules, routines, and demands of the workplace take priority over those of the home, the school, the community, and other aspects of social life. People think nothing of leaving their neighborhood, city, or state for a better job, disrupting family relationships, and undermining informal social control.
3. Economic language, standards, and norms penetrate noneconomic realms. Economic terms become part of the common vernacular: People want to get to the "bottom line." Spouses view themselves as "partners" who "manage" the household. Retired people say they want to "downsize" their household. We "outsource" home repairs instead of doing them ourselves. Corporate leaders run for public office promising to "run the country like a business."

According to Messner and Rosenfeld, the relatively high American crime rates can be explained by the interrelationship of culture and institutions. At the cultural level, the dominance of the American Dream mythology ensures that many people will develop desires for material goods that cannot be satisfied by legitimate means. Anomie becomes a norm, and extralegal means become a strategy for attaining material wealth. At the institutional level, the dominance of economic concerns weakens the informal social control exerted by family, church, and school. These institutions have lost their ability to regulate behavior and have instead become a conduit for promoting material success. Schools are evaluated not in terms of their effectively imparting knowledge but in terms of their ability to train students to get high-paying jobs. Social conditions reinforce each other: Culture determines institutions, and institutional change influences culture.[97] Crime rates may rise in a healthy economy because national prosperity heightens the attractiveness of monetary rewards, encouraging people to gain financial success by any means necessary, including illegal means. In this culture of competition, self-interest prevails and generates amorality, acceptance of inequality, and disdain for the less fortunate.[98]

RELATIVE DEPRIVATION THEORY

There is ample evidence that neighborhood-level income inequality is a significant predictor of neighborhood crime rates.[99] Sharp divisions between the rich and the poor create an atmosphere of envy and mistrust. Criminal motivation is fueled both by perceived humiliation and by the perceived right to humiliate a victim in return.[100] Psychologists warn that under these circumstances, young males will begin to fear and envy "winners" who are doing very well at their expense. If they fail to use risky aggressive tactics, they are surely going to lose out in social competition and have

Fact or Fiction?

Crime rates always go down in a healthy economy.

Fiction. Crime rates may rise in a healthy economy because prosperity makes monetary rewards more attractive, encouraging people to gain financial success by any means necessary.

institutional anomie theory
The view that anomie pervades U.S. culture because the drive for material wealth dominates and undermines social and community values.

American Dream
The goal of accumulating material goods and wealth through individual competition; the process of being socialized to pursue material success and to believe it is achievable.

little chance of future success.[101] These generalized feelings of **relative deprivation** are precursors to high crime rates.[102]

The concept of relative deprivation was proposed by sociologists Judith Blau and Peter Blau, who combined concepts from anomie theory with those derived from social disorganization models.[103] According to the Blaus, lower-class people may feel both deprived and embittered when they compare their life circumstances to those of the more affluent. People who feel deprived because of their race or economic class eventually develop a sense of injustice and discontent. The less fortunate begin to distrust the society that has nurtured social inequality and reduced their chances of progressing by legitimate means. The constant frustration that results from these feelings of inadequacy produces pent-up aggression and hostility, eventually leading to violence and crime. The effect of inequality may be greatest when the impoverished believe that they are becoming less able to compete in a society whose balance of economic and social power is shifting further toward the already affluent. Under these conditions, the relatively poor are increasingly likely to choose illegitimate life-enhancing activities. Crime rates may then spiral upward even if the relative size of the poor population does not increase.[104]

Relative deprivation is felt most acutely by African American youths because they consistently suffer racial discrimination and economic deprivation that inflict on them a lower status than that of other urban residents.[105] Wage inequality may motivate young African American males to enter the drug trade, an enterprise that increases the likelihood that they will become involved in violent crimes.[106]

In sum, according to the relative deprivation concept, people who perceive themselves as economically deprived relative to people they know, as well as to society in general, may begin to form negative self-feelings and hostility, which motivate them to engage in deviant and criminal behaviors.[107]

GENERAL STRAIN THEORY (GST)

Sociologist Robert Agnew's **general strain theory (GST)** helps identify the micro-level, or individual-level, influences of strain. Whereas Merton and Messner and Rosenfeld try to explain social class differences in the crime rate, Agnew tries to explain why individuals who feel stress and strain are likely to commit crimes. Agnew also offers a more general explanation of criminal activity among all elements of society, rather than restricting his views to crime among the lower socioeconomic classes.[108]

Multiple Sources of Strain Agnew suggests that criminality is the direct result of **negative affective states**—the anger and frustration that emerge in the wake of destructive social relationships. He finds that negative affective states are produced by a variety of sources of strain. These are described below and summarized in Figure 6.7.

▶ *Failure to achieve positively valued goals.* This cause of strain, similar to what Merton speaks of in his theory of anomie, is a result of the disjunction between aspirations and expectations. This type of strain occurs when someone aspires to wealth and fame but, lacking financial and educational resources, assumes that such goals are impossible to achieve; he or she then turns to crime and drug dealing.
▶ *Disjunction of expectations and achievements.* Strain can also be produced by a disjunction between expectations and achievements. When people compare themselves to peers who seem to be doing a lot better financially or socially (making more money, for example, or getting better grades), even those doing relatively well feel strain. For example, when a high school senior is accepted at a good college but not at a prestigious school, like some of her friends, she will feel strain. Perhaps she is not being treated fairly because the playing field is tilted against her: "Other kids have connections," she may say. Perceptions of inequity may result in many adverse reactions, ranging from running away from its source to lowering others' benefits through physical attacks or property vandalism.

relative deprivation
Envy, mistrust, and aggression resulting from perceptions of economic and social inequality.

general strain theory (GST)
The view that multiple sources of strain interact with an individual's emotional traits and responses to produce criminality.

negative affective states
Anger, frustration, and adverse emotions produced by a variety of sources of strain.

Figure 6.7 Elements of General Strain Theory (GST)

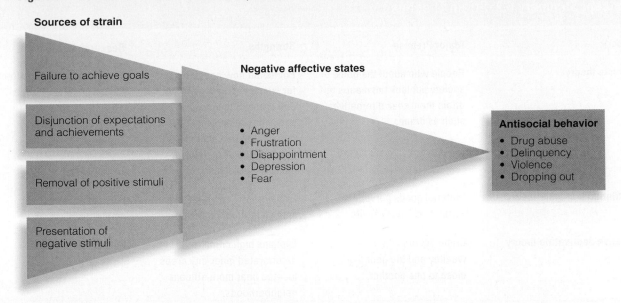

Sources of strain

- Failure to achieve goals
- Disjunction of expectations and achievements
- Removal of positive stimuli
- Presentation of negative stimuli

Negative affective states

- Anger
- Frustration
- Disappointment
- Depression
- Fear

Antisocial behavior

- Drug abuse
- Delinquency
- Violence
- Dropping out

▶ *Removal of positively valued stimuli.* Strain may occur because of the actual or anticipated loss of positively valued stimuli.[109] For example, the loss of a girlfriend or boyfriend can produce strain, as can the death of a loved one, or moving to a new neighborhood or school, or the divorce or separation of parents. The loss of positive stimuli may lead to delinquency as the adolescent tries to prevent the loss, retrieve what has been lost, obtain substitutes, or seek revenge against those responsible for the loss.

▶ *Presentation of negative stimuli.* Strain may also be caused by negative or noxious stimuli, such as child abuse or neglect, crime victimization, physical punishment, family or peer conflict, school failure, or stressful life events ranging from verbal threats to air pollution. The onset of delinquency has been linked to maltreatment through the rage and anger it generates. Children who are abused at home may take out their rage on younger children at school or become involved in violent delinquency.[110]

Although these sources of strain are independent of one another, they may overlap. For example, if a teacher insults a student, it may be viewed as an unfair application of negative stimuli that interferes with a student's academic aspirations. The greater the intensity and frequency of strain experiences, the greater their impact and the more likely they are to cause delinquency.

Consequences of Strain According to Agnew, each type of strain increases the likelihood of experiencing negative emotions such as disappointment, depression, fear, and (most important) anger. Anger increases perceptions of injury and of being wronged. It produces a desire for revenge, energizes individuals to take action, and lowers inhibitions. Violence and aggression seem justified if you have been wronged and are righteously angry. Because it produces these emotions, chronic, repetitive strain can be considered a predisposing factor for delinquency when it creates a hostile, suspicious, aggressive attitude. Individual strain episodes may trigger delinquency, such as when a particularly stressful event ignites a violent reaction.

Kids who report feelings of stress and anger are more likely to interact with delinquent peers and to engage in criminal behaviors.[111] They may join deviant groups and gangs whose law-violating activities produce even more strain and pressure to commit even more crime. For example, the angry youngster who gets involved with substance-abusing peers may feel forced to go on unwanted shoplifting sprees to pay for drugs.[112]

CONNECTIONS

The GST is not purely a structural theory because it focuses on how life events influence behavior. It therefore involves social psychological interactions and, in this regard, is reflective of the social process–based theories discussed in Chapter 7. However, Agnew's work is included here because it incorporates the view that social class position can be an important source of strain— and thus follows in the tradition of Merton's theory of anomie.

Concept Summary 6.2 Strain Theories

Theory	Major Premise	Strengths	Research Focus
Anomie theory	People who adopt the goals of society but lack the means to attain them seek alternatives, such as crime.	Points out how competition for success creates conflict and crime. Suggests that social conditions, and not personality, can account for crime. Explains high lower-class crime rates.	Frustration; anomie; effects of failure to achieve goals
Institutional anomie theory	Material goods pervade all aspects of American life.	Explains why crime rates are so high in American culture.	Frustration; effects of materialism
Relative deprivation theory	Crime occurs when the wealthy and the poor live close to one another.	Explains high crime rates in deteriorated inner-city areas located near more affluent neighborhoods.	Relative deprivation
General strain theory	Strain has a variety of sources. Strain causes crime in the absence of adequate coping mechanisms.	Identifies the complexities of strain in modern society. Expands on anomie theory. Shows the influence of social events on behavior over the life course. Explains middle-class crimes.	Strain; inequality; negative affective states; influence of negative and positive stimuli

Checkpoints

▶ Strain theories hold that economic deprivation causes frustration, which leads to crime.

▶ According to Merton's anomie theory, many people who desire material goods and other forms of economic success lack the means to achieve their goals. Some may turn to crime.

▶ Messner and Rosenfeld's institutional anomie theory argues that the goal of success at all costs has invaded every aspect of American life.

▶ Agnew's general theory of strain suggests that there is more than one source of anomie.

Coping with Strain Not all people who experience strain eventually resort to criminality. Some marshal their emotional, mental, and behavioral resources to cope with the anger and frustration produced by strain. Some individuals may be able to rationalize frustrating circumstances: Getting a good job is "just not that important"; they may be poor, but the "next guy is worse off"; if things didn't work out, they "got what they deserved." Others seek behavioral solutions, running away from adverse conditions or seeking revenge against those who caused the strain. Some try to regain emotional equilibrium with techniques ranging from physical exercise to drug abuse. Some people, especially those who are overly sensitive or emotional and who have an explosive temperament, low tolerance for adversity, and poor problem-solving skills, are less likely to cope well with strain.[113] As their perception of strain increases, so does their involvement in antisocial behaviors.[114]

Although these traits, which are linked to aggressive, antisocial behavior, seem to be stable over the life cycle, they may peak during adolescence.[115] This is a period of social stress caused by weakening parental supervision and the development of relationships with a diverse peer group. Many adolescents going through the trauma of family breakup and frequent changes in family structure feel a great deal of strain. They may react by becoming involved in precocious sexuality or by turning to substance abuse to mask the strain.[116]

As children mature, their expectations increase. Some are unable to meet academic and social demands. Adolescents are very concerned about their standing with peers. Teenagers who are deficient in these areas may find they are social outcasts, another source of strain. In adulthood, crime rates may drop because these sources of strain are reduced. New sources of self-esteem emerge, and adults seem more likely to align their goals with reality.

Evaluating GST Agnew's important work both clarifies the concept of strain and directs future research agendas. It also adds to the body of literature describing how social and life history events influence patterns of offending. Because sources of strain vary over the life course, so too do crime rates.

There is also empirical support for GST: [117]

▶ Indicators of strain—family breakup, unemployment, moving, feelings of dissatisfaction with friends and school, dropping out of school—are associated with criminality.[118]

▶ As predicted by GST, people who report feelings of stress and anger are more likely to interact with delinquent peers and to engage in criminal behaviors.[119]

▶ Minority group members are forced to live in difficult and unique social conditions that produce strain, and they may cope with strain and negative emotions through crime.[120]

▶ People who perceive strain because their success goals are blocked are more likely to engage in criminal activities.[121]

▶ The interactions predicted by GST have cross-cultural validity. Recent research conducted in South Korea found support for an association between strain factors and involvement in criminal acts. However, some culture-based differences were found, indicating that the factors that cause damaging strain may vary by time and place.[122]

Concept Summary 6.2 reviews major concepts and theories of the strain perspective.

▶ **Checkpoints**

Cultural Deviance Theory

The third branch of social structure theory combines the effects of social disorganization and strain to explain how people living in deteriorated neighborhoods react to social isolation and economic deprivation. Because their lifestyle is draining, frustrating, and dispiriting, members of the lower socioeconomic class create an independent subculture with its own set of rules and values. Whereas middle-class culture stresses hard work, delayed gratification, formal education, and being cautious, the lower-class subculture stresses excitement, toughness, taking risks, fearlessness, immediate gratification, and street smarts.

The subculture of the lower socioeconomic class is an attractive alternative because the urban poor find it impossible to meet the behavioral demands of middle-class society. However, subcultural norms often clash with conventional values. Urban dwellers must violate the law in order to obey the rules of the deviant culture with which they are in immediate contact (see Figure 6.8).

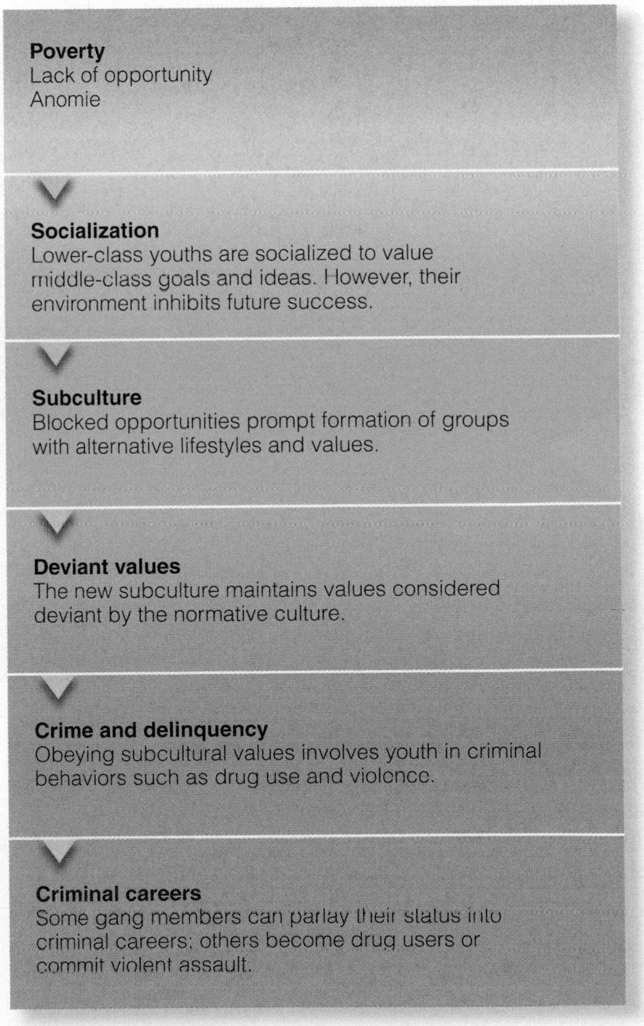

More than 50 years ago, sociologist Walter Miller identified the unique conduct norms that help define lower-class culture.[123] Miller referred to these norms as **focal concerns**, values that have evolved specifically to fit conditions in lower-class environments. The major lower-class focal concerns are set out in Exhibit 6.1.[124]

According to Miller, clinging to lower-class focal concerns promotes illegal or violent behavior. Toughness may mean displaying fighting prowess; street smarts may lead to drug deals; excitement may result in drinking, gambling, or drug abuse.[125] To illustrate, consider a recent study of violent young men in New York. Sociologist Jeffrey Fagan found that the most compelling function that violence served was to develop status as a "tough," an identity that helps young men acquire social power, while insulating them from becoming

focal concerns
Values, such as toughness and street smarts, that have evolved specifically to fit conditions in lower-class environments.

Figure 6.8 Elements of Cultural Deviance Theory

Poverty
Lack of opportunity
Anomie

Socialization
Lower-class youths are socialized to value middle-class goals and ideas. However, their environment inhibits future success.

Subculture
Blocked opportunities prompt formation of groups with alternative lifestyles and values.

Deviant values
The new subculture maintains values considered deviant by the normative culture.

Crime and delinquency
Obeying subcultural values involves youth in criminal behaviors such as drug use and violence.

Criminal careers
Some gang members can parlay their status into criminal careers; others become drug users or commit violent assault.

Exhibit 6.1 Miller's Lower-Class Focal Concerns

Trouble In lower-class communities, people are evaluated by their actual or potential involvement in making trouble. Getting into trouble includes such behaviors as fighting, drinking, and sexual misconduct. Dealing with trouble can confer prestige—for example, when a man establishes a reputation for being able to handle himself well in a fight. Not being able to handle trouble, and having to pay the consequences, can make a person look foolish and incompetent.

Toughness Lower-class males want local recognition of their physical and spiritual toughness. They refuse to be sentimental or soft and instead value physical strength, fighting ability, and athletic skill. Those who cannot meet these standards risk getting a reputation for being weak, inept, and effeminate.

Smartness Members of the lower-class culture want to maintain an image of being streetwise and savvy, using their street smarts, and having the ability to outfox and out-con the

opponent. Although formal education is not admired, knowing essential survival techniques (such as gambling, conning, and outsmarting the law) is a requirement.

Excitement Members of the lower class search for fun and excitement to enliven an otherwise drab existence. The search for excitement may lead to gambling, fighting, getting drunk, and sexual adventures. In between, the lower-class citizen may simply "hang out" and "be cool."

Fate Lower-class citizens believe their lives are in the hands of strong spiritual forces that guide their destinies. Getting lucky, finding good fortune, and hitting the jackpot are the daily dreams of most slum dwellers.

Autonomy Being independent of authority figures, such as the police, teachers, and parents, is required; losing control is an unacceptable weakness, incompatible with toughness.

SOURCE: Walter Miller, "Lower-Class Culture as a Generating Milieu of Gang Delinquency," *Journal of Social Issues* 14 (1958): 5–19.

A drug dealer openly sells marijuana on Liberty Street in the city of Newburgh, New York, on Thursday morning, August 13, 2009. According to cultural deviance theory, illegal acts such as drug dealing can become normative in some subcultures as a means of establishing financial success in an environment where conventional opportunities are blocked or nonexistent.

victims. Violence was also seen as a means to acquire the trappings of wealth (such as nice clothes, flashy cars, and access to clubs), control or humiliate another person, defy authority, settle drug-related disputes, attain retribution, satisfy the need for thrills or risk taking, and respond to challenges to one's manhood.[126]

To some criminologists, the influence of lower-class focal concerns and culture seems as relevant today as when it was first identified by Miller almost half a century ago. The accompanying Race, Culture, Gender, and Criminology feature discusses conflict as a recent version of the concept of cultural deviance.

THEORY OF DELINQUENT SUBCULTURES

Albert Cohen first articulated the theory of **delinquent subcultures** in his classic 1955 book *Delinquent Boys*.[127] Cohen's central argument was that delinquent behavior of lower-class youths is actually a protest against the norms and values of middle-class U.S. culture. Because social conditions prevent them from achieving success legitimately, lower-class youths experience a form of culture conflict that Cohen labels **status frustration**.[128] As a result, many of them join gangs and engage in behavior that is "nonutilitarian, malicious, and negativistic."[129]

Cohen viewed the delinquent gang as a separate subculture possessing a value system directly opposed

A widely cited view of the interrelationship of culture and behavior is Elijah Anderson's concept of the "code of the streets." He sees that life circumstances are tough for the "ghetto poor"—lack of jobs that pay a living wage, stigma of race, fallout from rampant drug use and drug trafficking, and alienation and lack of hope for the future. Living in such an environment places young people at special risk of crime and deviant behavior.

There are two cultural forces running through the neighborhood that shape these young people's reactions. "Decent values" are taught by families who are committed to middle-class values and to mainstream goals and standards of behavior. Although they may be better off financially than some of their street-oriented neighbors, they are generally "working

The Respect Game

Young men in poor inner-city neighborhoods build their self-image on the foundation of respect. It is understood that those who have "juice" (as respect is sometimes called on the street) can take care of themselves, even if it means resorting to violence. For street youths, losing respect on the street can be damaging and dangerous. Once they have demonstrated that they can be insulted, beaten up, or stolen from, they become an easy target. Kids from "decent" families may be able to keep their self-respect by getting good grades or a scholarship. Street kids do not have that luxury. With nothing to fall back on, they cannot walk away from an insult. They must retaliate with violence.

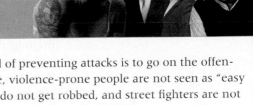

Race, Culture, Gender, and Criminology
The Code of the Streets

poor." They value hard work and self-reliance and are willing to sacrifice for their children; they harbor hopes that their sons and daughters will achieve a better future. Most go to church and take a strong interest in education. Some see their difficult situation as a test from God and derive great support from their faith and from the church community.

"Street values," by contrast, are born in the despair of inner-city life and are in opposition to those of mainstream society. The street culture has developed what Anderson calls a code of the streets, a set of informal rules setting down both proper attitudes and ways to respond if challenged. If the rules are violated, there are penalties and sometimes violent retribution.

At the heart of the code is the issue of respect—loosely defined as being treated "right." The code demands that disrespect be punished or else hard-won respect be lost. With the right amount of respect, a person can avoid "being bothered" in public. If he is bothered, not only may he be in physical danger, but he has been disgraced or "dissed" (disrespected). Some forms of dissing, such as maintaining eye contact for too long, may seem pretty mild. But to street kids who live by the code, these actions become serious indications of the other person's intentions and a warning of imminent physical confrontation.

These two orientations—decent values and street values—socially organize the community. Their coexistence means that kids who are brought up in "decent" homes must be able to successfully navigate the demands of the "street" culture. Even in decent families, parents recognize that the code must be obeyed or, at the very least, "negotiated"; it cannot simply be ignored.

One method of preventing attacks is to go on the offensive. Aggressive, violence-prone people are not seen as "easy prey." Robbers do not get robbed, and street fighters are not the favorite targets of bullies. A youth who communicates an image of not being afraid to die and not being afraid to kill has given himself a sense of power on the street.

Anderson's work has been well received by the criminological community. A number of researchers, including Timothy Brezina and his colleagues, are doing analyses to determine whether Anderson's observations are in fact valid. Using data on violence, their assessment finds a link between violent behavior and the social processes uncovered by Anderson.

CRITICAL THINKING

1. Does the code of the street, as described by Anderson, apply in the neighborhood in which you were raised? That is, is it universal?
2. Is there a form of "respect game" being played out on college campuses? If so, what is the substitute for violence?

SOURCES: Elijah Anderson, *Code of the Street: Decency, Violence, and the Moral Life of the Inner City* (New York: Norton, 2000); Elijah Anderson, "Violence and the Inner-City Street Code," in *Violence and Children in the Inner City*, ed. Joan McCord (New York: Cambridge University Press, 1998), pp. 1–30; Elijah Anderson, "The Code of the Streets," *Atlantic Monthly* 273 (May 1994): 80–94; Timothy Brezina, Robert Agnew, Francis T. Cullen, and John Paul Wright, "The Code of the Street: A Quantitative Assessment of Elijah Anderson's Subculture of Violence Thesis and Its Contribution to Youth Violence Research," *Youth Violence and Juvenile Justice* 2 (2004): 303–328.

to that of the larger society. He described the subculture as one that "takes its norms from the larger culture, but turns them upside down. The delinquent's conduct is right by the standards of his subculture precisely because it is wrong by the norms of the larger culture."[130]

According to Cohen, the development of the delinquent subculture is a consequence of socialization practices in lower-class environments. Here children lack the basic skills necessary to achieve social and economic success, including a proper education, which renders them incapable of developing the skills they need to succeed in society. Lower-class parents are incapable of teaching children the necessary techniques for entering the dominant middle-class culture. The consequences of this deprivation include developmental handicaps, poor speech and communication skills, and inability to delay gratification.

Middle-Class Measuring Rods One significant handicap that lower-class children face is the inability to positively impress authority figures, such as teachers, employers, or supervisors. In U.S. society, these positions tend to be held by members of the middle class, who have difficulty relating to the lower-class youngster. Cohen calls the standards set by these authority figures **middle-class measuring rods**.

The conflict and frustration that lower-class youths experience when they fail to meet these standards is a primary cause of delinquency. They may find themselves prejudged by others and not measuring up in the final analysis. Negative evaluations become part of a permanent "file" that follows an individual for the rest of his or her life. When the individual wants to improve, evidence of prior failures is used to discourage advancement.

Formation of Deviant Subcultures Cohen believes that lower-class boys rejected by middle-class decision makers usually join one of three existing subcultures: the corner boy, the college boy, or the delinquent boy.

The "corner boy" role is the most common response to middle-class rejection. The corner boy is not a chronic delinquent but may be a truant who engages in petty or status offenses, such as precocious sex and recreational drug abuse. His main loyalty is to his peer group, on which he depends for support, motivation, and interest. His values, therefore, are those of the group with which he is in close contact. The corner boy, well aware of his failure to achieve the standards of the American Dream, retreats into the comforting world of his lower-class peers and eventually becomes a stable member of his neighborhood, holding a menial job, marrying, and remaining in the community.

The "college boy" embraces the cultural and social values of the middle class. Rather than scorning middle-class measuring rods, he actively strives to succeed by those standards. Cohen views this type of youth as one who is embarking on an almost hopeless path because he is ill-equipped academically, socially, and linguistically to achieve the rewards of middle-class life.

The "delinquent boy" adopts a set of norms and principles that directly oppose middle-class values. He engages in short-run hedonism, living for today and letting "tomorrow take care of itself."[131] Delinquent boys strive for group autonomy. They resist efforts by family, school, or other sources of authority to control their behavior. Frustrated by their inability to succeed, these boys resort to a process to which Cohen attaches the psychoanalytic term **reaction formation**. This process includes overly intense responses that seem disproportionate to the stimuli that trigger them. For the delinquent boy, this takes the form of irrational, malicious, and unaccountable hostility to the enemy, which in this case is "the norms of respectable middle-class society."[132]

Cohen's approach skillfully integrates strain and social disorganization theories and has become an enduring element of criminological literature.

delinquent subculture
A value system adopted by lower-class youths that is directly opposed to that of the larger society.

status frustration
A form of culture conflict experienced by lower-class youths because social conditions prevent them from achieving success as defined by the larger society.

middle-class measuring rods
The standards by which authority figures, such as teachers and employers, evaluate lower-class youngsters and often prejudge them negatively.

reaction formation
Irrational hostility evidenced by young delinquents, who adopt norms directly opposed to middle-class goals and standards that seem impossible to achieve.

THEORY OF DIFFERENTIAL OPPORTUNITY

In their classic work *Delinquency and Opportunity*, written more than 50 years ago, Richard Cloward and Lloyd Ohlin combined strain and social disorganization principles to portray a gang-sustaining criminal subculture.[133]

The centerpiece of Cloward and Ohlin's theory is **differential opportunity**. According to this concept, people in all strata of society share the same success goals; however, those in the lower socioeconomic class have limited means of achieving them. People who perceive themselves as failures within conventional society will seek alternative or innovative ways to succeed. People who conclude that there is little hope for legitimate advancement may join like-minded peers to form a gang, which can provide them with emotional support. The youth who is considered a failure at school and is qualified for only a menial job at the minimum wage can earn thousands of dollars, plus the respect of his or her peers, by joining a gang and taking part in drug deals or armed robberies.

Cloward and Ohlin recognize that the opportunity for success in both conventional and criminal careers is limited. In stable areas, adolescents may be recruited by professional criminals, drug traffickers, or organized crime groups. Unstable areas, however, cannot support flourishing criminal opportunities. In these socially disorganized neighborhoods, adult role models are absent, and young criminals have few opportunities to join established gangs or learn the fine points of professional crime. Their most important finding, then, is that all opportunities for success, both illegal and conventional, are closed for the most disadvantaged youths. Because of differential opportunity, young people are likely to join one of three types of gangs.

▶ *Criminal gangs.* These gangs exist in stable neighborhoods where close connections among adolescent, young adult, and adult offenders create an environment for successful criminal enterprise.[134] Youths are recruited into established criminal gangs that provide training for a successful criminal career. Gang membership is a learning experience in which the knowledge and skills needed for success in crime are acquired. During this apprenticeship, older, more experienced members of the criminal subculture hold youthful trainees on tight reins, limiting activities that might jeopardize the gang's profits (for example, engaging in nonfunctional, irrational violence).

▶ *Conflict gangs.* These gangs develop in communities unable to provide either legitimate or illegitimate opportunities.[135] They attract tough adolescents who fight with weapons to win respect from rivals and engage in unpredictable and destructive assaults on people and property. Conflict gang members must be ready to fight to protect their own and their gang's integrity and honor. By doing so, they acquire a "rep," which gains them admiration from their peers and consequently helps them buttress their self-image.

▶ *Retreatist gangs.* Retreatists are double failures, unable to gain success through legitimate means and unwilling to do so through illegal ones. Members of the retreatist subculture constantly search for ways of getting high—alcohol, pot, heroin, unusual sexual experiences, music. To feed their habits, retreatists develop a "hustle"—pimping, conning, selling drugs, or committing petty crimes. Personal status in the retreatist subculture is derived from peer approval.

Cloward and Ohlin's theory integrates cultural deviance and social disorganization variables and recognizes different modes of criminal adaptation. The fact that criminal cultures can be supportive, rational, and profitable seems to reflect the actual world of the delinquent more realistically than Cohen's original view of purely negativistic, destructive delinquent youths who reject all social values.

Concept Summary 6.3 reviews the major concepts of cultural deviance theory.

▶ **Checkpoints**

Checkpoints

▶ Cultural deviance theory shows how subcultures develop with norms in opposition to the general society.

▶ Walter Miller describes the focal concerns that shape this subculture.

▶ Albert Cohen analyzes the lifestyle of delinquent boys, revealing how they obey an independent social code with its own values.

▶ Cohen shows how members of the lower class fail when they are judged by "middle-class measuring rods."

▶ Richard Cloward and Lloyd Ohlin find that deviant subcultures form when people believe that their legitimate opportunities are blocked or impaired.

▶ Crime prevention efforts have been aimed at increasing the conventional options for success open to members of the lower class.

differential opportunity
The view that lower-class youths, whose legitimate opportunities are limited, join gangs and pursue criminal careers as alternative means to achieve universal success goals.

Theory	Major Premise	Strengths	Research Focus
Miller's focal concern theory	Citizens who obey the street rules of lower-class life (focal concerns) find themselves in conflict with the dominant culture.	Identifies the core values of lower-class culture and shows their association to crime.	Cultural norms; focal concerns
Cohen's theory of delinquent gangs	Status frustration of lower-class boys, created by their failure to achieve middle-class success, causes them to join gangs.	Shows how the conditions of lower-class life produce crime. Explains violence and destructive acts. Identifies conflict of lower class with middle class.	Gangs; culture conflict; middle-class measuring rods; reaction formation
Cloward and Ohlin's theory of opportunity	Blockage of conventional opportunities causes lower-class youths to join criminal, conflict, or retreatist gangs.	Shows that even illegal opportunities are structured in society. Indicates why people become involved in a particular type of criminal activity. Presents a way of preventing crime.	Gangs; cultural norms; culture conflict; effects of blocked opportunity

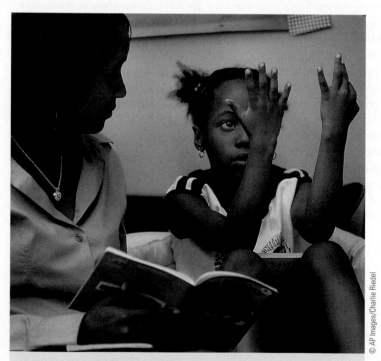

Public policy based on social structure theories may emphasize opening up opportunities to those who may not experience them in their current circumstances. Here, University of Missouri–Kansas City freshman Destiny Byers (left) watches first-grader Destiny Evans learning to count at the Santa Fe Accelerated Elementary School in Kansas City. Byers is one of 11 students in UMKC's Institute for Urban Education program, which trains inner-city students to become inner-city teachers.

© AP Images/Charlie Riedel

Social Structure Theory and Public Policy

Social structure theory has significantly influenced public policy. If the cause of criminality is viewed as a schism between lower-class individuals and conventional goals, norms, and rules, it seems logical that alternatives to criminal behavior can be provided by giving inner-city youth opportunities to share in the rewards of conventional society.

One approach is to give indigent people direct financial aid through public assistance or welfare. Although welfare has been curtailed under the Federal Welfare Reform Act of 1996, research shows that crime rates decrease when families receive supplemental income through public assistance payments.[136]

Efforts have also been made to reduce crime by improving the community structure in inner-city high-crime areas. Crime prevention efforts based on social structure precepts can be traced back to the Chicago Area Project supervised by Clifford Shaw. This program attempted to organize existing community structures to develop social stability in otherwise disorganized slums. The project sponsored recreation programs for neighborhood children, including summer camping. It campaigned for community improvements in education, sanitation, traffic safety, resource conservation, and law enforcement. Project members also worked with police and court agencies to supervise and treat gang youth and adult offenders.

Thinking Like a Criminologist

You have accepted a position in Washington as an assistant to the undersecretary of urban affairs. The secretary informs you that he wants to initiate a demonstration project in a major city to show that government can reduce poverty, crime, and drug abuse.

The area he has chosen is a large inner-city neighborhood in a midwestern city of more than 3 million people. It suffers disorganized community structure, poverty, and hopelessness. Predatory delinquent gangs run free, terrorizing local merchants and citizens. The school system has failed to provide opportunities and educational experiences sufficient to dampen enthusiasm for gang recruitment. Stores, homes, and public buildings are deteriorated and decayed. Commercial enterprise has fled the area, and civil

servants are reluctant to enter the neighborhood. There is an uneasy truce among the varied ethnic and racial groups that populate the area. Residents feel that little can be done to bring the neighborhood back to life. Merchants are afraid to open stores, and there is little outside development from major retailers or manufacturers. People who want to start their own businesses find that banks will not lend them money.

One of the biggest problems has been the large housing projects built in the 1960s. These are now overcrowded and deteriorated. Police are actually afraid to enter the buildings unless they arrive with a SWAT team. Each building is controlled by a gang whose members demand tribute from the residents.

Writing Assignment

Write a proposal outlining a redevelopment program to revitalize the area and eventually bring down the crime rate. In your essay, describe how the public or private sector can help with this overwhelming problem. Discuss how private industry can help in the struggle. What programs would you recommend to break the cycle of urban poverty?

Social structure concepts, especially Cloward and Ohlin's views, were a critical ingredient in the Kennedy and Johnson administrations' War on Poverty, begun in the early 1960s. War on Poverty programs—Head Start, Neighborhood Legal Services, and the Community Action Program—have continued to help people. Today the Weed and Seed program is a descendant of the social structure approach to crime prevention. This community-based strategy, sponsored by the U.S. Department of Justice (DOJ), involves a two-pronged approach: law enforcement agencies and prosecutors cooperate in "weeding out" violent criminals and drug abusers, and public agencies and community-based private organizations collaborate to "seed" much-needed human services, including prevention, intervention, treatment, and neighborhood restoration programs. A community-oriented policing component bridges the weeding and seeding elements. There are now more than 250 Weed and Seed sites that range in size from several neighborhood blocks to several square miles, with populations ranging from 3,000 to 50,000.[137]

Summary

1. Be familiar with the different elements of the U.S. social structure.

   People in the United States live in a stratified society; social strata are created by the unequal distribution of wealth, power, and prestige. There are now 37 million Americans living in poverty. The crushing lifestyle of lower-class areas produces a culture of poverty that is passed from one generation to the next and characterized by apathy, cynicism, helplessness, and mistrust of social institutions. Children in these areas are hit especially hard by poverty. The burdens of underclass life

   are often felt most acutely by minority group members. Almost 25 percent of African Americans and 22 percent of Latino Americans still live in poverty, compared to less than 10 percent of whites.

2. Describe the association between social structure and crime.

   According to social structure theory, the root cause of crime is the socioeconomic disadvantages that have become embedded in American society. People in the lower class are driven to desperate measures, such as crime and substance abuse, to cope with th economic plight. Aggravating this dynamic is the constant media bombardment linking material possessions to self-worth.

3. Know the elements of social disorganization theory.

This theory focuses on the urban conditions that affect crime rates. Crime occurs in disorganized areas where institutions of social control, such as the family, commercial establishments, and schools, have broken down and can no longer perform their expected or stated functions. Indicators of social disorganization include high unemployment and school dropout rates, deteriorated housing, low income levels, and large numbers of single-parent households. Residents in these areas experience conflict and despair, and as a result, antisocial behavior flourishes.

4. Be familiar with the views of Shaw and McKay.

Shaw and McKay explained crime and delinquency within the context of the changing urban environment and ecological development of the city. Poverty-ridden transitional neighborhoods suffer high rates of population turnover and often cannot induce residents to remain and defend the neighborhoods against criminal groups. The values that slum youths adopt often conflict with existing middle-class norms, which demand strict obedience to the legal code. Consequently, a value conflict further separates the delinquent youth and his or her peer group from conventional society; the result is a more solid embrace of deviant goals and behavior.

5. Know the various elements of ecological theory.

Crime rates and the need for police services are associated with community deterioration: disorder, poverty, alienation, disassociation, and fear of crime. In larger cities, neighborhoods with a high percentage of deserted houses and apartments experience high crime rates. As fear increases, quality of life deteriorates. People who live in neighborhoods that experience high levels of crime and civil disorder become suspicious, distrust authorities, and may develop a "siege mentality." As areas decline, residents flee to safer, more stable localities.

6. Be able to discuss the association between collective efficacy and crime.

Cohesive communities develop collective efficacy: mutual trust, a willingness to intervene in the supervision of children, and the maintenance of public order. Some elements of collective efficacy operate on the primary, or private, level and involve peers, families, and relatives. Communities that have collective efficacy attempt to use their local institutions to control crime. Stable neighborhoods are also able to arrange for external sources of social control.

7. Discuss the concept of strain.

Strain theorists argue that although people in all economic strata share similar social and economic goals, the ability to obtain these goals is class dependent. Most people in the United States desire wealth, material possessions, power, prestige, and other life comforts. Members of the lower class are unable to obtain these symbols of success through conventional means. Consequently, they feel anger, frustration, and resentment, referred to collectively as strain.

8. Know what is meant by the term "anomie."

Merton argues that in the United States, legitimate means to acquire wealth are stratified across class and status lines. Some people have inadequate means of attaining success; others who have the means reject societal goals. To resolve the goals–means conflict and relieve their sense of strain, some people innovate by stealing or extorting money; others retreat into drugs and alcohol; some rebel by joining revolutionary groups; and still others get involved in ritualistic behavior by joining a religious cult.

9. Discuss the concept of negative affective states.

Agnew suggests that criminality is the direct result of negative affective states—the anger, frustration, and adverse emotions that emerge in the wake of destructive social relationships. He finds that negative affective states are produced by a variety of sources of strain, including failure to achieve success, application of negative stimuli, and removal of positive stimuli.

10. Discuss the elements of cultural deviance theory.

Cultural deviance theory combines elements of both strain theory and social disorganization theory. A unique lower-class culture has developed in disorganized neighborhoods. These independent subcultures maintain unique values and beliefs that conflict with conventional social norms. Criminal behavior is an expression of conformity to lower-class subcultural values and traditions, not a rebellion from conventional society. Subcultural values are handed down from one generation to the next in a process called cultural transmission.

Key Terms

stratified society 136
social class 136
culture of poverty 137
underclass 137

social structure
    theory 139
social disorganization
    theory 142

strain theory 142
strain 142
cultural deviance
    theory 142

subculture 142
cultural transmission 142
transitional
    neighborhood 144

Critical Thinking Questions

1. Is there a "transitional" area in your town or city? Does the crime rate remain constant there, regardless of who moves in or out?

2. Is it possible that a distinct lower-class culture exists? Do you know anyone who has the focal concerns Miller talks about? Were there "focal concerns" in your high school or college experience?

3. Have you ever perceived anomie? What causes anomie? Is there more than one cause of strain?

4. How would Merton explain middle-class crime? How would Agnew?

5. Could "relative deprivation" produce crime among college-educated white-collar workers?

© AP Images/Gregory Smith

Chapter Outline

Social Process Theories

7

Teenager Genarlow Wilson was an honor student, a gifted athlete, attractive, popular, and outgoing. He had a 3.2 grade point average, he was All Conference in football, he was voted 11th-grade prom prince, and his senior year was capped off with a distinguished honor: He was elected Douglas County High's first-ever homecoming king. He was supposed to be a star athlete in college, but instead Wilson was sentenced to 10 years in a Georgia prison. His crime: engaging in consensual sex when he was 17 years old with a girl two years younger. Wilson was convicted of aggravated child molestation, even though he and the girl were both minors at the time and the sex was clearly consensual.

Wilson engaged in oral sex with the girl during a wild party involving a bunch of kids, marijuana, and alcohol—all captured on videotape. The tapes made it clear that the sex was voluntary and not coerced. Although the prosecutor favored leniency, Wilson refused to plea bargain because that would mean admitting he was a sexual predator—a charge he vehemently denied and that no one, including the prosecutor, believed was true. Ironically, if the couple had had sexual intercourse, it would have been considered a misdemeanor, but because oral sex was involved, the crime was considered a felony. An additional irony in the case is that soon after Wilson was convicted, the public outcry forced Georgia to change the law and make consensual oral sex a misdemeanor. But the new law does not apply retroactively, and Wilson was sent to prison hoping for some type of legal reprieve.[1] The case sparked a national outcry, and on October 26, 2007, the Georgia State Supreme Court, though not overturning the conviction itself, ruled that Wilson's sentence was cruel and unusual ("grossly disproportionate"). The crusade to free Genarlow worked, and he was released after serving over 2 years of his 10-year prison sentence in the Al Burruss Correctional Training Center in Forsyth, Georgia.

Fact or Fiction?

▶ No matter where kids live, even in a high-poverty area, having effective parents can reduce the lure of gangs and street crime.

▶ Parents today are too lenient. If they toughened up discipline, they could straighten out rebellious teens.

▶ High school dropouts are crime-prone troublemakers.

▶ Disturbed loners become delinquents; popular kids are too busy to commit crime.

▶ Being exposed to criminal parents and parental deviance is closely linked to crime.

▶ Criminals have a unique antisocial lifestyle that takes up all of their time.

▶ "Idle hands are the devil's workshop" is merely an old saying. Kids who work outside the home are the ones most likely to get into trouble.

Chapter Objectives

1. Be familiar with the concepts of social process and socialization.

2. Be able to discuss the differences among social learning theory, social control theory, and social reaction (labeling) theory.

3. Discuss the effect of family relationships on crime.

4. Understand how the educational setting influences crime.

5. Be aware of the link between peers and delinquency.

6. Be familiar with the association between beliefs and criminality.

7. Discuss the main types of social learning theory.

8. Be familiar with the principles of social control theory.

9. Know the basic elements of social reaction (labeling) theory.

10. Link social process theory to crime prevention efforts.

Genarlow Wilson's case shows how social interactions and processes shape crime and can label some people as criminals. He did not consider himself a criminal and, even in court, denied his culpability. Here is an exchange he had with the prosecutor during his trial:

Genarlow: . . . Aggravated child molestation is when like a 60-year—some old man like messing with 10-year-old girls. I'm 17, the girl was 15, sir. You call that child molestation, two years apart?

Barker: I didn't write the law.

Genarlow: I didn't write the law, either.

Barker: That's what the law states is aggravated child molestation, Mr. Wilson, not me.

Genarlow: Well, sir, I understand you're just doing your job. I don't blame you. . . . But do you think it's fair? . . . Would you want your son on trial for something like this?[2]

Should Genarlow Wilson ever have been labeled a "sexual predator"? If he had engaged in a different type of sex act, the case would never have been made public. The law itself was designed to protect young girls from being abused by much older men, not by members of their own peer group with whom they were socializing freely. And if the act itself was so bad, why was it legalized a short time later? The bottom line: If the party had occurred a few months later, Genarlow Wilson might have been playing football at Georgia State University instead of serving time in Georgia State Prison!

Genarlow Wilson was in fact labeled a sexual predator and sent to prison because those in power, who define the law and control its process, decided that his behavior constituted a serious crime, a felony. He was released when those in power decided that he was not really a felon and that the law was not intended to apply to his behavior.

social process theory
The view that criminality is a function of people's interactions with various organizations, institutions, and processes in society.

social learning theory
The view that people learn to be aggressive by observing others acting aggressively to achieve some goal or being rewarded for violent acts.

social control theory
The view that people commit crime when the forces binding them to society are weakened or broken.

social reaction (labeling) theory
The view that people become criminals when they are labeled as such and accept the label as a personal identity.

Some criminologists focus their attention on the social processes and interactions that occur in all segments of society. They believe that, rather than strictly being a product of their environment and their place in the social structure, most people are shaped by their interactions with social institutions such as schools and with social groups, such as family, peers, and neighbors. As we develop and are socialized over the life course, our relationships can be either positive and supportive, or dysfunctional and destructive. If the latter is the norm, then conventional success may be impossible for that individual to achieve. Criminal solutions may become the only feasible alternative. This view of crime is referred to as **social process theory**.

The social process approach has several independent branches. These are described briefly below and discussed in detail later in this chapter.

▶ **Social learning theory** suggests that people learn the techniques and attitudes of crime from close relationships with criminal peers: Crime is a learned behavior.
▶ **Social control theory** maintains that everyone has the potential to become a criminal, but most people are controlled by their bonds to society. Crime occurs when the forces that bind people to society are weakened or broken.
▶ **Social reaction (labeling) theory** holds that people become criminals when significant members of society label them as such and they accept those labels as a personal identity.

To put it another way, social learning theories assume that people are born good and learn to be bad; social control theory assumes that people are born bad and must be controlled in order to be good; and social reaction theory assumes that whether good or bad, people are shaped, directed, and influenced by the evaluations of others. Despite their apparent differences, social process theories share one basic concept: All people, regardless of their race, class, or gender, have the potential to become delinquents or criminals. Although members of the lower socioeconomic class bear the added burdens of poverty, racism, poor schools, and disrupted family lives, these social forces can be counteracted by positive peer relations, a supportive family, and educational success. And conversely, even the most affluent members of society may turn to antisocial behavior if their life experiences are damaging and/or destructive.

Institutions of Socialization

Social process theorists have long studied the critical elements of **socialization** to determine how they contribute to a burgeoning criminal career. Their view relies on the fact that interaction with key social institutions helps control human behavior. Prominent among these elements are the individual's family, peer group, school, and church.

FAMILY RELATIONS

Family relationships are considered a major determinant of behavior.[3] In fact, parenting factors, such as the ability to communicate and to provide proper discipline, may play a critical role in determining whether people misbehave as children and even later as adults. The family–crime relationship is significant across racial, ethnic, and gender lines, and this is one of the most replicated findings in the criminological literature.[4]

Parents who are supportive and who effectively control their children in a noncoercive way are more likely to raise children who refrain from delinquency; this phenomenon is referred to as **parental efficacy**.[5] Delinquency is reduced when parents provide the type of structure that integrates children into families, while giving them the ability to assert their individuality and regulate their own behavior.[6] Kids who report having troubled home lives also exhibit lower levels of self-esteem and are more prone to antisocial behaviors.[7]

In contrast, children who have warm and affectionate ties to their parents report greater levels of self-esteem beginning in adolescence and extending into their adulthood; high self-esteem is inversely related to criminal behavior.[8] As important as it is, parental efficacy is sometimes compromised by family disruption and separation. Divorce forces many kids to live in single-parent households that are more likely to suffer economic and other social problems that are less likely to plague intact families.[9] Figure 7.1 illustrates the percentage of children living in single-parent households by state.

The concept of family functioning and crime and the factors that disturb this interaction are discussed in the accompanying Current Issues in Crime feature on page 171.

Other family factors that have predictive value include the following:

▶ Marital distress and conflict are significantly related to harsh and hostile negative parenting styles. Adolescents who live in this type of environment develop poor emotional well-being, externalizing problems, and antisocial behavior.[10]
▶ Adolescents who do not receive affection from their parents during childhood are more likely to use illicit drugs and to be more aggressive as they mature.[11]

© AP Images/Nati Harnik

In July 2008, Nebraska adopted a "safe haven" law that allowed parents of children ages 18 and under to abandon them with impunity at local hospitals. The law was changed in November 2008, allowing only infants up to 30 days old to be abandoned. Before the law was amended, 36 children were dropped off in Nebraska hospitals over a four-month period, and none was an infant. Here, the mother of an 18-year-old daughter looks at a photograph in her daughter's room in Lincoln, Nebraska. She was one of the 36 parents who left children at a hospital; she acted in the hope that her daughter could get help. Would a safe haven law such as Nebraska's help or hinder the socialization process?

socialization
Process of human development and enculturation. Socialization is influenced by key social processes and institutions.

parental efficacy
The ability of parents to be supportive of their children and effectively control them in noncoercive ways.

Figure 7.1 Children Living in Single-Parent Households by State

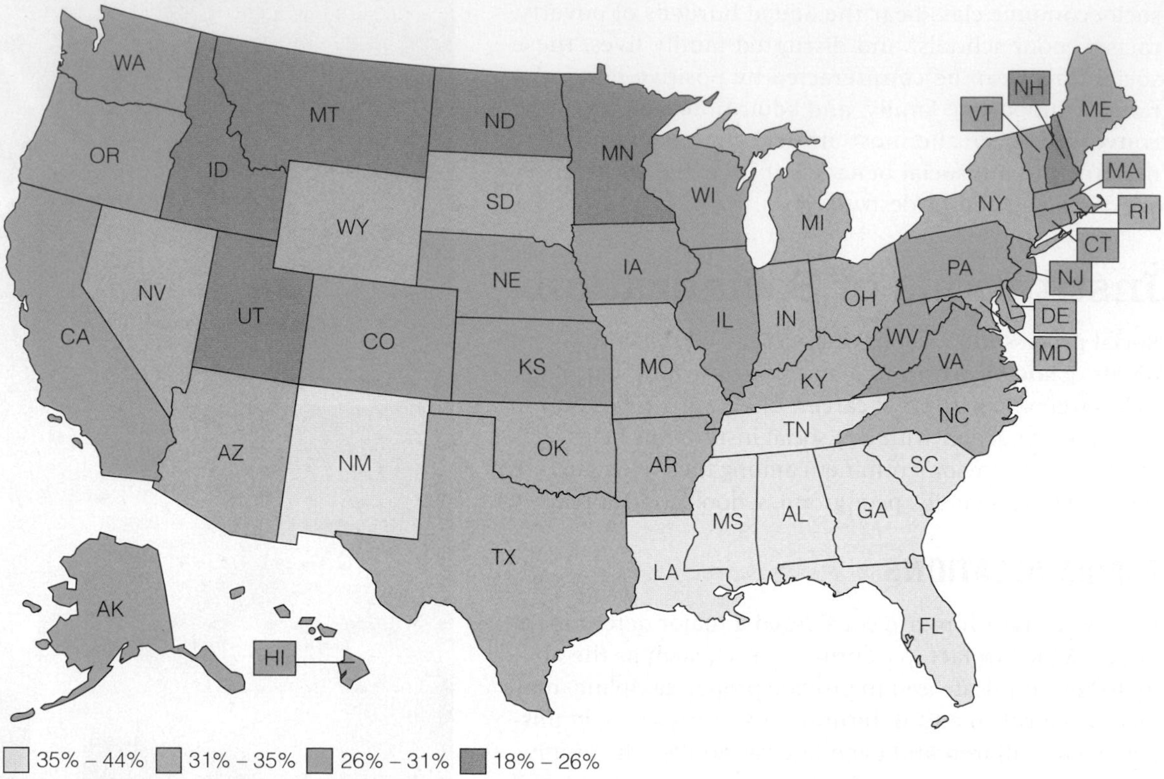

☐ 35% – 44% ☐ 31% – 35% ☐ 26% – 31% ☐ 18% – 26%

SOURCE: Annie E. Casey Foundation, Kids Count Data Center, 2009, http://datacenter.kidscount.org/data/acrossstates/Map.aspx?loct=2&ind=106&dtm=430&tf=18

Fact or Fiction?

No matter where kids live, even in a high-poverty area, having effective parents can reduce the lure of gangs and street crime.

Fact. Criminologists link parental efficacy and effectiveness to higher self-esteem and lower crime rates.

CONNECTIONS

Chapter 2's analysis of the relationship between socioeconomic class and crime showed why this relationship is still a hotly debated topic. Although serious criminals may be found disproportionately in lower-class areas, self-report studies show that criminality cuts across class lines. Middle-class use and abuse of recreational drugs, discussed in Chapter 13, suggests that law violators are not necessarily economically motivated.

▶ Children growing up in homes where a parent suffers mental impairment are also at risk for delinquency.[12]

▶ Children whose parents abuse drugs are more likely to become persistent substance abusers than the children of nonabusers.[13]

▶ Children (both males and females, both black and white) who experience abuse, neglect, or sexual abuse are believed to be more crime-prone and to suffer more from other social problems, such as depression, suicide attempts, and self-injurious behaviors.[14] Mental health and delinquency experts have found that abused kids experience mental and social problems across their life span, problems ranging from substance abuse to damaged personality.[15]

▶ Children who grow up in homes where parents use strict discipline, and where children lack parental warmth and involvement in their lives, are prone to antisocial behavior.[16] Links have been found among corporal punishment, delinquency, anger, spousal abuse, depression, and adult crime.[17]

The effects of family dysfunction are felt well beyond childhood. Kids who experience high levels of family conflict grow up to lead stressful adult lives, punctuated by periods of depression.[18] Children whose parents are harsh, angry, and irritable are likely to behave in the same way toward their own children, putting their own offspring at risk.[19] Thus, the seeds of adult dysfunction are planted early in childhood.

EDUCATIONAL EXPERIENCE

The educational process and adolescent school achievement have been linked to criminality. Children who do poorly in school, lack educational motivation, and feel alienated are the most likely to engage in criminal acts.[20] Children who fail in school offend more frequently than those who succeed. These children commit more serious and more violent offenses, and their criminal behavior regularly persists into adulthood.[21]

R and Conger is one of the nation's leading experts on family life. For the past two decades he has been involved with four major community studies that have examined the influence of economic stress on families, children, and adolescents; in sum these studies involve almost 1,500 families and over 4,000 individual family members who represent a diverse cross section of society. The extensive information that has been collected on all of these families over time includes reports by family members, videotaped discussions in the home, and data from schools and other community agencies.

One thing that Conger and his associates have learned is that in all of these different types of families, economic stress appears to have a harmful effect on parents and

turn, increase children's risk of suffering developmental problems, such as depressed mood, substance abuse, and engaging in delinquent behaviors. These economic stress processes also decrease children's ability to function in a competent manner in school and with peers.

The findings also show, however, that parents who remain supportive of one another, and who demonstrate effective problem-solving skills in spite of hardship, can disrupt this negative process and shield their children and themselves from these adverse consequences of economic stress. These parenting skills can be taught and used by human service professionals to assist families experiencing economic pressure or similar stresses in their lives.

Current Issues in Crime Family Functioning and Crime

children. According to his "Family Stress Model" of economic hardship, such factors as low income and income loss increase parents' sadness, pessimism about the future, anger, despair, and withdrawal from other family members. Economic stress has this impact on parents' social-emotional functioning through the daily pressures it creates for them, such as being unable to pay bills or acquire basic necessities such as adequate food, housing, clothing, and medical care. As parents become more emotionally distressed, they tend to interact with one another and their children in a more irritable and less supportive fashion. These patterns of behavior increase instability in the marriage and also disrupt effective parenting practices, such as monitoring children's activities and using consistent and appropriate disciplinary strategies. Marital instability and disrupted parenting, in

CRITICAL THINKING

To help deal with these problems, Conger advocates support for social policies that adequately aid families during stressful times as they recover from downturns in the economy. He also advocates educating parents about effective strategies for managing the economic, emotional, and family relationship challenges they will face when hardship occurs. What would you add to the mix to improve family functioning in America?

SOURCES: Rand Conger and Katherine Conger, "Understanding the Processes through Which Economic Hardship Influences Families and Children," in D. Russell Crane and Tim B. Heaton, *Handbook of Families and Poverty* (Thousand Oaks, CA: Sage Publications, 2008), pp. 64–81; Iowa State University, Institute for Social and Behavioral Research, The Research of Rand Conger, www.isbr.iastate.edu/staff/Personals/rdconger/

Dropping Out Even though national dropout rates are in decline, more than 10 percent of Americans aged 16 to 24 have left school permanently without a diploma; of these, more than 1 million withdrew before completing 10th grade. There are still ethnic racial gaps in graduation rates. Students from historically disadvantaged minority groups (American Indian, Hispanic, African American) have little more than a 50–50 chance of finishing high school with a diploma.[22] The research on the effect of dropping out is a mixed bag: Some research findings indicate that school dropouts face a significant chance of entering a criminal career, but other efforts using sophisticated methodological tools have failed to find a dropout effect.[23] If there *is* a "dropout effect," it is because those who do leave school early already have a long history of poor school performance and antisocial behaviors.[24] In other words, poor school performance predicts both dropping out and antisocial activity. Even if dropping out is not directly related to crime, it reduces earnings and dampens future life achievements.

Fact or Fiction?

Parents today are too lenient. If they toughened up discipline, they could straighten out rebellious teens.

Fiction. Most of the existing literature links strict discipline and corporal punishment to antisocial behavior. Effective parenting is the key to controlling youthful misbehavior.

Social process theories hold that socialization is a key element in the shaping of human behavior and that impaired socialization can have devastating effects. Peer group conflict, for example, can lead to disaster. Here Norman Keene, 35, stepfather of Jaheem Herrera, 11, embraces his daughter Ny'itsa Keene, 5, while discussing Jaheem's suicide at the family's apartment on April 20, 2009. Jaheem hanged himself with a belt after coming home from Dunaire Elementary School in DeKalb County, Georgia, where he was being bullied by fellow students. A photograph of Jaheem hangs on the family's front door above a poster that family, friends, and neighborhood residents have turned into a shrine in the boy's memory.

Getting Bullied Students are also subject to violence and intimidation on school grounds. Bullying is a sad but common occurrence in the U.S. educational system.[25] More than 15 percent of U.S. schoolchildren say they have been bullied by other students during the current school term.[26] School crime surveys yield estimates that about 1.5 million violent incidents occur in public elementary and secondary schools each year.[27] The presence of weapons and violence is not lost on the average student. Data from a recent survey of high school students found that almost half report having seen other students carry knives at school, roughly 1 in 10 reports having seen other students carry guns at school, and more than 1 in 5 report being fearful of weapon-associated victimization at school.[28]

PEER RELATIONS

Psychologists have long recognized that peer group relations have a powerful effect on human conduct and can dramatically influence decision making and behavior choices. Peer relations is a double-edged sword. Popular kids who hang out with their friends without parental supervision are at risk for delinquent behaviors mainly because they have more opportunity to get into trouble.[29] Less popular kids, who are routinely rejected by their peers, are more likely to display aggressive behavior and to disrupt group activities through bickering, bullying, or other antisocial behavior.[30] Those who report inadequate or strained peer relations, and who say they are not popular with the opposite sex, are prone to delinquent behaviors.[31]

Troubled kids find it tough to make friends; they choose delinquent peers out of necessity rather than desire.[32] Being a social outcast causes them to hook up with friends who are dangerous and get them into trouble.[33] Those who acquire delinquent friends may find that peer influence is a powerful determinant of behavior. Deviant peers may sustain or amplify antisocial behavior trends and reinforce delinquent careers.[34] The fear of punishment is diminished among kids who hang with delinquent friends, and loyalty to delinquent peers may outweigh the fear of punishment.[35]

Because delinquent friends tend to be, as criminologist Mark Warr puts it, "sticky" (once acquired, they are not easily lost), peer influence may continue through the life span.[36] People who maintain close relations with antisocial peers will sustain their own criminal behavior into adulthood.[37] In contrast, nondelinquent friends help to moderate delinquency.[38] Having prosocial friends who are committed to conventional success may help shield kids from crime-producing inducements in their environment.[39]

RELIGION AND BELIEF

Logic would dictate that people who hold high moral values and beliefs, who have learned to distinguish right from wrong, and who regularly attend religious services should also eschew crime and other antisocial behaviors. Religion binds people

Fact or Fiction?

High school dropouts are crime-prone troublemakers.

Fiction. It depends on why the individual drops out. Those who are having problems in school and are already involved in antisocial behaviors will commit more crime when they drop out. Kids who drop out to get a job or for other reasons are less crime-prone.

Figure 7.2 The Complex Web of Social Processes That Controls Human Behavior

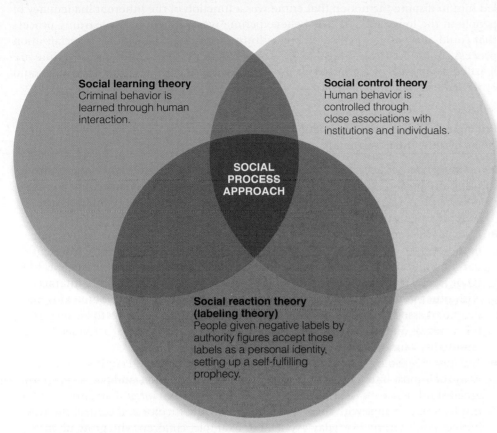

Social learning theory
Criminal behavior is learned through human interaction.

Social control theory
Human behavior is controlled through close associations with institutions and individuals.

SOCIAL PROCESS APPROACH

Social reaction theory (labeling theory)
People given negative labels by authority figures accept those labels as a personal identity, setting up a self-fulfilling prophecy.

CONNECTIONS

As you may recall from Chapter 2, most juveniles age out of crime and do not become adult offenders. Having delinquent friends may retard this process. According to the social process view, a chronic offender may have learned a delinquent way of life from his or her peer group members.

together and forces them to confront the consequences of their behavior. Committing crimes would violate the principles of all organized religions.

Recent research findings suggest that attending religious services does in fact have a significant negative impact on crime.[40] Kids living in disorganized, high-crime areas who attend religious services are better able to resist illegal drug use than nonreligious youths.[41] Interestingly, participation seems to be a more significant inhibitor of crime than merely having religious beliefs and values. That is, actually attending religious services has a more dramatic effect on behavior than merely holding religious beliefs.[42]

Figure 7.2 summarizes the relationship among the various elements of socialization.
▶ **Checkpoints**

Social Learning Theories

Social learning theorists believe that crime is a product of learning the norms, values, and behaviors associated with criminal activity. Social learning can involve the actual techniques of crime (how to hot-wire a car or roll a joint), as well as the psychological aspects of criminality (how to deal with the guilt or shame associated with illegal activities). This section briefly reviews two of the most prominent forms of social learning theory: differential association theory and neutralization theory.

DIFFERENTIAL ASSOCIATION THEORY

One of the most prominent social learning theories is Edwin H. Sutherland's **differential association theory**. Often considered the preeminent U.S. criminologist, Sutherland first put forth his theory in 1939 in *Principles of Criminology*.[43] The final version of the theory appeared in 1947. When Sutherland died in 1950, his longtime associate Donald Cressey continued his work until his own death in 1987.

Checkpoints

▶ Social process theories hold that the way people are socialized controls their behavior choices.

▶ Some criminologists maintain that crime is a learned behavior.

▶ Other criminologists view criminals as people whose behavior has not been controlled.

▶ Some view criminality as a function of labeling and stigma.

▶ There is strong evidence that social relations influence behavior.

▶ Children growing up with conflict, abuse, and neglect are at risk for crime and delinquency.

▶ Educational failure has been linked to criminality.

▶ Adolescents who associate with deviant peers are more likely to engage in crime than those who maintain conventional peer group relations.

Sutherland's research on white-collar crime, professional theft, and intelligence led him to dispute the notion that crime was a function of the inherent inadequacy of people in the lower classes.[44] He believed crime was a function of a learning process that could affect any individual in any culture. Acquiring a behavior is a socialization process, not a political or legal process. Skills and motives conducive to crime are learned as a result of contact with pro-crime values, attitudes, and definitions and other patterns of criminal behavior.

Principles of Differential Association Sutherland and Cressey explain the basic principles of differential association as follows:[45]

▶ *Criminal behavior is learned.* This statement differentiates Sutherland's theory from prior attempts to classify criminal behavior as an inherent characteristic of criminals. Sutherland implies that criminality is learned in the same manner as any other learned behavior, such as writing, painting, or reading.

▶ *Criminal behavior is learned as a by-product of interacting with others.* An individual does not start violating the law simply by living in a criminogenic environment or by manifesting personal characteristics associated with criminality, such as low IQ or family problems. People actively learn as they are socialized and interact with other individuals who serve as teachers and guides to crime. Some kids may meet and associate with criminal "mentors" who teach them how to be successful criminals and to reap the greatest benefits from their criminal activities.[46] Thus criminality cannot occur without the aid of others.

▶ *Learning criminal behavior occurs within intimate personal groups.* People's contacts with their most intimate social companions—family, friends, and peers—have the greatest influence on their development of deviant behavior and an antisocial attitude. Relationships with these influential individuals color and control the way individuals interpret everyday events. For example, children who grow up in homes where parents abuse alcohol are more likely to view drinking as socially and physically beneficial.[47]

▶ *Learning criminal behavior involves assimilating the techniques of committing crime, including motives, drives, rationalizations, and attitudes.* Young delinquents learn from their associates the proper way to pick a lock, shoplift, and obtain and use narcotics. In addition, novice criminals learn the proper terminology for their acts and acquire approved reactions to law violations. Criminals must learn how to react properly to their illegal acts, such as when to defend them, when to rationalize them, and when to show remorse for them.

▶ *The specific direction of motives and drives is learned from perceptions of various aspects of the legal code as favorable or unfavorable.* Because the reaction to social rules and laws is not uniform across society, people constantly meet others who hold different views on the utility of obeying the legal code. Some people admire others who may openly disdain or flout the law or ignore its substance. People experience what Sutherland calls **culture conflict** when they are exposed to opposing attitudes toward right and wrong or moral and immoral. The conflict of social attitudes and cultural norms is the basis for the concept of differential association.

▶ *A person becomes a criminal when he or she perceives more favorable than unfavorable consequences to violating the law.* According to Sutherland's theory, individuals become law violators when they are in contact with persons, groups, or events that produce an excess of definitions favorable toward criminality and are isolated from counteracting forces (see Figure 7.3). A definition favorable toward criminality occurs, for example, when a person hears friends talking about the virtues of getting high on drugs. A definition unfavorable toward crime occurs when friends or parents demonstrate their disapproval of crime.

▶ *Differential associations may vary in frequency, duration, priority, and intensity.* Whether a person learns to obey the law or to disregard it is influenced by the quality of that person's social interactions. Those of lasting duration have greater

differential association theory
The view that people commit crime when their social learning leads them to perceive more definitions favoring crime than favoring conventional behavior.

culture conflict
Result of exposure to opposing norms, attitudes, and definitions of right and wrong, moral and immoral.

Figure 7.3 Differential Associations

Differential association theory suggests that criminal behavior will occur when the definitions favorable to crime outweigh the unfavorable definitions.

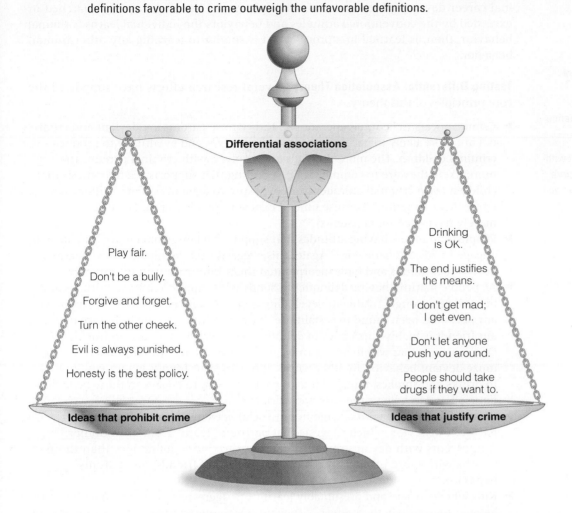

Differential associations

Play fair.

Don't be a bully.

Forgive and forget.

Turn the other cheek.

Evil is always punished.

Honesty is the best policy.

Ideas that prohibit crime

Drinking is OK.

The end justifies the means.

I don't get mad; I get even.

Don't let anyone push you around.

People should take drugs if they want to.

Ideas that justify crime

influence than those that are brief. Similarly, frequent contacts have greater effect than rare, haphazard contacts. "Priority" means the age of children when they first encounter definitions of criminality. Contacts made early in life probably have more influence than those developed later. Finally, "intensity" is generally interpreted to mean the importance and prestige attached to the individuals or groups from whom the definitions are learned. For example, the influence of a father, mother, or trusted friend far outweighs that of more socially distant figures.

▶ *The process of learning criminal behavior by association with criminal and anticriminal patterns involves all of the mechanisms that are involved in any other learning process.* Learning criminal behavior patterns is similar to learning nearly all other patterns and is not a matter of mere imitation.

▶ *Although criminal behavior expresses general needs and values, it is not excused by those general needs and values, because noncriminal behavior expresses the same needs and values.* This principle suggests that the motives for criminal behavior cannot logically be the same as those for conventional behavior. Sutherland rules out such motives as desire to accumulate money or social status, personal frustration, and low self-concept as causes of crime because they are just as likely to produce noncriminal behavior, such as getting a better education or working harder on a job. Only the learning of deviant norms through contact with an excess of definitions favorable toward criminality produces illegal behavior.

In sum, differential association theory holds that people learn criminal attitudes and behavior during their adolescence from close, trusted friends or relatives. A criminal career develops if learned antisocial values and behaviors are not matched or exceeded by the conventional attitudes and behaviors the individual learns. Criminal behavior, then, is learned in a process that is similar to learning any other human behavior.

Testing Differential Association Theory Several research efforts have supported the core principles of this theory.

▶ Crime appears to be intergenerational: Kids whose parents are deviant and criminal are more likely to become criminals themselves and eventually to produce criminal children. The more that kids are involved with criminal parents, the more likely they are to commit crime, a finding that supports the hypothesis that children learn criminal attitudes from exposure to deviant parents, rather than crime being inherited (because time of exposure predicts criminal behavior, not merely having criminal patents).[48]

▶ People who report having attitudes that support deviant behavior are also likely to engage in deviant behavior.[49] Again, this suggests that delinquents have learned deviant definitions and have incorporated them into their attitude structure.

▶ As people mature, having delinquent friends who support criminal attitudes and behavior is strongly related to developing criminal careers. Association with deviant peers has been found to sustain the deviant attitudes.[50] The influence of deviant friends is highly supportive of delinquency, regardless of race and/or class.[51] One reason is that within peer groups, high-status leaders will influence and legitimize deviant behavior. In other words, if one of your friends whom you look up to drinks and smokes, it makes it a lot easier for you to engage in those behaviors yourself and to believe they are appropriate.[52]

▶ Romantic partners who engage in antisocial activities may influence their partner's behavior, which suggests that partners "learn" from one another.[53] Adolescents with deviant romantic partners are more delinquent than those youths with more prosocial partners, regardless of friends' and parents' behavior.[54]

▶ Kids who associate and presumably learn from aggressive peers are more likely to behave aggressively themselves.[55] Deviant peers interfere with the natural process of aging out of crime by helping provide the support that keeps kids in criminal careers.[56]

▶ Scales measuring differential association have been significantly correlated with criminal behaviors among samples taken in other nations and cultures.[57]

▶ The more deviant an adolescent's social network and network of affiliations, including parents, peers, and romantic partners, the more likely that adolescent is to engage in antisocial behavior. It is likely that deviant affiliations provide definitions that incline adolescents toward delinquency.[58]

Analysis of Differential Association Theory Differential association theory is important because it does not specify that criminals come from a disorganized area or are members of the lower class. Outwardly law-abiding, middle-class parents can encourage delinquent behavior by their own drinking, drug use, or family violence. The influence of differential associations is not dependent on social class; deviant learning experiences can affect youths in all classes.[59]

There are, however, a number of valid criticisms of Sutherland's work. It fails to account for the origin of criminal definitions. How did the first "teacher" learn criminal attitudes and definitions in order to pass them on? Another criticism of differential association theory is that it assumes criminal and delinquent acts to be rational and systematic. This ignores spontaneous, wanton acts of violence and damage that appear to have little utility or purpose, such as the isolated psychopathic killing that is virtually unsolvable because of the killer's anonymity and lack of delinquent associations.

neutralization theory
The view that law violators learn to neutralize conventional values and attitudes, enabling them to drift back and forth between criminal and conventional behavior.

drift
Movement in and out of delinquency, shifting between conventional and deviant values.

neutralization techniques
Methods of rationalizing deviant behavior, such as denying responsibility or blaming the victim.

Some critics suggest that the reasoning behind the theory is circular: How can we know when a person has experienced an excess of definitions favorable toward criminality? When he or she commits a crime! Why do people commit crime? When they are exposed to an excess of criminal definitions!

NEUTRALIZATION THEORY

Neutralization theory is identified with the writings of Gresham Sykes and his associate David Matza.[60] These criminologists also view the process of becoming a criminal as a learning experience. They theorize that law violators must learn and master techniques that enable them to neutralize conventional values and attitudes, which enables them to drift back and forth between illegitimate and conventional behavior.

Neutralization theory points out that even the most committed criminals and delinquents are not involved in criminality all the time; they also attend schools, family functions, and religious services. Thus, their behavior falls along a continuum between total freedom and total restraint. This process of **drift**, or movement from one extreme to another, produces behavior that is sometimes unconventional or deviant and at other times constrained and sober.[61] Learning **neutralization techniques** equips a person to temporarily drift away from conventional behavior and become involved in antisocial behaviors, including crime and drug abuse.[62]

Neutralization Techniques Sykes and Matza suggest that people develop a distinct set of justifications for their law-violating behavior. Several observations form the basis of their theoretical model.[63]

► *Criminals sometimes voice guilt over their illegal acts.* If they truly embraced criminal or antisocial values, criminals would probably not exhibit remorse for their acts, apart from regret at being apprehended.

► *Offenders frequently respect and admire honest, law-abiding persons.* Those admired may include entertainers, sports figures, priests and other members of the clergy, parents, teachers, and neighbors.

► *Criminals define whom they can victimize.* Members of similar ethnic groups, churches, or neighborhoods are often off-limits. This practice implies that criminals are aware of the wrongfulness of their acts.

► *Criminals are not immune to the demands of conformity.* Most criminals frequently participate in the same social functions as law-abiding people—for example, school, church, and family activities.

Sykes and Matza conclude that criminals must first neutralize accepted social values before they are free to commit crimes; they do so by learning a set of techniques that allow them to counteract the moral dilemmas posed by illegal behavior.[64] Through their research, Sykes and Matza have identified the following techniques of neutralization:

► *Denial of responsibility.* Young offenders sometimes claim that their unlawful acts are not their fault—that such acts result from forces beyond their control or are accidents.

Differential association theory suggests that people learn the techniques and attitudes necessary to commit crime. Criminal knowledge is gained through experience, and then, after considering the outcomes of their past experiences, potential offenders decide which criminal acts will be profitable and which are dangerous and should be avoided. Here, a young man is shown photographing a drug deal on his cell phone. Is it possible that he is documenting the experience to have available, for future reference, a record of the best techniques of drug dealing?

Fact or Fiction?

Criminals have a unique antisocial lifestyle that takes up all of their time.

Fiction. Most criminals frequently participate in the same social functions as law-abiding people and then drift into crime and back again.

▶ *Denial of injury.* By denying the injury their acts cause, criminals neutralize illegal behavior. For example, stealing is viewed as borrowing; vandalism is considered mischief that has gotten out of hand. Offenders may find that their parents and friends support their denial of injury. In fact, parents and friends may claim that the behavior was merely a prank, which helps affirm the offender's perception that crime can be socially acceptable.

▶ *Denial of the victim.* Criminals sometimes neutralize wrongdoing by maintaining that the crime victim "had it coming." Vandalism may be directed against a disliked teacher or neighbor, or a gang may beat up homosexuals because they consider homosexual behavior offensive.

▶ *Condemnation of the condemners.* An offender views the world as a corrupt place with a dog-eat-dog code. Because police and judges are on the take, teachers show favoritism, and parents take out their frustrations on their children, offenders claim it is ironic and unfair for these authorities to condemn criminal misconduct. By shifting the blame to others, criminals repress their awareness that their own acts are wrong.

▶ *Appeal to higher loyalties.* Novice criminals often argue that they are caught in the dilemma of being loyal to their peer group while attempting to abide by the rules of society. The needs of the group take precedence because group demands are immediate and localized (see Figure 7.4).

In sum, neutralization theory states that people neutralize conventional norms and values by using excuses that enable them to drift into crime.

Testing Neutralization Theory Attempts have been made to verify neutralization theory empirically, but the results have been inconclusive.[65] One area of research has been directed at determining whether law violators really need to neutralize moral constraints. The thinking behind this research is that if criminals hold values in opposition to accepted social norms, there is really no need to neutralize. So far, the

Figure 7.4 Techniques of Neutralization

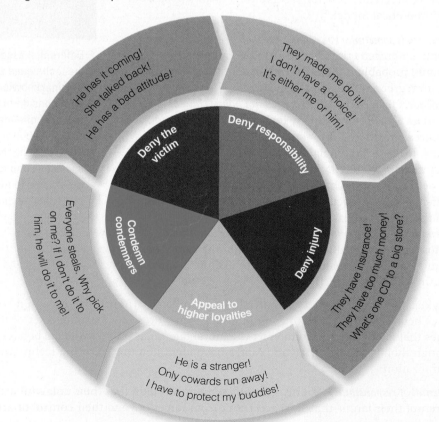

evidence is mixed. Some studies show that law violators approve of criminal behavior such as theft and violence, whereas other studies yield evidence that even though they may be active participants themselves, criminals voice disapproval of illegal behavior.[66] Some studies indicate that law violators approve of social values such as honesty and fairness; other studies support the opposite conclusion.[67]

Although the existing research findings are ambiguous, the weight of the evidence suggests that most adolescents generally disapprove of deviant behaviors such as violence, and that neutralizations do in fact enable youths to engage in socially disapproved behavior.[68] And, as Matza predicted, people seem to drift into and out of antisocial behavior, rather than being committed solely to a criminal way of life.[69]

Do Criminals Really Neutralize? Not all criminologists accept Matza's vision. Recently, criminologist Volkan Topalli conducted in-depth interviews with active criminals in St. Louis, Missouri, and found that street criminals living in disorganized, gang-ridden neighborhoods "disrespect authority, lionize honor and violence, and place individual needs above those of all others." Rather than having to neutralize conventional values in order to engage in deviant ones, these offenders do not experience guilt that requires neutralizations; they are "guilt free." There is no need for them to "drift" into criminality, Topalli finds, because their allegiance to nonconventional values and their lack of guilt perpetually leave them in a state of openness to crime. Rather than being embarrassed, they take great pride in their criminal activities and abilities. In fact, rather than neutralizing conventional values, these street kids may have to neutralize deviant values: They are expected to be "bad" and have to explain good behavior! Street criminals are also expected to seek vengeance if they themselves are the target of theft or violence. If they don't, their self-image is damaged and they look weak and ineffective. If they decide against vengeance, they must neutralize their decision by convincing themselves that they are being merciful out of respect for their enemies' friends and family.[70]

EVALUATING LEARNING THEORIES

Learning theories contribute significantly to our understanding of the onset of criminal behavior. Nonetheless, the general learning model has been criticized. One complaint is that learning theorists fail to account for the origin of criminal definitions. How did the first criminal learn the necessary techniques and definitions? Who came up with the original neutralization technique?

Learning theories imply that people systematically learn techniques that enable them to be active, successful criminals. However, as Topalli's research indicates, street criminals may be proud of their felonious exploits and have little need to neutralize their guilt. Learning theory also fails to adequately explain spontaneous, wanton acts of violence, damage, and other expressive crimes that appear to have little utility or purpose. Although principles of differential association can easily explain shoplifting, is it possible that a random shooting is caused by excessive deviant definitions? It is estimated that about 70 percent of all arrestees were under the influence of drugs and alcohol when they committed their crime. Do "crackheads" pause to neutralize their moral inhibitions before mugging a victim? Do drug-involved kids stop to consider what they have learned about moral values? Little evidence exists that people learn the techniques that enable them to become criminals before they actually commit criminal acts. It is equally plausible that people who are already deviant seek others with similar lifestyles to learn from. Early onset of deviant behavior is now considered a key determinant of criminal careers. It is difficult to see how very young children have had the opportunity to learn criminal behavior and attitudes within a peer group setting.

Despite these criticisms, learning theories have an important place in the study of delinquent and criminal behavior. They help explain the role that peers, family, and education play in shaping criminal and conventional behaviors. If crime were a matter of personal traits alone, these elements of socialization would not play such an important a role in determining human behavior. And unlike social structure theories, learning theories are not limited to explaining a single facet of antisocial activity;

CONNECTIONS
Denial of the victim may help explain hate crimes, in which people are victimized simply because they belong to the "wrong" race, religion, or ethnic group or because of their sexual orientation. Hate crimes are discussed in Chapter 10.

they explain criminality across all class structures. Even corporate executives may be exposed to pro-crime definitions and learn to neutralize moral constraints. Learning theories can thus be applied to a wide variety of criminal activity.

Social Control Theory

Social control theorists maintain that all people have the potential to violate the law and that modern society presents many opportunities for illegal activity. Criminal activities, such as drug abuse and car theft, are often exciting pastimes that hold the promise of immediate reward and gratification.

Considering the attractions of crime, social control theorists question why people obey the rules of society. They argue that people obey the law because behavior and passions are controlled by internal and external forces. Some individuals have **self-control**—a strong moral sense that renders them incapable of hurting others and violating social norms.

Other people have been socialized to have a **commitment to conformity**. They have developed a real, present, and logical reason to obey the rules of society, and they instinctively avoid behavior that will jeopardize their reputation and achievements.[71] The stronger people's commitment to conventional institutions, individuals, and processes, the less likely they are to commit crime. If that commitment is absent, there is little to lose, and people are free to violate the law.[72]

SELF-CONCEPT AND CRIME

Early versions of control theory speculated that criminality was a product of weak self-concept and poor self-esteem. Youths who are socialized to feel good about themselves and who maintain a positive attitude are able to control their own behavior and resist the temptations of the streets.

More than 50 years ago, sociologist Albert Reiss described delinquents as having weak egos and lacking the self-control to produce conforming behavior.[73] Scott Briar and Irving Piliavin noted that youths who believe criminal activity will damage their self-image and their relationships with others are likely to conform to social rules; in contrast, those less concerned about their social standing are free to violate the law.[74] Pioneering control theorist Walter Reckless argued that a strong self-image insulates a youth from the pressures of criminogenic influences in the environment.[75] In studies conducted within the school setting, Reckless and his colleagues found that students who were able to maintain a positive self-image were insulated from delinquency.[76]

These early works suggested that people who have a weak self-image and a damaged ego are crime-prone. They are immune from efforts to apply social control: Why obey the rules of society when you have no stake in the future and little to lose?

HIRSCHI'S SOCIAL CONTROL THEORY

The version of control theory articulated by Travis Hirschi in his influential 1969 book *Causes of Delinquency* is today the dominant version of control theory.[77] Hirschi links the onset of criminality to weakening of the ties that bind people to society. He assumes that all individuals are potential law violators, but most are kept under control because they fear that illegal behavior will damage their relationships with friends, family, neighbors, teachers, and employers. Without these **social bonds**, or ties, a person is free to commit criminal acts. Across all ethnic, religious, racial, and social groups, people whose bond to society is weak may fall prey to criminogenic behavior patterns.

Hirschi argues that the social bond a person maintains with society is divided into four main elements: attachment, commitment, involvement, and belief (see Figure 7.5).

▶ Attachment consists of a person's sensitivity to and interest in others.[78] Hirschi views parents, peers, and schools as the important social institutions with which a person should maintain ties. Attachment to parents is the most important. Even if

CONNECTIONS

The association of self-control and crime will be discussed more fully in Chapter 9 in the context of human development.

self-control
A strong moral sense that renders a person incapable of hurting others or violating social norms.

commitment to conformity
A strong personal investment in conventional institutions, individuals, and processes that prevents people from engaging in behavior that might jeopardize their reputation and achievements.

social bonds
The ties that bind people to society, including relationships with friends, family, neighbors, teachers, and employers. The elements of the social bond include commitment, attachment, involvement, and belief.

Figure 7.5 Elements of the Social Bond

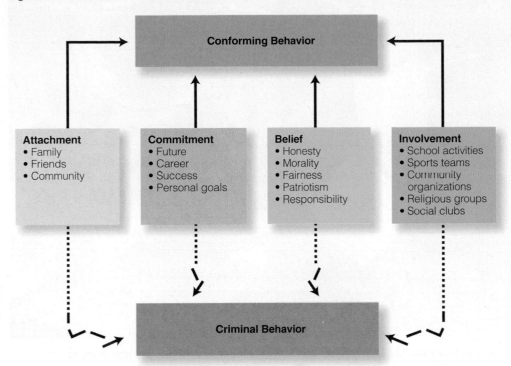

a family is shattered by divorce or separation, a child must retain a strong attachment to one or both parents. Without this attachment, it is unlikely that respect for other authorities will develop.

▶ Commitment involves the time, energy, and effort expended in conventional actions such as getting an education and saving money for the future. If people build a strong commitment to conventional society, they will be less likely to engage in acts that jeopardize their hard-won position. Conversely, the lack of commitment to conventional values may foreshadow a condition in which risk-taking behavior, such as crime, becomes a reasonable behavior alternative.

▶ People who live in the same social setting often share common moral beliefs; they may adhere to such values as sharing, sensitivity to the rights of others, and admiration for the legal code. If these beliefs are absent or weakened, individuals are more likely to participate in antisocial or illegal acts.

▶ Involvement in conventional activities such as sports, clubs, and school leaves little time for illegal behavior. Hirschi believes that involvement in school, recreation, and family insulates people from the lure of criminal behavior. Idleness, on the other hand, enhances that lure.

Hirschi further suggests that the interrelationship among the elements of the social bond controls subsequent behavior. For example, people who feel kinship and sensitivity to parents and friends should be more likely to adopt and work toward legitimate goals. A person who rejects such social relationships is more likely to lack commitment to conventional goals. Similarly, people who are highly committed to conventional acts and beliefs are more likely to be involved in conventional activities.

TESTING SOCIAL CONTROL THEORY: SUPPORTIVE RESEARCH

One of Hirschi's most significant contributions to criminology was his attempt to test the principal hypotheses of social control theory. He administered a detailed self-report survey to a sample of more than 4,000 junior and senior high school students in Contra Costa County, California.[79] In a detailed analysis of the data, Hirschi found

CONNECTIONS

Travis Hirschi, along with Michael Gottfredson, has restructured his concept of control by focusing on self-control and has woven his vision into a general theory of crime. Because this new theory is essentially developmental, it will be discussed more fully in Chapter 9.

According to Travis Hirschi, kids who are involved in productive activities are less likely to get involved in deviant activities. At La France Elementary School, fifth-graders Taylor Davis (left) and Blake Duncan complete worksheets about how to be kind to animals and people, while Tracy Grate (right) holds Abby, an SCDogs Therapy Group dog. The "Fix It Fido" program, which aims to curb bullying, finished its pilot year during the 2005–2006 school year. The program may enhance children's bonds to society and promote prosocial behaviors.

considerable evidence to support the control theory model. Among Hirschi's more important findings are the following:

► Youths who were strongly attached to their parents were less likely to commit criminal acts.
► Youths involved in conventional activity, such as homework, were less likely to engage in criminal behavior.
► Youths involved in unconventional behavior, such as smoking and drinking, were more prone to delinquency.
► Youths who maintained weak, distant relationships with people tended toward delinquency.
► Those who shunned unconventional acts were attached to their peers.
► Delinquents and nondelinquents shared similar beliefs about society.

Even when the statistical significance of Hirschi's findings was less than he expected, the direction of his research data was notably consistent. Only rarely did his findings contradict the theory's most critical assumptions. Hirschi's version of social control theory has been corroborated by numerous research studies showing that delinquent youths often feel detached from society.[80] What are some of the most important findings?

Attachment Kids who are attached to their families, friends, and school are less likely to get involved in a deviant peer group and consequently are less likely to engage in criminal activities.[81] Teens who are attached to their parents are also able to develop the social skills that equip them both to maintain harmonious social ties and to escape life stresses such as school failure.[82] In contrast, family detachment, including intra-family conflict, abuse of children, and lack of affection, supervision, and family pride, are predictive of delinquent conduct.

Attachment to education is equally important. Youths who are detached from the educational experience are at risk of criminality; those who are committed to school are less likely to engage in delinquent acts.[83] Detachment and alienation from school may be even more predictive of delinquency than school failure and/or educational underachievement.[84]

Belief Research efforts have shown that holding positive beliefs is inversely related to criminality. Children who are involved in religious activities and hold conventional religious beliefs are less likely to become involved in substance abuse.[85] Kids who live in areas marked by strong religious values and who hold strong religious beliefs themselves are less likely to engage in delinquent activities than adolescents who do not hold such beliefs or who live in less devout communities.[86]

Commitment As predicted by Hirschi, kids who are committed to school and educational achievement are less likely to become involved in delinquent behaviors than those who lack such commitment.[87] The association may be reciprocal: Kids who drink and engage in deviant behavior are more likely to fail in school; kids who fail in school are more likely to later drink and engage in deviant behavior.[88]

Involvement Research shows that youths who are involved in conventional leisure activities, such as supervised social activities and noncompetitive sports, are less likely to engage in delinquency than those who are involved in unconventional leisure activities and unsupervised, peer-oriented social pursuits.[89] Although there are gender differences in involvement, members of both sexes are less likely to commit crime if they are engaged in conventional activities.[90]

The accompanying Profiles in Crime feature describes a case that may rest on a frayed and tattered social bond.

CRITIQUING SOCIAL CONTROL THEORY

Few theoretical models in criminology have garnered as much attention as Hirschi's social control theory. And although there is a great deal of supportive research, a number of questions have been raised about the validity of his work.

The Influence of Friendship One significant concern is Hirschi's contention that delinquents are detached loners whose bond to friends has been broken. A number of researchers have argued that delinquents seem not to be "lone wolves" whose only personal relationships are exploitive; rather, their friendship patterns seem quite close to those of conventional youths.[91] Some types of offenders, such as drug abusers, have been found to maintain even more intimate relations with their peers than nonabusers do.[92] Hirschi would counter that what appears to be a close friendship is really a relationship of convenience and that "birds of a feather flock together" only when it suits their criminal activities. His view is supported by recent research conducted by criminologists Lisa Stolzenberg and Stewart D'Alessio, who found that most juvenile offenses are committed by individuals acting alone and that group offending, when it does occur, is incidental and of little importance to explaining the onset of delinquency.[93]

Failure to Achieve Hirschi argues that commitment to career and economic advancement reduces criminal involvement. But he does not deal with the issue of failure: What about kids who are committed to the future but fail in school and perceive few avenues for advancement? Some research indicates that people who are committed to success but fail to achieve it may be crime-prone.[94]

Fact or Fiction?

"Idle hands are the devil's workshop" is merely an old saying. Kids who work outside the home are the ones most likely to get into trouble.

Fiction. Old sayings are sometimes accurate. Kids who are involved in conventional leisure activities, such as supervised social activities and noncompetitive sports, are less likely to engage in delinquency.

Profiles in Crime Alpha Dog

Twenty-five-year-old Jesse James Hollywood (that is his real name) was enjoying a comfortable life in Brazil, teaching English and living in a fashionable neighborhood, when he was arrested in November 2005 and sent back to California, where he faces charges of kidnapping and killing a 15-year-old boy.

Even though Hollywood had never held a job, he was able, by age 19, to purchase a $200,000 house in West Hills, California, and a Mercedes. His place became a favorite hangout for local kids who came and went at all hours of the day. Jesse was a popular guy, an outgoing kid who, despite being short in stature, was an excellent athlete. How was Jesse able to do all this? Unknown to many, he was a large-scale marijuana dealer.

Jesse's world began to unravel when he came up with a scheme to get money owed to him by Benjamin Markowitz, 22, who was one of his customers. Hollywood and some friends headed for Markowitz's family home on August 6, 2000, planning to kidnap him and hold him for ransom. According to authorities, on the way there, Jesse and his friends spotted Markowitz's 15-year-old stepbrother, Nicholas, whom they forced into a van and transported to the home of another accomplice. After being held captive for a few days, Nick Markowitz was made to walk a mile into Los Padres National Forest before being shot nine times with a high-powered assault rifle and buried in a shallow grave. His body was discovered four days later by hikers.

Four other kids were tried and convicted in the case, but Hollywood escaped and became the subject of an international manhunt, his mug shot plastered on the FBI's website. He wound up in Brazil, where he used fake papers that identified him as Michael Costa Giroux, a native of Rio de Janeiro. Cooperating with the FBI, Brazilian authorities deported him as an illegal alien. Nine years after the killing, he was tried on murder charges. On July 8, 2009, a jury found him guilty of kidnapping and first-degree murder with special circumstances; afterward, Hollywood was sentenced to life in prison.

The 2006 film *Alpha Dog*, starring Bruce Willis, Justin Timberlake, and Sharon Stone, is based on the case.

CRITICAL THINKING

Jesse James Hollywood grew up in an affluent family and seemed to be popular and successful. How could he have become involved in a heinous, violent crime? How would a control theorist explain his actions?

SOURCE: Jeremiah Marquez, "Longtime Fugitive Jesse James Hollywood Captured in Brazil," March 11, 2005, http://sfgate.com/cgi-bin/article.cgi?file=/news/archive/2005/03/10/state/n085203S47.DTL; FBI Press Release, "Jesse James Hollywood, Fugitive in August 2000 Kidnap-Murder of Teenager, Arrested in Brazil," March 10, 2005, http://losangeles.fbi.gov/pressrel/2005/la031005.htm; Amy Silverstein, "Jesse James Hollywood Sentenced to Life," *Santa Barbara Independent*, July 14, 2009, www.independent.com/news/2009/jul/15/jesse-james-hollywood-sentenced-life/.

Deviant Involvement Adolescents who report high levels of involvement, which Hirschi suggests should reduce delinquency, actually report high levels of criminal behavior. Typically, these are kids who are involved in activities outside the home without parental supervision.[95] Kids who spend a lot of time hanging out with their friends, unsupervised by parents and/or other authority figures, and who own cars that give them the mobility to get into even more trouble, are the ones most likely to get involved in antisocial acts such as drinking and taking drugs.[96] This is especially true of dating relationships: Kids who date, especially if they have multiple partners, are the ones who are likely to get into trouble and engage in delinquent acts.[97] It is possible that although involvement is important, it depends on the behavior in which a person is involved!

Deviant Peers and Parents Perhaps the most controversial of Hirschi's conclusions is that any form of social attachment is beneficial, even attachment to deviant peers and parents. Despite Hirschi's claims, there is evidence that rather than deterring youths from delinquency, attachment to deviant peers and parents may support and nurture antisocial behavior.[98] A number of research efforts have found that youths attached to drug-abusing parents are more likely to use drugs themselves.[99] Attachment to deviant family members, peers, and associates may help motivate youths to commit crime and facilitate their antisocial acts.[100]

Mistaken Causal Order Hirschi's theory proposes that a weakened bond leads to delinquency, but Robert Agnew suggests that the chain of events may flow in the opposite direction: Perhaps youngsters who break the law find that their bonds to parents, schools, and society eventually become weak. Other studies have also found that criminal behavior weakens social bonds, and not vice versa.[101]

These criticisms are important, but Hirschi's views still constitute one of the preeminent theories in criminology.[102] Many criminologists consider social control theory the primary way of understanding the onset of youthful misbehavior. ▶ **Checkpoints**

Social Reaction (Labeling) Theory

The third type of social process theory, social reaction theory, also called labeling theory (the two terms are used interchangeably), explains criminal careers in terms of stigma-producing encounters. Social reaction theory has a number of key points:

▶ *Behaviors that are considered criminal are highly subjective.* Even such crimes as murder, rape, and assault are bad or evil only because people label them as such. The difference between a forcible rape and a consensual sexual encounter often rests on whom the members of a jury believe and how they interpret the events that took place. The difference between an excusable act and a criminal one is often subject to change and modification. Remember Genarlow Wilson: Was he a sex offender or a kid who partied too much? It depends on your viewpoint and the view of those in power. Acts such as performing an abortion, using marijuana, possessing a handgun, and gambling have been legal at some times and places and illegal at others.

▶ *Crime is defined by those in power.* The content and shape of criminal law is defined by the values of those who rule and is not an objective standard of moral conduct. Howard Becker refers to people who create rules as **moral entrepreneurs**. An example of a moral entrepreneur is someone who campaigns against violence in the media and wants laws passed to restrict the content of television shows.

▶ *Not only acts are labeled, but also people.* Labels define not just an act but also the actor. Valued labels, such as "smart," "honest," and "hardworking," suggest overall competence. Sometimes labels are highly symbolic, such as being named "most likely to succeed" or class valedictorian. People who hold these titles are automatically assumed to be leaders who are well on their way to success. Without meeting them, we know that they are hardworking, industrious, and bright. These positive labels can improve self-image and social standing. Research shows that people who are labeled with one positive trait, such as being physically attractive, are assumed to have other positive traits, such as being intelligent and competent.[103] In contrast, people who run afoul of the law or other authorities, such as school officials, are given negative labels, including "troublemaker," "mentally ill," and "stupid," that **stigmatize** them and reduce their self-image. Negative labels also define the whole person. People labeled "insane" are also assumed to be dangerous, dishonest, unstable, violent, strange, and otherwise unsound.

Checkpoints

▶ Social control theories maintain that behavior is a function of the attachment that people feel toward society. People who have a weak commitment to conformity are "free" to commit crime.

▶ A strong self-image may insulate people from crime.

▶ According to Travis Hirschi, social control is measured by a person's attachment, commitment, involvement, and belief.

▶ Significant research supports Hirschi's theory, but a number of criminologists question its validity.

moral entrepreneur
A person who creates moral rules that reflect the values of those in power rather than any objective, universal standards of right and wrong.

stigmatize
To apply negative labeling with enduring effects on a person's self-image and social interactions.

▶ *Both positive and negative labels involve subjective interpretation of behavior.* A "trouble-maker" is merely someone whom people label as "troublesome."

In a famous statement, Howard Becker sums up the importance of the audience's reaction:

> Social groups create deviance by making rules whose infractions constitute deviance, and by applying those rules to particular people and labeling them as outsiders. From this point of view, deviance is not a quality of the act a person commits, but rather a consequence of the application by others of rules and sanctions to an "offender." The deviant is one to whom the label has successfully been applied; deviant behavior is behavior that people so label.[104]

Even if some acts are labeled as bad or evil, those who participate in them can be spared a negative label. It is possible to take another person's life but not be considered a "murderer," because the killing was considered self-defense or even an accident. Acts have negative consequences only when they are labeled by others as being wrong or evil.

CONSEQUENCES OF LABELING

Although a label may be a function of rumor, innuendo, or unfounded suspicion, its adverse impact can be immense. If a devalued status is conferred by a significant other—a teacher, police officer, parent, or valued peer—the negative label may permanently harm the target. The degree to which a person is perceived as a social deviant may affect his or her treatment at home, at work, at school, and in other social situations. Children may find that their parents consider them a bad influence on younger brothers and sisters. School officials may limit them to classes reserved for people with behavioral problems. Likewise, when adults are labeled as "criminal," "ex-con," or "drug addict," they may find their eligibility for employment severely restricted. If the label is bestowed as the result of conviction for a criminal offense, the labeled person may also be subjected to official sanctions ranging from a mild reprimand to incarceration. The simultaneous effects of labels and sanctions reinforce feelings of isolation and detachment.

Public denunciation plays an important part in the labeling process. Condemnation is often carried out in "ceremonies" in which the individual's identity is officially transformed. One example of such a reidentification ceremony is a competency hearing in which a person is declared "mentally ill"; another is a public trial in which a person is found to be a "rapist" or "child molester." During the process, a permanent record is produced, such as an arrest or conviction record, so that the denounced person is ritually separated from a place in the legitimate order and set outside the world occupied by citizens of good standing. Harold Garfinkle has called transactions that produce irreversible, permanent labels **successful degradation ceremonies**.[105]

Self-Labeling According to labeling theory, depending on the visibility of the label and the manner and severity with which it is applied, negatively labeled individuals will become increasingly committed to a deviant career. Labeled persons may find themselves turning, for support and companionship, to others who have been similarly stigmatized.

Isolated from conventional society, labeled people may identify themselves as members of an outcast group and become locked into deviance. Kids who view themselves as delinquents after being labeled as such are giving an inner voice to their perceptions of how parents, teachers, peers, and neighbors view them. When they believe that others view them as antisocial or as troublemakers, they take on attitudes and roles that reflect this assumption; they expect to become suspects and then to be rejected.[106]

Joining Deviant Cliques People labeled as deviant may join with similarly outcast peers who facilitate their behavior. Eventually, antisocial behavior becomes habitual and automatic.[107] The desire to join deviant cliques and groups may stem from

successful degradation ceremony
A course of action or ritual in which someone's identity is publicly redefined and destroyed and he or she is thereafter viewed as socially unacceptable.

According to labeling theory, perceptions guide behavior. Would you want to invite this guy to lunch with your family? He is The Scary Guy (his real name), and he spends his time teaching students and adults about what they can do to change the world by taking responsibility for their own behavior. His mission is to eliminate hate, violence, and prejudice worldwide. He is shown here hammering home his message at Valencia Middle School in Tucson, Arizona. What do you think of him now?

Figure 7.6 The Labeling Process

Initial criminal act
People commit crimes for a number of reasons.

∨

Detection by the justice system
Arrest is influenced by racial, economic, and power relations.

∨

Decision to label
Some are labeled "official" criminals by police and court authorities.

∨

Creation of a new identity
Those labeled are known as troublemakers, criminals, and so on, and are shunned by conventional society.

∨

Acceptance of labels
Labeled people begin to see themselves as outsiders (secondary deviance, self-labeling).

∨

Deviance amplification
Stigmatized offenders are now locked into criminal careers.

self-rejecting attitudes ("At times, I think I am no good at all") that eventually weaken commitment to conventional values and behaviors. In turn, stigmatized individuals may acquire motives to deviate from social norms because they now share a common bond with similarly labeled social outcasts.[108]

Retrospective Reading Beyond any immediate results, labels tend to redefine the whole person. For example, the label "ex-con" may evoke in people's imaginations a whole series of behavior descriptions—tough, mean, dangerous, aggressive, dishonest, sneaky—that may or may not apply to a particular person who has been in prison. People react to the label and its connotations instead of reacting to the actual behavior of the person who bears it. The labeled person's past is reviewed and reevaluated to fit his or her current status—a process known as **retrospective reading**. For example, boyhood friends of an assassin or serial killer, interviewed by the media, report that the suspect was withdrawn, suspicious, and negativistic as a youth; they were always suspicious but never thought to report their concerns to the authorities. According to this retrospective reading, we can now understand what prompted his current behavior; therefore, the label must be accurate.[109]

Labels, then, become the basis of personal identity. As the negative feedback of law enforcement agencies, parents, friends, teachers, and other figures amplifies the force of the original label, stigmatized offenders may begin to reevaluate their own identities (see Figure 7.6). If they are not really evil or bad, they may ask themselves, "Why is everyone making such a fuss?" This process has been referred to as the "dramatization of evil."[110]

PRIMARY AND SECONDARY DEVIANCE

One of the better-known views of the labeling process is Edwin Lemert's concept of primary deviance and secondary deviance.[111] According to Lemert, **primary deviance** involves norm violations or crimes that have little influence on the actor

retrospective reading
The reassessment of a person's past to fit a current generalized label.

primary deviance
A norm violation or crime that has little or no long-term influence on the violator.

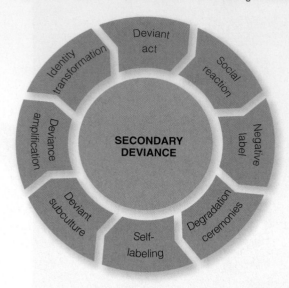

Figure 7.7 Secondary Deviance: The Labeling Process

Deviant act · Social reaction · Negative label · Degradation ceremonies · Self-labeling · Deviant subculture · Deviance amplification · Identity transformation

SECONDARY DEVIANCE

and can be quickly forgotten. For example, a college student successfully steals a textbook at the campus bookstore, gets an A in the course, graduates, is admitted to law school, and later becomes a famous judge. Because his shoplifting goes unnoticed, it is a relatively unimportant event that has little bearing on his future life.

In contrast, **secondary deviance** occurs when a deviant event comes to the attention of significant others or social control agents, who apply a negative label. The newly labeled offender then reorganizes his or her behavior and personality around the consequences of the deviant act. The shoplifting student is caught by a security guard and expelled from college. With his law school dreams dashed and his future cloudy, his options are limited; people say he lacks character, and he begins to share their opinion. He eventually becomes a drug dealer and winds up in prison (see Figure 7.7).

Secondary deviance involves resocialization into a deviant role. The labeled person is transformed into one who, according to Lemert, "employs his behavior or a role based upon it as a means of defense, attack, or adjustment to the overt and covert problems created by the consequent social reaction to him."[112] Secondary deviance produces a **deviance amplification** effect: Offenders feel isolated from the mainstream of society and become locked within their deviant role. They may seek others similarly labeled to form deviant groups. Ever more firmly enmeshed in their deviant role, they are trapped in an escalating cycle of deviance, apprehension, more powerful labels, and identity transformation. Lemert's concept of secondary deviance expresses the core of social reaction theory: Deviance is a process in which one's identity is transformed. Efforts to control offenders, whether by treatment or punishment, simply help to lock them in their deviant role.

CRIME AND LABELING

Because the process of becoming stigmatized is essentially interactive, labeling theorists blame the establishment of criminal careers on the social agencies originally designed for crime control, such as police, courts, and correctional agencies. These institutions, labeling theorists claim, are inflicting the very stigma that harms the people they are trying to treat or correct. As a result, they actually help to maintain and amplify criminal behavior.

Because crime and deviance are defined by the social audience's reaction to people and their behavior and by the subsequent effects of that reaction, these institutions form the audience that helps define behavior as evil or wrong, locking people into deviant identities.

secondary deviance
A norm violation or crime that comes to the attention of significant others or social control agents, who apply a negative label that has long-term consequences for the violator's self-identity and social interactions.

deviance amplification
Process whereby secondary deviance pushes offenders out of mainstream society and locks them into an escalating cycle of deviance, apprehension, labeling, and criminal self-identity.

DIFFERENTIAL ENFORCEMENT

An important principle of social reaction theory is that the law is differentially applied, benefiting those who hold economic and social power and penalizing the powerless. The probability of being brought under the control of legal authority is a function of a person's race, wealth, gender, and social standing. A core concept of social reaction theory is that police officers are more likely to formally arrest males, minority group members, and those in the lower socioeconomic class, and to use their discretionary powers to give beneficial treatment to more favored groups.[113] Minorities and the poor are more likely to be prosecuted for criminal offenses and to receive harsher punishments when convicted.[114] Judges may sympathize with white defendants and help them avoid criminal labels, especially if they seem to come from "good families," whereas minority youths are not afforded that luxury.[115] This helps to explain the significant racial and economic differences in the crime rate.

In sum, a major premise of social reaction theory is that the law is differentially constructed and applied, depending on the offender. It favors powerful members of society, who direct its content, and penalizes the powerless, such as minority group members and the poor, who demand equal rights.[116]

RESEARCH ON SOCIAL REACTION THEORY

Research on social reaction theory can be divided into two distinct categories. The first focuses on the characteristics of those offenders who are chosen for labeling. The theory predicts that they will be relatively powerless people who are unable to defend themselves against the negative labeling. The second type of research attempts to discover the effects of being labeled. Labeling theorists predict that people who are negatively labeled will view themselves as deviant and will commit increasing amounts of crime.

Targets of Labeling There is evidence that, just as predicted by labeling theory, poor and powerless people are victimized by the law and justice system. Labels are not equally distributed across class and racial lines. From the police officer's decision on whom to arrest, to the prosecutor's decision on whom to charge and how many and what kinds of charges to bring, to the court's decision on whom to release or free on bail or personal recognizance, to the grand jury's decision on indictment, to the judge's decision on sentence length—at every step, discretion works to the detriment of minorities.[117] The fact that labels are unfairly applied has focused attention on such practices as **racial profiling**, the practice of singling out minority group members for investigation, arrest, and prosecution simply on the basis of their racial characteristics.

Effects of Labeling Empirical evidence shows that negative labels may dramatically influence the self-image of offenders. Considerable evidence indicates that social sanctions lead to self-labeling and deviance amplification.[118] For example, children negatively labeled by their parents routinely suffer a variety of problems, including antisocial behavior and school failure.[119] This process has been observed in the United States and abroad, indicating that the labeling process is universal, especially in nations in which a brush with the law brings personal dishonor, such as China and Japan.[120]

This labeling process is important because once they are stigmatized as troublemakers, adolescents begin to reassess their self-image. Parents who label their children as troublemakers promote deviance amplification. Labeling alienates parents from their children, and negative labels reduce children's self-image and increase delinquency; this process is referred to as **reflected appraisals**.[121] Parental labeling is extremely damaging because it may cause adolescents to seek deviant peers whose behavior amplifies the effect of the labeling.[122]

As they mature, children are in danger of undergoing repeated, intensive, official labeling, which has been shown to produce self-labeling and to damage identities.[123] Kids who perceive that they have been negatively labeled by significant others, such as peers and teachers, are also more likely to self-report delinquent behavior and to adopt a deviant self-concept.[124] They are likely to make deviant friends and join gangs, associations that escalate their involvement in criminal activities.[125] Youngsters

CONNECTIONS

Fear of stigma has prompted efforts to reduce the impact of criminal labels through such programs as pretrial diversion and community treatment. In addition, some criminologists have called for noncoercive, "peacemaking" solutions to interpersonal conflict. This peacemaking or restorative justice movement is reviewed in Chapter 8.

racial profiling
The use of racial and ethnic characteristics by police in their determining whether a person is likely to commit a crime or engage in deviant and/or antisocial activities.

reflected appraisal
When parents are alienated from their children, their negative labeling reduces their children's self-image and increases delinquency.

Concept Summary 7.1 Social Process Theories

Theory	Major Premise	Strengths	Research Focus
Social Learning Theories			
Differential association theory	People learn to commit crime from exposure to antisocial definitions.	Explains onset of criminality. Explains the presence of crime in all elements of social structure. Explains why some people in high-crime areas refrain from criminality. Can apply to adults and juveniles.	Measuring definitions toward crime; influence of deviant peers and parents
Neutralization theory	Youths learn ways of neutralizing moral restraints and periodically drift in and out of criminal behavior patterns.	Explains why many delinquents do not become adult criminals. Explains why youthful law violators can participate in conventional behavior.	Do people who use neutralizations commit more crimes? Beliefs, values, and crime
Social Control Theory			
Hirschi's control theory	A person's bond to society prevents him or her from violating social rules. If the bond weakens, the person is free to commit crime.	Explains the onset of crime. Can apply to both middle- and lower-class crime. Explains its theoretical constructs adequately so they can be measured. Has been empirically tested.	The association among commitment, attachment, involvement, belief, and crime
Social Reaction Theory			
Labeling theory	People enter into law-violating careers when they are labeled and organize their personalities around the labels.	Explains society's role in creating deviance. Explains why some juvenile offenders do not become adult criminals. Develops concepts of criminal careers.	Measuring the association between self-concept and crime; differential application of labels; and the effect of stigma

labeled as troublemakers in school are the most likely to drop out, and dropping out has been linked to delinquent behavior.[126]

Even in adults, the labeling process can take its toll. Male drug users labeled as addicts by social control agencies eventually become self-labeled and increase their drug use.[127] People arrested in domestic violence cases, especially those with a low stake in conformity (for example, those who are jobless and unmarried), increase their offending after being given official labels.[128] And once in prison, inmates labeled high-risk are more likely to have disciplinary problems than those who are spared such negative labels.[129]

Empirical evidence supports the view that labeling plays a significant role in persistent offending.[130] Although labels may not cause adolescents to initiate criminal behaviors, experienced delinquents are significantly more likely to continue offending if they believe their parents and peers view them in a negative light.[131] Labeling, then, may help sustain criminality over time.

IS LABELING THEORY VALID?

Criminologists Raymond Paternoster and Leeann Iovanni have identified features of the labeling perspective that are important contributions to the study of criminality:[132]

▶ The labeling perspective identifies the role played by social control agents in crime causation. Criminal behavior cannot be fully understood if the agencies and individuals empowered to control and treat it are neglected.

▶ Labeling theory recognizes that criminality is not a disease or pathological behavior. It focuses attention on the social interactions and reactions that shape individuals and their behavior.

▶ Labeling theory distinguishes between criminal acts (primary deviance) and criminal careers (secondary deviance) and shows that these concepts must be interpreted and treated differently.

Labeling theory also contributes to understanding crime by focusing on interaction as well as the situation surrounding the crime. Rather than viewing the criminal as a robot-like creature whose actions are predetermined, it recognizes that crime often results from complex interactions and processes. The decision to commit crime involves actions of a variety of people, including peers, victim, police, and other key characters. Labels may foster crime by dictating the actions of all parties involved in these criminal interactions. Actions deemed innocent when performed by one person are considered provocative when performed by someone who has been labeled deviant. Similarly, labeled people may become quick to judge, take offense, or misinterpret others' behavior because of past experience. ▶ **Checkpoints**

Checkpoints

▶ According to labeling theory, stigma helps lock people into deviant careers.

▶ Labels amplify deviant behavior rather than deterring people from future criminality.

▶ Primary deviants view themselves as good people who have done a bad thing; secondary deviants accept a negative label as an identity.

▶ Labels are bestowed in a biased way. The poor and members of minority groups are more likely than others to receive negative labels.

Social Process Theory and Public Policy

Social process theories have had a major influence on public policy since the 1950s. Learning theories have greatly influenced the way criminal offenders are treated. The effect of these theories has been felt mainly by young offenders, who are viewed

According to social process theories, programs that aid children's socialization also help protect them from crime-producing influences in the environment. Here, as part of the ExCite/Head Start program, a retired professor spends time in the classroom with elementary students, teaching them the colors of the rainbow, reading stories, tying dangling shoelaces, and giggling over games.

Head Start is probably the best-known effort to help lower-class youths achieve proper socialization and, in so doing, reduce their potential for future criminality. Head Start programs were instituted in the 1960s as part of President Johnson's War on Poverty. In the beginning, Head Start was a two-month summer program for children who were about to enter a school that was aimed at embracing the "whole child." In embracing the whole child, the school offered comprehensive programming that helped improve physical health, enhance mental processes, and improve social and emotional development, self-image, and interpersonal relationships. Preschoolers were provided with an enriched educational environment to develop their learning and cognitive skills. They

immunizations; medical, dental, and mental health; and nutritional services.

- *Parent involvement.* An essential part of Head Start is the involvement of parents in parent education, program planning, and operating activities.

- *Social services.* Specific services are geared to each family, including community outreach, referrals, family need assessments, recruitment and enrollment of children, and emergency assistance and/or crisis intervention.

Today, with annual funding of more than $6 billion for more than 1,600 centers that service close to a million students, the Head Start program is administered by the Head Start Bureau, the Administration on Children, Youth,

Policy and Practice in Criminology Head Start

were given the opportunity to use pegs and pegboards, puzzles, toy animals, dolls, letters and numbers, and other materials that middle-class children take for granted. These opportunities gave the children a leg up in the educational process. The program is divided into four segments:

- *Education.* Head Start's educational program is designed to meet the needs of each child and of the community served, needs understood in the context of the community's ethnic and cultural characteristics. Every child receives a variety of learning experiences to foster intellectual, social, and emotional growth.
- *Health.* Head Start emphasizes the importance of the early identification of health problems. Every child is involved in a comprehensive health program, which includes

and Families (ACYF), the Administration for Children and Families (ACF), and the Department of Health and Human Services (DHHS). Head Start teachers strive to provide a variety of learning experiences appropriate to the child's age and development. These experiences encourage the child to read books, to understand cultural diversity, to express feelings, and to play with and relate to peers in an appropriate way. Students are guided in developing gross and fine motor skills and in achieving self-confidence. Health care is also an issue, and most children enrolled in the program receive comprehensive health screening, physical and dental examinations, and appropriate follow-up. Many programs provide meals and thus help children receive proper nourishment.

Head Start programs now serve parents in addition to their preschoolers. Some programs allow parents to enroll

as being more salvageable than hardened criminals. Advocates of the social learning approach argue that if people become criminal by learning definitions and attitudes favoring criminality, they can unlearn these attitudes by being exposed to definitions favoring conventional behavior.

This philosophy has been applied in numerous treatment facilities modeled in part on two early, pioneering efforts: the Highfields Project in New Jersey and the Silverlake Program in Los Angeles. These residential treatment programs, geared toward young male offenders, used group interaction sessions to attack criminal behavior orientations while promoting conventional modes of behavior. It is common today for residential and nonresidential programs to offer similar treatment, teaching children and adolescents to refuse drugs, to forgo delinquent behavior, and to stay in school. It is even common for celebrities to return to their old neighborhoods to urge young people to stay in school or stay off drugs. If learning did not affect behavior, such exercises would be futile.

Control theories have also influenced criminal justice and other social policies. Programs have been developed to increase people's commitment to conventional lines of action. Some focus on trying to create and strengthen bonds early in life before the onset of criminality. The educational system has hosted numerous programs designed to improve students' basic skills and create an atmosphere in which youths will develop a bond to their schools. See the accompanying Policy and Practice in Criminology feature.

in classes that cover parenting, literacy, nutrition and weight loss, domestic violence prevention, and other social issues. Social services, health, nutrition, and educational services are also available. An Early Head Start (EHS) program has been created for low-income infants, toddlers, pregnant women, and their families. EHS programs enhance children's physical, social, emotional, and intellectual development; help pregnant women to access comprehensive prenatal and postpartum care; support parents' efforts to fulfill their parental roles; and assist parents in moving toward self-sufficiency.

Head Start kids appear to have better health, immunization rates, and nutrition, as well as enhanced emotional characteristics, after leaving the program. Research also shows that the Head Start program can have psychological benefits for the mothers of participants, such as decreasing depression and anxiety and increasing feelings of life satisfaction. The best available evidence suggests several outcomes:

- Head Start is associated with short-term gains in cognitive skills as well as longer-term gains in school completion, and even greater gains are possible if children receive good follow-up in the early grades.
- Although Head Start centers vary in quality, on average they are better than privately run child care centers, have achieved short-term benefits, and would pay for themselves if they produced even a fraction of the long-term benefits associated with model programs.
- A seven-year national evaluation of Early Head Start found that the program promotes learning and the parenting that supports it within the first three years of life. Participating children perform significantly better in cognitive, language, and social-emotional development than their peers who do not participate. The program also had important impacts on many aspects of parenting and the home environment, and it supported parents' progress toward economic self-sufficiency.

If, as many experts believe, school performance, family life, and propensity toward crime are closely linked, programs such as Head Start can help some at-risk youths avoid problems with the law. By implication, their success indicates that programs that help socialize youngsters can be used to combat urban criminality. Although problems have been identified in individual centers, the government has shown its faith in Head Start as a socialization agent. Head Start's mission is to help low-income children start school ready to learn by providing early childhood education, promoting child development, and making available comprehensive health and social services.

Since 1965, local Head Start programs across the country have served more than 21 million children and built strong partnerships with parents and families.

CRITICAL THINKING

1. If crime were a matter of human traits, as some criminologists suggest, would a program such as Head Start help kids avoid criminal careers?
2. Can you suggest any other types of programs that might help parents or children avoid involvement in drugs or crime?
3. Were you in Head Start? If so, did it help you achieve your current academic success?

SOURCES: Head Start statistics can be accessed at the Head Start Bureau website, www.acf.hhs.gov/programs/ohs/ (accessed June 8, 2009); Mathematica Policy Research, Inc., "Making a Difference in the Lives of Infants and Toddlers and Their Families: The Impacts of Early Head Start," Vol. I: Final Technical Report, June 2002 (revisions made in January 2004), www.mathematica-mpr.com/publications/pdfs/ehsfinalvol1.pdf (accessed June 9, 2009); Katherine Magnuson, Christopher Ruhm, and Jane Waldfogel, "Does Prekindergarten Improve School Preparation and Performance?" National Bureau of Economic Research working paper, 2004, www.nber.org/digest/mar05/w10452.html.

Control theory's focus on the family has played a key role in programs designed to strengthen the bond between parent and child. Other programs attempt to repair bonds that have been broken and frayed. Examples of this approach are the career, work furlough, and educational opportunity programs being developed in the nation's prisons. These programs are designed to help inmates maintain a stake in society so they will be less willing to resort to criminal activity after their release.

Although labeling theorists caution that too much intervention can be harmful, programs aimed at reconfiguring an offender's self-image may help him or her develop revamped identities and desist from crime. With proper treatment, labeled offenders can cast off their damaged identities and develop new ones. As a result, they develop an improved self-concept that reflects the positive reinforcement they receive while in treatment.[133]

The influence of labeling theory can also be seen in diversion and restitution programs. **Diversion programs** remove both juvenile and adult offenders from the normal channels of the criminal justice process by placing them in rehabilitation programs. For example, a college student whose drunken driving hurts a pedestrian may, before trial, be placed for six months in an alcohol treatment program. If he successfully completes the program, charges against him will be dismissed; thus he avoids the stigma of a criminal label. Such programs are common throughout the United

diversion programs
Programs of rehabilitation that remove offenders from the normal channels of the criminal justice process, thus enabling them to avoid the stigma of a criminal label.

The state legislature is considering a bill that requires posting the names of people convicted of certain offenses (such as vandalism, soliciting a prostitute, and nonpayment of child support) in local newspapers under the heading "The Rogues Gallery." Those who favor the bill cite similar practices elsewhere: In Boston, men arrested for soliciting prostitutes are forced to clean streets. In Dallas, shoplifters are made to stand outside stores with signs stating their misdeeds.

Members of the state Civil Liberties Union have opposed the bill, stating, "It's simply needless humiliation of the individual." They argue that public shaming is inhumane and further alienates criminals who already have little stake in society, further ostracizing them from the mainstream. According to civil liberties attorneys, applying stigma helps criminals acquire a damaged reputation, which locks them more rigidly into criminal behavior patterns.

This "liberal" position is challenged by those who believe that convicted lawbreakers have no right to conceal their crimes from the public. Shaming penalties seem attractive as cost-effective alternatives to imprisonment. These critics ask what could be wrong with requiring a teenage vandal to personally apologize at the school he or she defaced and to wear a shirt with a big "V" on it while cleaning up the mess. If you do something wrong, they argue, you should have to face the consequences.

Writing Assignment

You have been asked to submit a position paper to the legislative committee on the issue of whether shaming could deter crime. What will you say? What are the advantages? What are the possible negative consequences?

States. They frequently offer counseling, medical advice, and vocational, educational, and family services.

Another popular label-avoiding innovation is **restitution**. Rather than face the stigma of a formal trial, an offender is asked either to pay back the victim of the crime for any loss incurred or to do some useful work in the community in lieu of receiving a court-ordered sentence.

restitution
Permitting an offender to repay the victim or do useful work in the community rather than facing the stigma of a formal trial and a court-ordered sentence.

Despite their good intentions, stigma-reducing programs have not met with great success. Critics charge that they substitute one kind of stigma for another—for instance, attending a mental health program in lieu of undergoing a criminal trial. In addition, diversion and restitution programs usually screen out violent and repeat offenders. Finally, there is little hard evidence that these alternative programs improve recidivism rates.

Concept Summary 7.1 on page 190 outlines the major concepts of social process theories.

Summary

1. Be familiar with the concepts of social process and socialization.

    Social process theories view criminality as a function of people's interaction with various organizations, institutions, and processes in society. People in all walks of life have the potential to become criminals if they maintain destructive social relationships. Improper socialization is a key component of crime.

2. Be able to discuss the differences among social learning theory, social control theory, and social reaction (labeling) theory.

    Social learning theory stresses that people learn how to commit crimes. It suggests that people learn criminal behaviors in much the same way as they learn conventional behavior. Social control theory analyzes the failure of society to control criminal tendencies.

    Labeling theory maintains that negative labels produce criminal careers.

3. Discuss the effect of family relationships on crime.

    Kids growing up in troubled families are crime-prone. Parental efficacy reduces crime. Divorce can strain families.

4. Understand how the educational setting influences crime.

    School failure is linked to delinquency. Dropping out may influence later criminality. School violence and conflict are also a problem.

5. Be aware of the link between peers and delinquency.

    Delinquent peers sustain individual offending patterns. Delinquent friends may help kids neutralize the fear of punishment. Both popular kids and loners can have problems.

6. Be familiar with the association between beliefs and criminality.

People with high moral standards can resist crime. Church attendance is related to low crime rates.

7. Discuss the main types of social learning theory.

Differential association theory was formulated by Edwin Sutherland. It holds that criminality is a result of a person's perceiving an excess of definitions in favor of crime. Gresham Sykes and David Matza formulated the theory of neutralization, which stresses that youths learn mental techniques that enable them to overcome societal values and hence break the law.

8. Be familiar with the principles of social control theory.

Control theory maintains that all people have the potential to become criminals, but their bonds to conventional society prevent them from violating the law. This view suggests that a person's self-concept enhances his or her commitment to conventional action. Travis Hirschi's social control theory describes the social bond as containing elements of attachment, commitment, involvement, and belief. Weakened bonds allow youths to behave antisocially.

9. Know the basic elements of social reaction (labeling) theory.

Social reaction or labeling theory holds that criminality is promoted by becoming negatively labeled by significant others. Such labels as "criminal," "ex-con," and "junkie" isolate people from society and lock them into lives of crime. Labels create expectations that the labeled person will act in a certain way, and labeled people are always watched and suspected. Eventually these people begin to accept their labels as personal identities, which may lock them irretrievably into lives of crime and deviance. Edwin Lemert suggests that people who accept labels are involved in secondary deviance, while primary deviants are able to maintain an undamaged identity.

10. Link social process theory to crime prevention efforts.

Social process theories have greatly influenced social policy. They have been applied in treatment orientations as well as community action policies. Some programs teach kids conventional attitudes and behaviors. Others are designed to improve the social bond.

Key Terms

social process theory 168
social learning theory 168
social control theory 168
social reaction (labeling) theory 168
socialization 169
parental efficacy 169
differential association theory 174

culture conflict 174
neutralization theory 176
drift 176
neutralization techniques 176
self-control 180
commitment to conformity 180

social bonds 180
moral entrepreneur 185
stigmatize 185
successful degradation ceremony 186
retrospective reading 187
primary deviance 187
secondary deviance 188

deviance amplification 188
racial profiling 189
reflected appraisal 189
diversion programs 193
restitution 194

Critical Thinking Questions

1. If criminal behavior is learned, who taught the first criminal? Have you ever been exposed to pro-crime definitions? How did you handle them? Did they affect your behavior?

2. Children who do well in school are less likely to commit criminal acts than those who are school failures. Which element of Hirschi's theory is supported by the school failure–delinquency link?

3. Have you ever been given a negative label, and, if so, did it cause you social harm? How did you lose the label, or did it become a permanent marker that still troubles you today?

4. If negative labels are damaging, do positive ones help insulate children from crime-producing forces in their environment? Has a positive label ever changed your life?

5. How would a social process theorist explain the fact that many children begin offending at an early age and then desist from crime as they mature? Are you involved in fewer antisocial acts in college than you were in high school? If so, how do you explain your behavioral changes?

© Reuters/STR/Landov

Chapter Outline

Social Conflict and Critical Criminology

8

In June of 2009, Amnesty International, the civil rights watchdog organization, published a report accusing the Sri Lankan government of a vicious cycle of civil rights abuse in its war against the Tamil Tiger rebel group. In addition, the Sri Lankan government was accused of failing to investigate civil rights violations, including disappearances and torture of political suspects, in their suppression of the Tamil independence movement. Even when the government formed Commissions of Inquiry to investigate disappearances and other human rights–related issues, Amnesty found that these commissions lacked credibility and actually delayed criminal investigations; very few prosecutions for human rights violations ever took place.

These allegations stemmed from the recently ended conflict between government forces and the Tamil Tigers (Liberation Tigers of Tamil Eelam, LTTE), a group that sought to carve out an independent state for the Tamil people, an ethnic/religious minority group. The conflict lasted more than 20 years, and enforced disappearances and extrajudicial executions reached vast proportions. But it was not just the rebels who were hunted and killed. There were more than 30,000 "disappearances" of people considered sympathetic to the Tamil cause, including businessmen, journalists, and individuals suspected of having "terrorist links"; even a vice chancellor of a university was a victim. Once they were taken into government hands, people suspected of aiding the rebels were often never seen again; they just "disappeared." In addition to this outrage, hundreds of thousands of innocent people were displaced from their homes.[1]

Fact or Fiction?

▶ It is illegal for the police to monitor people in public places with cameras and secretly record their activities.

▶ The CIA has sent terror suspects to foreign prisons where they can be subjected to harsh interrogation tactics.

▶ Racial profiling is a myth spread by antipolice radicals.

▶ Abuse of women increases as they get more power and men become envious and resentful of their success.

Chapter Objectives

1. Be familiar with the concept of social conflict and with how it shapes behavior.

2. Be able to discuss elements of conflict in the criminal justice system.

3. Be familiar with the basic ideas of critical criminology.

4. Define the concept of state (organized) crime.

5. Be able to discuss the difference between structural theory and instrumental theory.

6. Know the various techniques of critical research.

7. Be familiar with the critiques of critical criminology.

8. Know some of the basic ideas of critical feminism.

9. Explain the concept of left realism.

10. Discuss peacemaking criminology and restorative justice.

The civil rights violations and executions carried out in Sri Lanka are extreme examples of the social conflict that dominates and shapes contemporary society. We live in a world rife with political, social, and economic conflict in nearly every corner of the globe. Conflict comes in many forms, occurs at many levels of society, and involves a whole slew of adversaries: workers and bosses, the United States and its overseas enemies, religious zealots and apostates, citizens and police. It occurs within cities, in neighborhoods, and even within the family.

Conflict can be destructive when it leads to war, violence, and death; it can be functional when it results in positive social change. Conflict promotes crime by creating a social atmosphere in which the law is a mechanism for controlling dissatisfied, have-not members of society while the wealthy maintain their power. This is why crimes that are the province of the wealthy, such as illegal corporate activities, are sanctioned much more leniently than those, such as burglary, that are considered lower-class activities.

Conflict and Crime

As you may recall from Chapter 1, one of the roots of criminological theory is the political-economic vision created by philosopher Karl Marx. His vision of social change brought about by economic inequality and conflict had a profound influence on twentieth-century thought. Criminologists who view crime as a function of social conflict and economic rivalry have been known by a number of terms, including "conflict criminologists," "Marxist criminologists," and "radical criminologists," but here we will refer to them as critical criminologists and to their field of study as **critical criminology**.

Critical criminologists reject the notion that law is designed to maintain a tranquil, fair society and that criminals are malevolent people who wish to trample the rights of others. After all, the world is filled with acts and behaviors that damage the lives of countless people and cost millions of dollars (a short list includes racism, sexism, imperialism, environmental destruction, and exploitation of workers). Yet these behaviors are not considered "true crimes" because they are acts of the rich and powerful, who are able to control the content of the law and immunize themselves from its grasp. Because those in power shape the content of the law, it comes as no surprise that their behavior is often exempt from legal sanctions. Those who deserve the most severe sanctions (wealthy white-collar criminals whose crimes cost society billions of dollars) usually receive lenient punishments. In contrast, desperate acts of the helpless—petty burglaries, larcenies, and robberies that net a few dollars—are severely punished. Because they are committed by people without any political and social power, these crimes are considered a threat to the well-being of society. But in reality, the critical criminologists maintain, they are provoked by an extremely unfair social system and are more accurately interpreted as expressions of rage over unjust economic conditions than as actual crimes.[2]

This chapter reviews critical criminology—its development and principal ideas. Then it looks at policies that have been embraced by critical thinkers and that focus on peace and restoration rather than punishment and exclusion.

Origins of Critical Criminology

The social ferment of the 1960s gave birth to critical criminology (see Figure 8.1). In 1968, a group of British sociologists formed the National Deviancy Conference (NDC). With about 300 members, this organization sponsored several national symposiums and dialogues. Members came from all walks of life, but at its core was a group of academics who were critical of the positivist criminology being taught in British and American universities. More specifically, they rejected the conservative stance of criminologists and their close association with the government that funded many of their research projects.

critical criminology
The branch of criminology that holds that the cause of crime can be linked to economic, social, and political disparity. Some groups in society, particularly the working class and ethnic minorities, are seen as the most likely to suffer oppressive social relations based on class conflict and racism and hence to be more prone to criminal behavior.

Figure 8.1 The Branches of Critical Criminology

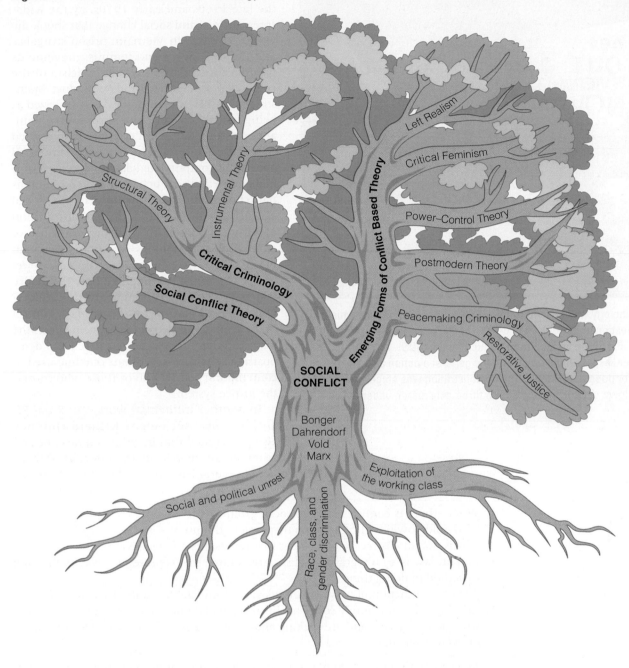

The NDC called attention to ways in which social control might actually *cause* deviance rather than just being a response to antisocial behavior. Many conference members became concerned about the political nature of social control.

In 1973, critical theory was given a powerful academic boost when British scholars Ian Taylor, Paul Walton, and Jock Young published *The New Criminology*.[3] This brilliant, thorough, and well-constructed critique of existing concepts in criminology called for the development of new methods of criminological analysis and critique. *The New Criminology* became the standard resource for scholars critical of both the field of criminology and the existing legal process. Since its publication, critical criminologists have established a tradition of focusing on the field itself and questioning the role criminology plays in supporting the status quo and collaborating in the oppression of the poor and powerless.[4]

Critical criminology was shaped by the social unrest of the 1960s, which led to the questioning of social and governmental power structures. Here, participants in a Students for a Democratic Society (SDS)–sponsored demonstration display signs protesting the general election as a "hoax" and calling for peace in Vietnam. The demonstration was staged on the steps of the Iowa capitol building after a three-mile march under police supervision.

U.S. scholars were also influenced, during the late 1960s and early 1970s, by the widespread unrest and social change that shook the world. The war in Vietnam, prison struggles, and the civil rights and feminist movements produced a climate in which criticism of the ruling class seemed a natural by-product. Mainstream, positivist criminology was criticized as being overtly conservative, pro-government, and antihuman. Critical criminologists scoffed when their fellow scholars used statistical analysis of computerized data to describe criminal and delinquent behavior. Several influential scholars embraced the idea that the social conflict produced by the unequal distribution of **power** and wealth was the root cause of crime. William Chambliss and Robert Seidman wrote the well-respected treatise *Law, Order and Power,* which documented how the justice system protects the rich and powerful.[5] Chambliss and Seidman's work showed how control of the political and economic system affects the way criminal justice is administered and demonstrated that the definitions of crime used in contemporary society favor those who control the justice system.

In another influential work, *The Social Reality of Crime*, sociologist Richard Quinney also proclaimed that in contemporary society, criminal law represents the interests of those who hold power in society.[6] He formulated several basic principles that inform the relationship between law, power, and crime:

1. Where there is conflict between social groups—the wealthy and the poor—those who hold power will create laws that benefit themselves and keep rivals in check.
2. Law is not an abstract body of rules that represents an objective moral code.
3. Rather, law is an integral part of society, a force that represents a way of life, and a method of doing things.
4. Crime is a function of power relations and an inevitable result of social conflict.
5. Criminals are not simply social misfits but people who have come up short in the struggle for success and are seeking alternative means of achieving wealth, status, or even survival.

As a group, these social thinkers began to show how, in our postindustrial, capitalist society, the economic system invariably produces haves and have-nots.[7] The mode of production shapes social life. Because economic competitiveness is the essence of capitalism, conflict increases and eventually destabilizes both social institutions and social groups.[8]

CONTEMPORARY CRITICAL CRIMINOLOGY

From these early roots a robust critical criminology has grown. Although critical criminologists still rely on Marx's identification of the social/economic/political forces that shape individual behavior, these views have morphed into a critical criminology that, at its core, questions the racial, gender, and economic inequalities that produce crime and criminality.[9]

Critical criminologists devote their attention to a number of important themes and concepts.

power
The ability of persons and groups to control the behavior of others, to shape public opinion, and to define deviance.

- Identifying the way social class, crime, and social control are connected[10]
- Explaining the role government plays in creating a criminogenic environment
- Identifying the relationship between personal or group power and the shaping of criminal law
- Examining race and gender bias in justice system operations
- Demystifying the relationship between a capitalistic, free-enterprise economy and crime rates
- Showing how people and institutions misuse their political/social/media power to control the behavior of others and shape public opinion. To critique the field/discipline of criminology, questioning the role that criminologists play in supporting the status quo and aiding in oppression of the poor and powerless[11]

Critical criminologists are also deeply concerned about the current state of the American political system and the creation of what they consider an American empire abroad. Ironically, recent events (such as the war in Iraq and the efforts to penalize immigrants and close the borders) have energized critical thinkers; their vision seems as pertinent today as it was during its heyday in the 1960s and 1970s.[12] The conservative agenda, they believe, calls for dismantling welfare and health programs, lowering labor costs through union busting, enacting tax cuts that favor the wealthy, ending affirmative action, and reducing environmental control and regulation. While spending is being cut on social programs, it is being raised on military expansion. The rapid buildup of the prison system and passage of draconian criminal laws that threaten civil rights and liberties—the death penalty, three strikes laws, and the USA PATRIOT Act—are other elements of the conservative agenda. Critical criminologists believe that they are responsible for informing the public about the dangers of these developments.[13]

The prevalence of racism and sexism is another key interest of critical thinkers. Some show how racism still pervades the American system and manifests itself in a wide variety of social practices, ranging from the administration of criminal justice to the "whitening" of the teaching force because the mechanism for filling its ranks rests upon a racially skewed selection process.[14]

Critical criminologists have turned their attention to the threat that competitive capitalism presents to the working class. They believe that in addition to perpetuating male supremacy and racialism, modern global capitalism helps destroy the lives of workers in less-developed countries. For example, capitalists hailed China's entry into the World Trade Organization in 2001 as a significant economic event. However, critical thinkers point out that the economic boom has significant costs: The average manufacturing wage in China is 20 to 25 cents per hour, and thousands of workers are killed at work each week and many more permanently or temporarily disabled.[15]

How Critical Criminologists Define Crime

According to critical theorists, crime is a political concept designed to protect the power and position of the upper classes at the expense of the poor. Part of the critical agenda, argues criminologist Robert Bohm, is to make the public aware that these behaviors "are crimes just as much as burglary and robbery."[16] Take, for instance, what Alette Smeulers and Roelof Haveman call *supranational crimes*: war crimes, crimes against humanity, genocide, and other human rights violations. Smeulers and Haveman believe that these types of crimes merit more attention by criminologists, and therefore they call for a separate specialization called **supranational criminology**, consisting of the study of war crimes, crimes against humanity, and the supranational penal system in which such crimes are prosecuted and tried.[17]

In our advanced technological society, those with economic and political power control the definition of crime and the manner in which the criminal justice system enforces the law.[18] Each stratum of the socioeconomic structure is involved with its own unique brand of criminality:

supranational criminology
The study of war crimes, crimes against humanity, and the supranational penal system.

- The poor are involved in "street crimes" (rape, murder, theft, and mugging) that are subject to police surveillance and severe sanctions.
- Members of the middle class engage in petty white-collar crime such as cheating on their taxes and petty corporate crime (employee theft)—acts that generate social disapproval but are rarely punished severely.
- The wealthy are involved in immoral acts that should be described as crimes but often are not, such as racism, sexism, and profiteering.

This system certainly favors the upper classes. Although regulatory laws control illegal business activities, these are rarely enforced, and violations are lightly punished. One reason is that an essential feature of capitalism is the need to expand business and create new markets. This goal often conflicts with laws designed to protect the environment and creates clashes with those who seek the enforcement of those laws. In our postindustrial society, the need for expansion usually triumphs. Corporate spokespeople and their political allies brand environmentalists as "tree huggers" who stand in the way of jobs and prosperity.[19]

The rich are insulated from street crimes because they live in areas far removed from crime. Those in power use the fear of crime as a tool to maintain their control over society. The poor are controlled through incarceration, and the middle class is diverted from caring about the crimes of the powerful by their fear of the crimes of the powerless.[20] Ironically, however, they may have more to lose from the economic crimes committed by the rich than from the street crimes of the poor. Stock market swindles and savings and loan scams cost the public billions of dollars, but they are typically settled with fines and probationary sentences.

Because private ownership of property is the true measure of success in American society (as opposed to being, say, a worthy person), the state becomes an ally of the wealthy in protecting their property interests. As a result, theft-related crimes are often punished more severely than acts of violence, because although the former may be interclass, the latter are typically intraclass.

STATE (ORGANIZED) CRIME

While mainstream criminologists focus on the crimes of the poor and powerless, critical criminologists focus their attention on the law violations of the powerful. One area of concern is referred to as **state (organized) crime**—acts defined by law as criminal and committed by state officials, both elected or appointed, while holding their positions as government representatives. Their actions, or in some cases their failure to act, amount to a violation of the criminal law they are bound by oath or duty to uphold.

Those who study state crime argue that these antisocial behaviors arise from efforts either to maintain governmental power or to uphold the race, class, and gender advantages of those who support the government. In industrial society, the state goes to great lengths to protect the property rights of the wealthy, while opposing the real interests of the poor. The government might even go to war to support the capitalist classes who need the wealth and resources of other nations. The desire for natural resources such as rubber, oil, and metals was one of the primary reasons for Japan's invasion of China and other Eastern nations, which sparked their entry into World War II. Fifty years later, the United States was accused by many media

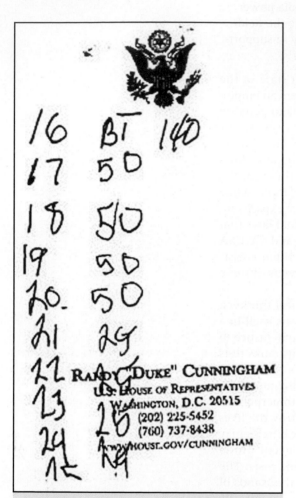

This document, submitted as evidence at the sentencing of Congressman Randy "Duke" Cunningham, was written in his own hand on congressional office stationery. The left column lists (in millions of dollars) the amount of government contracts; the right column lists (in thousands of dollars) the bribes Cunningham expected to get for his influence in securing them for contractors. For example, for $50,000 in bribes, Cunningham could promise $17 million, $18 million, and so on, of awarded contracts. "BT" is an abbreviation for "Buoy Toy," the $140,000 yacht ("140" to the right) that Cunningham received in exchange for $16 million in contracts. As the image indicates, once he had received $340,000 in bribes, Cunningham was willing to drop his rates to half price.

commentators and political pundits of invading Iraq in order to secure its oil for America's use.[21]

There are a number of different types of state crime and some of the most important are discussed in the following sections.[22]

Political Corruption Randy "Duke" Cunningham was a highly decorated Navy pilot who became a congressman representing California. However, he was forced to resign from the House of Representatives on November 28, 2005, after pleading guilty to accepting at least $2.4 million in bribes from defense contractors and failing to report his ill-got gains on his income tax returns (see the accompanying photo for a list of his "ill-got gains"). Cunningham's scheme was rather straightforward: As a member of the Defense Appropriations Subcommittee, he funneled government contracts to defense companies that paid him large bribes; the more money they gave him, the bigger the contract they received. On March 3, 2006, he was sentenced to eight years and four months in prison and ordered to pay $1.8 million in restitution.[23]

Cunningham's crimes are certainly not unique. State crimes such as his can involve violation of citizen trust through soliciting bribes (usually money or some other economic benefit, such as a gift or service). Some politicians, judges, police, and government regulators engage in corruption that damages public trust in the government and its processes. And unfortunately, when corruption is uncovered and the perpetrator brought to justice, it is difficult to determine whether a real criminal has been caught or a political opponent framed and punished.

Illegal Domestic Surveillance This occurs when government agents listen in on telephone conversations or intercept emails without proper approval in order to stifle dissent and monitor political opponents. Sometimes the true purpose of the surveillance is masked by claims of its importance to national security, whereas in reality it is illegal organizational policy and practice that has in some cases been sanctioned by heads of state for political purposes. The opportunities for illegal surveillance have been magnified by the routine use of closed-circuit TV cameras by metropolitan police agencies. Many cities, including Washington, New York, Chicago, and Los Angeles, have installed significant numbers of police-operated cameras trained on public spaces. Although they are ostensibly used to deter crime, once these surveillance facilities are in place, police departments can use them to record the faces of political demonstrators, to record what people are reading, and to store people's photographs on computer databases without their knowledge or permission. This capability worries civil libertarians as well as critical criminologists.[24]

Human Rights Violations Some governments, such as that of Iran, routinely deny their citizens basic civil rights, holding them without trial and using "disappearances" and summary executions to rid themselves of political dissidents. After students rioted against governmental controls in 1999, more than 70 simply disappeared, another 1,200–1,400 were detained, and dozens were killed when security forces broke up demonstrations.[25] Similar violent actions to break up demonstrations took place on the week of June 12, 2009, in the wake of the disputed election that returned President Mahmoud Ahmadinejad to power.

Another state crime involves becoming associated with correctional systems in nations that are notorious for depriving detainees of basic necessities and for inflicting hard labor and torture to punish political dissidents. The CIA has made use of their brutal regimes to soften up terror suspects for interrogation and has sent terror suspects to secret prisons abroad, without trial or indictment. Here they can be subjected to harsh interrogation tactics forbidden in the United States.[26]

Other human rights violations are directed against migrant laborers. For example, thousands of South Asian migrant workers are now working on a $27 billion island development in the United Arab Emirates. According to Human Rights Watch, in order to obtain the visas needed to work in the UAE, nearly all workers paid hefty

CONNECTIONS

We will revisit political crimes such as Cunningham's in the section on exploitation in Chapter 12.

Fact or Fiction?

It is illegal for the police to monitor people in public places with cameras and secretly record their activities.

Fiction. Since 9/11, local police in many cities in the United States have installed security cameras to monitor people in public places.

Fact or Fiction?

The CIA has sent terror suspects to foreign prisons where they can be subjected to harsh interrogation tactics.

Fact. President Bush admitted to having sent terror suspects to foreign prisons for interrogation in 2006.

state (organized) crime
Acts committed by state or government officials while holding their positions as government representatives.

fees to "labor-supply agencies"; many workers sold their homes or land or borrowed money at high rates of interest to pay the agencies' fees. Upon arrival in the UAE, the indebted workers, many of whom are illiterate, were required to sign contracts with the construction companies on much worse terms than they had been promised back home, ensuring that their debts can never be paid off. In the worst cases, they are subjected to what amounts to forced labor or virtual slavery.[27]

State–Corporate Crime This type of state crime is committed by individuals who abuse their state authority or who fail to exercise it when working with people and organizations in the private sector. These crimes may occur when a state institution such as an environmental agency fails to enforce laws, resulting in the pollution of public waterways. State–corporate crime is particularly alarming because regulatory laws aimed at controlling private corporations are being scaled back at a time when globalization has made corporations worldwide entities both in production and in advancing the consumption of their products.[28]

State Violence Sometimes governments engage in violence to maintain their power over dissident groups. An army of police officers may form **death squads**—armed vigilante groups that kill suspected political opponents or other undesirables. These groups commit assassinations and kidnappings, using extremely violent methods to intimidate the population and deter citizens from engaging in political activity against the government. For example, on January 24, 2009, Manoel Mattos, human rights activist and vice president of the workers' party in the state of Pernambuco, Brazil, was shot in his own home by intruders. Mattos had received repeated death threats as a result of his denouncing killings and abuses by death squads across northeast Brazil. Despite these threats, federal police had recently withdrawn the protection Mattos was receiving, because, they maintained, they believed it was no longer necessary.[29]

The use of death squads is common in developing countries, and even in Western industrialized nations, police violence and use of deadly force are not uncommon. In some nations, such as the Russian province of Chechnya during the civil war, nearly all political detainees were subjected to torture, including electric shocks, burnings, and severe beating with boots, sticks, plastic bottles filled with water or sand, and heavy rubber-coated cables. The rest were subjected to psychological pressure, such as intimidation via threats of sexual abuse or execution, as well as threats of harm to their relatives.[30]

State-sponsored violence is not restricted to death squads. The use of torture and waterboarding by U.S. interrogators to subdue terror suspects has become a subject of national debate and is the topic of the accompanying Current Issues in Crime feature.
▶ **Checkpoints**

How Critical Criminologists View the Cause of Crime

Critical thinkers believe that the key crime-producing element of modern corporate capitalism is the effort to create **surplus value**—the profits produced by the laboring classes that are accrued by business owners. Once accumulated, surplus value can be either reinvested or used to enrich the owners. To increase the rate at which surplus value accumulates, workers can be made to toil harder for less pay, be made more efficient, or be replaced by machines or technology. Therefore, economic growth does not benefit all elements of the population, and in the long run it may produce the same effect as a depression or recession.

As the rate of surplus value increases, more people are displaced from productive relationships, and the size of the marginal population swells. As corporations downsize to increase profits, high-paying labor and managerial jobs are lost to computer-driven machinery. Displaced workers are forced into service jobs at minimum wage. Many become temporary employees without benefits or a secure position.

Checkpoints

▶ Critical criminology focuses on identifying "real" crimes in U.S. society, such as profiteering, sexism, and racism.

▶ It seeks to evaluate how criminal law is used as a mechanism of social control.

It describes how power relations create inequities in U.S. society.

▶ Critical criminologists are concerned with the conservative control over American domestic and foreign policy.

▶ According to critical theory, crime is defined by those who hold power.

▶ The wealthy shield themselves from crime through their control over law.

▶ State crime consists of crimes committed by state officials in pursuit of their jobs as government representatives.

death squads
Covert military or paramilitary groups that carry out political assassinations.

surplus value
The difference between what workers produce and what they are paid, which goes to business owners as profits.

Of all state crimes, the use of torture to gain information from suspected political criminals is perhaps the most notorious. Most people loathe the thought of anyone being tortured, but some experts argue that torture can sometimes be justified in what they call the ticking bomb scenario. Suppose the government found out that a captured terrorist knew the whereabouts of a dangerous explosive device that was set to go off and kill thousands of innocent people. Would it be permissible to torture this single suspect if doing so would save the population of a city? Although the ticking bomb scenario is persuasive to some, opponents of torture believe that even imminent danger does not justify state violence. There is a danger that such state-sponsored violence would become calculated and premeditated; torturers would, by necessity, have to be trained, ready, and in place for the ticking bomb argument to apply.

for United States authorities to engage in indefinite detention or in torture, regardless of the end, the place, or the victim.[32]

The Waterboarding Controversy

Can a bright line be drawn between what is considered torture and what constitute firm but legal interrogation methods? This issue made headlines when it was revealed, in 2007, that the CIA made routine use of the waterboarding technique while interrogating suspected terrorists.[33] Waterboarding involves immobilizing a person on his or her back, with the head inclined downward, and pouring water over the face and into the breathing passages. This produces an immediate gag reflex and an experience akin to drowning; the subject believes that death is imminent.

The use of waterboarding is controversial because there seems to be no agreement on whether it is torture or a

Current Issues in Crime Torturing Terror Suspects

We couldn't be running around looking for torturers with a bomb set to go off, could we? Because torturers would be part of the government bureaucracy, there is no way to ensure that they would use their skills only in certain "morally justifiable" cases. What happens if a superior officer tells them to torture someone, but they believe the order is unjustified? Should they follow orders or risk a court martial for being disobedient? In addition, there is very little empirical evidence that torture provides any real benefits, and much more evidence suggests that it can create serious problems. It can damage civil rights and democratic institutions and cause the general public to have sympathy for the victims of torture, no matter their evil intent.[31]

Critics have complained that government agencies such as the Central Intelligence Agency (CIA), have used torture without legal authority. Despite the illegality of torture, enemy agents have been detained and physically abused in secret prisons around the world without the benefit of due process. In some cases, suspects have been held in foreign countries simply because the governments of those countries are not squeamish about using torture during interrogations. Shocking photo evidence of torture from detention facilities at the Guantanamo base in Cuba support their charges. Legal scholars have argued that these tactics violate both international treaties and domestic statutes prohibiting torture. Some maintain that the U.S. Constitution limits the authority of an executive agency such as the CIA to act against foreigners abroad and also that the government's right to use physical coercion is limited by the due process and self-incrimination clauses of the Fifth Amendment and by the Eighth Amendment prohibition of cruel and unusual punishments. Legally, it is not permissible

relatively harmless instrument of interrogation. Even though official U.S. government policy and government doctrine vehemently oppose torture, U.S. authorities have condoned harsh interrogation techniques that combine physical and psychological tactics, including head-slapping, waterboarding, and exposure to extreme cold. Waterboarding even became an issue during the 2008 presidential campaign, when Senator John McCain, a former prisoner of war who had experienced torture firsthand in a North Vietnamese prison camp, gave his opinion. McCain told the press, "All I can say is that it was used in the Spanish Inquisition, it was used in Pol Pot's genocide in Cambodia, and there are reports that it is being used against Buddhist monks today. . . . They should know what it is. It is not a complicated procedure. It is torture."[34]

JESSICA Wolfendale, "Training Torturers: A Critique of the 'Ticking Bomb' Argument," *Social Theory & Practice* 31 (2006): 269–287; Vittorio Bufacchi and Jean Maria Arrigo, "Torture, Terrorism and the State: A Refutation of the Ticking-Bomb Argument," *Journal of Applied Philosophy* 23 (2006): 355–373; Elizabeth Sepper, "The Ties That Bind: How the Constitution Limits the CIA's Actions in the War on Terror," *New York University Law Review* 81 (2006): 1,805–1,843; Scott Shane, David Johnston, and James Risen, "Secret U.S. Endorsement of Severe Interrogations," *New York Times*, October 4, 2007, www.nytimes.com/2007/10/04/washington/04interrogate.html?_r=1&oref=slogin (accessed May 17, 2009); Michael Cooper and Marc Santora, "McCain Rebukes Giuliani on Waterboarding Remark," *New York Times*, October 26, 2007, www.nytimes.com/2007/10/26/us/politics/26giuliani.html (accessed May 18, 2009); Alan M. Dershowitz, *Shouting Fire: Civil Liberties in a Turbulent Age* (New York: Little, Brown, 2002); Human Rights Watch, "The Twisted Logic of Torture," January 2005, http://hrw.org/wr2k5/darfurandabughraib/6.htm (accessed May 18, 2009).

Figure 8.2 Surplus Value and Crime

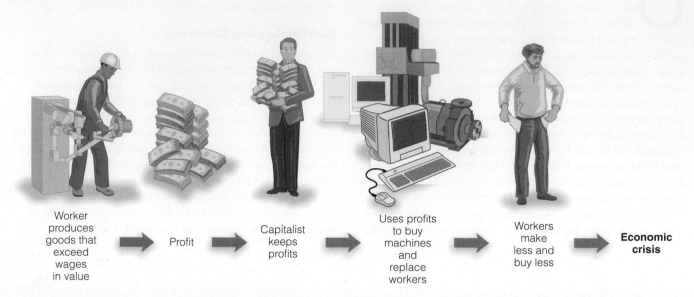

Worker produces goods that exceed wages in value → Profit → Capitalist keeps profits → Uses profits to buy machines and replace workers → Workers make less and buy less → **Economic crisis**

As more people are thrust outside the economic mainstream—a condition referred to as **marginalization**—a larger portion of the population is forced to live in areas conducive to crime. Once people are marginalized, commitment to the system declines, producing another criminogenic force: a weakened bond to society.[35] This process is illustrated in Figure 8.2.

The government may be quick to respond during periods of economic decline because those in power assume that poor economic conditions breed crime and social disorder. When unemployment is increasing, public officials assume the worst and devote greater attention to the criminal justice system, perhaps building new prisons to prepare for the coming "crime wave."[36] Empirical research confirms that economic downturns are indeed linked to government activities such as passing anticrime legislation that are meant to get tough on crime.[37] As the level of surplus value increases, so too do police expenditures, most likely because of the perceived or real need for the state to control those on the economic margin.[38]

GLOBALIZATION

The global economy is a particularly vexing development for critical theorists and their use of the concept of surplus value. **Globalization**, which usually refers to the process of creating transnational markets and political and legal systems, has shifted the focus of critical inquiry to a world perspective.

Globalization began when large companies decided to establish themselves in foreign markets by adapting their products or services to the local culture. The process took off with the fall of the Soviet Union, which opened new European markets. The development of China into an industrial superpower encouraged foreign investors to take advantage of China's huge supply of workers. As the Internet and communication revolution unfolded, companies established instant communications with their far-flung corporate empires, a technological breakthrough that further enhanced trade and foreign investments. A series of transnational corporate mergers and takeovers (such as Pfizer purchasing Wyeth for $68 billion) produced ever-larger transnational corporations.

Some experts believe that globalization can improve the standard of living in third world nations by providing jobs and training, but critical theorists question the altruism of multinational corporations. Their motives include exploiting natural resources, avoiding regulation, and taking advantage of desperate workers. When these giant corporations set up a factory in a developing nation, it is not to help the local

marginalization
Displacement of workers, pushing them outside the economic and social mainstream.

globalization
The process of creating a global economy through transnational markets and political and legal systems.

population but to get around environmental laws and take advantage of needy workers who may be forced to labor in substandard conditions.

In some cases, transnational companies take advantage of national unrest and calamity in order to engage in profiteering. For example, recent examinations of illegal mineral expropriation in the Democratic Republic of Congo (DRC) highlight the role that transnational corporations and international marketplaces played in the theft of Congolese gold. Perhaps these companies did not directly encourage the conflict or the massive human rights violations and crimes against humanity committed in the region, but they clearly took advantage of existing disorder and violence to reap huge profits.[39] Globalization has replaced imperialism and colonization as a new form of economic domination and oppression.

Globalization can present a number of threats to the world economy:

1. Growing global dominance and the reach of the free-market capitalist system, which disproportionately benefits wealthy and powerful organizations and individuals
2. Increasing vulnerability of indigenous peoples with a traditional way of life to the forces of globalized capitalism

Protesters march outside the Anglo American building in London on April 15, 2008. The protesters are accusing mining giant Anglo American of profiting at the expense of developing countries. According to the antipoverty charity War on Want, Anglo American's mining operations are worsening poverty, damaging the environment, and fueling conflict. Critics charge that poor communities in Colombia, the Philippines, the Democratic Republic of Congo, South Africa, Ghana, and Mali are being intimidated and repressed. Critical criminologists view such exploitation as the true cause of crime. Can we blame people who have been exploited if, in order to survive, they break the laws imposed by the ruling classes?

3. Growing influence and impact of international financial institutions (such as the World Bank) and the relative decline in the power of local or state-based institutions
4. Nondemocratic operation of international financial institutions [40]

Globalization may have a profound influence on the concept of surplus value. Workers in the United States who formerly held high-paying manufacturing jobs may be replaced not by machines but by foreign workers. Instant communication via the Internet and global communications, a development that Marx could not have foreseen, will speed this development immeasurably. Globalization will have a significant effect on the economy and, eventually, on crime rates.

Instrumental vs. Structural Theory

Not all critical thinkers share the same view of society and its control by the means of production. Instrumental theorists view criminal law and the criminal justice system solely as instruments for controlling the poor, have-not members of society. They view the state as the tool of capitalists. In contrast, structural theorists believe that the law is not the exclusive domain of the rich; rather, it is used to maintain the long-term interests of the capitalist system and to control members of *any* class who threaten its existence.

INSTRUMENTAL THEORY

According to the **instrumental theory**, the law and justice system serves the powerful and rich and enables them to impose their morality and standards of behavior on the entire society. Those who wield economic power can extend their self-serving

instrumental theory
The theory that criminal law and the criminal justice system are capitalist instruments for controlling the lower class.

definition of illegal or criminal behavior to encompass those who might threaten the status quo or interfere with their quest for ever-increasing profits.[41] The concentration of economic assets in the nation's largest industrial firms translates into the political power needed to control tax laws to limit the firms' tax liability.[42] Some companies have the economic clout to hire top attorneys to defend them against antitrust actions, making them almost immune to regulation.

According to this branch of critical theory, the poor may or may not commit more crimes than the rich, but they certainly are arrested and punished more often. Under the capitalist system, the poor are driven to crime because frustration naturally exists in a society in which affluence is well publicized but unattainable. When class conflict becomes unbearable, frustration can boil over in riots, such as the one that occurred in Los Angeles on April 29, 1992, which was described as a "class rebellion of the underprivileged against the privileged."[43] Class conflict generates a deep-rooted hostility among members of the lower class toward a social order they are not allowed to shape and whose benefits are unobtainable.[44]

Instrumental theorists consider it essential to **demystify** law and justice—that is, to unmask its true purpose. Criminological theories that focus on family structure, intelligence, peer relations, and school performance keep the lower classes servile by showing why they are more criminal, less intelligent, and more prone to school failure and family problems than the middle class. Demystification involves identifying the destructive intent of capitalist-inspired and -funded criminology. Instrumental theory's goal for criminology is to show how capitalist law preserves ruling-class power.[45]

STRUCTURAL THEORY

Structural theorists disagree with the view that the relationship between law and capitalism is unidirectional, always working for the rich and against the poor.[46] If law and justice were purely instruments of the wealthy, why would laws controlling corporate crimes, such as price fixing, false advertising, and illegal restraint of trade, have been created and enforced? Why would rich and powerful business executives from companies such as Enron and Worldcom now be serving prison sentences?

According to the **structural theory**, the law is designed to keep the system operating efficiently, and anyone, worker or owner, who rocks the boat is targeted for sanction. For example, antitrust legislation is designed to prevent any single capitalist from dominating the system. If the free-enterprise system is to function, no single person can become too powerful at the expense of the economic system as a whole. Structuralists would regard the efforts of the U.S. government to break up Microsoft as an example of a conservative government using its clout to keep the system on an even keel. The long prison sentences given to corporate executives who engage in insider trading is a warning to capitalists that they must play by the rules.

Research on Critical Criminology

Critical criminologists rarely use standard social science methodologies to test their views because many believe the traditional approach of measuring research subjects is antihuman and insensitive.[47] Critical thinkers believe that research conducted by mainstream liberal and positivist criminologists is often designed to unmask weak, powerless members of society so they can be better dealt with by the legal system. They are particularly offended by purely empirical studies, such as those designed to show that minority group members have lower IQs than whites, or that the inner city is the site of the most serious crime whereas middle-class areas are relatively free of crime. Critical scholars are more likely to examine historical trends and patterns than to do surveys and crunch numbers. Historian Michael Rustigan examined changes in criminal law by analyzing historical records revealing that law reform in nineteenth-century England was largely a response to pressure from the business community to increase punishment for property law violations to protect their rapidly increasing

demystify
To unmask the true purpose of law, justice, or other social institutions.

structural theory
The theory that criminal law and the criminal justice system are means of defending and preserving the capitalist system.

wealth.[48] Other research has focused on topics such as how the relationship between convict work and capitalism evolved in the nineteenth century. During this period, prisons became a profitable method of centralized state control over lower-class criminals, whose labor was exploited by commercial concerns. These criminals were forced to labor to pay off wardens and correctional administrators.[49]

Empirical research is not considered totally incompatible with critical criminology, and there have been some important efforts to test its fundamental assumptions. One area of critical research involves examining the criminal justice system to see whether it operates as an instrument of class oppression or as a fair, even-handed social control agency. Research has found that jurisdictions with significant levels of economic disparity are also the most likely to have large numbers of people killed by police officers. Police may act more forcefully in areas where class conflict creates the perception that extreme forms of social control are needed to maintain order.[50]

Empirical research also shows, as predicted by critical theory, that a suspect's race is an important factor in shaping justice system decision making. Using data from a national survey, Ronald Weitzer and Steven Tuch found that about 40 percent of African American respondents, compared to only 5 percent of whites, claimed they were stopped by police because of their race; almost 75 percent of young African American men, aged 18 to 34, said they were victims of profiling.[51] Recent research by Albert Meehan and Michael Ponder found that police are more likely to use racial profiling to stop black motorists as they travel farther into the boundaries of predominantly white neighborhoods: Black motorists driving in an all-white neighborhood attract such attention because they are "out of place."[52] It is not surprising to critical theorists that complaints of police brutality are highest in minority neighborhoods, especially those that experience relative deprivation (that is, where African American residents earn significantly less money than the European American majority).[53]

The conflict between police and the minority community can result in violence and charges of racism, a topic explored in the accompanying Profiles in Crime feature.

Criminal courts are also more likely to dole out harsh punishments to members of powerless, disenfranchised groups.[54] Both white and black offenders have been found to receive stricter sentences if their personal characteristics (single, young, urban, male) show them to be members of the "dangerous classes."[55] Unemployed racial minorities may be perceived as "social dynamite" who present a real threat to society and must be controlled and incapacitated.[56] Race also plays a role in prosecution and punishment. African American defendants are more likely to be prosecuted under habitual offender statutes when they commit crimes where there is greater likelihood of a white victim, such as larceny and burglary, than when they commit violent crimes that are largely intraracial; in other words, where there is a perceived "racial threat," punishment is enhanced.[57] Critical analysis also shows that despite legal controls, use of the death penalty seems to be skewed against racial minorities.[58]

Considering these examples of how conflict controls the justice process, it is not surprising when analysis of national population trends and imprisonment rates shows that as the percentage of minority group members increases in a population, the imprisonment rate does likewise.[59] Similarly, states with a substantial minority population have a much higher imprisonment rate than those with predominantly white populations.[60]

Some critical researchers have attempted to show how capitalism influences the distribution of punishment. Robert Weiss found that the expansion of the prison population is linked to the need for capitalists to acquire a captive and low-paid labor force to compete with overseas laborers and domestic immigrant labor. Employing immigrants has its political downside, because it displaces "American" workers and antagonizes their legal representatives. In contrast, using prison labor can be viewed as a humanitarian gesture. Weiss also observes that an ever-increasing prison population is politically attractive because it masks unemployment rates. Many inmates were chronically unemployed before their imprisonment; incarcerating the chronically unemployed allows politicians to claim they have lowered unemployment. When the millions of people who are on probation and parole and who must

CONNECTIONS

Enforcement of laws against illegal business activities such as price fixing, restraint of trade, environmental crimes, and false advertising is discussed in Chapter 12. Although some people are sent to prison for these white-collar offenses, many offenders are still punished just with a fine or economic sanction.

Fact or Fiction?

Racial profiling is a myth spread by antipolice radicals.

Fiction. Research shows that some police officers do in fact use racial profiling when they stop black motorists.

Mumia Abu-Jamal (born Wesley Cook, April 24, 1954) began his journalism career with the radical Black Panther Party in the 1960s. At 15, he was appointed Minister of Information for the Philadelphia chapter. After the party disbanded, he used his writing and speaking talent to become a local broadcaster, later becoming president of the Philadelphia Association of Black Journalists.

Then Mumia Abu-Jamal's life was turned upside down when he was charged with first-degree murder in the killing of police officer Daniel Faulkner. According to authorities, on December 9, 1981, Faulkner, then a 25-year-old Philadelphia police officer, stopped a car for driving the wrong way down the street. Calling for backup, he approached the car and asked the driver, Mr. William Cook, to exit the vehicle. A struggle ensued. According to prosecutors, Mumia Abu-Jamal, Cook's older brother, was sitting in a taxicab across the street watching the events unfold. Abu-Jamal approached Officer Faulkner and shot him in the back. Faulkner was able to draw his gun and fire one return shot that struck Abu-Jamal in the upper abdomen. Having fired this shot, Officer Faulkner fell to the sidewalk. While Faulkner lay helpless, Abu-Jamal approached him and shot him numerous times at close range, killing him.

At trial, four eyewitnesses testified that they saw Abu-Jamal kill Faulkner, experts testified that the gun that killed Faulkner was Abu-Jamal's, and jurors heard that a wounded Abu-Jamal was found at the scene of the crime. He was convicted and sentenced to death. Despite the conviction, the case has become a *cause célèbre* for many reasons. Supporters of Abu-Jamal claim that many procedural irregularities occurred during the trial and that the conviction violated his constitutional right to a fair trial. Among other things, Abu-Jamal was denied the right to represent himself at trial. Others claim that he was targeted and framed because of his radical political activities. The prosecution hid evidence, intimidated witnesses, and illegally excused potential African American jurors.

© AP Images/Chris Gardner

Abu-Jamal has now been on death row for more than 25 years. The case has attracted the attention of activists opposed to the death penalty from all over the world. Abu-Jamal has continued his political activism, has published a book titled *Live from Death Row*, has completed BA and MA degrees, and has made frequent radio broadcasts. The French have made him an honorary citizen of Paris and, in 2006, named a street *Rue Mumia Abu-Jamal* in his honor. Organizations including Amnesty International, Human Rights Watch, the European Parliament, and the Japanese Diet have demanded that he be awarded a new trial because of the flaws in the original case. However, there are also groups who are aghast at the attention being paid to someone they consider a coldblooded "cop killer." One group filed a lawsuit against the City of Paris that said in part, "awarding the honors of a city to a killer of a policeman is an immoral and irresponsible decision."

In 2008, a three-judge panel of the U.S. 3rd Circuit Court of Appeals upheld the murder conviction but ordered a new capital sentencing hearing over concerns that the jury was improperly instructed; Abu-Jamal is currently incarcerated at Pennsylvania's SCI Greene prison.

Critical criminologists view the Mumia Abu-Jamal case as an indicator of the social conflict that infects the nation's social and political systems. People are targeted because of their political views, minorities cannot get a fair trial, and people who are viewed as a threat to the system may find themselves behind bars or even on death row. Conflict rather than consensus rules and shapes society.

SOURCES: "Mumia Abu-Jamal's Freedom Journal," www.mumia.org/freedom.now/ (accessed June 4, 2006); Amnesty International, USA, "Mumia Abu-Jamal, Amnesty International Calls for Retrial," February, 17, 2000, http://web.amnesty.org/library/Index/engAMR510202000 (accessed June 4, 2009); "The Defense: Mumia Abu-Jamal's Legal Representation at Trial," www.amnestyusa.org/regions/americas/document.do?id=EB6C736A7369F3D78025686C00526C98 (accessed June 4, 2009); Cathy Ceïbe, "USA Sues Paris: From Death Row, Mumia Stirs Up More Controversy," *L'Humanité*, trans. Patrick Bolland, November 13, 2006, www.humaniteinenglish.com/article423.html (accessed June 12, 2009).

maintain jobs are added to the mix, it is clear that the correctional system is playing an ever-more-important role in suppressing wages and maintaining the profitability of capitalism.[61]

Critique of Critical Criminology

Critical criminology has been sharply criticized by some members of the criminological mainstream, who charge that its contribution has been "hot air, heat, but no real light."[62] In turn, critical thinkers have accused mainstream criminologists of being culprits in developing state control over individual lives and selling out their ideals for the chance to receive government funding.

Mainstream criminologists have also attacked the substance of critical thought. Some argue that critical theory simply rehashes the old tradition of helping the underdog, in which the poor steal from the rich to survive.[63] In reality, most theft is for luxury, not survival. Such critics maintain that although the wealthy do commit their share of illegal acts, these are nonviolent and leave no permanent injuries.[64] People do not live in fear of corrupt businessmen and stock traders; they fear muggers and rapists.

Other critics suggest that critical theorists unfairly neglect the capitalist system's efforts to regulate itself—for example, by instituting antitrust regulations and putting violators in jail. Similarly, they ignore efforts to institute social reforms aimed at helping the poor.[65] There seems to be no logic in condemning a system that helps the poor and empowers them to take on corporate interests in a court of law. Even inherently conservative institutions such as police departments have made attempts at self-regulation when they became aware of class- and race-based abuses such as the use of racial profiling in making traffic stops.[66]

Some argue that critical thinkers refuse to address the problems and conflicts that exist in socialist countries, such as the gulags and purges of the Soviet Union under Stalin. Similarly, they fail to explain why some highly capitalist countries, such as Japan, have extremely low crime rates. Critical criminologists are too quick to blame capitalism for every human vice without adequate explanation or regard for other social and environmental factors.[67] In so doing, they ignore objective reality and refuse to acknowledge that members of the lower classes tend to victimize one another. They ignore the plight of the lower classes, who must live in crime-ridden neighborhoods, while condemning the capitalist system from the security of the "ivory tower."

▶ **Checkpoints**

Left Realism

Some critical scholars are now addressing the need for the left wing to respond to the increasing power of right-wing conservatives. They are troubled by the emergence of a strict "law and order" philosophy that has as its centerpiece a policy of punishing juveniles severely in adult court. At the same time, these scholars find the focus of most left-wing scholarship—the abuse of power by the ruling elite—too narrow. It is wrong, they argue, to ignore inner-city gang crime and violence, which often target indigent people.[68] The approach of scholars who share these concerns is referred to as **left realism**.[69]

Left realism is most often connected to the writings of British scholars John Lea and Jock Young. In their well-respected 1984 book *What Is to Be Done about Law and Order?* they reject the utopian views of idealists who portray street criminals as revolutionaries.[70] They take the more "realistic" view that street criminals prey on the poor and disenfranchised, thus making the poor doubly abused, first by the capitalist system and then by members of their own class.

Lea and Young's view of crime causation borrows from conventional sociological theory and closely resembles the relative deprivation approach, which posits that experiencing poverty in the midst of plenty creates discontent and breeds crime. As they put it, "The equation is simple: relative deprivation equals discontent; discontent plus lack of political solution equals crime."[71]

In a more recent book, *Crime in Context: A Critical Criminology of Market Societies* (1999), Ian Taylor recognizes that anyone who expects an instant socialist revolution to take place is simply engaging in wishful thinking.[72] He uses data from both Europe

▶ Critical criminology tries to explain how the workings of the capitalist system produce inequality and crime.

▶ In this view, the state serves the interests of the ruling capitalist class.

▶ Criminal law is an instrument of economic oppression. Capitalism demands that the subordinate classes remain oppressed.

▶ The concept of surplus value means that capitalists exploit workers and keep the excess profits derived from workers' labors.

▶ Globalization has meant that capitalists can exploit foreign workers for labor and acquire foreign natural resources to maximize their profits.

▶ Instrumental theorists believe that the legal system supports the owners at the expense of the workers.

▶ Structural theorists believe that the law also ensures that no capitalist becomes too powerful. The law is used to maintain the long-term interests of the capitalist system.

▶ Critical research purports to show how capitalism creates large groups of people who turn to crime for survival.

left realism
Approach that sees crime as a function of relative deprivation under capitalism and favors pragmatic, community-based crime prevention and control.

and North America to show that the world is currently in the midst of multiple crises, which are shaping all human interaction, including criminality. These crises include lack of job creation, social inequality, social fear, political incompetence and failure, gender conflict, and family and parenting issues. These crises have led to a society in which the government seems incapable of creating positive social change. People have become more fearful and isolated from one another, and some are excluded from the mainstream because of racism and discrimination; manufacturing jobs have been exported overseas to nations that pay extremely low wages; and fiscal constraints inhibit the possibility of reform. These problems often fall squarely on the shoulders of young black men, who suffer from exclusion and poverty and who now feel the economic burden created by the erosion of manufacturing jobs due to the globalization of the economy. In response, they engage in a form of hypermasculinity, which increases their crime rates.[73]

CRIME PROTECTION

Left realists argue that crime victims in all classes need and deserve protection; crime control reflects community needs. They do not view police and the courts as inherently evil tools of capitalism whose tough tactics alienate the lower classes. In fact, they recognize that these institutions offer life-saving public services. The left realists wish, however, that police would reduce their use of force and increase their sensitivity to the public.[74]

Preemptive deterrence is an approach in which community organization efforts eliminate or reduce crime before police involvement becomes necessary. The reasoning behind this approach is that if the number of marginalized youths (those who feel they are not part of society and have nothing to lose by committing crime) could be reduced, then delinquency rates would decline.[75]

Although implementing a socialist economy might help eliminate the crime problem, left realists recognize that something must be done to control crime under the existing capitalist system. To develop crime control policies, left realists not only welcome critical ideas but also build on the work of strain theorists, social ecologists, and other mainstream views. Community-based efforts seem to hold the greatest promise of crime control.

Left realism has been criticized by critical thinkers as legitimizing the existing power structure: By supporting existing definitions of law and justice, it suggests that the "deviants," not the capitalist system, cause society's problems. Critics question whether left realists advocate the very institutions that "currently imprison us and our patterns of thought and action."[76] In rebuttal, left realists say that to speak of a socialist state lacking a police force or a system of laws and justice is unrealistic. They believe the criminal code does, in fact, represent public opinion.

Critical Feminist Theory

As is true of so many theories in criminology, most of the efforts of critical theorists have been devoted to explaining male criminality.[77] To remedy this theoretical lapse, a number of feminist writers have attempted to explain, from a critical perspective, the cause of crime, gender differences in crime rates, and the exploitation of female victims.

Critical feminism views gender inequality as stemming from the unequal power of men and women in a capitalist society, which leads to the exploitation of women by fathers and husbands. Under this system, women are considered a commodity worth possessing, much like land or money.[78]

The origin of gender differences can be traced to the development of private property and male domination of the laws of inheritance, which led to male control over property and power.[79] A **patriarchal** system developed in which men's work was valued and women's work was devalued. As capitalism came into its own, the division of labor by gender made women responsible for the unpaid maintenance and

preemptive deterrence
Efforts to prevent crime through community organization and youth involvement.

critical feminism
Approach that explains both victimization and criminality among women in terms of gender inequality, patriarchy, and the exploitation of women under capitalism.

patriarchal
Male-dominated.

reproduction of the current and future labor force, which was derisively called "domestic work." Although this unpaid work done by women is crucial and profitable for capitalists, who reap these free benefits, being consigned to such labor is exploitive and oppressive for women.[80] Even when women gained the right to work for pay, they were exploited as cheap labor. The dual exploitation of women within the household and in the labor market means that women produce far greater surplus value for capitalists than do men.

Patriarchy, or male supremacy, has been and continues to be supported by capitalists. This system sustains female oppression at home and in the workplace.[81] Although the number of traditional patriarchal families is in steep decline, in those that still exist, a wife's economic dependence ties men more securely to wage-earning jobs, further serving the interests of capitalists by undermining potential rebellion against the system.

PATRIARCHY AND CRIME

Critical feminists link criminal behavior patterns to the gender conflict created by the economic and social struggles common in postindustrial societies. In *Capitalism, Patriarchy, and Crime*, James Messerschmidt argues that capitalist society is marked by both patriarchy and class conflict. Capitalists control the labor of workers, and men control women both economically and biologically.[82] This "double marginality" explains why females in a capitalist society commit fewer crimes than males. Because they are isolated in the family, they have fewer opportunities to engage in elite deviance (white-collar and economic crimes). Although powerful females as well as males commit white-collar crimes, the female crime rate is restricted because of the patriarchal nature of the capitalist system.[83] Women are also denied access to male-dominated street crimes. Because capitalism renders lower-class women powerless, they tend to commit less serious, nonviolent, self-destructive crimes, such as abusing drugs.

Powerlessness also increases the likelihood that women will become targets of violent acts.[84] When lower-class males are shut out of the economic opportunity structure, they try to build their self-image through acts of machismo; such acts may involve violent abuse of women. This type of reaction accounts for a significant percentage of the female victims who are attacked by a spouse or intimate partner. According to this view, female victimization should decline as women's place in society is elevated, and they obtain more power at home, in the workplace, and in government. Empirical research seems to support this view. Cross-national studies of the educational and occupational status of women show that in nations where the status of women is generally high, sexual violence rates are significantly lower than in nations where women do not enjoy similar educational and occupational opportunities.[85] Women's victimization rates decline as they are empowered socially, economically, and legally.[86]

In *Masculinities and Crime*, Messerschmidt expands on these themes.[87] He suggests that in every culture, males try to emulate "ideal" masculine behaviors. In Western culture, this means being authoritative, in charge, combative, and controlling. Failure to adopt these roles leaves men feeling effeminate and unmanly. Their struggle to dominate women in order to prove their manliness is called "doing gender." Crime is a vehicle for men to "do gender" because it separates them from the weak and enables them to demonstrate physical bravery. Violence directed toward women is an especially economical way to demonstrate manhood. Would a weak, effeminate male ever attack a woman?

Feminist writers have supported this view by maintaining that in contemporary society, men achieve masculinity at the expense of women. In the best-case scenario, men must convince others that in no way are they feminine or that they have female qualities. For example, they are sloppy and don't cook or do housework because these are "female" activities. More ominously, men may work at excluding, hurting, denigrating, exploiting, or otherwise abusing women. Even in all-male groups, men often prove their manhood by treating the weakest member of the group as "woman-like" and abusing him accordingly. Men need to defend themselves at all costs from

Fact or Fiction?

Abuse of women increases as they get more power and men become envious and resentful of their success.

Fiction. Research shows that the rates of victimization of women decline as they are empowered socially, economically, and legally.

being contaminated with femininity, and these efforts begin in children's play groups and continue into adulthood and marriage.[88]

Exploitation and Criminality Feminists also focus on the social forces that shape women's lives and experiences to explain female criminality.[89] For example, they attempt to show how the sexual victimization of girls is a function of male socialization because so many young males learn to be aggressive and to exploit women. Males seek same-sex peer groups for social support; these groups encourage members to exploit and sexually abuse women. On college campuses, peers encourage sexual violence against women who are considered "teasers," "bar pickups," or "loose women." These derogatory labels allow the males to justify their actions; a code of secrecy then protects the aggressors from retribution.[90]

According to the critical feminist view, exploitation triggers the onset of female delinquent and deviant behavior. When female victims run away and abuse substances, they may be reacting to abuse they have suffered at home or at school. Their attempts at survival are labeled as deviant or delinquent behavior.[91] In a sense, the female criminal is herself a victim.

POWER–CONTROL THEORY

John Hagan and his associates have created a critical feminist model that uses gender differences to explain the onset of criminality.[92] Hagan's view is that crime and delinquency rates are a function of two factors: (1) class position (power) and (2) family functions (control).[93] The link between these two variables is that within the family, parents reproduce the power relationships they hold in the workplace; a position of dominance at work is equated with control in the household. As a result, parents' work experiences and class position influence the criminality of children.[94]

In **paternalistic families**, fathers assume the traditional role of breadwinners, while mothers tend to have menial jobs or remain at home to supervise domestic matters. Within the paternalistic home, mothers are expected to control the behavior of their daughters, while granting greater freedom to sons. In such a home, the parent–daughter relationship can be viewed as preparation for the "cult of domesticity," which makes girls' involvement in delinquency unlikely, whereas boys are freer to deviate because they are not subject to maternal control. Girls growing up in patriarchal families are socialized to fear legal sanctions more than are males; consequently, boys in these families exhibit more delinquent behavior than their sisters. The result is that boys not only engage in more antisocial behaviors but also have greater access to legitimate adult behaviors, such as working at part-time jobs or possessing their own transportation. In contrast, without these legitimate behavioral outlets, girls who are unhappy or dissatisfied with their status are forced to seek risky **role exit behaviors**, including such desperate measures as running away and contemplating suicide.

In **egalitarian families**—those in which the husband and wife share similar positions of power at home and in the workplace—daughters gain a kind of freedom that reflects reduced parental control. These families produce daughters whose law-violating behavior mirrors their brothers'. In an egalitarian family, girls may have greater opportunity to engage in legitimate adult-status behaviors and have less need to enact deviant role exits.[95]

Ironically, Hagan believes that these relationships also occur in female-headed households with absent fathers. Hagan and his associates found that when fathers and mothers hold equally valued managerial positions, the similarity between the rates of their daughters' delinquency and their sons' delinquency is greatest. By implication, middle-class girls are the most likely to violate the law because they are less closely controlled than their counterparts in the lower socioeconomic classes. In homes in which both parents hold positions of power, girls are more likely to have the same expectations of career success as their brothers. Consequently, siblings of both sexes will be socialized to take risks and engage in other behavior related to delinquency.

paternalistic families
Families in which the father is the breadwinner and rule maker, and the mother has a menial job or is a homemaker only. Sons are granted greater freedom than daughters.

role exit behaviors
Strategies, such as running away or contemplating suicide, that are used by young girls unhappy with their status in the family.

egalitarian families
Families in which the husband and wife share similar positions of power at home and in the workplace. Sons and daughters have equal freedom.

Evaluating Power–Control This **power–control theory** has received a great deal of attention in the criminological community because it encourages a new approach to the study of criminality—one that includes gender differences, class position, and the structure of the family. Empirical analysis of its premises has generally been supportive. Brenda Sims Blackwell's research supports a key element of power–control theory: Females in paternalistic households have learned to fear legal sanctions more than their brothers have.[96]

Not all research is as supportive.[97] Some critics have questioned its core assumption that power and control variables can explain crime.[98] More specifically, critics fail to replicate the finding that upper-class girls are more likely to deviate than their lower-class peers or that class and power interact to produce delinquency.[99] Some researchers have found few gender-based supervision and behavior differences in worker-dominated, manager-dominated, or owner-dominated households.[100] Research indicates that single-mother families may be different from two-parent egalitarian families, although Hagan's theory equates the two.[101]

The concept of family employed by Hagan may have to be reconsidered. Power–control theorists should consider the multitude of power and control relationships emerging in postmodern society: blended families, families where mothers hold managerial positions and fathers are blue-collar workers, and so forth.[102]

Finally, power and control may interact with other personal traits, such as personality and self-control, to shape behavior.[103] Further research is needed to determine whether power–control can have an independent influence on behavior and can explain gender differences in the crime rate.

Peacemaking Criminology

To members of the **peacemaking** movement, the main purpose of criminology is to promote a peaceful, just society. Rather than standing on empirical analysis of data, peacemaking draws its inspiration from religious and philosophical teachings ranging from Quakerism to Zen.[104] For example, rather than seeing socioeconomic status as a "variable" that is correlated with crime, as do mainstream criminologists, peacemakers view poverty as a source of suffering that is almost a "crime" in and of itself. Poverty enervates people, makes them suffer, and becomes a master status that subjects them to lives filled with suffering. From a peacemaking perspective, a key avenue for preventing crime is, in the short run, diminishing the suffering poverty causes and, in the long run, embracing social policies that reduce the prevalence of economic suffering in contemporary society.[105]

Peacemakers view the efforts of the state to punish and control as crime-encouraging rather than crime-discouraging. These views were first articulated in a series of books with an anarchist theme written by criminologists Larry Tifft and Dennis Sullivan in 1980.[106] Tifft argues, "The violent punishing acts of the state and its controlling professions are of the same genre as the violent acts of individuals. In each instance these acts reflect an attempt to monopolize human interaction."[107]

Sullivan stresses the futility of correcting and punishing criminals in the context of our

power–control theory
The view that gender differences in crime are a function of economic power (class position, one- versus two-earner families) and parental control (paternalistic versus egalitarian families).

peacemaking
Approach that considers punitive crime control strategies to be counterproductive and favors the use of humanistic conflict resolution to prevent and control crime.

© Emilien Camcet/AFP/Getty Images

Peacemakers abhor the use of violence in the name of justice. Here, members of Amnesty International and the French affiliate of ACAT (Action by Christians for the Abolition of Torture) pretend to be dead during a demonstration on July 2, 2009, at Place de la Concorde in Paris, to denounce the availability of the death penalty in the United States. People in white represent the U.S. states that have abolished the death penalty, people in black the states where the death penalty may be applied.

Theory	Major Premise	Strengths	Research Focus
Left realism	Crime is a function of relative deprivation; criminals prey on the poor.	Represents a compromise between conflict and traditional criminology.	Deterrence; protection
Critical feminist theory	The capitalist system creates partriarchy, which oppresses women.	Explains gender bias, violence against women, and repression.	Gender inequality; oppression; patriarchy
Power-control theory	Girls are controlled more closely than boys in traditional male-dominated households. There is gender equity in contemporary egalitarian homes.	Explains gender differences in the crime rate as a function of class and gender conflict.	Power and control; gender differences; domesticity
Peacemaking criminology	Peace and humanism can reduce crime; conflict resolution strategies can work.	Offers a new approach to crime control through mediation.	Punishment; nonviolence; mediation

Checkpoints

▶ Left realists are conflict scholars who believe the lower classes must be protected from predatory criminals until the social system changes and makes crime obsolete.

▶ Critical feminists study patriarchy and the oppression of women. They link female criminality to gender inequality.

▶ Power–control theory shows how family structure, women's economic status, and gender inequity interact to produce male/female differences in crime rates.

▶ Peacemaking criminologists seek nonviolent, humane alternatives to coercive punishment.

restorative justice
Using humanistic, nonpunitive strategies to right wrongs and restore social harmony.

conflict-ridden society: "The reality we must grasp is that we live in a culture of severed relationships, where every available institution provides a form of banishment but no place or means for people to become connected, to be responsible to and for each other."[108] Sullivan suggests that mutual aid rather than coercive punishment is the key to a harmonious society. In their newest volume, *Restorative Justice* (2001), Sullivan and Tifft reaffirm their belief that society must seek humanitarian forms of justice without resorting to brutal punishments:

> By allowing feelings of vengeance or retribution to narrow our focus on the harmful event and the person responsible for it—as others might focus solely on a sin committed and the "sinner"—we tell ourselves we are taking steps to free ourselves from the effects of the harm or the sin in question. But, in fact, we are putting ourselves in a servile position with respect to life, human growth, and the further enjoyment of relationships with others.[109] ▶ **Checkpoints**

Concept Summary 8.1 summarizes these subareas of critical criminology.

Critical Theory and Public Policy

Critical theorists argue that the "old methods" of punishment are a failure and that more than of two-thirds of all prison inmates recidivate soon after their release. They scoff at claims that the crime rate has dropped, because the number of people in prison is at an all-time high, and they counter these claims with studies showing that imprisonment rates are not at all related to crime rates; there is no consistent finding that locking people up helps reduce crimes.[110]

What can be done as an alternative? Rather than casting offenders aside, we must find ways to bring offenders back into the community. This approach to offender rehabilitation is now known as **restorative justice**. Springing both from academia and from reformers within the justice system itself, the restorative approach relies on nonpunitive strategies for crime prevention and control.[111] The next sections discuss the foundation and principles of restorative justice.

- Crime is an offense against human relationships.
- Victims and the community are central to justice processes.
- The first priority of justice processes is to assist victims.
- The second priority is to restore the community, to the degree possible.
- The offender has personal responsibility to victims and to the community for crimes committed.
- The offender will develop improved competency and understanding as a result of the restorative justice experience.

Exhibit 8.1 Basic Principles of Restorative Justice

- Stakeholders share responsibilities for restorative justice through partnerships for action.

SOURCE: Anne Seymour, "Restorative Justice/Community Justice," in *National Victim Assistance Academy Textbook* (Washington, DC: National Victim Assistance Academy, 2001).

THE CONCEPT OF RESTORATIVE JUSTICE

The term "restorative justice" is often hard to define because it encompasses a variety of programs and practices. According to a leading restorative justice scholar, Howard Zehr, restorative justice requires that society address victims' harms and needs, hold offenders accountable to put right those harms, and involve victims, offenders, and communities in the process of healing. Zehr maintains that the core value of the restoration process can be translated into respect for all, even those who are different from us, even those who seem to be our enemies. At its core, Zehr argues, restorative justice is a set of principles, a philosophy, and a fresh set of guiding questions that provide an alternative framework for thinking about wrongdoing.[112]

Restorative justice has grown out of a belief that the traditional justice system has done little to involve the community in the process of dealing with crime and wrongdoing. What has developed is a system of coercive punishments, administered by bureaucrats, that are inherently harmful to offenders and reduce the likelihood that offenders will ever become productive members of society. This system relies on punishment, stigma, and disgrace.

Restoration programs can take many forms. Regina Talbert and Anthony Belcher hand out food and clothing on skid row in Los Angeles on February 16, 2007. The two former addicts are part of the New Directions team, who perform outreach to addicted and alcoholic army, navy, and air force veterans in some of the city's most dangerous neighborhoods. Veterans of U.S. wars, including the current campaigns in Afghanistan and Iraq, are increasingly turning up with alarming signs of post-traumatic stress disorder and other serious mental conditions. Regina (left), who has been in recovery for nine years, hands out flyers about the New Directions treatment center. Would you consider this a "restoration"-based initiative?

© Charles Ommanney/Getty Images

Advocates of restorative justice argue that what is needed is a justice policy that repairs the harm caused by crime and that includes all parties who have suffered from that harm: the victim, the community, and the offender. They have made an ongoing effort to reduce the conflict created by the criminal justice system when it hands out harsh punishments to offenders, many of whom are powerless social outcasts. Based on the principle of reducing social harm, restorative justice advocates argue that the old methods of punishment are a failure; after all, upwards of two-thirds of all prison inmates recidivate soon after their release. And tragically, some inmates are never released. Some are given life sentences for relatively minor crimes under "three strikes" laws that mandate such a sentence for a third conviction, and some are given "life with no parole sentences," which are in actuality "death sentences."[113]

The principles of this approach are set out in Exhibit 8.1.

CONNECTIONS

Contrast the restorative justice approach with the crime control–deterrence policies advocated by rational choice theorists and discussed in Chapter 4.

THE PROCESS OF RESTORATION

The restoration process begins by redefining crime in terms of a conflict among the offender, the victim, and affected constituencies (families, schools, workplaces, and so forth). Therefore, it is vitally important that the resolution take place within the context in which the conflict originally occurred, rather than being transferred to a specialized institution that has no social connection to the community or group from which the conflict originated. In other words, most conflicts are better settled in the community than in a court.

By maintaining "ownership," or jurisdiction, over the conflict, the community can express its shared outrage about the offense. Shared community outrage is directly communicated to the offender. The victim is also given a chance to voice his or her story, and the offender can directly communicate his or her need for social reintegration and treatment. All restoration programs involve an understanding among victim, offender, and community. The processes involved differ in structure and style, but they generally include these elements:

▶ The offender is asked to recognize that he or she caused injury to personal and social relations and to accept responsibility (ideally accompanied by a statement of remorse). Only then can the offender be restored as a productive member of the community.

▶ Restoration involves turning the justice system into a "healing" agent rather than a distributor of retribution and revenge.

▶ Reconciliation is a big part of the restorative approach. Most people involved in offender–victim relationships actually know one another or were related in some way before the criminal incident took place. Instead of treating one of the involved parties as a victim deserving sympathy and the other as a criminal deserving punishment, it is more productive to address the issues that produced conflict between these people.[114]

▶ The effectiveness of justice ultimately depends on the stake a person has in the community (or a particular social group). If a person does not value his or her membership in the group, the person is unlikely to accept responsibility, show remorse, or repair the injuries caused by his or her actions. In contrast, people who have a stake in the community and its principal institutions (such as work, home, and school) find that their involvement enhances their personal and familial well-being.[115]

▶ A commitment to both material (monetary) restitution and symbolic reparation (an apology) is expected.

▶ A determination of community support and assistance for both victim and offender is involved.

The intended result of the process is to repair injuries suffered by the victim and the community, while ensuring reintegration of the offender.

RESTORATION PROGRAMS

Negotiation, mediation, consensus building, and peacemaking have been part of the dispute resolution process in European and Asian communities for centuries.[116] Native American and Native Canadian people have long used the type of community participation in the adjudication process (some examples are sentencing circles, sentencing panels, and elders panels) that the advocates of restorative justice are now embracing.[117]

In some Native American communities, people accused of breaking the law meet with community members, victims (if any), village elders, and agents of the justice system in a **sentencing circle**. Each member of the circle expresses his or her feelings about the act that was committed and raises questions or concerns. The accused can express regret about his or her actions and a desire to change the harmful behavior. People may suggest ways in which the offender can make things up to the community and those he or she harmed. A treatment program, such as Alcoholics Anonymous, can be suggested, if appropriate.

sentencing circle
A peacemaking technique in which offenders, victims, and other community members work together to formulate a sanction that addresses the needs of all.

Restorative justice is now being embraced on many levels within our society and the justice system:

Community Communities that isolate people and have few mechanisms for interpersonal interaction encourage and sustain crime. Those that implement forms of community dialogue to identify problems and plan tactics for eliminating them, guided by restorative justice practices and principles, may create a climate in which violent crime is less likely to occur.[118]

Schools Some schools have embraced restorative justice practices to deal with students involved in drug and alcohol abuse without having to resort to more punitive measures, such as expulsion. Schools in Minnesota, Colorado, and elsewhere are now trying to involve students in "relational rehabilitation" programs that strive to improve individuals' relationships with key figures in the community who may have been harmed by their actions.[119]

Police Restorative justice has also been implemented by police when crime is first encountered. The new community policing models that have been adapted around the country are an attempt to incorporate restorative concepts into law enforcement. Restorative justice relies on criminal justice policymakers listening and responding to the needs of those who are to be affected by their actions, and community policing relies on policies established via input from both officers and citizens, as well as exchanges between them.[120]

Courts Restorative programs in the courts typically involve diverting the case from the formal court process. These programs encourage meeting and reconciling the conflicts between offenders and victims via victim advocacy, mediation programs, and sentencing circles, in which crime victims and their families are brought together with offenders and their families in an effort to formulate a sanction that addresses the needs of each party. Victims are given a chance to voice their stories, and offenders can help compensate them financially or provide some service (such as repairing damaged property).[121] The goal is to enable offenders to appreciate the damage they have caused, to make amends, and to be reintegrated into society. In sum, restoration can be used at the following stages of the justice process:

▶ As diversion from prosecution
▶ As a pre-sentencing, post-conviction alternative to traditional sentencing
▶ As part of the sentencing process
▶ As a supplement to a community sentence (probation)
▶ As preparation for release from long-term imprisonment
▶ As a form of final warning to young offenders[122]

BALANCED AND RESTORATIVE JUSTICE (BARJ)

A number of restorative justice experts, including Gordon Bazemore and his associates, have suggested that restorative justice should be organized around the principle of balance.[123] According to this approach, the justice system should give equal weight to offender accountability, competency development, and community protection.

▶ *Holding offenders accountable to victims.* The term "offender accountability" refers specifically to the requirement that offenders make amends for the harm resulting from their crimes by repaying or restoring losses to victims and the community.
▶ *Providing competency development for offenders in the system so they can pursue legitimate endeavors after release.* Competency development, the rehabilitative goal for intervention, requires that people who enter the justice system should exit the system more capable of being productive and responsible in the community.
▶ *Ensuring community safety.* The community protection goal explicitly acknowledges and endorses a longtime public expectation—a safe and secure community.

The balanced approach means that justice policies and priorities should be designed to address each of the three goals *in each case* and that system balance should always be pursued. The goal of achieving balance suggests that no single objective can take precedence over any other without creating a system that is "out of balance" and implies that efforts to achieve one goal (such as offender accountability) should not undermine efforts to achieve other goals.

BARJ is founded on the belief that justice is best served when victim, community, and offender are viewed as equal clients of the justice system who will receive fair and balanced attention, will be actively involved in the justice process, and will gain tangible benefits from their interactions with the justice system. Most BARJ programs in operation today are located within the juvenile justice system.

The accompanying Policy and Practice in Criminology feature discusses one innovative community program based on the principles of restorative justice.

THE CHALLENGE OF RESTORATIVE JUSTICE

Restorative justice holds great promise. A recent scientific analysis of this approach, conducted by Lawrence Sherman and Heather Strang, compared outcomes to those achieved by conventional criminal justice programming. Sherman and Strang found that restoration

▶ Substantially reduced repeat offending for some but not all offenders
▶ Doubled (or more) the offenses brought to justice as diversion
▶ Reduced crime victims' post-traumatic stress symptoms and related costs
▶ Provided both victims and offenders with more satisfaction than traditional approaches
▶ Reduced crime victims' desire for violent revenge against their offenders
▶ Reduced the costs of criminal justice, when used as diversion
▶ Reduced recidivism *more than* prison (adults) or *as well as* prison (youths)[124]

These results are encouraging, but there are also some concerns:

▶ Is restorative justice a political movement or a treatment process? Some view it as a social movement rather than a method of rehabilitation.[125]
▶ Restorative justice programs must be mindful of the cultural and social differences that can be found throughout our heterogeneous society. What may be considered "restorative" in one subculture may be considered insulting and damaging in another.[126]
▶ There is still no single definition of what constitutes restorative justice.[127] Consequently, many diverse programs that call themselves restorative actually pursue objectives that seem remote from the restorative ideal.
▶ Restorative justice programs face the difficult task of balancing the needs of offenders with those of their victims. If programs focus solely on victims' needs, they may risk ignoring the offenders' needs and increase the likelihood of reoffending.
▶ Benefits may persist only in the short term, while long-term treatment needs are overlooked. Sharon Levrant and her colleagues suggest that restorative justice programs that feature short-term interactions with victims fail to help offenders learn prosocial ways of behaving. Restorative justice advocates may erroneously assume that relatively brief interludes of public shaming will change deeply rooted criminal predispositions.[128]

These are a few of the obstacles that restorative justice programs must overcome to be successful and productive. Yet because the method holds so much promise, criminologists are now conducting numerous demonstration projects to find the most effective means of returning the ownership of justice to the people and the community.[129]

There are a number of restorative justice programs in operation today. One that attempts to reconcile victims and offenders in Denver, Colorado, is described below.

The Victim Offender Reconciliation Program (VORP) of Denver began in 1993 in response to [a] summer of violence in [the] metro Denver area. VORP has collaborated with the justice system to provide Restorative Justice processes for our community as a way of addressing issues overlooked in a more traditional, adversarial justice system. VORP has been a catalyst for long-term answers to crime for offenders, victims, and our community. Each system has its role and provides part of the solution to the problem of administering justice. The VORP program, steeped in diverse cultural roots, gives an opportunity for reconciling and restoring relationships between victims, offenders, and our community.

were involved in and how they have been affected by this incident. This group will also include other juvenile shoplifters, their parents, community member, peer representative, and merchant representative, and will be facilitated by RESTORE Volunteers.

Part 3 – When the group sessions are complete, each youth and his/her parent or guardian review and sign a contract to repair the harm to the victim, the community, their family and themselves, including community service. They will sign up for a contract completion date and time to return to the RESTORE Council.

The amount of time to complete the contract varies from 12 to 20 hours, depending on the types of projects chosen by the youth.

RESTORE Session #2 will take approximately one half hour.

Policy and Practice in Criminology Victim Offender Reconciliation in Denver, Colorado

Programs are conducted by trained volunteers in Restorative Justice, mediation, facilitation, cultural competency, and communication. Currently VORP offers victim-offender mediation, community group conferencing, peace circles and a reparative panel as Restorative Justice tools. As needed, VORP staff and facilitators also work one on one with victims and offenders of crime.

VORP has three principal aims in furthering its mission:
1. Reduce recidivism
2. Restore and strengthen community relationships
3. Empower victims and our community

The Restore Progam

One of the Denver VORP programs is designed to help kids who have gotten into trouble by shoplifting from a local store. When a youth is referred by Juvenile Court, 191J, a RESTORE intake form is completed. The youth and a parent or guardian attend two RESTORE sessions and complete a contract, as described below.

RESTORE Session #1 has three parts and will take approximately 2 to 2½ hours.

Part 1 – During this session, the youth and their parents will listen to speakers discuss the impact of shoplifting on the merchant community, as well as the community-at-large. They will also hear other youth speak about how shoplifting has affected them, their peers, and their families.

Part 2 – Then, the youth and their parents will meet in smaller groups to talk about the shoplifting incidents they

The youth will return in one or two months to present their completed contract results and projects, including verification of community service and other contract items.

BY PARTICIPATING IN THE RESTORE PROGRAM, YOUTH CAN:
1. Learn more about shoplifting and how it affects victims and the community
2. Repair the harm done by the incident in a meaningful way
3. Make choices about the consequences for their actions
4. Have their theft charge dismissed upon successful completion of the program

The Restore program uses the principles of restorative justice to reintegrate young offenders back into their community. It is an example of turning theory into action.

CRITICAL THINKING

1. Could you design a program for recreational drug users applying the Restore Model?
2. Do you believe restorative justice programs can work? Or are they just a way for kids who commit crime to avoid legal responsiblity?

SOURCE: Victim Offender Reconciliation Program of Denver, 2009, www.denvervorp.org/index.html.

An interim evaluation of Restoration House's New Hope for Families program, a community-based residential treatment program for women with dependent children, shows that 70 percent of women who complete follow-up interviews six months after treatment have maintained abstinence or reduced their drug use. The other 30 percent, however, lapsed into their old habits.

The program relies on restorative justice techniques wherein people in the community meet with the women to discuss the harm that drug use can cause and how it can damage both them and their children. The community members show their support and help the women find a niche in the community.

Women who complete the Restoration House program improve their employment, reduce parenting stress, retain custody of their children, and restore their physical, mental, and emotional health. The program focuses not only on reducing drug and alcohol use but also on increasing health, safety, self-sufficiency, and positive attitudes.

Writing Assignment

Write an essay on how you would evaluate the Restoration House program and on what it would take before this program could be considered a success. In other words, what questions would have to be answered before it got your approval? What other approaches to helping women in need should be considered?

Summary

1. Be familiar with the concept of social conflict and with how it shapes behavior.

   Social conflict theorists view crime as a function of the conflict that exists in society. Conflict theorists suggest that crime in any society is caused by class conflict. Laws are created by those in power to protect their own rights and serve their own interests.

2. Be able to discuss elements of conflict in the criminal justice system.

   All criminal acts have political undertones. The justice system is biased against the poor and designed to protect the wealthy. Social and political oppression produce crime. Crime would disappear if equality, rather than discrimination, were the norm.

3. Be familiar with the basic ideas of critical criminology.

   Critical criminology views the competitive nature of the capitalist system as a major cause of crime. The poor commit crimes because of their frustration, anger, and need. The wealthy engage in illegal acts because they are used to competition and because they must do so to maintain their positions in society. Critical scholars have attempted to show that the law is designed to protect the wealthy and powerful and to control the poor, "have-not" members of society.

4. Define the concept of state (organized) crime.

   State crimes involve a violation of citizen trust. They are acts defined by law as criminal and committed by state officials while holding their positions as government representatives. Some state crimes are committed by individuals who abuse their state authority, or fail to exercise it, when working with people and organizations in the private sector. State–corporate crime involves the deviant activities by which the privileged classes strive to maintain or increase their power.

5. Be able to discuss the difference between structural theory and instrumental theory.

   Critical theorists subscribe to either instrumental theory or structural theory. Instrumental theorists hold that those in authority wield their power to control society and keep the lower classes in check. Structural theorists believe that the justice system is designed to maintain the status quo and is used to punish the wealthy, as well as members of the lower classes, when they break the rules governing capitalism.

6. Know the various techniques of critical research.

   Research on critical theory focuses on how the justice system was designed and how it operates to further class interests. Quite often, this research uses historical analysis to show how the capitalist classes have exerted control over the police, the courts, and correctional agencies.

7. Be familiar with the critiques of critical criminology.

   Critical criminology has been criticized by traditional criminologists. Some critics suggest that critical criminologists make fundamental errors in their concepts of ownership and class interest.

8. Know some of the basic ideas of critical feminism.

Critical feminist writers draw attention to the influence of patriarchal society on crime. According to power–control theory, gender differences in the crime rate can be explained by the structure of the family in a capitalist society.

9. Explain the concept of left realism.

Left realism sees crime as a function of relative deprivation under capitalism and views the justice system as necessary to protect the lower classes until a socialist society can be developed, which will end crime.

10. Discuss peacemaking criminology and restorative justice.

Peacemaking criminology brings a call for humanism to criminology. The restorative justice model holds that reconciliation rather than retribution should be applied to prevent and control crime. Restoration programs are now being used around the United States in schools, justice agencies, and community forums. They employ mediation, sentencing circles, and other techniques.

Key Terms

critical criminology 198
power 200
supranational
   criminology 201
state (organized)
   crime 202
death squads 204
surplus value 204

torture 205
ticking bomb
   scenario 205
marginalization 206
globalization 206
instrumental
   theory 207
demystify 208

structural theory 208
left realism 211
preemptive
   deterrence 212
critical feminism 212
patriarchal 212
paternalistic families 214
role exit behaviors 214

egalitarian
   families 214
power–control
   theory 215
peacemaking 215
restorative
   justice 216
sentencing circle 218

Critical Thinking Questions

1. How would a conservative reply to a call for more restorative justice? How would an advocate of restorative justice respond to a conservative call for more prisons?

2. Considering recent changes in American culture, how would a power–control theorist explain recent drops in the U.S. crime rate? Can they be linked to changes in the structure of the American family?

3. Is conflict inevitable in all cultures? If not, what can be done to reduce the level of conflict in our own society?

4. If Marx were alive today, what would he think about the prosperity enjoyed by the working class in industrial societies? Might he alter his vision of the capitalist system?

5. Has religious conflict replaced class conflict as the most important issue facing modern society? Can anything be done to heal the rifts between people of different faiths?

Cole Younger

Bob Young (rear

Jesse James

Frank James

The James Boys and the Younger Broth

© Corbis

Developmental Theories

Life-Course and Latent Trait

9

There is no more storied bad man in American history than the outlaw Jesse James. A true folk hero, James has been portrayed in books and films as a Southern gentlemen who took money from the rich and gave it to the needy. Loved by the "little people," he remained an active outlaw until April 3, 1882, when, while dusting a picture frame, he was shot in the back by Bob Ford, a fellow gang member who did the deed in order to claim a $5,000 reward.

Legend aside, James was in fact more of an impulsive killer than a latter-day Robin Hood. His rise to fame began in 1863, when at age 16 he joined his brother Frank in a band of pro-Confederate guerillas operating in the contested borderlands of Kansas and Missouri. These bushwhackers, or guerilla fighters, ambushed Union militias and assassinated civilians believed to be Union sympathizers. The James brothers eventually joined up with the notorious William Quantrill, a ruthless raider whose guerilla band savaged Unionists, killing people indiscriminately, burning homes, and destroying entire towns. On the morning of August 21, 1863, they attacked Lawrence, Kansas, burned the town, and killed 183 men and boys. In September 1864, Jesse and Frank, now riding with Bloody Bill Anderson, held up a train in the town of Centralia and helped to kill 22 unarmed Union soldiers on board.

After the war, Jesse James used the guerilla tactics he had learned during his bushwhacker days to stage robberies and murders. He carried out what is believed to have been the first daylight robbery of a bank in America, escaping from Liberty, Missouri, with $58,000 in 1866. Until his death in 1882, Jesse James left a long trail of dead lawmen, bank tellers, and railroad personnel. His exploits became fodder for a newly emerging media that used him as a symbol of Southern resistance to the postwar political order.

Fact or Fiction?

► The outlaw Jesse James was a romantic historical figure who stole from the rich and gave to the poor.

► People who commit crime have lots or problems and tend to die young.

► Most kids who get into serious trouble fall in with a bad crowd when they are teens.

► Getting married helps people stay out of trouble.

► Criminals are impulsive risk takers.

Chapter Objectives

1. Discuss the history of developmental theory.

2. Distinguish between the life-course theory and the latent trait theory.

3. Be familiar with the principles of the life-course theory.

4. Explain the term "problem behavior syndrome."

5. Be aware that there are different pathways to crime.

6. Discuss why age of onset is an important factor in crime.

7. Know the basic principles of Sampson and Laub's Age-Graded Theory.

8. Define the term "latent trait."

9. Be familiar with Wilson and Herrnstein's views on crime and human nature.

10. Understand the basic principles of the General Theory of Crime.

James didn't mind the publicity or the identification. On July 21, 1873, his gang wore Ku Klux Klan masks when they derailed the Rock Island train in Adair, Iowa, and stole approximately $3,000.[1]

Even though he died more than 100 years ago, the legend of Jesse James lives on. (He was played by Brad Pitt in a 2007 film, *The Assassination of Jesse James by the Coward Robert Ford*.) But James was no hero. His history of antisocial acts began in his youth and persisted into his adulthood, ending only in his premature death.

Fact or Fiction?

The outlaw Jesse James was a romantic historical figure who stole from the rich and gave to the poor.

Fiction. In reality, Jesse James was an impulsive killer who morphed from guerilla fighter into bank robber.

What causes someone like Jesse James to enter into a life of crime and then persist in it over his life span? He could have quit at any time (his brother Frank was actually acquitted of his crimes and lived a quiet life, dying from natural causes at age 72). But Jesse persisted in his antisocial activities until his death. What causes some people to begin a criminal career, persist in it, and even escalate their criminal activities throughout their lives, whereas most people either remain law-abiding citizens or **desist** and age out of crime as they mature? It is true that James's actions may in part reflect the turbulent period in which he lived, but relatively few of his cohort routinely engaged in guerilla warfare, massacres, train robberies, and murder.

Concern over these critical issues has prompted some criminologists to focus their attention on identifying and describing the developmental factors that explain the onset and continuation of a criminal career. Rather than focusing on the reasons why an individual may engage in crime, **developmental theories** attempt to explain the "natural history of a criminal career"—its onset, continuation, and termination.

Foundations of Developmental Theory

As you may recall, the research efforts of Sheldon and Eleanor Glueck formed the basis of today's developmental approach. Soon after the publication of their work, the Gluecks' methodology and their integration of biological, psychological, and social factors were sharply criticized, and for many years their work was ignored in criminology texts and overlooked in the academic curriculum.

During the 1990s, the Glueck legacy was rediscovered in a series of papers by criminologists Robert Sampson and John Laub, who used modern statistical techniques to reanalyze the Gluecks' carefully drawn empirical measurements. Sampson and Laub's findings, published in a series of books and articles, fueled the popularity of the developmental approach.[2]

The Philadelphia cohort research by Marvin Wolfgang and his associates also sparked interest in explaining criminal career development. Chapter 2 discussed how Wolfgang found that although many offenders commit a single criminal act and thereafter desist from crime, a small group of chronic offenders engage in frequent and repeated criminal activity and continue to do so across their life span. Wolfgang's research focused attention on criminal careers. His work prompted criminologists to ask this fundamental question: What prompts one person to engage in persistent criminal activity, while another, who on the surface suffers the same life circumstances, finds a way to steer clear of crime and travel a more conventional path?

A 1990 review paper by Rolf Loeber and Marc Le Blanc was another important event that spurred interest in a developmental criminology. In this landmark work, Loeber and LeBlanc proposed that criminologists should devote time and effort to understanding basic questions about the evolution of criminal careers. Rather than viewing criminality as static and constant—a person simply is either a criminal or a noncriminal—they viewed criminality as a dynamic process, with a beginning, middle, and end and changes all along the way. Loeber and Le Blanc challenged criminologists to answer these questions: Why do people begin committing antisocial acts? Why do some stop, whereas others continue? Why do some escalate the severity of their criminality (that is, go from shoplifting to drug dealing to armed robbery), whereas others deescalate and commit less serious crimes as they mature? If some terminate

desist
To spontaneously stop committing crime.

developmental theories
Theories that attempt to explain the "natural history" of a criminal career: its onset, the course it follows, and its termination.

their criminal activity, what (if anything) causes them to begin again? Why do some criminals specialize in certain types of crime, whereas others are generalists engaging in a variety of antisocial activities? According to Loeber and Le Blanc's developmental view, criminologists must pay attention to how a criminal career unfolds—how it begins, why it is sustained, and how it comes to an end.[3]

These scholarly advances created enormous excitement among criminologists and focused their attention on criminal career research. As research on criminal careers has evolved, two distinct developmental viewpoints have taken shape: the life-course view and the latent trait view. Those who subscribe to **life-course theories** view criminality as a dynamic process, influenced by a multitude of individual characteristics, traits, and social experiences. As people travel through the life course, they are constantly bombarded by changing perceptions and experiences, and as a result their behavior changes direction, sometimes for the better and sometimes for the worse. In contrast, proponents of **latent trait theories** (which are also called **propensity theories**) believe that human development is controlled by a "master trait," present at birth or soon after, that, in the case of criminals, endows them with an increased propensity to commit crime. Some criminologists believe that this master trait is inflexible, stable, and unchanging; others concede that under some circumstances, a latent trait can be altered, influenced, or changed by experiences and interactions. In either event, as people travel through their life course, this trait is always there, directing their behavior and shaping the course of their life. Because this master trait is enduring, the ebb and flow of criminal behavior is directed by the impact of external forces such as interpersonal interactions and criminal opportunity. In other words, people don't change their fundamental nature, but the world around them is constantly evolving. These two perspectives are discussed in detail in the following sections. ▶ **Checkpoints**

Life-Course Fundamentals

According to the life-course view, even as toddlers, people begin relationships and behaviors that will determine their adult life course. At first they must learn to conform to social rules and function effectively in society. Later they are expected to begin to think about careers, leave their parental homes, find permanent relationships, and eventually marry and begin their own families.[4] These transitions are expected to take place in order—completing school, then entering the workforce, next getting married, and then having children.

Some individuals, however, are incapable of maturing in a reasonable and timely fashion because of family, environmental, or personal problems. In some cases, transitions can occur too early, such as when an adolescent girl who engages in precocious sex gets pregnant and is forced to drop out of high school. In other cases, transitions may occur too late, such as when a teenage male falls in with the wrong crowd, goes to prison, and thereafter finds it difficult to break into the job market; he puts off getting married because of his diminished economic circumstances. Sometimes interruption of one trajectory can harm another. A teenager who has family problems may find that her educational and career development is upset. Because a transition from one stage of life to another can be a bumpy ride, the propensity to commit crimes is neither stable nor constant: It is a developmental process. A positive life experience may help some criminals desist from crime for a while, whereas a negative one may cause them to resume their activities.[5]

Life-course theories also recognize that as people mature, the factors that influence their behavior change.[6] As people make important life transitions—from child to adolescent, from adolescent to adult, from unwed to married—the nature of social interactions also changes.[7] At first, family relations may be most influential; it comes as no shock to life-course theorists when research shows that criminality runs in families and that having criminal relatives is a significant predictor of future misbehaviors.[8] In later adolescence, school and peer relations predominate; in adulthood, vocational achievement and marital relations may be the most critical influences. Some antisocial children who are in trouble throughout their adolescence manage to find stable work and maintain

▶ Pioneering criminologists Sheldon and Eleanor Glueck tracked the onset and termination of criminal careers.

▶ Their work led to the creation of developmental theories.

▶ Developmental theories attempt to provide a global vision of a criminal career that encompasses its onset, continuation, and termination.

▶ Developmental theories come in two different varieties.

▶ Life-course theories look at such issues as the onset of crime, escalation of offenses, continuity of crime, and desistance from crime.

▶ Latent trait theories assume that a "master trait" exists that guides human development.

life-course theories
Theories reflecting the view that criminality is a dynamic process, influenced by many characteristics, traits, and experiences, and that behavior changes accordingly, for better or worse, over the life course.

latent trait (propensity) theories
Theories reflecting the view that criminal behavior is controlled by a master trait, present at birth or soon after, that remains stable and unchanging throughout a person's lifetime.

Exhibit 9.1 Problem Behaviors

Social

- Family dysfunction
- Unemployment
- Educational underachievement
- School misconduct

Personal

- Substance abuse
- Suicide attempts
- Early sexuality

- Sensation seeking
- Early parenthood
- Accident-prone
- Medical problems
- Mental disease
- Anxiety
- Eating disorders (bulimia, anorexia)

Environmental

- High-crime area
- Disorganized area
- Racism
- Exposure to poverty

intact marriages as adults. These life events help them desist from crime. In contrast, less fortunate adolescents who develop arrest records and get involved with the wrong crowd may find themselves limited to menial jobs and at risk for criminal careers.

From these and similar efforts, a view of crime has emerged that incorporates personal change and growth. The factors that produce crime and delinquency at one point in the life cycle may not be relevant at another; as people mature, the social, physical, and environmental influences on their behavior are transformed. People may show a propensity to offend early in their lives, but the nature and frequency of their activities are often affected by forces beyond their control, which elevate and sustain their criminal activity.[9]

The following sections review some of the more important concepts associated with the developmental perspective and discuss some prominent life-course theories.

PROBLEM BEHAVIOR SYNDROME

The life-course view is that criminality may best be understood as one of many social problems faced by at-risk youth, referred to here as **problem behavior syndrome (PBS)**. In this view, crime is one among a group of interrelated antisocial behaviors that cluster together and typically involve family dysfunction, sexual and physical abuse, substance abuse, smoking, precocious sexuality and early pregnancy, educational underachievement, suicide attempts, sensation seeking, and unemployment.[10] People who suffer from one of these conditions typically exhibit many symptoms of the rest.[11] Problem behaviors have a cumulative, reciprocal effect: The more risk factors that individuals suffer, the greater the likelihood that they will engage in antisocial behaviors; and the more they engage in antisocial behaviors, the more likely they are to develop risk factors.[12] All varieties of criminal behavior, including violence, theft, and drug offenses, may be part of a generalized PBS, indicating that all forms of antisocial behavior have similar developmental patterns (see Exhibit 9.1).[13]

Those who exhibit PBS are prone to more difficulties than the general population.[14] They find themselves experiencing personal dilemmas ranging from drug abuse to being accident-prone, to requiring more health care and hospitalization, to becoming teenage parents, and to having mental health problems.[15] PBS has been linked to individual-level personality problems (such as impulsiveness, rebelliousness, and low ego); family problems (such as intrafamily conflict and parental mental disorder); substance abuse; and educational failure.[16]

Considering the types of problems that cluster together—as do mental illness, drug abuse, and hospitalization, for example—it is not surprising that people who have a long and varied criminal career are more likely than others to die early and to have greater than average mortality rates. Criminal conduct has been found to increase the chances of premature death due to both natural and unnatural causes, including deaths from accidents, homicide, and suicide. The more crime a person commits, the more likely he or she is to suffer premature death.[17]

Fact or Fiction?

People who commit crime have lots of problems and tend to die young.

Fact. Not surprisingly, criminals also manifest many other social programs and tend to die young.

---

problem behavior syndrome (PBS)
A cluster of antisocial behaviors that may include family dysfunction, substance abuse, smoking, precocious sexuality and early pregnancy, educational underachievement, suicide attempts, sensation seeking, and unemployment, as well as crime.

In sum, problem behavior syndrome portrays crime as a type of social problem rather than as the product of other social problems.[18] People involved in crime may fall prey to other social problems, ranging from poverty to premature death.[19]

PATHWAYS TO CRIME

Career criminals may travel more than a single road. Some may specialize in violence and extortion; some may be involved in theft and fraud; others may engage in a variety of criminal acts. Some offenders may begin their careers early in life, whereas others are late bloomers who begin committing crime when most people desist. Some are frequent offenders, and others travel a more moderate path.[20]

Some of the most important research on delinquent paths, or trajectories, has been conducted by Rolf Loeber and his associates. Using data from a longitudinal study of Pittsburgh youth, Loeber has identified three distinct paths to a criminal career (Figure 9.1).[21]

1. The **authority conflict pathway** begins at an early age with stubborn behavior. This leads to defiance (doing things one's own way, disobedience) and then to authority avoidance (staying out late, truancy, running away).

authority conflict pathway
Path to a criminal career that begins with early stubborn behavior and defiance of parents.

Figure 9.1 Loeber's Pathways to Crime

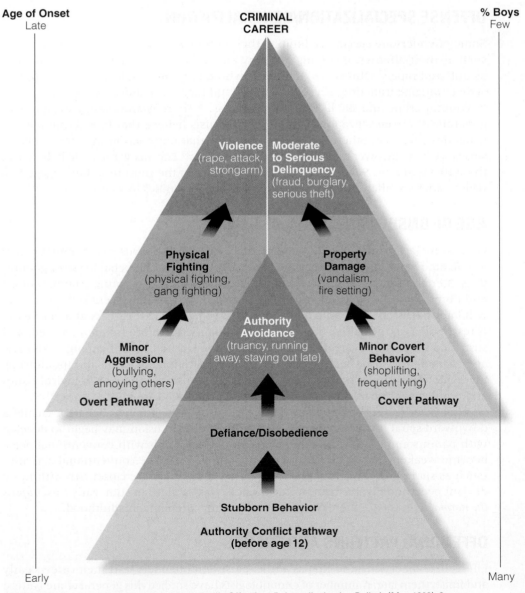

SOURCE: Rolf Loeber, "Serious and Violent Juvenile Offenders," *Juvenile Justice Bulletin* (May 1998): 3.

2. The **covert pathway** begins with minor, underhanded behavior (lying, shoplifting) that leads to property damage (setting nuisance fires, damaging property). This behavior eventually escalates to more serious forms of criminality, ranging from joyriding, pocket picking, larceny, and fencing stolen goods, to passing bad checks, using stolen credit cards, stealing cars, dealing drugs, and breaking and entering.
3. The **overt pathway** escalates to aggressive acts, beginning with aggression (annoying others, bullying), leading to physical (and gang) fighting and then to violence (attacking someone, forced theft).

The Loeber research indicates that each of these paths may lead to a sustained deviant career. Some people enter two or even three paths simultaneously: They are stubborn, lie to teachers and parents, are bullies, and commit petty thefts. These adolescents are the most likely to become persistent offenders as they mature. As adolescents they cheat on tests, bully kids in the schoolyard, take drugs, commit burglary, steal a car, and then shoplift from a store. Later, as adults, some specialize in a particular criminal activity such as drug trafficking, while others are involved in an assortment of deviant acts—selling drugs, committing robberies, and getting involved in break-ins—when the situation presents itself and the opportunities arise.[22]

The accompanying Profiles in Crime feature describes the path to murder taken by one band of notorious killers.

OFFENSE SPECIALIZATION/GENERALIZATION

Some offenders are specialists, limiting their criminal activities to a cluster of crimes such as theft offenses, including burglary and larceny, or violent offenses such as assault and rape.[23] Others are generalists who engage in a wide variety of criminal activity ranging from drug abuse to burglary and rape, depending on the opportunity to commit crime and the likelihood of success.[24] There is an ongoing debate over generalization/specialization. Some criminologists believe that most criminals are generalists, whereas others have found evidence that more serious offenders tend to specialize in a narrower range of antisocial activities.[25] The answer may lie in between these two positions. Some offenders may specialize in the short term but engage in a wider variety of offenses when presented with opportunities to commit crime.[26]

AGE OF ONSET/CONTINUITY OF CRIME

One of the key principles of life-course theory is that the seeds of a criminal career are planted early in life and that the early onset of antisocial behavior strongly predicts later and more serious criminality.[27] We know that most young criminals desist and do not become adult offenders.[28] The relatively few adolescent offenders who will later persist in crime into adulthood begin their deviant careers at a very early (preschool) age; the earlier the onset of criminality, the more frequent, varied, and sustained the criminal career.[29] What causes some kids to begin offending at an early age? Among the suspected root causes are poor parental discipline and monitoring, inadequate emotional support, distant peer relationships, and psychological issues and problems.[30] The psychic scars of a crippling childhood are hard to erase.[31]

Why is early onset so important? The early onset of delinquent behavior creates a downward spiral in a young person's life.[32] Thereafter, tension may begin to develop with parents and other family members, emotional bonds with conventional peers become weakened and frayed, and opportunities to pursue conventional activities (such as sports) dry up and wither away. Replacing them are closer ties with more deviant peers and involvement in a delinquent way of life.[33] In sum, early onset *upsets the normal course of life*, thereby directly influencing offending in adulthood.

OFFENDING PATTERNS AND TRENDS

Life-course theory suggests that as a rule, persistent offenders start their careers early and finish them late. A number of criminologists have studied this general crime pattern in order to identify different types of offenders according to their offending patterns.

covert pathway
Path to a criminal career that begins with minor underhanded behavior and progresses to fire starting and theft.

overt pathway
Path to a criminal career that begins with minor aggression, leads to physical fighting, and eventually escalates to violent crime.

In the hot summer months of 2004, Troy Victorino and friends Robert Cannon, Jerone Hunter, and Michael Salas were illegally squatting in a Deltona, Florida, home and using it as a "party house." The owners, who were spending the summer in Maine, asked their granddaughter, Erin Belanger, to check up on the property. When she saw what was going on, she called the police in order to get the squatters removed from the premises. Victorino (who was in jail on an unrelated matter at the time his friends were evicted) left behind an Xbox game system and some clothes, and Belanger took possession of these items. Once he was released from jail on bond, Victorino, feeling disrespected because the police had been called and his stuff confiscated, threatened Belanger and slashed the tires on her car. He warned her that unless she returned the items, he was going to come back and beat her with a baseball bat while she was sleeping. It was not an idle threat. On August 6, 2004, in what is now known either as the Xbox murders or the Deltona Massacre, Victorino and his friends Cannon, Hunter, and Salas armed themselves with aluminum bats, put on all-black clothing, covered their faces with scarves, kicked in the front door, and attacked Belanger and her roommates as they slept. All six victims, including Erin Belanger, were beaten and stabbed beyond recognition. All six died.

The perpetrators of the deadly attack left a trail of clues that resulted in their quick arrest and indictment on murder charges. It was a pretty sad bunch; they all seemed to have lived troubled lives. Michael Salas was abused even before his birth by his mother Doris, who used drugs during her pregnancy, traded food stamps for cocaine, and left her three sons alone for long periods during the winter. Child protective services found cigarette burns on the boys' bodies. Salas's father Roberto died of AIDS when Michael was 9. Hunter is a clinically depressed, mentally ill man whose parents were both committed to mental hospitals at the time of the massacre. As early as age 3, Hunter heard voices and claimed to have conversed with his identical twin brother Jeremy, who died from pneumonia at 6 months old. But it was Victorino, a 6-foot-6-inch, 300-pound career criminal, who most outraged the public. He had spent 8 of the last 11 years before the killings serving prison sentences for a variety of crimes, including auto theft, battery, arson, burglary, and theft. In 1996, he beat a man so severely that doctors needed 15 titanium plates to rebuild the victim's face. Not surprisingly, Victorino also had a long history of physical and sexual abuse, a torment that began when he was two years old. He suffered from neurological impairment that resulted in poor impulse control and the inability to manage his violent temper.

Despite their personal problems, on August 2, 2006, Victorino and Hunter were sentenced to death by lethal injection, and Cannon and Salas to life in prison without the possibility of parole. As of this writing, Victorino and Hunter remain on death row at the Florida State Prison in Starke (the average length of incarceration of a Florida inmate prior to execution is more than ten years).

The Xbox killers follow a classic developmental path: early abuse and problems in childhood leading to a long and sustained criminal career. These killers did not age out of crime but, rather, persisted and escalated their criminal involvement until it culminated in unspeakable tragedy.

SOURCES: "The Deltona Massacre," http://dic.academic.ru/dic.nsf/enwiki/6132751; News Journal on Line, "Terror at Telford Lane," www.news-journalonline.com/special/deltonadeaths/; CNN, "Probation Officers Fired after 'XBox killings'" August 10, 2004, http://www.cnn.com/2004/LAW/08/09/fla.killing.probation/index.html.

Troy Victorino

Michael Salas

Jerone Hunter

Troy Victorino, 29 (left), Michael Salas (center), and Jerone Hunter (right), both 20, killed six people in a revenge slaying over an Xbox video game system.

Adolescent-Limiteds and Life-Course Persisters According to psychologist Terrie Moffitt, most young offenders follow one of two paths, becoming either adolescent-limited offenders or life-course persisters. **Adolescent-limited offenders** may be considered "typical teenagers" who get into minor scrapes and engage in what might be considered rebellious teenage behavior with their friends.[34] As they reach their midteens, adolescent-limited delinquents begin to mimic the antisocial behavior of more troubled teens, only to reduce the frequency of their offending as they mature to around age 18.[35]

The second path is the one taken by a small group of **life-course persisters** who begin their offending career at a very early age and continue to offend well into adulthood.[36] Moffitt finds that life-course persisters combine family dysfunction with severe neurological problems that predispose them to antisocial behavior patterns. These afflictions can be the result of maternal drug abuse, poor nutrition, or exposure to toxic agents such as lead. It is not surprising, then, that life-course persisters display social and personal dysfunctions, including lower-than-average verbal ability, reasoning skills, learning ability, and school achievement.

There is evidence that the persistence patterns predicted by Moffitt are valid and accurate.[37] Life-course persisters offend more frequently and engage in a greater variety of antisocial acts than other offenders; they also manifest significantly more mental health problems, including psychiatric pathologies, than adolescent-limited offenders.[38] Life-course persisters are more likely to manifest traits such as low verbal ability and hyperactivity, they display a negative or impulsive personality, and they seem particularly impaired on spatial and memory functions.[39] Individual traits, rather than environment, seem to have the greatest influence on life-course persistence.[40]

Late Bloomers Criminologists Sarah Bacon, Raymond Paternoster, and Robert Brame have identified another subset of criminals, the "late bloomers." These persisters actually stay out of trouble in adolescence until late in their teenage years and then become violent chronic persisters. Bacon and her associates found that kids who started later in delinquency were actually the ones more likely to get involved in adult offending![41] These late bloomers combine psychopathology with risk-taking behavior and poor social skills; their behavior becomes increasingly violent over time.[42]

Theories of the Criminal Life Course

A number of systematic theories have been formulated that account for the onset, continuance, and termination of crime.[43] As a group, these theories integrate *personal factors* such as personality and intelligence, *social factors* such as income and neighborhood, *socialization factors* such as marriage and military service, *cognitive factors* such as information processing and attention/perception, and *situational factors* such as criminal opportunity, effective guardianship, and apprehension risk into complex multifactor explanations of human behavior. In this sense they are **integrated theories** because they incorporate social, personal, and developmental factors into complex explanations of human behavior. They do not focus on the relatively simple question of why people commit crime but, rather, on more complex issues: Why do some offenders persist in criminal careers, whereas others desist from or alter their criminal activity as they mature?[44] Why do some people continually escalate their criminal involvement, whereas others slow down and turn their lives around? Are all criminals similar in their offending patterns, or are there different types of offenders and paths to offending? Life-course theorists want to know not only why people enter a criminal way of life but also why, once they do, they alter the trajectory of their criminal involvement.

Perhaps the most important and most widely researched life-course theory is Robert Sampson and John Laub's **Age-Graded Theory**, which is discussed in some detail here.

adolescent-limited offender
One who follows the most common criminal trajectory, in which antisocial behavior peaks in adolescence and then diminishes.

life-course persister
One of the small group of offenders whose criminal careers continue well into adulthood.

integrated theories
Models of crime causation that weave social and individual variables into a complex explanatory chain.

Age-Graded Theory
According to Robert Sampson and John Laub, discrete factors influence people at different stages of their development, so the propensity to commit crimes is neither stable nor unyielding. The likelihood of committing crime is linked to the accumulation (or absence) of social capital, social control, and human decision making.

SAMPSON AND LAUB'S AGE-GRADED THEORY

If there are various pathways to crime and delinquency, are there trails back to conformity? In an important 1993 work, *Crime in the Making*, Robert Sampson and John Laub identify the **turning points** in a criminal career.[45] As devotees of the life-course perspective, Sampson and Laub find that the maintenance of a criminal career can be affected by events that occur later in life, even after a chronic delinquent career has been undertaken. They agree with other criminologists that formal and informal social controls restrict criminality and that crime begins early in life and continues over the life course, but they disagree with the idea that once this course is set, nothing can impede its progress.

To conduct their research, Laub and Sampson reanalyzed the data originally collected by the Gluecks more than 50 years ago. Using modern statistical analysis, Laub and Sampson found evidence supporting their developmental view. They found that discrete factors influence people at different stages of their development, and, therefore, the propensity to commit crimes is neither stable nor unyielding. Children who enter delinquent careers are those who have trouble at home and at school; their parents and family life are the greatest influence on their behavior. As adolescents, peer relations become all important, and kids who maintain deviant friends are the ones most at risk of committing crime. In adulthood, behavior choices are influenced by elements of informal social control such as marriage, family, and work.

Social Capital Laub and Sampson recognize the role of **social capital** and its influence on the trajectory of a criminal career. Social scientists have long recognized that people build social capital—positive relations with individuals and institutions that are life-sustaining. In the same manner that building financial capital improves the chances for personal success, building social capital supports conventional behavior and inhibits deviant behavior. Laub and Sampson find that at-risk kids who join the military and are honorably discharged significantly reduce the likelihood that they will become chronic offenders. A successful marriage (which creates social capital when it improves a person's stature, creates feelings of self-worth, and encourages people to trust the individual) also suppresses criminal activities. A successful career inhibits crime by creating a stake in conformity: Why commit crime when you are doing well at your job? The relationship is reciprocal. If people are chosen to be employees, they return the favor by doing the best job possible; if they are chosen as spouses, they blossom into devoted partners. In contrast, people who fail to accumulate social capital are more likely to commit criminal acts.[46] When faced with personal crisis, they lack the social supports that can help them reject criminal solutions and maintain a conventional behavior trajectory.

Trajectories, Transitions, and Turning Points One of Laub and Sampson's most important contributions is identifying the life events that enable adult offenders to desist from crime (Figure 9.2). According to them, trajectories are long-term patterns in life, and transitions are "short-term events embedded in trajectories."[47] Both transitions and trajectories can have a positive or a negative connotation. A positive transition, for example, might be graduating from college and getting a good job; a negative trajectory might be joining a gang.

A major concept in the Sampson and Laub theory is that criminal careers are a dynamic process in which an important life event can (1) produce a transition in the life course and (2) change the direction of a person's life-course trajectory. They refer to these as important life events as *turning points*. Two critical turning points are marriage and career. Adolescents who are at risk for crime can live conventional lives if they can find good jobs or achieve successful careers. Their success may hinge on a lucky break. Even those who have been in trouble with the law may turn from crime if employers are willing to give them a chance in spite of their records.

Fact or Fiction?

Getting married helps people stay out of trouble.

Fact. Marriage, according to Sampson and Laub, is one of those turning points that help people get out of a criminal career.

turning points
According to Laub and Sampson, the life events that alter the development of a criminal career.

social capital
Positive, life-sustaining relations with individuals and institutions.

Figure 9.2 Sampson and Laub's Age-Graded Theory

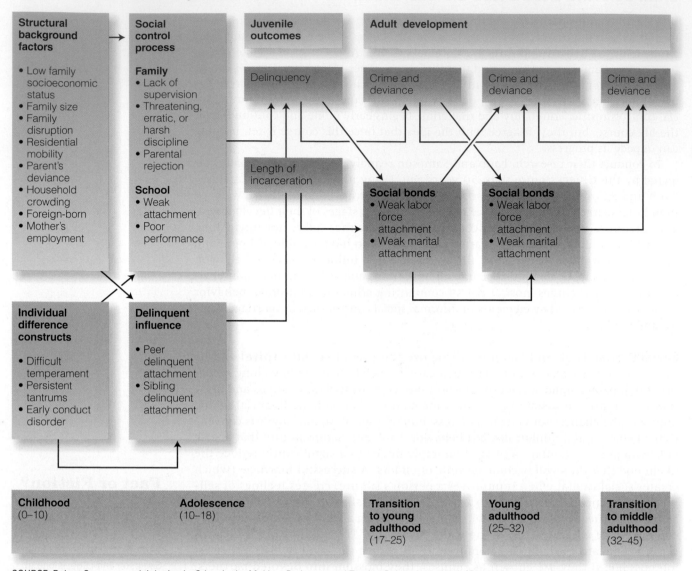

SOURCE: Robert Sampson and John Laub, *Crime in the Making: Pathways and Turning Points through Life* (Cambridge, MA: Harvard University, 1993), pp. 244–245.

When they achieve adulthood, adolescents who had significant problems with the law are able to desist from crime if they become attached to a spouse who supports and sustains them even when the spouse knows they were in trouble when they were young. Happy marriages are life-sustaining, and marital quality improves over time (as people work less and have fewer parental responsibilities).[48] Spending time in marital and family activities also reduces exposure to deviant peers, which in turn reduces the opportunity to become involved in delinquent activities.[49] People who cannot sustain secure marital relations are less likely than others to desist from crime. One key element of the theory is that marriage reduces criminal activities. This issue is explored in the Current Issues in Crime feature on page 236.

Testing the Age-Graded Theory Empirical research now shows that, just as Sampson and Laub predicted, people change over the life course, and the factors that predict delinquency in adolescence, such as weak social bonds, may have less of an impact on adult crime.[50] Criminality appears to be dynamic and is affected by behaviors that occur over the life course, such as accumulating deviant peers: The more deviant friends one accumulates over time, the more likely one is to get involved in crime.[51] Of critical importance is early labeling by the justice system: Adolescents who are convicted of crime at an early age are more likely to develop antisocial attitudes later in life. They later develop low educational achievement, declining occupational status, and unstable employment records.[52] People who get involved with the justice system as adolescents may find that their career paths are blocked well into adulthood.[53] The relationship is reciprocal: Men who are unemployed or underemployed report higher criminal participation rates than employed men.[54]

Evidence is also available that confirms Sampson and Laub's suspicion that criminal career trajectories can be reversed if life conditions improve.[55] For example, youths who have a positive high school experience, facilitated by occupationally oriented course work, small class size, and positive peer climates, are less likely to be incarcerated as adults than those who do not enjoy these social benefits.[56] Long-term exposure to poverty is associated with involvement in crime, but the involvement of such kids in crime will diminish if their life circumstances improve because their parents escape poverty and move to a more attractive environment. Recent research by Ross Macmillan and his colleagues shows that children whose mothers were initially poor but escaped from poverty were no more likely to develop behavior problems than children whose mothers were never poor. Gaining social capital, then, may help erase some of the damage caused by its absence.[57]

A number of research efforts have supported Sampson and Laub's position that accumulating social capital reduces crime rates. Youths who accumulate social capital in childhood (for example, by doing well in school or having a tightly knit family)

Age-Graded Theory suggests that kids who are on a trajectory toward delinquency can knife off that path if they experience positive life events and informal social control. Here Lamont Fowler, a star track athlete at Conrad Weiser High School in Robesonia, Pennsylvania, located about 10 miles west of Reading, competes in the 400-meter dash during the John H. Shaner Meet on May 2, 2009. Fowler, who set three meet records during the competition, struggled as a teen through a succession of foster families and a stint as a juvenile delinquent before discovering his talent for running in 2007 at the Glen Mills School, a facility for wayward boys about 20 miles west of Philadelphia. Peter Schaefer, Weiser High School's cross country coach and assistant track coach, welcomed Fowler into the family's home in September 2008 after becoming his legal guardian. Can such positive life events help other kids reject a delinquent way of life? Or is this story unique?

are also the most likely to maintain steady work as adults, and employment may help insulate them from crime.[58] Delinquents who enter the military, serve overseas, and receive veterans' benefits enhance their occupational status (social capital) while reducing their criminal involvement.[59] Similarly, high-risk adults who are fortunate enough to obtain good jobs are likely to reduce their criminal activities even if they have a prior history of offending.[60]

Future Research Directions Sampson and Laub's Age-Graded Theory has received enormous attention, but many research questions are still unanswered. Does a military career actually help reduce future criminality? Research by John Paul Wright and his colleagues found that Vietnam veterans significantly increased their involvement in substance abuse once they returned home. Considering the strong association

A key element of Sampson and Laub's Age-Graded Theory is that people who maintain a successful marriage and become parents are the most likely to mature out of crime. Marriage stabilizes people and helps them build social capital; it also may discourage crime by reducing contact with criminal peers. As criminologist Mark Warr puts it,

> For many individuals, it seems, marriage marks a transition from heavy peer involvement to a preoccupation with one's spouse. That transition is likely to reduce interaction with former friends and accomplices and thereby reduce the opportunities as well as the motivation to engage in crime.

Even people who have histories of criminal activity and have been convicted of serious offenses reduce the frequency of their offending if they live with spouses and maintain employment when they are in the community.

9-to-5 jobs, come home for dinner, take care of children if they have them, watch television, go to bed, and repeat that cycle over and over again. Single people have a lot of free time to do just what they want, especially if they are not employed. There's something about crossing the line of getting married that helps these men stay away from crime.

Marriage may also mark a physical/biological turning point in the life course. Kevin Beaver and his colleagues find that as people mature and go through biological changes, they slow down, and this prompts them to quit the hectic and strenuous criminal way of life and instead settle into a more comfortable and less taxing marital routine.

Why Do People Have Happy Marriages?

The marriage benefit may also be intergenerational. That is, children who grow up in two-parent families are more likely

Current Issues in Crime Love, Sex, Marriage, and Crime

Researchers Alex Piquero, John MacDonald, and Karen Parker tracked each of 524 men in their late teens and early twenties for seven years after they were paroled from the California Youth Authority during the 1970s and 1980s. They found that former offenders were far less likely to return to crime if they settled into the routines of a solid marriage. People who get married are more likely to have

to have happier marriages themselves than children who are the product of divorced or never-married parents. If people with marital problems are more crime-prone, their children will also suffer a greater long-term risk of marital failure and antisocial activity.

Because the marriage benefit is so great and long-lasting, it is troubling that 40–50 percent of first marriages,

Checkpoints

▶ Life-course theorists have identified a number of different concepts that influence human behavior.

▶ The concept of a problem behavior syndrome (PBS) suggests that criminality may be just one of a cluster of social, psychological, and physical problems.

▶ There is more than one pathway to crime.

cont.

latent trait
A stable feature, characteristic, property, or condition, present at birth or soon after, that makes some people crime-prone over the life course.

between drug abuse and crime, their research casts doubt on whether all types of military service can be beneficial, as Laub and Sampson suggest. Future research may profitably focus on individual experiences in the military and their effect on subsequent civilian behavior.[61]

Why are some troubled youths able to conform as they mature, whereas others cannot? If acquiring social capital—family, friends, education, marriage, and employment—aids in the successful recovery from crime, does the effect produce an actual change in the propensity to commit crime or does it merely reduce criminal opportunity?[62] To answer some of these questions, Laub and Sampson contacted the surviving members of the Glueck cohort, and some of their findings are discussed in the Current Issues in Crime feature on page 238. ▶ **Checkpoints**

Latent Trait Theories

In a critical 1990 article, David Rowe, D. Wayne Osgood, and W. Alan Nicewander proposed the concept of latent traits to explain the flow of crime over the life cycle. They suggested that a number of people in the population have a personal attribute or characteristic that controls their inclination or propensity to commit crimes.[63] This disposition, or **latent trait**, may be either present at birth or established early in life, and it can remain stable over time. Suspected latent traits include defective intelligence, damaged or impulsive personality, genetic abnormalities, the

67 percent of second marriages, and 74 percent of third marriages end in divorce. Sociologist Rand Conger and his colleagues have discovered that the seeds of divorce are planted early in childhood: Kids who grow up with warm, nurturing parents are the ones most likely to have intact marriages. Well-nurtured kids develop into warm and supportive marital partners who build marriages that are happy, satisfying, and likely to endure. The quality of the parents' marital relationship had no direct influence on the young adult romantic relationship. Rather, it is the quality of parenting, not the observation of adult romantic relations, that socializes a young person to engage in behaviors likely to promote successful and lasting romantic unions as an adult.

Sex, Love, and Crime

Is it marriage itself, or the promise of romantic love to which it is attached, that protects people from crime? When sociologists Bill McCarthy and Teresa Casey examined the association among love, sex, and delinquency in a sample of teens, they found that the closeness offered by adolescent romantic love may fill an important void between the weakening of bonds with parents and the onset of adult attachments, and this closeness may discourage an array of negative outcomes, including involvement in crime. Adolescent sexual activity without the promise of love, however, increases the likelihood of offending because it is associated with the strain inflicted by loveless relationships. McCarthy and Casey find that *romantic love has a deterrent effect that actually encourages youths who have offended to decrease their involvement in crime.* It is possible, they speculate, that romantic love discourages offending by strengthening the social bond. By contrast, the association between sex and crime is intensified in relationships short on love. It is possible that kids who engage in sex without love or romance are willing to partake in other risky and/or self-indulgent behaviors, including delinquency and drug use.

McCarthy and Casey's research indicates that just as marriage may help at-risk people "knife off" from crime, falling in love with a romantic partner may work equally well.

CRITICAL THINKING

1. Do you think that marriage is different from merely being in love? The McCarthy and Casey research indicates that having a romantic relationship may help reduce crime, but can marriage work better?
2. Even if we can show that married people are less likely to commit crime, does that fact prove that getting married is a cause of desistance? Isn't it possible that people who have already given up antisocial behaviors are ready to get married and therefore make more secure and steady marital companions?

SOURCES: Bill McCarthy and Teresa Casey, "Love, Sex, and Crime: Adolescent Romantic Relationships and Offending," *American Sociological Review* 73 (2008): 944–969; Kevin Beaver, John Paul Wright, Matt DeLisi, and Michael Vaughn, "Desistance from Delinquency: The Marriage Effect Revisited and Extended," *Social Science Research* 37 (2008): 736–752; Alex Piquero, John MacDonald, and Karen Parker, "Race, Local Life Circumstances, and Criminal Activity over the Life-Course," *Social Science Quarterly* 83 (2002): 654–671; Pamela Webster, Terri Orbuch, and James House, "Effects of Childhood Family Background on Adult Marital Quality and Perceived Stability," *American Journal of Sociology* 101 (1995): 404–432; Mark Warr, "Life-Course Transitions and Desistance from Crime," *Criminology* 36 (1998): 502–535; Divorce Statistics Collection, www.divorcereform.org/stats.html (accessed June 1, 2009).

physical-chemical functioning of the brain, and environmental influences on brain function, such as drugs, chemicals, and injuries.[64]

Regardless of gender or environment, those who maintain one of these suspect traits may be predisposed to crime and in danger of becoming career criminals; those who lack the traits have a much lower risk.[65]

ONSET AND PERSISTENCE OF CRIME

As you might imagine, those who believe in a master latent trait have a different view from that of life-course theorists on a key concept: the onset and persistence of crime. According to this view, people who begin to engage in crime at an early age do so because they maintain a preexisting latent trait that makes them crime-prone. Because latent traits are stable, people who are antisocial during adolescence are the most likely to persist in crime. The positive association between past and future criminality reflects the presence of this underlying criminogenic trait. That is, if low IQ contributes to delinquency in childhood, it should cause the same people to offend as adults because intelligence is usually stable over the life span.

Why do some people persist in criminal activity while others desist from it? *Whereas the propensity to commit crime is stable, the opportunity to commit crime fluctuates over time.* As a result, most people age out of crime. As they mature and develop, there are simply fewer opportunities to commit crimes and greater inducements to remain "straight."

Checkpoints (cont.)

▶ Adolescent-limited offenders begin offending late and age out of crime. Life-course persisters exhibit early onset of crime that persists into adulthood.

▶ There are a number of theories based on life-course events.

▶ According to Laub and Sampson's Age-Graded Theory, building social capital and strong social bonds reduces the likelihood of long-term deviance.

▶ Many criminals who desist from crime still face other risks, such as an early and untimely death.

Why are some delinquents destined to become persistent criminals as adults? John Laub and Robert Sampson have conducted a follow-up to their reanalysis of Sheldon and Eleanor Glueck's study that matched 500 delinquent boys with 500 nondelinquents. The individuals in the original sample were reinterviewed by the Gluecks at ages 25 and 32. Sampson and Laub located the survivors of the delinquent sample, the oldest 70 years old and the youngest 62, and reinterviewed this cohort.

Persistence and Desistance

Laub and Sampson found that delinquency and other forms of antisocial conduct in childhood are strongly related to adult delinquency and drug and alcohol abuse. Former delinquents also suffer consequences in other areas of social life, such as school, work, and family life. They are

60 percent had no arrests for predatory delinquency after age 31 (33 percent had none for total delinquency); and 79 percent had no arrests for predatory delinquency after age 40 (57 percent had none for total delinquency). Laub and Sampson concluded that desistance from delinquency is the norm and that most, if not all, serious delinquents desist from delinquency.

Why Do Delinquents Desist?

Laub and Sampson's earlier research indicated that building social capital through marriage and jobs was the key component of desistance from delinquency. In this new round of research, however, Laub and Sampson found out more about long-term desistance by interviewing 52 men as they approached age 70. The follow-up showed a dramatic drop in criminal activity as the men aged: Between 17 and

Current Issues in Crime Tracking Down the 500 Delinquent Boys

far less likely to finish high school than are nondelinquents and subsequently are more likely to be unemployed, to receive welfare, and to experience separation or divorce as adults.

In their latest research, Laub and Sampson address a key question posed by life-course theories: Is it possible for former delinquents to turn their lives around as adults? The researchers found that most antisocial children do not remain antisocial as adults. Of men in the study cohort who survived to 50 years of age, 24 percent had no arrests for delinquent acts of violence and property (predatory delinquency) after age 17 (6 percent had no arrests for total delinquency); 48 percent had no arrests for predatory delinquency after age 25 (19 percent had none for total delinquency);

24 years of age, 84 percent of the subjects had committed violent crimes; in their thirties and forties, that number dropped to 14 percent; it fell to 3 percent as the men reached their sixties and seventies. Property crimes and alcohol- and drug-related crimes showed significant decreases. The researchers found that men who desisted from crime were rooted in structural routines and had strong social ties to family and community. Drawing on the men's own words, they found that one important element for "going straight" is the "knifing off" of individuals from their immediate environment, offering the men a new script for the future. Joining the military can provide this knifing-off effect, as does marriage or changing one's residence. One former delinquent (age 69) told them,

They may obtain jobs, marry, and have children. The former delinquents' newfound adult responsibilities leave them little time to hang with their friends, abuse substances, and get into scrapes with the law. Thus, although their *propensity* to commit crime remains unchanged over the course of their life, their *opportunity* to do so has undergone radical change. Even if they wanted to engage in antisocial activities, as they age they either lack the opportunity and/or the energy to engage in criminal activities.

The Concept of State Dependence According to the concept of state dependence, kids who have the propensity to commit crime find that this latent trait profoundly and permanently disrupts normal socialization. And such disruptions in socialization thereafter increase the risk of prolonged antisocial behavior. In this view, early rule breaking increases the probability of future rule breaking because it weakens inhibitions to crime and/or strengthens criminal motivation. In other words, once kids get a taste of antisocial behavior, they like it and want to continue down a deviant path.[66]

I'd say the turning point was, number one, the Army. You get into an outfit, you had a sense of belonging, you made your friends. I think I became a pretty good judge of character. In the Army, you met some good ones, you met some foul balls. Then I met the wife. I'd say probably that would be the turning point. Got married, then naturally, kids come. So now you got to get a better job, you got to make more money. And that's how I got to the Navy Yard and tried to improve myself.

Former delinquents who "went straight" were able to put structure into their lives. Structure often led the men to disassociate from delinquent peers, reducing the opportunity to get into trouble. Getting married, for example, may limit the number of nights that men can "hang with the guys." As one wife of a former delinquent said, "It is not how many beers you have, it's who you drink with." Even multiple offenders who did time in prison were able to desist with the help of a stabilizing marriage.

Former delinquents who can turn their life around, who have acquired a degree of maturity by taking on family and work responsibilities, and who have forged new commitments are most likely to make a fresh start and find new direction and meaning in life. It seems that men who desisted also changed their identity, and this, in turn, affected their outlook and sense of maturity and responsibility. The ability to change did not reflect delinquency "specialty": Violent offenders followed the same path as property offenders.

Although many former delinquents desisted from delinquency, they still faced the risk of an early and untimely death. Thirteen percent ($N = 62$) of the delinquent subjects, compared to 6 percent ($N = 28$) of the nondelinquent subjects, died unnatural deaths, such as by violence, cirrhosis of the liver caused by alcoholism, poor self-care, or suicide. By 65 years of age, 29 percent ($N = 139$) of the delinquent and 21 percent ($N = 95$) of the nondelinquent subjects had died from natural causes. Frequent involvement in delinquency during adolescence and alcohol abuse were the strongest predictors of an early and unnatural death. Thus, although many troubled youths are able to reform, their early excesses may haunt them across their life span.

Policy Implications

Laub and Sampson found that youth problems—delinquency, substance abuse, violence, dropping out, teen pregnancy—often share common risk characteristics. Intervention strategies, therefore, should consider a broad array of antisocial, criminal, and deviant behaviors and not limit their focus to one subgroup or delinquency type. Because criminality and other social problems are linked, early prevention efforts that reduce delinquency will probably also reduce alcohol abuse, drunk driving, drug abuse, sexual promiscuity, and family violence. The best way to achieve these goals is through four significant life-changing events: marriage, joining the military, getting a job, and changing one's environment or neighborhood. What appears to be important about these processes is that they all involve, to varying degrees, the following items: a knifing off of the past from the present; new situations that provide both supervision and monitoring, as well as new opportunities for social support and growth; and new situations that provide the opportunity for transforming one's identity. Prevention of delinquency must be a policy at all times and at all stages of life.

CRITICAL THINKING

1. Do you believe that the factors that influenced the men in the original Glueck sample are still relevant for change—for example, a military career?

2. Would it be possible for men such as these to join the military today?

3. Do you believe that some sort of universal service program might be beneficial and help people turn their lives around?

SOURCES: John Laub and Robert Sampson, *Shared Beginnings, Divergent Lives: Delinquent Boys to Age 70* (Cambridge, MA: Harvard University Press, 2003); John Laub and Robert Sampson, "Understanding Desistance from Delinquency," in *Delinquency and Justice: An Annual Review of Research*, vol. 28, ed. Michael Tonry (Chicago: University of Chicago Press, 2001), pp. 1–71; John Laub and George Vaillant, "Delinquency and Mortality: A 50-Year Follow-Up Study of 1,000 Delinquent and Nondelinquent Boys," *American Journal of Psychiatry* 157 (2000): 96–102.

CRIME AND HUMAN NATURE

Latent trait theorists were encouraged when two prominent social scientists, James Q. Wilson and Richard Herrnstein, published *Crime and Human Nature* in 1985 and suggested that personal traits—such as genetic makeup, intelligence, and body build—may outweigh the importance of social variables as predictors of criminal activity.[67]

According to Wilson and Herrnstein, all human behavior, including criminality, is determined by its perceived consequences. A criminal incident occurs when an individual chooses criminal over conventional behavior (which Wilson and Herrnstein refer to as non-crime) after weighing the potential gains and losses associated with each: "The larger the ratio of net rewards of crime to the net rewards of non-crime, the greater the tendency to commit the crime."[68]

Wilson and Herrnstein's model assumes that both biological and psychological traits influence the choice between crime and non-crime. They see a close link between

Exhibit 9.2 Latent Trait Theories

Name Integrated Cognitive Antisocial Potential (ICAP) Theory

Principal Theorist David Farrington

Latent Trait Antisocial potential

Major Premise People maintain a range of "antisocial potential (AP)"—the potential to commit antisocial acts. AP can be viewed as both a long- and short-term phenomenon. Those with high levels of long-term AP are at risk for offending over the life course; those with low AP levels live more conventional lives. Though AP levels are fairly consistent over time, they peak in the teenage years because of the effects of maturational factors, such as increase in peer influence and decrease in family influence, that directly influence crime rates. Long-term AP can be reduced by life events such as marriage. Similarly, life events may increase a person's location on the AP continuum: A person with a relatively low long-term AP may suffer a temporary amplification if he is bored, angry, drunk, or frustrated. According to the ICAP theory, the commission of offenses and other types of antisocial acts depends on the interaction between the individual (with his or her immediate level of AP) and the social environment (especially criminal opportunities and victims).

Name Differential Coercion Theory

Principal Theorist Mark Colvin

Latent Trait Interpersonal/impersonal coercion

Major Premise Perceptions of coercion begin early in life when children experience punitive forms of discipline, including both physical attacks and psychological coercion such as negative commands, critical remarks, teasing, humiliation, whining, yelling, and threats. Through these destructive family interchanges, coercion becomes ingrained and guides reactions to adverse situations that arise in both family and nonfamily settings.

There are two sources of coercion: interpersonal and impersonal. Interpersonal coercion is direct, involving the use or threat of force and intimidation from parents, peers, and significant others. Impersonal coercion involves pressures beyond individual control, such as economic and social pressure caused by unemployment, poverty, or competition among businesses or other groups. High levels of coercion produce criminality, especially when the episodes of coercive behavior are inconsistent and random, because this teaches people that they cannot control their lives. Chronic offenders grew up in homes where parents used erratic control and applied it in an inconsistent way.

Name Control Balance Theory

Principal Theorist Charles Tittle

Latent Trait Control/balance

Major Premise The concept of control has two distinct elements: the amount of control one is subject to by others and the amount of control one can exercise over others. Conformity results when these two elements are in balance; control imbalances produce deviant and criminal behaviors.

People who sense a deficit of control turn to three types of behavior to restore balance: predation, defiance, or submission. Predation involves direct forms of physical violence, such as robbery, sexual assault, or other forms of physical violence. Defiance challenges control mechanisms but stops short of physical harm, for example, vandalism, curfew violations, and unconventional sex. Submission involves passive obedience to the demands of others, such as submitting to physical or sexual abuse without response.

An excess of control can result in crimes of exploitation, plunder, or decadence. Exploitation involves using others, such as contract killers or drug runners, to commit crimes; plunder involves using power without regard for others, such as committing a hate crime or polluting the environment; and decadence involves spur-of-the-moment, irrational acts such as child molesting.

SOURCES: David P. Farrington, "Developmental and Life-Course Criminology: Key Theoretical and Empirical Issues." Sutherland Award Address at the American Society of Criminology meeting in Chicago, November 2002, revised March 2003; Charles Tittle, *Control Balance: Toward a General Theory of Deviance* (Boulder, CO: Westview Press, 1995); Mark Colvin, *Crime and Coercion: An Integrated Theory of Chronic Criminality* (New York: Palgrave Press, 2000).

a person's decision to choose crime and such biosocial factors as low intelligence, mesomorphic body type, genetic influences (parental criminality), and possessing an autonomic nervous system that responds too quickly to stimuli. Psychological traits, such as an impulsive or extroverted personality or generalized hostility, also affect the potential to commit crime.

In their focus on the association between these constitutional and psychological factors and crime, Wilson and Herrnstein seem to be suggesting the existence of an elusive latent trait that predisposes people to commit crime.[69] Their vision helped inspire other criminologists to identify the elusive latent trait that causes criminal behavior. The most prominent latent trait theory is Gottfredson and Hirschi's General Theory of Crime. Exhibit 9.2 discusses some other important contributions to the latent trait model.

GENERAL THEORY OF CRIME

In their important work *A General Theory of Crime*, Michael Gottfredson and Travis Hirschi link the propensity to commit crime to two latent traits: an impulsive personality and a lack of self-control.[70]

Gottfredson and Hirschi attribute the tendency to commit crimes to a person's level of self-control. People with limited self-control tend to be impulsive; they are insensitive to other people's feelings, physical (rather than mental), risk takers, short-sighted, and nonverbal.[71] They have a here-and-now orientation and refuse to work for distant goals; they lack diligence, tenacity, and persistence. People lacking self-control tend to be adventure-some, active, physical, and self-centered. As they mature, they often have unstable marriages, jobs, and friendships.[72] They are less likely to feel shame if they engage in deviant acts and are more likely to find them pleasurable.[73] They are also more likely to engage in dangerous behaviors such as drinking, smoking, and reckless driving. All of these behaviors are associated with criminality.[74]

Because those with low self-control enjoy risky, exciting, or thrilling behaviors with immediate gratification, they are more likely to enjoy criminal acts, which require stealth, agility, speed, and power, than conventional acts, which demand long-term study and cognitive and verbal skills. As Gottfredson and Hirschi put it, they derive satisfaction from "money without work, sex without courtship, revenge without court delays."[75] Many of these individuals who have a propensity for committing crime also engage in other risky, impulsive behaviors such as smoking, drinking, gambling, and illicit sexuality.[76] Although these acts are not illegal, they too provide immediate, short-term gratification.

According to the General Theory of Crime, people who are impulsive and lack self-control are the ones most likely to engage in risky behavior, even if it is not always illegal.

What Causes Impulsivity/Low Self-Control to Develop? Gottfredson and Hirschi trace the root cause of poor self-control to inadequate child-rearing practices. Parents who refuse or are unable to monitor a child's behavior, to recognize deviant behavior when it occurs, and to punish that behavior will produce children who lack self-control. Children who are not attached to their parents, who are poorly supervised, and whose parents are criminal or deviant themselves are the most likely to develop poor self-control.

The "poor parenting produces low-self control in children" model may be inter-generational. That is, parents who themselves manifest low-self control are the ones most likely to use damaging and inappropriate supervision and punishment mechanisms, such as corporal punishment. And inappropriate discipline modes have been linked to lack of self-control in adolescence. These impulsive kids grow up to become poor parents who themselves use improper discipline, producing yet another generation of impulsive kids.[77]

Learning or Biology? The General Theory assumes that self-control is a function of socialization and parenting, but some criminologists maintain it may also have a biological basis. Measures of neuropsychological deficits, birth complications, and low birth weight have all been found to have significant direct or indirect effects on levels of self-control.[78] Recent research shows that children who suffer anoxia (oxygen

Fact or Fiction?

Criminals are impulsive risk takers.

Fact. According to the General Theory of Crime, criminals are impulsive people who lack the self-control to curb their criminal activities.

Figure 9.3 Gottfredson and Hirschi's General Theory of Crime

Criminal Offender

Impulsive personality
- Physical
- Insensitive
- Risk-taking
- Short-sighted
- Nonverbal

Low self-control
- Poor parenting
- Deviant parents
- Lack of supervision
- Active
- Self-centered

Weakening of social bonds
- Attachment
- Involvement
- Commitment
- Belief

Criminal Opportunity
- Presence of gangs
- Lack of supervision
- Lack of guardianship
- Suitable targets

Criminal Act
- Delinquency
- Smoking
- Drinking
- Underage sex
- Crime

+   **=**

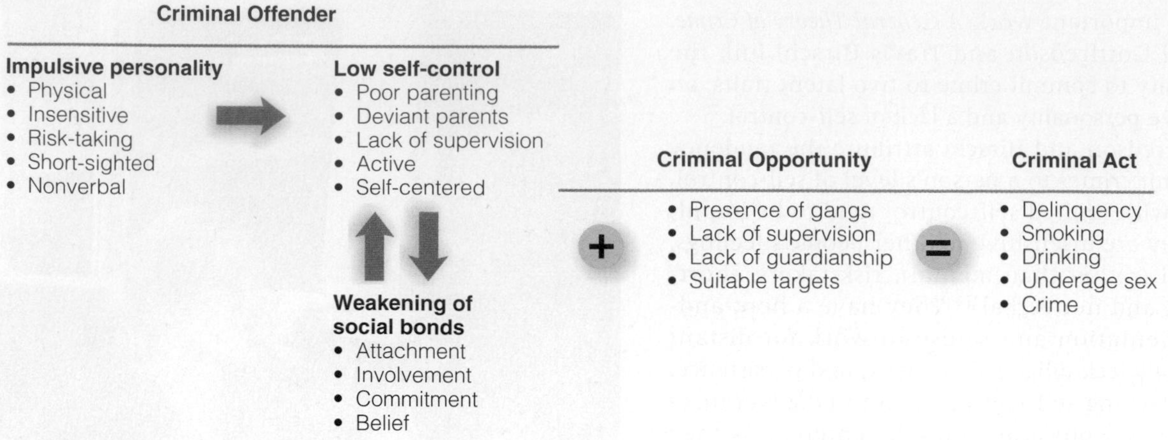

CONNECTIONS

In his original version of control theory, discussed in Chapter 7, Hirschi focused on the social controls that attach people to conventional society and insulate them from criminality. In this newer work, he concentrates on self-control as a stabilizing force. The two views are connected, however, because both social control (or social bonds) and self-control are acquired through early experiences with effective parenting.

General Theory of Crime (GTC)
Gottfredson and Hirschi's developmental theory, which modifies social control theory by integrating concepts from biosocial, psychological, routine activities, and rational choice theories.

self-control theory
Gottfredson and Hirschi's view that the cause of delinquent behavior is an impulsive personality. Kids who are impulsive may have a weak bond to society.

starvation) during the birthing process are the ones most likely to lack self-control later in life, which suggests that impulsivity may have a biological basis.[79] When Kevin Beaver and his associates examined impulsive personality and self-control in twin pairs, they discovered evidence that these traits may be inherited rather than developed. That might help explain the stability of these latent traits over the life course.[80]

The Act and the Offender Not all impulsive people become criminals, nor does impulsivity mean that someone is consistently antisocial. In their **General Theory of Crime (GTC)**, Gottfredson and Hirschi consider the criminal offender and the criminal act as separate concepts (Figure 9.3). On one hand, criminal acts, such as robberies or burglaries, are illegal events or deeds that offenders engage in when they perceive them to be advantageous. For example, burglaries are typically committed by young males looking for cash, liquor, and entertainment; the crime provides "easy, short-term gratification."[81]

On the other hand, criminal offenders are people predisposed to commit crimes. However, they are not robots who commit crime without restraint; their days are also filled with conventional behaviors, such as going to school, parties, concerts, and church. But given the same set of criminal opportunities, such as having a lot of free time for mischief and living in a neighborhood with unguarded homes containing valuable merchandise, crime-prone people have a much higher probability of violating the law than do noncriminals. It bears repeating: According to the GTC, the propensity to commit crimes remains stable throughout a person's life. Change in the frequency of criminal activity is purely a function of change in criminal opportunity.

Self-Control and Crime Gottfredson and Hirschi's General Theory relies on the concept of self-control: the ability to control one's emotions, desires, or actions by one's own will. They believe that such widely disparate crimes as burglary, robbery, embezzlement, drug dealing, murder, rape, and insider trading all stem from a deficiency of self-control. Likewise, gender, racial, and ecological differences in crime rates can be explained by discrepancies in self-control. To put it another way, the male crime rate is higher than the female crime rate because males have lower levels of self-control.

Gottfredson and Hirschi argue that, unlike other theoretical models that explain only narrow segments of criminal behavior (such as theories of teenage gang formation), their **self-control theory** applies equally to all crimes, ranging from murder to corporate theft. For example, Gottfredson and Hirschi maintain that white-collar crime rates remain low because people who lack self-control rarely attain the positions they would need to occupy to commit those crimes. However, relatively few white-collar criminals lack self-control to the same degree and in the same manner as criminals such as rapists and burglars. Although the criminal activity of individuals with low self-control also declines as those individuals mature, they maintain an offense rate that remains consistently higher than those with strong self-control.

Gottfredson and Hirschi help explain why some people who lack self-control escape criminality and, conversely, why some people who have self-control do not escape criminality. People who are at risk because they have impulsive personalities may forgo criminal careers because there are no criminal opportunities that satisfy their impulsive needs; instead, they may find other outlets for their impulsive personalities. In contrast, if the opportunity is strong enough, even people with relatively strong self-control may be tempted to violate the law; the incentives to commit crime may overwhelm self-control.

ANALYZING THE GENERAL THEORY OF CRIME

The GTC is one of the most important theoretical statements of the past two decades. It helps explain why some children enter into chronic offending, and others living in similar environments are able to resist criminal activity: The former lack self-control, whereas the latter possess it. The GTC can also help us understand why the corporate executive with a spotless record gets caught up in business fraud. Even a successful executive may find self-control inadequate if the potential for illegal gain is large. The driven executive, accustomed to both academic and financial success, may find that the fear of failure can overwhelm self-control. During tough economic times, the impulsive manager who fears dismissal may be tempted to circumvent the law to improve the bottom line.[82]

The GTC is truly a general theory. It attempts to explain all forms of crime and deviance, from lower-class gang delinquency to sexual harassment in the business community.[83] By integrating concepts of criminal choice, criminal opportunity, socialization, and personality, Gottfredson and Hirschi make a plausible argument that all deviant behaviors may originate at the same source. The GTC remains one of the cornerstones of contemporary criminological theory.

Since the publication of *A General Theory of Crime*, there have been few theories that have received as much attention. Numerous researchers have attempted to test the validity of Gottfredson and Hirschi's theoretical views. One approach involved identifying indicators of impulsiveness and self-control to determine whether scales measuring these factors correlate with measures of criminal activity. Numerous studies, conducted both in the United States and abroad, have confirmed this type of association.[84] Taken as a whole, they suggest that the lower a person's self-control, the more likely she or he is to engage in antisocial behaviors.[85] The lack of self-control may begin early in adolescence and be manifested in aggressive behavior that turns kids into school yard bullies. Aggressive bullies are rejected by other kids, marginalized, and prone to school failure, a path that winds up in a delinquent way of life.[86]

Recently, for example, Matt DeLisi and Michael Vaughn examined the association between low self-control and criminal careers.[87] They found that compared to non-career offenders, career criminals had significantly lower levels of self-control and that the lower the level of a person's self-control, the greater the chance of his or

© David McNew/Getty Images

One criticism of the General Theory of Crime is that people actually do change over their lifetime. Here are early photos of Stanley "Tookie" Williams, executed cofounder of the Crips gang, as seen in a memorial service program. Sentenced to prison for the 1979 murders of four people, Williams spent several years involved with violent activities in prison, but around 1993 he changed his behavior and became an antigang activist. Williams coauthored such books as *Life in Prison*, which encouraged kids to stay out of gangs, and his memoir *Blue Rage, Black Redemption*. Williams was nominated for the Nobel Peace Prize for his efforts. Do you believe that a gang leader such as "Tookie" Williams really can change? Or did his changing life circumstances simply prevent him from committing violent criminal acts? Regardless of his change, Williams was executed in 2005.

her becoming a career criminal. Notably, DeLisi and Vaughn discovered that low self-control was by far the strongest predictor of career criminality, exceeding the impact of age, race, ethnicity, gender, socioeconomic status, mental illness, attention-deficit/hyperactivity disorder diagnosis, and trauma experience. Moreover, when Alexander Vazsonyi and his associates analyzed self-control and deviant behavior in samples drawn from a number of different countries (Hungary, Switzerland, the Netherlands, the United States, and Japan), they found that low self-control is significantly related to antisocial behavior and that the association can be seen regardless of culture or national setting.[88] These results lend strong support to the GTC.

CRITIQUING THE GENERAL THEORY OF CRIME

Although the General Theory of Crime seems persuasive, a considerable body of published research has both examined and questioned its underlying premise. Several of these studies and issue are discussed next.

▶ *Tautological?* Some critics argue that the GTC is tautological, or involves circular reasoning: How do we know when people are impulsive? When they commit crimes! Are all criminals impulsive? Of course, or else they would not have broken the law![89]

Gottfredson and Hirschi counter by saying that impulsivity is not itself a propensity to commit crime but a condition that inhibits people from appreciating the long-term consequences of their behavior. Consequently, if given the opportunity, they are more likely to indulge in criminal acts than their nonimpulsive counterparts.[90] According to Gottfredson and Hirschi, impulsivity and criminality are neither identical nor equivalent. Some impulsive people may channel their reckless energies into noncriminal activity, such as trading on the commodities markets or speculating in real estate, and make a legitimate fortune for their efforts.

▶ *Different classes of criminals.* As you may recall, Moffitt has identified two classes of criminals, adolescent-limited and life-course persistent.[91] Other researchers have found that there may be different criminal paths, or trajectories. People differ in the pace at which they offend, commit different kinds of crimes, and are influenced by different external forces.[92] For example, most criminals tend to be "generalists," who engage in a wide variety of criminal acts. However, people who commit violent crimes may be different from nonviolent offenders who have maintained a unique set of personality traits and problem behaviors.[93] This would contradict the GTC vision that a single factor causes crime and that there is only a single class of offender.

▶ *Ecological differences.* The GTC also fails to address individual and ecological patterns in the crime rate. For example, if crime rates are higher in Los Angeles, California than in Albany, New York, can it be assumed that residents of Los Angeles are more impulsive than residents of Albany? There is little evidence of regional differences in impulsivity or self-control. There are also temporal differences that have little to do with impulsivity: Crime rates are higher in the summer and evening than in the winter and morning. Gottfredson and Hirschi might counter that these crime rate differences may reflect differences in criminal opportunity: One area may have more effective law enforcement, more draconian laws, and higher levels of guardianship. In their view, opportunity is controlled by economy and culture.

▶ *Racial and gender differences.* Although distinct gender differences in the crime rate exist, there is little evidence that males are more impulsive than females (although females and males differ in many other personality traits).[94] Some research efforts have found gender differences in the association between self-control and crime, but the GTC predicts that no such differences should occur.[95]

Looking that this relationship from another perspective, males who persist in crime exhibit different characteristics from those of female persisters. Women seem to be influenced by their place of residence, childhood and recent abuses, living

The General Theory of Crime seems to ignore moral beliefs and values. Can strengthening religious beliefs help kids refrain from committing crime? Here group members Lauren Ruggiero, Lori Saniuk, and Heather Kelly talk with each other at the Saint Mary's Life House in Dedham, Massachusetts. The Life House at Saint Mary's Catholic Church provides a place for young parishioners to hang out and discuss topics ranging from the burgeoning Catholic Church scandal to drugs and other issues related to growing up.

with a criminal partner, selling drugs, stress, depression, fearfulness, their romantic relationships, their children, and whether they have suicidal thoughts. In contrast, men are more likely to persist because of their criminal peer associations, carrying weapons, alcohol abuse, and aggressive feelings. Impulsivity alone may not be able to explain why males and females persist or desist at different rates.[96]

Similarly, Gottfredson and Hirschi explain racial differences in the crime rate as a failure of child-rearing practices in the African American community.[97] In so doing, they overlook issues of institutional racism, poverty, and relative deprivation, which have been shown to have a significant impact on crime rate differentials.

▶ *Moral beliefs.* The General Theory of Crime ignores the moral concept of right and wrong, or "belief," which Hirschi considered a cornerstone in his earlier writings on the social bond.[98] Does this mean that learning and assimilating moral values has little effect on criminality?[99] Recent research by Olena Antonaccio and Charles Tittle found that holding moral values may trump low self-control—that is, high moral standards can inhibit crime even among impulsive individuals.[100]

▶ *Peer influence.* A number of research efforts show that the quality of peer relations either enhances or controls criminal behavior and that these influences vary over time.[101] As children mature, peer influence continues to grow.[102] Research shows that kids who lack self-control also have trouble maintaining relationships with law-abiding peers. They may either choose (or be forced) to seek friends who are similarly limited in their ability to maintain self-control. But in the end, deviant peers enhance the propensity to commit crime that is created by a lack of self-control.[103]

Similarly, as they mature, they may seek romantic relationships with law-violating boyfriends and/or girlfriends, and these entanglements enhance the likelihood that they will get further involved in crime (girls seem to be more deeply influenced by their delinquent boyfriends than boys by their delinquent girlfriends).[104] This finding contradicts the GTC, which suggests that the influence of friends should be stable and unchanging and that a relationship established later in life (for example, making friends) should not influence criminal propensity. Gottfredson and Hirschi might counter that it should come as no surprise that impulsive kids, lacking in self-control, seek peers with similar personality characteristics.

▶ *People change.* One of the most important questions raised about the GTC concerns its assumption that criminal propensity (especially after age 10) does not change. Is it possible that human personality and behavior patterns remain unaltered over the life course? Research shows that changing life circumstances, such as starting and leaving school, abusing substances and then "getting straight," and starting or ending personal relationships, all influence the frequency of offending.[105] As people mature, they may be better able to control their impulsive behavior and reduce their criminal activities.[106] Although some people maintain the same level of self-control throughout their life span, for others it changes over time.[107]

Ronald Simons found that boys who were involved in deviant and oppositional behavior during childhood were able to turn their lives around if they later experienced improved parenting, increased school commitment, and/or reduced involvement with deviant peers. Thus, even though early childhood antisocial behavior may increase the chances of later criminality, even the most difficult children are at no greater risk for delinquency than their conventional counterparts if they later experience positive changes in their daily lives and increased ties with significant others and institutions.[108]

Although the Simons research seems to contradict the GTC, Gottfredson and Hirschi acknowledge that external factors such as parenting and school involvement may indeed reduce crime because they limit the opportunity to commit illegal acts. The child's criminal propensity remains the same, and if these external supports were once again weakened or removed, they would still be at risk for criminality.

▶ *Modest relationship.* Some research results support the proposition that self-control is a causal factor in criminal and other forms of deviant behavior but that the association is at best quite modest.[109] This would indicate that other forces also influence criminal behavior and that low self-control alone cannot predict the onset of a criminal or deviant career. Perhaps antisocial behavior is best explained by a condition that either develops subsequent to the development of self-control or is independent of a person's level of impulsivity.[110] This alternative quality, which may be the real stable latent trait, is still unknown.

▶ *Cross-cultural differences.* There is some evidence that criminals in other countries do not lack self-control, which suggests that the GTC may be culturally limited. For example, Otwin Marenin and Michael Resig found equal or higher levels of self-control in Nigerian criminals than in noncriminals.[111] Behavior that may be considered imprudent in one culture may be socially acceptable in another and therefore cannot be viewed as "lack of self-control."[112] There is, however, emerging evidence that the GTC may have validity in predicting criminality abroad.[113]

▶ *Misreads human nature.* According to Francis Cullen, John Paul Wright, and Mitchell Chamlin, the GTC makes flawed assumptions about human character.[114] It assumes that people are essentially selfish, self-serving, and hedonistic and must therefore be controlled, lest they gratify themselves at the expense of others. A more plausible view is that humans are inherently generous and kind; selfish hedonists may be a rare exception.

▶ *One of many causes.* Research shows that even if lack of self-control is a prerequisite to crime, so are other social, neuropsychological, and physiological factors.[115] Sociocultural factors have been found to make an independent contribution to criminal offending patterns.[116] Among the many psychological characteristics that set criminals apart from the general population is their lack of self-direction; rather than aiming at providing long-term benefits, their behavior has a here-and-now orientation.[117] Law violators exhibit lower resting heart rate and perform poorly on tasks that trigger cognitive functions.[118]

Part 2 Theories of Crime Causation

A real test of self-control theory is its ability to explain drug dealing, a crime that seems to reflect business enterprise and cunning, not impulsivity and lack of self control. In an important study, Steven Levitt and Sudhir Alladi Venkatesh studied the economic structure of a drug-dealing criminal gang. They examined the wage and revenue structure of the gang over a four-year period. Using this rather unique data source, Levitt and Venkatesh found that the gang's compensation structure is highly skewed in favor of the leaders, who make most of the money. Younger or lower-ranking gang members must "rise through the ranks" before earning high wages.

Levitt and Venkatesh found that the gang's "foot soldiers," who are "street-level drug sellers" and are "typically

the gang are sacrificing present wages for the hope of future gains. Listokin suggested that the gang is using the same compensation structure as one commonly used in law firms. The "foot soldiers," he concluded, are filling the role of law associates, a group not known for its impulsiveness. Moreover, foot soldiers seem acutely aware that they are making an investment in the future by forgoing present gains. As one foot soldier noted,

> You think I want a be selling drugs on the street my whole life? No way, But I know these n— [above me] are making more money. . . . So you know, I figure I got a chance to move up. But if not, s—, I get me a job doin' something else.

This quotation does not comport with the notion of a super-impulsive young criminal.

Current Issues in Crime Self-Control and Drug Dealing

from 16–22 years of age," are paid at an "hourly wage that is below the federal minimum wage," ranging between $2.50 and $7.10 per hour in inflation-adjusted 1995 dollars. In order to survive on this pittance, these young men hold second jobs in the legitimate world and are forced to live with their families in order to save money. In contrast, a gang leader earns 10 to 20 times as much as a foot soldier (between $32.50 and $97.20 per hour over the four years). Other high-level gang members also make considerably more than those at the bottom of the hierarchy, so overall, the average gang wage is four times higher than what a foot soldier makes. The gang leader's wages in particular are much higher than the wage that would be available to an individual with the same level of human capital in the legitimate sector. Gang leaders make far more than they possibly could in the legitimate world; for them, crime does pay.

Levitt and Venkatesh concluded that the economic aspects of the decision to join the gang are viewed as a "tournament" in which the participants vie for large awards that only a small fraction will eventually obtain. Members of the gang accept low wages in the present in the hope that they will advance in the gang and earn well above market wages in the future.

In his reanalysis of this data, Yair Listokin found that the tournament wage structure is strikingly inconsistent with the notion of present-oriented criminals. The supposedly impulsive, present-oriented 16- to 22-year-old foot soldiers of

Listokin believes that tournament-style compensation schemes are often used to ensure maximum effort by low-level employees. Executives (or gang leaders in this case) offer the new employee the promise of high future wages, as he rises in the hierarchy, to induce effort in the present. The prospect of high wages in the second period must suffice to induce effort in the first period. However, Listokin's analysis shows that few foot soldiers will ever become gang leaders and that the likelihood of their getting killed instead is quite high. Nonetheless, foot soldiers are willing to take the risk in order to earn a future benefit. This finding contradicts Gottfredson and Hirschi's vision of an impulsive criminal who lives for today without worrying about tomorrow.

CRITICAL THINKING

What other "professions" use the tournament approach? College professors and lawyers come to mind. Many are hired, but fewer get tenure or partnerships. Can you think of some other examples?

SOURCES: Steven Levitt and Sudhir Alladi Venkatesh, "An Economic Analysis of a Drug-Selling Gang's Finances," *Quarterly Journal of Economics* 13 (2000): 755–789; Yair Listokin, "Future-Oriented Gang Members? Gang Finances and the Theory of Present-Oriented Criminals," *The American Journal of Economics and Sociology* 64 (2005): 1,073–1,083.

Checkpoints

▶ Latent trait theories assume that a physical or psychological master trait makes some people crime-prone over the life course.

▶ Opportunity to commit crime varies, but latent traits remain stable.

▶ Gottfredson and Hirschi's General Theory of Crime says an impulsive personality is the key to criminal activity.

▶ Impulsive people have low self-control and a weak bond to society.

▶ Impulsive people often cannot resist criminal opportunities.

▶ *More than one kind of impulsivity.* Gottfredson and Hirschi assume that impulsivity is a singular construct: A person either is impulsive or is not. There may be more than one kind of impulsive personality, however. Some people may be impulsive because they are sensation seekers constantly looking for novel experiences, whereas other impulsive people simply lack deliberation and rarely think through problems. Some may give up easily, whereas others act without thinking when they get upset.[119]

▶ *Not all criminals are impulsive.* White-collar criminals, drug traffickers, and organized crime bosses seem more calculating than impulsive.[120] This issue is explored further in the Current Issues in Crime feature on page 247. ▶ **Checkpoints**

Public Policy Implications of Developmental Theory

Policies based on the premises of developmental theory have inspired a number of initiatives. These typically feature multisystemic treatment efforts designed to provide at-risk youths with personal, social, educational, and family services. For example, one program found that an intervention promoting academic success, social competence, and educational enhancement during the elementary grades can reduce risky sexual practices and their accompanying health consequences in early adulthood.[121]

Other programs are now employing multidimensional strategies and are aimed at targeting children in preschool through the early elementary grades to alter the direction of their life course. Many of the most successful programs are aimed at strengthening children's social-emotional competence and positive coping skills and suppressing the development of antisocial, aggressive behavior.[122] Research evaluations indicate that the most promising multicomponent crime and substance abuse prevention programs for youths, especially those at high risk, are designed to improve their developmental skills. They may include a school component, an after-school component, and a parent-involvement component. All of these components share the goal of increasing protective factors and decreasing risk factors in the areas of the family, the community, the school, and the individual.[123] One example is the Boys and Girls Clubs and School Collaborations' Substance Abuse Prevention Program, which includes a school component called SMART (skills mastery and resistance training); an after-school component called SMART Kids; and a parent-involvement component called SMART Parents. Each component is designed to reduce specific risk factors in the children's school, family, community, and personal environments.[124]

© Dave Darnell / The Commercial Appeal / Landov

Mentoring may provide the informal social control that life course theorists believe helps protect kids from criminal influences. The Southside Boys and Girls Clubs in Memphis are the hub of various activities involving kids and mentors. Kanesha Robinson, 10, concentrates during an exercise where all the people around the table talked about their favorite movies and the like. Do you think such programs can help kids like Kanesha achieve their greatest potential?

Gary L. Sampson, 41, a man addicted to alcohol and cocaine, was a deadbeat dad, a two-bit thief, and a bank robber with a long history of violence. On August 1, 2001, he turned himself in to the Vermont State Police after fleeing from pursuit for a string of three murders he committed in Massachusetts and New Hampshire.

Those who knew Sampson speculated that his murders were a desperate finale to a troubled life. During his early life in New England, he once bound, gagged, and beat three elderly women in a candy store; hijacked cars at knifepoint; and had been medically diagnosed as schizophrenic. In 1977 he married a 17-year-old girl he had impregnated; two months later he was arrested and charged with rape for having "unnatural intercourse with a child under 16." Although he was acquitted of that charge, his wife noticed that Sampson had developed a hair-trigger temper and had become increasingly violent; their marriage soon ended. As the years passed, Sampson had at least four failed marriages, was an absentee father to two children, and became an alcoholic and a drug user. He spent nearly half of his adult life behind bars.

Jumping bail after being arrested for theft from an antique store, he headed south to North Carolina and took on a new identity: Gary Johnson, a construction worker. He took up with Ricki Carter, a transvestite, but their relationship was anything but stable. Sampson once put a gun to Carter's head, broke his ribs, and threatened to kill his family. After his breakup with Carter, Sampson moved in with a new girlfriend, Karen Anderson, and began pulling bank jobs. When the police closed in, Sampson fled north. Needing transportation, he pulled three carjackings and killed the drivers, one a 19-year-old college freshman who had stopped to give Sampson a hand. In December 2003, Sampson received a sentence of death from a jury that was not swayed by his claim that he was mentally unfit.

Writing Assignment

Write an essay giving your opinion on whether Sampson should receive the death penalty or a sentence of life in prison. Were Sampson's crimes a product of his impaired development? And if so, should his life be spared?

Summary

1. Discuss the history of developmental theory.

   The foundation of this theory is Sheldon and Eleanor Glueck's integration of biological, psychological, and social factors. Later the Glueck data was rediscovered by criminologists Robert Sampson and John Laub. The Philadelphia cohort research by Marvin Wolfgang and his associates investigated criminal career development. Rolf Loeber and Marc Le Blanc proposed that criminologists should devote time and effort to understanding basic questions about the evolution of criminal careers.

2. Distinguish between the life-course theory and the latent trait theory.

   Life-course theorists view criminality as a dynamic process influenced by a multitude of individual characteristics, traits, and social experiences. Life-course theories look at such issues as the onset of crime, the escalation of offenses, the persistence of crime, and desistance from crime. Latent trait theorists believe that human development is controlled by a "master trait" that guides human development and gives some people an increased propensity to commit crime.

3. Be familiar with the principles of the life-course theory.

   At an early age, people begin relationships and behaviors that will determine their adult life course. Some individuals are incapable of maturing in a reasonable and timely fashion. A positive life experience may help some criminals desist from crime for a while, but a negative experience may cause them to resume their criminal activities. As people mature, the factors that influence their behavior change. The social, physical, and environmental influences on their behavior are transformed.

4. Explain the term "problem behavior syndrome."

   Crime is one of a group of interrelated antisocial behaviors that cluster together. Problem behaviors typically involve family dysfunction, sexual and physical abuse, substance abuse, smoking, precocious sexuality and early pregnancy, educational underachievement, suicide attempts, sensation seeking, and unemployment. People who suffer from one of these conditions typically exhibit many symptoms of the rest.

5. Be aware that there are different pathways to crime.

Some career criminals may specialize in violence and extortion; some may be involved in theft and fraud; some may engage in a variety of criminal acts. Some offenders may begin their careers early in life, whereas others are late bloomers who begin committing crime at about the time when most people desist.

6. Discuss why age of onset is an important factor in crime.

Early onset of antisocial behavior predicts later and more serious criminality. Adolescent offenders whose criminal behavior persists into adulthood are likely to have begun their deviant careers at a very early (pre-school) age. Early-onset kids tend to have poor parental discipline and monitoring, inadequate emotional support, distant peer relationships, and psychological issues and problems.

7. Know the basic principles of Sampson and Laub's Age-Graded Theory.

Sampson and Laub find that the maintenance of a criminal career can be affected by events that occur later in life. They recognize the role of social capital and its influence on the trajectory of a criminal career. When faced with personal crisis, offenders lack the social supports that can help them reject criminal solutions. Sampson and Laub view criminal careers as a dynamic process in which important life events can change the direction of a person's life-course trajectory; these key events are called turning points.

8. Define the term "latent trait."

A number of people in the population have a personal attribute or characteristic that controls their inclination or propensity to commit crimes. A latent trait is a stable feature, characteristic, property, or condition, present at birth or soon after, that guides and shapes behavior and may cause some people to become crime prone over their life course. Suspected latent traits include defective intelligence, damaged or impulsive personality, genetic abnormalities, the physical-chemical functioning of the brain, and environmental influences on brain function, such as drugs, chemicals, and injuries.

9. Be familiar with Wilson and Herrnstein's views on crime and human nature.

According to Wilson and Herrnstein, all human behavior, including criminality, is determined by its perceived consequences. A criminal incident occurs when an individual chooses criminal over conventional behavior. Wilson and Herrnstein assume that both biological and psychological traits influence the choice between crime and non-crime. Wilson and Herrnstein suggest the existence of an elusive latent trait that predisposes people to committing crime.

10. Understand the basic principles of the General Theory of Crime.

Gottfredson and Hirschi link the propensity to commit crime to an impulsive personality and a lack of self-control. People with limited self-control tend to be impulsive; they are insensitive to other people's feelings, predisposed toward physical (rather than mental) activities and solutions, risk takers, shortsighted, and nonverbal. Because those with low self-control enjoy risky, exciting, or thrilling behaviors with immediate gratification, they are more likely to enjoy criminal acts. Gottfredson and Hirschi trace the root cause of poor self-control to inadequate child-rearing practices.

Key Terms

desist 226
developmental theories 226
life-course theories 227
latent trait (propensity) theories 227

problem behavior syndrome (PBS) 228
authority conflict pathway 229
covert pathway 230
overt pathway 230

adolescent-limited offenders 232
life-course persisters 232
integrated theories 232
Age-Graded Theory 232
turning points 233

social capital 233
latent trait 236
General Theory of Crime (GTC) 242
self-control theory 242

Critical Thinking Questions

1. Do you consider yourself to have social capital? If so, what form does it take?

2. Someone you know gets a perfect score on the SAT. What personal, family, and social characteristics do you think this individual has? Another person becomes a serial killer. Without knowing this person, what personal, family, and social characteristics do you think this individual has? If "bad behavior" is explained by multiple problems, is "good behavior" explained by multiple strengths?

3. Do you believe it is a latent trait that makes a person crime-prone, or is crime a function of environment and socialization?

4. Do you agree with Loeber's multiple pathways model? Do you know people who have traveled down those paths?

5. Do people really change, or do they stay the same but appear to be different because their life circumstances have changed?

© AP Images/Wally Santana

Chapter Outline

Violent Crime

Personal and Political

On December 27, 2007, Pakastani political leader Benazir Bhutto was assassinated while leaving an election rally in Rawalpindi. The exact cause of her death remains a mystery, but there is no question that she was shot at by gunmen who then set off a bomb killing more than 20 other people and injuring many others. Bhutto, the daughter of a former prime minister, educated at Harvard and Oxford universities, had been elected prime minister in 1988 and again in1993. She had just returned to Pakistan after years in exile to run once again for public office. Her death was linked to Baitullah Mehsud, a militant leader who had orchestrated suicide attacks on government, military, and intelligence targets. Mehsud was also known to have run training camps, to have prepared and dispatched suicide bombers on both sides of the Afghanistan-Pakistan border, and to have links to Al Qaeda and other terror groups. Since Bhutto's death, Pakistan has been rocked by a series of violent incidents. For example, in March of 2009, Sri Lankan cricket players were attacked in Lahore on the way to a match against a Pakistani team; one month later, militants attacked a police training academy on the outskirts of Lahore, and a suicide bomber killed 20 worshipers in an Islamabad mosque.[1]

Fact or Fiction?

▶ Serial killers and other aggressive, violent people often begin their criminal careers by torturing the family dog.

▶ Guns don't cause crime, people do.

▶ Rape is essentially a sex crime.

▶ Many rapes go unreported because the woman is not sure whether she was actually raped.

▶ You can't be convicted of murder unless you participate in a killing.

▶ Robbers tend to look for vulnerable victims who can't fight back.

▶ Terrorists are mentally disturbed people who have been manipulated into performing violent acts.

Chapter Objectives

1. Be familiar with the various causes of violent crime.

2. Define rape and be familiar with why men commit rape.

3. Discuss the issues involving rape and the law.

4. Recognize that there are different types of murder.

5. Understand the nature and patterns of robbery.

6. Be able to discuss newly emerging forms of violence, such as stalking, hate crimes, and workplace violence.

7. Distinguish among terrorists, guerillas, insurgents, and revolutionaries.

8. Distinguish among the different forms that terrorism takes.

9. Discuss the motivations of terrorists.

10. Know about the various agencies that have been created or modified to fight terrorism and other forms of political violence.

The death of Benazir Bhutto is just one in a continuing string of international terrorist acts that have rocked the world since 9/11. No matter where they go, people may encounter violent acts. Some are **expressive violence**, acts that vent rage, anger, or frustration, and some are **instrumental violence**, acts designed to improve the financial or social position of the criminal—for example, through an armed robbery or murder for hire.

This chapter explores the concept of violence in some depth. It first focuses on interpersonal violence. Then it reviews some of the possible causes of violent crime and the various types of interpersonal violence, such as rape, homicide, assault, and robbery. Next, it addresses some newly recognized types of interpersonal violence, such as stalking and workplace violence. The second half of the chapter reviews politically motivated violence, including terrorism, guerilla warfare, insurgency, and revolutionary movements, covering definitions, motivations, goals, and efforts at control.

Causes of Violence

What sets off a violent person? Some experts suggest that a small number of inherently violence-prone individuals may themselves have been the victims of physical or psychological abnormalities. Another view is that violence and aggression are inherently human traits that can affect any person at any time. There may be violence-prone subcultures within society whose members value force, routinely carry weapons, and consider violence to have an acceptable place in social interaction.[2] A few of the most prominent factors discussed here are illustrated in Figure 10.1.

Figure 10.1 Sources of Violence

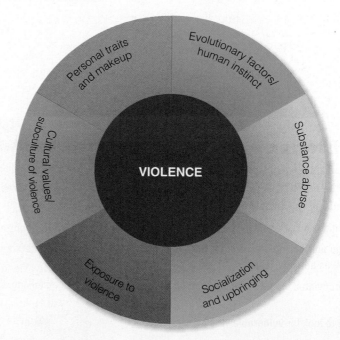

expressive violence
Acts that vent rage, anger, or frustration.

instrumental violence
Acts designed to improve the financial or social position of the criminal.

PERSONAL TRAITS

Research has shown that a significant number of people involved in violent episodes may be suffering from severe mental abnormalities.[3] Psychologist Dorothy Otnow Lewis and her associates found that murderous youths suffer signs of major neurological impairment (such as abnormal electroencephalograms (EEGs), multiple psychomotor impairments, and severe seizures); low intelligence as measured on standard IQ tests; psychotic close relatives; and psychotic symptoms such as paranoia, illogical thinking, and hallucinations.[4] In her book *Guilty by Reason of Insanity*, Lewis finds that death row inmates have a history of mental impairment and intellectual dysfunction.[5] Abnormal personality structures, including such traits as depression, impulsivity, aggression, dishonesty, pathological lying, lack of remorse, borderline personality syndrome, and psychopathology, have been associated with various forms of violence.[6] Considering this association, it is not surprising that a recent (2009) survey examining the association between early incidence of animal cruelty and later involvement with violence found that aggressive men had a long history of torturing and killing animals.[7] Animal cruelty has been associated with a number of psychiatric disorders, including antisocial personality disorder.[8]

INEFFECTIVE FAMILIES

Absent or deviant parents, inconsistent discipline, physical abuse, and lack of supervision have all been linked to persistent violent offending.[9] Although infants demonstrate individual temperaments, who they become may have a lot to do with how they are treated during their early years. Some children are less easy to soothe than others; in some cases, difficult infant temperament has been associated with later aggression and behavioral problems.[10] Parents who fail to set adequate limits or to use proper, consistent discipline reinforce a child's coercive behavior.[11] Inadequate parenting and early rejection may set the scene for violent behavior throughout life.[12]

Some parents abuse their children sexually and physically. Those exposed to even minimal amounts of physical punishment may be more likely one day to use violence themselves; if the abuse is prolonged, so are the effects.[13] Abused kids suffer from long-term mental, cognitive, and social dysfunctions.[14] They are more likely to physically abuse a sibling and later to engage in spouse abuse and other forms of criminal violence.[15] Abusive childhood experiences may be a key factor in the later development of relationship aggression.[16]

On February 12, 2009, Denver prosecutor Ken Kupfner begins his closing argument in the case of Alex Midyette, a man accused of killing his baby son Jason. Kupfner is shown here using a baby doll to illustrate the pulling and twisting that may have caused the broken bones that killed Jason Midyette. The argument was effective: Alex Midyette was found guilty of criminally negligent child abuse resulting in the death of his 11-week-old son. He was later sentenced to 16 years in prison. Kids who live through such abuse often grow up to become abusers themselves, creating a cycle of violence.

© AP Images/Mark Leffingwell, Pool

EVOLUTIONARY FACTORS/HUMAN INSTINCT

Perhaps violent responses and emotions are simply inherent in all humans, and the right spark can trigger them. Sigmund Freud believed that human aggression and violence are produced by instinctual drives.[17] Freud maintained that humans possess

CONNECTIONS

As you may recall from Chapter 5, biosocial theorists link violence to a number of biological irregularities, including but not limited to genetic influences and inheritance, the action of hormones, the functioning of neurotransmitters, brain structure, and diet. Psychologists link violent behavior to observational learning from violent TV shows, traumatic childhood experiences, low intelligence, mental illness, impaired cognitive processes, and abnormal (psychopathic) personality structure.

two opposing instinctual drives that interact to control behavior: **eros**, the life instinct, which drives people toward self-fulfillment and enjoyment; and **thanatos**, the death instinct, which impels toward self-destruction. Thanatos can be expressed externally (as violence and sadism) or internally (as suicide, alcoholism, or other self-destructive habits). Because aggression is instinctual, Freud saw little hope for its treatment.

A number of biologists and anthropologists have also speculated that instinctual violence-promoting traits may be common in the human species. One view is that aggression and violence are the result of instincts inborn in all animals, humans among them.[18] Unlike other animals, however, humans lack the inhibition against killing members of their own species, which protects animals from self-extinction, and are capable of killing their own kind in war or as a result of interpersonal conflicts.

EXPOSURE TO VIOLENCE

Kids who are constantly exposed to violence at home, at school, or in the environment may adopt violent methods themselves.[19] Exposure to violence can also occur at the neighborhood level when people are forced to live in violent, dangerous neighborhoods.[20] A report by Felton Earls and his associates finds that young teens who witness gun violence are more than twice as likely as nonwitnesses to commit violent crime.[21] Even a single exposure to firearm violence doubles the chance that a young person will later engage in violent behavior. Much of the difference between whites and racial minorities in crime rates can be explained by the fact that the latter are often forced to live in high-crime neighborhoods, which increases their risk of exposure to violence.[22] Children living in areas marked by extreme violence may in time become desensitized to the persistent neighborhood brutality and conflict they witness, eventually succumbing to violent behaviors themselves.[23] And not surprisingly, those children who are exposed to violence in the home and also live in neighborhoods with high violence rates are the ones most likely to engage in violent crime themselves.[24]

SUBSTANCE ABUSE

Substance abuse has been associated with violence on both the individual and social levels. Substance abusers have higher rates of violence than nonabusers. The National Survey on Drug Use and Health found that young people aged 12 to 17 who used any illicit drug in the past year were almost twice as likely to have engaged in violent behavior as those who did not use any illicit drug (50 versus 27 percent).[25]

Drug abuse rates are also associated with area violence rates: Neighborhoods with high levels of substance abuse also have higher violence.[26] Areas whose residents use drugs frequently also experience social disorganization, poverty, and unemployment, factors that further escalate violence rates.[27] Substance abuse influences violence in three ways:[28]

▶ A **psychopharmacological relationship** may be the direct consequence of ingesting mood-altering substances. Binge drinking, for example, has been closely associated with violent crime rates.[29] Heavy drinking reduces cognitive ability, information processing skills, and the ability to process and react to verbal and nonverbal behavior. As a result, miscommunication becomes more likely, and the capacity for rational dialogue is compromised.[30] It is not surprising that males involved in sexual assaults often claim that they were drinking and misunderstood their victim's intentions.[31]

▶ Drug ingestion may also cause **economic compulsive behavior**, in which drug users resort to violence to support their habit. Studies conducted in the United States and Europe show that addicts commit hundreds of crimes each year.[32]

▶ A **systemic link** between drugs and violence occurs when drug dealers turn violent in their competition with rival gangs. Studies of drug gangs show that their attempts to gain and secure drug markets result in a significant proportion of all urban homicides.[33]

eros
The life instinct, which drives people toward self-fulfillment and enjoyment.

thanatos
The death instinct, which impels toward self-destruction.

psychopharmacological relationship
In such a relationship, violence is the direct consequence of ingesting mood-altering substances.

economic compulsive behavior
Violence committed by drug users to support their habit.

systemic link
A link between drugs and violence that occurs when drug dealers turn violent in their competition with rival gangs.

FIREARM AVAILABILITY

Although firearm availability alone does not cause violence, it may be a facilitating factor. A petty argument can escalate into a fatal encounter if one party has a handgun. The nation has also been rocked by the recent slew of well-publicized school shootings. Research indicates that a significant number of kids routinely carry guns to school; those who have been the victims of crime themselves and those who hang with peers who carry weapons are most likely to bring guns to school.[34]

The Uniform Crime Report (UCR) indicates that two-thirds of all murders and about two-fifths of all robberies involve firearms.[35] Handguns kill two-thirds of all police who die in the line of duty. The presence of firearms in the home also significantly increases the risk of suicide among adolescents, regardless of how carefully the guns are secured or stored.[36]

CULTURAL VALUES

Areas that experience violence seem to cluster together.[37] To explain this phenomenon, criminologists Marvin Wolfgang and Franco Ferracuti formulated the famous concept that some areas are characterized by an independent **subculture of violence**.[38]

The subculture's norms are separate from society's central, dominant value system. In this subculture, a potent theme of violence influences lifestyles, the socialization process, and interpersonal relationships. Even though the members of the subculture share some of the dominant culture's values, they expect that violence will be used to solve social conflicts and dilemmas. In some cultural subgroups, then, violence has become legitimized by custom and norms. It is considered appropriate behavior within culturally defined conflict situations in which an individual who has been offended by a negative outcome in a dispute seeks reparations through violent means ("disputatiousness").[39]

Gangs are common in the subculture of violence. Gang boys routinely own guns and associate with violent peers who are also gun owners.[40] Violent gang friends support and sustain antisocial behavior.[41] The association between gang membership and violence has a number of roots. It can result from drug trafficking activities and turf protection, but it may also stem from personal vendettas and a perceived need for self-protection.[42] Violence is a core value of gang membership, and once kids leave the gang, the frequency of their violent activities rapidly declines.[43]

Why a subculture of violence exists in a particular area may have historical roots. Historian Eric Monkkonen analyzed nearly two centuries of Los Angeles homicide data and found that regional cultural differences contributed to relatively high rates of homicide.[44] Since the city's Old West days, Los Angelinos have accepted street justice, and the city has had high rates of "justifiable homicides." A considerable number of "executions" carried out by private citizens were initiated by individuals who "happened to be armed at the moment of need."[45] When Charis Kubrin and Ronald Weitzer studied homicide in St. Louis, Missouri, they discovered that in some neighborhoods residents resolve interpersonal conflicts informally—without calling the police—even if it means killing their opponent; neighbors understand and support their violent methods.[46] Because police and other agencies of formal social control are viewed as weak and devalued, understaffed, and/or corrupt, people are willing to take matters into their own hands and commit what they call "cultural retaliatory homicide."[47]

NATIONAL VALUES

Some nations—including the United States, Sri Lanka, Angola, Uganda, and the Philippines—have relatively high violence rates; others are much more peaceful. According to research by sociologist Jerome Neapolitan, a number of national characteristics are predictive of violence: a high level of social disorganization, economic stress, high

Fact or Fiction?

Guns don't cause crime, people do.

Fact. True, but guns facilitate violence and can turn a petty argument into a fatal encounter.

CONNECTIONS

It seems logical that banning the sale and ownership of firearms might help reduce violence, but as discussed in Chapter 2, those who support gun ownership do not agree. Some experts believe that taking guns away from citizens might endanger them if they are one day pitted against armed criminals.

CONNECTIONS

Delinquent subcultures were discussed in detail in Chapter 6. Recall that subculture theorists portray delinquents not as rebels from the normative culture but, rather, as people who act in accordance with the informal rules and values of their immediate culture. By adhering to their own cultural norms, they violate the law.

subculture of violence
A segment of society in which violence has become legitimized by the custom and norms of that group.

On April 12, 2009, a Jordanian man confessed to stabbing to death his pregnant sister and mutilating her body to protect the family honor. The 28-year-old married woman, who was five months pregnant, was stabbed repeatedly in the face, neck, abdomen, and back and then hacked up with a meat cleaver. She had moved back in with her family after an argument with her husband six months earlier. The brother believed that she had then started seeing other men and had gotten pregnant out of wedlock.

Honor killing and honor crime involve violence against women and girls, including such acts as beating, battering, and killing, by a family member or relative. The attacks are provoked by the belief or perception that an individual's or sexual activity, and even any suspicion that a girl or a woman was touched by another in a sexual manner, is enough to raise questions about the family's honor. Consequently, strict control of women and girls within the home and outside the home is justified. Women are restricted in their activities in the community, religion, and politics. These institutions, in turn, support the control of females. Williams believes that honor killing is designed to maintain male dominance. Submissiveness may be seen as a sign of sexual purity, and a woman's or girl's attempts to assert her rights can be seen as a violation of the family's honor that needs to be redressed. Rules of honor and threats against females who "violate" such rules reinforce the control of women and have a powerful impact on their lives. Honor

Race, Culture, Gender, and Criminology
The Honor Killing of Women and Girls

family's honor has been threatened by the actual or perceived sexual misconduct of the female. Honor killings are most common in traditional societies in the Middle East, Southwest Asia, India, China, and Latin America. However, the custom is now being exported around the world: In a crime that outraged Germany, a 24-year-old identified as Ahmad-Sobair O. killed his sister Morsal on May 15, 2008. He said he had objected to the pretty schoolgirl's lifestyle, her clothing, and her attempts to distance herself from her family. Germany is not alone. In 2008, a Lewisville, Texas, resident of Egyptian descent, Yaser Abdel Said, took his two teenaged daughters (under the guise of getting something to eat) to Irving, Texas, where he allegedly shot both girls to death. The reason: they had dated boys against his will.

Honor killing of a woman or girl by her father, brother, or other male relative may occur because of a suspicion that she engaged in sexual activities before or outside marriage and thus has dishonored the family. Even when rape of a woman or girl has occurred, this may be seen as violation of the honor of the family, for which the female must be killed. Wives' adultery and daughters' premarital "sexual activity," including rape, are seen as extreme violations of the codes of behavior and thus may result in the death of the female through this so-called "honor" killing. Honor killing/crime is based on the shame that a loss of control of the woman or girl brings to the family and to the male heads of the family.

According to sociologist Linda Williams, men consider honor killings culturally necessary, because any suspicion of killings/crimes serve to keep women and girls from "stepping out of line." The manner in which such behaviors silence women and destroy their spirit has led some to label honor killings/crimes more broadly as "femicide."

CRITICAL THINKING

1. Are there elements of American culture that might promote crimes against women? Is there anything in the media and or in sports that might cause sexual violence? What about our religious and/or political beliefs? If so, what can be done to change or alter the effect?

2. Is there an objective measure of morality? Should we condemn honor killings because they are unthinkable in our culture? Or should we respect the traditions of other cultures, no matter how strange or unpalatable?

SOURCES: Deutsche Welle, "Afghan-Born German Gets Life for Honor Killing of Sister," February 13, 2009, www.dw-world.de/dw/article/0,,4026518,00.html (accessed June 16, 2009); Dale Gavlak, "Jordan Honor Killing: Man Confesses to Brutally Stabbing to Death Pregnant Sister," *The Huffington Post*, April 12, 2009, www.huffingtonpost.com/2009/04/12/jordan-honor-killing-man-_n_185977.html# (accessed June 16, 2009); Linda M. Williams, "Honor Killings," in *Encyclopedia of Interpersonal Violence*, ed. Claire M. Renzetti and Jeffrey I. Edelson (Thousand Oaks, CA: Sage Publications, 2007); Dan Bilefsky, "How to Avoid Honor Killing in Turkey? Honor Suicide," *New York Times*, July 16, 2006, p. 3; Nadera Shalhoub-Kevorkian, "Reexamining Femicide: Breaking the Silence and Crossing 'Scientific' Borders," *Signs* 28 (2003): 581–608.

child abuse rates, approval of violence by the government, political corruption, and an inefficient justice system.[48] Children in high-violence nations are likely to be economically deprived and socially isolated, exposed to constant violence, and lacking in hope and respect for the law. Guns are common in these nations because, lacking an efficient justice system, people arm themselves or hire private security forces for protection.[49] In contrast, nations such as Japan have relatively low violence rates because of cultural and economic strengths. Japan boasts a system of exceptionally effective informal social controls that help reduce crime. It also has had a robust economy, which may alleviate the stresses that produce violence.[50] The accompanying Race, Culture, Gender, and Criminology feature discusses one type of culturally-based violent crime: the honor killing of women.

National values, as well as each of the factors just discussed, are believed to influence violent crime, including both traditional common-law crimes, such as rape, murder, assault, and robbery, and newly recognized problems, such as workplace violence, hate crimes, and political violence. Each of these forms of violent behavior is discussed in some detail in this chapter. ▶ **Checkpoints**

Forcible Rape

The common-law definition of **rape** (from the Latin *rapere*, "to take by force") is "the carnal knowledge of a female forcibly and against her will."[51] It is one of the most loathed, misunderstood, and frightening crimes. Under traditional common-law definitions, rape involves nonconsensual sexual intercourse inflicted on a female by a male. There are, of course, other forms of sexual assault, including male-on-male and female-on-male sexual assaults (some studies estimate that up to 25 percent of males have been the target of unwanted sexual advances by women), but these are not considered here within the traditional concept of rape.[52] However, recognizing these other forms of sexual assault, all but three states have now revised their rape statutes to make them gender neutral.[53]

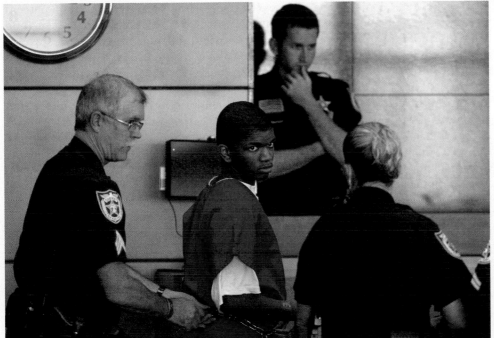
© AP Photo/Pool, Lannis Waters

Although many rapes involve acquaintances and even occur during dating relationships, others involve complete strangers. Here Sergeant Stephen Hatfield of the Palm Beach County Sheriff's Office escorts Avion Lawson into the courtroom to testify in West Palm Beach, Florida, on August 25, 2009. The teen defendant admitted that when he was a 14-year-old middle schooler, he participated in the gang rape of a mother and helped beat the woman's 12-year-old son in a horrific assault in which the two victims were forced to perform sex acts on each other.

Checkpoints

▶ There are a number of suspected causes of violence.

▶ Some violent criminals have personal traits that make them violence-prone, including mental impairment and intellectual dysfunction.

▶ Victims of severe child abuse and neglect may become violence-prone adults.

▶ Violence may have its roots in human evolution, being almost instinctual in some instances.

▶ Drug and alcohol abuse has been linked to violence through a psychopharmacological relationship, economic compulsive behavior, or a systemic link.

▶ Although guns do not cause violence, their presence can escalate its severity.

▶ Subcultures of violence encourage people to use aggressive tactics to solve disputes.

▶ Some nations have cultures that make them prone to violence.

rape
The carnal knowledge of a female forcibly and against her will.

Rape was often viewed as a sexual offense in the traditional criminological literature. It was presented as a crime that involved overwhelming lust, driving a man to force his attentions on a woman. Criminologists now consider rape a violent, coercive act of aggression, not a forceful expression of sexuality. Take for instance the use of rape in war crimes, a practice that became routine during the war in Bosnia; human rights groups have estimated that more than 30,000 women and young girls were sexually abused in the Balkan fighting.[54] Though shocking, the war crimes discovered in Bosnia have not deterred conquering armies from using rape as a weapon. More recently, pro-government militias in the Darfur region of Sudan were accused of using rape and other forms of sexual violence "as a weapon of war" to humiliate African women and girls as well as the rebels fighting the Sudanese government in Khartoum.[55]

In the United States, there has been a national campaign to alert the public to the seriousness of rape, offer help to victims, and change legal definitions to facilitate the prosecution of rape offenders. Such efforts have been only marginally effective in reducing rape, but significant progress has been made in overhauling rape laws and developing a vast social service network to aid victims.

INCIDENCE OF RAPE

According to the most recent UCR data, about 90,000 rapes or attempted rapes are now being reported each year—a rate of about 30 per 100,000 inhabitants or, more relevantly, 58 per 100,000 females.[56] As is true of other violent crimes, the rape rate has been in a decade-long decline, and current totals are significantly below 1992 levels, when 84 women per 100,000 were rape victims and more than 100,000 rapes were reported to police.

Population density influences the rape rate. Metropolitan areas today have rape rates significantly higher than rural areas; nonetheless, urban areas have experienced a much greater drop in rape reports than rural areas. The police make arrests in about 40 percent of all reported rape offenses. Of the offenders arrested, about 45 percent were under 25 years of age, and about two-thirds were Caucasian. The racial and age pattern of rape arrests has been fairly consistent for some time. Rape is a warm-weather crime—most incidents occur during July and August, with the lowest rates occurring during December, January, and February.

This data must be interpreted with caution. According to the National Crime Victimization Survey (NCVS), rape is frequently underreported. NCVS estimates that about 204,000 rapes and attempted rapes took place, suggesting that almost two-thirds of rape incidents are not reported to police.[57] Many people fail to report rape because they are embarrassed, believe nothing can be done, or blame themselves. Some victims of sexual assaults may even question whether they have really been "raped"; research indicates that when the assault involved a boyfriend, or if the woman was severely impaired by alcohol or drugs, or if the act involved oral or digital sex, the women were unlikely to label their experience as a "real" rape.[58] Some victims refuse to report rape because they have histories of excessive drinking and sexuality promiscuity, which may convince them that their intemperate and/or immoderate behavior contributed to their own victimization.[59] Thus, rape may be significantly underreported, and it is possible that more than 20 percent of females are rape victims.[60] But whether or not they acknowledge that their attack is a "real" rape, the experience can have devastating psychological effects that last long after the attack itself is over.[61]

TYPES OF RAPISTS

Some rapes are planned, whereas others are spontaneous; some focus on a particular victim, whereas others occur almost as an afterthought during the commission of another crime, such as a burglary. Some rapists commit a single crime, whereas others are multiple offenders; some attack alone, and others engage in group or gang rapes.[62]

Anger rape occurs when sexuality becomes a means of expressing and discharging pent-up anger and rage. The rapist uses far more brutality than would have been necessary if his real objective had been simply to have sex with his victim. His aim is to hurt his victim as much as possible; the sexual aspect of rape may be an afterthought. Often the anger rapist acts on the spur of the moment after an upsetting incident has caused him conflict, irritation, or aggravation. Surprisingly, anger rapes are less psychologically traumatic for the victim than might be expected. Because a woman is usually physically beaten during an anger rape, she is more likely to receive sympathy from her peers, relatives, and the justice system and consequently be immune from any suggestion that she complied with the attack.

Power rape involves an attacker who does not want to harm his victim as much as he wants to possess her sexually. His goal is sexual conquest, and he uses only the amount of force necessary to achieve his objective. The power rapist wants to be in control, to be able to dominate women and have them at his mercy. Yet it is not sexual gratification that drives the power rapist; in fact, he often has a consenting relationship with his wife or girlfriend. Rape is instead a way of putting personal insecurities to rest, asserting heterosexuality, and

Exhibit 10.1 Varieties of Forcible Rape

preserving a sense of manhood. The power rapist's victim is usually a woman equal in age to or younger than the rapist. The lack of physical violence may reduce the support given the victim by family and friends. Therefore, the victim's personal guilt over her rape experience is increased— perhaps, she thinks, she could have done something to get away.

Sadistic rape involves both sexuality and aggression. The sadistic rapist is bound up in ritual—he may torment his victim, bind her, or torture her. In the rapist's view, victims are usually related to a personal characteristic that he wants to harm or destroy. The rape experience is intensely exciting to the sadist; he gets satisfaction from abusing, degrading, or humiliating his captive. This type of rape is particularly traumatic for the victim. Victims of such crimes need psychiatric care long after their physical wounds have healed.

SOURCE: A. Nicholas Groth and Jean Birnbaum, *Men Who Rape* (New York: Plenum Press, 1979).

Because there is no single type of rape or rapist, criminologists have attempted to define and categorize the vast variety of rape situations.

Criminologists now recognize that there are numerous motivations for rape—and, consequently, various types of rapists. One of the best-known attempts to classify the personalities of rapists was that of A. Nicholas Groth, an expert on classifying and treating sex offenders. According to Groth, every rape encounter contains at least one of three elements: anger, power, or sadism.[63] Consequently, rapists can be classified according to one of the three dimensions described in Exhibit 10.1. In treating rape offenders, Groth found that about 55 percent represented the power type, about 40 percent the anger type, and about 5 percent the sadistic type. Groth's major contribution has been his recognition that rape is generally a crime of violence, not a sexual act. In all of these circumstances, rape involves a violent criminal offense in which a predatory criminal chooses to attack a victim.[64]

TYPES OF RAPE

In addition to the variety of types of rapists, there are also different categories of rapes.

Date Rape One disturbing trend involves people who are in some form of courting relationship—this is known as **date rape**. Some date rapes occur on first dates, others after a relationship has begun developing, and still others after the couple have been involved for some time. In long-term or close relationships, the male partner may feel he has invested so much time and money in his partner that he is owed sexual relations or that sexual intimacy is an expression or acknowledgment that the involvement is progressing.[65]

date rape
A rape that involves people who are in some form of courting relationship.

Date rape was first identified as a significant social problem in the 1980s when Mary Koss conducted surveys and found that a significant number of college-age women had been sexually assaulted by a dating partner; about 27 of the respondents had been the victim of rape or attempted rape. However, only about a quarter of the women called what had happened to them "rape"; the majority either blamed themselves or denied they had really been raped.[66]

Koss's research helped identify a social problem that all too long had remained below the radar. Nonetheless, despite her warning, fewer than 1 in 10 date rapes are being reported to police.[67] Some victims do not report the crime because they do not view their experience as a "real" rape, which, they believe, involves a strange man "jumping out of the bushes." Other victims are embarrassed and frightened. Many tell their friends about their rape while refusing to let authorities know what happened. Reporting is most common in the most serious cases, such as when a weapon is used; it is less common when drugs or alcohol is involved.[68]

Marital Rape Traditionally, a legally married husband could not be charged with raping his wife; this immunity was referred to as the **marital exemption**. However, research indicates that many women are raped each year by their husbands as part of an overall pattern of spousal abuse, and these women deserve the protection of the law. Many spousal rapes are accompanied by brutal, sadistic beatings and have little to do with normal sexual interests.[69] Not surprisingly, the marital exemption has undergone significant revision. In 1980, only three states had laws against marital rape; today almost every state recognizes marital rape as a crime.[70]

Statutory Rape The term **statutory rape** refers to sexual relations between an underage minor female and an adult male. Although the sex is not forced or coerced, the law says that young girls are incapable of giving informed consent, so the act is legally considered nonconsensual. Typically, a state's law cites an age of consent above which there can be no criminal prosecution for consensual sexual relations.[71]

CAUSES OF RAPE

What factors predispose some men to commit rape? Criminologists' responses to this question are almost as varied as the crime itself. However, most explanations can be grouped into a few consistent categories.

Evolutionary, Biological Factors One explanation for rape focuses on the evolutionary, biological aspects of the male sexual drive. This perspective suggests that rape may be instinctual, developed over the ages as a means of perpetuating the species. In more primitive times, forcible sexual contact may have helped spread genes and maximize offspring. Some believe that these prehistoric drives remain: Males still have a natural sexual drive that encourages them to have intimate relations with as many women as possible.[72] The evolutionary view is that the sexual urge corresponds to the unconscious need to preserve the species by spreading one's genes as widely as one can. Men who are sexually aggressive will have a reproductive edge over their more passive peers.[73]

Male Socialization In contrast to the evolutionary biological view, some researchers argue that rape is a function of socialization. Some men have been socialized to be aggressive with women and believe that the use of violence or force is legitimate if their sexual advances are rebuffed ("Women like to play hard to get and expect to be forced to have sex"). Those who have been socialized to believe that "no means yes" are more likely to be sexually aggressive.[74] The use of sexual violence is aggravated if pro-force socialization is reinforced by peers who share similar values.[75]

Diana Russell describes the **virility mystique**—the belief that males must separate their sexual feelings from their need for love, respect, and affection. She believes men are socialized to be the aggressors and expect to be sexually active with many women; consequently, male virginity and sexual inexperience are shameful.

marital exemption
The formerly accepted tradition that a legally married husband could not be charged with raping his wife.

statutory rape
Sexual relations between an underage minor female and an adult male.

virility mystique
The belief that males must separate their sexual feelings from their need for love, respect, and affection.

Similarly, sexually aggressive women frighten some men and cause them to doubt their own masculinity. Sexual insecurity may lead some men to commit rape to bolster their self-image and masculine identity.[76]

Psychological Abnormality Rapists may suffer from some type of personality disorder or mental illness. Research shows that a significant percentage of incarcerated rapists exhibit psychotic tendencies, and many others have hostile, sadistic feelings toward women.[77] A high proportion of serial rapists and repeat sexual offenders exhibit psychopathic personality structures.[78] There is evidence linking rape proclivity with **narcissistic personality disorder**, a pattern of traits and behaviors that indicate infatuation and fixation with one's self to the exclusion of all others and the egotistic and ruthless pursuit of one's own gratification, dominance, and ambition.[79]

Social Learning According to this perspective, men learn to commit rapes in much the same way they learn any other behavior. For example, sexual aggression may be learned through interaction with peers who articulate attitudes supportive of sexual violence.[80] Observing or experiencing sexual violence has also been linked to sexual aggression. Nicholas Groth found that 40 percent of the rapists he studied were sexually victimized as adolescents.[81] Experiencing sexual trauma has been linked with the desire to inflict sexual trauma on others.[82] Watching violent or pornographic films featuring women who are beaten, raped, or tortured has been linked to sexually aggressive behavior in men.[83]

Sexual Motivation Even though criminologists now consider rape a violent act without sexual motivation, there is evidence that at least some rapists have sexual feelings for their victim.[84] NCVS data reveals that rape victims tend to be young and that rapists prefer younger, presumably more attractive victims. Data show an association between the ages of rapists and those of their victims, indicating that men choose rape targets of approximately the same age as their consensual sex partners. And despite the fact that younger criminals are usually the most violent, older rapists tend to harm their victims more than younger rapists. This pattern indicates that older criminals may rape for motives of power and control, whereas younger offenders may be seeking sexual gratification. Victims may, therefore, suffer less harm from severe beatings and humiliation from younger attackers.

RAPE AND THE LAW

Unlike other crime victims, women may find that their claim of sexual assault is greeted with some skepticism by police and court personnel.[85] They will soon discover that they have to prove they did not engage in consensual sex and then develop remorse afterwards. However, police and courts are becoming more sensitive to the plight of rape victims and are now just as likely to investigate acquaintance rapes as they are **aggravated rape**s involving multiple offenders, weapons, and victim injuries. In some jurisdictions, the justice system takes all rape cases seriously and does not ignore those in which victim and attacker have had a prior relationship or those that did not involve serious injury.[86]

Proving Rape Proving guilt in a rape case is extremely challenging for prosecutors. Some judges also fear that women may charge men with rape because of jealousy, withdrawn marriage proposals, or pregnancy. There is also evidence that juries may consider the race of the victim and offender in their decision making; for example, they may believe victims and convict defendants more often in interracial rapes than when both parties are the same race.[87] Although the law does not recognize it, jurors are sometimes swayed by the insinuation that the rape was victim-precipitated; thus, the blame is shifted from rapist to victim. To get a conviction, prosecutors must establish that the act was forced and violent and that no question of voluntary compliance exists. They may be reluctant to prosecute cases where they have questions about the victim's moral character or if they believe the victim's demeanor and

CONNECTIONS
The social learning view will be explored further in Chapter 13 when the issue of pornography and violence is analyzed in greater detail. Most research does not show that watching pornography is directly linked to sexual violence, but there may be a link between sexual aggression and viewing movies with sexual violence as their theme.

narcissistic personality disorder A pattern of traits and behaviors indicating infatuation and fixation with one's self to the exclusion of all others, along with the egotistic and ruthless pursuit of one's own gratification, dominance, and ambition.

aggravated rape Rape involving multiple offenders, weapons, and victim injuries.

The law is cognizant that errors can occur in rape accusations. However, new scientific techniques can help ensure that the innocent go free. Here, Attorney Aliza Kaplan, deputy director of the Innocence Project, laughs as she puts her head on the shoulder of Dennis Maher, as they address members of the media on April 3, 2003, in Boston. Maher, who spent 19 years in prison for the rape of two women and the attempted rape of a third, walked out of a courthouse a free man after new DNA evidence proved that he could not have committed the crime.

attitude will turn off the jury and undermine the chance of conviction.[88] And there is always fear that a frightened and traumatized victim may later identify the wrong man, which happened in the case of Dennis Maher, a Massachusetts man freed in 2003 after spending more than 19 years in prison for rapes he did not commit. Even though three victims provided eyewitness identification at trial, DNA testing proved that Maher could not have been the rapist.[89]

Consent It is essential to prove that the attack was forced and that the victim did not give voluntary **consent** to her attacker. In a sense, the burden of proof is on the victim to show that her character is beyond question and that she in no way encouraged, enticed, or misled the accused rapist. A common defense tactic is to introduce, into the minds of the jury, suspicion that the woman may have consented to the sexual act and later regretted her decision or suspicion that her dubious moral character casts doubt on the veracity of her claims. Even the appearance of impropriety can undermine a case. When Kobe Bryant was accused of raping a young woman in 2003, the alleged victim was described in the press as being promiscuous, suicidal, mentally ill, a gold digger, and on drugs. She was also harrassed by Bryant's fans, and three men were actually jailed for making threats.[90] When she refused to testify, the charges were dropped; a civil suit was later settled out of court. Research shows that even when a defendant is found guilty in a sexual assault case, punishment is significantly reduced if the victim's personal characteristics are viewed as negative—for example, if she is a transient, a hitchhiker, or a substance abuser.[91] Proving the victim had good character is not a requirement in any other crime.

Legal Reform Because of the difficulty that rape victims have in obtaining justice, rape laws have been changing around the country. Reform efforts include changing the language of statutes, dropping the condition of victim resistance, and changing

consent
The victim of rape must prove that she in no way encouraged, enticed, or misled the accused rapist.

the requirement of *use* of force to include the *threat* of force or injury.[92] **Shield laws**, which protect women from being questioned about their sexual history unless it directly bears on the case, have become universal. Although some are quite restrictive, others grant the trial judge considerable discretion to admit prior sexual conduct in evidence if it is deemed relevant for the defense. In an important 1991 case, *Michigan v. Lucas*, the U.S. Supreme Court upheld the validity of shield laws and ruled that excluding evidence of a prior sexual relationship between the parties did not violate the defendant's right to a fair trial.[93]

In addition to requiring evidence that consent was not given, the common law of rape required corroboration that the crime of rape actually took place. This involved the need for independent evidence from police officers, physicians, and witnesses that the accused was actually the person who committed the crime, that sexual penetration took place, and that force was present and consent absent. This requirement shielded rapists from prosecution in cases where the victim delayed reporting the crime or physical evidence had been compromised or lost. Corroboration is no longer required except under extraordinary circumstances, such as when the victim is too young to understand the crime, has had a previous sexual relationship with the defendant, or gives a version of events that is improbable and self-contradictory.[94]

The federal government may have given rape victims another source of redress when it passed the Violence Against Women Act in 1994. This statute allows rape victims to sue in federal court on the grounds that sexual violence violates their civil rights; so far, the provisions of this act have been upheld by appellate courts.[95] Despite these reform efforts, prosecutors may be influenced in their decision to bring charges by the circumstances of a crime.[96]

Murder and Homicide

The common-law definition of **murder** is "the unlawful killing of a human being with malice aforethought."[97] It is the most serious of all common-law crimes and the only one, in the United States, that can still be punished by death. Western society's abhorrence of murderers is illustrated by the fact that there is no statute of limitations in murder cases. Whereas state laws limit prosecution of other crimes to a fixed period (usually 7 to 10 years), accused killers can be brought to justice at any time after their crimes were committed.

To legally prove that a murder has taken place, most state jurisdictions require prosecutors to show that the accused *maliciously* intended to kill the victim. "Express or actual malice" is the state of mind assumed to exist when someone kills another person in the absence of any apparent provocation. "Implied or constructive malice" is considered to exist when a death results from negligent or unthinking behavior. In these cases, even though the perpetrator did not wish to kill the victim, the killing resulted from an inherently dangerous act and therefore is considered murder. An unusual example of this concept is the case of Ignacio Perea, an AIDS-infected Miami man who kidnapped and raped an 11-year-old boy. Perea was convicted of attempted murder and sentenced to up to 25 years in prison when the jury agreed with the prosecutor's contention that the AIDS virus is a deadly weapon.[98]

DEGREES OF MURDER

There are different levels, or degrees, of homicide.[99] **First-degree murder** occurs when a person kills another after premeditation and deliberation. **Premeditation** means that the killing was considered beforehand and suggests that it was motivated by more than a simple desire to engage in an act of violence. **Deliberation** means the killing was planned after careful thought rather than carried out on impulse: "To constitute a deliberate and premeditated killing, the slayer must weigh and consider the question of killing and the reasons for and against such a choice; having in mind the consequences, he decides to and does kill."[100] The planning implied by this definition need not be a long process; it may be an almost instantaneous decision to

shield laws
Laws that protect women from being questioned about their sexual history unless such questioning directly bears on the case.

murder
The unlawful killing of a human being with malice aforethought.

first-degree murder
Killing a person after premeditation and deliberation.

premeditation
Considering the criminal act beforehand, which suggests that it was motivated by more than a simple desire to engage in an act of violence.

deliberation
Planning a criminal act after careful thought, rather than carrying it out on impulse.

take another's life. Also, a killing that accompanies a felony, such as robbery or rape, usually constitutes first-degree murder (**felony murder**).

Second-degree murder requires the killer to have malice aforethought but not premeditation or deliberation. A second-degree murder occurs when a person's wanton disregard for the victim's life and his or her desire to inflict serious bodily harm on the victim result in the victim's death. Homicide without malice is called **manslaughter** and is usually punished by anywhere from 1 to 15 years in prison. **Voluntary or nonnegligent manslaughter** refers to a killing committed in the heat of passion or during a sudden quarrel that provoked violence. Although intent may be present, malice is not. **Involuntary or negligent manslaughter** refers to a killing that occurs when a person's acts are negligent and without regard for the harm they may cause others. Most involuntary manslaughter cases involve motor vehicle deaths—for example, when a drunk driver kills a pedestrian.

Deliberate Indifference Murder Murder is often considered an intentional act, but a person can also be held criminally liable for the death of another even if she or he did not intend to injure another person but exhibited *deliberate indifference* to the danger her or his actions might cause. The deliberate indifference standard is met when a person knows of, and yet disregards or ignores, an excessive risk to another's health or safety. One of the most famous cases illustrating deliberate indifference murder occurred on January 26, 2001, when Diane Whipple, a San Francisco woman, died after two large dogs attacked her in the hallway of her apartment building. One of the dogs' owners/keepers, Robert Noel, was found guilty of manslaughter, and his wife Marjorie Knoller was convicted on charges of second-degree murder, because they knew that the dogs were highly dangerous but did little or nothing to control the animals' behavior. Their deliberate indifference put their neighbor at risk, with tragic consequences. After a long series of appeals, on June 1, 2007, the California Supreme Court ruled that a dog owner who knows the animal is a potential killer and exposes other people to that danger may be guilty of murder even though he or she did not intend that particular victim to be injured or killed. In a unanimous decision, the appellate court ruled that Knoller could be convicted of murder because she acted with "conscious disregard of the danger to human life." On September 22, 2008, the court sentenced Marjorie Knoller to serve 15 years to life for the death of Diane Whipple.[101]

NATURE AND EXTENT OF MURDER

It is possible to track the trends in U.S. murder rates from 1900 to the present with the aid of coroners' reports and UCR data. The murder rate peaked in 1933, a time of prolonged economic depression and lawlessness, and then fell until 1958. The homicide rate doubled from the mid-1960s to a peak in 1991 when almost 25,000 people were killed in a single year, a rate of about 10 per 100,000 people. The murder rate has since been in a decline. In 2008, there were about 16,000 murders, rate of about 5.4 per 100,000 population.

What else do official crime statistics tell us about murder today? Murder tends to be an urban crime. More than half of all homicides occur in cities with a population of 100,000 or more; nearly one-quarter of homicides occur in cities with a population of more than 1 million. Why is homicide an urban phenomenon? Large cities experience the greatest rates of structural disadvantage—poverty, joblessness, racial heterogeneity, residential mobility, family disruption, and income inequality—that are linked to high murder rates.[102] Not surprisingly, large cities are much more commonly the site of drug-related killings and gang-related murders and are relatively less likely to be the location of family-related homicides, including murders of intimates.

Murder victims and offenders tend to be males; about 80 percent of homicide victims and nearly 90 percent of offenders are male. Murder, like rape, tends to be an intraracial crime; about 90 percent of victims are slain by members of their own race. About half of all murder victims are African Americans.

felony murder
A killing that accompanies a felony, such as robbery or rape.

second-degree murder
A person's wanton disregard for the victim's life and his or her desire to inflict serious bodily harm on the victim, which results in the victim's death.

manslaughter
Homicide without malice.

voluntary or nonnegligent manslaughter
A killing committed in the heat of passion or during a sudden quarrel that provoked violence.

involuntary or negligent manslaughter
A killing that occurs when a person's acts are negligent and without regard for the harm they may cause others.

Approximately one-third of murder victims and almost half the offenders are under the age of 25. For both victims and offenders, the rate per 100,000 peaks in the 18- to 24-year-old age group. Some murders involve very young children, a crime referred to as **infanticide** (killing older children is called **filicide**), and others involve senior citizens, a crime referred to as **eldercide**.[103] The UCR indicates that about 500 children under 4 years of age are murdered each year. The younger the child, the greater the risk for infanticide. At the opposite end of the age spectrum, less than 5 percent of all homicides involve people age 65 or older. Males age 65 or older are more likely than females of the same age to be homicide victims. Although most of the offenders who committed eldercide were age 50 or younger, elderly females were more likely than elderly males to be killed by an elderly offender.[104]

Murderers typically have a long involvement in crime; few people begin a criminal career by killing someone. Research shows that people arrested for homicide are significantly more likely to have been in trouble with the law prior to their arrest than people arrested for other crimes.[105]

Today, few would deny that some relationship exists between social and ecological factors and murder. The following section explores some of the more important issues related to these factors.

MURDEROUS RELATIONS

Most murders are expressive—that is, motivated by rage or anger— and they typically involve friends, relatives, and acquaintances. In 2008, for example, of the 8,000 murders where the relationship between criminal and offender could be determined, only 1,700 involved complete strangers. Stranger homicides typically involve commission of another crime (such as a robbery, rape, or drug deal) where the perpetrator applied too much force in completing the crime.[106]

Murderous relations are also shaped by gender: Males are more likely to kill others of similar social standing in more public contexts, whereas women kill family members and intimate partners in private locations.[107] What other forms do murderous relations take?

Romantic Relations Many murders involve husbands and wives, boyfriends and girlfriends, and others involved in romantic relationships. Upwards of 40 percent of all murders in which the attacker can be identified involved an intimate partner, especially one who has young children.[108]

Research indicates that most females who kill their mates do so after suffering repeated violent attacks.[109] Perhaps the number of males killed by their partners has declined because alternatives to abusive relationships, such as shelters for battered women, are becoming more prevalent around the United States. Regions that provide greater social support for battered women and that have passed legislation to protect abuse victims also have lower rates of female-perpetrated homicide.[110]

Some people kill their mates because they find themselves involved in a *love triangle*.[111] Interestingly, women who kill out of jealousy aim their aggression at their partners; in contrast, men are more likely to kill their rivals (their mates' suitors). Love triangles tend to become lethal when the offenders believe they have been lied to or betrayed. Lethal violence is more common when (1) the rival initiated the affair, (2) the killer knew the spouse was already in a steady relationship outside the marriage, and (3) the killer was repeatedly lied to or betrayed.[112]

Personal Relations Most murders occur among people who are acquainted. Although on the surface the killing might seem senseless, it is often the result of a long-simmering dispute motivated by revenge, dispute resolution, jealousy, drug deals, racial bias, or threats to identity or status.[113] For example, a prior act of violence, motivated by profit or greed, such as when a buyer robs his dealer during a drug transaction, may generate revenge killing.

How do these murderous relations develop between two people who may have had little prior conflict? In a classic study, David Luckenbill examined murder transactions

CONNECTIONS

Men who perceive loss of face might aim their aggression at rivals who are competing with them for a suitable partner. Biosocial theory (Chapter 5) suggests that this behavior is motivated by the male's instinctual need to replenish the species and protect his place in the gene pool. Killing a rival would help a spouse maintain control over a potential mother for his children.

infanticide
Murder of a very young child.

filicide
Murder of an older child.

eldercide
Murder of a senior citizen.

CONNECTIONS

Recall from Chapter 3 the discussion of victim precipitation. The argument made by some criminologists is that murder victims help create the "transactions" that lead to their death.

to determine whether particular patterns of behavior are common between the killer and the victim.[114] He found that many homicides follow a sequential pattern. First, the victim makes what the offender considers an offensive move. The offender typically retaliates verbally or physically. An agreement to end things violently is forged with the victim's provocative response. The battle ensues, leaving the victim dead or dying. The offender's escape is shaped by his or her relationship to the victim or by the reaction of the audience, if any (Figure 10.2).

Stranger Relations In the past, people who killed tended to kill someone they knew or were related to, but over the last decade, the number of stranger homicides has increased. Today, about twenty percent of all murders involve strangers, a significant increase from years past. Stranger homicides occur most often as felony murders during rapes, robberies, and burglaries. Others are random acts of urban violence that fuel public fear. For example, a homeowner tells a motorist to move his car because it is blocking the driveway, an argument ensues, and the owner gets a pistol and kills the motorist. Or consider a young boy who kills a store manager because, he says, "Something came into my head to hurt the lady."[115]

Why do stranger killings now make up a greater percentage of all murders than in years past? Tough new sentencing laws, such as the "three strikes" laws used in California, and other habitual-criminal statutes could be responsible. These laws mandate that a "three-time loser" be given a life sentence if convicted of multiple felonies. It is possible, as Tomislav Kovandzic and his associates found, that these laws encourage criminals to kill while committing burglaries and robberies. "Why hesitate to kill now?" they may reason, because if they are caught, they will receive a life sentence anyway.[116]

Student Relations Sadly, violence in schools has become commonplace.[117] According to the latest national survey of crime in schools, more than 2 million nonfatal crimes occur on school grounds each year, including almost 800,000 violent acts. About 10 percent of male and 5 percent of female high school students reported being

Figure 10.2 Murder Transactions

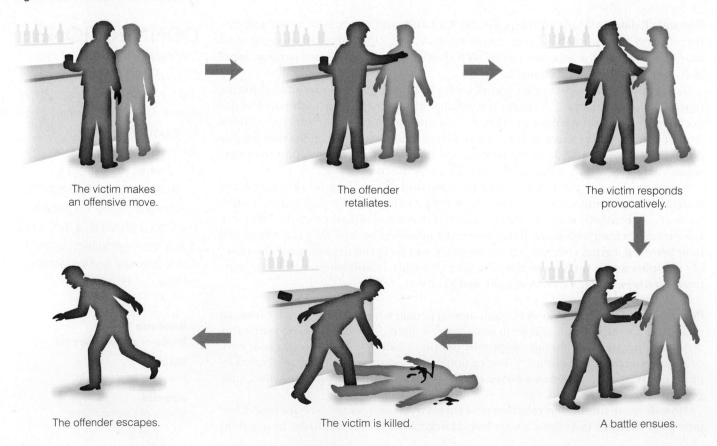

The victim makes an offensive move.

The offender retaliates.

The victim responds provocatively.

The offender escapes.

The victim is killed.

A battle ensues.

Violent episodes can occur anywhere. This poster shows Sophie Lancaster, who was kicked to death in England on August 2007 because she was a Goth. The poster reads, "Weirdo. Mosher. Freak. If only they'd stop at name calling." While walking through a park in Lancashire with her boyfriend, Robert Maltby, Sophie was attacked by a mob of adolescents who objected to their gothic attire. Sophie was repeatedly kicked in the head, and as a result of her severe head injuries she went into a coma, never regained consciousness, and later died. Some of the youths responsible were given long prison sentences. The kids involved were young teens who seemed oblivious to the damage they had caused.

threatened or injured with a weapon on school property in the past year. Of the violent acts, about 500,000 involved a weapon. These included 7,000 physical attacks, 600 robberies, and 4,500 rapes and sexual batteries.

Violence and bullying have become routine; surveys indicate that more than 16 percent of U.S. schoolchildren have been bullied by other students during the current school term, and approximately 30 percent of sixth- through tenth-grade students reported being involved in some aspect of moderate to frequent bullying, either as a bully or the target of bullying, or both.[118] Sometimes violence and bullying can escalate into a school shooting, such as the Columbine High School massacre, which resulted in the deaths of 15 people.

Though relatively rare, these incidents may be expected because up to 10 percent of students report bringing weapons to school on a regular basis.[119] Many of these kids have a history of being abused and bullied; many perceive a lack of support from peers, parents, and teachers.[120] Kids who have been the victims of crime themselves and who hang with peers who carry weapons are most likely to bring guns to school.[121] Troubled kids with little social support who are carrying deadly weapons make for an explosive situation.

Research shows that most shooting incidents occur around the start of the school day, the lunch period, or the end of the school day.[122] In most of the shootings (55 percent), a note, threat, or other action indicating risk for violence occurred before the event. Shooters were also likely to have expressed some form of suicidal behavior and to have been bullied by their peers.[123]

SERIAL KILLERS, MASS MURDERERS, AND SPREE KILLERS

For 31 years, citizens of Wichita, Kansas, lived in fear of the serial killer self-described as BTK (for Bind, Torture, Kill). During his murder spree, BTK sent taunting letters and packages to the police and the media. Suddenly, after committing some gruesome killings in the 1970s, he went underground and disappeared from view. Then after 25 years of silence, he renewed contact with a local news station. His last communication contained a computer disk, which was analyzed by the FBI and traced to 59-year-old Dennis Rader, who later confessed to ten murders in an effort to escape the death penalty.

Serial Killers Criminologists consider a **serial killer**, such as Rader, to be a person who kills three or more persons in three or more separate events. In between the murders, a serial killer reverts to his or her normal lifestyle.

Serial killers come from all walks of life. Two stereotypes surrounding serial killers are that they are almost always white males and that few African Americans are involved in serial killing. Research by Anthony Walsh found that in reality African Americans make up about 20 percent of all serial murderers and that their involvement is masked because the media rarely focus on black multiple murderers (the Atlanta child killer and D.C. snipers are two exceptions).[124]

There are different types of serial killers.[125] Some are sadists who gain satisfaction from torturing and killing their victims. Dr. Michael Swango, who is suspected of killing between 35 and 60 patients, described in his diary the "sweet, husky, close smell of indoor homicide" and wrote that murders were "the only way I have of reminding myself that I'm still alive."[126] In contrast, some serial killers think they are helping people when they put them to death. Harold Frederick Shipman, Britain's most notorious serial killer, was a general practitioner convicted of 15 murders, most involving elderly patients. After he committed suicide in 2004, further investigation found that he had actually killed at least 218 patients, and perhaps even more.[127]

Some experts have attempted to classify serial killers on the basis of their motivations and offense patterns.[128] According to James A. Fox and Jack Levin, there are at least three different types of serial killers:[129]

▶ "Thrill killers" strive for either sexual sadism or dominance. They enjoy the thrill, the sexual gratification, and the dominance they achieve over the lives of their

serial killer
A person who kills three or more persons in three or more separate events.

victims. Serial killers rarely use a gun because this method is too quick and would deprive them of their greatest pleasure—exulting in the victim's suffering. Extending the time it takes the victim to die increases the pleasure they experience from killing and prolongs their ability to ignore or enjoy their victims' suffering. They typically have a propensity for basking in the media limelight when apprehended for their crimes. Killing provides a way for them to feed their emotional hunger and reduce their anxiety levels.[130]

▶ "Mission killers" want to reform the world or have a vision that drives them to kill.

▶ "Expedience killers" are out for profit or want to protect themselves from a perceived threat.

Female Serial Killers An estimated 10 to 15 percent of serial killers are women. Criminologists Belea Keeney and Kathleen Heide investigated the characteristics of a sample of 14 female serial killers and found some striking differences between the way male and female killers carried out their crimes.[131] Males were much more likely than females to use extreme violence and torture. Whereas males used a "hands-on" approach, including beating, bludgeoning, and strangling their victims, females were more likely to poison or smother their victims. Men tracked or stalked their victims, but women were more likely to lure victims to their death.

There are also gender-based personality and behavior characteristics. Female killers, somewhat older than their male counterparts, abused both alcohol and drugs; males were not likely to be substance abusers. Women were diagnosed as having histrionic, manic-depressive, borderline, dissociative, and antisocial personality disorders; men were more often diagnosed as having antisocial personalities. Aileen Wuornos, executed for killing seven men, was diagnosed with a severe psychopathic personality, which probably arose from her horrific childhood marred by beatings, alcoholism, rape, incest, and prostitution.[132]

Thus, the typical female serial killer is a person who smothers or poisons someone she knows. During childhood she suffered from an abusive relationship in a disrupted family. Female killers' education levels are below average, and if they hold jobs, they are in low-status positions.

Mass Murderers In contrast to serial killings, **mass murder** involves the killing of four or more victims by one or a few assailants within a single event.[133] The Xbox killer Troy Victorino (Chapter 9) might be considered a mass murderer. The murderous incident can last but a few minutes or as long as several hours. In order to qualify as a mass murder, the incident must be carried out by one or a few offenders. Highly organized or institutionalized killings (such as war crimes and large-scale acts of political terrorism, as well as certain acts of highly organized crime rings), though atrocious, are not considered mass murder and are motivated by a totally different set of factors.

Fox and Levin define four types of mass murderers:

▶ "Revenge killers" want to get even with individuals or society at large. Their typical target is an estranged wife and "her" children or an employer and "his" employees.

▶ "Love killers" are motivated by a warped sense of devotion. They are often despondent people who commit suicide and take others, such as a wife and children, with them.

▶ "Profit killers" are usually trying to cover up a crime, eliminate witnesses, and carry out a criminal conspiracy.

▶ "Terrorist killers" are trying to send a message. Gang killings tell rivals to watch out; cult killers may actually leave a message behind to warn society about impending doom.[134]

Spree Killers Unlike mass murders, spree killing is not confined to a single outburst, and unlike serial killers, spree killers do not return to their normal identities in between killings. **Spree killers** engage in a rampage of violence over a period of days

mass murder
The killing of four or more victims by one or a few assailants within a single event.

spree killer
A killer of multiple victims whose murders occur over a relatively short span of time and often follow no discernible pattern.

or weeks. The most notorious spree killing to date occurred in October 2002, in the Washington, D.C. area.[135] John Lee Malvo, 17, a Jamaican citizen, and his traveling companion John Allen Muhammad, 41, an Army veteran with an expert's rating in marksmanship, went on a rampage that left more than ten people dead.

Some spree killers target a specific group or class. Joseph Paul Franklin targeted mixed-race couples (African Americans and Jews), committing over 20 murders in 12 states in an effort to instigate a race war. (Franklin also shot and paralyzed *Hustler* publisher Larry Flynt because he published pictures of interracial sex.)[136] Others, such as the D.C. snipers Malvo and Muhammad, kill randomly and do not seek a specific class of victim; their targets included the young and old, African Americans and whites, men and women.[137]

Assault and Battery

Although many people mistakenly believe that the phrase "assault and battery" refers to a single act, they are actually two separate crimes. **Battery** requires offensive touching, such as slapping, hitting, or punching a victim. **Assault** requires no actual touching but involves either attempted battery or intentionally frightening the victim by word or deed. Although common law originally intended these twin crimes to be misdemeanors, most jurisdictions now upgrade them to felonies either when a weapon is used or when they occur during the commission of a felony (for example, when a person is assaulted during a robbery).[138]

Under common law, battery required bodily injury, such as broken limbs or wounds. However, under modern law, an assault and battery occurs if the victim suffers a temporarily painful blow, even if no injury results. Battery can also involve offensive touching, such as a man kissing a woman against her will or putting his hands on her body. In some legal jurisdictions, biting someone when one is infected with AIDS is considered an aggravated assault; some people with AIDS have been convicted of aggravated assault for spitting on their victims.[139]

NATURE AND EXTENT OF ASSAULT

The pattern of criminal assault is quite similar to that of homicide and rape; one could say that the only difference is that the victim survives.[140] Assaults may be common in our society simply because of common life stresses. Motorists who assault each other have become such a familiar phenomenon that the term **road rage** has been coined. There have even been frequent incidents of violent assault among frustrated airline passengers who lose control while traveling.[141]

About 830,000 assaults are now being reported to police agencies annually—about 275 per 100,000 inhabitants. Just as for other violent crimes, the number of assaults has been in decline. It is down about one-third from its peak in 1993, when more than 1.1 million serious assaults were reported to the police. (People arrested for assault and those identified by victims are usually young, male (about 70 percent), and white, although the number of African Americans arrested for assault (30 percent) is disproportionate to their representation in the population. Assault victims tend to be male, but females also face a significant danger. Assault rates are highest in urban areas, during summer, and in southern and western regions. The weapons most commonly used in assaults are blunt instruments and hands and feet.

The NCVS indicates that more than 4 million assaults take place each year, about 840,000 are considered aggravated, and 3.3 million simple or weaponless assaults occur annually. Like that of other violent crimes, the number of assaults has been in steep decline—down more than 50 percent since 1998, according to the NCVS.

DOMESTIC VIOLENCE: ASSAULT IN THE HOME

Violent attacks in the home are one of the most frightening types of assault. Criminologists recognize that intrafamily violence is an enduring social problem in the United States and abroad.

battery
Offensive touching, such as slapping, hitting, or punching a victim.

assault
Either attempted battery or intentionally frightening the victim by word or deed (actual touching is not involved).

road rage
Violent assault by a motorist who loses control of their emotions while driving.

Child Abuse One area of intrafamily violence that has received a great deal of media attention is **child abuse**. This term describes any physical or emotional trauma inflicted on a child for which no reasonable explanation, such as an accident or ordinary disciplinary practices, can be found.[142] Child abuse can result from physical beatings administered to a child by hands, feet, weapons, belts, sticks, burning, and so on. Another form of abuse results from **neglect**—not providing a child with the care and shelter to which he or she is entitled.

Estimating the actual number of child abuse cases is difficult, because many incidents are never reported to the police. Child Protective Services (CPS) agencies throughout the United States receive more than 3 million reports of suspected child abuse or neglect per year. Of these, about 75 percent are considered unfounded, which leaves an estimated 800,000 children across the country who are victims of abuse or neglect; about 1,800 abuse-related deaths are recorded each year.[143] Who are abused kids?

▶ Children in the age group of birth to 1 year had the highest rate of victimization (22 per 1,000 children).

▶ About 52 percent of child victims were girls, and 48 percent were boys.

▶ Approximately half of all victims were white, 22 percent were African American, and 21 percent were Hispanic.

Although child abuse is still a serious social problem, child maltreatment rates are lower today than they were a decade ago. It is difficult to pinpoint the reason for the reduction in reported abuse, but it may be the result of better treatment strategies, lower substance abuse rates, reduced reliance on physical punishment, and the availability of abortion (which reduces the number of unwanted children).

Child sexual abuse is the exploitation of children through rape, incest, and molestation by parents or other adults. In a detailed study of child sexual exploitation in North America, Richard J. Estes and Neil Alan Weiner found that the problem of child sexual abuse is much more widespread than had previously been believed or documented.[144] Their research shows that each year in the United States, 25,000 children are subjected to some form of sexual exploitation, which often begins with sexual assaults by relatives and acquaintances, such as a teacher, a coach, or a neighbor. Sexual abuse is of particular concern because children who have been abused experience a long list of symptoms, including fear, post-traumatic stress disorder, behavior problems, sexualized behavior, and poor self-esteem.[145] As they mature, abused girls are more likely than other girls to drop out of high school, become teen parents, be obese, and experience psychiatric problems, substance dependence, and domestic violence.[146] Women who were abused as children are also at greater risk of being abused as adults than those who escaped childhood victimization.[147]

Causes of Child Abuse Why do parents physically assault their children? Such maltreatment is a highly complex problem with neither a single cause nor a readily available solution. It cuts across ethnic, religious, and socioeconomic lines. Abusive parents

Assault and battery in the home can involve child sexual and physical abuse. Few cases are as horrific as that of Josef Fritzl, shown here covering his face prior to the start of his trial for incest at the provincial courthouse in St. Poelten, Austria. Fritzl was accused of imprisoning his daughter for 24 years in a windowless cell in a house in Amstetten, Austria. On March 19, 2009, Fritzl was sentenced to life imprisonment, having been found guilty of a panoply of crimes, including the negligent murder of one of the seven children he fathered with his daughter. The jury at St. Poelten court found him guilty on all counts—guilty of negligent murder, enslavement, incest, rape, coercion, and false imprisonment. Fritzl quietly accepted the verdicts and waived his right to appeal.

child abuse
Any physical or emotional trauma to a child for which no reasonable explanation, such as an accident or ordinary disciplinary practices, can be found.

neglect
Not providing a child with the care and shelter to which he or she is entitled.

child sexual abuse
The exploitation of children through rape, incest, and molestation by parents or other adults.

Exhibit 10.2 Factors That Predict Spousal Abuse

- *Presence of alcohol:* Excessive alcohol use may turn otherwise docile husbands into wife abusers.
- *Access to weapon:* The perpetrator's access to a gun and previous threat with a weapon may lead to abuse.
- *Stepchild in the home:* Having a stepchild living in the home may provoke abuse because a parent may have a more limited bond to the child.
- *Estrangement:* Alienation or separation from a controlling partner and subsequent involvement with another partner are contributing factors in abuse.
- *Hostility toward dependency:* Some husbands who appear docile and passive may resent their dependence on their wives and react with rage and violence; this reaction has been linked to sexual inadequacy.
- *Excessive brooding:* Obsession with a wife's behavior, however trivial, can result in violent assaults.
- *Social learning:* Some males believe society approves of spouse or mate abuse and may use these beliefs to justify their violent behavior. Peer support helps shape their attitudes and behaviors.
- *Socioeconomic factors:* Men who fail as providers and are under economic stress may take their frustrations out on their wives.

- *Flashes of anger:* Research shows that a significant amount of family violence results from a sudden burst of anger after a verbal dispute.
- *Military service:* Spouse abuse among men who have served in the military is extremely high. Similarly, those serving in the military are more likely to assault their wives than are civilian husbands. The reasons for this phenomenon may be the violence promoted by military training and the close proximity in which military families live to one another.
- *Having been battered as children:* Husbands who assault their wives were generally battered as children.
- *Unpredictability:* Batterers are unpredictable, unable to be influenced by their wives, and impossible to prevent from battering once an argument has begun.

SOURCES: Christine Sellers, John Cochran, and Kathryn Branch, "Social Learning Theory and Partner Violence: A Research Note," *Deviant Behavior* 26 (2005): 379–395; Jacquelyn Campbell, Daniel Webster, Jane Koziol-McLain, Carolyn Block, Doris Campbell, Mary Ann Curry, Faye Gary, et al., "Risk Factors for Femicide in Abusive Relationships: Results from a Multisite Case Control Study," *American Journal of Public Health* 93 (2003): 1,089–1,097; Neil Jacobson and John Mordechai Gottman, *When Men Batter Women: New Insights into Ending Abusive Relationships* (New York: Simon and Schuster, 1998); Kenneth Leonard and Brian Quigley, "Drinking and Marital Aggression in Newlyweds: An Event-Based Analysis of Drinking and the Occurrence of Husband Marital Aggression," *Journal of Studies on Alcohol* 60 (1999): 537–541.

cannot be categorized by sex, age, or educational level, and they come from all walks of life.[148]

A number of factors have been commonly linked to abuse and neglect:

▶ Abusive parents may themselves have been abused, creating an intergenerational cycle of violence.

▶ Blended families, which include children living with an unrelated adult such as a stepparent or with another unrelated coresident, have higher incidence of abuse.[149]

▶ Parents may become abusive if they are isolated from friends, neighbors, or relatives who can help in times of crisis.[150]

▶ Abusive parents may be suffering from depression and other forms of psychological distress.[151]

Regardless of its cause, child abuse can have devastating long-term effects, ranging from depression to loss of self-esteem.[152] Not surprisingly, a history of childhood sexual and physical abuse is observed at a disproportionately high rate among persons with severe mental illness.[153]

Parental Abuse Parents are sometimes the target of abuse from their own children. The following facts emerge from studies of child-to-parent violence (CPV):

▶ The younger the child, the higher the rate of CPV.

▶ At all ages, more children were violent to mothers than to fathers.

▶ Both boys and girls hit mothers more than they hit fathers.

▶ At all ages, slightly more boys than girls hit parents.

Child-to-parent violence is associated with some form of earlier violence by parents: husband-to-wife, wife-to-husband, or child abuse.[154]

Spousal Abuse Spousal abuse has occurred throughout recorded history. By the mid-nineteenth century, severe wife beating fell into disfavor, and accused wife beaters were subject to public ridicule. Nonetheless, limited chastisement of abusers was still the rule. These ideas form the foundation of men's traditional physical control of women and have led to severe cases of spousal assault. Spouse abuse is still a significant problem. In their classic study of family violence, Richard Gelles and Murray Straus found that 16 percent of surveyed families had experienced husband-to-wife assaults.[155] The consequences of abuse can be significant, ranging from physical injury, to psychological trauma, to exposure to sexually transmitted disease.[156] Moreover, physical abuse is commonly accompanied by mental abuse and coercion that can have long-term damaging psychological effects.[157]

Not only married women are prone to being victimized by an intimate partner. Dating violence is quite common, and it is estimated that one high school girl in five may suffer sexual or physical abuse from a boyfriend. Dating violence has been linked to substance abuse, unsafe sex, and eating disorders.[158]

Women are not the only victims of spousal abuse. One recent study of 12,000 male abuse victims serving in the United States Army found that abused men were at greater risk than nonvictims for early army discharge and hospitalization—particularly hospitalization for depression, alcohol dependence, and mental health problems.[159]

In some instances, spousal abuse tragically leads to the death of the intimate partner. Factors that predict a lethal conclusion to domestic violence include the perpetrator's access to a gun and previous threat with a weapon; having a stepchild living in the home; estrangement, especially from a controlling partner; and subsequent involvement with another partner[160] (see Exhibit 10.2).

> **robbery**
> Taking or attempting to take anything of value from the care, custody, or control of a person or persons by force or threat of force or violence and/or by putting the victim in fear.

Robbery

The common-law definition of **robbery** (and the one used by the FBI) is "the taking or attempting to take anything of value from the care, custody, or control of a person or persons by force or threat of force or violence and/or by putting the victim in fear."[161] A robbery is considered a violent crime because it involves the use of force to obtain money or goods. Robbery is punished severely because the victim's life is put in jeopardy. In fact, the severity of punishment is based on the mount of force used during the crime, not on the value of the items taken.

The FBI records about 440,000 robberies a year, a rate of more than 145 per 100,000 population. As with most other violent crimes, there has been a significant reduction in the robbery rate during the past decade; the robbery rate is down almost 40 percent since 1991, when about 687,000 robberies were committed.

Robbery is considered a very serious crime because it can lead to murder. Here, a surveillance photo shows a masked gunman pointing his weapon inside the Illinois Service Federal Savings and Loan during a robbery on May 22, 2007. This robbery of the Chicago South Side bank exploded into gunfire, leaving a teller dead and two other people seriously wounded.

© AP Images/FBI-HO

The ecological pattern for robbery is similar to that of other violent crimes, with one significant exception: Northeastern states have the highest robbery rates by far. According to the NCVS, about 550,000 robberies were committed or attempted each year.

THE ARMED ROBBER

The typical armed robber is unlikely to be a professional who carefully studies targets while planning a crime. People walking along the street, convenience stores, and gas stations are much more likely robbery targets than banks or other highly secure environments. Robbers, therefore, seem to be diverted by modest defensive measures, such as having more than one clerk in a store or locating stores in strip malls; they are more likely to try an isolated store.[162]

Even though most robbers may be opportunistic rather than professional, that is not to suggest that armed robbery is a random act committed by an alcoholic or drug abuser. Marcus Felson describes robbers as foragers, predators who search for victims, preferably close to their homes, where numerous "nutritious" victims are abundant, where the robbers know the territory so that their prey cannot easily escape, and where their victims may be less vigilant because they are on their home turf.[163] Robbers, then, select targets that are *vulnerable, accessible,* and *profitable.*

One indicator is the fact that whereas most crime rates are higher in the summer, robberies seem to peak during the winter months. One reason may be that the cold weather allows for greater disguise; another reason is that robbers may be attracted to the large amounts of cash people and merchants carry during the Christmas shopping season.[164] Robbers may also be attracted to the winter because days are shorter, affording them greater concealment in the dark.

In their important book *Armed Robbers in Action: Stickups and Street Culture*, Scott Decker and Richard Wright interviewed active robbers in St. Louis, Missouri, and found that robbers are rational decision makers who look for easy prey. One ideal target is the married man who is looking for illicit sexual adventures and hires a prostitute, only to be robbed by her and her pimp. The robbers know that this victim will not be inclined to call the police and bring himself to their attention.

Because they realize that the risk of detection and punishment is the same whether the victim is carrying a load of cash or is penniless, experienced robbers use discretion in selecting targets. People whose clothing, jewelry, and demeanor mark them as carrying substantial amounts of cash make suitable targets; people who look like they can fight back are avoided. Some robbers station themselves at cash machines to spot targets who are flashing rolls of money.[165]

Wright and Decker are not the only researchers who found that most robbers seek out vulnerable victims. According to research by criminologist Jody Miller, female armed robbers are likely to choose female targets, reasoning that they will be more vulnerable and offer less resistance.[166] When robbing males, women "set them up" to catch them off guard; some feign sexual interest or prostitution to gain the upper hand.[167]

Although most robbers try to choose vulnerable victims, a small proportion prey on other criminals, most often drug dealers. Ripping off a dealer kills three birds with one stone, providing both money and drugs and, at the same time, targeting victims who are quite unlikely to call the police.[168]

Wright and Decker found that most armed robberies are motivated by a pressing need for cash. Many robbers career from one financial crisis to the next, prompted by their endless quest for stimulation and thrills. Interviewees described how they partied, gambled, drank, and abused substances until they were broke. Their partying not only provided excitement but also helped generate a street reputation as a "hip" guy who can "make things happen." Robbers had a "here and now" mentality and required a constant supply of cash to fuel their appetites.

ACQUAINTANCE ROBBERY

One type of robber may focus on people they know, a phenomenon referred to as **acquaintance robbery**. This seems puzzling, because victims can easily identify their

Fact or Fiction?

Robbers tend to look for vulnerable victims who can't fight back.

Fiction. Although most robbers look for easy prey, some like to rip off criminals, who tend to have cash and drugs on hand and who can't call the police.

acquaintance robbery
Robbery in which the victim or victims are people the robber knows.

attackers and report them to the police. However, despite this threat, acquaintance robbery may be attractive for a number of reasons:[169]

▶ Victims may be reluctant to report these crimes because they do not want to get involved with the police. They may be involved in crime themselves (drug dealers, for example), or they may fear retaliation if they report the crime. Some victims may be reluctant to gain the label of "rat" or "fink" if they go to the police.

▶ Some robberies are motivated by street justice. The robber has a grievance against the victim and settles the dispute by stealing the victim's property. In this instance, robbery may be considered a substitute for an assault—that is, the robber wants retribution and revenge rather than remuneration.[170]

▶ Because the robber knows the victim personally, the robber has inside information that there will be a "good take." Offenders may target people whom they know to be carrying a large amount of cash or who just purchased expensive jewelry.

▶ When a person in desperate need for immediate cash runs out of money, the individual may target people in close proximity simply because they are convenient targets.

When Richard Felson and his associates studied acquaintance robbery, they found that victims were more likely to be injured in acquaintance robberies than in stranger robberies, indicating that revenge rather than reward was the primary motive.[171] Similarly, robberies of family members were more likely to have a bigger pay-off than stranger robberies, an indication that the offender was aware that the target had a large amount of cash on hand. ▶ **Checkpoints**

Emerging Forms of Interpersonal Violence

Assault, rape, robbery, and murder are traditional forms of interpersonal violence. As more data has become available, criminologists have recognized relatively new subcategories of these types of crimes, such as serial murder and date rape. Additional new categories of interpersonal violence are also receiving attention in criminological literature; the next sections describe three of these forms of violent crime.

HATE CRIMES

On June 16, 2009, two Oregon men, Devan Klausegger and Gary Moss, were sent to prison for a hate crime they committed in 2008. In order to drive an African American family out of their neighborhood, the two poured a flammable liquid in the shape of a cross and the letters KKK on the front lawn of this family's residence and then used a small explosive device to start a fire on the lawn. Fortunately, a neighbor grabbed a garden hose and extinguished the fire before the victims' home could catch fire. Moss and Klausegger's acts were in violation of federal civil rights laws under the Fair Housing Act.[172]

Hate crimes, or **bias crimes**, are violent acts directed toward a particular person or members of a group merely because the targets share a discernible racial, ethnic, religious, or gender characteristic.[173] Such crimes range from desecration of a house of worship or cemetery to racially motivated murder.

Though normally associated with racially motivated attacks, hate crimes can involve convenient, vulnerable targets who are incapable of fighting back. There have been numerous reported incidents of teenagers attacking vagrants and the homeless in an effort to rid their town or neighborhood of people they consider undesirable.[174]

Another group targeted for hate crimes is gay men and women. The murder of Matthew Shepard, a gay college student who was kidnapped and beaten to death in Wyoming in 1998, was a grim reminder that gay bashing is all too common in America.[175] A 2009 national survey of gay, lesbian, and bisexual adults, conducted by psychologist Gregory Herek, found that approximately 20 percent of the sample reported having experienced a crime based on their sexual orientation; gay men were

Checkpoints

▶ Forcible rape has been known throughout history and is often linked with war and violence.

▶ Types of rape include date rape, marital rape, and statutory rape; types of rapists include serial rapists and sadists.

▶ Suspected causes of rape include male socialization, hypermasculinity, and biological determinism.

▶ Murder can involve either strangers or acquaintances. Typically, stranger murder occurs during a felony; acquaintance murder involves an interaction or interpersonal transaction between people who may be related romantically, through business dealings, or in other ways.

▶ Mass murder is the killing of numerous victims in a single outburst; serial killing involves numerous victims over an extended period of time. Spree killers attack multiple victims over a short period of time.

▶ Patterns of assault are quite similar to those for homicide.

▶ Millions of cases of child abuse and spousal abuse occur each year. There are also numerous cases of parent abuse.

▶ Robbers use force to steal. Some are opportunists looking for ready cash; others are professionals who have a long-term commitment to crime. Both types pick their targets carefully, which suggests that their crimes are calculated rather than spontaneous.

hate crimes (bias crimes)
Violent acts directed toward a particular person or members of a group merely because the targets share a discernible racial, ethnic, religious, or gender characteristic.

Hate crimes can have serious consequences, even when no bodily harm occurs. Here, on August 3, 2006, Myrna Francis sits in her vandalized home in York, Pennsylvania. Francis discovered just how much damage three gallons of deck stain can do in the hands of someone motivated by racist hatred. Someone who apparently wanted the black woman to move out of her mostly white neighborhood in the York suburbs broke into her home and did tens of thousands of dollars in damage.

significantly more likely than lesbians or bisexuals to experience violence and property crimes.[176] Exhibit 10.3 lists the factors that precipitate hate crimes.

Roots of Hate Why do people commit bias crimes? In a series of research studies, Jack McDevitt, Jack Levin, and Susan Bennett identify four motivations for hate crimes:[177]

▶ *Thrill-seeking hate crimes.* In the same way some kids like to get together to shoot hoops, hate-mongers join forces to have fun by bashing minorities or destroying property. Inflicting pain on others gives them a sadistic thrill.

▶ *Reactive (defensive)* hate crimes. Perpetrators of these crimes rationalize their behavior as a defensive stand taken against outsiders who they believe threaten their community or way of life. A gang of teens that attacks a new family in the neighborhood because they are the "wrong" race is committing a reactive hate crime.

▶ *Mission hate crimes.* Some disturbed individuals see it as their duty to rid the world of evil. Those "on a mission," such as skinheads, the Ku Klux Klan (KKK), and white supremacist groups, may seek to eliminate people who threaten their religious beliefs because they are members of a different faith, or threaten "racial purity" because they are of a different race.

▶ *Retaliatory hate crimes.* These offenses are committed in response to a hate crime either real or perceived; whether the original incident actually occurred is irrelevant. Sometimes a rumor of an incident may cause a group of offenders to exact vengeance, even if the original information was unfounded or inaccurate; the retaliatory crimes are perpetrated before anyone has had a chance to verify the accuracy of the original rumor. Attacks based on revenge tend to have the greatest potential for fueling and refueling additional hate offenses.

The research by McDevitt and his colleagues indicates that most hate crimes can be classified as thrill-motivated (66 percent), followed by defensive (25 percent) and retaliatory hate crimes (8 percent); few if any cases had mission-oriented offenders.

- Poor or uncertain economic conditions
- Racial stereotypes in films and on television
- Hate-filled discourse on talk shows or in political advertisements
- The use of racial code language, such as "welfare mothers" and "inner-city thugs"
- An individual's personal experiences with members of particular minority groups

Exhibit 10.3 Factors That Predict Hate Crimes

- Scapegoating—blaming a minority group for the misfortunes of society as a whole

SOURCE: "A Policymaker's Guide to Hate Crimes," *Bureau of Justice Assistance Monograph* (Washington, DC: Bureau of Justice Assistance, 1997).

Nature and Extent of Hate Crimes Each year the FBI now records almost 8,000 hate crime incidents—those motivated by a bias against a race, religion, disability, ethnicity, or sexual orientation—that involve about 10,000 victims and 7,000 offenders.[178] Most such incidents are motivated by race; a lesser proportion by religion (most often anti-Semitism), sexual orientation, or ethnicity; and about 1 percent by victim disability. Vandalism and property crimes were the products of hate crimes motivated by religion. However, criminals were more likely to turn to violent acts when race, ethnicity, and sexual orientation were the motivation. Most targets of hate crimes, especially the violent variety, were young white men. Similarly, the majority of known hate crime offenders were young white men.

In crimes where victims could identify the culprits, most victims reported that they were acquainted with their attackers or that their attackers were actually friends, coworkers, neighbors, or relatives.[179] Younger victims were more likely to be victimized by persons known to them. Hate crimes can occur in many settings, but most are perpetrated in public settings.

Controlling Hate Crimes Hate crime laws actually originated after the Civil War and were designed to safeguard the rights of freed slaves.[180] Today, almost every state jurisdiction has enacted some form of legislation designed to combat hate crimes. Thirty-nine states have passed laws against bias-motivated violence and intimidation; 19 states have statutes that specifically mandate the collection of hate crime data.

Some critics argue that it is unfair to punish criminals motivated by hate any more severely than those who commit similar crimes and whose motivation is revenge, greed, or anger. There is also the danger that what appears to be a hate crime, because the target is a minority group member, may actually be motivated by some other factor such as vengeance or monetary gain. Aaron McKinney, who is serving a life sentence for killing Matthew Shepard, told ABC News correspondent Elizabeth Vargas that he was high on methamphetamine when he killed Shepard, and that his intent was robbery, not hate. His partner, Russell Henderson, also claims that the killing was simply a robbery gone bad: "It was not because me and Aaron had anything against gays."[181]

However, in his important book *Punishing Hate: Bias Crimes under American Law,* Frederick Lawrence argues that criminals motivated by bias deserve to be punished more severely than those who commit identical crimes for other motives.[182] He suggests that a society dedicated to the equality of all its people must treat bias crimes differently than other crimes for several reasons.[183]

▶ Bias crimes are more likely to be violent and to involve serious physical injury to the victim.
▶ Bias crimes will have significant emotional and psychological impact on the victim; they result in a "heightened sense of vulnerability," which causes depression, anxiety, and feelings of helplessness.
▶ Bias crimes harm not only the victim but also the "target community."
▶ Bias crimes violate the shared value of equality among citizens and racial and religious harmony in a heterogeneous society.

Free Speech? Should symbolic acts of hate, such as drawing a swastika or burning a cross, be banned, or are they protected by the free speech clause of the First Amendment? The U.S. Supreme Court helped answer this question in the case of *Virginia v. Black* (2003) when it upheld a Virginia statute that makes it a felony "for any person . . ., with the intent of intimidating any person or group . . ., to burn . . . a cross on the property of another, a highway or other public place," and specifies that "[a]ny such burning . . . shall be prima facie evidence of an intent to intimidate a person or group." In its decision, the Court upheld Virginia's law, which criminalized cross burning. The Court ruled that cross burning was intertwined with the Ku Klux Klan and its reign of terror throughout the South. The Court has long held that statements in which the speaker communicates intent to commit an act of unlawful violence to a particular individual or group of individuals are not protected free speech and can be criminalized; the speaker need not actually intend to carry out the threat.[184]

WORKPLACE VIOLENCE

Workplace violence is now considered the third leading cause of occupational injury or death.[185] Who engages in workplace violence? The typical offender is a middle-aged white male who faces termination in a worsening economy. The fear of economic ruin is especially strong in agencies such as the U.S. Postal Service, where long-term employees fear job loss because of automation and reorganization. In contrast, when younger workers kill, it is usually while committing a robbery or some other felony. A number of factors precipitate workplace violence. One suspected cause is a management style that appears cold and insensitive to workers. As corporations cut their staffs because of an economic downturn or workers are summarily replaced with cost-effective technology, long-term employees may become irate and irrational; their unexpected layoff can lead to violent reactions.[186]

Not all workplace violence is triggered by management-induced injustice. In some incidents, coworkers have been killed because they refused romantic relationships with the assailants or reported them for sexual harassment. Others have been killed because they got a job the assailant coveted. Irate clients and customers have also killed because of poor service or perceived slights.[187] Hospital patients whose demands are not met may attack those people who are there to be caregivers. In fact, health care and social services workers have the highest rate of nonfatal assault injuries. Nurses are three times more likely to experience workplace violence than any other professional group.[188]

STALKING

In Wes Craven's popular movies *Scream 1–3*, the heroine Sydney (played by Neve Campbell) is stalked by a mysterious adversary who scares her half to death while killing off most of her peer group. Although obviously extreme even by Hollywood standards, the *Scream* movies focus on a newly recognized form of long-term and repeat victimization: **stalking**.[189]

A complex phenomenon, stalking can be defined as a course of conduct that is directed at a specific person and involves repeated physical or visual proximity, nonconsensual communication, or verbal, written, or implied threats sufficient to cause fear in a reasonable person.[190]

According to a leading government survey, stalking affects an estimated 1.4 million victims annually, although the actual numbers may be considerably higher.[191] One research effort estimates that 700,000 women are being stalked each year on college campuses alone.[192] Also undercounted may be juvenile stalkers who use text messages and emails, along with direct contact, to harass their victims. Some juvenile stalkers are bullies, and others are motivated by either romantic infatuation or retaliation for rejection.[193]

Although stalking usually stops within one or two years, victims experience its social and psychological consequences long afterward. About one-third seek

CONNECTIONS
Does the fact that salesclerks and police officers have the highest injury risk support routine activities theory? People in high-risk jobs who are out late at night and, in the case of salesclerks, do business in cash seem to have the greatest risk of injury on the job. See Chapter 3 for more on routine activities and crime.

workplace violence
Violence such as assault, rape, or murder committed at the workplace.

stalking
A course of conduct that is directed at a specific person and involves repeated physical or visual proximity, nonconsensual communication, or verbal, written, or implied threats sufficient to cause fear in a reasonable person.

psychological treatment, and about one-fifth lose time from work; indeed, some never return to work at all.

Even though stalking is a serious problem, research indicates that many cases are dropped by the courts despite the fact that stalkers often have extensive criminal histories and are frequently the subject of protective orders. A lenient response may be misplaced, considering that stalkers very often repeat their criminal activity within a short time after a stalking charge is lodged with police authorities.[194]

Political Violence and Terrorism

In addition to interpersonal violence, criminologists are also quite interested in the nature and extent of politically based violent acts. People who use violence to achieve political gains can be grouped into four categories:

1. *Terrorists.* Terrorism (from the Latin *terrere,* which means "to frighten") usually involves violence as a mechanism to promote change. **Terrorists** systematically murder and destroy or threaten violence to terrorize individuals, groups, communities, or governments into acceding to the terrorists' political demands.[195] Because terrorists lack large armies and formidable weapons, their use of subterfuge, secrecy, and hit-and-run tactics is designed to give them a psychological advantage and the power to neutralize the physical superiority of their opponents.

2. *Guerillas.* Spanish guerilla fighters, whose name derives from the Spanish term meaning "little war," fought against French troops after Napoleon's 1808 invasion of the Iberian Peninsula.[196] **Guerillas** are typically located in rural areas and attack military, police, and government targets in an effort to unseat or replace the existing government. Their organizations can grow quite large and eventually take the form of a conventional military force. However, guerilla fighters may also infiltrate urban areas in small bands.

3. *Insurgents.* During the Iraq war, the term **insurgents** began to be used to describe the forces opposed to American involvement. The typical goal of an insurgency is to confront the existing government in an effort to wrest away control of all or a portion of its territory, or to force political concessions in sharing political power.[197] Insurgents are typically organized into covert groups that engage in an orchestrated campaign of extreme violence that may often appear to be random and indiscriminate, causing the death of innocent civilians as well as government agents.[198]

   When insurgents use violence, it is designed to inspire support and gain converts, while at the same time destroying the government's ability to resist. It is easy to recruit supporters once the population believes that the government is incapable of fighting back. Insurgents represent a popular movement and may also seek external support from other nations to bring pressure on the government. A terror group, in contrast, neither requires nor has active support or sympathy from a large percentage of the population.

4. *Revolutionaries.* A revolution (from the Latin *revolutio,* "a revolving," and *revolvere,* "turn, roll back") is generally seen as a civil war fought between nationalists and a sovereign power that holds control of the land, or between the existing government and local groups over issues of ideology and power. Historically, the American Revolution may be considered an example of a struggle between nationalistic **revolutionaries** and an imperialistic overseas government. Classic examples of ideological rebellions include the French Revolution, which pitted the middle class and the urban poor against the aristocracy, and the Russian Revolution of 1917, during which the czarist government was toppled by the Bolsheviks. More recent ideological revolutions have occurred in China, Cuba, Nicaragua, and Chile, to name just a few.

CONTEMPORARY FORMS OF TERRORISM

Although politically inspired violence can include revolutionaries, insurgents, and guerillas, it is terrorists and terrorism that are the main focus of criminologists. We will concentrate on this form of political violence for the remainder of the chapter.

CONNECTIONS
Female students who are the victims of stalking tend to date more, go out at night to bars and parties, and live alone. Their lifestyle both brings them into contact with potential stalkers and makes them vulnerable to stalking. For more on lifestyle and victimization, go to Chapter 3.

terrorists
Individuals or groups that systematically attack or threaten violence to terrorize individuals, groups, communities, or governments into acceding to the terrorists' political demands.

guerillas
Fighters who are usually located in rural areas and attack military, police, and government targets in an effort to unseat or replace the existing government.

insurgents
Individuals or groups who confront the existing government for control of all or a portion of its territory, or to force political concessions in sharing political power.

revolutionaries
Either nationalists who struggle against a sovereign power that controls the land, or local groups that battle the existing government over issues of ideology and power.

Concept Summary 10.1 The Various Forms of Radical Political Groups

Group	Description	Example	Goals	Methods
Terrorist	Groups that engage in premeditated, politically motivated violence perpetrated against noncombatant targets	al Qaeda, Hamas	Seeks personal, criminal, or political gain or change	Small, clandestine cells that use systematic violence for purposes of intimidation
Guerilla	Armed groups operating in rural areas that attack the military, the police, and other government officials	Mao's People's Liberation Army; Ho Chi Minh's Viet Cong	Replace or overthrow existing government	Use unconventional warfare and mobile tactics. May grow large and use tactics similar to conventional military force
Insurgent	Groups that engage in armed uprising or revolt against an established civil or political authority	Iraqi insurgent groups	Win over the population by showing the government's incompetence. Force the government into political concessions and/or power sharing	May use violent (bombings and kidnappings) or nonviolent means (food distribution centers and creating schools)
Revolutionary	Engages in civil war against a sovereign power that holds control of the land	American Revolution, French Revolution, Russian Revolution	Gain independence or oust existing government or monarchy	Can use violent armed conflict, or nonviolent methods such as Ghandi used in India

Terrorist acts have been around for thousands of years. Zealots (Hebrew warrior groups) were active during the Roman occupation of Palestine during the first century C.E. A subgroup of the Zealots, the Sciari (literally translated as "daggermen"), were so named after the long curved knives they favored as a weapon to assassinate Romans or their sympathizers. The (Shi'ite) Muslim Order of the Assassins (*assassin* literally means "hashish-eater") was active in Persia, Syria, and Palestine from 1090 to 1272, killing a great number of their enemies.[199] However, the term "terrorist" first became popular during the French Revolution when it was used in reference to the Reign of Terror initiated by the revolutionary government against its political opponents. The Reign of Terror involved liberal use of the guillotine to eliminate those considered counter-revolutionaries.

Today the term "terrorism" encompasses many different behaviors and goals. Some of the more common forms are briefly described here.

Revolutionary Terrorists Revolutionary terrorists use violence to frighten those in power and their supporters in an effort to replace the existing government with a regime that holds acceptable political or religious views. Terrorist actions, such as kidnapping, assassination, and bombing, are designed to draw repressive responses from governments trying to defend themselves. These responses help revolutionaries to expose, through the skilled use of media coverage, the government's inhumane nature. The original reason for the government's harsh response may be lost as the effect of counterterrorist activities is felt by the public at large. For example, on October 12, 2002, a powerful bomb exploded in a nightclub on the Indonesian island of Bali, killing more than 180 foreign tourists. In the aftermath of the attack, the Indonesian government declared that the attack was the work of a fundamentalist Islamic group, Jemaah Islamiyah, which is a terrorist organization aligned with al Qaeda. Jemaah Islamiyah is believed to be intent on driving away foreign tourists and ruining the nation's economy so that it can usurp the government and set up a pan-Islamic nation in Indonesia and neighboring Malaysia.[200]

Political Terrorists Political terrorism is directed at people or groups who oppose the terrorists' political ideology or whom the terrorists define as "outsiders" who must be destroyed. Political terrorists may not want to replace the existing government but merely to shape it so that it accepts the terrorists' views.

U.S. political terrorists tend to be heavily armed groups organized around such themes as white supremacy, militant tax resistance, and religious revisionism. Over the nation's history, political terrorist groups have included the Aryan Covenant Church, the Aryan Nations, the New Order, and the Ku Klux Klan. Though unlikely to topple the government, the individualistic acts of terror that characterize political terrorism are difficult to predict or control. On April 19, 1995, the Oklahoma City bombing killed 168 people. This is the most severe example of political terrorism that has occurred in the United States.

Nationalist Terrorists Nationalist terrorism promotes the interests of a minority ethnic or religious group that believes it has been persecuted under majority rule and wishes to carve out its own independent homeland.

In the Middle East, terrorist activities have been linked to the Palestinians' desire to wrest their former homeland from Israel. For many years, the Palestinian Liberation Organization (PLO), led by Yasser Arafat, directed terrorist activities against Israel. Another active group, Hamas, was created in 1987 by Shaikh Ahmed Yassin and is known chiefly for suicide bombings and other attacks directed against Israeli civilians. Currently, Hamas has political control over the West Bank and the Gaza Strip and has continued to demand the destruction of Israel. In Lebanon, Iranian-backed Hezbollah is perpetuating the conflict with Israel and, in 2006, entered Israeli territory, killing a number of soldiers, capturing two, and setting off an Israeli incursion into Lebanon that left hundreds dead on both sides.

The Middle East is not the only source of nationalistic terrorism. The Chinese government has been trying to suppress separatist groups fighting for an independent state in the northwestern province of Xinjiang. The rebels are drawn from the region's Uyghur, most of whom practice Sufi Islam, speak a Turkic language, and wish to set up a Muslim state called Eastern Turkistan. During the past decade the Uyghur separatists have organized demonstrations, bombings, and political assassinations. The province has witnessed more than 200 attacks since 1990, which resulted in more than 150 deaths.[201] In Russia, Chechen terrorists have been intent on creating a free Chechen homeland and have been battling the Russian government to achieve their goal. And in Spain the ETA (Euskadi Ta Askatasuna, which means "Basque Fatherland and Liberty") uses terror tactics, including bombings and assassinations, in hopes of forming an independent Basque state in parts of northern Spain and southwestern France.

Cause-Based Terrorists Some terrorists espouse a particular social or religious cause and use violence to attract followers to their standard. They do not wish to set up their own homeland or topple a government but, rather, want to impose their social and religious code on others. The 9/11 attack on the World Trade Center in New York City is the most horrific example of cause-based terrorism in the United States to date. Similarly, antiabortion groups have demonstrated at abortion clinics, and some members have attacked clients, bombed offices, and killed doctors who perform abortions. On October 23, 1998, Dr. Barnett Slepian was shot by a sniper and killed in his Buffalo, New York, home. On June 1, 2009, Dr. George Tiller, who performed late-term abortions, was shot and killed while attending church in Wichita, Kansas. These physicians were part of a growing number of abortion providers believed to have been the victims of terrorists who ironically claim to be "pro-life."[202]

Some terrorists kill to support a cause or belief. Others show support for these killers' violent acts. A comment about the death of Dr. George Tiller is posted on a sign at the Spirit One Christian Center in Wichita, Kansas, on June 2, 2009. Tiller's alleged killer, Scott Roeder, was charged with first-degree murder in the shooting death of the abortion provider at a church in Wichita.

Environmental Terrorists There have been more than 1,500 terrorist acts committed by environmental groups during the past two decades. Radical environmentalists employ violence in an effort to slow down developers who they believe are threatening the environment or harming animals. Fires have also been set in government labs where animal research is conducted and spikes are driven into trees to prevent logging in fragile areas. One of the most active groups, the Earth Liberation Front (ELF), has conducted numerous operations in the United States and abroad. ELF claims that on March 2, 2008, it burned a row of luxury homes in Seattle, causing $7 million in damage. The multimillion-dollar homes had used green technology, but the development had attracted opposition because of fear that its septic systems could damage critical wetlands needed to protect an aquifer used by about 20,000 people in the area and could harm streams used by chinook salmon. Hence the attack. [203]

State-Sponsored Terrorists As you may recall from Chapter 8, state-sponsored political crime can involve violence when a repressive government regime forces its citizens into obedience, oppresses minorities, and stifles political dissent. **Death squads** and the use of government troops to destroy political opposition parties are often associated with Latin American political terrorism. Political prisoners are now being tortured in about 100 countries; people have disappeared or are being held in secret detention in about 20 countries; and government-sponsored death squads have been operating in more than 35 countries. Countries known for encouraging violent control of dissidents include Brazil, Colombia, Guatemala, Honduras, Peru, Iraq, and the Sudan.

Criminal Terrorists During the past decade, organized crime has become a major revenue source for terrorist groups worldwide. Criminal and terrorist groups appear to be learning from one another and adapting to each other's successes and failures. Sometimes terrorist groups become involved in common-law crimes such as drug dealing and kidnapping, even selling nuclear materials. Others form partnerships with crime groups for their mutual benefit. The Revolutionary Armed Forces of Colombia (FARC) has reportedly entered into alliances with criminal groups outside of Colombia, including Mexican drug traffickers, sending cocaine to Mexico in return for arms shipments.[204]

According to terrorism expert Chris Dishman, these illegal activities may on occasion become so profitable that they replace the group's original focus. Burmese insurgents continue to actively cultivate, refine, and traffic opium and heroin out of the Golden Triangle—the border shared by Myanmar (Burma), Thailand, and Laos—and some have even moved into the methamphetamine market.

In some instances, the line between being a terrorist organization with political support and vast resources and being an organized criminal group engaging in illicit activities for profit becomes blurred. What appears to be a politically motivated action, such as the kidnapping of a government official for ransom, may turn out to be a for-profit crime.[205]

WHAT MOTIVATES TERRORISTS AND TERRORISM?

In the aftermath of the September 11, 2001, destruction of the World Trade Center in New York City, many Americans asked themselves the same simple question: Why? What could motivate someone like Osama bin Laden to order the deaths of thousands of innocent people? How could someone who had never been to the United States or suffered personally at its hands develop such lethal hatred?

Psychological Disturbance One view is that terrorists are emotionally disturbed individuals who act out their psychosis within the confines of violent groups. According to this view, "terrorist" violence is not so much a political instrument as an end in itself; it is the result of compulsion or psychopathology. Terrorists do what they do because of a variety of emotional problems, including but not limited to self-destructive urges, disturbed emotions combined with problems with authority, and inconsistent and troubled parenting.[206] Appealing as it is, the psychological view is not universally accepted. After carefully reviewing existing evidence on the psychological state of terrorists, mental health expert Randy Borum concludes that

▶ Mental illness is not a critical factor in explaining terrorist behavior. Also, most terrorists are not "psychopaths."
▶ There is no "terrorist personality," nor is there any accurate profile— psychological or otherwise—of the terrorist.
▶ Histories of childhood abuse and trauma and themes of perceived injustice and humiliation often are prominent in terrorist biographies, but they do not really help to explain terrorism.[207]

death squads
Use of government troops to destroy political opposition parties.

The most recent case in which actual treason has been charged involves a 28-year-old California man, Adam Gadahn, also known as Azzam the American, who was indicted in 2006 for making a series of propaganda videotapes for al Qaeda, including one in which he praised the 9/11 hijackers and referred to the United States as "enemy soil."

Gadahn was raised in a counterculture atmosphere on a rural farm with his father, Philip Pearlstein, the son of a well-known Jewish doctor, and his mother, Jennifer, a computer whiz from Pennsylvania. His parents were self-sufficient and raised their son in a cabin with no running water; they produced their own electricity from solar panels. They hoped that by living in isolation and austerity, they could avoid the chaotic and destructive elements of contemporary society. Adam Gadahn became heavily involved in the death metal culture, but still feeling empty and alienated, he began studying Islam at age 17, at the Islamic Society of Orange County. He later moved to Pakistan and married an Afghan woman.

Gadahn appeared in a series of videotaped segments that were broadcast between October 2004 and September 11, 2006. In the first tape, Gadahn is shown wearing black sunglasses and a headdress wrapped around his face. He identified himself as Azzam the American and announced his relationship with al Qaeda. "The streets of America shall run red with blood," he claimed. In a broadcast in 2005, around the fourth anniversary of the 9/11 attacks, Gadahn called the attacks "blessed raids" and discussed the "jihad against America." In 2006, Gadahn appeared in a videotape that also contained statements from Osama bin Laden and Ayman al-Zawahiri and then made another propaganda broadcast aired on the fifth anniversary of 9/11. On May 29, 2007, Gadahn again made headlines when he issued another video that listed the following six actions that America must take in order to prevent future terrorist attacks.

- "Pull every last one of your soldiers, spies, security advisers, trainers, attachés . . . out of every Muslim land from Afghanistan to Zanzibar. . . . "
- End "all support and aid, military, political, economic, or otherwise, to the 56-plus apostate regimes of the Muslim world, and abandon them to their well-deserved fate."
- "End all support, moral, military, economic, political, or otherwise, to the bastard state of Israel, and ban your citizens, Zionist Jews, Zionist Christians, and the rest from traveling to occupied Palestine or settling there. Even one penny of aid will be considered sufficient justification to continue the fight."
- Leave all Muslims alone.

Adam Gadahn, also known as Azzam al-Amriki, is an American who grew up in southern California. He later converted to Islam and joined al Qaeda.

- Impose a blanket ban on all broadcasts to our region.
- Free all Muslim captives from your prisons, detention facilities, and concentration camps, regardless of whether they have been recipients of what you call a fair trial or not.

Gadahn warned, "Your failure to meet our demands . . . means that you and your people will, Allah willing, experience things which will make you forget about the horrors of September 11. This is not a call for negotiations. We do not negotiate with baby killers and war criminals like you." Gadahn also warned George Bush, "You will go down in history not only as the president who embroiled his nation in a series of unwinnable and bloody conflicts in the Islamic world but [also] as the president who set the United States upon its death march."

Gadahn is the first person to have been charged with treason against the United States in almost 50 years.

SOURCES: Craig Whitlock, "Converts to Islam Move Up in Cells, Arrests in Europe Illuminate Shift," *Washington Post* Foreign Service, September 15, 2007, p. A10, www.washingtonpost .com/wp-dyn/content/article/2007/09/14/AR2007091402265 .html?hpid=topnews; Federal Bureau of Investigation, "American Charged with Treason October 11, 2006," www.fbi.gov/page2/ oct2006/gadahn101106.htm (accessed January 18, 2008), video on Myzine.com, www.myzine.com/play.php?pid=10094; Raffi Khatchadourian, "Azzam the American: The Making of an Al Qaeda Homegrown," *The New Yorker*, January 22, 2007, www.newyorker .com/reporting/2007/01/22/070122fa_fact_khatchadourian.

The state legislature has asked you to prepare a report on statutory rape because of the growing number of underage girls who have been impregnated by adult men. Studies reveal that many teenage pregnancies result from affairs that underage girls have with older men, with age gaps ranging from 7 to 10 years. For example, the typical relationship prosecuted in California involves a 13-year-old girl and a 22-year-old male partner. Some outraged parents adamantly support a law that will provide state grants to counties to prosecute statutory rape. These grants would allow more vigorous enforcement of the law and could result in the conviction of more than 1,500 offenders each year.

However, some critics suggest that implementing statutory rape laws to punish males who have relationships with minor girls does not solve the problems of teenage pregnancies and out-of-wedlock births. Liberals dislike the idea of using criminal law to solve social problems, because doing so does not provide for the girls and their young children and focuses only on punishing offenders. In contrast, conservatives fear that such laws give the state power to prosecute people for victimless crimes, thereby increasing the government's ability to control people's private lives. Not all cases involve much older men, and critics ask whether we should criminalize the behavior of 17-year-old boys and their 15-year-old girlfriends.

Writing Assignment

Write an essay on statutory rape and how different states address sex with minors. Decide whether current laws should be changed to reflect current social behaviors.

Alienation Some experts believe that a lack of economic opportunity and recessionary economies are positively correlated with terrorism.[208] Because they are out of the political and social mainstream, young men and women are motivated to join violent political groups. Suffering alienation, they lack the tools to compete in a post-technological society. Many are relatively "ordinary" people who, alienated from modern society, believe that a suicide mission will cleanse them of the corruption of the modern world.[209]

Indoctrination into Extremism Another view is that terrorists hold extreme ideological beliefs that prompt their behavior (see the accompanying Profiles in Crime feature). Many have been educated in religious schools run by strong leaders who demand strict loyalty from their followers while indoctrinating them in political causes. This pattern is common among terror groups in Southeast Asia, where teachers command strong personal loyalty from their students. Once indoctrinated, the potential terrorists rely on the wisdom and experience of their leader/instructor. When he calls them to jihad, they are likely to follow, even if it means killing those who deny their faith or beliefs.[210]

Explaining State Terrorism How can state-sponsored terrorism be explained? After all, these violent acts are not directed at a foreign government or overseas adversaries but against natives of one's own country. In her book *Reigns of Terror*, Patricia Marchak finds that people willing to kill or maim their fellow countrymen are likely to be highly susceptible to unquestioning submission to authority. They are conformists who want to be part of the central group and who are quite willing to be part of a state regime. They are vulnerable to ideology that dehumanizes their targets and can utilize propaganda to distance themselves psychologically from those they are terrorizing.[211] Because the enemies of the state are considered traitors or agents of a foreign power, their status as fellow countrymen is neutralized and their death is warranted.

▶ Hate crimes are violent acts against targets selected because of their religion, race, ethnic background, gender, or sexual orientation.

▶ Some hate criminals are thrill seekers; others are motivated by hatred of outsiders; still others believe they are on a mission. More than 10,000 people are the targets of hate crimes each year in the United States.

▶ Workplace violence has become commonplace. It is believed to be related to a number of factors, including job stress and insensitive management style.

▶ Political crimes are committed when people believe that violence is the only means available to produce political change.

▶ Revolutionary terrorists seek to overthrow those in power; political terrorists oppose government policies; nationalist terrorists are minority group members who want to carve out a homeland; cause-based terrorists use violence to address their grievances; environmental terrorists aim at frightening off developers; state-sponsored terrorism is aimed at political dissenters or minority groups; criminal terrorists are more concerned with making profits from their cause than achieving some political purpose.

▶ The USA PATRIOT Act was passed to allow law enforcement agencies greater latitude in fighting terrorism.

USA PATRIOT Act (USAPA)

An act that gives sweeping new powers to domestic law enforcement and international intelligence agencies in an effort to fight terrorism, to expand the definition of terrorist activities, and to alter sanctions for violent terrorism.

RESPONSES TO POLITICAL VIOLENCE AND TERRORISM

In the wake of the 9/11 attacks, Congress moved quickly to pass the **USA PATRIOT Act (USAPA)**,[212] giving law enforcement agencies a freer hand to investigate and apprehend suspected terrorists. The bill, which is more than 340 pages long, created new laws and made changes to more than 15 existing statutes. Its aim was to give sweeping new powers to domestic law enforcement and international intelligence agencies in an effort to fight terrorism, to expand the definition of terrorist activities, and to alter sanctions for violent terrorism. Among its provisions, USAPA expands all four traditional tools of surveillance—wiretaps, search warrants, pen/trap orders (installing devices that record phone calls), and subpoenas. In addition, a director of national intelligence (DNI) was created and charged with coordinating data from the nation's primary intelligence-gathering agencies. The DNI serves as the principal intelligence adviser to the president and as the statutory intelligence adviser to the National Security Council.

Among the agencies reporting to the DNI are the National Counterterrorism Center (NCTC), which is staffed by terrorism experts from the CIA, the FBI, and the Pentagon; the Privacy and Civil Liberties Board; and the National Counterproliferation Center. The NCTC serves as the primary organization in the United States government for analyzing and integrating all intelligence possessed or acquired by the government pertaining to terrorism and counterterrorism, except for purely domestic counterterrorism information.

The FBI has announced a reformulation of its priorities, making protecting the United States from terrorist attack its number one commitment. It is now charged with coordinating intelligence collection with the Border Patrol, the Secret Service, and the CIA. The FBI must also work with and share intelligence with the National Counterterrorism Center (NCTC).

In addition to the FBI, the Department of Homeland Security (DHS) has been assigned the following mission:

▶ Prevent terrorist attacks within the United States.
▶ Reduce America's vulnerability to terrorism.
▶ Minimize the damage and recovery from attacks that do occur.

The DHS now has five independent branches:

1. Border and Transportation Security (BTS) is responsible for maintaining the security of our nation's borders and transportation systems.
2. Emergency Preparedness and Response (EPR) ensures that our nation is prepared for, and able to recover from, terrorist attacks and natural disasters.
3. Science and Technology (S&T) coordinates efforts in research and development, including preparing for and responding to the full range of terrorist threats involving weapons of mass destruction.
4. Information Analysis and Infrastructure Protection (IAIP) joins "under one roof" the capabilities to identify and assess intelligence information about threats to the homeland, to issue timely warnings, and to take appropriate preventive and protective action.
5. Management is responsible for budget, management, and personnel issues in the DHS.

The DHS's task is formidable, considering this country's large and porous border. In *Nuclear Terrorism* (2004), Graham Allison, an expert on nuclear weapons and national security, describes the almost superhuman effort it would take to seal the nation's borders from nuclear attack. Every day, 30,000 trucks, 6,500 rail cars, and 140 ships deliver more than 50,000 cargo containers to the United States. Fewer than 5 percent ever get screened, and those that do undergo nonphysical inspections that might not detect nuclear weapons or fissile material.[213] ▶ **Checkpoints**

Summary

1. Be familiar with the various causes of violent crime.

   Research has shown that a significant number of people involved in violent episodes may be suffering from severe mental abnormalities. Absent or deviant parents, inconsistent discipline, physical abuse, and lack of supervision have all been linked to persistent violent offending. A number of criminologists have speculated that instinctual violence-promoting traits may be common in the human species. Kids who are constantly exposed to violence at home, at school, or in the environment may adopt violent methods themselves. Substance abuse has been associated with violence on both the individual and social levels. Although firearm availability alone does not cause violence, it may be a facilitating factor. Furthermore, some areas contain an independent subculture of violence in which a potent theme of violence influences lifestyles, the socialization process, and interpersonal relationships. And some nations have cultures that support relatively high violence rates.

2. Define rape and be familiar with why men commit rape.

   The common-law definition of rape is "the carnal knowledge of a female forcibly and against her will." One explanation for rape focuses on the evolutionary, biological aspects of the male sexual drive. Some researchers argue that rape is a function of socialization. Rapists may suffer from some type of personality disorder or mental illness. Men may learn to commit rapes much as they learn any other behavior. Rape arises primarily from a desire to inflict pain and humiliation, but there is evidence that at least some rapists have sexual feelings for their victim.

3. Discuss the issues involving rape and the law.

   Proving guilt in a rape case is extremely challenging for prosecutors. It is essential to prove that the attack was forced and that the victim did not give voluntary consent to her attacker. Shield laws that protect women from being questioned about their sexual history unless it directly bears on the case have become universal.

4. Recognize that there are different types of murder.

   First-degree murder occurs when a person kills another after premeditation and deliberation. Second-degree murder is the charge when the killer had malice aforethought but not premeditation or deliberation. Voluntary or nonnegligent manslaughter is a killing committed in the heat of passion or during a sudden quarrel that provoked violence. Involuntary or negligent manslaughter is a killing that occurs when a person's acts are negligent and without regard for the harm they may cause others. Serial killers murder three or more persons in three or more separate events. Mass murder involves the killing of four or more victims by one or a few assailants within a single event. Spree killers engage in a rampage of violence over a period of days or weeks.

5. Understand the nature and patterns of robbery.

   The common-law definition of robbery is "the taking or attempting to take anything of value from the care, custody, or control of a person or persons by force or threat of force or violence and/or by putting the victim in fear. Some robbers are opportunists looking for ready cash; others are professionals who have a long-term commitment to crime. The typical armed robber is a rational decision maker. Many robbers choose victims who themselves are involved in illegal behavior, most often drug dealers. Female armed robbers are likely to choose female targets, reasoning that women will be more vulnerable and offer less resistance.

6. Be able to discuss newly emerging forms of violence, such as stalking, hate crimes, and workplace violence.

   Hate crimes, or bias crimes, are violent acts directed toward a particular person or members of a particular group merely because the targets share a discernible racial, ethnic, religious, or gender characteristic. Workplace violence is now considered the third leading cause of occupational injury or death. Stalking can be defined as conduct that is directed at a specific person and involves repeated physical or visual proximity, nonconsensual communication, and/or verbal, written, or implied threats sufficient to cause fear in a reasonable person.

7. Distinguish among terrorists, guerillas, insurgents, and revolutionaries.

   Terrorists engage in the illegal use of force against innocent people in an effort to achieve a political objective. The term "guerilla" refers to antigovernment forces located in rural areas that attack the military, the police, and government officials. The typical goal of insurgents is to confront the existing government for control of all or a portion of its territory, or to force political concessions in sharing political power. Revolutionaries wage a civil war between nationalists and a sovereign power that controls the land, or between the existing government and local groups over issues of ideology and power.

8. Distinguish among the different forms that terrorism takes.

   Revolutionary terrorists use violence to replace the existing government with a regime that holds acceptable political or religious views. Political terrorism is directed at people or groups who oppose the terrorists' political ideology. Nationalist terrorism promotes the interests of a minority ethnic or religious group that believes it has been persecuted under majority rule. Retributive terrorists want to impose their social and religious code on others. Al Qaeda is essentially a retributive terror organization. State-sponsored terrorism occurs when a repressive government regime forces its citizens into obedience, oppresses minorities, and stifles political dissent. Environmental terrorists employ violence in an effort to slow down developers who they believe are threatening the environment or harming animals. Criminal terrorist groups become involved in common-law crimes such as drug dealing and kidnapping.

9. Discuss the motivations of terrorists.

There is no single personality trait or behavior pattern that distinguishes the majority of terrorists. Some young men and women who join terror groups are alienated because they lack the tools to compete in a post-technological society. Some hold extreme ideological beliefs and have been indoctrinated in religious schools. People who engage in state-sponsored terrorism are highly susceptible to unquestioning submission to authority.

10. Know about the various agencies that have been created or modified to fight terrorism and other forms of political violence.

The Office of the Director of National Intelligence (DNI) is charged with coordinating data from the nation's primary intelligence-gathering agencies. The National Counterterrorism Center (NCTC) is responsible for analyzing and integrating all intelligence. The FBI has announced a reformulation of its priorities, making protecting the United States from terrorist attack its number one commitment. The Department of Homeland Security (DHS) is the federal agency responsible for preventing terrorist attacks within the United States.

Key Terms

expressive violence 254
instrumental violence 254
eros 256
thanatos 256
psychopharmacological relationship 256
economic compulsive behavior 256
systemic link 256
subculture of violence 257
rape 259
date rape 261
marital exemption 262
statutory rape 262

virility mystique 262
narcissistic personality disorder 263
aggravated rape 263
consent 264
shield laws 265
murder 265
first-degree murder 265
premeditation 265
deliberation 265
felony murder 266
second-degree murder 266
manslaughter 266

voluntary or nonnegligent manslaughter 266
involuntary or negligent manslaughter 266
infanticide 267
filicide 267
eldercide 267
serial killer 270
mass murder 271
spree killer 271
battery 272
assault 272
road rage 272
child abuse 273
neglect 273

child sexual abuse 273
robbery 275
acquaintance robbery 276
hate crimes (bias crimes) 277
workplace violence 280
stalking 280
terrorists 281
guerillas 281
insurgents 281
revolutionaries 281
death squads 285
USA PATRIOT Act (USAPA) 288

Critical Thinking Questions

1. Should the perpetrators of different types of rape receive different legal sanctions? For example, should someone who rapes a stranger be punished more severely than someone who is convicted of marital rape or date rape? If your answer is yes, do you think someone who kills a stranger should be punished more severely than someone who kills a spouse or a friend?

2. Is there a subculture of violence in your home city or town? If so, how would you describe the environment and values of that subculture?

3. There have been significant changes in rape law involving issues such as corroboration and shield laws. What other measures would you take to protect victims of rape when they have to testify in court?

4. Should hate crimes be punished more severely than crimes motivated by greed, anger, or revenge? Why should crimes be distinguished in terms of the motivations of the perpetrator? Is hate a more heinous motivation than revenge?

5. In light of the 9/11 attacks, should acts of terrorism be treated differently than other common-law violent crimes? For example, should terrorists be executed for attempting to commit violence even if no one is killed during their attack?

CRIME ALERT
LOS ANGELES POLICE DEPARTMENT
OFFICIAL PUBLICATION OF COMMERCIAL CRIMES DIVISION

$1 MILLION REWARD
STOLEN ART

Between September 2-3, 2009, a burglary occurred at a home along Angel[...] Drive in West L.A. Valuable art by Andy Warhol was removed from the walls. A $1 million reward is being offered for information leading to the recovery of th[...] paintings. NOTE: other Warhol originals exist for each of the images below, bu[...] with different colors.

Muhammad Ali

Chris Evert

Tom Seaver

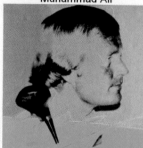

Jack Nicklaus

OJ Simpson

Kareem Abdul Jabbar

Pele

Willie Shoemaker

Dorothy Hamill

Rod Gilbert

Richard L. Weisman

Property Crimes

When William M. V. Kingsland died in 2006, New York City papers printed glowing obituaries describing him as an urbane upper-class gentleman, an intellectual, and an art expert.[1] His apartment was found to contain a vast and impressive collection of more than 300 works of art—paintings, sketches, sculptures, and other pieces by such artists as Pablo Picasso, John Singleton Copley, Alberto Giacometti, Giorgio Morandi, and Eugene Boudin. Because he named no heirs, New York's Public Administrator's office hired two auction houses—Christie's and Stair Galleries—to sell the art. One of his works, a Giacometti, was valued at $900,000 to $1.2 million, and a small painting by Giorgio Morandi would fetch about $600,000. There was a hitch, though. As Christie's researched the art to determine its provenance (history of ownership), the famed auction house discovered that many of the works had been reported stolen in the 1960s and 1970s. Upon further investigation, it turned out that the sophisticated Mr. Kingsland was actually born Melvyn Kohn, and that—contrary to his claims—he grew up in a small apartment rather than a manor house, did not attend either Groton or Harvard, and was never actually married to a member of the French royalty.

Kingsland, it turns out, was an art thief, and authorities have been trying for three years to figure out what was stolen and who the legitimate owners are. When a 1790 Copley portrait of the Second Earl of Bessborough was sold to an art dealer for $85,000, they soon found that it had been stolen in 1971 from the Fogg Art Museum at Harvard. The case had one more bizarre turn: A mover hired by New York's Public Administrator's Office to transport Kingsland's collection to a warehouse was charged with stealing two Picasso sketches, each valued at approximately $30,000. And moreover, it was not the first time those two sketches had been stolen: Before they ended up in Kingsland's collection, they had been filched from a New York art gallery![2]

Fact or Fiction?

▶ Professional theft gangs began in the American West during the nineteenth century.

▶ Most theft offenses are committed by trained professionals who know what they are doing and escape detection.

▶ Professional thieves tend to be specialists who apply their skills to a particular criminal act.

▶ To be convicted of larceny, you have to have taken the possession(s) of another person.

▶ Store owners are protected from lawsuits if they mistakenly arrest someone who they think has shoplifted.

▶ Once your home has been burgled you are safe from those thieves because they have already taken everything they think is valuable.

Chapter Objectives

1. Be familiar with the history of theft offenses.

2. Recognize the differences between professional and amateur thieves.

3. Know the similarities and differences between petty and grand larceny.

4. Understand the various forms of shoplifting.

5. Differentiate between fraud and embezzlement.

6. Compare the activities of professional and amateur car thieves.

7. Understand what it means to burgle a home.

8. Know what it takes to be a "good burglar."

9. Distinguish between the activities of male and female burglars.

10. Discuss why people commit arson for profit.

Even though professional art theft is relatively rare, each year millions of people suffer billions in losses to some form of theft. As a group, these theft offenses can be defined as acts that violate criminal law and are designed to bring financial reward to an offender. The range and scope of U.S. criminal activity motivated by the desire for financial gain are tremendous. Self-report studies show that property crime is widespread among the young in every social class. The National Crime Victimization Survey (NCVS) indicates that about 16 million personal and household thefts now occur annually.[3]

This chapter begins with some background information on the history and nature of theft as a crime. It then discusses larceny/theft and related offenses, including shoplifting, check forgery, credit card theft, and auto theft. There follows a discussion of other common theft crimes, including fraud, confidence games, receiving stolen property, and embezzlement. Next the discussion turns to a more serious form of theft, burglary, which involves forcible entry into a person's home or workplace for the purpose of theft. Finally, the crime of arson is discussed briefly. Chapter 12 is then devoted to white-collar crimes, cyber crimes, and economic crimes that involve criminal enterprise on an organized scale.

History of Theft

Theft is not unique to modern times; the theft of personal property has been known throughout recorded history. The Crusades of the eleventh century inspired peasants and downtrodden noblemen to leave the shelter of their estates to prey upon passing pilgrims.[4] Crusaders felt it was within their rights to appropriate the possessions of any infidels—Greeks, Jews, or Muslims—they happened to encounter during their travels. By the thirteenth century, returning pilgrims, not content to live as serfs on feudal estates, gathered in the forests of England and the Continent to poach game that was the rightful property of their lord or king and, when possible, to steal from passing strangers. By the fourteenth century, many such highwaymen and poachers were full-time thieves, stealing great numbers of cattle and sheep and terrorizing the countryside.[5]

The fifteenth and sixteenth centuries brought hostilities between England and France in the Hundred Years' War. Foreign mercenary troops fighting for both sides roamed the countryside; loot and pillage were viewed as a rightful part of their pay. As cities developed and a permanent class of propertyless urban poor came into being, theft became more professional.[6] By the eighteenth century, three separate groups of property criminals were active:

▶ *Skilled thieves* typically worked in the larger cities, such as London and Paris. This group included pickpockets, forgers, and counterfeiters, who operated freely. They congregated in "flash houses"— public meeting places, often taverns, that served as headquarters for gangs. Here deals were made, crimes were plotted, and the sale of stolen goods was negotiated.[7]

▶ *Smugglers* moved freely in sparsely populated areas and transported goods, such as spirits, gems, gold, and spices, without paying tax or duty.

▶ *Poachers* typically lived in the country and supplemented their diet and income with game that belonged to a landlord.

Property crimes have a long history. This painting illustrates fourteenth-century thieves plundering a home in Paris.

Roy 20 CVIII 41v British Library/Bridgeman Art Library

By the eighteenth century, professional thieves in the larger cities had banded to-gether into gangs to protect themselves, increase the scope of their activities, and help dispose of stolen goods. Jack Wild, perhaps London's most famous thief, perfected the process of buying and selling stolen goods and gave himself the title "Thief Taker General of Great Britain and Ireland." Before he was hanged, Wild controlled numer-ous gangs and dealt harshly with any thief who violated his strict code of conduct.[8] During this period, individual theft-related crimes began to be defined by common law. The most important of these categories are still used today.

Contemporary Thieves

Of the millions of property- and theft-related crimes that occur each year, most are committed by **occasional criminals** who do not define themselves by a criminal role or view themselves as committed career criminals. Other thefts are committed by skilled professional criminals.

OCCASIONAL THIEVES

Criminologists suspect that most economic crimes are the work of amateur occasional criminals, whose decision to steal is spontaneous and whose acts are unskilled, un-planned, and haphazard. Millions of thefts occur each year, and most are not re-ported to police agencies. Many of these theft offenses are committed by school-age youths who are unlikely to enter criminal careers and who drift between conven-tional and criminal behavior. Added to the pool of amateur thieves are the millions of adults whose behavior may occasionally violate the law—shoplifters, pilferers, tax cheats—but whose main source of income is conventional and whose self-identity is noncriminal. Added together, their behaviors form the bulk of theft crimes.

Occasional property crime occurs when there is an opportunity, or **situational inducement,** to commit crime.[9] Members of the upper class have the opportunity to engage in lucrative business-related crimes such as price-fixing, bribery, and em-bezzlement; lower-class individuals, lacking such opportunities, are overrepresented in street crime. Situational inducements are short-term influences on a person's be-havior that increase risk taking. They include psychological factors, such as financial problems, and social factors, such as peer pressure.

Occasional criminals may deny their criminality and instead view their transgres-sions as out of character. For example, they were only "borrowing" the car the police caught them with; they were going to pay for the merchandise they stole from the store—eventually. Because of their lack of commitment to a criminal lifestyle, occa-sional offenders may be the most likely to respond to the general deterrent effect of the law.

PROFESSIONAL THIEVES

Professional criminals make a significant portion of their income from crime. Pro-fessionals do not delude themselves with the belief that their acts are impulsive, one-time efforts, nor do they use elaborate rationalizations to excuse the harmfulness of their actions ("Shoplifting doesn't really hurt anyone"). Consequently, professionals pursue their craft with vigor, attempting to learn from older, experienced criminals the techniques that will enable them to "earn" the most money with the least risk. Although they are relatively few in number, professionals engage in crimes that in-flict the greater losses on society and perhaps cause the more significant social harm.

Professional theft consists of nonviolent forms of criminal behavior that are un-dertaken with a high degree of skill for monetary gain and that maximize financial opportunities and minimize the odds of apprehension. The most important categories have remained the same since they were classified many decades ago. They include pocket picking, burglary, shoplifting, forgery, counterfeiting, extortion, sneak theft, and confidence swindling (see Exhibit 11.1).[10]

Fact or Fiction?

Most theft offenses are committed by trained professionals who know what they are doing and escape detection.

Fiction. Most theft is the work of amateurs whose acts are spontaneous and unskilled.

occasional criminals
Offenders who do not define themselves by a criminal role or view themselves as committed career criminals.

situational inducement
Short-term influence on a person's behavior, such as financial problems or peer pressure, which increases risk taking.

professional criminals
Offenders who make a significant portion of their income from crime.

Exhibit 11.1 Categories of Professional Theft

- Pickpocket (cannon)
- Thief in rackets related to confidence games
- Forger
- Extortionist from those engaging in illegal acts (shakedown artist)

- Confidence game artist (con artist)
- Thief who steals from hotel rooms (hotel prowl)
- Jewel thief who substitutes fake gems for real ones (pennyweighter)
- Shoplifter (booster)
- Sneak thief from stores, banks, and offices (heel)

SOURCE: Edwin Sutherland and Chic Conwell, *The Professional Thief* (Chicago: University of Chicago Press, 1937).

Checkpoints

▶ Theft offenses have been common throughout recorded history.

▶ During the Middle Ages, poachers stole game, smugglers avoided taxes, and thieves worked as pickpockets and forgers.

▶ Occasional thieves are opportunistic amateurs who steal because of situational inducements.

▶ Professional thieves learn their trade and develop skills that help them avoid capture.

Fact or Fiction?

Professional thieves tend to be specialists who apply their skills to a particular criminal act.

Fact. Professionals tend to specialize in a particular crime, such as auto theft, stealing cargo, safecracking, or shoplifting.

larceny
Taking for one's own use the property of another, by means other than force or threats on the victim or forcibly breaking into a person's home or workplace; theft.

constructive possession
A legal fiction that applies to situations in which persons voluntarily give up physical custody of their property but still retain legal ownership.

Cargo Thieves Some professionals work in highly organized groups, targeting specific items and employing "specialists" who bring different sets of criminal skills to the table. Take professional cargo thieves whose base of operations is in truck yards, hubs for commercial freight carriers, airports, and port cities. These professionals prey upon the huge fleet of cargo ships, planes, and trucks that bring in a daily array of valuable cargoes. While other thieves target cash and jewels, these professionals make off with frozen shrimp, clothing, and electronic goods. There criminal activities cost the public somewhere between $15 billion and $30 billion a year. Cargo thieves use sophisticated operations with well-organized hierarchies of leadership. They employ specialists who carry out a variety of takes, including thieves and brokers, or fences, who help unload the stolen goods on the black market. "Lumpers" physically move the goods and work with drivers in transporting the stolen merchandise from the docks. Gangs usually employ a specialist who is an expert at foiling the antitheft locks on truck trailers. Cargo thieves heist whole truckloads of merchandise—the average freight on a trailer can be valued at up to $3 million.[11] ▶ **Checkpoints**

Larceny/Theft

Theft, or **larceny** (from *latrocinium*, Latin for "theft," and *latio*, "robber"), was one of the earliest common-law crimes created by English judges to define acts in which one person took for his or her own use the property of another.[12] According to common law, larceny was defined as "the trespassory taking and carrying away of the personal property of another with intent to steal."[13]

As originally construed, larceny involved taking property that was in the possession of the rightful owner. It would have been considered larceny for someone to sneak into a farmer's field and steal a cow. Thus, the original common-law definition required a "trespass in the taking"; that is, for an act to be considered larceny, goods had to have been taken from the physical possession of the rightful owner. In creating this definition of larceny, English judges were more concerned with disturbance of the peace than with theft itself. They reasoned that if someone tried to steal property from another's possession, the act could eventually lead to a physical confrontation and—possibly—to the death of one party or the other. Consequently, the original definition of larceny did not include the misappropriation of goods by trickery or deceit.

The definition of larceny evolved with the growth of manufacturing and the development of the free enterprise system. Because commercial enterprise often requires that property be entrusted to a second party, larceny evolved to include the misappropriation of goods that had come into a person's possession through legitimate means. For example, the commercial system would grind to a halt if people who were given merchandise to sell or transport could not be held liable for keeping the merchandise for their own use.

To get around the element of "trespass in the taking," English judges created the concept of **constructive possession**. This legal fiction applies to situations in which persons voluntarily give up temporary custody of their property but still believe that the property is legally theirs. If a person gives a jeweler her watch for repair, she still believes she owns the watch, in spite of the fact that she has handed it over to the jeweler. If the jeweler kept the watch or sold it, she would be guilty of larceny even though she did not "take" the watch; rather, it was given to her on a temporary basis. Similarly, when a person misplaces his wallet and someone else finds it and keeps it (even though identification of the owner can be plainly seen), the concept of constructive possession makes the person who has kept the wallet guilty of larceny. Thus, over the years, new forms of larceny have been created, including shoplifting, fraud, and auto theft.

Today, self-report studies indicate that a significant number of youths have engaged in theft. The FBI records more than 6 million acts of larceny annually, a rate of almost 2,200 per 100,000 persons. Larceny rates declined more than 20 percent between 1995 and 2008.[14] According to the NCVS, more than 12 million thefts occur each year. And like the UCR, the victim survey indicates that a steep decline (more than 33 percent) has occurred in the number and rate of larcenies during the past decade.[15]

COMMON LARCENY/THEFT OFFENSES

Most U.S. state criminal codes separate larceny into **petit** (or **petty**) **larceny** and **grand larceny**. The former involves small amounts of money or property and is punished as a misdemeanor. Grand larceny, involving merchandise of greater value, is a felony punished by a sentence to serve time in the state prison. Each state sets its own boundary between grand larceny and petty larceny, but $100 to $500 is not unusual. For example, in the Virginia Criminal Code, the main distinction between petit and grand larceny is the value of the item taken: Larceny of an item with a value of $200 or more is considered grand larceny, whereas taking something with a value of less than $200 is considered petit larceny. How the larceny is committed may also affect its definition: Stealing money or property worth $5 or more directly from a person is considered grand larceny, and taking a firearm from a home or car is automatically considered grand larceny. (The accompanying Profiles in Crime feature discusses one case—though hardly a typical example—of grand larceny.) In contrast, theft from the person of money or property with a value of less than $5 is petit larceny.[16]

How larceny is categorized can have a significant influence on the level of punishment. In Virginia, grand larceny is a felony with a specific punishment of not less than 1 year and not more than 20 years in prison, or, at the discretion of the jury (or judge) making the decision, it can also be punished with a jail sentence of not more than 12 months and/or a fine not to exceed $2,500. In contrast, petit larceny is a class 1 misdemeanor punishable by up to 12 months in jail and/or a fine of up to $2,500.[17] The distinction between petit and grand larceny can be especially significant in states, such as California, that employ "three strikes" laws mandating that someone convicted of a third felony be given a life sentence. The difference may not be lost on potential criminals: Research by John Worrall shows that larceny rates in California have been significantly lowered since passage of the three strikes law.[18]

Contemporary legal codes include a variety of theft offenses within the general category of larceny. The following sections cover the various forms of larceny that have been defined in law.

SHOPLIFTING

On January 24, 2008, law enforcement officers in Polk County, Florida, announced the arrest of 18 people in connection with a major shoplifting ring based in Longwood, Florida. Initial estimates were that the ring had stolen up to $100 million over the past five years! When detectives raided these criminals' homes, they found thousands of cosmetics and over-the-counter drugs that the ring had planned to sell at local flea markets or on the Internet. Police found out that the group had worked in pairs and cleared about $4,000 in three minutes. They used bags and purses with hidden compartments to conceal the stolen goods. They worked with maps and detailed plans so that they could avoid hitting any one store too often.[19]

petit (petty) larceny
Theft of a small amount of money or property, punished as a misdemeanor.

grand larceny
Theft of money or property of substantial value, punished as a felony.

In November 2004, New York Police investigated the Daniel George and Son Funeral Home in Brooklyn to check out what they considered to be a routine business dispute. But when they began looking around, they found a sealed room outfitted like an operating room, with a surgical table and overhead lights. They also found FedEx receipts made out to companies that purchase human tissue from cadavers for use in surgical procedures. The department's major case squad was called in, and they discovered that a former Manhattan dentist named Michael Mastromarino and three other men were running a multimillion-dollar body-snatching business that looted bones and tissue from more than a thousand corpses. The men then sold the body parts to legitimate companies that supplied hospitals around the United States. Hundreds of people in states as far away as Florida, Nebraska, and Texas received tissue and bone carved from looted corpses, including the cadaver of Alistair Cooke, the late host of PBS's *Masterpiece Theatre*. The tissue was used in such procedures as joint and heart-valve replacements, back surgery, dental implants, and skin grafts. After the case broke, victims rushed to doctors to be tested for tainted tissue. Some filed civil lawsuits. Mastromarino was charged with opening graves, body stealing, forgery, grand larceny, and racketeering.

Mastromarino had surrendered his dental license in 2000 because he was addicted to the painkiller Demerol. He started a career as a body harvester, opening Biomedical Tissue Services, an FDA-registered company that appeared completely legitimate. However, he got many of the corpses from Joseph Nicelli, an accomplice, who had been hired by funeral directors in New York, New Jersey, and Philadelphia to embalm the bodies. A single harvested body yielded $7,000 in salable parts. Nicelli helped Mastromarino sneak into the secret operating room at night to dissect corpses. To hide their crimes, Mastromarino replaced looted bones with plumbing pipes, and they stuffed their surgical gloves and

gowns into the bodies before stitching them back together.

On March 19, 2008, Mastromarino pled guilty to numerous charges of enterprise corruption, reckless endangerment, and body stealing. He admitted that he sold several tissue samples that were cancerous or infected with HIV and hepatitis and then disguised the truth with fake documentation. He is being sued by more than 900 of his victims, and prosecutors believe that thousands of patients may have tainted blood, bone, or tissue samples in their bodies. At his sentencing hearing on June 27, 2008, one of his victims, Dayna Ryan, who developed hepatitis from her bone transplant, told the court that "Mr. Mastromarino's sick, disgusting, appalling actions, all in the name of greed, have devastated my family to the point where we can never recover." The former dentist was then sentenced to 18 to 54 years in prison.

The body snatchers case illustrates the wide variety of schemes that can involve taking the possessions of another. In this case, the possessions were bodily organs, and the victims were dead!

SOURCES: Scott Shifrel, "Body-Snatch Ringleader Michael Mastromarino Gets 18–54 Years," *New York Daily News*, June 27, 2008, www.nydailynews.com/news/ny_crime/2008/06/27/2008–06–27_bodysnatch_ringleader_michael_mastromari.html; Michael Powell and David Segal, "In New York, a Grisly Traffic in Body Parts, Illegal Sales Worry Dead's Kin, Tissue Recipients," *Washington Post*, January 28, 2006, p. A03; William Sherman, "Clients Flee Biz Eyed in Ghoul Probe," *New York Daily News*, October 13, 2005.

While organized theft rings that average $20 million per year are not the norm, **shoplifting** is a very common form of larceny/theft involving the taking of goods from retail stores. Usually shoplifters try to snatch goods—such as jewelry, clothes, records, and appliances—when store personnel are otherwise occupied and to hide the goods on their bodies. The "five-finger discount" is an extremely common crime, and retailers lose upwards of 40 billion annually to inventory shrinkage.[20]

Retail security measures add to the already high cost of this crime, all of which is passed on to the consumer. Shoplifting incidents have increased dramatically in the past 20 years, and one reason is that the increasingly popular discount stores, such as Lowes, Wal-Mart, and Target, have minimal sales help and depend on highly visible merchandise displays to attract purchasers, all of which makes them particularly vulnerable to shoplifters.

shoplifting
The taking of goods from retail stores.

The Amateur Shoplifter In the early 1960s, Mary Owen Cameron conducted a classic study of shoplifting and found that the majority of shoplifters are amateur pilferers, called **snitches** in thieves' argot.[21] Snitches are otherwise respectable people who do not conceive of themselves as thieves but systematically steal merchandise for their own use. Some snitches are simply overcome by an uncontrollable urge to snatch something that attracts them, whereas others arrive at the store intending to steal. Some adolescents become shoplifters because they have been coerced by older kids into becoming "proxy shoplifters."[22]

Criminologists view amateur shoplifters as people who are likely to reform if apprehended. Cameron reasoned that because snitches are not part of a criminal subculture and do not think of themselves as criminals, they are deterred by initial contact with the law. Getting arrested traumatizes them, and they will not risk a second offense.[23]

Professional Shoplifters In her pioneering effort, Cameron found that about 10 percent of all shoplifters were professionals, like the Polk County ring, who derived the majority of their income from shoplifting. Called **boosters** or **heels**, professional shoplifters steal with the intention of reselling stolen merchandise to pawnshops or fences, usually at half the original price.[24]

These professionals can walk into a department store; fill up a cart with expensive medicines, DVDs, iPods, baby formula, and other high-cost items; and use deceptive techniques to slip past security guards.[25] Hitting several stores in a day and the same store once a month, a professional thief can make between $100,000 and $200,000 a year. Some enter a store carrying a "shopping list" provided by a fence who will pay them in cash or drugs. Fences later sell the merchandise in their own discount stores, at flea markets, or through online auctions. Some sell to higher-level fences who re-package—or scrub—the goods and pawn them off on retailers at prices that undercut legitimate distributors. Ironically, some stolen merchandise can actually make its way back onto the shelves of the chain store from which it was stolen.[26]

Controlling Shoplifting Fewer than 10 percent of shoplifting incidents are detected by store employees, and customers who notice boosters are unwilling to report even serious cases to managers.[27]

To encourage the arrest of shoplifters, a number of states have passed **merchant privilege laws** designed to offer retailers and their employees some protection from lawsuits stemming from improper or false arrests of suspected shoplifters.[28] These laws require that arrests be made on reasonable grounds or probable cause, that detention be short, and that store employees or security guards conduct themselves reasonably.

Retail stores are now initiating a number of strategies designed to reduce or eliminate shoplifting. **Target removal strategies** involve displaying dummy or disabled goods, while keeping the "real" merchandise locked up. For example, audio equipment is often displayed with parts missing, and only after items are purchased are the necessary components installed. Some stores sell from catalogs, keeping the merchandise in stockrooms.

Target hardening strategies involve locking goods into place or having them monitored by electronic systems. Clothing stores may use racks designed to prevent large quantities of garments from being slipped off easily. Store owners also rely on electronic article surveillance (EAS) systems, which feature tags with small electronic sensors that trip alarms if they are not removed by employees before the item leaves the store. These are used on highly desired yet small items, such as leather goods, perfume, and exclusive cosmetics. Some retailers use cables or hanger locks that require the assistance of a sales associate to unlock expensive clothing items before they can be worn.[29]

Security systems now feature source tagging, a process by which manufacturers embed the tag in the packaging or in the product itself. Thieves have trouble removing or defeating such tags, and retailers save on the time and labor needed to attach the tags at the store.[30]

These methods may control shoplifting, but stores must be wary of becoming overzealous in their enforcement policies. Those falsely accused have won significant

snitch
Amateur shoplifter who does not self-identify as a thief but who systematically steals merchandise for personal use.

booster (heel)
Professional shoplifter who steals with the intention of reselling stolen merchandise.

merchant privilege laws
Legislation that protects retailers and their employees from lawsuits if they arrest and detain a suspected shoplifter on reasonable grounds.

target removal strategy
Displaying dummy or disabled goods as a means of preventing shoplifting.

target hardening strategy
Locking goods into place or using electronic tags and sensing devices as means of preventing shoplifting.

Fact or Fiction?

Store owners are protected from lawsuits if they mistakenly arrest someone who they think has shoplifted.

Fiction. Falsely accused people can sue store owners and have won substantial amounts of money when they have been able to show that their arrest was based on racial profiling or some other extralegal factor.

judgments in civil actions when they have been able to prove that their arrest was unreasonable or based on extralegal factors.[31] In one case, a woman accused of shoplifting at a JCPenney store in Media, Pennsylvania, was awarded $250,000, having charged the store with false confinement and malicious prosecution after she was mistakenly taken for a shoplifter.[32] Stores may also be liable if security guards use excessive force when subduing a suspected shoplifter. There is also the danger of profiling based on gender, age, or racial or ethnic background, resulting in customers being targeted, detained, and searched for inappropriate reasons.[33] And of course searching and detaining customers based on stereotyping is legally indefensible: In 2009, eight African American plaintiffs sued the Dillard's Department store chain, claiming that employees and/or security workers questioned them while they were shopping in the stores and accused them of stealing merchandise solely on the basis of their race. And in a separate case, Dillard's was ordered to pay a $1.2 million verdict to an African American woman who was detained for shoplifting at a store in Overland Park, Kansas.[34]

CREDIT CARD THEFT

In 2008, federal authorities uncovered the largest credit card scam in history: Eleven people (three from Estonia, three from the Ukraine, two from China, and one from Belarus) stole 40 million credit and debit card numbers from companies such as Marshall's, T.J. Maxx, BJ's Wholesale Club, OfficeMax, and Barnes & Noble by hacking into their computer systems and installing "sniffer" programs designed to capture credit card numbers, passwords, and account information as they moved through the retailers' card-processing networks. The thieves then concealed the data in encrypted computer servers they controlled in the United States and eastern Europe. Some of the credit and debit card numbers were "cashed out" by encoding the numbers on the magnetic strips of blank cards and using these cards to withdraw tens of thousands of dollars at a time from automatic teller machines (ATMs).[35] This type of international credit card theft is not unique. A card stolen in Amsterdam can be used to make bogus online purchases in Prague within hours. Largely run by former Soviet Union residents, these international cartels cost the financial system billions each year.[36]

Use of stolen credit cards and credit card numbers has become a major problem in the United States as well, costing consumers and merchants hundreds of billions each year.[37] Most credit card abuse is the work of amateurs who acquire stolen cards through theft or mugging and then use them for two or three days at local stores. However, professional credit card rings may be getting into the act. One approach they use is first to obtain the victim's address and card number from a confederate, such as a store employee where the victim shops. They may then call the victim, claiming to be from the credit card company, and informing him or her that the account has been flagged because of suspicious activity. After offering credentials such as a bogus badge ID number, the thief tells the victim that someone has used the card to purchase a $1,500 television from a local store. When the consumer denies making the purchase, the scammer explains that he is starting a fraud investigation, gives the consumer a "confirmation number," and asks him or her for the three- or four-digit security number on the back of the card. Knowing this security code enables the thief to make purchases over the Internet or from local merchants.[38]

To curtail individual losses from credit card theft, in 1971 Congress limited a cardholder's liability to $50 per stolen card. Similarly, some states, such as California, have passed laws making it a misdemeanor to obtain property or services by means of cards that have been stolen, forged, canceled, or revoked, or whose use is unauthorized for any reason.[39] But even though the public is protected, merchants may have to foot the bill.

AUTO THEFT

Motor vehicle theft is another common larceny offense. Because of its frequency and seriousness, it is treated as a separate category in the Uniform Crime Report (UCR).

CONNECTIONS

Situational crime prevention measures, discussed in Chapter 4, are designed to make it more difficult to commit crimes. Some stores are now using these methods—for example, placing the most valuable goods in the least vulnerable places, posting warning signs to deter potential thieves, and using closed-circuit cameras.

Not all auto thefts are what they seem. Some reported crimes may actually be part of insurance fraud schemes. The hundreds of burned cars, trucks, and sport utility vehicles shown here on February 2, 2007, are stacked in an auto salvage lot in Henderson, Nevada. Las Vegas has one of the nation's highest rates of reported auto theft, but police estimate that at least 25 percent of all cars that are reported stolen there have actually been ignited and abandoned by their owners, who hope to cash in on fraudulent auto arson insurance claims.

The FBI now records slightly less than 1 million auto thefts per year, which account for a total loss of more than $6 billion. Just as for other crimes, there has been a significant reduction in motor vehicle theft rates over the past decade, and the number of car thefts has declined more than 25 percent. UCR projections on auto theft are similar to the projections of the NCVS, probably because almost every state requires owners to insure their vehicles, and auto theft is one of the most highly reported of all major crimes (75 percent of all auto thefts are reported to police).

Which Cars Are Taken Most? According to the Highway Loss Data Institute, the following cars have been stolen most frequently in the past few years:[40]

Honda S2000 convertible
2005–2007 models

Dodge Charger
2006–2007 models

Dodge Durango
2005–2007 models

Cadillac Escalade
2007 model

Hummer H2
2005–2007 models

Ford F-250 SuperCrew
2005–2007 models

Amateur Auto Thieves Amateur thieves steal cars for a number of reasons that involve some form of temporary personal use.[41] Among the reasons why an amateur would steal a car:

▶ *Joyriding*. Many car thefts are motivated by teenagers' desire to acquire the power, prestige, sexual potency, and recognition associated with an automobile. Joyriders steal cars not for profit or gain but to experience, even briefly, the benefits associated with owning an automobile.

- *Short-term transportation*. Auto theft for short-term transportation is similar to joyriding. It involves the theft of a car simply to go from one place to another. In more serious cases, the thief may drive to another city or state and then steal another car to continue the journey.
- *Long-term transportation*. Thieves who steal cars for long-term transportation intend to keep the cars for their personal use. Usually older than joyriders and from a lower-class background, these auto thieves may repaint and otherwise disguise cars to avoid detection.
- *Profit*. Auto theft for profit is motivated by the hope of monetary gain. Some amateurs hope to sell the stolen car, but most are auto strippers who steal batteries, tires, and wheel covers to sell or to re-equip their own cars.
- *Commission of another crime*. A few auto thieves steal cars to use in other crimes, such as robberies and thefts. This type of auto thief desires both mobility and anonymity.

Professional Car Thieves At one time, most auto theft was the work of amateurs, and most cars were taken by relatively affluent, middle-class teenagers looking for excitement.[42] But this pattern seems to have changed: Fewer cars are being taken today, and fewer stolen cars are being recovered. Part of the reason is an increase in the numbers of highly organized professionals who resell expensive cars after altering their identification numbers and falsifying their registration papers. Exporting stolen vehicles has become a global problem, and the emergence of capitalism in Eastern Europe has increased the demand for U.S.-made cars.[43] Some cars are now stolen in order to be sold to chop shops, for spare parts. Among the most attractive targets are the following parts:

- *Headlights*. Blue-white, high-intensity discharge headlights. New ones go for $500 and up per light, sometimes $3,000 per car.
- *Air bags*. About 10 percent of all theft claims involve an air bag. The bag on the driver's side, mounted in the steering wheel, is the easiest to remove and costs $500 to $1,000 to replace.
- *Wheels*. Custom rims are attractive to thieves, especially the "spinners" that keep revolving when the car is stopped. They go from $100 each up to $15,000 for a set of super-deluxe models.[44]

Car Cloning One new form of professional auto theft is called cloning: After stealing a luxury car from a mall or parking lot, car thieves later visit a large car dealership in another state and look for a car that is the exact same make and model (and even the same color) as the stolen one. The thieves jot down the vehicle identification number (VIN) stamped on the top of the dashboard and drive off. Then they remove the manufacturer-installed VIN plate from the stolen car and replace it with a homemade counterfeit that is similar to the original but bears the VIN of the legitimate vehicle. Phony ownership and registration documents complete the "cloning." At that point the stolen vehicle can be easily registered with a motor vehicle agency in another state and sold to an unwary buyer. In one case in Tampa, Florida, more than 1,000 cloned cars were sold to buyers in 20 states and several countries, with estimated losses of more than $25 million to consumers, auto insurers, and other victims.[45]

Combating Auto Theft There has been an ongoing effort to reduce the number of auto thefts by using situational crime prevention techniques. One approach has been to increase the risks of apprehension. Information hot lines offer rewards for information leading to the arrest of car thieves. Another approach has been to place fluorescent decals on windows indicating that the car is never used between 1:00 A.M. and 5:00 A.M.; if police spot a car with the decal being operated during this period, they know it is stolen.

The LoJack system installs a hidden tracking device in cars; the device gives off a signal that enables the police to pinpoint its location. Research evaluating the effectiveness of this device reveals that it significantly reduces crime.[46] Other prevention efforts involve making it more difficult to steal cars. Publicity campaigns have been directed at encouraging people to lock their cars. Parking lots have been equipped with theft-deterring closed-circuit TV cameras and barriers. Manufacturers have installed more sophisticated steering-column locking devices and other security systems that complicate theft.

A study by the Highway Loss Data Institute (HLDI) found that most car theft prevention methods, especially alarms, have little effect on theft rates. The most effective methods appear to be devices that immobilize a vehicle by cutting off the electrical power needed to start the engine when a theft is detected.[47] However, car thieves with modest resources—just a few hundred dollars' worth of off-the-shelf equipment—and some computer knowledge can crack the codes of millions of car keys and subvert their security systems.[48]

BAD CHECKS

Another form of larceny is cashing bad checks to obtain money or property. The checks are intentionally drawn on a nonexistent or underfunded bank account. In general, for a person to be guilty of passing a bad check, the bank the check is drawn on must refuse payment and the check casher must fail to make the check good within 10 days after finding out the check was not honored.

Edwin Lemert conducted the best-known study of check forgers more than 40 years ago.[49] Lemert found that the majority of check forgers—he calls them **naive check forgers**—are amateurs who do not believe their actions will hurt anyone. Most naive check forgers come from middle-class backgrounds and have little identification with a criminal subculture. They cash bad checks because of a financial crisis that demands an immediate resolution—perhaps they have lost money at the racetrack and have some pressing bills to pay.

Lemert found that a few professionals, whom he calls **systematic forgers**, make a substantial living passing bad checks. Estimating the number of such forgeries committed each year or the amounts involved is difficult. Stores and banks may choose not to press charges because it is not worth it to them to make the effort to collect the money due them. It is also difficult to separate the true check forger from the neglectful shopper.

Some of the different techniques used in check fraud schemes, which may cost retail establishments upwards of $1 billion per year, are set out in Exhibit 11.2.

FALSE PRETENSES/FRAUD

The crime of **false pretenses**, or **fraud**, involves misrepresenting a fact in a way that causes a victim to willingly give his or her property to the wrongdoer, who then keeps it.[50] In 1757, the English Parliament defined "false pretenses" to cover an area of law left untouched by larceny statutes. The first false pretenses law punished people who "knowingly and designedly by false pretense or pretenses, [obtained] from any person or persons, money, goods, wares or merchandise with intent to cheat or defraud any person or persons of the same."[51]

False pretense differs from traditional larceny because the victims willingly give their possessions to the offender, and the crime does not, as does larceny, involve a "trespass in the taking." One example of false pretenses is an unscrupulous merchant selling someone a chair by claiming it is an antique, knowing all the while that it is a cheap copy. Another example is a phony healer selling a victim a bottle of colored sugar water as an "elixir" to cure a disease. Swindlers have little shame when defrauding people out of their money; they often target the elderly, sick, and infirm. In the aftermath of Hurricane Katrina, in 2005, swindlers used the tragedy to solicit relief funds from charitable and well-meaning donors and then converted the money to their own use.[52] Today, about 250,000 people are arrested for fraud schemes each year, though that is probably only the tip of the iceberg.[53]

naive check forgers
Amateurs who cash bad checks because of some financial crisis but have little identification with a criminal subculture.

systematic forgers
Professionals who make a living by passing bad checks.

false pretenses (fraud)
Misrepresenting a fact in a way that causes a deceived victim to give money or property to the offender.

Exhibit 11.2 Check Fraud Schemes and Techniques

- **Forged Signatures** Legitimate blank checks with an imitation of the payor signature.

- **Forged Endorsements** The use of a stolen check, which is then endorsed and cashed or deposited by someone other than the payee.

- **Identity Assumption** Identity assumption occurs when criminals learn information about a financial institution customer, such as name, address, financial institution account number, Social Security number, home and work telephone numbers, or employer, and use the information to misrepresent themselves as the valid financial institution customer.

- **Counterfeit Checks** Counterfeit checks are presented based on fraudulent identification or are false checks drawn on valid accounts. Recent advancements in color copying and desktop publishing capabilities have made this the fastest-growing source of fraudulent checks today.

- **Altered Checks** After a legitimate maker creates a valid check to pay a debt, a criminal takes the good check and uses chemicals or other means to erase the amount or the name of the payee, so that new information can be entered. The new information can be added by typewriter, in handwriting, or with a laser printer or check imprinter.

- **Closed-Account Fraud** This type of fraud, which is based on writing checks against closed accounts, generally relies on the float time involved in transactions between financial institutions.

- **Check Kiting** Depositing a check from one bank account into a second bank account without sufficient funds to cover it.

SOURCES: Check Fraud Working Group, Washington, DC, "A Guide to Avoiding Losses," www.occ.treas.gov/chckfrd/chckfrd.pdf; National Check Fraud Center, Charleston, South Carolina, 2009, www.ckfraud.org/.

Confidence Games Some fraudulent schemes involve getting a mark (target) interested in some get-rich-quick scheme, which may have illegal overtones; this is known as a **confidence game** or **con game.** The criminal's hope is that when victims lose their money, they will be either too embarrassed or too afraid to call the police. There are hundreds of varieties of con games. Here is a small sample:

▶ Con artists read the obituary column and then send a surviving spouse bills supposedly owed by the person deceased. Or they deliver and request payment for an item, such as a Bible, that they say the deceased relative ordered just before he died. (The father-and-daughter team played by Ryan and Tatum O'Neal in the film *Paper Moon* ran this scam.)

▶ A con artist, posing as a bank employee, stops a customer as he or she is about to enter the bank. The con man claims to be an investigator who is trying to catch a dishonest teller. He asks the customer to withdraw cash to see whether he or she gets the right amount. After the cash is withdrawn, the con man asks that it be turned over to him so he can check the serial numbers. He promises to return the cash in a few minutes, gives the customer a receipt, and escapes through a back exit.

Third-Party Fraud In some instances of false pretenses, the "victim" is a third party, such as an insurance company that is forced to pay false claims. A common scheme involves fake auto accidents, including the ones described below.

▶ *The "swoop and squat."* Two vehicles work as a team to set up an accident. One vehicle pulls in front of a driver and the other alongside, blocking the victim in and preventing him or her from turning the car to avoid an accident. The lead car stops short, causing the victim to engage in a rear-end collision. After the "accident," everyone in the damaged car files bogus injury claims with the driver's insurance company. They may even go to crooked physical therapists, chiropractors, lawyers, or auto repair technicians to further exaggerate their bogus claims.

▶ *The drive down.* A driver is attempting to merge into a traffic lane, when suddenly another driver waves him or her forward, indicating willingness to let the car merge. But instead of letting the victim's car in, he slams into it, causing an accident. When the police arrive, the "injured" driver denies ever motioning, claims serious injury, and files an insurance claim with the victim's company.

▶ *The sideswipe.* As the victim rounds a corner at a busy intersection with multiple turn lanes, her or his car drifts slightly into the next lane. The fraudulent driver

confidence game (con game)
A swindle, often involving a get-rich-quick scheme, and often with illegal overtones so that the victim will be afraid or embarrassed to call the police.

of the car in that lane, waiting for just such an opportunity, steps on the gas and sideswipes the victim, producing an accident.

▶ *The T-bone.* A driver is crossing an intersection when a car coming from a side street accelerates and hits his or her car. When the police arrive, the driver of that car and several planted "witnesses" claim that the victim ran a red light or stop sign.[54]

How common are such fraudulent schemes? The FBI claims that staged accidents cost the insurance industry about $20 billion a year, increasing insurance rates on the average motorist between $100 and $300 extra per car per year.[55]

RECEIVING AND FENCING STOLEN PROPERTY

The crime of receiving stolen goods is a type of larceny/theft that involves the buying or acquiring possession of property by a person who knows (or should know) that the seller acquired it through theft, embezzlement, or some other illegal means. For this to constitute a crime, the receiver must know the goods were stolen at the time he receives them and must have the intent to aid the thief. Depending on the value of the property received, *receiving* stolen property is either a misdemeanor or a felony. *Fencing* is a crime that involves an ongoing effort to be a middleman or distributor of illegally received goods.

Today, the professional **fence**, who earns his or her living solely by buying and re-selling stolen merchandise, seems more like the "professional criminal" described by Sutherland earlier in the chapter than almost any other kind of criminal offender. Fences use stealth rather than violence, guile and knowledge rather than force or threat, as they buy and sell stolen merchandise ranging from diamonds to wheel rims.[56]

Sam Goodman, a fence interviewed by sociologists Darrell Steffensmeier and Jeffery Ulmer, purchased stolen goods from a wide variety of thieves and suppliers, including burglars, drug addicts, shoplifters, dockworkers, and truck drivers. To learn more about the life of Sam Goodman, read the accompanying Current Issues in Crime feature.

EMBEZZLEMENT

Embezzlement goes back at least to ancient Greece; the writings of Aristotle allude to theft by road commissioners and other government officials.[57] The crime of embezzlement was first codified into law by the English Parliament during the sixteenth century.[58] Until then, to be guilty of theft, a person had to take goods from the physical possession of another (trespass in the taking). In everyday commerce, store clerks, bank tellers, brokers, and merchants gain lawful possession but not legal ownership of other people's money. Embezzlement occurs when someone who is trusted with property fraudulently converts it—that is, keeps it for his or her own use or for the use of others. Most U.S. courts require a serious breach of trust before a person can be convicted of embezzlement. The mere act of moving property without the owner's consent, using it, or damaging it is not considered embezzlement. However, using it up, selling it, pledging it, giving it away, and holding it against the owner's will are all considered embezzlement.[59]

Although it is impossible to know how many embezzlement incidents occur annually, about 22,000 people are arrested for embezzlement each year—probably an extremely small percentage of all embezzlers. The number of people arrested for embezzlement has increased in the past decade, indicating that (1) more employees are willing to steal from their employers, (2) more employers are willing to report instances of embezzlement, and/or (3) law enforcement officials are more willing to prosecute embezzlers. There has also been a rash of embezzlement-type crimes around the world, especially in third world countries where poverty is all too common and the economy is poor and supported by foreign aid and loans. Government officials and businesspeople through whose hands this money passes may be tempted to convert it to their own use, a scenario that is sure to increase the likelihood of embezzlement.[60] ▶ **Checkpoints**

Checkpoints

▶ Larceny is the taking and carrying away of the constructive possessions of another.

▶ Shoplifting involves theft from a retail establishment by stealth and deception. Some shoplifters are impulsive; others are professionals who use elaborate means and devices.

▶ Passing bad checks without adequate funds is a form of larceny.

▶ Use of stolen credit cards and account numbers results in annual losses in the billions.

▶ Auto theft adds up to more than $7 billion in losses each year.

▶ Embezzlement occurs when trusted persons or employees take someone else's property for their own use.

fence
A buyer and seller of stolen merchandise.

embezzlement
A type of larceny in which someone who is trusted with property fraudulently converts it to his or her own use or for the use of others.

In their book *Confessions of a Dying Thief*, Darrell Steffensmeier and Jeffery Ulmer examine the dynamics of the criminal career of Sam Goodman, a veteran thief and fence and quasi-legitimate businessman. Goodman's criminal career spanned 50 years, beginning in his mid-teens and ending with his death when he was in his sixties. Steffensmeier and Ulmer find that, unlike amateur criminals who age out of crime, professional criminals such as Goodman (as well as skilled thieves, dealers in stolen goods, bookmakers, con artists, sex merchants, quasi-legitimate businessmen, local racketeers, and Mafiosi) frequently persist in their criminality until they are too old or feeble to do otherwise.

Their interviews with Goodman show that criminal opportunity is not merely passive: Professional criminals actively seek and create criminal opportunities that are

more positive attitudes toward legitimate people and associations (his employees, legitimate antiques dealers). Furthermore, the moonlighting phase of his career also saw some changes in Goodman's self-definition, as reflected in this assessment in the final weeks of his life:

> I never cared how the cops saw me but I wanted the public to see me in a different light. Not as a guy who did time, not as a burglar, not even as a fence, but as a businessman. *As a good joe.* In that way I knew what I done was wrong. . . . If they saw me as a crook, that I could handle. But not a [expletive] bum. I wanted the people to respect me as me. As a businessman taking care of business in my shop. (p. 375)

Deviants, even persistent criminals, are seldom deviant in all or even most aspects of their lives. Goodman comfortably rubbed shoulders with thieves, gamblers, and quasi-legitimate businessmen, but he also courted respectability

Current Issues in Crime Confessions of a Dying Thief

attractive. They support their careers by gaining different types of criminal knowledge:

- *Civil knowledge*: widely accessible general knowledge that can be put to criminal use
- *Preparatory knowledge*: prior familiarity with criminal orientations, language, attitudes, and skills often gained by "hanging around" with criminal associates and observing their lifestyles
- *Technical knowledge*: more esoteric knowledge or skills that can be obtained only via access to specialized settings and experienced criminal practitioners

Goodman had a strong commitment to crime throughout his life. The height of his personal commitment to crime was during the middle phase of his career, when he was a "big, wide-open" fence. Nonetheless, his favorable attitudes toward crime and other criminals remained in the later, "moonlighting" phase of his career, when he was less involved in crime. At that point, he also moved toward

and pledged allegiance to some major normative standards. Although he was in some respects remorseful for his life of crime, Sam Goodman did not regret his choices and may have been glad that he did not lead a more legitimate, respectable life, as these deathbed comments illustrate:

> I do not feel sad about my life. I did what I thought I had to do at the time. But I would not wish my life on somebody else. I made that very god damn plain to your students—a life in crime can be a bitch. . . . I done wrong, pulled some very rank shit. But helped a whole lot of people, too. If somebody needed something, came into my shop, I more or less gave it away. Anyone that worked for me, I dealt with fairly. Got paid a good dollar and helped them out in little ways. (p. 373)

The life of Sam Goodman shows that although most criminals age out of crime, many do not.

SOURCE: Darrell Steffensmeier and Jeffery Ulmer, *Confessions of a Dying Thief: Understanding Criminal Careers and Illegal Enterprise* (Chicago: Transaction-Aldine, 2005)

Burglary

burglary
Entering a home by force, threat, or deception with intent to commit a crime.

Under common law, the crime of **burglary** was defined as "the breaking and entering of a dwelling house of another in the nighttime with the intent to commit a felony within."[61] Burglary is considered a much more serious crime than larceny/theft because it involves entering another's home, which threatens occupants. Even though the home may be unoccupied at the time of the burglary, the potential for harm to the occupants is so significant that most state jurisdictions punish burglary as a felony.

The legal definition of burglary has undergone considerable change since its common-law origins. When first created by English judges during the late Middle Ages, laws against burglary were designed to protect people whose homes might be set upon by wandering criminals. Including the phrase "breaking and entering" in the definition protected people from unwarranted intrusions; if an invited guest stole something, it would not be considered a burglary. Similarly, the requirement that the crime be committed at nighttime was added because evening was considered the time when honest people might fall prey to criminals.[62]

More recent U.S. state laws have changed the requirements of burglary, and most have discarded the necessity of forced entry. Entry through deceit (for example, by posing as a deliveryman), through threat, or through conspiracy with others (such as guests or servants) is deemed legally equivalent to breaking and is called "constructive breaking." Many states now protect all structures, not just dwelling houses. A majority of states have also removed the nighttime element from their definitions of burglary. States commonly enact laws creating different degrees of burglary. The more serious, heavily punished crimes involve nighttime forced entry into the home; the least serious involve daytime entry into a nonresidential structure by an unarmed offender. Several legal gradations may be found between these extremes.

NATURE AND EXTENT OF BURGLARY

The FBI's definition of burglary is not restricted to burglary from a person's home; it includes any unlawful entry of a structure to commit a theft or felony. Burglary is further categorized into three subclasses: forcible entry, unlawful entry where no force is used, and attempted forcible entry.

According to the UCR, more than 2 million burglaries now occur each year. However, unlike the rates of other crimes, the burglary rate has increased about 6 percent since 1999.[63] As in the past, burglars targeted homes more often than nonresidential structures. In 2008 most burglaries were of residences, and about one-third were of nonresidential structures. Most residential burglaries occur during the day, from 6:00 A.M. to 6:00 P.M., when few people are home, whereas nonresidential structures are targeted in the evening, when businesses and shops are closed.

The average dollar loss per burglary offense is almost $2,000. Burglaries cost victims more than $4.6 billion dollars per year.

The NCVS reports that more than 3 million residential burglaries are either attempted or completed each year. Unlike the UCR, the NCVS indicates that the number of burglaries has declined significantly, dropping almost 8 million, or 22 percent, in the past decade.[64] According to the NCVS, those most likely to be burglarized are relatively poor Hispanic and African American families (annual income under $7,500). Owner-occupied and single-family residences had lower burglary rates than renter-occupied and multiple-family dwellings.

© AP Images/Ted S. Warren

Good burglars grasp the techniques of avoiding detection while getting away with the merchandise. Pat Gardiner is shown here in his empty airplane hangar in Bonners Ferry, Idaho, on October 5, 2009. Gardiner's Cesna T182T (shown in the photo he is holding) had been stolen from the hangar. The theft is similar to several other cases of stolen aircraft that authorities are speculating could be the work of Colton Harris-Moore, an accused serial burglar who, at the time of this writing, remains at large. Whenever police get near Harris-Moore, the teen seems to disappear; his crime spree seems reminiscent of the exploits of Frank Abagnale Jr., as played by Leonardo DiCaprio in the movie *Catch Me If You Can*. Since escaping from a halfway house in 2008, the 18-year-old Harris-Moore has been suspected of being involved in more than 50 burglaries and of stealing three airplanes.

TYPES OF BURGLARIES

Because it involves planning, risk, and skill, burglary has long been associated with professional thieves who painstakingly learn their craft.[65] Burglars must master the skills of their trade, learning to spot environmental cues that nonprofessionals fail to notice.[66] In an important book called *Burglars on the Job*, Richard Wright and Scott

Decker describe the working conditions of active burglars.[67] Most are motivated by the need for cash in order to get high; they want to enjoy the good life, "keep the party going," without having to work. They approach their job in a rational, businesslike fashion; still, their lives are controlled by their culture and environment. Unskilled and uneducated, urban burglars choose crime because they have few conventional opportunities for success.[68] Experienced burglars are more willing to travel to find rich targets. They have access to transportation, which enables them to select a wider variety of targets than younger, less experienced thieves.[69]

Residential Burglary Experienced burglars learn to avoid areas of the city in which most residents are renters and not home owners, reasoning that renters' homes are less likely to be suitable targets than the homes of more affluent owners.[70] Francis Hoheimer, an experienced professional burglar, has described how he learned the "craft of burglary" from a fellow inmate, Oklahoma Smith, when the two were serving time in the Illinois State Penitentiary. Smith recommended the following:

> Never wear deodorant or shaving lotion; the strange scent might wake someone up. The more people there are in a house, the safer you are. If someone hears you moving around, they will think it's someone else. . . . If they call, answer in a muffled sleepy voice. . . . Never be afraid of dogs, they can sense fear. Most dogs are friendly, snap your finger, they come right to you.[71]

Despite his elaborate preparations, Hoheimer spent many years in confinement. Burglars must master the skills of their "trade," learning to identify worthwhile, undefended targets.[72] They must learn which targets contain valuables worth stealing and which are most likely to prove to be dry holes. Research shows that burglary rates for student-occupied apartments are much lower than the rate for other residences in the same neighborhoods; burglars appear to have learned that students' apartments are ones to avoid![73] Burglars must learn to assess the value of the goods they take: what has good resale value and what should be avoided because the price is in decline. Obsolete audio equipment cannot be easily fenced; iPhones have greater value.[74]

Commercial Burglars Some burglars prefer to victimize commercial property rather than private homes, and a growing amount of research indicates that business premises are now being targeted for burglary.[75]

Of all business establishments, retail stores are the favorite target. Because they display merchandise, burglars know exactly what to look for, where it can be found, and, because the prices are also displayed, how much they can hope to gain from resale to a fence. Burglars can legitimately enter a retail store during business hours and see what the store contains and where the merchandise is stored; they can also check for security alarms and devices. Commercial burglars perceive retail establishments as ready sources of merchandise that can be sold easily.[76]

Other commercial establishments, such as service centers, warehouses, and factories, are less attractive targets because gaining legitimate access to plan the theft is more difficult. The burglar must use guile to scope out these places, perhaps posing as a delivery person. In addition, the merchandise is more likely to be used or more difficult to fence at a premium price. If burglars choose to attack factories, warehouses, or service centers, the most vulnerable properties are those located far from major roads and away from pedestrian traffic. In remote areas, burglar alarms are less effective because it takes police longer to respond than on more heavily patrolled thoroughfares, and an alarm is less likely to be heard by a pedestrian who would be able to call for help. Even in the most remote areas, however, burglars are wary of alarms, although their presence does suggest that there is something worth stealing.

Repeat Burglars Whether they specialize in residential or commercial targets, some burglars strike the same victim more than once.[77] Graham Farrell, Coretta Phillips, and Ken Pease suggest some reasons why burglars might want to hit the same target more than once:

CONNECTIONS

According to the rational choice approach discussed in Chapter 4, burglars make rational and calculated decisions before committing crimes. If circumstances and culture dictate their activities, their decisions must be considered a matter of choice.

- It takes less effort to burgle a home or apartment known to be a suitable target than to burgle an unknown or unsuitable one.
- The burglar is already aware of the target's layout.
- The ease of entry of the target has probably not changed, and escape routes are known.
- The lack of protective measures and the absence of nosy neighbors, which made the first burglary a success, have probably not changed.
- Goods have been observed that could not be taken out the first time.[78]

It is also likely that because burgled items are both indispensable (such as televisions and DVDs) and covered by insurance, burglars can safely assume that they will be quickly replaced, encouraging a second round of burglary![79]

CAREERS IN BURGLARY

Some criminals make burglary their career and continually develop new specialized skills. Neal Shover has studied the careers of professional burglars and uncovered the existence of a particularly successful type—the "good burglar."[80] Characteristics of the good burglar include technical competence, personal integrity, specialization in burglary, financial success, and the ability to avoid prison sentences. Shover found that to become "good burglars," novices must develop four key requirements of the trade:

- The good burglar must master the many skills needed to commit lucrative burglaries. These skills may include gaining entry into homes and apartment houses; selecting targets with high potential payoffs; choosing items with a high resale value; opening safes properly without damaging their contents; and using the proper equipment, including cutting torches, electric saws, explosives, and metal bars.
- The good burglar must be able to team up to form a criminal gang. Choosing trustworthy companions is essential if the obstacles to completing a successful job—police, alarms, secure safes—are to be overcome.
- The good burglar must have inside information. Without knowledge of what awaits them inside, burglars can spend a tremendous amount of time and effort on empty safes and jewelry boxes.
- The good burglar must cultivate fences or buyers for stolen wares. Once the burglar gains access to people who buy and sell stolen goods, he or she must also learn how to successfully sell these goods for a reasonable profit.

According to Shover, an older burglar teaches the novice how to handle such requirements of the trade as dealing with defense attorneys, bail bond agents, and other agents of the justice system. Apprentices must be known to have the appropriate character before they are accepted for training. Usually the opportunity to learn burglary comes as a reward for being a highly respected juvenile gang member; from knowing someone in the neighborhood who has made a living at burglary; or, more often, from having built a reputation for being solid while serving time in prison. Consequently, the opportunity to become a good burglar is not open to everyone.

The Female Burglar Most people arrested for burglary are males, so it is not surprising that burglary is considered a "male profession." But there are active female burglars, and research shows that they have offending patterns quite similar to those of males. For example, like their male peers, female burglars also engage in other forms of crime, such as shoplifting and assault.[81]

However, there are some differences between male and female burglars. Males are more likely to steal cars to supplement their income, a criminal activity shunned by females. Female burglars are much more likely to work with a partner, whereas males are more likely to go it alone. Males also begin their offending careers at an earlier age than females and are more likely to be repeat and recurrent offenders. Because the males started earlier and commit more crimes, it is not surprising that males have a much greater chance than females of getting caught and doing time.

Fact or Fiction?

Once your home has been burgled you are safe from those thieves because they have already taken everything they think is valuable.

Fiction. Repeat burglary is actually quite common. Thieves may want to come back to take what they missed the first time.

CONNECTIONS

Shover finds that the process of becoming a professional burglar is similar to the process described in Sutherland's theory of differential association, which is discussed in Chapter 7.

▶ Burglary is the breaking and entering of a structure in order to commit a felony, typically theft.

▶ Some burglars specialize in residential theft; others steal from commercial establishments.

▶ Some burglars repeatedly attack the same target, mainly because they are familiar with the layout and protective measures.

▶ Professional burglars have careers in which they learn the tricks of the trade from older, more experienced pros.

Female burglars can be divided into two groups: "accomplices" and "partners."[82] Accomplices commit burglaries because they were caught up in circumstances beyond their control. They feel compelled or pressured to commit crimes because of a relationship with another, more dominant person, typically a boyfriend or husband. Accomplices got into crime because they lacked legitimate employment, were drug dependent, or had alcohol problems. They exercise little control over their crimes and rely on others for planning and tactics; it is common for them to act as lookouts or drivers.

In contrast, "partners" plan and carry out crimes because they enjoy both the reward and the excitement of burglary. In planning their crimes, partners display cunning, planning, and rationality; they scope out targets, plan entries, and hatch escape plans. ▶ **Checkpoints**

Arson

Arson is the willful, malicious burning of a home, public building, vehicle, or commercial building. Although arson data can be sketchy, the FBI reports that about 65,000 arsons are now recorded annually, with an average cost of about $17,000 each. Arson attacks are not unique to the United States.

There are several motives for arson. Adult arsonists may be motivated by severe emotional turmoil or a disturbed personality.[83] Research on the background characteristics of juvenile fire setters shows that their acts are often associated with antisocial behavior and psychopathology.[84] These findings support the claim that arson should be viewed as a mental health problem, not a criminal act, and should be treated with counseling and other therapeutic measures, rather than with severe punishments.[85]

During the past decade, hundreds of jurisdictions across the nation have established programs to address the growing concern about juvenile fire setting. Housed primarily within the fire service, these programs are designed to identify, evaluate, and treat juvenile fire setters to prevent the recurrence of fire-setting behaviors. A promising approach is the FireSafe Families effort in Rhode Island, which combines a training curriculum for fire safety educators, a training program for community professionals to identify behavior that may lead to arson, and a cognitive behavioral therapy (CBT) program to treat not only children who are at risk to become juvenile fire starters but also their families.[86]

Not all fires are the work of emotionally disturbed youth; some are set by professionals who engage in arson for profit. People who want to collect insurance money but are afraid or unable to set the fires themselves hire professional arsonists who know how to set fires yet make the cause seem accidental (such as an electrical short circuit). Another form is arson fraud, which involves a business owner burning his or her property, or hiring someone to do it, to escape financial problems. Over the years, investigators have found that businesspeople are willing to become involved in arson to collect fire insurance or for these additional reasons:

© AP/Images/Kenneth Roberts

A helicopter drops water on a wildfire on March 11, 2007, near Anaheim Hills, California. The fast-moving brush fire scorched 1,000 acres of parched hillside and charred at least two homes, forcing authorities to evacuate more than 200 homes in Orange County. The fire was ignited by flames from a stolen car that was intentionally set ablaze during strong Santa Ana winds.

- To obtain money during a period of financial crisis
- To get rid of outdated or slow-moving inventory
- To destroy outmoded machines and technology
- To pay off legal and illegal debts
- To relocate or remodel a business—for example, a theme restaurant that has not been accepted by customers
- To take advantage of government funds available for redevelopment
- To apply for government building money, pocket it without making repairs, and then claim that fire destroyed the "rehabilitated" building
- To plan bankruptcies to eliminate debts after the merchandise supposedly destroyed was secretly sold before the fire
- To eliminate business competition by burning out rivals
- To employ extortion schemes that demand that victims pay up or the rest of their holdings will be burned
- To solve labor–management problems (this type of arson may be committed by a disgruntled employee)
- To conceal another crime, such as embezzlement

arson
The willful, malicious burning of a home, building, or vehicle.

Thinking Like a Criminologist

To reduce the risk of loss during the Christmas holidays, the Security Industry Association (SIA) suggests that you not display presents where they can be seen from a window or doorway and that you put gifts in a safe place before leaving the house or taking a trip. Closing drapes or blinds during even short trips away from home is a good habit.

It is important to trick burglars into believing someone is home. If you are away, the SIA suggests having lights on timers, stopping mail and newspaper delivery, and arranging, if possible, to have the walkways shoveled and a car parked in the driveway as additional security measures. Other suggestions include installing a good deadbolt lock

with at least a one-inch throat into a solid wood or steel door that fits securely into a sturdy frame, keeping doors locked, putting a chain-link fence around a yard, getting a dog, and having police inspect the house for security. Also, buy a weighted safe deposit box to secure items that cannot be replaced, and engrave your driver's license number and state of residence on your property to give police a way to contact you if your home is burglarized and the stolen items are later found.

Con artists may take advantage of people's generosity during the holidays by making appeals for nonexistent charities. The SIA suggests that you always ask for identification from solicitors.

Writing Assignment

As a criminologist, can you come up with any new ideas that the Security Industry Association failed to cover? What would you tell people who wanted to protect their homes from burglars?

Summary

1. Be familiar with the history of theft offenses.

   Common theft offenses include larceny, fraud, and embezzlement. These are common-law crimes, originally defined by English judges. *Skilled thieves* included pickpockets, forgers, and counterfeiters, who operated freely. *Smugglers* transported goods, such as spirits, gems, gold, and spices, without paying tax or duty. *Poachers* supplemented their diet and income with game that belonged to a landlord.

2. Recognize the differences between professional and amateur thieves.

   Economic crimes are designed to reap financial rewards for the offender. Opportunistic amateurs commit the majority of economic crimes. Economic crime has also attracted professional criminals. Professionals earn most of their income from crime, view themselves as criminals, and possess skills that aid them in their law-breaking behavior.

An example of the professional criminal is the fence who buys and sells stolen merchandise.

3. Know the similarities and differences between petty and grand larceny.

Larceny, the most common theft crime, involves taking the legal possessions of another. Petty (petit) larceny is typically theft between $100 and $500, depending on the state; grand larceny is theft over that amount. Grand larceny is a felony; petty larceny is a misdemeanor.

4. Understand the various forms of shoplifting.

Some shoplifters are amateurs who steal on the spur of the moment. These snitches are otherwise respectable persons who do not conceive of themselves as thieves but systematically steal merchandise for their own use. Some adolescents become shoplifters because they have been coerced by older kids. Called boosters or heels, professional shoplifters steal with the intention of reselling stolen merchandise to pawnshops or fences, usually at half the original price. Boosters know how to hit stores without being detected and have partners who can unload merchandise after it is stolen.

5. Differentiate between fraud and embezzlement.

Fraud involves tricking victims into giving up their goods or money under false pretenses, such as passing off counterfeit goods as the genuine article. Embezzlement involves people taking something that was temporarily entrusted to them. Bank tellers who take money out of the cash drawer and keep it for themselves are committing embezzlement.

6. Compare the activities of professional and amateur car thieves.

Auto theft usually involves amateur joyriders who "borrow" cars for short-term transportation. Some steal cars so they can commit other crimes. Professional auto thieves steal cars to sell the parts that are highly valuable. Car thieves take orders from chop shops and look for particular cars.

7. Understand what it means to burgle a home.

Under common law, the crime of burglary was defined as "the breaking and entering of a dwelling house of another in the nighttime with the intent to commit a felony within." Burglary is a serious crime because it involves entering another's home, which threatens occupants. More recent U.S. state laws have changed the requirements of burglary, and most have discarded the necessity of forced entry and the requirement that the crime take place in the evening to be considered a burglary.

8. Know what it takes to be a "good burglar."

Because burglary involves planning and risk, it attracts professional thieves. The most competent have technical skill and personal integrity, specialize in burglary, are financially successful, and avoid prison sentences. Professional burglars size up the value of a particular crime and balance it against the perceived risks. Many have undergone training in the company of older, more experienced burglars.

9. Distinguish between the activities of male and female burglars.

Both male and female burglars engage in other forms of crime, such as shoplifting and assault. Males are more likely to steal cars to supplement their income. Female burglars are much more likely to work with a partner, whereas males are more likely to go it alone. Males also begin their offending careers at an earlier age than females and are more likely to be repeat and recurrent offenders.

10. Discuss why people commit arson for profit.

Arson is the willful, malicious burning of a home, public building, vehicle, or commercial building. Most arsonists are teenage vandals. Professional arsonists specialize in burning commercial buildings for profit. The owners of commercial buildings may resort to arson to get rid of outdated inventory, to qualify for government redevelopment funds, to collect insurance money, to claim the loss of merchandise already sold, or to eliminate business competition (by burning a building owned by a competitor).

Key Terms

occasional criminals 295
situational
    inducement 295
professional criminals 295
larceny 296
constructive
    possession 296
petit (petty) larceny 297

grand larceny 297
shoplifting 298
snitch 299
booster (heel) 299
merchant privilege
    laws 299
target removal
    strategy 299

target hardening
    strategy 299
naive check forgers 303
systematic forgers 303
false pretenses
    (fraud) 303
confidence game (con
    game) 304

fence 305
embezzlement 305
burglary 306
arson 311

Critical Thinking Questions

1. Differentiate between an occasional and a professional criminal. Which one would be more likely to resort to violence?

2. What crime occurs when a person who owns an antiques store sells a client an "original" Tiffany lamp that she knows is a fake? Would it still be a crime if the seller were not aware that the lamp was a copy? Should antiques dealers have a duty to determine the authenticity of the products they sell?

3. What is the difference between a booster and a snitch? If caught, should they receive different punishments? What about naive and systematic check forgers?

4. What are the characteristics of the "good burglar"? Can you compare them to any other professionals?

© Jay Directo/AFP/Getty Images

Chapter Outline

Enterprise Crime

White-Collar Crime, Cyber Crime, and Organized Crime

In March of 2008, 22 people, including 12 Americans, were charged with participating in an international child pornography ring. Investigators confiscated more than 400,000 pictures, video files, and other images showing children engaged in sexual behavior. Some of the child victims were as young as five years old; many displayed innocent characteristics such as wearing their hair in pigtails. Originating in Australia, the ring had recruited pornographers from all over the world, including England, Canada, and Germany.

Although the ring was first discovered and infiltrated in 2006, it took more than two years to get indictments because of its technical sophistication, which included the use of encryption, background checks, and other security measures. One of the men indicted, 54-year-old Raymond Roy of San Juan Capistrano, California, posted videos of Thai children "to give everyone something to do for an afternoon." Another posting made on July 10, 2007, stated that "This one may offend here, so a word of caution, these girls are heavily drugged, Not much action to speak of, the girls are to [sic] [expletive deleted] up to move, or resist. Three girls, the first one being the youngest, around 8 or 9 yo." The yo stands for "years old."

The 12 men were charged with engaging in a child exploitation enterprise; illegally posting notices seeking to receive, exchange, and distribute child porn across state lines; and obstruction of justice. Several also were charged with producing the pornography, which means they had contact with the children who were exploited; more than half of those charged have already pled guilty and face 20-year prison sentences.[1]

Just a few years ago, this complex, global criminal enterprise could not have been contemplated, let alone transacted. Innovation brings change and with it new opportunities to commit crime, while making it more difficult to enforce the law. Technological change is an obstacle that enforcement agents must take on to

Fact or Fiction?

► White-collar crimes cost society far more than common-law crimes such as burglary and larceny.

► In order to avoid being cheated, you are better off going to a national franchise than to a local repair shop.

► Because you are not an employee yourself, it's OK to buy stock when your brother-in-law gives you a tip that the company he works for is about to be sold at a big profit.

► Most white-collar criminals get a slap on the wrist if they are convicted of crime.

► It will be difficult to defeat cyber criminals without inter-agency and international cooperation.

► Organized crime in the United States is controlled by five Mafia families in New York City and a few other, allied groups in Chicago, Los Angeles, and Miami.

Chapter Objectives

1. Know what is meant by the term "enterprise crime."
2. Be familiar with the various forms of white-collar crime.
3. Be aware of the causes that contribute to white-collar crime.
4. Discuss the special problems posed by cyber crime.
5. Be familiar with the different forms of cyber crime.
6. Discuss how the Internet is used for distributing obscene material.
7. Be familiar with the various forms of Internet-based copyright infringement violations.
8. Discuss the concept of identity theft.
9. Be aware of the various forms of cyber vandalism.
10. Discuss how the makeup of organized crime has evolved.

combat global crime groups whose schemes transcend national boundaries. Members of the transnational porn syndicate's illegal operation relied on Internet newsgroups, which are large file-sharing networks where text, software, pictures, and videos can be traded and shared; used sophisticated encryption methods to avoid detection; and traded more than 400,000 images and videos of child sexual abuse before their networks were dismantled after law enforcement infiltrated the group in August 2006.

The global scale of enforcement for what used to be a local problem can be seen in the agencies that cooperated in the investigation: the United States Department of Justice's U.S. Attorneys' Offices and the Criminal Division's Child Exploitation and Obscenity Section (CEOS); the FBI; the Queensland, Australia, Police Service; the Bundeskriminalamt (BKA) Child Pornography Unit in Germany; and the Child Exploitation and Online Protection Centre in the United Kingdom.

Enterprise Crime

It is now routine in our global free enterprise economy, for people to use complex and technologically sophisticated methods to secure illegal profits and/or provide criminal services. Sometimes these schemes are so complex that it takes enforcement agencies years to unravel them even after they become known. We refer here to these crimes of the marketplace as **enterprise crime**, because they mesh crime with business practices. In this chapter, crimes of illicit entrepreneurship are divided into three distinct categories. **White-collar crime** involves illegal activities of people and institutions whose acknowledged purpose is profit through legitimate business transactions. **Cyber crime** involves people using the instruments of modern technology for criminal purposes. **Organized crime** involves illegal activities of people and organizations whose acknowledged purpose is profit through illegitimate business enterprise.

CRIMES OF BUSINESS ENTERPRISE

White-collar crime, cyber crime, and organized crime are linked here because in each category, offenders twist the legal rules of commercial enterprise for criminal purposes. The three types of crime often overlap. Organized criminals may use the Internet to conduct fraud schemes and then seek legitimate enterprises to launder money, diversify their sources of income, increase their power and influence, and gain and enhance respectability.[2] Otherwise legitimate businesspeople may turn to organized criminals to help them with economic problems (such as breaking up a strike or dumping hazardous waste products), to stifle or threaten competition, and to increase their influence.[3] Whereas some corporate executives cheat to improve their company's position in the business world, others are motivated purely by personal gain, acting more like organized criminals than indiscreet businesspeople.[4]

Enterprise crimes taint and corrupt the free market system. They mix and match illegal and legal methods and legal and illegal products in all phases of commercial activity. Organized criminals often use illegal marketing techniques (including threats, extortion, and smuggling) to distribute otherwise legal products and services (lending money, conducting union activities, selling securities). They also engage in the distribution of products and services, such as drugs, sex, gambling, and prostitution, that have been outlawed. White-collar criminals use illegal business practices (embezzlement, price fixing, bribery, and so on) to market what are normally legitimate commercial products (securities, medical care, or online auctions, for example).[5] ▶ **Checkpoints**

White-Collar Crime

In the late 1930s, the distinguished criminologist Edwin Sutherland first used the phrase "white-collar crime" to describe the criminal activities of the rich and powerful. He defined white-collar crime as "a crime committed by a person of respectability and

enterprise crime
Use of illegal tactics to gain profit in the marketplace. Enterprise crimes can involve either the violation of law in the course of an otherwise legitimate occupation or the sale and distribution of illegal commodities.

white-collar crime
Illegal activities of people and institutions whose acknowledged purpose is profit through legitimate business transactions. White-collar crimes can involve theft, embezzlement, fraud, market manipulation, restraint of trade, and false advertising.

cyber crime
Use of the instruments of modern technology for criminal purposes.

organized crime
Illegal activities of people and organizations whose acknowledged purpose is profit through illegitimate business enterprise.

high social status in the course of his occupation."[6] As Sutherland saw it, white-collar crime involved conspiracies by members of the wealthy classes to use their positions in commerce and industry for personal gain without regard to the law. These actions were usually handled by civil courts, because injured parties were more concerned with recovering their losses than with seeing the offenders punished criminally. Consequently, Sutherland believed that the great majority of white-collar criminals avoided detection and that those who were caught generally avoided punishment.[7]

Sutherland focused on corporate criminality and crimes committed by wealthy industrialists. Contemporary criminologists have continued to study corporate crimes committed by unscrupulous executives who craft elaborate criminal conspiracies designed to improve market share or simply to siphon off corporate profits into their own pockets.[8] Contemporary definitions of white-collar crime are typically much broader than what Sutherland first envisioned. White-collar crime is now defined as any business-related act that uses deceit, deception, or dishonesty to carry out criminal enterprise. Included within the scope of white-collar crime are such diverse acts as income tax evasion, employee theft, soliciting bribes, accepting kickbacks, and embezzlement. Nor do criminologists restrict the definition to the wealthy and powerful; members of all social classes may engage in white-collar crimes.

Estimating the extent of white-collar crime and its influence on victims is difficult, because victims are often reluctant to report the crime to police, believing that nothing can be done and that getting further involved is pointless.[9] Experts place its total monetary value in the hundreds of billions of dollars, far outstripping the cost to society of any other type of crime. The FBI is currently pursuing more than 500 corporate fraud cases, several of which involve losses to public investors that exceed $1 billion. In 2009, investor Bernard Madoff was convicted of a fraudulent scheme that resulted in investor losses estimated at $65 billion; Robert Allen Stanford, owner of Stanford Financial Group and other affiliated companies, was charged with defrauding investors of approximately $7 billion.[10]

Components of White-Collar Crime

White-collar crime today represents a wide spectrum of behaviors involving individuals acting alone and within the context of a business structure. The victims of white-collar crime can be the general public, the organization that employs the offender, or a competing organization. Here we break down white-collar crime into a number of independent yet interrelated criminal activities, ranging from an individual using a business enterprise to commit theft-related crimes to a business enterprise engaging in activities that violate laws that regulate business and commerce.[11]

WHITE-COLLAR FRAUD

As you may recall from Chapter 11, one element of the common-law crime of larceny is *false pretenses*, in which a criminal uses trickery and deceit to separate victims from their money. Fraud can also be a white-collar enterprise crime when it involves people using their *institutional or business position* to trick others out of their money; these are essentially business-related frauds. Among business-related frauds are the following:

▶ *Pyramid schemes.* These schemes involve selling phony franchises. The investor buys a franchise to sell golf clubs or some other commodity, paying thousands of dollars, and is asked to recruit some friends to buy more franchises. The victim is promised a percentage of the sales of every new franchisee she or he recruits. Eventually there are hundreds of distributors but few customers, and the merchandise is typically unavailable. Those at the top make a lot of money before the pyramid collapses, but the newest investors at the bottom are bankrupted.

▶ *Repair frauds.* Shady contractors offer unusually low prices for expensive repairs and then use damaged or used merchandise on the job. For example, a driveway repair contractor gives a low bid but uses old motor oil rather than asphalt; it looks nice and shiny when the job is completed, but the first rain brings disaster.

Checkpoints

▶ Enterprise crimes involve illicit entrepreneurship and commerce.

▶ White-collar crime involves the illegal distribution of legal material.

▶ Cyber crime involves using technology to commit crime.

▶ Organized crime involves the illegal distribution of illegal material.

▶ White-collar crime and organized crime are linked because they involve entrepreneurship.

▶ Losses from enterprise crime may far outstrip those from any other type of crime.

▶ Enterprise crimes can cause deaths.

Fact or Fiction?

White-collar crimes cost society far more than common-law crimes such as burglary and larceny.

Fact. Losses due to white-collar crime are in the hundreds of billions each year and growing. Bernard Madoff alone swindled people out of $65 billion dollars.

CONNECTIONS

In Chapter 11, fraud was described as a common theft offense. Although common-law fraud and white-collar fraud are similar, common fraud involves a person using illegal methods to bilk another out of money, whereas white-collar fraud involves a person using his or her institutional or business position to achieve the same objective. Common-law fraud is typically a short-term transaction, whereas white-collar fraud involves a long-term criminal conspiracy. Although the ends are similar, the means are somewhat different.

Some crooked businessmen offer a low rate for a job that includes a "free" inspection. They then inform the client of an urgent need for expensive repairs, which are actually bogus.

▶ *Contract fraud.* In contract fraud, people are urged to sign long-term agreements but are not informed that the small print included on the sales contract obligates them to get high-priced services they did not really want in the first place. Another ploy is to trick the victim into thinking the contract is from a legitimate vendor because it has a familiar look: A business office receives an invoice in the mail with a self-addressed envelope that looks like it comes from the phone company (walking fingers on a yellow background). It appears to be a contract for an ad in the yellow pages. On the back, in small print, will be written, "By returning this confirmation, you're signing a contract to be an advertiser in the upcoming, and all subsequent, issues." If it returns the invoice, the business soon finds that it has agreed to a long-term contract to advertise in some private publication that is not widely distributed.

CHISELING

Chiseling involves regularly cheating an organization, its consumers, or both. Chiselers may be individuals who want to make quick profits in their own business, or

Fraud is not unique to American culture. Here pop music producer Tetsuya Komuro, 50, enters the Osaka District Court in Osaka, Japan, for his first court hearing in a fraud case in which he allegedly concluded a contract to sell music copyrights that did not belong to him and swindled an investor out of 500 million yen. Komuro is one of Japan's most successful music entrepreneurs. Singles that he composed have sold more than 70 million copies, and his songs have sold more than 42 million copies. On May 11, 2009, Komuro received a suspended three-year prison sentence, thanks to his acceptance of responsibility and the fact that restitution had been made to the victim.

© Kyodo via AP Images

chiseling
Using illegal means to cheat an organization, its consumers, or both, on a regular basis.

employees of large organizations who decide to cheat their own company or its clients by doing something contrary to either the law or company policy. For example, say a franchisee of a national auto repair company such as Jiffy Lube violates both the law and corporate policy by substituting cheaper generic products and charging customers for a more expensive name-brand product. (Perhaps the chiseler bills for a new Purolator or Mobil 1 oil filter but installs a cheaper generic model instead). Some unscrupulous franchisees may routinely charge for work that is not actually done, such as tire rotation and balancing. These illegal acts, which are almost impossible to detect, cheat customers while at the same time violating corporate policy and damaging customer relations.[12]

Professional Chiseling: Medical Crimes It is not uncommon for medical professionals to use their positions to chisel clients. Pharmacists have been known to alter prescriptions or substitute low-cost generic drugs for more expensive name brands.[13] In one recent case, Massachusetts pharmacy owner Monty Schwartz was sentenced to 20 months imprisonment and ordered to pay $459,000 in restitution for reselling drugs that had been returned by customers, as well as not-for-resale drug samples. He instructed his employees to remove the returned and sample drugs from their original packaging and put them back in stock bottles where they were used for filling new prescriptions. In this process, the lot numbers of the drugs were lost, leaving the store unable to track the pills in the event of a recall.[14]

The most notorious case of professional chiseling involved Kansas City pharmacist Robert R. Courtney, who was charged with fraud when it was discovered that he had been selling diluted mixtures of the medications Taxol, Gemzar, Paraplatin, and Platinol, which are used to treat cancer.[15] After he pled guilty, Courtney told authorities that his criminal activities affected the patients of 400 doctors, involved 98,000 prescriptions, and harmed approximately 4,200 patients.[16]

Professional Chiseling: Financial Crimes A great deal of chiseling takes place on the commodities and stock markets, where individuals engage in deceptive schemes to defraud clients. For example, dishonest investment counselors and insurance agents may use their positions to cheat individual clients by misleading them on the quality of their investments; financial organizations cheat their clients by promoting risky investments as being iron-clad safe. The greatest financial chiseler of all time is the subject of the accompanying Profiles in Crime feature on the next page.

Financial chiseling schemes can involve stockbrokers, mortgage brokers, bankers, and other fiduciary agents who violate accepted commercial practices. Their schemes include

▶ **Churning.** A stockbroker manipulates a client's account by repeated, excessive, and unnecessary buying and selling of stock.[17]
▶ **Front running.** A broker places personal orders ahead of a customer's large order to profit from the market effects of the trade.
▶ **Bucketing.** A broker confirms an order to a client without actually executing it and then waits to see how the stock performs. If the stock price increases, the customer is charged the higher price; if the stock price goes lower, the broker buys the stock at that price, places it in the customer's account at the higher price, and keeps the difference.[18]
▶ **Insider Trading.** It is illegal to use one's position of trust to profit from information unavailable to the public in order to buy and sell securities for personal profit. The law prohibiting insider trading was originally conceived to make it illegal for corporate employees with direct knowledge of market-sensitive information to use that information for their own benefit or that of their friends and relatives. For example, it would be illegal for employees to buy stock, using their insider information, in a company that their employer was about to take over at a much higher price. In recent years, the definition of insider trading has been expanded by federal courts to include employees of financial institutions, such as

churning
Repeated, excessive, and unnecessary buying and selling of a client's stock.

front running
Placing broker's personal orders ahead of a customer's large order to profit from the market effects of the trade.

bucketing
Skimming customer trading profits by falsifying trade information.

insider trading
Illegal buying of stock in a company on the basis of information provided by someone who has a fiduciary interest in the company, such as an employee or an attorney or accountant retained by the firm. Federal laws and the rules of the Securities and Exchange Commission require that all profits from such trading be returned and provide for both fines and a prison sentence.

On March 12, 2009, financier Bernard Madoff pled guilty to an 11-count criminal complaint, charging him with violating the antifraud provisions of the Securities Act of 1933, the Securities Exchange Act of 1934, and the Investment Advisers Act of 1940. At his hearing, Madoff admitted that he had defrauded thousands of investors in the nation's most elaborate financial crime. On June 29, 2009, Madoff was sentenced to 150 years in prison, a life sentence.

How did Madoff's scheme unfold? He founded the Wall Street firm Bernard L. Madoff Investment Securities LLC in 1960, and it soon became one of Wall Street's largest "specialist" trading firms. Madoff Investments specialized in investment management and advice, managing billions in assets. He became the darling of the jet set and was trusted by many wealthy people, including director Steven Spielberg; actors John Malkovich, acting couple Kevin Bacon and Kyra Sedgwick; and numerous sophisticated financial managers and investors. They were taken in by his promise of high returns and a long track record of success. But it all fell apart when the market crashed and people wanted their money back. It seems the asset management arm of Madoff's firm was a giant Ponzi scheme. Madoff had not invested *any* of the money he had taken in from investors but, instead, had deposited it in various banks, including New York's Chase Manhattan Bank. He used the interest and principal to pay off investors when they wanted to take money out of their accounts, but few did so because they were making fantastic paper profits. Madoff, of course, urged them to keep their profits in the account rather than asking for a distribution. But when they did attempt to withdraw in large numbers, his house of cards fell apart. Billions of dollars are missing—and authorities are still trying to figure out where it all went.

When the market melted down in 2007, time ran out and it proved impossible for Madoff to catch up to the paper profits. He finally told his sons what he had done, and they contacted the FBI. Madoff later claimed that he merely wanted to satisfy his clients' expectations of high returns and that their demands simply could not be met by legal

© Timothy A. Clary/AFP/Getty Images

means. Instead, he resorted to an illegal scheme involving false trading activities, illegal foreign transfers, and false SEC filings. He hoped that clients would simply reinvest their gains without requesting withdrawals until he could figure out a way to invest the money and actually make a profit! Madoff admitted he knew his day of reckoning was inevitable.

Madoff's Ponzi scheme has been estimated to have cost clients some *$65 billion*, maybe the largest criminal conspiracy in history. He will spend the rest of his life in prison while authorities try to find out what happened to the cash. Madoff has become a symbol of the greed run amok that almost destroyed the nation's financial system.

SOURCES: Securities and Exchange Commission, "SEC Charges Bernard L. Madoff for Multi-Billion Dollar Ponzi Scheme," December 11, 2008, www.sec.gov/news/press/2008/2008–293.htm (accessed April 30, 2009); Joe Lauria, "Life inside the Weird World of Bernard Madoff." Timesonline, March 22, 2009, http://business .timesonline.co.uk/tol/business/industry_sectors/banking_and_ finance/article5949961.ece (accessed April 28, 2009).

law or banking firms, who have access to confidential information about corporate clients.[19]

Recently, chiseling in the mortgage markets almost wrecked the U.S. economy. Chiseling scams involving subprime mortgages is the topic of the accompanying Current Issues in Crime feature.

During the period 2008–2009, the nation was rocked by fraudulent activity in the banking sector that threatened to destroy the financial system and create a 1929-style depression. The cornerstone of the crisis was the collapse of the subprime mortgage sector. A subprime mortgage lender is a business that lends to borrowers who do not qualify for loans from mainstream lenders. By 2006, subprimes had grown to 20 percent of the mortgage market, up from 2 percent a decade earlier; this means that an estimated $1.3 trillion of the total $4.5 trillion in outstanding U.S. mortgage loans is subprime.

Subprime lenders relied on continuing rises in real estate values to allow the borrowers to refinance or sell their properties before going into default. However, in 2008 when the real estate market collapsed and unemployment rose

result of these practices, some subprime lenders are being investigated by federal agencies for corporate fraud and insider trading. In one case, officers of Mercury Finance Company were convicted of intentionally misstating the company's financial records: They falsely reported a 1996 profit of more than $120 million instead of a loss of $30 million. Executives provided materially false financial statements to more than 20 financial institutions, enabling Mercury to obtain more than $1.5 billion in loan commitments and lines of credit. When the fraud was discovered, Mercury's stock price dropped significantly, costing shareholders nearly $2 billion in market value. A number of company officers went to prison, including former CEO John Brincat Sr., who pled guilty to wire fraud and

Current Issues in Crime The Subprime Mortgage Scandal

dramatically, many borrowers who were financially shaky to begin with could neither continue to make payments on their loans nor sell their homes. Loan defaults increased, while the ability to sell the new loans plummeted. As a result, mortgage companies experienced financial distress and bankruptcy.

Desperate for funds, some subprime lenders, in order to stave off regulators, falsified accounting entries and fraudulently inflated their assets and revenues. Some manipulated their reported loan portfolio risks and used various accounting schemes to inflate their financial reports. And in some cases, before these subprime lenders' stocks rapidly declined in value, executives with insider information sold their equity positions and profited illegally. As a

making a false statement to a bank and was sentenced to 10 years in prison.

CRITICAL THINKING

Should people who engage in white-collar chiseling that costs billions be sent to prison even though they are not dangerous, predatory criminals? Or should all their assets be confiscated, including those transferred to family members, while they are forced to work and surrender the majority of their wages to pay off debts or compensate victims?

SOURCE: FBI, "Financial Crimes," www.fbi.gov/publications/ financial/fcs_report2007/financial_crime_2007.htm#Mortgage

EXPLOITATION

Recently, an employee of the U.S. Army Corps of Engineers in Iraq and Afghanistan was charged with soliciting and receiving a $40,000 payment from a contractor, which was then awarded a $2.5 million project to build city parks in Kirkuk, Iraq. The engineer had responsibility for supervising various construction projects, including oil pipeline barriers, water projects, schools, and roads, so the contractor feared it would not get paid or would lose contracts if it failed to meet his demands for money.[20]

It is sad but true that some individuals exploit their position, even during times of war, in order to make an illegal profit. They use their power to take advantage of others who have an interest in how that power is used. A fire inspector who threatens a restaurant owner with a safety violation unless he is given a financial consideration is abusing his institutional position. In a recent case, an immigration officer demanded and received sexual favors from a woman after he threatened to withhold her green card.[21]

Exploitation occurs when the victim has a clear right to expect a service, and the offender threatens to withhold the service unless an additional payment or bribe is forthcoming. In the Iraq case, a contractor feared that it would be excluded from

exploitation
Forcing victims to pay for services or contracts to which they have a clear right.

military contracts unless it paid an inspector a bribe; the woman involved with the immigration officer feared that she would be deported unless she complied with his demands.

Exploitation can also occur in private industry. For example, a company employee might refuse to award a contract to a supplier unless it gave him or her a "piece of the action." Purchasing agents in large companies often demand payment for awarding contracts to suppliers and distributors. Managing agents in some of New York City's most luxurious buildings have been convicted on charges that they routinely extorted millions of dollars from maintenance contractors and building suppliers before awarding them contracts that they deserved on the merits of their service.[22]

INFLUENCE PEDDLING

Sometimes individuals who occupy important institutional positions sell power, influence, and information to outsiders who have an interest in influencing activities of the institution or receiving services that they do not deserve. Offenses within this category include government employees taking kickbacks from contractors in return for awarding contracts they could not have won on merit, and outsiders bribing government officials, such as those in the Securities and Exchange Commission, who might sell information about future government activities. Political leaders have been convicted of accepting bribes to rig elections that enable their party to control state politics.[23]

One major difference distinguishes those who engage in **influence peddling** from exploiters: Whereas exploiters force victims to pay for services *to which they have a clear right*, influence peddlers take bribes in order to use their positions to grant favors and/or sell information to which their co-conspirators are not entitled. The victims in crimes of institutional exploitation are the people who are threatened and forced to pay, whereas the victims in crimes of influence peddling are the organization compromised by its employees for their own interests and the people who pay for those organizations and expect them to be run in a fair and legal manner—that is, taxpayers.

Influence Peddling in Government It is unfortunately common for government workers and office holders to engage in official corruption, a circumstance that is particularly disturbing because society expects a higher standard of moral integrity from people empowered to uphold the law and judge their fellow citizens. On April 17, 2006, former Governor George Ryan of Illinois was convicted of steering government contracts to people who were willing to give him kickbacks and bribes. The prosecution said that Mr. Ryan and his family received fancy vacations, money, and other items worth at least $167,000, and in return he offered special political favors and state business in the dozen years that he served in the state's top roles.[24] But Illinois's problems did not end here. Ryan's successor Governor Rod Blagojevich was forced to resign after he was overheard, in federal wiretaps, speaking of his plan to sell President-elect Obama's seat in the United States Senate to the highest bidder.[25] Blagojevich was subsequently impeached and was removed from office on January 29, 2009; Blagojevich was also barred from ever again holding public office in the state of Illinois.

Influence Peddling in Criminal Justice Agents of the criminal justice system have also been accused of influence peddling. Police have routinely been accused and convicted of accepting bribes from individuals engaged in illegal activities. Some have been convicted on charges that they provided protection from and gave warning of planned raids on brothels, gambling dens, and drug houses.[26] Even customs inspectors have been convicted of being paid by drug cartels to look the other way when large shipments of illegal substances were smuggled across the border.[27]

Police are not the only justice officials who have been caught in the web of bribery and influence peddling. Sadly, judges have been accused of taking bribes paid to influence their decision making. For example, in 2009 Wayne G. Cresap, a Louisiana judge, was charged with accepting bribes to influence his bail decision making. Cresap

influence peddling
Using one's institutional position to grant favors and sell information to which one's co-conspirators are not entitled.

released defendants on their own recognizance, without requiring cash bail, if their lawyers would later give him a payoff in return.[28] Although Cresap's actions are troubling, they pale in comparison to what may be the most shocking case of judicial malfeasance on record. In 2009 two Pennsylvania judges, Mark Ciavarella and Michael Conahan, were indicted for accepting $2.6 million in payoffs to put juvenile offenders in lockups run by a privately managed youth detention corporation. Thousands of kids were put away for minor infractions so that the judges could earn millions in illegal payoffs; both eventually pled guilty and received seven-year prison sentences.[29]

Influence Peddling in Business Politicians and government officials are not the only ones accused of bribery; business has had its share of scandals. One form, known as **payola**, involves the practice of record companies paying radio stations to play songs without making listeners aware of the bribes. Some large companies have been caught in payola scandals; Sony paid $10 million to the State of New York to settle a claim that its promoters gave gifts to station managers to get songs played.[30]

In some foreign countries, soliciting bribes to do business is a common—even expected—practice. Not surprisingly, U.S. businesses have complained that stiff penalties in this country for bribery give foreign competitors an edge over them. In European countries, such as Italy and France, giving bribes to secure contracts is perfectly legal; and in West Germany, corporate bribes are actually tax-deductible.[31] Some government officials solicit bribes to allow American firms to do business in their countries.[32]

To limit bribing of foreign officials, Congress in 1977 passed the Foreign Corrupt Practices Act (FCPA), which made it a criminal offense to bribe foreign officials or to make other questionable overseas payments. Violations of the FCPA draw strict penalties for both the defendant company and its officers.[33] Moreover, all fines imposed on corporate officers are paid by them, not absorbed by the company. For violations of the antibribery provisions of the FCPA, a domestic corporation can be fined up to $1 million. Company officers, employees, or stockholders who are convicted of bribery may have to serve a prison sentence of up to five years and pay a $10,000 fine. Congressional dissatisfaction with the harshness and ambiguity of the bill has caused numerous revisions to be proposed. Despite the penalties imposed by the FCPA, corporations that deal in foreign trade have continued to give bribes to secure favorable trade agreements.[34] On June 16, 2004, Schering-Plough Corporation agreed to pay a civil penalty of $500,000 for violating provisions of the FCPA. An employee of Schering-Plough's Polish subsidiary made a payment to a charitable foundation headed by a Polish government official. The government charged that these "charitable" payments were designed to influence the official to purchase Schering-Plough's pharmaceutical products for his region's health fund.[35]

EMBEZZLEMENT AND EMPLOYEE FRAUD

Some individuals use their positions to embezzle company funds or appropriate company property for themselves. Here, the company or organization that employs the criminal, rather than an outsider, is the victim of white-collar crime.

Blue-Collar Fraud In 2002, three employees and a friend allegedly stole moon rocks from a NASA laboratory in Houston, Texas. FBI agents arrested them after they tried to sell the contraband to an undercover agent in Orlando, Florida. The would-be seller reportedly asked $2,000 per gram for the rocks at first but later bumped the price up to $8,000 per gram.[36] Although the theft of moon rocks does not happen very often, systematic theft of company property by employees, or **pilferage**, is common.[37]

Employee theft is most accurately explained by factors relevant to the work setting, such as job dissatisfaction and the workers' belief that they are being exploited by employers or supervisors; economic problems play a relatively small role in the decision to pilfer. Thus, although employers attribute employee fraud to economic conditions and declining personal values, workers themselves say they steal because of strain and conflict.

payola
The practice of record companies bribing radio stations to play songs without making listeners aware of the payment.

pilferage
Systematic theft of company property.

It is difficult to determine the value of goods taken by employees, but some recent surveys indicate it is substantial. In its most recent (2007) survey, Hayes International, a loss prevention firm, examined 24 large retail companies with 19,151 stores and over $689 billion in retail sales and got some sobering results.

▶ *Employee apprehensions.* 82,648 dishonest employees were apprehended in 2007, up 17 percent from 2006.
▶ *Employee recovery dollars.* Over $66 million was recovered from employee apprehensions in 2007, up 12 percent from 2006.
▶ *Rate of apprehension.* One in every 28 employees was apprehended for theft from their employer in 2007. (This figure is based on over 2.3 million employees.)
▶ *Putting it in context.* On a per-case average, dishonest employees steal a little over 6 times the amount stolen by shoplifters ($808.09 compared to $132.91).[38]

Management Fraud Blue-collar workers are not the only employees who commit corporate theft. Management-level fraud is also quite common. Such acts include converting company assets for personal benefit; fraudulently receiving increases in compensation (such as raises or bonuses); fraudulently increasing personal holdings of company stock; retaining one's present position within the company by manipulating accounts; and concealing unacceptable performance from stockholders.[39]

Management fraud has involved some of the nation's largest companies and richest people.

▶ *Tyco International Ltd.* In 2005, Tyco's chief executive officer L. Dennis Kozlowski and chief financial officer Marc Swartz were convicted on a variety of fraud and larceny charges, including misappropriating $170 million in company funds by hiding unauthorized bonuses and secretly forgiving loans to themselves. Kozlowski and Swartz were also accused of making more than $430 million by lying about Tyco's financial condition in order to inflate the value of their stock. Kozlowski was convicted of looting the company of $150 million and sentenced to 8–1/3 to 25 years in prison.[40]
▶ *Enron Corporation.* Executives of the oil and gas trading firm, once one of the largest companies in the United States, engaged in a massive fraud scheme that caused the company to go bankrupt. Chairman Kenneth L. Lay was charged with conspiracy, securities fraud, wire fraud, bank fraud, and making false statements. Enron CEO Jeffrey K. Skilling and former Enron chief accounting officer Richard Causey were also charged with money laundering and conspiracy. The government claimed that these executives oversaw a massive conspiracy to delude investors into believing that Enron was a growing company when, in fact, it was undergoing business setbacks. Why did they do it? Greed. Between 1998 and 2001, Lay received approximately $300 million from the sale of Enron stock options and restricted stock and made over $217 million in profit; he was also paid more than $19 million in salary and bonuses.[41]
▶ *WorldCom.* In 2005, WorldCom CEO Bernie Ebbers was found guilty of falsifying the company's financial statements by more than $9 billion. One of the most important elements of the case was the more than $400 million that WorldCom lent or guaranteed to lend Ebbers at an interest rate of 2.15 percent. When the market contracted, Ebbers was in no position to pay back the loans, and the company collapsed. On May 15, 2005, a federal jury in New York convicted Ebbers on all nine counts with which he was charged and sentenced him to 25 years in prison.[42]

CLIENT FRAUD

Some white-collar criminals scheme to defraud organizations that pay or reimburse them for services or advance credit to their clients. These offenses are linked because they involve cheating an organization (such as a government agency or insurance company) with many individual clients that the organization supports financially (such as welfare clients), reimburses for services provided (such as an insurance company reimbursing health care providers), covers losses of (such as insurance policyholders), or extends credit to (such as bank clients or taxpayers). Included in this category are insurance fraud, credit card fraud, fraud related to welfare and Medicare programs, and tax evasion.

Health Care Fraud Abusive and deceptive health care practices include such techniques as "ping-ponging" (referring patients to other physicians in the same office), "gang visits" (billing for multiple services that were not actually provided), and "steering" (directing patients to particular pharmacies that give the doctor a kickback). Doctors who abuse their Medicaid or Medicare patients in this way are liable to civil suits and criminal penalties.

In addition to physicians, health care providers have been accused of routinely violating the law to obtain millions in illegal payments. For example, on June 30, 2009, Jose Luis Perez and Reinaldo Guerra, owners of 21 corporations that supplied medical equipment to Medicare beneficiaries, were indicted on charges of submitting $179 million in fraudulent claims to Medicare for medical equipment that had not been prescribed or ordered by a physician or delivered to a Medicare beneficiary. Medicare paid the companies approximately $56 million. To carry out their scheme, Perez and Guerra used physicians' Medicare identification numbers without the physicians' authorization.[43]

The government has attempted to tighten control over the industry in order to restrict the opportunity for physicians to commit fraud. Health care companies providing services to federal health care programs are also regulated by federal laws that prohibit kickbacks and self-referrals. It is now a crime, punishable by up to five years in prison, to provide anything of value, money or otherwise, directly or indirectly, with the intent to induce the referral of a patient to a health care service. Liability attaches to both parties in the transaction—the entity or individual providing the kickbacks and the individual receiving payment for the referral.

Federal law also prohibits physicians and other health care providers from referring beneficiaries in federal health care programs to clinics or other facilities in which the physician or health care provider has a financial interest. It is illegal for a doctor to refer her patients to a blood-testing lab in which she has an ownership share. These practices—kickbacks and self-referrals—are prohibited under federal law because they

Health care fraud costs Americans billions each year. Here, federal agents escort suspects out of the FBI offices in Houston on July 29, 2009. Federal authorities arrested more than 30 suspects, including doctors, and were seeking other suspects in a major Medicare fraud bust in New York, Louisiana, Boston, and Houston.

would compromise a medical professional's independent judgment. Federal law prohibits arrangements that tend to corrupt medical judgment and tempt the prescriber to put the provider's bottom line ahead of the patient's well-being.[44]

Tax Evasion Another important aspect of client fraud is tax evasion. Here, the victim is the government that is cheated by one of its clients, the errant taxpayer to whom it extended credit by allowing the taxpayer to delay paying taxes on money he or she had already earned. Tax fraud is a particularly challenging area for criminological study because so many U.S. citizens regularly underreport their income, and it is often difficult to separate honest error from deliberate tax evasion.

The basic law on tax evasion is contained in the U.S. Internal Revenue Code, section 7201, which states that

> Any person who willfully attempts in any manner to evade or defeat any tax imposed by this title or the payment thereof shall, in addition to other penalties provided by law, be guilty of a felony and, upon conviction thereof, shall be fined not more than $100,000 or imprisoned not more than five years, or both, together with the costs of prosecution.

To prove tax fraud, the government must find that the taxpayer either underreported his or her income or did not report taxable income. No minimum dollar amount is stated before fraud exists, but the government can take legal action when there is a "substantial underpayment of tax." A second element of tax fraud is "willfulness" on the part of the tax evader. In the major case on this issue, willfulness was defined as a "voluntary, intentional violation of a known legal duty and not the careless disregard for the truth."[45] Finally, to prove tax fraud, the government must show that the taxpayer has purposely attempted to evade or defeat a tax payment. If the offender is guilty of passive neglect, the offense is a misdemeanor. "Passive neglect" means simply not paying taxes, not reporting income, or not paying taxes when due. On the other hand, "affirmative tax evasion," such as keeping double books, making false entries, destroying books or records, concealing assets, or covering up sources of income, constitutes a felony.

CORPORATE CRIME

Yet another component of white-collar crime involves situations in which powerful institutions or their representatives willfully violate the laws that restrain these institutions from doing social harm or require them to do social good. This is also known as **corporate**, or **organizational**, **crime**.

Interest in corporate crime first emerged in the early 1900s, when a group of writers known as muckrakers targeted the monopolistic business practices of John D. Rockefeller and other corporate business leaders. In a 1907 article, sociologist E. A. Ross described the "criminaloid": a business leader who, while enjoying immunity from the law, victimized an unsuspecting public.[46] Edwin Sutherland focused theoretical attention on corporate crime when he began his research on the subject in the late 1930s and 1940s. As we noted earlier, corporate crime was probably what he had in mind when he coined the phrase "white-collar crime."[47]

Corporate crimes are socially injurious acts committed to further the business interests of people who control companies. The target of these crimes can be the general public, the environment, or even company workers. What makes these crimes unique is that the perpetrator is a legal fiction—a corporation—and not an individual. In reality, it is company employees or owners who commit corporate crimes and who ultimately benefit through career advancement or greater profits.

Some of the acts included within corporate crime are price fixing and illegal restraint of trade, false advertising, and the use of company practices that violate environmental protection statutes. The variety of crimes contained within this category is great, and they cause vast damage. The following subsections examine some of the most important offenses.

corporate (organizational) crime
Powerful institutions or their representatives willfully violate the laws that restrain these institutions from doing social harm or require them to do social good.

Illegal Restraint of Trade A restraint of trade involves a contract or conspiracy designed to stifle competition, create a monopoly, artificially maintain prices, or otherwise interfere with free market competition.[48] The control of restraint-of-trade violations has its legal basis in the **Sherman Antitrust Act**, which subjects to criminal or civil sanctions any person "who shall make any contract or engage in any combination or conspiracy" in restraint of interstate commerce.[49] For violations of its provisions, this federal law created criminal penalties of up to three years' imprisonment and $100,000 in fines for individuals and $10 million in fines for corporations.[50] The act outlaws conspiracies between corporations that are designed to control the marketplace.

In most instances, the act lets the presiding court judge decide whether corporations have conspired to "unreasonably restrain competition." However, through the Sherman Antitrust Act, four types of market conditions considered inherently anticompetitive have been defined by federal courts as illegal per se, without regard to the facts or circumstances of the case:

▶ *Division of markets.* Firms divide a region into territories, and each firm agrees not to compete in the others' territories.
▶ *Tying arrangement.* A corporation requires customers of one of its services to use other services it offers. For example, it would be an illegal restraint of trade if a railroad required that companies doing business with it or supplying it with materials ship all goods they produce on trains owned by the rail line.[51]
▶ *Group boycott.* An organization or company boycotts retail stores that do not comply with its rules or desires.
▶ *Price fixing.* A conspiracy to set and control the price of a necessary commodity is considered an absolute violation of the act.

Price Fixing A violation of the Sherman Antitrust Act occurs when two or more business competitors conspire to sell the same or similar products or services at an agreed-on price. The purpose: to maximizing prices, reduce the costs of competition, and sell the product at a price higher than would be possible with normal competition.

An example of **price fixing** occurred in 2008, when executives from large electronics firms such as LG and Hitachi pled guilty to charges that they conspired to fix the prices of LCD screens sold to American companies such as Dell for use in desktop monitors and notebook computers.[52] They were not alone. In 2009, executives from 15 airlines were charged in a conspiracy to fix the cargo rates charged to customers for international air shipments, including to and from the United States. The companies paid criminal fines totaling more that $1.6 billion, and three airline executives were incarcerated. To carry out their scheme, the airline executives

▶ Participated in meetings, conversations and communications to discuss the cargo rates to be charged on certain routes to and from the United States
▶ Agreed, during those meetings, conversations, and communications, on certain components of the cargo rates to charge on shipments on certain routes to and from the United States
▶ Levied cargo rates in the United States and elsewhere in accordance with the agreements reached
▶ Engaged in meetings, conversations, and communications in the United States and elsewhere for the purpose of monitoring and enforcing adherence to the agreed-upon cargo rates[53]

Deceptive Pricing Even the largest U.S. corporations commonly use deceptive pricing schemes when they respond to contract solicitations. Deceptive pricing occurs when contractors provide the government or other corporations with incomplete or misleading information on how much it will actually cost to fulfill the contracts on which they are bidding, or use mischarges once the contracts are signed.[54] For example, defense contractors have been prosecuted for charging the government for costs

Sherman Antitrust Act
Federal law that subjects to criminal or civil sanctions any person "who shall make any contract or engage in any combination or conspiracy" in restraint of interstate commerce.

price fixing
The illegal control by agreement among producers or manufacturers of the price of a commodity to avoid price competition and deprive the consumer of reasumable prices.

incurred on work they are doing for private firms or for shifting the costs on fixed-price contracts to ones in which the government reimburses the contractor for all expenses ("cost-plus" contracts).

False Claims Advertising Executives in even the largest corporations sometimes face stockholders' expectations of ever-increasing company profits that seem to demand that sales be increased at any cost. At times they respond to this challenge by making claims about their products that cannot be justified by actual performance. However, there is a fine line between clever, aggressive sales techniques and fraudulent claims. It is traditional to show a product in its best light, even if that involves resorting to fantasy. Showing a delivery service vehicle taking off into outer space or implying that taking one sip of beer will make people feel they have just jumped into a freezer are not fraudulent. But it is illegal to knowingly and purposely advertise a product as possessing qualities that the manufacturer realizes it does not have, such as the ability to cure the common cold, grow hair, or turn senior citizens into rock stars (though some rock stars are senior citizens these days).

Worker Safety/Environmental Crimes Much attention has been paid to intentional or negligent environmental pollution caused by many large corporations. The numerous allegations in this area involve almost every aspect of U.S. business. There are many different types of environmental crimes. Some corporations have endangered the lives of their own workers by maintaining unsafe conditions in their plants and mines. It has been estimated that more than 20 million workers have been exposed to hazardous materials while on the job. Some industries have been hit particularly hard by complaints and allegations. The control of workers' safety in the United States has been the province of the Occupational Safety and Health Administration (OSHA), which sets industry standards for the proper use of such chemicals as benzene, arsenic, lead, and coke (from coal). Intentional violation of OSHA standards can result in criminal penalties.

© David Leeson/The Image Works

Environmental crimes include dumping toxic waste near water sources, a practice that can cause the severe illness or death of innocent people oblivious to the danger. Near Dallas, Texas, a city investigator looks for clues to the identity of the party that illegally discarded these barrels of toxic waste discovered in a wooded area. The investigator works for the water department and regularly checks for sources of ground water contamination.

The major enforcement arm against environmental crimes is the Environmental Protection Agency (EPA), which was given full law enforcement authority in 1988. The EPA has successfully prosecuted significant violations across all major environmental statutes, including data fraud cases (for instance, private laboratories submitting false environmental data to state and federal environmental agencies); indiscriminate hazardous waste dumping that resulted in serious injuries and death; industrywide ocean dumping by cruise ships; oil spills that caused significant damage to waterways, wetlands, and beaches; international smuggling of CFC refrigerants that damage the ozone layer and increase the risk of skin cancer; and illegal handling of hazardous substances such as pesticides and asbestos that exposed children, the poor, and other especially vulnerable groups to potentially serious illness.[55] Its Criminal Investigation Division (EPA CID) investigates allegations of criminal wrongdoing prohibited by various environmental statutes. Such investigations involve, but are not limited to, the following:

► Illegal disposal of hazardous waste
► Export of hazardous waste without the permission of the receiving country
► Illegal discharge of pollutants to a water of the United States
► Removal and disposal of regulated asbestos-containing materials in a manner inconsistent with the law and regulations
► Illegal importation of certain restricted or regulated chemicals into the United States
► Tampering with a drinking water supply
► Mail fraud
► Wire fraud
► Conspiracy and money laundering related to environmental criminal activities[56]
► **Checkpoints**

Theories of White-Collar Crime

Why do they do it? Why do otherwise respectable people decide to break the law? As noted, most criminal offenders begin their offending careers when they are quite young. Yet by its very nature, white-collar crime requires people to attain a position of some responsibility in the workplace before they can commit crime. Can the theories that predict common-law crime also apply to white-collar crime? There are a number of theories of white-collar crime. The next sections describe three of the most prominent.

RATIONALIZATION/NEUTRALIZATION VIEW

In his research on fraud, Donald Cressey found that the door to solving personal financial problems through criminal means is opened by the rationalizations people develop for white-collar crime: "Some of our most respectable citizens got their start in life by using other people's money temporarily"; "in the real estate business, there is nothing wrong about using deposits before the deal is closed"; "all people steal when they get in a tight spot."[57] Offenders use these and other rationalizations to resolve the conflict they experience over engaging in illegal behavior. Rationalizations allow offenders to meet their financial needs without compromising their values.

A recent study of Medicare/Medicaid fraud by speech, occupational, and physical therapists working in hospitals, in nursing homes, and with home health agencies found that these professionals frequently engaged in two fraudulent practices: cutting sessions short while charging for the entire session, and charging individual session rates for group therapy sessions.[58] When interviewed, the workers described using three techniques of neutralization that enabled them to defuse guilt over what they recognized as deviant practices: (1) Everyone else does it, (2) it's not my fault or responsibility, and (3) no one is hurt except insurance companies, and they are wealthy.

Checkpoints

► White-collar crime has a number of different subcategories.

► White-collar fraud involves people using their *institutional or business position* to trick others out of their money.

► Chiseling involves regular cheating of an organization or its customers.

► People who engage in exploitation demand payment for services to which victims are entitled by threatening consequences if their victims refuse. The victim here is the client.

► Influence peddling and bribery occur when a person in authority demands payment for a service to which the payer is clearly not entitled. The victim here is the organization.

► Embezzlement and employee fraud occur when a person uses a position of trust to steal from an organization.

► Client fraud involves theft from an organization that advances credit, covers losses, or reimburses for services.

► Organizational, or corporate, crime involves various illegal business practices, such as price fixing, restraint of trade, and false advertising.

CONNECTIONS

The view that white-collar crime is a learning process is reminiscent of Edwin Sutherland's description of how gang boys learn the techniques of drug dealing and burglary from older youths through differential association. See Chapter 7 for a description of this process.

CORPORATE CULTURE VIEW

The corporate culture view is that some business organizations promote white-collar criminality in the same way that lower-class culture encourages the development of juvenile gangs and street crime. According to the corporate culture view, some business enterprises cause crime by placing excessive demands on employees, while maintaining a business climate tolerant of employee deviance. New employees learn the attitudes and techniques needed to commit white-collar crime from their business peers.

The corporate culture theory can be invoked to explain the collapse of Enron. A new CEO had been brought in to revitalize the company, and he wanted to become part of the "new economy" based on the Internet. Layers of management were wiped out, and hundreds of outsiders were recruited. Huge cash bonuses and stock options were granted to top performers. Young managers were given authority to make $5 million decisions without higher approval. It became common for executives to change jobs two or three times in an effort to maximize their bonuses and pay. Seminars were conducted showing executives how to hide profits and avoid taxes.[59]

Those holding the corporate culture view would point to the Enron scandal as a prime example of what happens when people work in organizations in which the cultural values stress profit over fair play, government scrutiny is limited and regulators are viewed as the enemy, and senior members encourage newcomers to believe that "greed is good."

CONNECTIONS

As you may recall from Chapter 9, Gottfredson and Hirschi's General Theory of Crime holds that criminals lack self-control. Because Gottfredson and Hirschi believe all crime has a similar basis, the motivation and pressure to commit white-collar crime are the same as those that prompt any other form of crime.

SELF-CONTROL VIEW

Not all criminologists subscribe to corporate culture theory. Travis Hirschi and Michael Gottfredson take exception to the hypothesis that white-collar crime is a product of corporate culture.[60] If that were true, there would be much more white-collar crime than actually exists, and white-collar criminals would not be embarrassed by their misdeeds, as most seem to be. Instead, Hirschi and Gottfredson maintain that the motives that produce white-collar crimes—quick benefits with minimal effort—are the same as those that produce any other criminal behaviors.

White-collar criminals have low self-control and are inclined to follow momentary impulses without considering the long-term costs of such behavior.[61] White-collar crime is relatively rare because, as a matter of course, business executives tend to hire people with self-control, a practice that limits the number of potential white-collar criminals. Hirschi and Gottfredson have collected data showing that the demographic distribution of white-collar crime is similar to that of other crimes. For example, gender, race, and age ratios are the same for crimes such as embezzlement and fraud as they are for street crimes such as burglary and robbery.

White-Collar Crime and Law Enforcement Systems

On the federal level, detection of white-collar crime is primarily in the hands of administrative departments and agencies.[62] The decision whether to pursue these activities as criminal or civil violations is usually based on the seriousness of the case and the perpetrator's intent, on any actions taken to conceal the violation, and on the individual's prior record. Any evidence of criminal activity is then sent to the Department of Justice or the FBI for investigation. Some other federal agencies, such as the Securities and Exchange Commission and the U.S. Postal Service, have their own investigative arms. Enforcement is generally reactive (generated by complaints) rather than proactive (involving ongoing investigations or the monitoring of activities). Investigations are carried out by the various federal agencies and the FBI. If criminal prosecution is called for, the case will be handled by attorneys from the criminal, tax, antitrust, and civil rights divisions of the Justice Department. If insufficient evidence is available to warrant a criminal prosecution, the case will be handled civilly or administratively by some other federal agency. For example, the Federal Trade Commission can issue a cease and desist order in antitrust or merchandising fraud cases.

The number of state-funded technical assistance offices to help local prosecutors has increased significantly; more than 40 states offer such services. On the state and local levels, law enforcement officials have made progress in a number of areas, such as controlling consumer fraud. For example, the Environmental Crimes Strike Force in Los Angeles County, California, is considered a model for the control of illegal dumping and pollution.[63] Some of the more common environmental offenses investigated and prosecuted by the task force are

▶ Illegal transportation, treatment, storage, or disposal of hazardous waste
▶ Oil spills
▶ Fraudulent certification of automobile smog tests[64]

Nonetheless, although local agencies recognize the seriousness of enterprise-type crimes, they rarely have the funds necessary for effective enforcement.[65]

Local prosecutors pursue white-collar criminals more vigorously if the prosecutors are part of a team effort involving a network of law enforcement agencies.[66] National surveys of local prosecutors find that many do not consider white-collar crimes particularly serious problems. They are more willing to prosecute cases if the offense causes substantial harm and if other agencies fail to act. Relatively few prosecutors participate in interagency task forces designed to investigate white-collar criminal activity.[67]

CONTROLLING WHITE-COLLAR CRIME

The prevailing wisdom is that, unlike lower-class street criminals, white-collar criminals are rarely prosecuted and, when convicted, receive relatively light sentences. There have also been charges that efforts to control white-collar crime are biased against specific classes and races: Authorities seem to be less diligent when victims are poor or minority group members or when the crimes take place in areas populated largely by minority groups. When Michael Lynch and his associates studied whether petroleum refineries violating environmental laws in black, Latino, and low-income communities receive smaller fines than those refineries in white and affluent communities, they found that violations of the Clean Air Act, the Clean Water Act, and/or the Resource Conservation and Recovery Act in minority areas received much smaller fines than the same types of violations occuring in white areas ($108,563 compared to $341,590).[68]

Compliance vs. Deterrence What efforts have been made to bring violators of the public trust to justice? White-collar criminal enforcement typically involves two strategies designed to control organizational deviance: compliance and deterrence.[69]

Compliance strategies rely on the threat of economic sanctions or civil penalties to control potential violators. They attempt to create a marketplace incentive to obey the law. Under this system, the greater the violation, the larger the economic penalty. Compliance strategies also avoid stigmatizing and shaming businesspeople by focusing on the act, rather than the actor, in white-collar crime.[70] Compliance is regulated by administrative agencies set up to oversee business activity. For example, the Securities and Exchange Commission regulates Wall Street activities, and the Food and Drug Administration regulates drugs, cosmetics, medical devices, meats, and other foods. The legislation creating these agencies usually spells out the penalties for violating regulatory standards. This approach has been used to control environmental crimes by levying heavy fines based on the quantity and dangerousness of the pollution released into the environment.[71]

compliance strategies
Methods of controlling white-collar crime that rely on the threat of economic sanctions or civil penalties to control potential violators, creating a marketplace incentive to obey the law.

In contrast, **deterrence strategies** rely on the punishment of individual offenders to deter other would-be violators. Deterrence systems are oriented toward apprehending violators and punishing them, rather than creating conditions that induce conformity to the law. Law enforcement agencies and the courts have traditionally been reluctant to throw corporate executives in jail, but a number of well-publicized cases (such as that of Bernard Madoff) indicate that the gloves are off and the government is willing to punish high-profile white-collar criminals by seeking long prison sentences. Because the Madoff, Enron, Worldcom, and other scandals have deprived so many people of their life savings and caused such disruptions in the financial markets, both justice system personal and the general public now consider white-collar crimes as more serious than common-law theft offenses and believe that they should be punished accordingly.[72] Both fines and penalties have been increasing, and long prison sentences are being routinely handed out for white-collar crimes.[73] In fact, deterrence strategies have become so routine—and punishments so severe—that some commentators now argue that the government may actually be going overboard in its efforts to punish white-collar criminals, especially for crimes that are the result of negligent business practices rather than intentional criminal conspiracy.[74] ▶ **Checkpoints**

Cyber Crime

On May 15, 2008, a federal grand jury in Los Angeles indicted Lori Drew, a Missouri woman, for her alleged role in a MySpace hoax on a teenage neighbor who later committed suicide. Drew, along with others, created a fake online boy named

© AP Images/Nick Ut

Cyber bullying can have deadly consequences. Lori Drew, right, and her daughter Sarah Drew arrive at federal court on November 26, 2008, in Los Angeles. In a case that captured national attention, Drew, 50, was accused of participating in a cyber bullying scheme that targeted 13-year-old Megan Meier, who later committed suicide. The case against Drew hinged on her violating MySpace's terms-of-service agreement. Drew was convicted by the jury, but U.S. District Judge George Wu overturned the ruling, stating that the disallowed ruling "basically leaves it up to a website owner to determine what is a crime, and therefore it criminalizes what would be a breach of contract."

Josh Evans who established a cyber romance with 13-year-old Megan Meier. Later, after being spurned by "Josh," Megan took her own life. She had received several messages from "Josh" suggesting that she kill herself and that the "world would be better off without her." Drew was charged with one count of conspiracy and three counts of accessing protected computers without authorization to obtain information to inflict emotional distress, a violation of the Computer Fraud and Abuse Act. Drew was found guilty of a misdemeanor, but on July 2, 2009, a federal judge overturned her conviction on the grounds that although the computer fraud statute was intended to prohibit trespass and theft, it did not cover Drew's cyber bullying.[75]

This cyber bully case, though unusual, illustrates one of the newest trends in criminal behavior. The widespread use of both computers and the Internet has ushered in the age of **information technology (IT)** and made it an integral part of daily life in most industrialized societies.

IT can involve computer networking, the Internet, and/or advanced communications. It is the key to the economic system and will become more important as major industries shift their manufacturing plants to other areas of the world where production is much cheaper. IT is responsible for the **globalization** phenomenon, the process of creating transnational markets, politics, and legal systems—in other words, creating a global economy.

The cyber age has also generated an enormous amount of revenue. Annual spending on IT and telecommunications grows by more than 6 percent each year and will soon reach about $2 trillion.[76] Today more than 1 billion people are using email, and 240 million are mobile Internet users. Magnifying the importance of the Internet is the fact that many critical infrastructure functions, ranging from banking to control of shipping on the Mississippi River, are now being conducted online.[77]

This vast network has become a tool for illegal activities and enterprise. As a group, these activities are referred to as cyber crime—any act of criminal enterprise that involves the use of communication, computer, and Internet networks. **Cyber theft** schemes range from illegal copying of copyrighted material to using technology to commit traditional theft-based offenses such as larceny and fraud.

Cyber crime presents a compelling challenge for criminologists because (1) it is rapidly evolving, with new schemes being created daily, (2) it is difficult to detect through traditional law enforcement channels, and (3) planning or coordinating its control demands technical skills that match those of the perpetrators.[78] Cyber technology now allows people to steal information that is actually more valuable than the material and/or physical goods they may have filched in the past. Theft crimes can now be entirely virtual because the stolen information only exists in digital form; consequently, new laws must be developed to replace common law theft crimes that require that stolen material must be "taken and carried away." Some criminals can now cause damage by attacking a computer or computer network; this amounts to a new form of vandalism. The risk of detection is diminished because the crime can be performed on a laptop from the safe confines of one's own home. It may even be possible that the decade-long drop in UCR theft offenses such as burglary and larceny may be a result of cyber crime replacing traditional street crime. Instead of robbing a bank at gun point, a new group of contemporary thieves finds it easier to hack into accounts and transfer funds to offshore banks. Instead of shoplifting from a brick-and-mortar store, the contemporary cyber thief devises clever schemes to steal from etailers.

Not all cyber criminals seek profit; some are intent on causing damage and destroying computer networks for malicious reasons. Some cyber criminals are high-tech vandals; the property they destroy is electronic rather than physical. And some may combine theft and vandalism into politically based cyber terror attacks. But the rapid growth of cyber theft schemes now makes them a serious new entry into the world of enterprise crime. Some of the most common forms of cyber crime are briefly set out in Concept Summary 12.1 and described in more detail in the sections that follow.

information technology (IT)
A term that denotes all forms of technology used to create, store, retrieve, and exchange data in all its various forms, including electronic, voice, and still image.

globalization
The process of creating transnational markets, politics, and legal systems and thus forming a global economy.

cyber theft
Use of computer networks for criminal profits. Examples include copyright infringement, identity theft, and using technology to commit traditional theft-based offenses such as larceny and fraud.

Concept Summary 12.1 Cyber Crimes

Crime	Definition	Examples
Cyber theft	Use of cyber space either to distribute illegal goods and services or to defraud people for quick profits	Illegal copyright infringement, identity theft, Internet securities fraud, warez
Cyber vandalism	Use of cyberspace for revenge, for destruction, or to achieve a malicious intent	Website defacement, worms, viruses, cyber stalking, cyber bullying
Cyber terrorism	An effort by enemy forces to disrupt the intersection where the virtual electronic reality of computers meets the physical world	Logic bombs used to disrupt or destroy "secure" systems or networks; Internet used to communicate covertly with agents around the world

CYBER THEFT: CYBER CRIMES FOR PROFIT

The new computer-based technology enables criminals to operate in a more efficient and effective manner. Cyber thieves now have the luxury of remaining anonymous, living in any part of the world, conducting their business during the day or in the evening, working alone or in a group, and reaching a much greater number of potential victims than ever before. No longer are con artists and criminal entrepreneurs limited to fleecing victims in a particular geographic locale; the whole world can be their target. And the technology revolution has opened up new opportunities for cyber theft—ranging from the unlawful distribution of computer software to Internet fraud. Cyber thieves conspire to use cyber space either to distribute illegal goods and services or to defraud people for quick profits. Some of the most common methods are described below.

COMPUTER FRAUD

Computer fraud is not a unique offense but, rather, a common-law crime committed using contemporary technology. Consequently, many computer crimes are prosecuted under such traditional criminal statutes as those prohibiting larceny or fraud. However, not all computer crimes fall under common-law statutes, because the property stolen may be intangible—that is, electronic and/or magnetic impulse. Here are a few of these novel crimes:

▶ *Theft of information.* The unauthorized obtaining of information from a computer (such as via "hacking"), including software that is copied for profit.
▶ *The "Salami" fraud.* With this type of fraud, the perpetrator carefully "skims" small sums from the balances of a large number of accounts in order to bypass internal controls and escape detection.
▶ *Software theft.* The comparative ease of making copies of computer software has led to a huge illegal market, depriving authors of very significant revenues.
▶ *Manipulation of accounts/banking systems.* Similar to a "Salami" but on a much larger and usually more complex scale. Sometimes perpetrated as a "one-off kamikaze" fraud. These are but a few of the most common examples, and the list is as expansive as the imagination of the criminal mind.
▶ *Corporate espionage.* A company's trade secrets are stolen by one of its competitors, which can be either domestic or foreign. The rival's goal is to increase its own (or its nation's) competitive edge in the global marketplace.[79]

PORNOGRAPHY AND PROSTITUTION

The IT revolution has revitalized the "porn industry." The Internet is an ideal venue for selling and distributing adult materials; the computer is an ideal device for their storage and viewing. Because of their vast number, it is difficult to estimate how many websites feature sexual content, including nude photos, videos, live sex acts, and Webcam strip sessions, among other forms of "adult entertainment."[80] The number of pornography webpages has soared during the past six years, and there are now over 1.3 million such sites containing about 260 million pages of erotic content, all hoping to cash in on the billions in revenue spent on Internet porn annually.[81] The number of visits to pornographic sites surpasses those made to Internet search engines.

CONNECTIONS

We will revisit the nature and extent of Internet pornography in Chapter 13, when we discuss public order crimes.

DENIAL-OF-SERVICE ATTACK

A **denial-of-service attack** is an attempt to extort money from legitimate users of an Internet service by threatening to prevent the user from accessing the service.[82]

Examples include attempts to "flood" a computer network, thereby blocking out legitimate network traffic; attempts to disrupt connections within a computer network, thereby preventing access to a service; attempts to prevent a particular individual from accessing a service; and attempts to disrupt service to a specific system or person.

DISTRIBUTING DANGEROUS DRUGS

On May 1, 2009, a jury found employees of Jive Network, which sold controlled substances (mostly stimulants and depressants) using Internet websites, guilty of various drug trafficking crimes; among those convicted were medical doctors. Customers of Jive Network, who had no prescriptions, accessed its websites and purchased controlled substances such as valium, barbiturates, and steroids with a credit card or by money order. The customers were required to complete a short "health history."[83] But after reviewing the "health histories," the doctors employed by Jive, who had no face-to-face contact with the customers, approved orders for the controlled substances without verifying identities or ages, conducting any physical examinations or testing, or reviewing any medical records. For a fee, Jive Network doctors unlawfully approved and issued "prescription" drug orders outside the usual course of their professional practice and for no legitimate medical purpose. During the three-year conspiracy, the organization distributed approximately 5 million dosage units of Schedule III controlled substances (such as codeine, steroids, and Nalline) and approximately 39 million dosage units of Schedule IV controlled substances (such as Rohypnol and valium) to over 500,000 Internet customers who had no valid prescriptions. By this means, it illegally generated revenue in excess of $77 million.

As the Jive Network case illustrates, the Internet has become a prime purveyor of prescription drugs, some of which can be quite dangerous when they are used to excess or fall into the hands of minors. One recent (2008) national survey found 365 websites either advertising or offering controlled prescription drugs for sale online; only two of those sites were registered Internet pharmacy practice sites. More than 80 percent of sites offering drugs for sale required no prescription from a patient's physician. Of the 15 percent of sites offering drugs for sale that *do* indicate that a prescription is required, half simply ask that the prescription be faxed—increasing the risk of multiple use of one prescription or other fraud.[84]

ILLEGAL COPYRIGHT INFRINGEMENT

For the past decade, groups of individuals have been working together to obtain software illegally and then "crack" or "rip" its copyright protections, before posting it on the Internet for other members of the group to use. The resulting pirated software is called **warez**.

Frequently, these new pirated copies reach the Internet days or weeks before the legitimate product is commercially available. The government has actively pursued members of the warez community, and some have been charged and convicted under the Computer Fraud and Abuse Act (CFAA), which criminalizes accessing computer systems without authorization to obtain information.[85]

denial-of-service attack
Extorting money from Internet service users by threatening to prevent them from accessing the service.

warez
Pirated software illegally obtained, stripped of its copyright protections, and posted on the Internet to be downloaded or sold in violation of its license.

INTERNET SECURITIES FRAUD

Internet securities fraud involves using the Internet to intentionally manipulate the securities marketplace for profit. Three major types of Internet securities fraud are common today.

▶ *Market manipulation.* Stock market manipulation occurs when an individual tries to control the price of stock by interfering with the natural forces of supply and demand. There are two principal forms of this crime: the "pump and dump" and the "cyber smear." In a pump and dump scheme, erroneous and deceptive information is posted online to get unsuspecting investors interested in a stock, while those spreading the information sell previously purchased stock at an inflated price. The cyber smear is a reverse pump and dump: Negative information is spread online about a stock, driving down its price and enabling the schemers to buy it at an artificially low price before rebuttals by the company's officers reinflate the stock's price to its legitimate value.[86]

▶ *Fraudulent offerings of securities.* Some cyber criminals create websites specifically designed to sell securities fraudulently. To make the offerings look more attractive than they are, assets may be inflated, expected returns overstated, and risks understated. In these schemes, investors are promised abnormally high profits on their investments. No investment is actually made. Early investors are paid returns with the investment money received from the later investors. The system usually collapses, and the later investors do not receive dividends and lose their initial investment.

▶ *Illegal touting.* This crime occurs when individuals make securities recommendations and fail to disclose that they are being paid to disseminate their favorable opinions.

IDENTITY THEFT

Identity theft occurs when a person uses the Internet to steal someone's identity and/or impersonate the victim to open a new credit card account or conduct some other financial transaction. It is a type of cyber crime that has grown at surprising rates over the past few years.[87]

Identity thieves can destroy people's lives by manipulating credit records or stealing from their bank accounts. Some identity thieves create false emails and/or websites that look legitimate but are designed to gain illegal access to a victim's personal information. This is known as **phishing** (and also as *carding* and *spoofing*).

Phishing emails and websites have become even more of a problem now that cyber criminals can easily copy brand names, corporate personnel's names, and their insignia directly into the email. The look is so authentic that victims believe that the email comes from the advertised company. Most phishers send out spam emails to a large number of recipients, knowing that some of those recipients will have accounts with the company they are impersonating. Some phishing schemes involve job offers. Once the unsuspecting victims fill out the "application," answering personal questions and including their Social Security numbers, the phisher has them in his grasp.[88]

ETAILING FRAUD

New fraud schemes are evolving to reflect the fact that billions of dollars' worth of goods are sold on the Internet each year. **Etailing fraud** can involve illegally buying or selling merchandise—or both—on the Internet.

Some etailing scams involve failure to deliver on promised purchases or services, and others involve the substitution of cheaper or used material for higher-quality purchases.

identity theft
Using the Internet to steal someone's identity and/or impersonate the victim in order to conduct illicit transactions, such as committing fraud using the victim's name and identity.

phishing
Illegally acquiring personal information, such as bank passwords and credit card numbers, by masquerading as a trustworthy person or business in what appears to be an official electronic communication, such as an email or an instant message. The term "phishing" comes from the lures used to "fish" for financial information and passwords.

etailing fraud
Using the Internet to buy or sell merchandise illegally.

CYBER VANDALISM: CYBER CRIME WITH MALICIOUS INTENT

Some cyber criminals may be motivated not by greed or profit but by the desire for revenge, to cause destruction, and/or to achieve a malicious intent. Cyber vandalism ranges from sending destructive viruses and worms to mounting attacks designed to destroy important computer networks. Cyber vandals are motivated more by malice than by greed:

▶ Some cyber vandals target computers and networks seeking revenge for some perceived wrong.
▶ Some desire to exhibit their technical prowess and superiority.
▶ Some wish to highlight the vulnerability of computer security systems.
▶ Some desire to spy on other people's private financial and personal information ("computer voyeurism").
▶ Some want to destroy computer security because they believe in a philosophy of open access to all systems and programs.[89]

What forms of cyber vandalism currently exist?

▶ *Viruses.* A computer virus is one type of malicious software program (also called malware) that disrupts or destroys existing programs and networks, causing them to perform the task for which the virus was designed.[90] The virus is then spread from one computer to another when a user sends out an infected file through email, a network, or a disk.
▶ *Worms.* Computer worms are similar to viruses but use computer networks or the Internet to self-replicate and "send themselves" to other users, generally via email, without the aid of the operator.
▶ *Trojan horses.* Some hackers may introduce a Trojan horse program into a computer system. The Trojan horse looks like a benign application, but it contains illicit codes that can damage the system operations. Sometimes hackers with a sense of irony will install a Trojan horse and claim that it is an antivirus program. When it is opened, it spreads viruses in the computer system. Trojan horses do not replicate themselves as viruses do, but they can be just as destructive.
▶ *Web defacement.* Cyber vandals may target the websites of their victims. Web defacement is a type of cyber vandalism that occurs when a computer hacker intrudes on another person's website by inserting or substituting codes that expose visitors to the site to misleading or provocative information.

CYBER STALKING

Traditional stalking involves repeated harassing or threatening behavior, such as following a person, appearing at a person's home or place of business, making harassing phone calls, leaving written messages or objects, or vandalizing a person's property. **Cyber stalking** consists of using the Internet, email, or other electronic communications devices to stalk another person.[91] Some cyber stalkers pursue minors through online chat rooms, establish a relationship with the child, and later make contact for the purpose of engaging in criminal sexual activities. Today, Internet predators are more likely to meet their victims online, develop relationships with at-risk adolescents, and beguile underage teenagers, rather than using coercion and violence.[92]

CYBER BULLYING

The Lori Drew case exposed cyber bullies to the nation. Experts define bullying among children as repeated, negative acts committed by one or more children against another.[93] These negative acts may be physical or verbal in nature—for example, hitting or kicking, teasing or taunting—or they may involve indirect actions such as manipulating friendships or purposely excluding other children from activities. Although bullying is a problem that remains to be solved, it has now morphed from the physical to the virtual. Because of the creation of cyber space,

cyber stalking
Using the Internet, email, or other electronic communications devices to stalk or harass another person.

physical distance no longer limits the harm a bully can dole out to his or her victim.[94] Cyber bullying is willful and repeated harm inflicted through the medium of electronic text. Like their real-world counterparts, cyber bullies are malicious aggressors who seek implicit or explicit pleasure or profit through the mistreatment of other individuals. Although power in traditional bullying might be physical (stature) or social (competency or popularity), online power may simply stem from net proficiency. Cyber bullies who are able to navigate the Internet and utilize technology in a way that allows them to harass others are in a position of power relative to a victim. There are now two major formats that bullies can employ to harass their victims. (1) A bully can send harassing emails or instant messages; post obscene, insulting, and slanderous messages to online bulletin boards; or develop websites to promote and disseminate defamatory content. (2) A bully can send harassing text messages to the victim via cellular phones.[95]

CYBER TERRORISM: CYBER CRIME WITH POLITICAL MOTIVES

Criminologists have begun to identify and study attacks that integrate terrorist goals with cyber capabilities: cyber terrorism. Although the term may be difficult to define, cyber terrorism can be viewed as an effort by covert forces to disrupt the intersection where the virtual electronic reality of computers intersects with the physical world.[96]

Cyber terrorism has been defined as "the premeditated, politically motivated attack against information, computer systems, computer programs, and data which result in violence against noncombatant targets by sub-national groups or clandestine agents."[97] Cyber terrorism may involve the use of computer network tools to shut down critical national infrastructures or to coerce or intimidate a government or civilian population.[98]

Terrorist organizations are now beginning to understand the power that cyber crime can inflict on their enemies even though, ironically, many come from a region where computer databases and the Internet are not widely used. Terrorist organizations are now adopting IT into their arsenals, and agencies of the justice system have to be ready for a sustained attack on the nation's electronic infrastructure.

One form of attack is cyber espionage. This involves hacking secure computer networks at the enemies' most sensitive military bases, defense contractors, and aerospace companies in order to steal important data or to assess their defenses. Infrastructure attacks might also be aimed at water treatment plants, electric plants, dams, oil refineries, and nuclear power plants. These industries all provide vital services to society simply by enabling people to go about their daily lives. Terrorist computer hackers could cause a dam to overflow or do great property damage to oil refineries or nuclear plants by shutting down safeguards in the system that are designed to prevent catastrophic meltdowns.

Extent and Costs of Cyber Crime

How common are cyber crimes and how costly are cyber crimes to American businesses and the general public? The Internet has become a vast engine for illegal profits. Criminal entrepreneurs view this vast pool as a target for cyber crime, and although an accurate accounting of cyber crime will probably never be made because so many offenses go unreported there is little doubt that its incidence is growing rapidly.

Thousands of breaches occur each year, but most are not reported to local, state, or federal authorities. Some cyber crimes go unreported because they involve low-visibility acts (such as copying computer software in violation of copyright laws) that simply never get detected.[99] Some businesses choose not to report cyber crime because they fear revealing the weaknesses in their network security systems. However, the information that is available indicates that the profit reaped in cyber crime is vast and continually growing.[100] Losses are now in the billions and are rising with the continuing growth of e-commerce.

CONTROLLING CYBER CRIME

How has the justice system responded to cyber crime? Most of the efforts are being made at the federal level. The government is now operating a number of organizations that are coordinating their efforts to control cyber fraud. One approach is to create working groups that coordinate the activities of numerous agencies involved in investigating cyber crime. For example, the Interagency Telemarketing and Internet Fraud Working Group brings together representatives of numerous United States Attorneys' offices, the FBI, the Secret Service, the Postal Inspection Service, the Federal Trade Commission, the Securities and Exchange Commission, and other law enforcement and regulatory agencies to share information about trends and patterns in Internet fraud schemes. One of the most successful federal efforts is the New York Electronic Crimes Task Force (NYECTF), a partnership between the U.S. Secret Service and a host of other public safety agencies and private corporations. Today, the task force consists of over 250 individual members representing federal, state, and local law enforcement, the private sector, and computer science specialists from 18 different universities. Since 1995, the New York task force has charged over 1,000 individuals with electronic crime losses exceeding $1 billion. It has trained over 60,000 law enforcement personnel, prosecutors, and private industry representatives in prevention of cyber crime. Its success has prompted the establishment of similar task forces in Boston, Miami, Charlotte, Chicago, Las Vegas, San Francisco, Los Angeles, and Washington, DC.[101]

Other Specialized Enforcement Agencies Specialized enforcement agencies are being created to fight cyber crime. The Internet Fraud Complaint Center, based in Fairmont, West Virginia, is run by the FBI and the National White Collar Crime Center. It brings together about 1,000 state and local law enforcement officials and regulators. It then analyzes the fraud-related complaints for patterns, develops additional information on particular cases, and sends investigative packages to law enforcement authorities in the jurisdiction that appears likely to have the greatest investigative interest in the matter. In the first year of its operation, the center received 36,000 complaints, the majority involving auction fraud.

WHAT THE FUTURE HOLDS

The justice system's response to cyber crime and terrorism is constantly evolving. All too often it is moved by events, being reactive rather than proactive. For example, prior to 9/11, most local law enforcement agencies had little experience with terrorist-related incidents, and most did little to prepare for attacks. After 9/11, the country went on high alert. State and local agencies began to develop antiterror strategies and responses. In response to 9/11, criminal justice agencies increased the number of personnel engaged in emergency response planning and antiterror activities. They have updated plans for chemical, biological, or radiological attacks and, to a lesser extent, mutual aid agreements. They have reallocated internal resources and increased departmental spending to focus on terrorism preparedness.[102]

In the future, rather than merely reacting to events, the justice system may go on the offensive. Using technological prowess, efforts will be made to identify terrorists and cyber criminals and bring them to justice before they can carry out their attacks, rather than waiting for the attack and planning a reaction. To reach this goal, greater cooperation between agencies ranging from the FBI to the Department of Homeland Security, and from the National Counterterrorism Center to the Office of the Director of National Intelligence, will be critical.

Organized Crime

The third branch of enterprise crime involves organized crime—ongoing criminal enterprise groups whose ultimate purpose is personal economic gain through illegitimate means. Here, a structured enterprise system is set up to continuously supply

Fact or Fiction?

It will be difficult to defeat cyber criminals without interagency and international cooperation.

Fact. No one federal or state agency can hope to control cyber crime, so interagency cooperation is essential.

consumers with merchandise and services banned by criminal law but for which a ready market exists: prostitution, pornography, gambling, and narcotics. The system may resemble a legitimate business run by an ambitious chief executive officer, his or her assistants, staff attorneys, and accountants, with thorough, efficient accounts receivable and complaint departments.[103]

Because of its secrecy, power, and fabulous wealth, a great mystique has grown up about organized crime. Its legendary leaders—Al Capone, Meyer Lansky, Lucky Luciano—have been the subjects of books and films. The famous *Godfather* films popularized and humanized organized crime figures; Don Vito Corleone was the ultimate gentleman, who got into crime in order to protect his family.[104] The Corleone family was not the only Mafia clan to capture the public imagination: Watching the exploits of Tony Soprano and his family life became a national craze. *The Sopranos* further humanized organized criminals, making them out to be regular guys who saw therapists for their emotional problems, had kids in college, and dealt with social issues that plague the average suburban family, give or take a murder or two.

Because of this press and media coverage, nearly everyone is familiar with the terms mob, underworld, Mafia, wise guys, syndicate, and **La Cosa Nostra**, which refer to organized crime. Although most of us have neither met nor seen members of organized crime families, we feel sure that they exist, and we fear them. This section briefly defines organized crime, reviews its history, and discusses its economic effect and efforts to control it.

CHARACTERISTICS OF ORGANIZED CRIME

A precise description of the characteristics of organized crime is difficult to formulate, but here are some of its general traits:[105]

▶ Organized crime is a conspiratorial activity involving the coordination of numerous people in the planning and execution of illegal acts or in the pursuit of a legitimate objective by unlawful means (for example, threatening a legitimate business to get a stake in it). Organized crime involves continuous commitment by primary members, although individuals with specialized skills may be brought in as needed. Organized crime is usually structured along hierarchical lines—a chieftain supported by close advisers, lower subordinates, and so on.

▶ Organized crime has economic gain as its primary goal, although power and status may also be motivating factors. Economic gain is achieved through maintenance of a near-monopoly on illegal goods and services, including drugs, gambling, pornography, and prostitution.

▶ Organized crime activities are not limited to providing illicit services. They include such sophisticated activities as laundering illegally acquired money through legitimate businesses, land fraud, and computer crime.

▶ Organized crime employs predatory tactics, such as intimidation, violence, and corruption. It appeals to greed to accomplish its objectives and preserve its gains.

▶ By experience, custom, and practice, organized crime's conspiratorial groups are usually very quick and effective in controlling and disciplining their members, associates, and victims. The individuals involved know that any deviation from the rules of the organization will evoke a prompt response from the other participants. This response may range from a reduction in rank and responsibility to a death sentence.

▶ Organized crime is not synonymous with the Mafia, although this widespread assumption about organized crime is shared by many, including the federal government. Several families in the organization called the Mafia are important components of organized crime activities, but they do not have a monopoly on underworld activities.

▶ Organized crime does not include terrorists dedicated to political change. Although violent acts are a major tactic of organized crime, the use of violence per se does not necessarily mean that a group is part of a confederacy of organized criminals.

La Cosa Nostra
A national syndicate of some 25 Italian-dominated crime families who control organized crime in distinct geographic areas.

ACTIVITIES OF ORGANIZED CRIME

What are the main activities of organized crime? Its income is traditionally derived from (1) providing illicit materials and (2) using force to enter into and maximize profits in legitimate businesses.[106] Most organized crime income comes from narcotics distribution, loan-sharking (lending money at illegal rates), and prostitution. However, additional billions come from gambling, theft rings, pornography, and other illegal enterprises. Organized criminals have infiltrated labor unions and taken control of their pension funds and dues.[107] Hijacking of shipments and cargo theft are other sources of income. Underworld figures fence high-value items and maintain international sales territories. In recent years they have branched into cyber crime and into white-collar criminality. Organized crime figures have kept up with the information age by using computers and the Internet to sell illegal material such as pornography.

Organized crime figures are also involved in stock market manipulation. The FBI notes that organized crime groups target "small cap" or "micro cap" stocks, over-the-counter stocks, and other types of thinly traded stocks that can be easily manipulated and sold to elderly or inexperienced investors. The conspirators use offshore bank accounts to conceal their participation in the fraud scheme and to launder the illegal proceeds in order to avoid paying income tax.[108]

THE CONCEPT OF ORGANIZED CRIME

The term "organized crime" conjures up images of strong men in dark suits, machine gun–toting bodyguards, rituals of allegiance to secret organizations, professional "gangland" killings, and meetings of "family" leaders who chart the course of crime much as the board members at General Motors assess the country's transportation needs. These images have become part of what criminologists refer to as the **alien conspiracy theory** concept of organized crime. This is the belief, subscribed to by the federal government and many respected criminologists, that organized crime is a direct offshoot of a criminal society—the **Mafia**—that first originated in Italy and Sicily and now controls racketeering in major U.S. cities. A major premise of the alien conspiracy theory is that the Mafia is centrally coordinated by a national committee that settles disputes, dictates policy, and assigns territory.[109]

Not all criminologists believe in this narrow concept of organized crime, and many view the alien conspiracy theory as a figment of the media's imagination.[110] Their view depicts organized crime as a group of ethnically diverse gangs or groups who compete for profit in the sale of illegal goods and services or who use force and violence to extort money from legitimate enterprises. These groups are not bound by a central national organization but act independently on their own turf. We will now examine these perspectives in some detail.

CONTEMPORARY ORGANIZED CRIME GROUPS

Even such devoted alien conspiracy advocates as the U.S. Justice Department now view organized crime as a loose confederation of ethnic and regional crime groups, bound together by shared economic and political objectives.[111] Some of these groups are located in fixed geographic areas. Chicano crime families are found in areas with significant Latino populations, such as California and Arizona. White-ethnic crime organizations are found across the nation. Some Italian and Cuban groups operate internationally. Some have preserved their past identity, whereas others are constantly changing.

One important contemporary change in organized crime is the interweaving of ethnic groups into the traditional structure. African American, Latino, and Asian racketeers now compete with the more traditional groups, overseeing the distribution of drugs, prostitution, and gambling in a symbiotic relationship with old-line racketeers. For example, Asian organized crime includes traditional enterprises such as the Chinese Triads, Chinese Tong, and Japanese Boryokudan (also known as Yakuza), as well as more loosely organized groups such as the Big Boys Circle, the Asian Boyz Group,

alien conspiracy theory
The belief, subscribed to by the federal government and many respected criminologists, that organized crime is a direct offshoot of a criminal society that was imported into the United States from Europe and that crime cartels have a policy of restricting their membership to people of their own ethnic background.

Mafia
A group that originated in Italy and Sicily and now controls racketeering in major U.S. cities.

© AP Images/Itsuo Inouye

Although organized crime is on the wane in the United States, it is flourishing in Japan. Here, in Tokyo, former gangster boss Shinji Ishihara speaks to members of the press about his life with Yamaguchi-gumi, the biggest gangster syndicate in Japan, which has tens of thousands of members. Ishihara decided to retire after his latest prison stint ended five years ago. Unlike the situation in the Mafia, where it is said that the only way out is in a coffin, it is common for syndicate bosses to "wash their feet." Ishihara says, however, "There will always be a Yamaguchi-gumi."

and Vietnamese and Korean criminal enterprises. These criminal groups are involved in a range of illegal activities, including drug trafficking, extortion, murder, kidnapping, home invasions, prostitution, illegal gambling, loan-sharking, insurance/credit card fraud, stock fraud, and the theft of high-tech components. Chinese groups are also involved in human trafficking—bringing large numbers of Chinese migrants to North America and essentially enslaving them.

Eurasian Crime Groups Eastern gangs trace their origin to countries spanning the Baltics, the Balkans, Central/Eastern Europe, Russia, the Caucasus, and Central Asia. Although ethnically based, they work with other ethnic groups when perpetrating crimes. Trading in illegal arms, narcotics, pornography, and prostitution, they operate a multibillion-dollar transnational crime cartel. Organized groups prey upon women in the poorest areas of Europe—Romania, the Ukraine, Bosnia—and sell them into virtual sexual slavery. Many of these women are transported as prostitutes around the world, and some find themselves in the United States.

In addition, thousands of Russian immigrants are believed to be involved in criminal activity, primarily in Russian enclaves in New York City. Beyond extortion from immigrants, Russian organized crime groups have cooperated with Mafia families in narcotics trafficking, fencing stolen property, money laundering, and other traditional organized crime schemes.[112]

Have these newly emerging groups achieved the same level of control as traditional crime families? Some experts argue that new ethnic gangs will have a tough time developing the network of organized corruption (which involves working with government officials and unions) that traditional

crime families enjoyed.[113] For more on the Russian mob, see the accompanying Race, Culture, Gender, and Criminology feature on page 344.

CONTROLLING ORGANIZED CRIME

George Vold argued that the development of organized crime parallels early capitalist enterprises. Organized crime employs ruthless monopolistic tactics to maximize profits; it is also secretive, protective of its operations, and defensive against any outside intrusion.[114] Consequently, controlling its activities is extremely difficult.

Federal and state governments actually did little to combat organized crime until fairly recently. One of the first measures aimed directly at organized crime was the Interstate and Foreign Travel or Transportation in Aid of Racketeering Enterprises Act (Travel Act).[115] The Travel Act prohibits travel in interstate commerce or

Fact or Fiction?

Organized crime in the United States is controlled by five Mafia families in New York City and a few other, allied groups in Chicago, Los Angeles, and Miami.

Fiction. Organized crime has become multiethnic and now includes Asian, Latin, and European groups.

use of interstate facilities with the intent to promote, manage, establish, carry on, or facilitate an unlawful activity; it also prohibits the actual or attempted engagement in these activities. In 1970, Congress passed the Organized Crime Control Act. Title IX of the act, probably its most effective measure, has been called the **Racketeer Influenced and Corrupt Organization Act (RICO)**.[116]

RICO did not create new categories of crimes but rather new categories of offenses in racketeering activity, which it defined as involvement in two or more acts prohibited by 24 existing federal and 8 state statutes. The offenses listed in RICO include state-defined crimes, such as murder, kidnapping, gambling, arson, robbery, bribery, extortion, and narcotics violations; and federally defined crimes, such as bribery, counterfeiting, transmission of gambling information, prostitution, and mail fraud. RICO is designed to limit patterns of organized criminal activity by prohibiting involvement in acts intended to

- ▶ Derive income from racketeering or the unlawful collection of debts and use or investment of such income
- ▶ Acquire through racketeering an interest in or control over any enterprise engaged in interstate or foreign commerce
- ▶ Conduct business through a pattern of racketeering
- ▶ Conspire to use racketeering as a means of making income, collecting loans, or conducting business

An individual convicted under RICO is subject to 20 years in prison and a $25,000 fine. Additionally, the accused must forfeit to the U.S. government any interest in a business that is in violation of RICO. These penalties are much more potent than simple conviction and imprisonment.

RICO's success has shaped the way the FBI attacks organized crime groups. The agency now uses the **enterprise theory of investigation (ETI)** model as its standard investigative tool. Rather than investigating crimes after they are committed, under the ETI model the FBI focuses on criminal enterprise and attacks the structure of the criminal enterprise rather than criminal acts viewed as isolated incidents.[117] For example, a drug trafficking organization must get involved in such processes as transportation and distribution of narcotics, in financial activities such as money laundering, and in communication with clients and dealers. The FBI identifies and then targets each of these areas simultaneously, focusing on the subsystems that are considered the most vulnerable. ▶ **Checkpoints**

THE FUTURE OF ORGANIZED CRIME

Joseph Massino's nickname was "the Last Don." The name seemed quite apropos when in 2004 this boss of New York's Bonanno crime family was convicted on charges of murder and racketeering, ordered to pay fines of $9 million, and given two consecutive life sentences. Massino's greatest sin, however, may have been violating the Mafia's rule of *omerta*, the traditional "code of silence." While in prison, Massino cooperated with prosecutors, secretly taping a conversation with family *capo* Vincent "Vinnie Gorgeous" Basciano, who was outlining a plan to kill lead prosecutor Greg Andres. Massino's current circumstances are not unique. The heads of the four other New York Mafia families—Lucchese, Colombo, Gambino, and Genovese—have also been convicted and sentenced to prison terms.[118]

The successful prosecution of Massino and other high-ranking organized crime figures is an indication that the traditional organized crime syndicates are in decline. Law enforcement officials in Philadelphia, New Jersey, New England, New Orleans, Kansas City, Detroit, and Milwaukee all report that years of federal and state interventions have severely eroded the Mafia organizations in their areas.

What has caused this alleged erosion of Mafia power? First, a number of the reigning family heads are in their eighties or older, prompting some law enforcement officials to dub them "the Geritol gang."[119] A younger generation of mob leaders is

Checkpoints

▶ Organized crime is an ongoing criminal enterprise that employs illegal methods for personal gain.

▶ In some instances, organized crime involves the sale and distribution of illegal merchandise, such as drugs and pornography, whereas in other cases it uses illegitimate means to market legitimate services, such as lending money (loan-sharking) and selling stocks (market manipulation).

▶ Traditional, organized crime families were dominated by Italians and called La Cosa Nostra.

▶ Contemporary gangs are multicultural and multinational.

▶ Russian gangs are becoming more and more common.

▶ The government has used the Racketeer Influenced and Corrupt Organization Act (RICO) to go after organized crime gangs.

Racketeer Influenced and Corrupt Organization Act (RICO) Federal legislation that enables prosecutors to bring additional criminal or civil charges against people engaged in two or more acts prohibited by 24 existing federal and 8 state laws. RICO features monetary penalties that allow the government to confiscate all profits derived from criminal activities. Originally intended to be used against organized crime, RICO has also been used against white-collar criminals.

enterprise theory of investigation (ETI) A standard investigative tool of the FBI that focuses on criminal enterprise and attacks the structure of the criminal enterprise rather than criminal acts viewed as isolated incidents.

Since the collapse of the Soviet Union in 1991, criminal organizations in Russia and other former Soviet republics such as Ukraine have engaged in a variety of crimes: drugs and arms trafficking, stolen automobiles, trafficking in women and children, and money laundering. No area of the world seems immune to this menace, especially not the United States. America is apparently the land of opportunity for unloading criminal goods and laundering dirty money.

Unlike Colombian, Italian, Mexican, or other well-known forms of organized crime, Russian organized crime is not primarily based on ethnic or family structures. Instead, Russian organized crime is based on economic necessity wrought by the oppressive Soviet regime. Here, a professional criminal

criminal activities. For example, most businesses in Russia—legal, quasilegal, and illegal—must operate with the protection of a *krysha* (roof). The protection is often provided by police or security officials employed outside their "official" capacities for this purpose. In other cases, officials are "silent partners" in criminal enterprises that they, in turn, protect.
- The criminalization of the privatization process has resulted in the massive use of state funds for criminal gain. Valuable properties are purchased through insider deals for much less than their true value and then resold for substantial profits.
- Criminals have been able to directly influence the state's domestic and foreign policy to promote the interests

Race, Culture, Gender, and Criminology
Russian Organized Crime

class developed in Soviet prisons during the Stalinist period that began in 1924—the era of the gulag. These criminals adopted behaviors, rules, values, and sanctions that bound them together in what was called the thieves' world, led by the elite *vory v zakone*, criminals who lived according to the "thieves' law." This thieves' world, and particularly the *vory*, created and maintained the bonds and climate of trust necessary for carrying out organized crime.

The following are some specific characteristics of Russian organized crime in the post-Soviet era:

- Russian criminals make extensive use of the state governmental apparatus to protect and promote their

of organized crime, either by attaining public office themselves or by buying public officials.

Beyond these particular features, organized crime in Russia exhibits many characteristics that are common to organized crime elsewhere in the world:

- Systematic use of violence, including both the threat and the use of force
- Hierarchical structure
- Limited or exclusive membership
- Specialization in types of crime and a division of labor
- Military-style discipline, with strict rules and regulations for the organization as a whole

stepping in to take control of the families, and they seem to lack the skill and leadership of the older bosses. In addition, active government enforcement policies have halved what the estimated mob membership was 25 years ago, and a number of the highest-ranking leaders have been imprisoned.

Additional pressure comes from newly emerging ethnic gangs that want to muscle in on traditional syndicate activities, such as drug sales and gambling. For example, Chinese Triad gangs in New York and California have been active in the drug trade, loan-sharking, and labor racketeering. Other ethnic crime groups include black and Colombian drug cartels and the Sicilian Mafia, which operates independently of U.S. groups.

The U.S. Mafia has also been hurt by changing values in U.S. society. White, ethnic, inner-city neighborhoods, which were the locus of Mafia power, have been shrinking as families move to the suburbs. (It came as no surprise that fictional character Tony Soprano lived in suburban New Jersey and his daughter attended Columbia

- Possession of high-tech equipment, including military weapons; use of threats, blackmail, and violence to penetrate business management and assume control of commercial enterprises; or, in some instances, use of money derived from criminal activities to found their own enterprises

These activities have had several notable results.

- Russia has high rates of homicide that are now more than 20 times those in western Europe and approximately 3 times the rates recorded in the United States. The rates more closely resemble those of a country engaged in civil war or in conflict than those of a country 15 years into a transition.
- Corruption and organized crime are globalized. Russian organized crime is active in Europe, Africa, Asia, and North and South America.
- Massive money laundering is rampant. It enables Russian and foreign organized crime to flourish. In some cases, it is tied to terrorist funding.

The organized crime threat to Russia's national security is now becoming a global threat. Russian organized crime operates both on its own and in cooperation with foreign groups. The latter cooperation often comes in the form of joint money-laundering ventures. Russian criminals have become involved in killings for hire in central and western Europe, Israel, Canada, and the United States.

In the United States, with the exception of extortion and money laundering, Russians have had little or no involvement in some of the more traditional types of organized crime, such as drug trafficking, gambling, and loan-sharking. Instead, Russian criminal groups are extensively engaged in a broad array of frauds and scams, including health care fraud, insurance scams, stock frauds, antiquities swindles,

forgery, and fuel tax evasion schemes. Russians are believed to be the main purveyors of credit card fraud in the United States. Legitimate businesses, such as the movie business and textile industry, have become targets of criminals from the former Soviet Union, and they are often used for money laundering and extortion. The first significant conviction against the Russian mob in the United States occurred in 1996 when Vyacheslav Kirillovich Ivankov, who had been dispatched to act as the coordinating authority for all Russian organized crime activity in the United States, was convicted on extortion and conspiracy charges. Ivankov led an international criminal organization that operated mainly in New York, Toronto, London, Vienna, Budapest, and Moscow, but also in numerous other cities in the United States, Canada, and Europe, and specialized in extorting Russian business interests. Although Ivankov's conviction was a setback, Russian groups continue to thrive, engaging in Internet crimes, extortion, and white-collar criminality.

CRITICAL THINKING

The influence of new immigrant groups in organized crime seems to suggest that illegal enterprise is a common practice among "new" Americans. Do you believe that some aspect of American culture induces immigrants to choose a criminal lifestyle? Or does our open culture encourage criminal activities that may have been incubating in people's native lands?

SOURCES: Louise I. Shelley, "Crime and Corruption: Enduring Problems of Post-Soviet Development," *Demokratizatsiya* 11 (2003): 110–114; James O. Finckenauer and Yuri A. Voronin, *The Threat of Russian Organized Crime* (Washington, DC: National Institute of Justice, 2001); FBI, "Vyacheslav Kirillovich Ivankov, New York, New York," www.fbi.gov/hq/cid/orgcrime/casestudies/ivankov.htm (accessed July 4, 2009).

University.) Organized crime groups have consequently lost their political and social base of operations. In addition, the code of silence that protected Mafia leaders is now broken regularly by younger members (and even older ones like Massino) who turn informer rather than face prison terms. It is also possible that their very success has hurt organized crime families: Younger members are better educated than their forebears and are equipped to seek their fortunes through legitimate enterprise.[120]

If traditional organized gangs are in decline, that does not mean the end of organized crime. Russian, Caribbean, and Asian gangs seem to be thriving, and there are always new opportunities for illegal practices. Law enforcement officials believe that Internet gambling sites are a tempting target for enterprise criminals. It is not surprising that Illinois, Louisiana, Nevada, Oregon, and South Dakota have recently passed laws specifically banning Internet gambling.[121] It is unlikely, considering the demand for illegal goods and services and the emergence of newly constituted crime families, that organized criminal behavior will ever be eradicated.

As a criminologist and expert on white-collar crime, you are asked to help his legal defense team prepare a sentencing statement in support of Anthony J. Facciabrutto, 33, who has recently been convicted of numerous federal charges.

From 2004 through February 2009, Facciabrutto owned and operated Facciabrutto Holdings, Inc., a telemarketing company in the Los Angeles area. Facciabrutto Holdings raised approximately $31 million from more than 800 victims across the United States. Facciabrutto's investors received only a fraction of their total investment in the company. One victim invested in excess of $400,000 and received less than $10,000 in return.

It is alleged that Facciabrutto and the telemarketers he employed sold shares in restaurants and what were marketed as luxury resorts, which never generated profits. According to the indictment, the telemarketing operation was a scheme in which earlier investors were paid "dividend payments" derived from funds obtained from later investors.

Facciabrutto was the chief executive officer for Facciabrutto Holdings, Inc., and is alleged to have paid himself a 40 percent sales commission. Sales managers were paid 25 percent of total sales, and salespersons received a 25 percent commission. Facciabrutto is alleged to have misrepresented sales commissions and to have made false guarantees to customers. Facciabrutto misrepresented the company's imminent initial public offering, which never occurred. The SEC conducted a civil investigation into Facciabrutto's activities during 2009 and as a result, Facciabrutto was ordered to pay a $3 million judgment. This is his first offense, and he claims that overwhelming personal problems drove him to commit crime. Facciabrutto had large personal debts and had borrowed heavily from organized crime figures.

Writing Assignment

Prepare for the judge a brief that details why your client should not go to prison for his crimes. Employ data showing how people are punished for various crimes and why imprisoning Facciabrutto would be a miscarriage of justice.

Summary

1. Know what is meant by the term "enterprise crime."

   Enterprise crime involves illicit entrepreneurship and commerce. Such criminals make use of illegal tactics to amass profit in the marketplace. Enterprise crimes can involve the violation of law in the course of an otherwise legitimate occupation, as well as the sale and distribution of illegal commodities. White-collar crime, cyber crime, and organized crime are linked because they all involve entrepreneurship. Losses to society from enterprise crime may far outstrip losses from any other type of crime.

2. Be familiar with the various forms of white-collar crime.

   White-collar fraud involves using a business enterprise as a front to swindle people. Chiseling involves professionals who cheat clients. Embezzlement and employee fraud occur when a person uses a position of trust to steal from an organization. Client fraud involves theft from an organization that advances credit, covers losses, or reimburses for services. Corporate, or organizational, crime involves various illegal business practices such as price fixing, restraint of trade, and false advertising.

3. Be aware of the causes that contribute to white-collar crime.

   There are numerous explanations for white-collar crime. Some offenders are motivated by greed; others offend as a consequence of personal problems. They use rationalization to convince themselves that they are meeting their financial needs without compromising their values. Corporate culture theory suggests that some businesses actually encourage employees to cheat or cut corners. The self-control view is that white-collar criminals are like any other law violators: impulsive people who lack self-control.

4. Discuss the special problems posed by cyber crime.

   Cyber crime is a unique category of offenses that involve the theft and/or destruction of information, resources, or funds utilizing computers, computer networks, and the Internet. Cyber crime presents a challenge for the justice system because it is rapidly evolving, it is difficult to detect through traditional law enforcement channels, and to control it, agents of the justice system must develop technical skills that match those of the perpetrators.

5. Be familiar with the different forms of cyber crime.

Some cyber crimes use modern technology to accumulate goods and services (cyber theft). Cyber vandalism entails malicious attacks aimed at disrupting, defacing, and destroying technology that the attackers find offensive. Cyber terrorism is aimed at undermining the social, economic, and political system of an enemy nation by destroying its electronic infrastructure and disrupting its economy.

6. Discuss how the Internet is used for distributing obscene material.

The Internet has become an important venue for selling and distributing obscene material. Some sites cater to adult tastes within the law, but others cross the legal border by peddling access to obscene material or even child pornography. It is unlikely that any law enforcement efforts will put a dent in the Internet porn industry.

7. Be familiar with the various forms of Internet-based copyright infringement violations.

Warez consists of software that is obtained illegally, its copyright protections "cracked" or "ripped," and then posted on the Internet for other members of the criminal group responsible to use. File-sharing programs enable Internet users to download music and other copyrighted material without paying the artists and record producers the royalties they are entitled to.

8. Discuss the concept of identity theft.

Identity theft occurs when a person uses the Internet to steal someone's identity and/or impersonate the victim to open a new credit card account or conduct some other financial transaction. Identity theft can destroy peoples' reputation and credit rating and enable the thieves to steal from their bank accounts. Phishing involves the creation of false emails and/or websites that look legitimate but are designed to gain illegal access to a victim's personal information.

9. Be aware of the various forms of cyber vandalism.

Cyber vandalism ranges from the sending of destructive viruses and worms to hacker attacks designed to destroy important computer networks. A computer virus is one type of malicious software program that disrupts or destroys existing programs and networks, causing them to perform the task for which the virus was designed. Computer worms are similar to viruses but use computer networks or the Internet to self-replicate and send themselves to other users, generally via email, without the aid of the operator. A Trojan horse looks like a benign application but contains illicit codes that can damage the system operations.

10. Discuss how the makeup of organized crime has evolved.

Organized criminals used to be white ethnics—Jews, Italians, and Irish—but today African Americans, Latinos, and other groups have become involved in organized crime activities. The old-line "families" are now more likely to use their criminal wealth and power to buy into legitimate businesses. Eastern European crime families and Asian groups of racketeers are active abroad and in the United States. Russian organized crime has become a major problem for law enforcement agencies.

Key Terms

enterprise crime 316
white-collar crime 316
cyber crime 316
organized crime 316
chiseling 318
churning 319
front running 319
bucketing 319
insider trading 319
exploitation 321
influence peddling 322

payola 323
pilferage 323
corporate (organizational) crime 326
Sherman Antitrust Act 327
price fixing 327
compliance strategies 331
deterrence strategies 332

information technology (IT) 333
globalization 333
cyber theft 333
denial-of-service attack 335
warez 335
identity theft 336
phishing 336
etailing fraud 336
cyber stalking 337

La Cosa Nostra 340
alien conspiracy theory 341
Mafia 341
Racketeer Influenced and Corrupt Organization Act (RICO) 343
enterprise theory of investigation (ETI) 343

Critical Thinking Questions

1. How would you punish a corporate executive whose product killed people, if the executive had no knowledge that the product was potentially lethal? What if the executive did know about its potential lethality?

2. Is organized crime inevitable as long as immigrant groups seek to become part of the American Dream?

3. Do the media glamorize organized crime? Do they paint an inaccurate picture of noble crime lords fighting to protect their families?

4. Apply traditional theories of criminal behavior to white-collar and organized crime. Which one seems to best explain why someone would engage in these behaviors?

© Timothy A. Clary/AFP/Getty Images

Chapter Outline

Public Order Crimes

The tastefully crafted *Emperor's Club VIP* website stated, "Our goal is to make life more peaceful, balanced, beautiful and meaningful. We honor commitment to our clients as we covet long-term relationships of trust and mutual benefit. Experience for yourself a service of obvious distinction." The site also showed that hourly rates could approach $3,000 or up to $31,000 per day.

As we now know, the Emperor's Club was actually a high-priced call girl ring. One of the young women, known professionally as "Kristin," was 22-year-old Ashley Dupre, a high school dropout who knew what it was like to be broke, homeless, and in need of money. Ashley might have remained an anonymous "working girl" employed by a sex-for-hire organization that remained under the radar had it not been for a federal investigation of one of her clients, New York's hard-charging Governor Eliot Spitzer. Known in the club as Client 9, Spitzer had paid $80,000 for dates with Ashley and other escorts. When a federal investigation uncovered his involvement with the Emperor's Club, the scandal rocked the nation. Spitzer was forced to resign in disgrace in order to avoid prosecution.[1]

The Spitzer case is certainly not unique, and stories have circulated about students and suburban moms supplementing their income by advertising sexual and personal services on Internet sources such as craigslist. This practice is not without its risks: On April 14, 2009, aspiring model Julissa Brisman, who advertised her services as a masseuse on Craigslist, was killed in Boston, Massachusetts, by Philip Markoff, a 23-year-old Boston University medical student. Investigators later found that it was not the first time Markoff had assaulted a woman he had met via Craigslist and that he may have attacked at least two others.[2]

Fact or Fiction?

▶ Prostitution is a good example of a victimless crime.

▶ It is a crime to see a young child drowning and not jump in to help.

▶ More people die from the effects of using legal substances such as cigarettes and alcohol than die from using illegal drugs.

▶ Libraries receive more complaints about Harry Potter books than about any other work of fiction they carry on their shelves.

▶ Despite the sexual revolution, prostitution is still a booming business.

▶ Drugs cause crime.

Chapter Objectives

1. Understand the association between law and morality.
2. Be familiar with the term "social harm."
3. Discuss the activities of moral crusaders.
4. Be aware of the various forms of outlawed deviant sexuality.
5. Discuss the history of prostitution and indicate what the term means today.
6. Distinguish among the different types of prostitutes.
7. State the arguments for and against legalizing prostitution.
8. Explain what the terms "pornography" and "obscenity" mean.
9. Discuss the cause of substance abuse.
10. Compare and contrast the different methods of controlling the abuse of drugs.

Societies have long banned or limited behaviors believed to run contrary to social norms, customs, and values. These behaviors are often referred to as **public order crimes** and are sometimes called victimless crimes, although the latter term can be misleading, as the Craigslist killing tragically illustrates.[3] Public order crimes involve acts that interfere with the operations of society and the ability of people to function efficiently. To put it another way, whereas common-law crimes such as rape and robbery are banned because they cause social harm to a victim, other behaviors, such as prostitution and pornography, are outlawed because they conflict with social policy, prevailing moral rules, and current public opinion.

Statutes designed to uphold public order usually prohibit the manufacture and distribution of morally questionable goods and services such as erotic material, commercial sex, and mood-altering drugs. Prohibition of these acts can be controversial, in part because millions of otherwise law-abiding citizens often engage in these outlawed activities and consequently become criminals. These statutes are also controversial because they selectively prohibit desired goods, services, and behaviors; in other words, they outlaw sin and vice.

This chapter covers these public order crimes. It first briefly discusses the relationship between law and morality. Next, it addresses public order crimes of a sexual nature: prostitution, pornography, and deviant sex acts called paraphilias. The chapter concludes by focusing on the abuse of drugs and alcohol.

Law and Morality

Legislation of moral issues has continually frustrated lawmakers. There is little disagreement that the purpose of criminal law is to protect society and reduce social harm. When a store is robbed or a child assaulted, it is relatively easy to see and condemn the harm done to the victim. It is, however, more difficult to sympathize with or even identify the victims of immoral acts, such as pornography or prostitution, where the parties involved may be willing participants. Some of the "escorts" who worked for the Emperor's Club were paid more for a few days' work than a waitress or a teacher makes in a year. The "models" seemed willing and well paid. Can we consider them "victims"? People who employed these women, such as Governor Eliot Spitzer, were wealthy and powerful men who freely and voluntarily spent their money for sexual services. Certainly they were not victims here. If there is no victim, can there be a crime? Should acts be made illegal merely because they violate prevailing moral standards? And if so, who defines morality?

To answer these questions, we might first consider whether there is actually a victim in so-called **victimless crimes**. Some participants may have been coerced into their acts; if so, then they are victims. Opponents of pornography, such as Andrea Dworkin, charge that women involved in adult films, far from being highly paid stars, are "dehumanized—turned into objects and commodities."[4] Although taking drugs may be a matter of personal choice, it too has serious consequences. One study of crack cocaine–using women found that more than half had suffered a physical attack, one-third had been raped, and more than half had had to seek medical care for their injuries.[5] It has been estimated that women involved in street prostitution are 60 to 100 times more likely to be murdered than the average woman and that most of these murders, such as the Craigslist killing, result from a dispute over money rather than being sexually motivated.[6]

Some scholars argue that pornography, prostitution, and drug use erode the moral fabric of society and therefore should be prohibited and punished. They are crimes, according to the great legal scholar Morris Cohen, because "it is one of the functions of the criminal law to give expression to the collective feeling of revulsion toward certain acts, even when they are not very dangerous."[7]

According to this view, so-called victimless crimes are prohibited because one of the functions of criminal law is to express a shared sense of public morality.[8] However, basing criminal definitions on moral beliefs is often an impossible task. Who defines morality? Are we not punishing mere differences rather than social harm? As U.S. Supreme Court Justice William O. Douglas so succinctly put it, "What may

Fact or Fiction?

Prostitution is a good example of a victimless crime.

Fiction. Although they may be glamorized in films, most prostitutes can be viewed as victims likely to suffer coercion, rape, and physical attacks.

public order crime
Behavior that is outlawed because it threatens the general well-being of society and challenges its accepted moral principles.

victimless crime
Public order crime that violates the moral order but has no specific victim other than society as a whole.

be trash to me may be prized by others."[9] Would not any attempt to control or limit "objectionable" material eventually lead to the suppression of free speech and political dissent? Is this not a veiled form of censorship? Not so, according to social commentator Irving Kristol:

> If we start censoring pornography and obscenity, shall we not inevitably end up censoring political opinion? A lot of people seem to think this would be the case—which only shows the power of doctrinaire thinking over reality. We had censorship of pornography and obscenity for 150 years, until almost yesterday, and I am not aware that freedom of opinion in this country was in any way diminished as a consequence of this fact.[10]

CRIMINAL OR IMMORAL?

Acts that most of us deem highly immoral are not criminal. There are no laws banning *superbia* (hubris/pride), *avaritia* (avarice/greed), *luxuria* (extravagance or lust), *invidia* (envy), *gula* (gluttony), *ira* (wrath), and *acedia* (sloth), even though they are considered the "seven deadly sins." Nor is it a crime to ignore the pleas of a drowning child, even though to do so might be considered callous, coldhearted, and unfeeling. (Of course some people—lifeguards, paramedics, firefighters, police officers, and the parents—do have a legal duty to help save the child.)

Conversely, some acts that seem both well intentioned and moral are nonetheless considered criminal:

▶ It is a crime (euthanasia) to kill a loved one who is suffering from an incurable disease to spare him or her further pain; attempting to take your own life (attempted suicide) is also a crime.
▶ Stealing a rich person's money in order to feed a poor family is still considered larceny.
▶ Marrying more than one woman is considered a crime (bigamy), even though multiple marriage may conform to some groups' religious beliefs.[11]

As legal experts Wayne LaFave and Austin Scott Jr., put it, "A good motive will not normally prevent what is otherwise criminal from being a crime."[12]

Social Harm According to the theory of **social harm**, immoral acts can be distinguished from crimes on the basis of the injury they cause: Acts that cause harm or injury are outlawed and punished as crimes; acts, even those that are vulgar, offensive, and depraved, are not outlawed or punished if they harm no one.

The theory of social harm can explain most criminal acts, but not all of them. Some acts that cause enormous amounts of social harm are perfectly legal, whereas others that many people consider virtually harmless are outlawed and severely punished. It is now estimated that more than 500,000 deaths in the United States each year can be linked to the consumption of tobacco and alcohol, yet these "deadly substances" remain legal to produce and sell. Similarly, sports cars and motorcycles that can accelerate to more than 150 miles per hour are perfectly legal to sell and possess, even though almost 40,000 people die each year in car accidents. On the other hand, illegal drugs kill "only" about 17,000 people annually, and none of these fatalities are linked to marijuana. Yet the sale of marijuana and other recreational drugs is still banned and heavily punished.[13] According to the theory of social harm, if more people die each year from alcohol-, tobacco-, and automobile-related causes, whereas smoking pot is relatively safe, then marijuana should be legalized and Corvettes, scotch, and Marlboros outlawed. But they are not.

MORAL CRUSADERS AND MORAL CRUSADES

Public order crimes often trace their origin to moral crusaders who seek to shape the law to reflect their own way of thinking; Howard Becker calls them **moral entrepreneurs**. These rule creators, argues Becker, operate with an absolute certainty that their way is right and that they are justified in employing any means to

Fact or Fiction?

It is a crime to see a young child drowning and not jump in to help.

Fiction. Although you may be considered coldhearted and cruel if you do nothing to help, you are under no legal obligation to save a drowning child.

Fact or Fiction?

More people die from the effects of using legal substances such as cigarettes and alcohol than die from using illegal drugs.

Fact. Alcohol and tobacco, which can be purchased at the corner grocery store, are far more deadly than illegal drugs such as marijuana, the mere possession of which can earn you a prison sentence.

social harm
The injury caused to others by willful wrongful conduct.

moral entrepreneur
A person who creates moral rules, which thus reflect the values of those in power, rather than any objective, universal standards of right and wrong.

CONNECTIONS

Moral entrepreneurs are likely to use the interactionist definition of crime discussed in Chapter 1: Acts are illegal because they violate the moral standards of those in power and those who try to shape public opinion.

Checkpoints

▶ Societies can ban behaviors that lawmakers consider offensive. Critics question whether this amounts to censorship.

▶ The line between behaviors that are merely immoral and those that are criminal is often blurred.

▶ Immoral acts are considered crimes when they cause social harm.

▶ Although they are sometimes called victimless crimes, seemingly voluntary crimes such as pornography and prostitution do have victims, according to some.

▶ People who seek to control or criminalize deviant behaviors are called moral entrepreneurs. They often go on moral crusades.

▶ Abortion and gay marriage have been the focus of moral crusaders.

get their way: "The crusader is fervent and righteous, often self-righteous."[14] Today's moral crusaders take on such issues as prayer in school, gun ownership, gay marriage, abortion, and the distribution of sexually explicit books and magazines.

One popular target for moral crusaders is antismut campaigns that target books considered too "racy" or controversial to be suitable for a public school library. According to the American Library Association, between 2000 and 2006, the Harry Potter series topped the yearly list of books challenged by critics who demanded their removal from school library shelves. Most of the objections to J. K. Rowling's popular series about a young wizard in England centered on the charge that the series promotes Satanism and magic. In the last few years, complaints against Harry and his friends have been outpaced by those lodged against Peter Parnell and Justin Richardson's *And Tango Makes Three*, a children's book that tells the story of two male penguins who find an abandoned egg and raise a baby penguin chick. Because it is geared to a preschool audience, opponents suggest that the underlying theme of the book, learning to accept same-sex relationships (even among penguins) is morally unacceptable.[15]

The Gay Marriage Crusade One of the most heated "moral crusades" has been directed at influencing public acceptance of the gay lifestyle. One group of crusaders is determined to prevent the legalization of gay marriage; its objective is passage of an amendment to the U.S. Constitution declaring that marriage is between one man and one woman. The Defense of Marriage Act, which was passed in 1996 and defined marriage, for the purposes of federal law, as a union of one man and one woman, is one of this group's legal achievements.[16]

Opposing them are activists who have tirelessly campaigned for the civil rights of gay men and women. One of their most important victories occurred in 2003 when the U.S. Supreme Court delivered, in *Lawrence v. Texas*, a historic decision that made it impermissible for states to criminalize oral and anal sex (and all other forms of intercourse that are not conventionally heterosexual) under statutes prohibiting sodomy, deviant sexuality, or what used to be referred to as "buggery."[17] The *Lawrence* case involved two gay men who had been arrested in 1998 for having sex in the privacy of their Houston home. In overturning their convictions, the Court said this:

> Although the laws involved . . . here . . . do not more than prohibit a particular sexual act, their penalties and purposes have more far-reaching consequences, touching upon the most private human conduct, sexual behavior, and in the most private of places, the home. They seek to control a personal relationship that, whether or not entitled to formal recognition in the law, is within the liberty of persons to choose without being punished as criminals. The liberty protected by the Constitution allows homosexual persons the right to choose to enter upon relationships in the confines of their homes and their own private lives and still retain their dignity as free persons.

As a result of this decision, all sodomy laws in the United States were suddenly unconstitutional and unenforceable; acts that were once a crime were legalized. The *Lawrence* decision paved the way for states to rethink their marriage laws. In 2003 Massachusetts's highest court ruled that same-sex couples are legally entitled to wed under the state constitution and that the state may not "deny the protections, benefits, and obligations conferred by civil marriage to two individuals of the same sex who wish to marry."[18] A number of other states (to date Vermont, New Hampshire, Iowa, and Connecticut) have followed suit, and others have created legal unions that, although they are not being called marriage, extend all the rights and responsibilities of marriage under state law to same-sex couples. Other states either have granted limited rights or recognize the legality of same-sex marriages performed elsewhere. In California, the state supreme court ruled in May 2008 that the state constitution guaranteed gay and lesbian couples the "basic civil right" to marry. Moral crusaders opposed to gay marriage mounted a campaign that in 2008 resulted in the passage of Proposition 8, which added to the state constitution a new section that reads, "Only marriage between a man and a woman is valid or recognized in California," thus for the present outlawing gay marriage once again.[19]

The debate over gay marriage rages on: Is it fair to prevent one group of loyal tax-paying citizens from engaging in a behavior that is allowed others? Are there objective standards of morality or should society respect people's differences? After all, opponents charge, polygamy is banned and there are age standards for marriage in every state. If gay marriage is legalized, what about marriage to multiple partners, or with underage minors? How far should the law go in curbing human behaviors that do not cause social harm? Who controls the law and should the law be applied to shape morality?

The public order crimes discussed in this chapter are divided into two broad areas. The first relates to what conventional society considers deviant sexual practices: paraphilias, prostitution, and pornography. The second area concerns the use of substances that have been outlawed or controlled because of the harm they are alleged to cause: drugs and alcohol. ▶ **Checkpoints**

Sex-Related Offenses

On August 24, 2009, Phillip Garrido, a long-time sex offender left a four-page essay at FBI headquarters in San Francisco telling how he had overcome his sexual disorder and how his insights could help others. He also went to the University of California and asked whether he could hold a special Christian event on campus. When he returned the next day with two of his daughters, university officials became suspicious of Garrido and contacted his parole officer. He was asked to come in for an interview and arrived with his wife, two children, and a young woman named Allissa. After being separated from Garrido for a further interview, Allissa told authorities that she was really Jaycee Lee Dugard and that the two young girls were children that she had borne Garrido. Garrido, along with his wife, was placed under immediate arrest. As the nation soon learned, Jaycee Lee Dugard had been abducted on June 10, 1991, when she was 11 years old, at a school bus stop within sight of her home in South Lake Tahoe, California. After being grabbed off the street by Garrido, she had been held captive for 18 years, living in a tent in a walled-off compound on land that the Garridos owned in Antioch, California. Raped repeatedly, Dugard gave birth to daughters in 1994 and 1998; these girls were 15 and 11 at the time of Dugard's reappearance. Law enforcement officers had visited the residence at least twice in recent years but had failed to detect Jaycee or her children. Jaycee helped Garrido in his print shop, and over the years a number of neighbors and customers had spoken with her. On August 28, 2009, Garrido and his wife pled not guilty to charges that included kidnapping, rape, and false imprisonment.

The Jaycee Dugard story shocked the nation and had a chilling effect on the general public. How was a known sex offender able to grab a child off the street and keep her captive for 18 years? But this case is not unique. For example, on June 5, 2002, Elizabeth Smart was abducted from her bedroom in Salt Lake City, Utah, at the age of 14. She was found nine months later, on March 12, 2003, only 18 miles from her home. In a case that also made national headlines, Elizabeth had been kidnapped by Brian David Mitchell and Wanda Ileen Barzee, who were indicted for her kidnapping but were ruled mentally unfit to stand trial.[20]

Although these sex-related kidnappings are stunning in their sordidness, they are not unique or even rare. Each year thousands of children are abducted by strangers, and hundreds of

Pederasts prey on young children, fondling, kidnapping, raping, and even killing adolescent boys and girls. One of the most notorious cases involved 11-year-old Jaycee Lee Dugard, who was snatched from a bus stop in 1991. On August 26, 2009, 18 years later, Dugard's identity emerged when, on another matter, Phillip Craig Garrido brought her to the office of his parole officer in California. Garrido, 58, and his wife Nancy Garrido, 54, were arrested on kidnapping and other charges.

thousands are subjected to some form of sexual exploitation, including sexual abuse, prostitution, pornography, and molestation.[21] Because of these alarming statistics, and also because some sexual practices are believed to cause social harm, some forms of sexual conduct are outlawed and subject to state control. In the following sections, three of the most common such offenses—paraphilias, prostitution, and pornography—are discussed in some detail.

Paraphilias

On June 4, 2009, newspaper headlines around the world told the shocking story of actor David Carradine, who was found dead in a Thailand hotel. Authorities discovered the 72-year-old actor hanging in his closet, the victim of death resulting from engaging in an autoerotic practice known as *asphyxiophilia*, self-strangulation that restricts the supply of oxygen or blood to the brain in order to increase sexual intensity.[22]

Carradine's death was attributed to his involvement with a common **paraphilia**, a term derived from the Greek *para*, "to the side of," and *philos*, "loving." Paraphilias are bizarre or abnormal sexual practices that involve recurrent sexual urges focused on (1) nonhuman objects (such as underwear, shoes, or leather), (2) humiliation or the experience of receiving or giving pain (as in sadomasochism or bondage), or (3) children or others who cannot grant consent.[23] Paraphilias have existed and been recorded for thousands of years. Buddhist texts more than 2,000 years old contain references to sexually deviant behaviors among monastic communities, including sexual activity with animals and sexual interest in corpses. Richard von Krafft-Ebing's *Psychopathia Sexualis*, first published in 1887, was the first text to discuss such paraphilias as sadism, bestiality, and incest.[24]

When paraphilias, such as wearing clothes normally worn by the opposite sex (transvestite fetishism), are engaged in by adults in the privacy of their homes, they remain outside the law's reach. However, when paraphilias involve unwilling or underage victims, they are considered socially harmful and subject to criminal penalties. Outlawed paraphilias include

▶ *Frotteurism*. Rubbing against or touching a nonconsenting person in a crowd, elevator, or other public area
▶ *Voyeurism*. Obtaining sexual pleasure from spying on a stranger while he or she disrobes or engages in sexual behavior with another
▶ *Exhibitionism*. Deriving sexual pleasure from exposing the genitals to surprise or shock a stranger
▶ *Sadomasochism*. Deriving pleasure from receiving pain or inflicting pain on another
▶ *Pedophilia*. Attaining sexual pleasure through sexual activity with prepubescent children

PEDOPHILIA

Of all the commonly practiced paraphilias, pedophilia is the one that most concerns the general public. One focus of concern has been the on-going scandals that have rocked the Catholic Church. Numerous priests have been accused of sexually molesting young children, among the most notorious being Father James Porter, convicted of molesting at least 200 children of both sexes over a 30-year period. Porter was sentenced to an 18-to-20-year prison term and died of cancer while incarcerated.

The cause of pedophilia has not been determined, but suspected factors include abnormal brain structure, social maladaption, and neurological dysfunction. Research using brain scans shows that the central processing of sexual stimuli in pedophiles may be controlled by a disturbance in the prefrontal networks of the brain.[25] Brain trauma has also been linked to child molesting. And although injury may occur before or at birth, it is also possible that the damage caused by injury and/or accident can produce the brain malfunctions linked to pedophilia.[26] There is also some evidence that

paraphilia
Bizarre or abnormal sexual practices that may involve nonhuman objects, humiliation, or children.

Profiles in Crime The Jessica Lunsford Murder Case

On February 24, 2005, 9-year-old Jessica Lunsford was reported missing from her home. When a child is reported missing, the police typically check on all the known sex offenders in the area, who in this case included John Evander Couey. Couey, 46, was not living at the address where he was registered, a legal violation. When police located Couey and searched his room, they found nothing. But Couey had a long list of convictions, including burglary, carrying a concealed weapon, disorderly intoxication, driving under the influence, indecent exposure, disorderly conduct, fraud, insufficient funds, and larceny. A habitual drug abuser, in 1991 he had been arrested and charged with "fondling a child under the age of 16."

Nineteen days after Jessica Lunsford was first reported missing, detectives returned to Couey's home and this time found blood on the mattress. Couey had fled but was arrested in Georgia. While in police custody, Couey admitted that he had entered the Lunsford home at around 3 A.M. on February 24, 2005, and found Jessica asleep in her bed. He woke her and ordered her to be quiet. "Don't yell or nothing," he said and told her to follow him back to his sister's house, where he raped her repeatedly and kept her in a closet for three days. When he learned that detectives were searching for him, he panicked and buried her even though she was still alive. He showed investigators the shallow grave where they found Jessica's body inside two tied plastic garbage bags. Her wrists were bound, but she had managed to poke two fingers through the plastic in an attempt to free herself.

Couey was found guilty of murder on March 7, 2007, and a death penalty hearing was held soon after. In closing statements, prosecutor Ric Ridgway called the crime "evil" and asked jurors to remember how Jessica died by suffocating in the hole Couey dug, accompanied only by a stuffed toy she had grabbed as she was being abducted. "She was in pain. In the dark. She was certainly terrified," Ridgway said in his closing statement. "If this is not the person who deserves the death penalty, who does?"

© Brian LaPeter/Pool/Reuters/Landov

Defense lawyers pleaded for mercy, arguing that Couey deserved no more than a life sentence in prison because of mental retardation and mental illness, neglect as a child, and the effects of alcohol and drug abuse. "No matter what you do, John Couey is going to die in prison," said defense attorney Alan Fanter. "No child should have to die the way Jessica Lunsford did. But justice is not vengeance." The jury did not buy that argument and sentenced Couey to death on March 14, 2007. Couey died in prison on September 30, 2009, before his sentence could be carried out.

In the aftermath of Jessica Lunsford's abduction, Florida passed legislation that requires increased prison sentences, electronic tracking of all convicted sex offenders on probation, and the mandatory use of state databases by all local probation officials so that known sex offenders cannot avoid the scrutiny of law enforcement. Can such measures control the behavior of pedophiles such as Couey before they kill their innocent victims?

SOURCES: Court TV Crime Library, "Jessica Lunsford," www .crimelibrary.com/serial_killers/predators/jessica_lunsford/9.html (accessed April 26, 2009); *USA Today*, "Judge Throws Out Confession in Jessica Lunsford Case," June 30, 2006, www.usatoday.com/news/nation/2006–06–30-child-confession_x.htm (accessed April 26, 2009); Curt Anderson, "Death Sentence Endorsed in Lunsford Case," *Washington Post*, March 15, 2007, www.washingtonpost.com/wp-dyn/content/article/2007/03/15/AR2007031500518.html (accessed April 26, 2009).

pedophilia is heritable and that genetic factors are responsible for the development of pedophilia.[27] Other suspected connections range from cognitive distortions to exposure to pornography.[28] Whatever the cause, pedophilia is not a limited problem; research indicates that it is possible that up to 20 percent of males have at one time experienced sexual attraction to a minor.[29]

One of the most horrific cases of pedophilia involved the kidnapping and death of 9-year-old Jessica Lunsford, which is the subject of the accompanying Profiles in Crime feature.

Some predators prey upon young women involved in personal services. Here the notorious "Craigslist killer" and former Boston University medical student Philip Markoff, center, stands with his attorney John Salsberg, right, during his arraignment in Suffolk Superior Court on June 22, 2009, in Boston. Markoff was charged with first-degree murder in the April 23, 2009, shooting of Julissa Brisman, an aspiring actress and model. Brisman, whose financial problems induced her to advertise as a masseuse on Craigslist, was shot in a posh Boston hotel after a botched robbery. Markoff is also suspected of luring other women involved in personal services and sex work to hotels and then robbing them at gunpoint.

Prostitution

Prostitution has been known of for thousands of years. The term derives from the Latin *prostituere*, which means "to cause to stand in front of." The prostitute is viewed as publicly offering his or her body for sale. The earliest record of prostitution appears in ancient Mesopotamia, where priests engaged in sex to promote fertility in the community. All women were required to do temple duty, and passing strangers were expected to make donations to the temple after enjoying their services.[30]

Modern commercial sex appears to have its roots in ancient Greece, where Solon established licensed brothels in 500 B.C.E. The earnings of Greek prostitutes helped pay for the temple of Aphrodite. Famous men openly went to prostitutes to enjoy intellectual, aesthetic, and sexual stimulation; prostitutes, however, were prohibited from marrying.[31]

Today, **prostitution** can be defined as granting nonmarital sexual access for remuneration, under terms established by mutual agreement of the prostitutes, their clients, and their employers. Included in this process are the following elements:

▶ *Activity that has sexual significance for the customer.* This includes the entire range of sexual behavior, from sexual intercourse to exhibitionism, sadomasochism, oral sex, and so on.
▶ *Economic transaction.* Something of economic value, not necessarily money, is exchanged for the activity.
▶ *Emotional indifference.* The sexual exchange is simply for economic consideration. Although the participants may know one another, their interaction has nothing to do with affection for one another.[32]

INCIDENCE OF PROSTITUTION

It is difficult to assess the number of prostitutes operating in the United States. Fifty years ago, about two-thirds of non-college-educated men and one-quarter of college-educated men had visited a prostitute.[33] It is likely that the number of men who hire prostitutes has declined sharply since then.

How can these changes be accounted for? Changing sexual mores, brought about by the so-called sexual revolution, have liberalized sexuality. Men are less likely to use prostitutes because legitimate alternatives for sexuality are more open to them. In addition, the prevalence of sexually transmitted diseases has caused many men to avoid visiting prostitutes for fear of irreversible health hazards.[34] Although traditional forms of prostitution may be in decline, **ehooking**, in which prostitutes use the Internet to shield their identities and contact clients, may be responsible for a resurgence in sex for hire, especially in times of economic turmoil.[35]

Why do men still employ prostitutes? When interviewing a prostitute's clients, sociologist Monica Prasad found that the decision to employ a prostitute was not only shaped by sexuality but also influenced by (1) peer pressure to try something different and exciting, (2) the wish for a sexual exchange free from obligations, and (3) curiosity about the world of prostitution. Prasad found that most customers who became "regulars" began to view prostitution as a benign service and not an illicit activity.[36]

Despite such changes, the Uniform Crime Report (UCR) indicates that fewer than 80,000 prostitution arrests are now being made annually, with the gender ratio being

prostitution
The granting of nonmarital sexual access for remuneration.

ehooking
Using the Internet for purposes of prostitution in order to shield identities and contact clients.

about 2:1 female to male; in other words, about one-third of people arrested for prostitution are men. The number of prostitution arrests has been trending downward for some time; about 100,000 arrests were made in 1995. It is possible that fewer people are seeking the services of prostitutes, that police are reluctant to make arrests in prostitution cases, or that more sophisticated prostitutes who use the Internet or other forms of technology to "make dates" are better able to avoid detection by police.

But although prostitution arrests are down, that does not mean that the profession is on the decline. Indeed, the international sex trade is flourishing.

INTERNATIONAL SEX TRADE

Prostitution flourishes abroad. In some nations it is legal and regulated by the government, whereas other nations punish prostitution with the death penalty. An example of the former is Germany, which has a flourishing legal sex trade. Germany allows prostitutes to obtain regular work contracts, receive health insurance, and pay taxes; 400,000 people there work in the sex trade.[37] In contrast, many Islamic countries punish prostitution with death, a punishment that is sometimes carried out by stoning in the public square.[38]

There is also a troubling overseas trade in prostitution in which men from wealthy countries frequent marginally regulated sex areas in needy nations such as Thailand in order to procure young girls forced or sold into prostitution—a phenomenon known as *sex tourism*. In addition to sex tours, there has also been a soaring demand for pornography, strip clubs, lap dancing, escorts, and telephone sex in developing countries.[39] The international trade in prostitution is the subject of the accompanying Race, Culture, Gender, and Criminology feature on page 358.

TYPES OF PROSTITUTES

Several different types of prostitutes operate in the United States.

Streetwalkers Prostitutes who work the streets in plain sight of police, citizens, and customers are referred to as hustlers, hookers, or streetwalkers. Although glamorized by the Julia Roberts character in the film *Pretty Woman* (who winds up with multimillionaire Richard Gere), streetwalkers are considered the least attractive, lowest paid, most vulnerable men and women in the profession. Streetwalkers wear bright clothing, makeup, and jewelry to attract customers; they take their customers to hotels. The term "hooker," however, is derived not from streetwalkers using their charms to "hook" clients, but from the popular name given women who followed Union General "Fighting Joe" Hooker's army and serviced the troops during the Civil War.[40]

Research shows that there are a variety of working styles among women involved in street-based prostitution. Some are controlled by pimps who demand and receive a major share of their earnings. Others are independent entrepreneurs interested in building a stable group of steady clients. Still others manipulate and exploit their customers and may engage in theft and blackmail.[41]

Bar Girls B-girls, as they are also called, spend their time in bars, drinking and waiting to be picked up by customers. Although alcoholism

Sex trafficking has become an international scandal involving thousands of young men and women each year. Here, sex workers are seen at a red-light area in Mumbai, India, on August 4, 2009. Rights activists say thousands of poor women and girls are forced into prostitution every year, after being lured from villages to cities on false promises of jobs or marriage. Many other victims are teenagers sold to brothel owners by impoverished family members.

In the very popular 2008 film *Taken*, Brian Mills, a former CIA agent played by Liam Neeson, uses his skills to save his daughter Kim, who has been abducted while on a trip to Paris. Almost as soon as she arrives, Kim and a friend are kidnapped, drugged, and forced into the sex trade. As Brian searches frantically for his beloved daughter, he uncovers an international scheme in which young women are taken, abused, forcibly addicted to drugs, and used as sex slaves. Can these dreadful images be based on reality?

Unfortunately, they may be all too real. Every year, hundreds of thousands of women and children—primarily from Southeast Asia and eastern Europe—are lured by the promise of good jobs and then end up in the sex trade in industrialized countries. The data is notoriously unreliable, but estimates of

exploitation, and the victims are predominantly women and girls; about 20 percent of these victims are children.

Even though films such as *Taken* depict human traffickers as almost entirely men, the UN report found that the majority of sex traffickers are women. Many were in the sex trade themselves and were encouraged by their recruiter/trafficker to return home and recruit other women, often under the scrutiny of people working for the trafficker to make sure they don't try to escape.

Because it is a global enterprise, there is a great deal of cooperation in human trafficking. For example, a single gang in eastern Europe may include Russians, Moldavians, Egyptians, and Syrians. Cooperation makes it possible to traffic sex slaves not only to neighboring countries but all

Race, Culture, Gender, and Criminology
International Human Trafficking

the number of people trafficked internationally each year range between 600,000 and one million men, women, and children. Japan now has more than 10,000 commercial sex establishments with 150,000 to 200,000 foreign girls trafficked into the country each year. It is believed that traffickers import up to 50,000 women and children every year into the United States, despite legal efforts at control. According to a 2009 report prepared by the United Nations, the most common form of human trafficking (79 percent) is sexual

around the globe. The UN found that victims from East Asia were detected in more than 20 countries in regions throughout the world, including Europe, the Americas, the Middle East, Central Asia, and Africa.

Contributing Factors

Human trafficking is facilitated by social problems and disorder, such as disruptions in the global economy, war, and social unrest. Economic crisis hits young girls especially

may be a problem, B-girls usually work out an arrangement with the bartender whereby they are served diluted drinks or water colored with dye or tea, for which the customer is charged an exorbitant price. In some bars, the B-girl is given a credit for each drink she gets the customer to buy. It is common to find B-girls in towns with military bases and large transient populations.[42]

Brothel Prostitutes Also called bordellos, cathouses, sporting houses, and houses of ill repute, brothels flourished in the nineteenth and early twentieth centuries. They were large establishments, usually run by madams, that housed several prostitutes. A madam is a woman who employs prostitutes, supervises their behavior, and receives a fee for her services; her cut is usually 40 to 60 percent of the prostitutes' earnings. The madam's role may include recruiting women into prostitution and socializing them in the trade.[43]

Brothels declined in importance following World War II. The closing of the last brothel in Texas is chronicled in the play and film *The Best Little Whorehouse in Texas*. Today the best-known brothels exist in Nevada, where prostitution is legal outside large population centers.

Call Girls The aristocrats of prostitution are call girls. They charge customers thousands of dollar per night and may net more than $200,000 per year. Some gain clients through employment in escort services; others develop independent customer lists. Many call girls come from middle-class backgrounds and serve upper-class customers. Attempting to dispel the notion that their service is simply sex for money, they hard. Female victims are often poor and aspire to a better life. They may be forced, coerced, deceived, and psychologically manipulated into industrial or agricultural work, marriage, domestic servitude, organ donation, or sexual exploitation. Some traffickers exploit victims' frustration with low salaries in their home countries, and others take advantage of a crisis in the victim's family that requires her to make money abroad. The traffickers then promise the victim to take her abroad and find her a traditionally female service-sector job, such as waitress, salesperson, domestic worker, or au pair/babysitter.

Whereas victims often come from poorer countries, the market for labor and sex is found in wealthier countries or in countries that, though economically poor, cater to the needs of citizens from wealthy countries, of corporations, or of tourists.

Combating Human Trafficking

Recently, the United States made stopping the trafficking of women a top priority. In 1998, the "Memorandum on Steps to Combat Violence against Women and the Trafficking of Women and Girls" was issued. It directed the secretary of state, the attorney general, and the president's Interagency Council on Women to expand their efforts to combat violence against women to include working against the trafficking of women.

In the former Soviet Union, prevention education projects are aimed at potential victims of trafficking, and nongovernmental organizations have established hotlines for victims or women seeking information about the risks of accepting job offers abroad.

The UN report found that the number of convictions for human trafficking is increasing, especially in a handful of countries. Nonetheless, most countries' conviction rates rarely exceed 1.5 per 100,000 people, which is even below the level normally recorded for rare crimes such as kidnapping. As of 2007–2008, two out of every five countries covered by the UN Report had not recorded a single conviction for sex trafficking, so the problem still remains.

CRITICAL THINKING

1. If put in charge, what would you do to slow or end the international sex trade? Before you answer, remember the saying that prostitution is the world's oldest profession, which implies that curbing it may prove quite difficult.
2. Should men who hire prostitutes be punished very severely in order to deter them from getting involved in the exploitation of these vulnerable young women?

SOURCES: Mark Lusk and Faith Lucas, "The Challenge of Human Trafficking and Contemporary Slavery," *Journal of Comparative Social Welfare* 25 (2009): 49–57; United Nations Office on Drugs and Crime, "Global Reports on Trafficking in Persons," www.unodc .org/documents/Global_Report_on_TIP.pdf (accessed July 7, 2009); Shannon Devine, "Poverty Fuels Trafficking to Japan," *Herizons* 20 (2007): 18–22; Linda Williams and Jennifer Ngo, "Human Trafficking, "in *Encyclopedia of Interpersonal Violence,* ed. Claire Renzetti and Jeffrey Edleson (Thousand Oaks, CA: Sage Publications, 2007); Donna Hughes, "The 'Natasha' Trade: Transnational Sex Trafficking," *National Institute of Justice Journal* (January 2001), www .uri.edu/artsci/wms/hughes/natasha_nij.pdf (accessed March 15, 2009).

concentrate on making their clients feel important and attractive. Working exclusively via telephone "dates," call girls get their clients by word of mouth or by making arrangements with bellhops, cab drivers, and so on. They either entertain clients in their own apartments or visit clients' hotels and apartments. When she retires, a call girl can sell her date book, listing client names and sexual preferences, for thousands of dollars. Despite the lucrative nature of their business, call girls run considerable risk by being alone and unprotected with strangers. They often request the business cards of their clients to make sure they are dealing with "upstanding citizens."

Escort Services/Call Houses Some escort services are fronts for prostitution rings. Both male and female sex workers can be sent out after the client calls a number published in an ad in the yellow pages. How common are adult sexual services? In Los Angeles alone 216 escort services were recently listed in the yellow pages; New York City had 126.[44]

A relatively new phenomenon, the call house combines elements of the brothel and of call girl rings. A madam receives a call from a prospective customer, and if she finds the client acceptable, she arranges a meeting between the caller and a prostitute in her service. The madam maintains a list of prostitutes, who are on call rather than living together in a house. The call house insulates the madam from arrest because she never meets the client or receives direct payment.[45]

Circuit Travelers Prostitutes known as circuit travelers move around in groups of two or three to lumber, labor, and agricultural camps. They ask the foreman for permission to ply their trade, service the whole crew in an evening, and then move on. Some circuit travelers seek clients at truck stops and rest areas.

Sometimes young girls are forced to become circuit travelers by unscrupulous pimps who make them work for months as prostitutes in agricultural migrant camps. The young women are lured from developing countries such as Mexico with offers of jobs in landscaping, health care, housecleaning, and restaurants. But when they arrive in the United States, they are told that they owe their captors thousands of dollars and must work as prostitutes to pay off this debt. The young women are raped and beaten if they complain or try to escape.[46]

Cyber Prostitutes The technological revolution has begun to alter the world of prostitution. So-called cyber prostitutes set up personal websites or put listings on Web boards, such as "Adult Friendfinder" or Craigslist, that carry personals. They may use loaded phrases such as "looking for generous older man" in their self-descriptions. When contacted, they ask to exchange emails, chat online, or make voice calls with prospective clients. They may even exchange pictures. This enables them to select clients they want to be with and to avoid clients who may be threatening or dangerous. Some cyber prostitution rings offer customers the opportunity to choose women from their Internet page and then have them flown in from around the country.

BECOMING A PROSTITUTE

At 38, Lt. Cmdr. Rebecca Dickinson had risen from the enlisted ranks in the Navy to its officer corps. She had an assignment to the Naval Academy in Annapolis, Maryland, where she helped teach a leadership course. But faced with money and marital problems, Lt. Cmdr. Dickinson worked as a prostitute for some of the richest and most powerful men in Washington, DC. When asked why she did it, she replied, "I needed the money, yes I did." This desperate naval officer, whose career was destroyed in the scandal, was paid $130 for a 90-minute session.[47]

Why does someone turn to prostitution? Both male and female prostitutes often come from troubled homes marked by extreme conflict and hostility and from poor urban areas or rural communities. Divorce, separation, or death splits the family; most prostitutes grew up in homes without fathers.[48] Girls from the lower socioeconomic classes who get into "the life" report conflict with school authorities, poor grades, and an overly regimented school experience.[49]

Sexual abuse also plays a role in prostitution. Many prostitutes were initiated into sex by family members at ages as young as 10 to 12 years; they have long histories of sexual exploitation and abuse.[50] These early experiences with sex help teach them that their bodies have value and that sexual encounters can be used to obtain affection, power, or money.

Drug abuse, including heroin and cocaine addiction, is often a factor in the prostitute's life.[51] Surveys conducted in New York and Chicago have found that a significant portion of female prostitutes have substance abuse problems, and more than half claim that prostitution is how they support their drug habits; on the street, women who barter drugs for sex are called *skeezers*. Not all drug-addicted prostitutes barter sex for drugs, but those who do report more frequent drug abuse and sexual activity than other prostitutes.[52] Moreover, drug-abusing prostitutes are more likely than nonabusing prostitutes to have had a history of childhood abuse and neglect, school failure, and familial conflict.[53]

Although many prostitutes have a troubled past, not all do, and some (such as Lt. Cmdr. Dickinson) enter the life as a means of dealing with financial problems. Prostitution in this case may be a rational choice generated by personal problems and exigencies.

CONTROLLING PROSTITUTION

In the late nineteenth and early twentieth centuries, efforts were made to regulate prostitution in the United States through medical supervision and the licensing and zoning of brothels in districts outside residential neighborhoods.[54] After World War I, prostitution became associated with disease, and the desire to protect young servicemen from harm helped put an end to nearly all experiments with legalization in the United States.[55] Some reformers attempted to paint pimps and procurers as immigrants who used their foreign ways to snare unsuspecting American girls into prostitution. Such fears prompted passage of the federal Mann Act (1925), which prohibited bringing women into the country, or transporting them across state lines, for the purposes of prostitution. Often called the "white slave act," it carried penalties of a $5,000 fine, five years in prison, or both.[56]

Today, prostitution is considered a misdemeanor and is punishable by a fine or a short jail sentence. In practice, most law enforcement is uneven and aims at confining illegal activities to particular areas in the city.[57] Prostitution is illegal in all states except Nevada, where licensed and highly regulated brothels can operate as business enterprises in rural counties (population under 400,000 (this leaves out the counties in which Las Vegas and Reno are located). Until recently, in Rhode Island prostitution was not illegal so long as it occurred in a personal residence. However, in 2009 the Rhode Island legislature, bowing to pressure by moral crusaders, closed the loophole and banned all forms of prostitution.

LEGALIZE PROSTITUTION?

Feminists have articulated conflicting views of prostitution. One position is that women must become emancipated from male oppression and achieve sexual equality. The *sexual equality* view considers the prostitute a victim of male dominance. In patriarchal societies, male power is predicated on female subjugation, and prostitution is a clear example of this gender exploitation.[58] In contrast, for some feminists, the fight for equality depends on controlling all attempts by men or women to impose their will on women. The *free choice* view is that prostitution, if freely chosen, expresses women's equality and is not a symptom of subjugation.[59] Advocates of both positions argue that the penalties for prostitution should be reduced (in other words, the activity should be decriminalized), but neither side advocates outright legalization. Decriminalization would relieve already desperate women of the additional burden of severe legal punishment. However, legalization might be coupled with regulation by male-dominated justice agencies. For example, required medical examinations would mean increased male control over women's bodies.

Should prostitution be legalized in the United States? In her book *Brothel*, Alexa Albert makes a compelling case for legalization. A Harvard-trained physician who interviewed young women working at a legal brothel in Nevada, Albert found that the women remained HIV-free and felt safer working in a secure environment than alone on city streets. Despite long hours and rules that gave too much profit to the owners, the women actually took "pride" in their work. Besides benefiting from greater security, most were earning between $300 and $1,500 per day.[60]

While persuasive, Albert's vision is countered by research conducted by psychologist Melissa Farley, who surveyed brothel girls in Nevada and found that many suffered abuse and long-lasting psychological damage. Farley found that numerous brothel prostitutes are coerced into prostitution and that brothel owners are not much different from pimps who control them with an iron fist. Subject to sexual harassment, sexual exploitation, and rape, many fear for their lives. Moreover, legal prostitution does not protect women from the violence, verbal abuse, physical injury, and exposure to diseases such as HIV that occur in illegal prostitution.[61] Similarly, Roger Matthews, author of the recent book *Prostitution, Politics and Policy*, studied prostitution for more than two decades and found that sex workers were extremely desperate, damaged, and disorganized. Many are involved in substance abuse and experience beatings, rape, and other forms of violence on a regular basis. Prostitution is, he concludes, the world's most dangerous occupation. His solution is to treat the women forced into prostitution as victims and the men who purchase their services as the criminals. He applauds Sweden's decision to make buying sexual services a crime, thus criminalizing the "johns" rather than the women in prostitution. When governments legalize prostitution, it leads to a massive expansion of the trade, both legal and illegal.[62]

Pornography

The term **pornography** derives from the Greek *porne,* meaning "prostitute," and *graphein,* meaning "to write." In the heart of many major cities are stores that display and sell books, magazines, and films explicitly depicting every imaginable sex act. Suburban video stores also rent and sell sexually explicit tapes, which make up 15 to 30 percent of the home rental market. The purpose of this material is to provide sexual titillation and excitement for paying customers. Although material depicting nudity and sex is typically legal, protected by the First Amendment's provision limiting government control of speech, most criminal codes prohibit the production, display, and sale of obscene material.

Obscenity, derived from the Latin *caenum,* for "filth," is defined by Webster's dictionary as "deeply offensive to morality or decency . . . designed to incite to lust or depravity."[63] The problem of controlling pornography centers on this definition of obscenity. Police and law enforcement officials can legally seize only material that is judged obscene. "But who," critics ask, "is to judge what is obscene?" At one time, such novels as *Tropic of Cancer* by Henry Miller, *Ulysses* by James Joyce, and *Lady Chatterley's Lover* by D. H. Lawrence were prohibited because they were considered obscene; today they are considered works of great literary value. Thus, what is obscene today may be considered socially acceptable at a future time. After all, *Playboy* and other "men's magazines," which are sold openly in most bookstores, display nude models in all kinds of sexually explicit poses. The uncertainty surrounding this issue is illustrated by Supreme Court Justice Potter Stewart's famous 1964 statement on how he defined obscenity: "I know it when I see it." Because of this legal and moral ambiguity, the sex trade is booming around the United States.

IS PORNOGRAPHY HARMFUL?

Opponents of pornography argue that it degrades both the people who are photographed and members of the public who are sometimes forced to see obscene material. Pornographers exploit their models, who often include underage children. Investigations have found that many performers and models are victims of physical and psychological coercion.[64]

One uncontested danger of pornography is "kiddie porn." Each year more than a million children are believed to be used in pornography or prostitution, many of them runaways whose plight is exploited by adults. Sexual exploitation by these rings can devastate the child victims. Exploited children are prone to such acting-out behavior as setting fires and becoming sexually focused in the use of language, dress, and mannerisms; they also may suffer physical problems ranging from headaches and loss of appetite to genital soreness, vomiting, and urinary tract infections and psychological problems, including mood swings, withdrawal, edginess, and nervousness. There is also evidence linking kiddie porn to child sexual abuse: A recent study by Michael Bourke and Andres Hernandez compared a group of men who had been convicted of possessing child pornography but had no known history with "hands-on" sexual abuse, with a second group of consumers of child pornography who also had been convicted of sexual offending. The goal was to determine whether the former group of offenders were "merely" collectors of child pornography who presented no actual physical risk to children. Bourke and Hernandez found that the Internet offenders were significantly likely to have sexually abused a child via a hands-on contact, even though they had not been caught or convicted, and that they were likely to have offended against multiple victims.[65] Although this research doesn't prove that viewing child pornography is a cause of child molesting, it does indicate that there is a high correlation between viewing and acting out, regardless of whether the behavior has been detected or remains hidden.

pornography
Sexually explicit books, magazines, films, and DVDs intended to provide sexual titillation and excitement for paying customers.

obscenity
Material that violates community standards of morality or decency and has no redeeming social value.

DOES PORNOGRAPHY CAUSE VIOLENCE?

An issue critical to the debate over pornography is whether viewing it produces sexual violence or assaultive behavior. This debate reignited when serial killer Ted Bundy claimed his murderous rampage was fueled by reading pornography.

The scientific evidence linking sexually explicit material to violence is mixed.[66] Some research has found that viewing erotic material may act as a safety valve for those whose impulses might otherwise lead them to violence; in a sense, pornography reduces violence.[67] Viewing obscene material may have the unintended side effect of satisfying erotic impulses that otherwise might result in more sexually aggressive behavior. Thus, it is not surprising to some skeptics that convicted rapists and sex offenders report less exposure to pornography than control groups of nonoffenders.[68] The lack of a clear-cut connection between viewing pornography and violence is used to bolster the argument that all printed matter, no matter how sexually explicit, is protected by the First Amendment.

However, some research does find a link between consuming pornography and subsequent violent or controlling behavior.[69] There is also evidence that people exposed to adult films that portray violence, sadism, and women enjoying being raped and degraded are likely to be sexually aggressive toward female victims.[70] Laboratory experiments conducted by a number of leading authorities have found that men exposed to violent pornography are more likely to act aggressively toward women.[71] The evidence suggests that violence and sexual aggression are not linked to erotic or pornographic films per se but that erotic films depicting violence, rape, brutality, and aggression may evoke similar feelings in viewers. This finding is especially distressing because it is common for adult books and films to have sexually violent themes such as rape, bondage, and mutilation.[72] A leading critic of pornography, Diana Russell, contends that hatred of women is a principal theme in pornography and is often coupled with racism. Her research provides strong evidence linking pornography to misogyny (the hatred of women), an emotional response that often leads to rape.[73]

PORNOGRAPHY AND THE LAW

The First Amendment to the U.S. Constitution protects free speech and prohibits police agencies from limiting the public's right of free expression. However, the Supreme Court held, in the twin cases of *Roth v. United States* and *Alberts v. California*, that although the First Amendment protects all "ideas with even the slightest redeeming social importance—unorthodox ideas, controversial ideas, even ideas hateful to the prevailing climate of opinion. . ., implicit in the history of the First Amendment is the rejection of obscenity as utterly without redeeming social importance."[74] These decisions left unclear how obscenity is defined. If a highly erotic movie tells a "moral tale," must it be judged legal even if 95 percent of its content is objectionable? A spate of movies made after the *Roth* decision claimed that they were educational or warned the viewer about sexual depravity, so they could not be said to lack redeeming social importance. Many state obscenity cases were appealed to federal courts so that judges could decide whether the films totally lacked redeeming social importance. To rectify the situation, the Supreme Court redefined its concept of obscenity in the case of *Miller v. California*:

> The basic guidelines for the trier of fact must be (a) whether the average person applying contemporary community standards would find that the work taken as a whole appeals to the prurient interest; (b) whether the work depicts or describes, in a patently offensive way, sexual conduct specifically defined by the applicable state law, and (c) whether the work, taken as a whole, lacks serious literary, artistic, political or scientific value.[75]

To convict a person of obscenity under the *Miller* doctrine, the state or local jurisdiction must specifically define obscene conduct in its statute, and the pornographer must engage in that behavior. The Court gave some examples of what is considered

Pornography is a global phenomenon that involves billions of dollars annually. Here a potential customer considers buying a pirated pornographic DVD at a roadside shop in Lagos on May 26, 2008. There are hundreds of sellers of "pornos" in the sprawling city of Lagos, even though it is illegal to sell, market, or distribute pornographic material in Nigeria. In Lagos, Abuja, and Nigeria's other urban centers, the pirating, sale, and distribution of thousands of DVDs go virtually unhindered. The authorities responsible for controlling this pornographic material maintain that they are helpless to impede its flow, but it is widely suspected that when dealers brazenly break the law, the authorities very often look the other way.

obscene: "patently offensive representations or descriptions of masturbation, excretory functions and lewd exhibition of the genitals."[76] Obviously, a plebiscite cannot be held to determine the community's attitude for every trial concerning the sale of pornography. Works that are considered obscene in Omaha might be considered routine in New York, but how can we be sure? To resolve this dilemma, the Supreme Court in *Pope v. Illinois* articulated a reasonableness doctrine: A work is obscene if a reasonable person applying objective (national) standards would find the material to lack any social value.[77]

Congress attempted to control the growth of Internet porn when it passed the Child Pornography Prevention Act of 1996 (CPPA). This act expanded the federal prohibition on child pornography to include not only pornographic images made using actual children but also "any visual depiction, including any photograph, film, video, picture, or computer or computer-generated image or picture" that "is, or appears to be, of a minor engaging in sexually explicit conduct," and any sexually explicit image that is "advertised, promoted, presented, described, or distributed in such a manner that conveys the impression" that it depicts "a minor engaging in sexually explicit conduct." This language was used in order to ban "virtual child pornography," which appears to depict minors but is produced by means other than using real children, such as through the use of youthful-looking adults or computer-imaging technology. It also bans Web postings of material deemed "harmful to minors."[78] However, in 2002, the U.S. Supreme Court struck down some sections of the CPPA as being unconstitutionally deficient, especially those that ban "virtual porn":

Finally, the First Amendment is turned upside down by the argument that, because it is difficult to distinguish between images made using real children and those produced by computer imaging, both kinds of images must be prohibited. The overbreadth doctrine prohibits the Government from banning unprotected speech if a substantial amount of protected speech is prohibited or chilled in the process.[79]

CAN PORNOGRAPHY BE CONTROLLED?

Although politically appealing, law enforcement crusades do not necessarily obtain the desired effect. A get-tough policy could make sex-related goods and services scarce, driving up prices and making their sale even more desirable and profitable. Going after national distributors may help decentralize the adult movie and photo business and encourage local rings to expand their activities—for example, by making and marketing videos as well as still photos or distributing them through computer networks that originate abroad and are difficult to control.

An alternative approach has been to restrict the sale of pornography within acceptable boundaries. For example, New York City has enacted zoning that seeks to break up the concentration of peep shows, topless bars, and X-rated businesses in several neighborhoods, particularly in Times Square.[80] The law forbids sex-oriented businesses within 500 feet of residential zones, schools, churches, or day care centers. Sex shops cannot be located within 500 feet of each other, so concentrated "red light" districts must be dispersed. Rather than close their doors, sex shops got around the law by adding products such as luggage, cameras, T-shirts, and classic films. The courts have upheld the law, ruling that stores can stay in business if no more than 40 percent of their floor space and inventory are dedicated to adult entertainment.[81]

The biggest challenge to those seeking to control the sex-for-profit industry has been the technological change in the industry. Adult movie theaters are closing as people become able to download adult content off the Internet. There have been numerous attempts to control the spread of Internet pornography, but so far they have failed to withstand the First Amendment test of not abridging free speech. For example, Congress passed the Communications Decency Act (CDA), which made all Internet service providers, commercial online services, bulletin board systems, and electronic mail providers criminally liable whenever their services are used to transmit any material considered "obscene, lewd, lascivious, filthy, or indecent" (S 314, 1996). However, in *Reno v. ACLU* (1997), the Supreme Court ruled that the CDA unconstitutionally restricted free speech—yet another illustration of the difficulty that law enforcement encounters when trying to balance the need to control obscenity with leaving First Amendment protections intact.[82]
▶ **Checkpoints**

Substance Abuse

The problem of substance abuse stretches all across the United States. Large urban areas are beset by drug-dealing gangs, drug users who engage in crime to support their habits, and alcohol-related violence. Rural areas are important staging centers for the shipment of drugs across the country and are often the production sites for synthetic drugs and marijuana farming.[83]

Another indication of the concern about drugs has been the number of drug-related visits to hospital emergency rooms. Each year there are now more than 1 million emergency room (ER) visits related solely to illicit drug use. In a recent year,

▶ Cocaine was involved in 548,608 ER visits.
▶ Marijuana was involved in 290,563 ER visits.
▶ Heroin was involved in 189,780 ER visits.
▶ Stimulants, including amphetamines and methamphetamine, were involved in 107,575 ER visits.
▶ Visits related to other illicit drugs, such as PCP, Ecstasy, and GHB, were much less frequent than any of the above.[84]

Checkpoints

▶ Paraphilias are deviant sexual acts such as exhibitionism and voyeurism. Many are considered crimes.

▶ Prostitution has been common throughout recorded history. There are many kinds of prostitutes, including streetwalkers, bar girls, call girls, brothel prostitutes, and circuit travelers.

▶ It is feared that some girls are forced or tricked into prostitution against their will.

▶ A multibillion-dollar international sex trade involves tricking young girls from eastern Europe and Asia into becoming prostitutes.

▶ Pornography is a billion-dollar industry that is growing through technological advances such as the Internet.

▶ There is ongoing debate over whether obscene materials are harmful and related to violence.

▶ The Supreme Court has ruled that material is obscene if it has prurient sexual content and is devoid of social value.

▶ The First Amendment's guarantee of the right to free speech makes it difficult to control obscene material.

Drug- and alcohol-related ER visits have remained stable for the past few years but have increased significantly during the past two decades.

Despite the scope of the drug problem, some still view it as another type of victimless public order crime. There is heated debate over legalization of drugs and control of alcohol. Some consider drug use a private matter and drug control another example of government intrusion into people's private lives. Furthermore, legalization could reduce the profit of selling illegal substances, drive suppliers out of the market, and enable the government to regulate and control drugs, which might cut down on the substantial health risks associated with drug usage.[85] Others see these substances as dangerous, believing that the criminal activity of users makes the term "victimless" nonsensical. Still another position is that the possession and use of all drugs and alcohol should be legalized but that the sale and distribution of drugs should be heavily penalized. This would punish those profiting from drugs, while enabling users to be helped without fear of criminal punishment.

WHEN DID DRUG USE BEGIN?

Chemical substances have been used to change reality and provide stimulation, relief, or relaxation for thousands of years. Mesopotamian writings indicate that opium was used 4,000 years ago—it was known as the "plant of joy."[86] The ancient Greeks knew and understood the problem of drug use. At the time of the Crusades, the Arabs were using marijuana. In the Western Hemisphere, natives of Mexico and South America chewed coca leaves and used "magic mushrooms" in their religious ceremonies.[87] Drug use was also accepted in Europe well into the twentieth century. Recently uncovered pharmacy records from around 1900 to 1920 show sales of cocaine and heroin solutions to members of the British royal family; records from 1912 indicate that Winston Churchill, then a member of Parliament, was sold a cocaine solution while staying in Scotland.[88]

In the early years of the United States, opium and its derivatives were easily obtained. Opium-based drugs were used in various patent medicine cure-alls. Morphine was used extensively to relieve the pain of wounded soldiers in the Civil War. By the turn of the century, an estimated 1 million U.S. citizens were opiate users.[89]

ALCOHOL AND ITS PROHIBITION

The history of alcohol and the law in the United States has also been controversial and dramatic. At the turn of the century, a drive was mustered to prohibit the sale of alcohol. This **temperance movement** was fueled by the belief that the purity of the U.S. agrarian culture was being destroyed by the growth of cities. Urbanism was viewed as a threat to the lifestyle of the majority of the nation's population, then living on farms and in villages. The forces behind the temperance movement were such lobbying groups as the Anti-Saloon League led by Carrie Nation, the Women's Temperance Union, and the Protestant clergy of the Baptist, Methodist, and Congregationalist faiths.[90] They viewed the growing city, filled with newly arriving Irish, Italian, and eastern European immigrants, as centers of degradation and wickedness. Ratification of the Eighteenth Amendment in 1919, prohibiting the sale of alcoholic beverages, was viewed as a triumph of the morality of middle- and upper-class Americans over the threat posed to their culture by the "new Americans."[91]

Prohibition failed. It was enforced by the Volstead Act, which defined intoxicating beverages as those containing one-half of 1 percent, or more, alcohol.[92] What doomed Prohibition? One factor was the use of organized crime to supply illicit liquor. Also, the law made it illegal only to sell alcohol, not to purchase it, which reduced the deterrent effect. Finally, despite the work of Elliot Ness and his "Untouchables," law enforcement agencies were inadequate, and officials were likely to be corrupted by

temperance movement
The drive to prohibit the sale of alcohol in the United States, culminating in ratification of the Eighteenth Amendment in 1919.

Prohibition
The period from 1919 until 1933, when the Eighteenth Amendment to the U.S. Constitution outlawed the sale of alcohol; also known as the "noble experiment."

wealthy bootleggers.[93] In 1933, the Twenty-First Amendment to the Constitution repealed Prohibition, signaling the end of the "noble experiment."

EXTENT OF SUBSTANCE ABUSE

Despite continuing efforts at control, the use of mood-altering substances persists in the United States. What is the extent of the substance abuse problem today?

A number of national surveys attempt to chart trends in drug abuse in the general population. One important source of information on drug use is the annual Monitoring the Future (MTF) self-report survey of drug abuse among high school students conducted by the Institute of Social Research (ISR) at the University of Michigan.[94] This annual survey is based on the self-report responses of approximately 50,000 eighth-, tenth-, and twelfth-graders and is considered the most important source of data on adolescent drug abuse. As Figure 13.1 shows, MTF survey data indicates that drug use declined from a high point late in the 1970s until 1990, when it once again began to increase, finally stabilizing around 1996. Although drug use rates have stabilized, more than one-third of all high school seniors still report having used an illicit substance during the past 12 months, as do 27 percent of tenth-graders and more than 14 percent of eighth-graders.[95]

Another drug use survey, the National Household Survey (NHS) on Drug Abuse and Health sponsored by the federal government, also indicates the extent of drug use. As Figure 13.2 shows, this national survey also shows that drug use has stabilized. However, this still means that about 20 million Americans aged 12 or older were current (past-month) illicit drug users and had used an illicit drug during the prior month. This means that about 8.0 percent of the population aged 12 years old or older uses illicit drugs such as marijuana/hashish, cocaine (including crack), heroin, hallucinogens, inhalants, or prescription-type psychotherapeutics used nonmedically.[96] Thus, even though drug use appears to have stabilized, it is still a significant social problem.

Alcohol Abuse Both the MTF and NHS surveys indicate that alcohol abuse is quite common and that kids as young as 12 may be at risk for **binge drinking** and/or **heavy drinking**. According to the latest data from the National Household Survey,

Figure 13.1 Trends in Annual Prevalence of Teenage Illicit Drug Use

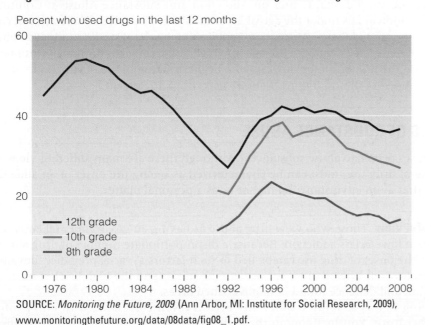

Percent who used drugs in the last 12 months

Legend:
— 12th grade
— 10th grade
— 8th grade

SOURCE: *Monitoring the Future, 2009* (Ann Arbor, MI: Institute for Social Research, 2009), www.monitoringthefuture.org/data/08data/fig08_1.pdf.

binge drinking
Having five or more drinks on the same occasion (that is, at the same time or within a couple of hours of each other) on at least 1 day in the past 30 days.

heavy drinking
Having five or more drinks on the same occasion on each of 5 or more days in the past 30 days.

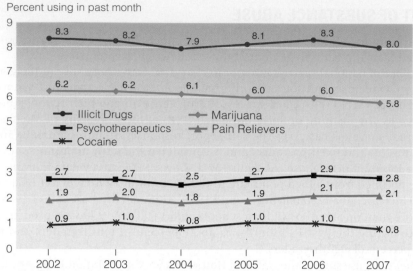

Figure 13.2 Past-Month Use of Selected Illicit Drugs among Persons Aged 12 or Older

SOURCE: National Survey on Drug Use and Health: National Findings, www.oas.samhsa.gov/NSDUH/2k7NSDUH/2k7results.cfm#Fig2-1.

▶ Slightly more than half of Americans aged 12 or older reported being current drinkers of alcohol. This means that about 127 million Americans drink regularly, many of them children.

▶ More than one-fifth of persons aged 12 or older participated in binge drinking at least once in the past 30 days.

▶ Heavy drinking was reported by 7 percent of the population aged 12 or older, or 17 million people.[97]

There also appears to be a trend for alcohol abuse to begin at an early age and remain an extremely serious problem over the life course. According to research conducted at the National Center on Addiction and Substance Abuse at Columbia University, individuals under the age of 21 drink about 19 percent of the alcohol consumed in the United States. More than 5 million high school students admit to binge drinking at least once a month. The age at which children begin drinking is dropping: Since 1975, the proportion of children who begin drinking in the eighth grade or earlier has jumped by almost a third, from 27 percent to 36 percent.[98]

CAUSES OF SUBSTANCE ABUSE

What causes people to abuse substances? Although there are many different views on the cause of drug use, most can be characterized as seeing the onset of an addictive career either as an environmental matter or as a personal matter.

Subcultural View Those who view drug abuse as having an environmental basis concentrate on lower-class addiction. Because a disproportionate number of drug abusers are poor, the onset of drug use can be tied to such factors as racial prejudice, devalued identities, low self-esteem, poor socioeconomic status, and the high level of mistrust, negativism, and defiance found in impoverished areas.

Residing in a deteriorated inner-city area is often correlated with entry into a drug subculture. Youths living in these depressed areas, where feelings of alienation and hopelessness run high, often meet established drug users who teach them that narcotics assuage their feelings of personal inadequacy and stress.[99]

The youths may join peers to learn the techniques of drug use and receive social support for their habit. Research shows that peer influence is a significant predictor of drug careers that actually grows stronger as people mature.[100] Shared feelings and a sense of intimacy lead the youths to become fully enmeshed in what has been described as the "drug-use subculture."[101] Some join gangs and enter into a career of using and distributing illegal substances, while also committing property and violent crimes.[102]

Psychological View Not all drug abusers reside in lower-class slum areas; the problem of middle-class substance abuse is very real. Consequently, some experts have linked substance abuse to psychological deficits such as impaired cognitive functioning, personality disturbance, and emotional problems that can strike people in any economic class.[103] These produce what is called a **drug-dependent personality**. Some teens may resort to drug abuse to reduce the emotional turmoil of adolescence or to cope with troubling impulses.[104]

Personality testing of known users suggests that a significant percentage suffer from psychotic disorders, including various levels of schizophrenia. Surveys show that youngsters with serious behavioral problems were more than seven times as likely as those with less serious problems to report that they were dependent on alcohol or illicit drugs. Youths with serious emotional problems were nearly four times more likely to report dependence on drugs than those without such issues.[105]

Genetic Factors Substance abuse may have a genetic basis. Evidence for this has been found in research showing that biological children of alcoholics reared by nonalcoholic adoptive parents develop alcohol problems more often than the biological children of the adoptive parents.[106] In a similar vein, a number of studies comparing alcoholism among identical twins and fraternal twins have found that the degree of concordance (both siblings behaving identically) is twice as high among the identical twin groups. These inferences are still inconclusive, because identical twins are more likely to be treated similarly than fraternal twins and are therefore more likely to be influenced by the same environmental conditions. Nonetheless, most children of abusing parents do not become drug dependent themselves, which suggests that even if drug abuse is heritable, environment and socialization must play some role in the onset of abuse.[107]

Social Learning Social psychologists suggest that drug abuse may also result from observing parental drug use. Parental drug abuse begins to have a damaging effect on children as young as 2 years old, especially when parents manifest drug-related personality problems such as depression or poor impulse control.[108] Children whose parents abuse drugs are more likely to have persistent abuse problems than the children of nonabusers.[109]

People who learn that drugs provide pleasurable sensations may be the most likely to experiment with illegal substances, and a habit may develop if the user experiences lower anxiety, fear, and tension levels.[110] Having a history of family drug and alcohol abuse has been found to be a characteristic of violent teenage sexual abusers.[111] Heroin abusers report an unhappy childhood that included harsh physical punishment and parental neglect and rejection.[112]

According to the social learning view, drug involvement begins with using tobacco and drinking alcohol at an early age, and this progresses to experimentation with marijuana and hashish and finally to cocaine and even heroin. Although most recreational users do not progress to "hard stuff," few addicts begin their involvement with narcotics without first experimenting with recreational drugs. By implication, if teen smoking and drinking could be reduced, the gateway to hard drugs would be narrowed. For example, one 2003 research study found that a 50 percent reduction in the number of teens who smoke cigarettes can cut marijuana use by 16 to 28 percent.[113]

Problem Behavior Syndrome (PBS) For many people, substance abuse is just one of many problem behaviors. Longitudinal studies show that drug abusers are maladjusted, alienated, and emotionally distressed and that their drug use is one among many social problems.[114] Having a deviant lifestyle begins early in life and is punctuated with criminal relationships, a family history of substance abuse, educational failure, and alienation. People who abuse drugs lack commitment to religious values, disdain education, spend most of their time in peer activities, engage in precocious sexual behavior, and experience school failure, family conflict, and similar social problems.[115]

Rational Choice Not all people who abuse drugs do so because of personal pathology. Some may use drugs and alcohol because they want to enjoy their effects: getting high, relaxation, improved creativity, escape from reality, and increased sexual responsiveness. Research indicates that adolescent alcohol abusers believe that getting high will make them powerful, increase their sexual performance, and facilitate their social behavior; they care little about negative future consequences.[116]

Substance abuse, then, may be a function of the rational but mistaken belief that drugs can benefit the user. The decision to use drugs involves evaluation of personal consequences (such as addiction, disease, and legal punishment) and of the expected benefits of drug use (such as peer approval, positive affective states, heightened awareness, and relaxation). Adolescents may begin using drugs because they believe their peers expect them to do so.[117]

Is There a Single "Cause" of Drug Abuse? There are many different views of why people take drugs, and no theory has proved adequate to explain all forms of substance abuse. Recent research efforts show that drug users suffer a variety of family and socialization difficulties, have addiction-prone personalities, and are generally at risk for many other social problems.[118] One long-held assumption is that addicts progress along a continuum from using so-called gateway drugs such as alcohol and marijuana to using ever more potent substances, such as cocaine and heroin; this is known as the *gateway hypothesis*.[119] A great deal of research has attempted to find out whether there is truly a drug gateway, but results so far have been mixed. One research effort by Andrew Golub and Bruce Johnson shows that many hard-core drug abusers have never smoked or used alcohol. And although many American youths have tried marijuana, few actually progress to crack or heroin abuse.[120] However, a recent longitudinal analysis by Cesar Rebellon and Karen Van Gundy found evidence that marijuana users are up to 5 times more likely than nonusers to escalate their drug abuse and try cocaine and heroin.[121] In sum, although most marijuana smokers do not become hard drug users, some do, and the risk of using dangerous substances may be increased by first engaging in recreational drug use.

DRUGS AND CRIME

One of the main reasons for the criminalization of particular substances is the significant association believed to exist between drug abuse and crime. Research suggests that many criminal offenders have extensive experience with alcohol and drug use and that abusers commit an enormous amount of crime.[122] Substance abuse appears to be an important precipitating factor in a variety of criminal acts, especially income-generating crimes such as burglary.[123]

A number of data sources provide powerful evidence of a drug–crime linkage:

▶ Surveys conducted with adolescent drug users show that they are more likely to self-report delinquency than abstainers. Kids who took drugs were more likely to report getting into a serious fight at school or work, carrying a handgun, selling illegal drugs, and/or stealing or trying to steal something worth $50 or more.[124]

▶ Adults who were arrested in the past year for any serious violent or property offense were more likely to have used an illicit drug in the past year than those who were not arrested for a serious offense (60.1 percent vs. 13.6 percent).[125]

▶ About 28 percent of the 5 million adults on probation report current drug use, compared to about 7 percent of adults not on probation.[126]

▶ Of the estimated 1.6 million adults aged 18 or older who were on parole or other supervised release from prison, about one-quarter were current illicit drug users, compared with 8 percent among adults who were not on parole or supervised release.[127]

What causes this linkage? Drug use interferes with maturation and socialization. Drug abusers are more likely to drop out of school, to be underemployed, to engage in premarital sex, and to become unmarried parents. These factors have been linked to a weakening of the social bond, which leads to antisocial behaviors.[128]

Although the connection between drug use and crime is powerful, the relationship is still uncertain because many users had a history of criminal activity before the onset of their substance abuse.[129] Nonetheless, even if drug use does not turn otherwise law-abiding citizens into criminals, it certainly amplifies the extent of their criminal activities.[130] And as addiction levels increase, so do the frequency and seriousness of criminality.[131]

In sum, research examining both the criminality of known narcotics users and the narcotics use of known criminals reveals a very strong association between drug use and crime. Even if the crime rate of drug users were actually only half that reported in the research literature, users would be responsible for a significant portion of the total criminal activity in the United States. ▶ **Checkpoints**

DRUGS AND THE LAW

The federal government first initiated legal action to curtail the use of some drugs early in the twentieth century.[132] In 1906, the Pure Food and Drug Act required manufacturers to list the amounts of habit-forming drugs in products on the labels but did not restrict their use. However, the act prohibited the importation and sale of opiates except for medicinal purposes. In 1914, the Harrison Narcotics Act restricted the importation, manufacture, sale, and dispensing of narcotics. It defined **narcotic** as any drug that produces sleep and relieves pain, such as heroin, morphine, and opium. The act was revised in 1922 to allow importation of opium and coca (cocaine) leaves for qualified medical practitioners. The Marijuana Tax Act of 1937 required registration and payment of a tax by all persons who imported, sold, or manufactured marijuana. Because marijuana was classified as a narcotic, those registering would also be subject to criminal penalty.

Subsequent federal laws were passed to clarify existing drug statutes and revise penalties. For example, the Boggs Act of 1951 provided mandatory sentences for violating federal drug laws. The Durham–Humphrey Act of 1951 made it illegal to dispense barbiturates and amphetamines without a prescription. The Narcotic Control Act of 1956 increased penalties for drug offenders. In 1965, the Drug Abuse Control Act set up stringent guidelines for the legal use and sale of mood-modifying drugs, such as barbiturates, amphetamines, LSD, and any other "dangerous drugs," except narcotics prescribed by doctors and pharmacists. Illegal possession was punished as a misdemeanor and manufacture or sale as a felony. And in 1970, the Comprehensive Drug Abuse Prevention and Control Act set up unified categories of illegal drugs and attached specific penalties to their sale, manufacture, or possession. The law gave the U.S. attorney general discretion to decide in which category to place any new drug.

Since then, various federal laws have attempted to increase penalties imposed on drug smugglers and to limit the manufacture and sale of newly developed substances. For example, the 1984 Controlled Substances Act set new, stringent penalties for drug dealers and created five categories of narcotic and nonnarcotic substances subject to federal laws.[133] The Anti–Drug Abuse Act of 1986 again set new standards for minimum and maximum sentences for drug offenders, increased penalties for most offenses, and created a new drug penalty classification for large-scale offenses (such as trafficking in more than one kilogram of heroin), for which the penalty for a first offense was ten years to life in prison.[134] With then-President George H. W. Bush's endorsement, Congress passed the Anti–Drug Abuse Act of 1988, which created a coordinated national drug policy under a "drug czar," set treatment and prevention priorities, and, clearly reflecting the government's hard-line stance against drug dealing, instituted availability of the death penalty for drug-related killings.[135]

For the most part, state laws mirror federal statutes. Some apply extremely heavy penalties for selling or distributing dangerous drugs, such as prison sentences of up to 25 years.

CONNECTIONS

Chapter 10 provides an analysis of the relationship between drugs and violence, which rests on three factors: (1) the psychopharmacological relationship, which is a direct consequence of ingesting mood-altering substances; (2) economic compulsive behavior, which occurs when drug users resort to violence to support their habit; and (3) a systemic link, which occurs when drug dealers battle for territories.

Checkpoints

▶ Substance abuse is an ancient practice dating back more than 4,000 years.

▶ A wide variety of drugs are in use today, and alcohol is a major problem.

▶ Drug use in the general population has increased during the past decade; about half of all high school seniors have tried illegal drugs at least once.

▶ There is no single cause of substance abuse. Some people may use drugs because they are predisposed to abuse.

▶ There is a strong link between drug abuse and crime. People who become addicts may increase their illegal activities to support their habits. Others engage in violence as part of their drug-dealing activities.

narcotic
A drug that produces sleep and relieves pain, such as heroin, morphine, and opium; a habit-forming drug.

© David Maung/epa/Corbis

Why is it difficult to stop the flow of illegal drugs to the United States? Perhaps because smugglers can bring them in by sea, by air, and even underground. Here, two U.S. Immigration and Customs Enforcement agents stand inside a descending section of a 2,400-foot drug-smuggling tunnel in San Diego, California, that links two warehouses, one in Tijuana, Mexico, and the other in the San Ysidro neighborhood of San Diego. On January 30, 2006, journalists were allowed to enter the U.S. side of the tunnel, which reaches a depth of 80 feet in some places. One tunnel found by authorities in 2009 measured 48 feet in the United States and 35 feet in Mexico. This tunnel contained side walls framed with 2-by-4 wooden studs and ceiling construction. It had electrical work wired into the Mexico side and a hose for ventilation and lighting.

DRUG CONTROL STRATEGIES

Substance abuse remains a major social problem in the United States. Politicians looking for a safe campaign issue can take advantage of the public's fear of drug addiction by calling for a war on drugs. Such wars have been declared even when drug use was stable or in decline.[136] Can these efforts pay off? Can illegal drug use be eliminated or controlled?

A number of different drug control strategies have been tried, with varying degrees of success. Some aim to deter people from using drugs by stopping the flow of drugs into the country, apprehending and punishing dealers, and cracking down on street-level drug deals. Others focus on preventing drug use by educating potential users to the dangers of substance abuse (convincing them to "say no to drugs") and by organizing community groups to work with the at-risk population in their area. Still another approach is to treat known users so they can control their addictions. Some of these efforts are discussed next.

Source Control One approach to drug control is to deter the sale and importation of drugs through the systematic apprehension of large-volume drug dealers, coupled with the enforcement of strict drug laws that carry heavy penalties. This approach is designed to capture and punish known international drug dealers and to deter others from entering the drug trade. A major effort has been made to cut off supplies of drugs by destroying overseas crops and arresting members of drug cartels in Central and South America, Asia, and the Middle East, where many drugs are grown and manufactured. The federal government has been in the vanguard of encouraging exporting nations to step up efforts to destroy drug crops and prosecute dealers. Three South American nations (Peru, Bolivia, and Colombia) have agreed with the United States to coordinate control efforts. However, translating words into deeds is a formidable task. Drug lords are willing and able to fight back through intimidation, violence, and corruption. The Colombian drug cartels do not hesitate to use violence and assassination to protect their interests. Mexico has been awash in blood as cartels compete for power and control of the drug trade.

The amount of narcotics grown each year is so vast that even if three-quarters of the opium crop were destroyed, the U.S. market would still require only 10 percent of the remainder to sustain the drug trade. The drug trade is an important source of foreign revenue for third world nations, and destroying the drug trade undermines their economies. More than a million people in developing nations depend on the cultivating and processing of illegal substances. Adding to the problem of source control is the fact that the United States has little influence in some key drug-producing areas, such as Vietnam, Cambodia, and Myanmar (formerly Burma).[137] War and terrorism also make source control strategies problematic. After the United States toppled Afghanistan's Taliban government, the remnants began to grow and sell poppy to support their insurgency; Afghanistan now supplies 90 percent of the world's opium.[138] And even though some guerillas may not be interested in joining or colluding with crime cartels, they finance their war against the government by aiding drug traffickers and "taxing" crops and sales.[139]

The federal government estimates that U.S. citizens spend more than $40 billion annually on illegal drugs, and much of this money is funneled overseas. Even if the government of one nation were willing to cooperate in vigorous drug suppression efforts, suppliers in other nations, eager to cash in on the "seller's market," would be encouraged to turn more acreage over to coca or poppy production. For example, enforcement efforts in Peru and Bolivia have been so successful that they altered cocaine cultivation patterns. As a consequence, Colombia became the premier coca-cultivating country, because the local drug cartels encouraged local growers to cultivate coca plants. When the Colombian government mounted an effective eradication campaign in the traditional growing areas, the cartels linked up with rebel groups in remote parts of the country for their drug supply.[140]

Interdiction Strategies Law enforcement efforts have also been directed at intercepting drug supplies as they enter the country. Border patrols and military personnel using sophisticated hardware have been involved in massive interdiction efforts; many impressive multimillion-dollar seizures have been made. Yet the U.S. borders are so vast and unprotected that meaningful interdiction is impossible. And even if all importation were shut down, homegrown marijuana and laboratory-made drugs, such as Ecstasy, LSD, and PCP, could become the drugs of choice. Even now, their easy availability and relatively low cost are increasing their popularity among the at-risk population.

Law Enforcement Strategies Local, state, and federal law enforcement agencies have been actively fighting drugs. One approach is to direct efforts at large-scale drug rings. The long-term consequence has been to decentralize drug dealing and encourage young independent dealers to become major suppliers. Ironically, it has proved easier for federal agents to infiltrate and prosecute traditional organized crime groups than to take on drug-dealing gangs. Consequently, some nontraditional groups have broken into the drug trade. Police can also target, intimidate, and arrest street-level dealers and users in an effort to make drug use so much of a hassle that consumption is cut back and the crime rate reduced. Approaches that have been tried include reverse stings, in which undercover agents pose as dealers to arrest users who approach them for a buy. Police have attacked fortified crack houses with heavy equipment to breach their defenses. They have used racketeering laws to seize the assets of known dealers. Special task forces of local and state police have conducted undercover operations and drug sweeps to discourage both dealers and users.[141]

Although some street-level enforcement efforts have succeeded, others are considered failures. Drug sweeps have clogged courts and correctional facilities with petty offenders, while draining police resources. There are also suspicions that a displacement effect occurs; that is, stepped-up efforts to curb drug dealing in one area or city simply encourage dealers to seek friendlier territory.[142]

Punishment Strategies Even if law enforcement efforts cannot produce a general deterrent effect, the courts may achieve the required result by severely punishing known drug dealers and traffickers. A number of initiatives have made the prosecution and punishment of drug offenders a top priority. State prosecutors have expanded their investigations into drug importation and distribution and assigned special prosecutors to focus on drug dealers. The fact that drugs such as crack are considered a serious problem may have convinced judges and prosecutors to expedite substance abuse cases.

However, these efforts often have their downside. Defense attorneys consider delay tactics sound legal maneuvering in drug-related cases. Courts are so backlogged that prosecutors are eager to plea-bargain. The consequence of this legal maneuvering is that many people convicted on federal drug charges are granted probation or some other form of community release. Even so, prisons have become jammed with inmates, many of whom were involved in drug-related cases. Many drug offenders sent to prison do not serve their entire sentences because they are released in an effort to relieve prison overcrowding.[143]

Community Strategies Another type of drug control effort relies on the involvement of local community groups to lead the fight against drugs. Representatives of various local government agencies, churches, civic organizations, and similar institutions are being brought together to create drug prevention and awareness programs.

Citizen-sponsored programs attempt to restore a sense of community in drug-infested areas, reduce fear, and promote conventional norms and values.[144] These efforts can be classified into one of four distinct categories.[145] The first involves efforts to aid law enforcement, which may include block watches, cooperative police–community efforts, and citizen patrols. These citizen groups are nonconfrontational: They simply observe or photograph dealers, write down their license plate numbers, and then notify police.

A second tactic is to use the civil justice system to harass offenders. Landlords have been sued for owning properties that house drug dealers; neighborhood groups have scrutinized drug houses for building code violations. Information acquired from these various sources is turned over to local authorities, such as police and housing agencies, for more formal action.

A third approach is through community-based treatment efforts in which citizen volunteers participate in self-help support programs, such as Narcotics Anonymous and Cocaine Anonymous, which have more than 1,000 chapters nationally. Other programs provide youths with martial arts training, dancing, and social events as alternatives to the drug life.

A fourth type of community-level drug prevention effort is designed to enhance the quality of life, improve interpersonal relationships, and upgrade the neighborhood's physical environment. Activities might include the creation of drug-free school zones (which encourage police to keep drug dealers away from the vicinity of schools). Consciousness-raising efforts include demonstrations and marches to publicize the drug problem and build solidarity among participants.

Drug Education and Prevention Strategies According to this view, substance abuse would decline if kids could be taught about the dangers of drug use. The most widely known drug education program, Drug Abuse Resistance Education (D.A.R.E.), is an elementary school course designed to give students the skills for resisting peer pressure to experiment with tobacco, drugs, and alcohol. It is unique because it employs uniformed police officers to carry the antidrug message to the students before they enter junior high school. But even though more than 40 percent of all school districts incorporate assistance from local law enforcement agencies in their drug prevention programming, reviews of the program have not been encouraging. Dennis Rosenbaum and his associates found that it had only a marginal impact on student drug use and attitudes.[146] A longitudinal study by psychologist Donald Lynam and his colleagues found that D.A.R.E. had no effect on students' drug use at any time through tenth grade, and a ten-year follow-up failed to find any hidden or delayed "sleeper" effects. At age 20, there were no differences in drug use between those who received D.A.R.E. and those who did not; the only difference was that those who received D.A.R.E. reported slightly lower levels of self-esteem at age 20, an effect that proponents were not aiming for.[147] These evaluations caused D.A.R.E. to revise its curriculum. It is now aimed at older students and relies more on helping them question their assumptions about drug use than on having them listen to lectures on the subject.

Drug-Testing Programs Drug testing of private employees, government workers, and criminal offenders is believed to deter substance abuse. In the workplace, employees are tested to enhance on-the-job safety and productivity. In some industries, such as mining and transportation, drug testing is considered essential because abuse can pose a threat to the public.[148] Business leaders have been enlisted in the fight against drugs. Mandatory drug-testing programs in government and industry are common; more than 40 percent of the country's largest companies, including IBM and AT&T, have drug-testing programs. The federal government requires employee testing in regulated industries such as nuclear energy and defense contracting. About 4 million transportation workers are subject to testing.

Criminal defendants are now routinely tested at all stages of the justice system, from arrest to parole. The goal is to reduce criminal behavior by detecting current users and curbing their abuse. Can such programs reduce criminal activity? Two evaluations of pretrial drug-testing programs found little evidence that monitoring defendants' drug use influenced their behavior.[149]

Treatment Strategies A number of approaches are taken to treat known users, getting them clean of drugs and alcohol and thereby reducing the at-risk population. One approach rests on the assumption that users have low self-esteem and that treatment efforts must focus on building a sense of self. For example, users have been placed in worthwhile programs of outdoor activities and wilderness training to create self-reliance and a sense of accomplishment.[150] More intensive efforts use group therapy, relying on group leaders who have been substance abusers; through such sessions, users get the skills and support to help them reject social pressure to use drugs. These programs are based on the Alcoholics Anonymous approach, which holds that users must find within themselves the strength to stay clean and that peer support from those who understand their experiences can help them achieve a drug-free life.

There are also residential programs for the more heavily involved, and a large network of drug treatment centers has been developed. Some detoxification units use medical procedures to wean patients from the more addicting drugs to other drugs, such as methadone, that can be more easily regulated. Methadone is a drug similar to heroin, and addicts can be treated at clinics where they receive methadone under controlled conditions. However, methadone programs have been undermined because some users sell their methadone in the black market, and others supplement their dosages with illegally obtained heroin. Other programs use drugs such as Naxalone, which counters the effects of narcotics and eases the trauma of withdrawal, but results have not been conclusive.[151]

Other therapeutic programs attempt to deal with the psychological causes of drug use in "therapeutic communities." Hypnosis, aversion therapy (getting users to associate drugs with unpleasant sensations, such as nausea), counseling, biofeedback, and other techniques are often used. Some programs report significant success with clients who are able to complete the full course of the treatment.[152]

The long-term effects of treatment on drug abuse are still uncertain. Critics charge that a stay in a residential program can help stigmatize people as addicts even if they never used hard drugs; and in treatment they may be introduced to hard-core users with whom they will associate after release. Users do not often enter these programs voluntarily and have little motivation to change. Supporters of treatment argue that many addicts are helped by intensive inpatient and outpatient treatment, and the cost saving is considerable.[153] Moreover, it is estimated that less than half of the 5 million people who need drug treatment actually get it, so treatment strategies have not been given a fair trial.

Employment Programs Research indicates that drug abusers who obtain and keep employment are likely to end or reduce the incidence of their substance abuse.[154] Not surprisingly, then, there have been a number of efforts to provide vocational rehabilitation for drug abusers. One approach is the supported work program, which typically involves jobsite training, ongoing assessment, and jobsite intervention. Rather than teaching work skills in a classroom, support programs rely on helping drug abusers deal with real work settings. Other programs provide training to overcome barriers to employment, including help with motivation, education, experience, the job market, job-seeking skills, and personal issues. For example, female abusers may be unaware of child care resources that would enable them to seek employment opportunities. Another approach is to help addicts improve their interviewing skills so that once a job opportunity can be identified, they are equipped to convince potential employers of their commitment and reliability.

Concept Summary 13.1 Drug-Control Strategies

Control Strategy	Main Focus	Problems/Issues
Source control	Destroy overseas crops and drug labs	Drug profits hard to resist; drug crops in hostile nations are off limits
Interdiction	Seal borders; arrest drug couriers	Extensive U.S. borders hard to control
Law enforcement	Police investigation and arrest of dealers	New dealers are recruited to replace those in prison
Punishment	Deter dealers with harsh punishments	Crowded prisons promote bargain justice
Community programs	Help community members deal with drug problems on the local level	Relies on community cohesion and efficacy
Drug education	Teach kids about the harm of taking drugs	Evaluations do not show programs are effective
Drug testing	Threaten employees with drug tests to deter use	Evaluations do not show drug testing is effective; people cheat on tests
Treatment	Use of therapy to get people off drugs	Expensive, requires motivation; clients associate with other users
Employment	Provide jobs as an alternative to drugs	Requires that former addicts become steady employees
Legalization	Decriminalize or legalize drugs	Political hot potato; danger of creating more users

LEGALIZATION OF DRUGS

In terms of weight and availability, there is still no commodity whose sale is more lucrative than illegal drugs. They cost relatively little to produce, and they provide dealers and traffickers with large profit margins. At the current average street price of $125 per gram in the United States, a metric ton of pure cocaine is worth more than $100 million; cutting it to reduce its purity can double or triple the value.[155] With that kind of profit to be made, can any strategy, whether treatment- or punishment-oriented, reduce the lure of drug trafficking? The futility of drug control efforts is illustrated by the fact that despite massive long-term efforts, the price of illegal narcotics such as crack cocaine and heroin has drifted downward as supplies have become more plentiful.

Considering these problems, some commentators have called for the legalization or decriminalization of restricted drugs. The so-called war on drugs has cost more than $500 billion over the past 20 years—money that could have been spent on education and economic development.[156]

Legalization is warranted, according to drug expert Ethan Nadelmann, because the use of mood-altering substances is customary in nearly all human societies; people have always wanted—and will always find ways of obtaining—psychoactive drugs.[157] Banning drugs creates networks of manufacturers and distributors, many of whom use violence as part of their standard operating procedures. Although some believe that drug use is immoral, Nadelmann questions whether it is any worse than the unrestricted use of alcohol and cigarettes, both of which are addicting and unhealthful. Far more people die each year because they abuse these legal substances than are killed in drug wars or die from abusing illegal substances.

Nadelmann also states that just as Prohibition failed to stop the flow of alcohol in the 1920s, while simultaneously increasing the power of organized crime, the policy of prohibiting drugs is similarly doomed to failure. When drugs were legal and freely

You have been called upon by the director of the Department of Health and Human Services to give your opinion on a recent national survey that found that serious mental illness is highly correlated with illicit drug use. Among adults who used an illicit drug in the past year, 17.1 percent had serious mental illness in that year, whereas the rate of serious mental illness was 6.9 percent among adults who did not use an illicit drug. Among adults with serious mental illness, 28.9 percent used an illicit drug in the past year, whereas the rate of illicit drug use was 12.7 percent among those without serious mental illness. The relationship is illustrated in Figure A.

Among adults with serious mental illness, 23.2 percent (4 million) were dependent on or abused alcohol or illicit drugs, whereas the rate of dependence or abuse among adults without serious mental illness was only 8.2 percent. Adults with serious mental illness were more likely than those without serious mental illness to be dependent on or to abuse illicit drugs (9.6 percent versus 2.1 percent) and more likely to be dependent on or to abuse alcohol (18 percent versus

Figure A Rates of Serious Mental Illness Correlated with Illicit Drug, Alcohol, and Cigarette Use among Adults Aged 18 or Older

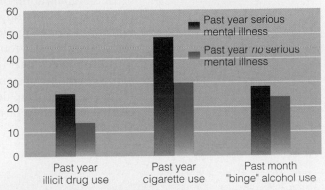

Percent using

SOURCE: *National Household Survey on Drug Abuse, 2002* (Washington, DC: U.S. Department of Health and Human Services, 2003).

7 percent). Among adults with substance dependence or abuse, 20.4 percent had serious mental illness. The rate of serious mental illness was 7 percent among adults who did not have substance abuse or dependence.

Writing Assignment

The director realizes that one possible explanation of this data is that drugs cause people to become mentally ill. He asks you to comment on other possible explanations. Write an essay spelling out what you will tell him.

---

available early in the twentieth century, the proportion of Americans who used drugs was not much greater than it is today. Most users led normal lives, largely because of the legal status of their drug use.

If drugs were legalized, the argument goes, price and distribution could be controlled by the government. This would reduce addicts' cash requirements, so crime rates would drop because users would no longer need the same cash flow to support their habits. Drug-related deaths would decline because government control would reduce needle sharing and the spread of AIDS. Legalization would also destroy the drug-importing cartels and gangs. Because drugs would be bought and sold openly, the government would reap a tax windfall both from taxes on the sale of drugs and from income taxes paid by drug dealers on profits that have been part of the hidden economy. Of course, as with alcohol, drug distribution would be regulated, keeping drugs away from adolescents, public servants such as police and airline pilots, and known felons. Those who favor legalization point to the Netherlands as a country that has legalized drugs and remains relatively free of crime.[158]

This approach might indeed have the short-term effect of reducing the association between drug use and crime, but it might also have grave social consequences. Legalization might increase the nation's rate of drug usage, creating an even larger group of nonproductive, drug-dependent people who must be cared for by the rest of society.[159] In countries such as Iran and Thailand, where drugs are cheap and readily available, the rate of narcotics use is quite high. Historically, the availability of cheap narcotics has preceded drug use epidemics, as was the case when British and American merchants sold opium in nineteenth-century China.

If juveniles, criminals, and members of other at-risk groups were forbidden to buy drugs, who would be the customers? Noncriminal, nonabusing, middle-aged adults? And would not those prohibited from legally buying drugs create an underground market almost as vast as the current one? If the government tried to raise money by taxing legal drugs, as it now does with liquor and cigarettes, that might encourage drug smuggling to avoid tax payments; these "illegal" drugs might then fall into the hands of adolescents.

Decriminalization or legalization of controlled substances is unlikely in the near term, but further study is warranted. What effect would a policy of partial decriminalization (for example, legalizing small amounts of marijuana) have on drug use rates? Would a get-tough policy help to "widen the net" of the justice system and thus (through contact with users during incarceration) actually deepen some youths' involvement in substance abuse? Can society provide alternatives to drugs that will reduce teenage drug dependency?[160] The answers to these questions have proved elusive. The different types of drug control strategies are summarized in Concept Summary 13.1.

Summary

1. Understand the association between law and morality.

   Public order crimes are acts considered illegal because they conflict with social policy, accepted moral rules, and/or public opinion. There is usually great debate over public order crimes. Some charge that they are not really crimes at all and that it is foolish to try to legislate morality. Others view such acts as prostitution, gambling, and drug abuse as harmful and therefore subject to public control.

2. Be familiar with the term "social harm."

   According to the theory of social harm, acts become crimes when they cause injury and produce harm to others. However, some dangerous activities are not considered crimes, and some activities that do not appear harmful are criminalized.

3. Discuss the activities of moral crusaders.

   Moral crusaders seek to shape the law to reflect their own way of thinking. These moral entrepreneurs go on moral crusades to take on such issues as prayer in schools, gun ownership, gay marriage, abortion, and the distribution of sexually explicit books. Two of the most vigorous moral crusades have been directed at influencing public acceptance of the gay lifestyle. One group of crusaders is determined to prevent the legalization of gay marriage; their objective is passage of a constitutional amendment declaring that marriage is between one man and one woman. Opposing them are activists who have tirelessly campaigned for the civil rights of gay men and women.

4. Be aware of the various forms of outlawed deviant sexuality.

   The outlawed sexual behaviors known as paraphilias include frotteurism (rubbing against or touching a nonconsenting person), voyeurism (obtaining sexual pleasure from spying on a stranger while he or she disrobes or engages in sexual behavior with another), exhibitionism (deriving sexual pleasure from exposing the genitals to surprise or shock a stranger), sadomasochism (deriving pleasure from receiving pain or inflicting pain on another), and pedophilia (attaining sexual pleasure through sexual activity with prepubescent children).

5. Discuss the history of prostitution and indicate what the term means today.

   Prostitution has been known for thousands of years. The earliest record of prostitution appears in ancient Mesopotamia, where priests engaged in sex to promote fertility in the community. Modern commercial sex appears to have its roots in ancient Greece. Today, prostitution can be defined as granting nonmarital sexual access, established by mutual agreement of the prostitutes, their clients, and their employers, for remuneration.

6. Distinguish among the different types of prostitutes.

   Prostitutes who work the streets in plain sight of police, citizens, and customers are referred to as hustlers, hookers, or streetwalkers. B-girls spend their time in bars, drinking and waiting to be picked up by customers. Brothel prostitutes live in a house with a madam who employs them, supervises their behavior, and receives a fee for her services. Call girls work via telephone "dates" and get their clients by word of mouth or by making arrangements with bellhops, cab drivers, and so on. Some escort services are fronts for prostitution rings. Prostitutes known as circuit travelers move around in groups of two or three to lumber, labor, and agricultural camps. Cyber prostitutes set up personal websites or put listings on Web boards such as craigslist that carry personal ads.

7. State the arguments for and against legalizing prostitution.

The *sexual equality* view considers the prostitute a victim of male dominance. The *free choice* view is that prostitution, if freely chosen, expresses women's equality and is not a symptom of subjugation. Advocates of both positions argue that prostitution should be decriminalized in order to relieve already desperate women from the additional burden of severe legal punishment. However, decriminalizing prostitution does not protect women from the violence, verbal abuse, physical injury, and diseases (such as HIV, AIDS) to which they are exposed in illegal prostitution.

8. Explain what the terms "pornography" and "obscenity" mean.

Pornography is written or visual material that provides sexual titillation and excitement for paying customers. Although material depicting nudity and sex is typically legal, most criminal codes prohibit the production, display, and sale of obscene material, which is "deeply offensive to morality or decency and designed to incite to lust or depravity." Legally, something is considered obscene if the average person applying contemporary contemporary standards would find that the work, taken as a whole, appeals to prurient interest; that the work depicts or describes prohibited sexual conduct; that the work, taken as a whole, lacks serious literary, artistic, political, or scientific value.

9. Discuss the cause of substance abuse.

The onset of drug use can be tied to such factors as racial prejudice, devalued identities, low self-esteem, poor socioeconomic status, and the high level of mistrust, negativism, and defiance typically found in impoverished areas. Some experts have linked substance abuse to psychological deficits such as impaired cognitive functioning, personality disturbance, and emotional problems. Substance abuse may have a genetic basis. Social psychologists suggest that drug abuse may also result from observing parental drug use. Substance abuse may be just one of many social problem behaviors. Some may use drugs and alcohol because they want to enjoy their effects: getting high, relaxation, improved creativity, escape from reality, and increased sexual responsiveness.

10. Compare and contrast the different methods of controlling the abuse of drugs.

A number of different drug control strategies have been tried, with varying degrees of success. Some aim to deter drug use by stopping the flow of drugs into the country, apprehending and punishing dealers, and cracking down on street-level drug deals. Others focus on preventing drug use by educating potential users to the dangers of substance abuse (convincing them to "say no to drugs") and by organizing community groups to work with the at-risk population in their area. Still another approach is to treat known users so that they become able to control their addictions.

Key Terms

public order crime 350

victimless crime 350

social harm 351

moral entrepreneur 351

paraphilia 354

prostitution 356

ehooking 356

pornography 362

obscenity 362

temperance movement 366

Prohibition 366

binge drinking 367

heavy drinking 367

drug-dependent personality 369

narcotic 371

Critical Thinking Questions

1. Why do you think people take drugs? Do you know anyone with an addiction-prone personality, or do you believe that is a myth?

2. What might be the best strategy to reduce teenage drug use: source control, reliance on treatment, national education efforts, or community-level enforcement?

3. Under what circumstances, if any, might the legalization or decriminalization of sex-related material be beneficial to society?

4. Do you consider alcohol a drug? Should greater control be imposed on the sale of alcohol?

5. Is prostitution really a crime? Should men or women have the right to sell sexual favors if they so choose?

© Mark Wilson/Getty Images

Chapter Outline

The Criminal Justice System

Savana Redding was a 13-year-old eighth-grade honor student at Safford Middle School, located about 127 miles from Tucson, Arizona, when on October 3, 2003, she was taken out of class by the school's vice principal. It seems that one of Redding's classmates had been caught possessing prescription-strength ibuprofen (400 mg, the strength of two Advils). When asked where she got the pills, this girl blamed Redding, who had no history of disciplinary issues or drug abuse.

Savanna claimed that she had no knowledge of the pills, but because the school has a zero-tolerance policy for all over-the-counter medication (which students could not possess without prior written permission), she was subjected to a strip-search by the school nurse and another female employee. During the search, she was forced to strip to her underwear, and her bra and underpants were pulled away from her body. Again, no drugs were found. Redding later told authorities, "The strip search was the most humiliating experience I have ever had. I held my head down so that they could not see that I was about to cry."

After a trial court ruled that the search was legal, Savanna sought help from the American Civil Liberties Union, who helped her bring an appeal to the 9th Circuit Court of Appeals. Here the judges ruled the search "traumatizing" and illegal, stating in its opinion that "Common sense informs us that directing a 13-year-old girl to remove her clothes, partially revealing her breasts and pelvic area, for allegedly possessing ibuprofen . . . was excessively intrusive." It went on to say that "The overzealousness of school administrators in efforts to protect students has the tragic impact of traumatizing those they claim to serve. And all this to find prescription-strength ibuprofen." However, rather than let the court decision stand, the school district appealed the case to the United States Supreme Court, complaining that restrictions on conducting student

Fact or Fiction?

▶ The prison population is clearly declining, because the crime rate has been down for ten years.

▶ Police officers routinely use force when they stop a suspect.

▶ Only the rich can afford competent legal counsel.

▶ Most people released from prison quickly fail on the outside and are returned to prison.

▶ A police officer must inform a suspect that "You are under arrest" in order for the arrest to be legal.

▶ Most criminal defendants receive a jury trial.

Chapter Objectives

1. Discuss the formation of the criminal justice system.
2. Discuss the role of police and law enforcement.
3. Be familiar with the structure and function of the criminal court system.
4. Be familiar with the various elements and institutions of the correctional system.
5. Understand the size and scope of the contemporary justice system.
6. Trace the formal criminal justice process.
7. Know what is meant by the term "criminal justice assembly line."
8. Discuss the role of discretion in the criminal justice system.
9. Understand the role of law in the criminal justice system.
10. Be familiar with the various perspectives on justice.

searches would cast a "roadblock to the kind of swift and effective response that is too often needed to protect the very safety of students, particularly from the threats posed by drugs and weapons."[1]

On June, 25, 2009, the Supreme Court held that Savanna's Fourth Amendment rights were violated when school officials searched her underwear for nonprescription painkillers.[2] With Justice Souter writing for the majority, the Court agreed that search measures used by school officials to root out contraband must be "reasonably related to the objectives of the search and not excessively intrusive in light of the age and sex of the student and the nature of the infraction." In Samantha's case, school officials did not have enough suspicion to warrant extending the search to her underwear. The majority found that in the present case, school officials could not be held personally liable because the law was unclear prior to the Court's decision on the matter. In a separate opinion, Justice John Paul Stevens agreed that the strip search was unconstitutional but also expressed his belief that the school administrators should be held personally liable: "It does not require a constitutional scholar to conclude that a nude search of a 13-year-old child is an invasion of constitutional rights of some magnitude." The only justice to disagree with the main finding was Clarence Thomas, who concluded that the judiciary should not meddle with decisions of school administrators that are intended to be in the interest of school safety.

The Redding case illustrates the role that the criminal justice system plays in the everyday lives of citizens. In this case, a young girl relied on a fair and objective court system to grant her justice—and they did. If it were not for the justice system, how could an individual such as Savanna hope to receive fair treatment when confronted by a large and powerful institution such as the school system? And how would it be possible for individuals to protect themselves from violent gangs and predatory criminals? If it were not for the justice system, we would have to return to the days of the Old West, where carrying firearms and vigilante justice were the norm. The public relies on the agencies of the criminal justice system to provide solutions to the crime problem and to shape the direction of crime policy. This loosely coupled collection of agencies is charged with (among other matters) protecting the public, maintaining order, enforcing the law, identifying transgressors, bringing the guilty to justice, and treating criminal behavior.

Although firmly entrenched in our culture, common criminal justice agencies have existed for only 150 years or so. This chapter reviews these agencies, describes the criminal justice process, and briefly discusses the various visions of justice that control how this process operates in contemporary society.

What is the Criminal Justice System?

The **criminal justice system** consists of the agencies of government charged with enforcing law, adjudicating crime, and correcting criminal conduct. It is essentially an instrument of social control: Society considers some behaviors so dangerous and destructive that it either strictly controls their occurrence or outlaws them outright. The agencies of justice are designed to prevent social harm by apprehending, trying, convicting, and punishing those who have already violated the law, as well as deterring those who may be contemplating future wrongdoing. Society maintains other types of informal social control, such as parental and school discipline, but these are designed to deal with moral, not legal, misbehavior. Only the criminal justice system maintains the power to control crime and punish those who violate the law.

Because of its varied and complex mission, the contemporary criminal justice system in the United States is monumental in size. As Figure 14.1 shows, the cost of law enforcement, courts, and correctional agencies has increased significantly during the past 25 years.

criminal justice system
The agencies of government—police, courts, and corrections—that are responsible for apprehending, adjudicating, sanctioning, and treating criminal offenders.

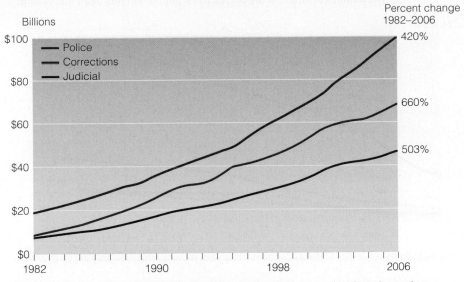

Figure 14.1 Direct Expenditure for Each of the Major Criminal Justice Functions

SOURCE: Justice Expenditure and Employment Extracts, www.ojp.usdoj.gov/bjs/glance/exptyp.htm.

It now costs federal, state, and local governments more than $215 billion per year to administer civil and criminal justice, up more than 300 percent since 1982. (One reason why the justice system is so expensive to run is that it employs more than 2 million people. There are now almost 18,000 U.S. law enforcement agencies employing more than 1 million people; of these, more than 800,000 are full-time sworn law enforcement officers, and the remainder are part-time officers and civilian employees.[3] There are nearly 17,000 courts, more than 8,000 prosecutorial agencies, about 6,000 correctional institutions, and more than 3,500 probation and parole departments.

In addition to personnel, there are also capital costs. State jurisdictions are now conducting a massive correctional building campaign, adding tens of thousands of prison cells. It costs about $100,000 to build a prison cell, and about $25,000 per year is needed to keep an inmate in prison; juvenile institutions cost about $30,000 per year per resident. In all, each U.S. citizen pays more than $650 per year to support justice system agencies.

The system is massive because it must process, treat, and care for millions of people. Although the crime rate has declined substantially, more than 14 million people are still being arrested each year, including more than 2 million for serious felony offenses.[4] In addition, about 1.5 million juveniles are handled by the juvenile courts. Today, state and federal courts convict a combined total of over 1 million adults a year on felony charges.[5]

Considering the massive proportions of this system, it does not seem surprising that more than 7.3 million people are under some form of correctional supervision, including 2.3 million men and women in the nation's jails and prisons and an additional 5 million adult men and women being supervised in the community while on probation or parole. Even though the crime rate has been in decline for most of the past decade, the correctional population continues to grow, and the number of people in the correctional system has trended upward (Figure 14.2). How can this trend be explained? Although crime rates have been in decline for the past decade, people are more likely to be convicted than in the past and, if sent to prison or jail, are likely to serve more of their sentence.

The major components of this immense system—the police, courts, and correctional agencies—are described in the sections that follow. What are their duties? What are the major stages in the formal criminal justice process, and how are decisions made at these critical junctures? What is the informal justice process, and how does it operate? These important questions are addressed next.

Fact or Fiction?

The prison population is clearly declining, because the crime rate has been down for ten years.

Fiction. The prison population has continued to increase. There is less crime, but people are more likely to be convicted than in the past and, if sent to prison or jail, are likely to serve more of their sentence.

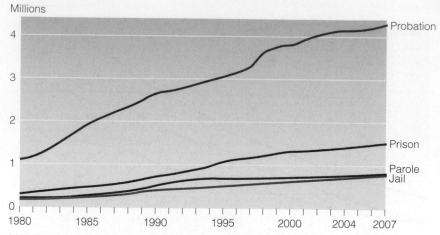

Figure 14.2 Adult Correctional Populations
The number of adults in the correctional population has been increasing.

SOURCE: Bureau of Justice Statistics Correctional Surveys, www.ojp.usdoj.gov/bjs/glance/corr2.htm.

POLICE AND LAW ENFORCEMENT

Most departments are municipal, general-purpose police forces, numbering about 12,000 in all. In addition, local jurisdictions maintain more than 1,000 special police units, including park rangers, harbor police, transit police, and campus security agencies at local universities. At the county level, there are approximately 3,000 sheriff's departments, which, depending on the jurisdiction, provide police protection in unincorporated areas of a county, perform judicial functions such as serving subpoenas, and maintain the county jail and detention facilities. Every state except Hawaii maintains a state police force. The federal government has its own law enforcement agencies, including the FBI and Secret Service.

Law enforcement agencies are charged with peacekeeping, deterring potential criminals, and apprehending law violators.[6] Whereas the traditional police role involved maintaining order through patrolling public streets and highways, responding to calls for assistance, investigating crimes, and identifying criminal suspects, it has gradually expanded to include a variety of human service functions, from preventing youth crime and diverting juvenile offenders from the criminal justice system, to resolving family conflicts. It is not unusual to see the contemporary patrol officer routinely facilitating the movement of people and vehicles, preserving civil order during emergencies, providing emergency medical care, and striving to improve police–community relations.

Police are the most visible agents of the justice process. They are continually scrutinized and routinely criticized for being too harsh or too lenient, too violent or too passive. Police response to minority groups, youths, political protesters, and union workers is closely watched by the media. Widely publicized cases of police brutality (such as the Rodney King beating in Los Angeles) and police corruption have prompted calls for the investigation and prosecution of police officers. Police departments have made noteworthy efforts to control both corruption and brutality, and the evidence suggests that significant progress has been made.

Police and Force The police officer's job is dangerous and can involve both force and violence. The most recent national survey on police contacts with civilians found that in a single year, about 44 million citizens, or 19 percent of U.S. residents age 16 or older, had face-to-face contacts with police. Here are some other things the survey revealed:

► Contact between police and the public was more common among males, whites, and younger residents.

- Overall, about 9 out of 10 persons who had contact with police felt the police acted properly.
- An estimated 2 percent of people stopped by police had force used or threatened against them during their most recent contact.
- Blacks and Hispanics experienced police use of force at higher rates than whites.[7]

The data indicates that (1) relatively few contacts with police and the public involve physical force, but (2) there seem to be racial and ethnic differences in the rate at which force is applied.

Community Policing Despite efforts to improve police–community relations, many citizens still report having negative attitudes toward police.[8] To remedy this situation while improving the quality of their services, police departments have experimented with new forms of law enforcement, which are collectively referred to as **community policing (COP)** and **problem-oriented policing**. These models are proactive rather than reactive: Rather than just responding to crime after it occurs, police departments are now shaping their forces into community change agents in order to prevent crimes before they occur.

Community programs involve police in such activities as citizen crime patrols and councils that identify crime problems. Community policing often involves decentralized units that operate on the neighborhood level in order to be more sensitive to the particular concerns of the public; community policing creates a sense of security in a neighborhood and improves residents' opinions of the police.[9] In neighborhoods that maintain collective efficacy, police work closely with existing neighborhood groups to implement crime reduction programs; programs in these areas seem quite successful.[10] In more disorganized areas, police use aggressive tactics to reduce crime and "take back the streets" before building relationships with community leaders.[11]

Community policing efforts have produced numerous benefits, such as reducing disorder and lowering neighborhood crime rates.[12] The most successful programs give officers time to meet with local residents, to talk about crime in the neighborhood, and to use personal initiative to solve problems. Where it is employed, citizens seem to like community policing initiatives, and those who volunteer and get involved in community crime prevention programs report higher confidence in local police agencies and their ability to create a secure environment.[13] They may find that officers are more respectful of citizens, a condition that helps lower the number of complaints and improves community relations.[14]

On the other hand, there is no clear-cut evidence that community policing (COP) is highly successful at reducing crime across the board. Crime rate reductions in cities that have used COP may be a result of an overall downturn in the nation's crime rate, rather than a result of community policing efforts. Researchers have also found that it is difficult to change the traditional values and attitudes of police officers involved in the programs.[15] Police managers still face resistance from some experienced officers who hold traditional law-and-order values and question the utility of community policing models. It is unlikely that these innovative programs can enjoy long-term success unless veteran officers make a commitment to the values of community policing.[16]

THE CRIMINAL COURT SYSTEM

Many people consider the criminal courts to be the core element in the administration of criminal justice. The court is a complex social agency with many independent but interrelated subsystems—clerk, prosecutor, defense attorney, judge, and probation department—each having a role in the court's operation. It is also the scene of many important elements of criminal justice decision making—detention, jury selection, trial, and sentencing. Ideally, the judicatory process operates with absolute fairness and equality. The entire process—from filing the initial complaint to final sentencing of the defendant—is governed by precise rules of law designed to ensure fairness. No defendant tried before a U.S. court should suffer or benefit because of his or her personal characteristics, beliefs, or affiliations.

Fact or Fiction?

Police officers routinely use force when they stop a suspect.

Fiction. Relatively few contacts with police involve force.

CONNECTIONS

As you may recall, the concept of collective efficacy was discussed in Chapter 6. Neighborhoods with collective efficacy use community resources to exert informal social control over people who might otherwise disrupt the social order.

community policing (COP) (problem-oriented policing) A proactive form of policing: Rather than merely responding to crime after it occurs, police departments are shaping their forces into community change agents in order to prevent crimes before they occur.

© AP Images/Stefano Medici

In a case that has made headlines around the world, U.S. citizen Amanda Knox is seen at a hearing in a courthouse in Perugia, Italy, on September 19, 2009, during her trial for the murder of Meredith Kercher, a British student with whom Knox shared a rented flat in the Italian city of Perugia. Knox and her Italian boyfriend, Raffaele Sollecito, were accused of killing Kercher during a "sex game" that went awry. On December 4, 2009, both were found guilty of murder, sexual violence, and other charges. Knox, now 22, was sentenced to 26 years in prison, while Sollecito, 25, received 25 years. During the trial, Knox claimed she had been beaten by police and that the case has been handled in a fashion that would violate the legal standards that protect people accused of crime in the U.S. court system. For example, she was interrogated for hours by the Italian police without the benefit of an attorney. The Italian media sensationalized the case, portraying Knox as a femme fatale and sex fiend. The fact that she admitted sleeping with her boyfriend the night of the crime horrified sexually conservative Italians. Her supporters believe her conviction was a miscarriage of justice without any basis in fact; the prosecution relied on DNA evidence that had been tainted; there was little real evidence of her guilt; and another person, Rudy Guédé, had already been convicted of the murder and sentenced to 30 years in prison. The Knox case is a reminder that the American legal system, for all its flaws, provides criminal defendants an unmatched level of due process of law.

However, U.S. criminal justice can be selective. **Discretion** accompanies defendants through every step of the process, determining what will happen to them and how their cases will be resolved. Discretion means that two people committing similar crimes may receive highly dissimilar treatment. Almost one-third of all people convicted of serious felonies receive a probation sentence; only 40 percent go to prison. Probation is used even in the most serious felony cases: Although most people convicted on sexual assault and rape charges are incarcerated, about 20 percent get probation only; about 5 percent of people convicted on murder charges receive probation as a sole sentence.[17] And as Figure 14.3 shows, a sizable number of defendants with prior felony convictions are not sentenced to prison when convicted of another felony offense.

Court Structure The typical state court structure is illustrated in Figure 14.4.

Most states employ a multitiered court structure. Lower courts try misdemeanors and conduct the preliminary processing of felony offenses. Superior trial courts try felony cases. Appellate courts review the criminal procedures of trial courts to determine whether offenders were treated fairly. Superior appellate courts or state supreme courts, used in about half the states, review lower appellate court decisions.

The independent federal court system has three tiers, as shown in Figure 14.5. The U.S. district courts are the trial courts of the system; they have jurisdiction over cases involving violations of federal law, such as interstate transportation of stolen vehicles and racketeering. Appeals from the district court are heard in one of the intermediate federal courts of appeal. The highest federal appeals court, the U.S. Supreme Court, is the court of last resort for all cases tried in the various federal and state courts.

The Supreme Court The U.S. Supreme Court is composed of nine members, who are appointed for lifetime terms by the president with the approval of Congress. In general, the Court hears only cases it deems important and appropriate. When the Court decides to hear a case, it usually grants a *writ of certiorari*, a court order requesting a transcript of the case proceedings for review.

The Supreme Court can word a decision in such a way that it becomes a precedent that must be honored by all lower courts. If the Court grants a particular litigant the right to counsel at a police lineup, then all people in similar situations must be given the same right. This type of ruling is usually referred to as a **landmark decision**. The use of precedent in the legal system gives the Supreme Court power to influence and mold the everyday operating procedures of police agencies, trial courts, and correctional institutions.

Prosecution and Defense Within the structure of the court system, the prosecutor and defense attorney are opponents in what is known as the **adversary system**. These two parties oppose each other in a hotly disputed contest—the

Figure 14.3 Effect of Criminal History on Sentences Given Defendants Convicted of a Felony

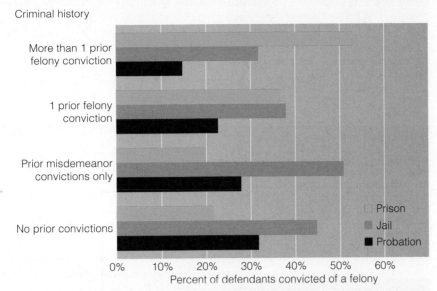

SOURCE: Tracey Kyckelhahn and Thomas H. Cohen, *Felony Defendants in Large Urban Counties, 2004* (Washington, DC: Bureau of Justice Statistics, 2008), www.ojp.usdoj.gov/bjs/pub/pdf/fdluc04.pdf.

criminal trial—in accordance with rules of law and procedure. In every criminal case, the state acts against the defendant, and the defense attorney acts for the defendant before an impartial judge or jury, with each side trying to bring forward evidence and arguments to advance its case. Theoretically, the ultimate objective of the adversary system is to seek the truth, determining the guilt or innocence of the defendant from the formal evidence presented at the trial. The adversary system is designed to ensure that each defendant gets a fair trial, that the relevant facts of the case emerge, and that an impartial decision is reached.

Criminal Prosecution The **prosecutor** is the public official who represents the government and presents its case against the **defendant**, who is charged with a violation of the criminal law. Traditionally, the prosecutor is a local attorney whose area of jurisdictional responsibility is limited to a particular county or city. The prosecutor is known variously as a district attorney or a prosecuting attorney and is either an elected or an appointed official. On the state level, the prosecutor may be referred to as the attorney general; in the federal jurisdiction, the prosecutor's title is United States attorney.

The prosecutor is responsible not only for charging the defendant with the crime but also for bringing the case to trial and to a final conclusion. The prosecutor's authority ranges from determining the nature of the charge to reducing the charge by negotiation or recommending that the complaint be dismissed. The prosecutor also participates in bail hearings, presents cases before a grand jury, and appears for the state at arraignments. In sum, the prosecutor is responsible for presenting the state's case from the time of the defendant's arrest through conviction and sentencing in the criminal court.

The prosecutor, like the police officer, exercises a great deal of discretion; he or she can decide initially whether to file a criminal charge and can determine what charge to bring or explore the availability of noncriminal dispositions.[18] Prosecutorial discretion would not be as important as it is if it were desirable to prosecute all violations of the law. However, full enforcement of every law is not practical, because police officers and prosecutors ordinarily lack sufficient resources, staff, and support services to attain that goal. Therefore, it makes sense to screen out cases where the accused is obviously innocent, where the evidence is negligible, or where criminal sanctions may seem inappropriate: The case must have **convictability**—it must stand a good

discretion
The use of personal decision making by those carrying out police, judicial, and sanctioning functions within the criminal justice system.

landmark decision
A ruling by the U.S. Supreme Court that serves as a precedent for similar legal issues; it often influences the everyday operating procedures of police agencies, trial courts, and correctional institutions.

adversary system
The U.S. method of criminal adjudication, in which prosecution (the state) and defense (the accused) each try to bring forward evidence and arguments, with guilt or innocence ultimately decided by an impartial judge or jury.

prosecutor
Public official who represents the government in criminal proceedings, presenting the case against the accused.

defendant
In criminal proceedings, the person accused of violating the law.

convictability
Existence of conditions surrounding a criminal case that indicate it has a good chance of resulting in a conviction.

Figure 14.4 Structure of a State Judicial System

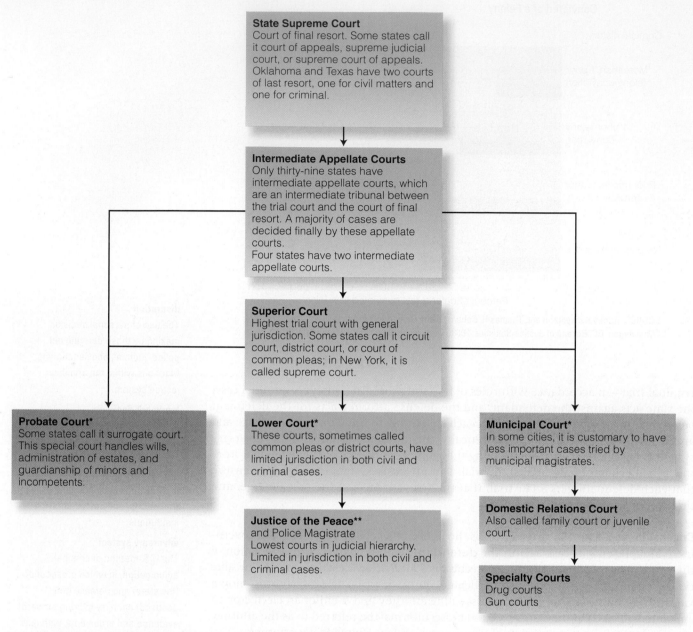

State Supreme Court
Court of final resort. Some states call it court of appeals, supreme judicial court, or supreme court of appeals. Oklahoma and Texas have two courts of last resort, one for civil matters and one for criminal.

Intermediate Appellate Courts
Only thirty-nine states have intermediate appellate courts, which are an intermediate tribunal between the trial court and the court of final resort. A majority of cases are decided finally by these appellate courts.
Four states have two intermediate appellate courts.

Superior Court
Highest trial court with general jurisdiction. Some states call it circuit court, district court, or court of common pleas; in New York, it is called supreme court.

Probate Court*
Some states call it surrogate court. This special court handles wills, administration of estates, and guardianship of minors and incompetents.

Lower Court*
These courts, sometimes called common pleas or district courts, have limited jurisdiction in both civil and criminal cases.

Municipal Court*
In some cities, it is customary to have less important cases tried by municipal magistrates.

Justice of the Peace**
and Police Magistrate
Lowest courts in judicial hierarchy. Limited in jurisdiction in both civil and criminal cases.

Domestic Relations Court
Also called family court or juvenile court.

Specialty Courts
Drug courts
Gun courts

Notes: *Courts of special jurisdiction, such as family, probate, and juvenile courts, and the so-called inferior courts, such as common pleas and municipal courts, may be separate courts or part of the trial court of general jurisdiction.
**Justices of the peace do not exist in all states. Where they do exist, their jurisdictions vary greatly from state to state.
SOURCE: American Bar Association, *Law and the Courts* (Chicago: ABA, 1974), p. 20. Updated information provided by West Publishing, Eagen, Minnesota.

defense attorney
Person responsible for protecting the constitutional rights of the accused and presenting the best possible legal defense; represents a defendant from initial arrest through trial, sentencing, and any appeal.

right to counsel
The right of a person accused of crime to the assistance of a defense attorney in all criminal prosecutions.

chance of resulting in a conviction. Instead of total or automatic law enforcement, a process of selective or discretionary enforcement exists; as a result, the prosecutor must make many decisions that significantly influence police operations and control the actual number of cases processed through the court and correctional systems.

Criminal Defense The **defense attorney** is responsible for providing legal representation of the defendant. This role involves two major functions: (1) protecting the constitutional rights of the accused and (2) presenting the best possible legal defense for the defendant.

The defense attorney represents a client from initial arrest through the trial stage, during the sentencing hearing, and, if needed, through the process of appeal. The defense attorney is also expected to enter into plea negotiations and

Figure 14.5 The Federal Judicial System

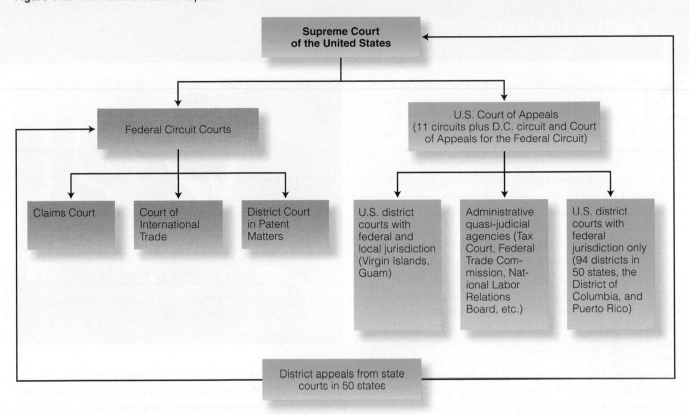

SOURCE: American Bar Association, *Law and the Courts* (Chicago: ABA, 1974), p. 20. Updated information provided by the Federal Courts Improvement Act of 1982 and West Publishing, Eagen, Minnesota.

obtain for the defendant the most suitable bargain regarding type and length of sentence.

Any person accused of a crime may obtain the services of a private attorney if he or she can afford to do so. One of the most critical questions in the criminal justice system has been whether an indigent (poor) defendant has a **right to counsel**. The federal court system has long provided counsel to the indigent on the basis of the Sixth Amendment to the U.S. Constitution, which gives the accused the right to have the assistance of defense counsel. Through a series of landmark U.S. Supreme Court decisions, beginning with *Powell v. Alabama* in 1932 and continuing with *Gideon v. Wainwright* in 1963 and *Argersinger v. Hamlin* in 1972, the right of a criminal defendant to have counsel has become fundamental to the U.S. system of criminal justice.[19] Today, state courts must provide counsel to indigent defendants charged with criminal offenses where the possibility of incarceration exists. Consequently, more than 1,000 **public defender** agencies have been set up around the United States to provide free legal counsel to indigent defendants. In other jurisdictions, defense lawyers volunteer their services, a practice referred to as working **pro bono**, and are assigned to criminal defendants. A few rural counties have defense lawyers under contract who handle all criminal matters.

The Supreme Court has ruled that in addition to having an attorney, every defendant is entitled to a legally competent defense, even those who may engage in particularly heinous or distasteful criminal acts (see the accompanying Profiles in Crime feature). A conviction can be overturned if it can be shown that an attorney did not meet this standard. To prove that her legal assistance was legally ineffective, a defendant must show that her lawyer's performance was deficient and that this deficiency prejudiced the defense. Performance is deficient if it falls below an objective standard of reasonableness—for example, if an attorney does not conduct a reasonable investigation of the facts of the case.[20]

Fact or Fiction?

Only the rich can afford competent legal counsel.

Fiction. The Supreme Court has interpreted the Sixth Amendment to guarantee that all people accused of crime have the right to a competent attorney.

public defender
Attorney employed by the state whose job is to provide free legal counsel to indigent defendants.

pro bono
Literally, done without compensation, "for the public good"; free legal counsel provided to indigent defendants by private attorneys as a service to the profession and the community.

NFL quarterback Michael Vick (in photo) is perhaps the most famous celebrity convicted for his involvement with dog fighting, but he is by no means alone. In July 2009, after a year-long investigation by federal, state, and local law enforcement agencies, 30 people across five states were arrested for their involvement in a multistate dog fighting ring. Among those arrested were Robert Hackman, who operated "Shake Rattle and Roll Kennel"; Jack Ruppel of "Ozark Hillbillys Kennel"; Michael Morgan, aka "Missouri Mike," who operated "Cannibal Kennel"; and Ronald Creach, who operated "Hard Goodbye Kennel." In addition to the arrests, about 350 dogs—mostly pit bull terriers—were seized in Missouri, Texas, Illinois, Iowa, and Oklahoma. Those arrested for their involvement face felony charges that carry maximum sentences of five years in prison and fines of up to $250,000. Dog fighting is banned throughout the country and is a felony in all 50 states.

According to the indictments, the defendants acquired, bred, and trained pit bull dogs for the purpose of fighting. When dogs were injured during fights, the defendants denied them adequate medical treatment, and they "routinely" destroyed dogs—sometimes by electrocution—that became severely injured after fighting.

The fights were often so violent and bloody that some of the defendants were designated as "sponge men"—they provided the dogs' handlers with sponges to wipe blood from their dogs or to cool them down during the fight. One of the defendants allegedly used a .22-caliber rifle to shoot and kill two dogs who fought but didn't perform up to his expectations.

© AP Images/Gerald Herbert

On September 18, 2009, five of the men pled guilty, and on December 8, 2009, two were sentenced to more than a year in prison; the remainder are awaiting sentencing or trial. Clearly, although the Vick case alerted the nation to the brutality of dog fighting, it did not end the practice.

SOURCES: United States Attorney's Office, Eastern District of Missouri, "Five Charged, More Than 150 Dogs Seized in Raids on Dog Fighting Rings," July 8, http://stlouis.fbi.gov/dojpressrel/pressrel09/sl070809.htm (accessed July 11, 2009); FBI, "Canine Cruelty: Five-State Dog Fighting Ring Busted," July 7, 2009, www.fbi.gov/page2/july09/dogfighting_070909.html (accessed July 11, 2009).

CORRECTIONS

After conviction and sentencing, the offender enters the correctional system. Correctional agencies administer the post-adjudicatory care given to offenders, which can range from informal monitoring in the community to solitary confinement in a maximum-security prison, depending on the seriousness of the crime and the individual needs of the offender.

Probation Because the gap between what correctional programs promise to deliver and their actual performance is often significant, many jurisdictions have instituted community-based correctional facilities. The most common correctional treatment, **probation**, is a legal disposition that allows the convicted offender to remain in the community, subject to conditions imposed by court order, under the supervision of a probation officer. This lets the offender continue working and avoids the crippling effects of **incarceration**.

Traditional probation programs have been supplemented with intermediate community sanctions featuring such elements as house arrest enhanced by electronic

probation
Conditional release of a convicted offender into the community under the supervision of a probation officer and subject to certain conditions.

incarceration
Confinement in jail or prison.

monitoring. The concept is to provide more secure monitoring than traditional probation, while maintaining offenders in the community where they can access treatment programs. For those defendants who require more secure correctional care, a variety of small neighborhood residential centers and halfway houses have been developed. Experts believe that only a small percentage of criminal defendants require maximum security and that most can be more effectively rehabilitated in community-based facilities. Rather than totally confining offenders in an impersonal, harsh prison, such programs offer them the opportunity to maintain normal family and social relationships, while providing rehabilitative services and resources at a lower cost to taxpayers.

Correctional Institutions Criminal defendants who are sentenced to a year or less for misdemeanors are typically held in **jails**, or houses of correction. Jails are also used to detain those awaiting trial or involved in other proceedings, such as grand jury deliberations, arraignments, and preliminary hearings. Many of these institutions for short-term detention are administered by county governments. Little is done to treat inmates because the personnel and facilities lack the qualifications, services, and resources.

State and federally operated facilities that receive felony offenders sentenced by the criminal courts are called **prisons** or **penitentiaries**. They may be minimum-, medium-, or maximum-security institutions. Prison facilities vary throughout the country. Some have high walls, cells, and large, heterogeneous inmate populations; others offer much freedom, progressive correctional programs, and small, homogeneous populations.

Both the jail and prison populations have been steadily increasing despite a reduction in the crime rate, probably because sentences have been increasing and the proportion of those convicted who are sentenced to prison has been increasing (see Figure 14.6). In addition, legislative **truth-in-sentencing** initiatives that require inmates to serve a greater percentage of their sentences behind bars have also contributed to prison overcrowding.

Parole Most inmates do not serve their entire sentence and are released back into the community via **parole**, a system whereby eligible inmates can earn early release and serve the remainder of their sentence in the community under the supervision of a parole officer. The main purpose of parole is to help the ex-inmate bridge the gap between institutional confinement and a positive adjustment within the community. All parolees must adhere to a set of rules of behavior while they are "on the

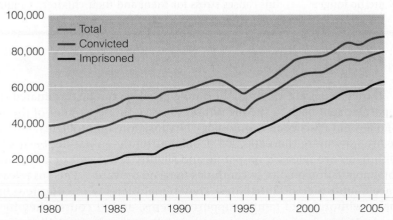

Figure 14.6 Outcomes for Defendants in Cases Concluded in U.S. District Court

SOURCE: Bureau of Justice Statistics data, www.ojp.usdoj.gov/bjs/glance/fedipc.htm (accessed July 11, 2009).

jail
Institution, usually run by the county, for short-term detention of those convicted of misdemeanors and those awaiting trial or other judicial proceedings.

prison (penitentiary)
State or federally operated facility for the incarceration of felony offenders sentenced by the criminal courts.

truth in sentencing
The requirement that inmates serve a greater percentage of their time behind bars before they are eligible for early release mechanisms such as parole.

parole
Conditional early release from prison, with the offender serving the remainder of the sentence in the community under the supervision of a parole officer.

Because of America's two-decade-long imprisonment boom, more than 500,000 inmates are now being released back into the community each year. As criminologist Joan Petersilia warns, a number of unfortunate consequences occur, because many of those being released have not received adequate treatment and are unprepared for life in conventional society. The risks they present to the community include increases in child abuse, family violence, the spread of infectious diseases, homelessness, and community disorganization.

The increased risks associated with reentry can be tied to legal changes in how people are released from prison. In the past, offenders were granted early release only if a parole board believed they were rehabilitated and had ties welcome in subsidized public housing complexes. This is a consequence of the U.S. Department of Housing and Urban Development's "one strike and you're out" policy, where all members of the household are evicted if even a single member is involved in crime. One year after release, as many as 60 percent of former inmates are not employed in the regular labor market, and there is increasing reluctance among employers to hire ex-offenders. Ex-offenders are commonly barred from working in fields in which most jobs are being created, such as child care, education, security, nursing, and home heath care. More jobs are also now unionized, and many unions exclude ex-offenders.

Being barred from work opportunities produces chronic unemployment, a status closely related to drug and alcohol

Policy and Practice in Criminology Problems of Reentry

to the community—such as a family or a job. Inmates were encouraged to enter treatment programs to earn parole. Changes in sentencing law have resulted in the growth of mandatory release and limits on discretionary parole. People now serve a fixed sentence, and the discretion of parole boards has been blunted. Inmates may be discouraged from seeking involvement in rehabilitation programs (which no longer affect the chance of parole being granted), and this lack of incentive means that fewer inmates leaving prison have participated in programs to address work, education, and substance use deficiencies. Nor does the situation improve upon release. Many inmates are not assigned to supervision caseloads once they are back in the community. About 200,000 released inmates go unsupervised each year, three-quarters of whom have been released after completing their maximum sentence and therefore are not obligated to be supervised.

Work-Related Issues

Most people leave prison with no savings, no immediate entitlement to unemployment benefits, and few employment prospects. Upon release, some find that they are no longer abuse. Losing a job can lead to substance abuse, which in turn is related to child and family violence.

Family Issues

Recidivism may be a by-product of the disruptive effect a prison experience has on personal relationships. Ex-inmates may find their home life torn and disrupted when they are finally released. Recent research by Beth Heubner shows that incarceration significantly reduces the chances of marriage for all men released from prison. Because marriage has proved a significant neutralizer of future criminality, the suppression effect on marriage that a prison sentence inflicts may help explain high recidivism rates. And even if they do marry, former inmates may be restricted in their choice of mates. Their circumstances may force them to choose partners with equally checkered backgrounds—a circumstance that may enhance rather than reduce the likelihood of future criminality.

Being released from prison is not just harmful to men. Mothers released from prison have difficulty finding services such as housing, employment, and child care, and this causes stress for them and their children. Children of

outside." If these rules are violated, the parole privilege can be terminated (revoked) and the parolee sent back to the institution to serve the remainder of the sentence. See the Policy and Practice in Criminology box for more on problems of parole.

There are now more than 800,000 people currently on parole. Each year about 500,000 inmates are released on parole and slightly fewer exit or complete parole, so the total population on parole continues to trend upward.[21] Persons released from prison face a multitude of difficulties. They remain largely uneducated, unskilled, and usually without solid family support systems, and of course they have criminal records. Not surprisingly, most parolees fail, and rather quickly; rearrests are most common in the first six months after release.[22] In all, more than 60 percent of incarcerated and released parents may suffer confusion, sadness, and social stigma, and these feelings often result in difficulties in school, low self-esteem, aggressive behavior, and general emotional dysfunction. If the parents are negative role models, children fail to develop positive attitudes toward work and responsibility. They are five times more likely to serve time in prison than children whose parents were never incarcerated.

Physical and Mental Problems

Prisoners have significantly more physical and mental health problems than the general population. More than three-fourths of the inmates who leave prison report a history of drug and/or alcohol abuse in the following year. Furthermore, inmates with mental illness (about 16 percent of all inmates) are increasingly being imprisoned—and then released. Even when public mental health services are available, many mentally ill individuals fail to use them because they fear institutionalization, deny they are mentally ill, or distrust the mental health system. The situation will become more serious as more and more parolees are released into the disorganized communities whose deteriorated conditions contributed to their original involvement in crime.

Effect on Communities

Parole expert Richard Seiter notes that when there were only a few hundred thousand prisoners, and a few thousand released per year, the issues surrounding the release of offenders did not overly challenge communities. Families could house ex-inmates, job-search organizations could find them jobs, and community social service agencies could respond to their individual needs for mental health or substance abuse treatment. Today, the sheer number of reentering inmates severely taxes the communities to which they are returning. Charles Kubrin and Eric Stewart have found that communities that already suffer the greatest social and economic disadvantages are those that produce the highest recidivism rates. Obviously, the influx of returning inmates can magnify their problems.

Reentry and Crime

Research now shows, then, that high rates of prison admissions produce high crime rates. Fear of a prison stay has

less of an impact on behavior than ever before. As the prison population grows, the negative impact of incarceration may be lessening. In neighborhoods where "doing time" is more the rule than the exception, it becomes less of a stigma and more of a badge of acceptance. It also becomes a way of life from which some ex-convicts do rebound. Teens may encounter older men who have gone to prison and have returned to begin their lives again. With the proper skills and survival techniques, prison is considered "manageable." Although a prison stay is still unpleasant, it has lost its aura of shame and fear. By becoming commonplace and mundane, the "myth" of the prison experience has been exposed and its deterrent power reduced. Clearly, the national policy of relying on prison as a deterrent to crime may produce results that policymakers had not expected or desired.

CRITICAL THINKING

1. All too often, government leaders jump on the incarceration bandwagon as a panacea for the nation's crime problem. Is it a "quick fix" whose long-term consequences may be devastating for the nation's cities, or are these problems counterbalanced by the crime-reducing effect of putting large numbers of high-rate offenders behind bars?

2. If you agree that incarceration undermines neighborhoods, can you think of some other, indirect ways in which high incarceration rates help increase crime rates?

SOURCES: Bruce Way, Donald Sawyer, Stephanie Lilly, Catherine Moffitt, and Barbara Stapholz, "Characteristics of Inmates Who Received a Diagnosis of Serious Mental Illness upon Entry to New York State Prison," *Psychiatric Services* 59 (2008): 1,335–1,337; Beth Huebner, "Racial and Ethnic Differences in the Likelihood of Marriage: The Effect of Incarceration," *Justice Quarterly* 24 (2007): 156–183; Charles Kubrin and Eric Stewart, "Predicting Who Reoffends: The Neglected Role of Neighborhood Context in Recidivism Studies," *Criminology* 44 (2006): 165–197; Joan Petersilia, *When Prisoners Come Home: Parole and Prisoner Reentry* (New York: Oxford University Press, 2003); Joan Petersilia, "Hard Time Ex-offenders Returning Home after Prison," *Corrections Today* 67 (2005): 66–72; Joan Petersilia, "When Prisoners Return to Communities: Political, Economic, and Social Consequences," *Federal Probation* 65 (2001): 3–9; Richard Seiter, "Prisoner Reentry and the Role of Parole Officers," *Federal Probation* 66 (2002).

parolees return to prison within three years of their release, and the failure rate has actually increased during the past 30 years. The cost of this recidivism is acute. One federal survey of 156,000 parole violators who had been sent back to prison concluded that these offenders committed at least 6,800 murders, 5,500 rapes, 8,800 assaults, and 22,500 robberies during the first year they were under supervision in the community.[23]

Other ways in which an offender may be released from an institution include mandatory release upon completion of his or her sentence and the pardon, a form of executive clemency. ▶ **Checkpoints**

▶ The concept of a criminal justice system is relatively new.

▶ The system is vast, costing taxpayers about $150 billion a year.

▶ The police are the largest component of the system. They identify law violators, keep the peace, and provide emergency services.

▶ The court system dispenses fair and even-handed justice.

▶ Prosecutors bring the criminal charge, and defense attorneys represent the accused.

▶ Correctional agencies incarcerate and treat millions of convicted offenders.

▶ Included within corrections are closed institutions, such as prisons and jails, and community correctional efforts, such as probation.

▶ Most inmates are eventually paroled, but the rate of offender failure on parole is still acute, and more than half are considered failures.

Fact or Fiction?

A police officer must inform a suspect that "You are under arrest" in order for the arrest to be legal.

Fiction. Actually, a police officer does not have to say anything to make an arrest legal. Some suspects may be unconscious or intoxicated when they are arrested, and others may not understand English or another language the arresting officer can speak.

arrest
The taking into police custody of an individual suspected of a crime.

probable cause
Evidence of a crime, and of a suspect's involvement in it, sufficient to warrant an arrest.

booking
Fingerprinting, photographing, and recording personal information of a suspect in police custody.

The Process of Justice

In addition to viewing the criminal justice system as a collection of agencies, it is possible to see it as a series of decision points through which offenders flow. This process, illustrated in Figure 14.7, begins with initial contact with police and ends with the offender's reentering society. At any point in the process, a decision may be made to drop further proceedings and allow the accused back into society without further penalty. In a classic statement, political scientist Herbert Packer described this process as follows:

> The image that comes to mind is an assembly line conveyor belt down which moves an endless stream of cases, never stopping, carrying them to workers who stand at fixed stations and who perform on each case as it comes by the same small but essential operation that brings it one step closer to being a finished product, or to exchange the metaphor for the reality, a closed file. The criminal process is seen as a screening process in which each successive stage—pre-arrest investigation, arrest, post-arrest investigation, preparation for trial, or entry of plea, conviction, disposition—involves a series of routinized operations whose success is gauged primarily by their tendency to pass the case along to a successful conclusion.[24]

Although each jurisdiction is somewhat different, a comprehensive view of the processing of a felony offender would probably contain the following decision points.

1. *Initial contact.* The initial contact an offender has with the justice system occurs when police officers observe a criminal act during patrol of city streets, parks, or highways. They may also find out about a crime through a citizen or victim complaint. Similarly, an informer may alert them about criminal activity in return for financial or other consideration. Sometimes political officials, such as the mayor or city council, ask police to look into ongoing criminal activity, such as gambling, and during their subsequent investigations police officers encounter an illegal act.

2. *Investigation.* Regardless of whether the police observe, hear of, or receive a complaint about a crime, they may investigate to gather sufficient facts, or evidence, to identify the perpetrator, justify an arrest, and bring the offender to trial. An investigation may take a few minutes, as when patrol officers see a burglary in progress and apprehend the burglar at the scene of the crime. Other investigations may take years to complete and involve numerous investigators. When federal agents tracked and captured Theodore Kaczynski (known as the Unabomber) in 1996, his arrest completed an investigation that had lasted more than a decade.

3. *Arrest.* An **arrest** occurs when the police take into custody a person who is alleged to have committed a criminal act. An arrest is legal when all of the following conditions exist: (a) the officer believes there is sufficient evidence (**probable cause**) that a crime is being or has been committed and that the suspect committed the crime; (b) the officer deprives the individual of freedom; and (c) the suspect believes that he or she is in the custody of a police officer and cannot voluntarily leave. The police officer is not required to use the word "arrest" or any similar word to initiate an arrest; nor does the officer first have to bring the suspect to the police station. For all practical purposes, a person who has been deprived of liberty is under arrest. Arrests can be made at the scene of a crime or after a warrant is issued by a magistrate.

4. *Custody.* After arrest, the suspect remains in police custody. The person may be taken to the police station to be fingerprinted and photographed and to have personal information recorded—a procedure popularly referred to as **booking**. (In the past the information was recorded in a book; it is now entered into a computer database). Witnesses may be brought in to view the suspect in a lineup, and further evidence may be gathered on the case. Suspects may be interrogated by police officers to get their side of the story, they may be asked to sign a confession of guilt, or they may be asked to identify others involved in the crime. The

Figure 14.7 Critical Stages of the Justice Process

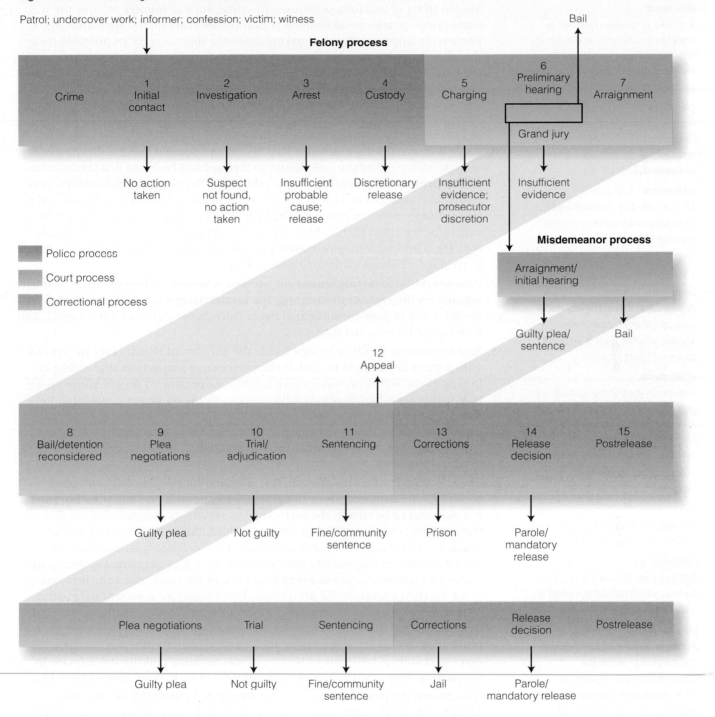

Patrol; undercover work; informer; confession; victim; witness

Felony process

| | 1 Initial contact | 2 Investigation | 3 Arrest | 4 Custody | 5 Charging | 6 Preliminary hearing | 7 Arraignment |
| Crime | | | | | | | |

Bail

Grand jury

- No action taken
- Suspect not found, no action taken
- Insufficient probable cause; release
- Discretionary release
- Insufficient evidence; prosecutor discretion
- Insufficient evidence

Misdemeanor process

Arraignment/ initial hearing

- Guilty plea/ sentence
- Bail

- Police process
- Court process
- Correctional process

12 Appeal

| 8 Bail/detention reconsidered | 9 Plea negotiations | 10 Trial/ adjudication | 11 Sentencing | 13 Corrections | 14 Release decision | 15 Postrelease |

- Guilty plea
- Not guilty
- Fine/community sentence
- Prison
- Parole/ mandatory release

| Plea negotiations | Trial | Sentencing | Corrections | Release decision | Postrelease |

- Guilty plea
- Not guilty
- Fine/community sentence
- Jail
- Parole/ mandatory release

law allows suspects to have their lawyer present whenever police conduct an in-custody **interrogation**.

5. *Complaint/charging.* After police turn the evidence in a case over to the prosecutor, who represents the state at any criminal proceedings, a decision is made whether to file charges against the accused. In determining whether to file charges, the prosecution weighs the evidence to determine whether there are sufficient facts to support the accusation. Such factors as witness reliability, the quality and validity of police procedures, and the victim's statements are considered. If, in its discretion, the prosecutor's office believes there is insufficient evidence to move the case forward, it issues a **nolle prosequi** declaration, which signifies its decision to drop the case from further prosecution.

interrogation
The questioning of a suspect in police custody.

nolle prosequi
A declaration that expresses the prosecutor's decision to drop a case from further prosecution.

indictment

A written accusation returned by a grand jury charging an individual with a specified crime, based on the prosecutor's demonstration of probable cause.

grand jury

A group of citizens chosen to hear testimony in secret and to issue formal criminal accusations (indictments).

information

A filing before an impartial lower-court judge who decides whether the case should go forward (this filing is an alternative to the use of a grand jury).

preliminary hearing

Alternative to a grand jury, in which an impartial lower-court judge decides whether there is probable cause sufficient for a trial.

arraignment

The step in the criminal justice process in which the accused is brought before the trial judge, formal charges are read, defendants are informed of their rights, a plea is entered, bail is considered, and a trial date is set.

bail

A money bond intended to ensure that the accused will return for trial.

recognizance

Pledge by the accused to return for trial, which may be accepted in lieu of bail.

plea bargain

Agreement between prosecution and defense in which the accused pleads guilty in return for a reduction of charges, a more lenient sentence, or some other consideration.

hung jury

A jury that is unable to agree on a decision, thus leaving the case unresolved and open for a possible retrial.

disposition

Sentencing of a defendant who has been found guilty; usually involves a fine, probation, or incarceration.

6. *Preliminary hearing/grand jury.* Because it is a tremendous personal and financial burden to stand trial for a serious felony crime, such as murder or rape, the U.S. Constitution provides that before a person can be charged, the state must first prove to an impartial decision-making authority that there exists probable cause that the accused committed the crime and that there is sufficient evidence to try the person as charged. In about half the states and in the federal system, the decision is made via an **indictment** issued by a **grand jury**, which considers the case in a closed hearing during which only the prosecutor is permitted to present evidence. If sufficient facts are presented, the grand jury will issue a "true bill of indictment"; insufficient evidence will result in a "no bill." In the remaining states, a criminal **information** is filed before an impartial lower-court judge, who decides whether the case should go forward and be heard in a felony court. At this **preliminary hearing** (or probable cause hearing), the defendant is permitted to appear and dispute the prosecutor's charges. In both procedures, if the prosecution's evidence is found to be factual and sufficient, the suspect will be summoned to stand trial for his or her crime. (In misdemeanor cases, the term typically used in charging is "criminal complaint," an allegation made to a court in writing by either a victim or a police officer.)

7. *Arraignment.* At an **arraignment** the accused is brought before the court that will actually try the case. At this hearing, the formal charges are read, and defendants are informed of their constitutional rights (such as the right to legal counsel). Bail is considered, and a trial date is set.

8. *Bail or detention.* **Bail** is a money bond, the amount of which is set by judicial authority; it is intended to ensure the presence of suspects at trial, while allowing them their freedom until that time. Suspects who do not show up for trial forfeit their bail. Suspects who cannot afford bail or are considered too dangerous or too great a flight risk may be required to remain in detention until trial. Many jurisdictions now allow defendants awaiting trial to be released on their own **recognizance**, without bail, if they are stable members of the community.

9. *Plea bargaining.* After arraignment, it is common for the prosecutor to meet with the defendant and his or her attorney to discuss a possible **plea bargain**. If a bargain can be struck, the accused pleads guilty as charged, thus ending the criminal trial process. In return for the plea, the prosecutor may reduce charges, request a lenient sentence, or grant the defendant some other consideration. The public and the media tend to view plea bargains as contests in which defense attorneys use every legal trick in the book to get the best outcome for their clients, while prosecutors try to convince reluctant defendants or threaten them into "taking the deal," but the reality may be quite different. Research shows that plea bargaining reflects a degree of cooperation between prosecutors and defense attorneys; they work together in the vast majority of cases to achieve a favorable outcome.[25] Pleas bargains end the trial process in upwards of 90 percent of all cases, including serious felonies (see Exhibit 14.1).

10. *Adjudication.* If a plea bargain cannot be arranged, a criminal trial takes place. This involves a full-scale inquiry into the facts of the case before a judge, a jury, or both. The defendant can be found guilty or not guilty, or the jury can fail to reach a decision (**hung jury**), thereby leaving the case unresolved and open for a possible retrial. The fact that most Americans believe that every citizen is entitled to a fair trial, no matter what their financial or social status is the cornerstone of the justice process and a key element of the democratic system.

11. *Disposition.* After a criminal trial, a defendant who is found guilty as charged is sentenced by the presiding judge. **Disposition** usually involves a fine, a term of community supervision (probation), a period of incarceration in a penal institution, or some combination of these penalties. In the most states, it is also possible to sentence the offender to death. Dispositions are usually made after the sentencing judge considers evidence presented by the probation department, victim testimony, expert opinions, and the defendant's own statement at a

Although almost all cases are settled with a plea, a few proceed to a full-blown trial. What factors influence the decision to plead or not to plead?

- Court-appointed lawyers may want to gain trial experience. They convince their clients not to accept favorable bargains, fearing that the case will be settled out of court and they will lose the opportunity to try the case.

- Both the prosecution and the defense may be overly optimistic about their abilities and skills. Overconfidence in their abilities may cloud their judgment, causing them

either to refuse to offer a bargain in the case of the prosecution, or to refuse to accept in the case of the defense.

- Some defendants falsely assume they are so charismatic and appealing that a jury will never reach a conviction.

SOURCE: Stephanos Bibas, "Plea Bargaining outside the Shadow of Trial," *Harvard Law Review* 117 (2004): 2,464–2,543.

separate sentencing hearing. As Figure 14.8 shows, about two-thirds of all defendants convicted of felonies receive incarceration sentences. Of course, this means that many people convicted of serious criminal offenses, including murder and rape, are granted a community sentence—that is, probation.

12. *Postconviction remedies.* After conviction, if the defendant believes he or she was not treated fairly by the justice system, the individual may **appeal** the conviction. An appellate court reviews trial procedures to determine whether an error was made. Such issues as whether evidence was used properly, whether the judge conducted the trial in an approved fashion, whether the jury was representative, and whether the attorneys in the case acted appropriately may be the basis for an appeal. In most instances, if the appellate court rules in favor of the defendant, she or he is granted a new trial. Outright release can also be ordered if the state prosecuted the case in violation of the double jeopardy clause of the U.S. Constitution or if it violated the defendant's right to a speedy trial.

In some jurisdictions, arraignments have gone high-tech and defendants do not have to be in court to be arraigned. Here Tina Page (seated, right) is arraigned for a misdemeanor by videoconference in front of Kanawha County magistrate Jeanie Moore (left screen) without having to leave the South Central Regional Jail in Charleston, West Virginia. Assisting Page is corrections officer C. D. Fleming (left position on right screen) and First Sgt. R. E. Rogers (center of right screen).

13. *Correctional treatment.* Offenders who are found guilty and are formally sentenced come under the jurisdiction of correctional authorities. They may serve a term of community supervision under control of the county probation department; they may spend time in a community correctional center; or they may be incarcerated in a large penal institution.

14. *Release.* At the end of the correctional sentence, the offender is released into the community. Most incarcerated offenders are granted parole before the expiration of the maximum term given them by the court, and therefore they finish their prison sentences in the community under supervision of the parole department. Offenders sentenced to community supervision, if successful, simply finish their terms and resume their lives unsupervised by court authorities.

15. *Postrelease/aftercare.* After termination of correctional treatment, the offender must successfully return to the community. This adjustment is usually aided by

appeal
Taking a criminal case to a higher court on the grounds that the defendant was found guilty because of legal error or violation of his or her constitutional rights; a successful appeal may result in a new trial.

Figure 14.8 Felony Sentencing Outcomes in State Court
Over two-thirds of the felons convicted in state courts are sentenced to prison or jail.

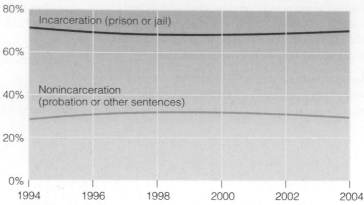

SOURCE: *Felony Sentences in State Courts, 2004,* www.ojp.usdoj.gov/bjs/glance/felpct.htm.

corrections department staff members, who attempt to counsel the offender through the period of reentry into society. The offender may be asked to spend some time in a community correctional center, which acts as a bridge between a secure treatment facility and absolute freedom. Offenders may find that their conviction has cost them some personal privileges, such as the right to hold certain kinds of jobs. These privileges may be restored by court order once the offenders have proved their trustworthiness and willingness to adjust to society's rules. Successful completion of the postrelease period marks the end of the criminal justice process.

DISCRETION AND THE CRIMINAL JUSTICE PROCESS

At every stage of the criminal justice process, an agency of criminal justice decides whether to send the case farther down the line or "kick it" from the system. An investigation may be pursued for a few days, and if a suspect is not identified, the case is dropped. A prosecutor may decide not to charge a person in police custody because he or she believes there is insufficient evidence to sustain a finding of guilt. A grand jury may fail to hand down an indictment because it finds that the prosecutor presented insufficient evidence. A jury may fail to convict the accused because it doubts his or her guilt. A parole board may decide to release one inmate but to deny another's request for early release. Decisions to proceed through trial may transform the identity of the individual passing through the system from an accused to a defendant, convicted criminal, inmate, and ex-con. Conversely, if decision makers take no action, people accused of crime can return to their daily lives with minimal interference in their lives or change in their identities. Their friends and neighbors may not even know that they were once the subject of criminal investigation.

Because decision making and discretion mark each stage of the system, the criminal justice process serves as a funnel in which a great majority of cases are screened out before trial. As Figure 14.9 shows, cases are dismissed at each stage of the system, and relatively few actually reach trial. Those that do are more likely to be handled with a plea bargain than with a criminal trial. The funnel indicates that the justice system does not treat all felonies alike; only the relatively few serious cases make it through to the end of the formal process.[26]

Figure 14.9 The Criminal Justice Funnel

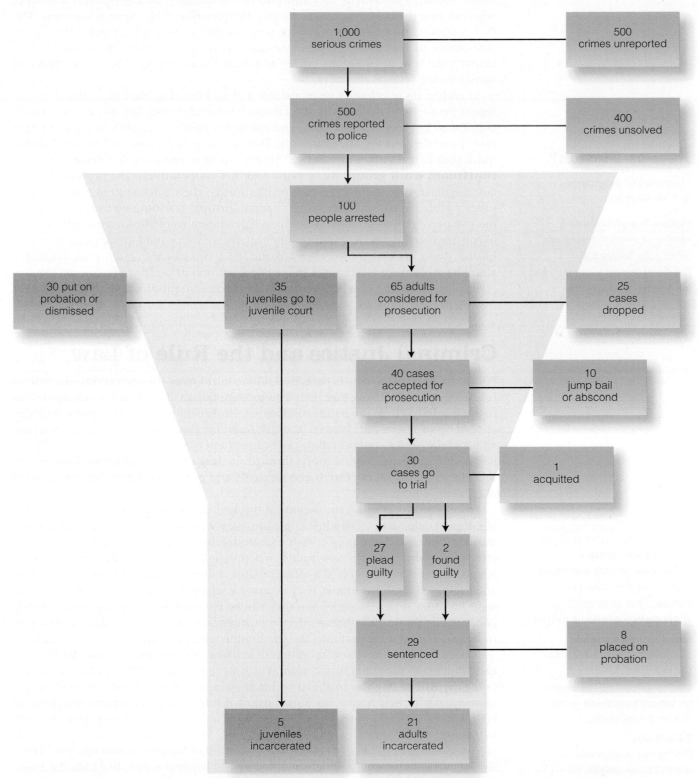

SOURCES: Tracey Kyckelhahn and Thomas H. Cohen, *Felony Defendants in Large Urban Counties, 2004* (Washington, DC: Bureau of Justice Statistics, 2008); Matthew Durose and Patrick Langan, *Felony Sentences in State Courts, 2004* (Washington, DC: Bureau of Justice Statistics, 2007)

COURTROOM WORK GROUP

Public perceptions about criminal justice are often formed on the basis of what happens in a few celebrated cases that receive widespread media attention. Some involve wealthy clients who can afford to be represented by high-power attorneys who can hire the best experts to convince the jury that their client is innocent. The O. J. Simpson murder case remains the best example of the celebrity defendant. Other defendants, such as Scott Peterson, become celebrities when they are accused of particularly heinous or notorious crimes and draw the attention of both the press and accomplished defense attorneys.

In reality, these celebrity cases are few and far between. Most defendants are indigent people who cannot afford a comprehensive defense. The system is actually dominated by judges, prosecutors, and public defenders who work in concert to get cases processed quickly and efficiently. Trials are rare; most cases are handled with a quick plea bargain and sentencing. This pattern of cooperation is referred to as the **courtroom work group**. By working together cooperatively, the prosecution and defense make sure that the cases flowing through the justice system proceed in an orderly and effective manner. Such "bargain justice" is estimated to occur in more than 90 percent of all criminal cases. If each defendant were afforded the full measure of constitutional rights, including a jury trial, the system would quickly become overloaded. Court dockets are too crowded and funds too scarce to grant each defendant a full share of justice.[27] Although the criminal court system is founded on the concept of equality before the law, poor and wealthy citizens unquestionably receive different treatment when they are accused of crimes.

Criminal Justice and the Rule of Law

For many years, U.S. courts exercised little control over the operations of criminal justice agencies, believing that their actions were not an area of judicial concern. This policy is referred to as the hands-off doctrine. However, in the 1960s, under the guidance of Chief Justice Earl Warren, the U.S. Supreme Court became more active in the affairs of the justice system. Today, each component of the justice system is closely supervised by state and federal courts through the **law of criminal procedure**, which sets out and guarantees citizens certain rights and privileges when they are accused of crime.

Procedural law controls the actions of the agencies of justice and define the rights of criminal defendants. They first come into play when people are suspected of committing crimes and the police wish to investigate them, search their property, or interrogate them. Here the law dictates whether police can search the homes of or interrogate unwilling suspects. If a formal charge is filed, procedural laws guide pretrial and trial activities; for example, they determine when and whether people can obtain state-financed attorneys and when they can be released on bail. If a person is found guilty of committing a criminal offense, procedural laws guide the posttrial and correctional processes; for example, they determine when a conviction can be appealed.

Procedural laws have several different sources. Most important are the first ten amendments to the U.S. Constitution, which were ratified in 1791 and are generally called the **Bill of Rights**. Included within these amendments are the right of people to be secure in their homes from unwarranted intrusion by government agents, to be free from self-incrimination, and to be protected against cruel punishments, such as torture.

The guarantees of freedom contained in the Bill of Rights initially applied only to the federal government and did not affect the individual states. In 1868, the Fourteenth Amendment made the first ten amendments to the Constitution binding on the state governments. However, it has remained the duty of state and federal court systems to interpret constitutional law and develop a body of case law that spells out the exact procedural rights to which a person is entitled. Thus, it is the U.S. Supreme Court that interprets the Constitution and sets out the procedural laws that must be

courtroom work group
Prosecution, defense, and judges working together to resolve criminal cases quickly and efficiently through plea bargaining.

law of criminal procedure
Judicial precedents that define and guarantee the rights of criminal defendants and control the various components of the criminal justice system.

Bill of Rights
The first ten amendments to the U.S. Constitution, including guarantees against unreasonable search and seizure, self-incrimination, and cruel punishment.

followed by the lower federal and state courts. If the Supreme Court has not ruled on a procedural issue, the lower courts are free to interpret the Constitution as they see fit.

Today, procedural rights protect defendants from illegal searches and seizures and from overly aggressive police interrogations. According to the **exclusionary rule**, illegally seized evidence cannot be used during a trial. This procedure is illustrated by an important 2009 case, *Arizona v. Gant*. Rodney Gant, a motorist, was arrested for driving with a suspended license, handcuffed, and put in the back of a patrol car.[28] Police officers then searched his car and discovered cocaine in the pocket of a jacket on the back seat. He was sentenced to three years in prison. But Gant appealed, arguing that the search was unconstitutional because he posed no threat to the officers after he was handcuffed in the patrol car. The state argued that the search was legal under a previous Supreme Court decision, *New York v. Belton* (453 U.S. 454), that allowed a vehicle search after an occupant was arrested, even though the arrestee was outside his vehicle at the time of the search. However, the U.S. Supreme Court ruled that because Gant could not have accessed his car to retrieve weapons or evidence at the time of the search, the case differed from *Belton*, in which the defendant might have been able to access the car and retrieve a weapon. Therefore, the evidence in *Gant* was excluded from trial. This ruling illustrates one of the ways in which the Supreme Court can shape the operations of the justice system. ▶ **Checkpoints**

Checkpoints

▶ The criminal justice process can be best understood as a series of decision points.

▶ At each stage of the system, a decision is reached whether to process an offender to the next stage or terminate the case.

▶ Although a few celebrity cases receive the full range of justice procedures, most cases are handled in a cursory fashion and are settled with a plea bargain.

▶ The justice system is bound by the rule of law, which ensures that criminal defendants are protected from violations of their civil rights.

Concepts of Justice

Many justice system operations are controlled by the rule of law, but they are also influenced by the various philosophies or viewpoints held by its practitioners and policymakers. These, in turn, have been influenced by criminological theory and research. Knowledge about crime, its causes, and its control has significantly affected perceptions of how criminal justice should be managed.

Not surprisingly, many competing views of justice exist simultaneously in U.S. culture. Those in favor of one position or another try to win public opinion to their side, hoping to influence legislative, judicial, or administrative decision making. Over the years, different philosophical viewpoints tend to predominate for a while, only to fall into disfavor as programs based on their principles fail to prove effective.

The remainder of this chapter briefly discusses the most important concepts of criminal justice.

CRIME CONTROL MODEL

Those who support the **crime control model** believe that the overriding purpose of the justice system is to protect the public, deter people from engaging in criminal behavior, and incapacitate known criminals. People want protection from dangerous criminals and expect the government to do what is necessary—punish criminals so that the public feels secure. Crime control is assumed to be part of the democratic process.[29]

Those who embrace its principles view the justice system as a barrier between destructive criminal elements and conventional society. Speedy, efficient justice, unencumbered by legal red tape and followed by punishment designed to fit the crime, is the goal of advocates of the crime control model. Its disciples promote such policies as increasing the size of police forces, maximizing the use of discretion, building more prisons, using the death penalty, and reducing legal controls on the justice system. Police departments, they would argue, would be more effective crime fighters if they employed a proactive, aggressive law enforcement style, improved their response time (the time it takes them to respond to a criminal incident), and increased the number of officers on patrol in the community.[30]

One impediment to effective crime control is the legal roadblocks set up by the courts to protect the due process rights of criminal defendants. Thousand of criminals go free every year in cases that are dropped because police officers violated the

exclusionary rule
The rule that evidence against a defendant may not be presented in court if it was obtained in violation of the defendant's rights.

crime control model
View that the overriding purpose of the justice system is to protect the public, deter people from criminal behavior, and incapacitate known criminals; favors speedy, efficient justice and punishment.

suspects' right to remain silent or failed to remind suspects that they have the right to an attorney during police interrogations—protections known as the suspects' **Miranda rights**.[31] Crime control advocates lobby for abolition of the exclusionary rule, which requires that illegally seized evidence be barred from criminal proceedings. Their voice has been heard: A more conservative Supreme Court has given police greater latitude to search for and seize evidence and has eased restrictions on how police operate. In this permissive environment, it is not surprising to find research showing that police routinely violate suspects' rights when searching for evidence.[32]

The crime control philosophy emphasizes protecting society and compensating victims. The criminal is responsible for his or her actions, has broken faith with society, and has chosen to violate the law for reasons such as anger, greed, or revenge. Therefore, money spent should be directed not at making criminals more comfortable but at increasing the efficiency of police in apprehending them, of the courts in trying them effectively, and of the corrections system in meting out criminal punishment. This last element of justice is critical, because punishment symbolizes the legitimate social order and the power societies have to regulate behavior and punish those who break social rules.[33]

The crime control philosophy has become a dominant force in U.S. justice. A number of important reviews claimed that treatment and rehabilitation efforts directed at known criminals just do not work.[34] There is more evidence that most criminals recidivate after their release from prison and that their reentry into society can destabilize the neighborhoods to which they return. Therefore, a get-tough approach is the only way to control crime.

The lack of clear evidence that criminals can be successfully treated has produced a climate in which conservative, hard-line solutions to the crime problem are being sought. The results of this swing can be seen in such phenomena as increasing use of the death penalty, erosion of the exclusionary rule, prison overcrowding, and attacks on the insanity defense. In the past few years, a number of states (including Tennessee, Utah, Iowa, Ohio, and West Virginia) have changed their juvenile codes, making it easier to try juveniles as adults. Other states have expanded their control over ex-offenders by requiring registration of sex offenders. And although efforts to abolish the death penalty have succeeded in a number of states (such as New York and Illinois), other states have expanded the circumstances under which a person may be eligible for the death penalty.[35]

Can such measures deter crime? Crime control advocates point to one fact they claim is indisputable: As the number of people behind bars has increased, crime rates have decreased, proving that getting tough on crime can have an appreciable beneficial effect.

DUE PROCESS MODEL

In *The Limits of the Criminal Sanction*, Herbert Packer contrasted the crime control model with an opposing view that he refers to as the **due process model**.[36] According to Packer, the due process model combines elements of liberal/positivist criminology with the legal concept of procedural fairness for the accused. Those who adhere to due process principles believe in individualized justice, legal protections, and civil rights. If discretion exists in the criminal justice system, it should be used to evaluate the treatment of offenders by police agents. Most important, the civil rights of the accused should be protected at all costs. This emphasis calls for strict scrutiny of police search and interrogation procedures, review of sentencing policies, and development of prisoners' rights.

Advocates of the due process model have demanded that competent defense counsel, jury trials, and other procedural safeguards be offered to every criminal defendant. They have also called for making public the operations of the justice system and imposing controls over its discretionary power.

Due process advocates see themselves as protectors of a criminal suspect's rights. They view overzealous police as violators of basic constitutional rights. They are skeptical about the intentions of social workers, whose treatments often entail

CONNECTIONS

The crime control model is rooted in choice theory, discussed in Chapter 4. Fear of criminal sanctions is viewed as the primary deterrent to crime. Because criminals are rational and choose to commit crime, it stands to reason that their activities can be controlled if the costs of crime become too high. Swift, sure, and efficient justice is considered an essential element of an orderly society.

Miranda rights
Rights of criminal defendants, including the right against self-incrimination and the right to counsel, spelled out in the case of *Miranda v. Arizona*.

due process model
View that focuses on protecting the civil rights of those accused of crime.

greater confinement and penalties than punishment does. Their concern is magnified by data showing that poor and minority group members are often maltreated in the criminal justice system. In some jurisdictions, such as Washington, DC, nearly half of all African American young men are under the control of the justice system. Is it possible that this reflects racism, discrimination, and a violation of their civil rights?[37] Research shows that in at least some states, African Americans are more likely to be sent to prison than European Americans; these racial differences in the incarceration rate cannot be explained by the fact that blacks are arrested more often than whites.[38] The accompanying Race, Culture, Gender, and Criminology feature explores the issue of racial discrimination in the sentencing process.

Due process exists to protect citizens—both from those who wish to punish them and from those who wish to treat them without regard for their legal and civil rights. Advocates of the due process model worry about the government's expanding ability to use computers to intrude into people's private lives. In 1996, for example, the federal government announced plans for a computerized registry of sex offenders; there are plans for nationwide computer-based mug shot and fingerprint systems. These measures can erode privacy and civil liberties, although research shows that they may have relatively little impact on controlling crime.[39]

What is the true meaning of due process? Here, on January 28, 2009, inmate David Miles, who claims it nearly triggered a riot when he was assigned to what traditionally had been a Hispanic bunk at the Sierra Conservation Center, is seen sitting on his bunk at the facility in Jamestown, California. Despite efforts by California prison officials to end one of the nation's last vestiges of institutionalized, government-mandated racial segregation, powerful race-based gangs violently oppose attempts to desegregate prison housing units. Is it simply prudent to house inmates on the basis of ethnicity and race? Or is this practice a violation of due process of law?

Advocates of the due process orientation are quick to point out that the justice system remains an adversary process that pits the forces of an all-powerful state against those of a solitary individual accused of crime. If an overriding concern for justice and fairness did not exist, the defendant who lacked resources could easily be overwhelmed. Take, for instance, the right to a fair trial guaranteed by the Sixth Amendment. This right is a cornerstone of the justice process, and yet receiving a fair trial is getting increasingly difficult because finding impartial jurors, especially in this age of instant media coverage, is becoming impossible. For many cases, most potential jurors have read or heard about the case on an overabundance of cable TV and Internet news sources. And even after they are seated on the jury, the problem does not end. They are able to turn to their BlackBerrys and iPhones to seek information about almost *any* case. They can Google the defendant and witnesses on the Internet, go to Facebook, and share information not presented at trial with other jurors. Even though they are expressly forbidden to do this, one commentator notes that the practice is "wreaking havoc on trials around the country, upending deliberations and infuriating judges."[40] There is no officially tally of the number of cases compromised by jurors' Internet research, but the number is certainly growing. One Florida case involving illegally selling prescription drugs was upended because jurors researched the case on their own and were able to discover information not presented at trial. After their actions came to light, the judge had no choice but to declare a mistrial.[41] Due process advocates are concerned about these events and how they will affect the future of the jury trial.

Nothing is more disturbing to due process advocates than an innocent person being found guilty. They point to miscarriages of justice such as the case of Jeffrey Blake, who went to prison for a double murder in 1991 and spent seven years behind bars before his conviction was overturned in 1998. The prosecution's star witness conceded

Critics of American race relations may think otherwise, but research on sentencing has failed to show a definitive pattern of racial discrimination. Although some research does indicate that a defendant's race has a direct impact on sentencing outcomes, other efforts show that the influence of race on sentencing is less clear-cut than anticipated. In fact, as John Wooldredge has found recently, in some contexts minority group members actually get lesser sentences than whites. It is possible that the disproportionate number of minority group members in prison is a result of crime and arrest patterns, not of racial bias by judges when they hand out criminal sentences. Racial and ethnic minorities commit more crime, the argument goes, and

- African Americans receive longer sentences for drug crimes than whites because (1) they are more likely to be arrested for crack possession and sales, and (2) crack dealing is more severely punished by state and federal laws than other drug crimes.

It is also possible that some research efforts miss a racial effect because they use invalid measures of race. Some may combine Anglo and Hispanic cases into a single category of "white" defendants and then compare them with the sentencing of black defendants. Darrell Steffensmeier and Stephen Demuth's analysis of sentencing in Pennsylvania found that Hispanics are punished considerably more

Race, Culture, Gender, and Criminology
Does Racial Bias Exist in Criminal Sentencing?

therefore they are more likely to constitute a disproportionate share of the prison population.

Why does the critical issue of racial disparity remain so murky? One reason may be that if disparity is a factor in sentencing, its cause may lie outside of judicial sentencing practices. Consider the following:

- African Americans are more likely to be detained before trial than whites.

- Prosecutors are less likely to divert minorities from the legal system than they are whites.

- Minorities have less money for bail and private attorneys.

- Minorities live in poor communities, and people living in poor areas get harsher sentences, regardless of their race.

severely than non-Hispanic Anglos and that combining the two groups masks the ethnic differences in sentencing.

Where Race and Sentencing Collide

The relationship between race and sentencing may be difficult to establish because of external factors that shroud the association. Race may have an impact on sentencing because some race-specific crimes are punished more harshly than others. African Americans receive longer sentences for drug crimes than Anglos because, as noted above, (1) they are more likely to be arrested for crack possession and sales, and (2) crack dealing is more severely punished by state and federal laws than other drug crimes. Because whites are more likely to use marijuana and methamphetamines, prosecutors are more willing to plea-bargain and offer shorter jail terms.

that he had lied on the stand, forcing Blake to spend a quarter of his life in prison for a crime he did not commit.[42] His wrongful conviction would have been even more tragic if he had been executed for his alleged crime. What can prevent wrongful convictions? Having an attorney who puts on a spirited defense may mean the difference between life and death. Research by Talia Roitberg Harmon and William Lofquist, which compared (1) people who had been falsely convicted of murder and were later exonerated with (2) people who were most likely innocent but had been executed, found that the exonerated defendants employed private defense attorneys who were able to present a robust defense at trial.[43] Is it fair that a life-or-death outcome may rest on the ability to afford private counsel?

rehabilitation model
View that criminals are victims of social injustice, poverty, and racism and that appropriate treatment can change them into productive, law-abiding citizens.

REHABILITATION MODEL

The **rehabilitation model** embraces the idea that given the proper care and treatment, criminals can be changed into productive, law-abiding citizens. Influenced by positivist criminology, the rehabilitation school suggests that people commit crimes

The Victim's Race Is the Key

Racial bias has also been linked to victim–offender status. Minority defendants are sanctioned more severely if their victim is white than if their target is a fellow minority group member; minorities who kill whites are more likely to get the death penalty than those who kill other minorities. Judges may base sentencing decisions on the race of the victim and not the race of the defendant.

Financial Effects

Racial status influences sentencing partly because minority group members have a lower income than whites and are more likely to be unemployed. Being poor also affects sentencing in other ways. Defendants who can afford bail receive more lenient sentences than those who remain in pretrial detention; minority defendants are less likely to make bail because they suffer a higher degree of income inequality. Sentencing outcome is also affected by the defendant's ability to afford a private attorney and mount a vigorous legal defense that makes use of high-paid expert witnesses.

Thus, even though efforts to limit racial disparity have been ongoing, research studies still find that on many occasions, minorities receive longer sentences and more punitive treatment than white defendants who are convicted of committing similar crimes. Whatever the cause, the effects can be devastating. As Bruce Western warns, by marginalizing and incarcerating so many African American men, whole communities are being destabilized. And doing prison time can turn minor offenders into hardened criminals, undermining any chance of rehabilitation and later opportunities. The prison boom, Western writes, "may be a self-defeating strategy for crime control."

CRITICAL THINKING

Do you feel that sentences should be influenced by the fact that one ethnic or racial group is more likely to commit that crime? For example, federal sentencing guidelines have been changed to reduce the provisions that punish crack possession more heavily than possession of powdered cocaine because of complaints that the law discriminated against African Americans who are more likely to use crack (while whites are more likely to use powdered cocaine). Do you approve of such a change? Remember, because of the lingering problem of racial and class bias in the sentencing process, one primary goal of the criminal justice system in the 1990s was to reduce disparity by creating new forms of criminal sentences that limit judicial discretion and are aimed at achieving uniformity and fairness.

SOURCES: John Wooldredge, "Neighborhood Effects on Felony Sentencing," *Journal of Research in Crime and Delinquency* 44 (2007): 238–263; Bruce Western, *Punishment and Inequality in America* (New York: Russell Sage Foundation, 2006). Sara Steen, Rodney Engen, and Randy Gainey, "Images of Danger and Culpability: Racial Stereotyping, Case Processing, and Criminal Sentencing," *Criminology* 43 (2005): 435–468; Stephanie Bontrager, William Bales, and Ted Chiricos, "Race, Ethnicity, Threat, and the Labeling of Convicted Felons," *Criminology* 43 (2005): 589–622; Pauline Brennan, "Sentencing Female Misdemeanants: An Examination of the Direct and Indirect Effects of Race/Ethnicity," *Justice Quarterly* 23 (2006): 60–95; Mitchell Ojmarrh, "A Meta-Analysis of Race and Sentencing Research: Explaining the Inconsistencies," *Journal of Quantitative Criminology* 21 (2005): 439–466; Shawn Bushway and Anne Morrison Piehl, "Judging Judicial Discretion: Legal Factors and Racial Discrimination in Sentencing," *Law and Society Review* 35 (2001): 733–765; Barbara Koons-Witt, "The Effect of Gender on the Decision to Incarcerate before and after the Introduction of Sentencing Guidelines," *Criminology* 40 (2002): 97–129; Marian R. Williams and Jefferson E. Holcomb, "Racial Disparity and Death Sentences in Ohio," *Journal of Criminal Justice* 29 (2001): 207–218; Rodney Engen and Randy Gainey, "Modeling the Effects of Legally Relevant and Extra-legal Factors under Sentencing Guidelines: The Rules Have Changed," *Criminology* 38 (2000) 1,207–1,230; Darrell Steffensmeier and Stephen Demuth, "Ethnicity and Judges' Sentencing Decisions: Hispanic-Black-White Comparisons," *Criminology* 39 (2001): 145–178; Tracy Nobiling, Cassia Spohn, and Miriam DeLone, "A Tale of Two Counties: Unemployment and Sentence Severity," *Justice Quarterly* 15 (1998): 459–486;

through no fault of their own. Instead, criminals themselves are the victims of social injustice, poverty, and racism; their acts are a response to a society that has betrayed them. And because of their disturbed and impoverished upbringing, they may be suffering psychological problems and personality disturbances that further enhance their crime-committing capabilities. Although the general public wants protection from crime, the argument goes, it also favors programs designed to help unfortunate people who commit crime because of emotional or social problems.[44]

Dealing effectively with crime requires attacking its root causes. Funds must be devoted to equalizing access to conventional means of success. This requires supporting such programs as public assistance, educational opportunity, and job training. When individuals run afoul of the law, efforts should be made to treat them, not punish them, by emphasizing counseling and psychological care in community-based treatment programs. Whenever possible, offenders should be placed on probation in halfway houses or in other rehabilitation-oriented programs.

This view of the justice system portrays it as a method for dispensing "treatment" to needy "patients." Also known as the medical model, it portrays offenders as

From the rehabilitation model perspective, even the most hardened criminal may be helped by effective institutional treatment plans and services. Here, prison inmate Stephanie Walker works with her Labrador retriever puppy "Gage" during guide dog training at Metro State Prison in Atlanta, Georgia. The IMPACT program (Inmates Providing Animal Care and Training) teams inmates with puppies provided by Southeastern Guide Dog, Inc., for a 16-month program of training with a volunteer obedience instructor. The Georgia Department of Corrections then returns the dogs for advanced training, ultimately providing guide dogs to people with impaired vision.

CONNECTIONS

The rehabilitation model is linked to social structure and social process theories because it assumes that if lifestyle and socialization could be improved, crime rates would decline. See Chapters 6 and 7 for more on these theories.

equal justice model
View that emphasizes fairness and equal treatment in criminal procedures and sentencing.

people who, because they have failed to exercise self-control, need the help of the state. The medical model rejects the crime control philosophy on the grounds that it ignores the needs of offenders, who are people whom society has failed to help.

Research evidence suggests that some criminal justice–based treatment programs can have an important influence on offenders.[45] Given the proper treatment, offenders can significantly lower their rates of recidivism.[46] Community intervention programs have had significant success with drug offenders.[47] Programs that teach interpersonal skills and use individual counseling and behavioral modification techniques have produced positive results both in the community and within correctional institutions.[48] And although some politicians call for a strict law-and-order approach, the general public is quite supportive of treatment programs such as early childhood intervention and services for at-risk children.[49]

EQUAL JUSTICE MODEL

According to the **equal justice model**, it is futile to rehabilitate criminals, both because treatment programs are ineffective and because they deny people equal protection under the law.[50] It is unfair when two people commit the same crime but receive different sentences because only one is receptive to treatment. The consequence is a sense of injustice in the criminal justice system.

Beyond these problems, advocates of the equal justice model question the crime control perspective's reliance on deterrence. Is it fair to punish or incarcerate based on predictions of what offenders will do in the future or on whether their punishment will deter others from committing crime? Advocates of the equal justice model are also concerned with unfairness in the system, such as racism and discrimination that causes sentencing disparity and unequal treatment before the law.[51]

As an alternative, the equal justice model calls for fairness in criminal procedure. This would require **determinate sentencing**, in which all offenders in a particular crime category would receive the same sentence. Prisons would be viewed as places of just, evenhanded punishment, not rehabilitation. Discretionary parole would be abolished and replaced with mandatory release dates in order to avoid any unfairness associated with that mechanism of early release.

The equal justice model has had an important influence on criminal justice policy. Some states have adopted determinate sentencing statutes and have limited the use of parole. There is a trend toward giving prison sentences because people deserve punishment rather than because the sentences will rehabilitate them or deter others.

NONINTERVENTION MODEL

In the late 1960s and 1970s, both the rehabilitation ideal and the due process movement were viewed suspiciously by experts concerned about the stigmatization of offenders. Regardless of the purpose, the more the government intervenes in the lives of people, the greater the harm done to their future behavior patterns. Once arrested and labeled, the offender is placed at a disadvantage at home, at school, and in the job market.[52] Rather than deterring such individuals from committing crime, the stigma of a criminal label erodes their social capital and jeopardizes their future success and achievement.

The **nonintervention model** calls for limiting government intrusion into the lives of people (especially minors) who run afoul of the law.[53] Noninterventionists advocate deinstitutionalization of nonserious offenders, diversion from formal court processes into informal treatment programs, and decriminalization of nonserious offenses, such as possessing small amounts of marijuana. Under this concept, the justice system should interact as little as possible with offenders. Police, courts, and correctional agencies would concentrate their efforts on diverting law violators out of the formal justice system, thereby helping them avoid the stigma of formal labels such as "delinquent" or "ex-con." Programs instituted under this model include mediation (instead of trial), diversion (instead of formal processing), and community-based corrections (instead of secure corrections).

Nonintervention advocates are also skeptical about the creation of laws that criminalize acts that were previously legal, thus expanding the reach of justice and creating new classes of offenders. An example is the growing popularity of expanding control over youthful offenders by passing local curfew laws that make it a crime for young people to be out at night after a certain hour, such as 11:00 P.M. An adolescent who was formerly a night owl is now a criminal![54]

There are many examples of nonintervention ideas in practice. The juvenile justice system has made a major effort to remove youths from adult jails and to reduce the use of pretrial detention. Mediation programs have proved successful alternatives to the formal trial process. In the adult system, pretrial release programs (alternatives to bail) are now the norm instead of an experimental innovation. And although the prison population is rising, probation and community treatment have become the most common forms of criminal sanction.

The noninterventionist philosophy also has its critics. There is little evidence that alternative programs reduce recidivism. Some critics charge that alternative programs actually result in "widening the net."[55] That is, efforts to remove people from the justice system enmesh them further within it by ordering them to spend more time in treatment than they would have had to spend in the formal legal process.

In the future, the appeal of the nonintervention philosophy will be aided by the rising cost of justice. Although low-impact, nonintrusive programs may work no better than prison, they are certainly cheaper, and program costs may receive greater consideration than program effectiveness.

determinate sentencing
The principle that all offenders who commit the same crime should receive the same sentence.

nonintervention model
View that arresting and labeling offenders does more harm than good, that youthful offenders in particular should be diverted into informal treatment programs, and that minor offenses should be decriminalized.

Perspective on Justice	Main Beliefs
Crime Control Perspective	• The purpose of the justice system is to deter crime through the application of punishment. • The more efficient the system, the greater its effectiveness.
Rehabilitation Perspective	• In the long run, it is better to treat than to punish. • Helping others is part of the American culture.
Due Process Perspective	• Every person deserves the full array of constitutional rights and privileges. • Because of potential errors, decisions made within the justice system must be carefully reviewed.
Nonintervention Perspective	• The justice process stigmatizes offenders. • Less is better. Decriminalize, divert, and deinstitutionalize whenever possible.
Equal Justice Perspective	• People should receive equal treatment for equal crimes. • Whenever possible, individual discretion must be reduced and controlled.
Restorative Justice Perspective	• Offenders should be reintegrated into society. • The justice system must become more humane.

RESTORATIVE JUSTICE MODEL

Some justice scholars believe that the true purpose of the criminal justice system is to promote a peaceful, just society; they advocate peacemaking, not punishment.[56] This vision has become known as restorative justice.

The **restorative justice model** draws its inspiration from religious and philosophical teachings ranging from Quakerism to Zen. Advocates of restorative justice say that state efforts to punish and control encourage crime. The violent punishing acts of the state, they claim, are not unlike the violent acts of individuals.[57] Whereas the advocates of crime control associate lower crime rates with increased punishment, restorative justice advocates counter that punitive methods of correction (such as jail) are no more effective than more humanitarian efforts (such as probation with treatment).[58] Therefore, mutual aid rather than coercive punishment is the key to a harmonious society. Without the capacity to restore damaged social relations, society's response to crime has been almost exclusively punitive.

Restorative justice is guided by three essential principles: (1) community "ownership" of conflict (including crime), (2) material and symbolic reparation for crime victims, and (3) social reintegration of the offender.[59] Maintaining ownership, or jurisdiction, over the conflict means that the conflict between criminal and victim should be resolved in the community in which it originated, not in some faraway prison. The victim should be given a chance to voice his or her story, and the offender should help compensate the victim financially or by providing some service. The goal is to enable the offender to appreciate the damage caused, to make amends, and to be reintegrated into society.

Restorative justice programs are geared to these principles. The ability of police officers to mediate disputes rather than resort to formal arrest has long been recognized; it is an essential element of community policing.[60] Mediation and conflict resolution programs are now common in efforts to resolve harmful human interactions ranging from domestic violence to hate crimes.[61] Financial and community-service restitution programs as an alternative to imprisonment have been in operation for more than two decades.

Although restorative justice has become an important perspective in recent years, there are so many diverse programs calling themselves "restorative" that there is still

CONNECTIONS

The basis of restorative justice was reviewed in Chapter 8, on critical criminology.

restorative justice model
View that emphasizes the promotion of a peaceful, just society through reconciliation and reintegration of the offender into society.

no single definition of what constitutes restorative justice.[62] Restorative justice programs must also be aware of the cultural and social differences that can be found throughout our heterogeneous society. What may be considered restorative in one subculture may be considered insulting and damaging in another.[63]

CONCEPTS OF JUSTICE TODAY

The various philosophies of justice compete today for dominance in the criminal justice system. See Concept Summary 14.1.

Each perspective has supporters who lobby diligently for their positions. At the time of this writing, it seems that the crime control and equal justice models have captured the support of legislators and the general public. There is a growing emphasis on protecting the public by increasing criminal sentences and swelling prison populations.[64] Yet the association between adoption of crime control programs and reduction in the crime rate may be misleading. It is possible that the crime rate is merely undergoing a natural pull-back from the abnormally high, unprecedented increases brought about by the crack cocaine epidemic in the 1980s; if so, the success of get-tough crime control programs may be illusory. Locking more and more people up may have a harmful effect in the long run: Most offenders eventually return to society, and most eventually reoffend. Their chances of success in the legitimate world have, if anything, been severely diminished by their prison experiences. As rehabilitation advocates suggest, punishment may produce short-term reductions in the crime rate, but only rehabilitation and treatment can produce long-term improvement.

Therefore, despite the demand for punishing serious, chronic offenders, the door to treatment for nonviolent, nonchronic offenders has not been closed. The number of nonintervention and restorative justice programs featuring restitution and nonpunitive sanctions is growing. As the cost of justice skyrockets and the correctional system becomes increasingly overcrowded, alternatives such as house arrest, electronic monitoring, intensive probation supervision, and other cost-effective programs have come to the forefront. ▶ Checkpoints

Checkpoints

▶ The U.S. Supreme Court maintains legal control over the justice system through its application of the Bill of Rights.

▶ There are a number of models of justice.

▶ The most conservative view is the crime control model, which holds that the justice system is designed to protect the public and deter people from engaging in criminal behavior.

▶ In contrast, the rehabilitation model holds that the justice system can help treat needy people and help them turn their lives around.

▶ Advocates of the equal justice model believe that the system must be on the lookout for disparate or unequal treatment.

▶ The restorative justice model holds that the justice system is an ideal venue for reconciliation and healing.

▶ The due process model is concerned with providing and protecting civil rights.

▶ The nonintervention model focuses on limiting stigma and negative labels.

Thinking Like a Criminologist

You have been appointed assistant to the president's drug czar, who is in charge of coordinating the nation's drug control policy. She has asked you to develop a plan to reduce drug abuse by 25 percent within three years.

You realize that multiple perspectives of justice exist and that the agencies of the criminal justice system can apply a number of different strategies to reduce drug trafficking and the use of drugs. It might be possible to control the drug trade through a strict crime control effort—for example, using law enforcement officers to cut off supplies of drugs by destroying crops and arresting members of drug cartels in drug-producing countries. Border patrols and military personnel armed with sophisticated hardware could also help prevent drugs from entering the country.

According to the equal justice model, if drug violations were punished with criminal sentences commensurate with their harm, then the rational drug trafficker might look for a new line of employment. The adoption of mandatory sentences for drug crimes to ensure that all offenders receive similar punishment for their acts might reduce crime. The rehabilitation model suggests that strategies should be aimed at reducing the desire to use drugs and at increasing incentives for users to eliminate substance abuse. A nonintervention strategy might call for the legalization of drugs so that distribution could be controlled by the government. Crime rates would be cut because drug users would no longer need the same cash flow to support their habit.

Writing Assignment

Considering these different approaches, write an essay on how you would you shape drug control policy. Discuss both the strategies you think might work and those that are doomed to failure.

Summary

1. Discuss the formation of the criminal justice system.

   There was little in the way of a formal criminal justice system until the nineteenth century when the first police agencies were created. The term "criminal justice system" became prominent around 1967, when the President's Commission on Law Enforcement and the Administration of Justice launched a nationwide study of the nation's crime problem. Criminal justice is a field that uses knowledge from various disciplines in an attempt to understand what causes people to commit crimes and how to deal with the crime problem.

2. Discuss the role of police and law enforcement.

   Law enforcement agencies are charged with peacekeeping, deterring potential criminals, and apprehending law violators. The traditional police role involved maintaining order through patrolling public streets and highways, but it has gradually expanded to include a variety of human service functions, which range from preventing youth crime and diverting juvenile offenders from the criminal justice system to resolving family conflicts.

3. Be familiar with the structure and function of the criminal court system.

   The court is a complex social agency with many independent but interrelated subsystems. It is also the scene of many important elements of criminal justice decision making. Within the criminal court system, the entire process is governed by precise rules of law designed to ensure fairness. The prosecutor and defense attorney are opponents in what is known as the adversary system.

4. Be familiar with the various elements and institutions of the correctional system.

   Probation is a legal disposition that allows the convicted offender to remain in the community, subject to conditions imposed by court order, under the supervision of a probation officer. Criminal defendants sentenced to a year or less for misdemeanors are typically held in jails, which are also used to detain those awaiting trial. State and federally operated facilities that hold felony offenders are called prisons or penitentiaries. Most inmates are released back into the community via parole.

5. Understand the size and scope of the contemporary justice system.

   The contemporary criminal justice system in the United States is monumental in size. Administering civil and criminal justice now costs federal, state, and local governments more than $200 billion per year. The criminal justice system employs more than 2 million people. The system is massive because it must process, treat, and care for millions of people. More than 14 million people are still being arrested each year. There are more than 7 million people in the correctional system.

6. Trace the formal criminal justice process.

   The process consists of the actual steps the offender takes from the initial investigation through trial, sentencing, and appeal. The justice process includes 15 stages, each of which is a *decision point* through which cases flow. Each of these decisions can have a critical effect on the defendant, the justice system, and society.

7. Know what is meant by the term "criminal justice assembly line."

   Some experts believe that the justice system processes cases in a routine, ritualized manner resembling an assembly line. Because justice is often dispensed in a hasty fashion, an innocent person may suffer or a dangerous individual may be released to continue to prey upon society. The system acts as a "funnel": Most people who commit crime escape detection, and of those who do not, relatively few are bound over for trial, convicted, and eventually sentenced to prison.

8. Discuss the role of discretion in the criminal justice system.

   At every stage of the criminal justice process, discretion is used by criminal justice agencies and officials, who must decide whether to send the case farther down the line or "kick it" from the system. These decisions can transform the individual passing through the system from an accused to a defendant, convicted criminal, inmate, and ex-con. In many cases, criminal justice agents work together to settle the case, even though they are supposedly adversaries.

9. Understand the role of law in the criminal justice system.

   Today, each component of the justice system is closely supervised by state and federal courts through the law of criminal procedure, which sets out and guarantees citizens certain rights and privileges when they are accused of crime. Procedural laws control the actions of the agencies of justice and define the rights of criminal defendants. Procedural laws have several different sources. Most important are the first ten amendments to the U.S. Constitution, which were ratified in 1791 and are generally called the Bill of Rights. Included within these amendments are the rights of the people to be secure in their homes from unwarranted intrusion by government agents, to be free from self-incrimination, and to be protected against cruel punishments, such as torture.

10. Be familiar with the various perspectives on justice.

    The role of criminal justice can be interpreted in many ways. People who study the field or work in its agencies bring their own ideas and feelings to bear when they try to decide on the right course of action to take or recommend. Thus, there are a number of different perspectives on criminal justice today. The crime control perspective is oriented toward deterring people from committing crime and incapacitating serious criminal offenders. The due process perspective sees the justice system as a legal process. The rehabilitation model views the justice system as a treatment agency.

The equal justice model is concerned with making the system equitable. The nonintervention model is concerned about stigma and helping defendants avoid a widening net of justice. The restorative justice model focuses on finding peaceful and humanitarian solutions to crime.

Key Terms

criminal justice
   system 382
community policing (COP)
   (problem-oriented
   policing) 385
discretion 387
landmark decision 387
adversary system 387
prosecutor 387
defendant 387
convictability 387
defense attorney 388
right to counsel 388
public defender 389

pro bono 389
probation 390
incarceration 390
jail 391
prison (penitentiary) 391
truth in sentencing 391
parole 391
arrest 394
probable cause 394
booking 394
interrogation 395
nolle prosequi 395
indictment 396
grand jury 396

information 396
preliminary hearing 396
arraignment 396
bail 396
recognizance 396
plea bargain 396
hung jury 396
disposition 396
appeal 397
courtroom work
   group 400
law of criminal
   procedure 400
Bill of Rights 400

exclusionary rule 401
crime control model 401
Miranda rights 402
due process model 402
rehabilitation model 404
equal justice model 406
determinate
   sentencing 407
nonintervention
   model 407
restorative justice
   model 408

Critical Thinking Questions

1. Describe the differences between the formal and informal justice systems. Is it fair to treat some offenders informally?
2. What are the basic elements of each model of justice or perspective on justice? Which best represents your own point of view?
3. How would each perspective on criminal justice consider the use of the death penalty as a sanction for first-degree murder? In your opinion, does the death

penalty serve as a deterrent to murder? If not, why not?
4. Discuss the trends that will influence policing during the coming decade.
5. Why does the problem of sentencing disparity exist? Do programs exist that can reduce disparate sentences? If so, what are they?
6. Should all people who commit the same crime receive the same sentence?

Notes

Chapter 1. Crime and Criminology

1. Federal Bureau of Investigation, "Norman Hsu Pleads Guilty to Investment Fraud," May 7, 2009, http://new york.fbi.gov/dojpressrel/pressrel09/nyfo050709.htm (accessed on May 10, 2009).

2. John Hagan and Alberto Palloni, "Sociological Criminology and the Mythology of Hispanic Immigration and Crime," *Social Problems* 46 (1999): 617–632.

3. Irvin Wolfgang and Franco Ferracuti, *The Subculture of Violence* (London: Social Science Paperbacks, 1967), p. 20.

4. Tatia M. C. Lee, Siu-Ching Chan, and Adrian Raine, "Hyperresponsivity to Threat Stimuli in Domestic Violence Offenders: A Functional Magnetic Resonance Imaging Study," *Journal of Clinical Psychiatry* 70 (2009): 36–45.

5. Marvin Wolfgang, *Patterns in Criminal Homicide* (Philadelphia: University of Pennsylvania Press, 1958).

6. Edwin Sutherland, *White-Collar Crime: The Uncut Version* (New Haven, CT: Yale University Press, 1983).

7. Randy Borum, *Psychology of Terrorism* (Tampa: University of South Florida, 2004), www.ncjrs.gov/pdffiles1/nij/grants/208552.pdf (accessed May 10, 2009).

8. Samuel Gross, Kristen Jacoby, Daniel Matheson, Nicholas Montgomery, and Sujata Patil, "Exonerations in the United States 1989 through 2003," *Journal of Criminal Law & Criminology* 95 (2005): 523–559.

9. Hans von Hentig, *The Criminal and His Victim* (New Haven, CT: Yale University Press, 1948); Stephen Schafer, *The Victim and His Criminal* (New York: Random House, 1968).

10. Linda Teplin, Gary McClelland, Karen Abram, and Darinka Mileusnic, "Early Violent Death among Delinquent Youth: A Prospective Longitudinal Study," *Pediatrics* 115 (2005): 1586–1593.

11. Eugene Weber, *A Modern History of Europe* (New York: W. W. Norton, 1971), p. 398.

12. Marvin Wolfgang, *Patterns in Criminal Homicide* (Philadelphia: University of Pennsylvania Press, 1958).

13. Nicole Rafter, "The Murderous Dutch Fiddler: Criminology, History, and the Problem of Phrenology," *Theoretical Criminology* 9 (2005): 65–97.

14. Described in David Lykken, "Psychopathy, Sociopathy, and Crime," *Society* 34 (1996): 29–38.

15. See Peter Scott, "Henry Maudsley," in *Pioneers in Criminology*, ed. Hermann Mannheim (Montclair, NJ: Prentice-Hall, 1981).

16. Nicole Hahn Rafter, "Criminal Anthropology in the United States," *Criminology* 30 (1992): 525–547.

17. Ibid., p. 535.

18. See, generally, Robert Nisbet, *The Sociology of Emile Durkheim* (New York: Oxford University Press, 1974).

19. L. A. J. Quetelet, *A Treatise on Man and the Development of His Faculties* (Gainesville, FL: Scholars' Facsimiles and Reprints, 1969), pp. 82–96.

20. Ibid., p. 85.

21. Emile Durkheim, *Rules of the Sociological Method*, reprint ed., trans. W. D. Halls (New York: Free Press, 1982).

22. Emile Durkheim, *The Division of Labor in Society*, reprint ed. (New York: Free Press, 1997).

23. Robert Park and Ernest Burgess, *The City* (Chicago: University of Chicago Press, 1925).

24. Karl Marx and Friedrich Engels, *Capital: A Critique of Political Economy*, trans. E. Aveling (Chicago: Charles Kern, 1906); Karl Marx, *Selected Writings in Sociology and Social Philosophy*, trans. P. B. Bottomore (New York: McGraw-Hill, 1956). For a general discussion of Marxist thought, see Michael Lynch and W. Byron Groves, *A Primer in Radical Criminology* (New York: Harrow and Heston, 1986), pp. 6–26.

25. Sheldon Glueck and Eleanor Glueck, *Unraveling Juvenile Delinquency* (Cambridge, MA: Harvard University Press, 1950).

26. Ibid., p. 48.

27. Charles McCaghy, *Deviant Behavior* (New York: Macmillan, 1976), pp. 2–3.

28. Edward Brecher, *Licit and Illicit Drugs* (Boston: Little, Brown, 1972), pp. 413–416.

29. Hearings on H.R. 6385 April 27, 28, 29, 30, and May 4, 1937, www.druglibrary.org/schaffer/hemp/taxact/anslng1.htm (accessed April 10, 2004).

30. www.dpf.org/drugwar (accessed April 12, 2004).

31. Edwin Sutherland and Donald Cressey, *Criminology*, 8th ed. (Philadelphia: J. B. Lippincott, 1960), p. 8.

32. Howard Becker, *Outsiders: Studies in the Sociology of Deviance* (New York: Free Press, 1963), p. 9.

33. Ibid.

34. Oliver Wendell Holmes, *The Common Law*, ed. Mark De Wolf (Boston: Little, Brown, 1881), p. 36.

35. National Institute of Justice, *Project to Develop a Model Anti-Stalking Statute* (Washington, DC: National Institute of Justice, 1994).

36. Associated Press, "Judge Upholds State's Sexual Predator Law," *Bakersfield Californian*, October 2, 1996.

37. *Lawrence et al. v. Texas*, No. 02-102, June 26, 2003.

38. Joachim Savelsberg, Ryan King, and Lara Cleveland, "Politicized Scholarship? Science on Crime and the State," *Social Problems* 49 (2002): 327–349.

39. See, for example, Michael Hindelang and Travis Hirschi, "Intelligence and Delinquency: A Revisionist Review," *American Sociological Review* 42 (1977): 471–486.

40. Richard Herrnstein and Charles Murray, *The Bell Curve* (New York: Free Press, 1994).

41. Dermot Feenan, "Legal Issues in Acquiring Information about Illegal Behaviour through Criminological Research," *British Journal of Criminology* 42 (2002): 762–781.

42. Anthony Petrosino, Carolyn Turpin-Petrosino, and James Finckenauer, "Well-Meaning Programs Can Have Harmful Effects! Lessons from Experiments on Programs Such as Scared Straight," *Crime and Delinquency* 46 (2000): 354–379.

43. Victor Boruch, Timothy Victor, and Joe Cecil, "Resolving Ethical and Legal Problems in Randomized Experiments," *Crime and Delinquency* 46 (2000): 330–353.

44. Ida Dupont, "Beyond Doing No Harm: A Call for Participatory Action Research with Marginalized Populations in Criminological Research," *Critical Criminology* 16 (2008): 197–207.

Chapter 2. The Nature and Extent of Crime

1. Fox News, "Georgia Professor Who Killed Wife [and] 2 Others Died after Shooting Himself in Head," May 12, 2009, www.foxnews.com/story/0,2933,519897,00.html.

2. Federal Bureau of Investigation, *Crime in the United States, 2008* (Washington, DC: U.S. Government Printing Office, 2009). http://www.fbi.gov/ucr/cius2008/index.html

3. Lynn Addington, "The Effect of NIBRS Reporting on Item Missing Data in Murder Cases," *Homicide Studies* 8 (2004): 193–213.

4. Michael Rand, *Criminal Victimization, 2008* (Washington, DC: Bureau of Justice Statistics, 2009), www.ojp.usdoj.gov/bjs/pub/pdf/cv08.pdf.

5. Michael Rand and Shannan Catalano, *Criminal Victimization, 2006* (Washington, DC: Bureau of Justice Statistics, 2007), www.ojp.usdoj.gov/bjs/pub/pdf/cv06.pdf.

6. Lynn Addington and Callie Marie Rennison, "Rape Co-occurrence: Do Additional Crimes Affect Victim Reporting and Police Clearance of Rape?" *Journal of Quantitative Criminology* 24 (2008): 205–226.

7. L. Edward Wells and Joseph Rankin, "Juvenile Victimization: Convergent Validation of Alternative Measurements," *Journal of Research in Crime and Delinquency* 32 (1995): 287–307.

8. Robert M. Groves and Daniel L. Cork, *Surveying Victims: Options for Conducting the National Crime Victimization Survey* (Washington, DC: National Research Council, 2008), www.nap.edu/catalog/12090.html (accessed June 26, 2008).

9. A pioneering effort in self-report research is A. L. Porterfield, *Youth in Trouble* (Fort Worth, TX: Leo Potishman Foundation, 1946); for a review, see Robert Hardt and George Bodine, *Development of Self-Report Instruments in Delinquency Research: A Conference Report* (Syracuse, NY: Syracuse University Youth Development Center, 1965). See also Fred Murphy, Mary Shirley, and Helen Witner, "The Incidence of Hidden Delinquency," *American Journal of Orthopsychology* 16 (1946): 686–696.

10. See John Paul Wright and Francis Cullen, "Juvenile Involvement in Occupational Delinquency," *Criminology* 38 (2000): 863–896.

11. Christiane Brems, Mark Johnson, David Neal, and Melinda Freemon, "Childhood Abuse History and Substance Use among Men and Women Receiving Detoxification Services," *American Journal of Drug & Alcohol Abuse* 30 (2004): 799–821.

12. Leonore Simon, "Validity and Reliability of Violent Juveniles: A Comparison of Juvenile Self-Reports with Adult Self-Reports Incarcerated in Adult Prisons." Paper presented at the annual meeting of the American Society of Criminology, Boston, November 1995, p. 26.

13. Stephen Cernkovich, Peggy Giordano, and Meredith Pugh, "Chronic Offenders: The Missing Cases in Self-Report Delinquency Research," *Journal of Criminal Law and Criminology* 76 (1985): 705–732.

14. Terence Thornberry, Beth Bjerregaard, and William Miles, "The Consequences of Respondent Attrition in Panel Studies: A Simulation Based on the Rochester Youth Development Study," *Journal of Quantitative Criminology* 9 (1993): 127–158.

15. See Spencer Rathus and Larry Siegel, "Crime and Personality Revisited: Effects of MMPI Sets on Self-Report Studies," Criminology 18 (1980): 245–251; John Clark and Larry Tifft, "Polygraph and Interview Validation of Self-Reported Deviant Behavior," *American Sociological Review* 31 (1966): 516–523.

16. Mallie Paschall, Miriam Ornstein, and Robert Flewelling, "African-American Male Adolescents' Involvement in the Criminal Justice System: The Criterion Validity of Self-Report Measures in Prospective Study," *Journal of Research in Crime and Delinquency* 38 (2001): 174–187.

17. Lloyd Johnston, Patrick O'Malley, and Jerald Bachman, *Monitoring the Future, 8* (Ann Arbor, MI: Institute for Social Research, 2009); http://monitoringthefuture.org/.

18. United States Census Bureau, Data Set: 2005–2007 American Community Survey 3-Year Estimates, http://factfinder.census.gov/servlet/STTable?_bm=y&-geo_id=01000US&-qr_name=ACS_2007_3YR_G00_S0101&-ds_name=ACS_2007_3YR_G00_.

19. Jennifer Roberts, Edward Mulvey, Julie Horney, John Lewis, and Michael Arter, "A Test of Two Methods of Recall for Violent Events," *Journal of Quantitative Criminology* 21 (2005): 175–193.

20. Lila Kazemian and David Farrington, "Comparing the Validity of Prospective, Retrospective, and Official Onset for Different Offending Categories," *Journal of Quantitative Criminology* 21 (2005): 127–147.

21. Barbara Warner and Brandi Wilson Coomer, "Neighborhood Drug Arrest Rates: Are They a Meaningful Indicator of Drug Activity? A Research Note," *Journal of Research in Crime and Delinquency* 40 (2003): 123–139.

22. Alfred Blumstein, Jacqueline Cohen, and Richard Rosenfeld, "Trend and Deviation in Crime Rates: A Comparison of UCR and NCVS Data for Burglary and Robbery," *Criminology* 29 (1991): 237–248. See also Michael Hindelang, Travis Hirschi, and Joseph Weiss, *Measuring Delinquency* (Beverly Hills, CA: Sage, 1981).

23. Clarence Schrag, *Crime and Justice: American Style* (Washington, DC: U.S. Government Printing Office, 1971), p. 17.

24. Rand, *Criminal Victimization, 2008.*

25. James A. Fox, *Trends in Juvenile Violence: A Report to the United States Attorney General on Current and Future Rates of Juvenile Offending* (Boston: Northeastern University, 1996).

26. Steven Levitt, "The Limited Role of Changing Age Structure in Explaining Aggregate Crime Rates," *Criminology* 37 (1999): 581–599.

27. Darrell Steffensmeier and Miles Harer, "Making Sense of Recent U.S. Crime Trends, 1980 to 1996/1998: Age Composition Effects and Other Explanations," *Journal of Research in Crime and Delinquency* 36 (1999): 235–274.

28. Ibid., p. 265.

29. Ellen Cohn, "The Effect of Weather and Temporal Variations on Calls for Police Service," *American Journal of Police* 15 (1996): 23–43.

30. R. A. Baron, "Aggression as a Function of Ambient Temperature and Prior Anger Arousal," *Journal of Personality and Social Psychology* 21 (1972): 183–189.

31. Brad Bushman, Morgan Wang, and Craig Anderson, "Is the Curve Relating Temperature to Aggression Linear or Curvilinear? Assaults and Temperature in Minneapolis Reexamined," *Journal of Personality & Social Psychology* 89 (2005): 62–66.

32. Paul Bell, "Reanalysis and Perspective in the Heat–Aggression Debate," *Journal of Personality & Social Psychology* 89 (2005): 71–73.

33. Ellen Cohn, "The Prediction of Police Calls for Service: The Influence of Weather and Temporal Variables on Rape and Domestic Violence," *Journal of Environmental Psychology* 13 (1993): 71–83.

34. John Simister and Cary Cooper, "Thermal Stress in the U.S.A.: Effects on Violence and on Employee Behaviour," *Stress and Health* 21 (2005): 3–15.

35. Amie Nielsen, Ramiro Martinez, and Richard Rosenfeld, "Firearm Use, Injury, and Lethality in Assaultive Violence: An Examination of Ethnic Differences," *Homicide Studies* 9 (2005): 83–108.

36. See generally Franklin Zimring and Gordon Hawkins, *Crime Is Not the Problem: Lethal Violence in America* (New York: Oxford University Press, 1997).

37. Ibid., p. 36.

38. Gary Kleck and Marc Gertz, "Armed Resistance to Crime: The Prevalence and Nature of Self-Defense with a Gun," *Journal of Criminal Law and Criminology* 86 (1995): 219–249.

39. Robert Nash Parker, "Bringing 'Booze' Back In: The Relationship between Alcohol and Homicide," *Journal of Research in Crime and Delinquency* 32 (1995): 3–38.

40. Victoria Brewer and M. Dwayne Smith, "Gender Inequality and Rates of Female Homicide Victimization across U.S. Cities," *Journal of Research in Crime and Delinquency* 32 (1995): 175–190.

41. Syed Moniruzzaman and Ragnar Andersson, "Age and Sex-Specific Analysis of Homicide Mortality as a Function of Economic Development: A Crossnational Comparison." *Scandinavian Journal of Public Health* 33 (2005): 464–471.

42. Charles Tittle and Robert Meier, "Specifying the SES/Delinquency Relationship," *Criminology* 28 (1990): 271–301; R. Gregory Dunaway, Francis Cullen, Velmer Burton, and T. David Evans, "The Myth of Social Class and Crime Revisited: An Examination of Class and Adult Criminality," *Criminology* 38 (2000): 589–632.

43. Judith Blau and Peter Blau, "The Cost of Inequality: Metropolitan Structure and Violent Crime," *American Sociological Review* 147 (1982): 114–129; Richard Block, "Community Environment and Violent Crime," *Criminology* 17 (1979): 46–57; Robert Sampson, "Structural Sources of Variation in Race-Age-Specific Rates of Offending across Major U.S. Cities," *Criminology* 23 (1985): 647–673.

44. Robert J. Sampson, "Disparity and Diversity in the Contemporary City: Social (Dis)order Revisited," *British Journal of Sociology* 60 (2009): 1–31.

45. Travis Hirschi and Michael Gottfredson, "Age and the Explanation of Crime," *American Journal of Sociology* 89 (1983): 552–584, at p. 581.

46. Darrell Steffensmeier and Cathy Streifel, "Age, Gender, and Crime across Three Historical Periods: 1935, 1960 and 1985," *Social Forces* 69 (1991): 869–894.

47. Hirschi and Gottfredson, "Age and the Explanation of Crime."

48. Robert Agnew, "An Integrated Theory of the Adolescent Peak in Offending," *Youth & Society* 34 (2003): 263–302.

49. Margo Wilson and Martin Daly, "Life Expectancy, Economic Inequality, Homicide, and Reproductive Timing in Chicago Neighbourhoods," *British Journal of Medicine* 314 (1997): 1,271–1,274.

50. Edward Mulvey and John LaRosa, "Delinquency Cessation and Adolescent Development: Preliminary Data," *American Journal of Orthopsychiatry* 56 (1986): 212–224.

51. James Q. Wilson and Richard Herrnstein, *Crime and Human Nature* (New York: Simon & Schuster, 1985), pp. 126–147.

52. Ibid., p. 219.

53. Erich Labouvie, "Maturing Out of Substance Use: Selection and Self-Correction," *Journal of Drug Issues* 26 (1996): 457–474.

54. Kevin Beaver, John Paul Wright, Matt DeLisi, and Michael Vaughn, "Desistance from Delinquency: The Marriage Effect Revisited and Extended," *Social Science Research* 37 (2008): 736–752.

55. Paul Tracy, Kimberly Kempf-Leonard, and Stephanie Abramoske-James. "Gender Differences in Delinquency and Juvenile Justice Processing: Evidence from National Data, *Crime and Delinquency* 55 (2009): 171–215.

56. Janet Lauritsen, Karen Heimer, James Lynch, "Trends In The Gender Gap In Violent Offending: New Evidence From The National Crime Victimization Survey" *Criminology* 47 (2009): 361–399.

57. Cesare Lombroso, *The Female Offender* (New York: Appleton, 1920), p. 122.

58. Ibid.

59. Alan Booth and D. Wayne Osgood, "The Influence of Testosterone on Deviance in Adulthood: Assessing and Explaining the Relationship," *Criminology* 31 (1993): 93–118.

60. Jean Bottcher, "Social Practices of Gender: How Gender Relates to Delinquency in the Everyday Lives of High-Risk Youths," *Criminology* 39 (2001): 893–932.

61. Debra Kaysen, Miranda Morris, Shireen Rizvi, and Patricia Resick, "Peritraumatic Responses and Their Relationship to Perceptions of Threat in Female Crime Victims," *Violence against Women* 11 (2005): 1,515–1,535.

62. Freda Adler, *Sisters in Crime* (New York: McGraw-Hill, 1975); Rita James Simon, *The Contemporary Woman and Crime* (Washington, DC: U.S. Government Printing Office, 1975).

63. David Rowe, Alexander Vazsonyi, and Daniel Flannery, "Sex Differences in Crime: Do Mean and Within-Sex Variation Have Similar Causes?" *Journal of Research in Crime and Delinquency* 32 (1995): 84–100; Michael Hindelang, "Age, Sex, and the Versatility of Delinquency Involvements," *Social Forces* 14 (1971): 525–534; Martin Gold, *Delinquent Behavior in an American City* (Belmont, CA: Brooks/Cole, 1970); Gary Jensen and Raymond Eve, "Sex Differences in Delinquency: An Examination of Popular Sociological Explanations," *Criminology* 13 (1976): 427–448.

64. Knut Steen and Steinar Hunskaar, "Gender and Physical Violence," *Social Science & Medicine* 59 (2004): 567–571.

65. Finn-Aage Esbensen and Elizabeth Piper Deschenes, "A Multisite Examination of Youth Gang Membership: Does Gender Matter?" *Criminology* 36 (1998): 799–828.

66. Darrell Steffensmeier, Jennifer Schwartz, Hua Zhong, and Jeff Ackerman, "An Assessment of Recent Trends in Girls' Violence Using Diverse Longitudinal Sources: Is the Gender Gap Closing?" *Criminology* 43 (2005): 355–406.

67. Susan Miller, Carol Gregory, and Leeann Iovanni, "One Size Fits All? A Gender-Neutral Approach to a Gender-Specific Problem: Contrasting Batterer Treatment Programs for Male and Female Offenders," *Criminal Justice Policy Review* 16 (2005): 336–359.

68. Johnston, O'Malley, and Bachman, *Monitoring the Future*, pp. 102–104.

69. Miriam Sealock and Sally Simpson, "Unraveling Bias in Arrest Decisions: The Role of Juvenile Offender Type-Scripts," *Justice Quarterly* 15 (1998): 427–457.

70. Robin Shepard Engel and Jennifer Calnon, "Examining the Influence of Drivers' Characteristics during Traffic Stops with Police: Results from a National Survey," *Justice Quarterly* 21 (2004): 49–90.

71. Richard Lundman and Brian Kowalski, "Speeding While Black? Assessing the Generalizability of Lange et al.'s (2001, 2005) New Jersey Turnpike Speeding Survey Findings" *Justice Quarterly* 26 (2009): 504–527.

72. Terrance Taylor, David Holleran, and Volkan Topalli, "Racial Bias in Case Processing: Does Victim Race Affect Police Clearance of Violent Crime Incidents?" *Justice Quarterly* 26 (2009): 562–591.

73. James Comer, "Black Violence and Public Policy," in *American Violence and Public Policy*, ed. Lynn Curtis (New Haven, CT: Yale University Press, 1985), pp. 63–86.

74. Michael Leiber and Jayne Stairs, "Race, Contexts and the Use of Intake Diversion," *Journal of Research in Crime and Delinquency* 36 (1999): 56–86; Darrell Steffensmeier, Jeffery Ulmer, and John Kramer, "The Interaction of Race, Gender, and Age in Criminal Sentencing: The Punishment Cost of Being Young, Black, and Male," *Criminology* 36 (1998): 763–798.

75. David Eitle and Susanne Monahan, "Revisiting the Racial Threat Thesis: The Role of Police Organizational Characteristics in Predicting Race-Specific Drug Arrest Rates," *Justice Quarterly*, 26 (2009): 528–561.

76. Bradley Keen and David Jacobs, "Racial Threat, Partisan Politics, and Racial Disparities in Prison Admissions," *Criminology* 47 (2009): 209–238.

77. Karen Parker, Briam Stults, and Stephen Rice, "Racial Threat, Concentrated Disadvantage and Social Control: Considering the Macro-Level Sources of Variation in Arrests," *Criminology* 43 (2005): 1,111–1,134; Lisa Stolzenberg, J. Stewart D'Alessio, and David Eitle, "A Multilevel Test of Racial Threat Theory," *Criminology* 42 (2004): 673–698.

78. Michael Leiber and Kristan Fox, "Race and the Impact of Detention on Juvenile Justice Decision Making," *Crime and Delinquency* 51 (2005): 470–497; Traci Schlesinger, "Racial and Ethnic Disparity in Pretrial Criminal Processing," *Justice Quarterly* 22 (2005): 170–192.

79. Tracy Nobiling, Cassia Spohn, and Miriam DeLone, "A Tale of Two Counties: Unemployment and Sentence Severity," *Justice Quarterly* 15 (1998): 459–486.

80. Robert Sampson, Jeffrey Morenoff, and Stephen Raudenbush, "Social Anatomy of Racial and Ethnic Disparities in Violence," *American Journal of Public Health* 95 (2005): 224–233; Joanne Kaufman, "Explaining the Race/Ethnicity–Violence Relationship: Neighborhood Context and Social Psychological Processes," *Justice Quarterly* 22 (2005): 224–251.

81. Karen Parker and Patricia McCall, "Structural Conditions and Racial Homicide Patterns: A Look at the Multiple Disadvantages in Urban Areas," *Criminology* 37 (1999): 447–469.

82. Gary LaFree and Richard Arum, "The Impact of Racially Inclusive Schooling on Adult Incarceration Rates among U.S. Cohorts of African Americans and Whites since 1930," *Criminology* 44 (2006): 73–103.

83. R. Kelly Raley, "A Shortage of Marriageable Men? A Note on the Role of Cohabitation in Black–White Differences in Marriage Rates," *American Sociological Review* 61 (1996): 973–983.

84. Julie Phillips, "Variation in African-American Homicide Rates: An Assessment of Potential Explanations," *Criminology* 35 (1997): 527–559.

85. Gary LaFree and Richard Arum, "The Impact of Racially Inclusive Schooling"; Robert Sampson, Jeffrey Morenoff, and Stephen Raudenbush, "Social Anatomy of Racial and Ethnic Disparities in Violence."

86. Marvin Wolfgang, Robert Figlio, and Thorsten Sellin, *Delinquency in a Birth Cohort* (Chicago: University of Chicago Press, 1972).

87. See Thorsten Sellin and Marvin Wolfgang, *The Measurement of Delinquency* (New York: Wiley, 1964), p. 120.

88. Paul Tracy and Robert Figlio, "Chronic Recidivism in the 1958 Birth Cohort." Paper presented at the American Society of Criminology meeting, Toronto, October 1982; Marvin Wolfgang, "Delinquency in Two Birth Cohorts," in *Perspective Studies of Crime and Delinquency*, ed. Katherine Teilmann Van Dusen and Sarnoff Mednick (Boston: Kluwer-Nijhoff, 1983), pp. 7–17. The following sections rely heavily on these sources.

89. Lyle Shannon, *Criminal Career Opportunity* (New York: Human Sciences Press, 1988).

90. D. J. West and David P. Farrington, *The Delinquent Way of Life* (London: Heinemann, 1977).

91. Michael Schumacher and Gwen Kurz, *The 8% Solution: Preventing Serious Repeat Juvenile Crime* (Thousand Oaks, CA: Sage, 1999).

92. Peter Jones, Philip Harris, James Fader, and Lori Grubstein, "Identifying Chronic Juvenile Offenders," *Justice Quarterly* 18 (2001): 478–507.

93. Michael Ezell and Amy D'Unger, "Offense Specialization among Serious Youthful Offenders: A Longitudinal Analysis of a California Youth Authority Sample" (Durham, NC: Duke University, 1998, unpublished report).

Chapter 3. Victims and Victimization

1. New England News, "Authorities Develop Case against Bouncer in Grad Student Slaying," March 24, 2006, www1.whdh.com/news/articles/local/BO16577/.

2. Ibid.

3. Children's Safety Network Economics and Insurance Resource Center, "State Costs of Violence Perpetrated by Youth," www.csneirc.org/pubs/tables/youth-viol.htm (accessed July 12, 2000).

4. Ted Miller, Mark Cohen, and Brian Wiersema, *The Extent and Costs of Crime Victimization: A New Look* (Washington, DC: National Institute of Justice, 1996).

5. Ted R. Miller, Mark A. Cohen, and Brian Wiersema, *Victim Costs and Consequences: A New Look* (Washington, DC: National Institute of Justice, 1996), p. 9, table 2.

6. Ross Macmillan, "Adolescent Victimization and Income Deficits in Adulthood: Rethinking the Costs of Criminal Violence from a Life-Course Perspective," *Criminology* 38 (2000): 553–588.

7. James Anderson, Terry Grandison, and Laronistine Dyson, "Victims of Random Violence and the Public Health Implication: A Health Care of Criminal Justice Issue," *Journal of Criminal Justice* 24 (1996): 379–393.

8. Amy Rose Grubb and Julie Harrower, "Understanding Attribution of Blame in Cases of Rape: An Analysis of Participant Gender, Type of Rape and Perceived Similarity to the Victim," *Journal of Sexual Aggression* 15 (2009): 63–81.

9. Courtney Ahrens, "Being Silenced: The Impact of Negative Social Reactions on the Disclosure of Rape," *American Journal of Community Psychology* 38 (2006): 263–274.

10. Rebecca Campbell and Sheela Raja, "Secondary Victimization of Rape Victims: Insights from Mental Health Professionals Who Treat Survivors of Violence," *Violence and Victims* 14 (1999): 261–274.

11. Min Xie, Greg Pogarsky, James Lynch, and David McDowall, "Prior Police Contact and Subsequent Victim Reporting: Results from the NCVS," *Justice Quarterly* 23 (2006): 481–501.

12. Angela Scarpa, Sara Chiara Haden, and Jimmy Hurley, "Community Violence Victimization and Symptoms of Posttraumatic Stress Disorder: The Moderating Effects of Coping and Social Support," *Journal of Interpersonal Violence* 21 (2006): 446–469.

13. Heather Littleton and Craig Henderson, "If She Is Not a Victim, Does That Mean She Was Not Traumatized? Evaluation of Predictors of PTSD Symptomatology among College Rape Victims," *Violence against Women* 15 (2009): 148–167.

14. Catherine Grus, "Child Abuse: Correlations with Hostile Attributions," *Journal of Developmental & Behavioral Pediatrics* 24 (2003): 296–298.

15. Kim Logio, "Gender, Race, Childhood Abuse, and Body Image among Adolescents," *Violence against Women* 9 (2003): 931–955.

16. Jeanne Kaufman and Cathy Spatz Widom, "Childhood Victimization, Running Away, and Delinquency," *Journal of Research in Crime and Delinquency* 36 (1999): 347–370.

17. N. N. Sarkar and Rina Sarkar, "Sexual Assault on Woman: Its Impact on Her Life and Living in Society," *Sexual & Relationship Therapy* 20 (2005): 407–419.

18. Michael Wiederman, Randy Sansone, and Lori Sansone, "History of Trauma and Attempted Suicide among Women in a Primary Care Setting," *Violence and Victims* 13 (1998): 3–11; Susan Leslie Bryant and Lillian Range, "Suicidality in College Women Who Were Sexually and Physically Abused and Physically Punished by Parents," *Violence and Victims* 10 (1995): 195–215; William Downs and Brenda Miller, "Relationships between Experiences of Parental Violence during Childhood and Women's Self-Esteem," *Violence and Victims* 13 (1998): 63–78; Sally Davies-Netley, Michael Hurlburt, and Richard Hough, "Childhood Abuse as a Precursor to Homelessness for Homeless Women with Severe Mental Illness," *Violence and Victims* 11 (1996): 129–142.

19. Jane Siegel and Linda Williams, "Risk Factors for Sexual Victimization of Women," *Violence against Women* 9 (2003): 902–930.

20. Michael Miner, Jill Klotz Flitter, and Beatrice Robinson. "Association of Sexual Revictimization with Sexuality and Psychological Function," *Journal of Interpersonal Violence* 21 (2006): 503–524.

21. Lana Stermac and Emily Paradis, "Homeless Women and Victimization: Abuse and Mental Health History among Homeless Rape Survivors," *Resources for Feminist Research* 28 (2001): 65–81.

22. Gregory Stuart, Todd M. Moore, Kristina Coop Gordon, Susan Ramsey, and Christopher Kahler, "Psychopathology in Women Arrested for Domestic Violence," *Journal of Interpersonal Violence* 21 (2006): 376–389; Caron Zlotnick, Dawn Johnson, and Robert Kohn, "Intimate Partner Violence and Long-Term Psychosocial Functioning in a National Sample of American Women," *Journal of Interpersonal Violence* 21 (2006): 262–275.

23. K. Daniel O'Leary, "Psychological Abuse: A Variable Deserving Critical Attention in Domestic Violence," *Violence and Victims* 14 (1999): 1–21.

24. Ron Acierno, Alyssa Rheingold, Heidi Resnick, and Dean Kilpatrick, "Predictors of Fear of Crime in Older Adults," *Journal of Anxiety Disorders* 18 (2004): 385–396.

25. Ibid.

26. Susan Brison, *Aftermath: Violence and the Remaking of a Self* (Princeton, NJ: Princeton University Press, 2001).

27. Pamela Wilcox Rountree, "A Reexamination of the Crime–Fear Linkage," *Journal of Research in Crime and Delinquency* 35 (1998): 341–372.

28. Min Xie and David McDowall, "Escaping Crime: The Effects of Direct and Indirect Victimization on Moving," *Criminology* 46 (2008): 809–840.

29. Mirka Smolej and Janne Kivivuori, "The Relation between Crime News and Fear of Violence," *Journal of Scandinavian Studies in Criminology & Crime Prevention* 7 (2006): 211–227.

30. Matthew Lee and Erica DeHart, "The Influence of a Serial Killer on Changes in Fear of Crime and the Use of Protective Measures: A Survey-Based Case Study of Baton Rouge," *Deviant Behavior* 28 (2007): 1–28.

31. Timothy Ireland and Cathy Spatz Widom, *Childhood Victimization and Risk for Alcohol and Drug Arrests* (Washington, DC: National Institute of Justice, 1995).

32. Brigette Erwin, Elana Newman, Robert McMackin, Carlo Morrissey, and Danny Kaloupek, "PTSD, Malevolent Environment, and Criminality among Criminally Involved Male Adolescents," *Criminal Justice and Behavior* 27 (2000): 196–215.

33. Min Jung Kim, Emiko Tajima, Todd Herrenkohl, and Bu Huang, "Early Child Maltreatment, Runaway Youths, and Risk of Delinquency and Victimization in Adolescence: A Mediational Model," *Social Work Research*, 33 (2009): 19–28.

34. Ulrich Orth, Leo Montada, and Andreas Maercker, "Feelings of Revenge, Retaliation Motive, and Post-traumatic Stress Reactions in Crime Victims," *Journal of Interpersonal Violence* 21 (2006): 229–243.

35. Cathy Spatz Widom, *The Cycle of Violence* (Washington, DC: National Institute of Justice, 1992), p. 1.

36. Chris Melde, Finn-Aage Esbensen, and Terrance Taylor, "'May Piece Be with You': A Typological Examination of the Fear and Victimization Hypothesis of Adolescent Weapon Carrying," *Justice Quarterly* 26 (2009): 348–376.

37. Chris Gibson, Zara Morris, and Kevin Beaver, "Secondary Exposure to Violence during Childhood and Adolescence: Does Neighborhood Context Matter?" *Justice Quarterly* 26 (2009): 30–57.

38. Pamela Wilcox, Marie Skubak Tillyer, and Bonnie S. Fisher, "Gendered Opportunity? School-Based Adolescent Victimization," *Journal of Research in Crime and Delinquency* 46 (2009): 245–269.

39. Bureau of Justice Statistics, "Indicators of School Crime and Safety, 2008," www.ojp.usdoj.gov/bjs/abstract/iscs08.htm.

40. Victoria Titterington, "A Retrospective Investigation of Gender Inequality and Female Homicide Victimization," *Sociological Spectrum* 26 (2006): 205–231.

41. David, Finkelhor, Heather Turner, and Richard Ormrod, "Kid's Stuff: The Nature and Impact of Peer and Sibling Violence on Younger and Older Children," *Child Abuse & Neglect* 30 (2006): 1401–1421.

42. Lamar Jordan, "Law Enforcement and the Elderly: A Concern for the 21st Century," *FBI Law Enforcement Bulletin* 71 (2002): 20–24.

43. Tracy Dietz and James Wright, "Age and Gender Differences and Predictors of Victimization of the Older Homeless," *Journal of Elder Abuse & Neglect* 17 (2005): 37–59.

44. Karin Wittebrood and Paul Nieuwbeerta, "Criminal Victimization during One's Life Course: The Effects of Previous Victimization and Patterns of Routine Activities," *Journal of Research in Crime and Delinquency* 37 (2000): 91–122; Janet Lauritsen and Kenna Davis Quinet, "Repeat Victimizations among Adolescents and Young Adults," *Journal of Quantitative Criminology* 11 (1995): 143–163.

45. Denise Osborn, Dan Ellingworth, Tim Hope, and Alan Trickett, "Are Repeatedly Victimized Households Different?" *Journal of Quantitative Criminology* 12 (1996): 223–245.

46. Graham Farrell, "Predicting and Preventing Revictimization," in *Crime and Justice: An Annual Review of Research,* ed. Michael Tonry and David Farrington, vol. 20 (Chicago: University of Chicago Press, 1995), pp. 61–126.

47. Ibid., p. 61.

48. David Finkelhor and Nancy Asigian, "Risk Factors for Youth Victimization: Beyond a Lifestyles/Routine Activities Theory Approach," *Violence and Victimization* 11 (1996): 3–19.

49. Graham Farrell, Coretta Phillips, and Ken Pease, "Like Taking Candy: Why Does Repeat Victimization Occur?" *British Journal of Criminology* 35 (1995): 384–399.

50. Christopher Innes and Lawrence Greenfeld, *Violent State Prisoners and Their Victims* (Washington, DC: Bureau of Justice Statistics, 1990).

51. Hans Von Hentig, *The Criminal and His Victim: Studies in the Sociobiology of Crime* (New Haven, CT: Yale University Press, 1948), p. 384.

52. Marvin Wolfgang, *Patterns of Criminal Homicide* (Philadelphia: University of Pennsylvania Press, 1958).

53. Menachem Amir, *Patterns in Forcible Rape* (Chicago: University of Chicago Press, 1971).

54. Susan Estrich, *Real Rape* (Cambridge, MA: Harvard University Press, 1987).

55. Pamela Wilcox, Marie Skubak Tillyer, and Bonnie S. Fisher, "Gendered Opportunity? School-Based Adolescent Victimization," *Journal of Research in Crime and Delinquency* 46 (2009): 245–269.

56. Edem Avakame, "Female's Labor Force Participation and Intimate Femicide: An Empirical Assessment of the Backlash Hypothesis," *Violence and Victims* 14 (1999): 277–283.

57. Martin Daly and Margo Wilson, *Homicide* (New York: Aldine de Gruyter, 1988).

58. Wilcox, Tillyer, and Fisher, "Gendered Opportunity?"

59. Christopher Schreck, Eric Stewart, and Bonnie Fisher, "Self-Control, Victimization, and Their Influence on Risky Lifestyles: A Longitudinal Analysis Using Panel Data," *Journal of Quantitative Criminology* 22 (2006): 319–340.

60. Lening Zhang, John W. Welte, and William F. Wieczorek, "Deviant Lifestyle and Crime Victimization," *Journal of Criminal Justice* 29 (2001): 133–143.

61. Dan Hoyt, Kimberly Ryan, and Mari Cauce, "Personal Victimization in a High-Risk Environment: Homeless and Runaway Adolescents," *Journal of Research in Crime and Delinquency* 36 (1999): 371–392.

62. See, generally, Gary Gottfredson and Denise Gottfredson, *Victimization in Schools* (New York: Plenum Press, 1985).

63. Gary Jensen and David Brownfield, "Gender, Lifestyles, and Victimization: Beyond Routine Activity Theory," *Violence and Victims* 1 (1986): 85–99.

64. Dana Haynie and Alex Piquero. "Pubertal Development and Physical Victimization in Adolescence," *Journal of Research in Crime and Delinquency* 43 (2006): 3–35.

65. Michael Ezell and Emily Tanner-Smith, "Examining the Role of Lifestyle and Criminal History Variables on the Risk of Homicide Victimization," *Homicide Studies* 13 (2009): 144–173; Rolf Loeber, Mary DeLamatre, George Tita, Jacqueline Cohen, Magda Stouthamer-Loeber, and David Farrington, "Gun Injury and Mortality: The Delinquent Backgrounds of Juvenile Offenders," *Violence and Victim* 14 (1999): 339–351.

66. Adam Dobrin, "The Risk of Offending on Homicide Victimization: A Case Control Study," *Journal of Research in Crime and Delinquency* 38 (2001): 154–173.

67. Bonnie Fisher, John Sloan, Francis Cullen, and Chunmeng Lu, "Crime in the Ivory Tower: The Level and Sources of Student Victimization," *Criminology* 36 (1998): 671–710.

68. Bonnie Fisher, Francis Cullen, and Michael Turner, *The Sexual Victimization of College Women* (Washington, DC: National Institute of Justice, 2001).

69. Elizabeth Reed, Hortensia Amaro, Atsushi Matsumoto, and Debra Kaysen, "The Relation between Interpersonal Violence and Substance Use among a Sample of University Students: Examination of the Role of Victim and Perpetrator Substance Use," *Addictive Behaviors* 34 (2009): 316–318.

70. S. Farrall and S. Maltby, "The Victimisation of Probationers," *Howard Journal of Criminal Justice* 42 (2003): 32–55.

71. Rolf Loeber, Larry Kalb, and David Huizinga, *Juvenile Delinquency and Serious Injury Victimization* (Washington, DC: Office of Juvenile Justice and Delinquency Prevention, 2001).

72. Christopher Schreck, Eric Stewart, and D. Wayne Osgood, "A Reappraisal of the Overlap of Violent Offenders and Victims, *Criminology* 46 (2008): 872–906.

73. Maryse Richards, Reed Larson, and Bobbi-Viegas Miller, "Risky and Protective Contexts and Exposure to Violence in Urban African American Young Adolescents" *Journal of Clinical Child and Adolescent Psychology* 33 (2004): 138–148.

74. James Garofalo, "Reassessing the Lifestyle Model of Criminal Victimization," in *Positive Criminology*, ed. Michael Gottfredson and Travis Hirschi (Newbury Park, CA: Sage, 1987), pp. 23–42.

75. Terance Miethe and David McDowall, "Contextual Effects in Models of Criminal Victimization," *Social Forces* 71 (1993): 741–759.

76. Rodney Stark, "Deviant Places: A Theory of the Ecology of Crime," *Criminology* 25 (1987): 893–911.

77. Ibid., p. 902.

78. Pamela Wilcox Rountree, Kenneth Land, and Terance Miethe, "Macro–Micro Integration in the Study of Victimization: A Hierarchical Logistic Model Analysis across Seattle Neighborhoods," paper presented at the annual meeting of the American Society of Criminology, Phoenix, Arizona, November 1993.

79. Lawrence Cohen and Marcus Felson, "Social Change and Crime Rate Trends: A Routine Activities Approach," *American Sociological Review* 44 (1979): 588–608.

80. For a review, see James LeBeau and Thomas Castellano, "The Routine Activities Approach: An Inventory and Critique," unpublished paper, Center for the Studies of Crime, Delinquency, and Corrections, Southern Illinois University, Carbondale, 1987.

81. Teresa LaGrange, "The Impact of Neighborhoods, Schools, and Malls on the Spatial Distribution of Property Damage," *Journal of Research in Crime and Delinquency* 36 (1999): 393–422.

82. Denise Gottfredson and David Soulé, "The Timing of Property Crime, Violent Crime, and Substance Use among Juveniles," *Journal of Research in Crime and Delinquency* 42 (2005): 110–120.

83. Marcus Felson, *Crime and Everyday Life: Insights and Implications for Society,* 3rd ed. (Thousand Oaks, CA: Sage, 2002).

84. Amy Anderson and Lorine Hughes, "Exposure to Situations Conducive to Delinquent Behavior: The Effects of Time Use, Income, and Transportation," *Journal of Research in Crime and Delinquency* 46 (2009): 5–34.

85. Lawrence Cohen, Marcus Felson, and Kenneth Land, "Property Crime Rates in the United States: A Macrodynamic Analysis, 1947–1977, with Ex-ante Forecasts for the Mid-1980s," *American Journal of Sociology* 86 (1980): 90–118.

86. Steven Messner, Lawrence Raffalovich, and Richard McMillan, "Economic Deprivation and Changes in Homicide Arrest Rates for White and Black Youths, 1967–1998: A National Time Series Analysis," *Criminology* 39 (2001): 591–614.

87. Melanie Wellsmith and Amy Burrell, "The Influence of Purchase Price and Ownership Levels on Theft Targets: The Example of Domestic Burglary," *British Journal of Criminology* 45 (2005): 741–764.

88. Terence Miethe and Robert Meier, *Crime and Its Social Context: Toward an Integrated Theory of Offenders, Victims, and Situations* (Albany, NY: State University of New York Press, 1994).

89. Richard Felson, "Routine Activities and Involvement in Violence as Actor, Witness, or Target," *Violence and Victimization* 12 (1997): 209–223.

90. Georgina Hammock and Deborah Richardson, "Perceptions of Rape: The Influence of Closeness of Relationship, Intoxication, and Sex of Participant," *Violence and Victimization* 12 (1997): 237–247.

91. Wittebrood and Nieuwbeerta, "Criminal Victimization during One's Life Course," pp. 112–113.

92. Patricia Resnick, "Psychological Effects of Victimization: Implications for the Criminal Justice System," *Crime and Delinquency* 33 (1987): 468–478.

93. Dean Kilpatrick, Benjamin Saunders, Lois Veronen, Connie Best, and Judith Von, "Criminal Victimization: Lifetime Prevalence, Reporting to Police, and Psychological Impact," *Crime and Delinquency* 33 (1987): 479–489.

94. U.S. Department of Justice, *Report of the President's Task Force on Victims of Crime* (Washington, DC: U.S. Government Printing Office, 1983).

95. Ibid., pp. 2–10; "Review on Victims: Witnesses of Crime," *Massachusetts Lawyers Weekly,* April 25, 1983, p. 26.

96. Robert Davis, *Crime Victims: Learning How to Help Them* (Washington, DC: National Institute of Justice, 1987).

97. This section leans heavily on Albert Roberts, "Delivery of Services to Crime Victims: A National Survey," *American Journal of Orthopsychiatry* 6 (1991): 128–137; see also Albert Roberts, *Helping Crime Victims: Research, Policy, and Practice* (Newbury Park, CA: Sage, 1990).

98. Randall Schmidt, "Crime Victim Compensation Legislation: A Comparative Study," *Victimology* 5 (1980): 428–437.

99. Ibid.

100. Office for Victims of Crime, 2009 Crime Victims Fund Compensation and Assistance Allocations, www.ojp.usdoj.gov/ovc/fund/cvfa2009.html.

101. Rebecca Campbell, "Rape Survivors' Experiences with the Legal and Medical Systems: Do Rape Victim Advocates Make a Difference?" *Violence against Women* 12 (2006): 30–45.

102. Ulrich Orth and Andreas Maercker, "Do Trials of Perpetrators Retraumatize Crime Victims?" *Journal of Interpersonal Violence* 19 (2004): 212–228.

103. *Payne v. Tennessee,* 111 S.Ct. 2597, 115 L.Ed.2d 720 (1991).
104. Robert Davis and Barbara Smith, "The Effects of Victim Impact Statements on Sentencing Decisions: A Test in an Urban Setting," *Justice Quarterly* 11 (1994): 453–469; Edna Erez and Pamela Tontodonato, "The Effect of Victim Participation in Sentencing on Sentence Outcome," *Criminology* 28 (1990): 451–474.
105. Douglas E. Beloof, "Constitutional Implications of Crime Victims as Participants," *Cornell Law Review* 88 (2003): 282–305.
106. Pater Jaffe, Marlies Sudermann, Deborah Reitzel, and Steve Killip, "An Evaluation of a Secondary School Primary Prevention Program on Violence in Intimate Relationships," *Violence and Victims* 7 (1992): 129–145.
107. Good Samaritan Program, www.ojp.usdoj.gov/ovc/publications/infores/Good_Samaritans/welcome.html (accessed May 28, 2009).
108. Andrew Karmen, "Victim–Offender Reconciliation Programs: Pro and Con," *Perspectives of the American Probation and Parole Association* 20 (1996): 11–14.
109. National Center for Victims of Crime, www.ncvc.org/policy/issues/rights/ (accessed September 24, 2003).
110. Alesha Durfee, "Victim Narratives, Legal Representation, and Domestic Violence Civil Protection Orders," *Feminist Criminology* 4 (2009): 7–31.
111. http://www.nsopr.gov/ (accessed on March 27, 2006).
112. European Union, "The Rights of Crime Victims," http://europa.eu/scadplus/leg/en/lvb/l33091.htm (accessed May 28, 2009).

Chapter 4. Choice Theory: Because They Want To

1. Reuters News Service, "T. Boone Pickens' Son Gets Probation in Fraud Case," December 10, 2007, www.cnbc.com/id/22183588/; Federal Bureau of Investigation, "Hot Stock Tip, Anyone? The Case of the Phony Faxes," 11/20/06, www.fbi.gov/page2/nov06/stock_scam112006.htm.
2. Bob Roshier, *Controlling Crime* (Chicago: Lyceum Books, 1989), p. 10.
3. Gary Becker, "Crime and Punishment: An Economic Approach," *The Journal of Political Economy* 76 (1968) 169–217.
4. James Q. Wilson, *Thinking about Crime,* rev. ed. (New York: Vintage Books, 1983), p. 260.
5. See, generally, Derek Cornish and Ronald Clarke, eds., *The Reasoning Criminal: Rational Choice Perspectives on Offending* (New York: Springer Verlag, 1986); Philip Cook, "The Demand and Supply of Criminal Opportunities," in *Crime and Justice,* vol. 7, ed. Michael Tonry and Norval Morris (Chicago: University of Chicago Press, 1986), pp. 1–28; Ronald Clarke and Derek Cornish, "Modeling Offenders' Decisions: A Framework for Research and Policy," in *Crime and Justice,* vol. 6, ed. Michael Tonry and Norval Morris (Chicago: University of Chicago Press, 1985), pp. 147–187; Morgan Reynolds, *Crime by Choice: An Economic Analysis* (Dallas: Fisher Institute, 1985).
6. Hung-en Sung and Linda Richter, "Rational Choice and Environmental Deterrence in the Retention of Mandated Drug Abuse Treatment Clients," *International Journal of Offender Therapy and Comparative Criminology* 51 (2007): 686–702.
7. Melanie Wellsmith and Amy Burrell, "The Influence of Purchase Price and Ownership Levels on Theft Targets: The Example of Domestic Burglary," *British Journal of Criminology* 45 (2005): 741–764.
8. Jeffrey Bouffard, "Predicting Differences in the Perceived Relevance of Crime's Costs and Benefits in a Test of Rational Choice Theory," *International Journal of Offender Therapy and Comparative Criminology,* 51 (2007): 461–485.
9. George Rengert and John Wasilchick, *Suburban Burglary: A Time and Place for Everything* (Springfield, IL: Charles C Thomas, 1985).
10. Carlo Morselli and Marie-noële Royer, "Criminal Mobility and Criminal Achievement," *Journal of Research in Crime and Delinquency* 45 (2008): 4–21.
11. Bouffard, "Predicting Differences."
12. Ross Matsueda, Derek Kreager, and David Huizinga, "Deterring Delinquents: A Rational Choice Model of Theft and Violence," *American Sociological Review,* 71 (2006): 95–122.
13. Derek Cornish and Ronald Clarke, "Understanding Crime Displacement: An Application of Rational Choice Theory," *Criminology* 25 (1987): 933–947.
14. Michael Gottfredson and Travis Hirschi, *A General Theory of Crime* (Stanford, CA: Stanford University Press, 1990).
15. Jeannette Angell, "Confessions of an Ivy League Hooker," *Boston Magazine,* August 2004, pp. 120–134.
16. Christopher Uggen and Melissa Thompson, "The Socioeconomic Determinants of Ill-Gotten Gains: Within-Person Changes in Drug Use and Illegal Earnings," *American Journal of Sociology* 109 (2003): 146–185.
17. Pierre Tremblay and Carlo Morselli, "Patterns in Criminal Achievement: Wilson and Abrahmse Revisited," *Criminology* 38 (2000): 633–660.
18. Steven Levitt and Sudhir Alladi Venkatesh, "An Economic Analysis of a Drug-Selling Gang's Finances," NBER Working Papers 6592 (Cambridge, MA: National Bureau of Economic Research, 1998).
19. Bill McCarthy, "New Economics of Sociological Criminology," *Annual Review of Sociology* (2002): 417–442.
20. Ronald Akers, "Rational Choice, Deterrence and Social Learning Theory in Criminology: The Path Not Taken," *Journal of Criminal Law and Criminology* 81 (1990): 653–676.
21. Neal Shover, *Aging Criminals* (Beverly Hills, CA: Sage, 1985).
22. Robert Agnew, "Determinism, Indeterminism, and Crime: An Empirical Exploration," *Criminology* 33 (1995): 83–109.
23. Ibid., pp. 103–104.
24. Bruce Jacobs, Volkan Topalli, and Richard Wright. "Carjacking, Street Life, and Offender Motivation," *British Journal of Criminology* 43 (2003): 673–688.
25. Bruce Jacobs and Jody Miller, "Crack Dealing, Gender, and Arrest Avoidance," *Social Problems* 45 (1998): 550–566.
26. Leanne Fiftal Alarid, James Marquart, Velmer Burton, Francis Cullen, and Steven Cuvelier, "Women's Roles in Serious Offenses: A Study of Adult Felons," *Justice Quarterly* 13 (1996): 431–454, at p. 448.
27. Bruce Jacobs, "Crack Dealers' Apprehension Avoidance Techniques: A Case of Restrictive Deterrence," *Justice Quarterly* 13 (1996): 359–381.
28. Ibid., p. 367.

29. Ibid., p. 372.

30. Paul Cromwell, James Olson, and D'Aunn Wester Avary, *Breaking and Entering: An Ethnographic Analysis of Burglary* (Newbury Park, CA: Sage, 1989), p. 24.

31. Ibid., pp. 30–32.

32. George Rengert and John Wasilchick, *Space, Time, and Crime: Ethnographic Insights into Residential Burglary* (Washington, DC: National Institute of Justice, 1989); see also Rengert and Wasilchick, *Suburban Burglary*.

33. Matthew Robinson, "Lifestyles, Routine Activities, and Residential Burglary Victimization," *Journal of Criminal Justice* 22 (1999): 27–52.

34. Patrick Donnelly and Charles Kimble, "Community Organizing, Environmental Change, and Neighborhood Crime," *Crime and Delinquency* 43 (1997): 493–511.

35. Ronald Clarke and Marcus Felson, "Introduction: Criminology, Routine Activity and Rational Choice," in *Routine Activity and Rational Choice* (New Brunswick, NJ: Transaction, 1993), pp. 1–14.

36. Associated Press, "Thrift Hearings Resume Today in Senate," *Boston Globe*, January 2, 1991, p. 10.

37. Ronald Clarke and Patricia Harris, "Auto Theft and Its Prevention," in *Crime and Justice: An Annual Edition*, ed. Michael Tonry and Norval Morris (Chicago: University of Chicago Press, 1992), pp. 1–54, at pp. 20–21.

38. Wellsmith and Burrell, "The Influence of Purchase Price and Ownership Levels on Theft Targets."

39. Wim Bernasco and Paul Nieuwbeerta, "How Do Residential Burglars Select Target Areas? A New Approach to the Analysis of Criminal Location Choice," *British Journal of Criminology* 45 (2005): 296–315.

40. Gordon Knowles, "Deception, Detection, and Evasion: A Trade Craft Analysis of Honolulu, Hawaii's Street Crack Cocaine Traffickers," *Journal of Criminal Justice* 27 (1999): 443–455.

41. John Petraitis, Brian Flay, and Todd Miller, "Reviewing Theories of Adolescent Substance Use: Organizing Pieces in the Puzzle," *Psychological Bulletin* 117 (1995): 67–86.

42. George Rengert, *The Geography of Illegal Drugs* (Boulder, CO: Westview Press, 1996).

43. Levitt and Venkatesh, "An Economic Analysis of a Drug-Selling Gang's Finances."

44. Richard Felson and Steven Messner, "To Kill or Not to Kill? Lethal Outcomes in Injurious Attacks," *Criminology* 34 (1996): 519–545, at p. 541.

45. Richard Wright and Scott Decker, *Armed Robbers in Action: Stickups and Street Culture* (Boston: Northeastern University Press, 1997).

46. Ibid., p. 52.

47. William Smith, Sharon Glave Frazee, and Elizabeth Davison, "Furthering the Integration of Routine Activity and Social Disorganization Theories: Small Units of Analysis and the Study of Street Robbery as a Diffusion Process," *Criminology* 38 (2000): 489–521.

48. Paul Bellair, "Informal Surveillance and Street Crime: A Complex Relationship," *Criminology* 38 (2000): 137–167.

49. John Gibbs and Peggy Shelly, "Life in the Fast Lane: A Retrospective View by Commercial Thieves," *Journal of Research in Crime and Delinquency* 19 (1982): 229–230.

50. Gary Kleck and Don Kates, *Armed: New Perspectives on Guns* (Amherst, NY: Prometheus Books, 2001).

51. Elizabeth Ehrhardt Mustaine and Richard Tewksbury, "Predicting Risks of Larceny Theft Victimization: A Routine Activity Analysis Using Refined Lifestyle Measures," *Criminology* 36 (1998): 829–858.

52. Bruce A. Jacobs, *Robbing Drug Dealers: Violence beyond the Law* (Hawthorne, NY: Aldine de Gruyter, 2000).

53. Bruce A. Jacobs and Richard Wright, "Moralistic Street Robbery," *Crime and Delinquency* 54 (2008): 511–531.

54. Andy Hochstetler, "Opportunities and Decisions: Interactional Dynamics in Robbery and Burglary Groups," *Criminology* 39 (2001): 737–763.

55. Peter Wood, Walter Gove, James Wilson, and John Cochran, "Nonsocial Reinforcement and Habitual Criminal Conduct: An Extension of Learning," *Criminology* 35 (1997): 335–366.

56. Jeff Ferrell, "Criminological Verstehen: Inside the Immediacy of Crime," *Justice Quarterly* 14 (1997): 3–23, at p. 12.

57. Jack Katz, *Seductions of Crime* (New York: Basic Books, 1988).

58. Bill McCarthy, "Not Just 'For the Thrill of It': An Instrumentalist Elaboration of Katz's Explanation of Sneaky Thrill Property Crime," *Criminology* 33 (1995): 519–539.

59. Timothy Brezina, "Delinquent Problem-Solving: An Interpretive Framework for Criminological Theory and Research," *Journal of Research in Crime and Delinquency* 37 (2000): 3–30; Andy Hochstetler, "Opportunities and Decisions: Interactional Dynamics in Robbery and Burglary Groups," *Criminology* 39 (2001): 737–763.

60. Patricia Brantingham, Paul Brantingham, and Wendy Taylor, "Situational Crime Prevention as a Key Component in Embedded Crime Prevention," *Canadian Journal of Criminology & Criminal Justice* 47 (2005): 271–292.

61. Ronald Clarke, *Situational Crime Prevention: Successful Case Studies* (Albany, NY: Harrow and Heston, 1992).

62. Derek Cornish and Ronald Clarke, "Opportunities, Precipitators and Criminal Decisions: A Reply to Wortley's Critique of Situational Crime Prevention," *Crime Prevention Studies* 16 (2003): 41–96; Ronald Clarke and Ross Homel, "A Revised Classification of Situational Prevention Techniques," in *Crime Prevention at a Crossroads*, ed. Steven P. Lab (Cincinnati: Anderson Publishing, 1997).

63. Nancy LaVigne, "Gasoline Drive-Offs: Designing a Less Convenient Environment," in *Crime Prevention Studies*, vol. 2, ed. Ronald Clarke (Monsey, NY: Criminal Justice Press, 1994), pp. 91–114.

64. Barry Webb, "Steering Column Locks and Motor Vehicle Theft: Evaluations for Three Countries," in *Crime Prevention Studies*, vol. 2, ed. Ronald Clarke (Monsey, NY: Criminal Justice Press, 1994), pp. 71–89.

65. Andrew Fulkerson, "Blow and Go: The Breath-Analyzed Ignition Interlock Device as a Technological Response to DWI," *American Journal of Drug and Alcohol Abuse* 29 (2003): 219–235.

66. Marcus Felson, "Those Who Discourage Crime," in *Crime and Place, Crime Prevention Studies*, vol. 4, ed. John Eck and David Weisburd (New York: Criminal Justice Press, 1995), pp. 53–66.

67. John Eck, "Drug Markets and Drug Places," in *Problem-Oriented Policing: Crime-Specific Problems, Critical Issues and Making POP Work*, Vol. II, ed. Corina Solé Brito and Tracy Allan (Washington, DC: Police Executive Research Forum, 1999), p. 29.

68. William Bratton with Peter Knobler, *Turnaround: How America's Top Cop Reversed the Crime Epidemic* (New York: Random House, 1998).

69. Brandon Welsh and David Farrington, "Effects of Closed-Circuit Television on Crime," *Annals of the American Academy of Political and Social Science* 587 (2003): 110–136.

70. "Pervert's Tough Sign-tence," *The Sun Newspaper*, March 26, 2008. www.thesun.co.uk/sol/homepage/news/article960199.ece.

71. Ronald Clarke, "Deterring Obscene Phone Callers: The New Jersey Experience," in *Situational Crime Prevention*, ed. Ronald Clarke (Albany, NY: Harrow and Heston, 1992), pp. 124–132.

72. Ronald Clarke and David Weisburd, "Diffusion of Crime Control Benefits: Observations of the Reverse of Displacement," in *Crime Prevention Studies*, vol. 2, ed. Ronald Clarke (New York: Criminal Justice Press, 1994).

73. David Weisburd and Lorraine Green, "Policing Drug Hot Spots: The Jersey City Drug Market Analysis Experiment," *Justice Quarterly* 12 (1995): 711–734.

74. Lorraine Green, "Cleaning Up Drug Hot Spots in Oakland, California: The Displacement and Diffusion Effects," *Justice Quarterly* 12 (1995): 737–754.

75. Robert Barr and Ken Pease, "Crime Placement, Displacement, and Deflection," in *Crime and Justice, A Review of Research*, vol. 12, ed. Michael Tonry and Norval Morris (Chicago: University of Chicago Press, 1990), pp. 277–319.

76. Clarke, *Situational Crime Prevention*, p. 27.

77. Robert Apel, Greg Pogarsky, and Leigh Bates, "The Sanctions–Perceptions Link in a Model of School-Based Deterrence," *Journal of Quantitative Criminology* 25 (2009): 201–226.

78. Daniel Nagin and Greg Pogarsky, "Integrating Celerity, Impulsivity, and Extralegal Sanction Threats into a Model of General Deterrence: Theory and Evidence," *Criminology* 39 (2001): 865–892.

79. Robert Bursik, Harold Grasmick, and Mitchell Chamlin, "The Effect of Longitudinal Arrest Patterns on the Development of Robbery Trends at the Neighborhood Level," *Criminology* 28 (1990): 431–450; Theodore Chiricos and Gordon Waldo, "Punishment and Crime: An Examination of Some Empirical Evidence," *Social Problems* 18 (1970): 200–217.

80. Etienne Blais and Jean-Luc Bacher, "Situational Deterrence and Claim Padding: Results from a Randomized Field Experiment," *Journal of Experimental Criminology*, 3 (2007): 337–352.

81. R. Steven Daniels, Lorin Baumhover, William Formby, and Carolyn Clark-Daniels, "Police Discretion and Elder Mistreatment: A Nested Model of Observation, Reporting, and Satisfaction," *Journal of Criminal Justice* 27 (1999): 209–225.

82. Daniel Nagin and Greg Pogarsky, "Integrating Celerity, Impulsivity, and Extralegal Sanction Threats into a Model of General Deterrence: Theory and Evidence."

83. Daniel Nagin, "Criminal Deterrence Theory at the Outset of the Twenty-First Century," in *Crime and Justice: An Annual Review of Research*, vol. 23, ed. Michael Tonry (Chicago: University of Chicago Press, 1998), pp. 51–92; for an opposing view, see Robert Bursik, Harold Grasmick, and Mitchell Chamlin, "The Effect of Longitudinal Arrest Patterns on the Development of Robbery Trends at the Neighborhood Level," *Criminology* 28 (1990): 431–450.

84. Daniel Nagin and Greg Pogarsky, "An Experimental Investigation of Deterrence: Cheating, Self-Serving Bias and Impulsivity," *Criminology* 41 (2003): 167–195.

85. Michael White, James Fyfe, Suzanne Campbell, and John Goldkamp, "The Police Role in Preventing Homicide: Considering the Impact of Problem-Oriented Policing on the Prevalence of Murder," *Journal of Research in Crime and Delinquency* 40 (2003): 194–226.

86. Tomislav V. Kovandzic and John J. Sloan, "Police Levels and Crime Rates Revisited: A County-Level Analysis from Florida (1980–1998)," *Journal of Criminal Justice* 30 (2002): 65–76; Steven Levitt, "Using Electoral Cycles in Police Hiring to Estimate the Effect of Police on Crime," *American Economic Review* 87 (1997): 270–291.

87. Thomas Marvell and Carlisle Moody, "Specification Problems, Police Levels, and Crime Rates," *Criminology* 34 (1996): 609–646; Colin Loftin and David McDowall, "The Police, Crime, and Economic Theory: An Assessment," *American Sociological Review* 47 (1982): 393–401.

88. Richard Timothy Coupe and Laurence Blake, "The Effects of Patrol Workloads and Response Strength on Arrests at Burglary Emergencies," *Journal of Criminal Justice* 33 (2005): 239–255.

89. Antonio Tavares, Silvia Mendes, and Claudia Costa, "The Impact of Deterrence Policies on Reckless Driving: The Case of Portugal," *European Journal on Criminal Policy & Research* 14 (2008): 417–429; Greg Pogarsky, "Identifying 'Deterrable' Offenders: Implications for Research on Deterrence," *Justice Quarterly* 19 (2002): 431–453.

90. Ed Stevens and Brian Payne, "Applying Deterrence Theory in the Context of Corporate Wrongdoing: Limitations on Punitive Damages," *Journal of Criminal Justice* 27 (1999): 195–209; Jeffrey Roth, *Firearms and Violence* (Washington, DC: National Institute of Justice, 1994); Thomas Marvell and Carlisle Moody, "The Impact of Enhanced Prison Terms for Felonies Committed with Guns," *Criminology* 33 (1995): 247–281; Gary Green, "General Deterrence and Television Cable Crime: A Field Experiment in Social Crime," *Criminology* 23 (1986): 629–645.

91. Richard D. Clark, Celerity and Specific Deterrence: A Look at the Evidence, *Canadian Journal of Criminology* 30 (1988): 109–122.

92. Nagin and Pogarsky, "An Experimental Investigation of Deterrence."

93. Silvia Mendes, "Certainty, Severity, and Their Relative Deterrent Effects: Questioning the Implications of the Role of Risk in Criminal Deterrence Policy," *Policy Studies Journal* 32 (2004): 59–74.

94. Ernest Van Den Haag, "The Criminal Law as a Threat System," *Journal of Criminal Law and Criminology* 73 (1982): 709–785.

95. David Lykken, "Psychopathy, Sociopathy, and Crime," *Society* 34 (1996): 30–38.

96. George Lowenstein, Daniel Nagin, and Raymond Paternoster, "The Effect of Sexual Arousal on Expectations of Sexual Forcefulness," *Journal of Research in Crime and Delinquency* 34 (1997): 443–473.

97. Lyn Exum, "The Application and Robustness of the Rational Choice Perspective in the Study of Intoxicated and Angry Intentions to Aggress," *Criminology* 40 (2002): 933–967.

98. David Klinger, "Policing Spousal Assault," *Journal of Research in Crime and Delinquency* 32 (1995): 308–324.

99. James Williams and Daniel Rodeheaver, "Processing of Criminal Homicide Cases in a Large Southern City," *Sociology and Social Research* 75 (1991): 80–88.

100. Greg Pogarsky, "Identifying 'Deterrable' Offenders: Implications for Deterrence Research."

101. Nagin and Pogarsky, "Integrating Celerity, Impulsivity, and Extralegal Sanction Threats into a Model of General Deterrence: Theory and Evidence."

102. Anthony Braga, "Pulling Levers Focused Deterrence Strategies and the Prevention of Gun Homicide," *Journal of Criminal Justice* 36 (2008): 332–343.

103. Dieter Dolling, Horst Entorf, Dieter Hermann, and Thomas Rupp, "Deterrence Effective? Results of a Meta-Analysis of Punishment," *European Journal on Criminal Policy & Research* 15 (2009): 201–224.

104. Michael Tonry, "Learning from the Limitations of Deterrence Research," *Crime & Justice: A Review of Research* 37 (2008): 279–311.

105. James Q. Wilson, *Thinking about Crime* (New York: Basic Books, 1975).

106. James Q. Wilson and Richard Herrnstein, *Crime and Human Nature* (New York: Simon & Schuster, 1985), p. 494.

107. Lawrence Sherman and Richard Berk, "The Specific Deterrent Effects of Arrest for Domestic Assault," *American Sociological Review* 49 (1984): 261–272.

108. J. David Hirschel, Ira Hutchison, and Charles Dean, "The Failure of Arrest to Deter Spouse Abuse," *Journal of Research in Crime and Delinquency* 29 (1992): 7–33; Franklyn Dunford, David Huizinga, and Delbert Elliott, "The Role of Arrest in Domestic Assault: The Omaha Experiment," *Criminology* 28 (1990): 183–206.

109. Lawrence Sherman, Janell Schmidt, Dennis Rogan, Patrick Gartin, Ellen Cohn, Dean Collins, and Anthony Bacich, "From Initial Deterrence to Long-Term Escalation: Short-Custody Arrest for Domestic Violence," *Criminology* 29 (1991): 821.

110. Andrew Klein and Terri Tobin, "A Longitudinal Study of Arrested Batterers, 1995–2005: Career Criminals," *Violence against Women* 14 (2008): 136–157.

111. Christina DeJong, "Survival Analysis and Specific Deterrence: Integrating Theoretical and Empirical Models of Recidivism," *Criminology* 35 (1997): 561–576; Paul Tracy and Kimberly Kempf-Leonard, *Continuity and Discontinuity in Criminal Careers* (New York: Plenum Press, 1996).

112. Allen Beck and Bernard Shipley, *Recidivism of Prisoners Released in 1983* (Washington, DC: Bureau of Justice Statistics, 1989).

113. Cassia Spohn and David Holleran, "The Effect of Imprisonment on Recidivism Rates of Felony Offenders: A Focus on Drug Offenders," *Criminology* 40 (2002): 329–359; Raymond Paternoster and Alex Piquero, "Reconceptualizing Deterrence: An Empirical Test of Personal and Vicarious Experiences," *Journal of Research in Crime and Delinquency* 32 (1995): 251–258.

114. David Lovell, L. Clark Johnson, and Kevin Cain, "Recidivism of Supermax Prisoners in Washington State," *Crime & Delinquency* 53 (2007): 633–656.

115. Greg Pogarsky and Alex R. Piquero, "Can Punishment Encourage Offending? Investigating the 'Resetting' Effect," *Journal of Research in Crime and Delinquency* 40 (2003): 92–117.

116. Bruce Arrigo and Jennifer Bullock, "The Psychological Effects of Solitary Confinement on Prisoners in Supermax Units: Reviewing What We Know and Recommending What Should Change," *International Journal of Offender Therapy and Comparative Criminology* 52 (2008): 622–640.

117. Jeffrey Fagan and Tracey Meares, "Deterrence and Social Control: The Paradox of Punishment in Minority Communities," *Ohio State Journal of Criminal Law* 6 (2008): 173–229.

118. Pew Charitable Trust, *One in 100: Behind Bars in America 2008* (Washington, DC: Pew Charitable Trusts, 2008),www.pewcenteronthestates.org/uploadedFiles/One%20in%20100.pdf.

119. See, generally, Raymond Paternoster, "Absolute and Restrictive Deterrence in a Panel of Youth: Explaining the Onset, Persistence/Desistance, and Frequency of Delinquent Offending," *Social Problems* 36 (1989): 289–307; Raymond Paternoster, "The Deterrent Effect of Perceived Severity of Punishment: A Review of the Evidence and Issues," *Justice Quarterly* 42 (1987): 173–217.

120. Isaac Ehrlich, "Participation in Illegitimate Activities: An Economic Analysis," *Journal of Political Economy* 81 (1973): 521–567; Lee Bowker, "Crime and the Use of Prisons in the United States: A Time Series Analysis," *Crime and Delinquency* 27 (1981): 206–212.

121. David Greenberg, "The Incapacitative Effects of Imprisonment: Some Estimates," *Law and Society Review* 9 (1975): 541–580.

122. Reuel Shinnar and Shlomo Shinnar, "The Effects of the Criminal Justice System on the Control of Crime: A Quantitative Approach," *Law and Society Review* 9 (1975): 581–611.

123. William Spelman, "Specifying the Relationship between Crime and Prisons," *Journal of Quantitative Criminology* 24 (2008): 149–178.

124. Steven D. Levitt and Stephen J. Dubner, *Freakonomics: A Rogue Economist Explores the Hidden Side of Everything* (New York: William Morrow, 2006).

125. Steven Levitt, "Why Do Increased Arrest Rates Appear to Reduce Crime: Deterrence, Incapacitation, or Measurement Error?" *Economic Inquiry* 36 (1998): 353–372; see also Thomas Marvell and Carlisle Moody, "The Impact of Prison Growth on Homicide," *Homicide Studies* 1 (1997): 205–233.

126. John Wallerstedt, *Returning to Prison, Bureau of Justice Statistics Special Report* (Washington, DC: U.S. Department of Justice, 1984).

127. James Marquart, Victoria Brewer, Janet Mullings, and Ben Crouch, "The Implications of Crime Control Policy on HIV/AIDS-Related Risk among Women Prisoners," *Crime and Delinquency* 45 (1999): 82–98.

128. Jose Canela-Cacho, Alfred Blumstein, and Jacqueline Cohen, "Relationship between the Offending Frequency of Imprisoned and Free Offenders," *Criminology* 35 (1997): 133–171.

129. Kate King and Patricia Bass, "Southern Prisons and Elderly Inmates: Taking a Look Inside," paper presented at the American Society of Criminology meeting, San Diego, 1997.

130. James Lynch and William Sabol, "Prisoner Reentry in Perspective," Urban Institute: www.urban.org/publications/410213.html (accessed March 15, 2007).

131. Thomas Marvell and Carlisle Moody, "The Impact of Out-of-State Prison Population on State Homicide Rates: Displacement and Free-Rider Effects," *Criminology* 36 (1998): 513–538; Thomas Marvell and Carlisle Moody, "The Impact of Prison Growth on Homicide," *Homicide Studies* 1 (1997): 205–233.

132. Ilyana Kuziemko and Steven D. Levitt, "An Empirical Analysis of Imprisoning Drug Offenders," NBER Working Papers 8489 (Cambridge, MA: National Bureau of Economic Research, 2001).

133. Marc Mauer, testimony before the U.S. Congress, House Judiciary Committee, on "Three Strikes and You're Out," March 1, 1994.

134. James Stephan and Tracy Snell, *Capital Punishment, 1994* (Washington, DC: Bureau of Justice Statistics, 1996), p. 8.

135. Cass R. Sunstein and Adrian Vermeule, "Is Capital Punishment Morally Required? Acts, Omissions, and Lifetime Tradeoffs," *Stanford Law Review* 58 (2006): 703–750 at p. 749.

Chapter 5. Trait Theory

1. Ian Urbina and Manny Fernandez, "Memorial Services Held in U.S. and Around World," *New York Times*, April 21, 2007.

2. Raymond Hernandez, "A Friend, a 'Good Listener' and a Victim in a Day of Tragedy," *New York Times*, April 17, 2007.

3. Ibid.

4. Abbie Boudreau and Scott Zamost, "Girlfriend: Shooter Was Taking Cocktail of 3 Drugs," CNN, February 20, 2008, www.cnn.com/2008/CRIME/02/20/shooter .girlfriend/ (accessed February 25, 2008).

5. Lee Ellis, "A Discipline in Peril: Sociology's Future Hinges on Curing Biophobia," *American Sociologist* 27 (1996): 21–41.

6. Edmund O. Wilson, *Sociobiology: The New Synthesis* (Cambridge, MA: Harvard University Press, 1975).

7. Per-Olof Wikstrom and Rolf Loeber, "Do Disadvantaged Neighborhoods Cause Well-Adjusted Children to Become Adolescent Delinquents?" *Criminology* 38 (2000): 1,109–1,142.

8. Bernard Rimland, *Dyslogic Syndrome: Why Today's Children Are "Hyper," Attention Disordered, Learning Disabled, Depressed, Aggressive, Defiant, or Violent—And What We Can Do About It* (London, England: Jessica Kingsley Publishers, 2008).

9. Anthony Walsh, "Behavior Genetics and Anomie/Strain Theory," *Criminology* 38 (2000): 1,075–1,108.

10. Israel Nachshon, "Neurological Bases of Crime, Psychopathy and Aggression," in *Crime in Biological, Social and Moral Contexts,* ed. Lee Ellis and Harry Hoffman (New York: Praeger, 1990), p. 199.

11. John Cloud, "Harvey Milk: People Told Him No Openly Gay Man Could Win Political Office. Fortunately, He Ignored Them," *Time,* June 14, 1999, www.time.com/ time/time100/heroes/profile/milk01.html.

12. F. T. Crews, A. Mdzinarishvili, D. Kim, J. He, and K. Nixon, "Neurogenesis in Adolescent Brain Is Potently Inhibited by Ethanol," *Neuroscience* 137 (2006): 437–445.

13. G. B. Ramirez, O. Pagulayan, H. Akagi, A. Francisco Rivera, L. V. Lee, A. Berroya, M. C. Vince Cruz, and D. Casintahan, "Tagum Study II: Follow-Up Study at Two Years of Age after Prenatal Exposure to Mercury," *Pediatrics* 111 (2003): 289–295.

14. D. K. L. Cheuk and Virginia Wong, "Attention deficit hyperactivity disorder and blood mercury level: A case-control study in Chinese children," *Neuropediatrics, 37* (2006): 234–240.

15. G. B. Ramirez et al., "Tagum Study II."

16. Eric Konofal, Samuele Cortese, Michel Lecendreux, Isabelle Arnulf, and Marie Christine Mouren, "Effectiveness of Iron Supplementation in a Young Child with Attention-Deficit/Hyperactivity Disorder," *Pediatrics* 116 (2005): 732–734.

17. Alexandra Richardson and Paul Montgomery, "The Oxford-Durham Study: A Randomized Controlled Trial of Dietary Supplementation with Fatty Acids in Children with Developmental Coordination Disorder," *Pediatrics* 115 (2005): 1,360–1,366.

18. Courtney Van de Weyer, "Changing Diets, Changing Minds: How Food Affects Mental Well-Being and Behaviour," Sustain: The Alliance for Better Food and Farming, www.sustainweb.org/pdf/MHRep_LowRes.pdf (accessed March 26, 2006).

19. Crystal Haskell, Andrew Scholey, Philippa Jackson, Jade Elliott, Margaret Defeyter, Joanna Greer, Bernadette Robertson, Tom Buchanan, Brian Tiplady, and David Kennedy, "Cognitive and Mood Effects in Healthy Children during 12 Weeks' Supplementation with Multi-Vitamin/Minerals," *British Journal of Nutrition* 100 (2008): 1,086–1,096.

20. Diana Fishbein, "Neuropsychological Function, Drug Abuse, and Violence: A Conceptual Framework," *Criminal Justice and Behavior* 27 (2000): 139–159.

21. Matti Virkkunen, "Reactive Hypoglycemic Tendency among Habitually Violent Offenders," *Nutrition Reviews Supplement* 44 (1986): 94–103.

22. Stephanie H. M. van Goozen, Walter Matthys, Peggy Cohen-Kettenis, Jos Thijssen, and Herman van Engeland, "Adrenal Androgens and Aggression in Conduct Disorder Prepubertal Boys and Normal Controls," *Biological Psychiatry* 43 (1998): 156–158.

23. Paul Bernhardt, "Influences of Serotonin and Testosterone in Aggression and Dominance: Convergence with Social Psychology," *Current Directions in Psychological Science* 6 (1997): 44–48.

24. Christy Miller Buchanan, Jacquelynne Eccles, and Jill Becker, "Are Adolescents the Victims of Raging Hormones? Evidence for Activational Effects of Hormones on Moods and Behavior at Adolescence," *Psychological Bulletin* 111 (1992): 62–107.

25. Alan Booth and D. Wayne Osgood, "The Influence of Testosterone on Deviance in Adulthood: Assessing and Explaining the Relationship," *Criminology* 31 (1993): 93–117.

26. Celina Cohen-Bendahan, Jan Buitelaar, Stephanie van Goozen, Jacob Orlebeke, and Peggy Cohen-Kettenis, "Is There an Effect of Prenatal Testosterone on Aggression and Other Behavioral Traits? A Study Comparing Same-Sex and Opposite-Sex Twin Girls," *Hormones and Behavior, 47* (2005): 230–237.

27. Albert Reiss and Jeffrey Roth, eds., *Understanding and Preventing Violence* (Washington, DC: National Academy Press, 1993), p. 118.

28. Anthony Walsh, "Genetic and Cytogenetic Intersex Anomalies: Can They Help Us to Understand Gender Differences in Deviant Behavior?" *International Journal of Offender Therapy and Comparative Criminology* 39 (1995): 151–166.

29. Walter Gove, "The Effect of Age and Gender on Deviant Behavior: A Biopsychosocial Perspective," in *Gender and the Life Course*, ed. A. S. Rossi (New York: Aldine, 1985), pp. 115–144.

30. For a review of this concept, see Anne E. Figert, "The Three Faces of PMS: The Professional, Gendered, and Scientific Structuring of a Psychiatric Disorder," *Social Problems* 42 (1995): 56–72.

31. Katharina Dalton, *The Premenstrual Syndrome* (Springfield, IL: Charles C Thomas, 1971).

32. Julie Horney, "Menstrual Cycles and Criminal Responsibility," *Law and Human Nature* 2 (1978): 25–36.

33. Diana Fishbein, "Selected Studies on the Biology of Antisocial Behavior," in *New Perspectives in Criminology*, ed. John Conklin (Needham Heights, MA: Allyn & Bacon, 1996), pp. 26–38.

34. Patricia Weiser Easteal, "Women and Crime: Premenstrual Issues," *Trends & Issues in Crime and Criminal Justice* 31, Australian Institute of Criminology, 2005, www.aic.gov.au/publications/tandi/tandi31.html (accessed June 1, 2009).

35. David C. Bellinger, "Lead," *Pediatrics* 113 (2004): 1,016–1,022; Herbert Needleman, Christine McFarland, Roberta Ness, Stephen Fienberg, and Michael Tobin, "Bone Lead Levels in Adjudicated Delinquents: A Case Control Study," *Neurotoxicology and Teratology* 24 (2002): 711–717.

36. Jeff Evans, "Asymptomatic, High Lead Levels Tied to Delinquency," *Pediatric News* 37 (2003): 13.

37. Mark Opler, Alan Brown, Joseph Graziano, Manisha Desai, Wei Zheng, Catherine Schaefer, Pamela Factor-Litvak, and Ezra S. Susser, "Prenatal Lead Exposure, [Delta]-Aminolevulinic Acid, and Schizophrenia," *Environmental Health Perspectives* 112 (2004): 548–553.

38. Paul Stretesky and Michael Lynch, "The Relationship between Lead Exposure and Homicide," *Archives of Pediatric Adolescent Medicine* 155 (2001): 579–582.

39. Rick Nevin "Understanding International Crime Trends: The Legacy of Preschool Lead Exposure," *Environmental Research* 104 (2007): 315–336.

40. Paul Stewart, Edward Lonky, Jacqueline Reihman, James Pagano, Brooks Gump, and Thomas Darvill, "The Relationship between Prenatal PCB Exposure and Intelligence (IQ) in 9-Year-Old Children," *Environmental Health Perspectives* 116 (2008): 1,416–1,422.

41. Lilian Calderón-Garcidueñas et al., "Air Pollution, Cognitive Deficits and Brain Abnormalities: A Pilot Study with Children and Dogs," *Brain and Cognition* 68 (2008): 117–127.

42. Terrie Moffitt, "The Neuropsychology of Juvenile Delinquency: A Critical Review," in *Crime and Justice: An Annual Review*, vol. 12, ed. Norval Morris and Michael Tonry (Chicago: University of Chicago Press, 1990), pp. 99–169.

43. Terrie Moffitt, Donald Lynam, and Phil Silva, "Neuropsychological Tests Predicting Persistent Male Delinquency," *Criminology* 32 (1994): 277–300; Elizabeth Kandel and Sarnoff Mednick, "Perinatal Complications Predict Violent Offending," *Criminology* 29 (1991): 519–529; Sarnoff Mednick, Ricardo Machon, Matti Virkkunen, and Douglas Bonett, "Adult Schizophrenia Following Prenatal Exposure to an Influenza Epidemic," *Archives of General Psychiatry* 44 (1987): 35–46; C. A. Fogel, S. A. Mednick, and N. Michelson, "Hyperactive Behavior and Minor Physical Anomalies," *Acta Psychiatrica Scandinavia* 72 (1985): 551–556.

44. Nathaniel Pallone and James Hennessy, "Brain Dysfunction and Criminal Violence," *Society* 35 (1998): 21–27.

45. Jean Seguin, Robert Pihl, Philip Harden, Richard Tremblay, and Bernard Boulerice, "Cognitive and Neuropsychological Characteristics of Physically Aggressive Boys," *Journal of Abnormal Psychology* 104 (1995): 614–624; Deborah Denno, "Gender, Crime and the Criminal Law Defenses," *Journal of Criminal Law and Criminology* 85 (1994): 80–180.

46. Adrian Raine, Monte Buchsbaum, and Lori LaCasse, "Brain Abnormalities in Murderers Indicated by Positron Emission Tomography," *Biological Psychiatry* 42 (1997): 495–508.

47. Kevin Beaver, John Paul Wright, and Matt DeLisi, "Self-Control as an Executive Function: Reformulating Gottfredson and Hirschi's Parental Socialization Thesis," *Criminal Justice and Behavior* 34 (2007): 1,345–1,361.

48. J. Arturo Silva, Gregory B. Leong, and Michelle M. Ferrari, "A Neuropsychiatric Developmental Model of Serial Homicidal Behavior," *Behavioral Sciences and the Law* 22 (2004): 787–799.

49. Alice Jones, Kristin Laurens, Catherine Herba, Gareth Barker, and Essi Viding, Amygdala Hypoactivity to Fearful Faces in Boys with Conduct Problems and Callous-Unemotional Traits," *American Journal of Psychiatry* 166 (2009): 95–102.

50. Brian Perron and Matthew Howard, "Prevalence and Correlates of Traumatic Brain Injury among Delinquent Youths," *Criminal Behaviour and Mental Health* 18 (2008): 243–255.

51. Stephen Faraone et al., "Intellectual Performance and School Failure in Children with Attention Deficit Hyperactivity Disorder and in Their Siblings," *Journal of Abnormal Psychology* 102 (1993): 616–623.

52. Simon, "Does Criminal Offender Treatment Work?"

53. Ibid.

54. Molina Pelham, Jr., "Childhood Predictors of Adolescent Substance Use in a Longitudinal Study of Children with ADHD," *Journal of Abnormal Psychology* 112 (2003): 497–507; Peter Muris and Cor Meesters, "The Validity of Attention Deficit Hyperactivity and Hyperkinetic Disorder Symptom Domains in Nonclinical Dutch Children," *Journal of Clinical Child & Adolescent Psychology* 32 (2003): 460–466.

55. Elizabeth Hart et al., "Criterion Validity of Informants in the Diagnosis of Disruptive Behavior Disorders in Children: A Preliminary Study," *Journal of Consulting and Clinical Psychology* 62 (1994): 410–414.

56. Russell Barkley, Mariellen Fischer, Lori Smallish, and Kenneth Fletcher, "Young Adult Follow-Up of Hyperactive Children: Antisocial Activities and Drug Use," *Journal of Child Psychology and Psychiatry* 45 (2004): 195–211.

57. Susan Young, Andrew Smolen, Robin Corley, Kenneth Krauter, John De-Fries, Thomas Crowley, and John Hewitt, "Dopamine Transporter Polymorphism Associated with Externalizing Behavior Problems in Children," *American Journal of Medical Genetics* 114 (2002): 144–149.

58. Avshalom Caspi, Joseph McClay, Terrie E. Moffitt, Jonathan Mill, Judy Martin, Ian W. Craig, Alan Taylor, and Richie Poulton, "Role of Genotype in the Cycle of Violence in Maltreated Children," *Science* 297 (2002): 851–854.

59. M. Skondras, M. Markianos, A. Botsis, E. Bistolaki, and G. Christodoulou, "Platelet Monoamine Oxidase Activity and Psychometric Correlates in Male Violent Offenders Imprisoned for Homicide or Other Violent Acts," *European Archives of Psychiatry and Clinical Neuroscience* 254 (2004): 380–386.

60. Lee Ellis, "Monoamine Oxidase and Criminality: Identifying an Apparent Biological Marker for Antisocial Behavior," *Journal of Research in Crime and Delinquency* 28 (1991): 227–251.

61. Matti Virkkunen, David Goldman, and Markku Linnoila, "Serotonin in Alcoholic Violent Offenders," *The Ciba Foundation Symposium: Genetics of Criminal and Antisocial Behavior* (Chichester, England: Wiley, 1995).

62. Lee Ellis, "Left- and Mixed-Handedness and Criminality: Explanations for a Probable Relationship," in *Left-Handedness: Behavioral Implications and Anomalies*, ed. S. Coren (Amsterdam: Elsevier, 1990), pp. 485–507.

63. Lee Ellis, "Arousal Theory and the Religiosity–Criminality Relationship," in *Contemporary Criminological Theory*, ed. Peter Cordella and Larry Siegel (Boston: Northeastern University, 1996), pp. 65–84.

64. Adrian Raine, Peter Venables, and Sarnoff Mednick, "Low Resting Heart Rate at Age 3 Years Predisposes to Aggression at Age 11 Years: Evidence from the Mauritius Child Health Project," *Journal of the American Academy of Adolescent Psychiatry* 36 (1997): 1,457–1,464.

65. David Rowe, "As the Twig Is Bent: The Myth of Child-Rearing Influences on Personality Development," *Journal of Counseling and Development* 68 (1990): 606–611; David Rowe, Joseph Rogers, and Sylvia Meseck-Bushey, "Sibling Delinquency and the Family Environment: Shared and Unshared Influences," *Child Development* 63 (1992): 59–67; Gregory Carey and David DiLalla, "Personality and Psychopathology: Genetic Perspectives," *Journal of Abnormal Psychology* 103 (1994): 32–43.

66. Anita Thapar, Kate Langley, Tom Fowler, Frances Rice, Darko Turic, Naureen Whittinger, John Aggleton, Marianne Van den Bree, Michael Owen, and Michael O'Donovan, "Catechol O-methyltransferase Gene Variant and Birth Weight Predict Early-Onset Antisocial Behavior in Children with Attention-Deficit/Hyperactivity Disorder," *Archives of General Psychiatry* 62 (2005): 1,275–1,278.

67. For an early review, see Barbara Wooton, *Social Science and Social Pathology* (London: Allen & Unwin, 1959); John Laub and Robert Sampson, "Unraveling Families and Delinquency: A Reanalysis of the Gluecks' Data," *Criminology* 26 (1988): 355–380.

68. D. J. West and D. P. Farrington, "Who Becomes Delinquent?" in *The Delinquent Way of Life*, ed. D. J. West and D. P. Farrington (London: Heinemann, 1977), pp. 1–28; D. J. West, *Delinquency: Its Roots, Careers, and Prospects* (Cambridge, MA: Harvard University Press, 1982).

69. West, *Delinquency*, p. 114.

70. David Farrington, "Understanding and Preventing Bullying," in *Crime and Justice*, vol. 17, ed. Michael Tonry (Chicago: University of Chicago Press, 1993), pp. 381–457.

71. David Rowe and David Farrington, "The Familial Transmission of Criminal Convictions," *Criminology* 35 (1997): 177–201.

72. R. J. Cadoret, C. Cain, and R. R. Crowe, "Evidence for a Gene–Environment Interaction in the Development of Adolescent Antisocial Behavior," *Behavior Genetics* 13 (1983): 301–310.

73. Barry Hutchings and Sarnoff A. Mednick, "Criminality in Adoptees and Their Adoptive and Biological Parents: A Pilot Study," in *Biological Bases in Criminal Behavior*, ed. S. A. Mednick and K. O. Christiansen (New York: Gardner Press, 1977).

74. Michael Lyons, Karestan Koenen, Francisco Buchting, Joanne Meyer, Lindon Eaves, Rosemary Toomey, Seth Eisen, et al., "A Twin Study of Sexual Behavior in Men," *Archives of Sexual Behavior* 33 (2004): 129–136.

75. Sarnoff Mednick and Jan Volavka, "Biology and Crime," in *Crime and Justice*, ed. Norval Morris and Michael Tonry (Chicago: University of Chicago Press, 1980), pp. 85–159 at p. 94.

76. Edwin J. C. G. van den Oord, Frank Verhulst, and Dorret Boomsma, "A Genetic Study of Maternal and Paternal Ratings of Problem Behaviors in 3-Year-Old Twins," *Journal of Abnormal Psychology* 105 (1996): 349–357.

77. Ping Qin, "The Relationship of Suicide Risk to Family History of Suicide and Psychiatric Disorders," *Psychiatric Times* 20 (2003), www.psychiatrictimes.com/p031262 .html.

78. Jane Scourfield, Marianne Van den Bree, Neilson Martin, and Peter McGuffin, "Conduct Problems in Children and Adolescents: A Twin Study," *Archives of General Psychiatry* 61 (2004) 489–496; Jeanette Taylor, Bryan Loney, Leonardo Bobadilla, William Iacono, and Matt McGue, "Genetic and Environmental Influences on Psychopathy Trait Dimensions in a Community Sample of Male Twins," *Journal of Abnormal Child Psychology* 31(2003): 633–645.

79. Ginette Dionne, Richard Tremblay, Michel Boivin, David Laplante, and Daniel Perusse, "Physical Aggression and Expressive Vocabulary in 19-Month-Old Twins," *Developmental Psychology* 39 (2003): 261–273.

80. Sara R. Jaffee, Avshalom Caspi, Terrie Moffitt, Kenneth Dodge, Michael Rutter, Alan Taylor, and Lucy Tully, "Nature × Nurture: Genetic Vulnerabilities Interact with Physical Maltreatment to Promote Conduct Problems," *Development and Psychopathology* 17 (2005): 67–84.

81. Essi Viding, James Blair, Terrie Moffitt, and Robert Plomin, "Evidence for Substantial Genetic Risk for Psychopathy in 7-Year-Olds," *Journal of Child Psychology and Psychiatry* 46 (2005): 592–597.

82. Alice Gregory, Thalia Eley, and Robert Plomin, "Exploring the Association between Anxiety and Conduct Problems in a Large Sample of Twins Aged 2–4," *Journal of Abnormal Child Psychology* 32 (2004): 111–123.

83. Marshall Jones and Donald Jones, "The Contagious Nature of Antisocial Behavior," *Criminology* 38 (2000): 25–46.

84. Lawrence Cohen and Richard Machalek, "A General Theory of Expropriative Crime: An Evolutionary Ecological Approach," *American Journal of Sociology* 94 (1988): 465–501.

85. For a general review, see Martin Daly and Margo Wilson, "Crime and Conflict: Homicide in Evolutionary Psychological

Theory," in *Crime and Justice: An Annual Edition*, ed. Michael Tonry (Chicago: University of Chicago Press, 1997), pp. 51–100.

86. Lee Ellis, "The Evolution of Violent Criminal Behavior and Its Nonlegal Equivalent," in *Crime in Biological, Social and Moral Contexts*, ed. Lee Ellis and Harry Hoffman (New York: Praeger, 1990), pp. 63–65.

87. David Rowe, Alexander Vazsonyi, and Aurelio Jose Figuerdo, "Mating-Effort in Adolescence: A Conditional Alternative Strategy," *Personal Individual Differences* 23 (1997): 105–115.

88. Ibid., p. 101.

89. Todd Shackelford, "Risk of Multiple-Offender Rape–Murder Varies with Female Age," *Journal of Criminal Justice* 30 (2002): 135–142.

90. Margo Wilson, Holly Johnson, and Martin Daly, "Lethal and Nonlethal Violence against Wives," *Canadian Journal of Criminology* 37 (1995): 331–361.

91. Deborah Denno, "Sociological and Human Developmental Explanations of Crime: Conflict or Consensus?" *Criminology* 23 (1985): 711–741.

92. Kevin Beaver, John Paul Wright, and Matt DeLisi, "Delinquent peer group formation: evidence of a gene x environment correlation," *Journal of Genetic Psychology* 169 (2008): 227–244.

93. Theodore Beauchaine, Emily Neuhaus, Sharon Brenner, and Lisa Gatzke-Kopp, "Ten Good Reasons to Consider Biological Processes in Prevention and Intervention Research," *Development and Psychopathology* 20 (2008): 745–774.

94. Glenn Walters and Thomas White, "Heredity and Crime: Bad Genes or Bad Research?" *Criminology* 27 (1989): 455–486, at p. 478.

95. Edwin Driver, "Charles Buckman Goring," in *Pioneers in Criminology*, ed. Hermann Mannheim (Montclair, NJ: Patterson Smith, 1970), p. 440.

96. Gabriel Tarde, *Penal Philosophy*, trans. R. Howell (Boston: Little, Brown, 1912).

97. See, generally, Donn Byrne and Kathryn Kelly, *An Introduction to Personality* (Englewood Cliffs, NJ: Prentice-Hall, 1981).

98. See, generally, D. A. Andrews and James Bonta, *The Psychology of Criminal Conduct* (Cincinnati, OH: Anderson, 1994), pp. 72–75.

99. John Bowlby, *Maternal Care and Mental Health*, World Health Organization Monograph, WHO Monographs Series No. 2 (Geneva: World Health Organization, 1951).

100. Eric Wood and Shelley Riggs, "Predictors of Child Molestation: Adult Attachment, Cognitive Distortions, and Empathy," *Journal of Interpersonal Violence* 23 (2008): 259–275.

101. Karen L. Hayslett-McCall and Thomas J. Bernard, "Attachment, Masculinity, and Self-Control: A Theory of Male Crime Rates," *Theoretical Criminology* 6 (2002): 5–33.

102. This discussion is based on three works by Albert Bandura: *Aggression: A Social Learning Analysis* (Englewood Cliffs, NJ: Prentice-Hall, 1973); *Social Learning Theory* (Englewood Cliffs, NJ: Prentice-Hall, 1977; and "The Social Learning Perspective: Mechanisms of Aggression," in *Psychology of Crime and Criminal Justice*, ed. Hans Toch (New York: Holt, Rinehart & Winston, 1979), pp. 198–236.

103. Amy Street, Lynda King, Daniel King, and David Riges, "The Associations among Male-Perpetrated Partner Violence, Wives' Psychological Distress and Children's Behavior Problems: A Structural Equation Modeling Analysis," *Journal of Comparative Family Studies* 34 (2003): 23–46.

104. David Phillips, "The Impact of Mass Media Violence on U.S. Homicides," *American Sociological Review* 48 (1983): 560–568.

105. Kenneth Dodge, "A Social Information Processing Model of Social Competence in Children," in *Minnesota Symposium in Child Psychology*, vol. 18, ed. M. Perlmutter (Hillsdale, NJ: Erlbaum, 1986), pp. 77–125.

106. Tony Ward and Claire Stewart, "The Relationship between Human Needs and Criminogenic Needs," *Psychology, Crime & Law* 9 (2003): 219–225.

107. David Ward, Mark Stafford, and Louis Gray, "Rational Choice, Deterrence, and Theoretical Integration," *Journal of Applied Social Psychology* 36 (2006): 571–585.

108. L. Huesman and L. Eron, "Individual Differences and the Trait of Aggression," *European Journal of Personality* 3 (1989): 95–106.

109. Rolf Loeber and Dale Hay, "Key Issues in the Development of Aggression and Violence from Childhood to Early Adulthood," *Annual Review of Psychology* 48 (1997): 371–410.

110. Vincent Marziano, Tony Ward, Anthony Beech, and Philippa Pattison, "Identification of Five Fundamental Implicit Theories Underlying Cognitive Distortions in Child Abusers: A Preliminary Study," *Psychology, Crime & Law* 12 (2006): 97–105.

111. See, generally, Walter Mischel, *Introduction to Personality*, 4th ed. (New York: Holt, Rinehart & Winston, 1986).

112. Edelyn Verona and Joyce Carbonell, "Female Violence and Personality," *Criminal Justice and Behavior* 27 (2000): 176–195.

113. Gerhard Blickle, Alexander Schlegel, Pantaleon Fassbender, and Uwe Klein, "Some Personality Correlates of Business White-Collar Crime," *Applied Psychology: An International Review* 55 (2006): 220–233.

114. Hans Eysenck and M. W. Eysenck, *Personality and Individual Differences* (New York: Plenum, 1985).

115. Catrien Bijleveld and Jan Hendriks, "Juvenile Sex Offenders: Differences between Group and Solo Offenders," *Psychology, Crime & Law* 9 (2003): 237–246.

116. Laurie Frost, Terrie Moffitt, and Rob McGee, "Neuropsychological Correlates of Psychopathology in an Unselected Cohort of Young Adolescents," *Journal of Abnormal Psychology* 98 (1989): 307–313.

117. David Lykken, "Psychopathy, Sociopathy, and Crime," *Society* 34 (1996): 30–38.

118. Avshalom Caspi, Terrie Moffitt, Phil Silva, Magda Stouthamer-Loeber, Robert Krueger, and Pamela Schmutte, "Are Some People Crime-Prone? Replications of the Personality–Crime Relationship across Countries, Genders, Races and Methods," *Criminology* 32 (1994): 163–195.

119. Lykken, "Psychopathy, Sociopathy, and Crime."

120. Kent Kiehl, Andra Smith, Adrianna Mendrek, Bruce Forster, Robert Hare, and Peter F. Liddle, "Temporal Lobe Abnormalities in Semantic Processing by Criminal Psychopaths as Revealed by Functional Magnetic Resonance Imaging," *Psychiatry Research: Neuroimaging* 130 (2004): 27–42.

121. James Blair, Derek Mitchell, and Karina Blair, *The Psychopath: Emotion and the Brain* (London: Wiley Blackwell, 2005).

122. Henry Goddard, *Efficiency and Levels of Intelligence* (Princeton, NJ: Princeton University Press, 1920); Edwin Sutherland, "Mental Deficiency and Crime," in *Social Attitudes,* ed. Kimball Young (New York: Henry Holt, 1931), chap. 15.

123. William Healy and Augusta Bronner, *Delinquency and Criminals: Their Making and Unmaking* (New York: Macmillan, 1926).

124. Joseph Lee Rogers, H. Harrington Cleveland, Edwin van den Oord, and David Rowe, "Resolving the Debate over Birth Order, Family Size and Intelligence," *American Psychologist* 55 (2000): 599–612.

125. Sutherland, "Mental Deficiency and Crime."

126. Travis Hirschi and Michael Hindelang, "Intelligence and Delinquency: A Revisionist Review," *American Sociological Review* 42 (1977): 471–586.

127. Anna Elmund, Lennart Melin, Anne-Liis von Knorring, Lemm Proos, and Torsten Tuvemo, "Cognitive and Neuropsychological Functioning in Transnationally Adopted Juvenile Delinquents," *Acta Paediatrica* 93 (2004): 1,507–1,513; Deborah Denno, "Sociological and Human Developmental Explanations of Crime: Conflict or Consensus?" *Criminology* 23 (1985): 711–741.

128. James Q. Wilson and Richard Herrnstein, *Crime and Human Nature* (New York: Simon & Schuster, 1985), p. 148.

129. Richard Herrnstein and Charles Murray, *The Bell Curve: Intelligence and Class Structure in American Life* (New York: Free Press, 1994).

130. H. D. Day, J. M. Franklin, and D. D. Marshall, "Predictors of Aggression in Hospitalized Adolescents," *Journal of Psychology* 132 (1998): 427–435; Scott Menard and Barbara Morse, "A Structuralist Critique of the IQ–Delinquency Hypothesis: Theory and Evidence," *American Journal of Sociology* 89 (1984): 1,347–1,378; Denno, "Sociological and Human Developmental Explanations of Crime."

131. Ulric Neisser et al., "Intelligence: Knowns and Unknowns," *American Psychologist* 51 (1996): 77–101, at p. 83.

132. Aaron Beck, Neil Rector, Neal Stolar, and Paul Grant, *Schizophrenia: Cognitive Theory, Research, and Therapy* (New York, Guilford Press, 2008).

133. Paige Crosby Ouimette, "Psychopathology and Sexual Aggression in Nonincarcerated Men," *Violence and Victimization* 12 (1997): 389–397.

134. Ellen Kjelsberg, "Gender- and Disorder-Specific Criminal Career Profiles in Former Adolescent Psychiatric In-Patients," *Journal of Youth & Adolescence* 33 (2004): 261–270.

135. Barbara Maughan, Richard Rowe, Julie Messer, Robert Goodman, and Howard Meltzer, "Conduct Disorder and Oppositional Defiant Disorder in a National Sample: Developmental Epidemiology," *Journal of Child Psychology & Psychiatry & Allied Disciplines* 45 (2004): 609–621.

136. Jennifer Beyers and Rolf Loeber, "Untangling Developmental Relations between Depressed Mood and Delinquency in Male Adolescents," *Journal of Abnormal Child Psychology* 31 (2003): 247–267.

137. Dorothy Espelage, Elizabeth Cauffman, Lisa Broidy, Alex Piquero, Paul Mazerolle, and Hans Steiner, "A Cluster-Analytic Investigation of MMPI Profiles of Serious Male and Female Juvenile Offenders," *Journal of the American Academy of Child & Adolescent Psychiatry* 42 (2003): 770–777.

138. Robert Vermeiren, "Psychopathology and Delinquency in Adolescents: A Descriptive and Developmental Perspective," *Clinical Psychology Review* 23 (2003): 277–318.

139. David Vinkers, Edwin de Beurs, and Marko Barendregt, "Psychiatric Disorders and Repeat Offending," *American Journal of Psychiatry* 166 (2009): 489.

140. Jacques Baillargeon, Ingrid Binswanger, Joseph Penn, Brie Williams, and Owen Murray, "Psychiatric Disorders and Repeat Incarcerations: The Revolving Prison Door," *American Journal of Psychiatry* 166 (2009): 103–109.

141. John Monahan, *Mental Illness and Violent Crime* (Washington, DC: National Institute of Justice, 1996).

142. Eric Silver, "Mental Disorder and Violent Victimization: The Mediating Role of Involvement in Conflicted Social Relationships," *Criminology* 40 (2002): 191–212.

143. Eric Silver, "Extending Social Disorganization Theory: A Multilevel Approach to the Study of Violence among Persons with Mental Illness," *Criminology* 38 (2000): 1,043–1,074.

144. B. Lögdberg, L-L. Nilsson, M. T. Levander, and S. Levander, "Schizophrenia, Neighbourhood, and Crime," *Acta Psychiatrica Scandinavica* 110 (2004): 92–97; Stacy DeCoster and Karen Heimer, "The Relationship between Law Violation and Depression: An Interactionist Analysis," *Criminology* 39 (2001): 799–837.

145. Courtenay Sellers, Christopher Sullivan, Bonita Veysey, and Jon Shane, "Responding to Persons with Mental Illnesses: Police Perspectives on Specialized and Traditional Practices," *Behavioral Sciences & the Law* 23 (2005): 647–657.

146. Susan Pease and Craig T. Love, "Optimal Methods and Issues in Nutrition Research in the Correctional Setting," *Nutrition Reviews Supplement* 44 (1986): 122–131.

147. Mark O'Callaghan and Douglas Carroll, "The Role of Psychosurgical Studies in the Control of Antisocial Behavior," in *The Causes of Crime: New Biological Approaches,* ed. Sarnoff Mednick, Terrie Moffitt, and Susan Stack (Cambridge: Cambridge University Press, 1987), pp. 312–328.

148. Reiss and Roth, *Understanding and Preventing Violence,* p. 389.

149. Kathleen Cirillo, B. E. Pruitt, Brian Colwell, Paul M. Kingery, Robert S. Hurley, and Danny Ballard, "School Violence: Prevalence and Intervention Strategies for At-Risk Adolescents," *Adolescence* 33 (1998): 319–331.

Chapter 6. Social Structure Theory

1. Arian Campo-Flores, "The Most Dangerous Gang in the United States," *Newsweek,* March 28, 2006; Ricardo Pollack, "Gang Life Tempts Salvador Teens," BBC News, http://news.bbc.co.uk/1/hi/world/americas/4201183.stm (accessed April 3, 2006).

2. FBI, "The MS-13 Threat, A National Assessment," January 14, 2008, www.fbi.gov/page2/jan08/ms13_011408.html.

3. Steven Messner and Richard Rosenfeld, *Crime and the American Dream* (Belmont, CA: Wadsworth, 1994), p. 11.

4. U.S. Census Bureau Data, United States Census, www.census.gov/prod/2008pubs/p60-235.pdf (accessed May 15, 2009).

5. Merrill Lynch, "World Wealth Report," 2008, www.us.capgemini.com/DownloadLibrary/files/Capgemini_FS_WWR08.pdf.

6. Oscar Lewis, "The Culture of Poverty," *Scientific American* 215 (1966): 19–25.

7. Gunnar Myrdal, *The Challenge of World Poverty* (New York: Vintage Books, 1970).

8. Jeanne Brooks-Gunn and Greg J. Duncan, "The Effects of Poverty on Children," *Future of Children* 7 (1997): 34–39.

9. Greg Duncan, W. Jean Yeung, Jeanne Brooks-Gunn, and Judith Smith, "How Much Does Childhood Poverty Affect the Life Chances of Children?" *American Sociological Review* 63 (1998): 406–423.

10. Ibid., p. 409.

11. Maria Velez, Lauren Krivo, and Ruth Peterson, "Structural Inequality and Homicide: An Assessment of the Black-White Gap in Killings," *Criminology* 41 (2003): 645–672.

12. U.S. Department of Census Data, "Poverty Highlights," www.census.gov/hhes/www/poverty/poverty07/pov07hi.html.

13. U.S. Department of Labor, "The Employment Situation: April 2009," www.bls.gov/news.release/pdf/empsit.pdf.

14. Michael Leiber and Joseph Johnson, "Being Young and Black: What Are Their Effects on Juvenile Justice Decision Making?" *Crime & Delinquency* 54 (2008): 560–581.

15. Pew Foundation, "One in 100: Behind Bars in America 2008," www.pewcenteronthestates.org/uploadedFiles/8015PCTS_Prison08_FINAL_2-1-1_FORWEB.pdf.

16. National Center for Education Statistics, 2008, http://nces.ed.gov/fastfacts/display.asp?id=16.

17. Ronald Mincy, ed., *Black Males Left Behind* (Washington, DC: Urban Institute, 2006); Erik Eckholm, "Plight Deepens for Black Men, Studies Warn," *New York Times*, March 20, 2006.

18. James Ainsworth-Darnell and Douglas Downey, "Assessing the Oppositional Culture Explanation for Racial/Ethnic Differences in School Performances," *American Sociological Review* 63 (1998): 536–553.

19. Julie A. Phillips, "White, Black, and Latino Homicide Rates: Why the Difference?" *Social Problems* 49 (2002): 349–374.

20. Jonathan Crane, "The Epidemic Theory of Ghettos and Neighborhood Effects on Dropping Out and Teenage Childbearing," *American Journal of Sociology* 96 (1991): 1,226–1,259; see also Rodrick Wallace, "Expanding Coupled Shock Fronts of Urban Decay and Criminal Behavior: How U.S. Cities Are Becoming 'Hollowed Out,'" *Journal of Quantitative Criminology* 7 (1991): 333–355.

21. Barbara Warner, "The Role of Attenuated Culture in Social Disorganization Theory," *Criminology* 41 (2003): 73–97.

22. Jeffrey Fagan and Garth Davies, "The Natural History of Neighborhood Violence," *Journal of Contemporary Criminal Justice* 20 (2004): 127–147.

23. Justin Patchin, Beth Huebner, John McCluskey, Sean Varano, Timothy Bynum, "Exposure to Community Violence and Childhood Delinquency," *Crime & Delinquency* 52 (2006): 307–332.

24. See Ruth Kornhauser, *Social Sources of Delinquency* (Chicago: University of Chicago Press, 1978), p. 75.

25. Kerryn E. Bell, "Gender and Gangs: A Quantitative Comparison," *Crime & Delinquency* 55 (2009): 363–387.

26. Arlen Egley and Christina O'Donnell, *Highlights of the 2007 National Youth Gang Survey* (Washington, DC: Office of Juvenile Justice and Delinquency Prevention, 2009), www.nationalgangcenter.gov/documents/2007-survey-highlights.pdf.

27. John M. Hagedorn, *A World of Gangs: Armed Young Men and Gangsta Culture* (Minneapolis: University of Minnesota Press, 2008).

28. Clifford R. Shaw and Henry D. McKay, *Juvenile Delinquency and Urban Areas*, rev. ed. (Chicago: University of Chicago Press, 1972).

29. Ibid., p. 52.

30. Ibid., p. 171.

31. Claire Valier, "Foreigners, Crime and Changing Mobilities," *British Journal of Criminology* 43 (2003): 1–21.

32. The best known of these critiques is Kornhauser, *Social Sources of Delinquency*.

33. For a general review, see James Byrne and Robert Sampson, eds., *The Social Ecology of Crime* (New York: Springer Verlag, 1985).

34. See, generally, Robert Bursik, "Social Disorganization and Theories of Crime and Delinquency: Problems and Prospects," *Criminology* 26 (1988): 521–539.

35. D. Wayne Osgood and Jeff Chambers, "Social Disorganization outside the Metropolis: An Analysis of Rural Youth Violence," *Criminology* 38 (2000): 81–117.

36. William Spelman, "Abandoned Buildings: Magnets for Crime?" *Journal of Criminal Justice* 21 (1993): 481–493.

37. Keith Harries and Andrea Powell, "Juvenile Gun Crime and Social Stress: Baltimore, 1980–1990," *Urban Geography* 15 (1994): 45–63.

38. Ellen Kurtz, Barbara Koons, and Ralph Taylor, "Land Use, Physical Deterioration, Resident-Based Control, and Calls for Service on Urban Streetblocks," *Justice Quarterly* 15 (1998): 121–149.

39. Matthew Lee and Terri Earnest, "Perceived Community Cohesion and Perceived Risk of Victimization: A Cross-National Analysis," *Justice Quarterly* 20 (2003): 131–158.

40. Pamela Wilcox, Neil Quisenberry, and Shayne Jones, "The Built Environment and Community Crime Risk Interpretation," *Journal of Research in Crime and Delinquency* 40 (2003): 322–345.

41. Yili Xu, Mora Fiedler, and Karl Flaming, "Discovering the Impact of Community Policing: The Broken Windows Thesis, Collective Efficacy, and Citizens' Judgment," *Journal of Research in Crime and Delinquency* 42 (2005): 147–186.

42. Stephanie Greenberg, "Fear and Its Relationship to Crime, Neighborhood Deterioration, and Informal Social Control," in *The Social Ecology of Crime*, ed. James Byrne and Robert Sampson (New York: Springer Verlag, 1985), pp. 47–62.

43. C. L. Storr, C.-Y. Chen, and J. C. Anthony, "'Unequal Opportunity': Neighborhood Disadvantage and the Chance to Buy Illegal Drugs," *Journal of Epidemiology and Community Health* 58 (2004): 231–238.

44. Pamela Wilcox Rountree and Kenneth Land, "Burglary Victimization, Perceptions of Crime Risk, and Routine Activities: A Multilevel Analysis across Seattle Neighborhoods and Census Tracts," *Journal of Research in Crime and Delinquency* 33 (1996): 147–180.

45. Ted Chiricos, Ranee McEntire, and Marc Gertz, "Social Problems, Perceived Racial and Ethnic Composition of Neighborhood and Perceived Risk of Crime," *Social Problems* 48 (2001): 322–341; Wesley Skogan, "Fear of Crime and Neighborhood Change," in *Communities and Crime*, ed. Albert Reiss and Michael Tonry (Chicago: University of Chicago Press, 1986), pp. 191–232.

46. Catherine E. Ross, John Mirowsky, and Shana Pribesh, "Powerlessness and the Amplification of Threat: Neighborhood Disadvantage, Disorder, and Mistrust," *American Sociological Review* 66 (2001): 568–580.

47. Jodi Lane and James Meeker, "*Social Disorganization* Perceptions, Fear of Gang Crime, and Behavioral Precautions among Whites, Latinos, and Vietnamese," *Journal of Criminal Justice,* 32 (2004): 49–62.

48. John Hagan, Carla Shedd, and Monique Payne, "Race, Ethnicity, and Youth Perceptions of Criminal Injustice," *American Sociological Review* 70 (2005): 381–407.

49. Jane Sprott and Anthony Doob, "The Effect of Urban Neighborhood Disorder on Evaluations of the Police and Courts," *Crime & Delinquency* 55 (2009): 339–362.

50. William Terrill and Michael Reisig, "Neighborhood Context and Police Use of Force," *Journal of Research in Crime and Delinquency* 40 (2003): 291–321.

51. Finn-Aage Esbensen and David Huizinga, "Community Structure and Drug Use: From a Social Disorganization Perspective," *Justice Quarterly* 7 (1990): 691–709.

52. Karen Parker, Brian Stults, and Stephen Rice, "Racial Threat, Concentrated Disadvantage, and Social Control: Considering the Macro-Level Sources of Variation in Arrests," *Criminology* 43 (2005): 1,111–1,134.

53. Bridget Freisthler, Elizabeth Lascala, Paul Gruenewald, and Andrew Treno, "An Examination of Drug Activity: Effects of Neighborhood Social Organization on the Development of Drug Distribution Systems," *Substance Use & Misuse* 40 (2005): 671–686.

54. Micere Keels, Greg Duncan, Stefanie Deluca, Ruby Mendenhall, James Rosenbaum, "Fifteen Years Later: Can Residential Mobility Programs Provide a Long-Term Escape from Neighborhood Segregation, Crime, and Poverty?" *Demography* 42 (2005): 51–72.

55. Allen Liska and Paul Bellair, "Violent-Crime Rates and Racial Composition: Convergence over Time," *American Journal of Sociology* 101 (1995): 578–610.

56. Patricia McCall and Karen Parker, "A Dynamic Model of Racial Competition, Racial Inequality, and Interracial Violence," *Sociological Inquiry* 75 (2005): 273–294.

57. Steven Barkan and Steven Cohn, "Why Whites Favor Spending More Money to Fight Crime: The Role of Racial Prejudice," *Social Problems* 52 (2005): 300–314.

58. Leo Scheurman and Solomon Kobrin, "Community Careers in Crime," in *Communities and Crime*, ed. Albert Reiss and Michael Tonry (Chicago: University of Chicago Press, 1986), pp. 67–100.

59. Ibid.

60. Paul Stretesky, Amie Schuck, and Michael Hogan, "Space Matters: An Analysis of Poverty, Poverty Clustering, and Violent Crime," *Justice Quarterly* 21 (2004): 817–841.

61. Gregory Squires and Charis Kubrin, "Privileged Places: Race, Uneven Development and the Geography of Opportunity in Urban America," *Urban Studies* 42 (2005): 47–68; Matthew Lee, Michael Maume, and Graham Ousey, "Social Isolation and Lethal Violence across the Metro/Nonmetro Divide: The Effects of Socioeconomic Disadvantage and Poverty Concentration on Homicide," *Rural Sociology* 68 (2003): 107–131.

62. Lee, Maume, and Ousey, "Social Isolation and Lethal Violence across the Metro/Nonmetro Divide"; Charis E. Kubrin, "Structural Covariates of Homicide Rates: Does Type of Homicide Matter?" *Journal of Research in Crime and Delinquency* 40 (2003): 139–170; Darrell Steffensmeier and Dana Haynie, "Gender, Structural Disadvantage, and Urban Crime: Do Macrosocial Variables Also Explain Female Offending Rates?" *Criminology* 38 (2000): 403–438.

63. Kyle Crowder and Scott South, "Spatial Dynamics of White Flight: The Effects of Local and Extralocal Racial Conditions on Neighborhood Out-Migration," *American Sociological Review* 73 (2008): 792–812.

64. Paul Jargowsky and Yoonhwan Park, "Cause or Consequence? Suburbanization and Crime in U.S. Metropolitan Areas," *Crime & Delinquency* 55 (2009): 28–50.

65. Jeffrey Morenoff, Robert Sampson, and Stephen Raudenbush, "Neighborhood Inequality, Collective Efficacy, and the Spatial Dynamics of Urban Violence," *Criminology* 39 (2001): 517–560.

66. Scott Menard and Delbert Elliott, "Self-Reported Offending, Maturational Reform, and the Easterlin Hypothesis," *Journal of Quantitative Criminology* 6 (1990): 237–268.

67. Elijah Anderson, *Streetwise: Race, Class and Change in an Urban Community* (Chicago: University of Chicago Press, 1990), pp. 243–244.

68. Jeffrey Michael Cancino, "The Utility of Social Capital and Collective Efficacy: Social Control Policy in Nonmetropolitan Settings," *Criminal Justice Policy Review* 16 (2005): 287–318; Chris Gibson, Jihong Zhao, Nicholas Lovrich, and Michael Gaffney, "Social Integration, Individual Perceptions of Collective Efficacy, and Fear of Crime in Three Cities," *Justice Quarterly* 19 (2002): 537–564; Felton Earls, *Linking Community Factors and Individual Development* (Washington, DC: National Institute of Justice, 1998).

69. Robert J. Sampson and Stephen W. Raudenbush, *Disorder in Urban Neighborhoods: Does It Lead to Crime?* (Washington, DC: National Institute of Justice, 2001).

70. Andrea Altschuler, Carol Somkin, and Nancy Adler, "Local Services and Amenities, Neighborhood Social Capital, and Health," *Social Science and Medicine* 59 (2004): 1,219–1,230.

71. Michael Reisig and Jeffrey Michael Cancino, "Incivilities in Nonmetropolitan Communities: The Effects of Structural Constraints, Social Conditions, and Crime," *Journal of Criminal Justice* 32 (2004): 15–29.

72. Robert Sampson, Jeffrey Morenoff, and Felton Earls, "Beyond Social Capital: Spatial Dynamics of Collective Efficacy for Children," *American Sociological Review* 64 (1999): 633–660.

73. Donald Black, "Social Control as a Dependent Variable," in *Toward a General Theory of Social Control*, ed. D. Black (Orlando, FL: Academic Press, 1990).

74. Jennifer Beyers, John Bates, Gregory Pettit, and Kenneth Dodge, "Neighborhood Structure, Parenting Processes, and the Development of Youths' Externalizing Behaviors: A Multilevel Analysis," *American Journal of Community Psychology* 31 (2003): 35–53.

75. Ronald Simons, Leslie Gordon Simons, Callie Harbin Burt, Gene Brody, and Carolyn Cutrona, "Collective Efficacy, Authoritative Parenting and Delinquency: A Longitudinal Test of a Model Integrating Community and Family-Level Processes," *Criminology* 43 (2005): 989–1,029.

76. April Pattavina, James Byrne, and Luis Garcia, "An Examination of Citizen Involvement in Crime Prevention in High-Risk versus Low- to Moderate-Risk Neighborhoods," *Crime & Delinquency* 52 (2006): 203–231.

77. Paul Bellair, "Informal Surveillance and Street Crime: A Complex Relationship," *Criminology* 38 (2000): 137–170.

78. Skogan, *Disorder and Decline: Crime and the Spiral of Decay in American Neighborhoods* (New York: Free Press, 1990), pp. 15–35.

79. Robert Sampson and W. Byron Groves, "Community Structure and Crime: Testing Social Disorganization Theory," *American Journal of Sociology* 94 (1989): 774–802; Denise Gottfredson, Richard McNeill, and Gary Gottfredson, "Social Area Influences on Delinquency: A Multilevel Analysis," *Journal of Research in Crime and Delinquency* 28 (1991): 197–206.

80. Fred Markowitz, Paul Bellair, Allen Liska, and Jianhong Liu, "Extending Social Disorganization Theory: Modeling the Relationships between Cohesion, Disorder, and Fear," *Criminology* 39 (2001): 293–320.

81. Robert Bursik and Harold Grasmick, "The Multiple Layers of Social Disorganization," paper presented at the annual meeting of the American Society of Criminology, New Orleans, November 1992.

82. George Capowich, "The Conditioning Effects of Neighborhood Ecology on Burglary Victimization," *Criminal Justice and Behavior* 30 (2003): 39–62.

83. Ruth Peterson, Lauren Krivo, and Mark Harris, "Disadvantage and Neighborhood Violent Crime: Do Local Institutions Matter?" *Journal of Research in Crime and Delinquency* 37 (2000): 31–63.

84. Maria Velez, "The Role of Public Social Control in Urban Neighborhoods: A Multi-Level Analysis of Victimization Risk," *Criminology* 39 (2001): 837–864.

85. David Klinger, "Negotiating Order in Patrol Work: An Ecological Theory of Police Response to Deviance," *Criminology* 35 (1997): 277–306.

86. Rodney Stark, "Deviant Places: A Theory of the Ecology of Crime," *Criminology* 25 (1987): 893–911.

87. Robert Kane, "Compromised Police Legitimacy as a Predictor of Violent Crime in Structurally Disadvantaged Communities," *Criminology* 43 (2005): 469–498.

88. Robert Bursik and Harold Grasmick, "Economic Deprivation and Neighborhood Crime Rates, 1960–1980," *Law and Society Review* 27 (1993): 263–278.

89. Delbert Elliott, William Julius Wilson, David Huizinga, Robert Sampson, Amanda Elliott, and Bruce Rankin, "The Effects of Neighborhood Disadvantage on Adolescent Development," *Journal of Research in Crime and Delinquency* 33 (1996): 389–426.

90. James DeFronzo, "Welfare and Homicide," *Journal of Research in Crime and Delinquency* 34 (1997): 395–406.

91. John Worrall, "Reconsidering the Relationship between Welfare Spending and Serious Crime: A Panel Data Analysis with Implications for Social Support Theory," *Justice Quarterly* 22 (2005): 364–391.

92. Ibid., p. 414.

93. Peterson, Krivo, and Harris, "Disadvantage and Neighborhood Violent Crime: Do Local Institutions Matter?".

94. Robert Merton, *Social Theory and Social Structure*, enlarged ed. (New York: Free Press, 1968).

95. Albert Cohen, "The Sociology of the Deviant Act: Anomie Theory and Beyond," *American Sociological Review* 30 (1965): 5–14.

96. Messner and Rosenfeld, *Crime and the American Dream*.

97. Jon Gunnar Bernburg, "Anomie, Social Change and Crime: A Theoretical Examination of Institutional-Anomie Theory," *British Journal of Criminology* 42 (2002): 729–743.

98. John Hagan, Gerd Hefler, Gabriele Classen, Klaus Boehnke, and Hans Merkens, "Subterranean Sources of Subcultural Delinquency beyond the American Dream," *Criminology* 36 (1998): 309–340.

99. Morenoff, Sampson, and Raudenbush, "Neighborhood Inequality, Collective Efficacy, and the Spatial Dynamics of Urban Violence."

100. John Braithwaite, "Poverty, Power, White-Collar Crime and the Paradoxes of Criminological Theory," *Australian and New Zealand Journal of Criminology* 24 (1991): 40–58.

101. Margo Wilson and Martin Daly, "Life Expectancy, Economic Inequality, Homicide, and Reproductive Timing in Chicago Neighbourhoods," *British Journal of Medicine* 314 (1997): 1,271–1,274.

102. Judith Blau and Peter Blau, "The Cost of Inequality: Metropolitan Structure and Violent Crime," *American Sociological Review* 147 (1982): 114–129.

103. Ibid.

104. Tomislav Kovandzic, Lynne Vieraitis, and Mark Yeisley, "The Structural Covariates of Urban Homicide: Reassessing the Impact of Income Inequality and Poverty in the Post-Reagan Era," *Criminology* 36 (1998): 569–600.

105. Scott South and Steven Messner, "Structural Determinants of Intergroup Association," *American Journal of Sociology* 91 (1986): 1,409–1,430; Steven Messner and Scott South, "Economic Deprivation, Opportunity Structure, and Robbery Victimization," *Social Forces* 64 (1986): 975–991.

106. Richard Fowles and Mary Merva, "Wage Inequality and Criminal Activity: An Extreme Bounds Analysis for the United States 1975–1990," *Criminology* 34 (1996): 163–182.

107. Beverly Stiles, Xiaoru Liu, and Howard Kaplan, "Relative Deprivation and Deviant Adaptations: The Mediating Effects of Negative Self Feelings," *Journal of Research in Crime and Delinquency* 37 (2000): 64–90.

108. Robert Agnew, "Foundation for a General Strain Theory of Crime and Delinquency," *Criminology* 30 (1992): 47–87.

109. Ibid., p. 57.
110. Timothy Brezina, "Adolescent Maltreatment and Delinquency: The Question of Intervening Processes," *Journal of Research in Crime and Delinquency* 35 (1998): 71–99.
111. Paul Mazerolle, Velmer Burton, Francis Cullen, T. David Evans, and Gary Payne, "Strain, Anger, and Delinquent Adaptations Specifying General Strain Theory," *Journal of Criminal Justice* 28 (2000): 89–101; Paul Mazerolle and Alex Piquero, "Violent Responses to Strain: An Examination of Conditioning Influences," *Violence and Victimization* 12 (1997): 323–345.
112. George E. Capowich, Paul Mazerolle, and Alex Piquero, "General Strain Theory, Situational Anger, and Social Networks: An Assessment of Conditioning Influences," *Journal of Criminal Justice* 29 (2001): 445–461.
113. Robert Agnew, Timothy Brezina, John Paul Wright, and Francis T. Cullen, "Strain, Personality Traits, and Delinquency: Extending General Strain Theory," *Criminology* 40 (2002): 43–71.
114. Lee Ann Slocum, Sally Simpson, and Douglas Smith, "Strained Lives and Crime: Examining Intra-Individual Variation in Strain and Offending in a Sample of Incarcerated Women," *Criminology* 43 (2005): 1,067–1,110.
115. Robert Agnew, "Stability and Change in Crime over the Life Course: A Strain Theory Explanation," in *Advances in Criminological Theory: Vol. 7, Developmental Theories of Crime and Delinquency*, ed. Terence Thornberry (New Brunswick, NJ: Transaction Books, 1995), pp. 113–137.
116. Lawrence Wu, "Effects of Family Instability, Income, and Income Instability on the Risk of Premarital Birth," *American Sociological Review* 61 (1996): 386–406.
117. Robert Agnew and Helene Raskin White, "An Empirical Test of General Strain Theory," *Criminology* 30 (1992): 475–499.
118. John Hoffman and Alan Miller, "A Latent Variable Analysis of General Strain Theory," *Journal of Quantitative Criminology* 13 (1997): 111–113; Raymond Paternoster and Paul Mazerolle, "General Strain Theory and Delinquency: A Replication and Extension," *Journal of Research in Crime and Delinquency* 31 (1994): 235–263; G. Roger Jarjoura, "The Conditional Effect of Social Class on the Dropout–Delinquency Relationship," *Journal of Research in Crime and Delinquency* 33 (1996): 232–255.
119. Mazerolle, Burton, Cullen, Evans, and Payne, "Strain, Anger, and Delinquent Adaptations: Specifying General Strain Theory."
120. Joanne Kaufman, Cesar Rebellon, Sherod Thaxton, and Robert Agnew, "A General Strain Theory of Racial Differences in Criminal Offending," *The Australian and New Zealand Journal of Criminology* 41 (2008): 421–437.
121. Stephen Cernkovich, Peggy Giordano, and Jennifer Rudolph, "Race, Crime and the American Dream," *Journal of Research in Crime and Delinquency* 37 (2000): 131–170.
122. Byongook Moon, Merry Morash, Cynthia Perez McCluskey, and Hye-Won Hwang, "A Comprehensive Test of General Strain Theory: Key Strains, Situational- and Trait-Based Negative Emotions, Conditioning Factors, and Delinquency," *Journal of Research in Crime and Delinquency* 46 (2009): 182–212.
123. Walter Miller, "Lower-Class Culture as a Generating Milieu of Gang Delinquency," *Journal of Social Issues* 14 (1958): 5–19.
124. Ibid., pp. 14–17.
125. Fred Markowitz and Richard Felson, "Social-Demographic Attitudes and Violence," *Criminology* 36 (1998): 117–138.
126. Jeffrey Fagan, *Adolescent Violence: A View from the Street*, NIJ Research Preview (Washington, DC: National Institute of Justice, 1998).
127. Albert Cohen, *Delinquent Boys* (New York: Free Press, 1955).
128. Ibid., p. 25.
129. Ibid., p. 28.
130. Ibid.
131. Ibid., p. 30.
132. Ibid., p. 133.
133. Richard Cloward and Lloyd Ohlin, *Delinquency and Opportunity* (New York: Free Press, 1960).
134. Ibid., p. 171.
135. Ibid., p. 73.
136. James DeFronzo, "Welfare and Burglary," *Crime and Delinquency* 42 (1996): 223–230.
137. Weed and Seed, www.ojp.usdoj.gov/ccdo/ws/welcome.html (accessed on June 1, 2009).

Chapter 7. Social Process Theories

1. Wright Thompson, "Outrageous Injustice," ESPN online, http://sports.espn.go.com/espn/eticket/story?page=wilson;"Free Genarlow Wilson Now," *New York Times*, December 21, 2006, www.nytimes.com/2006/12/21/opinion/21thu4.html?ei=5088&en=d3a8cf6d030c60b7&ex=1324357200&partner=rssnyt&emc=rss&pagewanted=print.
2. Chandra Thomas, "Why Is Genarlow Wilson in Prison?" *Atlanta Magazine* online, www.atlantamagazine.com/article.php?id=158.
3. Sheldon Glueck and Eleanor Glueck, *Unraveling Juvenile Delinquency* (Cambridge, MA: Harvard University Press, 1950); Ashley Weeks, "Predicting Juvenile Delinquency," *American Sociological Review* 8 (1943): 40–46.
4. Alexander Vazsonyi and Lloyd Pickering, "The Importance of Family and School Domains in Adolescent Deviance: African American and Caucasian Youth," *Journal of Youth and Adolescence* 32 (2003): 115–129; Denise Kandel, "The Parental and Peer Contexts of Adolescent Deviance: An Algebra of Interpersonal Influences," *Journal of Drug Issues* 26 (1996): 289–315; Ann Goetting, "The Parenting–Crime Connection," *Journal of Primary Prevention* 14 (1994): 167–184.
5. John Paul Wright and Francis Cullen, "Parental Efficacy and Delinquent Behavior: Do Control and Support Matter?" *Criminology* 39 (2001): 677–706.
6. Carter Hay, "Parenting, Self-Control, and Delinquency: A Test of Self-Control Theory," *Criminology* 39 (2001): 707–736.
7. Robert Vermeiren, Jef Bogaerts, Vladislav Ruchkin, Dirk Deboutte, and Mary Schwab-Stone, "Subtypes of Self-Esteem and Self-Concept in Adolescent Violent and Property Offenders," *Journal of Child Psychology and Psychiatry* 45 (2004): 405–411.
8. Robert Roberts and Vern Bengston, "Affective Ties to Parents in Early Adulthood and Self-Esteem across 20 Years," *Social Psychology Quarterly* 59 (1996): 96–106.

9. Cesar Rebellon, "Reconsidering the Broken Homes/Delinquency Relationship and Exploring Its Mediating Mechanism(s)," *Criminology* 40 (2002): 103–135.

10. Ming Cui and Rand D. Conger, "Parenting Behavior as Mediator and Moderator of the Association between Marital Problems and Adolescent Maladjustment," *Journal of Research on Adolescence* 18(2008): 261–284.

11. Tiffany Field, "Violence and Touch Deprivation in Adolescents," *Adolescence* 37 (2002): 735–749.

12. Robert Johnson, S. Susan Su, Dean Gerstein, Hee-Choon Shin, and John Hoffman, "Parental Influences on Deviant Behavior in Early Adolescence: A Logistic Response Analysis of Age- and Gender-Differentiated Effects," *Journal of Quantitative Criminology* 11 (1995): 167–192.

13. Thomas Ashby Wills, Donato Vaccaro, Grace McNamara, and A. Elizabeth Hirky, "Escalated Substance Use: A Longitudinal Grouping Analysis from Early to Middle Adolescence," *Journal of Abnormal Psychology* 105 (1996): 166–180.

14. Kristi Holsinger and Alexander Holsinger, "Differential Pathways to Violence and Self-Injurious Behavior: African American and White Girls in the Juvenile Justice System," *Journal of Research in Crime and Delinquency* 42 (2005): 211–242; Carolyn Smith and Terence Thornberry, "The Relationship between Childhood Maltreatment and Adolescent Involvement in Delinquency," *Criminology* 33 (1995): 451–479.

15. Fred Rogosch and Dante Cicchetti, " Child Maltreatment and Emergent Personality Organization: Perspectives from the Five-Factor Model," *Journal of Abnormal Child Psychology* 32 (2004): 123–145.

16. Eric Slade and Lawrence Wissow, "Spanking in Early Childhood and Later Behavior Problems: A Prospective Study of Infants and Young Toddlers," *Pediatrics* 113 (2004): 1,321–1,330; Ronald Simons, Chyi-In Wu, Kuei-Hsiu Lin, Leslie Gordon, and Rand Conger, "A Cross-Cultural Examination of the Link between Corporal Punishment and Adolescent Antisocial Behavior," *Criminology* 38 (2000): 47–79.

17. Murray A. Straus, "Spanking and the Making of a Violent Society: The Short- and Long-Term Consequences of Corporal Punishment," *Pediatrics* 98 (1996): 837–843.

18. Todd Herrenkohl, Rick Kosterman, David Hawkins, and Alex Mason, "Effects of Growth in Family Conflict in Adolescence on Adult Depressive Symptoms: Mediating and Moderating Effects of Stress and School Bonding," *Journal of Adolescent Health* 44 (2009): 146–152.

19. Rand Conger, Institute for Social and Behavioral Research, Iowa State University, www.isbr.iastate.edu/staff/Personals/rdconger/ (accessed May 15, 2009).

20. *The Forgotten Half: Pathways to Success for America's Youth and Young Families* (Washington, DC: William T. Grant Foundation, 1988); Lee Jussim, "Teacher Expectations: Self-Fulfilling Prophecies, Perceptual Biases, and Accuracy," *Journal of Personality and Social Psychology* 57 (1989): 469–480.

21. Eugene Maguin and Rolf Loeber, "Academic Performance and Delinquency," in *Crime and Justice: A Review of Research*, vol. 20, ed. Michael Tonry (Chicago: University of Chicago Press, 1995), pp. 145–264.

22. Christopher B. Swanson, *Who Graduates? Who Doesn't? A Statistical Portrait of Public High School Graduation, Class of 2001* (Washington, DC: Urban Institute, 2004).

23. Gary Sweeten, Shawn D. Bushway, and Raymond Paternoster, "Does Dropping Out of School Mean Dropping into Delinquency?" *Criminology* 47 (2009): 47–91; G. Roger Jarjoura, "Does Dropping Out of School Enhance Delinquent Involvement? Results from a Large-Scale National Probability Sample," *Criminology* 31 (1993): 149–172; Terence Thornberry, Melanie Moore, and R. L. Christenson, "The Effect of Dropping Out of High School on Subsequent Criminal Behavior," *Criminology* 23 (1985): 3–18.

24. Sweeten, Bushway, and Paternoster, "Does Dropping Out of School Mean Dropping into Delinquency?"

25. Catherine Dulmus, Matthew Theriot, Karen Sowers, and James Blackburn, "Student Reports of Peer Bullying Victimization in a Rural School," *Stress, Trauma & Crisis: An International Journal* 7 (2004): 1–15.

26. Tonja Nansel, Mary Overpeck, and Ramani Pilla, "Bullying Behaviors among U.S. Youth: Prevalence and Association with Psychosocial Adjustment," *JAMA* 285 (2001): 2,094–3,100.

27. Jill DeVoe, Katharin Peter, Sally Ruddy, Amanda Miller, Mike Planty, Thomas Snyder, and Michael Rand, *Indicators of School Crime and Safety, 2003* (Washington, DC: U.S. Department of Education and Bureau of Justice Statistics, 2004).

28. Ben Brown and William Reed Benedict, "Bullets, Blades, and Being Afraid in Hispanic High Schools: An Exploratory Study of the Presence of Weapons and Fear of Weapon-Associated Victimization among High School Students in a Border Town," *Crime & Delinquency* 50 (2004): 372–395.

29. Amy Anderson and Lorine Hughes, "Exposure to Situations Conducive to Delinquent Behavior: The Effects of Time Use, Income, and Transportation," *Journal of Research in Crime and Delinquency* 46 (2009): 5–34.

30. Delbert Elliott, David Huizinga, and Suzanne Ageton, *Explaining Delinquency and Drug Use* (Beverly Hills, CA: Sage, 1985); Helene Raskin White, Robert Padina, and Randy La-Grange, "Longitudinal Predictors of Serious Substance Use and Delinquency," *Criminology* 6 (1987): 715–740.

31. Robert Agnew and Timothy Brezina, "Relational Problems with Peers, Gender and Delinquency," *Youth and Society* 29 (1997): 84–111.

32. Paul Friday, Xin Ren, Elmar Weitekamp, Hans-Jürgen Kerner, and Terrance Taylor, "A Chinese Birth Cohort: Theoretical Implications," *Journal of Research in Crime and Delinquency* 42 (2005): 123–146.

33. Daneen Deptula and Robert Cohen, "Aggressive, Rejected, and Delinquent Children and Adolescents: A Comparison of Their Friendships," *Aggression & Violent Behavior* 9 (2004): 75–104; Stephen W. Baron, "Self-control, Social Consequences, and Criminal Behavior: Street Youth and the General Theory of Crime," *Journal of Research in Crime and Delinquency* 40 (2003): 403–425.

34. Sylive Mrug, Betsy Hoza, and William Bukowski. "Choosing or Being Chosen by Aggressive-Disruptive Peers: Do They Contribute to Children's Externalizing and Internalizing Problems?" *Journal of Abnormal Child Psychology* 32 (2004): 53–66; Terence Thornberry and Marvin Krohn, "Peers, Drug Use and Delinquency," in *Handbook of Antisocial Behavior*, ed. David Stoff, James Breiling, and Jack Maser (New York: Wiley, 1997), pp. 218–233.

35. Shelley Keith Matthews and Robert Agnew, "Extending Deterrence Theory: Do Delinquent Peers Condition the

Relationship between Perceptions of Getting Caught and Offending?" *Journal of Research in Crime and Delinquency* 45 (2008): 91–118.

36. Mark Warr, "Age, Peers, and Delinquency," *Criminology* 31 (1993): 17–40.

37. David Fergusson, L. John Horwood, and Daniel Nagin, "Offending Trajectories in a New Zealand Birth Cohort," *Criminology* 38 (2000): 525–551.

38. Sara Battin, Karl Hill, Robert Abbott, Richard Catalano, and J. David Hawkins, "The Contribution of Gang Membership to Delinquency beyond Delinquent Friends," *Criminology* 36 (1998): 93–116.

39. John Paul Wright and Francis Cullen, "Employment, Peers, and Life-Course Transitions," *Justice Quarterly* 21 (2004): 183–205.

40. Colin Baier and Bradley Wright, "If You Love Me, Keep My Commandments": A Meta-Analysis of the Effect of Religion on Crime," *Journal of Research in Crime and Delinquency* 38 (2001): 3–21; Byron Johnson, Sung Joon Jang, David Larson, and Spencer De Li, "Does Adolescent Religious Commitment Matter? A Reexamination of the Effects of Religiosity on Delinquency," *Journal of Research in Crime and Delinquency* 38 (2001): 22–44.

41. Sung Joon Jang and Byron Johnson, "Neighborhood Disorder, Individual Religiosity, and Adolescent Use of Illicit Drugs: A Test of Multilevel Hypothesis," *Criminology* 39 (2001): 109–144.

42. T. David Evans, Francis Cullen, R. Gregory Dunaway, and Velmer Burton Jr., "Religion and Crime Reexamined: The Impact of Religion, Secular Controls, and Social Ecology on Adult Criminality," *Criminology* 33 (1995): 195–224.

43. Edwin H. Sutherland, *Principles of Criminology* (Philadelphia: Lippincott, 1939).

44. See, for example, Edwin Sutherland, "White-Collar Criminality," *American Sociological Review* 5 (1940): 2–10.

45. See Edwin Sutherland and Donald Cressey, *Criminology*, 8th ed. (Philadelphia: Lippincott, 1970), pp. 77–79.

46. Carlo Morselli, Pierre Tremblay, and Bill McCarthy, "Mentors and Criminal Achievement," *Criminology* 44 (2006): 17–43.

47. Sandra Brown, Vicki Creamer, and Barbara Stetson, "Adolescent Alcohol Expectancies in Relation to Personal and Parental Drinking Patterns," *Journal of Abnormal Psychology* 96 (1987): 117–121.

48. Terence P. Thornberry, "The Apple Doesn't Fall Far from the Tree (Or Does It?): Intergenerational Patterns of Antisocial Behavior—The American Society of Criminology 2008 Sutherland Address," *Criminology* 47 (2009): 297–325; Terence Thornberry, Adrienne Freeman-Gallant, Alan Lizotte, Marvin Krohn, and Carolyn Smith, "Linked Lives: The Intergenerational Transmission of Antisocial Behavior," *Journal of Abnormal Child Psychology* 31 (2003): 171–184.

49. Paul Vowell and Jieming Chen, "Predicting Academic Misconduct: A Comparative Test of Four Sociological Explanations," *Sociological Inquiry* 74 (2004): 226–249.

50. Andy Hochstetler, Heith Copes, and Matt DeLisi, "Differential Association in Group and Solo Offending," *Journal of Criminal Justice* 30 (2002): 559–566.

51. Wesley Church II, Tracy Wharton, and Julie Taylor, "An Examination of Differential Association and Social Control Theory: Family Systems and Delinquency," *Youth Violence and Juvenile Justice* 7 (2009): 3–15.

52. Wesley Younts, "Status, Endorsement and the Legitimacy of Deviance," *Social Forces* 87 (2008): 561–590.

53. Dana Haynie, Peggy Giordano, Wendy Manning, and Monica Longmore, "Adolescent Romantic Relationships and Delinquency Involvement," *Criminology* 43 (2005): 177–210.

54. Robert Lonardo, Peggy Giordano, Monica Longmore, and Wendy Manning, "Parents, Friends, and Romantic Partners: Enmeshment in Deviant Networks and Adolescent Delinquency Involvement," *Journal of Youth and Adolescence* 38, (2009): 367–383.

55. Joel Hektner, Gerald August, and George Realmuto, "Effects of Pairing Aggressive and Nonaggressive Children in Strategic Peer Affiliation," *Journal of Abnormal Child Psychology* 31 (2003): 399–412; Matthew Ploeger, "Youth Employment and Delinquency: Reconsidering a Problematic Relationship," *Criminology* 35 (1997): 659–675; William Skinner and Anne Fream, "A Social Learning Theory Analysis of Computer Crime among College Students," *Journal of Research in Crime and Delinquency* 34 (1997): 495–518; Denise Kandel and Mark Davies, "Friendship Networks, Intimacy, and Illicit Drug Use in Young Adulthood: A Comparison of Two Competing Theories," *Criminology* 29 (1991): 441–467.

56. Warr, "Age, Peers, and Delinquency."

57. Clayton Hartjen and S. Priyadarsini, "Gender, Peers, and Delinquency," *Youth & Society* 34 (2003): 387–414.

58. Lonardo et al., "Parents, Friends, and Romantic Partners."

59. Craig Reinerman and Jeffrey Fagan, "Social Organization and Differential Association: A Research Note from a Longitudinal Study of Violent Juvenile Offenders," *Crime and Delinquency* 34 (1988): 307–327.

60. Gresham Sykes and David Matza, "Techniques of Neutralization: A Theory of Delinquency," *American Sociological Review* 22 (1957): 664–670; David Matza, *Delinquency and Drift* (New York: John Wiley, 1964).

61. Matza, *Delinquency and Drift*, p. 51.

62. Sykes and Matza, "Techniques of Neutralization"; see also David Matza, "Subterranean Traditions of Youths," *Annals of the American Academy of Political and Social Science* 378 (1961): 116.

63. Sykes and Matza, "Techniques of Neutralization."

64. Ibid.

65. Ian Shields and George Whitehall, "Neutralization and Delinquency among Teenagers," *Criminal Justice and Behavior* 21 (1994): 223–235; Robert A. Ball, "An Empirical Exploration of Neutralization Theory," *Criminologica* 4 (1966): 22–32. See also M. William Minor, "The Neutralization of Criminal Offense," *Criminology* 18 (1980): 103–120; Robert Gordon, James Short, Desmond Cartwright, and Fred Strodtbeck, "Values and Gang Delinquency: A Study of Street Corner Groups," *American Journal of Sociology* 69 (1963): 109–128.

66. Michael Hindelang, "The Commitment of Delinquents to Their Misdeeds: Do Delinquents Drift?" *Social Problems* 17 (1970): 500–509; Robert Regoli and Eric Poole, "The Commitment of Delinquents to Their Misdeeds: A Reexamination," *Journal of Criminal Justice* 6 (1978): 261–269.

67. Larry Siegel, Spencer Rathus, and Carol Ruppert, "Values and Delinquent Youth: An Empirical Reexamination of Theories of Delinquency," *British Journal of Criminology* 13 (1973): 237–244.

68. Robert Agnew, "The Techniques of Neutralization and Violence," *Criminology* 32 (1994): 555–580.

69. Jeffrey Fagan, *Adolescent Violence: A View from the Street*, NIJ Research Preview (Washington, DC: National Institute of Justice, 1998).

70. Volkan Topalli, "When Being Good Is Bad: An Expansion of Neutralization Theory," *Criminology* 43 (2005): 797–836.

71. Scott Briar and Irving Piliavin, "Delinquency: Situational Inducements and Commitment to Conformity," *Social Problems* 13 (1965–1966): 35–45.

72. Lawrence Sherman and Douglas Smith, with Janell Schmidt and Dennis Rogan, "Crime, Punishment, and Stake in Conformity: Legal and Informal Control of Domestic Violence," *American Sociological Review* 57 (1992): 680–690.

73. Albert Reiss, "Delinquency as the Failure of Personal and Social Controls," *American Sociological Review* 16 (1951): 196–207.

74. Briar and Piliavin, "Delinquency."

75. Walter Reckless, *The Crime Problem* (New York: Appleton-Century Crofts, 1967), pp. 469–483.

76. Among the many research reports by Reckless and his colleagues are Walter Reckless, Simon Dinitz, and Ellen Murray, "Self-Concept as an Insulator against Delinquency," *American Sociological Review* 21 (1956): 744–746; Walter Reckless, Simon Dinitz, and Barbara Kay, "The Self-Component in Potential Delinquency and Potential Non-Delinquency," *American Sociological Review* 22 (1957): 566–570; Walter Reckless, Simon Dinitz, and Ellen Murray, "The Good Boy in a High Delinquency Area," *Journal of Criminal Law, Criminology, and Police Science* 48 (1957): 12–26; Frank Scarpitti, Ellen Murray, Simon Dinitz, and Walter Reckless, "The Good Boy in a High Delinquency Area: Four Years Later," *American Sociological Review* 23 (1960): 555–558; Walter Reckless and Simon Dinitz, "Pioneering with Self-Concept as a Vulnerability Factor in Delinquency," *Journal of Criminal Law, Criminology, and Police Science* 58 (1967): 515–523.

77. Travis Hirschi, *Causes of Delinquency* (Berkeley: University of California Press, 1969).

78. Ibid., p. 231.

79. Ibid., pp. 66–74.

80. Michael Wiatroski, David Griswold, and Mary K. Roberts, "Social Control Theory and Delinquency," *American Sociological Review* 46 (1981): 525–541.

81. Helen Garnier and Judith Stein, "An 18-Year Model of Family and Peer Effects on Adolescent Drug Use and Delinquency," *Journal of Youth and Adolescence* 31 (2002): 45–56; Bobbi Jo Anderson, Malcolm Holmes, and Erik Ostresh, "Male and Female Delinquents' Attachments and Effects of Attachments on Severity of Self-Reported Delinquency," *Criminal Justice and Behavior* 26 (1999): 435–452.

82. Teresa LaGrange and Robert Silverman, "Perceived Strain and Delinquency Motivation: An Empirical Evaluation of General Strain Theory." Paper presented at the American Society of Criminology meeting, Boston, November 1995.

83. Allison Ann Payne, "A Multilevel Analysis of the Relationships among Communal School Organization, Student Bonding, and Delinquency," *Journal of Research in Crime and Delinquency* 45 (2008): 429–455.

84. Norman White and Rolf Loeber, "Bullying and Special Education as Predictors of Serious Delinquency," *Journal of Research in Crime and Delinquency* 45 (2008): 380–397.

85. John Cochran and Ronald Akers, "An Exploration of the Variable Effects of Religiosity on Adolescent Marijuana and Alcohol Use," *Journal of Research in Crime and Delinquency* 26 (1989): 198–225.

86. Mark Regnerus and Glen Elder, "Religion and Vulnerability among Low-Risk Adolescents," *Social Science Research* 32 (2003): 633–658; Mark Regnerus, "Moral Communities and Adolescent Delinquency: Religious Contexts and Community Social Control," *The Sociological Quarterly* 44 (2003): 523–554.

87. Eugene Maguin and Rolf Loeber, "Academic Performance and Delinquency," *Justice Review* 28 (2003): 254–277.

88. Robert Crosnoe, "The Connection between Academic Failure and Adolescent Drinking in Secondary School," *Sociology of Education* 79 (2006): 44–60.

89. Jonathan Zaff, Kristin Moore, Angela Romano Papillo, and Stephanie Williams, "Implications of Extracurricular Activity Participation during Adolescence on Positive Outcomes," *Journal of Adolescent Research* 18 (2003): 599–631; Robert Agnew and David Peterson, "Leisure and Delinquency," *Social Problems* 36 (1989): 332–348.

90. Jeb Booth, Amy Farrell, and Sean Varano, "Social Control, Serious Delinquency, and Risky Behavior: A Gendered Analysis," *Crime & Delinquency* 54 (2008): 423–456.

91. Peggy Giordano, Stephen Cernkovich, and M. D. Pugh, "Friendships and Delinquency," *American Journal of Sociology* 91 (1986): 1,170–1,202.

92. Denise Kandel and Mark Davies, "Friendship Networks, Intimacy, and Illicit Drug Use in Young Adulthood: A Comparison of Two Competing Theories," *Criminology* 29 (1991): 441–467.

93. Lisa Stolzenberg and Stewart D'Alessio, "Co-Offending and the Age–Crime Curve," *Journal of Research in Crime and Delinquency* 45 (2008): 65–86.

94. Stephen Cernkovich, Peggy Giordano, and Jennifer Rudolph, "Race, Crime and the American Dream," *Journal of Research in Crime and Delinquency* 37 (2000): 131–170.

95. Velmer Burton, Francis Cullen, T. David Evans, R. Gregory Dunaway, Sesha Kethineni, and Gary Payne, "The Impact of Parental Controls on Delinquency," *Journal of Criminal Justice* 23 (1995): 111–126.

96. Amy Anderson and Lorine Hughes, "Exposure to Situations Conducive to Delinquent Behavior: The Effects of Time Use, Income, and Transportation," *Journal of Research in Crime and Delinquency* 46 (2009): 5–34.

97. Patrick Seffrin, Peggy Giordano, Wendy Manning, Monica Longmore, "The Influence of Dating Relationships on Friendship Networks, Identity Development, and Delinquency," *Justice Quarterly* 26 (2009): 238–267.

98. Michael Hindelang, "Causes of Delinquency: A Partial Replication and Extension," *Social Problems* 21 (1973): 471–487.

99. Gary Jensen and David Brownfield, "Parents and Drugs," *Criminology* 21 (1983): 543–554. See also M. Wiatrowski, D. Griswold, and M. Roberts, "Social Control Theory and Delinquency," *American Sociological Review* 46 (1981): 525–541.

100. Leslie Samuelson, Timothy Hartnagel, and Harvey Krahn, "Crime and Social Control among High School Dropouts," *Journal of Crime and Justice* 18 (1990): 129–161.

101. Alan E. Liska and M. D. Reed, "Ties to Conventional Institutions and Delinquency: Estimating Reciprocal Effects," *American Sociological Review* 50 (1985): 547–560.

102. Wiatrowski, Griswold, and Roberts, "Social Control Theory and Delinquency."

103. Linda Jackson, John Hunter, and Carole Hodge, "Physical Attractiveness and Intellectual Competence: A Meta-Analytic Review," *Social Psychology Quarterly* 58 (1995): 108–122.

104. Howard Becker, *Outsiders: Studies in the Sociology of Deviance* (New York: Macmillan, 1963), p. 9.

105. Harold Garfinkle, "Conditions of Successful Degradation Ceremonies," *American Journal of Sociology* 61 (1956): 420–424.

106. Stacy DeCoster and Karen Heimer, "The Relationship between Law Violation and Depression: An Interactionist Analysis," *Criminology* 39 (2001): 799–837.

107. Karen Heimer and Ross Matsueda, "Role-Taking, Role-Commitment and Delinquency: A Theory of Differential Social Control," *American Sociological Review* 59 (1994): 365–390.

108. See, for example, Howard Kaplan and Hiroshi Fukurai, "Negative Social Sanctions, Self-Rejection, and Drug Use," *Youth and Society* 23 (1992): 275–298; Howard Kaplan and Robert Johnson, "Negative Social Sanctions and Juvenile Delinquency: Effects of Labeling in a Model of Deviant Behavior," *Social Science Quarterly* 72 (1991): 98–122; Howard Kaplan, Robert Johnson, and Carol Bailey, "Deviant Peers and Deviant Behavior: Further Elaboration of a Model," *Social Psychology Quarterly* 30 (1987): 277–284.

109. John Lofland, *Deviance and Identity* (Englewood Cliffs, NJ: Prentice-Hall, 1969).

110. Frank Tannenbaum, *Crime and the Community* (New York: Columbia University Press, 1938), pp. 19–20.

111. Edwin Lemert, *Social Pathology* (New York: McGraw-Hill, 1951).

112. Ibid., p. 75.

113. Christy Visher, "Gender, Police Arrest Decision, and Notions of Chivalry," *Criminology* 21 (1983): 5–28.

114. Marjorie Zatz, "Race, Ethnicity and Determinate Sentencing," *Criminology* 22 (1984): 147–171.

115. Christina DeJong and Kenneth Jackson, "Putting Race into Context: Race, Juvenile Justice Processing, and Urbanization," *Justice Quarterly* 15 (1998): 487–504.

116. Joan Petersilia, "Racial Disparities in the Criminal Justice System: A Summary," *Crime and Delinquency* 31 (1985): 15–34.

117. Carl Pope and William Feyerherm, "Minority Status and Juvenile Justice Processing," *Criminal Justice Abstracts* 22 (1990): 327–336. See also Carl Pope, "Race and Crime Revisited," *Crime and Delinquency* 25 (1979): 347–357; National Minority Council on Criminal Justice, *The Inequality of Justice* (Washington, DC: National Minority Advisory Council on Criminal Justice, 1981), p. 200.

118. Howard Kaplan and Robert Johnson, "Negative Social Sanctions and Juvenile Delinquency: Effects of Labeling in a Model of Deviant Behavior," *Social Science Quarterly* 72 (1991): 98–122.

119. Ruth Triplett, "The Conflict Perspective, Symbolic Interactionism, and the Status Characteristics Hypothesis," *Justice Quarterly* 10 (1993): 540–558.

120. Lening Zhang, "Official Offense Status and Self-Esteem among Chinese Youths," *Journal of Criminal Justice* 31 (2003): 99–105.

121. Ross Matsueda, "Reflected Appraisals, Parental Labeling, and Delinquency: Specifying a Symbolic Interactionist Theory," *American Journal of Sociology* 97 (1992): 1,577–1,611.

122. Xiaoru Liu, "The Conditional Effect of Peer Groups on the Relationship between Parental Labeling and Youth Delinquency," *Sociological Perspectives* 43 (2000): 499–515.

123. Suzanne Ageton and Delbert Elliott, *The Effect of Legal Processing on Self-Concept* (Boulder, CO: Institute of Behavioral Science, 1973).

124. Mike Adams, Craig Robertson, Phyllis Gray-Ray, and Melvin Ray, "Labeling and Delinquency," *Adolescence* 38 (2003): 171–186.

125. Jón Gunnar Bernburg, Marvin Krohn, and Craig Rivera, "Official Labeling, Criminal Embeddedness, and Subsequent Delinquency: A Longitudinal Test of Labeling Theory," *Journal of Research in Crime and Delinquency* 43 (2006): 67–88.

126. Christine Bowditch, "Getting Rid of Troublemakers: High School Disciplinary Procedures and the Production of Dropouts," *Social Problems* 40 (1993): 493–507.

127. Melvin Ray and William Downs, "An Empirical Test of Labeling Theory Using Longitudinal Data," *Journal of Research in Crime and Delinquency* 23 (1986): 169–194.

128. Sherman and Smith, with Schmidt and Rogan, "Crime, Punishment, and Stake in Conformity."

129. Lawrence Bench and Terry Allen, "Investigating the Stigma of Prison Classification: An Experimental Design," *Prison Journal* 83 (2003): 367–382.

130. Charles Tittle, "Two Empirical Regularities (Maybe) in Search of an Explanation: Commentary on the Age/Crime Debate," *Criminology* 26 (1988): 75–85.

131. Robert Sampson and John Laub, "A Life-Course Theory of Cumulative Disadvantage and the Stability of Delinquency," in *Developmental Theories of Crime and Delinquency,* ed. Terence Thornberry (New Brunswick, NJ: Transaction Press, 1997), pp. 133–161; Douglas Smith and Robert Brame, "On the Initiation and Continuation of Delinquency," *Criminology* 4 (1994): 607–630.

132. Raymond Paternoster and Leeann Iovanni, "The Labeling Perspective and Delinquency: An Elaboration of the Theory and an Assessment of the Evidence," *Justice Quarterly* 6 (1989): 358–394.

133. Shadd Maruna, Thomas Lebel, Nick Mitchell, and Michelle Maples, "Pygmalion in the Reintegration Process: Desistance from Crime through the Looking Glass," *Psychology, Crime & Law* 10 (2004): 271–281.

Chapter 8. Social Conflict and Critical Criminology

1. Amnesty International, "Injustice Fuels Sri Lanka's Cycle of Abuse and Impunity" June 11, 2009, www.amnesty.org/en/news-and-updates/report/injustice-fuels-sri-lankas-cycle-abuse-and-impunity-20090611; Asian Human Rights commission, Sri Lanka: A Disappearance Every Five Hours Is a Result of Deliberate Removal of All Legal Safeguards against Illegal Detention, Murder and Illegal Disposal of Bodies, February 2, 2007, www.ahrchk.net/statements/mainfile.php/2007statements/912/.

2. Michael Lynch and W. Byron Groves, *A Primer in Radical Criminology*, 2nd ed. (Albany, NY: Harrow & Heston, 1989), pp. 32–33.

3. Ian Taylor, Paul Walton, and Jock Young, *The New Criminology: For a Social Theory of Deviance* (London: Routledge & Kegan Paul, 1973).

4. Biko Agozino, "Imperialism, Crime and Criminology: Towards the Decolonisation of Criminology," *Crime, Law, and Social Change* 41 (2004): 343–358.

5. William Chambliss and Robert Seidman, *Law, Order, and Power* (Reading, MA: Addison-Wesley, 1971), p. 503.

6. Richard Quinney, *The Social Reality of Crime* (Boston: Little, Brown, 1970).

7. This section borrows heavily from Richard Sparks, "A Critique of Marxist Criminology," in *Crime and Justice*, vol. 2, ed. Norval Morris and Michael Tonry (Chicago: University of Chicago Press, 1980), pp. 159–208.

8. Barbara Sims, "Crime, Punishment, and the American Dream: Toward a Marxist Integration," *Journal of Research in Crime and Delinquency* 34 (1997): 5–24.

9. Gregg Barak, "Revisionist History, Visionary Criminology, and Needs-Based Justice," *Contemporary Justice Review* 6 (2003): 217–225.

10. Michael Lynch, "Rediscovering Criminology: Lessons from the Marxist Tradition," in *Marxist Sociology: Surveys of Contemporary Theory and Research,* ed. Donald McQuarie and Patrick McGuire (New York: General Hall Press, 1994).

11. Agozino, "Imperialism, Crime and Criminology."

12. Barak, "Revisionist History, Visionary Criminology, and Needs-Based Justice."

13. Tony Platt and Cecilia O'Leary, "Patriot Acts," *Social Justice* 30 (2003): 5–21.

14. Kitty Kelley Epstein, "The Whitening of the American Teaching Force: A Problem of Recruitment or a Problem of Racism?" *Social Justice* 32 (2005): 89–102.

15. Garrett Brown, "The Global Threats to Workers' Health and Safety on the Job," *Social Justice* 29 (2002): 12–25.

16. Robert Bohm, "Radical Criminology: Back to the Basics." Paper presented at the annual meeting of the American Society of Criminology, Phoenix, Arizona, November 1993, p. 2.

17. Alette Smeulers and Roelof Haveman, eds., *Supranational Criminology: Towards a Criminology of International Crimes* (Antwerp, Belguim: Intersentia, 2008).

18. Jeffery Reiman, *The Rich Get Richer and the Poor Get Prison* (New York: Wiley, 1984), pp. 43–44.

19. Rob White, "Environmental Harm and the Political Economy of Consumption," *Social Justice* 29 (2002): 82–102.

20. Sims, "Crime, Punishment, and the American Dream."

21. Greg Palast, "Secret US Plan for Iraqi Oil," BBC News, March 17, 2005, http://news.bbc.co.uk/1/hi/programmes/newsnight/4354269.stm.

22. Jeffrey Ian Ross, *The Dynamics of Political Crime* (Thousand Oaks, CA: Sage, 2003).

23. Lois Romano, "Cunningham Friends Baffled by His Blunder into Bribery: Navy Ace-Turned-Congressman Didn't Act Like Big Spender," December 4, 2005, www.washingtonpost.com/wp-dyn/content/article/2005/12/03/AR2005120301046.html (accessed May 18, 2009); CNN, "Crooked Congressman Going to Prison," www.cnn.com/2006/LAW/03/03/cunningham.sentenced/index.html.

24. American Civil Liberties Union, "What's Wrong with Public Video Surveillance? The Four Problems with Public Video Surveillance," www.aclu.org/privacy/spying/14863res20020225.html (accessed May 18, 2009).

25. BBC News, "Six Days That Shook Iran," July 11, 2000, http://news.bbc.co.uk/2/hi/middle_east/828696.stm.

26. MSNBC News, Bush Acknowledges Secret CIA Prisons," September 6, 2006, www.msnbc.msn.com/id/14689359/ (accessed June 12, 2009); American Civil Liberties Union, "FBI Inquiry Details Abuses Reported by Agents at Guantanamo," January 3, 2007, www.aclu.org/safefree/torture/27816prs20070103.html.

27. Human Rights Watch, "UAE: Exploited Workers Building 'Island of Happiness,'" May 19, 2009, www.hrw.org/en/news/2009/05/18/uae-exploited-workers-building-island-happiness (accessed May 20, 2009).

28. Ross, *The Dynamics of Political Crime.*

29. Amnesty International, "Brazil: One More Human Rights Defender Lost to the Scourge of 'Death-Squads,'" January 26, 2009, www.amnesty.org/en/for-media/press-releases/brazil-one-more-human-rights-defender-lost-scourge-death-squads-20090126.

30. Human Rights Watch, "Chechnya: Research Shows Widespread and Systematic Use of Torture," http://hrw.org/english/docs/2006/11/13/russia14557_txt.htm.

31. Vittorio Bufacchi and Jean Maria Arrigo, "Torture, Terrorism and the State: A Refutation of the Ticking-Bomb Argument," *Journal of Applied Philosophy* 23 (2006): 355–373.

32. Elizabeth Sepper, "The Ties That Bind: How the Constitution Limits the CIA's Actions in the War on Terror," *New York University Law Review* 81 (2006): 1805–1843.

33 Scott Shane, David Johnston, and James Risen, "Secret U.S. Endorsement of Severe Interrogations," *New York Times*, October 4, 2007, www.nytimes.com/2007/10/04/washington/04interrogate.html?_r=1&oref=slogin (accessed January 17, 2008).

34. Michael Cooper and Marc Santora, "McCain Rebukes Giuliani on Waterboarding Remark," *New York Times*, October 26, 2007, www.nytimes.com/2007/10/26/us/politics/26giuliani.html (accessed January 18, 2008).

35. Michael Lynch, "Assessing the State of Radical Criminology: Toward the Year 2000." Paper presented at the annual meeting of the American Society of Criminology, Phoenix, Arizona, November 1993.

36. Steven Box, *Recession, Crime, and Unemployment* (London: Macmillan, 1987).

37. David Barlow, Melissa Hickman-Barlow, and W. Wesley Johnson, "The Political Economy of Criminal Justice Policy: A Time-Series Analysis of Economic Conditions, Crime, and Federal Criminal Justice Legislation, 1948–1987," *Justice Quarterly* 13 (1996): 223–241.

38. Mahesh Nalla, Michael Lynch, and Michael Leiber, "Determinants of Police Growth in Phoenix, 1950–1988," *Justice Quarterly* 14 (1997): 144–163.

39. Dawn L. Rothe, Jeffrey Ian Ross, Christopher W. Mullins, David Friedrichs, Raymond Michalowski, Gregg Barak, David Kauzlarich, and Ronald C. Kramer, "That Was Then, This Is Now, What about Tomorrow? Future Directions in State Crime Studies," *Critical Criminology* 17 (2009): 3–13.

40. David Friedrichs and Jessica Friedrichs, "The World Bank and Crimes of Globalization: A Case Study," *Social Justice* 29 (2002): 13–36.

41. Gresham Sykes, "The Rise of Critical Criminology," *Journal of Criminal Law and Criminology* 65 (1974): 211–229.

42. David Jacobs, "Corporate Economic Power and the State: A Longitudinal Assessment of Two Explanations," *American Journal of Sociology* 93 (1988): 852–881.

43. Deanna Alexander, "Victims of the L.A. Riots: A Theoretical Consideration." Paper presented at the annual meeting of the American Society of Criminology, Phoenix, Arizona, November 1993.

44. Richard Quinney, "Crime Control in Capitalist Society," in *Critical Criminology*, ed. Ian Taylor, Paul Walton, and Jock Young (London: Routledge & Kegan Paul, 1975), p. 199.

45. Ibid.

46. John Hagan, *Structural Criminology* (New Brunswick, NJ: Rutgers University Press, 1989), pp. 110–119.

47. Roy Bhaskar, "Empiricism," in *A Dictionary of Marxist Thought*, ed. T. Bottomore (Cambridge, MA: Harvard University Press, 1983), pp. 149–150.

48. Michael Rustigan, "A Reinterpretation of Criminal Law Reform in Nineteenth-Century England," in *Crime and Capitalism*, ed. D. Greenberg (Palo Alto, CA: Mayfield, 1981), pp. 255–278.

49. Rosalind Petchesky, "At Hard Labor: Penal Confinement and Production in Nineteenth-Century America," in *Crime and Capitalism*, ed. D. Greenberg (Palo Alto, CA: Mayfield, 1981), pp. 341–357; Paul Takagi, "The Walnut Street Jail: A Penal Reform to Centralize the Powers of the State," *Federal Probation* 49 (1975): 18–26.

50. David Jacobs and David Britt, "Inequality and Police Use of Deadly Force: An Empirical Assessment of a Conflict Hypothesis," *Social Problems* 26 (1979): 403–412.

51. Ronald Weitzer and Steven Tuch, "Perceptions of Racial Profiling: Race, Class and Personal Experience," *Criminology* 40 (2002): 435–456.

52. Albert Meehan and Michael Ponder, "Race and Place: The Ecology of Racial Profiling African American Motorists," *Justice Quarterly* 29 (2002): 399–431.

53. Malcolm Homes, "Minority Threat and Police Brutality: Determinants of Civil Rights Criminal Complaints in U.S. Municipalities," *Criminology* 38 (2000): 343–368.

54. Darrell Steffensmeier and Stephen Demuth, "Ethnicity and Judges' Sentencing Decisions: Hispanic-Black-White Comparisons," *Criminology* 39 (2001): 145–178; Alan Lizotte, "Extra-Legal Factors in Chicago's Criminal Courts: Testing the Conflict Model of Criminal Justice," *Social Problems* 25 (1978): 564–580.

55. Terance Miethe and Charles Moore, "Racial Differences in Criminal Processing: The Consequences of Model Selection on Conclusions about Differential Treatment," *Sociological Quarterly* 27 (1987): 217–237.

56. Tracy Nobiling, Cassia Spohn, and Miriam DeLone, "A Tale of Two Counties: Unemployment and Sentence Severity," *Justice Quarterly* 15 (1998): 459–485.

57. Charles Crawford, Ted Chiricos, and Gary Kleck, "Race, Racial Threat, and Sentencing of Habitual Offenders," *Criminology* 36 (1998): 481–511.

58. Michael Lenza, David Keys, and Teresa Guess, "The Prevailing Injustices in the Application of the Missouri Death Penalty (1978 to 1996)," *Social Justice* 32 (2005): 151–166.

59. Thomas Arvanites, "Increasing Imprisonment: A Function of Crime or Socioeconomic Factors?" *American Journal of Criminal Justice* 17 (1992): 19–38.

60. David Greenberg and Valerie West, "State Prison Populations and Their Growth, 1971–1991," *Criminology* 39 (2001): 615–654.

61. Robert Weiss, "Repatriating Low-Wage Work: The Political Economy of Prison Labor Reprivatization in the Postindustrial United States," *Criminology* 39 (2001): 253–292.

62. Jack Gibbs, "An Incorrigible Positivist," *Criminologist* 12 (1987): 2–3.

63. Jackson Toby, "The New Criminology Is the Old Sentimentality," *Criminology* 16 (1979): 513–526.

64. Richard Sparks, "A Critique of Marxist Criminology," in *Crime and Justice*, vol. 2, ed. Norval Morris and Michael Tonry (Chicago: University of Chicago Press, 1980), pp. 159–208.

65. Carl Klockars, "The Contemporary Crises of Marxist Criminology," in *Radical Criminology: The Coming Crisis*, ed. J. Inciardi (Beverly Hills, CA: Sage, 1980), pp. 92–123.

66. Matthew Petrocelli, Alex Piquero, and Michael Smith, "Conflict Theory and Racial Profiling: An Empirical Analysis of Police Traffic Stop Data," *Journal of Criminal Justice* 31 (2003): 1–10.

67. Ibid.

68. Tony Platt, "Criminology in the 1980s: Progressive Alternatives to 'Law and Order,'" *Crime and Social Justice* 21–22 (1985): 191–199.

69. See, generally, Roger Matthews and Jock Young, eds., *Confronting Crime* (London: Sage, 1986); for a thorough review of left realism, see Martin Schwartz and Walter DeKeseredy, "Left Realist Criminology: Strengths, Weaknesses, and the Feminist Critique," *Crime, Law, and Social Change* 15 (1991): 51–72.

70. John Lea and Jock Young, *What Is to Be Done about Law and Order?* (Harmondsworth, England: Penguin, 1984).

71. Ibid., p. 88.

72. Ian Taylor, *Crime in Context: A Critical Criminology of Market Societies* (Boulder, CO: Westview Press, 1999).

73. Ibid, pp. 30–31.

74. Richard Kinsey, John Lea, and Jock Young, *Losing the Fight against Crime* (London: Blackwell, 1986).

75. Martin Schwartz and Walter DeKeseredy, *Contemporary Criminology* (Belmont, CA: Wadsworth, 1993), p. 249.

76. Schwartz and DeKeseredy, "Left Realist Criminology."

77. For a general review of this issue, see Kathleen Daly and Meda Chesney-Lind, "Feminism and Criminology," *Justice Quarterly* 5 (1988): 497–538; Douglas Smith and Raymond Paternoster, "The Gender Gap in Theories of Deviance: Issues and Evidence," *Journal of Research in Crime and Delinquency* 24 (1987): 140–172; and Pat Carlen, "Women, Crime, Feminism, and Realism," *Social Justice* 17 (1990): 106–123.

78. Herman Schwendinger and Julia Schwendinger, *Rape and Inequality* (Newbury Park, CA: Sage, 1983).

79. Daly and Chesney-Lind, "Feminism and Criminology."

80. Janet Saltzman Chafetz, "Feminist Theory and Sociology: Underutilized Contributions for Mainstream Theory," *Annual Review of Sociology* 23 (1997): 97–121.

81. Ibid.

82. James Messerschmidt, *Capitalism, Patriarchy, and Crime* (Totowa, NJ: Rowman & Littlefield, 1986); for a critique of this work, see Herman Schwendinger and Julia Schwendinger, "The World According to James Messerschmidt," *Social Justice* 15 (1988): 123–145.

83. Kathleen Daly, "Gender and Varieties of White-Collar Crime," *Criminology* 27 (1989): 769–793.

84. Jane Roberts Chapman, "Violence against Women as a Violation of Human Rights," *Social Justice* 17 (1990): 54–71.

85. Carrie Yodanis, "Gender Inequality, Violence against Women, and Fear," *Journal of Interpersonal Violence* 19 (2004): 655–675.

86. Victoria Titterington, "A Retrospective Investigation of Gender Inequality and Female Homicide Victimization," *Sociological Spectrum* 26 (2006): 205–236.

87. James Messerschmidt, *Masculinities and Crime: Critique and Reconceptualization of Theory* (Lanham, MD: Rowman & Littlefield, 1993).

88. Angela P. Harris, "Gender, Violence, Race, and Criminal Justice," *Stanford Law Review* 52 (2000): 777–810.

89. Suzie Dod Thomas and Nancy Stein, "Criminality, Imprisonment, and Women's Rights in the 1990s," *Social Justice* 17 (1990): 1–5.

90. Walter DeKeseredy and Martin Schwartz, "Male Peer Support and Woman Abuse: An Expansion of DeKeseredy's Model," *Sociological Spectrum* 13 (1993): 393–413.

91. Daly and Chesney-Lind, "Feminism and Criminology." See also Drew Humphries and Susan Caringella-MacDonald, "Murdered Mothers, Missing Wives: Reconsidering Female Victimization," *Social Justice* 17 (1990): 71–78.

92. Hagan, *Structural Criminology*.

93. John Hagan, A. R. Gillis, and John Simpson, "The Class Structure and Delinquency: Toward a Power–Control Theory of Common Delinquent Behavior," *American Journal of Sociology* 90 (1985): 1,151–1,178; John Hagan, John Simpson, and A. R. Gillis, "Class in the Household: A Power–Control Theory of Gender and Delinquency," *American Journal of Sociology* 92 (1987): 788–816.

94. John Hagan, Bill McCarthy, and Holly Foster, "A Gendered Theory of Delinquency and Despair in the Life Course," *Acta Sociologica* 45 (2002): 37–47.

95. Brenda Sims Blackwell, Christine Sellers, and Sheila Schlaupitz, "A Power–Control Theory of Vulnerability to Crime and Adolescent Role Exits—Revisited," *Canadian Review of Sociology and Anthropology* 39 (2002): 199–219.

96. Brenda Sims Blackwell, "Perceived Sanction Threats, Gender, and Crime: A Test and Elaboration of Power–Control Theory," *Criminology* 38 (2000): 439–488.

97. Christopher Uggen, "Class, Gender, and Arrest: An Intergenerational Analysis of Workplace Power and Control," *Criminology* 38 (2001): 835–862.

98. Gary Jensen, "Power–Control versus Social-Control Theory: Identifying Crucial Differences for Future Research." Paper presented at the annual meeting of the American Society of Criminology, Baltimore, Maryland, November 1990.

99. Gary Jensen and Kevin Thompson, "What's Class Got to Do with It? A Further Examination of Power–Control Theory," *American Journal of Sociology* 95 (1990): 1,009–1,023. For some critical research, see Simon Singer and Murray Levine, "Power–Control Theory, Gender and Delinquency: A Partial Replication with Additional Evidence on the Effects of Peers," *Criminology* 26 (1988): 627–648.

100. Kevin Thompson, "Gender and Adolescent Drinking Problems: The Effects of Occupational Structure," *Social Problems* 36 (1989): 30–38.

101. Kristin Mack and Michael Leiber, "Race, Gender, Single-Mother Households, and Delinquency: A Further Test of Power-Control Theory," *Youth & Society* 37 (2005): 115–144.

102. See, generally, Uggen, "Class, Gender, and Arrest."

103. Brenda Sims Blackwell and Alex Piquero, "On the Relationships between Gender, Power Control, Self-Control, and Crime," *Journal of Criminal Justice* 33 (2005): 1–17.

104. Liz Walz, "One Blood," *Contemporary Justice Review* 6 (2003): 25–36.

105. John F. Wozniak, "Poverty and Peacemaking Criminology: Beyond Mainstream Criminology," *Critical Criminology* 16 (2008): 209–223.

106. See, for example, Tifft and Sullivan, *The Struggle to Be Human*; Dennis Sullivan, *The Mask of Love* (Port Washington, NY: Kennikat Press, 1980).

107. Larry Tifft, "Foreword," in Sullivan, *The Mask of Love*, p. 6.

108. Sullivan, *The Mask of Love*, p. 141.

109. Dennis Sullivan and Larry Tifft, *Restorative Justice* (Monsey, NY: Willow Tree Press, 2001).

110. Tomislav Kovandzic and Lynne Vieraitis, "The Effect of County-Level Prison Population Growth on Crime Rates," *Criminology & Public Policy* 5 (2006): 213–244; Robert DeFina and Thomas Arvanites, "The Weak Effect of Imprisonment on Crime: 1971–1998," *Social Science Quarterly* 83 (2002): 635–654.

111. Kathleen Daly and Russ Immarigeon, "The Past, Present and Future of Restorative Justice: Some Critical Reflections," *Contemporary Justice Review* 1 (1998): 21–45.

112. Howard Zehr, *The Little Book of Restorative Justice* (Intercourse, PA: Good Books, 2002): 1–10.

113. Alfred Villaume, "'Life without Parole' and 'Virtual Life Sentences': Death Sentences by Any Other Name," *Contemporary Justice Review* 8 (2005): 265–277.

114. Gene Stephens, "The Future of Policing: From a War Model to a Peace Model," in *The Past, Present and Future of American Criminal Justice*, ed. Brendan Maguire and Polly Radosh (Dix Hills, NY: General Hall, 1996), pp. 77–93.

115. Rick Shifley, "The Organization of Work as a Factor in Social Well-Being," *Contemporary Justice Review* 6 (2003): 105–126.

116. Kay Pranis, "Peacemaking Circles: Restorative Justice in Practice Allows Victims and Offenders to Begin Repairing the Harm," *Corrections Today* 59 (1997): 74–78.

117. Carol LaPrairie, "The 'New' Justice: Some Implications for Aboriginal Communities," *Canadian Journal of Criminology* 40 (1998): 61–79.

118. Diane Schaefer, "A Disembodied Community Collaborates in a Homicide: Can Empathy Transform a Failing Justice System?" *Contemporary Justice Review* 6 (2003): 133–143.

119. David R. Karp and Beau Breslin, "Restorative Justice in School Communities," *Youth & Society* 33 (2001): 249–272.

120. Paul Jesilow and Deborah Parsons, "Community Policing as Peacemaking," *Policing & Society* 10 (2000): 163–183.

121. Gordon Bazemore and Curt Taylor Griffiths, "Conferences, Circles, Boards, and Mediations: The 'New Wave' of Community Justice Decision Making," *Federal Probation* 61 (1997): 25–37.

122. Lawrence W. Sherman and Heather Strang, *Restorative Justice: The Evidence* (London, England: Smith Institute, 2007), www.sas.upenn.edu/jerrylee/RJ_full_report.pdf.

123. This section is based on Gordon Bazemore and Mara Schiff, "Paradigm Muddle or Paradigm Paralysis? The Wide and Narrow Roads to Restorative Justice Reform (Or, a Little Confusion May Be a Good Thing)," *Contemporary Justice Review* 7 (2004): 37–57.

124. Sherman and Strang, *Restorative Justice: The Evidence.*

125. John Braithwaite, "Setting Standards for Restorative Justice," *British Journal of Criminology* 42 (2002): 563–577.

126. David Altschuler, "Community Justice Initiatives: Issues and Challenges in the U.S. Context," *Federal Probation* 65 (2001): 28–33.

127. Lois Presser and Patricia Van Voorhis, "Values and Evaluation: Assessing Processes and Outcomes of Restorative Justice Programs," *Crime & Delinquency* 48 (2002): 162–189.

128. Sharon Levrant, Francis Cullen, Betsy Fulton, and John Wozniak, "Reconsidering Restorative Justice: The Corruption of Benevolence Revisited?" *Crime & Delinquency* 45 (1999): 3–28.

129. Edward Gumz, "American Social Work, Corrections and Restorative Justice: An Appraisal," *International Journal of Offender Therapy & Comparative Criminology* 48 (2004): 449–460.

Chapter 9. Developmental Theories: Life-Course and Latent Trait

1. T. J. Stiles, *Jesse James, Last Rebel of the Civil War* (New York: Vintage, 2003); Ted Yeatman, *Frank & Jesse James: The Story behind the Legend* (Nashville, TN: Cumberland House, 2003).

2. See, generally, John Laub and Robert Sampson, "The Sutherland–Glueck Debate: On the Sociology of Criminological Knowledge," *American Journal of Sociology* 96 (1991): 1,402–1,440; John Laub and Robert Sampson, "Unraveling Families and Delinquency: A Reanalysis of the Gluecks' Data," *Criminology* 26 (1988): 355–380.

3. Rolf Loeber and Marc Le Blanc, "Toward a Developmental Criminology," in *Crime and Justice,* vol. 12, ed. Norval Morris and Michael Tonry (Chicago: University of Chicago Press, 1990), pp. 375–473; Rolf Loeber and Marc Le Blanc, "Developmental Criminology Updated," in *Crime and Justice,* vol. 23, ed. Michael Tonry (Chicago: University of Chicago Press, 1998), pp. 115–198.

4. Marvin Krohn, Alan Lizotte, and Cynthia Perez, "The Interrelationship between Substance Use and Precocious Transitions to Adult Sexuality," *Journal of Health and Social Behavior* 38 (1997): 87–103, at p. 88.

5. Bradley Entner Wright, Avshalom Caspi, Terrie Moffitt, and Phil Silva, "The Effects of Social Ties on Crime Vary by Criminal Propensity: A Life-Course Model of Interdependence," *Criminology* 39 (2001): 321–352.

6. Gerald Patterson, Barbara DeBaryshe, and Elizabeth Ramsey, "A Developmental Perspective on Antisocial Behavior," *American Psychologist* 44 (1989): 329–335.

7. Robert Sampson and John Laub, "Crime and Deviance in the Life Course," *American Review of Sociology* 18 (1992): 63–84.

8. David Farrington, Darrick Jolliffe, Rolf Loeber, Magda Stouthamer-Loeber, and Larry Kalb, "The Concentration of Offenders in Families, and Family Criminality in the Prediction of Boys' Delinquency," *Journal of Adolescence* 24 (2001): 579–596.

9. Raymond Paternoster, Charles Dean, Alex Piquero, Paul Mazerolle, and Robert Brame, "Generality, Continuity, and Change in Offending," *Journal of Quantitative Criminology* 13 (1997): 231–266.

10. Magda Stouthamer-Loeber and Evelyn Wei, "The Precursors of Young Fatherhood and Its Effect on Delinquency of Teenage Males," *Journal of Adolescent Health* 22 (1998): 56–65; Richard Jessor, John Donovan, and Francis Costa, *Beyond Adolescence: Problem Behavior and Young Adult Development* (New York: Cambridge University Press, 1991); Xavier Coll, Fergus Law, Aurelio Tobias, Keith Hawton, and Joseph Tomas, "Abuse and Deliberate Self-Poisoning in Women: A Matched Case-Control Study," *Child Abuse and Neglect* 25 (2001): 1,291–1,293.

11. Richard Miech, Avshalom Caspi, Terrie Moffitt, Bradley Entner Wright, and Phil Silva, "Low Socioeconomic Status and Mental Disorders: A Longitudinal Study of Selection and Causation during Young Adulthood," *American Journal of Sociology* 104 (1999): 1,096–1,131; Krohn, Lizotte, and Perez, "The Interrelationship between Substance Use and Precocious Transitions to Adult Sexuality," p. 88; Richard Jessor, "Risk Behavior in Adolescence: A Psychosocial Framework for Understanding and Action," in *Adolescents at Risk: Medical and Social Perspectives,* ed. D. E. Rogers and E. Ginzburg (Boulder, CO: Westview Press, 1992).

12. Rolf Loeber, Dustin Pardini, D. Lynn Homish, Evelyn Wei, Anne Crawford, David Farrington, Magda Stouthamer-Loeber, Judith Creemers, Steven Koehler, and Richard Rosenfeld, "The Prediction of Violence and Homicide in Young Men," *Journal of Consulting and Clinical Psychology* 73 (2005): 1,074–1,088.

13. Deborah Capaldi and Gerald Patterson, "Can Violent Offenders Be Distinguished from Frequent Offenders? Prediction from Childhood to Adolescence," *Journal of Research in Crime and Delinquency* 33 (1996): 206–231; D. Wayne Osgood, "The Covariation among Adolescent Problem Behaviors." Paper presented at the annual meeting of the American Society of Criminology, Baltimore, November 1990.

14. Terence Thornberry, Carolyn Smith, and Gregory Howard, "Risk Factors for Teenage Fatherhood," *Journal of Marriage and the Family* 59 (1997): 505–522; Todd Miller, Timothy Smith, Charles Turner, Margarita Guijarro, and Amanda Hallet, "A Meta-Analytic Review of Research on Hostility and Physical Health," *Psychological Bulletin* 119 (1996): 322–348; Marianne Junger, "Accidents and Crime," in *The Generality of Deviance,* ed. T. Hirschi and M. Gottfredson (New Brunswick, NJ: Transaction Books, 1993).

15. James Marquart, Victoria Brewer, Patricia Simon, and Edward Morse, "Lifestyle Factors among Female Prisoners with Histories of Psychiatric Treatment," *Journal of Criminal Justice* 29 (2001): 319–328; Rolf Loeber, David Farrington, Magda Stouthamer-Loeber, Terrie

Moffitt, Avshalom Caspi, and Don Lynam, "Male Mental Health Problems, Psychopathy, and Personality Traits: Key Findings from the First 14 Years of the Pittsburgh Youth Study," *Clinical Child and Family Psychology Review* 4 (2002): 273–297.

16. Robert Johnson, S. Susan Su, Dean Gerstein, Hee-Choon Shin, and John Hoffman, "Parental Influences on Deviant Behavior in Early Adolescence: A Logistic Response Analysis of Age and Gender-Differentiated Effects," *Journal of Quantitative Criminology* 11 (1995): 167–192; Judith Brook, Martin Whiteman, and Patricia Cohen, "Stage of Drug Use, Aggression, and Theft/Vandalism," in *Drugs, Crime and Other Deviant Adaptations: Longitudinal Studies,* ed. Howard Kaplan (New York: Plenum Press, 1995), pp. 83–96.

17. Paul Nieuwbeerta and Alex Piquero, "Mortality Rates and Causes of Death of Convicted Dutch Criminals 25 Years Later," *Journal of Research in Crime and Delinquency* 45 (2008): 256–286.

18. David Fergusson, L. John Horwood, and Elizabeth Ridder, "Show Me the Child at Seven II: Childhood Intelligence and Later Outcomes in Adolescence and Young Adulthood," *Journal of Child Psychology & Psychiatry & Allied Disciplines* 46 (2005): 850–859.

19. Krysia Mossakowski, "Dissecting the Influence of Race, Ethnicity, and Socioeconomic Status on Mental Health in Young Adulthood," *Research on Aging* 30 (2008): 649–671.

20. Margit Wiesner and Ranier Silbereisen, "Trajectories of Delinquent Behaviour in Adolescence and Their Covariates: Relations with Initial and Time-Averaged Factors," *Journal of Adolescence* 26 (2003): 753–771.

21. Rolf Loeber, Phen Wung, Kate Keenan, Bruce Giroux, Magda Stouthamer-Loeber, Wemoet Van Kammen, and Barbara Maughan, "Developmental Pathways in Disruptive Behavior," *Development and Psychopathology* (1993): 12–48.

22. Sheila Royo Maxwell and Christopher Maxwell, "Examining the 'Criminal Careers' of Prostitutes within the Nexus of Drug Use, Drug Selling, and Other Illicit Activities," *Criminology* 38 (2000): 787–809.

23. Jacqueline Schneider, "The Link between Shoplifting and Burglary: The Booster Burglar," *British Journal of Criminology* 45 (2005): 395–401.

24. Glenn Deane, Richard Felson, and David Armstrong, "An Examination of Offense Specialization Using Marginal Logit Models," *Criminology* 43 (2005): 955–988.

25. Christopher Sullivan, Jean Marie McGloin, Travis Pratt, and Alex Piquero, "Rethinking the 'Norm' of Offender Generality: Investigating Specialization in the Short Term," *Criminology* 44 (2006): 199–233.

26. Jean Marie McGloin, Christopher J. Sullivan, and Alex R. Piquero, "Aggregating to Versatility? Transitions among Offender Types in the Short Term," *British Journal of Criminology* 49 (2009): 243–264.

27. Alex R. Piquero and He Len Chung, "On the Relationships between Gender, Early Onset, and the Seriousness of Offending," *Journal of Criminal Justice* 29 (2001): 189–206.

28. Lila Kazemian, David Farrington, and Marc Le Blanc, "Can We Make Accurate Long-term Predictions About Patterns of De-escalation in Offending Behavior?" *Journal of Youth and Adolescence* 38 (2009): 384–400.

29. David Nurco, Timothy Kinlock, and Mitchell Balter, "The Severity of Preaddiction Criminal Behavior among Urban, Male Narcotic Addicts and Two Nonaddicted Control Groups," *Journal of Research in Crime and Delinquency* 30 (1993): 293–316.

30. Mary Campa, Catherine Bradshaw, John Eckenrode, and David Zielinski, "Patterns of Problem Behavior in Relation to Thriving and Precocious Behavior in Late Adolescence," *Journal of Youth and Adolescence* 37 (2008): 627–640; Alex Mason, Rick Kosterman, J. David Hawkins, Todd Herrenkohl, Liliana Lengua, and Elizabeth McCauley, *Journal of the American Academy of Child & Adolescent Psychiatry* 43 (2004): 307–315; Rolf Loeber and David Farrington, "Young Children Who Commit Crime: Epidemiology, Developmental Origins, Risk Factors, Early Interventions, and Policy Implications," *Development and Psychopathology* 12 (2000): 737–762; Patrick Lussier, Jean Proulx, and Marc Le Blanc, "Criminal Propensity, Deviant Sexual Interests and Criminal Activity of Sexual Aggressors against Women: A Comparison of Explanatory Models," *Criminology* 43 (2005): 249–281; Glenn Clingempeel and Scott Henggeler, "Aggressive Juvenile Offenders Transitioning into Emerging Adulthood: Factors Discriminating Persistors and Desistors," *American Journal of Orthopsychiatry* 73 (2003): 310–323.

31. David Gadd and Stephen Farrall, "Criminal Careers, Desistance and Subjectivity: Interpreting Men's Narratives of Change," *Theoretical Criminology* 8 (2004): 123–156.

32. W. Alex Mason, Rick Kosterman, J. David Hawkins, Todd Herrenkohl, Liliana Lengua, and Elizabeth McCauley, "Predicting Depression, Social Phobia, and Violence in Early Adulthood from Childhood Behavior Problems," *Journal of the American Academy of Child & Adolescent Psychiatry* 43 (2004): 307–315; Ronald Prinz and Suzanne Kerns, "Early Substance Use by Juvenile Offenders," *Child Psychiatry and Human Development* 33 (2003): 263–268.

33. Sarah Bacon, Raymond Paternoster, and Robert Brame, "Understanding the Relationship between Onset Age and Subsequent Offending during Adolescence," *Journal of Youth and Adolescence* 38 (2009): 301–311.

34. Alex Piquero and Timothy Brezina, "Testing Moffitt's Account of Adolescent-Limited Delinquency," *Criminology* 39 (2001): 353–370.

35. Terrie Moffitt, "Adolescence-Limited and Life-Course Persistent Antisocial Behavior: A Developmental Taxonomy," *Psychological Review* 100 (1993): 674–701.

36. Terrie Moffitt, "Natural Histories of Delinquency," in *Cross-National Longitudinal Research on Human Development and Criminal Behavior,* ed. Elmar Weitekamp and Hans-Jurgen Kerner (Dordrecht, Netherlands: Kluwer, 1994), pp. 3–65.

37. Andrea Donker, Wilma Smeenk, Peter van der Laan, and Frank Verhulst, "Individual Stability of Antisocial Behavior from Childhood to Adulthood: Testing the Stability Postulate of Moffitt's Developmental Theory," *Criminology* 41 (2003): 593–609.

38. Robert Vermeiren, "Psychopathology and Delinquency in Adolescents: A Descriptive and Developmental Perspective," *Clinical Psychology Review* 23 (2003): 277–318; Paul Mazerolle, Robert Brame, Ray Paternoster, Alex Piquero, and Charles Dean, "Onset Age, Persistence, and Offending Versatility: Comparisons across Sex," *Criminology* 38 (2000): 1,143–1,172.

39. Adrian Raine, Rolf Loeber, Magda Stouthamer-Loeber, Terrie Moffitt, Avshalom Caspi, and Don Lynam, "Neurocognitive Impairments in Boys on the Life-Course

Persistent Antisocial Path," *Journal of Abnormal Psychology* 114 (2005): 38–49.

40. Per-Olof Wikstrom and Rolf Loeber, "Do Disadvantaged Neighborhoods Cause Well-Adjusted Children to Become Adolescent Delinquents? A Study of Male Juvenile Serious Offending, Individual Risk and Protective Factors, and Neighborhood Context," *Criminology* 38 (2000): 1,109–1,142.

41. Bacon, Paternoster, and Brame, "Understanding the Relationship between Onset Age and Subsequent Offending."

42. Victor van der Geest, Arjan Blokland, and Catrien Bijleveld, "Delinquent Development in a Sample of High-Risk Youth: Shape, Content, and Predictors of Delinquent Trajectories from Age 12 to 32," *Journal of Research in Crime and Delinquency* 46 (2009): 111–143.

43. Robert Agnew, *Why Do Criminals Offend? A General Theory of Crime and Delinquency* (Los Angeles: Roxbury Publishing, 2005); Terence Thornberry, "Toward an Interactional Theory of Delinquency," *Criminology* 25 (1987): 863–891; Richard Catalano, J. David Hawkins, "The Social Development Model: A Theory of Antisocial Behavior," in *Delinquency & Crime: Current Theories*, ed. J. David Hawkins (New York: Cambridge University Press, 1996): pp. 149–197.

44. Stephen Farrall and Benjamin Bowling, "Structuration, Human Development, and Desistance from Crime," *British Journal of Criminology* 39 (1999): 253–268.

45. Robert Sampson and John Laub, *Crime in the Making: Pathways and Turning Points through Life* (Cambridge, MA: Harvard University Press, 1993); John Laub and Robert Sampson, "Turning Points in the Life Course: Why Change Matters to the Study of Crime." Paper presented at the annual meeting of the American Society of Criminology, New Orleans, November 1992.

46. Daniel Nagin and Raymond Paternoster, "Personal Capital and Social Control: The Deterrence Implications of a Theory of Criminal Offending," *Criminology* 32 (1994): 581–606.

47. John Laub, Robert J. Sampson, and Gary Sweeten, "Assessing Sampson and Laub's Life-course Theory of Crime," in *Taking Stock: The Status of Criminological Theory, vol. 15, Advances in Criminological Theory*, ed. Francis T. Cullen, John Paul Wright, and Kristie R. Blevins (New Brunswick, NJ: Transaction, 2006), p. 314.

48. Terri Orbuch, James House, Richard Mero, and Pamela Webster, "Marital Quality over the Life Course," *Social Psychology Quarterly* 59 (1996): 162–171; Lee Lillard and Linda Waite, "'Til Death Do Us Part': Marital Disruption and Mortality," *American Journal of Sociology* 100 (1995): 1,131–1,156.

49. Mark Warr, "Life-Course Transitions and Desistance from Crime," *Criminology* 36 (1998): 183–216.

50. Leonore M. J. Simon, "Social Bond and Criminal Record History of Acquaintance and Stranger Violent Offenders," *Journal of Crime and Justice* 22 (1999): 131–146.

51. Raymond Paternoster and Robert Brame, "Multiple Routes to Delinquency? A Test of Developmental and General Theories of Crime," *Criminology* 35 (1997): 49–84.

52. Spencer De Li, "Legal Sanctions and Youths' Status Achievement: A Longitudinal Study," *Justice Quarterly* 16 (1999): 377–401.

53. Shawn Bushway, "The Impact of an Arrest on the Job Stability of Young White American Men," *Journal of Research on Crime and Delinquency* 35 (1999): 454–479.

54. Candace Kruttschnitt, Christopher Uggen, and Kelly Shelton, "Individual Variability in Sex Offending and Its Relationship to Informal and Formal Social Controls." Paper presented at the American Society of Criminology meeting, San Diego, 1997; Mark Collins and Don Weatherburn, "Unemployment and the Dynamics of Offender Populations," *Journal of Quantitative Criminology* 11 (1995): 231–245.

55. Robert Hoge, D. A. Andrews, and Alan Leschied, "An Investigation of Risk and Protective Factors in a Sample of Youthful Offenders," *Journal of Child Psychology and Psychiatry* 37 (1996): 419–424.

56. Richard Arum and Irenee Beattie, "High School Experience and the Risk of Adult Incarceration," *Criminology* 37 (1999): 515–540.

57. Ross Macmillan, Barbara J. McMorris, and Candace Kruttschnitt, "Linked Lives: Stability and Change in Maternal Circumstances and Trajectories of Antisocial Behavior in Children," *Child Development* 75 (2004): 205–220.

58. Avshalom Caspi, Terrie Moffitt, Bradley Entner Wright, and Phil Silva, "Early Failure in the Labor Market: Childhood and Adolescent Predictors of Unemployment in the Transition to Adulthood," *American Sociological Review* 63 (1998): 424–451.

59. Robert Sampson and John Laub, "Socioeconomic Achievement in the Life Course of Disadvantaged Men: Military Service as a Turning Point, circa 1940–1965," *American Sociological Review* 61 (1996): 347–367.

60. Christopher Uggen, "Ex-Offenders and the Conformist Alternative: A Job Quality Model of Work and Crime," *Social Problems* 46 (1999): 127–151.

61. John Paul Wright, David E. Carter, and Francis T. Cullen, "A Life-Course Analysis of Military Service in Vietnam," *Journal of Research in Crime and Delinquency* 42 (2005): 55–83.

62. Eloise Dunlop and Bruce Johnson, "Family and Human Resources in the Development of a Female Crack-Seller Career: Case Study of a Hidden Population," *Journal of Drug Issues* 26 (1996): 175–198.

63. David Rowe, D. Wayne Osgood, and W. Alan Nicewander, "A Latent Trait Approach to Unifying Criminal Careers," *Criminology* 28 (1990): 237–270.

64. Lee Ellis, "Neurohormonal Bases of Varying Tendencies to Learn Delinquent and Criminal Behavior," in *Behavioral Approaches to Crime and Delinquency*, ed. E. Morris and C. Braukmann (New York: Plenum, 1988), pp. 499–518.

65. David Rowe, Alexander Vazsonyi, and Daniel Flannery, "Sex Differences in Crime: Do Means and Within-Sex Variation Have Similar Causes?" *Journal of Research in Crime and Delinquency* 32 (1995): 84–100.

66. Bacon, Paternoster, and Brame, "Understanding the Relationship between Onset Age and Subsequent Offending."

67. James Q. Wilson and Richard Herrnstein, *Crime and Human Nature* (New York: Simon & Schuster, 1985).

68. Ibid., p. 44.

69. Ibid., p. 171.

70. Michael Gottfredson and Travis Hirschi, *A General Theory of Crime* (Stanford, CA: Stanford University Press, 1990).

71. Ibid., p. 90.

72. Ibid., p. 89.

73. Alex Piquero and Stephen Tibbetts, "Specifying the Direct and Indirect Effects of Low Self-Control and Situational Factors in Offenders' Decision Making: Toward a More

Complete Model of Rational Offending," *Justice Quarterly* 13 (1996): 481–508.

74. David Forde and Leslie Kennedy, "Risky Lifestyles, Routine Activities, and the General Theory of Crime," *Justice Quarterly* 14 (1997): 265–294.

75. Gottfredson and Hirschi, *A General Theory of Crime*, p. 112.

76. Ibid.

77. Stacey Nofziger, "The 'Cause' of Low Self-Control: The Influence of Maternal Self-Control," *Journal of Research in Crime and Delinquency* 45 (2008): 191–224.

78. Marie Ratchford and Kevin Beaver, "Neuropsychological Deficits, Low Self-Control, and Delinquent Involvement: Toward a Biosocial Explanation of Delinquency," *Criminal Justice and Behavior* 36 (2009): 147–162.

79. Kevin Beaver and John Paul Wright, "Evaluating the Effects of Birth Complications on Low-Control in a Sample of Twins," *International Journal of Offender Therapy & Comparative Criminology* 49 (2005): 450–472.

80. Kevin M. Beaver, J. Eagle Shutt, Brian Boutwell, Marie Ratchford, Kathleen Roberts, and J. C. Barnes, "Genetic and Environmental Influences on Levels of Self-Control and Delinquent Peer Affiliation: Results from a Longitudinal Sample of Adolescent Twins," *Criminal Justice and Behavior* 36 (2009): 41–60.

81. Gottfredson and Hirschi, *A General Theory of Crime*, p. 27.

82. Michael Benson and Elizabeth Moore, "Are White-Collar and Common Offenders the Same? An Empirical and Theoretical Critique of a Recently Proposed General Theory of Crime," *Journal of Research in Crime and Delinquency* 29 (1992): 251–272.

83. Kevin Thompson, "Sexual Harassment and Low Self-Control: An Application of Gottfredson and Hirschi's General Theory of Crime." Paper presented at the annual meeting of the American Society of Criminology, Phoenix, Arizona, November 1993.

84. David Brownfield and Ann Marie Sorenson, "Self-Control and Juvenile Delinquency: Theoretical Issues and an Empirical Assessment of Selected Elements of a General Theory of Crime," *Deviant Behavior* 14 (1993): 243–264; Harold Grasmick, Charles Tittle, Robert Bursik, and Bruce Arneklev, "Testing the Core Empirical Implications of Gottfredson and Hirschi's General Theory of Crime," *Journal of Research in Crime and Delinquency* 30 (1993): 5–29; John Cochran, Peter Wood, and Bruce Arneklev, "Is the Religiosity–Delinquency Relationship Spurious? A Test of Arousal and Social Control Theories," *Journal of Research in Crime and Delinquency* 31 (1994): 92–123; Marc Le Blanc, Marc Ouimet, and Richard Tremblay, "An Integrative Control Theory of Delinquent Behavior: A Validation, 1976–1985," *Psychiatry* 51 (1988): 164–176.

85. Sullivan, McGloin, Pratt, and Piquero, "Rethinking the 'Norm' of Offender Generality"; Daniel Nagin and Greg Pogarsky, "Time and Punishment: Delayed Consequences and Criminal Behavior," *Journal of Quantitative Criminology* 20 (2004): 295–317.

86. Norman White and Rolf Loeber, "Bullying and Special Education as Predictors of Serious Delinquency," *Journal of Research in Crime and Delinquency* 45 (2008): 380–397.

87. Matt DeLisi and Michael Vaughn, "The Gottfredson-Hirschi Critiques Revisited: Reconciling Self-Control Theory, Criminal Careers, and Career Criminals,"

International Journal of Offender Therapy and Comparative Criminology 52 (2008): 520–537.

88. Alexander Vazsonyi, Janice Clifford Wittekind, Lara Belliston, and Timothy Van Loh, "Extending the General Theory of Crime to 'The East': Low Self-Control in Japanese Late Adolescents," *Journal of Quantitative Criminology* 20 (2004): 189–216; Alexander Vazsonyi, Lloyd Pickering, Marianne Junger, and Dick Hessing, "An Empirical Test of a General Theory of Crime: A Four-Nation Comparative Study of Self-Control and the Prediction of Deviance," *Journal of Research in Crime and Delinquency* 38 (2001): 91–131.

89. Ronald Akers, "Self-Control as a General Theory of Crime," *Journal of Quantitative Criminology* 7 (1991): 201–211.

90. Gottfredson and Hirschi, *A General Theory of Crime*, p. 88.

91. Moffitt, "Adolescence-Limited and Life-Course Persistent Antisocial Behaviors."

92. Alex Piquero, Robert Brame, Paul Mazerolle, and Rudy Haapanen, "Crime in Emerging Adulthood," *Criminology* 40 (2002): 137–170.

93. Donald Lynam, Alex Piquero, and Terrie Moffitt, "Specialization and the Propensity to Violence: Support from Self-Reports But Not Official Records," *Journal of Contemporary Criminal Justice* 20 (2004): 215–228.

94. Alan Feingold, "Gender Differences in Personality: A Meta-Analysis," *Psychological Bulletin* 116 (1994): 429–456.

95. Charles Tittle, David Ward, and Harold Grasmick, "Gender, Age, and Crime/Deviance: A Challenge to Self-Control Theory," *Journal of Research in Crime and Delinquency* 40 (2003): 426–453.

96. Brent Benda, "Gender Differences in Life-Course Theory of Recidivism: A Survival Analysis," *International Journal of Offender Therapy & Comparative Criminology* 49 (2005): 325–342.

97. Gottfredson and Hirschi, *A General Theory of Crime*, p. 153.

98. Ann Marie Sorenson and David Brownfield, "Normative Concepts in Social Control." Paper presented at the annual meeting of the American Society of Criminology, Phoenix, Arizona, November 1993.

99. Brent Benda, "An Examination of Reciprocal Relationship between Religiosity and Different Forms of Delinquency within a Theoretical Model," *Journal of Research in Crime and Delinquency* 34 (1997): 163–186.

100. Olena Antonaccio and Charles Tittle, "Morality, Self-Control, and Crime," *Criminology* 46 (2008): 479–510.

101. Delbert Elliott and Scott Menard, "Delinquent Friends and Delinquent Behavior: Temporal and Developmental Patterns," in *Crime and Delinquency: Current Theories*, ed. J. David Hawkins (Cambridge: Cambridge University Press, 1996).

102. Graham Ousey and David Aday, "The Interaction Hypothesis: A Test Using Social Control Theory and Social Learning Theory." Paper presented at the American Society of Criminology Meeting, Boston, 1995.

103. Jean Marie McGloin and Lauren O'Neill Shermer, "Self-Control and Deviant Peer Network Structure," *Journal of Research in Crime and Delinquency* 46 (2009): 35–72.

104. Dana Haynie, Peggy Giordano, Wendy Manning, and Monica Longmore, "Adolescent Romantic Relationships and Delinquency Involvement," *Criminology* 43 (2005): 177–210.

105. Julie Horney, D. Wayne Osgood, and Ineke Haen Marshall, "Criminal Careers in the Short-Term: Intra-Individual Variability in Crime and Its Relations to Local

Life Circumstances," *American Sociological Review* 60 (1995): 655–673; Martin Daly and Margo Wilson, "Killing the Competition," *Human Nature* 1 (1990): 83–109.

106. Charles R. Tittle and Harold G. Grasmick, "Criminal Behavior and Age: A Test of Three Provocative Hypotheses," *Journal of Criminal Law and Criminology* 88 (1997): 309–342.

107. L. Thomas Winfree Jr., Terrance Taylor, Ni He, and Finn-Aage Esbensen, "Self-Control and Variability over Time: Multivariate Results Using a 5-Year, Multisite Panel of Youths," *Crime & Delinquency* 2006 (52): 253–286.

108. Ronald Simons, Christine Johnson, Rand Conger, and Glen Elder, "A Test of Latent Trait versus Life-Course Perspectives on the Stability of Adolescent Antisocial Behavior," *Criminology* 36 (1998): 217–244.

109. Carter Hay, "Parenting, Self-Control, and Delinquency: A Test of Self-Control Theory," *Criminology* 39 (2001): 707–736; Douglas Longshore, "Self-Control and Criminal Opportunity: A Prospective Test of the General Theory of Crime," *Social Problems* 45 (1998): 102–114; Finn-Aage Esbensen and Elizabeth Piper Deschenes, "A Multisite Examination of Youth Gang Membership: Does Gender Matter?" *Criminology* 36 (1998): 799–828.

110. Raymond Paternoster and Robert Brame, "The Structural Similarity of Processes Generating Criminal and Analogous Behaviors," *Criminology* 36 (1998): 633–670.

111. Otwin Marenin and Michael Resig, "A General Theory of Crime and Patterns of Crime in Nigeria: An Exploration of Methodological Assumptions," *Journal of Criminal Justice* 23 (1995): 501–518.

112. Bruce Arneklev, Harold Grasmick, Charles Tittle, and Robert Bursik, "Low Self-Control and Imprudent Behavior," *Journal of Quantitative Criminology* 9 (1993): 225–246.

113. Peter Muris and Cor Meesters, "The Validity of Attention Deficit Hyperactivity and Hyperkinetic Disorder Symptom Domains in Nonclinical Dutch Children," *Journal of Clinical Child and Adolescent Psychology* 32 (2003): 460–466.

114. Francis Cullen, John Paul Wright, and Mitchell Chamlin, "Social Support and Social Reform: A Progressive Crime Control Agenda," *Crime and Delinquency* 45 (1999): 188–207.

115. Alex Piquero, John MacDonald, Adam Dobrin, Leah Daigle, and Francis Cullen, "Self-Control, Violent Offending, and Homicide Victimization: Assessing the General Theory of Crime," *Journal of Quantitative Criminology* 21 (2005): 55–71.

116. Ibid.

117. Richard Wiebe, "Reconciling Psychopathy and Low Self-Control," *Justice Quarterly* 20 (2003): 297–336.

118. Elizabeth Cauffman, Laurence Steinberg, and Alex Piquero, "Psychological, Neuropsychological and Physiological Correlates of Serious Antisocial Behavior in Adolescence: The Role of Self-Control," *Criminology* 43 (2005): 133–176.

119. Donald Lynam and Joshua Miller, "Personality Pathways to Impulsive Behavior and Their Relations to Deviance: Results from Three Samples," *Journal of Quantitative Criminology* 20 (2004): 319–341.

120. Yair Listokin, "Future-Oriented Gang Members? Gang Finances and the Theory of Present-Oriented Criminals," *The American Journal of Economics and Sociology* 64 (2005): 1,073–1,083.

121. Heather Lonczk, Robert Abbott, J. David Hawkins, Rick Kosterman, and Richard Catalano, "Effects of the Seattle Social Development Project on Sexual Behavior, Pregnancy, Birth, and Sexually Transmitted Disease Outcomes by Age 21 Years," *Archive of Pediatrics and Adolescent Medicine* 156 (2002): 438–447.

122. Kathleen Bodisch Lynch, Susan Rose Geller, and Melinda G. Schmidt, "Multi-Year Evaluation of the Effectiveness of a Resilience-Based Prevention Program for Young Children," *Journal of Primary Prevention* 24 (2004): 335–353.

123. This section leans on Thomas Tatchell, Phillip Waite, Renny Tatchell, Lynne Durrant, and Dale Bond, "Substance Abuse Prevention in Sixth Grade: The Effect of a Prevention Program on Adolescents' Risk and Protective Factors," *American Journal of Health Studies* 19 (2004): 54–61.

124. Nancy Tobler and Howard Stratton, "Effectiveness of School Based Drug Prevention Programs: A Meta-Analysis of the Research," *Journal of Primary Prevention* 18 (1997): 71–128.

Chapter 10. Violent Crime: Personal and Political

1. CNN, "At Least 20 Feared Dead in Pakistan Mosque Blast," May 5, 2009, www.cnn.com/2009/WORLD/asiapcf/04/05/pakistan.blast/index.html?eref=rss_topstories.

2. Robert Nash Parker and Catherine Colony, "Relationships, Homicides, and Weapons: A Detailed Analysis." Paper presented at the annual meeting of the American Society of Criminology, Montreal, November 1987.

3. Rokeya Farrooque, Ronnie Stout, and Frederick Ernst, "Heterosexual Intimate Partner Homicide: Review of Ten Years of Clinical Experience," *Journal of Forensic Sciences* 50 (2005): 648–651; Miltos Livaditis, Gkaro Esagian, Christos Kakoulidis, Maria Samakouri, and Nikos Tzavaras, "Matricide by Person with Bipolar Disorder and Dependent Overcompliant Personality," *Journal of Forensic Sciences* 50 (2005): 658–661.

4. Dorothy Otnow Lewis, Ernest Moy, Lori Jackson, Robert Aaronson, Nicholas Restifo, Susan Serra, and Alexander Simos, "Biopsychosocial Characteristics of Children Who Later Murder," *American Journal of Psychiatry* 142 (1985): 1,161–1,167.

5. Dorothy Otnow Lewis, *Guilty by Reason of Insanity* (New York: Fawcett Columbine, 1998).

6. Richard Rogers, Randall Salekin, Kenneth Sewell, and Keith Cruise, "Prototypical Analysis of Antisocial Personality Disorder," *Criminal Justice and Behavior* 27 (2000): 234–255; Amy Holtzworth-Munroe and Gregory Stuart, "Typologies of Male Batterers: Three Subtypes and the Differences among Them," *Psychological Bulletin* 116 (1994): 476–497.

7. Christopher Hensley and Suzanne Tallichet, "Childhood and Adolescent Animal Cruelty Methods and Their Possible Link to Adult Violent Crimes," *Journal of Interpersonal Violence* 24 (2009): 147–158.

8. Roman Gleyzer, Alan Felthous, Charles Holzer, "Animal Cruelty and Psychiatric Disorders," *Journal of the American Academy of Psychiatry and the Law* 30 (2002): 257–265.

9. Todd Herrenkhol, Bu Huan, Emiko Tajima, and Stephen Whitney, "Examining the Link between Child Abuse

and Youth Violence," *Journal of Interpersonal Violence* 18 (2003): 1,189–1,208; Pamela Lattimore, Christy Visher, and Richard Linster, "Predicting Rearrest for Violence among Serious Youthful Offenders," *Journal of Research in Crime and Delinquency* 32 (1995): 54–83.

10. Rolf Loeber and Dale Hay, "Key Issues in the Development of Aggression and Violence from Childhood to Early Adulthood," *Annual Review of Psychology* 48 (1997): 371–410.

11. Deborah Capaldi and Gerald Patterson, "Can Violent Offenders Be Distinguished from Frequent Offenders? Prediction from Childhood to Adolescence," *Journal of Research in Crime and Delinquency* 33 (1996): 206–231.

12. Adrian Raine, Patricia Brennan, and Sarnoff Mednick, "Interaction between Birth Complications and Early Maternal Rejection in Predisposing Individuals to Adult Violence: Specificity to Serious, Early-Onset Violence," *American Journal of Psychiatry* 154 (1997): 1,265–1,271.

13. Eric Slade and Lawrence Wissow, "Spanking in Early Childhood and Later Behavior Problems: A Prospective Study of Infants and Young Toddlers," *Pediatrics* 113 (2004): 1,321–1,330; Timothy Ireland, Carolyn Smith, and Terence Thornberry, "Developmental Issues in the Impact of Child Maltreatment on Later Delinquency and Drug Use," *Criminology* 40 (2002): 359–401.

14. Richard Reading, "The Enduring Effects of Abuse and Related Adverse Experiences in Childhood: A Convergence of Evidence from Neurobiology and Epidemiology," *Child: Care, Health & Development* 32 (2006): 253–256.

15. Murray Straus, "Discipline and Deviance: Physical Punishment of Children and Violence and Other Crime in Adulthood," *Social Problems* 38 (1991): 133–154.

16. Alan Rosenbaum and Penny Leisring, "Beyond Power and Control: Towards an Understanding of Partner Abusive Men," *Journal of Comparative Family Studies* 34 (2003): 7–26.

17. Sigmund Freud, *Beyond the Pleasure Principle* (London: Inter-Psychoanalytic Press, 1922).

18. Konrad Lorenz, *On Aggression* (New York: Harcourt Brace Jovanovich, 1966).

19. Wade Myers, *Sexual Homicide by Juveniles* (London: Academic Press, 2002).

20. Justin Patchin, Beth Huebner, John McCluskey, Sean Varano, and Timothy Bynum, "Exposure to Community Violence and Childhood Delinquency," *Crime & Delinquency* 52 (2006): 307–332.

21. Jeffrey B. Bingenheimer, Robert T. Brennan, and Felton J. Earls, "Firearm Violence Exposure and Serious Violent Behavior," *Science* 308 (2005): 1,323–1,326; "Witnessing Gun Violence Significantly Increases Likelihood That a Child Will Also Commit Violent Crime; Violence May Be Viewed as Infectious Disease," *AScribe Health News Service*, May 26, 2005.

22. Joanne Kaufman, "Explaining the Race/Ethnicity–Violence Relationship: Neighborhood Context and Social Psychological Processes," *Justice Quarterly* 22 (2005): 224–251; David Farrington, Rolf Loeber, and Magda Stouthamer-Loeber, "How Can the Relationship between Race and Violence be Explained?" in *Violent Crimes: Assessing Race and Ethnic Differences*, ed. D. F. Hawkins (New York: Cambridge University Press, 2003), pp. 213–237.

23. Eric Stewart, Ronald Simons, and Rand Conger, "Assessing Neighborhood and Social Psychological Influences on Childhood Violence in an African-American Sample," *Criminology* 40 (2002): 801–830.

24. Farrington, Loeber, and Stouthamer-Loeber, "How Can the Relationship between Race and Violence Be Explained?"

25. National Survey on Drug Use and Health (NSDUH), "Youth Violence and Illicit Drug Use, 2006," www.oas.samhsa.gov/2k6/youthViolence/youthViolence.htm (accessed February 8, 2006).

26. Amie Nielsen, Ramiro Martinez, and Matthew Lee, "Alcohol, Ethnicity, and Violence: The Role of Alcohol Availability for Latino and Black Aggravated Assaults and Robberies," *Sociological Quarterly* 46 (2005): 479–502; Chris Allen, "The Links between Heroin, Crack Cocaine and Crime: Where Does Street Crime Fit In?" *British Journal of Criminology* 45 (2005): 355–372.

27. Steven Messner, Glenn Deane, Luc Anselin, and Benjamin Pearson-Nelson, "Locating the Vanguard in Rising and Falling Homicide Rates across Cities," *Criminology* 43 (2005): 661–696.

28. Paul Goldstein, Henry Brownstein, and Patrick Ryan, "Drug-Related Homicide in New York: 1984–1988," *Crime and Delinquency* 38 (1992): 459–476.

29. Robert Brewer and Monica Swahn, "Binge Drinking and Violence," *JAMA: Journal of the American Medical Association* 294 (8/3/2005): 16–20.

30. Tomika Stevens, Kenneth Ruggiero, Dean Kilpatrick, Heidi Resnick, and Benjamin Saunders, "Variables Differentiating Singly and Multiply Victimized Youth: Results from the National Survey of Adolescents and Implications for Secondary Prevention," *Child Maltreatment* 10 (2005): 211–223; James Collins and Pamela Messerschmidt, "Epidemiology of Alcohol-Related Violence," *Alcohol Health and Research World* 17 (1993): 93–100.

31. Antonia Abbey, Tina Zawacki, Philip Buck, Monique Clinton, and Pam McAuslan, "Sexual Assault and Alcohol Consumption: What Do We Know about Their Relationship and What Types of Research Are Still Needed?" *Aggression and Violent Behavior* 9 (2004): 271–303.

32. Martin Grann and Seena Fazel, "Substance Misuse and Violent Crime: Swedish Population Study," *British Medical Journal* 328 (2004): 1,233–1,234; Susanne Rogne Gjeruldsen, Bjørn Myrvang, and Stein Opjordsmoen, "Criminality in Drug Addicts: A Follow-Up Study over 25 Years," *European Addiction Research* 10 (2004): 49–56; Kenneth Tardiff, Peter Marzuk, Kira Lowell, Laura Portera, and Andrew Leon, "A Study of Drug Abuse and Other Causes of Homicide in New York," *Journal of Criminal Justice* 30 (2002): 317–325.

33. Paul Goldstein, Patricia Bellucci, Barry Spunt, and Thomas Miller, "Volume of Cocaine Use and Violence: A Comparison between Men and Women," *Journal of Drug Issues* 21 (1991): 345–367.

34. Pamela Wilcox and Richard Clayton, "A Multilevel Analysis of School-Based Weapon Possession," *Justice Quarterly* 18 (2001): 509–542.

35. FBI, *Crime in the United States, 2008* (Washington, DC: U.S. Government Printing Office, 2009).

36. David Brent, Joshua Perper, Christopher Allman, Grace Moritz, Mary Wartella, and Janice Zelenak, "The Presence

and Accessibility of Firearms in the Home and Adolescent Suicides," *Journal of the American Medical Association* 266 (1991): 2,989–2,995.

37. Robert Baller, Luc Anselin, Steven Messner, Glenn Deane, and Darnell Hawkins, "Structural Covariates of U.S. County Homicide Rates Incorporating Spatial Effects," *Criminology* 39 (2001): 561–590.

38. Marvin Wolfgang and Franco Ferracuti, *The Subculture of Violence* (London: Tavistock, 1967).

39. David Luckenbill and Daniel Doyle, "Structural Position and Violence: Developing a Cultural Explanation," *Criminology* 27 (1989): 419–436.

40. Daneen Deptula and Robert Cohen, "Aggressive, Rejected, and Delinquent Children and Adolescents: A Comparison of Their Friendships," *Aggression and Violent Behavior* 9 (2004): 75–104; Beth Bjerregaard and Alan Lizotte, "Gun Ownership and Gang Membership," *Journal of Criminal Law and Criminology* 86 (1995): 37–58.

41. Sylive Mrug, Betsy Hoza, and William Bukowski, "Choosing or Being Chosen by Aggressive-Disruptive Peers: Do They Contribute to Children's Externalizing and Internalizing Problems?" *Journal of Abnormal Child Psychology* 32 (2004): 53–66.

42. Daniel Neller, Robert Denney, Christina Pietz, and R. Paul Thomlinson, "Testing the Trauma Model of Violence," *Journal of Family Violence* 20 (2005): 151–159; James Howell, "Youth Gang Homicides: A Literature Review," *Crime and Delinquency* 45 (1999): 208–241.

43. Rachel Gordon, Benjamin Lahey, Eriko Kawai, Rolf Loeber, Magda Stouthamer-Loeber, and David Farrington, "Antisocial Behavior and Youth Gang Membership," *Criminology* 42 (2004): 55–88.

44. Eric Monkkonen, "Homicide in Los Angeles, 1827–2002," *Journal of Interdisciplinary History* 36 (2005): 167–183.

45. Ibid., 177–178.

46. Charis Kubrin and Ronald Weitzer, "Retaliatory Homicide: Concentrated Disadvantage and Neighborhood Culture," *Social Problems* 50 (2003): 157–180.

47. Robert J. Kane, "Compromised Police Legitimacy as a Predictor of Violent Crime in Structurally Disadvantaged Communities," *Criminology* 43 (2005): 469–499.

48. Jerome Neapolitan, "A Comparative Analysis of Nations with Low and High Levels of Violent Crime," *Journal of Criminal Justice* 27 (1999): 259–274.

49. Ibid., p. 271.

50. Aki Roberts and Gary Lafree, "Explaining Japan's Postwar Violent Crime Trends," *Criminology* 42 (2004): 179–210.

51. William Green, *Rape* (Lexington, MA: Lexington Books, 1988), p. 5.

52. Barbara Krah, Renate Scheinberger-Olwig, and Steffen Bieneck, "Men's Reports of Nonconsensual Sexual Interactions with Women: Prevalence and Impact," *Archives of Sexual Behavior* 32 (2003): 165–176.

53. Siegmund Fred Fuchs, "Male Sexual Assault: Issues of Arousal and Consent," *Cleveland State Law Review* 51 (2004): 93–108.

54. Marlise Simons, "Bosnian Serb Pleads Guilty to Rape Charge before War Crimes Tribunal," *New York Times*, March 10,1998, p. 8.

55. Marc Lacey, "Amnesty Says Sudan Militias Use Rape as Weapon," *New York Times*, July 19, 2004, p. A9.

56. Uniform Crime Reports, *Crime in the United States, 2008* (Washington, DC: Federal Bureau of Investigation, 2009), www.fbi.gov/ucr/cius2008/index.html. Crime data in this chapter comes from this source.

57. Michael Rand, *Criminal Victimization 2008* (Washington, DC: Bureau of Justice Statistics, 2009), www.ojp.usdoj .gov/bjs/pub/pdf/cv08.pdf.

58. Carol Vanzile-Tamsen, Maria Testa, and Jennifer Livingston, "The Impact of Sexual Assault History and Relationship Context on Appraisal of and Responses to Acquaintance Sexual Assault Risk," *Journal of Interpersonal Violence* 20 (2005): 813–822; Arnold Kahn, Jennifer Jackson, Christine Kully, Kelly Badger, and Jessica Halvorsen, "Calling It Rape: Differences in Experiences of Women Who Do or Do Not Label Their Sexual Assault as Rape," *Psychology of Women Quarterly* 27 (2003): 233–242.

59. Amy Buddie and Maria Testa, "Rates and Predictors of Sexual Aggression among Students and Nonstudents," *Journal of Interpersonal Violence* 20 (2005): 713–725.

60. For an analysis of the validity of rape data, see Bonnie S. Fisher, "The Effects of Survey Question Wording on Rape Estimates: Evidence from a Quasi-Experimental Design," *Violence against Women* 15 (2009): 133–147.

61. Heather Littleton and Craig Henderson, "If She Is Not a Victim, Does That Mean She Was Not Traumatized? Evaluation of Predictors of PTSD Symptomatology among College Rape Victims," *Violence against Women* 15 (2009): 148–167.

62. Mark Warr, "Rape, Burglary and Opportunity," *Journal of Quantitative Criminology* 4 (1988): 275–288.

63. A. Nicholas Groth and Jean Birnbaum, *Men Who Rape* (New York: Plenum Press, 1979).

64. For another typology, see Raymond Knight, "Validation of a Typology of Rapists," in *Sex Offender Research and Treatment: State-of-the-Art in North America and Europe*, ed. W. L. Marshall and J. Frenken (Beverly Hills, CA: Sage, 1997), pp. 58–75.

65. R. Lance Shotland, "A Model of the Causes of Date Rape in Developing and Close Relationships," in *Close Relationships*, ed. C. Hendrick (Newbury Park, CA: Sage, 1989), pp. 247–270.

66. Mary Koss, "Hidden Rape: Sexual Aggression and Victimization in a National Sample of Students in Higher Education," in *Rape and Sexual Assault*, vol. 2, ed. Anne Wolbert Burgess (New York: Garland Publishing, 1988), p. 824.

67. Kimberly Tyler, Dan Hoyt, and Les Whitbeck, "Coercive Sexual Strategies," *Violence and Victims* 13 (1998): 47–63.

68. Bonnie Fisher, Leah Daigle, Francis Cullen, and Michael Turner, "Reporting Sexual Victimization to the Police and Others: Results from a National-Level Study of College Women," *Criminal Justice and Behavior* 30 (2003): 6–39.

69. David Finkelhor and K. Yllo, *License to Rape: Sexual Abuse of Wives* (New York: Holt, Rinehart and Winston, 1985).

70. Jill Elaine Hasday, "Contest and Consent: A Legal History of Marital Rape," *California Law Review* 88 (2000): 1,373–1,433.

71. Sharon Elstein and Roy Davis, *Sexual Relationships between Adult Males and Young Teen Girls: Exploring the Legal and Social Responses* (Chicago: American Bar Association, 1997).

72. Donald Symons, *The Evolution of Human Sexuality* (Oxford: Oxford University Press, 1979).

73. Lee Ellis and Anthony Walsh, "Gene-Based Evolutionary Theories in Criminology," *Criminology* 35 (1997): 229–276.

74. Suzanne Osman, "Predicting Men's Rape Perceptions Based on the Belief That 'No' Really Means 'Yes,'" *Journal of Applied Social Psychology* 33 (2003): 683–692.

75. Martin Schwartz, Walter DeKeseredy, David Tait, and Shahid Alvi, "Male Peer Support and a Feminist Routine Activities Theory: Understanding Sexual Assault on the College Campus," *Justice Quarterly* 18 (2001): 623–650.

76. Diana Russell and Rebecca M. Bolen, *The Epidemic of Rape and Child Sexual Abuse in the United States* (Thousand Oaks, CA: Sage, 2000).

77. Paul Gebhard, John Gagnon, Wardell Pomeroy, and Cornelia Christenson, *Sex Offenders: An Analysis of Types* (New York: Harper & Row, 1965), pp. 198–205; Richard Rada, ed., *Clinical Aspects of the Rapist* (New York: Grune & Stratton, 1978), pp. 122–130.

78. Stephen Porter, David Fairweather, Jeff Drugge, Huues Herve, Angela Birt, and Douglas Boer, "Profiles of Psychopathy in Incarcerated Sexual Offenders," *Criminal Justice and Behavior* 27 (2000): 216–233.

79. Brad Bushman, Angelica Bonacci, Mirjam van Dijk, and Roy Baumeister, "Narcissism, Sexual Refusal, and Aggression: Testing a Narcissistic Reactance Model of Sexual Coercion," *Journal of Personality and Social Psychology* 84 (2003): 1,027–1,040.

80. Schwartz, DeKeseredy, Tait, and Alvi, "Male Peer Support and a Feminist Routine Activities Theory."

81. Groth and Birnbaum, *Men Who Rape*, p. 101.

82. See, generally, Edward Donnerstein, Daniel Linz, and Steven Penrod, *The Question of Pornography* (New York: Free Press, 1987); Diana Russell, *Sexual Exploitation* (Beverly Hills, CA: Sage, 1985), pp. 115–116.

83. Neil Malamuth and John Briere, "Sexual Violence in the Media: Indirect Effects on Aggression against Women," *Journal of Social Issues* 42 (1986): 75–92.

84. Richard Felson and Marvin Krohn, "Motives for Rape," *Journal of Research in Crime and Delinquency* 27 (1990): 222–242.

85. Laura Monroe, Linda Kinney, Mark Weist, Denise Spriggs Dafeamekpor, Joyce Dantzler, and Matthew Reynolds, "The Experience of Sexual Assault: Findings from a Statewide Victim Needs Assessment," *Journal of Interpersonal Violence* 20 (2005): 767–776.

86. Julie Horney and Cassia Spohn, "The Influence of Blame and Believability Factors on the Processing of Simple versus Aggravated Rape Cases," *Criminology* 34 (1996): 135–163.

87. Patricia Landwehr, Robert Bothwell, Matthew Jeanmard, Luis Luque, Roy Brown III, and Marie-Anne Breaux, "Racism in Rape Trials," *Journal of Social Psychology* 142 (2002): 667–670.

88. Cassia Spohn, Dawn Beichner, and Erika Davis-Frenzel, "Prosecutorial Justifications for Sexual Assault Case Rejection," *Social Problems* 48 (2001): 206–235.

89. "Man Wrongly Convicted of Rape Released 19 Years Later," *The Forensic Examiner* (May-June 2003): 44.

90. Kirk Johnson, "Prosecutors Drop Kobe Bryant Rape Case," *New York Times*, September 2, 2004, www.nytimes.com/2004/09/02/national/02kobe.html.

91. Rodney Kingsworth, Randall MacIntosh, and Jennifer Wentworth, "Sexual Assault: The Role of Prior Relationship and Victim Characteristics in Case Processing," *Justice Quarterly* 16 (1999): 276–302.

92. Susan Estrich, *Real Rape* (Cambridge, MA: Harvard University Press, 1987), pp. 58–59.

93. *Michigan v. Lucas* 90-149 (1991); Comment, "The Rape Shield Paradox: Complainant Protection amidst Oscillating Trends of State Judicial Interpretation," *Journal of Criminal Law and Criminology* 78 (1987): 644–698.

94. Andrew Karmen, *Crime Victims* (Pacific Grove, CA: Brooks/Cole, 1990), p. 252.

95. "Court Upholds Civil Rights Portion of Violence against Women Act," *Criminal Justice Newsletter* 28 (December 1, 1997), p. 3.

96. Cassia Spohn and David Holleran, "Prosecuting Sexual Assault: A Comparison of Charging Decisions in Sexual Assault Cases Involving Strangers, Acquaintances, and Intimate Partners," *Justice Quarterly* 18 (2001): 651–688; Colleen Fitzpatrick and Philip Reichel, "Conceptions of Rape and Perceptions of Prosecution." Paper presented at the American Society of Criminology meeting, San Diego, 1997.

97. Donald Lunde, *Murder and Madness* (San Francisco: San Francisco Book, 1977), p. 3.

98. Lisa Baertlein, "HIV Ruled Deadly Weapon in Rape Case," *Boston Globe,* March 2, 1994, p. 3.

99. The legal principles here come from Wayne LaFave and Austin Scott, *Criminal Law* (St. Paul, MN: West, 1986; updated 1993). The definitions and discussion of legal principles used in this chapter rely heavily on this work.

100. LaFave and Scott, *Criminal Law.*

101. Bob Egelko, "State's Top Court OKs Dog Maul Murder Charge, Judge Ordered to Reconsider Owner's Original Conviction," *San Francisco Chronicle*, June 1, 2007, www.sfgate.com/cgi-bin/article.cgi?f=/c/a/2007/06/01/BAGIPQ5KE51.DTL (accessed June 20, 2007); Evelyn Nieves, "Woman Gets 4-Year Term in Fatal Dog Attack," *New York Times,* July 16, 2002, p.1.

102. Dana Haynie and David Armstrong, "Race and Gender-Disaggregated Homicide Offending Rates: Differences and Similarities by Victim-Offender Relations across Cities," *Homicide Studies* 10 (2006): 3–32.

103. Todd Shackelford, Viviana Weekes-Shackelford, and Shanna Beasley, "An Exploratory Analysis of the Contexts and Circumstances of Filicide-Suicide in Chicago, 1965–1994," *Aggressive Behavior* 31 (2005): 399–406.

104. Ibid.

105. Philip Cook, Jens Ludwig, and Anthony Braga, "Criminal Records of Homicide Offenders," JAMA: *Journal of the American Medical Association* 294 (2005): 598–601.

106. C. Gabrielle Salfati and Paul Taylor, "Differentiating Sexual Violence: A Comparison of Sexual Homicide and Rape," *Psychology, Crime & Law* 12 (2006): 107–125.

107. Terance Miethe and Wendy Regoeczi with Kriss Drass, *Rethinking Homicide: Exploring the Structure and Process Underlying Deadly Situations* (Cambridge, MA: Cambridge University Press, 2004).

108. Victoria Frye, Vanessa Hosein, Eve Waltermaurer, Shannon Blaney, and Susan Wilt, "Femicide in New York City: 1990 to 1999," *Homicide Studies* 9 (2005): 204–228.

109. Linda Saltzman and James Mercy, "Assaults between Intimates: The Range of Relationships Involved," in *Homicide: The Victim/Offender Connection,* ed. Anna Victoria

Wilson (Cincinnati, OH: Anderson Publishing, 1993), pp. 65–74.

110. Angela Browne and Kirk Williams, "Exploring the Effect of Resource Availability and the Likelihood of Female-Perpetrated Homicides," *Law and Society Review* 23 (1989): 75–94.

111. Richard Felson, "Anger, Aggression, and Violence in Love Triangles," *Violence and Victimization* 12 (1997): 345–363.

112. Ibid., p. 361.

113. Scott Decker, "Deviant Homicide: A New Look at the Role of Motives and Victim–Offender Relationships," *Journal of Research in Crime and Delinquency* 33 (1996): 427–449.

114. David Luckenbill, "Criminal Homicide as a Situational Transaction," *Social Problems* 25 (1977): 176–186.

115. Margaret Zahn and Philip Sagi, "Stranger Homicides in Nine American Cities," *Journal of Criminal Law and Criminology* 78 (1987): 377–397.

116. Tomislav Kovandzic, John Sloan, and Lynne Vieraitis, "Unintended Consequences of Politically Popular Sentencing Policy: The Homicide Promoting Effects of 'Three Strikes' in U.S. Cities (1980–1999)," *Criminology and Public Policy* 3 (2002): 399–424.

117. National Center for Education Statistics, "Indicators of School Crime and Safety: 2008," http://nces.ed.gov/programs/crimeindicators/crimeindicators2008/tables/table_06_1.asp?referrer=report.

118. Tonja Nansel, Mary Overpeck, and Ramani Pilla, "Bullying Behaviors among US Youth: Prevalence and Association with Psychosocial Adjustment," *Journal of the American Medical Association* 285 (2001): 2,094–3,100.

119. Christine Kerres Malecki and Michelle Kilpatrick Demaray, "Carrying a Weapon to School and Perceptions of Social Support in an Urban Middle School," *Journal of Emotional and Behavioral Disorders* 11 (2003): 169–178.

120. Ibid.

121. Pamela Wilcox and Richard Clayton, "A Multilevel Analysis of School-Based Weapon Possession," *Justice Quarterly* 18 (2001): 509–542.

122. Mark Anderson, Joanne Kaufman, Thomas Simon, Lisa Barrios, Len Paulozzi, George Ryan, Rodney Hammond, William Modzeleski, Thomas Feucht, Lloyd Potter, and the School-Associated Violent Deaths Study Group, "School-Associated Violent Deaths in the United States, 1994–1999," *Journal of the American Medical Association* 286 (2001): 2,695–2,702.

123. Bryan Vossekuil, Marisa Reddy, Robert Fein, Randy Borum, and William Modzeleski, *Safe School Initiative, An Interim Report on the Prevention of Targeted Violence in Schools* (Washington, DC: United States Secret Service, 2000).

124. Anthony Walsh, "African Americans and Serial Killing in the Media: The Myth and the Reality," *Homicide Studies* 9 (2005): 271–291.

125. Alasdair Goodwill and Laurence Alison, "Sequential Angulation, Spatial Dispersion and Consistency of Distance Attack Patterns from Home in Serial Murder, Rape and Burglary," *Journal of Psychology, Crime & Law* 11 (2005): 161–176.

126. www.crimelibrary.com/serial_killers/weird/swango/pleasure_8.html (accessed September 3, 2005).

127. Aneez Esmail, "Physician as Serial Killer—The Shipman Case," *New England Journal of Medicine* 352 (2005): 1,483–1,844.

128. Christopher Ferguson, Diana White, Stacey Cherry, Marta Lorenz, and Zhara Bhimani, "Defining and Classifying Serial Murder in the Context of Perpetrator Motivation," *Journal of Criminal Justice* 31 (2003): 287–293.

129. James Alan Fox and Jack Levin, "Multiple Homicide: Patterns of Serial and Mass Murder," in *Crime and Justice: An Annual Edition*, vol. 23, ed. Michael Tonry (Chicago: University of Chicago Press, 1998): 407–455. See also James Alan Fox and Jack Levin, *Overkill: Mass Murder and Serial Killing Exposed* (New York: Plenum, 1994); James Alan Fox and Jack Levin, "A Psycho-Social Analysis of Mass Murder," in *Serial and Mass Murder: Theory, Policy, and Research*, ed. Thomas O'Reilly-Fleming and Steven Egger (Toronto: University of Toronto Press, 1993); James Alan Fox and Jack Levin, "Serial Murder: A Survey," in *Serial and Mass Murder*; Jack Levin and James Alan Fox, *Mass Murder* (New York: Plenum Press, 1985).

130. Terry Whitman and Donald Akutagawa, "Riddles in Serial Murder: A Synthesis," *Aggression and Violent Behavior* 9 (2004) 693–703.

131. Belea Keeney and Kathleen Heide, "Gender Differences in Serial Murderers: A Preliminary Analysis," *Journal of Interpersonal Violence* 9 (1994): 37–56.

132. Wade Myers, Erik Gooch, and Reid Meloy, "The Role of Psychopathy and Sexuality in a Female Serial Killer" *Journal of Forensic Sciences* 50 (2005): 652–658.

133. Fox and Levin, "Multiple Homicide: Patterns of Serial and Mass Murder"; Fox and Levin, *Overkill: Mass Murder and Serial Killing Exposed*; James Alan Fox, Jack Levin, and Kenna Quinet, *The Will to Kill: Making Sense of Senseless Murder*, 2nd ed. (Boston: Allyn & Bacon, 2004); Fox and Levin, "A Psycho-Social Analysis of Mass Murder

134. Ibid.

135. Elissa Gootman, "The Hunt for a Sniper: The Victim; 10th Victim Is Recalled as Motivator on Mission," *New York Times*, October 14, 2002, p. A15; Sarah Kershaw, "The Hunt for a Sniper: The Investigation; Endless Frustration But Little Evidence in Search for Sniper," *New York Times*, October 14, 2002, p. A1.

136. "Mugshots, "Court TV's Criminal Biography Series Profiles Racist Serial Killer Joseph Paul Franklin," www.courttv.com/archive/press/Franklin.html (accessed September 3, 2005).

137. Francis X. Clines with Christopher Drew, "Prosecutors to Discuss Charges As Rifle Is Tied to Sniper Killings," *New York Times*, October 25, 2002, p. A1.

138. FBI, *Crime in the United States, 2000* (Washington, DC: U.S. Government Printing Office, 2001), p. 34.

139. Associated Press, "Woman with HIV Gets 3 Years for Spitting in Face," www.11alive.com/news/watercooler/story.aspx?storyid=118948&catid=186 (accessed June 9, 2009).

140. Salfati Gabrielle and Paul Taylor, "Differentiating Sexual Violence: A Comparison of Sexual Homicide and Rape," *Psychology, Crime and Law* 12 (2006): 107–125; Keith Harries, "Homicide and Assault: A Comparative Analysis of Attributes in Dallas Neighborhoods, 1981–1985," *Professional Geographer* 41 (1989): 29–38.

141. Laurence Zuckerman, "The Air-Rage Rage: Taking a Cold Look at a Hot Topic," *New York Times*, October 4, 1998, p. A3.

142. See, generally, Ruth S. Kempe and C. Henry Kempe, *Child Abuse* (Cambridge, MA: Harvard University Press, 1978).

143. U.S. Department of Health and Human Services, Administration for Children and Families, Children's Bureau, *Child Maltreatment, 2007* (Washington, DC: 2008), www.acf.hhs.gov/programs/cb/pubs/cm07/summary.htm.

144. Richard Estes and Neil Alan Weiner, "The Commercial Sexual Exploitation of Children in the U.S., Canada and Mexico," (Philadelphia: University of Pennsylvania, 2001).

145. Eva Jonzon and Frank Lindblad, "Adult Female Victims of Child Sexual Abuse," *Journal of Interpersonal Violence* 20 (2005): 651–666.

146. Jennie Noll, Penelope Trickett, William Harris, and Frank Putnam, "The Cumulative Burden Borne by Offspring Whose Mothers Were Sexually Abused as Children: Descriptive Results from a Multigenerational Study," *Journal of Interpersonal Violence* 24 (2009): 424–449,

147. Jane Siegel and Linda Williams, "Risk Factors for Sexual Victimization of Women," *Violence against Women* 9 (2003): 902–930.

148. Glenn Wolfner and Richard Gelles, "A profile of violence toward children: A national study," *Child Abuse and Neglect* 17 (1993): 197–212.

149. Martin Daly and Margo Wilson, "Violence against Step Children," *Current Directions in Psychological Science* 5 (1996): 77–81.

150. Ruth Inglis, *Sins of the Fathers: A Study of the Physical and Emotional Abuse of Children* (New York: St. Martins Press, 1978), p. 53.

151. Cindy Schaeffer, Pamela Alexander, Kimberly Bethke, and Lisa Kretz, "Predictors of Child Abuse Potential among Military Parents: Comparing Mothers and Fathers," *Journal of Family Violence* 20 (2005): 123–129.

152. April Chiung-Tao Shen, "Self-Esteem of Young Adults Experiencing Interparental Violence and Child Physical Maltreatment: Parental and Peer Relationships as Mediators," *Journal of Interpersonal Violence* 24 (2009): 770–794.

153. Christina Meade, Trace Kershaw, Nathan Hansen, and Kathleen Sikkema, "Long-Term Correlates of Childhood Abuse among Adults with Severe Mental Illness: Adult Victimization, Substance Abuse, and HIV Sexual Risk Behavior," *AIDS and Behavior* 13 (2009): 207–216.

154. Arina Ulman and Murray Straus, "Violence by Children against Mothers in Relation to Violence between Parents and Corporal Punishment by Parents," *Journal of Comparative Family Studies* 34 (2003): 41–63.

155. Richard Gelles and Murray Straus, "Violence in the American Family," *Journal of Social Issues* 35 (1979): 15–39.

156. Lauren Josephs and Eileen Mazur Abel, "Investigating the Relationship between Intimate Partner Violence and HIV Risk-Propensity in Black/African-American Women," *Journal of Family Violence* 24 (2009): 221–229.

157. Maureen Outlaw, "No One Type of Intimate Partner Abuse: Exploring Physical and Non-Physical Abuse among Intimate Partners," *Journal of Family Violence* 24 (2009): 263–272.

158. Jay Silverman, Anita Raj, Lorelei Mucci, and Jeanne Hathaway, "Dating Violence against Adolescent Girls and Associated Substance Abuse, Unhealthy Weight Control, Sexual Risk Behavior, Pregnancy and Suicidality," *Journal of the American Medical Association* 286 (2001): 572–579.

159. Nicole Bell, "Health and Occupational Consequences of Spouse Abuse Victimization among Male U.S. Army Soldiers," *Journal of Interpersonal Violence* 24 (2009): 751–769.

160. Jacquelyn Campbell, Daniel Webster, Jane Koziol-McLain, Carolyn Block, Doris Campbell, Mary Ann Curry, Faye Gary, et al., "Risk Factors for Femicide in Abusive Relationships: Results from a Multisite Case Control Study," *American Journal of Public Health* 93 (2003): 1,089–1,097.

161. FBI, *Crime in the United States, 2000*, p. 29.

162. James Calder and John Bauer, "Convenience Store Robberies: Security Measures and Store Robbery Incidents," *Journal of Criminal Justice* 20 (1992): 553–566.

163. Marcus Felson, *Crime and Nature* (Thousand Oaks, CA: Sage, 2006).

164. Peter Van Koppen and Robert Jansen, "The Time to Rob: Variations in Time of Number of Commercial Robberies," *Journal of Research in Crime and Delinquency* 36 (1999): 7–29.

165. Richard Wright and Scott Decker, *Armed Robbers in Action: Stickups and Street Culture* (Boston: Northeastern University Press, 1997).

166. Jody Miller, "Up It Up: Gender and the Accomplishment of Street Robbery," *Criminology* 36 (1998): 37–67.

167. Ibid., pp. 54–55.

168. Volkan Topalli, Richard Wright, and Robert Fornango, "Drug Dealers, Robbery and Retaliation: Vulnerability, Deterrence and the Contagion of Violence," *British Journal of Criminology* 42 (2002): 337–351.

169. Richard Felson, Eric Baumer, and Steven Messner, "Acquaintance Robbery," *Journal of Research in Crime and Delinquency* 37 (2000): 284–305.

170. Ibid., p. 287.

171. Ibid.

172. Department of Justice Press Release, "Two Medford Men Sentenced for Role in Federal Hate Crime: Defendants Admit to Cross-Burning Incident at Medford Residence on May 26, 2008," June 16, 2009, http://portland.fbi.gov/dojpressrel/pressrel09/pd061609.htm.

173. James Garofalo, "Bias and Non-Bias Crimes in New York City: Preliminary Findings." Paper presented at the annual meeting of the American Society of Criminology, Baltimore, November 1990.

174. "Boy Gets 18 Years in Fatal Park Beating of Transient," *Los Angeles Times*, December 24, 1987, p. 9B.

175. James Brooke, "Gay Student Who Was Kidnapped and Beaten Dies," *New York Times*, October 13, 1998, p. A1.

176. Gregory Herek, "Hate Crimes and Stigma-Related Experiences among Sexual Minority Adults in the United States: Prevalence Estimates from a National Probability Sample," *Journal of Interpersonal Violence* 24 (2009): 54–74.

177. Jack McDevitt, Jack Levin, and Susan Bennett, "Hate Crime Offenders: An Expanded Typology," *Journal of Social Issues* 58 (2002): 303–318; Jack Levin and Jack McDevitt, *Hate Crimes: The Rising Tide of Bigotry and Bloodshed* (New York: Plenum, 1993).

178. FBI, *Hate Crime Statistics, 2007*, www.fbi.gov/ucr/hc2007/table_01.htm (accessed June 11, 2009).

179. Gregory Herek, Jeanine Cogan, and Roy Gillis, "Victim Experiences in Hate Crimes Based on Sexual Orientation," *Journal of Social Issues* 58 (2002): 319–340.

180. Brian Levin, "From Slavery to Hate Crime Laws: The Emergence of Race- and Status-Based Protection in American Criminal Law," *Journal of Social Issues* 58 (2002): 227–246.

181. Felicia Lee, "Gays Angry over TV Report on a Murder," *New York Times*, November 26, 2004, A3.

182. Frederick M. Lawrence, *Punishing Hate: Bias Crimes under American Law* (Cambridge, MA: Harvard University Press, 1999).

183. Ibid., p. 3.

184. *Virginia v. Black et al.*, No. 01-1107, 2003.

185. James Alan Fox and Jack Levin, "Firing Back: The Growing Threat of Workplace Homicide," *Annals* 536 (1994): 16–30.

186. John King, "Workplace Violence: A Conceptual Framework." Paper presented at the annual meeting of the American Society of Criminology, Phoenix, Arizona, November 1993.

187. Robert Simon, *Bad Men Do What Good Men Dream* (Washington, DC: American Psychiatric Press, 1999).

188. Janet R. Copper, "Response to 'Workplace Violence in Health Care: Recognized but Not Regulated' by Kathleen M. McPhaul and Jane A. Lipscomb (September 30, 2004)," *Online Journal of Issues in Nursing* 10 (2005): 53–55.

189. The following sections rely heavily on Patricia Tjaden, *The Crime of Stalking: How Big Is the Problem?* (Washington, DC: National Institute of Justice, 1997). See also Robert M. Emerson, Kerry O. Ferris, and Carol Brooks Gardner, "On Being Stalked," *Social Problems* 45 (1998): 289–298.

190. Patrick Kinkade, Ronald Burns, and Angel Ilarraza Fuentes, "Criminalizing Attractions: Perceptions of Stalking and the Stalker," *Crime and Delinquency* 51 (2005): 3–25.

191. Tjaden, *The Crime of Stalking: How Big Is the Problem?*

192. Bonnie Fisher, Francis Cullen, and Michael Turner, "Being Pursued: Stalking Victimization in a National Study of College Women," *Criminology and Public Policy* 1 (2002): 257–309.

193. Rosemary Purcell, Bridget Moller, Teresea Flower, and Paul Mullen, "Stalking among Juveniles," *British Journal of Psychiatry* 194 (2009): 451–455.

194. Carol Jordan, T. K. Logan, and Robert Walker, "Stalking: An Examination of the Criminal Justice Response," *Journal of Interpersonal Violence* 18 (2003): 148–165.

195. Paul Wilkinson, *Terrorism and the Liberal State* (New York: Wiley, 1977), p. 49.

196. Robert Friedlander, *Terrorism* (Dobbs Ferry, NY: Oceana Publishers, 1979), p. 14.

197. "Terrorism," www.terrorism-research.com/insurgency/.

198. Andrew Silke, "Holy Warriors: Exploring the Psychological Processes of Jihadi Radicalization," *European Journal of Criminology* 5 (2008), 99–123.

199. This section relies heavily on Friedlander, *Terrorism*, pp. 8–20.

200. Associated Press, "Malaysia Arrests Five Militants," *New York Times*, October 15, 2002, p. A2.

201. Chung Chien-Peng, "China's War on Terror," *Foreign Affairs* 81 (July–August 2002): 8–13.

202. Stephanie Simon and Miguel Bustillo, "Abortion Provider Is Shot Dead," *Wall Street Journal*, June 1, 2009, http://online.wsj.com/article/SB124379172024269869.html.

203. Steve Miletich, "Hunt Is On: Who Torched the Street of Dreams?" *Seattle Times*, March 4, 2008, http://seattletimes.nwsource.com/cgi-bin/PrintStory.pl?document_id=2004258337&zsection_id=2003749379&slug=arson04m&date=20080304.

204. Tamara Makarenko, "The Crime-Terror Continuum: Tracing the Interplay between Transnational Organised Crime and Terrorism." *Global Crime* 6 (2004): 129–145.

205. Chris Dishman, "Terrorism, Crime, and Transformation," *Studies in Conflict & Terrorism* 24 (2001): 43–56.

206. Mark Jurgensmeyer, *Terror in the Mind of God* (Berkeley and Los Angeles: University of California Press, 2000).

207. Randy Borum, *Psychology of Terrorism* (Tampa: University of South Florida, 2004), www.ncjrs.gov/pdffiles1/nij/grants/208552.pdf (accessed January 12, 2008).

208. Ethan Bueno de Mesquita, "The Quality of Terror," *American Journal of Political Science* 49 (2005): 515–530.

209. Haruki Murakami, *Underground* (New York: Vintage Books, 2001).

210. Ibid.

211. Patricia Marchak, *Reigns of Terror* (Montreal: McGill-Queen's University Press, 2003).

212. "Hunting Terrorists Using Confidential Informant Reward Programs," *FBI Law Enforcement Bulletin* 71 (2002): 26–28; Sara Sun Beale and James Felman, "The Consequences of Enlisting Federal Grand Juries in the War on Terrorism: Assessing the USA Patriot Act's Changes to Grand Jury Secrecy," *Harvard Journal of Law and Public Policy* 25 (2002): 699–721.

213. Graham Allison, *Nuclear Terrorism: The Ultimate Preventable Catastrophe* (New York: Times Books, 2004).

Chapter 11. Property Crimes

1. "William Kingsland, City 'Gazetteer,' Is Dead," April 13, 2006, www.nysun.com/arts/william-kingsland-city-gazetteer-is.../30926/.

2. FBI News Release, "Stolen Art Uncovered: Is It Yours?" August 11, 2008.

3. Michael Rand, National Crime Victimization Survey, Criminal Victimization 2008 (Washington, DC: Bureau of Justice Statistics, 2009), www.ojp.usdoj.gov/bjs/pub/pdf/cv08.pdf.

4. Andrew McCall, *The Medieval Underworld* (London: Hamish Hamilton, 1979), p. 86.

5. Ibid., p. 104.

6. J. J. Tobias, *Crime and Police in England, 1700–1900* (London: Gill and Macmillan, 1979).

7. Ibid., p. 9.

8. Marilyn Walsh, *The Fence* (Westport, CT: Greenwood Press, 1977), pp. 18–25.

9. John Hepburn, "Occasional Criminals," in *Major Forms of Crime*, ed. Robert Meier (Beverly Hills, CA: Sage, 1984), pp. 73–94.

10. James Inciardi, "Professional Crime," in *Major Forms of Crime*, ed. Robert Meier (Beverly Hills, CA: Sage, 1984), p. 223.

11. FBI, "Cargo Theft's High Cost: Thieves Stealing Billions Annually," July 21, 2006, www.fbi.gov/page2/july06/cargo_theft072106.htm (accessed June 24, 2009).

12. This section depends heavily on a classic book: Wayne La Fave and Austin Scott, *Handbook on Criminal Law* (St. Paul, MN: West, 1972).

13. La Fave and Scott, *Handbook on Criminal Law*, p. 622.

14. FBI, *Crime in the United States, 2008* (Washington, DC: U.S. Government Printing Office, 2009), www.fbi.gov/ucr/cius2008/index.html.

15. Michael Rand, "Criminal Victimization, 2008" (Bureau of Justice Statistics, 2009), www.ojp.usdoj.gov/bjs/pub/pdf/cv07.pdf (accessed October 15, 2009).

16. Virginia Crime Codes, www.vcsc.state.va.us/VCC_book_fel.pdf (accessed June 15, 2009).

17. Ibid.

18. John Worrall, "The Effect of Three-Strikes Legislation on Serious Crime in California," *Journal of Criminal Justice* 32 (2004): 283–296.

19. "Operation 'Beauty Stop' Nabs 18 in $100 Million Theft Ring," January 24, 2008, www.wftv.com/news/15130764/detail.html (accessed June 25, 2009).

20. FBI, "Organized Retail Theft: New Initiative to Tackle the Problem," April 6, 2007, www.fbi.gov/page2/april07/retail040607.htm (accessed June 24, 2009).

21. Mary Owen Cameron, *The Booster and the Snitch* (New York: Free Press, 1964).

22. Janne Kivivuori, "Crime by Proxy: Coercion and Altruism in Adolescent Shoplifting," *British Journal of Criminology* 47 (2007): 817–833.

23. Lawrence Cohen and Rodney Stark, "Discriminatory Labeling and the Five-Finger Discount: An Empirical Analysis of Differential Shoplifting Dispositions," *Journal of Research on Crime and Delinquency* 11 (1974): 25–35.

24. Ibid., p. 57.

25. FBI, "Organized Retail Theft."

26. Ibid.

27. Erhard Blankenburg, "The Selectivity of Legal Sanctions: An Empirical Investigation of Shoplifting," *Law and Society Review* 11 (1976): 109–129.

28. George Keckeisen, *Retail Security versus the Shoplifter* (Springfield, IL: Charles Thomas, 1993), pp. 31–32.

29. "Tesco Trials Electronic Product Tagging," *Computing and Control Engineering* 14 (2003): 3.

30. Jill Jordan Siedfer, "To Catch a Thief, Try This: Peddling High-Tech Solutions to Shoplifting," *U.S. News & World Report*, September 23, 1996, p. 71.

31. Shaun Gabbidon and Patricia Patrick, "Characteristics and Outcomes of Shoplifting Cases in the U.S. Involving Allegations of False Arrest," *Security Journal* 18 (2005): 7–18.

32. *Ruditys v. J.C. Penney Co.*, No. 02-4114 (Delaware Co., Pa., Ct. C.P. 2003).

33. Dean Dabney, Laura Dugan, Volkan Topalli, and Richard Hollinger, "The Impact of Implicit Stereotyping on Offender Profiling: Unexpected Results from an Observational Study of Shoplifting," *Criminal Justice and Behavior* 33 (2006): 646–674.

34. "Lawsuit Claims Dillard's Used Racial Profiling to Fight Shoplifting," February 6, 2009, Security Information Watch, www.securityinfowatch.com/root+level/1280619.

35. CNN Money.com, "11 Charged in Theft of More than 40M Card Numbers," August 6, 2008, http://money.cnn.com/2008/08/05/news/companies/card_fraud/index.htm.

36. Matt Richtell, "Credit Card Theft Is Thriving Online as Global Market," *New York Times*, May 13, 2002, p. A1.

37. Jennifer Conlin, "Credit Card Fraud Keeps Growing on the Net," *New York Times*, May 11, 2007, www.nytimes.com/2007/05/11/your-money/11iht-mcredit.1.5664687.html (accessed June 30, 2009).

38. Kimberly Palmer, "Beware the Latest Credit Card Scam," *U.S. News & World Report*, May 15, 2008, www.usnews.com/blogs/alpha-consumer/2008/05/15/beware-the-latest-credit-card-scam.html (accessed June 15, 2009).

39. La Fave and Scott, *Handbook on Criminal Law*, p. 672.

40. Information provided by Highway Loss Data Institute, www.iihs.org/.

41. Charles McCaghy, Peggy Giordano, and Trudy Knicely Henson, "Auto Theft," *Criminology* 15 (1977): 367–381.

42. Donald Gibbons, *Society, Crime and Criminal Careers* (Englewood Cliffs, NJ: Prentice-Hall, 1977), p. 310.

43. Kim Hazelbaker, "Insurance Industry Analyses and the Prevention of Motor Vehicle Theft," in *Business and Crime Prevention*, ed. M. Felson and R Clarke (Monsey, NY: Criminal Justice Press, 1997), pp. 283–315.

44. "Hot Cars: Parts Crooks Love Best," *BusinessWeek*, September 15, 2003, p. 104.

45. FBI, "Steering Clear of Car Cloning: Some Advice and Solutions," 2009, www.fbi.gov/page2/march09/cloning_032409.html.

46. Ian Ayres and Steven D. Levitt, "Measuring Positive Externalities from Unobservable Victim Precaution: An Empirical Analysis of Lojack," *Quarterly Journal of Economics* 113 (1998): 43–78.

47. Hazelbaker, "Insurance Industry Analyses and the Prevention of Motor Vehicle Theft," p. 289.

48. P. Weiss, "Outsmarting the Electronic Gatekeeper: Code Breakers Beat Security Scheme of Car Locks, Gas Pumps," *Science News* 167 (2005): 86.

49. Edwin Lemert, "An Isolation and Closure Theory of Naive Check Forgery," *Journal of Criminal Law, Criminology and Police Science* 44 (1953): 297–298.

50. La Fave and Scott, *Handbook on Criminal Law*, p. 655.

51. 30 Geo. III, C.24 (1975).

52. Internet Crime Complaint Center, "Fraudulent Sites Capitalizing on Relief Efforts of Hurricane Katrina," www.ifccfbi.gov/strategy/katrina_warning.pdf (accessed June 11, 2006).

53. FBI, *Uniform Crime Reports, 2007*, Table 29, www.fbi.gov/ucr/cius2007/data/table_29.html.

54. FBI, "A Cautionary Tale. Staged Auto Accident Fraud: Don't Let It Happen to You," www.fbi.gov/page2/feb05/stagedauto021805.htm (accessed April, 1, 2009).

55. Ibid.

56. Carl Klockars, *The Professional Fence* (New York: Free Press, 1976); Darrell Steffensmeier, *The Fence: In the Shadow of Two Worlds* (Totowa, NJ: Rowman and Littlefield, 1986); Walsh, *The Fence*, pp. 25–28.

57. Jerome Hall, *Theft, Law and Society* (Indianapolis, IN: Bobbs-Merrill, 1952), p. 36.

58. La Fave and Scott, *Handbook on Criminal Law*, p. 644.

59. Wayne La Fave and Austin Scott, *Handbook on Criminal Law* (St. Paul: West Publishing, 1972), p. 649.

60. Dawit Kiros Fantaye, "Fighting Corruption and Embezzlement in Third World Countries," *Journal of Criminal Law* 68 (April 2004): 170.

61. Ibid., p. 708.

62. William Blackstone, *Commentaries on the Laws of England* (London: Clarendon Press, 1769), p. 224.

63. FBI, *Crime in the United States, 2008*, www.fbi.gov/ucr/cius2008/offenses/property_crime/burglary.html.

64. Michael Rand, *Criminal Victimization, 2008*.

65. Frank Hoheimer, *The Home Invaders: Confessions of a Cat Burglar* (Chicago: Chicago Review, 1975).

66. Richard Wright, Robert Logie, and Scott Decker, "Criminal Expertise and Offender Decision Making: An Experimental Study of the Target Selection Process in Residential Burglary," *Journal of Research in Crime and Delinquency* 32 (1995): 39–53.

67. Richard Wright and Scott Decker, *Burglars on the Job: Streetlife and Residential Break-ins* (Boston: Northeastern University Press, 1994).

68. Matthew Robinson, "Accessible Targets, But Not Advisable Ones: The Role of 'Accessibility' in Student Apartment Burglary," *Journal of Security Administration* 21 (1998): 28–44.

69. Brent Snook, "Individual Differences in Distance Travelled by Serial Burglars," *Journal of Investigative Psychology & Offender Profiling* 1 (2004): 53–66.

70. Elizabeth Groff and Nancy LaVigne, "Mapping an Opportunity Surface of Residential Burglary," *Journal of Research in Crime and Delinquency* 38 (2001): 257–278.

71. Hoheimer, *The Home Invaders: Confessions of a Cat Burglar*.

72. Wright, Logie, and Decker, "Criminal Expertise and Offender Decision Making."

73. Matthew Robinson, "Accessible Targets, but Not Advisable Ones."

74. Melanie Wellsmith and Amy Burrell, "The Influence of Purchase Price and Ownership Levels on Theft Targets: The Example of Domestic Burglary," *British Journal of Criminology* 45 (2005): 741–764.

75. Matt Hopkins, "Crimes against Businesses: The Way Forward for Future Research," *British Journal of Criminology* 42 (2002): 782–797.

76. Simon Hakim and Yochanan Shachmurove, "Spatial and Temporal Patterns of Commercial Burglaries," *American Journal of Economics and Sociology* 55 (1996): 443–457.

77. Roger Litton, "Crime Prevention and the Insurance Industry," in *Business and Crime Prevention*, ed. Marcus Felson and Ronald Clarke (Monsey, NY: Criminal Justice Press, 1997), p. 162.

78. Graham Farrell, Coretta Phillips, and Ken Pease, "Like Taking Candy: Why Does Repeat Victimization Occur?" *British Journal of Criminology* 35 (1995): 384–399, at p. 391.

79. Ronald Clarke, Elizabeth Perkins, and Donald Smith, "Explaining Repeat Residential Burglaries: An Analysis of Property Stolen," in *Repeat Victimization, vol 12, Crime Prevention Studies*, ed. Graham Farrell and Ken Pease (Monsey, NY: Criminal Justice Press, 2001), pp. 119–132.

80. See, generally, Neal Shover, "Structures and Careers in Burglary," *Journal of Criminal Law, Criminology and Police Science* 63 (1972): 540–549.

81. Scott Decker, Richard Wright, Allison Redfern, and Dietrich Smith, "A Woman's Place Is in the Home: Females and Residential Burglary," *Justice Quarterly* 10 (1993): 143–163.

82. Ibid.

83. Nancy Webb, George Sakheim, Luz Towns-Miranda, and Charles Wagner, "Collaborative Treatment of Juvenile Firestarters: Assessment and Outreach," *American Journal of Orthopsychiatry* 60 (1990): 305–310.

84. Pekka Santtila, Helina Haikkanen, Laurence Alison, and Carrie Whyte, "Juvenile Firesetters: Crime Scene Actions and Offender Characteristics," *Legal and Criminological Psychology* 8 (2003): 1–20.

85. John Taylor, Ian Thorne, Alison Robertson, and Ginny Avery, "Evaluation of a Group Intervention for Convicted Arsonists with Mild and Borderline Intellectual Disabilities," *Criminal Behaviour and Mental Health* 12 (2002): 282–294.

86. Scott Turner, "Funding Sparks Effort to Cut Juvenile Arson Rate," *George Street Journal* 27 (January 31, 2003): 1. Available at www.brown.edu/Administration/George_Street_Journal/vol27/27GSJ16f.html.

Chapter 12. Enterprise Crime: White-Collar Crime, Cyber Crime, and Organized Crime

1. Department of Justice, "Seven Defendants Convicted for Participation in International Child Exploitation Enterprise," January 14, 2009, www.projectsafechildhood.gov/docs/PensacolaFL_01142009.pdf (accessed April 30, 2009; Associated Press, "International Child Porn Ring Uncovered," *New York Times*, March 4, 2008, www.nytimes.com/aponline/us/AP-Porn-Ring.html?_r=1&scp=1&sq=International+Child+Porn+Ring+Uncovered&st=nyt&oref=slogin.

2. Nikos Passas and David Nelken, "The Thin Line between Legitimate and Criminal Enterprises: Subsidy Frauds in the European Community," *Crime, Law, and Social Change* 19 (1993): 223–243.

3. For a thorough review, see David Friedrichs, *Trusted Criminals* (Belmont, CA: Wadsworth, 1996).

4. Kitty Calavita and Henry Pontell, "Savings and Loan Fraud as Organized Crime: Toward a Conceptual Typology of Corporate Illegality," *Criminology* 31 (1993): 519–548.

5. Mark Haller, "Illegal Enterprise: A Theoretical and Historical Interpretation," *Criminology* 28 (1990): 207–235.

6. Edwin Sutherland, *White-Collar Crime: The Uncut Version* (New Haven, CT: Yale University Press, 1983).

7. Edwin Sutherland, "White-Collar Criminality," *American Sociological Review* 5 (1940): 2–10.

8. Ronald Kramer and Raymond Michalowski, "State-Corporate Crime." Paper presented at the annual meeting of the American Society of Criminology, Baltimore, Maryland, November 1990.

9. Natalie Taylor, "Under-Reporting of Crime against Small Business: Attitudes towards Police and Reporting Practices," *Policing and Society* 13 (2003): 79–90.

10. FBI, "Ponzi Scheme Indictments: Five Charged in $7 Billion Ploy," June 19, 2009, www.fbi.gov/page2/june09/stanford_061909.html (accessed July 2, 2009).

11. This structure is based on an analysis contained in Mark Moore, "Notes toward a National Strategy to Deal with White-Collar Crime," in *A National Strategy for Containing White-Collar Crime*, ed. Herbert Edelhertz and Charles Rogovin (Lexington, MA: Lexington Books, 1980), pp. 32–44.

12. Joel Grover and Matt Goldberg, "Jiffy Lube Reacts to Hidden Camera Report," NBC LA News, October 17, 2008, www.nbclosangeles.com/Jiffy_Lube_Reacts_to_Hidden_Camera_Report.html. See also Channel 6 News, "Buried Secret: Quick Lube Chain Cheats Customers; Customers Pay Premium for Low-Priced Oil." November 1, 2007, www.theindychannel.com/news/14479142/detail.html (accessed July 3, 2009).

13. Richard Quinney, "Occupational Structure and Criminal Behavior: Prescription Violation of Retail Pharmacists," *Social Problems* 11 (1963): 179–185. See also John Braithwaite, *Corporate Crime in the Pharmaceutical Industry* (London: Routledge and Kegan Paul, 1984).

14. Department of Justice News Release, "Former Springfield Pharmacist Sentenced for Selling Recycled and Sample Drugs," July 11, 2007, http://boston.fbi.gov/dojpressrel/pressrel07/drugsamples071107.htm (accessed July 3, 2009).

15. Pam Belluck, "Prosecutors Say Greed Drove Pharmacist to Dilute Drugs," *New York Times*, August 18, 2001, p. 3.

16. FBI press release, April 22, 2002, Kansas City Division.

17. James Armstrong et al., "Securities Fraud," *American Criminal Law Review* 33 (1995): 973–1,016.

18. Scott McMurray, "Futures Pit Trader Goes to Trial," *Wall Street Journal*, May 8, 1990, p. C1; Scott McMurray, "Chicago Pits' Dazzling Growth Permitted a Free-for-All Mecca," *Wall Street Journal*, August 3, 1989, p. A4.

19. *Carpenter v. United States* 484 U.S. 19 (1987). See also John Boland, "The SEC Trims the First Amendment," *Wall Street Journal*, December 4, 1986, p. 28.

20. U.S. Department of Justice, "U.S. Charges Bolingbrook, Illinois Man with Bribery in Connection with Army Corps of Engineers Contract in Iraq," May 4, 2009, http://chicago.fbi.gov/dojpressrel/pressrel09/cg050409.htm.

21. CNN.com, "Officer Charged with Demanding Sex for Green Card," www.cnn.com/2008/CRIME/03/21/immigration.officer/index.html, March 21, 2008 (accessed July 3, 2009).

22. Charles V. Bagli, "Kickback Investigation Extends to Middle-Class Buildings in New York," *New York Times*, October 14, 1998, p. A19.

23. United Press International, "Minority Leader in N.Y. Senate Is Charged," *Boston Globe*, September 17, 1987, p. 20.

24. Monica Davey and John O'Neil, "Ex-Governor of Illinois Is Convicted on All Charges," *New York Times*, April 18, 2006, p.1.

25. MSNBC, "Feds: Governor Tried to 'Auction' Obama's Seat," December 9, 2008, www.msnbc.msn.com/id/28139155/ (accessed July 3, 2009).

26. See, for example, Justice Department News Release, "Former Laredo Police Officers Sentenced In Bribery Scheme," February 15, 2008, http://sanantonio.fbi.gov/dojpressrel/pressrel08/briberyscheme021508.htm (accessed July 4, 2009).

27. FBI, "Abuse of Trust: The Case of the Crooked Border Official," June 8, 2009, www.fbi.gov/page2/june09/border060809.html (accessed July 4, 2009).

28. Justice Department News Release, "St. Bernard Parish Judge Wayne Cresap, Two Lawyers Charged in Bribery Scheme," July 1, 2009, http://neworleans.fbi.gov/dojpressrel/2009/no070109a.htm (accessed July 4, 2009).

29. MSNBC, "Pa. Judges Accused of Jailing Kids for Cash: Judges Allegedly Took $2.6 Million in Payoffs to Put Juveniles in Lockups," February 11, 2009, www.msnbc.msn.com/id/29142654/ (accessed July 4, 2009).

30. Disclosure of Payments to Individuals Connected with Broadcasts, U.S. Criminal Code, Title 47 > Chapter 5 > Subchapter V > § 508.

31. Marshall Clinard and Peter Yeager, *Corporate Crime* (New York: Free Press, 1980), p. 67.

32. Ibid.

33. Public Law No. 95-213, 101-104, 91 Stat. 1494.

34. Thomas Burton, "The More Baxter Hides Its Israeli Boycott Role, the More Flak It Gets," *Wall Street Journal*, April 25, 1991, p. 1.

35. Foreign Corrupt Practices Act Update, "Schering-Plough Settles FCPA Case with SEC for Payments to Charity Headed by Government Official," http://wilmer.admin.hubbardone.com/files/tbl_s29Publications%5CFileUpload5665%5C4421%5CFCPA%2006-30-04.pdf (accessed June 30, 2004).

36. Adrian Cho, "Hey Buddy … Wanna Buy a Moon Rock?" *Science Now*, July 7, 2002, p. 1.

37. Charles McCaghy, *Deviant Behavior* (New York: Macmillan, 1976), p. 178.

38. Highlights from Jack L. Hayes International, Inc.'s 20th Annual Retail Theft Survey, www.hayesinternational.com/thft_srvys.html (accessed July 3, 2009).

39. J. Sorenson, H. Grove, and T. Sorenson, "Detecting Management Fraud: The Role of the Independent Auditor," in *White-Collar Crime, Theory and Research*, ed. G. Geis and E. Stotland (Beverly Hills, CA: Sage, 1980), pp. 221–251.

40. MSNBC, "Ex-Tyco Executives Get Up to 25 Years in Prison," September 20, 2005; "Kozlowski, Swartz Punished for Stealing Hundreds of Millions of Dollars," www.msnbc.msn.com/id/9399803/ (accessed July 3, 2009).

41. Kurt Eichenwald, "Ex-Andersen Partner Pleads Guilty in Record-Shredding," *New York Times*, April 12, 2002, p. C1; John A. Byrne, "At Enron, the Environment Was Ripe for Abuse," *BusinessWeek* (February 25, 2002): 12; Peter Behr and Carrie Johnson, "Govt. Expands Charges against Enron Execs," *Washington Post*, May 1, 2003, p.1.

42. Krysten Crawford, CNN, "Ex-WorldCom CEO Ebbers Guilty," March 15, 2006, http://money.cnn.com/2005/03/15/news/newsmakers/ebbers/index.htm; MSNBC, "Ebbers Sentenced to 25 Years in Prison, Ex-WorldCom CEO Guilty of Directing Biggest Accounting Fraud," July 13, 2005, www.msnbc.msn.com/id/8474930; Lynne W. Jeter, "Disconnected: Deceit and Betrayal at WorldCom (New York: Wiley, 2003).

43. Department of Justice, "Two Miami Men Indicted for $179 Million Medicare Fraud Scheme," http://miami.fbi.gov/dojpressrel/pressrel09/mm070209.htm (accessed July 4, 2009).

44. 42 USC 1320a-7b(b); 42 USC 1320a-7b(b)(3); 42 CFR 1001.952 (regulatory safe harbors). 42 USC 1395nn (codifying "Stark I" and "Stark II" statutes).

45. *United States v. Bishop*, 412 U.S. 346 (1973).

46. Cited in Nancy Frank and Michael Lynch, *Corporate Crime, Corporate Violence* (Albany, NY: Harrow & Heston, 1992), pp. 12–13.

47. Sutherland, "White-Collar Criminality."

48. Kylie Cooper and Adrienne Dedjinou, "Antitrust Violations," *American Criminal Law Review* 42 (2005): 179–221.

49. 15 U.S.C. section 1 (1994).

50. 15 U.S.C. 1–7 (1976).

51. *Northern Pacific Railways v. United States*, 356 U.S. 1 (1958).

52. Grant Gross, "LG Display Executive Pleads Guilty in LCD Price-Fixing Case," *PC World*, April 28, 2009, www.pcworld.com/article/164007/lg_display_executive_pleads_guilty_in_lcd_pricefixing_case.html.

53. Department of Justice, "Dutch Airline Executive Agrees to Plead Guilty for Fixing Prices on Air Cargo Shipments: Martinair Holland Executive Agrees to Serve Jail Time," April 29, 2009, http://washingtondc.fbi.gov/dojpressrel/pressrel09/wfo042909.htm (accessed May 4, 2009).

54. Tim Carrington, "Federal Probes of Contractors Rise for Year," *Wall Street Journal*, February 23, 1987, p. 50.

55. Environmental Protection Agency, Criminal Investigation Division, www.epa.gov/compliance/criminal/index.html.

56. Andrew Oliveira, Christopher Schenck, Christopher Cole, and Nicole Janes, "Environmental Crimes (Annual Survey of White-Collar Crime)," *American Criminal Law Review* 42 (2005): 347–380.

57. Donald Cressey, *Other People's Money: A Study of the Social Psychology of Embezzlement* (Glencoe, IL: Free Press, 1973), p. 96.

58. Rhonda Evans and Dianne Porche, "The Nature and Frequency of Medicare/Medicaid Fraud and Neutralization Techniques among Speech, Occupational, and Physical Therapists," *Deviant Behavior* 26 (2005): 253–271.

59. John A. Byrne, "At Enron, the Environment Was Ripe for Abuse," *BusinessWeek* (February 25, 2002): 14.

60. Travis Hirschi and Michael Gottfredson, "Causes of White-Collar Crime," *Criminology* 25 (1987): 949–974.

61. Michael Gottfredson and Travis Hirschi, *A General Theory of Crime* (Stanford, CA: Stanford University Press, 1990), p. 191.

62. This section relies heavily on Daniel Skoler, "White-Collar Crime and the Criminal Justice System: Problems and Challenges," in *A National Strategy for Containing White-Collar Crime*, ed. Herbert Edelhertz and Charles Rogovin (Lexington, MA: Lexington Books, 1980), pp. 57–76.

63. Theodore Hammett and Joel Epstein, *Prosecuting Environmental Crime: Los Angeles County* (Washington, DC: National Institute of Justice, 1993).

64. Information provided by Los Angeles County District Attorney's Office, April 2003.

65. Ronald Burns, Keith Whitworth, and Carol Thompson, "Assessing Law Enforcement Preparedness to Address Internet Fraud," *Journal of Criminal Justice* 32 (2004): 477–493.

66. Michael Benson, Francis Cullen, and William Maakestad, "Local Prosecutors and Corporate Crime," *Crime and Delinquency* 36 (1990): 356–372.

67. Ibid., pp. 369–370.

68. Michael Lynch, Paul Stretesky, and Ronald Burns, "Slippery Business," *Journal of Black Studies* 34 (2004): 421–440.

69. This section relies heavily on Albert Reiss Jr., "Selecting Strategies of Social Control over Organizational Life," in *Enforcing Regulation*, ed. Keith Hawkins and John M. Thomas (Boston: Kluwer, 1984), pp. 25–37.

70. Michael Benson, "Emotions and Adjudication: Status Degradation among White-Collar Criminals," *Justice Quarterly* 7 (1990): 515–528; John Braithwaite, *Crime, Shame, and Reintegration* (Sydney, Australia: Cambridge University Press, 1989).

71. John Braithwaite, "The Limits of Economism in Controlling Harmful Corporate Conduct," *Law and Society Review* 16 (1981–1982): 481–504.

72. Sean Rosenmerkel, "Wrongfulness and Harmfulness as Components of Seriousness of White-Collar Offenses," *Journal of Contemporary Criminal Justice* 17 (2001): 308–328.

73. Jonathan Lechter, Daniel Posner, and George Morris, "Antitrust Violations," *American Criminal Law Review* 39 (2002): 225–273.

74. Mark Cohen, "Environmental Crime and Punishment: Legal/Economic Theory and Empirical Evidence on Enforcement of Federal Environmental Statutes," *Journal of Criminal Law and Criminology* 82 (1992): 1,054–1,109.

75. Fox News, "Missouri Woman Indicted in MySpace Cyber-Bullying Case That Ended in Teen's Suicide," May 15, 2008, www.foxnews.com/printer_friendly_story/0,3566,356056,00.html.

76. Ed Frauenheim, "IDC: Cyberterror and Other Prophecies," CNET News.com, December 12, 2002, http://news.com.com/2100-1001-977780.html (accessed June 11, 2005).

77. Giles Trendle, "An e-jihad against Government?" *EGOV Monitor*, September 2002.

78. Statement of Michael A. Vatis, Director, National Infrastructure Protection Center, FBI, on cyber crime, before the Senate Judiciary Committee, Criminal Justice Oversight Subcommittee and House Judiciary Committee, Crime Subcommittee, Washington, DC, February 29, 2000, www.cybercrime.gov/vatis.htm (accessed July 12, 2005).

79. VoGon International, www.vogon-international.com/ (accessed April 20, 2007).

80. Andreas Philaretou, "Sexuality and the Internet," *Journal of Sex Research* 42 (2005): 180–181.

81. N2H2 communication, www.n2h2.com/index.php.

82. This section relies heavily on CERT® Coordination Center Denial of Service Attacks, www.cert.org/tech_tips/denial_of_service.html (accessed September 8, 2005).

83. Department of Justice, "Fourteen Convicted on Charges of Internet Trafficking in Controlled Substances as Well as Money Laundering," May 1, 2009, http://tampa.fbi.gov/dojpressrel/2009/ta050109.htm (accessed May 5, 2009).

84. National Center on Addiction and Substance Abuse at Columbia University, "You've Got Drugs! V: Prescription Drug Pushers on the Internet," May 2008, www.casacolumbia.org/articlefiles/531-2008%20You've%20Got%20Drugs%20V.pdf.

85. The Computer Fraud and Abuse Act (CFAA), 18 U.S.C. §1030 (1998).

86. Jim Wolf, "Internet Scams Targeted in Sweep: A 10-Day Crackdown Leads to 62 Arrests and 88 Indictments," *Boston Globe*, May 22, 2001, p. A2.

87. These sections rely on Anti-Phishing Working Group, "Phishing Activity Trends Report, June 2005," (2005), www.ncjrs.org/spotlight/identity_theft/publications.html#phishing (accessed August 30, 2005); U.S. Department of Justice Criminal Division, "Special Report on 'Phishing,'" (2004), www.ncjrs.org/spotlight/identity_theft/publications.html#phishing (accessed August 30, 2005).

88. Identity Theft Resource Center (ITRC), "Scams and Consumer Alerts," www.idtheftcenter.org (accessed April 15, 2008).

89. Anne Branscomb, "Rogue Computer Programs and Computer Rogues: Tailoring Punishment to Fit the Crime," *Rutgers Computer and Technology Law Journal* 16 (1990): 24–26.

90. Heather Jacobson and Rebecca Green, "Computer Crimes," *American Criminal Law Review* 39 (2002): 272–326.

91. United States Department of Justice, "Cyberstalking: A New Challenge for Law Enforcement and Industry," A Report from the Attorney General to the Vice President Washington, DC, 1999, www.usdoj.gov/criminal/cyber crime/cyberstalking.htm (accessed September 12, 2005).

92. Janis Wolak, David Finkelhor, Kimberly Mitchell, and Michele Ybarra, "Online 'Predators' and Their Victims: Myths, Realities, and Implications for Prevention and Treatment," *American Psychologist* 63 (2008): 111–128.

93. Jane Ireland and Rachel Monaghan, "Behaviours Indicative of Bullying among Young and Juvenile Male Offenders: A Study of Perpetrator and Victim Characteristics," *Aggressive Behavior* 32 (2006): 172–180.

94. This section leans heavily on Justin Patchin and Sameer Hinduja, "Bullies Move beyond the Schoolyard: A Preliminary Look at Cyberbullying," *Youth Violence and Juvenile Justice* 4 (2006): 148–169.

95. Justin Patchin and Sameer Hinduja, "Bullies Move Beyond the Schoolyard."

96. Barry C. Collin (2004), "The Future of CyberTerrorism: Where the Physical and Virtual Worlds Converge." http://afgen.com/terrorism1.html (accessed August 14, 2005).

97. Mark Pollitt, "Cyberterrorism—Fact or Fancy?" FBI Laboratory, www.cs.georgetown.edu/~denning/infosec/pollitt.html (accessed August 17, 2005).

98. Ibid.

99. Clyde Wilson, "Software Piracy: Uncovering Mutiny on the Cyberseas," *Trial* 32 (1996): 24–31.

100. Deloitte, 2005 Global Security Survey, www.deloitte .com/dtt/cda/doc/content/dtt_financialservices_2005Glo balSecuritySurvey_2005-07-21.pdf (accessed September, 14, 2005).

101. Statement of Mr. Bob Weaver, Deputy Special Agent in Charge, New York Field Office, United States Secret Service, before the House Financial Services Committee Subcommittee on Financial Institutions and Consumer Credit and the Subcommittee on Oversight and Investigations, U.S. House of Representatives April 3, 2003.

102. Rand Corporation, Research in Brief, "How Prepared Are State and Local Law Enforcement for Terrorism?" www.rand.org/publications/RB/RB9093/ (accessed July 13, 2005).

103. See, generally, President's Commission on Organized Crime, *Report to the President and the Attorney General, The Impact: Organized Crime Today* (Washington, DC: U.S. Government Printing Office, 1986). Herein cited as *Organized Crime Today*.

104. Frederick Martens and Michele Cunningham-Niederer, "Media Magic, Mafia Mania," *Federal Probation* 49 (1985): 60–68.

105. *Organized Crime Today*, pp. 7–8.

106. Alan Block and William Chambliss, *Organizing Crime* (New York: Elsevier, 1981).

107. Alan Block, *East Side/West Side* (New Brunswick, NJ: Transaction Books, 1983), pp. vii, 10–11.

108. Statement for the record of Thomas V. Fuentes, Chief, Organized Crime Section, Criminal Investigative Division, FBI, "Organized Crime," before the House Subcommittee on Finance and Hazardous Materials, September 13, 2000.

109. Donald Cressey, *Theft of the Nation* (New York: Harper & Row, 1969).

110. Dwight Smith, *The Mafia Mystique* (New York: Basic Books, 1975).

111. *Organized Crime Today*, p. 11.

112. Omar Bartos, "Growth of Russian Organized Crime Poses Serious Threat," *CJ International* 11 (1995): 8–9.

113. Robert Kelly and Rufus Schatzberg, "Types of Minority Organized Crime: Some Considerations." Paper presented at the annual meeting of the American Society of Criminology, Montreal, November 1987.

114. George Vold, *Theoretical Criminology*, 2nd ed., rev. Thomas Bernard (New York: Oxford University Press, 1979).

115. 18 U.S.C. 1952 (1976).

116. Public Law 91-452, Title IX, 84 Stat. 922 (1970) (codified at 18 U.S.C. 1961–68, 1976).

117. Richard McFeely, "Enterprise Theory of Investigation," *FBI Law Enforcement Bulletin* 70 (2001): 19–26.

118. National Legal Policy Center, "Bonanno Crime Boss Gets Two Life Terms," August 17, 2005, www.nlpc.org/view .asp?action=viewArticle&aid=975.

119. Selwyn Raab, "A Battered and Ailing Mafia Is Losing Its Grip on America." *New York Times*, October 22, 1990, p. 1.

120. Ibid., p. B7.

121. Rebecca Porter, "Prosecutors, Plaintiffs Aim to Curb Internet Gambling," *Trial* 40 (August 2004): 14.

Chapter 13. Public Order Crimes

1. "Emperors Club: All about Eliot Spitzer's Alleged Prostitution Ring," *Huffington Post*, March 10, 2008, www .huffingtonpost.com/2008/03/10/emperors-club-all-about-_n_90768.html.

2. Emily Friedman and Michele McPhee, "'Craigslist Killer' Appears in Court, Shouts 'Not Guilty,'" ABC News, June 22, 2009, http://abcnews.go.com/US/story?id=7897975 (accessed July 4, 2009).

3. Edwin Schur, *Crimes without Victims* (Englewood Cliffs, NJ: Prentice-Hall, 1965).

4. Andrea Dworkin, quoted in "Where Do We Stand on Pornography?" *Ms* (January-February 1994), p. 34.

5. Russel Falck, Jichuan Wang, and Robert Carlson, "The Epidemiology of Physical Attack and Rape among Crack-Using Women," *Violence and Victims* 16 (2001): 79–89.

6. C. Gabrielle Salfati, Alison James, and Lynn Ferguson, "Prostitute Homicides: A Descriptive Study," *Journal of Interpersonal Violence* 23 (2008): 505–543.

7. Morris Cohen, "Moral Aspects of the Criminal Law," *Yale Law Journal* 49 (1940): 1017.

8. See Joel Feinberg, *Social Philosophy* (Englewood Cliffs, NJ: Prentice-Hall, 1973), chaps. 2, 3.

9. *United States v. 12 200-ft Reels of Super 8mm Film*, 413 U.S. 123 (1973), at p. 137.

10. Irving Kristol, "Liberal Censorship and the Common Culture," *Society* 36 (1999, September): 5.

11. Wayne La Fave and Austin Scott Jr., *Criminal Law* (St. Paul, MN: West, 1986), p. 12.

12. Ibid.

13. Ali Mokdad, James Marks, Donna F. Stroup, and Julie Gerberding, "Actual Causes of Death in the United States, 2000," *Journal of the American Medical Association* 291 (2004): 1,238–1,241.

14. Howard Becker, *Outsiders* (New York: Macmillan, 1963), pp. 13–14.

15. American Library Association, *Frequently Challenged Books*, www.ala.org/ala/aboutala/offices/oif/bannedbooksweek/challengedbanned/frequentlychallengedbooks.cfm.

16. US Code, Title 1 § 7. Definition of "marriage" and "spouse."

17. *Lawrence et al. v. Texas*, No. 02-102, June 26, 2003.

18. *Hillary Goodridge et al. vs. Department of Public Health and Another*, SJC-08860, November 18, 2003.

19. CNN News, "California Ban on Same-Sex Marriage Struck Down," May 16, 2008, www.cnn.com/2008/US/05/15/same.sex.marriage/index.html (accessed July 4, 2009); Huffington Post, "California Gay Marriage Banned As Proposition 8 Passes," November 5, 2008, www.huffingtonpost.com/2008/11/05/california-gay-marriage-b_n_141429.html (accessed July 4, 2009).

20. David Gardner, "I Feel Guilty: Girl Held for 18 Years 'Bonded with Kidnapper,'" *London Evening Standard*, August 28, 2009, www.thisislondon.co.uk/standard/article-23737833-i-feel-guilty-girl-held-for-18-years-bonded-with-kidnapper.do.

21. Richard Estes and Neil Alan Weiner, *The Commercial Sexual Exploitation of Children in the U.S., Canada, and Mexico* (Philadelphia: University of Pennsylvania Press, 2001).

22. Associated Press, "David Carradine Found Dead in Thailand Hotel" MSNBC.com, June 4, 2009, www.msnbc.msn.com/id/31103217/ (accessed July 7, 2009).

23. See, generally, Spencer Rathus and Jeffery Nevid, *Abnormal Psychology* (Englewood Cliffs, NJ: Prentice-Hall, 1991), pp. 373–411.

24. W. P. de Silva, "Sexual Variations," *British Medical Journal* 318 (1999): 654–655.

25. Boris Schiffer, Thomas Paul, Elke Gizewski, Michael Forsting, Norbert Leygraf, Manfred Schedlowski, and Tillmann H. C. Kruger, "Functional Brain Correlates of Heterosexual Paedophilia," *Neuroimage* 41 (2008): 80–91.

26. Ray Blanchard, Bruce K. Christensen, Scott M. Strong, James M. Cantor, Michael E. Kuban, Philip Klassen, Robert Dickey, and Thomas Blak, "Retrospective Self-Reports of Childhood Accidents Causing Unconsciousness in Phallometrically Diagnosed Pedophiles," *Archives of Sexual Behavior* 31 (2002): 111–127.

27. Michael Allan and Randolph Grace, "Psychometric Assessment of Dynamic Risk Factors for Child Molesters," *Sexual Abuse: A Journal of Research* 19 (2007): 347–367.

28. For an analysis of this issue, see Theresa Gannon and Devon Polaschek, "Cognitive Distortions in Child Molesters: A Re-examination of Key Theories and Research," *Clinical Psychology Review* 26 (2006): 1000–1019.

29. Kathy Smiljanich and John Briere, "Self-Reported Sexual Interest in Children: Sex Differences and Psychosocial Correlates in a University Sample," *Violence and Victims* 11 (1996): 39–50.

30. See, generally, V. Bullogh, *Sexual Variance in Society and History* (Chicago: University of Chicago Press, 1958), pp. 143–144.

31. Spencer Rathus, *Human Sexuality* (New York: Holt, Rinehart and Winston, 1983), p. 463.

32. Charles McCaghy, *Deviant Behavior* (New York: Macmillan, 1976), pp. 348–349.

33. Ibid.

34. Michael Waldholz, "HTLV–I Virus Found in Blood of Prostitutes," *Wall Street Journal*, January 5, 1990, p. B2.

35. Scott Shuger, "Hookers.com: How E-commerce Is Transforming the Oldest Profession," *Slate Magazine*, www.slate.com/id/73797/ (accessed April 15, 2009).

36. Monica Prasad, "The Morality of Market Exchange: Love, Money, and Contractual Justice," *Sociological Perspectives* 42 (1999): 181–187.

37. Mark Lander, "World Cup Brings Little Pleasure to German Brothels," *New York Times*, July 3, 2006, www.nytimes.com/2006/07/03/world/europe/03berlin.html?ex=1309579200&en=e28e47eba8978d37&ei=5089&partner=rssyahoo&emc=rss.

38. Associated Press, "Iran Stones Six to Death," October 26, 1997, APO 10, www.uri.edu/artsci/wms/hughes/stoned_to_death.

39. Elizabeth Bernstein, "The Meaning of the Purchase: Desire, Demand, and the Commerce of Sex," *Ethnography* 2 (2001): 389–420.

40. Charles Winick and Paul Kinsie, *The Lively Commerce* (Chicago: Quadrangle, 1971), p. 58.

41. Celia Williamson and Lynda Baker, "Women in Street-Based Prostitution: A Typology of Their Work Styles," *Qualitative Social Work* 8 (2009): 27–44.

42. Winick and Kinsie, *The Lively Commerce*, pp. 172–173.

43. Paul Goldstein, "Occupational Mobility in the World of Prostitution: Becoming a Madam," *Deviant Behavior* 4 (1983): 267–279.

44. http://www.yellowpages.com/Los-Angeles-CA/Escort-Service?search_terms=escort+services (accessed July 4, 2009).

45. Ibid.

46. Mireya Navarro, "Group Forced Illegal Aliens into Prostitution, U.S. Says," *New York Times*, April 24, 1998, p. A10.

47. Ginger Thompson and Philip Shenon, "Navy Officer Describes Working as a Prostitute," *New York Times*, April 12, 2008, www.nytimes.com/2008/04/12/us/12officer.html?ex=1365652800&en=65a734ab30a26c33&ei=5088&partner=rssnyt&emc=rss.

48. D. Kelly Weisberg, *Children of the Night: A Study of Adolescent Prostitution* (Lexington, MA: Lexington Books, 1985), pp. 44–55.

49. N. Jackman, Richard O'Toole, and Gilbert Geis, "The Self-Image of the Prostitute," in *Sexual Deviance*, ed. J. Gagnon and W. Simon (New York: Harper & Row, 1967), pp. 152–153.

50. Gerald Hotaling and David Finkelhor, *The Sexual Exploitation of Missing Children* (Washington, DC: U.S. Department of Justice, 1988).

51. Weisberg, *Children of the Night*, p. 98.

52. Paul Goldstein, Lawrence Ouellet, and Michael Fendrich, "From Bag Brides to Skeezers: A Historical Perspective on Sex-for-Drugs Behavior," *Journal of Psychoactive Drugs* 24 (1992): 349–361.

53. Kara Marie Brawn and Dominique Roe-Sepowitz, "Female Juvenile Prostitutes: Exploring the Relationship to Substance Use," *Children and Youth Services Review* 30 (2008): 1,395–1,402.

54. Barbara G. Brents and Kathryn Hausbeck, "State-Sanctioned Sex: Negotiating Formal and Informal Regulatory Practices

in Nevada Brothels," *Sociological Perspectives* 44 (2001): 307–335.

55. Ibid.

56. Mara Keire, "The Vice Trust: A Reinterpretation of the White Slavery Scare in the United States, 1907–1917," *Journal of Social History* 35 (2001): 5–42.

57. Ronald Weitzer, "The Politics of Prostitution in America," in *Sex for Sale*, ed. R. Weitzer (New York: Routledge, 2000), pp. 159–180.

58. Andrea Dworkin, *Pornography* (New York: Dutton, 1989).

59. Annette Jolin, "On the Backs of Working Prostitutes: Feminist Theory and Prostitution Policy," *Crime and Delinquency* 40 (1994): 60–83, at pp. 76–77.

60. Alexa Albert, *Brothel: Mustang Ranch and Its Women* (New York: Random House, 2001).

61. Melissa Farley, *Prostitution and Trafficking in Nevada: Making the Connections* (San Francisco, CA: Prostitution Research & Education, 2007); Melissa Farley, "Trafficking for Prostitution: Making the Connections," American Psychological Association, 115th Annual Convention, August 17, 2007, San Francisco.

62. Roger Matthews, *Prostitution, Politics and Policy* (London, Routledge-Cavendish, 2008).

63. *Merriam-Webster Dictionary* (New York: Pocket Books, 1974), p. 484.

64. Attorney General's Commission, Report on Pornography, *Final Report* (Washington, DC: U.S. Government Printing Office, 1986), pp. 837–901. Hereafter cited as Pornography Commission.

65. Michael Bourke and Andres Hernandez, "The 'Butner Study' Redux: A Report of the Incidence of Hands-on Child Victimization by Child Pornography Offenders," *Journal of Family Violence* 24 (2009): 183–191.

66. *Report of the Commission on Obscenity and Pornography* (Washington, DC: U.S. Government Printing Office, 1970).

67. Berl Kutchinsky, "The Effect of Easy Availability of Pornography on the Incidence of Sex Crimes," *Journal of Social Issues* 29 (1973): 95–112.

68. Michael Goldstein, "Exposure to Erotic Stimuli and Sexual Deviance," *Journal of Social Issues* 29 (1973): 197–219.

69. Catherine Simmons, Peter Lehmann, and Shannon Collier-Tenison, "Linking Male Use of the Sex Industry to Controlling Behaviors in Violent Relationships: An Exploratory Analysis," *Violence against Women* 14 (2008): 406–417.

70. See Edward Donnerstein, Daniel Linz, and Steven Penrod, *The Question of Pornography* (New York: Free Press, 1987).

71. Edward Donnerstein, "Pornography and Violence against Women," *Annals of the New York Academy of Science* 347 (1980): 277–288; E. Donnerstein and J. Hallam, "Facilitating Effects of Erotica on Aggression against Women," *Journal of Personality and Social Psychology* 36 (1977): 1,270–1,277; Seymour Fishbach and Neil Malamuth, "Sex and Aggression: Proving the Link," *Psychology Today* 12 (1978): 111–122.

72. Donald Smith, "Sexual Aggression in American Pornography: The Stereotype of Rape," paper presented at the annual meeting of the American Sociological Association, Salt Lake City, Utah, August 1976.

73. Diana Russel, *Dangerous Relationships: Pornography, Misogyny, and Rape* (Thousand Oaks, CA: Sage, 1998).

74. 354 U.S. 476; 77 S.Ct. 1304 (1957).

75. 413 U.S. 15 (1973).

76. R. George Wright, "Defining Obscenity: The Criterion of Value," *New England Law Review* 22 (1987): 315–341.

77. *Pope v. Illinois*, 107 S.Ct. 1918 (1987).

78. ACLU, "*ACLU v. Reno*, Round 2: Broad Coalition Files Challenge to New Federal Net Censorship Law," News Release, October 22, 1998.

79. *Ashcroft, Attorney General, et al. v. Free Speech Coalition et al.*, No. 00- 795, April 16, 2002.

80. Thomas J. Lueck, "At Sex Shops, Fear That Ruling Means the End Is Near," *New York Times*, February 25, 1998, p. 1.

81. David Rohde, "In Giuliani's Crackdown on Porn Shops, Court Ruling Is a Setback," *New York Times*, August 29, 1998, p. A11.

82. ACLU, *Reno v. ACLU*, No. 96-511.

83. Ralph Weisheit, "Studying Drugs in Rural Areas: Notes from the Field," *Journal of Research in Crime and Delinquency* 30 (1993): 213–232.

84. U.S. Department of Health and Human Services, Substance Abuse and Mental Health Services Administration Drug Abuse Warning Network, 2006, "National Estimates of Drug-Related Emergency Department Visits," http://dawninfo.samhsa.gov/files/ED2006/DAWN2k6ED.htm (accessed April 20, 2009).

85. Richard Dembo, Steven Belenko, Kristina Childs, and Jennifer Wareham, "Drug Use and Sexually Transmitted Diseases among Female and Male Arrested Youths," *Journal of Behavioral Medicine* 32 (2009): 129–141.

86. James Inciardi, *The War on Drugs* (Palo Alto, CA: Mayfield, 1986), p. 2.

87. See, generally, David Pittman, "Drug Addiction and Crime," in *Handbook of Criminology*, ed. D. Glazer (Chicago: Rand McNally, 1974), pp. 209–232; Board of Directors, National Council on Crime and Delinquency, "Drug Addiction: A Medical, Not a Law Enforcement, Problem," *Crime and Delinquency* 20 (1974): 4–9.

88. Associated Press, "Records Detail Royals' Turn-of-Century Drug Use," *Boston Globe*, August 29, 1993, p. 13.

89. See Edward Brecher, *Licit and Illicit Drugs* (Boston: Little, Brown, 1972).

90. James Inciardi, *Reflections on Crime* (New York: Holt, Rinehart and Winston, 1978), pp. 8–10; see also A. Greeley, William McCready, and Gary Theisen, *Ethnic Drinking Subcultures* (New York: Praeger, 1980).

91. Joseph Gusfield, *Symbolic Crusade* (Urbana: University of Illinois Press, 1963), chap. 3.

92. McCaghy, *Deviant Behavior*, p. 280.

93. Ibid.

94. The annual survey is conducted by Lloyd Johnston, Jerald Bachman, Patrick O'Malley, and John Schulenberg of the Institute of Social Research, University of Michigan, Ann Arbor, www.monitoringthefuture.org/pubs/monographs/overview2008.pdf.

95. Monitoring the Future, 2008, "Data from In-School Surveys of 8th-, 10th-, and 12th-Grade Students," www.monitoringthefuture.org/data/08data.html#2008data-drugs.

96. Department of Health and Human Services, "Results from the 2007 National Survey on Drug Use and Health: National Findings," www.oas.samhsa.gov/nsduh/2k7nsduh/2k7Results.cfm#TOC (accessed April 20, 2009).

97. Department of Health and Human Services, "Results from the 2007 National Survey on Drug Use and Health: National Findings."

98. National Center on Addiction and Substance Abuse, *Teen Tipplers: America's Underage Drinking Epidemic,* rev. ed. (New York City: Author, 2003).

99. C. Bowden, "Determinants of Initial Use of Opioids," *Comprehensive Psychiatry* 12 (1971): 136–140.

100. Marvin Krohn, Alan Lizotte, Terence Thornberry, Carolyn Smith, and David McDowall, "Reciprocal Causal Relationships among Drug Use, Peers, and Beliefs: A Five-Wave Panel Model," *Journal of Drug Issues* 26 (1996): 205–228.

101. R. Cloward and L. Ohlin, *Delinquency and Opportunity: A Theory of Delinquent Gangs* (Glencoe, IL: Free Press, 1960).

102. Lening Zhang, John Welte, and William Wieczorek, "Youth Gangs, Drug Use and Delinquency," *Journal of Criminal Justice* 27 (1999): 101–109.

103. Peter Giancola, "Constructive Thinking, Antisocial Behavior, and Drug Use in Adolescent Boys with and without a Family History of a Substance Use Disorder," *Personality and Individual Differences* 35 (2003): 1,315–1,331.

104. Amy Young, Carol Boyd, and Amy Hubbell, "Social Isolation and Sexual Abuse among Women Who Smoke Crack," *Journal of Psychosocial Nursing* 39 (2001): 16–19.

105. Substance Abuse and Mental Health Services Administration, Office of Applied Studies, "The Relationship between Mental Health and Substance Abuse among Adolescents," Analytic Series: A-9, 1999.

106. D. W. Goodwin, "Alcoholism and Genetics," *Archives of General Psychiatry* 42 (1985): 171–174.

107. For a thorough review of this issue, see John Petraitis, Brian Flay, and Todd Miller, "Reviewing Theories of Adolescent Substance Use: Organizing Pieces in the Puzzle," *Psychological Bulletin* 117 (1995): 67–86.

108. Judith Brook and Li-Jung Tseng, "Influences of Parental Drug Use, Personality, and Child Rearing on the Toddler's Anger and Negativity," *Genetic, Social and General Psychology Monographs* 122 (1996): 107–128.

109. Thomas Ashby Wills, Donato Vaccaro, Grace McNamara, and A. Elizabeth Hirky, "Escalated Substance Use: A Longitudinal Grouping Analysis from Early to Middle Adolescence," *Journal of Abnormal Psychology* 105 (1996): 166–180.

110. Denise Kandel and Mark Davies, "Friendship Networks, Intimacy, and Illicit Drug Use in Young Adulthood: A Comparison of Two Competing Theories," *Criminology* 29 (1991): 441–471.

111. J. S. Mio, G. Nanjundappa, D. E. Verlur, and M. D. DeRios, "Drug Abuse and the Adolescent Sex Offender: A Preliminary Analysis," *Journal of Psychoactive Drugs* 18 (1986): 65–72.

112. D. Baer and J. Corrado, "Heroin Addict Relationships with Parents during Childhood and Early Adolescent Years," *Journal of Genetic Psychology* 124 (1974): 99–103.

113. The National Center on Addiction and Substance Abuse, "Reducing Teen Smoking Can Cut Marijuana Use Significantly," Press Release, September 16, 2003.

114. John Wallace and Jerald Bachman, "Explaining Racial/Ethnic Differences in Adolescent Drug Use: The Impact of Background and Lifestyle," *Social Problems* 38 (1991): 333–357.

115. John Donovan, "Problem-Behavior Theory and the Explanation of Adolescent Marijuana Use," *Journal of Drug Issues* 26 (1996): 379–404.

116. A. Christiansen, G. T. Smith, P. V. Roehling, and M. S. Goldman, "Using Alcohol Expectancies to Predict Adolescent Drinking Behavior after One Year," *Journal of Counseling and Clinical Psychology* 57 (1989): 93–99.

117. Icek Ajzen, *Attitudes, Personality and Behavior* (Homewood, IL: Dorsey Press, 1988).

118. Judith Brook, Martin Whiteman, Elinor Balka, and Beatrix Hamburg, "African-American and Puerto Rican Drug Use: Personality, Familial, and Other Environmental Risk Factors," *Genetic, Social, and General Psychology Monographs* 118 (1992): 419–438.

119. Bu Huang, Helene Raskin White, Rick Kosterman, Richard Catalano, and J. David Hawkins, "Developmental Associations between Alcohol and Interpersonal Aggression during Adolescence," *Journal of Research in Crime and Delinquency* 38 (2001): 64–83.

120. Andrew Golub and Bruce D. Johnson, *The Rise of Marijuana as the Drug of Choice among Youthful Adult Arrestees* (Washington, D.C.: National Institute of Justice, 2001).

121. Cesar Rebellon and Karen Van Gundy, "Can Social Psychological Delinquency Theory Explain the Link between Marijuana and Other Illicit Drug Use? A Longitudinal Analysis of the Gateway Hypothesis," *Journal of Drug Issues* 36 (2006): 515–540.

122. Marvin Dawkins, "Drug Use and Violent Crime among Adolescents," *Adolescence* 32 (1997): 395–406.

123. Denise Gottfredson, Brook Kearley, Shawn Bushway, "Substance Use, Drug Treatment, and Crime: An Examination of Intra-Individual Variation in a Drug Court Population," *Journal of Drug Issues* 38 (2008): 601–630.

124. "Overview of Findings from the 2002 National Survey on Drug Use and Health," www.oas.samhsa.gov/nhsda/2k2nsduh/Overview/2k2Overview.htm#chap5 (accessed April 27, 2007).

125. National Surveys on Drug Use and Health, "Illicit Drug Use among Persons Arrested for Serious Crimes," www.oas.samhsa.gov/2k5/arrests/arrests.cfm (accessed April 27, 2007).

126. Department of Health and Human Services, "Results from the 2007 National Survey on Drug Use and Health: National Findings."

127. Ibid.

128. Marvin Krohn, Alan Lizotte, and Cynthia Perez, "The Interrelationship between Substance Use and Precocious Transitions to Adult Sexuality," *Journal of Health and Social Behavior* 38 (1997): 87–103, at p. 88; Richard Jessor, "Risk Behavior in Adolescence: A Psychosocial Framework for Understanding and Action," in *Adolescents at Risk: Medical and Social Perspectives,* ed. D. E. Rogers and E. Ginzburg (Boulder, CO: Westview Press, 1992).

129. George Speckart and M. Douglas Anglin, "Narcotics Use and Crime: An Overview of Recent Research Advances," *Contemporary Drug Problems* 13 (1986): 741–769; Charles Faupel and Carl Klockars, "Drugs–Crime Connections: Elaborations from the Life Histories of Hard-Core Heroin Addicts," *Social Problems* 34 (1987): 54–68.

130. M. Douglas Anglin, Elizabeth Piper Deschenes, and George Speckart, "The Effect of Legal Supervision on Narcotic Addiction and Criminal Behavior," paper presented at the annual meeting of the American Society of Criminology, Montreal, November 1987, p. 2.

131. Speckart and Anglin, "Narcotics Use and Crime," p. 752.

132. See Kenneth Jones, Louis Shainberg, and Carter Byer, *Drugs and Alcohol* (New York: Harper & Row, 1979) pp. 137–146.

133. Controlled Substance Act, 21 U.S.C. 848 (1984).

134. Anti–Drug Abuse Act of 1986, Pub. L. No. 99-570, U.S.C. 841 (1986).

135. Anti–Drug Abuse Act of 1988, Pub. L. No. 100-690; 21 U.S.C. 1501; Subtitle A–Death Penalty, Sec. 7001, Amending the Controlled Substances Abuse Act, 21 U.S.C. 848.

136. Eric Jensen, Jurg Gerber, and Ginna Babcock, "The New War on Drugs: Grass Roots Movement or Political Construction?" *Journal of Drug Issues* 21 (1991): 651–667.

137. George Rengert, *The Geography of Illegal Drugs* (Boulder, CO: Westview Press, 1996), p. 2.

138. Office of National Drug Control Policy, *Drug Facts, 2009,* www.whitehousedrugpolicy.gov/DrugFact/index.html.

139. Francisco Gutierrez, "Institutionalizing Global Wars: State Transformations in Colombia, 1978–2002: Colombian Policy Directed at Its Wars, Paradoxically, Narrows the Government's Margin of Maneuver Even As It Tries to Expand It," *Journal of International Affairs* 57 (2003): 135–152.

140. U.S. Department of State, *1998 International Narcotics Control Strategy Report,* February 1999.

141. David Hayeslip, "Local-Level Drug Enforcement: New Strategies," *NIJ Reports* (1989, March/April): 1.

142. Mark Moore, *Drug Trafficking* (Washington, DC: National Institute of Justice, 1988).

143. Peter Rossi, Richard Berk, and Alec Campbell, "Just Punishments: Guideline Sentences and Normative Consensus," *Journal of Quantitative Criminology* 13 (1997): 267–283.

144. Robert Davis, Arthur Lurigio, and Dennis Rosenbaum, eds., *Drugs and the Community* (Springfield, IL: Charles C Thomas, 1993), pp. xii–xv.

145. Saul Weingart, "A Typology of Community Responses to Drugs," in *Drugs and the Community,* ed. Robert Davis, Arthur Lurigio, and Dennis Rosenbaum (Springfield, IL: Charles C Thomas, 1993), pp. 85–105.

146. Dennis Rosenbaum, Robert Flewelling, Susan Bailey, Chris Ringwalt, and Deanna Wilkinson, "Cops in the Classroom: A Longitudinal Evaluation of Drug Abuse Resistance Education (D.A.R.E.)," *Journal of Research in Crime and Delinquency* 31 (1994): 3–31.

147. Donald R. Lynam, Rich Milich, Rick Zimmerman, Scott Novak, T. K. Logan, Catherine Martin, Carl Leukefeld, and Richard Clayton, "Project D.A.R.E.: No Effects at 10-Year Follow-Up," *Journal of Consulting and Clinical Psychology* 67 (1999): 590–593.

148. Mareanne Zawitz, *Drugs, Crime, and the Justice System* (Washington, D.C.: U.S. Government Printing Office, 1992), pp. 115–122.

149. John Goldkamp and Peter Jones, "Pretrial Drug-Testing Experiments in Milwaukee and Prince George's County: The Context of Implementation," *Journal of Research in Crime and Delinquency* 29 (1992): 430–465; Chester Britt, Michael Gottfredson, and John Goldkamp, "Drug Testing and Pretrial Misconduct: An Experiment on the Specific Deterrent Effects of Drug Monitoring Defendants on Pretrial Release," *Journal of Research in Crime and Delinquency* 29 (1992): 62–78. See, generally, Peter Greenwood and Franklin Zimring, *One More Chance* (Santa Monica, CA: Rand Corporation, 1985).

150. See, generally, Greenwood and Zimring, *One More Chance*.

151. Tracy Beswick, David Best, Jenny Bearn, Michael Gossop, Sian Rees, and John Strang, "The Effectiveness of Combined Naloxone/Lofexidine in Opiate Detoxification: Results from a Double-Blind Randomized and Placebo-Controlled Trial," *American Journal on Addictions* 12 (2003): 295–306.

152. George De Leon, Stanley Sacks, Graham Staines, and Karen McKendrick, "Modified Therapeutic Community for Homeless Mentally Ill Chemical Abusers: Treatment Outcomes," *American Journal of Drug and Alcohol Abuse* 26 (2000): 461–480.

153. Michael French, H. J. Jeanne Salome, Jody Sindelar, and A. Thomas McLellan, "Benefit–Cost Analysis of Ancillary Social Services in Publicly Supported Addiction Treatment," February 1, 1999, data supplied by the Center for Substance Abuse Research (CESAR), College Park, MD 20740.

154. The following section is based on material found in Jerome Platt, "Vocational Rehabilitation of Drug Abusers," *Psychological Bulletin* 117 (1995): 416–433.

155. Arthur Fries, Robert W. Anthony, Andrew Cseko Jr., Carl C. Gaither, and Eric Schulman, *The Price and Purity of Illicit Drugs: 1981–2007* (Alexandria, VA: Institute for Defense Analysis, 2008), www.whitehousedrugpolicy.gov/publications/price_purity/price_purity07.pdf.

156. Office of National Drug Control Policy, *National Drug Control Strategy: FY 2004 Budget Summary* (Washington, DC: Author, 2003).

157. Ethan Nadelmann, "The U.S. Is Addicted to War on Drugs," *Globe and Mail,* May 20, 2003, p. 1; Ethan Nadelmann, "America's Drug Problem," *Bulletin of the American Academy of Arts and Sciences* 65 (1991): 24–40.

158. See, generally, Ralph Weishcit, *Drugs, Crime and the Criminal Justice System* (Cincinnati, OH: Anderson, 1990).

159. David Courtwright, "Should We Legalize Drugs? History Answers No," *American Heritage* (1993, February/March): 43–56.

160. Kathryn Ann Farr, "Revitalizing the Drug Decriminalization Debate," *Crime and Delinquency* 36 (1990): 223–237.

Chapter 14. The Criminal Justice System

1. *Safford United School District No. 1 v. Redding* [08-479].
2. *Safford v. Redding*.
3. Bureau of Justice Statistics, www.ojp.usdoj.gov/bjs/sandlle.htm (accessed February 10, 2009).
4. Federal Bureau of Investigation, *Crime in the United States, 2007* (Washington, DC: Government Printing Office, 2006), Table 29.
5. Matthew R. Durose and Patrick A. Langan, *Felony Sentences in State Courts, 2002* (Washington, DC: Bureau of Justice Statistics, 2004).

6. See Albert Reiss, *Police and the Public* (New Haven, CT: Yale University Press, 1972).

7. Matthew Durose and Patrick Langan, *Contacts between Police and the Public: Findings from the 2005 National Survey* (Washington, DC: Bureau of Justice Statistics, 2007).

8. Wesley Skogan, "Asymmetry in the Impact of Encounters with Police," *Policing & Society* 16 (2006): 99–126.

9. James Hawdon and John Ryan, "Police-Resident Interactions and Satisfaction with Police: An Empirical Test of Community Policing Assertions," *Criminal Justice Policy Review* 14 (2003): 55–74.

10. Yili Xu, Mora Fiedler, and Karl Flaming, "Discovering the Impact of Community Policing: The Broken Windows Thesis, Collective Efficacy, and Citizens' Judgment," *Journal of Research in Crime and Delinquency* 42 (2005): 147–186.

11. James Nolan, Norman Conti, and Jack McDevitt, "Situational Policing: Neighbourhood Development and Crime Control," *Policing & Society* 14 (2004): 99–118.

12. Xu, Fiedler, and Flaming, "Discovering the Impact of Community Policing."

13. Ling Ren, Liqun Cao, Nicholas Lovrich, and Michael Gaffney, "Linking Confidence in the Police with the Performance of the Police: Community Policing Can Make a Difference," *Journal of Criminal Justice* 33 (January/February 2005): 55–66.

14. Robert Davis, Pedro Mateu-Gelabert, and Joel Miller, "Can Effective Policing Also Be Respectful? Two Examples in the South Bronx," *Police Quarterly* 8 (2005): 229–247.

15. Jihong Zhao, Ni He, and Nicholas Lovrich, "Value Change among Police Officers at a Time of Organizational Reform: A Follow-Up Study using Rokeach Values," *Policing* 22 (1999): 152–170.

16. Kevin Ford, Daniel Weissbein, and Kevin Plamondon, "Distinguishing Organizational from Strategy Commitment: Linking Officers' Commitment to Community Policing to Job Behaviors and Satisfaction," *Justice Quarterly* 20 (2003): 159–186.

17. Tracey Kyckelhahn and Thomas H. Cohen, *Felony Defendants in Large Urban Counties, 2004* (Washington, DC: Bureau of Justice Statistics, 2008), www.ojp.usdoj.gov/bjs/pub/pdf/fdluc04.pdf.

18. Cassia Spohn, Dawn Beichner, and Erika Davis-Frenzel, "Prosecutorial Justifications for Sexual Assault Case Rejection: Guarding the 'Gateway to Justice,'" *Social Problems* 48 (2001): 206–235.

19. *Powell v. Alabama*, 287 U.S. 45, 53 S.Ct. 55, 77 L.Ed. 158 (1932); *Gideon v. Wainwright*, 372 U.S. 335, 83 S.Ct. 792, 9 L.Ed. 2d 799 (1963); *Argersinger v. Hamlin*, 407 U.S. 25, 92 S.Ct. 2006, 32 L.Ed. 2d 530 (1972).

20. *Wiggins v. Smith, Warden*, No. 02-311 [decided June 26, 2003].

21. Lauren Glaze and Thomas Bonczar, *Probation and Parole in the United States, 2007* (Washington, DC: Bureau of Justice Statistics, 2008), Statistical Table 5, www.ojp.usdoj.gov/bjs/pub/pdf/ppus07st.pdf.

22. Patrick A. Langan and David J. Levin, *Recidivism of Prisoners Released in 1994* (Washington, DC: Bureau of Justice Statistics, 2002).

23. Robyn L. Cohen, *Probation and Parole Violators in State Prison, 1991: Survey of State Prison Inmates, 1991* (Washington, DC: Bureau of Justice Statistics, 1995).

24. Herbert L. Packer, *The Limits of the Criminal Sanction* (Stanford, CA: Stanford University Press, 1968), p. 159.

25. Deirdre M. Bowen, "Calling Your Bluff: How Prosecutors and Defense Attorneys Adapt Plea Bargaining Strategies to Increased Formalization," *Justice Quarterly* 26 (2009): 2–29.

26. Barbara Boland, Catherine Conly, Paul Mahanna, Lynn Warner, and Ronald Sones, *The Prosecution of Felony Arrests, 1987* (Washington, DC: Bureau of Justice Statistics, 1990), p. 3.

27. See Donald Newman, *Conviction: The Determination of Guilt or Innocence without Trial* (Boston: Little, Brown, 1966).

28. *Arizona v. Gant*, No. 07-542. April 21, 2009.

29. *Vanessa Barker*, "The Politics of Punishing," *Punishment & Society* 8 (2006): 5–32.

30. Richard Timothy Coupe and Laurence Blake, "The Effects of Patrol Workloads and Response Strength on Arrests at Burglary Emergencies," *Journal of Criminal Justice* 33 (2005): 239–255.

31. Paul Cassell, "How Many Criminals Has Miranda Set Free?" *Wall Street Journal*, March 1, 1995, p. A15.

32. Jon Gould and Stephen Mastrofski, "Suspect Searches: Assessing Police Behavior under the U.S. Constitution," *Criminology & Public Policy* 3 (2004): 315–362.

33. David Garland, *Punishment and Modern Society* (Chicago: University of Chicago Press, 1990).

34. The most often cited of these is Douglas Lipton, Robert Martinson, and Judith Wilks, *The Effectiveness of Correctional Treatment: A Survey of Treatment Evaluation Studies* (New York: Praeger, 1975).

35. "Many State Legislatures Focused on Crime in 1995, Study Finds," *Criminal Justice Newsletter*, January 17, 1996, pp. 1–2.

36. Packer, *The Limits of the Criminal Sanction*.

37. Eric Lotke, "Hobbling a Generation: Young African-American Men in Washington, D.C.'s Criminal Justice System—Five Years Later," *Crime and Delinquency* 44 (1998): 355–366.

38. Roy Austin and Mark Allen, "Racial Disparity in Arrest Rates as an Explanation of Racial Disparity in Commitment to Pennsylvania's Prisons," *Journal of Research in Crime and Delinquency* 37 (2000): 200–220.

39. Anthony Petrosino and Carolyn Petrosino, "The Public Safety Potential of Megan's Law in Massachusetts: An Assessment from a Sample of Criminal Sexual Psychopaths," *Crime and Delinquency* 43 (1999): 140–158; "New Laws Said to Raise Demands on Justice Information Systems," *Criminal Justice Newsletter*, September 17, 1996, pp. 3–4.

40. John Schwartz, "As Jurors Turn to Web, Mistrials Are Popping Up," *New York Times* (March 17, 2009), www.nytimes.com/2009/03/18/us/18juries.html?_r=1&emc=eta1 (accessed March 27, 2009).

41. Patrick Danner, "Charges Dismissed in South Florida Internet Drug Case," *Miami Herald*, April 4, 2009, www.miamiherald.com/living/health/costs/story/989862.html (accessed July 10, 2009).

42. Jim Yardley, "Convicted in Murder Case, Man Cleared 7 Years Later," *New York Times*, October 29, 1998, p. 11.

43. Talia Roitberg Harmon and William S. Lofquist, "Too Late for Luck: A Comparison of Post-Furman Exonerations and Executions of the Innocent," *Crime and Delinquency* 51 (2005): 498–520.

44. Richard McCorkle, "Research Note: Punish and Rehabilitate? Public Attitudes Toward Six Common Crimes," *Crime and Delinquency* 39 (1993): 240–252.

45. D. A. Andrews, Ivan Zinger, R. D. Hoge, James Bonta, Paul Gendreau, and Francis Cullen, "Does Correctional Treatment Work? A Clinically-Relevant and Psychologically-Informed Meta-Analysis," *Criminology* 28 (1990): 369–404.

46. John Hepburn, "Recidivism among Drug Offenders Following Exposure to Treatment," *Criminal Justice Policy Review* 16 (2005): 237–259.

47. Denise Gottfredson, "Participation in Drug Treatment Court and Time to Rearrest," *Justice Quarterly* 21 (2004): 637–658.

48. Mark Lipsey and David Wilson, "Effective Intervention for Serious Juvenile Offenders: A Synthesis of Research," in *Serious and Violent Juvenile Offenders: Risk Factors and Successful Interventions,* ed. Rolf Loeber and David Farrington (Thousand Oaks, CA: Sage, 1998), pp. 39–53.

49. Francis Cullen, John Paul Wright, Shayna Brown, Melissa Moon, Michael Blankenship, and Brandon Applegate, "Public Support for Early Intervention Programs: Implications for a Progressive Policy Agenda," *Crime and Delinquency* 44 (1998): 187–204.

50. David Fogel, *We Are the Living Proof* (Cincinnati, OH: Anderson, 1975). See also David Fogel, *Justice as Fairness* (Cincinnati, OH: Anderson, 1980).

51. Travis Pratt, "Race and Sentencing: A Meta-Analysis of Conflicting Empirical Research Results," *Journal of Criminal Justice* 26 (1998): 513–525.

52. Shawn Bushway, "The Impact of an Arrest on the Job Stability of Young White American Men," *Journal of Research in Crime and Delinquency* 35 (1998): 454–479.

53. Edwin M. Lemert, "The Juvenile Court—Quest and Realities," in President's Commission on Law Enforcement and the Administration of Justice, *Task Force Report: Juvenile Delinquency and Youth Crime* (Washington, DC: U.S. Government Printing Office, 1967).

54. Craig Hemmens and Katherine Bennett, "Juvenile Curfews and the Courts: Judicial Response to a Not-So-New Crime Control Strategy," *Crime and Delinquency* 45 (1999): 99–121.

55. James Austin and Barry Krisberg, "The Unmet Promise of Alternatives to Incarceration," *Crime and Delinquency* 28 (1982): 3–19. For an alternative view, see Arnold Binder and Gilbert Geis, "Ad Populum Argumentation in Criminology: Juvenile Diversion as Rhetoric," *Criminology* 30 (1984): 309–333.

56. Herbert Bianchi, *Justice as Sanctuary* (Bloomington: Indiana University Press, 1994); Nils Christie, "Conflicts as Property," *British Journal of Criminology* 17 (1977): 1–15; L. Hulsman, "Critical Criminology and the Concept of Crime," *Contemporary Crises* 10 (1986): 63–80.

57. Larry Tifft, "Foreword," in Dennis Sullivan, *The Mask of Love* (Port Washington, NY: Kennikat Press, 1980), p. 6.

58. Robert Davis, Barbara Smith, and Laura Nickles, "The Deterrent Effect of Prosecuting Domestic Violence Misdemeanors," *Crime and Delinquency* 44 (1998): 434–442.

59. John Braithwaite, "Setting Standards for Restorative Justice," *British Journal of Criminology* 42 (2002): 563–577.

60. Christopher Cooper, "Patrol Police Officer Conflict Resolution Processes," *Journal of Criminal Justice* 25 (1997): 87–101.

61. Robert Coates, Mark Umbreit, and Betty Vos, "Responding to Hate Crimes through Restorative Justice Dialogue," *Contemporary Justice Review* 9 (2006): 7–21; Kathleen Daly and Julie Stubbs, "Feminist Engagement with Restorative Justice," *Theoretical Criminology* 10 (2006): 9–28.

62. Lois Presser and Patricia Van Voorhis, "Values and Evaluation: Assessing Processes and Outcomes of Restorative Justice Programs," *Crime and Delinquency* 48 (2002): 162–189.

63. David Altschuler, "Community Justice Initiatives: Issues and Challenges in the U.S. Context," *Federal Probation* 65 (2001): 28–33.

64. Elliott Currie, *Crime and Punishment in America* (New York: Henry Holt, 1998). See also Elliott Currie, *Confronting Crime: An American Challenge* (New York: Pantheon, 1985); Elliott Currie, *Reckoning: Drugs, the Cities, and the American Future* (New York: Hill and Wang, 1993).

Glossary

acquaintance robbery Robbery in which the victim or victims are people the robber knows.

active precipitation Aggressive or provocative behavior of victims that results in their victimization.

adolescent-limited offender One who follows the most common criminal trajectory, in which antisocial behavior peaks in adolescence and then diminishes.

adversary system The U.S. method of criminal adjudication, in which prosecution (the state) and defense (the accused) each try to bring forward evidence and arguments, with guilt or innocence ultimately decided by an impartial judge or jury.

Age-Graded Theory According to Robert Sampson and John Laub, discrete factors influence people at different stages of their development, so the propensity to commit crimes is neither stable nor unyielding. The likelihood of committing crime is linked to the accumulation (or absence) of social capital, social control, and human decision making.

aggravated rape Rape involving multiple offenders, weapons, and victim injuries.

aging out Phrase used to express the fact that people commit less crime as they mature.

alien conspiracy theory The belief, subscribed to by the federal government and many respected criminologists, that organized crime is a direct offshoot of a criminal society that was imported into the United States from Europe and that crime cartels have a policy of restricting their membership to people of their own ethnic background.

American Dream The goal of accumulating material goods and wealth through individual competition; the process of being socialized to pursue material success and to believe it is achievable.

androgens Male sex hormones.

anomie A lack of norms or clear social standards. Because of rapidly shifting moral values, the individual has few guides to what is socially acceptable.

anomie theory The view that anomie results when socially defined goals (such as wealth and power) are universally mandated but access to legitimate means (such as education and job opportunities) is stratified by class and status.

antisocial personality Combination of traits, such as hyperactivity, impulsivity, hedonism, and inability to empathize with others, that make a person prone to deviant behavior and violence; also referred to as sociopathic or psychopathic personality.

appeal Taking a criminal case to a higher court on the grounds that the defendant was found guilty because of legal error or violation of his or her constitutional rights; a successful appeal may result in a new trial.

appellate court Court that reviews trial court procedures to determine whether they have complied with accepted rules and constitutional doctrines.

arousal theory The view that people seek to maintain a preferred level of arousal but vary in how they process sensory input. A need for high levels of environmental stimulation may lead to aggressive, violent behavior patterns.

arraignment The step in the criminal justice process in which the accused is brought before the trial judge, formal charges are read, defendants are informed of their rights, a plea is entered, bail is considered, and a trial date is set.

arrest The taking into police custody of an individual suspected of a crime.

arson The willful, malicious burning of a home, building, or vehicle.

assault Either attempted battery or intentionally frightening the victim by word or deed (actual touching is not involved).

attachment theory Bowlby's theory that being able to form an emotional bond to another person is an important aspect of mental health throughout the life span.

attention-deficit/hyperactivity disorder (ADHD) A developmentally inappropriate lack of attention, along with impulsivity and hyperactivity.

authority conflict pathway Path to a criminal career that begins with early stubborn behavior and defiance of parents.

bail A money bond intended to ensure that the accused will return for trial.

battery Offensive touching, such as slapping, hitting, or punching a victim.

behavior modeling The process of learning behavior (notably, aggression) by observing others. Aggressive models may be parents, criminals in the neighborhood, or characters on television or in movies.

behavior theory The view that all human behavior is learned through a process of social reinforcement (rewards and punishment).

Bill of Rights The first ten amendments to the U.S. Constitution, including guarantees against unreasonable search and seizure, self-incrimination, and cruel punishment.

binge drinking Having five or more drinks on the same occasion (that is, at the same time or within a couple of hours of each other) on at least 1 day in the past 30 days.

biosocial theory Approach to criminology that focuses on the interaction between biological and social factors as they are related to crime.

bipolar disorder An emotional disturbance in which moods alternate between periods of wild elation and deep depression; also known as manic-depression.

booking Fingerprinting, photographing, and recording personal information of a suspect in police custody.

booster (heel) Professional shoplifter who steals with the intention of reselling stolen merchandise.

bucketing Skimming customer trading profits by falsifying trade information.

burglary Entering a home by force, threat, or deception with intent to commit a crime.

capable guardians Effective deterrents to crime, such as police or watchful neighbors.

capital punishment The execution of criminal offenders; the death penalty.

Chicago School Group of urban sociologists who studied the relationship between environmental conditions and crime.

child abuse Any physical or emotional trauma to a child for which no reasonable explanation, such as an accident or ordinary disciplinary practices, can be found.

child sexual abuse The exploitation of children through rape, incest, and molestation by parents or other adults.

chiseling Using illegal means to cheat an organization, its consumers, or both, on a regular basis.

chronic offenders (career criminals) The small group of persistent offenders who account for a majority of all criminal offenses.

churning Repeated, excessive, and unnecessary buying and selling of a client's stock.

classical criminology Theoretical perspective suggesting that (1) people have free will to choose criminal or conventional behaviors; (2) people choose to commit crime for reasons of greed or personal need; and (3) crime can be controlled only by the fear of criminal sanctions.

cleared crimes Crimes are considered cleared when at least one person is arrested, charged, and turned over to the court for prosecution or when some element beyond police control (such as the offender having left the country) precludes the physical arrest of an offender.

Code of Hammurabi The first written criminal code, developed in Babylonia about 2000 BC.

cognitive theory Psychological perspective that focuses on the mental processes by which people perceive and represent the world around them and solve problems.

collective efficacy Social control exerted by cohesive communities and based on mutual trust, including intervention in the supervision of children and maintenance of public order.

commitment to conformity A strong personal investment in conventional institutions, individuals, and processes that prevents people from engaging in behavior that might jeopardize their reputation and achievements.

common law Early English law, developed by judges, which became the standardized law of the land in England and eventually formed the basis of the criminal law in the United States.

community policing (problem-oriented policing) A proactive form of policing: Rather than merely responding to crime after it occurs, police departments are shaping their forces into community change agents in order to prevent crimes before they occur.

compensation Financial aid awarded to crime victims to repay them for their loss and injuries; may cover medical bills, loss of wages, loss of future earnings, and/or counseling.

compliance strategies Methods of controlling white-collar crime that rely on the threat of economic sanctions or civil penalties to control potential violators, creating a marketplace incentive to obey the law.

conduct disorder (CD) A pattern of repetitive behavior in which the rights of others or social norms are violated.

concentration effect As working- and middle-class families flee inner-city poverty-ridden areas, the most disadvantaged population is consolidated in urban ghettos.

confidence game (con game) A swindle, often involving a get-rich-quick scheme, and often with illegal overtones so that the victim will be afraid or embarrassed to call the police.

conflict theory The view that human behavior is shaped by interpersonal conflict and that those who maintain social power will use it to further their own ends.

conflict view The belief that criminal behavior is defined by those in power in such as way as to protect and advance their own self-interest.

consensus view The belief that the majority of citizens in a society share common values and agree on what behaviors should be defined as criminal.

consent The victim of rape must prove that she in no way encouraged, enticed, or misled the accused rapist.

constructive possession A legal fiction that applies to situations in which persons voluntarily give up physical custody of their property but still retain legal ownership.

contagion effect People become deviant when they are influenced by others with whom they are in close contact.

convictability Existence of conditions surrounding a criminal case that indicate it has a good chance of resulting in a conviction.

corporate (organizational) crime Powerful institutions or their representatives willfully violate the laws that restrain these institutions from doing social harm or require them to do social good.

courtroom work group Prosecution, defense, and judges working together to resolve criminal cases quickly and efficiently through plea bargaining.

covert pathway Path to a criminal career that begins with minor underhanded behavior and progresses to fire starting and theft.

crime An act, deemed socially harmful or dangerous, that is specifically defined, prohibited, and punished under the criminal law.

crime control model View that the overriding purpose of the justice system is to protect the public, deter people from criminal behavior, and incapacitate known criminals; favors speedy, efficient justice and punishment.

crime discouragers People who serve as guardians of property or people.

criminal justice system The agencies of government—police, courts, and corrections—that are responsible for apprehending, adjudicating, sanctioning, and treating criminal offenders.

criminal law The written code that defines crimes and their punishments.

Criminological Enterprise The various subareas included within the scholarly discipline of criminology, which, taken as a whole, define the field of study.

criminology The scientific study of the nature, extent, cause, and control of criminal behavior.

crisis intervention Emergency counseling for crime victims.

Critical Criminologists Members of a branch of criminology that focuses on the oppression of the poor, women, and minorities, thereby linking class conflict, sexism, and racism to crime rates. Critical criminologists examine how those who hold political and economic power shape the law to uphold their self-interests.

critical criminology The branch of criminology that holds that the cause of crime can be linked to economic, social, and political disparity. Some groups in society, particularly the working class and ethnic minorities, are seen as the most likely to suffer oppressive social relations based on class conflict and racism and hence to be more prone to criminal behavior.

critical feminism Approach that explains both victimization and criminality among women in terms of gender inequality, patriarchy, and the exploitation of women under capitalism.

cultural deviance theory Branch of social structure theory that sees strain and social disorganization together resulting in a unique lower-class culture that conflicts with conventional social norms.

cultural transmission Process whereby values, beliefs, and traditions are handed down from one generation to the next.

culture conflict Result of exposure to opposing norms, attitudes, and definitions of right and wrong, moral and immoral.

culture of poverty A separate lower-class culture, characterized by apathy, cynicism, helplessness, and mistrust of social institutions such as schools, government agencies, and the police, that is passed from one generation to the next.

cyber crime Any act of criminal enterprise that involves the use of communication, computer, and Internet networks.

cyber stalking Using the Internet, email, or other electronic communications devices to stalk or harass another person.

cyber theft Use of computer networks for criminal profits. Examples include copyright infringement, identity theft, and using technology to commit traditional theft-based offenses such as larceny and fraud.

cycle of violence Victims of crime, especially victims of childhood abuse, are more likely to commit crimes themselves.

date rape A rape that involves people who are in some form of courting relationship.

death squads Covert military or paramilitary groups that carry out political assassinations.

decriminalized Having criminal penalties reduced rather than eliminated.

defendant In criminal proceedings, the person accused of violating the law.

defense attorney Person responsible for protecting the constitutional rights of the accused and presenting the best possible legal defense; represents a defendant from initial arrest through trial, sentencing, and any appeal.

defensible space The principle that crime can be prevented or displaced by modifying the physical environment to reduce the opportunity that individuals have to commit crime.

deliberation Planning a criminal act after careful thought, rather than carrying it out on impulse.

delinquent subculture A value system adopted by lower-class youths that is directly opposed to that of the larger society.

demystify To unmask the true purpose of law, justice, or other social institutions.

denial-of-service attack Extorting money from Internet service users by threatening to prevent them from accessing the service.

desist To spontaneously stop committing crime.

determinate sentencing The principle that all offenders who commit the same crime should receive the same sentence.

deterrence strategies Methods of controlling white-color crime that rely on the punishment of individual offenders to deter other would-be violators.

developmental theories Theories that attempt to explain the "natural history" of a criminal career: its onset, the course it follows, and its termination. These theories maintain that criminality is a dynamic process, influenced by social experiences as well as individual characteristics.

deviance Behavior that departs from the social norm but is not necessarily criminal.

deviance amplification Process whereby secondary deviance pushes offenders out of mainstream society and locks them into an escalating cycle of deviance, apprehension, labeling, and criminal self-identity.

deviant place theory The view that victimization is primarily a function of where people live.

differential association theory The view that people commit crime when their social learning leads them to perceive more definitions favoring crime than favoring conventional behavior.

differential opportunity The view that lower-class youths, whose legitimate opportunities are limited, join gangs and pursue criminal careers as alternative means to achieve universal success goals.

diffusion An effect that occurs when efforts to prevent one crime unintentionally prevent another.

discouragement An effect that occurs when crime control efforts targeting a particular locale help reduce crime in surrounding areas and populations.

discretion The use of personal decision making by those carrying out police, judicial, and sanctioning functions within the criminal justice system.

displacement An effect that occurs when crime control efforts simply move, or redirect, offenders to less heavily guarded alternative targets.

disposition Sentencing of a defendant who has been found guilty; usually involves a fine, probation, or incarceration.

diversion programs Programs of rehabilitation that remove offenders from the normal channels of the criminal justice process, thus enabling them to avoid the stigma of a criminal label.

dizygotic (DZ) twins Fraternal (nonidentical) twins.

drift Movement in and out of delinquency, shifting between conventional and deviant values.

drug-dependent personality A personal trait characterized by a pervasive psychological dependence on mood-altering substances.

due process model View that focuses on protecting the civil rights of those accused of crime.

early onset The view that repeat offenders begin their criminal careers at a very young age.

economic compulsive behavior Violence committed by drug users to support their habit.

edgework The excitement or exhilaration of successfully executing illegal activities in dangerous situations.

egalitarian families Families in which the husband and wife share similar positions of power at home and in the workplace. Sons and daughters have equal freedom.

ego The part of the personality developed in early childhood that helps control the id and keep people's actions within the boundaries of social convention.

ehooking Using the Internet for purposes of prostitution in order to shield identities and contact clients.

eldercide Murder of a senior citizen.

embezzlement A type of larceny in which someone who is trusted with property fraudulently converts it to his or her own use or for the use of others.

enterprise crime Use of illegal tactics to gain profit in the marketplace. Enterprise crimes can involve either the violation of law in the course of an otherwise legitimate occupation or the sale and distribution of illegal commodities.

enterprise theory of investigation (ETI) A standard investigative tool of the FBI that focuses on criminal enterprise and attacks the structure of the criminal enterprise rather than criminal acts viewed as isolated incidents.

equal justice model View that emphasizes fairness and equal treatment in criminal procedures and sentencing.

equipotentiality The view that all humans are born with equal potential to learn and achieve.

eros The life instinct, which drives people toward self-fulfillment and enjoyment.

etailing fraud Using the Internet to buy or sell merchandise illegally.

exclusionary rule The rule that evidence against a defendant may not be presented in court if it was obtained in violation of the defendant's rights.

exploitation Forcing victims to pay for services or contracts to which they have a clear right.

expressive crimes Offenses committed not for profit or gain but to vent rage, anger, or frustration.

expressive violence Acts that vent rage, anger, or frustration.

extinction An effect that occurs when crime reduction programs produce a short-term positive effect, but benefits dissipate as criminals adjust to new conditions.

false pretenses (fraud) Misrepresenting a fact in a way that causes a deceived victim to give money or property to the offender.

felony A serious offense that carries a penalty of imprisonment, usually for one year or more, and may entail loss of political rights.

felony murder A killing that accompanies a felony, such as robbery or rape.

fence A buyer and seller of stolen merchandise.

filicide Murder of an older child.

first-degree murder Killing a person after premeditation and deliberation.

focal concerns Values, such as toughness and street smarts, that have evolved specifically to fit conditions in lower-class environments.

front running Placing broker's personal orders ahead of a customer's large order to profit from the market effects of the trade.

general deterrence A crime control policy that depends on the fear of criminal penalties, convincing the potential law violator that the pains associated with crime outweigh its benefits.

general strain theory (GST) The view that multiple sources of strain interact with an individual's emotional traits and responses to produce criminality.

General Theory of Crime (GTC) Gottfredson and Hirschi's developmental theory, which modifies social control theory by integrating concepts from biosocial, psychological, routine activities, and rational choice theories.

globalization The process of creating transnational markets, politics, and legal systems and thus forming a global economy.

grand jury A group of citizens chosen to hear testimony in secret and to issue formal criminal accusations (indictments).

grand larceny Theft of money or property of substantial value, punished as a felony.

guerillas Fighters who are usually located in rural areas and attack military, police, and government targets in an effort to unseat or replace the existing government.

hate crimes (bias crimes) Violent acts directed toward a particular person or members of a group merely because the targets share a discernible racial, ethnic, religious, or gender characteristic.

heavy drinking Having five or more drinks on the same occasion on each of 5 or more days in the past 30 days.

hung jury A jury that is unable to agree on a decision, thus leaving the case unresolved and open for a possible retrial.

hypoglycemia A condition that occurs when glucose (sugar) in the blood falls below levels necessary for normal and efficient brain functioning.

id The primitive part of people's mental makeup, present at birth, that represents unconscious biological drives for food, sex, and other life-sustaining necessities. The id seeks instant gratification without concern for the rights of others.

identity theft Using the Internet to steal someone's identity and/or impersonate the victim in order to conduct illicit transactions, such as committing fraud using the victim' name and identity.

incapacitation effect Placing offenders behind bars during their prime crime years reduces their opportunity to commit crime and helps lower the crime rate.

incarceration Confinement in jail or prison.

indictment A written accusation returned by a grand jury charging an individual with a specified crime, based on the prosecutor's demonstration of probable cause.

infanticide Murder of a very young child.

influence peddling Using one's institutional position to grant favors and sell information to which one's co-conspirators are not entitled.

information A filing before an impartial lower-court judge who decides whether the case should go forward (this filing is an alternative to the use of a grand jury).

information-processing theory Theory that focuses on how people process, store, encode, retrieve, and manipulate information to make decisions and solve problems.

information technology (IT) A term that denotes all forms of technology used to create, store, retrieve, and exchange data in all its various forms, including electronic, voice, and still image.

insider trading Illegal buying of stock in a company on the basis of information provided by someone who has a fiduciary interest in the company, such as an employee, attorney, or accountant retained by the firm. Federal laws and the rules of the Securities and Exchange Commission require that all profits from such trading be returned and provide for both fines and a prison sentence.

institutional anomie theory The view that anomie pervades U.S. culture because the drive for material wealth dominates and undermines social and community values.

instrumental crimes Offenses designed to improve the financial or social position of the criminal.

instrumental theory The theory that criminal law and the criminal justice system are capitalist instruments for controlling the lower class.

instrumental violence Acts designed to improve the financial or social position of the criminal.

insurgents Individuals or groups who confront the existing government for control of all or a portion of its territory, or to force political concessions in sharing political power.

integrated theories Models of crime causation that weave social and individual variables into a complex explanatory chain.

interactionist view The belief that those with social power are able to impose their values on society as a whole, and these values then define criminal behavior.

interdisciplinary Involving two or more academic fields.

interrogation The questioning of a suspect in police custody.

involuntary or negligent manslaughter A killing that occurs when a person's acts are negligent and without regard for the harm they may cause others.

jail Institution, usually run by the county, for short-term detention of those convicted of misdemeanors and those awaiting trial or other judicial proceedings.

La Cosa Nostra A national syndicate of some 25 Italian-dominated crime families who control organized crime in distinct geographic areas.

landmark decision A ruling by the U.S. Supreme Court that serves as a precedent for similar legal issues; it often influences the everyday operating procedures of police agencies, trial courts, and correctional institutions.

larceny Taking for one's own use the property of another, by means other than force or threats on the victim or forcibly breaking into a person's home or workplace; theft.

latent trait A stable feature, characteristic, property, or condition, present at birth or soon after, that makes some people crime-prone over the life course.

latent trait (propensity) theories Theories reflecting the view that criminal behavior is controlled by a master trait, present at birth or soon after, that remains stable and unchanging throughout a person's lifetime.

law of criminal procedure Judicial precedents that define and guarantee the rights of criminal defendants and control the various components of the criminal justice system.

left realism Approach that sees crime as a function of relative deprivation under capitalism and favors pragmatic, community-based crime prevention and control.

liberal feminist theory A view of crime that suggests that the social and economic role of women in society controls their crime rates.

life-course persister One of the small group of offenders whose criminal careers continue well into adulthood.

life-course theories Theories reflecting the view that criminality is a dynamic process, influenced by many characteristics, traits, and experiences, and that behavior changes accordingly, for better or worse, over the life course.

lifestyle theories Views on how people become crime victims because of lifestyles that increase their exposure to criminal offenders.

Mafia A group that originated in Italy and Sicily and now controls racketeering in major U.S. cities.

mandatory sentences A statutory requirement that a certain penalty shall be carried out in all cases of conviction for a specified offense or series of offenses.

manslaughter Homicide without malice.

marginalization Displacement of workers, pushing them outside the economic and social mainstream.

marital exemption The formerly accepted tradition that a legally married husband could not be charged with raping his wife.

masculinity hypothesis The view that women who commit crimes have biological and psychological traits similar to those of men.

mass murder The killing of four or more victims by one or a few assailants within a single event.

merchant privilege laws Legislation that protects retailers and their employees from lawsuits if they arrest and detain a suspected shoplifter on reasonable grounds.

middle-class measuring rods The standards by which authority figures, such as teachers and employers, evaluate lower-class youngsters and often prejudge them negatively.

Miranda rights Rights of criminal defendants, including the right against self-incrimination and the right to counsel, spelled out in the case of *Miranda v. Arizona*.

misdemeanor A minor crime usually punished by a short jail term and/or a fine.

monozygotic (MZ) twins Identical twins.

mood disorder A condition in which the prevailing emotional mood is distorted or inappropriate to the circumstances.

moral entrepreneur A person who creates moral rules, which thus reflect the values of those in power, rather than any objective, universal standards of right and wrong.

Mosaic Code The laws of the ancient Israelites, found in the Old Testament of the Judeo-Christian Bible.

motivated offenders People willing and able to commit crimes.

murder The unlawful killing of a human being with malice aforethought.

naive check forgers Amateurs who cash bad checks because of some financial crisis but have little identification with a criminal subculture.

narcissistic personality disorder A pattern of traits and behaviors indicating infatuation and fixation with one's self to the exclusion of all others, along with the egotistic and ruthless pursuit of one's own gratification, dominance, and ambition.

narcotic A drug that produces sleep and relieves pain, such as heroin, morphine, and opium; a habit-forming drug.

National Crime Victimization Survey (NCVS) The ongoing victimization study conducted jointly by the Justice Department and the U.S. Census Bureau that surveys victims about their experiences with law violation.

National Incident-Based Reporting System (NIBRS) Program that requires local police agencies to provide a brief account of each incident and arrest within 22 crime patterns, including incident, victim, and offender information.

nature theory The view that intelligence is largely determined genetically and that low intelligence is linked to criminal behavior.

negative affective states Anger, frustration, and adverse emotions produced by a variety of sources of strain.

neglect Not providing a child with the care and shelter to which he or she is entitled.

neurophysiology The study of brain activity.

neurotransmitter A chemical substance, such as dopamine, that transmits nerve impulses from one neuron to another (neurons are specialized cells that make up the body's nervous system).

neutralization techniques Methods of rationalizing deviant behavior, such as denying responsibility or blaming the victim.

neutralization theory The view that law violators learn to neutralize conventional values and attitudes, enabling them to drift back and forth between criminal and conventional behavior.

nolle prosequi A declaration that expresses the prosecutor's decision to drop a case from further prosecution.

nonintervention model View that arresting and labeling offenders does more harm than good, that youthful offenders in particular should be diverted into informal treatment programs, and that minor offenses should be decriminalized.

nurture theory The view that intelligence is not inherited but is largely a product of environment. Low IQ scores do not cause crime but may result from the same environmental factors.

obscenity Material that violates community standards of morality or decency and has no redeeming social value.

occasional criminals Offenders who do not define themselves by a criminal role or view themselves as committed career criminals.

offender-specific crime A crime in which offenders evaluate their skills, motives, needs, and fears before deciding to commit the criminal act.

offense-specific crime A crime in which the offender reacts selectively to the characteristics of a particular criminal act.

oppositional defiant disorder (ODD) A pattern of negativistic, hostile, and defiant behavior, during which a child often loses her or his temper, often argues with adults, and often actively defies or refuses to comply with adults' requests or rules.

organized crime Illegal activities of people and organizations whose acknowledged purpose is profit through illegitimate business enterprise.

overt pathway Path to a criminal career that begins with minor aggression, leads to physical fighting, and eventually escalates to violent crime.

paraphilia Bizarre or abnormal sexual practices that may involve nonhuman objects, humiliation, or children.

parental efficacy Parents who are supportive and effectively control their children in a noncoercive way.

parole Conditional early release from prison, with the offender serving the remainder of the sentence in the community under the supervision of a parole officer.

Part I crimes The eight most serious offenses included in the UCR: murder, rape, assault, robbery, burglary, arson, larceny, and motor vehicle theft.

Part II crimes All other crimes, aside from the eight Part I crimes, included in the UCR arrest data. Part II crimes include drug offenses, sex crimes, and vandalism, among others.

passive precipitation Personal or social characteristics of victims that make them attractive targets for criminals; such victims may unknowingly either threaten or encourage their attackers.

paternalistic families Families in which the father is the breadwinner and rule maker, and the mother has a menial job or is a homemaker only. Sons are granted greater freedom than daughters.

patriarchal Male-dominated.

payola The practice of record companies bribing radio stations to play songs without making listeners aware of the payment.

peacemaking Approach that considers punitive crime control strategies to be counterproductive and favors the use of humanistic conflict resolution to prevent and control crime.

penology Subarea of criminology that focuses on the correction and control of criminal offenders.

personality The reasonably stable patterns of behavior, including thoughts and emotions, that distinguish one person from another.

petit (petty) larceny Theft of a small amount of money or property, punished as a misdemeanor.

phishing Illegally acquiring personal information, such as bank passwords and credit card numbers, by masquerading as a trustworthy person or business in what appears to be an official electronic communication, such as an email or an instant message. The term "phishing" comes from the lures used to "fish" for financial information and passwords.

pilferage Systematic theft of company property.

plea bargain Agreement between prosecution and defense in which the accused pleads guilty in return for a reduction of charges, a more lenient sentence, or some other consideration.

population All people who share a particular characteristic, such as all high school students or all police officers.

pornography Sexually explicit books, magazines, films, and DVDs intended to provide sexual titillation and excitement for paying customers.

positivism The branch of social science that uses the scientific method of the natural sciences and suggests that human behavior is a product of social, biological, psychological, or economic forces.

post-traumatic stress disorder Psychological reaction to a highly stressful event; symptoms may include depression, anxiety, flashbacks, and recurring nightmares.

power The ability of persons and groups to control the behavior of others, to shape public opinion, and to define deviance.

power–control theory The view that gender differences in crime are a function of economic power (class position, one- versus two-earner families) and parental control (paternalistic versus egalitarian families).

precedent A rule derived from previous judicial decisions and applied to future cases; the basis of common law.

preemptive deterrence Efforts to prevent crime through community organization and youth involvement.

preliminary hearing Alternative to a grand jury, in which an impartial lower-court judge decides whether there is probable cause sufficient for a trial.

premeditation Considering the criminal act beforehand, which suggests that it was motivated by more than a simple desire to engage in an act of violence.

premenstrual syndrome (PMS) Condition, postulated by some theorists, wherein several days before and during menstruation, excessive amounts of female sex hormones stimulate antisocial, aggressive behavior.

price fixing The illegal control by agreement among producers or manufacturers of the price of a commodity to avoid price competition and deprive the consumer of reasonable prices.

primary deviance A norm violation or crime that has little or no long-term influence on the violator.

prison (penitentiary) State or federally operated facility for the incarceration of felony offenders sentenced by the criminal courts.

probable cause Evidence of a crime, and of a suspect's involvement in it, sufficient to warrant an arrest.

probation Conditional release of a convicted offender into the community under the supervision of a probation officer and subject to certain conditions.

problem behavior syndrome (PBS) A cluster of antisocial behaviors that may include family dysfunction, substance abuse, smoking, precocious sexuality and early pregnancy, educational underachievement, suicide attempts, sensation seeking, and unemployment, as well as crime.

pro bono Literally, done without compensation, "for the public good"; free legal counsel provided to indigent defendants by private attorneys as a service to the profession and the community.

professional criminals Offenders who make a significant portion of their income from crime.

Prohibition The period from 1919 until 1933, when the Eighteenth Amendment to the U.S. Constitution outlawed the sale of alcohol; also known as the "noble experiment."

prosecutor Public official who represents the government in criminal proceedings, presenting the case against the accused.

prostitution The granting of nonmarital sexual access for remuneration.

psychodynamic (psychoanalytic) theory Theory, originated by Freud, that the human personality is controlled by unconscious mental processes that develop early in childhood and involve the interaction of id, ego, and superego.

psychopharmacological relationship In such a relationship, violence is the direct consequence of ingesting mood-altering substances.

public defender Attorney employed by the state whose job is to provide free legal counsel to indigent defendants.

public order crime Behavior that is outlawed because it threatens the general well-being of society and challenges its accepted moral principles.

racial profiling The use of racial and ethnic characteristics by police in their determining whether a person is likely to commit a crime or engage in deviant and/or antisocial activities.

racial threat theory As the size of the black population increases, the perceived threat to the white population increases, resulting in a greater amount of social control imposed on blacks.

Racketeer Influenced and Corrupt Organization Act (RICO) Federal legislation that enables prosecutors to bring additional criminal or civil charges against people engaged in two or more acts prohibited by 24 existing federal and 8 state laws. RICO features monetary penalties that allow the government to confiscate all profits derived from criminal activities. Originally intended to be used against organized crime, RICO has also been used against white-collar criminals.

rape The carnal knowledge of a female forcibly and against her will.

rational choice theory (choice theory) The view that crime is a function of a decision-making process in which the potential offender weighs the potential costs and benefits of an illegal act.

reaction formation Irrational hostility evidenced by young delinquents, who adopt norms directly opposed to middle-class goals and standards that seem impossible to achieve.

recidivism Repetition of criminal behavior.

recognizance Pledge by the accused to return for trial, which may be accepted in lieu of bail.

reflected appraisal When parents are alienated from their children, their negative labeling reduces their children's self-image and increases delinquency.

rehabilitation Treatment of criminal offenders that is aimed at preventing future criminal behavior.

rehabilitation model View that criminals are victims of social injustice, poverty, and racism and that appropriate treatment can change them into productive, law-abiding citizens.

relative deprivation Envy, mistrust, and aggression resulting from perceptions of economic and social inequality.

reliable measure A measure that produces consistent results from one measurement to another.

replacement An effect that occurs when criminals try new offenses they had previously avoided because situational crime prevention programs neutralized their crime of choice.

restitution Permitting an offender to repay the victim or do useful work in the community rather than facing the stigma of a formal trial and a court-ordered sentence.

restorative justice Using humanistic, nonpunitive strategies to restore social harmony. This view emphasizes the promotion of a peaceful, just society through reconciliation and reintegration of the offender into society.

retrospective reading The reassessment of a person's past to fit a current generalized label.

revolutionaries Either nationalists who struggle against a sovereign power that controls the land, or local groups that battle the existing government over issues of ideology and power.

right to counsel The right of a person accused of crime to the assistance of a defense attorney in all criminal prosecutions.

road rage Violent assault by a motorist who loses control of his or her emotions while driving.

robbery Taking or attempting to take anything of value from the care, custody, or control of a person or persons by force or threat of force or violence and/or by putting the victim in fear.

role exit behaviors Strategies, such as running away or contemplating suicide, that are used by young girls unhappy with their status in the family.

routine activities theory The view that victimization results from the interaction of three everyday factors: the availability of suitable targets, the absence of capable guardians, and the presence of motivated offenders.

sampling Selecting a limited number of people for study as representative of a larger group.

schizophrenia A severe disorder marked by hearing nonexistent voices, seeing hallucinations, and exhibiting inappropriate responses.

scientific method The use of verifiable principles and procedures for the systematic acquisition of knowledge. Typically involves formulating a problem, creating hypotheses, and collecting data, through observation and experiment, to verify the hypotheses.

secondary deviance A norm violation or crime that comes to the attention of significant others or social control agents, who apply a negative label that has long-term consequences for the violator's self-identity and social interactions.

second-degree murder A person's wanton disregard for the victim's life and his or her desire to inflict serious bodily harm on the victim, which results in the victim's death.

seductions of crime The situational inducements or immediate benefits that draw offenders into law violations.

self-control A strong moral sense that renders a person incapable of hurting others or violating social norms.

self-control theory Gottfredson and Hirschi's view that the cause of delinquent behavior is an impulsive personality. Kids who are impulsive may have a weak bond to society.

self-report survey A research approach that requires subjects to reveal their own participation in delinquent or criminal acts.

sentencing circle A peacemaking technique in which offenders, victims, and other community members work together to formulate a sanction that addresses the needs of all.

serial killer A person who kills three or more persons in three or more separate events.

Sherman Antitrust Act Federal law that subjects to criminal or civil sanctions any person "who shall make any contract or engage in any combination or conspiracy" in restraint of interstate commerce.

shield laws Laws that protect women from being questioned about their sexual history unless such questioning directly bears on the case.

shoplifting The taking of goods from retail stores.

situational crime prevention A method of crime prevention that seeks to eliminate or reduce particular crimes in specific settings.

situational inducement Short-term influence on a person's behavior, such as financial problems or peer pressure, which increases risk taking.

snitch Amateur shoplifter who does not self-identify as a thief but who systematically steals merchandise for personal use.

social bonds The ties that bind people to society, including relationships with friends, family, neighbors, teachers, and employers. The elements of the social bond include commitment, attachment, involvement, and belief.

social capital Positive, life-sustaining relations with individuals and institutions.

social class Segment of the population whose members are at a relatively similar economic level and who share attitudes, values, norms, and an identifiable lifestyle.

social control theory The view that people commit crime when the forces binding them to society are weakened or broken.

social disorganization theory Branch of social structure theory that focuses on the breakdown, in inner-city neighborhoods, of institutions such as the family, school, and employment.

social harm The injury caused to others by willful wrongful conduct.

socialization Process of human development and enculturation. Socialization is influenced by key social processes and institutions.

social learning theory The view that people learn to be aggressive by observing others acting aggressively to achieve some goal or being rewarded for violent acts.

social process theory The view that criminality is a function of people's interactions with various organizations, institutions, and processes in society.

social reaction (labeling) theory The view that people become criminals when they are labeled as such and accept the label as a personal identity.

social structure theory The view that disadvantaged economic class position is a primary cause of crime.

sociobiology The view that human behavior is motivated by inborn biological urges to survive and preserve the species.

sociological criminology Approach to criminology, based on the work of Quetelet and Durkheim, that focuses on the relationship between social factors and crime.

specific deterrence The view that criminal sanctions should be so powerful that offenders will never repeat their criminal acts.

spree killer A killer of multiple victims whose murders occur over a relatively short span of time and often follow no discernible pattern.

stalking A course of conduct that is directed at a specific person and involves repeated physical or visual proximity, nonconsensual communication, or verbal, written, or implied threats sufficient to cause fear in a reasonable person.

state (organized) crime Acts committed by state or government officials while holding their positions as government representatives.

status frustration A form of culture conflict experienced by lower-class youths because social conditions prevent them from achieving success as defined by the larger society.

statutory crimes Crimes defined by legislative bodies in response to changing social conditions, public opinion, and custom.

statutory rape Sexual relations between an underage minor female and an adult male.

stigmatize To apply negative labeling with enduring effects on a person's self-image and social interactions.

strain The anger, frustration, and resentment experienced by people who believe they cannot achieve their goals through legitimate means.

strain theory Branch of social structure theory that sees crime as a function of the conflict between people's goals and the means available to obtain them.

stratified society People grouped according to economic or social class; characterized by the unequal distribution of wealth, power, and prestige.

structural theory The theory that criminal law and the criminal justice system are means of defending and preserving the capitalist system.

subculture A set of values, beliefs, and traditions unique to a particular social class or group within a larger society.

subculture of violence A segment of society in which violence has become legitimized by the custom and norms of that group.

successful degradation ceremony A course of action or ritual in which someone's identity is publicly redefined and destroyed and he or she is thereafter viewed as socially unacceptable

suitable targets Objects of crime (persons or property) that are attractive and readily available.

superego Incorporation within the personality of the moral standards and values of parents, community, and significant others.

supranational criminology The study of war crimes, crimes against humanity, and the supranational penal system.

surplus value The difference between what workers produce and what they are paid, which goes to business owners as profits.

systematic forgers Professionals who make a living by passing bad checks.

systemic link A link between drugs and violence that occurs when drug dealers turn violent in their competition with rival gangs.

target hardening strategy Locking goods into place or using electronic tags and sensing devices as means of preventing shoplifting.

target removal strategy Displaying dummy or disabled goods as a means of preventing shoplifting.

temperance movement The drive to prohibit the sale of alcohol in the United States, culminating in ratification of the Eighteenth Amendment in 1919.

terrorists Individuals or groups that systematically attack or threaten violence to terrorize individuals, groups, communities, or governments into acceding to the terrorists' political demands.

testosterone The principal male hormone.

thanatos The death instinct, which impels toward self-destruction.

"three strikes" laws Laws that require offenders to serve life in prison after they are convicted of a third felony.

trait theory The view that criminality is a product of abnormal biological or psychological traits.

transitional neighborhood An area undergoing a shift in population and structure, usually from middle-class residential to lower-class mixed-use.

truly disadvantaged The lowest level of the underclass; urban, inner-city, socially isolated people who occupy the bottom rung of the social ladder and are the victims of discrimination.

truth in sentencing The requirement that inmates serve a greater percentage of their time behind bars before they are eligible for early release mechanisms such as parole.

turning points According to Laub and Sampson, the life events that alter the development of a criminal career.

underclass The lowest social stratum in any country, whose members lack the education and skills needed to function successfully in modern society.

Uniform Crime Report (UCR) Large database, compiled by the FBI, of crimes reported and arrests made each year throughout the United States.

USA PATRIOT Act (USAPA) An act that gives sweeping new powers to domestic law enforcement and international intelligence agencies in an effort to fight terrorism, to expand the definition of terrorist activities, and to alter sanctions for violent terrorism.

utilitarianism The view that people's behavior is motivated by the pursuit of pleasure and the avoidance of pain.

valid measure A measure that actually measures what it purports to measure; a measure that is factual.

victimless crime Public order crime that violates the moral order but has no specific victim other than society as a whole.

victim–offender reconciliation programs Mediated face-to-face encounters between victims and their attackers, designed to produce restitution agreements and, if possible, reconciliation.

victimologists Criminologists who focus on the victims of crime.

victimology The study of the victim's role in criminal events.

victim precipitation theory The view that victims may initiate, either actively or passively, the confrontation that leads to their victimization.

victim–witness assistance programs Government programs that help crime victims and witnesses; may include compensation, court services, and/or crisis intervention.

virility mystique The belief that males must separate their sexual feelings from their need for love, respect, and affection.

voluntary or nonnegligent manslaughter A killing committed in the heat of passion or during a sudden quarrel that provoked violence.

warez Pirated software illegally obtained, stripped of its copyright protections, and posted on the Internet to be downloaded or sold in violation of its license.

white-collar crime Illegal activities of people and institutions whose acknowledged purpose is profit through legitimate business transactions. White-collar crimes can involve theft, embezzlement, fraud, market manipulation, restraint of trade, and false advertising.

workplace violence Violence such as assault, rape, or murder committed at the workplace.

Name Index

Subject Index

misdemeanors, 19
mission killers, 271
Mitchell, Brian David, 353
monamine oxidase (MAO), 115
Monitoring the Future survey, 35
monozygotic (MZ) twins, 117–118
mood disorders, 128–129
moral beliefs. *See* beliefs
moral crusaders, 351–353
moral entrepreneurs, 185, 351–352
More than Just Race (Wilson), 141
Morgan, Michael "Missouri Mike," 390
Mosaic Code, 18
Moscone, George, 110
Moss, Gary, 277
motivated offenders, 71, 72
motor vehicle theft, 29, 41, 89, 300–303
MS-13 gang, 135–136
Muhammad, John Allen, 272
murder
    defined, 29, 265
    degrees of, 265–266
    deliberate indifference, 266
    deliberation in, 265–266
    eldercide, 267
    expressive, 267
    felony murder, 266
    filicide, 267
    first-degree, 265
    homicide trends, 38, 39, 40
    honor killing, 258
    infanticide, 267
    involuntary or negligent manslaughter, 29, 266
    manslaughter, 266
    mass murderers, 271
    nature and extent of, 266–267
    personal relations and, 267–268
    romantic relations and, 267
    second-degree, 266
    serial killers, 270–271
    spree killers, 271–272
    stranger relations and, 268
    student relations and, 268, 270
    transactions, 268
    voluntary or nonnegligent manslaughter, 29, 266
MZ (monozygotic) twins, 117–118

Nahimana, Benita, 112
naive check forgers, 303
narcissistic personality disorder, 263
narcotic, 371
Narcotic Control Act, 371
Nation, Carrie, 366
National Counterterrorism Center (NCTC), 288
National Crime Victimization Survey (NCVS), 32–33, 36, 38, 40
National Deviancy Conference (NDC), 198
National Incident-Based Reporting System (NIBRS), 31
national terrorists, 283
nature theory, 127
negative affective states, 154
neglect, defined, 273
negligent manslaughter, 266
neurophysiological factors in crime
    ADHD, 113–115
    arousal theory, 116
    brain chemistry, 115
    conduct disorder (CD), 113, 114, 129
    summary of, 120
neurophysiology, 113
neurotransmitters, 49, 115
neutralization techniques, 176, 177–178
neutralization theory, 176, 177–179, 190
neutralization view of white-collar crime, 329
New Criminology (Taylor, Walton, Young), 199
New York Electronic Crimes Task Force (NYECTF), 339
New York v. Belton, 401
Nicelli, Joseph, 298

Noel, Robert, 266
nolle prosequi declaration, 395
nonintervention model, 407, 408
nonnegligent manslaughter, 29, 266
Nuclear Terrorism (Allison), 288
nurture theory, 127–128

Obama, Barack, 52
obscenity, 362
observational research, 38
occasional criminals, 295
Occupational Safety and Health Administration (OSHA), 328
offender-specific crime, 86
offense specialization/generalization, 230
offense-specific crime, 86
Omnibus Victim and Witness Protection Act, 75
oppositional defiant disorder (ODD), 128–129
organizational (corporate) crime, 326–329. *See also* white-collar crime
organized crime. *See also* state (organized) crime
    activities of, 341
    cargo thieves, 296
    characteristics of, 340
    concepts of, 341
    contemporary groups, 341–342
    controlling, 342–343
    defined, 316
    Eurasian groups, 342
    future of, 343–345
    mystique of, 340
    overview, 339–340
    Russian, 344–345
    shoplifting rings, 297–298
Örko, Ella, 54
overt pathway, 230

paraphilias, 354
parental abuse, 274
parental efficacy, 169
parole, 391–393
Part I/Part II crimes, 28–29
particular deterrence, 99–100, 102
passive precipitation, 68, 69
paternalistic families, 214
pathways to crime, 229–230
patriarchal system, 212–213
Patterns in Criminal Homicide (Wolfgang), 7
payola, 323
PBS (problem behavior syndrome), 228–229, 369–370
PCBs (polychlorinated biphenyls), 113
peacemaking, 215
pedophilia, 355
peers
    deviant, 185
    GTC and, 245
    socialization by, 172
penitentiary (prison), 391
penology, 7–8
Perea, Ignacio, 265
Perez, Jose Luis, 325
persistence of delinquency, 238–239
personality
    antisocial, 126–127
    criminal traits, 125–127
    defined, 125
    drug-dependent, 369
    extroverted *vs.* introverted, 126
    narcissistic disorder, 263
    psychopathic, 126–127
    traits linked to violence, 255
personal relations and murder, 267–268
petit (petty) larceny, 297
phishing, 336
Pickens, Michael, 83, 84
pilferage, 323–324
place for crime, rational choice in, 87–88

plea bargain, 396
PMS (premenstrual syndrome), 112
poachers, 294
police. *See also* law enforcement
    community policing (COP), 385
    deterrent effect of, 96
    force and, 384–385
    restorative justice by, 219
policy. *See* public policy
political corruption, 203
political terrorists, 283
political violence. *See* terrorism and political violence
polychlorinated biphenyls (PCBs), 113
Ponzi schemes, 3
Pope v. Illinois, 364
population for surveys, 31
pornography
    controlling, 365
    cyber crime, 334–335
    defined, 362
    harmfulness of, 362
    kiddie porn, 15, 315–316, 362
    law and, 363–365
    obscenity, definitional problems of, 362
    sexual violence and, 363
positivism, 10
positivist criminology, 10–11
postconviction remedies, 397
postrelease/aftercare, 397–398
post-traumatic stress disorder (PTSD), 61–62
poverty
    in children, 137
    concentration effect, 148
    crime and, 12, 139, 145, 147, 235
    crime-rate patterns and, 48, 53
    culture of, 137
    expressive crimes and, 48
    extent of, 43, 136, 137, 138, 139
    inner-city, 140
    in minority groups, 137, 139
    peacemaking view of, 215
    rehabilitation model and, 404, 405
    in social disorganization theory, 143
    in transitional neighborhoods, 144
Powell v. Alabama, 389
power, 200
power rape, 261
power-control theory, 214–215, 216
precedents, 19
preemptive deterrence, 212
preliminary hearing, 396
premeditation, 265
premenstrual syndrome (PMS), 112
prevention. *See* deterrence
price fixing, 327
primary deviance, 187–188
primary prevention programs, 129–130
prison (penitentiary), 391
prisoner reentry, crime trends and, 46, 393
probable cause, 394
probation, 390–391
problem behavior syndrome (PBS), 228–229, 369–370
problem-oriented policing, 385
pro bono, 389
process perspective, 14
professional criminals, 295. *See also* chronic offenders
profit killers, 271
Prohibition, 366–367
propensity theories. *See* latent trait theories
property crimes. *See also specific kinds*
    arson, 29, 310–311
    burglary, 29, 41, 306–310
    larceny/theft, 29, 89, 293–306
    Part I crimes, 28, 29
    pilferage, 323–324